T0137016

Lecture Notes in Computer Science　　10735

Commenced Publication in 1973
Founding and Former Series Editors:
Gerhard Goos, Juris Hartmanis, and Jan van Leeuwen

Editorial Board

David Hutchison
　Lancaster University, Lancaster, UK
Takeo Kanade
　Carnegie Mellon University, Pittsburgh, PA, USA
Josef Kittler
　University of Surrey, Guildford, UK
Jon M. Kleinberg
　Cornell University, Ithaca, NY, USA
Friedemann Mattern
　ETH Zurich, Zurich, Switzerland
John C. Mitchell
　Stanford University, Stanford, CA, USA
Moni Naor
　Weizmann Institute of Science, Rehovot, Israel
C. Pandu Rangan
　Indian Institute of Technology Madras, Chennai, India
Bernhard Steffen
　TU Dortmund University, Dortmund, Germany
Demetri Terzopoulos
　University of California, Los Angeles, CA, USA
Doug Tygar
　University of California, Berkeley, CA, USA
Gerhard Weikum
　Max Planck Institute for Informatics, Saarbrücken, Germany

More information about this series at http://www.springer.com/series/7409

Bing Zeng · Qingming Huang
Abdulmotaleb El Saddik · Hongliang Li
Shuqiang Jiang · Xiaopeng Fan (Eds.)

Advances in Multimedia Information Processing – PCM 2017

18th Pacific-Rim Conference on Multimedia
Harbin, China, September 28–29, 2017
Revised Selected Papers, Part I

 Springer

Editors
Bing Zeng
University of Electronic Science
  and Technology of China
Chengdu
China

Qingming Huang (iD)
University of Chinese Academy of Sciences
Beijing
China

Abdulmotaleb El Saddik
University of Ottawa
Ottawa, ON
Canada

Hongliang Li
University of Electronic Science
  and Technology of China
Chengdu
China

Shuqiang Jiang
Chinese Academy of Sciences
Beijing
China

Xiaopeng Fan
Harbin Institute of Technology
Harbin
China

ISSN 0302-9743   ISSN 1611-3349   (electronic)
Lecture Notes in Computer Science
ISBN 978-3-319-77379-7   ISBN 978-3-319-77380-3   (eBook)
https://doi.org/10.1007/978-3-319-77380-3

Library of Congress Control Number: 2018935899

LNCS Sublibrary: SL3 – Information Systems and Applications, incl. Internet/Web, and HCI

© Springer International Publishing AG, part of Springer Nature 2018
This work is subject to copyright. All rights are reserved by the Publisher, whether the whole or part of the material is concerned, specifically the rights of translation, reprinting, reuse of illustrations, recitation, broadcasting, reproduction on microfilms or in any other physical way, and transmission or information storage and retrieval, electronic adaptation, computer software, or by similar or dissimilar methodology now known or hereafter developed.
The use of general descriptive names, registered names, trademarks, service marks, etc. in this publication does not imply, even in the absence of a specific statement, that such names are exempt from the relevant protective laws and regulations and therefore free for general use.
The publisher, the authors and the editors are safe to assume that the advice and information in this book are believed to be true and accurate at the date of publication. Neither the publisher nor the authors or the editors give a warranty, express or implied, with respect to the material contained herein or for any errors or omissions that may have been made. The publisher remains neutral with regard to jurisdictional claims in published maps and institutional affiliations.

Printed on acid-free paper

This Springer imprint is published by the registered company Springer International Publishing AG
part of Springer Nature
The registered company address is: Gewerbestrasse 11, 6330 Cham, Switzerland

Preface

On behalf of the Organizing Committee, it is our great pleasure to welcome you to the proceedings of the 2017 Pacific-Rim Conference on Multimedia (PCM 2017). PCM serves as an international forum to bring together researchers and practitioners from academia and industry to discuss research on state-of-the-art Internet multimedia processing, multimedia service, analysis, and applications. PCM 2017 was the 18th in the series that has been held annually since 2000. In 2017, PCM was held in Harbin, China.

Consistent with previous editions of PCM, we prepared a very attractive technical program with two keynote talks, one best paper candidate session, nine oral presentation sessions, two poster sessions, and six oral special sessions. Moreover, thanks to the co-organization with IEEE CAS Beijing chapter, this year's program featured a panel session titled "Advanced Multimedia Technology." Social and intellectual interactions were enjoyed among students, young researchers, and leading scholars.

We received 264 submissions for regular papers this year. These submissions cover the areas of multimedia content analysis, multimedia signal processing and systems, multimedia applications and services, etc. We thank our 104 Technical Program Committee members for their efforts in reviewing papers and providing valuable feedback to the authors. From the total of 264 submissions and based on at least two reviews per submission, the Program Chairs decided to accept 48 oral papers (18.2%) and 96 poster papers, i.e, the overall acceptance ratio for regular paper is 54.9%. Among the 48 oral papers, two papers received the Best Paper and the Best Student Paper award. Moreover, we accepted six special sessions with 35 papers.

The technical program is an important aspect but only delivers its full impact if surrounded by challenging keynotes. We are extremely pleased and grateful to have two exceptional keynote speakers, Wenwu Zhu and Josep Lladós, accept our invitation and present interesting ideas and insights at PCM 2017. We would also like to express our sincere gratitude to all the other Organizing Committee members, the general chairs, Bing Zeng, Qingming Huang, and Abdulmotaleb El Saddik, the program chair, Hongliang Li, Shuqiang Jiang, and Xiaopeng Fan, the panel chairs, Zhu Li and Debin Zhao, the organizing chairs, Shaohui Liu, Liang Li, and Yan Chen, the publication chairs, Shuhui Wang and Wen-Huang Cheng, the sponsorship chairs, Wangmeng Zuo, Luhong Liang, and Ke Lv, the registration and finance chairs, Guorong Li and Weiqing Min, among others. Their outstanding effort contributed to this extremely rich and complex main program that characterizes PCM 2017. Last but not the least, we thank all the authors, session chairs, student volunteers, and supporters. Their contributions are much appreciated.

We sincerely hope that you will enjoy reading the proceedings of PCM 2017.

September 2017

Bing Zeng
Qingming Huang
Abdulmotaleb El Saddik
Hongliang Li
Shuqiang Jiang
Xiaopeng Fan

Organization

Organizing Committee

General Chairs

Bing Zeng — University of Electronic Science and Technology of China

Qingming Huang — University of Chinese Academy of Sciences, China

Abdulmotaleb El Saddik — University of Ottawa, Canada

Program Chairs

Hongliang Li — University of Electronic Science and Technology of China

Shuqiang Jiang — ICT, Chinese Academy of Sciences, China

Xiaopeng Fan — Harbin Institute of Technology, China

Organizing Chairs

Shaohui Liu — Harbin Institute of Technology, China

Liang Li — University of Chinese Academy Sciences, China

Yan Chen — University of Electronic Science and Technology of China

Panel Chairs

Zhu Li — University of Missouri-Kansas City, USA

Debin Zhao — Harbin Institute of Technology, China

Technical Committee

Publication Chairs

Shuhui Wang — ICT, Chinese Academy of Sciences, China

Wen-Huang Cheng — Taiwan Academia Sinica, Taiwan

Tongwei Ren — Nanjing University, China

Lu Fang — Hong Kong University of Science and Technology, SAR China

Special Session Chairs

Yan Liu — The Hong Kong Polytechnic University, SAR China

Yu-Gang Jiang — Fudan University, China

Wen Ji — ICT, Chinese Academy of Sciences, China

Jinqiao Shi — Chinese Academy Sciences, China

Feng Jiang — Harbin Institute of Technology, China

Tutorial Chairs

Zheng-jun Zha	Hefei Institute of Intelligent Machines, Chinese Academy of Sciences, China
Siwei Ma	Peking University, China
Chong-Wah Ngo	City University of Hong Kong, SAR China
Ruiqin Xiong	Peking University, China

Publicity Chairs

Liang Lin	Sun Yat-sen University, China
Luis Herranz	Computer Vision Center, Spain
Cees Snoek	University of Amsterdam and Qualcomm Research, The Netherlands
Shin'ichi Satoh	National Institute of Informatics, Japan
Zi Huang	The University of Queensland, Australia

Sponsorship Chairs

Wangmeng Zuo	Harbin Institute of Technology, China
Luhong Liang	ASTRI, Hong Kong, SAR China
Ke Lv	University of Chinese Academy of Sciences, China

Registration Chairs

Guorong Li	University of Chinese Academy of Sciences, China
Shuyuan Zhu	University of Electronic Science and Technology of China
Wenbin Yin	Harbin Institute of Technology, China

Finance Chairs

Weiqing Min	ICT, Chinese Academy of Sciences, China
Wenbin Che	Harbin Institute of Technology, China

Contents – Part I

Image Super-Resolution, Debluring, and Dehazing

Person Identity and Emotion

Tracking and Action Recognition

Detection and Classification

Multimedia Signal Reconstruction and Recovery

Text and Line Detection/Recognition

3D and Panoramic Vision

Deep Learning for Signal Processing and Understanding

Contents – Part II

Best Paper Candidate

Deep Graph Laplacian Hashing for Image Retrieval

Jiancong Ge[1(✉)], Xueliang Liu[1], Richang Hong[1], Jie Shao[2], and Meng Wang[1]

[1] Hefei University of Technology, Hefei, China
jiancongge@mail.hfut.edu.cn, liuxueliang@hfut.edu.cn
[2] University of Electronic Science and Technology, Chengdu, China

Abstract. Due to the storage and retrieval efficiency, hashing has been widely deployed to approximate nearest neighbor search for fast image retrieval on large-scale datasets. It aims to map images to compact binary codes that approximately preserve the data relations in the Hamming space. However, most of existing approaches learn hashing functions using the hand-craft features, which cannot optimally capture the underlying semantic information of images. Inspired by the fast progress of deep learning techniques, in this paper we design a novel Deep Graph Laplacian Hashing (DGLH) method to simultaneously learn robust image features and hash functions in an unsupervised manner. Specifically, we devise a deep network architecture with graph Laplacian regularization to preserve the neighborhood structure in the learned Hamming space. At the top layer of the deep network, we minimize the quantization errors, and enforce the bits to be balanced and uncorrelated, which makes the learned hash codes more efficient. We further utilize back-propagation to optimize the parameters of the networks. It should be noted that our approach does not require labeled training data and is more practical to real-world applications in comparison to supervised hashing methods. Experimental results on three benchmark datasets demonstrate that DGLH can outperform the state-of-the-art unsupervised hashing methods in image retrieval tasks.

Keywords: Image retrieval · Deep hashing learning · Graph Laplacian

1 Introduction

With the explosive growth of online images in recent years, large-scale image retrieval has attracted increasing attention [4,16,21], which tries to return visually similar images that match the visual query from a large database. However, retrieving the exact nearest neighbors is computationally impracticable when the reference database becomes very large. To alleviate this problem, hashing [20] has been widely used to speed up the query process. The basic idea of hashing approach is to transform the high dimensional data into compact binary codes, which preserve the semantic information. Then the distance between data points in high dimensional space can be approximated by Hamming distance.

© Springer International Publishing AG, part of Springer Nature 2018
B. Zeng et al. (Eds.): PCM 2017, LNCS 10735, pp. 3–13, 2018.
https://doi.org/10.1007/978-3-319-77380-3_1

Existing hashing methods can be classified into two categories: unsupervised hashing methods and supervised hashing methods. Unsupervised hashing methods only exploit unlabeled data to learn hash functions, such as Locality Sensitive Hashing (LSH) [1], Spectral Hashing (SH) [22], Iterative Quantization (ITQ) [2], Spherical Hashing (SpH) [9], and Discrete Graph Hashing (DGH) [13]. Different from unsupervised methods, supervised methods utilize label information to learn the hash codes, which can preserve the similarity relationships among data points in Hamming space, like Binary Reconstructive Embedding (BRE) [7], Minimal Loss Hashing (MLH) [17], and Kernel-based Supervised Hashing (KSH) [14]. However, these traditional hashing methods learn hash functions using hand-crafted features, like GIST [18] or SIFT [15], which are not sufficient to represent the visual content, hence these methods result in suboptimal hashing codes.

In recent years, with the rapid development of deep learning [6], it has become a hot topic to combine deep learning and hashing methods [27]. Some deep hashing methods, like CNNH [23], DNNH [8], DHN [28] and DPSH [10], have shown better performance than the traditional hashing methods because the deep architectures generate more discriminative feature representations.

However, most existing deep hashing methods are designed in the supervised scenario, which relies on the label information of data points to preserve the semantic similarity. With the rapid growth of visual data on the web, most of the online data do not have label annotations. In addition, labeling data is also very expensive, which means it is difficult to acquire sufficient semantic labels in real applications. Thus it is more acceptable to develop unsupervised hashing methods which can exploit unlabeled data directly. But the existing unsupervised hashing methods depend on hand-crafted features which cannot effectively capture the semantic information of images.

To alleviate the above problems, in this paper, we propose a novel unsupervised deep hashing method, named Deep Graph Laplacian Hashing (DGLH), to simultaneously learn the deep feature representation and the compact binary codes. We design a graph-based objective function [24–26] at the top layer of the deep network to preserve the adjacency relation of images without using the label information. We also minimize the quantization loss between the real-valued Euclidean distance and the Hamming distance. Moreover, we enforce the bits to be balanced and uncorrelated, which makes the learned hash codes more effective. Finally, the model parameters are learned by back propagation algorithm. The proposed DGLH is an end-to-end learning method, which means that we can directly obtain hash codes from the input images by utilizing DGLH directly. We compare the proposed DGLH method with state-of-the-art unsupervised hashing methods on several commonly-used image retrieval benchmarks, and the experimental results demonstrate the effectiveness of the proposed method.

The rest of this paper is organized as follows: The proposed DGLH method is introduced in Sect. 2. Section 3 presents the experimental results and analysis, followed by a conclusion in Sect. 4.

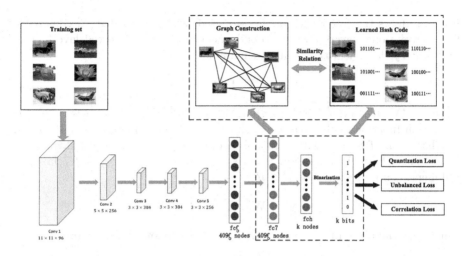

Fig. 1. Deep Graph Laplacian Hashing (DGLH) model with a hash layer *fch*. The *fc7* layer extracts the deep features for the input images, which are also used for graph constructing. We enforce four objectives on the neurons at the top layer of the network to learn compact binary codes: (1) we use graph Laplacian criterion to preserve the adjacency relation of images from the original feature space to the Hamming space, (2) the bits should be uncorrelated, (3) the bits should be balanced, and (4) the quantization loss should be minimized.

2 The Proposed Approach

In this paper, we use bold and uppercase letters, like $\mathbf{X}$, to denote matrices. Bold and lowercase letters, like $\mathbf{x}$, are used to denote vectors. $\mathbf{1}$ and $\mathbf{0}$ are used to denote the vectors with all ones and zeros, respectively. $\mathbf{I}_k$ is used to denote the $k \times k$ identity matrix. Further, the Frobenius norm $\| \cdot \|_F$ is written as $\| \cdot \|$.

2.1 Deep Hashing Model

Given a set of n data points $\mathbf{X} = [\mathbf{x}_1, \mathbf{x}_2, \ldots, \mathbf{x}_n]$ where $\mathbf{x}_i \in R^D$ is the feature vector of the i-th data point, we aim to learn a set of nonlinear hash functions to map the $\mathbf{X}$ into compact k-bit hash codes $\mathbf{H} = [\mathbf{h}_1, \mathbf{h}_2, \ldots, \mathbf{h}_n]$ where $\mathbf{h}_i \in \{-1, 1\}^k$. During the projection, we should preserve the similarity relation among the data points in the Hamming space, which means the similar data points should have the similar hash codes. We denote $\mathbf{S}_{ij}$ as the similarity between $\mathbf{x}_i$ and $\mathbf{x}_j$. So the similarity constraints are preserved as:

$$\mathbf{S}_{ij} < \mathbf{S}_{kl} \Rightarrow D(\mathbf{h}_i, \mathbf{h}_j) < D(\mathbf{h}_k, \mathbf{h}_l), \tag{1}$$

where $D(\mathbf{h}_i, \mathbf{h}_j)$ is the Hamming distance between $\mathbf{h}_i$ and $\mathbf{h}_j$.

In order to simultaneously learn robust feature representation and compact hash codes, we utilize a deep neural network, the AlexNet [6], in this work.

Figure 1 shows the framework of the proposed method. AlexNet [6] consists of five convolutional layers (*conv1–conv5*) and three fully connected layers (*fc6–fc8*). Each *fc* layer learns a nonlinear mapping as follows:

$$\mathbf{f}_i^l = p^l(\mathbf{W}^l \mathbf{f}_i^{l-1} + \mathbf{b}^l), \tag{2}$$

where $\mathbf{f}_i^l$, $\mathbf{W}^l$, $\mathbf{b}^l$, and p^l are the output, the weight and bias parameters and the activation function of the *l*-th layer respectively. To learn compact hash codes, we change the *fc8* layer with a new full-connected layer *fch* of k hidden units to compact the 4096-dimensional representation $\mathbf{f}_i^7 \in R^{4096 \times 1}$ of *fc7* layer to k-dimensional representation $\mathbf{y}_i \in R^k$.

$$\mathbf{y}_i = \mathbf{W}^{fch} \mathbf{f}_i^7 + \mathbf{b}^{fch}. \tag{3}$$

Finally we can obtain the binary code $\mathbf{h}_i \in R^k$ by following function:

$$\mathbf{h}_i = sgn(\mathbf{y}_i), \tag{4}$$

where

$$sgn(i) = \left\{ \begin{array}{l} 1, i > 0 \\ -1, i \leq 0 \end{array} \right. . \tag{5}$$

2.2   Objective Function

In this work, we learn the compact hashing codes by a deep neural network with graph Laplacian constraint. In our method, we use spectral hashing method [22] to map the deep feature extracted from the each training sample $\mathbf{x}_i$ to a binary hash code $\mathbf{h}_i$. Besides, to obtain more robust feature, the learned hash codes should be balanced and uncorrelated. To this end, our objective function is defined as follows:

$$\arg\min_{\mathbf{W},b} \mathbf{C} = \arg\min_{\mathbf{W},b} \{\mathbf{G} + \alpha \mathbf{B} + \beta \mathbf{U}\}. \tag{6}$$

There are three terms in Eq. (6). The first term is used to preserve the similarity among the data points in Hamming space:

$$\mathbf{G} = \sum_{i,j=1}^{n} \|\mathbf{h}_i - \mathbf{h}_j\|^2 \mathbf{S}_{ij}, \tag{7}$$

where $\mathbf{S}_{ij}$ is the similarity matrix. For an image dataset, it could be computed by:

$$\mathbf{S}_{ij} = \exp^{\frac{-\|\mathbf{f}_i^7 - \mathbf{f}_j^7\|^2}{\rho}}. \tag{8}$$

In Eq. (8), $\rho > 0$ is the bandwidth parameter, $\mathbf{f}_i^7$ and $\mathbf{f}_j^7$ are the 4096-dimensional representation extracted from *fc7* layer for $\mathbf{x}_i$ and $\mathbf{x}_j$ respectively.

For similarity, we define the graph Laplacian matrix: $\mathbf{L} = \mathbf{D} - \mathbf{S}$, where $\mathbf{D}$ is the diagonal degree matrix with $\mathbf{D}_{ii} = \sum_j \mathbf{S}_{ij}$. And Eq. (7) could be rewritten as:

$$\mathbf{G} = \sum_{i,j=1}^{n} \|\mathbf{h}_i - \mathbf{h}_j\|^2 \mathbf{S}_{ij} = tr(\mathbf{HLH}^T). \tag{9}$$

The second term in Eq. (6) is to enforce the hash codes to be balanced. According to the information theory, to maximize the information capacity of the hash codes, each bit should have a 50% chance to be 1 or -1. In another words, an ideal hashing code $\mathbf{h}_i$ has $\sum_{i=1}^{n} \mathbf{h}_i = 0$. On the learned hashing matrix H, we define the unbalanced loss as follows:

$$\mathbf{B} = \|\sum_{i=1}^{n} \mathbf{h}_i\|^2 = \|\mathbf{H1}\|^2. \tag{10}$$

Moreover, the hash codes should be uncorrelated and different hashing code is desired to be independent to each other, to minimize the redundancy among the bits.

We use the last term in Eq. (6) to measure the correlation among the hashing codes, which could be defined as:

$$\mathbf{U} = \|\sum_{i=1}^{n} \mathbf{h}_i \mathbf{h}_i^T - n\mathbf{I}_k\|^2 = \|\mathbf{HH}^T - n\mathbf{I}_k\|^2. \tag{11}$$

With $\mathbf{G}$, $\mathbf{B}$ and $\mathbf{U}$, the objective function could be rewritten as:

$$\min_{\mathbf{W},\mathbf{b}} \mathbf{C} = \min_{\mathbf{W},\mathbf{b}} \{\mathbf{G} + \alpha\mathbf{B} + \beta\mathbf{U}\} = tr(\mathbf{HLH}^T) + \alpha\|\mathbf{H1}\|^2 + \beta\|\mathbf{HH}^T - n\mathbf{I}_k\|^2 \tag{12}$$

$$s.t. \quad \mathbf{H} \in \{-1, 1\}^{k \times n},$$

where the $\alpha > 0$ and $\beta > 0$ are the balanced parameters of regularization terms.

Note that the above-mentioned optimization problem defined in Eq. (12) is a discrete optimization problem (NP hard problem) that is hard to solve. To tackle the challenging problem, inspired by [10], we relax Eq. (4) as $\mathbf{h}_i = \mathbf{y}_i$. Then, the discrete optimization problem can be solved by a constraint approach. We reformulate the problem as:

$$\min_{\mathbf{W},\mathbf{b}} \mathbf{C} = tr(\mathbf{YLY}^T) + \alpha\|\mathbf{Y1}\|^2 + \beta\|\mathbf{YY}^T - n\mathbf{I}_k\|^2 + \varphi\|\mathbf{Y} - \mathbf{H}\|^2 \tag{13}$$

$$s.t. \quad \mathbf{H} \in \{-1, 1\}^{k \times n},$$

where $\mathbf{Y} \in R^{k \times n}$ is the output matrix of *fch* layer: $\mathbf{Y} = \{\mathbf{y}_i\}_{i=1}^{n}$, and $\mathbf{y}_i = \mathbf{W}^{fch}\mathbf{f}_i^7 + \mathbf{b}^{fch}$. The last term in Eq. (13) is to minimize the quantization loss, and the parameter $\varphi > 0$ is the regularization parameter.

2.3   Learning

In the DGLH model, we need to learn the parameters of the deep neural network, which could be solved by stochastic gradient descent algorithm. In each iteration we select a mini-batch of images from the training set to optimize the model parameters.

And the derivative of the objective function in Eq. (13) with respect to $\mathbf{Y}$ is computed as:

$$\frac{\partial \mathbf{C}}{\partial Y} = 2\mathbf{YL} + 2\alpha\mathbf{Y}\mathbf{1}\mathbf{1}^T + 4\beta(\mathbf{Y}\mathbf{Y}^T - n\mathbf{I}_k)\mathbf{Y} + 2\varphi(\mathbf{Y} - \mathbf{H}). \qquad (14)$$

Then we can update the parameters $\mathbf{W}^{fch}$, $\mathbf{b}^{fch}$ and the parameters of five convolutional layers (conv1–conv5) and two fully connected layers (fc6–fc7) by back propagation method.

3   Experiments

To evaluate the proposed method, we conduct large-scale similarity search experiments on three benchmark datasets: **CIFAR-10**, **CIFAR-100**, **Flickr-25K**, and compare the proposed DGLH method with five unsupervised hashing methods, including Locality Sensitive Hashing (LSH) [1], Spectral Hashing (SH) [22], Spherical Hashing (SpH) [9], Density Sensitive Hashing (DSH) [11] and PCA-Iterative Quantization (PCA-ITQ) [2].

3.1   Datasets and Setting

The **CIFAR-10** [5] dataset consists of 60000 color images in 10 classes with size of 32×32 (6000 images per class). We randomly select 1000 images (100 images per class) as the query set, and the remaining 59000 images as the database for image retrieval.

The **CIFAR-100** [5] dataset consists of 60000 color images in 100 classes (600 images per class). The size of each image is also 32×32. We randomly select 10000 images (100 images per class) as the query set, and the remaining 50000 images as the database for image retrieval.

The **Flickr-25K** [3] dataset consists of 25000 images collected from Flickr. The dataset are annotated by 24 topics such as bird, sky, night, and people. We randomly select 2000 images as the test query set, and the remaining images as the database for image retrieval. We resize each image in all dataset into 224×224 to feed the proposed neural network.

For DGLH method, we directly use the image pixels as input. For other compared unsupervised hashing methods, we represent each image in 4096-dimensional deep features extracted by the AlexNet [6] with pre-trained model on ImageNet dataset.

We implement the DGLH model based on the MatConvNet [19]. Specifically, we employ the AlexNet architecture [6], and reuse the parameters of convolutional layers $conv1$–$conv5$ and full-connect layers $fc6$–$fc7$ from the pre-trained model on ImageNet dataset, and train the last hashing layer fch from scratch. The bandwidth parameter is set as $\rho = 4$. The two hyper-parameters $\alpha = 0.006$, $\beta = 0.18$. We set $\varphi = 100$ for **CIFAR** dataset, and $\varphi = 1000$ for **Flickr-25K**.

3.2   Experimental Results and Analysis

To evaluate the performance of different hashing methods on image retrieval, we follow [12] to use the mean Average Precision (mAP), precision and recall at top-K positions (Precision@K, Recall@K) as evaluation metrics.

Table 1 shows the mAP results of DGLH and other comparing unsupervised hashing methods on **CIFAR-10**,**CIFAR-100** and **Flickr-25K** when learning 32, 48 and 64 bits hashing codes. Figures 2, 3 and 4 show the results of precision and recall curves with 48 and 64 bits for DGLH and other comparing unsupervised hashing methods on **CIFAR-10**, **CIFAR-100** and **Flickr-25K** respectively. As above experimental results shown, it could be concluded that the proposed DGLH approach outperforms the comparing hashing methods.

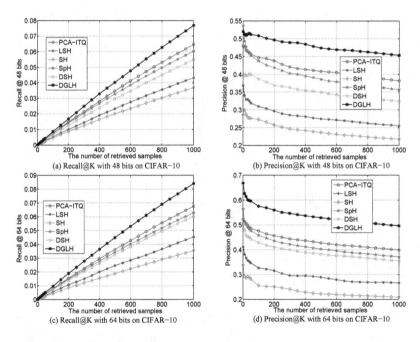

Fig. 2. The results of precision curves and recall curves with 48 and 64 bits hashing on the **CIFAR-10**.

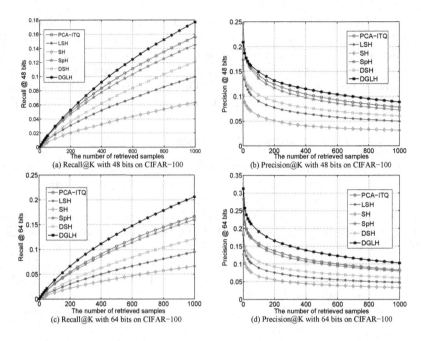

Fig. 3. The results of precision curves and recall curves with 48 and 64 bits hashing on the **CIFAR-100**.

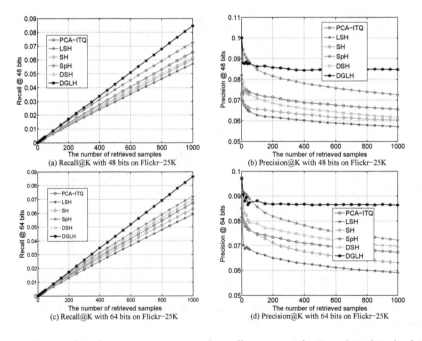

Fig. 4. The results of precision curves and recall curves with 48 and 64 bits hashing on the **Flickr-25K**.

Table 1. mAP comparison results using Hamming ranking on three datasets with different hash bits.

Methods	CIFAR-10			CIFAR-100			Flickr-25K		
	32 bits	48 bits	64 bits	32 bits	48 bits	64 bits	32 bits	48 bits	64 bits
DGLH	**0.2893**	**0.3326**	**0.3407**	**0.0675**	**0.0811**	**0.0968**	**0.0914**	**0.0926**	**0.0950**
LSH	0.1513	0.1759	0.1737	0.0270	0.0376	0.0356	0.0644	0.0673	0.0698
SH	0.1389	0.1501	0.1459	0.0313	0.0250	0.0259	0.0726	0.0696	0.0757
SpH	0.2205	0.2281	0.2357	0.0508	0.0592	0.0668	0.0858	0.0856	0.0857
DSH	0.2311	0.2197	0.2460	0.0395	0.0466	0.0474	0.0684	0.0735	0.0816
PCA-ITQ	0.2541	0.2611	0.2677	0.0589	0.0672	0.0743	0.0743	0.0760	0.0782

4   Conclusion

In this paper, we propose a novel unsupervised deep hashing method for large-scale image retrieval. In this method, unlike most previous unsupervised hashing methods, we design a graph-based deep hashing network to simultaneously learn robust feature representation and compact hashing codes, which preserves the adjacency relation of images without using the label information. When training the model, we relax the discrete optimization problem and reduce quantization loss when learning the hashing code. We also use other two constraints to optimize the binary code learning to make the learned hash codes more effective. The proposed DGLH method is an end-to-end model, which can learn the hashing code from image pixels directly. Experimental results on three image retrieval datasets demonstrate that the DGLH method outperforms other state-of-the-art unsupervised hashing methods.

Acknowledgments. This work was supported in part by the National Natural Science Foundation of China (NSFC) under grants 61472116 and 61502139, in part by Natural Science Foundation of Anhui Province under grants 1608085MF128, and in part by the Open Projects Program of National Laboratory of Pattern Recognition under grant 201600006.

References

1. Andoni, A., Indyk, P.: Near-optimal hashing algorithms for approximate nearest neighbor in high dimensions. Commun. ACM **51**(1), 117–122 (2008)
2. Gong, Y., Lazebnik, S.: Iterative quantization: a procrustean approach to learning binary codes. In: IEEE Conference on Computer Vision and Pattern Recognition, pp. 817–824 (2011)
3. Huiskes, M.J., Lew, M.S.: The MIR Flickr retrieval evaluation. In: ACM International Conference on Multimedia Information Retrieval (2008)
4. Jiang, S., Song, X., Huang, Q.: Relative image similarity learning with contextual information for internet cross-media retrieval. Multimed. Syst. **20**(6), 645–657 (2014)

5. Krizhevsky, A., Hinton, G.: Learning multiple layers of features from tiny images. Technical report, University of Toronto (2009)
6. Krizhevsky, A., Sutskever, I., Hinton, G.E.: Imagenet classification with deep convolutional neural networks. In: Advances in Neural Information Processing Systems, pp. 1097–1105 (2012)
7. Kulis, B., Darrell, T.: Learning to hash with binary reconstructive embeddings. In: Advances in Neural Information Processing Systems, pp. 1042–1050. Curran Associates Inc. (2009)
8. Lai, H., Pan, Y., Liu, Y., Yan, S.: Simultaneous feature learning and hash coding with deep neural networks. CoRR, abs/1504.03410 (2015)
9. Lee, Y.: Spherical hashing. In: IEEE Conference on Computer Vision and Pattern Recognition, pp. 2957–2964 (2012)
10. Li, W., Wang, S., Kang, W.: Feature learning based deep supervised hashing with pairwise labels. CoRR, abs/1511.03855 (2015)
11. Lin, Y., Cai, D., Li, C.: Density sensitive hashing. CoRR, abs/1205.2930 (2012)
12. Liu, H., Ji, R., Wu, Y., Liu, W.: Towards optimal binary code learning via ordinal embedding. In: AAAI Conference on Artificial Intelligence, pp. 1258–1265 (2016)
13. Liu, W., Mu, C., Kumar, S., Chang, S.-F.: Discrete graph hashing. In: Advances in Neural Information Processing Systems, pp. 3419–3427 (2014)
14. Liu, W., Wang, J., Ji, R., Jiang, Y.-G., Chang, S.-F.: Supervised hashing with kernels. In: IEEE Conference on Computer Vision and Pattern Recognition, pp. 2074–2081 (2012)
15. Lowe, D.G.: Distinctive image features from scale-invariant keypoints. Int. J. Comput. Vis. **60**(2), 91–110 (2004)
16. Nie, L., Yan, S., Wang, M., Hong, R., Chua, T.-S.: Harvesting visual concepts for image search with complex queries. In: ACM International Conference on Multimedia, pp. 59–68. ACM (2012)
17. Norouzi, M., Blei, D.M.: Minimal loss hashing for compact binary codes. In: International Conference on Machine Learning, pp. 353–360 (2011)
18. Oliva, A., Torralba, A.: Modeling the shape of the scene: a holistic representation of the spatial envelope. Int. J. Comput. Vis. **42**(3), 145–175 (2001)
19. Vedaldi, A., Lenc, K.: MatConvNet: Convolutional neural networks for MATLAB. In: ACM International Conference on Multimedia, pp. 689–692 (2015)
20. Wang, J., Shen, H.T., Song, J., Ji, J.: Hashing for similarity search: a survey. CoRR, abs/1408.2927 (2014)
21. Wang, S., Jiang, S.: INSTRE: a new benchmark for instance-level object retrieval and recognition. ACM Trans. Multimed. Comput. Commun. Appl. **11**(3), 37 (2015)
22. Weiss, Y., Torralba, A., Fergus, R.: Spectral hashing. In: Advances in Neural Information Processing Systems, pp. 1753–1760 (2009)
23. Xia, R., Pan, Y., Lai, H., Liu, C., Yan, S.: Supervised hashing for image retrieval via image representation learning. In: AAAI Conference on Artificial Intelligence, pp. 2156–2162 (2014)
24. Liu, X., Wang, M., Yin, B.-C., Huet, B., Li, X.: Event-based media enrichment using an adaptive probabilistic hypergraph model. IEEE Trans. Cybern. **45**(11), 2461–2471 (2015)
25. Yan, J., Cho, M., Zha, H., Yang, X., Chu, S.M.: Multi-graph matching via affinity optimization with graduated consistency regularization. IEEE Trans. Pattern Anal. Mach. Intell. **38**(6), 1228–1242 (2016)
26. Yan, J., Yin, X.-C., Lin, W., Deng, C., Zha, H., Yang, X.: A short survey of recent advances in graph matching. In: ACM on International Conference on Multimedia Retrieval, pp. 167–174. ACM (2016)

27. Zhang, H., Shen, F., Liu, W., He, X., Luan, H., Chua, T.-S.: Discrete collaborative filtering. In: International ACM SIGIR Conference on Research and Development in Information Retrieval, pp. 325–334 (2016)
28. Zhu, H., Long, M., Wang, J., Cao, Y.: Deep hashing network for efficient similarity retrieval. In: AAAI Conference on Artificial Intelligence, pp. 2415–2421 (2016)

Deep Video Dehazing

Wenqi Ren⬤ and Xiaochun Cao$^{(\boxtimes)}$

State Key Laboratory of Information Security (SKLOIS), Institute of Information
Engineering, Chinese Academy of Sciences, Beijing 100093, China
{renwenqi,caoxiaochun}@iie.ac.cn

Abstract. Haze is a major problem in videos captured in outdoors.
Unlike single-image dehazing, video-based approaches can take advantage of the abundant information that exists across neighboring frames.
In this work, assuming that a scene point yields highly correlated transmission values between adjacent video frames, we develop a deep learning
solution for video dehazing, where a CNN is trained end-to-end to learn
how to accumulate information across frames for transmission estimation. The estimated transmission map is subsequently used to recover
a haze-free frame via atmospheric scattering model. To train this network, we generate a dataset consisted of synthetic hazy and haze-free
videos for supervision based on the NYU depth dataset. We show that
the features learned from this dataset are capable of removing haze that
arises in outdoor scene in a wide range of videos. Extensive experiments
demonstrate that the proposed algorithm performs favorably against the
state-of-the-art methods on both synthetic and real-world videos.

Keywords: Video dehazing · Defogging · Transmission map
Convolutional Neural Network

1 Introduction

Outdoor images and videos often suffer from limited visibility due to haze, fog,
smoke and other small particles in the air that scatter the light in the atmosphere.
Haze has two effects on the captured videos: it attenuates the signal of the
viewed scene, and it introduces an additive component to the image, termed the
atmospheric light (the color of a scene point at infinity). The image degradation
caused by haze increases with the distance from the camera, since the scene
radiance decreases and the atmospheric light magnitude increases. Thus, a single
hazy image or frame can be modeled as a per-pixel combination of a haze-free
image, scene transmission map and the global atmospheric light as follow [1],

$$\boldsymbol{I}(x) = \boldsymbol{J}(x)t(x) + \boldsymbol{A}(1 - t(x)), \tag{1}$$

where $\boldsymbol{I}(x)$ and $\boldsymbol{J}(x)$ are the observed hazy image and the clear scene radiance,
$\boldsymbol{A}$ is the global atmospheric light, and $t(x)$ is the scene transmission describing
the portion of light that is not scattered and reaches the camera sensors.

© Springer International Publishing AG, part of Springer Nature 2018
B. Zeng et al. (Eds.): PCM 2017, LNCS 10735, pp. 14–24, 2018.
https://doi.org/10.1007/978-3-319-77380-3_2

Our goal is to recover the haze-free frames and the corresponding transmission maps. This is an ill-posed problem that has an under-determined system [2,3] of three equations and at least four unknowns per pixel, with inherent ambiguity between haze and object radiance [4]. To handle this highly under-constrained problem, some previous works use additional information such as more images, while others assumed an image prior to solve the problem from a single image.

The most successful video dehazing approaches use information from neighboring frames to estimate transmission maps from the input video [5], taking advantage of a hazy video is temporally coherent and thus the transmission values of an object are similar between adjacent image frames. Based on this assumption, one can design the temporal coherence constraint and add it to the loss costs. Then, the optimal transmission values for each frame can be obtained by minimizing the overall cost [5]. Previous work [6] has shown significant improvement over traditional single image based dehazing approaches. One of the main challenges associated with aggregating information across multiple frames in previous work is that the differently hazy frames must be aligned. This can be done by using optical flow [7]. However, warping-based alignment is not robust around dis-occlusions and areas with low texture, and often yields warping artifacts. In addition to the alignment computation cost, methods that rely on warping have to therefore disregard information from mis-aligned content or warping artifacts, which can be hard by looking at local image patches alone.

To this end, we present the first end-to-end data driven approach to video dehazing, the results of which can be seen in Sect. 5. We train specifically hazy videos synthesized by the NYU depth dataset [8] that comprised of indoor images, however we show that our dehazing method extends to outdoor hazy videos as well. In addition, we show good dehazing results without any alignment at all. Our main contribution is an end-to-end solution to train a deep neural network to learn how to dehaze videos via a short stack of neighboring video frames. To train the deep network, we create a hazy video dataset using the image sequence and the corresponding depth map from the NYU depth dataset [8]. We compare qualitatively to real videos previously used for video dehazing, and quantitatively with synthesized dataset with ground truth.

2   Related Work

There exist two main approaches for dehazing: clear image priors based methods, and approaches that rely on multi-image aggregation or fusion.

Dehaze using priors: Most existing single-image dehazing approaches [1,2,9,11] jointly estimate a transmission map and the underlying haze-free image via designing clear image priors. For example, Fattal [10] proposes a refined image formation model for surface shading and scene transmission estimation. Based on this model, the scene transmission can be inferred. He et al. [1] propose a single image dehazing method based on the statistical observation of the dark channel, which allows a rough estimation of the transmission map. Then, they use the expensive matting strategy to refine the final transmission map. Zhu et al. [11] find that the difference between brightness and saturation in a clear image should be very small. Therefore, they propose a new color attenuation prior based on this observation for haze removal from a single input hazy image. Recently, Berman et al. [4] introduce a non-local method for single image dehazing. This approach is based on the assumption that an image can be faithfully represented with just a few hundreds of distinct colors.

All of the above approaches strongly rely on the accuracy of the assumed image priors, thus may perform poorly when the hand-crafted priors are insufficient to describe real data. As a result, these approaches tend to be more fragile than aggregation-based methods [12], and often introduce undesirable artifacts such as amplified noises.

Multi-image aggregation: Multi-image aggregation methods directly combine multiple images in either spatial or other domains (e.g., chromatic, luminance and saliency) without solving any inverse problem. Most existing works merge multiple low quality images into the final result [5,12]. Kim et al. [5] assume that a scene point yields highly correlated transmission values between adjacent image frames, then add the temporal coherence cost to the contrast cost and the truncation loss cost to define the overall cost function. However, the pixel-level processing increases the computational complexity, therefore, may not be suitable for handling videos. Zhang et al. [13] first dehaze videos frame by frame, and then use optical flow to improve the temporal coherence based on Markov Random Field (MRF). Ancuti et al. [12] derive two different inputs (a white balanced image and a contrast enhanced image) from the original hazy image, and then filter their important features by computing three measures.

All the above approaches have explicit formulations on how to fuse multiple images. In this work, we instead adopt a data-driven approach to learn how multiple images should be aggregated to generate a transmission map.

Data-driven approaches: Recently, CNNs have been applied to achieve leading results on a wide variety of reconstruction problems. These methods tend to work best when large training datasets are easily constructed. Such as image denoising [14] and image deblurring [7]. However, these approaches address a different problem, with its own set of challenges. In this work we focus on video dehazing, where neighboring hazy frames can provide abundant information for transmission map estimation.

CNNs have also been used for single image dehazing based on synthetic training data [15,16]. Ren et al. [15] propose a multi-scale CNN for transmission map estimation. Cai et al. [16] present an end-to-end system for single image dehazing. However, these algorithms focus on static image dehazing, and may yield flickering artifacts due to the lack of temporal coherence when applied to video dehazing. In our experiments, we show that multi frame transmission maps can be directly estimated by leveraging multiple video frames and our proposed deep network.

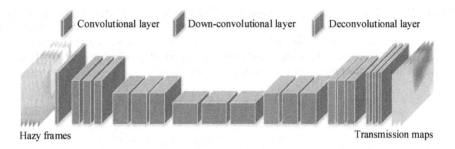

Fig. 1. Our proposed VDHNet. Proposed encoder-decoder style architecture that takes in five consecutive hazy frames stack and produces central three transmission maps. The depth of each block represents the number of features after convolution.

3   Our Method

In this section, we train an end-to-end system for video dehazing, where the input is a stack of five neighboring frames and the output are the estimated transmission maps of central three frames in the stack. The estimated transmission maps are subsequently used to recover a haze-free video via atmospheric scattering model. We do not use any alignment algorithm since the warp errors will dominate the final performance of the restoration procedure [7]. In the following, we first present our neural network architecture, and then describe a number of experiments for evaluating its effectiveness and comparing with existing dehazing methods [1,9,16,17]. The key advantage of our method is the allowance of lessening the requirements for accurate alignment, a fragile component of prior work, but implicitly enforces the temporal coherence of estimated transmission maps of neighboring frames.

3.1   Network Architecture

We use an encoder-decoder style network, which have been shown to produce good results for a number of generative tasks [7]. To keep the temporal coherence of neighboring transmission maps, We perform an early fusion of neighboring hazy frames by concatenating five consecutive images in the input layer. The output of the network is the central three transmission maps of the neighboring five hazy frames. The training loss is MSE to the synthetic ground truth transmission maps as

$$L(t_i(x), t_i^*(x)) = \frac{1}{pq} \sum_{v=1}^{p} \sum_{f=1}^{q} ||t_i(x) - t_i^*(x)||^2, \tag{2}$$

where f is the frame index and v denotes the video index, p and q is the number of training videos and frames in each video, respectively. We refer to this network as VideoDehazeNet, or VDHNet, and show a diagram of it in Fig. 1. It consists of three types of layers: down-convolutional layers, that compress the

Table 1. Specifications of the proposed VDHNet model. After each convolutional and deconvolutional layer, except the last one, there is a rectified linear unit. We pad all convolutional layers with zeros such that the output size is the same as the input size when using a stride of 1. All output sizes refer the original image width W and height H, as the model can process images of any resolution.

Layer	Kernel size	Stride	Output size
Input	–	–	$15 \times H \times W$
Conv 0	5×5	1×1	$32 \times H \times W$
Down conv 1	3×3	2×2	$64 \times H/2 \times W/2$
Conv 1-1	3×3	1×1	$64 \times H/2 \times W/2$
Conv 1-2	3×3	1×1	$64 \times H/2 \times W/2$
Down conv 2	3×3	2×2	$128 \times H/2 \times W/2$
Conv 2-1	3×3	1×1	$128 \times H/4 \times W/4$
Conv 2-2	3×3	1×1	$128 \times H/4 \times W/4$
Down conv 3	3×3	2×2	$256 \times H/8 \times W/8$
Conv 3-1	3×3	1×1	$256 \times H/8 \times W/8$
Conv 3-2	3×3	1×1	$256 \times H/8 \times W/8$
Up conv 1	4×4	$1/2 \times 1/2$	$128 \times H/4 \times W/4$
Conv 4-1	3×3	1×1	$128 \times H/4 \times W/4$
Conv 4-2	3×3	1×1	$128 \times H/4 \times W/4$
Up conv 2	4×4	$1/2 \times 1/2$	$64 \times H/2 \times W/2$
Conv 5-1	3×3	1×1	$64 \times H/2 \times W/2$
Conv 5-2	3×3	1×1	$64 \times H/2 \times W/2$
Up conv 3	4×4	$1/2 \times 1/2$	$32 \times H \times W$
Conv 6-1	3×3	1×1	$32 \times H \times W$
Conv 6-2	3×3	1×1	$32 \times H \times W$
Output	–	–	$3 \times H \times W$

spatial resolution of the features while increasing the spatial support of subsequent layers; the deconvolutional layers, that increase the spatial resolution; and convolutional layers. We use convolutions after both down-convolutional and deconvolution layers to further sharpen the activation results. Please refer to Table 1 for detailed configurations of the layers.

With the designed VDHNet, we estimate transmission maps directly from input hazy frames. After estimating the transmission maps for the inputed video frames, we use the method in [9] to compute atmospheric light and recover final dehazed frames based on the atmospheric scattering model (1).

Fig. 2. Synthetic hazy videos for training. The top row is the haze-free frames of two videos from NYU Depth dataset [8], and the bottom two rows are our synthetic hazy frames with different haze thickness.

3.2 Implementation Details

During training we use a batch size of 10, and patch size of $15 \times 256 \times 256$, where 15 is the total number of RGB channels stacked from the crops of 5 consecutive video frames. We observed that a patch size of 256 was sufficient to provide enough overlapping content in the stack even if the frames are not aligned, which has also been reported in [7]. We use ADAM for optimization, and initialize the learning rate as 0.001 and halve it every 10,000 iterations. For all the results reported in the paper we train the network for 50,000 iterations, which takes about 40 h on a NVidia K20 GPU. Default values of β_1 and β_2 are used, which are 0.9 and 0.999 respectively, and we set weight decay to 0.00001. Since our approach dehazes frames in a single forward pass, it is computationally very efficient. Using a NVidia K20 GPU, we can process three 640×480 frames within 0.2 s. Previous approaches took on average 26 s [1] and 3 s [9] per frame on CPUs. The recent video dehazing method [17] takes more than 100 s for each frame.

4   Training Dataset

Generating realistic training data is a major challenge for video dehazing task in which ground truth data cannot be easily collected. To train our deep network, we generate a dataset with synthesized hazy videos and their corresponding transmission maps and haze-free videos. The NYU Depth dataset [8] contains 587 video clips and corresponding depth values. We randomly sample 100 clean video clips and the corresponding depth maps to construct the training set. Given a clear frame $J(x)$ and the ground truth depth $d(x)$, we synthesize a hazy image using the physical model (1). We generate the random atmospheric light $A = [k, k, k]$, where $k \in [0.8 \ 1.0]$. We synthesize transmission map for each frame based on the ground truth depth map $d(x)$,

$$t(x) = e^{-\beta d(x)}. \tag{3}$$

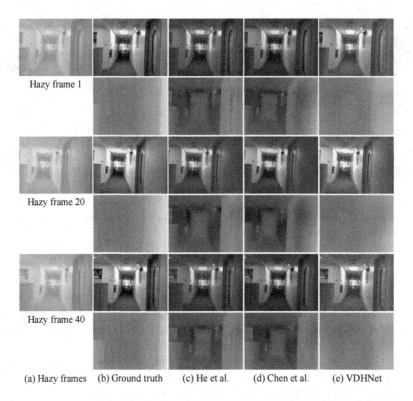

(a) Hazy frames   (b) Ground truth   (c) He et al.   (d) Chen et al.   (e) VDHNet

Fig. 3. Dehazed results (odd rows) and estimated transmission maps (even rows) on our synthetic videos. Both single image dehazing method [1] and the recent video dehazing method [17] tend to over-estimate haze concentration and result in dark results. In contrast, our approach performs better than the state-of-the-art methods.

Table 2. Average PSNR and SSIM of dehazed results on the 20 synthetic videos.

	He et al. [1]	Chen et al. [15]	Our VDHNet
PSNR	19.79	20.28	**22.32**
SSIM	0.67	0.66	**0.83**

Mathematically, β and depth $d(x)$ in (3) have equal effects on the generated transmission map. We sample four random $\beta \in [0.5\ 1.5]$ in (3) for every video clip. Therefore, we have 400 hazy videos and the corresponding haze-free videos (100 videos $\times$ 4 medium extinction coefficients β) in the training set. Examples of the dataset are shown in Fig. 2.

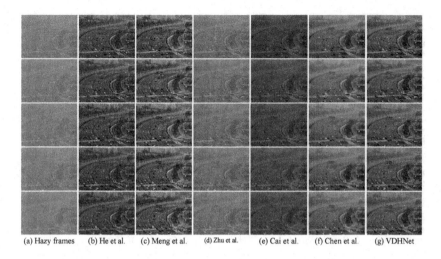

(a) Hazy frames   (b) He et al.   (c) Meng et al.   (d) Zhu et al.   (e) Cai et al.   (f) Chen et al.   (g) VDHNet

Fig. 4. Dehazed results on *crossroad* video.

5   Experimental Results

In this section, we conduct a series of experiments to evaluate the effectiveness of the learned model.

5.1   Quantitative Evaluation

In this section, we compare our proposed VDHNet with the state-of-the-art single image dehazing method [1] and the recent video dehazing method [17]. For quantitative performance evaluation, we construct a new testing hazy video dataset. We select 20 video clips and their depth maps from the NYU Depth dataset [8] (different from those that used for training) to synthesize 20 transmission map sequence and corresponding hazy videos.

Figure 3 shows some dehazed frames by different methods. The estimated transmission maps by He et al. [1] are overestimated in some slight hazy regions. Therefore, the dehazed results tend to be darker than the ground truth images in some regions, e.g., the ceiling in Fig. 3(c). We note that the dehazed results in Fig. 3(d) by the video dehazing method [17] are similar to those by He et al. [1] in Fig. 3(c) since the method [17] also use the dark channel prior. The final dehazed frames are darker then the ground truth in Fig. 3(b). Figure 3(e) shows the estimated transmission maps and the final recovered images by the proposed VDHNet. Overall, the dehazed results by the proposed algorithm have higher visual quality and less color distortions. The qualitative results are also reflected by the quantitative PSNR and SSIM metrics shown in Table 2.

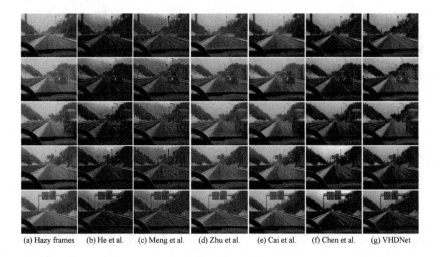

(a) Hazy frames   (b) He et al.   (c) Meng et al.   (d) Zhu et al.   (e) Cai et al.   (f) Chen et al.   (g) VHDNet

Fig. 5. Dehazed results on *highway* video.

5.2   Real Videos

Although our proposed VDHNet is trained on synthetic indoor videos, we note that it can be applied for outdoor images as well since we could increase the haze concentration by adjusting the value of the medium extinction coefficient β in (3). Therefore, our synthesized transmission maps cover the range of values in real transmission maps as illustrated in [15].

We evaluate the proposed algorithm against the state-of-the-art image and video dehazing methods [1,9,11,16,17] using challenging real videos as shown in Figs. 4 and 5. In Figs. 4 and 5, the dehazed frames by He et al. [1] are too dark since this method tends to overestimate transmission maps as mentioned in Sect. 5.1. The dehazed frames by Meng et al. [9] have significant color distortions and miss most details as shown in Figs. 4 and 5(c), especially the distant road. The dehazing methods of Zhu et al. [11] and Cai et al. [16] tend to under-estimate the thickness of the haze. Thus, the dehazed videos still have some remaining haze as shown in Figs. 4 and 5(d) and (e). The method by Chen et al. [17] can enhance the image visibility. However, the dehazed results are over-smoothed and much fine details in the recovered images are removed. For example, the *distant buildings* are over smoothed. In contrast, the dehazed results by the proposed VDHNet in Figs. 4 and 5(g) are visually more pleasing in dense haze regions without color distortions or artifacts.

6   Conclusions

In this paper, we proposed a novel deep learning approach for video dehazing in an encoder-decoder style. We show that the temporal coherence of consecutive transmission maps can be automatically learned in a trainable end-to-end system without special design. Our method generates results that are as good as or superior to the state-of-the-art dehazing approaches, without parameter tuning or the requirement of challenging image alignment.

Although we successfully applied the VHDNet for consecutive transmission maps estimation, we still use the traditional method for computing atmospheric light. Therefore, we can design a network for estimate transmission and atmospheric light in a unified network in future.

Acknowledgments. This work is supported by the National Key R&D Program of China (Grant No. 2016YFB0800603), National Natural Science Foundation of China (No. 61422213, U1605252), Beijing Natural Science Foundation (4172068).

References

1. He, K., Sun, J., Tang, X.: Single image haze removal using dark channel prior. In: IEEE Conference on Computer Vision and Pattern Recognition, pp. 1956–1963. IEEE Press (2009)
2. Li, N., Liu, Z., Lei, J., Song, M., Bu, J.: Automatic color image enhancement using double channels. In: Chen, E., Gong, Y., Tie, Y. (eds.) PCM 2016. LNCS, vol. 9917, pp. 74–83. Springer, Cham (2016). https://doi.org/10.1007/978-3-319-48896-7_8
3. Ren, W., Cao, X., Pan, J., Guo, X., Zuo, W., Yang, M.-H.: Image deblurring via enhanced low-rank prior. IEEE Trans. Image Process. **25**(7), 3426–3437 (2017)
4. Berman, D., Treibitz, T., Avidan, S.: Non-local image dehazing. In: IEEE Conference on Computer Vision and Pattern Recognition, pp. 1674–168. IEEE Press (2016)
5. Kim, J.-H., Jang, W.-D., Park, Y., Lee, D.-H., Sim, J.-Y., Kim, C.-S.: Temporally x real-time video dehazing. In: 19th IEEE International Conference on Image Processing, pp. 969–972. IEEE Press (2012)
6. Lv, X., Chen, W., Shen, I.: Real-time dehazing for image and video. In: 18th Pacific Conference on Computer Graphics and Applications, pp. 62–69. IEEE Press (2010)
7. Su, S., Delbracio, M., Wang, J., Sapiro, G., Heidrich W., Wang O.: Deep video deblurring. In: IEEE Conference on Computer Vision and Pattern Recognition. IEEE Press (2017)
8. Silberman, N., Hoiem, D., Kohli, P., Fergus, R.: Indoor segmentation and support inference from RGBD images. In: Fitzgibbon, A., Lazebnik, S., Perona, P., Sato, Y., Schmid, C. (eds.) ECCV 2012. LNCS, vol. 7576, pp. 746–760. Springer, Heidelberg (2012). https://doi.org/10.1007/978-3-642-33715-4_54
9. Meng, G., Wang, Y., Duan, J., Xiang, S., Pan C.: Efficient image dehazing with boundary constraint and contextual. In: IEEE International Conference on Computer Vision, pp. 617–624. IEEE Press (2013)
10. Fattal, R.: Single image dehazing. ACM Trans. Graph. **27**(3), 72 (2008)
11. Zhu, Q., Mai, J., Shao, L.: A fast single image haze removal algorithm using color attenuation prior. IEEE Trans. Image Process. **24**(11), 3522–3533 (2015)
12. Ancuti, C.O., Ancuti, C.: Single image dehazing by multi-scale fusion. IEEE Trans. Image Process. **22**(8), 3271–3282 (2013)
13. Zhang, J., Li, L., Zhang, Y., Yang, G., Cao, X., Sun, J.: Video dehazing with spatial and temporal coherence. Vis. Comput. **27**(6), 749–757 (2011)

14. Zhang, K., Zuo, W., Chen, Y., Meng, D., Zhang, L.: Beyond a Gaussian denoiser: residual learning of deep CNN for image denoising. IEEE Trans. Image Process. **26**(7), 3142–3155 (2017)
15. Ren, W., Liu, S., Zhang, H., Pan, J., Cao, X., Yang, M.-H.: Single image dehazing via multi-scale convolutional neural networks. In: Leibe, B., Matas, J., Sebe, N., Welling, M. (eds.) ECCV 2016. LNCS, vol. 9906, pp. 154–169. Springer, Cham (2016). https://doi.org/10.1007/978-3-319-46475-6_10
16. Cai, B., Xu, X., Jia, K., Qing, C., Tao, D.: DehazeNet: an end-to-end system for single image haze removal. IEEE Trans. Image Process. **25**(11), 5187–5198 (2016)
17. Chen, C., Do, M.N., Wang, J.: Robust image and video dehazing with visual artifact suppression via gradient residual minimization. In: Leibe, B., Matas, J., Sebe, N., Welling, M. (eds.) ECCV 2016. LNCS, vol. 9906, pp. 576–591. Springer, Cham (2016). https://doi.org/10.1007/978-3-319-46475-6_36

Image Tagging by Joint Deep Visual-Semantic Propagation

Yuexin Ma[1(✉)], Xinge Zhu[2], Yujing Sun[1], and Bingzheng Yan[3]

[1] University of Hong Kong, Hong Kong, China
{yxma,yjsun}@cs.hku.hk
[2] University of Chinese Academy of Sciences, Beijing, China
zhuxinge15@mails.ucas.ac.cn
[3] National University of Defense Technology, Changsha, China
bingzhengyan93@gmail.com

Abstract. Image tagging has attracted much research interest due to its wide applications. Many existing methods have gained impressive results, however, they have two main limitations: (1) only focus on tagging images, but ignore the tags' influences on visual feature modeling. (2) model the tag correlation without considering visual contents of image. In this paper, we propose a joint visual-semantic propagation model (JVSP) to address these two issues. First, we leverage a joint visual-semantic modeling to harvest integrated features which can accurately reflect the relationship between tags and image regions. Second, we introduce a visual-guided LSTM to capture the co-occurrence relation of the tags. Third, we also design a diversity loss to enforce that our model learns to focus on different regions. Experimental results on three challenging datasets demonstrate that our proposed method leads to significant performance gains over existing methods.

Keywords: Image tagging · CNN-LSTM · Visual-semantic

1 Introduction

Automatic image tagging aims to associate images with appropriate tags which reflect visual contents in the image. The problem is difficult because every real-world image usually contains multiple labels and has intricately spatial layout. Since the scale of visual data is growing fast and manually tagging images is expensive and time-consuming, there is a huge demand for image tagging.

Every tag is closely related to specific region of image. Modeling the connection between the tag and corresponding image region plays an important role in image tagging. Existing methods that model the relationship between images and tags can be roughly divided into parametric and non-parametric methods. One of the most popular parametric methods is the generative model [1], which is usually dedicated to maximize generative likelihood of image features and tags. On the other hand, many non-parametric nearest neighbor models [13] have been

© Springer International Publishing AG, part of Springer Nature 2018
B. Zeng et al. (Eds.): PCM 2017, LNCS 10735, pp. 25–35, 2018.
https://doi.org/10.1007/978-3-319-77380-3_3

proposed. They transfer tags from nearest neighbor images to the query image based on the assumption that visually similar images are more likely to share common labels. However, most existing approaches leave the tag information in the input feature space untouched and ignore the tags' influences on visual feature modeling. They are not rich enough to mine the complicated relationships between local image regions and tags. Moreover, different regions of the image have different weights with respect to different tags. Without considering tags' effect, these methods giving whole image the same weights are hard to recognize some objects, especially some small objects.

There is an observation that the tags associated with natural images do not appear in isolation, they appear correlatively and interact with each other. We refer it as tag correlation. For instance, the probability of an image being labeled with "sea" would be high if the image has been annotated with "boat" and "island". Instead of simply learning independent binary classifiers for each tag, many methods try to exploit tag correlation for improving tagging performance. These methods consider the tag correlation as additional information, which can be learned via sparse learning [1], graphical model [11], or dictionary learning [14]. However, two main drawbacks of these models mining the tag correlation need to be concerned. First, they explore the tag correlation in semantic level without considering visual contents of image. This manner causes the tag correlation less flexible when recognizing particular image, and has a negative effect if there exists remarkable tag correlation discrepancy between the training and test sets. Second, due to huge computational complexity, most methods only model the pairwise tag correlation rather than long range correlation among tags. It can not be able to well capture the intricate tag correlation.

Inspired by the great success from convolutional neural network (CNN) in image classification [5], many methods try to extend the CNN to multi-label image tagging [7]. In addition, recurrent neural networks have proven to be able to model the long range temporal dependencies [17]. Therefore, recent works [8] try to employ the RNN to model tag correlation for multi-label problem. However, these methods also suffer from aforementioned problems, including leaving the relationship between tags and visual features untouched in the input feature space and ignoring the effects of visual contents in the image during tag correlation exploitation.

In this paper, we propose a joint visual-semantic propagation (JVSP) model to address the foregoing problems. First, to sufficiently exploit the tag information in the input feature space, we introduce a joint visual-semantic modeling to explore the tag representation and visual features, and make them benefit from each other in a collaborative way. There are two steps in this process: (1) we incorporate the tag embedding into image features to obtain the integrated visual features, which characterize the relationship between tag and corresponding image region. (2) based on step one, we in turn refine the tag representation by fusing the integrated visual features into tag embedding. The refined tag representation will be less ambiguous and have a stronger connection with visual content of the image. Second, we introduce a visual-guided LSTM to model the tag correlation. Unlike previous methods that model tag correlation without considering image contents, we leverage the integrated visual features as an instruction, and feed it into LSTM with refined tag representation together to capture the complex correlation among tags. Third, we design a diversity loss to enforce the proposed model concentrates on different image regions for extracting more discriminative features with respect to different labels. Finally, in this way, we cast the image tagging task into a visual-semantic propagation problem. Based on corresponding image regions and tag relation, we can propagate multiple tags by the visual-guided LSTM in an iterative way. We conduct extensive experiments on three large-scale datasets, showing that JVSP consistently outperforms the existing methods.

2 Proposed Method

We show an example pipeline of the proposed model in Fig. 1. As shown in Fig. 1, the overall architecture of the model consists of three components: feature extraction, joint visual-semantic modeling, and tag propagation.

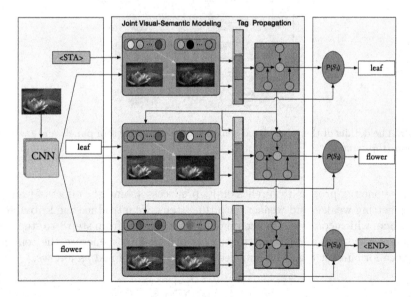

Fig. 1. Schematic of the proposed model. We unfold a complete tag propagation procedure of a two-label image to get three steps. As the pipeline shows, our model first extracts the image features from CNN and computes the tag embedding, then the joint visual-semantic modeling explores and integrates both of them. Finally, the visual-guided LSTM is applied to model the tag correlation and perform the tag propagation. In this way, we build an automatic framework to propagate tags in an iterative manner.

2.1   Joint Visual-Semantic Modeling

To overcome the issue existing in most previous methods: ignoring the effect of tags on image feature representation, we introduce the joint visual-semantic modeling. Figure 2 describes the detailed structure of the joint visual-semantic modeling and tag propagation module. At time step t, a tag k is represented as a one-hot vector e_k. There are two different tag embedding matrices, U_l and U_f. Tag embeddings can be obtained by multiplying these two tag embedding matrices.

$$w_k = U_l e_k, w_f = U_f e_k \tag{1}$$

where w_k is used as the semantic guidance and w_f is applied to form the refined tag representation.

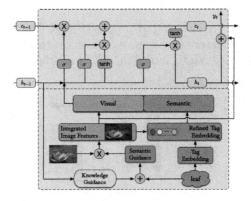

Fig. 2. The details of the joint visual-semantic modeling (bottom panel) and tag propagation (top panel).

Since one tag propagation relies on its predecessors and the effect of previous tags is getting weaker and weaker with time steps, we introduce the **knowledge guidance**, which consists of preceding hidden states h_i (from step 1 to step $t-1$) to enhance the role of previous tags. It is beneficial to generate the semantic guidance for current tag. The knowledge guidance is defined as follows:

$$K_t = \frac{1}{t-1}(W_h \sum_{i=1}^{t-1} \lambda_i h_i) \tag{2}$$

where λ_i is the maximum tag probability at time step i. Learnable matrix W_h is used to embed the knowledge guidance into the same vector space as w_k. We then obtain the **semantic guidance vector** g_t:

$$g_t = w_k + K_t \tag{3}$$

We regard the semantic guidance as a weighted mask, and then earn the integrated image features by following function:

$$V_t = \Phi(C(I) \odot g_t) \tag{4}$$

where V_t is the integrated image features at time step t, and $C(I)$ is the original image features extracted from CNN. $\odot$ represents the element-wise multiplication, and $\Phi(\cdot)$ denotes a non-linear transfer function, $i.e.$, Softmax, which is chosen based on cross-validation. As shown in Fig. 2, the integrated image features have high activations on specific regions of image under the semantic guidance.

After generating integrated image features, we in turn utilize it to refine the tag embedding. The operation can be expressed in the following steps:

$$\hat{g}_t = W_{gt}^T \tanh(w_f + U_{ig}V_t) \tag{5}$$

$$T_t = \Phi(w_f \odot \hat{g}_t) \tag{6}$$

where U_{ig} and W_{gt} are learnable weight matrices. V_t is the integrated image features obtained from Eq. 4. Furthermore, V_t is a visual guidance to refine the tag embedding. For a label of multiple senses, $e.g.$, "mouse", the direct tag embedding will always project it into same vector regardless of its senses in the image. In contrast, V_t can guide the tag embedding with its real senses in the image because of the differences in visual features. Thus, we get the weighted vector $\hat{g}_t$ by incorporating the integrated image features. We also apply dropout on $U_{ig}V_t$ in the training phase to overcome overfitting problem. Then we compute the refined tag representation T_t according to Eq. 6.

Finally, we combine the integrated image features and refined tag representation into a feature concatenation.

$$X_t = [V_t, T_t] \tag{7}$$

where $[\cdot]$ is the concatenation operation on two vectors.

2.2 Tag Propagation by Visual-Guided LSTM

Unlike the normal LSTM which only takes the text representation as the input, we introduce a visual-guided LSTM, which accepts the integrated image features as the guidance in both the input and output space to instruct the tag propagation. [17] points out that as the time step continues, the generation result of LSTM becomes "blind", for the reason that the role of image representation, which is only fed once at the beginning, becomes weaker and weaker. To figure out this problem, they extend the LSTM with semantic information which is a global guidance and does not change with time step. In our model, we employ the integrated image features as the visual guidance and feed it into LSTM at each time step. More importantly, the visual guidance is different from the global guidance mentioned above because it is relevant to current tag which is varying with time step.

The visual-guided LSTM neuron in our implementation is illustrated in the top panel of Fig. 2. The interaction between states and gates is defined as follows:

$$
\begin{aligned}
i_t &= \sigma(W_{iv}V_t + W_{it}T_t + W_{ih}h_{t-1}) \\
f_t &= \sigma(W_{fv}V_t + W_{ft}T_t + W_{fh}h_{t-1}) \\
o_t &= \sigma(W_{ov}V_t + W_{ot}T_t + W_{oh}h_{t-1}) \\
c_t &= f_t \odot c_{t-1} + i_t \odot \delta(W_{cv}V_t \\
&\quad + W_{ct}T_t + W_{ch}h_{t-1}) \\
h_t &= o_t \odot \delta(c_t)
\end{aligned}
\tag{8}
$$

where i_t stands for the input gate, f_t for the forget gate, o_t for the output gate. c_t denotes the state of the memory cell and h_t encodes the hidden state. All these variables are the key points to learn long-term correlation. $\sigma(\cdot)$ represents the sigmoid function and $\delta(\cdot)$ denotes the hyperbolic tangent function. $W_{[\cdot]}$ stand for the learnable weight matrices. The visual guidance V_t is the integrated image features, and T_t is the refined tag representation. Both of them are obtained from Eq. 7.

The visual-guided LSTM generates label scores based on the hidden state h_t and visual guidance V_t. As the visual guidance is capable of describing the high-level visual concepts from specific regions, it is conducive to the tag prediction.

$$
y_t = W_s^T(h_t + V_t)
\tag{9}
$$

where y_t represents the score vector of labels at time step t and W_s is a projection matrix. The predicted tag probability can be computed using the Softmax on the score y_t.

2.3   Diversity Loss

To make the focused region vary with time steps, we propose the diversity loss to compute the correlation between neighboring integrated image features:

$$
\mathcal{L}_V = \frac{1}{T-1}\sum_{t=2}^{T}\sum_{i=1}^{M} V_{t-1,i} \cdot V_{t,i}
\tag{10}
$$

$$
s.t. \quad V_{[\cdot,\cdot]} \geq \beta
$$

where $V_{t,i}$ is the i-th value of the integrated image features at time step t. T denotes the total number of time steps and M represents the length of integrated image features. β is a given threshold. Values larger than β can be regarded as high activation. In general, $\mathcal{L}_V$ will get a large value if the focused regions between two temporally adjacent image features are similar. We then apply the negative log probability as the classification loss. The final loss function is obtained by combining both of them:

$$
L = \frac{1}{T}\sum_{t=1}^{T} -\log\frac{\exp(\hat{y}_t)}{\sum_{j=1}^{\phi}\exp(y_t^j)} + \alpha\mathcal{L}_V
\tag{11}
$$

where y_t follows Eq. (9) and the formulation of $\mathcal{L}_V$ follows Eq. (10). $\hat{y}_t$ is the score of the predicted tag at time step t. ϕ is the size of label vocabulary. α is a constant weighting factor.

3 Experiments

We evaluate our proposed model on three widely used datasets for image tagging: ESP Game dataset [16], NUS-WIDE dataset [6] and MS-COCO dataset [15].

For fairness of comparison, we follow previous work [13] to evaluate methods. The precision (P) and recall (R) of all labels are applied as evaluation metrics. Based on these two measures, we also compute the F1-score $F1 = 2*P*R/(P+R)$, which takes care of the trade-off between precision and recall. Additionally, the number of tags with non-zero recall value ($N+$) and the mean average precision (MAP) measure are reported for evaluation.

3.1 Implementation Details

The visual features are extracted from VGG network [3] pretrained on the ImageNet dataset [4]. The dimensionality of image features and tag embedding are both set to 512. We apply fixed input state dimension of 1024 and hidden state dimension of 512 for all visual-guided LSTM neurons. Learning rate is scheduled as 10^{-3} and a staircase weight decay is applied after a few epochs. β_1, β_2 in adam are set to 0.8 and 0.999. We set the threshold $\beta = 0.01$ and the weighting factor $\alpha = 0.5$ based on cross-validation. Dropout with rate 0.5 is applied on the top of output state in the LSTM neuron. For testing images, we annotate each of them with top k labels.

3.2 Performance on NUS-WIDE

NUS-WIDE dataset is widely used as the benchmark for image tagging and multimedia retrieval due to its large amount of images and high quality annotations. As each label has enough training images, we put the more frequency tags before the less frequency ones in the training time. Not only the precision and recall scores (C-P and C-R) over all classes, but we also report the overall

Table 1. Performance evaluation on NUS-WIDE dataset for $k = 3$.

Method	C-P	C-R	C-F1	O-P	O-R	O-F1	MAP
Multi-edge graph [2]	–	–	–	35.0	37.0	36.0	–
KNN [6]	32.6	19.3	24.3	42.9	53.4	47.6	–
Softmax	31.7	31.2	31.4	47.8	59.5	53.0	–
WARP [7]	31.7	35.6	33.5	48.6	60.5	53.9	–
CNN-RNN [8]	**40.5**	30.4	34.7	49.9	61.7	55.2	56.1
JVSP	33.1	**46.2**	**38.5**	**52.9**	**65.8**	**58.6**	**68.5**

precision (O-P), overall recall (O-R) and overall F1 (O-F1) scores, where the average is taken over all testing images.

We compare the performance of our method against several state-of-the-art approaches, *i.e.* KNN [6], WARP [7], CNN-RNN [8]. Table 1 shows the comparison results. Comparing with these methods using the learning to rank framework *i.e.* WARP [7], the proposed method obtains superior results in all evaluation terms. As compared with [8] that proposes a CNN-RNN based model, our approach can gain a favorable performance improvement, which indicates the effectiveness of jointly considering visual features and tag representation. In particular, we can see our method achieves 16% higher recall and 12% higher MAP than the CNN-RNN based method, because our model can focus on local image regions to precisely recognize some objects, especially small objects, which is the key to significantly improve the performance. Furthermore, we also quantitatively verify the capability of recognizing small objects in Sect. 3.3.

3.3   Performance on MS-COCO

In the MS-COCO dataset, we view the object annotations as the labels. There are 80 object types and each label has enough training images, so we use the same frequent-first strategy as in the NUS-WIDE dataset. As the number of objects per image varies considerably, we do not set the limitation of minimum k time steps during tag propagation in the testing stage. We measure the performance in the same setting as NUS-WIDE dataset.

Table 2 compares the performance of the proposed method to existing approaches on MS-COCO dataset. Several competitors participate in the comparison, including WARP [7], multi-label binary cross entropy, and CNN-RNN model [8]. From Table 2, it is obvious that the proposed method achieves better performances compared with other methods.

Table 2. Performance evaluation on MS-COCO dataset.

Method	C-P	C-R	C-F1	O-P	O-R	O-F1	MAP
Softmax	59.0	57.0	58.0	60.2	62.1	61.1	47.4
WARP [7]	59.3	52.5	55.7	59.8	61.4	60.7	49.2
Binary cross-entropy	59.3	**58.6**	58.9	61.7	65.0	63.3	–
No RNN [8]	65.3	54.5	59.3	68.5	61.3	65.7	57.2
CNN-RNN [8]	66.0	55.6	60.4	69.2	**66.4**	67.8	61.2
JVSP	**67.6**	58.1	**62.5**	**72.3**	65.7	**68.8**	**62.7**

Most previous methods give the whole image the same weights. This setting harms the performances, especially when the image contains some small objects. Rather than using the whole image with uniform weights, our model incorporates tag information into the visual features to highlight different regions conditioned on different tags. To verify the efficiency of recognizing small objects in our model, we sample some small objects in the MS-COCO dataset, including "bottle", "cell phone", "bowl", "spoon", "fork", "knife" and "mouse", then compare their per-class precision and recall scores with the CNN-RNN [8]. The comparison results are shown in Fig. 3. It can be observed that JVSP gains a significant improvement than CNN-RNN [8] among these small objects.

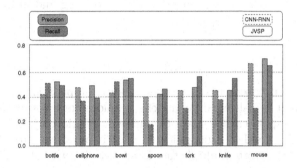

Fig. 3. Performances on small objects between CNN-RNN [8] and JVSP.

3.4 Performance on ESP Game

ESP Game dataset contains 268 different labels, and some labels include only less than 100 training images. Since some rare labels are easier to be ignored, we raise the priority of the rarer labels in the training stage and apply a rare-first order of labels. For a fair comparison, we annotate each image with 5 tags. Table 3 shows the results of the proposed model and existing approaches on ESP Game dataset. Comparing with these models [12,13] leaving the tag correlation untouched, JVSP has gained marked improvement on R, $F1$ and $N+$. Different from these methods [1,14] which explore tag correlations without studying the

Table 3. Performance evaluation on ESP Game dataset for $k = 5$.

Method	Features	P	R	F1	N+
TagProp [13]	HC	39	27	32	239
2PKNN [12]	HC	**51**	23	31.7	245
SFR [1]	HC	37	24	29	238
SLED [14]	HC	49	30	37	253
CNN-R [10]	Caffe-Net	44.5	28.5	34.7	248
2PKNN	VGG-16	40	23	29	250
RIA [9]	VGG-16	32	32	31	249
CCA-KNN [10]	VGG-16	46	36	40.4	**260**
JVSP	VGG-16	50.3	**36.4**	**42.2**	258

visual contents of image, our model utilizes the visual-guided LSTM to capture tag co-occurrence correlation. All above methods use the hand-crafted features, and we also compare with the methods [10,12] which use deep visual features. We can see our model outperforms all other deep models in most evaluation terms. Compared with these methods [9] which applied the RNN to model the tag relation, our proposed model also achieves much better performance since we consider the tags' influences on image feature modeling and utilizes the visual features to guide the tag propagation.

4   Conclusion

In this paper, we proposed a joint visual-semantic propagation model for image tagging. The joint visual-semantic modeling exploits tag information and image features in the input feature space to mine the relationship between tag and local image region, and a visual-guided LSTM is introduced to model the tag correlation and propagate multiple tags in an iterative way. We train our model with a novel diversity loss in an end-to-end manner. We conducted experiments on three benchmark datasets. The experimental results demonstrated that our model achieves superior performance to the state-of-the-art methods, especially for some small objects.

References

1. Sun, F., Tang, J., Li, H., Qi, G.J., Huang, T.S.: Multi-label image categorization with sparse factor representation. IEEE TIP **23**(3), 1028–1037 (2014)
2. Liu, D., Yan, S., Rui, Y., Zhang, H.J.: Unified tag analysis with multi-edge graph. In: Proceedings of the 18th ACM International Conference on Multimedia, pp. 25–34 (2010)
3. Simonyan, K., Zisserman, A.: Very deep convolutional networks for large-scale image recognition. arXiv preprint arXiv:1409.1556 (2014)
4. Deng, J., Dong, W., Socher, R., Li, L.J., Li, K., Fei-Fei, L.: ImageNet: a large-scale hierarchical image database. In: CVPR 2009, pp. 248–255 (2009)
5. He, K., Zhang, X., Ren, S., Sun, J.: Deep residual learning for image recognition. In: Proceedings of CVPR, pp. 770–778 (2015)
6. Chua, T.S., Tang, J., Hong, R., Li, H., Luo, Z., Zheng, Y.: NUS-WIDE: a real-world web image database from National University of Singapore. In: Proceedings of the ACM International Conference on Image and Video Retrieval, p. 48 (2009)
7. Gong, Y., Jia, Y., Leung, T., Toshev, A., Ioffe, S.: Deep convolutional ranking for multilabel image annotation. arXiv preprint arXiv:1312.4894 (2013)
8. Wang, J., Yang, Y., Mao, J., Huang, Z., Huang, C., Xu, W.: CNN-RNN: a unified framework for multi-label image classification. In: Proceedings of the IEEE CVPR, pp. 2285–2294 (2016)
9. Jin, J., Nakayama, H.: Annotation order matters: recurrent image annotator for arbitrary length image tagging. arXiv preprint arXiv:1604.05225 (2016)
10. Murthy, V.N., Maji, S., Manmatha, R.: Automatic image annotation using deep learning representations. In: Proceedings of the 5th ACM on ICMR, pp. 603–606 (2015)

11. Wang, H., Huang, H., Ding, C.: Image annotation using multi-label correlated green's function. In: IEEE ICCV (2009)
12. Verma, Y., Jawahar, C.V.: Image annotation using metric learning in semantic neighbourhoods. In: Fitzgibbon, A., Lazebnik, S., Perona, P., Sato, Y., Schmid, C. (eds.) ECCV 2012. LNCS, vol. 7574, pp. 836–849. Springer, Heidelberg (2012). https://doi.org/10.1007/978-3-642-33712-3_60
13. Guillaumin, M., Mensink, T., Verbeek, J., Schmid, C.: TagProp: discriminative metric learning in nearest neighbor models for image auto-annotation. In: ICCV, pp. 309–316 (2009)
14. Cao, X., Zhang, H., Guo, X., Liu, S., Meng, D.: SLED: semantic label embedding dictionary representation for multilabel image annotation. IEEE TIP **24**(9), 2746–2759 (2015)
15. Lin, T.-Y., et al.: Microsoft COCO: common objects in context. In: Fleet, D., Pajdla, T., Schiele, B., Tuytelaars, T. (eds.) ECCV 2014. LNCS, vol. 8693, pp. 740–755. Springer, Cham (2014). https://doi.org/10.1007/978-3-319-10602-1_48
16. Von Ahn, L., Dabbish, L.: Labeling images with a computer game. In: Proceedings of the SIGCHI Conference on Human Factors in Computing Systems, pp. 319–326. ACM (2004)
17. Jia, X., Gavves, E., Fernando, B., Tuytelaars, T.: Guiding the long-short term memory model for image caption generation. In: ICCV, pp. 2407–2415 (2015)

Exploiting Time and Frequency Diversities for High-Quality Linear Video Transmission: A MCast Framework

Chaofan He[1], Huiying Wang[1], Yang Hu[1(✉)], Yan Chen[1(✉)], and Houqiang Li[2]

[1] School of Electronic Engineering, University of Electronic Science and Technology of China, Chengdu, China
{yanghu,eecyan}@uestc.edu.cn
[2] Department of Electronic Engineering and Information Science, University of Science and Technology of China, Hefei, China

Abstract. Uncoded linear video transmission has recently gained much attention. However, the received quality may not be good enough due to the channel fluctuation. In this paper, we propose a framework, named MCast, to exploit the time and frequency diversities by transmitting the data multiple times for better reconstruction. The key problem in MCast is how to assign channels and allocate power for the data blocks. We derive a close-form optimal power allocation solution for any given channel assignment. Then we propose a suboptimal channel assignment scheme, where we sort the channels with their powers and assign the channels one-by-one to the blocks that can reduce the most reconstruction error. Finally, simulations show that MCast can achieve better performance compared with existing methods.

Keywords: Uncoded linear video transmission · Power allocation Channel assignment

1 Introduction

With the rapid development of mobile communication, wireless video is gradually to be the new generation of application for wireless networks. It is estimated that the volume of wireless videos will increase manyfold. How people can more easily enjoy high definition wireless video becomes an important issue, and as a result, substantial efforts have been made to improve the wireless video quality.

Traditionally, as a general framework, videos are compressed into a bit stream and transmitted over channels which go through quantization, entropy coding, channel coding and modulation, etc. [10,14]. However, with the prevalence of wireless networks and mobile devices, the weakness of traditional framework

This work was partly supported by the 111 Project No. B17008, the National Natural Science Foundation of China under Grant 61672137 and 61602090, and the Thousand Youth Talents Program of China (to Yan Chen).

© Springer International Publishing AG, part of Springer Nature 2018
B. Zeng et al. (Eds.): PCM 2017, LNCS 10735, pp. 36–46, 2018.
https://doi.org/10.1007/978-3-319-77380-3_4

becomes obvious. The main weakness is the cliff effect due to the mismatches between the estimated channel condition and the actual channel condition. For the multi-user scenario where different users encounter different channel conditions, the traditional framework will choose the bit rate conservatively to satisfy the user under the worst channel condition. In such a case, those users under good channel conditions cannot enjoy better video quality. Furthermore, wireless medium unavoidably suffers from errors due to both interference and channel noise. The traditional framework utilizes the forward error correction (FEC) [17,20,21] to correct errors without retransmission. Besides, since different packets contribute differently in video reconstruction, it is beneficial to classify them based on their importance and provide different levels of protection through unequal error protection (UEP) [6,9,15,16,18]. Nevertheless, in spite of these efforts, errors can still happen, and the whole packet will be discarded once one single bit error happens after channel decoding.

To tackle the above challenges, cross-layer joint source and channel coding approaches have been proposed to improve the received video quality. A pseudo-analog scalable video delivery scheme, known as SoftCast [8], skips quantization, entropy coding and channel coding, simply uses 3D-DCT to de-correlate the video source and transmits the uncoded DCT coefficients directly. Since only linear operations are used in the entire process, the received video quality varies with the channel quality smoothly. Therefore, there is no cliff effect. Also, with Softcast, the packet with errors will not be discarded. Instead, it is optimally reconstructed by the linear minimal mean square error estimator [19]. However, the reconstructed video quality by Softcast may not be good enough especially when the signal-to-noise-ratio (SNR) is low. This is mainly due to two reasons: Softcast fails to fully exploit the redundancy of the source and the channel information is not utilized in Softcast. To improve the reconstructed video quality, many efforts have been made in the literature. In [4,5], Fan et al. proposed a Dcast framework to exploit the inter-frame redundancy with the distributed video coding theory [2,7]. The Parcast in [11] considered the transmission over the multiple-input multiple-output (MIMO) wireless channels and proposed to transmit high-energy DCT components in high-gain channels.

While the aforementioned approaches have achieved promising performance, most of them assume that the transmission is real-time. However, due to the fluctuation of the wireless channels, the source data may need to be transmitted across multiple time slots and multiple channels. The key problem here is how to optimally allocate the power and assign the channels at each time slot to the source data such that the overall performance is maximized. To resolve the problem, in this paper, we propose a framework, named MCast, to utilize the time and frequency diversities to achieve high-quality linear video transmission. Specifically, we first derive a close-form optimal power allocation solution for any given channel assignment. With the optimal power allocation, we then propose a suboptimal channel assignment scheme, where we sort the channels with their powers and assign the channel one-by-one to the corresponding block that can reduce the most reconstruction error. Finally, simulations are conducted to show that the proposed MCast system can achieve better performance compared with existing methods.

The rest of this paper is organized as follows. The system model and problem formulation is described in detail in Sect. 2. The joint power allocation and channel assignment for the proposed MCast system is discussed in Sect. 3. The simulation results are shown in Sect. 4 while the conclusions are drawn in Sect. 5.

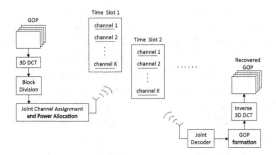

Fig. 1. System model of the MCast system.

2   System Model

As shown in Fig. 1, in this paper, we consider a multiple time slots joint source and channel coding system, which we call "MCast" system. In the MCast system, a group of pictures (GOP) is first converted into frequency domain through 3D DCT transform and divided into blocks. Then, the blocks will be transmitted through multiple time slots and multiple channels to the receiver by exploiting the time and frequency diversities. The key problem here is how to assign channels and allocate power among different blocks to achieve the best quality.

Here, we assume that the GOP data is transmitted across L time slots, and each time slot there are K channels. Let X_P denote the GOP data to be transmitted to the receiver. With the 3D DCT transform, X_P is converted to the frequency representation, denoted as X_F. Then, these DCT coefficients are divided into blocks with equal size, which are represented by $\{X_1, X_2, ..., X_B\}$. These blocks will be re-scaled and transmitted through different channels across different time slots. Specifically, let us assume that there are n_{ij} channels allocated to block X_i at the jth time slot, denoted as $H_{ij} = \{h_{ij1}, h_{ij2}, ..., h_{ijn_{ij}}\}$. The corresponding power weights are denoted as $G_{ij} = \{g_{ij1}, g_{ij2}, ..., g_{ijn_{ij}}\}$, where g_{ijk} is the re-scale power weight of channel h_{ijk}.

At the receiver, for each block X_i, multiple distorted copies will be received

$$Y_{ijk} = h_{ijk} g_{ijk} X_i + Z_{ijk}, \tag{1}$$

where Z_{ijk} is the AWGN with zero mean and variance $\sigma_{z_i}^2$.

Let $\mathbf{Y}_i = [Y_{i11}, ..., Y_{i1n_{i1}}, ..., Y_{iL1}, ..., Y_{iLn_{iL}}]^T$, $\mathbf{C}_i = [h_{i11}g_{i11}, ..., h_{i1n_{i1}}g_{i1n_{i1}}, ..., h_{iL1}g_{iL1}, ..., h_{iLn_{iL}}g_{iLn_{iL}}]^T$, and $\mathbf{Z}_i = [Z_{i11}, ..., Z_{i1n_{i1}}, ..., Z_{iL1}, ..., Z_{iLn_{iL}}]^T$. Then, (1) can be re-written in a vector form as

$$\mathbf{Y}_i = \mathbf{C}_i X_i + \mathbf{Z}_i. \tag{2}$$

According to (2), we can see that the observations are the sum of a term linear in X_i and AWGN noise. Therefore, at the receiver, an optimal linear minimal mean square error estimator can be performed to estimate X_i as follows [3]

$$\hat{X}_i = \frac{\sigma_{x_i}^2}{\sigma_{x_i}^2 \parallel \mathbf{C}_i \parallel^2 + \sigma_{z_i}^2} \mathbf{C}_i^T \mathbf{Y}_i, \tag{3}$$

where $\sigma_{x_i}^2$ is the variance of X_i, and the corresponding expected estimation error can also be derived as follows

$$\epsilon(\hat{X}_i, X_i) = E(\hat{X}_i - X_i)^2 = \frac{\sigma_{x_i}^2 \sigma_{z_i}^2}{\sigma_{x_i}^2 \parallel \mathbf{C}_i \parallel^2 + \sigma_{z_i}^2}. \tag{4}$$

After obtaining the estimate of each block $\hat{X}_i$, we rearrange the estimated blocks back to the 3D DCT domain, represented as $\hat{X}_F$. Finally, we obtain the reconstruction of the original GOP $\hat{X}_P$ by taking the inverse 3D DCT of $\hat{X}_F$.

3   Joint Channel Assignment and Power Allocation

Our objective is to minimize the end-to-end distortion, i.e., the mean square error (MSE) between the original video X_P and the reconstructed video $\hat{X}_P$. Since X_F and $\hat{X}_F$ are the 3D DCT versions of X_P and $\hat{X}_P$, respectively, and the 3D DCT is a linear operation, minimizing the MSE between X_P and $\hat{X}_P$ is the same as minimizing the MSE between X_F and $\hat{X}_F$.

While the blocks can be transmitted through multiple time slots to exploit the time-frequency diversities, the actual transmission is slot-by-slot since the channels may vary slot-by-slot. In such a case, the power allocation and channel assignment should be performed slot-by-slot. For each time slot, there is a total power constraint for all channels at that time slot as follows

$$\sum_{i=1}^{B} \sum_{k=1}^{n_{ij}} g_{ijk}^2 \sigma_{x_i}^2 \le P_t, \ \forall j = 1, ..., L, \tag{5}$$

where P_t is the total power constraint at each time slot.

Moreover, since there are K channels at each time slot, the channel assigned to all blocks at each time slot should not exceed K

$$\sum_{i=1}^{B} n_{ij} \le K, \ \forall j = 1, ..., L. \tag{6}$$

In practice, the channel information is obtained slot-by-slot, thus the problem needs to be solved slot-by-slot. With the power constraint in (5) and the channel constraint in (6), the joint channel assignment and power allocation at the jth time slot can be written as

$$\min_{\mathbf{H}_j, \mathbf{G}_j} \quad \sum_{i=1}^{B} \frac{\sigma_{x_i}^2 \sigma_{z_i}^2}{\sigma_{x_i}^2 \parallel \mathbf{C}_i^j \parallel^2 + \sigma_{z_i}^2},$$

$$\text{subject to} \quad \sum_{i=1}^{B} n_{ij} \leq K, \tag{7}$$

$$\sum_{i=1}^{B} \sum_{k=1}^{n_{ij}} g_{ijk}^2 \sigma_{x_i}^2 \leq P_t,$$

where $\mathbf{H}_j = \{H_{1j}, ..., H_{Bj}\}$, $\mathbf{G}_j = \{G_{1j}, ..., G_{Bj}\}$, and $\mathbf{C}_i^j = [h_{i11}g_{i11}, ...,$ $h_{i1n_{i1}}g_{i1n_{i1}}, ..., h_{ij1}g_{ij1}, ..., h_{ijn_{ij}}g_{ijn_{ij}}]^T$.

The optimization problem in (7) is obviously not convex due to the coupling between $\mathbf{H}_j$ and $\mathbf{G}_j$. In the following, we first discuss the power allocation problem by treating $\mathbf{H}_j$ as parameters. Then, we discuss how to perform the channel assignment.

3.1 Optimal Power Allocation

When the channel assignment is given, we can expand $||\mathbf{C}_i^j||^2$ as follows

$$\parallel \mathbf{C}_i^j \parallel^2 = \sum_{m=1}^{j-1} \sum_{k=1}^{n_{im}} |h_{imk}|^2 g_{imk}^2 + \sum_{k=1}^{n_{ij}} |h_{ijk}|^2 g_{ijk}^2,$$

$$= b_{ij} + \sum_{k=1}^{n_{ij}} |h_{ijk}|^2 g_{ijk}^2, \tag{8}$$

where $b_{ij} = \sum_{m=1}^{j-1} \sum_{k=1}^{n_{im}} |h_{imk}|^2 g_{imk}^2$, if $j > 1$, and $b_{ij} = 0$ if $j = 1$, which is fixed at time slot j.

Since the objective function in (7) is monotonically decreasing in term of g_{ijk}^2, the equality in the power constraint should be hold. Then let $u_{ijk} = g_{ijk}^2$, and by substituting (8) into (7), the optimization problem in (7) can be re-written as

$$\min_{\mathbf{U}_j} \quad J(\mathbf{U}_j) = \sum_{i=1}^{B} \frac{\sigma_{z_i}^2}{\sum_{k=1}^{n_{ij}} |h_{ijk}|^2 u_{ijk} + b_{ij} + \sigma_{z_i}^2/\sigma_{x_i}^2},$$

$$\text{subject to} \quad \sum_{i=1}^{B} \sum_{k=1}^{n_{ij}} u_{ijk} \sigma_{x_i}^2 = P_t, \text{and} \quad u_{ijk} \geq 0. \tag{9}$$

Obviously, this is a convex optimizaiton problem and to solve it, we first derive the following theorem.

Theorem 1. *Under the optimal channel assignment, the number of channel assigned to each block cannot exceed one at each time slot.*

Proof. Let us assume that under optimal channel assignment, two channels h_{ij1} and h_{ij2} are assigned to the ith block at j^{th} time slot, where the corresponding optimal power allocation is u_{ij1} and u_{ij2}. Without loss of generality, we assume that $|h_{ij1}|^2 > |h_{ij2}|^2$. Then, let us consider another channel assignment, where only channel h_{ij1} is assigned to the ith block at j^{th} time slot with the allocated power $u_{ij1} + u_{ij2}$. Obviously, both these two assignment schemes share the same constraint in (9), and we have

$$\frac{\sigma_{z_i}^2}{|h_{ij1}|^2 \sum_{k=1}^{2} u_{ijk} + b_{ij} + \sigma_{z_i}^2/\sigma_{x_i}^2} < \frac{\sigma_{z_i}^2}{\sum_{k=1}^{2} |h_{ijk}|^2 u_{ijk} + b_{ij} + \sigma_{z_i}^2/\sigma_{x_i}^2}. \quad (10)$$

From the above inequality, we can see that the new assignment scheme achieves better performance, which contradicts with the assumption. Therefore, under the optimal channel assignment, the number of channel assigned to each block cannot exceed one at each time slot.

With Theorem 1, the optimization in (9) can be simplified as follows

$$\min_{\mathbf{U}_j} \ J(\mathbf{U}_j) = \sum_{i=1}^{B} \frac{\sigma_{z_i}^2}{|h_{ij}|^2 u_{ij} + b_{ij} + \sigma_{z_i}^2/\sigma_{x_i}^2},$$

$$\text{subject to } \sum_{i=1}^{B} u_{ij}\sigma_{x_i}^2 = P_t, \text{and} \ \ u_{ij} \geq 0. \quad (11)$$

With the Lagrange multipliers, the optimal power allocation can be derived

$$u_{ij}^* = \left(\frac{\sigma_{z_i}}{\sqrt{\lambda}\sigma_{x_i}|h_{ij}|} - \frac{b_{ij}\sigma_{x_i}^2 + \sigma_{z_i}^2}{\sigma_{x_i}^2|h_{ij}|^2} \right)^+, \quad (12)$$

where $(x)^+$ is equal to x, if $x > 0$, and equal to 0 if $x \leq 0$, and λ is a parameter satisfies $\sum_{i=1}^{B} u_{ij}^*\sigma_{x_i}^2 = P_t$.

3.2   Channel Assignment

With the optimal power allocation in the previous subsection, we discuss in this subsection about the channel assignment. Finding the optimal channel assignment in (7) is NP-hard [12] as all the possible permutations of available channels at j^{th} time slot need to be evaluated, which is computationally infeasible. To resolve the problem, we propose a suboptimal channel assignment scheme, where we first sort the channels with their powers and then assign the channel one-by-one to the corresponding block that can reduce the most MSE.

Without loss of generality, let us assume $|h_{1j}|^2 > |h_{2j}|^2 > ... > |h_{Kj}|^2$ and suppose that we are now assigning channel h_{ij}. According to Theorem 1, each block will be assigned at most one channel under optimal channel assignment. Thus, denoting $S_i = \{x_1, ..., x_{i-1}\}$ be the block set containing those blocks which have been assigned channels, and $\bar{S}_i$, the complementary of S_i, be the block set containing the blocks which can be assigned to channel h_{ij}. To choose a proper block for channel h_{ij}, we define a measure γ_{il} for each block $l \in \bar{S}_i$ as follows

$$\gamma_{il} = \frac{\sigma_{z_l}^2 \sigma_{x_l}^2}{b_{lj}\sigma_{x_l}^2 + \sigma_{z_l}^2} - \frac{\left(\sum_{d=1}^{i-1} \frac{\sigma_{z_d}\sigma_{x_d}}{|h_{dj}|} + \frac{\sigma_{z_l}\sigma_{x_l}}{|h_{ij}|}\right)^2}{P_t + \sum_{d=1}^{i-1} \frac{b_{dj}\sigma_{x_d}^2 + \sigma_{z_d}^2}{|h_{dj}|^2} + \frac{b_{lj}\sigma_{x_l}^2 + \sigma_{z_l}^2}{|h_{ij}|^2}}, \tag{13}$$

and the block that maximizes γ_{il} will be chosen for channel h_{ij}, i.e.,

$$x_i = \arg\max_{l \in \bar{S}_i} \gamma_{il} \tag{14}$$

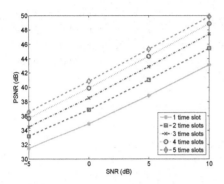

Fig. 2. The PSNR performance of the proposed MCast system: *foreman* sequence.

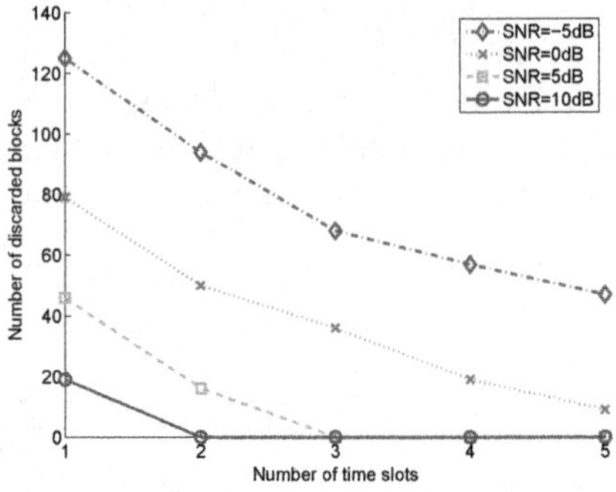

Fig. 3. The number of discarded blocks with different SNRs and time slots.

4   Simulation Results

To evaluate the performance of the proposed MCast system, we conduct multiple simulations under different settings in this section. We also compare with four other approaches to demonstrate the superiority of the proposed MCast system. These four approaches, Softcast+average, Softcast+joint, Parcast+average, and Parcast+joint, are direct extensions of Softcast [8] and Parcast [11], where "average" means that the receiver decodes the received signal of each time slot independently and average the results while "joint" means that the receiver jointly decodes the received signals of all time slots.

4.1   Simulation Settings

The test videos are chosen from Xiph [1], which are in standard CIF format (352 × 288 pixels, 30 fps). Therefore, the source bandwidth is 3.04 MHz. The size of GOP is set to be 16 frames, which is processed as a whole through 3D-DCT. After 3D-DCT, the DCT coefficients are equally divided into 192 blocks, each of which contains 88 × 72 pixels. Similar to most of the traditional wireless communication systems [13], the Rayleigh fading channels are assumed in our MCast system. We further assume that there are 192 channels, however, some deep fading channels may not be used with our channel assignment algorithm.

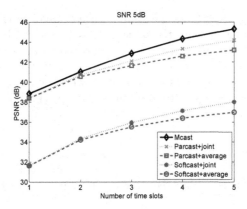

Fig. 4. The PSNR performance comparison among different approaches with SNR = 5 dB.

4.2 Performances of the Proposed MCast System

In this subsection, we conduct simulations to study the performance of the proposed MCast system. We assume current time slot is the jth time slot and the channel assignments and power allocation in all previous time slots is known.

We first evaluate the quality of the reconstructed sequences versus the transmitted SNR when the video sequences are transmitted across different number of time slots, and the results are shown in Fig. 2. We can see that the PSNR increases as the channel SNR increases when the number of used time slots is fixed. This is reasonable since the reconstruction will be better with better channel condition. From Fig. 2, we can also observe that with any fixed channel SNR, the PSNR increases as the number of time slots increases, but the increment becomes smaller when the number of time slots is larger. Such a phenomenon is because that with more time slots, we can exploit better time and frequency diversities to improve the reconstruction, but the benefit will saturate when there are too many diversities.

In Fig. 3, we illustrate the number of discarded blocks, i.e., the blocks with zero power allocation, versus the number of time slots with different SNRs. We can see that the number of discarded blocks decreases as the number of time slots increases and/or the SNR increases. When the SNR is 10 dB, all blocks are transmitted if more than one time slot is utilized for transmission. However, when the SNR is −5 dB, there are about 50 blocks discarded even if five time slots are utilized for transmission. That is because when the channel condition is not good, assigning good channels to a few important blocks with large power and discarding some less important blocks can lead to smaller total MSE.

4.3 Comparison with Other Systems

In this subsection, we compare the performance of the MCast system with those of Parcast+joint, Parcast+average, Softcast+joint and Softcast+average. In the

Parcast+joint and Parcast+average systems, the channel assignment and power allocation at each time slot are the same as those employed by Parcast. Specifically, at each time slot, both the channels and blocks are sorted in a descend order according to the channel powers and block energy, respectively. Then, each channel is assigned to the corresponding block with the same sorted order, i.e., higher gain channel is assigned to more important block. According to [11], the power allocated to each channel is $g_i = \sqrt{\dfrac{P_t}{\sigma_{x_i}|h_i|\sum_j(\sigma_{x_i}/|h_i|)}}$.

In Softcast+joint and Softcast+average systems, there is no channel assignment procedure and the power allocation at each time slot is the same as that in Softcast [8], where the allocated power only depends on the energy of each block as $g_i = \sqrt{\dfrac{P_t}{\sigma_{x_i}\sum_j\sigma_{x_i}}}$.

The PSNR performance comparisons versus the number of time slots that are utilized for transmission at SNR $= 5$ dB is shown in Fig. 4. We can see the Softcast+average performs worst, and Softcast+joint performs slightly better with joint decoding, especially when the number of time slots utilized increases. By utilizing the channel information in both the channel assignment and power allocation, Parcast+average and Parcast+joint can greatly improve the PSNR performance, and again the joint decoding can further improve the performance. By exploiting the time and frequency diversities across multiple time slots, the proposed MCast system can achieve the best PSNR performance. The performance improvement is larger when the number of time slots utilized increases. This is because when the number of time slots utilized is large, there are more diversities to exploit and thus the performance gain is larger.

5   Conclusion

In this paper, we propose a MCast system to exploit the time and frequency diversities to achieve high-quality linear video transmission. The MCast system solves the problem of how to optimally allocate the power and assign the channels at each time slot to the source data to maximize the overall performance. Specifically, a close-form optimal power allocation solution is derived when the channel assignment is given. With the optimal power allocation, a suboptimal channel assignment scheme is proposed, where the channels are first sorted according to their powers and then assigned one-by-one to the source data that can reduce the most distortion. Simulation results show that compared with existing schemes, the proposed MCast system can better exploit the time and frequency diversities to achieve better performance.

References

1. Xiph.org media. https://media.xiph.org/video/derf
2. Aaron, A., Zhang, R., Girod, B.: Wyner-ziv coding of motion video. In: Conference Record of the Thirty-Sixth Asilomar Conference on Signals, Systems and Computers, vol. 1, pp. 240–244, November 2002
3. Cui, H., Luo, C., Chen, C.W., Wu, F.: Robust linear video transmission over rayleigh fading channel. IEEE Trans. Commun. **62**(8), 2790–2801 (2014)
4. Fan, X., Wu, F., Zhao, D., Au, O.C.: Distributed wireless visual communication with power distortion optimization. IEEE Trans. Circuits Syst. Video Techn. **23**(6), 1040–1053 (2013)
5. Fan, X., Wu, F., Zhao, D., Au, O.C., Gao, W.: Distributed soft video broadcast (DCAST) with explicit motion. In: Storer, J.A., Marcellin, M.W. (eds.) 2012 Data Compression Conference, Snowbird, UT, USA, 10–12 April 2012, pp. 199–208. IEEE Computer Society (2012)
6. Gallant, M., Kossentini, F.: Rate-distortion optimized layered coding with unequal error protection for robust internet video. IEEE Trans. Circuits Syst. Video Techn. **11**(3), 357–372 (2001)
7. Girod, B., Aaron, A.M., Rane, S., Rebollo-Monedero, D.: Distributed video coding. Proc. IEEE **93**(1), 71–83 (2005)
8. Jakubczak, S., Katabi, D.: A cross-layer design for scalable mobile video. In: Ramanathan, P., Nandagopal, T., Levine, B.N. (eds.) Proceedings of the 17th Annual International Conference on Mobile Computing and Networking, MOBICOM 2011, Las Vegas, Nevada, USA, 19–23 September 2011, pp. 289–300. ACM (2011)
9. Kim, J., Mersereau, R.M., Altunbasak, Y.: Error-resilient image and video transmission over the internet using unequal error protection. IEEE Trans. Image Process. **12**(2), 121–131 (2003)
10. Kolmogorov, A.N.: On the shannon theory of information transmission in the case of continuous signals. IRE Trans. Inf. Theory **2**(4), 102–108 (1956)
11. Liu, X.L., Hu, W., Pu, Q., Wu, F., Zhang, Y.: Parcast: soft video delivery in MIMO-OFDM wlans. In: Akan, Ö.B., Ekici, E., Qiu, L., Snoeren, A.C. (eds.) The 18th Annual International Conference on Mobile Computing and Networking, Mobicom 2012, Istanbul, Turkey, 22–26 August 2012, pp. 233–244. ACM (2012)
12. Pistikopoulos, E.N.: C.A. floudas, nonlinear and mixed-integer optimization. fundamentals and applications. J. Global Optim. **12**(1), 108–110 (1998)
13. Rappaport, T.S., et al.: Wireless Communications: Principles and Practice, vol. 2. Prentice Hall PTR, New Jersey (1996)
14. Shannon, C.E.: A mathematical theory of communication. ACM SIGMOBILE Mob. Comput. Commun. Rev. **5**(1), 3–55 (2001)
15. Stankovic, V., Hamzaoui, R., Charfi, Y., Xiong, Z.: Real-time unequal error protection algorithms for progressive image transmission. IEEE J. Sel. Areas Commun. **21**(10), 1526–1535 (2003)
16. Tan, W., Zakhor, A.: Video multicast using layered FEC and scalable compression. IEEE Trans. Circuits Syst. Video Techn. **11**(3), 373–386 (2001)
17. Taubman, D.S., Thie, J.: Optimal erasure protection for scalably compressed video streams with limited retransmission. IEEE Trans. Image Process. **14**(8), 1006–1019 (2005)
18. Thomos, N., Boulgouris, N.V., Strintzis, M.G.: Wireless image transmission using turbo codes and optimal unequal error protection. IEEE Trans. Image Process. **14**(11), 1890–1901 (2005)

19. Tse, D., Viswanath, P.: Fundamentals of Wireless Communication. Cambridge University Press, Cambridge (2005)
20. Xiong, R., Taubman, D., Sivaraman, V.: Optimal PET protection for streaming scalably compressed video streams with limited retransmission based on incomplete feedback. IEEE Trans. Image Process. **19**(9), 2382–2395 (2010)
21. Xiong, R., Taubman, D.S., Sivaraman, V.: PET protection optimization for streaming scalable videos with multiple transmissions. IEEE Trans. Image Process. **22**(11), 4364–4379 (2013). https://doi.org/10.1109/TIP.2013.2272516

Light Field Image Compression with Sub-apertures Reordering and Adaptive Reconstruction

Chuanmin Jia[1], Yekang Yang[1], Xinfeng Zhang[2], Shiqi Wang[3],
Shanshe Wang[1], and Siwei Ma[1(✉)]

[1] Institute of Digital Media, Peking University, Beijing, China
swma@pku.edu.cn
[2] Rapid-Rich Object Search (ROSE) Lab,
Nanyang Technological University, Singapore, Singapore
[3] Department of Computer Science, City University of Hong Kong,
Kowloon Tong, Hong Kong

Abstract. Light field (LF) attracts tremendous attention due to its capability of recording the intensity of scene objects as well as the direction of the light ray, which also dramatically increases the amount of redundant data. In this paper, we explore the structure of the light field images, and propose a pseudo-sequence based light field image compression with sub-aperture reordering and adaptive reconstruction to efficiently improve the coding performances. In the proposed method, we firstly decompose the lenslet image into sub-aperture images, and then design an optimized sub-aperture scan order to rearrange them sequentially as a pseudo-sequence. Third, we take advantage of the state-of-the-art video codec to compress the pseudo-sequence by leveraging both intra- and inter-view correlations. Considering the interpolation and transform induced by the reconstruction procedure from sub-aperture images to lenslet image, we propose an enhanced reconstruction method by applying region-based non-local adaptive filters which extracts the non-local similarities for collaborative filtering to promote the quality of reconstructed lenslet images. Extensive experimental results show that the proposed method achieves up to 15.7% coding gain in terms of BD-rate.

Keywords: Light Field · Image compression
Sub-apertures arrangement · Adaptive reconstruction

1 Introduction

Light field (LF) image compression and the standardization progress of JPEG pleno [1] have attracted tremendous attentions recently. Light field is able to capture the intensity of objects and record the information of light rays. However, due to the dense sampling during LF imaging, large amount of redundant data

© Springer International Publishing AG, part of Springer Nature 2018
B. Zeng et al. (Eds.): PCM 2017, LNCS 10735, pp. 47–55, 2018.
https://doi.org/10.1007/978-3-319-77380-3_5

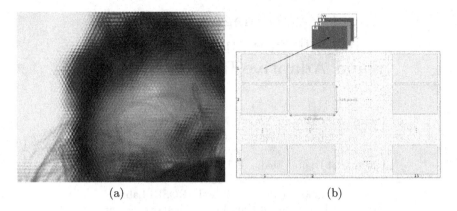

Fig. 1. (a) Crop of an uncompressed lenslet image in RGB. (b) LF structure produced by the LF toolbox [10], dimension: $15 \times 15 \times 434 \times 625 \times 4$.

are introduced which show less hospitality for transmission, storage and further LF applications. To address this issue, high efficiency compression methods for LF image are urgently required.

Conventional light field image compression schemes [2–4] treat LF as a natural image with large amount of intra-redundancy, and optimizes intra prediction for redundancy removal, which do not dive into the structure of LF. In other words, better compression performance can be achieved by taking LF characteristics into consideration.

For better understanding of the LF characteristics, two concepts widely used in LF are introduced in this paragraph: elemental images and LF structures. As for elemental images, a micro lens array is placed in front of the image sensor, which optically subdivides the image sensor into a matrix of sub-images. We refer to such sub-images as elemental images (EI). Figure 1(a) shows a crop of lenslet image in RGB for the illustration of EI. The LF structures, however, is a 5-*Dimension* representation of image data: the first two dims denote the number of sub-apertures in row and column of lenslet image respectively while the following two dims indicate the resolution of each sub-aperture. The last dimension is the number of color channels. Given EI and LF structures, the sub-aperture images can be generated by resampling pixels who have the same horizontal and vertical location within each EI. The only difference among each sub-aperture is that different sub-aperture records different angles of light ray during imaging. Figure 1(b) illustrates the sub-apertures obtained by decomposition with LF MATLAB Toolbox [10].

Once sub-apertures are obtained, intra prediction in LF compression can be naturally converted to inter prediction since we have already transferred intra redundancy in the form of inter correlations. Hence, inter prediction in existing video codecs can be adopted to achieve better coding performance. Generally, all sub-apertures can be arranged as a pseudo-sequence for both intra- and inter-redundancy removal [9,11,13]. However, the compression performances of LF sub-apertures is sensitive to the sub-apertures arrangement mechanism, as different arrangement methods reveal different reference relationships and inter prediction capabilities. For the lenslet decomposition procedure from lenslet image to sub-apertures, the affine transform and interpolation make this process irreversible, which limit the quality of reconstructed lenslet image.

In this paper, we explore the structure of LF, and propose a pseudo-sequence based LF compression with sub-aperture reordering and adaptive reconstruction. To reduce the intra- and inter-view redundancies as much as possible, we first decompose the lenslet image into sub-apertures, and rearrange them into a pseudo-sequence according to the proposed optimal scan order for sub-apertures. Subsequently, the elaborately designed video coding methods, e.g., HEVC, can be directly utilized to reduce these redundancies via intra and inter predictions. To alleviate the distortions generated in lenslet image decomposition and reconstruction, we propose a region-based adaptive non-local filtering technique for the reconstructed lenslet image by searching non-local similar patches to arrange them as groups and designing low-pass filters for the groups in transform domain. Based on our experiments, the proposed algorithm achieves obvious improvement in terms of bit-rate reduction.

The rest of the paper is organized as follows. Section 2 briefly reviews related work in LF image compression. Section 3 introduces the proposed sub-aperture reordering scheme and non-local adaptive reconstruction for lenslet image. Extensive experimental results are reported in Sects. 4 and 5 concludes this paper.

2   Related Work

Many specific compression methods for LF images have been proposed in literatures, which can be roughly classified into two categories: (i) non-local intra prediction based compression [2–4] and (ii) sub-apertures based compression [11–13].

Intra Prediction Based Compression. Methods in this category focus on directly compressing the lenslet images. Li *et al.* [2] proposed an intra prediction algorithm by combining a sparse image set and its associated disparities for the prediction of highly correlated EIs. To further reduce the redundancy, Conti *et al.* [4] formulated a self-similarity model into HEVC by searching similar blocks in a nonlocal reconstructed region for prediction. Zhong *et al.* [3] proposed a super-pixel based L1 norm linear weighted intra prediction scheme for lenslet compression. However, the intrinsic LF structure of the above methods has been largely ignored.

Sub-apertures Based Compression. As for the sub-aperture based compression, LF image is firstly decomposed into sub-apertures by its calibration information, and then those sub-apertures are rearranged sequentially as a pseudo-sequence for further compression. Liu *et al.* [11] proposed a reference management and rate allocation scheme for sub-apertures. However, the complexity of reference scheme may limit the usage in practical LF coding scenario. Chen *et al.* [12] integrated the sparse coding into LF compression and selected key sub-apertures to train sparse dictionary for coding. This algorithm is efficient under low bit rate coding circumstance, which may lack its generalization ability. Zhao *et al.* [13] provided a hybrid arrangement order for sub-apertures by combing z scan order and U-shape order. Though promising performance has been achieved, in-depth performance analyses are still required to further leverage the prediction structure for coding efficiency improvement.

In this work, we propose a sub-apertures arrangement algorithm to deal with two main problems in LF image coding. First, a novel sub-apertures reordering scheme is proposed to deal with the lack of inter-prediction precision in conventional z-scan. Second, non-local adaptive reconstruction for lenslet image is also proposed to compensate the irreversible distortion induced by affine transform and interpolation during lenslet decomposition. Experimental results show that the proposed algorithm achieves obvious bit-rate reduction.

3   Sub-aperture Reordering and Adaptive Reconstruction

In this section, we first introduce the generation of sub-apertures and pseudo-sequence via proposed scan order. Then, we describe the details of proposed non-local adaptive reconstruction for lenslet image.

3.1   Sub-apertures Generation

To explore the correlations between sub-apertures, the lenslet images are converted into 5-D LF using MATLAB LF Toolbox [10]. The conversion process is listed as follows. (i) affine transform for lenslet images based on the camera calibration information, (ii) interpolation and (iii) resamping pixels in each EI to generate sub-apertures. The test LF images are chosen from EPFL LF dataset [14] with resolution 7728×5368 in YUV420 color space. After the decomposition process, the shape of 5-D LF structure is in $15 \times 15 \times 434 \times 625 \times 4$, which has been illustrated in Fig. 1(b). The resolution of each sub-aperture is 434×625.

3.2   Pseudo-sequence Generation

Since the scan order of subapertures will directly affect the inter-prediction efficiency. In this subsection, we design an optimized scan order for sub-apertures to generate the pseudo-sequence for compression. According to the Call for Proposal (CfP) for LF coding [1], we mainly consider the inner 13×13 views, which means the total frame numbers of generated pseudo-sequence is 169.

It is obvious that different sub-apertures reordering methods lead to different inter prediction capability such that coding efficiency varies for different reordering methods. To promote the coding efficiency, similar sub-apertures should be temporally adjacent for better inter prediction. Our proposed method gathers similar sub-apertures during pseudo-sequence generation. In view of this, a new sub-apertures arrangement mechanism is proposed, as shown in Fig. 2(b).

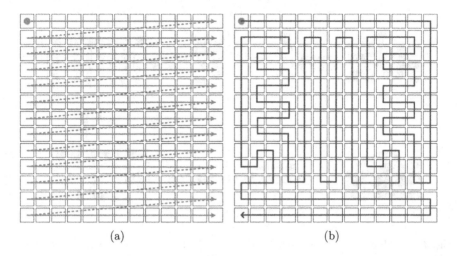

Fig. 2. (a) The anchor sub-apertures scan order in [1]. (b) The proposed scan order.

3.3   Non-local Adaptive Reconstruction for Lenslet

This subsection describes the lenslet reconstruction from sub-aperture images. For lenslet reconstruction, our method conducts inverse decomposition to reconstruct lenslet from the coded pseudo sequence. We first convert the pseudo sequence back to 5-D LF structures by arranging each frame of pseudo sequence with proposed reordering method. Since the pseudo sequence only contains $13 \times 13 = 169$ frames. The outer most sub-apertures of 5-D LF structures are filled with their nearest sub-aperture. However, the transform during decomposition makes the lenslet reconstruction irreversible therefore the upper bound of reconstructed lenslet quality is limited. To address this issue, region based adaptive reconstruction is proposed into the method by drawing lessons from the high efficiency of in-loop filters in video coding [5,6].

Recently, non-local structure filters [7,8] provide significant coding performance promotion in video coding. We illustrate the proposed non-local adaptive reconstruction algorithm in Fig. 3 which can be categorized into four stages, patch extraction & matching, group construction, low-pass filtering and weighted reconstruction. First, the whole constructed lenslet image can be overlaply divided into small patches whose size is $\sqrt{B_s} \times \sqrt{B_s}$ (small red square). Then for each patch, we find K nearest neighbors according to the Euclidean distance between different image patches within a search window $W_s \times W_s$ (dashed blue square).

$$d(x_i, x_j) = \parallel x_i - x_j \parallel_2^2, \tag{1}$$

The patch group X_{G_i} can be generated by vectorizing K patches and forming a two-dimension matrix whose size is $B_s \times K$.

$$X_{G_i} = [x_{G_i,1}, x_{G_i,2}, ..., x_{G_i,K}], \tag{2}$$

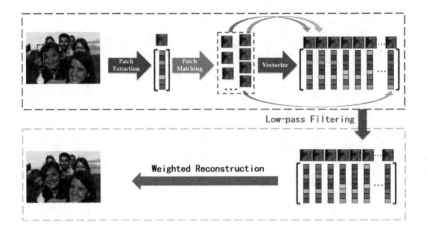

Fig. 3. The flowchart of proposed non-local adaptive reconstruction. (Color figure online)

After a singular value decomposition (SVD) procedure to patch group, the low-pass filtering can be performed with the singular values.

$$X_{G_i} = U_{G_i} \Sigma_{G_i} V_{G_i}^T, \tag{3}$$

where Σ_{G_i} is a diagonal matrix namely as singular value matrix. The low-pass filtering process is done by hard thresholding each element of the singular value matrix as follows,

$$\alpha_{G_i} = hard(\Sigma_{G_i,k}, \tau), \tag{4}$$

where k in Eq. 4 denotes the index for singular value in singular value matrix and τ is the hard threshold. For simplicity, we use the filtering threshold proposed in [8]. Since the filtering process is applied to all patch groups X_{G_i}, we finally average all group patches and reconstruct the filtered image. The non-local adaptive reconstruction is applied for both luma and chroma channels.

4   Experimental Results

In this section, we first describe the dataset and configurations we use in our experiment. Second, the performances of the proposed sub-aperture reordering and non-local adaptive reconstruction are provided. The bit-rate reduction for luma channel is reported in this paper.

4.1   Dataset

As mentioned in previous section, all lenslet images are selected from EPFL LF dataset [14] which contains 12 single frame lenslet images with resolution 7728×5368. The 5-D LF structure can be acquired by decomposing lenslet image with MATLAB toolbox [10]. According to JPEG call for proposal [1], inner $13 \times 13 \times 434 \times 625 \times 4$ sub-apertures out of the $15 \times 15 \times 434 \times 625 \times 4$ LF structure are re-arranged to generate the pseudo-sequence for compression. When reconstructing lenslet from pseudo-sequence, the outer sub-apertures of the $15 \times 15 \times 434 \times 625 \times 4$ LF structure are filled with its nearest sub-aperture.

4.2 Test Configuration

The configuration follows the common test condition (CTC) of HEVC [16]. All tests are conducted with random access (RA) configuration with four QP values: 22, 27, 32, 37. To investigate the performance of the proposed two coding tools, we set 5 experiments to illustrate the coding efficiency of reordering and non-local adaptive reconstruction, the details of which will be discussed in the next subsection. The BD-rate performances are calculated using the method described in [17]. The peak-signal-noise-ratio (PSNR) is calculated between original lenslet and reconstructed lenslet. We report the BD-rate in luminance channel.

Table 1. Rate distortion performances of proposed method

Test image	Test 1	Test 2	Test 3	Test 4	Test 5
I01 Bikes	−4.0%	−3.8%	−9.2%	−9.0%	−12.7%
I02 Danger de Mort	−3.1%	−7.1%	−8.5%	−8.6%	−15.0%
I03 Flowers	−5.8%	−2.2%	−4.8%	−5.2%	−10.7%
I04 Stone Pillars Outside	−3.9%	−4.3%	−9.0%	−9.5%	−13.0%
I05 Vespa	−1.5%	−1.4%	−12.4%	−12.3%	−13.6%
I06 Ankylosaurus & Diplodocus 1	−4.0%	−4.0%	−14.3%	−14.3%	−14.2%
I07 Desktop	−1.2%	−2.6%	−4.1%	−4.4%	−6.7%
I08 Magnets 1	−1.1%	0.0%	−10.8%	−10.8%	−10.8%
I09 Fountain & Vincent 2	−1.8%	−3.4%	−3.8%	−3.8%	−7.1%
I10 Friends 1	−2.1%	−1.0%	−13.8%	−13.9%	−15.7%
I11 Color Chart 1	−1.7%	−1.0%	−7.7%	−7.7%	−7.7%
I12 ISO Chart 12	−2.0%	−1.9%	−9.8%	−9.9%	−11.6%
Average	**−2.7%**	**−2.7%**	**−9.0%**	**−9.1%**	**−11.6%**

4.3 Evaluation

This subsection provides the details of each experiment in Table 1. Test 1 shows the performance of proposed region-based non-local adaptive reconstruction with z scan for sub-apertures reordering, in which the anchor of test 1 is z scan for sub-apertures and no non-local adaptive reconstruction to the reconstructed lenslet. As for test 2, the anchor is proposed scan order with the non-local adaptive reconstruction turning OFF, while the proposed method is sub-apertures with proposed scan order (in Fig. 2(b)) with the non-local adaptive reconstruction turning ON. From the first 2 tests, we can learn that the proposed non-local adaptive reconstruction filters bring similar performances when different sub-apertures scan order is used. The average coding performances for test 1 and test 2 are 2.7% and 2.7% respectively which show the robustness of proposed non-local adaptive reconstruction algorithm.

For test 3 and test 4, these two tests provide the coding performances of proposed reordering scheme for sub-apertures. The anchor of test 3 is z scan while the proposed method of test 3 is with proposed scan order. It is worth noting that the adaptive reconstruction is turned OFF in test 3. Further, to show the performance of proposed scan order when non-local reconstruction turns ON. We conduct test 4. The anchor of test 4 is reordering all sub-apertures with z scan while the proposed method for test 4 is with proposed scan order. Both of the anchor and proposed methods in test 4 are with non-local adaptive reconstruction applied to the reconstructed lenslet. Generally speaking, the proposed scan manner achieves 9.1% bit-rate saving with adaptive reconstruction while 9.0% bit-rate can be reduced when there is no adaptive reconstruction. Similar to the first two tests, the test 3 and test 4 also provides the robustness for proposed scan order for sub-apertures.

For the last evaluation, test 5 shows the combination performances of proposed reordering scheme and non-local adaptive reconstruction. The anchor of test 5 is reordering all sub-apertures with z scan and without non-local adaptive reconstruction to reconstructed lenslet. Up to 15.7% bit-rate reduction can be achieved when applying both the proposed scan order and adaptive reconstruction. It is worth noting that the performance of reordering and non-local adaptive reconstruction is addable, which means that further coding performances can be achieved by using both of the two coding tools.

5   Conclusion

In this paper, we propose a pseudo-sequence based light field image compression algorithm by reordering sub-apertures as well as applying the adaptive reconstruction filters for lenslet to promote the reconstruction quality. The proposed compression method first utilizes the HEVC codec to compress the pseudo-sequence, which is constructed by decomposing the lenslet image into sub-apertures and rearranging them according to a special designed order. Then, we propose a region-based non-local filters to further promote the quality of reconstructed lenslet image according to LF structures. Experimental results demonstrate that our proposed scheme can obviously improve the quality of the reconstructed lenslet LF images, and achieve significant coding gains.

Acknowledgement. This work was supported in part by the National High-tech R&D Program of China (863 Program, 2015AA015903) National Natural Science Foundation of China (61632001, 61571017, 61421062), and the Top-Notch Young Talents Program of China, which are gratefully acknowledged.

References

1. JPEG Pleno Final Call for Proposals on Light Field Coding. https://jpeg.org/items/20170208_cfp_pleno.html
2. Li, Y., Sjostrom, M., Olsson, R., Jennehag, U.: Efficient intra prediction scheme for light field image compression. In: 2014 IEEE International Conference on Acoustics, Speech and Signal Processing, pp. 539–543 (2014)
3. Zhong, R., Wang, S., Cornelis, B., Zheng, Y., Yuan, J., Munteanu, A.: L1-optimized linear prediction for light field image compression. In: 2016 IEEE Picture Coding Symposium, pp. 1–5 (2016)
4. Conti, C., Nunes, P., Soares, L.D.: HEVC-based light field image coding with bi-predicted self-similarity compensation. In: 2016 IEEE International Conference on Multimedia and Expo Workshops, pp. 1–4 (2016)
5. Zhang, X., Xiong, R., Ma, S., Gao, W.: Adaptive loop filter with temporal prediction. In: 2012 IEEE Picture Coding Symposium (PCS), pp. 437–440 (2012)
6. Zhang, X., Xiong, R., Lin, W., Zhang, J., Wang, S., Ma, S., Gao, W.: Low-rank based nonlocal adaptive loop filter for high efficiency video compression. IEEE Trans. Circ. Syst. Video Technol. (2016)
7. Ma, S., Zhang, X., Zhang, J., Jia, C., Wang, S., Gao, W.: Nonlocal in-loop filter: the way toward next-generation video coding? IEEE Multimed. **23**(2), 16–26 (2016)
8. Zhang, J., Jia, C., Ma, S., Gao, W.: Non-local structure-based filter for video coding. In: 2015 IEEE International Symposium on Multimedia, pp. 301–306 (2015)
9. Li, L., Li, Z., Li, B., Liu, D., Li, H.: Pseudo sequence based 2-D hierarchical reference structure for light-field image compression. arXiv preprint arXiv:1612.07309
10. Dansereau, D.G.: Light Field Toolbox for Matlab. Software Manual (2015)
11. Liu, D., Wang, L., Li, L., Xiong, Z., Wu, F., Zeng, W.: Pseudo-sequence-based light field image compression. In: 2016 IEEE International Conference on Multimedia and Expo Workshops, pp. 1–4 (2016)
12. Chen, J., Hou, J., Chau, L.P.: Light field compression with disparity guided sparse coding based on structural key views. arXiv preprint arXiv:1610.03684
13. Zhao, S., Chen, Z., Yang, K., Huang, H.: Light field image coding with hybrid scan order. In: 2016 IEEE Visual Communications and Image Processing, pp. 1–4 (2016)
14. Rerabek, M., Yuan, L., Authier, L.A., Ebrahimi, T.: EPFL light-field image dataset. ISO/IEC JTC 1/SC 29/WG1 (2015)
15. Tsai, C.-Y., et al.: Adaptive loop filtering for video coding. IEEE J. Selected Top. Sig. Process. **7**(6), 934–945 (2013)
16. Bossen, F., Flynn, D., Shring, K.: HEVC reference software manual. JCTVC-D404, Daegu, Korea (2011)
17. Bjontegaard, G.: Calculation of average PSNR differences between RD-curves. ITU SG16 Document VCEG-M33, April 2001
18. Girod, B.: The efficiency of motion-compensating prediction for hybrid coding of video sequences. IEEE J. Sel. Areas Commun. **5**(7), 1140–1154 (1987)

Video Coding

Fast QTBT Partition Algorithm
for JVET Intra Coding Based on CNN

Zhipeng Jin, Ping An$^{(\boxtimes)}$, and Liquan Shen

School of Communication and Information Engineering,
Shanghai University, Shanghai 200072, China
anping@shu.edu.cn

Abstract. The latest Joint Video Exploration Team (JVET) employs
quad-tree plus binary-tree (QTBT) block partitioning structure, which
can improve coding performance significantly than HEVC with hugely
increased encoding complexity. Aiming at alleviating the encoding complexity, we propose a novel fast coding unit (CU) depth decision method
based on convolution neural networks (CNN) in this paper. Specially,
the QTBT partition depth range is modeled as a 5-class classification
problem, and design a single CNN classifier try to predict the depth
range of CU directly, rather than to judge split or not at each depth
level. The proposed fast scheme has the advantage that it can make the
trade-off between the RD performance and time saving by setting different partition method; our "RD Maintaining" setting can achieve 43.69%
complexity reduction with only 0.77% Bjontegaard Delta bitrate (BD-
rate) increase. And our "Low Complexity" setting can achieve 62.96%
complexity reduction with 2.06% BD-rate increase.

Keywords: JVET · QTBT partition · Coding Units (CU)
Fast intra coding · Convolutional Neural Networks (CNN)

1 Introduction

Recognizing High Definition (HD) and Ultra-High Definition (UHD) videos are
becoming more popular, the joint video exploration team (JVET) working for
next video coding standard was founded in October 2015. JVET with a compression capability that significantly exceeds that of the HEVC (including its
extensions to screen content coding and high dynamic range coding) [1].

In JVET, the biggest change is the replacement of quad-tree (QT) structure by quad-tree plus binary-tree (QTBT) partition structure. Compared with
HM16.9, JEM 5.0 can provide 20% Luma BD-rate reduction under All-Intra
(AI) configuration, with the encoding complexity increasing by about 63 times
[2]. So, it is a hot research topic to investigate fast encoder decision methods.

This work is supported in part by the Natural Science Foundation of China, under
Grants U1301257, 61571285, and 61422111.

© Springer International Publishing AG, part of Springer Nature 2018
B. Zeng et al. (Eds.): PCM 2017, LNCS 10735, pp. 59–69, 2018.
https://doi.org/10.1007/978-3-319-77380-3_6

Due to the high flexibility of the QTBT structure, it is challenging for the design of a fast CU decision algorithm. Specifically, (1) In QTBT structure, a CU can have either a square or rectangular shape, and supports a wide variety of sizes {e.g. 128×128, 64×64, 32×32, 16×32, 8×32, 4×32, 16×16, 8×16, 4×16, 8×8, 4×8, and 4×4 in intra coding}. It may be not desirable for fast algorithms to judge split or not on each depth level. (2) A coding tree units (CTU) is firstly partitioned by a QT structure. The QT leaf nodes are further partitioned by a binary-tree (BT) structure. The CUs will be used for prediction and transform without any further partitioning. This implies that existing fast algorithms for QT structure used in HEVC cannot be directly applied to QTBT structure.

These challenges motivate us to develop a novel fast QTBT partition algorithm based on convolutional neural networks. As powerful end-to-end nonlinear classifiers, deep learning strategies (such as CNN) generate more discriminative representations directly from raw data [10], suitable to the complex classification task of QTBT optimization. The remaining of this paper is organized as follows. Section 2 reviews the related work. Section 3 introduces the QTBT structure, and category analysis. In Sect. 4, the proposed CNN architecture and raining details is presented. Section 5 describes the fast QTBT depth decision algorithm based on CNNs. In Sect. 6, experimental results and discussions are presented. Section 7 concludes the paper with a summary.

2   Related Works on Fast CU Decision Methods

To alleviate the CU depth decision complexity, a lot of fast intra encoding methods have been proposed for HEVC encoder. We divide these methods into the following three categories.

A. Traditional Method Based on Statistical Correlation Analysis. Shen et al. [3] exploit RD cost and mode correlations among different depth levels and spatially neighboring CUs. The depth levels that are rarely chosen as the optimal depth in spatially neighboring CUs are skipped. In [4], Zhang exploits the early CU split termination algorithm by using the approximate aggregated RD cost with sub-CUs' RDO results. In [5], a fast CU size decision algorithm based on global and local edge complexities is proposed. In [6], Lei et al. proposes a fast intra prediction method. CUs are classified into natural content CUs and screen content CUs, based on the statistic characteristics of the content. These methods are efficient in reducing the computational complexity. However, these approaches highly depend on the global statistical information of previously coded CUs, which may be difficult to handle complex situations.

B. Classification Method Based on Machine Learning. In [7], the CUs mode decision is modeled as a binary classification problem of SKIP/non-SKIP. Shen and Yu [8], proposed a two-level binary classification based approach, where the RD cost increment caused by misclassifications was modeled as weights in support vector machine (SVM) training. In [9], Zhang et al. models the CU depth decision problem as a hierarchical binary classification problem for different sizes $\{64 \times 64, 32 \times 32, 16 \times 16\}$, where a joint classifier consisting of multiple SVM classifiers is proposed by considering the risk of false prediction. In addition, a RD-complexity model is derived to optimize the coding complexity and RD performance. The performances of those machine learning methods highly depending on the hand-crafted features, to design and extract some useful encoding features is critical.

C. End-to-End Learning Method Based on Deep Neural Networks.
Recently, convolutional neural networks (CNNs) have achieved significant success for various visual tasks, such as image classification [11], semantic segmentation [12], and so on. However, fast CU decision algorithms using deep learning methods are very limited in the literature.

One of the latest literatures is [13], where a CNN oriented fast intra CU mode decision algorithm is proposed. In order to share the same CNN architecture, 32×32 and 16×16 CU are first averaging and subsampling to 8×8 matrix, and then sent into the CNN nets. The return value of CNN nets is "HOMO" or "SPLIT" indicate whether needing to split at the current depth level. This work reveals the power potential of the CNN used for the fast CU decision. However, the average increase of BD-rate is 4.79%, might be far from the state-of-the-art results.

All of the aforementioned fast encoding algorithms are well developed for QT structure, but not suitable for the new QTBT structure utilized in JVET.

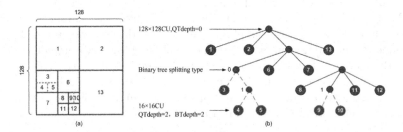

Fig. 1. An example of QTBT partitioning for I slice. (a) CTU block partitioning shape by using QTBT, (b) illustrates the corresponding QTBT tree structure.

3   QTBT Structure and Category Analysis

3.1   Quad-Tree Plus Binary-Tree (QTBT) Block Structure

QTBT block structure can support much more flexible partitioning shapes, so can better match the local characteristics of video data. Figure 1 illustrates an example of QTBT partition structure. JEM encoder will try every possible combination of QTBT partitioning structures, and choose the optimal QTBT partitioning structure with the minimum RD cost, expressed as

$$RDCost(s,c) = \arg \min_{m} \{SSD(s,c) + \lambda_m(QP) \cdot R(s,c,m)\} \qquad (1)$$

where, QP is quantization parameter, and $\lambda_m(QP)$ is the Lagrangian multiplier, $SSD(s,c)$ is the sum of squared difference between the original CU pixels s and the reconstructed pixels c, $R(s,c,m)$ represents the rate costs which is needed to encode the mode m and QP. This traverse calculation strategy is of extremely high complexity and make it difficult for real-time implementation.

3.2   Category Design and Training Samples Collection

In this work, the QTBT partition depth range is modeled as a multi classification problem. We set classes according to the max QTBT partition depth of sub CUs in a 32×32 CU. Considering the QTBT parameters setting (maxBTSize is 32×32 pixels for I slice) [2], we use 32×32 CUs as the basis for classification, which can cover all of the depth of BT partition, also can expand to the larger size of QT partition flexibility, see Sect. 5 for details.

$$class\_depth = \arg\max(QTBTDepth_{sub\_CU_i})$$
$$QTBTDepth_{CU_i} = 2 \times QTDepth_{CU_i} + BTDepth_{CU_i} \tag{2}$$

where, $QTBTDepth_{CU_i}$ is the final QTBT partitioning depth of sub_CU_i. And $class\_depth$ is the max QTBT partition depth within a 32×32 CU, which represents the minimum splitting shapes. Considering spatial correlations, the minimum splitting shapes often reflect the texture richness of the whole 32×32 CU.

Training samples are collected by the original JEM 3.1 encoder. Six sequences with various resolutions and properties were encoded, including "Kebia", "BQMall", "Johnny", "Cactus", "Traffic", and "Tango". For simplicity, to avoid similar frames and duplicate samples in the training dataset, we extract 13 sample frames to encoding from each sequence with TemporalSubsampleRatio=8.

In the training dataset, we eliminate such samples which the RD cost difference between the candidate CUs mode is too small, since such samples will make the nets trapped in an ill-conditions in the training [13]. For that reason, the samples with $|\Delta RDCost| \leq 0.01$ are discarded.

$$\Delta RDCost = \frac{RDCost_{opt} - RDCost_{sub}}{RDCost_{opt} + RDCost_{sub}} \tag{3}$$

where, $RDCost_{opt}$ and $RDCost_{sub}$ denominate the RD costs of the optimal 32×32 CUs partition structure and sub-optimal structure, respectively. About 200k samples were collected in total, eighty percent of them used for training, and the remaining was used as the cross validation set.

4   CNN Architecture and Training

We design a CNN network for QTBT depth classification, as shown by Fig. 2. The front part of the proposed network is mainly used to extract image features, which is mainly based on the framework of ResNets [11]. The feature map extracted by the residual units can be calculated as follows:

$$x^{l+1} = [\max(0, x^l \cdot w_0^l + b_0^l) \cdot w_1^l + b_1^l] + x^l \tag{4}$$

Here, x^l and x^{l+1} are input and output of the *l-th* residual units, w and b represent weights matrix and bias respectively, and $max(0, x^l \cdot w_0 + b_0)$ is a rectified linear unit (ReLU) activation functions.

The latter part of the proposed network is used to realize the nonlinear fusion of image features and *QP*. Here, we employ 1×1 convolutional, which is used for strengthening the connection between different feature channels. Then, *QP* and image feature vectors are sent into the multilayer perception layer for nonlinear fusion, and finally output classification results.

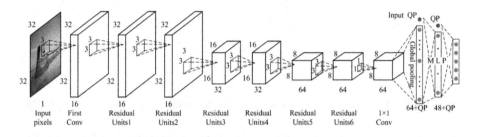

Fig. 2. Architecture of the proposed convolutional neural network.

We implement our proposed network based on the Caffe [14]. During training, we don't make any kind preprocessing on the import pixels. This enables the nets to extract and deliver more useful information from the raw data. In addition, we found that using the L2 HingeLoss as objective function yields a better classification accuracy in this task. We apply a two-stage training procedure to effectively reduce the difficulty of training. We first pre-training the network by using the samples only collected under QP 27, by using the stochastic gradient descent with Nesterov momentum of 0.9, and fixed weight decay 0.0005. All weights of convolutional filters are initialized using the Xavier normalized initialization procedure, and all bias are initialized with constant 0. A batch size of 50 and an initial learning rate of 0.002 was used. On the second training stage, samples collected under all QPs{22, 27, 32, and 37} are applied for fine-tuning, to ensure the networks adapt to the natural distributions of classes.

5   Fast QTBT Partition Method Based on CNN Classifier

5.1   Framework of the Proposed Fast QTBT Partition Algorithm

In this work, the QTBT structure optimization process is modeled as a multi classification problem, and the candidate depth range for each 32×32 CUs is adaptively determined around the online classification results. Each CTU will be processed according to the workflow in Fig. 3. Described as follows:

First, each CTU (128×128) is evenly divided into a set of small patches with 32×32 pixels before QTBT partition, each patch just like a 32×32 CUs. That is, a CTU is comprised of 16 small patches and fed into CNN classifier.

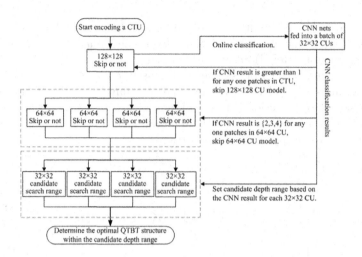

Fig. 3. Flowchart of the proposed fast QTBT mode decision algorithm based on CNNs.

Second, feature extraction and classification are performed by the CNN networks for each input patch, based on the QP and properties of the current CU itself without other hand-crafted features.

Third, we propose two encoding settings schemes with different candidate search ranges around the classifier results for RDO calculation, which are explained as follows:

Step 1: If the classification result is greater than "1" for anyone patches in 128 × 128 CTU, it means that the CTU contains some textures or not very homogeneous, suitable for partitioning into smaller CUs. Hence, skipping 128 × 128 CU's RD cost calculation, directly.

Step 2: If CNN classification result is "2", "3" or "4" for anyone patches in a 64 × 64 CU, it means that current 64 × 64 CU contains some detail textures. So, skipping 64 × 64 CU's RD cost calculation. Otherwise, calculate the RD cost of the 64 × 64 CU, and then go into step 3, to calculate the RD cost of each sub CUs, and finally determine the optimal QTBT partition structure.

Step 3: When entering the 32 × 32 CU level, encoder will calculate RD cost for each partition depth within the candidate depth range. Candidate partition depth range (QT and BT depth) for 32 × 32 CUs as shown in Table 1, which can make the trade-off between the RD performance and time saving.

5.2 Two Trade-Off Settings for Candidate QTBT Depth Range

Firstly, a same partition shape can be generated by different QTBT partition methods, as shown in Fig. 4. What's more, we design categories according to the maximum QTBT partition depth, which represents the minimum splitting shapes. As a result, each category exists with different QTBT partition methods, with the same class label.

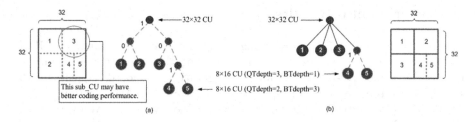

Fig. 4. An instance of the same partition shape generated by different QTBT partition methods. (a) Combinations of binary-tree splitting straightforward, (b) Combinations of quad-tree plus binary-tree splitting indirectly.

Secondly, though splitting shapes are identical for the two splitting methods, the coding performance is differ from each other under intra coding. As shown in Fig. 4a, when adopt combinations of binary-tree splitting partition straightforward, the upper-right sub-CU may have better prediction quality, which mainly results from different processing orders leading to different reference samples as well as prediction signals.

Thirdly, When restrict the maxBTDepth=2, we can also obtain similar block partition results through the combination of quad-tree plus binary-tree splitting indirectly, as shown in Fig. 4b. This avoids the most time consuming partition (BTDepth=3).

Based above analysis, our proposed method provides two different candidate depth range settings around the CNN classifier results, by considering the trade-off between the RD performance and computational complexity. Namely "RD maintaining" setting and "Low complexity", as shown in Table 1. Our insight is that you need to bypass much more BT partition modes checking, leading to more computational complexity savings. In general, the design can be adjusted flexibly according to practical requirements.

Table 1. Candidate QTBT partition depth range for 32 × 32 CUs

Class label	RD maintaining	Low complexity
0	QTDepth=2, BTDepth=0-1	QTDepth=2, BTDepth=0-1
	QTDepth=3, BTDepth=0	
1	QTDepth=2, BTDepth=0-3	QTDepth=2, BTDepth=0-2
	QTDepth=3, BTDepth=0-1	QTDepth=3, BTDepth=0
2	QTDepth=2, BTDepth=0-3	QTDepth=2, BTDepth=0-2
	QTDepth=3, BTDepth=0-2	QTDepth=3, BTDepth=0-1
3	QTDepth=3, BTDepth=0-3	QTDepth=3, BTDepth=0-2
	QTDepth=4, BTDepth=0	QTDepth=4, BTDepth=0-1
4	QTDepth=3, BTDepth=0-3	QTDepth=3, BTDepth=0-2
	QTDepth=4, BTDepth=0-2	QTDepth=4, BTDepth=0-2

6   Experimental Results

The proposed fast QTBT decision algorithm has been integrated into JEM 3.1. Experiments are conducted strictly following the common test condition (CTC) [15], under All-Intra (AI) main configuration. Standard sequences with 100 frames were used, and four QPs{22, 27, 32, and 37}. Average time saving (ATS) is employed to measure the encoding complexity saving. And CNN classifier time (NetT) is employed to measure the computational burden of CNN classification in the proposed algorithm.

$$ATS = average\left\{(T_{JEM} - T_{proposed})/T_{JEM} \times 100\%\right\} \tag{5}$$

$$NetT = average(T_{Net}/T_{proposed} \times 100\%) \tag{6}$$

Experimental results are given in Table 2, where "BR" column stand for BD-rate. Compared with anchor JEM 3.1, our proposed fast QTBT partition mode decision framework can achieve an averaged complexity reduction of 43.69% under "RD Maintaining" setting with 0.77% negligible BD-rate increase. Under "Low Complexity" setting, we achieve 62.96% average complexity reduction with 2.06% acceptable BD-rate increase.

The main difference between "RD maintaining" and "Low complexity" setting lies in the different candidate BT partition depth. Comparing the RD performance and time saving of these two settings, we can get the preliminary conclusion that binary tree partition can achieve much better compression performance at the expense of largely increased encoding computational complexity.

In addition, our deep learning model shows good generalization ability to various sequences. In Table 2, sequences with * are those videos whose 13 frames were used in the training phase. We observe comparable BD-rate increase and similar complexity reduction, when we compare sequences used for training and sequences that are not used for training.

Table 2 "AC" column indicates CU depth decision accuracy within the candidate depth range. We achieve 88.46% and 77.08% on average under "RD Maintaining" and "Low Complexity" setting respectively. It is important to realize that, when class "3" was misclassified as "4", the encoder still can fine the optimal partition depth through RDO in the end, since the optimal partition depth still inside the candidate depth range of class "4".

We also can be clear from the Table 2 "NetT" column, that the computational complexity added to the encoder associated with the CNN classifier is account 2.95% and 4.51% on average under "RD Maintaining" and "Low Complexity" setting respectively. These computational burdens are fully acceptable compared with the overall encoding time saving.

To further verify the proposed scheme, we compare it with the method proposed in the JVET-D0077 [16]. In [16], fast algorithms includes the re-use of split decision and intra prediction mode is proposed, if the same block in the other partition choices have the same neighboring coded blocks. The method in D0077 can provide 11.38% encoding time saving with 0.05% BD-rate increase. Compared with the method in D0077, the contribution of our algorithm is to

Table 2. Performance of the propose fast QTBT partition algorithm

Test sequence		RD maintaining				Low complexity				D0077 [16]	
		BR (%)	AC (%)	ATS (%)	NetT (%)	BR (%)	AC (%)	ATS (%)	NetT (%)	BR (%)	ATS (%)
Class A 2560 × 1600	Traffic*	0.69	86.38	43.41	2.78	2.34	71.25	64.75	4.35	–	–
	SteamTrain	0.73	81.77	39.91	2.50	1.21	70.34	65.74	4.48	–	–
	NebutaFestiv	0.66	79.50	40.11	2.02	0.92	68.97	65.38	3.04	–	–
	PeopleOnStre	0.62	88.12	44.02	2.66	2.34	72.64	63.87	4.04	–	–
Class A1 4K	Tango*	1.18	90.49	45.76	4.53	1.78	84.10	62.26	6.93	0.01	11.83
	Drums100	0.68	86.40	39.78	2.66	1.42	76.29	63.73	5.12	0.01	12.26
	CampfirePart	1.40	86.07	42.07	3.10	2.75	77.66	61.37	5.65	0.07	10.56
	ToddlerFount	0.89	82.76	40.10	2.02	2.10	68.67	65.13	3.04	0.01	9.46
Class B 1920 × 1080	Cactus*	0.88	87.16	41.23	2.18	2.63	72.06	62.88	4.55	0.04	11.61
	Kimono	0.60	94.16	47.50	5.30	1.00	90.27	66.59	7.84	0.04	12.30
	ParkScene	0.99	86.45	42.98	2.14	2.24	71.41	63.93	3.43	0.03	12.76
	BQTerrace	0.66	89.31	45.24	2.41	1.82	77.90	60.32	3.35	0.06	12.22
Class C 832 × 480	BQMall*	0.64	89.52	44.60	2.26	2.39	74.13	62.46	3.27	0.04	10.47
	Flowervase	0.86	94.32	44.55	5.22	2.87	87.54	60.64	7.21	–	–
	PartyScene	0.29	93.14	43.61	1.38	1.09	78.15	62.31	1.85	0.05	11.71
	RaceHorses	0.54	87.72	45.70	2.17	1.63	74.34	62.34	3.01	0.02	12.04
Class D 416 × 240	Kebia*	0.65	85.26	44.55	2.21	2.37	73.24	63.19	3.48	–	–
	BlowingBubb	0.94	83.38	46.03	1.56	2.24	71.81	62.08	2.20	0.04	11.17
	RaceHorses	0.66	87.85	48.30	1.77	1.73	74.85	63.26	2.60	0.09	10.44
	BQSquare	0.61	92.96	41.19	1.53	1.05	85.62	59.96	1.98	0.06	7.47
Class E 1280 × 720	Johnny*	0.72	94.67	45.12	5.80	2.54	86.87	61.84	8.15	0.06	10.94
	KristenandSa	1.05	91.27	42.89	4.77	2.53	83.12	61.37	7.01	0.07	13.14
	FourPeople	0.63	91.78	47.95	3.49	2.79	77.85	63.91	5.22	0.07	13.16
	vidyo1	0.91	92.49	42.03	4.40	2.86	80.85	61.64	6.53	–	–
Overall		0.77	88.46	43.69	2.95	2.06	77.08	62.96	4.51	0.05	11.38

Notes: Sequences with * are those videos whose 13 frames were used for training.

significantly reduce the coding complexity. The time saving of our proposed algorithm is 3.8–5.5 times as much as that of D0077. Based on accurate classification and depth range prediction, our proposed fast scheme can skip or early termination some unnecessary partition iterations which outside the scope of candidate QT and BT depth ranges, thus greatly saving encoding time.

7   Conclusion

In this paper, we propose a novel fast QTBT mode decision method based on CNNs for JVET, in which the candidate QTBT partition depth range is adaptively determined, based on the properties of the current CU itself without other hand-crafted features. The main contributions of this paper can be summarized as following: (1) We propose an end-to-end fast QTBT block partition framework, and set candidate QTBT partition depth according to the online classification results. (2) We design a single CNN classifier try to predict the depth range within 32 × 32 CUs directly, rather than to judge split or not at each depth of CU, which can effectively reduce the complexity of encoding. (3) The proposed fast scheme also has the advantage that it can make the trade-off between the RD performance and time saving by setting different partition method. Experimental results demonstrate that the proposed algorithm exhibiting applicability to various types of video sequences.

References

1. Chen, J., Alshina, E., Sullivan, G.J.: Algorithm Description of Joint Exploration Test Model 1, JVET-A1001, JVET 1st Meeting, Geneva (2015)
2. Karczewicz, M., Alshina, E.: JVET AHG Report: Tool Evaluation (AHG1). JVET-F0001, JVET 6th Meeting, Hobart, 31 March 2017
3. Shen, L.Q., Zhang, Z.Y., An, P.: Fast CU size decision and mode decision algorithm for HEVC intra coding. IEEE Trans. Consum. Electron. **59**(1), 207–213 (2013)
4. Zhang, H., Ma, Z.: Fast intra mode decision for high efficiency video coding (HEVC). IEEE Trans Circuits Syst. Video Technol. **24**(4), 660–668 (2014)
5. Min, B., Cheung, R.C.C.: A fast CU size decision algorithm for the HEVC intra encoder. IEEE Trans. Circuits Syst. Video Technol. **25**(5), 892–896 (2015)
6. Lei, J.J., Li, D.Y., Pan, Z.Q., Sun, Z.Y., Kwong, S., Hou, C.P.: Fast intra prediction based on content property analysis for low complexity HEVC-based screen content coding. IEEE Trans. Broadcast. **63**(1), 48–58 (2017)
7. Hu, Q., Zhang, X.Y., Shi, Z.R., Gao, Z.Y.: Neyman-Pearson-based early mode decision for HEVC encoding. IEEE Trans. Multimed. **18**(3), 379–391 (2016)
8. Shen, X.L., Yu, L.: CU splitting early termination based on weighted SVM. EURASIP J. Image Video Process. (2013)
9. Zhang, Y., Kwong, S., Wang, X., Yuan, H., Pan, Z.Q., Xu, L.: Machine learning-based coding unit depth decisions for flexible complexity allocation in high efficiency video coding. IEEE Trans. Image Process. **24**(7), 2225–2238 (2015)
10. LeCun, Y., Bengio, Y., Hinton, G.: Deep learning. Nature **521**(7553), 436–444 (2015)

11. He, K., Zhang, X., Ren, S., Sun, J.: Deep residual learning for image recognition. CoRR, abs/1512.03385 (2015)
12. Long, J., Shelhamer, E., Darrell, T.: Fully convolutional networks for semantic segmentation. In: Proceedings of CVPR, pp. 3431–3440. IEEE (2015)
13. Liu, Z.Y., Yu, X.Y., Gao, Y., Chen, S.L., Ji, X.Y., Wang, D.S.: CU partition mode decision for HEVC hardwired intra encoder using convolution neural network. IEEE Trans. Image Process. **25**(11), 5088–5103 (2016)
14. Jia, Y., Shelhamer, E., Donahue, J., Karayev, S., Long, J., Girshick, R., Guadarrama, S., Darrell, T.: Caffe: convolutional architecture for fast feature embedding. arXiv preprint arXiv:1408.5093 (2014)
15. Suehring, K., Li, X.: JVET Common Test Conditions and Software Reference Configurations, B1010, JVET 2nd Meeting, San Diego, February 2016
16. Huang, H., Shan, L., Huang, Y.W.: AHG5: Speed-Up for JEM-3.1. JVET-D0077, JVET 4th Meeting, Chengdu, 15–21 October 2016

A Novel Saliency Based Bit Allocation and RDO for HEVC

Jiajun Xu, Qiang Peng$^{(\boxtimes)}$, Bing Wang, Changbin Li, and Xiao Wu

School of Information Science and Technology, Southwest Jiaotong University,
Chengdu 611756, China
{jjxu,bwang}@my.swjtu.edu.cn, qpeng@home.swjtu.edu.cn,
mailoflichangbin@163.com, wuxiaohk@gmail.com

Abstract. In this paper, an efficient rate control algorithm is proposed which is based on saliency map for high-efficiency video coding (HEVC). The aim of the proposed algorithm is increasing the amount bits assigned in saliency region. To begin with, the Context-Aware model is used to obtain the saliency map. With the saliency information, a novel scheme is proposed to guide the LCU (Largest Coding Unit) level bit-allocation. Based on that, a novel perceptual rate distortion model is proposed, which takes saliency weight into consideration when performing rate-distortion optimization (RDO). Finally, the experimental results show our algorithm significantly improves the subjective quality of videos compressed by HEVC and gains of 0.61 dB in Y-PSNR.

Keywords: HEVC · Saliency map · Bit-allocation
Rate-Distortion Optimization (RDO)

1 Introduction

With the study of human visual system (HVS), the research of perceptual video coding becomes more and more popular. Perception model can improve the video coding efficiency [1,2]. Additionally, in [3], the perceptual video coding methods are classified into three categories: vision-model based approach, signal-driven approach, and hybrid approach. At the same time, the techniques for computational visual-model have been extensively explored. When people observe the scenes, the visual attention is affected by two manners, top-down visual attention and bottom-up visual attention. Top-down attention is task-dependent, volition-controlled and knowledge-based, while bottom-up attention is task-independent and stimulus-based. Meanwhile, Itti [4] proposes a computational visual attention model based on the feature integration theory to analyze the attention region in the visual scene. Then, different attention models are proposed and utilized in perceptual video coding.

Rate control is an important topic in video coding, which aims to optimize visual quality via reasonably allocating bits to various frames and blocks using a given bit-rate. In recent years, rate control algorithms for perceptual video

© Springer International Publishing AG, part of Springer Nature 2018
B. Zeng et al. (Eds.): PCM 2017, LNCS 10735, pp. 70–78, 2018.
https://doi.org/10.1007/978-3-319-77380-3_7

coding have also gained much attention. Milani et al. [5] use the object detection algorithm to generate saliency metric and optimize the object edge bits allocation. In [6], a rate control scheme based on region of interest (ROI) is proposed for H.264/AVC, aiming at allocating more bit resource to ROI and still maintaining the accuracy of the output bit-rate. Hadizadeh et al. [7] develops a method for saliency estimation in the DCT domain to reduce attention-grabbing coding artifacts. Li et al. [8] utilize the saliency map calculated from the computational visual attention model to adjust bits allocation for better perceptual quality. However, most of these algorithms are designed for H.264/AVC, which could not be directly applied to HEVC. Because the coding structure of HEVC is different from H.264/AVC and some advanced technologies which adopted in HEVC are not suitable for these algorithms.

In this paper, a saliency-based rate control algorithm for HEVC is proposed which contains follows steps. First, an efficient method is used to generate a saliency map for each frame. Second, with the saliency information, a visual weight bit-allocation scheme is proposed to allow the encoder to allocate bits for LCUs. Finally, we take saliency weight into consideration by this novel scheme, when performing RDO. The proposed rate control algorithm is compared with the existing rate control method in HEVC. The results show that our method gains a better performance in preserving the information contained in saliency region and makes the actual encoding bit-rate meet the target bit-rate.

The remainder of the paper is organized as follows: in Sect. 2, we introduce a saliency model. Section 3 proposed a bit-allocation scheme. The improved RDO is in Sect. 4. Experimental results and conclusion are given in Sects. 5, and 6, respectively.

2   Context-Aware Saliency Map

According to the visual stimulus, saliency refers to the indication of the probability of human attention. Among the existing bottom-up computational models of visual attention, the Context-Aware model [9] can achieve a good performance. Thus, we use this method to get the saliency maps in our algorithm. Figure 1 is the framework of Context-Aware model.

Fig. 1. Framework of the Context-Aware model

In our algorithm, saliency map for each frame is generated using the Context-Aware model before encoding the video sequence. Figure 2 shows the saliency maps of one frame for 6 videos.

The property of HVS indicates that people pay more attention to saliency region. In HEVC, the ill-suited bits allocation problem may cause an unsatisfactory visual perception performance, since it does not take the unequal perceptual

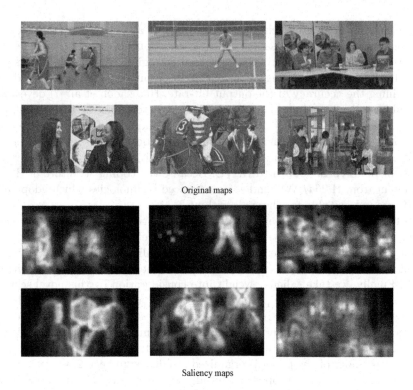

Original maps

Saliency maps

Fig. 2. Context-Aware saliency maps of one frame for 6 videos

weights between the saliency and non-saliency regions into consideration when allocating the bits in video coding. Therefore, a reasonable approach is to allocate more bits in saliency regions and less bits in non-saliency regions, which can improve the quality of human experience (QoE) in the same situation. In the next section, we will introduce a bit-allocation scheme in our algorithm.

3   Saliency Map Based Bits Allocation Scheme

One of the most important tasks of video coding is bit-allocation, which aims at finding some improved balance between video quality and bit-rate. In [10], a linear R-λ model based rate control algorithm is proposed, which is the recommended rate control algorithm in the present HEVC reference software. The λ is the Lagrange multiplier in the RDO, and defined as

$$\lambda = \alpha \times R^{\beta} \tag{1}$$

Where R is the target bits. α, β are parameters related to video content.

In HEVC, target bits allocation of one frame is determined by frame-level rate control. Then LTU level bit-allocation is performed based on MAD (Mean

Absolute Difference). When the target bits for a frame $T_{currpic}$ is obtained, the Lagrange multiplier of a frame λ_{pic} is obtained by Eq. (1). The texture-complexity weight of the ith LTU is bit weight (BW), the $BW_{LTU}(i)$ is obtained by Eq. (2). According to Eqs. (1) and (2), the target bits allocation of the ith LTU is defined by Eq. (3) where M is the number of the macroblock in current frame, $\alpha_{LTU}(i)$ and $\beta_{LTU}(i)$ are renew based on [10].

$$BW_{LTU}(i) = (\frac{\lambda_{pic}}{\alpha_{LTU}(i)})^{\frac{1}{\beta_{LTU}(i)}} \tag{2}$$

$$T_{LTU}(i) = T_{currpic} \times \frac{BW_{LTU}(i)}{\sum_{j=0}^{M-1} BW_{LTU}(j)} \tag{3}$$

Nevertheless, this bit-allocation scheme does not consider the HVS. In order to be consistent with the HVS, it is essential to proposing an efficient method which allocate the bits more reasonably. According to Sect. 2, the saliency maps can be obtained using the Context-Aware model. In a Saliency map, $S_{r,c}$ is the saliency weight of pixel(r,c), $S(i)$ is the saliency weight for the CTU of index i.

$$S(i) = \frac{\sum_{(r,c) \in LTU_i} S_{r,c}}{N_{LTU_i}} \tag{4}$$

where N_{LTU_i} is the sum of pixels for ith LTU. Based on Eqs. (3) and (4), the saliency weight is taken into consideration. Therefore, $T_{LTU}(i)$ is updated by Eq. (5)

$$T_{LTU}(i) = T_{currpic} \times ((1 - \varphi) \times \frac{BW_{LTU}(i)}{\sum_{j=0}^{M-1} BW_{LTU}(j)} + \varphi \times \frac{S(i)}{\sum_{j=0}^{M-1} S(j)}) \tag{5}$$

where φ is the ratio of saliency weight to texture-complexity weight, which is related to bit-rate. It is defined by Eq. (6).

$$\varphi = min((\frac{C_1}{R_c} + C_2), 1) \tag{6}$$

where R_c is the bit-rate of sequence, C_1 and C_2 are related with video content. We set $C_1 = 100$, $C_2 = 0.5$ in our algorithm. When the bit-rate is very low, φ is more likely equals to 1, it means the saliency weight plays the key role. Allocating more bits to saliency region can achieve a higher quality of experience. The bit-allocation scheme is called Weighted Bit Allocation (WBA).

4 Proposed Perceptual RDO

In HEVC, numerous modes are provided to adapt to video content variation. The different mode represents the different partitions of an LCU. An LCU can be split into four quad-tree structured coding unit (CU). For the LCUs with low texture-complexity video content, the large size mode is preferred. On the contrary, the LCUs with high textured video content may benefit from the small partitions. The decision of the best mode recurs to RDO. RDO tries to achieve a tradeoff between the bit cost and visual quality degradation usually measured by MSE. Traditional RDO is formulated as:

$$J = D + \lambda R \tag{7}$$

where D represents the distortion and R is the bit cost for coding a CU. With the same distortion, the mode with the least bit cost would be the best mode. Equivalently, the mode with the least MSE would be the best mode under the same bit cost.

According to Sect. 3, saliency region is more sensitive to noise. When a CU contains saliency region, it needs to be chosen a mode with less distortion. Hence, we consider modifying the distortion of each CU with the saliency weight $d\omega(i)$. The RDO process in each CU can be improved by $d\omega(i)$ as:

$$J = D(\mu + \delta \times d\omega(i)) + \lambda R \tag{8}$$

$$d\omega(i) = \frac{1}{N_{CU_i}} \times \sum_{(r,c) \in CU_i} S_{r,c} \tag{9}$$

where N_{CU_i} is the sum of pixels for the ith CU, $(\mu + \delta \times d\omega(i))$ is a linear statistical model, which is obtained based on the experimental results. It indicates that the CU can tolerate more or less MSE distortion. μ is set to 0.5, δ is set to 1 in our algorithm. The improved RD performance is discussed in the next section. The modified RDO fixed by weighted distortion is called WDRDO.

5   Experiment

We firstly compare the WDRDO with WBA and HM 16.7 (with rate control algorithm in [10]), WDRDO is performed based on WBA. We use 6 test sequences from HEVC test database with "low delay P configuration" and all sequences are in 4:2:0 format and the other configuration is in Table 1.

Table 1. The configuration of test sequences

Sequence	Resolution	Framerate (fps)	Frames	Bit-rate (kb/s)				
BasketballDrive (BD)	1920 × 1080	50	250	256	512	1024	2048	4096
Tennis	1920 × 1080	24	240	256	512	1024	2048	4096
FourPeople (FP)	1280 × 720	60	600	128	256	512	1024	2048
KristenAndSara (KS)	1280 × 720	60	600	128	256	512	1024	2048
RaceHorses (RH)	832 × 480	30	300	128	256	512	1024	2048
BQMall (BQM)	832 × 480	60	600	128	256	512	1024	2048

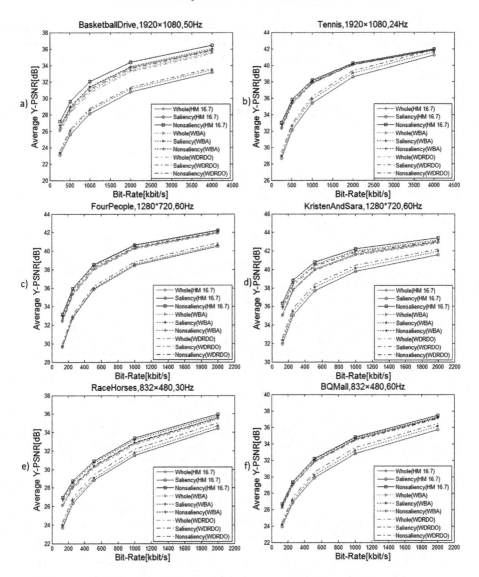

Fig. 3. Rate distortion performance comparison over saliency, non-saliency, and whole regions between the HM 16.7 and our algorithm on compressing 6 sequences. (a) BD, (b) Tennis, (c) FP, (d) KS, (e) RH, (f) BQM.

5.1 Objective Experiment

The results of our objective experiments are shown in Fig. 3 and Table 2. Figure 3 shows the rate distortion performance between the HM 16.7 and our algorithm on compressing 6 sequences. Table 2 lists the experimental results of different sequences with different target bit-rate. According to the experimental results, we can easily see that the average Y-PSNR of WDRDO in saliency region increases 0.61dB compared to HM 16.7 and the bit-rate accuracy with a negligible mismatch, which indicates WDRDO achieve a better performance than HM 16.7.

Table 2. Bit-rate, sal and non-sal region PSNR of HM 16.7 with rate control and the WD

Sequence	R_{target} (kbps)	HM16.7 with RC in [10]				Proposed algorithm of WDRDO				ΔPSNR (dB)	
		R_{actual} (kbps)	Sal region PSNR	Non-sal region PSNR	Bit-rate error ratio	R_{actual} (kbps)	Sal region PSNR	Non-sal region PSNR	Bit-rate error ratio	Sal	Non-sal
BD	256	257.62	23.07	27.17	0.0063	257.64	23.67	26.42	0.0064	0.60	−0.75
	512	513.29	25.61	29.63	0.0025	513.35	26.25	28.67	0.0026	0.64	−0.97
	1000	997.10	28.15	32.05	0.0029	1000.55	28.77	31.06	0.0005	0.62	−0.99
	2000	1994.68	30.75	34.42	0.0027	1999.59	31.35	33.62	0.0002	0.60	−0.8
	4000	3995.85	33.13	36.43	0.0010	4000.64	33.64	35.82	0.0002	0.51	−0.61
BD$_{average}$			28.14	31.94	0.0031		28.74	31.12	0.0020	0.60	−0.82
Tennis	256	257.12	28.64	33.01	0.0044	257.10	29.41	32.51	0.0043	0.77	−0.5
	512	513.07	32.14	35.83	0.0021	512.98	32.94	35.47	0.0019	0.80	−0.36
	1000	999.69	35.42	38.18	0.0003	997.03	36.20	37.90	0.0030	0.79	−0.27
	2000	2001.39	38.57	40.26	0.0007	2001.36	39.35	40.08	0.0007	0.77	−0.19
	4000	4002.95	41.23	41.96	0.0007	4001.86	41.89	41.79	0.0005	0.66	−0.18
Tennis$_{average}$			35.20	37.85	0.0016		35.96	37.55	0.0021	0.76	−0.30
FP	128	129.92	29.66	33.19	0.0150	129.94	30.02	32.77	0.0152	0.36	−0.42
	256	257.91	32.80	35.93	0.0075	257.91	33.14	35.54	0.0075	0.34	−0.39
	512	513.90	35.87	38.54	0.0037	513.85	36.23	38.25	0.0036	0.36	−0.29
	1000	1002.03	38.45	40.66	0.0020	1001.80	38.82	40.42	0.0018	0.37	−0.24
	2000	2001.92	40.52	42.25	0.0010	2001.85	40.88	42.07	0.0009	0.36	−0.17
FP$_{average}$			35.46	38.11	0.0058		35.82	37.81	0.0058	0.36	−0.3
KS	128	130.02	32.00	36.32	0.0158	130.03	32.64	35.70	0.0159	0.64	−0.62
	256	258.00	35.03	38.84	0.0078	258.11	35.76	38.27	0.0082	0.73	−0.57
	512	514.00	37.71	40.80	0.0039	514.24	38.40	40.35	0.0044	0.69	−0.45
	1000	1002.02	39.79	42.23	0.0020	1002.33	40.44	41.85	0.0023	0.64	−0.38
	2000	2002.12	41.56	43.42	0.0011	2002.28	42.17	43.01	0.0011	0.61	−0.41
KS$_{average}$			37.22	40.32	0.0061		37.88	39.84	0.0064	0.66	−0.49
RH	128	128.97	23.70	26.92	0.0076	128.99	24.31	26.54	0.0077	0.60	−0.39
	256	256.97	26.32	28.78	0.0038	256.97	26.96	28.31	0.0038	0.64	−0.47
	512	512.97	28.84	30.90	0.0019	513.04	29.47	30.46	0.0020	0.63	−0.44
	1000	1001.01	31.52	33.38	0.0010	1001.09	32.16	32.93	0.0011	0.63	−0.45
	2000	2001.00	34.41	35.97	0.0005	2001.15	35.05	35.57	0.0006	0.64	−0.41
RH$_{average}$			28.96	31.19	0.0030		29.59	30.76	0.0051	0.63	−0.43
BQM	128	128.94	23.92	26.66	0.0073	129.94	24.45	26.34	0.0152	0.53	−0.32
	256	257.98	26.80	29.35	0.0077	258.00	27.47	29.00	0.0078	0.67	−0.34
	512	513.94	29.87	32.16	0.0038	513.98	30.53	31.86	0.0039	0.66	−0.3
	1000	1001.97	32.80	34.83	0.0020	1002.03	33.53	34.50	0.0020	0.73	−0.33
	2000	2001.98	35.73	37.43	0.0010	2002.03	36.45	37.08	0.0010	0.73	−0.35
BQM$_{average}$			29.82	32.09	0.0044		30.49	31.76	0.0060	0.66	−0.33
ALL$_{AVERAGE}$			32.47	35.25	0.0040		33.08	34.80	0.0042	0.61	−0.44

5.2 Subjective Experiment

The subjective experiment is designed in agreement with the recommendation of ITU-R BT.500-13 [11]. 22 participants, between 18 and 35 years old, are involved in the subjective experiments. All participants are volunteer and non-experts. We use the Double-Stimulus Continue Quality-Scale (DSCQS) as our assessment methodology. The mean opinion score (MOS) scales for the DSCQS protocol range from 0 to 100 for the quality from bad to excellent: excellent (100-81), good (80-61), fair (60-41), poor (40-21), bad (20-1).

Table 3. The difference mean opinion score (DMOS) of subjective experiment

Sequence	Resolution	Bitrate (kb/s)	HM16.7	WBA	WDRDO
BasketballDrive (BD)	1920 × 1080	1000	27.15	23.08	22.69
Tennis	1920 × 1080	1000	26.46	22.77	22.38
FourPeople (FP)	1280 × 720	256	44.00	34.17	32.17
KristenAndSara (KS)	1280 × 720	256	26.46	22.77	22.38
RaceHorses (RH)	832 × 480	128	56.69	51.46	47.54
BQMall (BQM)	832 × 480	128	73.54	68.08	65.08

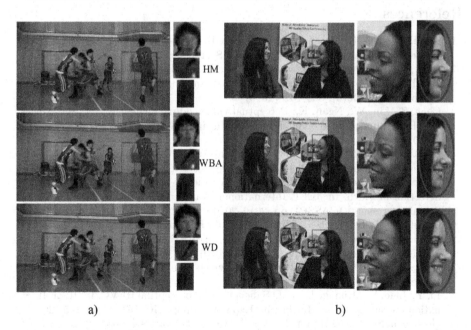

a)   b)

Fig. 4. Subjective visual quality comparison between HM 16.7, WBA and WDRDO. (a) Analysis of the 106th frame of BasketballDrive (1920 × 1080). (b) Analysis of the 34th frame of KristenAndSara (1280 × 720).

The difference MOS (DMOS) is then calculated as the difference between the MOS of the original video and the reconstructed video for each representation. The smaller DMOS indicates that the subjective quality is closer to the original video and represents the better visual quality. The subjective experimental result is reported in Table 3. Two examples of subjective visual quality comparison are shown in Fig. 4. It can be seen that the proposed algorithm achieves significant improvement in perceptual quality.

Both the objective and subjective experiments demonstrate our algorithm achieve better perceptual performance than HM 16.7.

6   Conclusion

In this paper, we have proposed a rate control algorithm for HEVC. A novel bit-allocation scheme in our algorithm is proposed, for improving the subjective visual quality of video on the HEVC platform. Then we propose a perceptual RDO based model. The experimental results demonstrate that our algorithm can improve the visual quality of encoded video compared to the rate control algorithm in HM 16.7. In the future, we will explore the more perceptually-friendly distortion metric instead of the conventional MSE in the RDO cost function. So that might bring a better performance to our algorithm.

References

1. Harel, J., Koch, C., Perona, P.: Graph-based visual saliency. In: 20th Annual Conference on Neural Information Processing Systems (NIPS), pp. 545–552 (2007)
2. Chen, Z., Guillemot, C., et al.: Perceptually-friendly H. 264/AVC video coding based on foveated just-noticeable-distortion model. IEEE Trans. Circuits Syst. Video Technol. **20**(6), 806–819 (2010)
3. Chen, Z., Lin, W., Ngan, K.: Perceptual video coding: challenges and approaches. In: IEEE International Conference on Multimedia Expo (ICME), pp. 784–789 (2010)
4. Itti, L.: Automatic foveation for video compression using a neurobiological model of visual attention. IEEE Trans. Image Process. **13**(10), 1304–1318 (2004)
5. Milani, S., Bernardini, R., Rinaldo, R.: A saliency-based rate control for people detection in video. In: IEEE International Conference on Acoustics, Speech and Signal Processing (ICASSP), pp. 2016–2020 (2013)
6. Chiang, J.-C., Hsieh, C.-S., Chang, G., et al.: Region of interest based rate control scheme with flexible quality on demand. In: IEEE International Conference on Multimedia Expo (ICME), pp. 238–242 (2010)
7. Hadizadeh, H., Bajic, I.: Saliency-aware video compression. IEEE Trans. Image Process. **23**(1), 19–33 (2014)
8. Li, Y., Liao, W., Huang, J., et al.: Saliency based perceptual HEVC. In: IEEE International Conference on Multimedia Expo Workshops (ICMEW), pp. 1–5 (2014)
9. Goferman, S., Zelnik-Manor, L., Tal, A.: Context-Aware saliency detection. IEEE Trans. Pattern Anal. Mach. Intell. **34**(10), 1915–1926 (2012)
10. Li, B., Li, H., Li, L., et al.: Lambda domain rate control algorithm for high efficiency video coding. IEEE Trans. Image Process. **23**(9), 3841–3854 (2014)
11. Recommendation ITU-R BT.500-13. Methodology for the Subjective Assessment of the Quality of Television Pictures. ITU-R, Geneva (2012)

Light Field Image Compression Scheme Based on MVD Coding Standard

Xinpeng Huang, Ping An$^{(\boxtimes)}$, Liquan Shen, and Kai Li

School of Communication and Information Engineering, Shanghai University,
No. 149 Yanchang Road, Shanghai 200072, China
xinpeng_huang@163.com,
{anping,jsslq,kailee}@t.shu.edu.cn

Abstract. In this paper, we propose a new Light Field Image (LFI) compression scheme based on Multiview Video plus Depth (MVD) coding architecture. Through LF function analysis, we preliminarily estimate depth map according to the concept of Epipolar Plane Image (EPI). Such a rough estimation causes some error pixels within initial depth map, so we design a weighting mean filter to smooth the inaccurate region. The final estimated depth maps can be encoded by MVD coding standard jointly with a small number of viewpoint images in LFI, so as to improve compression efficiency of LFI. Ultimately, massive experiments are conducted on 4 LFIs to verify the effectiveness of the proposed compression scheme. The simulated results demonstrate that our LFI compression scheme can achieve a high LFI compression performance and outperform the-state-of-art coding solution.

Keywords: LFI compression · MVD · EPI

1 Introduction

With the rapid commercialization and industrialization of hand-held light field camera in recent years, the field of auto-stereoscopic display system is increasingly populated by Light Field Image (LFI). Because light field camera can simultaneously capture both spatial light information and angular light by one shot, the LFI contains much larger volume of data than conventional camera picture [1]. Since microlens array is put in front of the sensor and the focal plane of the microlens array is on the sensor, LF data can be preserved in the large matrices of Micro-Images (MIs) which record not only the light intensity in each spatial position but the light rays directions, thus it is a full representation of a real stereoscopic scene [2].

Two representations of LFI are illustrated in Fig. 1. It is evident from Fig. 1(b) that the raw format is composed of a huge number of MIs. For the sub-aperture format, each of the sub-aperture images, which can be considered as a viewpoint image, is obtained from the raw light image, and a slightly small disparity exists in these viewpoint images, as shown in Fig. 1(d). In addition, the redundancy in sub-aperture format is much more than that in raw format and a huge amount of data limits the storage and transmission of LFI. Taken together, LFI compression faces a major challenge of data volume reduction, which triggers more investigations on sub-aperture LFI. To reduce

© Springer International Publishing AG, part of Springer Nature 2018
B. Zeng et al. (Eds.): PCM 2017, LNCS 10735, pp. 79–88, 2018.
https://doi.org/10.1007/978-3-319-77380-3_8

the bitrates of coding LFI in sub-aperture format, we originally utilize Multiview Video plus Depth (MVD) coding scheme to compress LFI efficiently.

Fig. 1. The two types of LFI; (a) raw format; (b) close-up of (a); (c) sub-aperture format; (d) close-up of (c)

An outline of this article is organized as follows. In Sect. 2 the related works about sub-aperture LFI are described. Section 3 provides our proposed LFI compression algorithm. The simulated experimental results and analysis are exhibited in Sect. 4. Ultimately, this paper is concluded in Sect. 5.

2   Related Works

For the sub-aperture format, some algorithms convert the LFI into a single viewpoint video and encode using video coding standard [3–6]. This manner is efficient, but not developed for the type of correlation within LFIs. Multiview Video Coding (MVC) structure is quite feasible to tackle the increasing number of viewpoint images, but more bitrates reduction by MVC is still required [7–9]. MVD coding structure accomplishes significantly low bitrates for multiview video, because it can synthesize intermediate view at decoder side using a small number of depth map and corresponding texture video [10, 11]. It is, therefore, expected that MVD can be a good alternative coding approach for eliminating redundancy of LF data. In terms of depth map estimation, an accurate depth map estimation algorithm for LFI is proposed in [12], where a disparity interpolation approach is utilized to improve the precision of depth estimation. Additionally, a novel 4D LF depth estimation method is presented in [13] based on the linear scheme of Epipolar Plane Image (EPI) and Locally Linear Embedding (LLE). But only a few depth estimation algorithms have been proposed for LFI captured from hand-hold LF camera.

Admittedly, researchers have made great efforts to compress LFI by numerous coding methods. However, it is still lack of investigation on LFI compression using MVD architecture. Motivated by the abovementioned issues, we propose a new compression method for LFI using estimated depth map. The proposed approach can render depth map with high precision and reduce the bitrates of coding LFI extremely.

3 Proposed Scheme

3.1 LF Function Analysis

A four-dimensional function $LF(u, v, s, t)$ is used widely to represent light field. More specifically, a light ray must go through two parallel planes successively if no obstacle, as illustrated in Fig. 2. When a light ray emanates from image plane to camera plane, the two intersection points firstly locate at image plane, and then at camera plane. As shown in Fig. 2, the distance between image plane and camera plane is denoted as f and the depth from object to camera plane is marked as D. According to similar triangle theorem, we can derive a proportional relation as follow.

$$D = \frac{f}{1 - \frac{dist_u}{dist_s}} \tag{1}$$

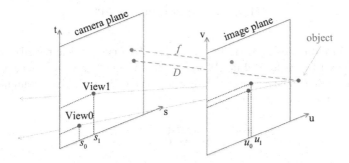

Fig. 2. Diagram of the four-dimensional light field function

where $dist_u$ and $dist_s$ express the distances of intersection points at image and camera plane, respectively. Due to f is a constant value, it is obvious from Eq. (1) that the depth value D is only related with the ratio $dist_u/dist_s$. In other word, if an object is far away from the cameras, it will have a larger $dist_u/dist_s$ than the object that is nearer to cameras. Based on this observation, the depth map of LFI can be estimated, which is demonstrated in detail in the following.

3.2 Depth Map Estimation Using EPI

Because viewpoint images in sub-aperture LFI are arranged in a grid, only horizontal or vertical disparities exist between two adjacent viewpoint images. The value of $dist_u$ and $dist_s$ in sub-aperture LFI can be considered in horizontal or vertical direction, and the relation between them can be clear via a multiview transformation method, namely, EPI [14].

Figure 3 depicts a process of EPI transformation. The left side of Fig. 3 implies that viewpoint images in sub-aperture LFI are stacked as a cube and cut by a horizontal plane. A part of achieved EPI is shown in the right side of Fig. 3, where the EPI is achieved by cutting viewpoint images stack. The slope of each pixel in EPI can be expressed as $\tan \alpha = dist_u/dist_s$, so according to Eq. (1) the depth information of arbitrary pixels can be deduced using the angle α.

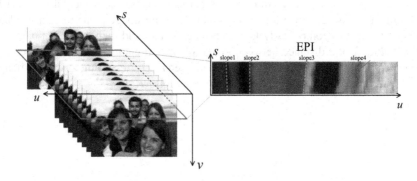

Fig. 3. Transforming LFI into EPI

Inspired by this observation, the best angle $\alpha^*(p)$ can be determined from a candidate angle set for each pixel in EPI. For a certain sample $p = (u, s)$ locating at EPI, the optimal angle can be decided if the Mean Squared Error (MSE) is minimal for this angle. The expression is formulated as follow.

$$\alpha^*(p) = \underset{\alpha \in (-45°, 45°)}{\arg \min} \ MSE(\alpha, p) \tag{2}$$

where $MSE(\alpha, p)$ indicates the MSE of the angle α for the sample. Due to the constraint condition is $0 < Var_u < Var_s$, α ranges from $-45°$ to $45°$. The detail computational process of $MSE(\alpha, p)$ is demonstrated as follow.

$$MSE(\alpha, p) = \sum_{i=-\frac{N}{2}}^{\frac{N}{2}} \omega_i \left(V_{u,s} - V_{u+i \cdot \tan \alpha, s+i}\right)^2 \Big/ \sum_{i=-\frac{N}{2}}^{\frac{N}{2}} \omega_i \tag{3}$$

where N stands for the number of views. Note that if N is an odd number, $\frac{N}{2}$ is rounded down for an integer. $V_{u,s}$ and $V_{u+i \cdot \tan \alpha, s+i}$ denote the gray value of current pixel and candidate pixel. Moreover, ω_i is a weighting factor, which is assigned to 0 if the candidate pixel is inaccurate; otherwise, ω_i is equal to 1.

After calculating the optimal angle of each sample in EPI, the depth values of the total samples in all views can be obtained according to Eq. (1). Because this paper adopts MVD strategy to compress LFI, the value of depth map to be coded is limited between 0 and 255. Accordingly, Min-Max Normalization function (MMN) is employed to maintain the linear structure of depth values. By means of EPI and MMN process, consequently, the depth map can be generated preliminarily by our proposed method.

3.3 Error Pixel Repairing

An available depth map is characterized by large homogenous region, where the pixels have almost the same depth value. However, for these areas, because of non-unique of $\alpha^*(p)$ in Eq. (2), it is difficult to decide which the optimal slope is in such region. Not surprisingly, the textureless region is full of error pixels. To eliminate these error pixels in initial estimated depth map, a weighting mean filter, formulated in Eq. (4), is exploited for flat areas.

$$D_e = \sum_{n \in N(e)} \gamma_n D_n \tag{4}$$

where D_e and D_n signify the depth values of error pixel and its neighboring pixels, respectively. $N(e)$ represents a pixel set containing the adjacent pixels around this error pixel. Additionally, γ_n denotes the weighting factor achieved from Eq. (5), which ensures $\sum_{n \in N(e)} \gamma_n = 1$.

$$\gamma_n = \frac{(D_e - D_n)^2}{\sum_{n \in N(e)} (D_e - D_n)^2} \tag{5}$$

It is possible that a few pixels around the error pixel are also inaccurate, hence, the straight mean filter likely results in error spread. As we add the weighting factor into mean filter, a high weight value can be yielded when the detected pixel is correct and a low weight value can be generated if the tested pixel is also error. By this manner, the pixel to be repaired can keep a good consistency with its neighboring pixels.

3.4 Viewpoint Images Transformation for MVD Architecture

If each viewpoint image in sub-aperture LFI is regarded as one viewpoint, it will increase the computational burden with substantial header information within the massive viewpoints. Simply organizing viewpoint images as a single viewpoint video sequence can decrease the number of views adequately; however, it dramatically sacrifices the relationship between frames. Therefore, it is expected to adopt MVD architecture, a 3D extension of HEVC, in this paper.

Here we extract 7 columns from a sub-aperture LFI and transform them into 7 viewpoint video sequences from top to bottom as illustrated in Fig. 4. The red part is regarded as center viewpoint, and its left and right side columns are considered as dependent views (marked as blue). The center viewpoint is also referred to the independent view, so its texture image and associated depth map are coded independently using a conventional HEVC video coder. Except for the independent view and dependent views, the remaining white parts are synthesized by 3D-HEVC, instead of being coded.

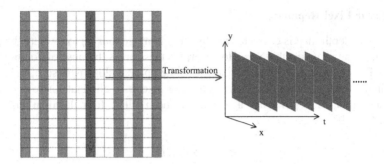

Fig. 4. Diagram of viewpoint selection and transformation (Color figure online)

4 Experimental Results and Analysis

4.1 Test Condition

To evaluate the compression performance of our presented approach, we choose 4 LFIs from the MMSPG-EPFL LFI Dataset to be tested, as illustrated in Fig. 5. Meanwhile, as the sub-aperture LFI has been prevalent study object, simulated experiments in this section are conducted on the LFIs in sub-aperture format. In order to be coded by standard coding solutions, all the 15×15 viewpoint images (including available and unavailable views) are cut into the resolution of 624×432, resulting in the sub-aperture LFI with the size of 9360×6480.

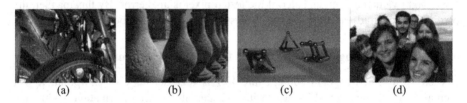

| (a) | (b) | (c) | (d) |

Fig. 5. Test LFIs in this paper. (a) Bikes; (b) Stone_Pillars_Outside; (c) Magnets_1; (d) Friends_1

4.2 Assessment for Estimated Depth Map

To compare with other depth map estimation methods, the approaches we selected in this paper are the Efficient Large Scale Stereo (ELSS) [15] and the Line-Assisted Graph Cut (LAGC) [16].

Based on the comparative experiments on the test LFIs illustrated in Fig. 6, our proposed method outperforms other three approaches significantly. We can see that for the Magnets_1 and Stone_Pillars_Outside with large flat regions, ELSS, LAGC and Lytro Desktop fail to estimate a high precise depth map, while our method obtains a relative high performance. As it was expected, in respect of the LFI with large complex texture areas, such as the Bikes and Friends_1, our depth map estimation method gains an impressive result, especially for the preservation of complicated texture contour. Because LFI contains dense views whose disparity is slightly small, the algorithms ELSS and LAGC cannot render the depth map accurately. Instead, our algorithm is proper for such format. Although the depth map acquired by Lytro Desktop software possesses much smooth areas and sharp edges, it cannot distinguish objects that have similar depth value. Therefore, our depth map estimation method based on EPI can obtain a good performance while preserving contour region of different objects compared to other depth map estimation methods, and it verifies that the depth map estimated by our method can be utilized in 3D-HEVC structure.

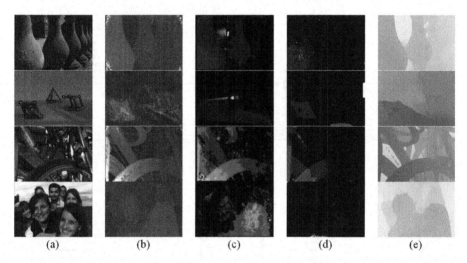

(a)   (b)   (c)   (d)   (e)

Fig. 6. Experiments on the test LFIs. (a) center view; (b) ours; (c) ELSS; (d) LAGC; (e) Lytro Desktop software

4.3   Evaluation of the Proposed Compression Method

To evaluate the compression performance, the still sub-aperture LFI compression is regarded as the benchmarking. We also compare the proposed scheme with existing the-state-of-art sub-aperture LFI compression approach [4], labeled as LSM for line scan mapping and RSM rotation scan mapping. Besides, the 3D-HEVC test model (HTM) reference software HTM 16.0 has been utilized for our proposed scheme and the quantization parameters are set to 22, 27, 32 and 37, respectively. The coding performance throughout this paper is jointly measured by Peak Signal to Noise Ratio (PSNR) and bitrate.

From Fig. 7 it is observed that due to converting LFI into video sequence, both LSM and RSM can improve coding performance extremely compared with compressing static LFI by HEVC under All-Intra configuration. Meanwhile, it is should be noted that the compression performance of our compression scheme is better than that of the algorithm in [4]. Because the depth maps of the entire viewpoint images are accurately estimated by our proposed algorithm, MVD architecture can be implemented with coding a few viewpoint images and their corresponding depth maps. Great reduction of data volume can alleviate the computational burden dramatically. Therefore, this comparative experimental result indicates that the proposed LFI compression method can achieve a better compression performance compared to the-state-of-art algorithm.

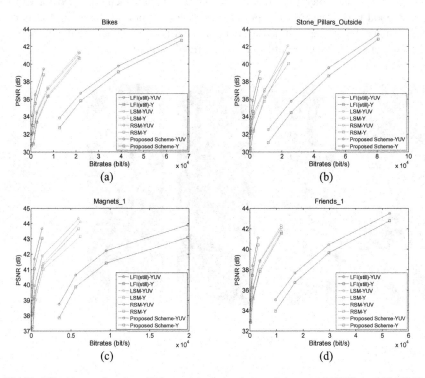

Fig. 7. RD curves of various LFI compression solutions in terms of YUV- and Y-PSNR

4.4   Key Viewpoint Images Quality Assessment

For assessing compressed LFI quality, we select 9 key viewpoint images as samples according to [17]. Due to space constraints, only objective comparison is discussed here. Viewpoint 2, 5 and 8 are from independent view which is independently coded by traditional HEVC encoder. The remaining views are synthesized by the neighboring texture images and their associated depth maps. So from Fig. 8 we can find that the quality of viewpoint 2, 5 and 8 is little higher than that of other viewpoints, but all viewpoints in one LFI have almost the same performance.

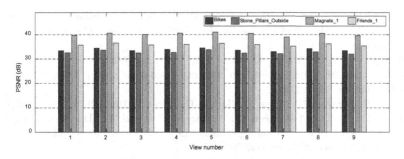

Fig. 8. Key viewpoint image quality

5 Conclusion

MVD coding structure is employed in this paper to improve LFI compression efficiency originally. Inspired by EPI, we propose an accurate depth map estimation method that can precisely calculate depth value of each pixel in LFI. We choose a few viewpoint images as multiview video sequence and utilize MVD to code the selected viewpoints. The experimental results show that our proposed scheme can obtain a great improvement in terms of LFI compression efficiency compared to the-state-of-art LFI compression algorithm.

Acknowledgement. This work was supported in part by the National Natural Science Foundation of China, under Grants 61571285 and U1301257.

References

1. Assuncao, P.A.A.: Evolution from 3D video to light-field coding and transmission over future media networks. In: Mediterranean Electrotechnical Conference, pp. 1–5 (2016)
2. Pereira, F., Silva, E.A.B.D.: Efficient plenoptic imaging representation: Why do we need it? In: IEEE International Conference on Multimedia and Expo, pp. 1–6 (2016)
3. Helin, P., Astola, P., Rao, B., Tabus, I.: Sparse modelling and predictive coding of subaperture images for lossless plenoptic image compression. In: 3DTV-Conference: the True Vision - Capture, Transmission and Display of 3D Video, pp. 1–4 (2016)
4. Dai, F., Zhang, J., Ma, Y., Zhang, Y.: Lenselet image compression scheme based on subaperture images streaming. In: IEEE International Conference on Image Processing, pp. 4733–4737 (2015)
5. Dricot, A., Jung, J., Cagnazzo, M., Pesquet, B.: Integral images compression scheme based on view extraction. In: Signal Processing Conference, pp. 101–105 (2015)
6. Liu, D., Wang, L., Li, L., Xiong, Z., Wu, F., Zeng, W.: Pseudo-sequence-based light field image compression. In: IEEE International Conference on Multimedia & Expo Workshops, pp. 1–4 (2016)
7. Vetro, A., Wiegand, T., Sullivan, G.J.: Overview of the stereo and multiview video coding extensions of the H.264/MPEG-4 AVC standard. Proc. IEEE **99**(4), 626–642 (2011)

8. Hannuksela, M.M., Yan, Y., Huang, X., Li, H.: Overview of the multiview high efficiency video coding (MV-HEVC) standard. In: IEEE International Conference on Image Processing, pp. 2154–2158 (2015)
9. Tech, G., Chen, Y., Müller, K., Ohm, J.R., Vetro, A., Wang, Y.K.: Overview of the multiview and 3D extensions of high efficiency video coding. IEEE Trans. Circuits Syst. Video Technol. **26**(1), 1 (2015)
10. Müller, K., Schwarz, H., Marpe, D., Bartnik, C., Bosse, S., Brust, H., Hinz, T., Lakshman, H., Merkle, P., Rhee, F.H., Tech, G., Winken, M., Wiegand, T.: 3D high-efficiency video coding for multi-view video and depth data. IEEE Trans. Image Process. **22**(9), 3366–3378 (2013). https://doi.org/10.1109/TIP.2013.2264820
11. Chen, Y., Zhao, X., Zhang, L., Kang, J.W.: Multiview and 3D video compression using neighboring block based disparity vectors. IEEE Trans. Multimed. **18**(4), 576–589 (2016). https://doi.org/10.1109/TMM.2016.2525010
12. Navarro, J., Buades, A.: Robust and dense depth estimation for light field images. IEEE Trans. Image Process. **26**(4), 1873–1886 (2017). https://doi.org/10.1109/TIP.2017.2666041
13. Zhang, Y., Lv, H., Liu, Y., Wang, H., Wang, X., Huang, Q., Xiang, X., Dai, Q.: Light-field depth estimation via epipolar plane image analysis and locally linear embedding. IEEE Trans. Circuits Syst. Video Technol. **27**(4), 739–747 (2017). https://doi.org/10.1109/TCSVT.2016.2555778
14. Bolles, R.C., Baker, H.H., Marimont, D.H.: Epipolar-plane image analysis: An approach to determining structure from motion. Int. J. Comput. Vis. **1**(1), 7–55 (1987)
15. Geiger, A., Roser, M., Urtasun, R.: Efficient large-scale stereo matching. In: Kimmel, R., Klette, R., Sugimoto, A. (eds.) ACCV 2010. LNCS, vol. 6492, pp. 25–38. Springer, Heidelberg (2011). https://doi.org/10.1007/978-3-642-19315-6_3
16. Yu, Z., Guo, X., Ling, H., Lumsdaine, A., Yu, J.: Line assisted light field triangulation and stereo matching. In: 2013 IEEE International Conference on Computer Vision, 1–8 Dec 2013, pp. 2792–2799 (2013)
17. Alves, G., Pereira, F., Silva, E.A.B.D.: Light field imaging coding: performance assessment methodology and standards benchmarking. In: IEEE International Conference on Multimedia & Expo Workshops, pp. 1–6 (2016)

A Real-Time Multi-view AVS2 Decoder on Mobile Phone

Yingfan Zhang[1], Zhenan Lin[1], Weilun Feng[1], Jun Sun[1,2](✉),
and Zongming Guo[1,2]

[1] Institute of Computer Science and Technology,
Peking University, Beijing, China
{zhangyingfan, zhenanlin, fengweilun, jsun,
guozongming}@pku.edu.cn
[2] Cooperative Medianet Innovation Center, Shanghai, China

Abstract. This demonstration provides a real-time AVS2 decoder, which is able to decode two 1080p videos in different views and render videos in red-blue 3D on mobile phones. The newly-published second generation of Audio-video coding standard (AVS2) is the successor to Audio-video coding standard (AVS). AVS2 improves video coding efficiency at the cost of significant complexity, making it hard to promote applications on mobile devices. In this paper, we firstly introduce our implementation on three levels: framework-level optimization, frame-level threading and data-level paralleling. Then, we evaluate the performance on mobile phones via experiments, which demonstrate our decoder achieves up to 142.382 fps when decoding 720p videos. At last, our decoder is integrated into a multi-view system. Although there have been lots of related work on the coetaneous standard HEVC and several implementations for AVS2, it is the first real-time multi-view AVS2 decoder on mobile phones so far.

Keywords: Real-time decoder · Mobile application · Multi-view system

1 Introduction

The second generation of Audio-video coding standard for video has been conducted as an industry standard of China GY/T 299.1-2016 [1] and published as a national standard of China GB/T 33475.2-2016 [2] to meet the demand of higher coding efficiency for high-definition videos. With enhanced coding tools introduced, AVS2 is expected to achieve about 50% bitrate reduction for equal perceptual video quality in AVS. However, the significant complexity has become a burning issue for real-time applications over modern processors. Since mobile video traffic now accounts for more than half of all mobile data traffic [3], the demand of high performance video decoders on mobile devices becomes more and more intense. As a newly-published standard, AVS2 has a reference software RD [8] without intensive optimization, failing to utilize the parallel computing capability provided by processors.

To meet the requirement of real-time decoding and promote AVS2 applications on mobile devices, we implement an optimized AVS2 decoder for mobile phones, which has the capability to decode two 1080p videos in different views and render videos in

© Springer International Publishing AG, part of Springer Nature 2018
B. Zeng et al. (Eds.): PCM 2017, LNCS 10735, pp. 89–95, 2018.
https://doi.org/10.1007/978-3-319-77380-3_9

red-blue 3D on general mobile phones. Although there has been lots of related work
[4, 5] on the coetaneous standard HEVC [6] and several implementations [7] on x86
architecture for AVS2, but there is no public well-designed AVS2 decoder on
ARM-based architecture so far.

The rest of this paper is organized as follows. Section 2 describes the implementation of our AVS2 decoder. Section 3 provides performance analysis through experiments. Section 4 presents the multi-view decoding and rendering system and Sect. 5
make a conclusion for this demonstration.

2 Decoder Implementation

A high performance decoder could be well-designed on three levels: framework level,
task parallel level and data parallel level. In this section, we analyze key issues of
implementation and present our design for each level.

2.1 Framework Level Optimization

To accord with the standard, the decoder should be able to reconstruct all conformance
bitstreams correctly. Furthermore, the decoding speed, memory usage and robustness
are important criteria in framework design. We decouple decoding processes into 8
different modules, each module has the same input/output data structure and executes
similar process to improve memory access performance and make it easier to achieve
error concealment.

Bitstream Buffering: This module is used for buffering incoming bitstream as the
inputted segment may be part of the full bitstream and not enough to execute a
complete decoding process.

Bitstream Decomposing: This module decomposes buffered bitstream into network
abstract layer unit (NALU). Although the decoding process is expected to process
NALUs one by one, we can make up access unit (AU) with NALUs to support frame
level parallel.

NALU Reading: The smallest data unit for storage is byte, but the decoding process
usually reads several bits from NALUs each time. This module is used to access data in
bit level and to support parallel reading.

AEC Decoding: The arithmetic entropy coding (AEC) decodes binary bins according
to contexts specified by syntax and bits read from NALUs. This module accepts the
related context and needed bits to decode binary bins, then parse values of corresponding syntax and update the status of the context.

CU Decoding: The coding unit (CU) decoding process is recursively called to decode
largest coding units, determine CU partitioning, decide prediction modes, calculate the
inverse quantization and perform the integer transform. In this module, the decoded
information in coding blocks is organized and stored in well-design data structure,
which can improve memory access performance and reduce memory usage.

Loop Filtering: Each reconstructed frame should be filtered before being outputted or referred. AVS2 includes three in-loop filters: de-blocking filter (DBF), Sample Adaptive Offset (SAO) and Adaptive Loop Filter (ALF). We only need to backup pixels on necessary instead of copying the whole frame to save time and memory.

Picture Buffering: The standard has specified a decoded picture buffer (DPB) to store decoded picture that has not been outputted or is still being referred. The amount of pictures in the decoder cannot exceed the maximum number specified by the standard. The handle of a picture removed from DPB will be recycled to the decoded picture recycler (DPR) and allocated to the following picture, reducing the frequency of memory allocation and destroy.

Scheduling: This module works for memory allocation and thread management.

2.2 Frame Level Threading

We implement a thread pool with first-in-first-out (FIFO) mechanism to achieve frame level threading. In this implementation, the decoding context in each thread is the same as that in serial decoding. In addition, the DPR can guarantee sustained decoding processes when being out of memory.

As illustrated in Fig. 1, we create a thread pool containing two threads (denoted as T0, T1) and assume there is only enough memory for storing three picture handles (denoted as H0, H1, H2). The dashed arrow presents dependence among pictures (denoted as P0, P1, P2...), while the full arrow presents the corresponding handle referring.

(a) At the beginning, the decoder allocates H0/H1 for P0/P1, T0/T1 take the responsibility to decode P0/P1.
(b) When P0 decoded, H0 is released from T0. The decoder allocates H2 for P2, T0 takes the responsibility to decode P2.
(c) When P1 decoded, H1 is released form T1, P2 is under reconstruction and refers to P0/P1. There is no enough memory to allocate for P3, T0 is still working while T1 becomes idle.
(d) When P2 decoded, H2 is released form T0, P0 ~ P2 have been outputted and will not be referred anymore, so H0 ~ H2 are recycled into DPR. Then the decoder allocates H0/H1 for P3/P4, T1/T0 take the responsibility to decode P3/P4. There are two working threads again.

2.3 Data Level Paralleling

NEON [9] enables the same operation on multiple data in parallel on ARM-based processors. Within a single instruction, the same operation can be performed on the multiple data stored in a wide register. For example, a 128-bit register can be used to store four 32-bit integers, eight 16-bit integers or sixteen 8-bit integers. Hence, up to 16

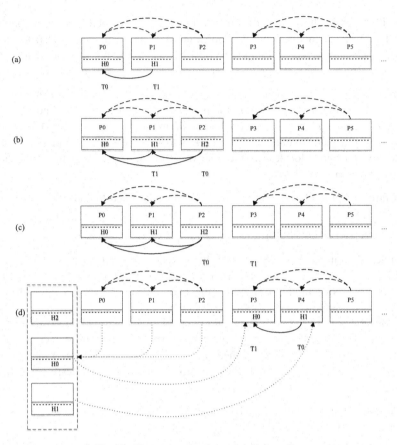

Fig. 1. Illustration for frame level threading

identical operations can be executed simultaneously within a single instruction. For easily using these instructions, a series of intrinsic functions, called as intrinsics [10], are provided to automatically generate corresponding instructions.

In order to identify the most time-consuming modules in AVS2 decoder, we breakdown execution time of reference decoder into different modules, including motion compensation (MC), adaptive loop filter (ALF), transform, entropy, deblock, memory operation and others. Though the reference decoder is not performance optimized, but it can fairly represent the complexity of various module in AVS2. Bitstreams of 720p standard test sequences (City and Crew with QPI 27/32/38/45 in Common Test Condition - Random Access) are selected. The average breakdown execution time is illustrated in Fig. 2, from which we can observe that MC, transform and ALF are the most time-consuming modules in the reference decoder. NEON intrinsics are applied to improve the computational performance of these modules.

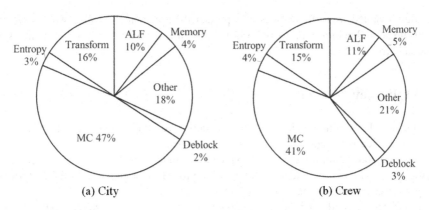

Fig. 2. Breakdown execution time of decoder modules in reference decoder

3   Performance Analysis

We develop the AVS2 decoder over ARM-based processors based on proposed implementation. The experimental results are carried out on smartphone MI Note Pro (with a Qualcomm Snapdragon 810 processor and 4 GB memory) and compared to the decoder in reference software RD17.0. We encode four 720p videos in different bitrates for decoding experiments. The overall acceleration shown in Table 1 indicates that the proposed AVS2 decoder (denoted as Prop.) is about 10 times faster than the reference

Table 1. Decoding speed comparison between proposed decoder and reference decoder

Seq.	Bitrate (kbps)	Decoding speed (fps)			Speedup	
		RD	Prop.	M.T.	Prop.	M.T.
City	4802.520	2.376	21.522	41.769	9.058	17.580
	2178.231	2.512	30.284	58.983	12.056	23.480
	1001.896	2.876	38.735	80.891	13.468	28.126
	443.911	4.754	48.901	108.569	10.286	22.837
Crew	4183.702	3.554	18.654	43.051	5.249	12.113
	2077.131	4.009	24.319	47.752	6.066	11.911
	1017.790	4.187	31.412	71.395	7.502	17.052
	464.807	4.517	38.916	90.715	8.615	20.083
Vidyo 1	1166.070	4.348	23.219	81.540	5.340	18.753
	653.840	4.808	33.051	104.369	6.874	21.707
	367.527	5.731	55.778	124.725	9.733	21.763
	195.054	6.194	58.431	**142.382**	9.433	22.987
Vidyo 3	1415.497	3.020	40.771	88.793	13.500	29.402
	788.049	3.389	48.318	109.115	14.257	32.197
	446.656	3.960	57.042	121.187	14.405	30.603
	236.902	5.106	61.771	138.250	12.098	27.076
Average	–	–	–	–	9.871	22.354

decoder (denoted as RD). Besides, the proposed implementation also works well in multi-thread and achieves up to 142.382 fps real-time decoding for 720p HD videos in 4 threads (denoted as M.T.).

4 Multi-view System

We integrated into a multi-view system to decode two 1080p videos in different views and render videos in red-blue 3D on mobile phones.

In the encoder end, there are multiple cameras to capture 1080p videos in different views. Each view is encoded in AVS2 baseline profile. Bitstreams from different views are packed and sent into network via UDP.

In the decoder end, there is a mobile phone running an app to listen the network and download video packets. Received packets are demuxed into bitstreams in different

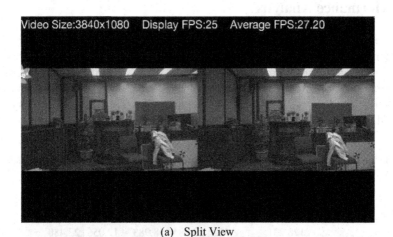

(a) Split View

(b) 3D View

Fig. 3. Decoded picture in different views (Color figure online)

views, two of which are selected and sent into two independent proposed decoders. Decoded pictures are sync up and send to the render in two forms:

(a) Split View: videos from different views are spliced and displayed synchronously, we can see the video made up of two different views as shown in Fig. 3(a).
(b) 3D View: R/G component from one view and B component form the other view are mixed, we can see 3D effect through red-blue glasses as shown in Fig. 3(b).

5 Conclusion

This demonstration provides a real-time AVS2 decoder, which is able to decode two 1080p videos in different views and render videos in red-blue 3D on general mobile phones. We firstly introduce the implementation on three aspects: framework-level optimization, frame-level threading and da-ta-level paralleling. Then, we evaluate the performance on mobile phones via experiments, which demonstrate our decoder achieves up to 142.382 fps when decoding 720p videos. At last, our decoder is integrated into a multi-view system and becomes a real-time multi-view AVS2 decoder on mobile phones, popularizing video applications in AVS2.

Acknowledgement. This work was supported by National Natural Science Foundation of China under contract No. 61671025 and National Key Technology R&D Program of China under Grant 2015AA011605.

References

1. State Administration of Press, Publication, Radio, Film and Television of P.R.C. "High efficiency coding of audio and video - Part 1: Video", GY/T 299.1-2016
2. Standardization Administration of P.R.C. "Information technology - High efficiency media coding - Part 2: Video", GB/T 33475.2-2016
3. Cisco: "Cisco visual networking index: global mobile data traffic forecast update (2016–2021). http://www.cisco.com/c/en/us/solutions/collateral/service-provider/visual-networking-index-vni/mobile-white-paper-c11-520862.pdf
4. Yan, L., Duan, Y., Sun, J., Guo, Z.: An optimized real-time multi-thread HEVC decoder. In: IEEE Visual Communications and Image Processing (VCIP) (2012)
5. Yan, L., Duan, Y., Sun, J., Guo, Z.: Implementation of HEVC decoder on x86 processors with SIMD optimization. In: IEEE Visual Communications and Image Processing (VCIP) (2012)
6. Sullivan, G.J., Ohm, J.-R., Han, W.-J., Wiegand, T.: Overview of the high efficiency video coding (HEVC) standard. IEEE Trans. Circuits Syst. Video Technol. **22**(12), 1649–1668 (2012)
7. Peking University: "uAVS2 Encoder". http://media.pkusz.edu.cn/index.php/2-uncategorised/159-avs2-high-resolution
8. AVS Workgroup: "AVS2 reference software source code". http://www.avs.org.cn/AVS2_download
9. ARM: "NEON Programmer's Guide", DEN0018A, June 2013
10. ARM: "NEON Intrinsics Reference", IHI0073A, May 2014

Compressive Sensing Depth Video Coding via Gaussian Mixture Models and Object Edges

Kang Wang[1], Xuguang Lan[1(✉)], Xiangwei Li[2], Meng Yang[1], and Nanning Zheng[1]

[1] Institute of Artificial Intelligence and Robotics,
Xi'an Jiaotong University, Xi'an, China
xglan@mail.xjtu.edu.cn
[2] Xi'an Institute of Optics and Precision Mechanics,
Chinese Academy of Sciences, Xi'an, China

Abstract. In this paper, we propose a novel compressive sensing depth video (CSDV) coding scheme based on Gaussian mixture models (GMM) and object edges. We first compress several depth videos to get CSDV frames in the temporal direction. A whole CSDV frame is divided into a set of non-overlap patches in which object edges is detected by Canny operator to reduce the computational complexity of quantization. Then, we allocate variable bits for different patches based on the percentages of non-zero pixels in every patch. The GMM is used to model the CSDV frame patches and design product vector quantizers to quantize CSDV frames. The experimental results show that our compression scheme achieves a significant Bjontegaard Delta (BD)-PSNR improvement about 2–10 dB when compared to the standard video coding schemes, e.g. Uniform Scalar Quantization-Differential Pulse Code Modulation (USQ-DPCM) and H.265/HEVC.

Keywords: Gaussian mixture models · Depth video coding
Compressive sensing · View synthesis

1 Introduction

Depth video coding from stereo is one of the most developed research areas in computer vision because the quality of each synthesized virtual view highly depends on the depth video [1]. Once a reconstructed depth video is available, it can be used in several fields, such as 3-D TV, movie and so on. There are two main challenges of the depth video technology: one is storing the large data of depth videos; another one is reconstructing accurate frames with the minimal distortion [1, 2]. This is why researching the depth videos remains a hot topic of research till the moment.

Depth video is gray-scale data containing the depth information. The size of raw depth data is typically one third of raw color data. An ordinary approach for depth video coding is just applying the state-of-the-art texture video coding algorithm [2], e.g. H.265/HEVC and Uniform Scalar Quantization-Differential Pulse Code Modulation (USQ-DPCM) [13]. However, it has already been widely researched that the depth

© Springer International Publishing AG, part of Springer Nature 2018
B. Zeng et al. (Eds.): PCM 2017, LNCS 10735, pp. 96–104, 2018.
https://doi.org/10.1007/978-3-319-77380-3_10

video is totally different from the texture video [4–6]. Usually, depth videos contain larger area of slowly varying values within objects, as well as fewer sharp edges at object edges [3]. The traditional video coding methods cannot produce the satisfactory coding performance for depth videos [5]. Motivated by this limitation, Byung et al. [2] proposed a newly defined rendering view distortion function to improve the quality of synthesized virtual views. Karsten et al. [3] presented efficient coding tools for depth video in depth-enhanced video formats. However, these methods are not taking the sparsity and object edges of depth videos into account.

Compressive sensing (CS) was proposed as a new theory by Cands and Donoho [12]. It is a specialized method to compress the sparse signals. Different from the traditional Nyquist sampling theory, CS can reconstruct the original signal accurately with the less sampling rate. Moreover, compared with the texture video, the depth video is much sparser. The characteristic of depth videos makes the CS more suitable for it. However, the redundancy of the compressive sensing depth video (CSDV) acquired by compressing depth videos in temporal direction is still huge. It is reasonable to further compress these compressed signals rather than storing these signals directly.

In this paper, we propose a new coding method for CSDV frames, which uses Gaussian mixture models (GMM) and object edges. We use CS to compress depth videos to get CSDV frames in the temporal direction [7, 8]. Based on the law of large numbers, the probability distribution of a CSDV frame satisfies the Gaussian mixture distribution. Therefore, the GMM is used to model CSDV frames and design product vector quantizers (PVQs) using our work [7]. To reduce the computational complexity, we divide CSDV frames into a set of non-overlap patches and extract object edges for every patch. Then, we calculate the percentages of non-zero pixels in every patch and allocate variable bits. Experimental results demonstrate that our coding scheme leads to higher Bjontegaard Delta (BD)-PSNR when compared to the state-of-the-art schemes, e.g. USQ-DPCM and H.265/HEVC.

The rest of this paper is organized as follows. In Sect. 2, we give a brief description about how to use the GMM to model a CSDV frame and design PVQs. The proposed coding scheme based on the object edges is presented in Sect. 3. Experimental results are discussed in Sect. 4. Finally, we draw a conclusion in Sect. 5.

2 CSDV Modeling and PVQs Design

In this section, we describe two basic processes: (1) getting a CSDV frame and using the GMM to model it; (2) utilizing the GMM to design PVQs. The framework of this Section is shown in Fig. 1. The block of D represents the depth video without compression, Y indicates the CSDV frame after using the CS. The block of GMM is one of our models, it is used to model the CSDV frame and structure PVQs. The symbol $\sum_k$ denotes the kth covariance matrix of the GMM and it is utilized to design the kth PVQ. The details of these blocks are discussed in the following.

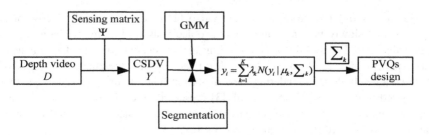

Fig. 1. Block diagram of CSDV modeling and PVQs design.

2.1   CSDV Modeling for Depth Video

In general, a depth video can be expressed by $D \in \mathbb{R}^{N_x \times N_y \times T}$, where N_x and N_y denote the height and width of the input video respectively, T indicates the temporal frames. The CSDV frame is represented by $Y \in \mathbb{R}^{N_x \times N_y}$. We choose the random mask Ψ as sensing matrix. The CSDV acquisition process is expressed as [12]

$$Y = \Psi D \tag{1}$$

In order to reduce the computational complexity of the system, we divide the depth video data D into L non-overlap patches of the size $S \times S \times T$ [8], where S represents the spatial resolution of the patches in the horizontal and vertical directions. Similarly, the CSDV frame Y is divided into a set of patches of the size $S \times S$. After vectorizing the ith patch's data of D to $d_i \in \mathbb{R}^{(S^2 T) \times 1}$ and Y to $y_i \in \mathbb{R}^{(S^2) \times 1}$, the CSDV acquisition process for each patch can be formulized as

$$y_i = \varphi_i d_i + \varepsilon_i \tag{2}$$

where $\varphi_i \in \{0,1\}^{(S^2) \times (S^2 T)}$ indicates the ith patch of the sensing matrix Ψ, ε_i is the Gaussian white noise. We assume ε_i satisfies the Gaussian distribution with zero-mean.

Assume that $y_i \in \mathbb{R}^p$ ($p = S^2$) in Eq. (2) is composed of a GMM with K Gaussian components [9, 14].

$$y_i \sim \sum_{k=1}^{K} \lambda_k N\left(y_i | \mu_k, \sum k\right), \quad \forall i = 1, \ldots, L \tag{3}$$

where $\mu_k \in \mathbb{R}^p$ is the mean value, $\sum_k \in \mathbb{R}^{p \times p}$ is the covariance matrix, λ_k is the weight of the kth Gaussian component ($\lambda_k > 0$ and $\sum_{k=1}^{K} \lambda_k = 1$). All these parameters can be estimated by the expectation-maximization algorithm, based on training video patches.

2.2   PVQs Design via GMM

We utilize K covariance matrixes of the GMM to design PVQs [7]. Let B_{tot} denote the total number of bits used to quantize y_i in Eq. (3). The number of bits allocated to the kth PVQ is indicated by B_k. The optimal bit allocation among K PVQs is given by [10]

$$2^{B_k} = 2^{B_{tot}} \left(\lambda_k \sigma_k^2\right)^{p/(p+2)} / \sum\nolimits_{k=1}^{K} \left(\lambda_k \sigma_k^2\right)^{p/(p+2)}, k = 1,\dots,\text{K} \qquad (4)$$

where σ_k^2 is the geometric mean of the eigenvalues of $\sum_k$, λ_k represents the weight of the kth Gaussian component of y_i.

The number of bits allocated to the ith sub-quantizer of PVQ is expressed by b_i. The standard high-resolution bit allocation scheme allocates bits among the sub-quantizers as follows [11]

$$b_i = B_k/p + log_2\left(\gamma_i/\sigma^2\right)/2, i = 1,\dots,p \qquad (5)$$

where γ_i is the ith eigenvalue of $\sum_k$, σ^2 is the geometric mean of the eigenvalue of $\sum_k$.

3 Proposed Coding Scheme

We propose an effective CSDV frames coding scheme based on object edges of the CSDV frame and GMM. Firstly, object edges of the CSDV frame are detected by Canny operator. Then, we allocate variable bits for different patches based on the percentages of non-zero pixels in every patch (the second model in our work). The adaptive bits allocation combines with the GMM mentioned in Sect. 2 to design adaptive PVQs. Finally, the coding scheme based on PVQs is proposed. The block diagram of the proposed scheme is shown in Fig. 2.

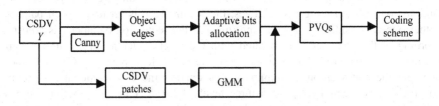

Fig. 2. Block diagram of the proposed scheme.

3.1 Adaptive Bits Allocation Based on Object Edges

In our work, we simply select Canny operator to detect the object edges of CSDV frames. The object edges of a CSDV frame is shown in Fig. 3. We can see that the edges frame contains larger areas of slowly varying values within objects, as well as fewer sharp edges at object boundaries. We divide the CSDV frame into two portions: smooth regions and boundaries regions. Through lots of numerical statistics, we find that the pixels of boundaries regions take percentage of about 33.3 in average for a CSDV frame. For a patch of the smooth regions, we can reduce the bits allocation. On the contrary, we can increase the bits allocation on the boundaries regions.

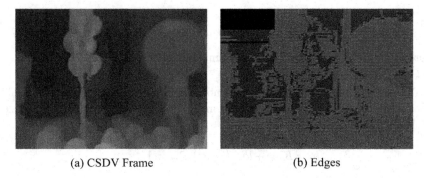

(a) CSDV Frame   (b) Edges

Fig. 3. A typical example of a CSDV frame and the corresponding object edges of *Balloons*. (a) A CSDV frame of depth videos; (b) Object edges of the CSDV frame.

3.2 Coding Scheme

For a given patch y_i of CSDV frames in Eq. (2), we extract object edges and calculate the percentage of non-zero pixels indicated by α. We introduce variable β as a regulation parameter, the equation of (4) can be expressed as

$$2^{B_k} = 2^{\beta B_{tot}} \left(\lambda_k \sigma_k^2\right)^{p/(p+2)} / \sum_{k=1}^{K} \left(\lambda_k \sigma_k^2\right)^{p/(p+2)}, k = 1,\ldots, K \qquad (6)$$

where B_{tot} is the total number of bits used to quantize y_i. β is used for regulating the bits allocated to every patch based on the parameter α. The bits allocated to different patches based on the product of B_{tot} with β. In order to compare, we consider two solutions: one is neglecting object edges, the parameter β is set to 1 for all patches; another one is considering the edge information, the regulation parameter is adjusted according to the value of α. Compared with the original depth video without compression, the sparsity of CSDV frames is much less. The less sparsity of CSDV frames, the larger the computational complexity. Considering the computational complexity and precision, we empirically set β three levels 0.2, 0.5, 1 in our experiments. The correlation of the weights α and β is shown in Table 1.

Table 1. The correlation of α and β.

α	<0.4	0.4–0.7	>0.7
β	0.2	0.5	1

We utilize K PVQs proposed in Sect. 2 to quantize the patch y_i of CSDV frame. The quantizer whose distortion is minimal is selected as the final PVQ. Its quantization result is chosen as the best reconstruction vector y_i^q. The reconstruction vector y_i^q and the corresponding PVQ index (from 1 to K) are regarded as the output symbols for transmission. Furthermore, we make use of the temporal correlation between adjacent

CSDV frames. Instead of transmitting the original output symbols, we transmit the differences of the adjacent CSDV frames. Then, we apply the arithmetic coding solution to further decrease data redundancy among the differences of output symbols. Moreover, we train a set of quantizers for several specific bits in advance, such as 10 bits, 20 bits and so on. When allocating these bits for various patches, we can just load the corresponding quantizer without training online.

4 Experimental Results

We perform tests on various depth videos to evaluate the performance of our coding schemes in comparison with other coding solutions. Four test depth sequences are selected for the evaluation, e.g. *Balloons* and *Book Arrival* (1024 × 768), *Champagne* and *Pantomime* (1280 × 960). The GMM parameters in Eq. (3) are trained by the sequences of *Ballet*, *Kendo*, *Dancer* and *Newspaper*. Each test video sequence contains 80 depth videos frames at 30 fps, and the corresponding CSDV frames are 10 frames at 3.75 fps. The number of Gaussian components K in Eq. (6) is set to 16, the temporal frames T is set to 8. In all the tests, the corresponding correlation of the weights α and β in Eq. (6) is mentioned in Table 1.

We use two quality measures in the comparisons. The first one is the Peak Signal to Noise Ratio (PSNR) between the input CSDV frames and the decoded CSDV frames, while the second is the quality of synthesized view visually. In our experimental studies, two proposed depth video coding are examined for all the test sequences: (1) GMM only, (2) GMM and object edges. We choose three compression schemes for comparison studies e.g. USQ-DPCM, H.265/HEVC Intra and H.265/HEVC.

The results of those experiments on the CSDV frames are shown in Fig. 4. We can see that the PSNR values obtained from the two proposed methods are much higher than USQ-DPCM and H.265/HEVC Intra. Compared with the H.265/HEVC, the PSNR values of our coding scheme based on GMM and object edges are higher for *Balloons* and *Book Arrival* no matter in what rate they are. And for *Pantomime* and *Champagne*, in high rate, the PSNRs of H.265/HEVC are higher than our scheme with considering edges, whereas are lower than our scheme in low rate. Synthesizing all the rates, we can find that the BD-PSNR of our scheme based on the GMM and object edges is higher than H.265/HEVC. Similarly, compared with the scheme that only considering the GMM, the proposed scheme based on GMM and object edges achieves a significant BD-PSNR improvement about 2–3 dB in average. Note that the scene complexity and motion amplitude of *Balloons* and *Book Arrival* are larger than *Pantomime* and *Champagne*. Therefore, our schemes are more suitable for high complexity and motion amplitude.

To show the improvement visually, we present two results of the view synthesis (*Balloons* and *Champagne*) in Fig. 5. The ground truths are synthesized by using the original texture videos and depth videos without coding. Others are synthesized by using the original texture videos and various compressed depth videos. For the two synthesized sequences, we only choose the 35th frames of the sequences. The rates of the two synthesized sequences are about 1220 kbps and 1196 kbps respectively. We can see that our proposed coding method with edge information has the least visual

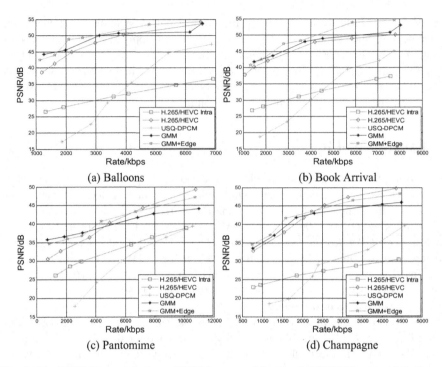

(a) Balloons

(b) Book Arrival

(c) Pantomime

(d) Champagne

Fig. 4. The PSNR between the input CSDV frames and the decoded CSDV frames. (a) *Balloons*. (b) *Book Arrival*. (c) *Pantomime*. (d) *Champagne*.

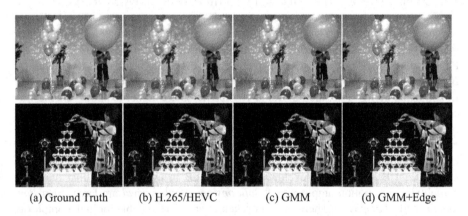

(a) Ground Truth   (b) H.265/HEVC   (c) GMM   (d) GMM+Edge

Fig. 5. The resulting view synthesized using the original texture video and various compressed depth videos. From up till down: *Balloons* and *Champagne*. These images are chosen from the 35th frames of test sequences.

effects in the synthesized frames. Moreover, it also has the closest output to that of the ground truth depth videos in Fig. 5. Note that the PSNR of the H.265/HEVC is higher than our two schemes in high rate (see Fig. 4c and 4d). However, its subjective quality of synthesized virtual views is much worse than our schemes (see Fig. 5b) and the

Table 2. The time consumption of various schemes.

Scheme	H.265/HEVC	H.265/HEVC Intra	USQ-DPCM	GMM	GMM + Edge Online	GMM + Edge Off-line
Time/s	1067.5	340.4	232.6	223.9	1130.7	235.3

Table 3. The experimental results of the four sequences (~ 1220 kbps).

Sequence	Balloons	Book arrival	Champagne	Pantomime
GMM + Edge Online(dB)	43.52	41.46	34.79	37.57
GMM + Edge Off-line(dB)	43.01	40.97	34.08	36.60

BD-PSNR of H.265/HEVC is lower than our scheme based on the GMM and object edges. The result proves that the traditional coding schemes are not suitable for the CSDV frames.

In all the experiments, the coding scheme based on GMM and object edges gets the highest values of the PSNR in average. And the visual errors of this scheme are the lowest. The results of USQ-DPCM and our two schemes are measured in Matlab, whereas H.265/HEVC is implemented with C/C++. We apply the following test conditions to roughly compare the running time: 10 CSDV frames of *Balloons* sequence, Intel Core i7-4790 CPU at 3.6 GHz, 32 GB RAM, and the rate is about 1220 kbps. The time consumption is shown in Table 2. We can see that the value of GMM and object edges based scheme (online) is much larger than others. For different patches, the parameter α is different and we need to allocate variable bits. Therefore, we have to design quantizers repetitively. This is the main reason of time consumption. As mentioned in Sect. 3.2, we can train a set of quantizers for special bits in advance. In this way, the time consumption is similar to the GMM. However, compared with the online, the BD-PSNR of off-line is lower about 0.5–1 dB for four test sequences. The experimental results of the four sequences are listed in Table 3.

5   Conclusions

In this paper, we propose a novel depth video coding technique based on GMM and object edges. The method first use the CS to compress several depth images into ones to get a CSDV frame. The GMM is then introduced to model the CSDV frame and design PVQs. For simplicity, we segment this CSDV frame and allocate various bits for different patches based on the percentages of non-zeros pixels in every patch. The experiments show that the proposed coding scheme has the best result than the standard video coding algorithms, e.g. USQ-DPCM and H.265/HEVC. This is because our coding scheme takes object edges of the CSDV frame into account.

In the future, we will integrate a suitable coding scheme that can apply to the arbitrary bits and project a novel operator to detect edges accurately.

Acknowledgement. This work is supported in part by the key projects of Trico-Robot plan of NSFC under grant No.91748208, National Key Research and Development Program of China under grant 2016YFB1000903, NSFC No. 61573268 and Program 973 No. 2012CB316400.

References

1. Michel, S., Diepold, K.: Depth map compression via compressed sensing. In: 16th IEEE International Conference on Image Processing. IEEE (2009)
2. Oh, B., Lee, J., Park, D.: Depth map coding based on synthesized view distortion function. IEEE J. Sel. Top. Sign. Proces. **5**(7), 1344–1352 (2011)
3. Karsten, M., et al.: 3D video coding with depth modeling modes and view synthesis optimization. In: Asia-Pacific Signal & Information Processing Association Annual Summit and Conference (APSIPA ASC). IEEE (2012)
4. Godwin, S., et al.: Edge-aware intra prediction for depth-map coding. In: 2010 IEEE International Conference on Image Processing. IEEE (2010)
5. Oh, K., Vetro, A., Ho, Y.: Depth coding using a boundary reconstruction filter for 3-D video systems. IEEE Trans. Circuits Syst. Video Technol. **21**(3), 350–359 (2011)
6. Yannick, M., Farin, D.: Platelet-based coding of depth maps for the transmission of multiview images. In: International Society for Optics and Photonics, Electronic Imaging (2006)
7. X. Li, et al.: Efficient compressive sensing video compression method based on Gaussian mixture models. In: Visual Communication and Image Processing. IEEE (2016)
8. Yang, J., et al.: Gaussian mixture model for video compressive sensing. In: IEEE International Conference on Image Processing. IEEE (2013)
9. Yang, J., et al.: Video compressive sensing using Gaussian mixture models. IEEE Trans. Image Process. **23**(11), 4863–4878 (2014)
10. Anand, S., Rao, B.: PDF optimized parametric vector quantization of speech line spectral frequencies. IEEE Trans. Speech Audio Process. **11**(2), 130–142 (2003)
11. Gersho, A., Gray, R.: Vector Quantization and Signal Compression. Springer, New York (1992). https://doi.org/10.1007/978-1-4615-3626-0
12. Candes, E.J.: Compressive sampling. In: Proceedings of the International Congress of Mathematicians. Madrid, Spain, pp. 1433–1452 (2006)
13. Liu, H., Song, B., Tian, F., Qin, H.: Joint sampling rate and bit-depth optimization in compressive video sampling. IEEE T-MM **16**(6), 1549–1562 (2014)
14. Li, X., et al.: Efficient lossy compression for compressive sensing acquisition of images in compressive sensing imaging system. Sensors **14**(12), 23398–23418 (2014)

Image Super-Resolution, Debluring, and Dehazing

AWCR: Adaptive and Weighted Collaborative Representations for Face Super-Resolution with Context Residual-Learning

Tao Lu[1,2,3(✉)], Lanlan Pan[1], Jiaming Wang[1], Yanduo Zhang[1], Zhongyuan Wang[4], and Zixiang Xiong[1,2,3]

[1] School of Computer Science and Engineering, Wuhan Institute of Technology, Wuhan 430073, China
lut@wit.edu.cn
[2] Department of Electrical and Computer Engineering, Texas A&M University, College Station, TX 77843, USA
[3] Monash University, Melbourne, Australia
[4] School of Computer Science, Wuhan University, Wuhan 430072, China

Abstract. Owing to the ill-posed nature of the image super-resolution (SR) problem, learning-based approaches typically employ regularization terms in the representation. Current local-patch based face SR approaches weight representation coefficients to obtain adaptive and accurate priors. However, they ignore the fact that heteroskedasticity generally exists both in the observed data and representation coefficients. In this paper, we present a novel adaptive and weighted representation framework for face SR to further exploit adaptive and accurate prior information for different content inputs. Moreover, we enrich patch priors by sampling context patches, and learn the residual high-frequency components for better reconstruction performance. Experiments on the CAS-PEAL-R1 face database show that our proposed approach outperforms state-of-the-arts that include other deep learning based methods.

Keywords: Face super-resolution · Local-face · Context patch
Adaptive and weighted collaborative representation · Residual-learning

1 Introduction

Face super-resolution (SR), so called "face hallucination" which enhances the quality and resolution of low-resolution (LR) input facial images, is widely used in face recognition, face portrait, identification and so on [1]. It is a research hot topic which attracts scholars' attentions. Wang *et al.* [1] distinguished face hallucinations into three categories: interpolation-based, reconstruction-based and learning-based approaches. Among them, learning-based approaches incorporate image prior from training samples and achieve satisfactory objective and subjective performance.

© Springer International Publishing AG, part of Springer Nature 2018
B. Zeng et al. (Eds.): PCM 2017, LNCS 10735, pp. 107–116, 2018.
https://doi.org/10.1007/978-3-319-77380-3_11

Baker and Kanade [2] first proposed face SR problem and developed coupled multi-resolution Gaussian pyramids for patch matching to infer the missing high-frequency information.

Generally speaking, face SR can be divided into global- and local- face image methods by the manner of how to represent image prior.

Global-face SR treat one facial image as a whole to exploit the structure information. Intensive global face SR [3–7] were consecutively proposed in recent years. Although global-face SR is prone to robust to noise or outliers in inputs, high dimensions of whole images bring under-fitting problem. Accurate representing large images requires exponential number of training samples, however, sufficient training samples are always not available and impractical.

Local-face SR samples the facial image by overlapped patches for pursuing accurate prior. In this scenario, in order to overcome under-fitting or over-fitting of optimal coefficients, different regularization methods are commonly used in least squares schemes. Chang *et al.* [8] first introduced local linear embedding (LLE) method into SR by the k-nearest neighbor patches. Ma *et al.* [9] proposed a position-patch based least squares representation approach for face position patch prior. Then, sparse representation [10–13], low-rank representation [14] are used in face SR for the accurate prior from samples. Furthermore, Wang *et al.* [15] pointed out that heteroskedasticity of coefficient domain brings bias in noise scenario. And considering the adaptive prior for inputs signal, locality-constrained representation [16], weighted patch representation [17], and Tikhonov regularized representation [18] emphasized on the adaption of coefficient domain by introducing locality constraints.

While aforementioned position-patch based approaches achieved good performance since position-patch contains structural prior after aligning, we find its limitations in two aspects: first it only considers heteroskedasticity of representation coefficients domain for adaptive prior; second, it only utilizes local patch information for accurate prior. Recently, Dong *et al.* [19] proposed an end-to-end convolutional network for image SR to obtain accurate prior. Kim *et al.* [20] proofed very deep structure was good for accurate residual prediction, and used large receptive field for exploiting context information.

In order to address above issues, based on the nature of heteroskedasticity generally comes from observed data and coexists in representation coefficients domain [21], we propose a novel method to practically resolve the issues.

Adaptive Prior. Different from aforementioned representation based approaches, we consider adaptive prior both from input data and representation coefficients. Since the heteroskedasticities of observe data and representation coefficients are tamed for obtaining adaptive priors, diversity of input and local adaptation between input and dictionary atoms are simultaneously satisfied to guarantee appropriate and meaningful image representation and reconstruction.

Accurate Prior. Inspired by aforementioned deep learning based approaches, we extend position patch into context-patch for acquiring more context information (more accurate prior than position patch) for representation and reconstruction of patch-level prior. Moreover we adopt residual-learning instead of pixel-wised feature learning for accurately predicting high frequency information for reconstruction.

Contributions. Overall, in this paper, we proposed an adaptive and weighted collaborative representation based face SR, termed AWCR, which weight reconstruction error and adapt representation coefficients simultaneously for adaptive prior. Traditional position-patch based approach is extended into context-patch which effectively exploits context information as additional prior rather than local position-patch for accurate prior. In addition, we use residual-learning to replace the pixel-wised feature predicting for accurate high frequent information.

2   Preliminaries

2.1   Weighted Least Squares Representation

Given an input patch vector $x \in \Re^{p \times 1}$, with a dictionary $L \in \Re^{p \times K}$, where p is the dimension of vector and K is the number of dictionary atoms. Representation learning is to obtain a coefficient vector α by following objective function:

$$\alpha^* = \arg \min_{\alpha}\{||\epsilon||_2^2 + \lambda\Phi(\alpha)\}, s.t.\, \epsilon = x - L\alpha, \tag{1}$$

where the first term is referred as reconstruction error, $\Phi(\alpha)$ is the regularization term, λ is a nonnegative constant which controls the balance between reconstruction error and regularization term.

Suppose ϵ with zero mean, i.e. $E(\epsilon|L) = 0$. If their variance $Var(\epsilon|L) = \sigma$, σ is constant, then the residuals is homoskedastic and it can be solved by ordinary least squares. Generally, each observation varies so the variance $Var(\epsilon|L) = \Omega$, and Ω are independent variables that determines the particular heteroskedasticity. In this case, it is called as "Generalized least square" (GLS). GLS minimizes its squared Mahalanobis distance to estimate its representation coefficients:

$$\alpha^*_{(GLS)} = \arg \min_{\alpha}\{(x - L\alpha)^T \Omega^{-1} (x - L\alpha)\}. \tag{2}$$

This simplifies to weighted least squares representation (WLSR) in case Ω is diagonal and has analytical solution:

$$\alpha^*_{(WLSR)} = \left(L^T \Omega^{-1} L\right)^{-1} L^T \Omega^{-1} x. \tag{3}$$

2.2   Patch Based Face Super-Resolution

In patch-based face SR scenario, suppose $\{A_i, B_i\}_{i=1}^N$ indicates coupled LR and HR training database pairs, where $A_i \in \Re^{m \times n}$ and $B_i \in \Re^{tm \times tn}$, t is the scale factor, N is the number of training samples. Given an input LR image $X \in \Re^{m \times n}$, the goal of SR is to infer an output HR image $Y \in \Re^{tm \times tn}$ with the help of training samples. We divide images into overlapped patches, for input patches $\{x_i\}_{i=1}^p$, p is the number of patches. Then for each input patch x_i, a coupled LR and HR dictionary pair (L_i, H_i) can be learnt from training samples with same manner to obtaining patches. Thus, patch-based face SR can be summarized into two-steps:

LR Representation Learning: is to obtain the representation coefficients α_i^* by formulate with different regularization term configuration.

HR Reconstruction: based on manifold consistency assumption, the latent HR image patch can be rendered by:

$$y_i = H_i \alpha_i^*, \tag{4}$$

where i is the index of patches. As the result, the whole HR image Y can be stitched by all p patches.

3 Proposed Method

3.1 Dictionary Learning from Context-Patch

Different from the position-patch based methods, we leverage all the contextual patches around the i-th position to enrich the LR and HR dictionaries [22]. In the proposed method, we define the contextual patches as size of $ps \times ps$ within a bigger window of size $ws \times ws$ centered at this patch. In this bigger window we use step size ss to sample multiple patches, the number of context-patches c can be obtained by the window size ws, the patch size ps and the step size ss:

$$c = \left(1 + \frac{ws + ps}{ss}\right)^2. \tag{5}$$

For the i-th patch (vector form) $x_i \in \Re^{ps^2 \times 1}$, it has $c \times N$ LR training pool $C_i^L = [c_1^L, c_2^L, \ldots, c_{c \times N}^L] \in \Re^{ps^2 \times (c \times N)}$ for representation, and its HR version $C_i^H = [c_1^H, c_2^H, \ldots, c_{c \times N}^H] \in \Re^{(ps \times t^2)^2 \times (c \times N)}$ for reconstruction. Once context patches are obtained, for x_i, we use hard threshold by Euclidean distance to find K nearest neighbor patches L_i from LR patch pool C_i^L. And then we use the same index to find the K nearest neighbors patches H_i from the HR corresponding patch pool C_i^H. Here, $L_i \in \Re^{ps^2 \times K}$ is used for LR input representation and $H_i \in \Re^{(ps \times t^2)^2 \times K}$ is for HR output reconstruction, K is the number of the dictionary atoms.

3.2 Adaptive and Weighted Collaborative Representations (AWCR)

In order to get accurate representation coefficients from supporting dictionaries, we weight reconstruction error and representation coefficient simultaneously, then traditional collaborative representation becomes adaptively by content and locality constraints:

$$\alpha_i^* = \arg\min_{\alpha_i}\{(x_i - L_i\alpha_i)^T \Omega^{-1}(x_i - L_i\alpha_i) + \lambda||\Gamma\alpha_i||_2^2\}, \tag{6}$$

here, Ω is a diagonal matrix for weighting reconstruction error, and Γ is a diagonal locality constraint matrix. These two matrices are supported to be known in advance. In particular, we use ordinary LSR to obtain initial estimation of representation residual, then diagonal matrix Ω has its diagonal elements by absolute value of residuals:

$$\Omega = diag\left(|\epsilon|\right), \epsilon = x_i - L_i\alpha_{i(LSR)}^{*}. \tag{7}$$

For Γ, we obtain it by calculating the diagonal matrix of the distance between the dictionary L_i and the input patch x_i:

$$\Gamma = diag(||l_1 - x_i||_2, ||l_2 - x_i||_2, \ldots, || l_K - x_i||_2), \tag{8}$$

where l_j is the j-th atom in dictionary L_i. Once weighted matrices Ω and Γ are obtained, then formulate (AWCR) can be solved by least square approach as:

$$\alpha_{i(AWCR)}^{*} = \left(L_i^T \Omega^{-1} L_i + \lambda \left(\Gamma^T \Gamma\right)\right)^{-1} L_i^T \Omega^{-1} x_i. \tag{9}$$

From above, we can observe that AWCR is a general form of different representation approaches:

(1) If $\Omega = I$ and $\Gamma = 0$, the proposed method is simplifies to LSR [23];
(2) If $\Omega \neq I$ and $\Gamma = I$, the proposed method is simplifies to weighted CR;
(3) If $\Omega = I$ and $\Gamma = diag(||l_1 - x_i||_2, ||l_2 - x_i||_2, \ldots, ||l_K - x_i||_2)$, the proposed method is simplifies to TR [24].
(4) If $\Omega = I$ and $\Gamma = diag(||l_1 - x_i||_2, ||l_2 - x_i||_2, \ldots, ||l_K - x_i||_2), s.t. \sum_{j=1}^{K} \alpha_i[j] = 1$, here $\alpha_i[j]$ indicates the i-th coefficient vector the j-th element. Then the proposed method is simplifies to LCR [13].

3.3   Context Residual-Learning

As we know, representation based SR approaches have one basic assumption: HR and LR manifolds share similar geometry structure, *i.e.*, representation coefficients are isometric. So the correlation between HR and LR coefficients play an important role in reconstruction. While interpolating LR images into same size of HR always brings better correlation for LR and HR coefficients, this manner are widely used in images SR [19]. Moreover, predicting residuals are common for image SR to get accurate high frequent components [20, 25]. In this paper, we use context patch residual-learning to replace traditional pixel-wised learning scheme. This simple modification boosts SR performance.

Overall, the proposed face SR approach is described in Algorithm 1.

Algorithm 1. AWCR for face SR

Input: HR and LR training images $\{A_i\}_{i=1}^N$ and $\{B_i\}_{i=1}^N$, LR input image X, scale
    factor t, regularization parameter λ, patch size ps, window size ws and step size ss,
    number of dictionary atoms K.
Dictionry learning:
 1: Prepare LR training data $\{A_i\}_{i=1}^N$, and residual training HR data $\{B_i - A_i\}_{i=1}^N$.
 2: Form two context patch pools, for each input patch x_i and its interpolated version
    x_i^*, learn HR and LR dictionaries L_i and H_i.
AWCR:
for each patch: i=1 to p.
 3: Compute weighted matrices Ω and Γ by using (7) and (8).
 4: Compute the weights $\alpha_{i(AWCR)}^*$ by using (9), and reconstruct HR residual $r(y_i)$ by
    using(4).
end.
 5: HR patch $y_i = r(y_i) + x_i^*$, integrate all p HR patches to form Y.
Output: The target HR image Y.

---

4   Experimental Results

We conduct experiments on CAS-PEAL-R1 Face Database [26], which has 30871
images of 1040 subjects. We only use 1040 frontal face images: 1000 images are
randomly selected as training data and the rest 40 images for testing. Therefore,
all the test subjects are not in present in the training database. Peak signal to
noise ratio (PSNR) and structural similarity (SSIM) are used as evaluation metrics. The HR image is 112×96 pixels, then LR images are formed by average
blur (blur kernel is 4 pixels) and down-sampling (scale factor is 4) from corresponding HR images, thus the size of LR face images is 28×24 pixels, after that
we interpolate LR images into size of HR. LR and HR patches are 12×12 with
4 pixels overlapped.

4.1   Parameter Selection

The Effects of the Regulatory Parameter λ. We plot average PSNR and
SSIM of all 40 testing images in Fig. 2. Here, it is easy to observe that the
regulatory parameter λ plays an important role in reconstruction performance.

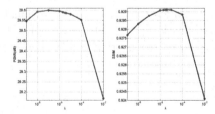

Fig. 1. The average PSNR and SSIM values of the proposed method with different λ.

With the increase of the regulatory parameter λ, much benefit can be gained which means λ is effective for the experiment performance. In the proposed method, we set the regularization parameter λ at 10^{-7} for the best performance (Fig. 1).

The Effects of the Number Dictionary Atoms K. In order to verify the effects of the number of dictionary atoms K, we plot the average PSNR and SSIM values of all test images with different K. As show in Fig. 2, we can see the number dictionary atoms K has a significant influence of performance. As the number dictionary atoms K increase, the performance of the proposed method will be increased. When the number dictionary atoms K is between 500 and 1000, the proposed method can continually obtain a stable and good performance. Thus we set the number dictionary atoms K at a stable range. In the proposed method we set the number dictionary atoms K at 800.

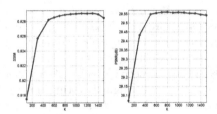

Fig. 2. The average PSNR and SSIM of the proposed method with different K.

4.2   Roles of the Weighted Matrix Ω and Γ

In formulate (6), if the weighted items Ω is Identity matrix, then AWCR will lose the weighted function, and if $\lambda = 0$, AWCR will lose adaptive function. In Table 1, there are four different configurations: for the first column, AWCR is degraded into LSR [9]; for the second column, AWCR is equivalent to WLSR; for the third column, AWCR is same with TR [18]; the last column is AWCR. Experiments are conducted on pixel-wise domain, without Γ, Ω improves PSNR 0.40 dB; without Ω, Γ improves PSNR 0.59 dB; however, with both Ω and Γ, PSNR improves 0.78 dB. This phenomenon proofs that weighting matrix Ω and the adaptive matrix Γ are helpful for image reconstruction.

Table 1. The average PSNR(dB) and SSIM of different configurations on Ω and Γ

Configurations	$\Omega = I, \lambda = 0$	$\Omega \neq I, \lambda = 0$	$\Omega = I, \lambda \neq 0$	$\Omega \neq I, \lambda \neq 0$
PSNR	27.04	27.44	27.63	27.82
SSIM	0.875	0.884	0.885	0.889

4.3   Comparison with State-of-the-Art Methods

We compared the results with some state-of-the-art methods including: SRCNN [19], VDSR [20] (The best performance of deep learning based approach), LCR [16] (The best performance of position based approach), CLNE [27] (The best performance of iterative representation based approach), LLE [8], WSR [15], LSR [9]. All the parameters are set as their best performance according to their papers. Because the SRCNN and VDSR methods have to remove image border for their best performance, for a fair competition, we compare traditional competitors with border, and deep learning based approaches without border. We list average PSNR and SSIM of all 40 LR testing images in Table 2, our proposed approach outperforms traditional face SR by a significant margin, *i.e.*, 1.48 dB (PSNR) and 0.033 (SSIM) compared with the second best performance position-based face SR approach. Comparing with VDSR, our methods has gains of 0.35 dB and 0.01 on PSNR and SSIM respectively. In particular, we show the results of AWCR with position-patch and context-patch respectively. Context information improves 1.19 dB on PSNR and 0.021 on SSIM, and residual-learning brings promotion of 0.59 dB and 0.019.

We select two representative images (one is aligned to training data, the other one is not) to show the subjective quality of different face SR approaches in Fig. 3. The first row of Fig. 3 is aligned testing image, and the second one is unaligned testing image, it is obvious that details of our proposed algorithm (red frame parts) are more clear. In addition, for position-based approaches, there are aliasing effects on unaligned reconstructed image due to unsuitable position dictionaries providing inaccurate patch prior. SRCNN and VDSR use random patch for reconstruction, so they are robust to unaligned inputs. Thus

Table 2. The average of PSNR(dB) and SSIM values with different methods.

Methods	LSR	WSR	LLE	LCR	CLNE	AWCR		Remove border		
						Position	Context	SRCNN	VDSR	AWCR
PSNR	27.04	27.20	27.58	27.61	28.12	28.41	29.60	29.28	30.38	30.73
SSIM	0.875	0.874	0.886	0.887	0.896	0.908	0.929	0.914	0.927	0.937
Gains of PSNR	2.56	2.40	2.02	1.99	1.48	1.19	–	1.35	0.35	–
Gains of SSIM	0.054	0.055	0.044	0.042	0.033	0.021	–	0.023	0.010	–

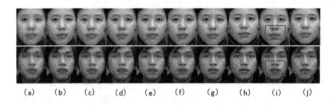

(a)   (b)   (c)   (d)   (e)   (f)   (g)   (h)   (i)   (j)

Fig. 3. Visual face SR results with different SR approaches. (a) Input LR images, (b) LSR, (c) SR, (d) LLE, (e) LCR, (f) CLNE, (g) SRCNN, (h) VDSR, (i) our method, (j) Original HR image. (Color figure online)

our method utilize context-patch information which obtains context information in larger region than patch to get better reconstruction performance. We list results of all 40 testing images in supplement material.

5 Conclusion

In this work, we have presented a face SR using adaptive and weighted collaborative representation, which can be regarded as a general form of LSR, TR, WLSR and LCR. In addition, we extend position patch based face SR into context patch scheme for accurate patch prior, then context residual-learning is used to further predict accurate high frequent information for better images reconstruction. Experimental results on CAS-PEAL-R1 face database indicate our approach outperforms position-based approaches by a significant margin. We believe this approach is readily applicable to other image restoration problems, *e.g.*, denoising and general image SR.

Acknowledgments. This work is supported by the grant of China Scholarship Council, the National Natural Science Foundation of China (61502354,61501413), the Natural Science Foundation of Hubei Province of China (2012FFA099, 2012FFA134, 2013CF125, 2014CFA130, 2015CFB451), Scientific Research Foundation of Wuhan Institute of Technology.

References

1. Wang, N., Tao, D., Gao, X., Li, X., Li, J.: A comprehensive survey to face hallucination. Int. J. Comput. Vis. **106**, 9–30 (2014)
2. Baker, S., Kanade, T.: Hallucinating faces. In: 2000 IEEE International Conference on Automatic Face and Gesture Recognition, pp. 83–88, March 2000
3. Wang, X., Tang, X.: Hallucinating face by eigentransformation. IEEE Trans. Syst. Man Cybern. Part C (Appl. Rev.) **35**, 425–434 (2005)
4. Lu, T., Hu, R., Han, Z., Jiang, J., Zhang, Y.: From local representation to global face hallucination: a novel super-resolution method by nonnegative feature transformation. In: 2013 Visual Communications and Image Processing (VCIP), pp. 1–6, November 2013
5. Zhou, H., Hu, J., Lam, K.M.: Global face reconstruction for face hallucination using orthogonal canonical correlation analysis. In: 2015 Asia-Pacific Signal and Information Processing Association Annual Summit and Conference (APSIPA), pp. 537–542, December 2015
6. Zhuang, Y., Zhang, J., Wu, F.: Hallucinating faces: LPH super-resolution and neighbor reconstruction for residue compensation. Pattern Recogn. **40**(11), 3178–3194 (2007)
7. Lan, C., Hu, R., Han, Z., Wang, Z.: A face super-resolution approach using shape semantic mode regularization. In: 2010 IEEE International Conference on Image Processing, pp. 2021–2024, September 2010
8. Chang, H., Yeung, D.-Y., Xiong, Y.: Super-resolution through neighbor embedding. IEEE Trans. Syst. Man Cybern. Part C: Appl. Rev. **1**(3), I (2004)

9. Ma, X., Zhang, J., Qi, C.: Hallucinating face by position-patch. Pattern Recogn. **43**(6), 2224–2236 (2010)
10. Jung, C., Jiao, L., Liu, B., Gong, M.: Position-patch based face hallucination using convex optimization. IEEE Sig. Process. Lett. **18**, 367–370 (2011)
11. Yang, J., Wright, J., Huang, T., Ma, Y.: Image super-resolution as sparse representation of raw image patches. In: 2008 IEEE Conference on Computer Vision and Pattern Recognition (CVPR), pp. 1–8, June 2008
12. Wang, Z., Hu, R., Wang, S., Jiang, J.: Face hallucination via weighted adaptive sparse regularization. IEEE Trans. Circ. Syst. Video Technol. **24**(5), 802–813 (2014)
13. Jung, C., Jiao, L., Liu, B., Gong, M.: Position-patch based face hallucination using convex optimization. IEEE Sig. Process. Lett. **18**(6), 367–370 (2011)
14. Gao, G., Jing, X.Y., Huang, P., Zhou, Q., Wu, S., Yue, D.: Locality-constrained double low-rank representation for effective face hallucination. IEEE Access **4**, 8775–8786 (2016)
15. Wang, Z., Hu, R., Jiang, J., Han, Z., Shao, Z.: Heteroskedasticity tuned mixed-norm sparse regularization for face hallucination. Multimedia Tools Appl. **75**(24), 17273–17301 (2016)
16. Jiang, J., Hu, R., Wang, Z., Han, Z.: Noise robust face hallucination via locality-constrained representation. IEEE Trans. Multimedia **16**(5), 1268–1281 (2014)
17. Zhang, Y., Zhang, Z., Hu, G., Hancock, E.R.: Face image super-resolution via weighted patches regression. In: 2016 23rd International Conference on Pattern Recognition (ICPR), pp. 3881–3886 (2016)
18. Jiang, J., Chen, C., Huang, K., Cai, Z., Hu, R.: Noise robust position-patch based face super-resolution via Tikhonov regularized neighbor representation. Inf. Sci. **367**, 354–372 (2016)
19. Dong, C., Loy, C.C., He, K., Tang, X.: Image super-resolution using deep convolutional networks. IEEE Trans. Pattern Anal. Mach. Intell. **38**, 295–307 (2016)
20. Kim, J., Kwon Lee, J., Mu Lee, K.: Accurate image super-resolution using very deep convolutional networks. In: The IEEE Conference on Computer Vision and Pattern Recognition (CVPR Oral), June 2016
21. Timofte, R., Gool, L.V.: Adaptive and weighted collaborative representations for image classification. Pattern Recogn. Lett. **43**, 127–135 (2014)
22. Romano, Y., Elad, M.: Con-patch: when a patch meets its context. IEEE Trans. Image Process. **25**, 3967–3978 (2016)
23. Zhang, L., Yang, M., Feng, X.: Sparse representation or collaborative representation: which helps face recognition? In: Proceedings, vol. 2011, no. 5, pp. 471–478 (2011)
24. Tikhonov, A.N., Arsenin, V.Y.: Solution of ill-posed problems. Math. Comput. **32**(144), 491 (1978)
25. Timofte, R., Rothe, R., Gool, L.V.: Seven ways to improve example-based single image super resolution. In: 2016 IEEE Conference on Computer Vision and Pattern Recognition (CVPR), pp. 1865–1873, June 2016
26. Gao, W., Cao, B., Shan, S., Chen, X., Zhou, D., Zhang, X., Zhao, D.: The CAS-PEAL large-scale Chinese face database and baseline evaluations. IEEE Trans. Syst. Man Cybern. - Part A: Syst. Hum. **38**, 149–161 (2008)
27. Jiang, J., Hu, R., Wang, Z., Han, Z., Ma, J.: Facial image hallucination through coupled-layer neighbor embedding. IEEE Trans. Circ. Syst. Video Technol. **26**, 1674–1684 (2016)

Single Image Haze Removal Based on Global-Local Optimization for Depth Map

Hongda Zhang[1], Yuanyuan Gao[1], Hai-Miao Hu[1,2(✉)],
Qiang Guo[1], and Yukun Cui[1]

[1] Beijing Key Laboratory of Digital Media, School of Computer Science
and Engineering, Beihang University, Beijing 100083, China
frank0139@163.com
[2] State Key Laboratory of Virtual Reality Technology and Systems,
Beihang University, Beijing 100191, China

Abstract. With the wide application of computer vision system, image haze removal has become a new challenge. A great number of image dehazing methods are proposed, which have varying degrees of dehazing effects and different shortcomings. The color attenuation prior for image haze removal presents a new way based on depth map estimation. The novel method performs well with little distortion and natural colors. This paper discusses the color attenuation prior for image haze removal and proposes the haze removal method based on global-local optimization for depth map. Regarding the halo artifacts in dehazing images, we combine the minimum filter and minimum-maximum filter to detect the potential areas of the halo artifacts and suppress them. For the case of the underestimation of depth information, we take advantage of the atmospheric light estimation to perform global optimization for final depth map. Experimental results demonstrate excellent performance of the proposed method.

Keywords: Image haze removal · Global-local optimization
Minimum-Maximum filter · Depth map

1 Introduction

Single image haze removal is important for many practical applications, such as intelligent vehicles, satellite imaging, and aerial imagery [1, 2]. The conventional contrast enhancement algorithms fail to achieve an appropriate result and will introduce the color distortion, which cannot meet the requirement of practical applications [2, 3]. Therefore, image dehazing remains a challenge due to the unknown scene depth.

In order to extract depth information for image dehazing, researchers focused on image dehazing by using additional information [4, 5] or multiple images [6–12]. Recently, many single image haze removal algorithms [13–15] have been proposed by using reasonable priors/assumptions [16, 17] and the widely-used haze imaging model proposed in [9, 10].

In 2008, Fattal [16] recovered the hazy images based on Independent Component Analysis (ICA). The method cannot be used for grayscale image dehazing and has high time complexity. In 2009, He *et al.* firstly proposed the dark channel prior (DCP) for

© Springer International Publishing AG, part of Springer Nature 2018
B. Zeng et al. (Eds.): PCM 2017, LNCS 10735, pp. 117–127, 2018.
https://doi.org/10.1007/978-3-319-77380-3_12

image dehazing based on statistics of a large number of haze-free images [17]. However, the method cannot work well with some cases, especially the sky.

In 2015, the image haze removal based on color attenuation prior (IHRCAP) was presented in Zhu *et al.* [18]. According to experimental results, we find that there are two aspects of IHRCAP that could be improved. First, the dehazing image may possess obvious halo artifacts at sharp edges. Second, IHRCAP works well with moderately hazy images, but cannot achieve appropriate results to the others.

In 2016, Berman *et al.* [19] developed a novel approach based on non-local prior. The algorithm can achieve appropriate results by utilizing the assumption that a haze-free image can be well structured by a few hundred distinct colors. In 2017, Gao *et al.* [20] proposed an illumination estimation method based on Retinex, which works well with dense-haze images.

In order to further improve the dehazing effect, this paper firstly introduces IHR-CAP proposed in [18]. Then, the local optimization by combining the minimum filter and minimum-maximum filter is proposed to detect the potential areas of halo artifacts and suppress the halo artifacts. In addition, we find that IHRCAP tends to underestimate depth information to some images, leading to inappropriate effect. To improve it, the global optimization based on atmospheric light estimation is proposed to refine the depth map. The experimental results show that the proposed dehazing method improves both subjective and objective effect compared to IHRCAP.

2   Related Work and Observation

In this section, IHRCAP is introduced and analyzed through experiments.

2.1   Image Haze Removal Based on Color Attenuation Prior

IHRCAP is proposed based on experiments on various hazy images. The main ideas of IHRCAP are as follows:

Color Attenuation Prior. Zhu *et al.* [18] find that as the concentration of the haze increases, the difference between brightness and saturation tends to increase. In addition, based on the assumption that the scene depth is positively correlated with the concentration of the haze, the above law can be used to estimate the depth information of the scene in hazy images.

The Linear Model Definition. IHRCAP defines a linear model to calculate depth information, as follows:

$$d(x) = \alpha + \beta v(x) + \gamma s(x) + \varepsilon(x) \tag{1}$$

where x is the pixel point, d is the scene depth, v is the brightness component, s is the saturation component, α, β, γ are the unknown linear coefficients, ε is a random variable representing the random error of the model and is regarded as a Gaussian density with zero mean and variance σ.

Estimation of the Atmospheric Light and Scene Radiance Recovery. IHRCAP selects the brightest pixels in the top 0.1% from the depth map and utilizes the pixel with highest intensity in the corresponding position of the hazy image as the atmospheric light.

When the depth of the scene and the atmospheric light are known, the scene radiance can be easily restored according to the atmospheric scattering model which is proposed by McCartney in 1976 [21] and further derived by Narasimhan and Nayar [9–11, 22].

2.2 Observations Aiming at IHRCAP

Although IHRCAP can achieve outstanding results on moderate hazy images, it may result in local halo artifacts and inaccuracy of global depth estimation.

Local Halo Artifacts. The guided filter is a smoothing filter proposed by He *et al.* [13]. Figure 1 shows a hazy image and the dehazing images with different filter radii of the guided filter. As can be seen, there are different intensities of halo artifacts at the edges of the foreground leaves. As the filter radius decreases, the halo artifacts become more obvious at the sharp edges and the dehazing effect is better at the smooth areas (see the wall in Fig. 1).

(a)   (b)   (c)   (d)

Fig. 1. Results using different guided filtering radii. (a) A hazy image. (b) The final result with $r = 15$. (c) The final result with $r = 30$. (d) The final result with $r = 60$.

Obviously, employing a larger guided filtering radius can overcome the halo artifacts appearing at the sharp edges markedly, meanwhile, it would result in worse dehazing effect at the smooth areas. If the halo artifacts can be removed, using a smaller guided filter radius will be a better choice.

Global Depth Information. Figure 2(a) and (d) give two hazy images, Fig. 2(b) and (e) show the corresponding depth maps refined by the guided filter, and Fig. 2(c) and (f) display the restored images. As can be seen from Fig. 2(c) and (f), IHRCAP works well with Fig. 2(a), but cannot achieve appropriate result to Fig. 2(d). According to Fig. 2(b), the depth information is richly layered, in which the depth values become larger as the distance increases. As can be seen in Fig. 2(d), the depth map is too simplex which cannot reflect the actual depth information, leading to inappropriate effect.

| (a) | (b) | (c) | (d) | (e) | (f) |

Fig. 2. Refined depth maps and dehazing images in different cases. (a), (d) The hazy images. (b), (e) Corresponding refined depth maps with guided filter. (c), (f) The dehazing images.

3 Proposed Method

3.1 Local Optimization by Combining Minimum Filter and Minimum-Maximum Filter

Disposing the raw depth map with minimum filter can effectively overcome the issue of white object, but it could cause the edge of the object to extend from the side with lower depth value to another side, resulting in inaccurate estimation of the depth information at the edges. The extension at the sharp edge would cause bad influence in the subsequent processes, leading to the halo artifacts indirectly.

The locations where may possess the halo artifacts usually are the sharp edges in depth map. In order to locate those positions, we process the minimum-filter depth map with maximum filter and median filter. Then, we compare the values of the two kind of depth map to judge whether the position would possess the halo artifacts. We give the following decision method:

$$\max_{y \in \Omega_{r(x)}} d_{min}(y) - \underset{z \in \Omega_{r(x)}}{median} \, d_{min}(z) > d_{threshold} \tag{2}$$

where $\Omega_r(x)$ is an $r * r$ neighborhood centered at x, d_{min} is the depth map with the minimum filter, the $d_{threshold}$ is empirically set as 0.2. Locations with halo artifacts always satisfy the above condition.

As can be seen in Fig. 3(b), the result with a radius $r = 15$ guided filter radius in IHRCAP has obvious halo artifacts at the edge of the front mountain. As can be seen in Fig. 3(c), the halo artifacts areas can be detected using the expression (2). Then, we use the minimum-maximum filter at those locations, and employ the minimum filter at other positions. As shown in Fig. 3(d), the halo artifacts can be effectively removed with the local optimization for depth map.

3.2 Global Optimization for Depth Estimation Based on Atmospheric Light Estimation

Typically, the depth values of pixels should be very close to 1 at sky region. In IHRCAP, the depth information tends to be underestimated in some cases and the

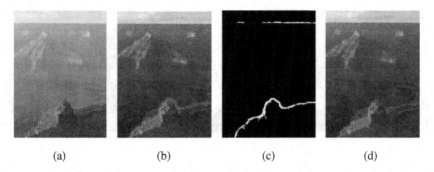

| (a) | (b) | (c) | (d) |

Fig. 3. Locate the position with halo artifacts. (a) The hazy image. (b) The result with $r = 15$ guided filter radius in IHRCAP. (c) The halo artifacts areas detection. (d) The result with local optimization in proposed approach.

depth values of sky region are far less than 1, leading to inappropriate result. Based on a large number of experiments, we find that the images with inappropriate results in IHRCAP always have a low atmospheric light value. Thus, we calculate the *average* value of the sky region as the scale to adaptively optimize the depth map, as follows:

$$average = max \left\{ \frac{1}{n} \sum_{i=1}^{n} \max_{c \in \{R,G,B\}} I^c(i), floor \right\} \tag{3}$$

where n is the total number of the pixels in sky region, c is the channel of RGB color space, I is the hazy image, *floor* is the lower limit and empirically set as 0.7. In addition, we estimate the sky region by choosing the pixels in hazy image which are the top 0.1% remotest pixels in corresponding depth map. Because some images do not contain sky region, so we set a *floor* value to avoid the average value being too small. Then we use the *average* value to optimize the depth map as follows:

$$d_{opt}(x) = d(x) \times 255/average \tag{4}$$

where x represents the pixel in depth map, d represents the original depth map before optimization, d_{opt} is the optimized depth map.

As Fig. 4(b) shows, the original depth map tends to be dark. The depth values of the remotest area are close to that of the middle distance area, so that it cannot reflect the actual depth information properly. As shown in Fig. 4(c), the depth information of optimized depth map is closer to the actual depth information. Figure 4(d) and (e) show the result of IHRCAP and the result after global optimization for depth map. As can be seen, the optimized result has better visual effect (see the road).

122   H. Zhang et al.

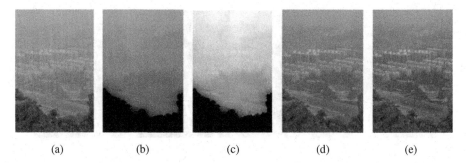

(a)   (b)   (c)   (d)   (e)

Fig. 4. Global optimization for depth map. (a) The hazy image. (b) The original depth map. (c) The optimized depth map. (d) The result with IHRCAP. (e) The result with global optimization for depth map.

4 Experimental Results

In this section, we compare results of conventional and the proposed approaches. Figures 5, 6, 7 and 8 show the results and close-ups of Fattal [16], DCP [17], IHRDCP [18] and the proposed algorithm on real-world hazy images. Note that, the parameters of these approaches are set according to [16–18]. The guided filter radii of IHRCAP and the proposed method are both set as 15.

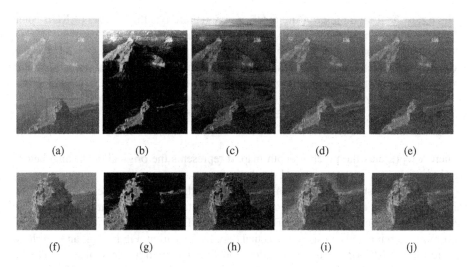

(a)   (b)   (c)   (d)   (e)

(f)   (g)   (h)   (i)   (j)

Fig. 5. Results for image *Mountains*. (a) The hazy image. (b) Result of Fattal. (c) Result of DCP. (d) Result of IHRCAP. (e) Result of the proposed algorithm. (f–j): Close-ups of (a–e).

As shown in Fig. 5, restored image of Fattal has serious distortion in which the sky area becomes white and the closer areas tend to be dark. Result of DCP looks too dark. Result of IHRCAP is more natural and has little distortion, but there are halo artifacts at

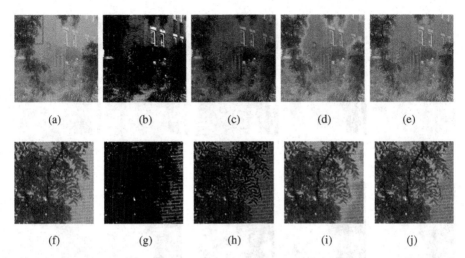

Fig. 6. Results for image *House*. (a) The hazy image. (b) Result of Fattal. (c) Result of DCP. (d) Result of IHRCAP. (e) Result of the proposed algorithm. (f–j): Close-ups of (a–e).

Fig. 7. Results for image *Trees*. (a) The hazy image. (b) Result of Fattal. (c) Result of DCP. (d) Result of IHRCAP. (e) Result of the proposed algorithm. (f–j): Close-ups of (a–e).

the edge of the front mountain, while result of the proposed approach preserves the advantages of IHRCAP and removes the halo artifacts markedly.

As can be seen in Fig. 6, result of Fattal has the similar problem to Fig. 5(b) (see the black branches) and DCP produces the over-saturated image. IHRCAP and the proposed method achieve natural results, but there are serious halo artifacts in the result of IHRCAP. As we can observe in Fig. 7(f–j), approach of Fattal performs well at foreground, but produces white area at background leading to information loss. Result of IHRCAP produces agglomerate haze at the edges of branches in foreground, while the proposed method has more balanced performance than others. As can be seen in Fig. 8(f–j), Fattal and DCP both make the person look too dark, so that the texture information is lost. IHRCAP presents uneven color effect, while the proposed approach

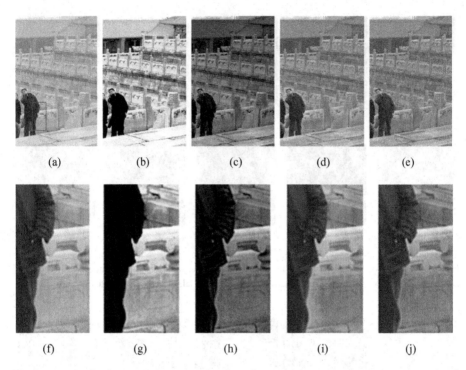

(a)   (b)   (c)   (d)   (e)

(f)   (g)   (h)   (i)   (j)

Fig. 8. Results for image *Palace*. (a) The hazy image. (b) Result of Fattal. (c) Result of DCP. (d) Result of IHRCAP. (e) Result of the proposed algorithm. (f–j): Close-ups of (a–e).

achieves appropriate result. In summary, results of the proposed algorithm are more natural and have less distortion than others.

To objectively assess the quality of the results, we make the use of one-dimensional color image information entropy and the gray-scale image structural similarity (SSIM) [23]. The one-dimensional color image information entropy is defined as:

$$H = - \sum\nolimits_{c \in \{R,G,B\}} \sum\nolimits_{i=0}^{255} p_{(c,i)} log p_{(c,i)} \tag{5}$$

where c is the channel of RGB color space, $p_{(c,i)}$ represents the probability of grayscale i in channel c. The information entropy reflects the amount of the information in an image and the higher entropy value usually indicates more details. The SSIM evaluates the ability of the algorithm to retain structural information. It should be noted that the greater value of SSIM means the higher similarity between two images, but it is not equal to the better dehazing effect.

Table 1 demonstrates the information entropy and the SSIM of the 4 groups of images in Figs. 5, 6, 7 and 8. As can be seen in Table 1, the proposed method has similar entropy values to IHRCAP, and the two approaches obtain higher values than Fattal and DCP. As to the SSIM, the averages of Fattal and DCP are both lower than 0.6 which means serious loss of structural information. The proposed algorithm and

IHRCAP achieve close SSIM values which are both higher than 0.8. Combing the subjective comparison and SSIM, it can be seen that the proposed method achieves promising visual effect under the condition of little structural information loss.

Table 1. Color image information entropy and SSIM of results.

Images	Eval. Meth.	Fattal [16]	DCP [17]	IHRCAP [18]	Proposed
Mountains	Inf. Entropy	5.44	15.54	15.63	15.64
	SSIM	0.21	0.45	0.85	0.84
House	Inf. Entropy	3.70	13.61	16.79	16.76
	SSIM	0.13	0.59	0.96	0.96
Trees	Inf. Entropy	13.16	13.48	14.98	15.00
	SSIM	0.74	0.69	0.97	0.96
Palace	Inf. Entropy	11.81	15.10	15.61	15.55
	SSIM	0.68	0.64	0.91	0.91
Average	Inf. Entropy	8.53	14.43	15.75	15.74
	SSIM	0.44	0.59	0.92	0.92

5 Conclusions

In this paper, we discuss IHRCAP and propose two optimization methods for depth map to improve it. With regard to the halo artifacts appearing at the edges of objects, we propose the local optimization for depth map by combining minimum filter and the minimum-maximum filter. The approach effectively removes the halo artifacts. As for the underestimation to depth information, we present the global optimization for depth map based on atmospheric light estimation. Using the statistics of sky region intensity, we optimize the depth map to make it more approximate to actual depth information. Combining the above two optimization methods, we improve the dehazing effect of IHRCAP to a certain extent. Experiments on real-world hazy images demonstrate the effectiveness of the proposed method.

Acknowledgements. This work was partially supported by the National Key Research and Development Program of China (Grant No. 2016YFC0801003), the National Natural Science Foundation of China (No. 61370121, No. 61421003).

References

1. Woodell, G.A., Jobson, D.J., Rahman, Z.U., Hines, G.D.: Advanced image processing of aerial imagery. In: Visual Information Processing, p. 62460E (2006). https://doi.org/10.1117/12.666767
2. Gao, Y., Hu, H., Wang, S., Li, B.: A fast image dehazing algorithm based on negative correction. Sig. Process. **103**, 380–398 (2014). https://doi.org/10.1016/j.sigpro.2014.02.016

3. Ancuti, C.O., Ancuti, C., Hermans, C., Bekaert, P.: A fast semi-inverse approach to detect and remove the haze from a single Image. In: Asian Conference on Computer Vision, pp. 501–514 (2010). https://doi.org/10.1007/978-3-642-19309-5_39
4. Kopf, J., Neubert, B., Chen, B., Cohen, M., Cohen-Or, D., Deussen, O., Uyttendaele, M., Lischinski, D.: Deep photo: model-based photograph enhancement and viewing. ACM Trans. Graph. 27(5), 116 (2008). https://doi.org/10.1145/1457515.1409069
5. Narasimhan, S.G., Nayar, S.K.: Interactive (de) weathering of an image using physical models. In: IEEE Workshop on Color and Photometric Methods in Computer Vision (2003)
6. Schechner, Y.Y., Narasimhan, S.G., Nayar, S.K.: Instant dehazing of images using polarization. In: Proceedings of CVPR. IEEE Press, vol. 1, p. I (2001). https://doi.org/10.1109/cvpr.2001.990493
7. Schechner, Y.Y., Narasimhan, S.G., Nayar, S.K.: Polarization-based vision through haze. Appl. Opt. 42(3), 511–525 (2003). https://doi.org/10.1364/AO.42.000511
8. Shwartz, S., Namer, E., Schechner, Y.Y.: Blind haze separation. In: Proceedings of CVPR. IEEE Press, vol. 2, pp. 1984–1991 (2006). https://doi.org/10.1109/cvpr.2006.71
9. Narasimhan, S.G., Nayar, S.K.: Chromatic framework for vision in bad weather. In: Proceedings of CVPR. IEEE Press, vol. 1, pp. 598–605 (2000). https://doi.org/10.1109/cvpr.2000.855874
10. Narasimhan, S.G., Nayar, S.K.: Vision and the atmosphere. Int. J. Comput. Vision 48(3), 233–254 (2002). https://doi.org/10.1023/A:1016328200723
11. Narasimhan, S.G., Nayar, S.K.: Contrast restoration of weather degraded images. IEEE Trans. Pattern Anal. Mach. Intell. 25(6), 713–724 (2003). https://doi.org/10.1109/TPAMI.2003.1201821
12. Hu, H., Wu, J., Li, B., Guo, Q., Zheng, J.: An adaptive fusion algorithm for visible and infrared videos based on entropy and the cumulative distribution of gray levels. IEEE Trans. Multimedia 99, 2706–2719 (2017). https://doi.org/10.1109/tmm.2017.2711422
13. He, K., Sun, J., Tang, X.: Guided image filtering. IEEE Trans. Pattern Anal. Mach. Intell. 35(6), 1397–1409 (2013). https://doi.org/10.1109/TPAMI.2012.213
14. Xiao, C., Gan, J.: Fast image dehazing using guided joint bilateral filter. Vis. Comput. 28(6–8), 713–721 (2012). https://doi.org/10.1007/s00371-012-0679-y
15. Xie, B., Guo, F., Cai, Z.: Improved single image dehazing using dark channel prior and multi-scale retinex. In: International Conference on Intelligent System Design and Engineering Application, vol. 1, pp. 848–851 (2010). https://doi.org/10.1109/isdea.2010.141
16. Fattal, R.: Single image dehazing. ACM Trans. Graph. 27(3), 72 (2008). https://doi.org/10.1145/1360612.1360671
17. He, K., Sun, J., Tang, X.: Single image haze removal using dark channel prior. In: Proceedings of CVPR. IEEE Press, pp. 1956–1963 (2009). https://doi.org/10.1109/cvpr.2009.5206515
18. Zhu, Q., Mai, J., Shao, L.: A fast single image haze removal algorithm using color attenuation prior. IEEE Trans. Image Process. 24(11), 3522–3533 (2015). https://doi.org/10.1109/TIP.2015.2446191
19. Berman, D., Treibitz, T., Avidan, S.: Non-local image dehazing. In: Proceedings of CVPR. IEEE Press, pp. 1674–1682 (2016). https://doi.org/10.1109/cvpr.2016.185
20. Gao, Y., Hu, H., Li, B., Guo, Q.: Naturalness preserved non-uniform illumination estimation for image enhancement based on retinex. IEEE Trans. Multimedia (2017). https://doi.org/10.1109/TMM.2017.2740025
21. McCartney, E.J.: Optics of the atmosphere: scattering by molecules and particles. Wiley, New York, USA (1976)

22. Narasimhan, S.G., Nayar, S.K.: Removing weather effects from monochrome images. In: Proceedings of CVPR, pp. II-186–II-193. IEEE Press (2001). https://doi.org/10.1109/cvpr. 2001.990956
23. Wang, Z., Bovik, A.C., Sheikh, H.R., Simoncelli, E.P.: Image quality assessment: from error visibility to structural similarity. IEEE Trans. Image Process. **13**(4), 600–612 (2004). https:// doi.org/10.1109/TIP.2003.819861

Single Image Dehazing Using Deep Convolution Neural Networks

Shengdong Zhang[1], Fazhi He[1(✉)], and Jian Yao[2]

[1] State Key Laboratory of Software Engineering, School of Computer Science,
Wuhan University, Wuhan, China
`fzhe@whu.edu.cn`
[2] School of Remote Sensing and Information Engineering, Wuhan University,
Wuhan, China

Abstract. Haze removal is urgently desired in multi-media system. A deep learning-based method, called dehazingCNN, is proposed to estimate an approximate clear image. The proposed learning model is different from traditional learning based method. We adopts Deep Convolution Neural Networks (CNN) to take a hazy image as the input and outputs the corresponding clear image directly. The output of the network is high quality except some block artifacts and color distortions. We can remove the color distortion in the approximate clear image via atmospheric scattering model and guided filter effectively. Experimental results on different type of images, such as synthetic and benchmark of hazy images, demonstrate that the proposed method is comparative to and even better than many complex state-of-the-art methods.

Keywords: Haze removal · Image restoration
Deep Convolution Neural Networks

1 Introduction

Haze removing or defogging is urgently needed in computer vision applications and commercial/computational photography. However defogging or haze removal is a challenging problem due to the fog formulation which depends on the unknown depth information of the scene. Three equations can be provided for the pixels in a single input image, while there exists four unknown quantities to be recovered. Therefore, in the past decades, a lot of methods have been proposed by using additional data or multiple images [1,2].

However, removing haze from single input image is more difficult and has more wide applications than multiple images methods. Traditional single image dehazing methods [3–11] have been applied to single image dehazing successfully. Because our method is a learning-based method, we focus on comparing with learning-based methods [10,12–14].

In [12], Tang et al. investigate the different haze-relevant feature of hazy image, and use best suitable feature combination to estimate the corresponding

© Springer International Publishing AG, part of Springer Nature 2018
B. Zeng et al. (Eds.): PCM 2017, LNCS 10735, pp. 128–137, 2018.
https://doi.org/10.1007/978-3-319-77380-3_13

transmission map for a hazy image. In [10], Zhu et al. propose a learning-based method which considers the transmission as a linear combination of the saturation and brightness of pixels in a hazy image. The most relative works to ours are references [13,14], which are deep learning-based methods to estimate transmission map. In [14], Ren et al. propose a multi-scale deep convolutional neural networks for dehazing. Our main contributions are three folds. First, to the best of our knowledge, this work is the first one to remove haze from single image without estimating transmission map. Second, we convert the problem from color domain to detail domain, in which the direct haze removing without estimating transmission map becomes possible. Third, a lot of experiments demonstrate that our method can achieve the state-of-the-art performance.

2 Haze Removal

The proposed method consists of three essential steps: (1) preprocessing to get $\mathbf{I}_A(x)$; (2) estimating clear image with Deep Convolution Neural Networks; (3) removing color distortion and block artifacts (see Algorithm 1).

Modeling of Haze Images: Haze model [15] is widely used :

$$\mathbf{I}(i,j) = \mathbf{J}(i,j) * t(i,j) + (1 - t(i,j)) * \mathbf{A}, \tag{1}$$

where $\mathbf{I}$ represents the haze image, $\mathbf{J}$ represents the haze free image, $\mathbf{A}$ represents the global atmospheric light, t represents the transmission describing the probability of the light that is not scattered and absorption by air particle or mist and arrives at the camera. To remove haze from the hazy image is equal to solve the $\mathbf{A}$, t from $\mathbf{I}$.

Notation: We estimate A using one of the previous methods [7,16]. We define $I_{A},r(x)$ and J_A as follows:

$$\mathbf{I}_A(x) = \mathbf{I}(x) - \mathbf{A} \tag{2}$$

$$r(x) = ||\mathbf{I}_A(x)|| \tag{3}$$

$$\mathbf{J}_A(x) = \mathbf{J}(x) - \mathbf{A} \tag{4}$$

$$\tilde{r}(x) = ||\mathbf{J}_A(x)|| \tag{5}$$

Where $\mathbf{I}_A$ translates the 3D RGB coordinate of hazy image to sphere coordinate, in which the airlight is at the origin, $r(x)$ represents the distance in RGB space of each pixel in hazy image to the airlight, $\mathbf{J}_A$ translate a clear image $\mathbf{J}$ to sphere coordinate, $\tilde{r}(x)$ represents the distance in RGB space of each pixel in haze-free image to the airlight.

Formulation: Considering a single hazy image, we first get $\mathbf{I}_A(x)$ by using Eq. 2, which is the preprocessing we perform. Our goal is to recover from $\mathbf{I}_A(x)$ the init clear image patch $F(\mathbf{I}_A)$, which is as similar as possible to the truth clear image patch $\mathbf{J}_A$. For the ease of presentation, we still call $\mathbf{I}_A(x)$ a hazy image, although it is $\mathbf{I}(x) - \mathbf{A}$.

Fig. 1. The CNN architecture used for haze removal experiments.

In order to estimate clear image exactly, our goal is expressed as following:

$$\min \|F(\mathbf{I}_A) - \mathbf{J}_A\|^2, \tag{6}$$

$F(\mathbf{I}_A)$ represents the output of the network, X represents the truth $\mathbf{J}_A$.

We utilize a preprocessing, which converts the problem from image color domain to image details domain. DCNN method can benefit from this preprocessing, which makes our network easy to train.

It is hard to train a network for predicting a haze-free image from hazy image directly. We first attempt to train such a network, and test the output of network. We find that the output can not be regarded as haze-free image. So our method benefits from learning $\mathbf{J}_A$ from $\mathbf{I}_A$, which makes our method remove haze from hazy image without estimating transmission.

Estimating Initial Clear Image: Because weights sharing allows for larger interactive range than other fully connected structures, we choose convolutional neural network (CNN) architecture. As shown in Fig. 1, our CNN architecture is simple for implementation. We denote Y as $\mathbf{I}_A(x)$. It is expressed as :

$$F^0(Y) = Y, \tag{7}$$

$$F^n(Y) = \max(W^n * F^{(n-1)}(Y) + B^n, 0), n = 1, \dots, 5 \tag{8}$$

$$F_W(Y) = W^n * F^{(n-1)}(Y) + B^n, n = 6 \tag{9}$$

n represents the layers, which ranges from 1 to 5. Our architecture consists of five layers and contains four hidden layers for convolution generation. The bottom layer with index 0 is the input layer and is expressed in Eq. 7.

Each intermediate layer in Eq. 8 represents a convolution process for the nodes. $*$ represents the convolution operation, W^n represents the convolution kernel and B^n is the bias. The top layer with $F_W(Y)$ in Eq. 9 generates the $\tilde{\mathbf{J}}_A(x)$ from the network.

Once $\tilde{\mathbf{J}}_A(x)$ is predicted, it is added with $\mathbf{A}(x)$, which can generate a high quality image dehazing result. Although our dehazing result is very similar to haze-free image, it contains block artifacts.

Remove Color Distortion and Block Artifacts: We apply an regularization operation to remove the block artifacts and color distortion. Because we recover $\mathbf{J}_A(x)$ from $\mathbf{I}(x)_A(x)$, we can use this information and $\mathbf{I}_A(x)$ to recover the initial transmission of each pixel using following Eq. 10.

$$\tilde{t}(x) = r(x)/\tilde{r}(x), \tag{10}$$

then we use guided filter to get a smooth transmission map $t(x)$.

Dehazing: Once the transmission map is estimated, we can recover the haze-free image using Eq. 1 as follows :

$$J(x) = \frac{\mathbf{I}(x) - \mathbf{A}}{t(x)} + \mathbf{A} \tag{11}$$

In Fig. 2, we show an example of our method, which is summarized in Algorithm 1. Figure 2(a) shows the input hazy image. Our haze removal result is shown in Fig. 2(b). Figure 2(c) shows the distance in RGB space of every pixel in the hazy image to the airlight. Figure 2(d) shows the estimated distance of clear pixel to the airlight. Since larger values are represented by brighter colors, this indicates that the distance to the airlight is increased. Figure 2(e) shows the initial transmission calculate using Eq. 10. Figure 2(f) shows the final transmission.

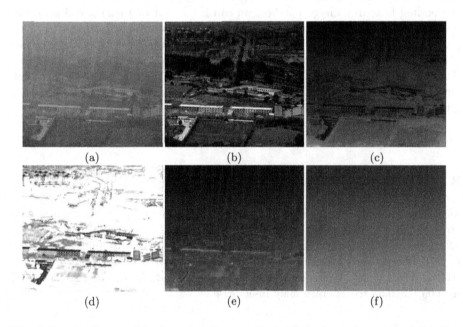

Fig. 2. Intermediate and final results of our method: (a) An input hazy image; (b) The output image; (c) The distance $r(x)$ of every pixel of the hazy image to the airlight; (d) The estimate distance $\tilde{r}(x)$; (e) The init $\tilde{t}(x)$; (f) The final $t(x)$.

Train Data Preparation and Train DehazeCNN Network: It is hard to collect the vast amount of labelled data for training DehazingCNN [13]. Therefore we adopt same strategy as [10,12,13], which is based on two assumptions [12]. First, the transmission in a local patch is constant. Second, image content has no relation with the transmission. Given a haze-free image patch, we assume that the transmission for this patch is constant with value t. We use the Eq. 1

Algorithm 1. Our proposed single image dehazing framework.

Input: The hazy image.
Output: The haze free image.

1: Compute the atmospheric light using Meng et al.'s method;
2: $\mathbf{I}_A(x) = \mathbf{I}(x) - \mathbf{A}$;
3: Compute $r(x)$ using Eq. 3;
4: Compute $\tilde{\mathbf{J}}_A(x)$ using deep convolutional network;
5: Compute $\tilde{r}(x)$ using Eq. 5.
6: Compute transmission:$\tilde{t} = r(x)/\tilde{r}(x)$.
7: Get the final transmission $t(x)$ map using guided filter.
8: Get the finial dehazing result using Eq. 11.

to get a hazy image patch. After we get the hazy image patches and the corresponding haze-free image patches, we can get a pair of $\mathbf{I}_A(x)$ and $\mathbf{J}_A(x)$, we use these data to train our network. We train a model for each value of A. The patch size is 16×16. We implements our CNN architecture using Caffe package [17], which is a popular tool of deep learning. We use stochastic gradient descent (SGD) to train DehazingCNN. We provide demo with a model train with $A = [0.78, 0.78, 0.78]$ and $A = [0.5, 0.6, 1]$, which can be found on https://github.com/killsking/DehazingCNN.

The constant assumption on transmission in a local patch will result in block artifacts [7]. We use guided filter [18] to eliminate the block artifacts.

3   Experiment Results

We evaluate our method on both synthetic and natural images and compare with state-of-the-art methods [7,13,14,19,20]. We use the $L1err = \frac{1}{N}\sum_{c \in R,G,B}|\mathbf{J}^c - \mathbf{G}^c|$ as metric. We convert the dehazing result and ground truth image into range of $[0,1]$. We generate an indoor hazy image dataset, which is based on the indoor RGBD dataset [21]. We use $\mathbf{A} = [0.78, 0.78, 0.78]$ and choose three value for β as $0.06, 0.3, 0.54$ to generate hazy image [14].

3.1   Synthetic Hazy Images

Although our deep network is trained on synthetic outdoor images, it can be applied for indoor images as well.

An outdoor synthetic hazy images dataset was introduced by [19] and is available online. For this dataset, we sum all L1 error as quality standard. As shown in Table 1a, we can see that our results are best. We also compare our method with some state-of-art methods [7,19,20] on some images in dataset. As shown in Fig. 3, OurJ is the result of adding $\mathbf{A}$ to $\mathbf{J}_A(x)$, which is the output of our DCNN.

We compare our method with other state-of-art methods [14,20]. We use our synthetic hazy images to evaluate our performance as shown in Table 1b.

Table 1. Overall comparison. Red color indicates the best results and blue indicates the second.

type	He	Fattal	Berman	Our
outdoor	5.77	4.54	5.96	3.87

(a) Fattal's dataset.

type	Ren	Berman	Our
indoor	1.58e+03	1.05e+03	0.85e+03

(b) Our dataset.

Outdoor Hazy Images: In this part, we also compare our method with other state-of-art methods [7,19,20] on images in dataset. We show the results in Table 2. As we can see from the results, our method can get a very similar results to the ground truths in general and also can get high quality result for particular image. Figure 3 shows some results on two hazy images. Our network output is very similar to haze-free image.

Fig. 3. Comparison on outdoor hazy images.

Indoor Hazy Images: In this part, we compare our method with Ren et al. [14] and Berman et al. [20]. The structural similarity (SSIM) image quality assessment index [22] is used to evaluate performance of the methods. The higher value of SSIM shows that the dehazing result is better. First, we compare all images in our dataset, where we can get highest SSIM score for 2393 images in 4347 image. Second, we show some results use SSIM and L1Err (Fig. 4).

3.2   Quantitative Evaluation on Benchmark Natural Images Dataset

In this subsection, we compare our method with state-of-the-art methods. As previously pointed by [7], the image after dehazing might look dim because the scene radiance is usually not as bright as the airlight. For display, we perform a global linear contrast stretch on the output, clipping 0.05% of the pixel values in both the shadows and the highlights. In Fig. 5, we compare our method with state-of-the-art methods. Some of the results are provided by Fattal [19], Berman [20] and Cai [13], which are online. We also get some results via the program provided by Ren [14]. As shown in Fig. 5, Ancuti et al.'s method [23] can't

Table 2. Quantitative comparison. Red color indicates the best results and blue indicates the second.

image	He	Fattal	Berman	Our
D1	0.135	0.130	0.308	0.127
D2	0.117	0.107	0.116	0.113
D3	0.112	0.083	0.170	0.087
S10	0.140	0.160	0.127	0.130
S25	0.164	0.291	0.171	0.174
S50	0.226	0.400	0.241	0.226
church	0.117	0.107	0.116	0.113

(a) Church.

image	He	Fattal	Berman	Our
D1	0.150	0.0915	0.299	0.086
D2	0.142	0.084	0.060	0.062
D3	0.152	0.050	0.107	0.074
S10	0.146	0.094	0.072	0.077
S25	0.165	0.156	0.122	0.116
S50	0.213	0.269	0.224	0.186
lawn1	0.142	0.086	0.060	0.062

(b) Lawn1.

image	He	Fattal	Berman	Our
D1	0.92	0.067	0.267	0.072
D2	0.085	0.052	0.100	0.052
D3	0.088	0.036	0.198	0.044
S10	0.080	0.065	0.115	0.060
S25	0.089	0.106	0.146	0.084
S50	0.149	0.159	0.190	0.134
mansion	0.085	0.049	0.100	0.052

(c) Mansion.

image	He	Fattal	Berman	Our
D1	0.121	0.08	0.300	0.106
D2	0.101	0.069	0.080	0.083
D3	0.093	0.055	0.148	0.056
S10	0.115	0.081	0.090	0.093
S25	0.142	0.139	0.125	0.121
S50	0.202	0.243	0.192	0.179
road1	0.101	0.069	0.080	0.083

(d) Road1.

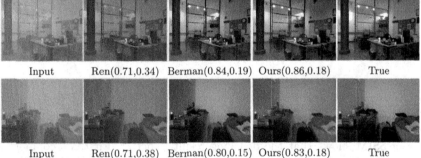

Input   Ren(0.71,0.34)   Berman(0.84,0.19)   Ours(0.86,0.18)   True

Input   Ren(0.71,0.38)   Berman(0.80,0.15)   Ours(0.83,0.18)   True

Fig. 4. Comparison on indoor hazy images. The number in left is SSIM value and the right is L1ERR

remove haze completely, while Meng et al.'s method [16] has the problem of overenhancement. The result of Luzón-González et al. [24] can't deal with the boundary of segments well and results in a lot of artifacts. He et al.'s method can yield an excellent result in general but lacks some micro-contrast details when compared to [19] and ours. This is obvious in the zoomed-in buildings shown in Cityscape results. In our result and [19], the windows are more clear than that in [7]. We also find that the result of Ren et al. losses some details of tree in

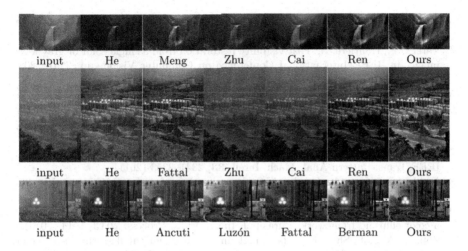

Fig. 5. Comparison on natural images: [Left] input images. [Right] our result. Middle columns display results by several methods, since each paper reports results on a different set of images.

Cityscape. In contrast, our method can deal this area well. The results of velly show that our method get a high quality result, which can recover more image details and vivid color than other state-of-the-art methods.

4 Conclusions

This paper addresses the haze removal problem using a deep network which learns effective features to estimate the corresponding haze-free image. The proposed learning method restores the haze-free image directly from hazy image without estimating of transmission map. Experimental results on synthetic outdoor and indoor images and real images demonstrate the effectiveness of the proposed algorithm. In future work, we will accelerate the proposed algorithm with GPU computing and intelligent computing [25–28]. We also want to extend the idea to other areas of graphics and image processing [29–37].

Acknowledgement. National Science Foundation of China (Grant No. 61472289) and National Key Research and Development Project of China (Grant No. 2016YFC0106305).

References

1. Schechner, Y.Y., Narasimhan, S.G., Nayar, S.K.: Instant dehazing of images using polarization. In: IEEE Conference on Computer Vision and Pattern Recognition, vol. 1, pp. 325–332. IEEE (2001)
2. Kopf, J., Neubert, B., Chen, B., Cohen, M., Cohen-Or, D., Deussen, O., Uyttendaele, M., Lischinski, D.: Deep photo: model-based photograph enhancement and viewing. ACM Trans. Graph. (TOG) **27**, 116 (2008)

3. Tan, R.T.: Visibility in bad weather from a single image. In: IEEE Conference on Computer Vision and Pattern Recognition, pp. 1–8. IEEE (2008)
4. Tarel, J.P., Hautiere, N.: Fast visibility restoration from a single color or gray level image. In: IEEE International Conference on Computer Vision, pp. 2201–2208. IEEE (2009)
5. Fattal, R.: Single image dehazing. ACM Trans. Graph. (TOG) **27**, 1–9 (2008)
6. Kratz, L., Nishino, K.: Factorizing scene albedo and depth from a single foggy image. In: IEEE International Conference on Computer Vision, vol. 30, pp. 1701–1708 (2009)
7. He, K., Sun, J., Tang, X.: Single image haze removal using dark channel prior. IEEE Trans. Pattern Anal. Mach. Intell. **33**, 2341–2353 (2011)
8. Nishino, K., Kratz, L., Lombardi, S.: Bayesian defogging. Int. J. Comput. Vis. **98**, 263–278 (2012)
9. Gibson, K.B., Nguyen, T.Q.: An analysis of single image defogging methods using a color ellipsoid framework. Eurasip J. Image Video Process. **2013**, 1–14 (2013)
10. Zhu, Q., Mai, J., Shao, L.: A fast single image haze removal algorithm using color attenuation prior. IEEE Trans. Image Process. **24**, 3522–3533 (2015)
11. Li, Z., Zheng, J.: Edge-preserving decomposition-based single image haze removal. IEEE Trans. Image Process. **24**, 5432–5441 (2015)
12. Tang, K., Yang, J., Wang, J.: Investigating haze-relevant features in a learning framework for image dehazing. In: IEEE Conference on Computer Vision and Pattern Recognition (CVPR), pp. 2995–3002. IEEE (2014)
13. Cai, B., Xu, X., Jia, K., Qing, C., Tao, D.: Dehazenet: An end-to-end system for single image haze removal. arXiv preprint arXiv:1601.07661 (2016)
14. Ren, W., Liu, S., Zhang, H., Pan, J., Cao, X., Yang, M.-H.: Single image dehazing via multi-scale convolutional neural networks. In: Leibe, B., Matas, J., Sebe, N., Welling, M. (eds.) ECCV 2016. LNCS, vol. 9906, pp. 154–169. Springer, Cham (2016). https://doi.org/10.1007/978-3-319-46475-6_10
15. Harald, K.: Theorie der horizontalen Sichtweite: Kontrast und Sichtweite, vol. 12. Keim & Nemnich, Munich (1924)
16. Meng, G., Wang, Y., Duan, J., Xiang, S., Pan, C.: Efficient image dehazing with boundary constraint and contextual regularization. In: IEEE International Conference on Computer Vision, pp. 617–624 (2013)
17. Jia, Y., Shelhamer, E., Donahue, J., Karayev, S., Long, J., Girshick, R., Guadarrama, S., Darrell, T.: Caffe: convolutional architecture for fast feature embedding. In: ACM International Conference on Multimedia, pp. 675–678. ACM (2014)
18. He, K., Sun, J., Tang, X.: Guided image filtering. IEEE Trans. Pattern Anal. Mach. Intell. **35**, 1397–1409 (2013)
19. Fattal, R.: Dehazing using color-lines. ACM Trans. Graph. (TOG) **34**, 13 (2014)
20. Berman, D., Treibitz, T., Avidan, S.: Non-local image dehazing. In: IEEE Conference on Computer Vision and Pattern Recognition (CVPR), pp. 1674–1682 (2016)
21. Silberman, N., Hoiem, D., Kohli, P., Fergus, R.: Indoor segmentation and support inference from RGBD images. In: Fitzgibbon, A., Lazebnik, S., Perona, P., Sato, Y., Schmid, C. (eds.) ECCV 2012. LNCS, vol. 7576, pp. 746–760. Springer, Heidelberg (2012). https://doi.org/10.1007/978-3-642-33715-4_54
22. Wang, Z., Bovik, A.C., Sheikh, H.R., Simoncelli, E.P.: Image quality assessment: from error visibility to structural similarity. IEEE Trans. Image Process. **13**, 600–612 (2004)

23. Ancuti, C.O., Ancuti, C., Hermans, C., Bekaert, P.: A fast semi-inverse approach to detect and remove the haze from a single image. In: Kimmel, R., Klette, R., Sugimoto, A. (eds.) ACCV 2010. LNCS, vol. 6493, pp. 501–514. Springer, Heidelberg (2011). https://doi.org/10.1007/978-3-642-19309-5_39

24. Luzón-González, R., Nieves, J.L., Romero, J.: Recovering of weather degraded images based on RGB response ratio constancy. Appl. Opt. **54**, B222–B231 (2015)

25. Zhou, Y., He, F., Qiu, Y.: Dynamic strategy based parallel ant colony optimization on GPUs for TSPs. Sci. China Inf. Sci. **60**, 068102 (2017)

26. Zhou, Y., He, F., Qiu, Y.: Optimization of parallel iterated local search algorithms on graphics processing unit. J. Supercomput. **72**, 2394–2416 (2016)

27. Yan, X., He, F., Hou, N.: A novel hardware/software partitioning method based on position disturbed particle swarm optimization with invasive weed optimization. J. Comput. Sci. Technol. **32**, 340–355 (2017)

28. Yan, X., He, F., Hou, N., Ai, H.: An efficient particle swarm optimization for large scale hardware/software co-design system. Int. J. Coop. Inf. Syst. (2017). https://doi.org/10.1142/S0218843017410015

29. Zhang, D., He, F., Soonhung, H., Li, X.: Quantitative optimization of interoperability during feature-based data exchange. Integr. Comput. Aided Eng. **23**, 31–51 (2016)

30. Cheng, Y., He, F., Wu, Y., Zhang, D.: Meta-operation conflict resolution for human-human interaction in collaborative feature-based CAD systems. Clust. Comput. **19**, 237–253 (2016)

31. Li, K., He, F., Chen, X.: Real time object tracking via compressive feature selection. Front. Comput. Sci. **10**, 689–701 (2016)

32. Wu, Y., He, F., Zhang, D., Li, X.: Service-oriented feature-based data exchange for cloud-based design and manufacturing. IEEE Trans. Serv. Comput. (2015). https://doi.org/10.1109/TSC.2015.2501981

33. Chen, Y., He, F., Wu, Y., Hou, N.: A local start search algorithm to compute exact Hausdorff distance for arbitrary point sets. Pattern Recognit. **67**, 139–148 (2017)

34. Zhang, D., He, F., Han, S., Zou, L., Wu, Y., Chen, Y.: An efficient approach to directly compute the exact Hausdorff distance for 3D point sets. Integr. Comput. Aided Eng. **24**, 261–277 (2017)

35. Li, K., He, F., Yu, H.: Robust visual tracking based on convolutional features with illumination and occlusion handling. J. Comput. Sci. Technol. **33**, 223–236 (2017). https://doi.org/10.1007/s11390-017-1764-5

36. Huang, Z., He, F., Cai, X., Zhou, Z., Liu, J., Liang, M., Chen, X.: Efficient random saliency map detection. Sci. China Inf. Sci. **54**, 1207–1217 (2011)

37. Li, X., He, F., Cai, X., Zhang, D., Chen, Y.: A method for topological entity matching in the integration of heterogeneous CAD systems. Integr. Comput. Aided Eng. **20**, 15–30 (2013)

SPOS: Deblur Image by Using Sparsity Prior and Outlier Suppression

Yiwei Zhang[1], Ge Li[1(✉)], Xiaoqiang Guo[2], Wenmin Wang[1],
and Ronggang Wang[1]

[1] School of Electronic and Computer Engineering,
Peking University Shenzhen Graduate School, Lishui Road 2199,
Nanshan District, Shenzhen 518055, Guangdong Province, China
yuriyzhang@pku.edu.cn, gli@pkusz.edu.cn
[2] Academy of Broadcasting Science, SAPPRET, China Fuxingmen Outer Street 2,
Xicheng District, Beijing 100866, China

Abstract. In this paper, we propose an effective and robust method SPOS (Sparsity Prior and Outlier Suppression) for blurry image restoration. First, we combine histogram equalization and prior constrain to obtain the salient structure which contains main texture of image. Second, kernel is estimated by salient structure and sparsity constrain. Final, the blurry image is restored by non-blind deconvolution. The contributions of SPOS lie in two aspects: (1) we combine histogram equalization and sparsity suppression to obtain salient structure; (2) we take kernel outliers into consideration and introduce L_0 norm to suppress kernel's shape. The experiment results show that SPOS has the better performance compared with the state-of-the-art methods.

Keywords: Histogram equalization · Salient structure · Outliers
L_0-norm · Sparsity suppression

1 Introduction

The motion-blur is a phenomenon caused by camera shake when capturing an image. Over the past decades, restoring blurry image has become an important topic, as the image quality directly affect analysis and processing on computer vision. As a pre-processing, the relative algorithms [1–3, 7, 18, 20, 24] have been utilized in many research fields, such as object detection, object segmentation, foreground segmentation, behavior analysis, etc. Due to imprecise motion estimation, artifacts ringing often occurs in the restored image when performing deconvolution. Hence, an accurate blur kernel estimation is the key to further improve image quality. By applying the prior [4] that the gradient of natural

This project was supported by Shenzhen Peacock Plan (20130408-183003656), Science and Technology Planning Project of Guangdong Province, China (No. 2014B090910001) and China 863 project under Grant (No. 2015AA015905).

© Springer International Publishing AG, part of Springer Nature 2018
B. Zeng et al. (Eds.): PCM 2017, LNCS 10735, pp. 138–148, 2018.
https://doi.org/10.1007/978-3-319-77380-3_14

image follows the rule of heavy-tail, a few algorithms [4,7,20], adopt Maximum a Posterior (MAP) and Maximum Expectation (EM) to perform kernel estimation. Furthermore, Levin [10] proposed an advanced MAP_k, pointing out that conventional $MAP_{x,k}$ is a no-blur explanation and cause a failure for the kernel estimation. Besides, based on the convolutional property of delta kernel, Michaeli [14] pointed out that the down-sampled blurry image has the tendency to be clear and its textures are similar to original image. However, the accuracy of kernel estimation is also heavily related to edge information, which could contaminate kernel when the scale of the texture is smaller than that of the kernel. To solve this problem, some literatures [2,22] use salient structure to estimate kernel before deconvolution. And also, the image quality will been contaminated even if there exists very few outliers in kernel shown in Fig. 3(b). Nevertheless, this founding is ignored in existing algorithms, and is first considered in the proposed method.

In this paper, we propose an effective and robust method called SPOS by using sparsity and outlier suppression to deblur single image. First, we combine histogram equalization and prior constrain to obtain the salient structure which contains main texture of image. By constraining the sparsity of salient structure, trivial edges of structure is removed. Second, we use salient structure and sparsity constrain to estimate kernel. And the inconsecutive kernel outliers are further suppressed by the L_0 norm. Final, blurry image is restored by non-blind deconvolution. The contributions of SPOS lie in two aspects: (1) we combine histogram equalization and sparsity suppression to obtain salient structure; (2) we take kernel outliers into consideration and introduce L_0 norm to suppress kernel's shape. The experiment results show that SPOS has better performance compared with the state-of-the-art methods.

2 SPOS Overview

As shown in Fig. 1, SPOS consists of two major steps: salient structure and kernel estimation. As an input, the blurry image I^0 is down-scaled (red arrows in Fig. 1) to n smaller images $I^1, ..., I^n$. First, I^n and initialed k^n are utilized to obtain the salient structure. In this process, the main texture is extracted by histogram equalization and prior constrain. Second, the kernel k^{n-1} corresponding to I^{n-1} is estimated. Due to the kernel outliers are devils to restore blurry image, suppressing it is the key in this section. Then, iterate the former two steps (green arrows in Fig. 1) until the kernel k^0 estimation completes. Final, restore the I^0 by non-blind deconvolution (blue arrows in Fig. 1).

3 The Proposed Method

For single image, we apply SPOS to uniform model. And it is also hold for non-uniform model supposed image can be segmented into several uniform patches. Generally, the camera shake can be modeled as a convolution process, and the

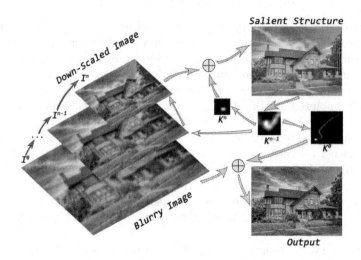

Fig. 1. The flowchart of SPOS (Color figure online)

blurry image can be considered as an output by convolving clear image and blur kernel shown in Eq. 1.

$$I = L \otimes k + \eta \qquad (1)$$

Where I, L, k and η represent blurry image, clear image, blur kernel and unknown sensor noise respectively, $\otimes$ denotes the convolution operator. For simplicity, we suppose that η is Additive White Gaussian Noise (AWGN). The blind deconvolution is a process that recover L from I with unknown k, so it is an ill-posed problem. In this paper, we utilize a salient structure to estimate blur kernel, then to perform non-blind deconvolution. Well, the SPOS mainly performs following steps: salient structure and kernel estimation.

3.1   Salient Structure Estimation

Though previous literatures [2,22] have the process to estimate salient structure, we propose a new and robust method to reinforce this process. [2,22] both utilize shock filter to obtain it in their literatures. In our method, we combine histogram equalization and prior constrain. Supposed salient structure obeys heavy-tail rule, we constrain the smooth region and texture region in it with L_2 and L_0 respectively. The process of salient structure estimation is modeled as Eq. 2.

$$\min_{S} ||S \otimes k - I||_2^2 + \lambda_1 ||\nabla S||^\alpha + \lambda_2 ||\nabla S \circ M||_0 + \lambda_3 ||\nabla S \circ (1 - M)||_2^2 \qquad (2)$$

Where S denotes the salient structure, $\nabla = (\partial_h, \partial_v)^T$ is a gradient operator in horizontal and vertical directions, $\circ$ is a element-wise operator, α controls the distribution of gradient, M is a $2D$ binary matrix which indexes texture region in S, $\mathbf{1}$ is all 1's matrix. λ_1 controls the weight of distribution, λ_2, λ_3 adjust the

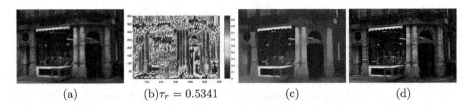

(a)   (b)$\tau_r = 0.5341$ (c)   (d)

Fig. 2. (a) Blurry image. (b) Energy diagram of r and corresponding $\tau_r = 0.5341$. (c) Salient structure. (d) Restored image by SPOS. (Color figure online)

proportion between texture region and smooth region in S. Due to there exists noise in smooth region, we utilize L_2 norm to suppress it. Based on the property of convolution, the process of deconvolution will be failed when the texture size is smaller than that of kernel. So we design a metric M to index resultful texture and utilize it to constrain S. The model of M follows Eq. 3.

$$M = H(r - \tau_r) \tag{3}$$

Where $H(\cdot)$ is a Heaviside step function, $r \in [0,1]^{size(r)}$ is a score matrix which determines the score that corresponding pixels belong to resultful texture, τ_r is the score threshold. Some methods, for example, shock filter [2,15,22], can be used to compute r. However, the most important is how to set τ_r. So we use histogram equalization to obtain a statistic score and compute its expectation shown in Eq. 4.

$$\tau_r = \frac{\sum\limits_{r(x) \in D(r)} r(x) \cdot c(x)}{\sum\limits_{r(x) \in D(r)} c(x)} \tag{4}$$

Where $D(r)$ denotes the histogram distribution of r, $r(x)$ denotes the score of pixel x, $c(x)$ denotes the pixel amount in interval where r(x) locates. As shown in Fig. 2(b), blue denotes the smooth, red denotes the resultful texture, and green denotes the trivial texture. Compared with Fig. 2(a), it is clear to see that M has the power to distinguish resultful texture and other regions.

Now, consider the problem of salient structure in Eq. 2. With L_0-norm and α existing, it is not a convex optimization problem. Inspired by half-quadratic penalty method [5], we introduce two auxiliary variables u and w to selectively substitute ∇S. And the problem is modified as Eq. 5.

$$\min_{S,u,w} ||S \otimes k - I||_2^2 + \lambda_1 ||w||^\alpha + \lambda_2 ||u \circ M||_0 + \lambda_3 ||u \circ (1 - M)||_2^2 + \beta ||u - \nabla S||_2^2 + \gamma ||w - \nabla S||_2^2 \tag{5}$$

Notice that $u = \nabla S$, $w = \nabla S$ when $\beta \to \infty$, $\gamma \to \infty$. So it is clear that Eq. 5 is equivalent to Eq. 2. In [5], the problem can be solved by iteration. Similar to it, we optimize Eq. 5 by iteratively updating u, w and S. And each variable can be computed by fixing other variables. For variable u, the L_0 optimization problem has been introduced in [23], and we use it to obtain the solution of u. For variable w, the way to solve the subproblem is decided by α. Suppose that ∇S obeys Laplacian distribution, then $\alpha = 1$, and the subproblem is converted to a convex optimization. When $\alpha \neq 1$, the subproblem can be solved by lookup table and analytic solution proposed in [8]. For variable S, we adopt FFT to solve the subproblem because there exists convolution operation. Based on the Parseval's theorem, S can be computed by Eq. 6.

$$S = \mathcal{F}^{-1}\left(\frac{\mathcal{F}(I) \circ \overline{\mathcal{F}(k)} + \beta\mathcal{F}(u) \circ \overline{\mathcal{F}(\nabla)} + \gamma\mathcal{F}(w) \circ \overline{\mathcal{F}(\nabla)}}{\mathcal{F}(k) \circ \overline{\mathcal{F}(k)} + \beta\mathcal{F}(\nabla) \circ \overline{\mathcal{F}(\nabla)} + \gamma\mathcal{F}(\nabla) \circ \overline{\mathcal{F}(\nabla)}}\right) \qquad (6)$$

3.2 Kernel Estimation

The existing methods [2,16,19] only adopt a singe L_2 norm to guarantee the kernel sparsity, which results in some discontinuous outliers. And this will degrade the kernel, which is ignored by previous literatures. As shown in Fig. 3(b), the outliers in the estimated kernel are devils to restore the blurry image. By founding this, we use L_0 sparsity constrain to control the kernel shape and L_2 norm to suppress noise. And ∇S is utilized to minimizing the following energy function:

$$\min_{k} ||\nabla S \otimes k - \nabla I||_2^2 + \psi_1||k||_2^2 + \psi_2||\nabla k||_0$$
$$s.t. \quad k \geq 0, ||k||_1 = 1 \qquad (7)$$

| (a) | (b) | (c) | (d) |

Fig. 3. (a) Blurry image. (b) Restored image by Fergus [4] and estimated kernel. (c) Salient structure in our method. (d) Restored image by SPOS and estimated kernel.

Where ψ_1 controls kernel smooth, ψ_2 controls the weight to suppress outliers. Similar, half-quadratic penalty method [5] can be adopted to solve the problem in Eq. 7. So we introduce variable v to substitute ∇k and the kernel estimation is modified as Eq. 8.

$$\min_{k,v} ||\nabla S \otimes k - \nabla I||_2^2 + \psi_1||k||_2^2 + \psi_2||v||_0 + \varphi||v - \nabla k||_2^2 \qquad (8)$$

When $\varphi \to \infty$, $v = \nabla k$, then Eq. 8 is equivalent to Eq. 7. So the optimization problem in Eq. 8 can be solved by iteratively updating. For variable v, we solve it by L_0 optimization[]. For variable k, we use FFT to compute it in Eq. 9.

$$k = \mathcal{F}^{-1}\left(\frac{\mathcal{F}(\nabla I) \circ \overline{\mathcal{F}(\nabla S)} + \varphi \mathcal{F}(v) \circ \overline{\mathcal{F}(\nabla)}}{\mathcal{F}(\nabla S) \circ \overline{\mathcal{F}(\nabla S)} + \psi_1 + \varphi \mathcal{F}(\nabla) \circ \overline{\mathcal{F}(\nabla)}}\right) \tag{9}$$

In Fig. 3(d), we can observe that our estimated kernel nearly has no outliers and the restored image has the better performance. Besides, to verify the convergence of kernel estimation, we record the Sum of Squared Differences Error (SSDE) for 4 different kernel shown in Fig. 4. Though the kernel estimation is not convergent in a few iterations, it comes to convergence in the final iteration. Hence, we believe that our kernel estimation is valid.

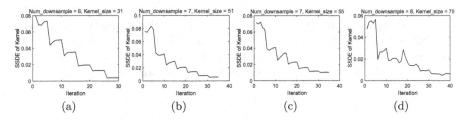

(a)   (b)   (c)   (d)

Fig. 4. (a)–(d) are the SSDE of kernel when the kernel size is 31, 51, 55, 75 respectively. And the $Num\_downsample$ denotes the number of downsampled images, $Kernel\_size$ denotes the size of kernel.

4   Image Restoration

We restore blurry image with estimated kernel by non-blind deconvolution. As mentioned above, it is an ill-posed problem to restore a blurry image, since the estimated kernel may be imprecise. To overcome this difficulty, we adopt iterative algorithm to optimize the salient structure and blur kernel. In the meantime, the initialization of kernel is the key to avoid local optimum. Considering the down-sampled blurry image has more similar texture with corresponding clear image, we apply the smallest down-sampled blurry image as initial input. And delta kernel is utilized as the initial value.

5   Experiment

We apply both synthetic motion blur images and real blurry images to test our method. In the salient structure estimation, we set $\lambda_1 = 0.001$, $\lambda_2 = 0.001$, $\lambda_3 = 0.001$, initialed $\beta = 0.5$, and for the simplicity, γ is set the same value with β. In the start of each iteration, β and γ are multiplied by a constant to update their value. In the kernel estimation, we set $\psi_1 = 0.001$, $\psi_2 = 0.002$ and $\varphi = 10$. To further verify the robustness of SPOS, we perform non-blind deconvolution with Total Variation[] and Hyper Laplacian [8], which we call $SPOS_{TV}$ and $SPOS_{Lp}$ respectively. Different form previous methods which analyzing results from the view of synthetic and real image, our experiments are evaluated by both objective and subjective method.

5.1   Objective Analysis and Evaluation

In our experiments, we use PSNR, SSIM, FSIM as objective metrics to measure restored image generated by 11 methods. And Dataset [21] is utilized. In Table 1, we list average scores of these metrics. By comparison, our method $SPOS_{TV}$, $SPOS_{Lp}$ have the highest score. What may be confused is that scores evaluated under three metrics are not high. The reason is that there exists noise in restored images, and for simplicity, we do not perform any post-processing to remove corresponding noise. Besides, we use quantitative evaluation on benchmark datases [21] shown in Fig. 5. It is clear that SPOS has the highest success ratio among the compared methods. Figure 6 shows the vision comparison among 11 methods and it is obvious that SPOS has better performance especially in text areas.

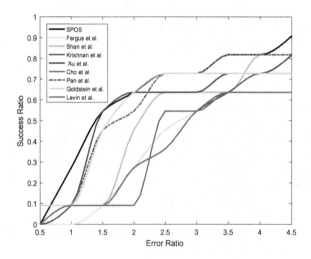

Fig. 5. Quantitative evaluation

5.2   Subjective Analysis and Evaluation

When there is no benchmark, it is impossible to evaluate the objective quality of image. So we adopt two no-reference metrics LR [13], BIBLE [12] to evaluate

Table 1. Image quality evaluation on benchmark dataset [21]

Metric	Method										
	Fergus	Shan	Krishnan	Xu	Cho	Levin	Goldstein	Pan	Zhang	$SPOS_{TV}$	$SPOS_{Lp}$
PSNR	15.86	17.03	15.95	17.89	15.85	15.99	18.10	17.94	18.53	**18.62**	18.55
SSIM	0.5488	0.6531	0.5988	0.7079	0.6120	0.6073	0.6961	0.7277	0.7383	0.7443	**0.7445**
FSIM	0.6915	0.7692	0.7027	0.8134	0.6994	0.7363	0.7881	0.8191	0.8325	**0.8363**	0.8350
$K_{size} = 27$ BIBLE	4.04	5.39	4.12	5.66	5.46	3.45	4.10	4.56	**5.79**	5.78	5.71
LR	−11.67	−9.66	−9.95	−8.72	−8.44	−11.19	−10.32	−9.57	−8.24	-8.47	**-8.19**
$K_{size} = 23$ BIBLE	3.74	5.39	3.56	5.04	5.39	3.20	3.77	4.46	5.70	5.77	**5.81**
LR	−12.71	−10.67	−11.75	−8.87	−9.12	−12.00	−11.78	−9.95	−8.56	−8.60	**−8.35**

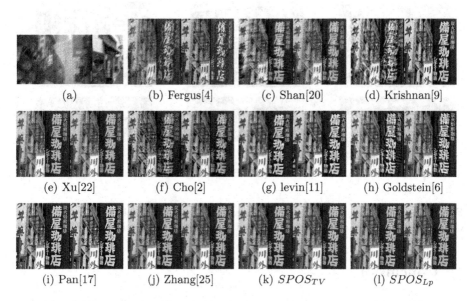

(a)   (b) Fergus[4]   (c) Shan[20]   (d) Krishnan[9]

(e) Xu[22]   (f) Cho[2]   (g) levin[11]   (h) Goldstein[6]

(i) Pan[17]   (j) Zhang[25]   (k) $SPOS_{TV}$ (l) $SPOS_{Lp}$

Fig. 6. (a) Blurry image in benchmark dataset [12]. (b–l) 11 compared methods in our experiments. In each image except (a), the left: kernel size is 23 in benchmark, the right: kernel size is 27 in benchmark.

both synthetic and real image. We use 11 methods to deblur image contaminated by two kernel, and the kernel size is 23 and 27 respectively. The statistical result is shown in Table 1, and it indicates that our method has the best score under LR and considerable score under BIBLE. The vision comparison is shown in Fig. 7.

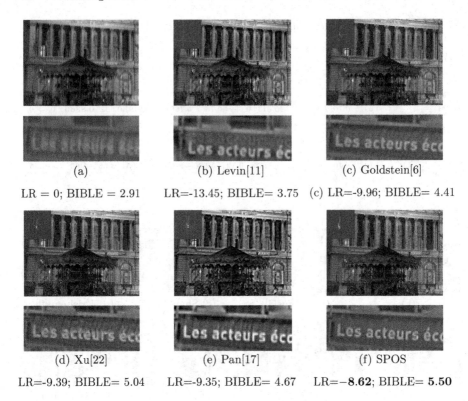

(a)

LR = 0; BIBLE = 2.91

(b) Levin[11]

LR=-13.45; BIBLE= 3.75

(c) Goldstein[6]

(c) LR=-9.96; BIBLE= 4.41

(d) Xu[22]

LR=-9.39; BIBLE= 5.04

(e) Pan[17]

LR=-9.35; BIBLE= 4.67

(f) SPOS

LR=−**8.62**; BIBLE= **5.50**

Fig. 7. (a) Real blurry image. (b–f) Restoration and estimated kernel by Levin [11], Goldstein [6], Xu [22], Pan [17] and our method SPOS respectively.

6   Conclusion

In this paper, we propose an effective and robust method called SPOS by using sparsity and outlier suppression to deblur single image. First, we combine histogram equalization and prior constrain to obtain the salient structure. Second, we use salient structure and sparsity constrain to estimate kernel. Final, blurry image is restored by non-blind deconvolution. The contributions of SPOS lie in two aspects: (1) we combine histogram equalization and sparsity suppression to obtain salient structure; (2) we take kernel outliers into consideration and introduce L_0 norm to suppress kernel's shape. The experiment results show that SPOS has better performance compared with state-of-the-art methods both on synthetic image and real image.

References

1. Beck, A., Teboulle, M.: Fast gradient-based algorithms for constrained total variation image denoising and deblurring problems. IEEE Trans. Image Process. **18**(11), 2419–2434 (2009)
2. Cho, S., Lee, S.: Fast motion deblurring. ACM Trans. Graph. (TOG) **28**, 145 (2009)
3. Cho, S., Wang, J., Lee, S.: Handling outliers in non-blind image deconvolution. In: 2011 International Conference on Computer Vision, pp. 495–502. IEEE (2011)
4. Fergus, R., Singh, B., Hertzmann, A., Roweis, S.T., Freeman, W.T.: Removing camera shake from a single photograph. ACM Trans. Graph. (TOG) **25**, 787–794 (2006)
5. Geman, D., Yang, C.: Nonlinear image recovery with half-quadratic regularization. IEEE Trans. Image Process. **4**(7), 932–946 (1995)
6. Goldstein, A., Fattal, R.: Blur-kernel estimation from spectral irregularities. In: Fitzgibbon, A., Lazebnik, S., Perona, P., Sato, Y., Schmid, C. (eds.) ECCV 2012. LNCS, vol. 7576, pp. 622–635. Springer, Heidelberg (2012). https://doi.org/10.1007/978-3-642-33715-4_45
7. Jia, J.: Single image motion deblurring using transparency. In: 2007 IEEE Conference on Computer Vision and Pattern Recognition, pp. 1–8. IEEE (2007)
8. Krishnan, D., Fergus, R.: Fast image deconvolution using hyper-laplacian priors. In: Advances in Neural Information Processing Systems, pp. 1033–1041 (2009)
9. Krishnan, D., Tay, T., Fergus, R.: Blind deconvolution using a normalized sparsity measure. In: 2011 IEEE Conference on Computer Vision and Pattern Recognition (CVPR), pp. 233–240. IEEE (2011)
10. Levin, A., Weiss, Y., Durand, F., Freeman, W.T.: Understanding and evaluating blind deconvolution algorithms. In: IEEE Conference on Computer Vision and Pattern Recognition, CVPR 2009, pp. 1964–1971. IEEE (2009)
11. Levin, A., Weiss, Y., Durand, F., Freeman, W.T.: Efficient marginal likelihood optimization in blind deconvolution. In: 2011 IEEE Conference on Computer Vision and Pattern Recognition (CVPR), pp. 2657–2664. IEEE (2011)
12. Li, L., Lin, W., Wang, X., Yang, G., Bahrami, K., Kot, A.C.: No-reference image blur assessment based on discrete orthogonal moments. IEEE Trans. Cybern. **46**(1), 39–50 (2016)
13. Liu, Y., Wang, J., Cho, S., Finkelstein, A., Rusinkiewicz, S.: A no-reference metric for evaluating the quality of motion deblurring. ACM Trans. Graph. **32**(6), 175–1 (2013)
14. Michaeli, T., Irani, M.: Blind deblurring using internal patch recurrence. In: Fleet, D., Pajdla, T., Schiele, B., Tuytelaars, T. (eds.) ECCV 2014. LNCS, vol. 8691, pp. 783–798. Springer, Cham (2014). https://doi.org/10.1007/978-3-319-10578-9_51
15. Osher, S., Rudin, L.I.: Feature-oriented image enhancement using shock filters. SIAM J. Numer. Anal. **27**(4), 919–940 (1990)
16. Pan, J., Liu, R., Su, Z., Gu, X.: Kernel estimation from salient structure for robust motion deblurring. Sig. Process. Image Commun. **28**(9), 1156–1170 (2013)
17. Pan, J., Liu, R., Su, Z., Liu, G.: Motion blur kernel estimation via salient edges and low rank prior. In: 2014 IEEE International Conference on Multimedia and Expo (ICME), pp. 1–6. IEEE (2014)
18. Perrone, D., Favaro, P.: Total variation blind deconvolution: the devil is in the details. In: 2014 IEEE Conference on Computer Vision and Pattern Recognition, pp. 2909–2916. IEEE (2014)

19. Ren, W., Cao, X., Pan, J., Guo, X., Zuo, W., Yang, M.H.: Image deblurring via enhanced low-rank prior. IEEE Trans. Image Process. **25**(7), 3426–3437 (2016)
20. Shan, Q., Jia, J., Agarwala, A.: High-quality motion deblurring from a single image. ACM Trans. Graph. (TOG) 27, 73 (2008)
21. Lai, W.-S., Huang, J.-B., Hu, Z., Ahuja, N., Yang, M.H.: A comparative study for single image blind deblurring (2016)
22. Xu, L., Jia, J.: Two-phase kernel estimation for robust motion deblurring. In: Daniilidis, K., Maragos, P., Paragios, N. (eds.) ECCV 2010. LNCS, vol. 6311, pp. 157–170. Springer, Heidelberg (2010). https://doi.org/10.1007/978-3-642-15549-9_12
23. Xu, L., Lu, C., Xu, Y., Jia, J.: Image smoothing via L0 gradient minimization. ACM Trans. Graph. (TOG) **30**, 174 (2011)
24. Xu, L., Zheng, S., Jia, J.: Unnatural L0 sparse representation for natural image deblurring. In: Proceedings of the IEEE Conference on Computer Vision and Pattern Recognition, pp. 1107–1114 (2013)
25. Zhang, X., Wang, R., Tian, Y., Wang, W., Gao, W.: Image deblurring using robust sparsity priors. In: 2015 IEEE International Conference on Image Processing (ICIP), pp. 138–142. IEEE (2015)

Single Image Super-Resolution Using Multi-scale Convolutional Neural Network

Xiaoyi Jia, Xiangmin Xu$^{(\boxtimes)}$, Bolun Cai, and Kailing Guo

School of Electronic and Information Engineering,
South China University of Technology, Guangzhou, China
xy_jia@foxmail.com, xmxu@scut.edu.cn, caibolun@gmail.com,
eecollinguo@gmail.com

Abstract. Methods based on convolutional neural network (CNN) have demonstrated tremendous improvements on single image super-resolution. However, the previous methods mainly restore images from one single area in the low-resolution (LR) input, which limits the flexibility of models to infer various scales of details for high-resolution (HR) output. Moreover, most of them train a specific model for each up-scale factor. In this paper, we propose a multi-scale super resolution (MSSR) network. Our network consists of multi-scale paths to make the HR inference, which can learn to synthesize features from different scales. This property helps reconstruct various kinds of regions in HR images. In addition, only one single model is needed for multiple up-scale factors, which is more efficient without loss of restoration quality. Experiments on four public datasets demonstrate that the proposed method achieved state-of-the-art performance with fast speed.

Keywords: Super-resolution · Convolutional neural network
Multi-scale

1 Introduction

The task of single image super-resolution aims at restoring a high-resolution (HR) image from a given low-resolution (LR) one. Super-resolution has wide applications in many fields where image details are on demand, such as medical, remote sensing imaging, video surveillance, and entertainment. In the past decades, super-resolution has attracted much attention from computer vision communities. Early methods include bicubic interpolation [5], Lanczos resampling [9], statistical priors [15], neighbor embedding [4], and sparse coding [23].

This work is supported by the National Natural Science Foundation of China (61171142, 61401163, U1636218), the Science and technology Planning Project of Guangdong Province of China (2014B010111003, 2014B010111006), Guangzhou Key Lab of Body Data Science (201605030011).

© Springer International Publishing AG, part of Springer Nature 2018
B. Zeng et al. (Eds.): PCM 2017, LNCS 10735, pp. 149–157, 2018.
https://doi.org/10.1007/978-3-319-77380-3_15

However, super-resolution is highly ill-posed since the process from HR to LR contains non-invertible operation such as low-pass filtering and subsampling.

Deep convolutional neural networks (CNNs) have achieved state-of-the-art performance in computer vision, such as image classification [20], object detection [10], and image enhancement [3]. Recently, CNNs are widely used to address the ill-posed inverse problem of super-resolution, and have demonstrated superiority over traditional methods [4,9,15,23] with respect to both reconstruction accuracy and computational efficiency. Dong et al. [6,7] successfully design a super-resolution convolutional neural network (SRCNN) to demonstrate that a CNN can be applied to learn the mapping from LR to HR in an end-to-end manner. A fast super-resolution convolutional neural network (FSRCNN) [8] is proposed to accelerate the speed of SRCNN [6,7], which takes the original LR image as input and adopts a deconvolution layer to replace the bicubic interpolation. In [19], an efficient sub-pixel convolution layer is introduced to achieve real time performance. Kim et al. [14] uses a very deep super-resolution (VDSR) network with 20 convolutional layers, which greatly improves the accuracy of the model.

The previous methods based on CNN has achieved great progress on the restoration quality as well as efficiency. However, there are some limitations mainly coming from the following aspects:

– CNN based methods make efforts to enlarge the receptive field of the models as well as stack more layers. They reconstruct any type of contents from LR images using only single-scale region, thus ignore the various scales of different details. For instance, restoring the detail in the sky probably relies on a larger image region, while the tiny text may only be relevant to a small patch.
– Most previous approaches learn a specific model for one single up-scale factor. Therefore, the model learned for one up-scale factor cannot work well for another. That is, many scale-specific models should be trained for different up-scale factors, which is inefficient both in terms of time and memory. Though [14] trains a model for multiple up-scales, it ignores the fact that a single receptive field may contain different information amount in various resolution versions.

In this paper, we propose a multi-scale super resolution (MSSR) convolutional neural network to issue these problems – there are two folds of meaning in the term multi-scale. First, the proposed network combines multi-path subnetworks with different depth, which correspond to multi-scale regions in the input image. Second, the multi-scale network is capable to select a proper receptive field for different up-scales to restore the HR image. Only one single model is trained for multiple up-scale factors by multi-scale training.

2   Multi-scale Super-Resolution

Given a low-resolution image, super-resolution aims at restoring its high-resolution version. For this ill-posed recovery problem, it is probably an effective

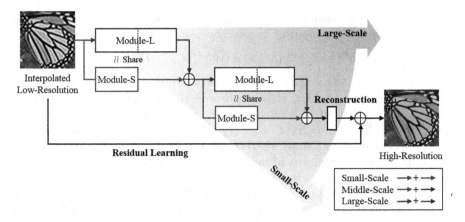

Fig. 1. The network architecture of MSSR. We cascade convolutional layers and nonlinear layers (ReLU) repeatedly. An interpolated low-resolution image goes through MSSR and transforms into a high-resolution image. MSSR consists of two convolution modules (Module-L and Module-S), streams of three different scales (Small/Middle/Large-Scale), and a reconstruction module with residual learning.

way to estimate a target pixel by taking into account more context information in the neighborhood. In [6,7,14], authors found that larger receptive field tends to achieve better performance due to richer structural information. However, we argue that the restoration process is not only depending on single-scale regions with large receptive field.

Different kinds of components in an image may be relevant to different scales of neighborhood. In [26], multi-scale neighborhood has been proven effective for super-resolution, which simultaneously integrates local and non-local sparse priors. Multi-scale feature extraction [3,24] is also effective to represent image patterns. For example, the inception architecture in GoogLeNet [21] uses parallel convolutions with varying filter sizes, and better addresses the issue of aligning objects in input images, resulting in state-of-the-art performance in object recognition. Motivated by this, we propose a multi-scale super-resolution convolutional neural network to improve the performance (see as Fig. 1): low-resolution image is first up-sampled to the desired size by bicubic interpolation, and then MSSR is implemented to predict the detail.

2.1 Multi-scale Architecture

With fixed filter size larger than 1, the receptive field is going larger when network stacks more layers. The proposed architecture is composed of two parallel paths as illustrated in Fig. 1. The upper path (Module-L) stacks N_L convolutional layers which is able to catch a large region of information in the LR image. The other path (Module-S) contains N_S ($N_S < N_L$) convolutional layers to ensure a relatively small receptive filed. The response of the k-th convolutional layer in Module-L/S for input h^k is given by

$$h^{k+1} = f^{k+1}(h^k) = \sigma(W^{k+1} * h^k + b^{k+1}), \qquad (1)$$

where W^{k+1} and b^{k+1} are the weights and bias respectively, and $\sigma(\cdot)$ represents nonlinear operation (ReLU). Here we denote the interpolated low-resolution image as x. The output of Module-L is $H_L(x) = f^{N_L}(f^{N_L-1}(...f^1(x)))$, and the output of Module-S is $H_S(x) = f^{N_S}(f^{N_S-1}(...f^1(x)))$.

For saving consideration, parameters between Module-S and the front part of Module-L are shared. Outputs of the two modules are fused into one, which can take various functional forms (e.g. connection, weighting, and summation). We find that simply summation is efficient enough for our purpose, and the fusion result is generated as $H_f(x) = H_L(x) + H_S(x)$. To further vary the spatial scales of the ensemble architecture, a similar subnetwork is cascaded to the previous one as $F(x) = H_f(H_f(x))$. A final reconstruction module with N_r convolutional layers is employed to make the prediction. Following [20], size of all convolutional kernels is set to 3×3 with zero-padding. With respect to the local information involved in LR image, there are streams of three scales (Small/Middle/Large-Scale) corresponding to $2 \times (N_S + N_S + N_r) + 1$, $2 \times (N_S + N_L + N_r) + 1$ and $2 \times (N_L + N_L + N_r) + 1$, respectively. Each layer consists of 64 filters except for the last reconstruction layer, which contains only one single filter without nonlinear operation.

2.2   Multi-scale Residual Learning

High-frequency content is more important for HR restoration, such as gradient features taken into account in [1,2,4]. Since the input is highly similar to the output in super-resolution problem, the proposed network (MSSR) focuses on high-frequency details estimation through multi-scale residual learning.

The given training set $\{x_s^{(i)}, y^{(i)}\}_{\{i,s\}=\{1,1\}}^{\{N,S\}}$ includes N pairs of multi-scale LR images $x_s^{(i)}$ with S scale factors and HR image $y^{(i)}$. Multi-scale residual image for each sample is computed as $r_s^{(i)} = y^{(i)} - x_s^{(i)}$. The goal of MSSR is to learn the nonlinear mapping $F(x)$ from multi-scale LR images $x_s^{(i)}$ to predict the residual image $r_s^{(i)}$. The network parameters $\Theta = \{W^k, b^k\}$ are achieved through minimizing the loss function as

$$
\begin{aligned}
L(\Theta) &= \frac{1}{2NS} \sum_{i=1}^{N} \sum_{s=1}^{S} \left\| r_s^{(i)} - F\left(x_s^{(i)}; \Theta\right) \right\|^2 \\
&= \frac{1}{2NS} \sum_{i=1}^{N} \sum_{s=1}^{S} \left\| y^{(i)} - \left(x_s^{(i)} + F\left(x_s^{(i)}; \Theta\right)\right) \right\|^2
\end{aligned}
\qquad (2)
$$

With multi-scale residual learning, we only train a general model for multiple up-scale factors. For LR images $x_s^{(i)}$ with different down sampling scales s, even the same region size in LR images may contain different information content. In the work of Dong et al. [8], a small patch in LR space could cover almost all information of a large patch in HR. For multiple up-scale samples, a model with only one single receptive field cannot make the best of them all simultaneously. However, our multi-scale network is capable of handling this problem. The advantages of multi-scale learning include not only memory and time saving, but also a way to adapt the model for different down sampling scales.

3   Experiments

3.1   Datasets

Training Dataset. The model is trained on 91 images from Yang et al. [23] and 200 images from the training set of Berkeley Segmentation Dataset (BSD) [17], which are widely used for super-resolution problem [7,8,14,18]. As in [8], to make full use of the training data, we apply data augmentation in two ways: (1) Rotate the images with the degree of 90°, 180° and 270°. (2) Downscale the images with the factor of 0.9, 0.8, 0.7 and 0.6. Following the sample cropping in [14], training images are cropped into sub-images of size 41 × 41 with non-overlapping. In addition, to train a general model for multiple up-scale factors, we combine LR-HR pairs of three up-scale size (×2, ×3, ×4) into one.

Test Dataset. The proposed method is evaluated on four publicly available benchmark datasets: Set5 [1] and Set14 [25] provide 5 and 14 images respectively; B100 [17] contains 100 natural images collected from BSD; Urban100 [12] consists of 100 high-resolution images rich of structures in real-world. Following previous works [8,12,14], we transform the images to YCbCr color space and only apply the algorithm on the luminance channel, since human vision is more sensitive to details in intensity than in color.

3.2   Experimental Settings

In the experiments, the *Caffe* [13] package is implemented to train the proposed MSSR with Adam [16]. To ensure varying receptive field scales, we set $N_L = 9$, $N_S = 2$ and $N_r = 2$ respectively. That is, each Module-L in Fig. 1 stacks 9 convolutional layers, while Module-S stacks 2 layers. The reconstruction module is built of 2 layers. Thus, the longest path in the network consists of 20 convolutional layers totally, and there are streams of three different scales corresponding to 13, 27 and 41. Model weights are initialized according to the approach described in [11]. Learning rate is initially set to 10^{-4} and decreases by the factor of 10 after 80 epochs. Training phase stops at 100 epochs. We set the parameters of batch-size, momentum and weight decay to 64, 0.9 and 10^{-4} respectively.

3.3   Results

To quantitatively assess the proposed model, MSSR is evaluated for three different up-scale factors from 2 to 4 on four testing datasets aforementioned. We compute the Peak Signal-to-Noise Ratio (PSNR) and structural similarity (SSIM) of

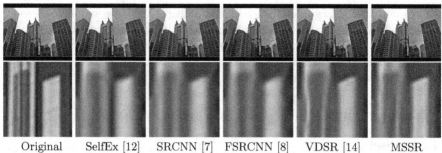

Original	SelfEx [12]	SRCNN [7]	FSRCNN [8]	VDSR [14]	MSSR
PSNR/SSIM	25.69/0.7940	25.48/0.7712	25.63/0.7815	26.58/0.8285	27.01/0.8391

Fig. 2. Super-resolution results of *img099* (Urban100) with scale factor x3. Line is straightened and sharpened in MSSR, whereas other methods give blurry or distorted lines.

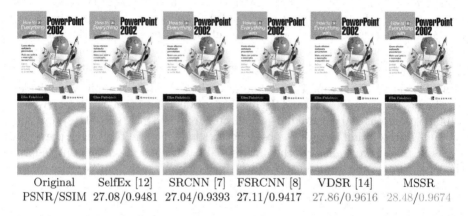

Original	SelfEx [12]	SRCNN [7]	FSRCNN [8]	VDSR [14]	MSSR
PSNR/SSIM	27.08/0.9481	27.04/0.9393	27.11/0.9417	27.86/0.9616	28.48/0.9674

Fig. 3. Super-resolution results of *ppt3* (Set14) with scale factor x3. Texts in MSSR are sharp and legible, while character edges are blurry in other methods.

the results to compare with some recent competitive methods, including A+ [22], SelfEx [12], SRCNN [7], FSRCNN [8] and VDSR [14]. As shown in Table 1, we can see that the proposed MSSR outperforms other methods almost on every up-scale factor and each test set. The only suboptimal result is the PSNR on B100 of up-scale factor 4, which is slightly lower than VDSR [14], but still competitive with a higher SSIM. Visual comparisons can be found in Figs. 2 and 3.

As for effectiveness, we evaluate the execution time using the public code of state-of-the-art methods. The experiments are conducted with an Intel CPU (Xeon E5-2620, 2.1 GHz) and an NVIDIA GPU (GeForce GTX 1080). Figure 4 shows the PSNR performance of several state-of-the-art methods for super-resolution versus the execution time. The proposed MSSR network achieves better super-resolution quality than existing methods, and are tens of times faster.

Table 1. Average PSNR/SSIM for scale factors x2, x3 and x4 on datasets Set5 [1], Set14 [25], B100 [17] and Urban100 [12]. Red color indicates the best performance and blue color indicates the second best performance. (All the output images are cropped to the same size as SRCNN [7] for fair comparisons.)

Dataset	Scale	A+ [22]	SelfEx [12]	SRCNN [7]	FSRCNN [8]	VDSR [14]	MSSR
Set5	x2	36.54/0.9544	36.49/0.9537	36.66/0.9542	37.00/0.9558	37.53/0.9587	37.62/0.9592
	x3	32.58/0.9088	32.58/0.9093	32.75/0.9090	33.16/0.9140	33.66/0.9213	33.82/0.9226
	x4	30.28/0.8603	30.31/0.8619	30.49/0.8628	30.71/0.8657	31.35/0.8838	31.42/0.8849
Set14	x2	32.28/0.9056	32.22/0.9034	32.45/0.9067	32.63/0.9088	33.03/0.9124	33.11/0.9133
	x3	29.13/0.8188	29.16/0.8196	29.30/0.8215	29.43/0.8242	29.77/0.8314	29.86/0.8332
	x4	27.32/0.7491	27.40/0.7518	27.50/0.7513	27.59/0.7535	28.01/0.7674	28.05/0.7686
B100	x2	31.21/0.8863	31.18/0.8855	31.36/0.8879	31.50/0.8906	31.90/0.8960	31.94/0.8966
	x3	28.29/0.7835	28.29/0.7840	28.41/0.7863	28.52/0.7893	28.82/0.7976	28.85/0.7985
	x4	26.82/0.7087	26.84/0.7106	26.90/0.7103	26.96/0.7128	27.29/0.7251	27.28/0.7256
Urban100	x2	29.20/0.8938	29.54/0.8967	29.51/0.8946	29.85/0.9009	30.76/0.9140	30.84/0.9149
	x3	26.03/0.7973	26.44/0.8088	26.24/0.7991	26.42/0.8064	27.14/0.8279	27.20/0.8295
	x4	24.32/0.7183	24.79/0.7374	24.52/0.7226	24.60/0.7258	25.18/0.7524	25.19/0.7535

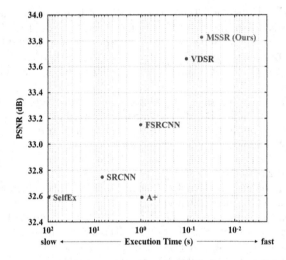

Fig. 4. Our MSSR achieves more accurate and efficient results for scale factor x3 on dataset Set5 in comparison to the state-of-the-art methods.

4   Conclusion

In this paper, we highlight the importance of scales in super-resolution problem, which is neglected in the previous work. Instead of simply enlarge the size of input patches, we proposed a multi-scale convolutional neural network for single image super-resolution. Combining paths of different scales enables the model to synthesize a wider range of receptive fields. Since different components in images may be relevant to a diversity of neighbor sizes, the proposed network can benefit from multi-scale features. Our model generalizes well across different up-scale factors. Experimental results reveal that our approach can achieve state-of-the-art results on standard benchmarks with a relatively high speed.

References

1. Bevilacqua, M., Roumy, A., Guillemot, C., Alberi-Morel, M.L.: Low-complexity single-image super-resolution based on nonnegative neighbor embedding (2012)
2. Bevilacqua, M., Roumy, A., Guillemot, C., Morel, M.L.A.: Super-resolution using neighbor embedding of back-projection residuals. In: 18th International Conference on Digital Signal Processing (DSP), pp. 1–8. IEEE (2013)
3. Cai, B., Xu, X., Jia, K., Qing, C., Tao, D.: DehazeNet: an end-to-end system for single image haze removal. IEEE Trans. Image Process. **25**(11), 5187–5198 (2016)
4. Chang, H., Yeung, D.Y., Xiong, Y.: Super-resolution through neighbor embedding. In: Proceedings of the 2004 IEEE Computer Society Conference on Computer Vision and Pattern Recognition (CVPR 2004), vol. 1, p. 1. IEEE (2004)
5. De Boor, C.: Bicubic spline interpolation. Stud. Appl. Math. **41**(1–4), 212–218 (1962)
6. Dong, C., Loy, C.C., He, K., Tang, X.: Learning a deep convolutional network for image super-resolution. In: Fleet, D., Pajdla, T., Schiele, B., Tuytelaars, T. (eds.) ECCV 2014. LNCS, vol. 8692, pp. 184–199. Springer, Cham (2014). https://doi.org/10.1007/978-3-319-10593-2_13
7. Dong, C., Loy, C.C., He, K., Tang, X.: Image super-resolution using deep convolutional networks. IEEE Trans. Pattern Anal. Mach. Intell. **38**(2), 295–307 (2016)
8. Dong, C., Loy, C.C., Tang, X.: Accelerating the super-resolution convolutional neural network. In: Leibe, B., Matas, J., Sebe, N., Welling, M. (eds.) ECCV 2016. LNCS, vol. 9906, pp. 391–407. Springer, Cham (2016). https://doi.org/10.1007/978-3-319-46475-6_25
9. Duchon, C.E.: Lanczos filtering in one and two dimensions. J. Appl. Meteorol. **18**(8), 1016–1022 (1979)
10. Girshick, R., Donahue, J., Darrell, T., Malik, J.: Rich feature hierarchies for accurate object detection and semantic segmentation. In: Proceedings of the IEEE Conference on Computer Vision and Pattern Recognition, pp. 580–587 (2014)
11. He, K., Zhang, X., Ren, S., Sun, J.: Delving deep into rectifiers: surpassing human-level performance on ImageNet classification. In: Proceedings of the IEEE International Conference on Computer Vision, pp. 1026–1034 (2015)
12. Huang, J.B., Singh, A., Ahuja, N.: Single image super-resolution from transformed self-exemplars. In: Proceedings of the IEEE Conference on Computer Vision and Pattern Recognition, pp. 5197–5206 (2015)
13. Jia, Y., Shelhamer, E., Donahue, J., Karayev, S., Long, J., Girshick, R., Guadarrama, S., Darrell, T.: Caffe: convolutional architecture for fast feature embedding. In: Proceedings of the 22nd ACM International Conference on Multimedia, pp. 675–678. ACM (2014)
14. Kim, J., Kwon Lee, J., Mu Lee, K.: Accurate image super-resolution using very deep convolutional networks. In: Proceedings of the IEEE Conference on Computer Vision and Pattern Recognition, pp. 1646–1654 (2016)
15. Kim, K.I., Kwon, Y.: Single-image super-resolution using sparse regression and natural image prior. IEEE Trans. Pattern Anal. Mach. Intell. **32**(6), 1127–1133 (2010)

16. Kingma, D., Ba, J.: Adam: a method for stochastic optimization. arXiv preprint arXiv:1412.6980 (2014)
17. Martin, D., Fowlkes, C., Tal, D., Malik, J.: A database of human segmented natural images and its application to evaluating segmentation algorithms and measuring ecological statistics. In: Proceedings of the Eighth IEEE International Conference on Computer Vision (ICCV 2001), vol. 2, pp. 416–423. IEEE (2001)
18. Schulter, S., Leistner, C., Bischof, H.: Fast and accurate image upscaling with super-resolution forests. In: Proceedings of the IEEE Conference on Computer Vision and Pattern Recognition, pp. 3791–3799 (2015)
19. Shi, W., Caballero, J., Huszár, F., Totz, J., Aitken, A.P., Bishop, R., Rueckert, D., Wang, Z.: Real-time single image and video super-resolution using an efficient sub-pixel convolutional neural network. In: Proceedings of the IEEE Conference on Computer Vision and Pattern Recognition, pp. 1874–1883 (2016)
20. Simonyan, K., Zisserman, A.: Very deep convolutional networks for large-scale image recognition. arXiv preprint arXiv:1409.1556 (2014)
21. Szegedy, C., Liu, W., Jia, Y., Sermanet, P., Reed, S., Anguelov, D., Erhan, D., Vanhoucke, V., Rabinovich, A.: Going deeper with convolutions. In: Proceedings of the IEEE Conference on Computer Vision and Pattern Recognition, pp. 1–9 (2015)
22. Timofte, R., De Smet, V., Van Gool, L.: A+: adjusted anchored neighborhood regression for fast super-resolution. In: Cremers, D., Reid, I., Saito, H., Yang, M.-H. (eds.) ACCV 2014. LNCS, vol. 9006, pp. 111–126. Springer, Cham (2015). https://doi.org/10.1007/978-3-319-16817-3_8
23. Yang, J., Wright, J., Huang, T.S., Ma, Y.: Image super-resolution via sparse representation. IEEE Trans. Image Process. **19**(11), 2861–2873 (2010)
24. Zeng, L., Xu, X., Cai, B., Qiu, S., Zhang, T.: Multi-scale convolutional neural networks for crowd counting. arXiv preprint arXiv:1702.02359 (2017)
25. Zeyde, R., Elad, M., Protter, M.: On single image scale-up using sparse-representations. In: Boissonnat, J.-D., Chenin, P., Cohen, A., Gout, C., Lyche, T., Mazure, M.-L., Schumaker, L. (eds.) Curves and Surfaces 2010. LNCS, vol. 6920, pp. 711–730. Springer, Heidelberg (2012). https://doi.org/10.1007/978-3-642-27413-8_47
26. Zhang, K., Gao, X., Tao, D., Li, X.: Multi-scale dictionary for single image super-resolution. In: IEEE Conference on Computer Vision and Pattern Recognition (CVPR), pp. 1114–1121. IEEE (2012)

Person Identity and Emotion

Complexity and Emotion

A Novel Image Preprocessing Strategy for Foreground Extraction in Person Re-identification

Daiyin Wang, Wenbin Yao, and Yuesheng Zhu$^{(\boxtimes)}$

Communication and Information Security Lab, Shenzhen Graduate School,
Institute of Big Data Technologies, Peking University, Shenzhen, China
{1501213964,wbyao}@sz.pku.edu.cn, zhuys@pkusz.edu.cn

Abstract. Foreground extraction can help to improve the performance of person re-identification. In this paper, we propose a novel image preprocessing strategy for foreground extraction. First, we propose that the appropriate background information of the images should be increased in the cropped pedestrian images to improve the saliency detection performance. Second, an Adaptive Multi-layer Cellular Automata model (AMCA) is put forward to extract the foregrounds. Experiments on the VIPeR show that AMCA outperforms other existing methods both on saliency detection and re-identification performance. Furthermore, in order to verify the effectiveness of the proposed strategy, we build a new dataset named Looser Cropped Pedestrian Recognition Dataset (LCPeR), which simultaneously provides the compact-cropped images and the loose-cropped images. Experiments on the LCPeR show that the proposed strategy can further improve the saliency detection and re-identification performance.

Keywords: Saliency detection · Foreground extraction
Person re-identification

1 Introduction

Person re-identification aims to automatically find the same person that appears in non-overlapping camera networks. It is a very challenging task because of the impact of background interference, low resolution, illumination, and viewpoint change, etc.

For the past few years, many approaches have been proposed for person re-identification [1]. Among them, most of the existing approaches focus on designing a robust feature representation [2–4] or learning a discriminative distance or similarity function [4–6], which relatively ignore the preprocessing of the images themselves. However, images of the same person appearing in different cameras have significantly different backgrounds, and the background could be similar in images of different person. Hence, background information can interfere with feature representation, which could lead to the mismatching in the following re-identification [7].

To handle this problem, foreground extraction, as a common preprocessing procedure, is often used. And image saliency detection has widely used as a pre-processing step in computer vision [8], which is also usually proposed for foreground extraction in

© Springer International Publishing AG, part of Springer Nature 2018
B. Zeng et al. (Eds.): PCM 2017, LNCS 10735, pp. 161–171, 2018.
https://doi.org/10.1007/978-3-319-77380-3_16

person re-identification. In retrospect, Farenzena et al. [2] utilized STEL segmentation model [9] to extract the image foreground. Then, the STEL model was also used in [3, 10]. Nguyen et al. [7] presented background removal methods by using an adaptive local salience detection method to improve salience-based re-identification performance. Ma et al. [11] used a pre-attentive spectral saliency model to get global saliency maps, which are further developed to generalize eye fixation maps for refining the appearance of pedestrians. However, there is only a relatively low performance improvement or even worse by using the foregrounds extracted by these methods, such as STEL, since the extracted foregrounds are not accurate enough.

In recent years, more and more bottom-up saliency detection methods [12–16] are proposed and have achieved the state-of-the-art performance in the field of saliency detection. Specifically, In BFS [12], saliency maps are detected via background and foreground seed selection. In BSCA [13], saliency maps are detected firstly based on the clustered boundary seeds and then are optimized by Cellular Automata. In DSR [14], saliency maps are attained via dense and sparse reconstruction, in which the background templates in images boundaries are selected as likely cues. In MAP [15], saliency maps are detected by Markov absorption probabilities via using partial boundaries as background cues and then are improved by a series of optimization techniques. In RRWR [16], saliency maps first are detected by incorporating local grouping cues and boundary priors and then are refined with erroneous boundary removal and regularized random walks ranking. In general, all of these methods have the advantage of background information, assuming that regions along the image boundary are more likely to be the background to some extent. Indeed, as proved in [8], the image border is more likely to be the background for images in the general saliency detection scenario. However, for the compact-cropped pedestrian images in the person re-identification scenario, it is no longer a valid assumption. Therefore, these saliency detection methods are no longer applicable directly.

In this paper, we propose a novel image preprocessing strategy for foreground extraction in person identification. First, for the images themselves, we present a novel idea that the appropriate background information should be increased in the cropped pedestrian images to enhance the performance of saliency detection when we automatically detect or manually crop pedestrian images from surveillance video, so as to further improve the person re-identification performance. Second, in order to obtain a more favorable and robust pedestrian foreground, based on MCA [13], we propose an Adaptive Multi-layer Cellular Automata model (AMCA) to integrate multiple saliency maps detected by different saliency methods and generate the final pedestrian foreground. In AMCA, a new adaptive threshold method is proposed for binarization.

Since the existing re-identification datasets only provide the compact-cropped pedestrian images with a very small amount of fixed background information, to verify the effectiveness of the proposed strategy, we build a new dataset named Looser Cropped Pedestrian Recognition Dataset (LCPeR), which simultaneously provides the compact-cropped images and the loose-cropped images for comparison. Meanwhile, the validity of AMCA is also proved in VIPeR, an existing re-identification dataset.

In addition, since our proposed strategy is a separated process from feature extraction and similarity estimation in person re-identification, we can choose any feature representation and similarity estimation method to achieve person re-identification task based on the generated foreground images.

2   A Novel Image Preprocessing Strategy

2.1   Increasing the Appropriate Background Information

In order to increase the appropriate background information on the cropped pedestrian images, we can make a looser processing on the original images when we automatically detect or manually crop pedestrian images from surveillance video.

If pedestrian images are cropped manually, we first crop compactly the pedestrian images just like the other existing re-identification datasets, such as VIPeR. Then, according to the border position of the compact-cropped pedestrian images on original pedestrian images, we extend the border out with an appropriate parameter ω to get the loose-cropped pedestrian images. If pedestrian images are detected automatically through a pedestrian detection algorithm [17], it is also easy to achieve a looser processing by adjusting the four coordinates of the detected pedestrian (that is, compact-cropped image) with an appropriate parameter ω.

The parameter ω is of great significance both for saliency detection and person re-identification. On the one hand, in order to enhance the performance of saliency detection, we need to expand the boundaries through ω to increase background information. On the other hand, for an image scaled to the same size, the lager value of ω means that the image has fewer effective pedestrian feature areas, which can affect person re-identification performance. Empirically, ω is recommended to be set to 10% of the corresponding compact-cropped image's width.

As shown in Fig. 1, the loose-cropped images have more background information than the compact-cropped images. And intuitively, the compact-cropped images are more likely to lose partial pedestrian regions, such as head, arm, leg, and foot. It can be explained mainly because the object appeared on the image boundary is more likely to be regarded as background [8]. In general, the generated pedestrian foregrounds of the loose-cropped images are better than that of the compact-cropped images.

2.2   Adaptive Multi-layer Cellular Automata

We extend Multi-layer Cellular Automata (MCA) [13] to integrate M saliency maps generated by M different saliency detection methods into a more accurate and powerful saliency map, and then use SaliencyCut [18] and morphological image processing to refine the results and obtain the final pedestrian foreground image. We denote this extended model as Adaptive Multi-layer Cellular Automata (AMCA).

Firstly, we employ the same initial settings as those proposed in MCA. Each of the preliminary saliency maps serves as a layer of Cellular Automata. Each cell represents a pixel, and we use the saliency value of each pixel to represent the state of each cell. The number of all cells in an image is denoted as H. In addition, cells with the same coordinates in different masks are defined as neighbors. That is, for any cell on a saliency map, it may have $M - 1$ neighbors on other saliency maps. And we assume

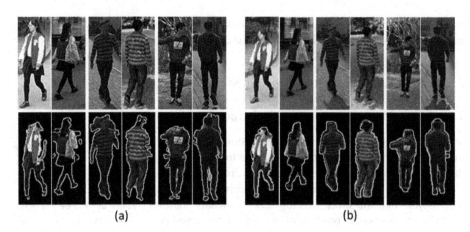

Fig. 1. Some examples of the extracted foregrounds by AMCA of (a) compact-cropped images and (b) loose-cropped images in LCPeR. All images are normalized to 128×48 pixels.

that all neighbors have the same influential power to determine the cell's next state. The saliency value of cell i stands for its probability to be the foreground F, denoted as $P(i \in F) = S_i$, while $1 - S_i$ stands for its possibility to be the background B, denoted as $P(i \in B) = 1 - S_i$.

Then, we propose a new adaptive threshold τ'_m for binarization as follows:

$$B_m(x, y) = \begin{cases} 0, & S_m(x, y) < \tau_m \\ 1, & S_m(x, y) \geq \tau_m \end{cases} \tag{1}$$

$$\tau'_m = \frac{1}{N} \sum_{x=1}^{W} \sum_{y=1}^{H} (1 - B_m(x, y)) \cdot S_m(x, y) \tag{2}$$

where the subscript m represents the m-th saliency map, $S_m(x, y)$ is the saliency value of the pixel at position (x, y), τ_m is the threshold generated by OTSU [19]. $B_m(x, y)$ is the corresponding binarized value. N is the number of all pixels of $B_m(x, y) = 0$, W and H are the width and the height of the saliency map S_m in pixels, respectively. The threshold τ'_m is only related to the initial m-th saliency map and remains the same all the time.

For the detected saliency maps without obvious bimodal distribution between foreground and background, such as the examples in Fig. 2(b)–(f), compared with using τ_m directly, the problem, that large portions of the pedestrian body with relatively low saliency values would be regarded directly as the background, can be avoided to some extent by using our new threshold τ'_m.

After binarization, we set $\sigma_i = +1$ if the cell i is measured as foreground and $\sigma_i = -1$ if it is measured as background. If cell i belongs to the foreground, the probability that one of its neighboring cell j (with the same coordinates on another masks) is measured as foreground is $\lambda = P(\sigma_j = +1 | i \in F)$. Correspondingly, the probability $\mu = P(\sigma_j = -1 | i \in B)$ represents that the cell j is measured as background

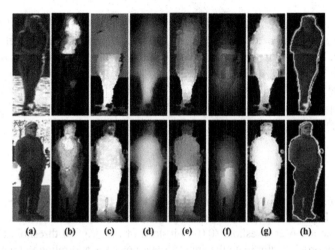

Fig. 2. Two examples of foreground extraction via AMCA. (a) Input image. (b)–(f) Saliency maps detected respectively by BFS [12], BSCA [13], DSR [14], MAP [15] and RRWR [16]. (g) The integrated saliency maps. (h) The final foreground images.

under the condition that cell i belongs to the background. It is reasonable to assume that both λ and μ are constants. Then the posterior probability $P(i \in F | \sigma_j = +1)$ can be calculated as follows:

$$P(i \in F | \sigma_j = +1) \propto P(i \in F)P(\sigma_j = +1 | i \in F) = S_i \cdot \lambda \qquad (3)$$

In order to avoid the normalizing constant, the prior and posterior ratio $\Lambda(i \in F)$ and $\Lambda(i \in F) | \sigma_j = +1$ are defined as:

$$\Lambda(i \in F) = \frac{P(i \in F)}{P(i \in B)} = \frac{S_i^t}{1 - S_i^t} \qquad (4)$$

$$\Lambda(i \in F | \sigma_j = +1) = \frac{P(i \in F | \sigma_j = +1)}{P(i \in B | \sigma_j = +1)} = \frac{S_i^{t+1}}{1 - S_i^{t+1}} = \frac{S_i^t}{1 - S_i^t} \cdot \frac{\lambda}{1 - \mu} \qquad (5)$$

where S_i^t denotes the saliency value of cell i at time t. Notice that the prior ratio is easier to deal with the logarithm of Λ. So we have:

$$l(i \in F | \sigma_j = +1) = l(i \in F) + ln\left(\frac{\lambda}{1 - \mu}\right) \qquad (6)$$

And we define the synchronous updating rule $f : S^{m-1} \rightarrow S$ as:

$$l(S_m^{t+1}) = l(S_m^t) + \sum_{\substack{k = 1 \\ k \neq m}}^{M} sign(S_k^t - \tau_k \cdot 1) \cdot ln\left(\frac{\lambda}{1 - \lambda}\right) \qquad (7)$$

where $S_m^t = \left[S_{m1}^t, S_{m2}^t, \cdots, S_{mH}^t \right]^T$ represents the saliency value of all cells on the m-th map at time t, and the matrix $1 = [1, 1, \cdots, 1]^T$ has H elements. Intuitively, if a cell observes that its neighbors are binarized as foreground, it ought to increase its saliency value.

Therefore, Eq. (7) requires $\lambda > 0.5$ and then $ln\left(\frac{\lambda}{1-\lambda}\right) > 0$. In this paper, similar to [19], we empirically set $ln\left(\frac{\lambda}{1-\lambda}\right) = 0.15$. After N_2 time steps, the final integrated saliency map S^{N_2} is calculated as:

$$S^{N_2} = \frac{1}{M} \sum_{m=1}^{M} S_m^{N_2} \qquad (8)$$

After that, we employ the SaliencyCut algorithm to separate the foreground and background. In order to avoid the lack of pedestrian edge with relatively low saliency values, we use a looser threshold (0.001) instead of the original threshold (0.275).

Finally, in order to eliminate the small isolated patches and refine the binary mask, we generate the final masks of pedestrian images through holes filling, grayscale erosion and dilation operation with a 3×3 square. And we can directly use the final masks to generate the foreground images by a pixel-wise operation.

In this paper, we use ACMA to integrate five saliency maps detected by BFS [12], BSCA [13], DSR [14], MAP [15] and RRWR [16] respectively for each pedestrian image. Two examples of foreground extraction via AMCA are shown in Fig. 2. Apparently, the integrated saliency maps are evenly highlighted and more accurate.

3 Person Re-identification Pipeline

The typical pipeline of hand-crafted approach in person re-identification can be divided into three steps: **preprocessing**, **feature extraction** and **similarity estimation**. After generating the foreground images by our proposed strategy, we can use any state-of-the-art feature extraction method and similarity estimation method to perform person re-identification. In this paper, we extract the Local Maximal Occurrence (LOMO) [4] feature as the feature representation. The LOMO feature is a discriminative and robust feature representation for re-identification, and it can be extracted quickly. Then, we utilize the Cross-view Quadratic Discriminant Analysis (XQDA) [4] algorithm, which recently is commonly used in person re-identification [1], to estimate the similarity rank between images.

4 Experiments

4.1 Datasets and Settings

VIPeR [20] is the most popular dataset for person re-identification. It contains 632 person pairs taken from arbitrary viewpoints. All images are scaled to 128×48 pixels. Additionally, we provide the manual mask of each image as ground truth (GT). We adopt the most widely used experimental protocol on this dataset that is to randomly divide all the pairs of images into half for training and the other half for testing, and repeat 10 times to get an average performance.

LCPeR[1], a new re-identification dataset, is built by us to verify the proposed strategy since the existing datasets only provide the compact-cropped pedestrian images. LCPeR contains 206 pedestrian image pairs with large viewpoint changes, which are randomly obtained from the surveillance videos captured by six disjoint cameras in the campus. For each pedestrian, two compact-cropped images and two loose-cropped images are provided simultaneously. The loose-cropped images are developed by increasing approximately 10% of the corresponding compact-cropped image's width so that they have more appropriate background information. All images are scaled to 128 × 48 pixels. Some examples are shown in the first row of Fig. 1. In addition, for each image, we also provide a manual mask as ground truth (GT). In our Experiments, we take the same experimental protocol as VIPeR dataset does.

4.2 Evaluation Metrics

We adopt mean absolute error (MAE) [21] and F-measure [22] to evaluate the performance of saliency detection and foreground extraction. The MAE indicates how similar a saliency map is to the ground truth, and is of great significance for the application of image segmentation. The F-measure is put forward as a weighted average between precision and recall and usually regarded as the overall performance measurement.

Furthermore, the Cumulated Matching Characteristic (CMC) [23] is usually used for evaluating the re-identification performance. The most important value in CMC curve is the probability matching at rank-1.

4.3 Experiments on VIPeR

Comparison of Different Saliency Detection Methods. We compare our proposed AMCA with six saliency detection methods (BFS [12], BSCA [13], DSR [14], MAP [15], RRWR [16] and MCA [13]). In addition, the CMC result of the LOMO + XQDA method (No Mask) is added to Fig. 3 for comparison.

As shown in Tables 1 and 2, compared to the other methods, AMCA has achieved the best results. In detail, AMCA can detect saliency maps that are closer to ground truth, and generate more accurate binary masks.

As shown in Fig. 3, AMCA performs best and have achieved 41.52% at rank-1, with an improvement of 1.52% than No Mask, while the other methods perform worse than No Mask, which experimentally proves that these existing saliency detection methods are no longer directly applicable to VIPeR.

Comparison with the Existing Re-identification Methods. We compare our approach with the existing re-identification methods, which have taken advantage of

---

[1] The dataset can be downloaded in http://pan.baidu.com/s/1c229w44, password: vbyn.

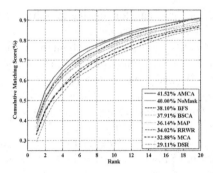

Fig. 3. CMC curves and rank-1 identification rates on VIPeR

Table 1. MAE on VIPeR

Method	BFS	BSCA	DSR	MAP	RRWR	MCA	AMCA
MAE	0.4369	0.3397	0.3860	0.3725	0.3552	0.2986	*0.2207*

Table 2. F-measure on VIPeR

Method	BFS	BSCA	DSR	MAP	RRWR	MCA	AMCA
F-measure	0.6929	0.7834	0.7013	0.7668	0.7184	0.7936	*0.8625*

foreground extraction. From Table 3, our approach performs best and achieves 41.52% at rank-1, outperforming the second best one SCNCD by 3.72%.

Table 3. CMC results (%) of the existing re-identification methods on VIPeR.

Method	rank = 1	rank = 10	rank = 20
SP [11]	18.70	50.63	63.10
SDALF [2]	19.87	49.37	65.73
SMWH&SC [10]	21.50	56.67	69.53
BR [7]	24.81	58.35	73.64
SCNCD [3]	37.80	81.20	90.40
AMCA (ours)	*41.52*	*81.23*	*91.04*

4.4 Experiments on LCPeR

We compare AMCA with six saliency detection methods (BFS, BSCA, DSR, MAP, RRWR and MCA) on the compact-cropped images and the loose-cropped images in LCPeR respectively. The experimental results are listed in Fig. 4, Tables 4 and 5.

Horizontal Contrast. We analyze the results of the compact-cropped images and the loose-cropped images in LCPeR, respectively. Compared to the other saliency detection methods, our proposed AMCA performs best whether it is the detected saliency

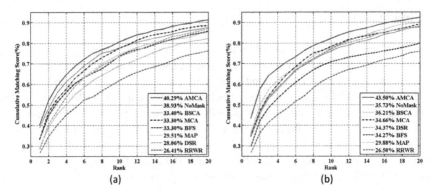

Fig. 4. CMC curves and rank-1 identification rates on the LCPeR dataset with (a) compact-cropped images and (b) loose-cropped images.

Table 4. MAE on LCPeR

Method	BFS	BSCA	DSR	MAP	RRWR	MCA	AMCA
Compact	0.3188	0.2250	0.2491	0.2741	0.2425	0.2293	*0.1529*
Loose	**0.2164**	**0.1461**	**0.1596**	**0.2048**	**0.1608**	**0.1504**	*0.1112*

Table 5. F-measure on LCPeR

Method	BFS	BSCA	DSR	MAP	RRWR	MCA	AMCA
Compact	0.7463	0.8262	0.7799	0.8077	0.7713	0.7899	*0.8654*
Loose	**0.8031**	**0.8661**	**0.8232**	**0.8164**	**0.8161**	**0.8460**	*0.8816*

maps or the generated binary masks or the person re-identification results, which is the same conclusion as in VIPeR.

Vertical Contrast. We compare the results of the compact-cropped images and the loose-cropped images in LCPeR. In general, for all the saliency detection methods, all the results of the loose-cropped images are better than those of the compact-cropped images. Especially, from Fig. 4, without foreground extraction (that is, No mask), there is a worse performance with 3.2% on the loose-cropped images than that on the compact-cropped images. But after foreground extraction by AMCA, the result of the loose-cropped images achieves the optimal performance at rank-1 with 43.50% in LCPeR because of the significant improvement of 7.77%. These results indicate that increasing the appropriate background information works well.

To sum up, our proposed strategy can obviously further improve the saliency detection and re-identification performance.

5 Conclusion

This paper has presented a novel image preprocessing strategy for foreground extraction in Person Re-identification. The proposed strategy includes a novel idea of increasing the appropriate background information in the cropped pedestrian images and an AMCA model for foreground extraction. Experiments on VIPeR and LCPeR demonstrate that the proposed strategy contributes to extract better saliency maps and image foregrounds, so as to further improve the performance of re-identification. Since this preprocessing strategy is a separated process, in the future, we will test the performance when it is combined with other feature extraction and similarity estimation method, and work on extracting more accurate foreground images.

Acknowledgement. This work is supported by the Shenzhen Municipal Development and Reform Commission (Disciplinary Development Program for Data Science and Intelligent Computing), and the Shenzhen Engineering Laboratory of Broadband Wireless Network Security.

References

1. Zheng, L., Yi, Y., Hauptmann, A.G.: Person re-identification: past, present and future. arXiv preprint arXiv:1610.02984 (2016)
2. Bazzani, L., Cristani, M., Murino, V.: SDALF: modeling human appearance with symmetry-driven accumulation of local features. In: Gong, S., Cristani, M., Yan, S., Loy, C.C. (eds.) Person Re-Identification. ACVPR, pp. 43–69. Springer, Cham (2014). https://doi.org/10.1007/978-1-4471-6296-4_3
3. Yang, Y., Yang, J., Yan, J., Liao, S., Yi, D., Li, S.Z.: Salient color names for person re-identification. In: Fleet, D., Pajdla, T., Schiele, B., Tuytelaars, T. (eds.) ECCV 2014. LNCS, vol. 8689, pp. 536–551. Springer, Cham (2014). https://doi.org/10.1007/978-3-319-10590-1_35
4. Liao, S., Hu, Y., Zhu, X., Li, S.Z.: Person re-identification by local maximal occurrence representation and metric learning. In: CVPR, pp. 2197–2206 (2015)
5. Koestinger, M., Hirzer, M., Wohlhart, P., Roth, P.M., Bischof, H.: Large scale metric learning from equivalence constraints. In: CVPR, pp. 2288–2295 (2012)
6. Chen, D., Yuan, Z., Chen, B., Zheng, N.: Similarity learning with spatial constraints for person re-identification. In: CVPR, pp. 1268–1277 (2016)
7. Nguyen, T.B., Pham, V.P., Le, T.L., Le C.V.: Background removal for improving saliency-based person re-identification. In: KSE, pp. 339–344 (2016)
8. Borji, A., Cheng, M.M., Jiang, H., Li, J.: Salient object detection: a benchmark. IEEE Trans. Image Process. **24**, 5706–5722 (2015)
9. Jojic, N., Perina, A., Cristani, M., Murino, V., Frey, B.: Stel component analysis: modeling spatial correlations in image class structure. In: CVPR, pp. 2044–2051 (2009)
10. Liu, Y., Shao, Y., Sun, F.: Person re-identification based on visual saliency. In: ISDA, pp. 884–889 (2012)
11. Ma, C., Miao, Z., Li, M.: Saliency preprocessing for person re-identification images. In: ICASSP, pp. 1941–1945 (2016)
12. Wang, J., Lu, H., Li, X., Tong, N., Liu, W.: Saliency detection via background and foreground seed selection. Neurocomputing **152**, 359–368 (2015)

13. Qin, Y., Lu, H., Xu, Y., Wang, H.: Saliency detection via cellular automata. In: CVPR, pp. 110–119 (2015)
14. Li, X., Lu, H., Zhang, L., Ruan, X., Yang, M.H.: Saliency detection via dense and sparse reconstruction. In: ICCV, pp. 2976–2983 (2013)
15. Sun, J., Lu, H., Liu, X.: Saliency region detection based on markov absorption probabilities. IEEE Trans. Image Process. **24**, 1639–1649 (2015)
16. Li, C., Yuan, Y., Cai, W., Xia, Y., Feng, D.D.: Robust saliency detection via regularized random walks ranking. In: CVPR, pp. 2710–2717 (2015)
17. Ren, S., He, K., Girshick, R., Sun, J.: Faster R-CNN: towards real-time object detection with region proposal networks. In: Neural Information Processing Systems, pp. 91–99 (2015)
18. Cheng, M.M., Mitra, N.J., Huang, X., Torr, P.H., Hu, S.M.: Global contrast based salient region detection. IEEE Trans. PAMI **37**, 569–582 (2015)
19. Otsu, N.: A threshold selection method from gray-level histograms. Automatica **11**, 23–27 (1975)
20. Gray, D., Brennan, S., Tao, H.: Evaluating appearance models for recognition, reacquisition, and tracking. In: PETS, vol. 3 (2007)
21. Perazzi, F., Krahenbuhl, P., Pritch, Y., Hornung, A.: Saliency filters: contrast based filtering for salient region detection. In: CVPR, pp. 733–740 (2012)
22. Achanta, R., Hemami, S., Estrada, F., Susstrunk, S.: Frequency-tuned salient region detection. In: CVPR, pp. 1597–1604 (2009)
23. Wang, X., Doretto, G., Sebastian, T., Rittscher, J., Tu, P.: Shape and appearance context modeling. In: ICCV, pp. 1–8 (2007)

Age Estimation via Pose-Invariant 3D Face Alignment Feature in 3 Streams of CNN

Li Sun$^{(\boxtimes)}$, Song Qiu, Qingli Li, Hongying Liu, and Mei Zhou

Shanghai Key Laboratory of Multidimensional Information Processing,
East China Normal University, Shanghai 200241, China
sqiu@ee.ecnu.edu.cn

Abstract. This paper proposes an algorithm for age estimation intentionally considering the pose variation and local deformation of faces. Pose-invariant patches are extracted in face region, and they are located from the landmarks' neighborhood in 2D image coordinate. The landmarks can be regarded as the projections of the points on 3D face model, and the projection parameters are estimated by Convolution Neural Network (CNN). Two different structures of CNN are designed for age estimation task. One way is to stack individual patch in the spatial domain, and the stacked image is given to a CNN to make the estimation. The second is to design CNN for each particular patch and CNNs for different patches do not share weights. Together with another CNN trained on the original face region, the three streams for age estimation are combined by late fusion of the output layer. Experiments show that the proposed scheme outperforms other state-of-the-art methods.

1 Introduction

The computer vision application based on facial image has been an active research topic. Particularly, face recognition has been used in varieties of computer vision systems such as security control, surveillance monitoring or human-computer interaction. Human face provides an amount of important information not only about the identity, but also about emotion, ethnicity, gender or age. In all these characteristics, age is one of the most useful one, and the automatic age estimation can improve the human-computer interface greatly. For examples, a video system can automatically identify teenagers and prevent them from watching unsuitable contents. The vending machine can keep the under ages away from cigarettes or alcohol. Therefore, age estimation attracts researchers' attention not only for fun, but also for its practical applications.

Age estimation is a challenging task for following reasons. First, it is hard to obtain the annotated data like other computer vision tasks. The real age of a person in a given photo depends on the dates of both birth and photo acquisition.

This work was supported in part by the National Natural Science Foundation of China under Project 61302125, 61671376 and in part by Natural Science Foundation of Shanghai under Project 17ZR1408500.

© Springer International Publishing AG, part of Springer Nature 2018
B. Zeng et al. (Eds.): PCM 2017, LNCS 10735, pp. 172–183, 2018.
https://doi.org/10.1007/978-3-319-77380-3_17

So it is impossible to know the real age of a face in the existing dataset such as LFW [14] or FRVT [18]. In order to enlarge the size of useful data for age estimation task, instead of real age, researchers begin to use apparent age. As defined, it is the labeled age given by several volunteers for the single individual in image, according to the appearance of the face. Compared with real age, the annotated apparent age is somehow arbitrary, but the mean of the labels from different annotators becomes relatively stable. In this paper, we adopt the CACD dataset [1] in which the face age is labeled in this way. But datasets with real age, such as FGNet [13] or Morph [10], are also used to train and test the model.

Second, although accurate age estimation is regarded as a classical regression problem, it is still difficult to find reliable features to reflect age. People under the same age may have large differences on facial appearances. On the other hand, people of largely different ages may also look about the same. To overcome the age ambiguity, some researchers choose to perform age group estimation rather than accurate age estimation. Gallagher and Chen [4] propose a dataset which consists of Flick face images labeled with 7 age categories. Shan [21] proposes to adopt Adaboost to learn the discriminative local features to represent age, such as boosted LBP or Gabor, and they classify the age group by SVM based on these features. Yan et al. [23] give a age group estimation scheme based on Convolution Neural Network (CNN). Features from different layers of CNN are extracted and fed into SVM classifier to estimate the age group.

Accurate age estimation can be divided into three types, which are based on anthropometric model [11,12], subspace learning [5,6] and regression [3,7,24]. In the first type, Kwon and Lobo [12] propose an anthropometric model based on geometric ratios of human face. They calculate several types of distance ratios defined by the landmarks, and use them as features to estimate age. In [11], Koruga et al. extend the model by calculating more distance ratios. These methods need to locate the landmark first, which is often a more difficult task than age estimation. Another type of methods of age estimation are based on subspace learning. In [6], Geng et al. proposes the aging pattern subspace method which models a sequence of individual aging face images by learning a subspace representation. The age of a test face is determined by the projections in the subspace that can best reconstruct the face image. They extend their work in [5] by inculpating nonlinear kernel method into subspace learning. With respect to the third types, in [24], Yan et al. treat age estimation as a nonlinear regression task with uncertain non-negative labels. They use kernel trick to implicitly transform features into high-dimensional space, and solve the problem with semi-definite programming algorithm. Chen et al. [3] propose to make the combination of accurate age estimation and ranking, by jointly learning an embedded age subspace via the semi-supervised method. [7] simultaneously considers the feature space learning and regression. They adopt manifold learning to extract expressive features for support vector regression.

Recently, researchers begin to explore the problem by the powerful tool of Convolution Neural Network (CNN), and they try to merge the feature space learning with regression. In [26], Yi et al. propose an algorithm based on the locally aligned patches in face region. Each patch is given to sub-network with 3 layers. Finally, a fully-connected layer makes the fusion of multiple outputs of sub-network to regress the age. Levi and Hassncer [15] propose an age and gender estimation scheme by a small scale CNN with 3 convolution layers and 2 fully connected layers. The face images, which they use to train and test the model, are from Audience benchmark, in which more challenges are considered. Yang et al. [25] regard age estimation as label distribution learning task, and they solve the problem with two different deep CNN models which are built as two streams. They fine-tune the networks with multiple data-sets.

In spite that previous works in [15,25] consider face images with less constrained conditions, none of them particularly focuses on the effect of pose or expression variation on age estimation task. Intuitively, humans can give a good estimation on the frontal view of face with a neutral expression, but not on the side view with exaggerated expressions. In order to look young, many people like to take photos from up to down at 45° angle, which also demonstrates that pose affects apparent age. This paper investigates the age estimation problem based on pose-invariant 3D face alignment feature. Specifically, we perform not only global pose alignment but also local warping before age estimation to get rid of the effect of pose variation. The method proposed in [9] is adopted here to estimate the pose of the face by fitting the 3D Morphable Model (3DMM) onto image. The 3DMM is an universal face model defined by a set of vertexes on the 3D face shape surface. The model is determined by a series of parameters, including the description of the pose, identities and expressions. To estimate the parameters, the cascaded structure of several CNNs is used to iteratively update the value. After that, multiple patches are cropped in the neighbourhood of 3D landmarks defined by four vertexes in 3DMM using Piecewise Affine Warped Feature (PAWF), similar with [26]. Cropped patches are normalized into the same size, and two types of CNN are constructed based on them. First, these patches can be stacked in a fixed order in 2D spatial coordinate and given to one type of CNN as input. Second, each patch can be fully exploited as the input for CNN defined on an individual part. A third stream is another CNN takes the original image as the input, and also plays a role to estimates age. Features from the three streams are fully connected into output layer in which 100 neurons represents the age from 0 to 99. Compared to existing works, the contributions of proposed algorithm lie in following aspects.

- We conspicuously consider the deformation of face caused by both pose and expression variations with the help of 3DMM. Previous works such as [16,23,25] only perform preprocessing steps such as simple alignment, which is not enough to give robust estimation results.
- We employ local patches in face region as a cue for age estimation. Unlike [8,26], which only selects the neighbourhood of patch without considering the deformation, we make full use of the 3DMM to help selecting patches and they are being warped before cropped, so that those with the same index ranking in different images can cover the exactly the same local region on faces. More accurate alignment improves the performance of age estimation.

– The structure of three streams of CNN and their fusion way to estimate age is another contribution of this paper. One stream uses the original whole image, and the second adopts the local patches stacked in the predefined order, and the third defines on individual patch based CNN without sharing parameters with other patches. All the three streams play a role in age estimation.

We organize the remainder of the paper as follows. Technical details of our scheme are given in Sect. 2. Results of experiment compared with other works are given in Sect. 3. Brief conclusions are finally given in Sect. 4.

2 Proposed Algorithm

In the proposed algorithm, there are three streams of CNN. As usual, one of them uses the original global face region as input, and this type is named as CNN-Global. The other two take advantage of 3DMM, and uses either the spatially stacked local patches as the input, named as CNN-Stacked, or designs the CNN on individual patch, named as CNN-Local. The flowchart of the algorithm is given in Fig. 1. During training, each stream is firstly trained independently for age estimation task. And then, by breaking the last fully connected (FC) layer of individual stream and adding a bigger FC layer on the concatenated features of each stream, all streams are finetuned together under a single loss. Details about the structure of CNN are given in Sect. 2.2.

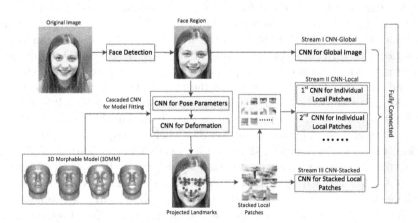

Fig. 1. Flowchart of the proposed algorithm.

2.1 3D Morphable Model Fitting

To give an accurate estimation, image patches on predefined landmarks, laterly used for CNN-Stacked and CNN-Local, need to be located from the image. We first adopt the method in [17] to detect the face region in the image. The located image patches come from the model fitting results. In this paper, 3D Morphable

Model (3DMM) is used to represent a dense 3D shape of an individual face. The 3DMM has a collection of 3D face surfaces to represent different types (identities) and different expressions of faces. Each 3D surface is composed of a set of 3D points. Fitting the 3DMM is actually to estimate a series of parameters to characterize face image. Suppose the 3D face surface matrix is $\mathbf{A} = \{\mathbf{x}_1, \mathbf{x}_2, \cdots, \mathbf{x}_Q\}$ with its size $3 \times Q$, in which there are Q vertexes and each of them is a 3D vector which represents the coordinate $(x, y, z)^T$ of a point on the surface. The matrix $\mathbf{A}$ of any person in the image can be represented as the linear combination of several predefined templates like in (1).

$$\mathbf{A} = \mathbf{A}_0 + \sum_{i=1}^{N_{id}} p_{id}^i \mathbf{A}_{id}^i + \sum_{i=1}^{N_{exp}} p_{exp}^i \mathbf{A}_{exp}^i \qquad (1)$$

Here $\mathbf{A}_0$ is the mean shape with the neutral expression. $\mathbf{A}_{id}^i$ with $i = 1, \cdots, N_{id}$ and $\mathbf{A}_{exp}^i$ with $i = 1, \cdots, N_{exp}$ can be regarded as the templates. $\mathbf{A}_{id}^i$ is the ith identity eigen base surface, and $\mathbf{A}_{exp}^i$ is the ith expression eigen base surface. p_{id}^i and p_{exp}^i are the coefficients corresponding to $\mathbf{A}_{id}^i$ and $\mathbf{A}_{exp}^i$, respectively. These coefficients form vectors $\mathbf{p}_{id}$ and $\mathbf{p}_{exp}$. Since N_{id} and N_{exp} are the number of bases, and all together $N = N_{id} + N_{exp} = 228$, so one task of model fitting is to estimate the high dimensional vectors including $\mathbf{p}_{id}$ and $\mathbf{p}_{exp}$. Another task in model fitting is to estimate the projection vector $\mathbf{m}$, composed by a vector of 6 parameters $\mathbf{m} = (s, \alpha, \beta, \gamma, t_\mathbf{x}, t_\mathbf{y})^T$ under affine projection assumption. $\mathbf{m}$ describes the global pose of the face. s is a scale parameter. α, β and γ are 3 rotation angles with respect to the coordinates in 3D space, which can further determine the rotation matrix $\mathbf{R}$. $t_\mathbf{x}$ and $t_\mathbf{y}$ are two parameters which can form a translational vector $\mathbf{t}$. $\mathbf{m}$ links the 3D vertexes with its projection 2D coordinates.

The method of cascaded CNN proposed in [9] is adopted to estimate $\mathbf{p}_{id}$, $\mathbf{p}_{exp}$ and $\mathbf{m}$. The idea is to first divide the model fitting task into two types, including the $\mathbf{m}$ and $\mathbf{p}$ ($\mathbf{p}_{id}$ and $\mathbf{p}_{exp}$) estimation respectively. Then it iteratively specifies the value of $\mathbf{m}$ and $\mathbf{p}$. Instead of directly giving the absolute value of $\mathbf{m}$ and $\mathbf{p}$, we choose to update them based on their corresponding values in the previous iteration. Specifically, there are 6 cascaded CNNs, and each of them refines the model parameter based on its previous value. Here we organize two types of CNN alternatively, and the CNN estimating $\mathbf{m}$, with a 6 dimensions (all elements in $\mathbf{m}$) vector at the output layer, is followed by the estimation of $\mathbf{p}$, with a $N = 228$ dimensions vector at the output layer. Note that the input of first CNN is an entire face region cropped by the bounding box given by [17] and resized to 100×100, but the inputs for the second to sixth CNN are stacked patches arrays with 20×20 pose-invariant feature patches, extracted from the current estimated 2D landmarks. The first and second CNNs are designed for the estimation of $\mathbf{m}$ and then the alternation of two types of CNN begins. So there are 4 CNNs for $\mathbf{m}$ estimation and 2 for $\mathbf{p}$ estimation. All the 6 CNNs in model fitting step are trained by Euclidean loss. Note that the stacked images given to the second to sixth CNNs are generated by the same method [9].

2.2   Three Streams of CNN

There are totally three streams of CNN used in the proposed algorithm as is shown in Fig. 1. All streams of CNN treat age estimation as a direct classification task with 100 neurons representing the probability distribution from 0 to 99, and they get trained by minimize the soft-max loss. The CNN-Global and CNN-Stacked have totally the same structure as is shown in Fig. 3. It has 3 convolutional (CONV) layers, where each one is followed by a pooling layer, and it also has two FC layers at the top. The spatial extent for the first two CONV layers is 5×5 and it shrinks to 3×3 at the third CONV. In all the CONV layers, we do not perform padding and the strides all equal 1. In CNN-Global, which is defined on the original cropped face region, the input given to CNN is resized to 100×100, the same size as CNN-Stacked.

We now focus on the stream of CNN-Stacked and CNN-Local. The basic idea is that aligned local patches in face region are important cues for many applications such as the facial landmark regression method [9] used in Sect. 2.1. Stacking each aligned patch in 2D and forming a re-organized aligned image is one simple option. Another way is to design a CNN for each patch. As is discussed in the Sect. 2.1, with the help of 3DMM, we can know both the global pose $\mathbf{m}$ and the deformation parameter $\mathbf{p}_{id}$ and $\mathbf{p}_{exp}$. Thus, all the 3D points on the face surface are obtained, so it is easy to project a 3D vertex onto the 2D image plane. Here, we choose to project several important vertexes so that 2D landmarks in the image can be obtained. There are 25 points in total, indicating the start/end or corner point at eyes, nose, mouth, and eyebrows. Figure 2 visualizes several different feature maps from CNN-Global before the FC layer. We can see that the region with large values is rather limited, which demonstrates patches not the whole image should play a role in age estimation.

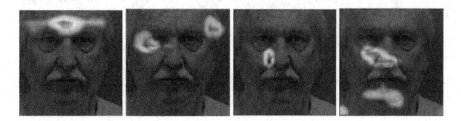

Fig. 2. Visualization of the feature map in CNN-Global. Feature maps are from the last pooling layer just before the first FC layer. Large values are shown in warm color.

To generate aligned patches used as the input for CNN, the 2D landmarks needs to be located, and these landmarks provide not only pixels but also the aligned semantics in it. One way for selecting them is to simply crop squares with the same size surrounding the 2D landmarks as in [26]. But due to the pose variation caused by 3D to 2D projection, it is impossible to make sure that the extracted local patch from one image corresponding to the one in another image, even though both of them are at the same 2D landmark. Intuitively, patches at the same landmark should cover the same local regions of the face. Again, with the help of 3DMM, this pose effect can be easily removed if **m** is known. We give the following simple steps to locate local patches. Other complex methods such as in [9] also work. According to the nth landmarks, we first find M nearest vertexes on 3D face surface. Then we rotate the face model based on **m** so that the normal of the landmark towards the camera. We select 4 among the rotated M vertexes so that they have the minimum or maximum projection coordinate. The 4 vertexes without rotation is projected onto the image and the located patch is finally warped into square with predefined size which is 20×20.

25 landmarks are used in this paper, so that we can collect 25 patches. These patches are stacked with a fixed order to form the input image for CNN-Stacked. The structure of CNN-Stacked, the same as CNN-Global, is given in Fig. 3. The dimensions of feature maps are also given in Fig. 3. CNN-Local, which uses the individual local patch as the input, is also designed for age estimation task. Given the fact that each patch is only 20×20, CNN-Local has only 2 CONV layers and each of them is followed by pooling layer. The spatial sizes of the two CONV layers are 3×3 and the stride and padding are all 1. Note that CNN-Local is actually a series of CNNs defined on a particular patch, in other words, the patches given to CNN-Local are not only aligned but also with a concrete meaning, such as left eye, nose, etc. Fig. 4 shows the architecture of CNN-Local.

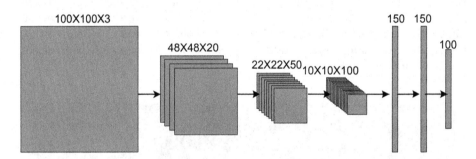

Fig. 3. The structure of CNN-Stacked and CNN-Global. The input can be the stacked local patches or the original image.

2.3   Fusion of Three Streams

3 streams of CNN all predict the age probability distribution of the given face region. In this section, we try to make the fusion of the 3 streams. Our scheme is to break the last FC layer of each stream, and concatenate all features before FC layer. Furthermore, we add another FC-layer with 100 neurons predicting the score of each age between 0 and 99. By softmax loss, it is easy to finetune all the parameters of all streams.

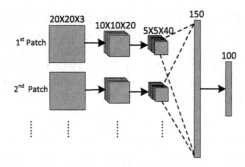

Fig. 4. The structure of CNN-Local. The input is the aligned local patches with pre-defined size 20×20.

3 Experiments

In this section, we present the experimental evaluation of the proposed algorithm. First, a brief overview of all the data-sets and the implementation details are given. Then we report the results of quantitative metrics on the testing data-sets.

3.1 Data-Sets and Implementation Details

There are about 55,000 face images of more than 13,000 subjects in Morph-II. Age ranges from 16 to 77 years in Morph-II. It is the most widely used data-set for age estimation task. But the main problem of it is its uneven distribution of gender and ethnicity. Another problem is this data-set contains the frontal face only, and most of them are with neutral expression, which is not suitable for age estimation under different pose or deformation. Another data-set that we use is FGnet aging database. It is also a public available database for age estimation, and contains 1002 high-resolution color or grey scale face images with relatively large variation of lighting, pose, and expression. It is actually an album of the same person under different age. The main problem of FGnet is that young person images are almost of the same old style. For example, most of the face images, with age under 5 years old, are in grey scale. Thus, age patterns learning from FGnet may not be reflected by facial region. CACD2000 is a data-set in which there are nearly 160000 image with 2000 subjects. It contains the largest pose and expression variation in all data-sets. But the age labels are not very accurate in it. In ChaLearn, 3,615 face images, 2479 in the training data-set and 1136 in the test data-set, with their apparent ages and standard deviations are provided. For the Morph-II, FGnet and CACD2000, we randomly use 75% of them to train and 25% of them to test. Face regions in all images are first detected by [17] and then the method in [9] is used to locate the local patches.

In order to release the simultaneous training procedure of 3 streams, each of them is first pre-trained independently. Then they are combined and 3 streams are fine-tuned based on a single loss function. For the pre-training of the CNN-Stack and CNN-Global, we set the base learning rate to 0.01 and reduce the learning rate by polynomial with gamma value equals to 0.5, while the pre-training of CNN-Local uses a larger initial learning rate of 0.02. For the fine-tuning of the CNN for all streams, the initial learning rate is of 0.001. All experiments are conducted on 12 GB Titan-X GPU. Both the pre-training and fine-tuning are completed by mini-batch stochastic gradient decent (SGD) with the size of mini-batch 100.

3.2   Evaluations

We conduct a comprehensive evaluation on the testing data-sets. The evaluation is performed on each stream of CNN and their fusion, as we proposed in Sect. 2.3. To compare different schemes in the output layer, there are also 2 typical options for loss functions, which are the softmax loss used for 0/1 label encoding classification, the softmax loss used for Gaussian label encoding classification. In the 0/1 label schemes, we use the label vector with the only one entry indicated by 1 and all the others are 0 during training. This is the most common scheme in classification. Gaussian label scheme encodes the label vector by Gaussian distribution with its mean position annotated manually. And σ in Gaussian distribution, which is a hyper-parameter determined by validation, equals $\sigma = 2$. These two schemes treat the age estimation as the classification task and minimize the softmax loss.

To compare different schemes, numerical metrics of mean absolute error (MAE) is applied to FGnet, Morph-II and CACD2000, and ϵ-score is used on ChaLearn. ϵ-score is defined as $\epsilon = 1 - \exp(-(p-g)^2/\sigma^2)$, in which p is the predicted age, g is the ground truth age label, averaging from at least 10 opinions of volunteers, and σ is the standard deviation of all gauged ages for the given image. Table 1 gives the metrics comparison for two label encoding schemes. To give a clear evaluation on the each individual stream, we also list the performances which are obtained only by CNN-Global, CNN-Stacked and CNN-Local. From Table 1, we can see that the performance achieves the best by making the fusion of three streams. Also, it is obvious that the label of Gaussian encoding achieves better results than 0/1 encoding. It is also clear that the stream of stacked aligned local patch outperforms the global image.

Table 1. The MAE (or ϵ-score) of the proposed algorithm with different forms labels including 0/1 encoding and Gaussian encoding.

	0/1 encoding				Gaussian encoding			
	Global	Stacked	Local	Fusion	Global	Stacked	Local	Fusion
FGnet	3.82	3.07	3.42	3.03	3.59	3.26	3.38	**2.98**
MORPH-II	3.64	3.11	3.28	3.06	3.57	3.03	3.35	**2.95**
CACD2000	4.96	3.54	4.02	**3.28**	4.48	3.61	4.13	3.32
ChaLearn	0.332	0.288	0.308	0.283	0.320	0.258	0.278	**0.257**

Table 2. The comparison of MAE (or ϵ-score) between the proposed algorithm and algorithms in the reference.

	Our algorithm	[26]	[16]	[22]	[19]	[2]	[20]
FGnet	2.98	–	–	–	–	–	3.09
MORPH-II	2.95	3.63	–	3.03	–	–	2.68
CACD2000	3.28	–	–	–	–	–	4.79
ChaLearn	0.257	–	0.290	–	0.278	0.297	0.265

Table 2 demonstrates the comparisons among our results and other state-of-the-art methods. Note that we only list the fusion results with Gaussian encoding labels. In Table 2, we can see that our results outperform all the listed methods on 3 data-sets, while it is slightly worse than [20] on MORPH-II. Note that MORPH-II is relatively easy without significant pose and expression variation, so it is not challenge enough to exploit the pose-invariant alignment patch feature.

4 Conclusions

This paper investigates the age estimation problem by the combination of three streams of CNN. One of them directly estimates based on the global image, while the other two either use the stacked local patches or individual local patches as the input for CNN. These patches are located in the surrounding region of 2D landmarks. Under the help of 3DMM, the extracted patches are aligned even with the existence of the pose or expression variation. Each stream is first trained indecently, and then. Experiments show that our algorithm is more accurate than other state-of-the-art method.

References

1. Chen, B.-C., Chen, C.-S., Hsu, W.H.: Cross-age reference coding for age-invariant face recognition and retrieval. In: Fleet, D., Pajdla, T., Schiele, B., Tuytelaars, T. (eds.) ECCV 2014. LNCS, vol. 8694, pp. 768–783. Springer, Cham (2014). https://doi.org/10.1007/978-3-319-10599-4_49
2. Chen, J.C., Kumar, A., Ranjan, R., Patel, V.M., Alavi, A., Chellappa, R.: A cascaded convolutional neural network for age estimation of unconstrained faces. In: IEEE 8th International Conference on Biometrics Theory, Applications and Systems (BTAS), pp. 1–8, September 2016
3. Chen, Y.L., Hsu, C.T.: Subspace learning for facial age estimation via pairwise age ranking. IEEE Trans. Inf. Forensics Secur. 8(8), 2164–2176 (2013)
4. Gallagher, A.C., Chen, T.: Understanding images of groups of people. In: IEEE Conference on Computer Vision and Pattern Recognition (CVPR 2009), pp. 256–263 (2009)
5. Geng, X., Smith-Miles, K., Zhou, Z.H.: Facial age estimation by nonlinear aging pattern subspace. In: International Conference on Multimedia, Vancouver, pp. 721–724, October 2008

6. Geng, X., Zhou, Z.H., Zhang, Y., Li, G., Dai, H.: Learning from facial aging patterns for automatic age estimation. In: ACM International Conference on Multimedia, Santa Barbara, pp. 307–316, October 2006

7. Guo, G., Fu, Y., Dyer, C.R., Huang, T.S.: Image-based human age estimation by manifold learning and locally adjusted robust regression. IEEE Trans. Image Process. **17**(7), 1178–1188 (2008). A Publication of the IEEE Signal Processing Society

8. Guo, G., Mu, G., Fu, Y., Huang, T.S.: Human age estimation using bio-inspired features. In: IEEE Conference on Computer Vision and Pattern Recognition (CVPR 2009), pp. 112–119 (2009)

9. Jourabloo, A., Liu, X.: Large-pose face alignment via CNN-based dense 3D model fitting. In: Proceedings of the IEEE Computer Vision and Pattern Recognition (2016)

10. Ricanek Jr., K., Tesafaye, T.: Morph: a longitudinal image database of normal adult age-progression. In: International Conference on Automatic Face and Gesture Recognition, pp. 341–345 (2006)

11. Koruga, P., Bača, M., Ševa, J.: Application of modified anthropometric model in facial age estimation. In: Proceedings of ELMAR, pp. 17–20 (2011)

12. Kwon, Y.H., Lobo, N.D.V.: Age classification from facial images. Comput. Vis. Image Underst. **74**(1), 1–21 (1999)

13. Lanitis, A.: Comparative evaluation of automatic age-progression methodologies. EURASIP J. Adv. Signal Process. **2008**(1), 10 (2008)

14. Learned-Miller, E., Huang, G.B., RoyChowdhury, A., Li, H., Hua, G.: Labeled faces in the wild: a survey. In: Kawulok, M., Celebi, M.E., Smolka, B. (eds.) Advances in Face Detection and Facial Image Analysis, pp. 189–248. Springer, Cham (2016). https://doi.org/10.1007/978-3-319-25958-1_8

15. Levi, G., Hassncer, T.: Age and gender classification using convolutional neural networks. In: IEEE Conference on Computer Vision and Pattern Recognition Workshops, pp. 34–42 (2015)

16. Liu, X., Li, S., Kan, M., Zhang, J.: AgeNet: deeply learned regressor and classifier for robust apparent age estimation. In: IEEE International Conference on Computer Vision Workshop, pp. 258–266 (2015)

17. Mathias, M., Benenson, R., Pedersoli, M., Van Gool, L.: Face detection without bells and whistles. In: Fleet, D., Pajdla, T., Schiele, B., Tuytelaars, T. (eds.) ECCV 2014. LNCS, vol. 8692, pp. 720–735. Springer, Cham (2014). https://doi.org/10.1007/978-3-319-10593-2_47

18. Phillips, P.J., Grother, P., Micheals, R., Blackburn, D.M., Tabassi, E., Bone, M.: Face recognition vendor test 2002. In: IEEE International Workshop on Analysis and Modeling of Faces and Gestures, p. 44 (2003)

19. Rothe, R., Timofte, R., Gool, L.V.: DEX: deep expectation of apparent age from a single image. In: IEEE International Conference on Computer Vision Workshop (ICCVW), pp. 252–257, December 2015

20. Rothe, R., Timofte, R., Gool, L.V.: Deep expectation of real and apparent age from a single image without facial landmarks. Int. J. Comput. Vis. 1–14 (2016)

21. Shan, C.: Learning local features for age estimation on real-life faces. In: ACM International Workshop on Multimodal Pervasive Video Analysis, pp. 23–28 (2010)

22. Tan, Z., Zhou, S., Wan, J., Lei, Z., Li, S.Z.: Age estimation based on a single network with soft softmax of aging modeling. In: Lai, S.-H., Lepetit, V., Nishino, K., Sato, Y. (eds.) ACCV 2016. LNCS, vol. 10113, pp. 203–216. Springer, Cham (2017). https://doi.org/10.1007/978-3-319-54187-7_14

23. Yan, C., Lang, C., Wang, T., Du, X., Zhang, C.: Age estimation based on convolutional neural network. In: Ooi, W.T., Snoek, C.G.M., Tan, H.K., Ho, C.-K., Huet, B., Ngo, C.-W. (eds.) PCM 2014. LNCS, vol. 8879, pp. 211–220. Springer, Cham (2014). https://doi.org/10.1007/978-3-319-13168-9_22
24. Yan, S., Wang, H., Tang, X., Huang, T.S.: Learning auto-structured regressor from uncertain nonnegative labels. In: IEEE International Conference on Computer Vision, pp. 1–8 (2007)
25. Yang, X., Gao, B.B., Xing, C., Huo, Z.W.: Deep label distribution learning for apparent age estimation. In: IEEE International Conference on Computer Vision Workshop, pp. 344–350 (2015)
26. Yi, D., Lei, Z., Li, S.Z.: Age estimation by multi-scale convolutional network. In: Cremers, D., Reid, I., Saito, H., Yang, M.-H. (eds.) ACCV 2014. LNCS, vol. 9005, pp. 144–158. Springer, Cham (2015). https://doi.org/10.1007/978-3-319-16811-1_10

Face Alignment Using Local Probabilistic Features

Qing Lu[1], Jun Yu[1], and Zengfu Wang[1,2(✉)]

[1] Department of Automation, University of Science and Technology of China,
Hefei, China
ustclq@mail.ustc.edu.cn, {harryjun,zfwang}@ustc.edu.cn
[2] Institute of Intelligent Machines, Chinese Academy of Sciences, Hefei, China

Abstract. Random forest is an effective tool for locating facial landmarks. In this paper, we propose a novel random forest based face alignment method using local probabilistic features (LPF). Here, the LPF has the property of calculating the probability of a sample belonging to the leaf nodes of a tree. The obtained LPF is then used to train a regression model for approximating to the real location of facial landmarks. The above procedure is repeated several times step-by-step in a cascaded form until the model converges. In the end, various convergent results are combined to overcome the instability of a single one. By this way, our method markedly outperforms the state-of-the-art methods. Experimental results show the effectiveness of our algorithm on various face alignment datasets.

Keywords: Random forest · Face alignment
Local probabilistic features · Cascaded form

1 Introduction

Face alignment aims to locate facial landmarks, such as mouth corners, nose tip, pupil and chin. It is a fundamental component in many applications (e.g., facial attribute inference [15], face recognition [13], face verification [17] and facial animation [18]). With the rapid growth in image data nowadays, a highly efficient and accurate face alignment method is in great demand. Though great success has been achieved in this field, accurate and robust alignment of facial landmarks is still a formidable challenge due to partial occlusion and large variations of head pose.

Active appearance model (AAM) [7] solves the task of face landmarks detection by reconstructing entire face using an appearance model and minimizing model parameter errors in training phase. The model of AAM may not work well on unseen faces as the limited expressive power to model texture space. It is also well known that AAM can not handle large variations of expression, illumination and initialization. To solve this problem, local feature based methods such as active shape model (ASM) [8] and constrained local model (CLM) [9]

© Springer International Publishing AG, part of Springer Nature 2018
B. Zeng et al. (Eds.): PCM 2017, LNCS 10735, pp. 184–193, 2018.
https://doi.org/10.1007/978-3-319-77380-3_18

have been proposed, which only model the local appearance around the landmarks instead of the entire face. The results show better generalization ability and stability performance. However, the local features sampled from the current facial landmarks are still not robust enough to adapt to large deformation, pose variation and occlusions.

The vast majority of face alignment approaches proposed in recent years are on the basis of shape regression [6,10,11,14,21]. The advantages of these methods are reflected in the ability of adaptively enforcing shape constrains and the capability of effectively leveraging large bodies of training data. The shape regression algorithm is frequently used in a cascaded manner. Cascaded shape regression (CSR) is first put forward in [6]. Without using a fixed parametric shape model, the inherent shape constraint in [6] is encoded into a cascaded regression framework and implemented from coarse to fine during the test phase. Beginning with an initial shape calculated from the average facial landmarks of the training datasets, the face shape is optimized stage-by-stage by adding a shape increment. In each stage, features are extracted from the images and then used in a regression method to calculate the current location of the facial landmarks.

The selection of features is crucial to the results of regression, so a series of algorithms on it is gradually put forward. The efficiency can be obviously improved by employing the shape-indexed feature [6]. In [26], SIFT (scale-invariant feature transform) feature is used to achieve a robust representation against illumination. Sun et al. [24] takes the advantage of the deep structures of convolutional networks to learn the features. In [21], local binary features (LBF) are presented for extremely accurate and fast face alignment. The obtained LBF is incorporated into CSR framework to learn a linear regression. Due to the simplicity of the pixel based feature, LBF is an exceedingly efficient tool for facial landmarks location. Nevertheless, it is more sensitive to noise compared with other conventional methods, such as HOG (histogram of oriented gradient) and SIFT.

In this paper, we propose a method using local probabilistic features (LPF), which is an optimization of LBF. The proposed LPF has the ability of modeling the probability of a test sample belonging to each leaf node. In the process of tree node split, we employ the average pixel difference value of three pairs of pixels, which can not only guarantee the accuracy of the algorithm, but also improve the speed of the algorithm. In order to obtain the optimized output results, various convergent models are combined to contribute their respective advantages.

The main contributions of our method are:

1. As an extension of local binary features [21], we focus on the important role of the probability for improving the learning effectiveness and efficiency in random forest at the first time. The method synthesizes not only the efficient performance of LBF, but also the probability of a sample reaching each leaf node. Qualitative and quantitative results show the superiority of our algorithm by blending them together.

2. Traditionally, the results of facial landmarks detection are determined by a single regression model [6,10,14,21]. We overcome this limitation by combining various convergent models, since each model has its unique advantages. By integrating them together, we can overcome the instability of a single one.

2   Related Work

2.1   The Cascade Shape Regressors

In recent years, the concept of cascade shape regression gradually shows its superior quality in the research field of face alignment. All these methods take face alignment as a regression problem. Cascade shape regressors generally employ N regressors in series form. The vector S consists of the x, y-coordinates of L facial landmarks. Beginning with an image and a raw initial face shape S^0, S is optimized by a shape increment δS^n, which is calculated by the regressor R^n, n $= 1, 2, ..., $N, stage-by-stage:

$$S^n = S^{n-1} + \delta S^n \qquad (1)$$

where S^n is the current shape estimation, S^{n-1} is the shape estimated by the previous stage, δS^n is calculated as follow:

$$\delta S^n = W^n \Phi^n(I, S^{n-1}) \qquad (2)$$

where W^n is a matrix for global linear projection, Φ^n is a feature mapping function.

2.2   Random Forest

In recent years, random forests [4] play a great role in many classic pattern recognition problems, such as image classification [3], data clustering [23] and shape regression [21]. This approach has many advantages: (a) efficiency in both training and prediction, (b) the ability to handle a large number of input variables, (c) the ability to detect the interaction between features, and (d) suitable for multi-classification problem.

3   Method

In the training phase, we first augment our training data to meet the diversity of different situations. Then the local probabilistic features are generated from the random forest. After that we learn a global linear projection W^n by dual coordinate descent method [12]. The above procedure is repeated N times step-by-step in a cascaded form. The overview of our training algorithm is shown in Table 1.

The proposed local probabilistic features are extracted from conventional random forest. Following the framework proposed by [20], one facial landmark

Table 1. Training of cascade face alignment with local probabilistic features

---

Algorithm 1 Training of cascade face alignment with local probabilistic features

---

Input: training datasets (images I_i, ground truth shapes $\widehat{S}_i$ and initial shapes S_i^0),
the number of stages N, the numbe of trees in each stage T, the tree depth D, the
number of landmarks L
Output: W^n, Φ^n
for n=1 to N **do**
1: expand training samples
    augment training samples with multiple initializations for one image, use an
    augmentation of 5 times
2: train random forest
    follow the framework proposed by [4]
3: extract local probabilistic features
    for l=1 to L **do**
    extract local probabilistic features ϕ_l^n
    end for
    $\Phi^n=[\phi_1^n; \phi_2^n; ...; \phi_L^n]$
4: learn the global regressionW^n
    follow the framework proposed by [21]
5: update shapes using W^n, Φ^n of this stage
    $S_i^n=S_i^{n-1}+W^n\Phi^n(I,S^{n-1})$
end for

---

corresponds to one random forest, which is composed of 10 trees. For each leaf
node, we calculate the local probabilistic features as follow:

$$p'(i) = \frac{num(i)}{\sum_{i=1}^{I} num(i)} \quad (3)$$

where $p'(i)$ is the initial probability value of the ith leaf node of a tree, $num(i)$
is the number of training samples falling into the leaf node.

$$p(i) = \begin{cases} lowTh, & \text{if } p'(i) < \text{lowTh} \\ p'(i), & \text{if lowTh} \leq p'(i) < \text{highTh} \\ highTh, & \text{if } p'(i) \geq \text{highTh} \end{cases} \quad (4)$$

where $p(i)$ is the final probability value of the ith leaf node of a tree, $lowTh$ and
$highTh$ are the lower threshold and the upper threshold, respectively.

For each facial landmark, we train a random forest through the method
proposed by [4]. Figure 1 roughly illustrates the process of producing local probabilistic features from random forest. Each leaf node contains a pixel difference
feature f [6], a local probabilistic feature $p(i)$, and a threshold.

When all of the local feature mapping functions ϕ_i^n, $i=1,...,L$, have been
established, high-dimensional probabilistic features are formed by concatenating
all local probabilistic features. Details are shown in Fig. 2.

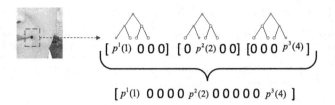

Fig. 1. The process of producing local probabilistic features from random forest. For the parameter $p^i(j)$, i denotes the ith tree in its random forest and j denotes the jth leaf node in its tree.

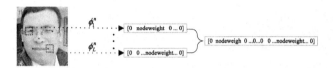

Fig. 2. The high-dimensional probabilistic features are formed by concatenating all local probabilistic features.

The process of testing is same as that for training, but we add an optimization strategy by combining various models to overcome the instability of a single one.

$$S = \frac{1}{M} \sum_{i=1}^{M} S_i = \frac{1}{M} \sum_{i=1}^{M} \sum_{j=1}^{L} s_i(x_j, y_j) \qquad (5)$$

where M is the number of models, S_i is the shape calculated by the ith model, $s_i(x_j, y_j)$ denotes the location of jth landmark.

4   Experiments of Alignment

In this section, we first confirm the selection of some parameters, which are critical to our experimental performance. Then, we show the effectiveness of our method on two datasets, 300 W and Helen.

4.1   Datasets

Helen [16] consists of 2000 training and 330 test web images. The high resolution images are useful for accurate location. In order to achieve rapid results, we employ 68 landmarks instead of 194 landmarks to show the performance of our method. **300 W** [22] is short for 300 faces in the wild. It is created from classical datasets, including LFPW [2], Helen [16], AFW [20], XM2VTS [19] and IBUG. Our training images are composed of the training sets of Helen and LFPW, and the whole AFW dataset. Our testing images are composed of the test sets of LFPW and Helen, which are also called the common test set, and the whole IBUG dataset, which is also called the challenging test set.

4.2   Selection of Parameters

In our experiments, a multi-pose V.J. detector is used for detecting face rectangles, and the mean shape of the training data is chosen as the initial shape of test image.

For the proposed method, the number of cascade stages N and the number of trees T in every random forest are crucial parameters. Figure 3 shows the mean errors as a function of the number of cascade stage. We can see that when N increases to 7, the performance of the algorithm achieve an ideal state. Figure 4 shows the mean errors as a function of the number of trees. With the growth of this parameter, the performance is fluctuating and the test time is increasing.

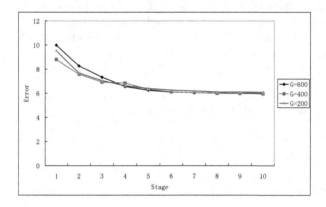

Fig. 3. The mean error at each stage of the cascade is plotted. Using many stages of regressors is fairly useful, regardless of the number of dot group, G, in each forest.

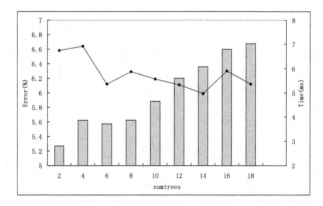

Fig. 4. The mean error as a function of the number of trees T in each random forest (line chart). The test time as a function of T (bar chart).

4.3 Results and Discussion

Our method is implemented in C++ and tested on a i7-6700 CPU. The results of other compared approaches are from the reports in original papers. When the parameter T is set to 2, we can see that the alignment rate of our method is better than others from Table 2.

To evaluate the effectiveness of the local probabilistic features, we take our experiments on two frequently-used datasets, Helen and 300 W, and compare our results with other excellent methods. The parameters are set as follows: $N = 7$, $D = 5$ and $M = 6$.

On the Helen dataset, to keep consistent with other methods, we use 68 landmarks to evaluate our algorithm. From Table 3, we can find that our algorithm achieves a satisfactory result. We believe this all due to the effectiveness of the LPF and the high performance of federated models.

On the 300-W dataset, Table 4 shows the experimental results of our and the competitors' methods. We can see the superiority of our method in the

Table 2. Runtime (in FPS) on 300-W. Our parameter T is set to 2, and the results of other approaches are quoted from the original theses.

Method	CFSS [31]	CFAN [28]	TCDCN [29]	SDM [26]	RCPR [5]	ESR [6]	LBF [21]	Proposed
FPS	25	44	56	70	80	120	320	356

Table 3. Mean errors (percent) on Helen dataset (68 landmarks)

Method	RCPR [5]	SDM [26]	CFAN [28]	CDM [27]	GN-DPM [25]	CFSS [31]	TCDCN [29]	Proposed
Error	5.93	5.50	5.53	9.90	5.69	4.63	4.60	4.98

Table 4. Mean errors (percent) on 300-W dataset (68 landmarks)

Method	Common subset	Challenging subset	Fullset	FPS
CDM [27]	10.10	19.54	11.94	-
DRMF [1]	6.65	19.79	9.22	-
RCPR [5]	6.18	17.26	8.35	80
GN-DPM [25]	5.78	-	-	-
CFAN [28]	5.50	16.78	7.69	44
ESR [6]	5.28	17.00	7.58	120
SDM [26]	5.57	15.40	7.50	70
ERT [14]	-	-	6.40	**1000**
LBF [21]	4.95	11.98	6.32	320
CFSS [31]	4.73	9.98	5.76	25
TCDCN [30]	4.80	8.60	5.54	56
Proposed	**4.61**	**8.38**	**5.35**	33

Fig. 5. Example alignment results on 300-W. The first row shows the challenging sets, the second row shows the Helen dataset of common sets, and the last row shows the LFPW dataset of common sets.

challenging subset as well as the common subset and fullset. As a result of the mechanism of combining various convergent models to predict the final shapes, the proposed method is imperfect relative to other methods in term of speed. Exemplary alignment results of our method are depicted in Fig. 5.

We provide a demo of our method at https://pan.baidu.com/s/1hsqjZqW.

5   Conclusion

In this paper, we propose a novel local probabilistic features based method for face alignment, under cascaded framework. The local probabilistic features contribute to modelling the probability of a test sample reaching each leaf node. This makes the prediction more realistic and theoretical. The cascade framework also obviously enhances the performance of our experiments. By combining various convergent models to overcome the instability of a single one, the regression accuracy of our method is superior to state-of-the-art methods. We demonstrate the efficiency and accuracy of the proposed method on two classical face alignment datasets. Furthermore, it is worth applying the local probabilistic features to many regression problems.

Acknowledgements. This work is supported by the National Natural Science Foundation of China (No. 61472393, No. 61572450 and No. 61303150), the Fundamental Research Funds for the Central Universities (WK2350000002).

References

1. Asthana, A., Zafeiriou, S., Cheng, S., Pantic, M.: Robust discriminative response map fitting with constrained local models, vol. 9, no. 4, pp. 3444–3451 (2013)
2. Belhumeur, P.N., Jacobs, D.W., Kriegman, D.J., Kumar, N.: Localizing parts of faces using a consensus of exemplars. In: IEEE Conference on Computer Vision and Pattern Recognition, pp. 545–552 (2011)
3. Bosch, A., Zisserman, A., Munoz, X.: Image classification using random forests and ferns. In: IEEE International Conference on Computer Vision, pp. 1–8 (2007)

4. Breiman, L.: Random forests. Mach. Learn. **45**(1), 5–32 (2001)
5. Burgos-Artizzu, X.P., Perona, P., Dollar, P.: Robust face landmark estimation under occlusion. In: IEEE International Conference on Computer Vision, pp. 1513–1520 (2013)
6. Cao, X., Wei, Y., Wen, F., Sun, J.: Face alignment by explicit shape regression. Int. J. Comput. Vis. **107**(2), 177–190 (2014)
7. Cootes, T.F., Edwards, G.J., Taylor, C.J.: Active appearance models. IEEE Trans. Patt. Anal. Mach. Intell. **23**(6), 681–685 (2001)
8. Cootes, T.F., Taylor, C.J., Cooper, D.H., Graham, J.: Active shape models-their training and application. Comput. Vis. Image Underst. **61**(1), 38–59 (1995)
9. Cristinacce, D., Cootes, T.F.: Feature detection and tracking with constrained local models. In: 2006 British Machine Vision Conference, Edinburgh, UK, September, pp. 929–938 (2006)
10. Dantone, M., Gall, J., Fanelli, G., Van Gool, L.: Real-time facial feature detection using conditional regression forests. In: IEEE Conference on Computer Vision and Pattern Recognition, pp. 2578–2585 (2012)
11. Dollar, P., Welinder, P., Perona, P.: Cascaded pose regression, vol. 238, no. 6, pp. 1078–1085. IEEE (2010)
12. Fan, R.E., Chang, K.W., Hsieh, C.J., Wang, X.R., Lin, C.J.: Liblinear: a library for large linear classification. J. Mach. Learn. Res. **9**, 1871–1874 (2008)
13. Huang, Z., Zhao, X., Shan, S., Wang, R., Chen, X.: Coupling alignments with recognition for still-to-video face recognition. In: IEEE International Conference on Computer Vision, pp. 3296–3303 (2013)
14. Kazemi, V., Sullivan, J.: One millisecond face alignment with an ensemble of regression trees. In: Computer Vision and Pattern Recognition, pp. 1867–1874 (2014)
15. Kumar, N., Belhumeur, P., Nayar, S.: FaceTracer: a search engine for large collections of images with faces. In: Forsyth, D., Torr, P., Zisserman, A. (eds.) ECCV 2008. LNCS, vol. 5305, pp. 340–353. Springer, Heidelberg (2008). https://doi.org/10.1007/978-3-540-88693-8_25
16. Le, V., Brandt, J., Lin, Z., Bourdev, L., Huang, T.S.: Interactive facial feature localization. In: Fitzgibbon, A., Lazebnik, S., Perona, P., Sato, Y., Schmid, C. (eds.) ECCV 2012. LNCS, vol. 7574, pp. 679–692. Springer, Heidelberg (2012). https://doi.org/10.1007/978-3-642-33712-3_49
17. Lu, C., Tang, X.: Surpassing human-level face verification performance on LRW with Gaussian face. Computer Science (2014)
18. Luo, C., Jiang, C., Yu, J., Wang, Z.: Expressive facial animation from videos. In: IEEE International Conference on Image Processing, pp. 4617–4621 (2014)
19. Messer, K., Matas, J., Kittler, J., Jonsson, K., Luettin, J., Maitre, G.: XM2VTSDB: the extended M2VTS database. In: Proceedings of the Second International Conference on Audio- and Video-Based Biometric Person Authentication, pp. 72–77 (2000)
20. Ramanan, D., Zhu, X.: Face detection, pose estimation, and landmark localization in the wild. In: Computer Vision and Pattern Recognition, pp. 2879–2886 (2012)
21. Ren, S., Cao, X., Wei, Y., Sun, J.: Face alignment at 3000 fps via regressing local binary features. IEEE Trans. Image Process. **25**(3), 1685–1692 (2014)
22. Sagonas, C., Tzimiropoulos, G., Zafeiriou, S., Pantic, M.: A semi-automatic methodology for facial landmark annotation. In: IEEE Conference on Computer Vision and Pattern Recognition Workshops, pp. 896–903 (2013)
23. Schölkopf, B., Platt, J., Hofmann, T.: Fast discriminative visual codebooks using randomized clustering forests. In: NIPS, pp. 985–992 (2007)

24. Sun, Y., Wang, X., Tang, X.: Deep convolutional network cascade for facial point detection, vol. 9, no. 4, pp. 3476–3483 (2013)
25. Tzimiropoulos, G., Pantic, M.: Gauss-Newton deformable part models for face alignment in-the-wild. In: 2014 IEEE Conference on Computer Vision and Pattern Recognition (CVPR), pp. 1851–1858 (2014)
26. Xiong, X., Torre, F.D.L.: Supervised descent method and its applications to face alignment. In: Computer Vision and Pattern Recognition, pp. 532–539 (2013)
27. Yu, X., Huang, J., Zhang, S., Yan, W., Metaxas, D.N.: Pose-free facial landmark fitting via optimized part mixtures and cascaded deformable shape model. In: IEEE Transactions on Software Engineering, pp. 1944–1951 (2013)
28. Zhang, J., Shan, S., Kan, M., Chen, X.: Coarse-to-fine auto-encoder networks (CFAN) for real-time face alignment. In: Fleet, D., Pajdla, T., Schiele, B., Tuytelaars, T. (eds.) ECCV 2014. LNCS, vol. 8690, pp. 1–16. Springer, Cham (2014). https://doi.org/10.1007/978-3-319-10605-2_1
29. Zhang, Z., Luo, P., Loy, C.C., Tang, X.: Facial landmark detection by deep multi-task learning. In: Fleet, D., Pajdla, T., Schiele, B., Tuytelaars, T. (eds.) ECCV 2014. LNCS, vol. 8694, pp. 94–108. Springer, Cham (2014). https://doi.org/10.1007/978-3-319-10599-4_7
30. Zhang, Z., Luo, P., Chen, C.L., Tang, X.: Learning deep representation for face alignment with auxiliary attributes. IEEE Trans. Patt. Anal. Mach. Intell. **38**(5), 918 (2016)
31. Zhu, S., Li, C., Chen, C.L., Tang, X.: Face alignment by coarse-to-fine shape searching. In: CVPR, pp. 4998–5006 (2015)

Multi-modal Emotion Recognition with Temporal-Band Attention Based on LSTM-RNN

Jiamin Liu[1]([✉]), Yuanqi Su[2], and Yuehu Liu[1,3]

[1] Institute of Artificial Intelligence and Robotics, Xi'an Jiaotong University,
Xi'an, China
ljm.168@stu.xjtu.edu.cn, liuyh@mail.xjtu.edu.cn
[2] Department of Computer Science and Technology, Xi'an Jiaotong University,
Xi'an, China
yuanqisu@mail.xjtu.edu.cn
[3] Shaanxi Key Laboratory of Digital Technology and Intelligent System,
Xi'an, China

Abstract. Emotion recognition is a key problem in Human-Computer Interaction (HCI). The multi-modal emotion recognition was discussed based on untrimmed visual signals and EEG signals in this paper. We propose a model with two attention mechanisms based on multi-layer Long short-term memory recurrent neural network (LSTM-RNN) for emotion recognition, which combines temporal attention and band attention. At each time step, the LSTM-RNN takes the video and EEG slice as inputs and generate representations of two signals, which are fed into a multi-modal fusion unit. Based on the fusion, our network predicts the emotion label and the next time slice for analyzing. Within the process, the model applies different levels of attention to different frequency bands of EEG signals through the band attention. With the temporal attention, it determines where to analyze next signal in order to suppress the redundant information for recognition. Experiments on Mahnob-HCI database demonstrate the encouraging results; the proposed method achieves higher accuracy and boosts the computational efficiency.

Keywords: Emotion recognition · LSTM-RNN · Temporal attention
Band attention · Multi-modal fusion

1 Introduction

Emotions are the short-lived human affective phenomena that are elicited as a result of stimuli [3]. Recently, with the development of HCI technologies, automatic emotion recognition becomes available. However, the results show that accuracy or efficiency of existing methods still need for improvement. Emotion recognition can be implemented based on the emotional data from visual

© Springer International Publishing AG, part of Springer Nature 2018
B. Zeng et al. (Eds.): PCM 2017, LNCS 10735, pp. 194–204, 2018.
https://doi.org/10.1007/978-3-319-77380-3_19

(e.g. video), audio (e.g. speech) or physiological channel (e.g. heart rate and EEG signals). Comparing with the uni-modal method, the multi-modal method which utilizes data from different modalities can benefit from each other [1]. However, many existing methods for multi-modal recognition lack efficiency and accuracy, when they deal with the raw, untrimmed emotional data (e.g. raw videos and speeches of subjects) [14,17,18].

In this paper, the proposed model aims to improve both accuracy and efficiency for multi-modal emotion recognition. We consider expression emotions extracted from videos and neural emotions taken from EEG signals. Additionally, the emotions are represented as discrete labels in the arousal (calm vs. excited) and valence (negative vs. positive) space respectively [10].

There are two main challenges in our work. The first one arises from the representation of EEG signals. The ref. [2] has demonstrated that the raw EEG signals could be transformed into a sequence of images on three frequency bands of brain wave, i.e. the α wave, β wave and θ wave separately. In this way, transforming EEG data into "video" data based on spatial information simplifies the process to generate and combine the feature of EEG data and video data. However, there is no work focusing on applying different weights to different critical frequency bands based on previous data/information. To effectively utilize EEG signals, we consider this problem while proposing the band attention.

Secondly, in the field of emotion recognition, it is difficult to rapidly localize the useful information in the untrimmed emotional data which have a large portion of redundant information. For instance, in a 2-min video recording the spontaneous response of a man watching a funny video, there is only around 10-s in which the man is laughing. Accordingly, most of frames in this video are useless for recognition and reduce efficiency. Most previous works [9,14,17,18] run models exhaustively over the whole time-series. Thus, it is hard to achieve both high accuracy and efficiency. In this paper, we introduce a temporal attention mechanism which learns to jump to the next time point for analysis. This mechanism successfully reduces the computational load comparing with the existing ones.

Driven by above challenges, we propose a multi-layer LSTM-RNN based model with two attention mechanisms. The model takes emotional data of both modalities as inputs and automatically outputs emotion prediction. At each time step, the model first employs VGG-16 network to extract features from inputs. It's worth noting that while processing the EEG signals, the proposed model applies different attentions to different frequency bands by using the band attention. Then, the multi-layer LSTM-RNN takes features from both modalities as inputs and outputs the hidden state. With the hidden state from LSTM-RNN, the model then determines the next frame to be analyzed by using the temporal attention. At the final time step, a emotion prediction is given by considering temporally accumulated knowledge from LSTM-RNN.

In summary, the main contributions of this paper are three-fold.

- We propose a novel multi-layer LSTM-RNN based model with two attention mechanisms, which achieves high accuracy and boost the computational efficiency of emotion recognition.

- We introduce a band attention mechanism which can dynamically assign different attentions to different frequency bands of EEG signals at each time step for effectively utilizing EEG signals.
- We design a temporal attention that can directly skip the redundant information in the emotional data for boosting the efficiency.

2   Related Work

There are extensive literatures, addressing the problem of emotion recognition [5,7,9]. We will review the works that are relevant to our research in the following part.

2.1   Multi-modal Emotion Recognition

Recently, due to the excellent performance of deep learning approaches, a lot of works for multi-modal emotion recognition have emerged to use the Deep Neural Network (DNN), like the Convolutional Neural Network (CNN) [2], Deep Belief Network (DBN) [19] and LSTM-RNN [5]. He et al. [5] propose a fully automatic way which is based on LSTM-RNN model with decision-level fusion mechanism. It demonstrates that LSTM-RNN exceeded non-sequential models for emotion recognition by analyzing sequential emotional data.

All the mentioned models directly analyze the raw emotional data exhaustively which include a large portion of redundant information. To exclude the redundant information, the "peak frames" are defined which are vital for the emotion recognition. In order to only explore peak frames, some researchers have proposed the three-phase model. In [18], Zhalehpour et al. utilize maximum dissimilarity-based method to extract peak frames from the videos. Then the model implements the emotion recognition separately for videos and speeches. Afterwards, the model fuses the audio and visual modality in decision-level and gives the prediction.

However, a notable fact is that all of the methods mentioned is by scanning through a complete sequence of data (including the methods of analyzing peak frames which scan the whole data whiling picking peak frames). In contrast, our model is designed to directly skip the redundant information.

2.2   Transformation of EEG Signals

There are many existing works for emotion recognition based on EEG signals. Liu et al. [11] employ fractal dimension based method for real-time emotion recognition. Zheng et al. [19] introduce DBN for EEG-based emotion recognition. In [2], Bashivan et al. have demonstrated that the raw EEG time series signals could be transformed into a sequence of images on three frequency bands of brain wave, i.e. α wave, β wave and θ wave separately. In this way, transforming EEG-based emotion recognition into computer vision simplifies the process and generates the generalized features.

However, there is no work focusing on dynamically assigning different attentions to different critical frequency bands. In order to effectively utilize EEG signals, we consider this problem while designing our model.

2.3 Attention Mechanisms

Recently, attention mechanisms have been introduced to neural network, which influences the area of deep learning. These mechanisms permit the system to pay attention to the pertinent piece of information, rather than all of the information. By far, attention mechanisms are broadly utilized in neural machine translation [12], image caption [16] and action recognition [13,15]. [13] propose a visual attention based method which applies different attentions on spatial regions of images. This method can also be used for analyzing the facial expressions.

3   Method

As shown in Fig. 1, the overall network consists of three subnetworks: visual subnetwork, EEG signals subnetwork and LSTM-RNN subnetwork. The band attention module is included in EEG signals subnetwork and the temporal attention module is used in the LSTM-RNN subnetwork. In this paper, there are two such networks used for arousal and valence of emotion, respectively.

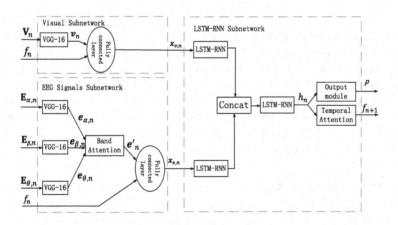

Fig. 1. The proposed network for multi-modal emotion recognition.

3.1   Visual Subnetwork

As shown in Fig. 1, the visual subnetwork includes a VGG-16 network and a fully connected layer with the learnable parameters $\boldsymbol{\theta}_v$. At each time step n, there are two inputs for the visual subnetwork. The first one is the normalized temporal location of current frame $f_n \in [0,1]$ indicating its location in the video. The location indexes of the frames are normalized to $[0, 1]$. The second input is an image $\mathbf{V}_n \in \mathbb{R}^{256 \times 256}$ of cropped face in the video frame indexed by f_n. In this paper, we always resize $\mathbf{V}_n$ into size 265×256 and extract a 4096-dimensional FC-7 layer feature $\mathbf{v}_n \in \mathbb{R}^{4096}$ of $\mathbf{V}_n$ from the VGG-16 network. Next, we combine $\mathbf{v}_n$ and f_n with the fully connected layer. Then we can obtain a 1024-dimensional vector $\mathbf{x}_{v,n} \epsilon \mathbb{R}^{1024}$ as the output of this subnetwork.

3.2   EEG Signals Subnetwork

As the EEG signals subnetwork, its consists of three VGG-16 networks with sharing weights, the band attention module and a fully connected layer.

At each time step n, the inputs of the EEG signals subnetwork are divided into two parts. The first part is the normalized temporal location f_n. The second part is three channels of images $\mathbf{E}_{\alpha,n}, \mathbf{E}_{\beta,n}, \mathbf{E}_{\theta,n} \in \mathbb{R}^{256 \times 256}$ related to f_n, where $\mathbf{E}_{\alpha,n}, \mathbf{E}_{\beta,n}, \mathbf{E}_{\theta,n}$ denote the images on three frequency bands of brain wave, i.e. α wave, β wave and θ wave transformed from the raw EEG time-series signals.

In detail, we extract three 4096-dimensional FC-7 layer feature vectors $\mathbf{e}_{\alpha,n}$, $\mathbf{e}_{\beta,n}$, $\mathbf{e}_{\theta,n} \in \mathbb{R}^{4096}$ of $\mathbf{E}_{\alpha,n}, \mathbf{E}_{\beta,n}, \mathbf{E}_{\theta,n}$ from the VGG-16 networks respectively. Next, we calculate a weighted summation $\mathbf{e}'_n \in \mathbb{R}^{4096}$ as the result of the band attention module. Subsequently, we combine $\mathbf{e}'_n$ and f_n with the fully connected layer. Finally, we obtain a 1024-dimensional vector $\mathbf{x}_{e,n} \epsilon \mathbb{R}^{1024}$ as the output.

We will separately explain the transformation of EEG time-series signals and the band attention module in the following parts.

Transformation of EEG Signals. We adopted the method of [2] which obtain image sequences from the raw EEG time-series. We first divide each EEG time-series signals of each group into T segments. Each segment lasts 0.125 s in order to synchronize with the 8 fps video. Then, during the tth segment, we extract spectral power within three prominent frequency bands for 16 electrodes on scalp and use these to form topographical images. Afterwards, the three channels of images $\mathbf{E}_{\alpha,t}$, $\mathbf{E}_{\beta,t}$, $\mathbf{E}_{\theta,t}$ are obtained that are the three inputs of the EEG signal subnetwork where $t = Tf_n$.

Band Attention Module. At each time step n, the band attention module is used for combining $\mathbf{e}_{\alpha,n}, \mathbf{e}_{\beta,n}, \mathbf{e}_{\theta,n}$ with different attentions.

The weights $\boldsymbol{\theta}_{en} = (\theta_{en,1}, \theta_{en,2}, \theta_{en,3})$ is derived from softmax over the three bands. They assign different levels of attention to different frequency bands. $\theta_{en,1}, \theta_{en,2}, \theta_{en,3}$ correspond to the weights for α wave, β wave and θ wave respectively.

$$\theta_{en,i} = \frac{\exp\left(\mathbf{W}_{h,i}\boldsymbol{h}_{n-1} + b_{h,i}\right)}{\sum_{j=1}^{3} \exp\left(\mathbf{W}_{h,j}\boldsymbol{h}_{n-1} + b_{h,j}\right)} \qquad i = 1, 2, 3 \qquad (1)$$

Where $\mathbf{W}_{h,i}$ are the learnable weights matrixes to the ith weight, $b_{h,i}$ is the bias parameter to the ith weight. $\boldsymbol{h}_{n-1} \in \mathbb{R}^{2048}$ represents the hidden state of the multi-layer LSTM-RNN from last time step $n - 1$. The output of the band attention module $\mathbf{e}'_n \in \mathbb{R}^{4096}$ is computed by,

$$\mathbf{e}'_n = \mathbf{e}_{\alpha,n}\theta_{en,1} + \mathbf{e}_{\beta,n}\theta_{en,2} + \mathbf{e}_{\theta,n}\theta_{en,3} \tag{2}$$

3.3 LSTM-RNN Subnetwork

The LSTM-RNN subnetwork consists of a multi-layer LSTM-RNN, the prediction module and the temporal attention module. At each time step n, this subnetwork takes $\mathbf{x}_{v,n}$ and $\mathbf{x}_{e,n}$ as inputs. It is used for multi-modal fusion in middle level and calculating the frame f_{n+1} to be analyzed in the next time step. At the final time step N, it is used for computing the emotion prediction $\boldsymbol{p}$.

Multi-layer LSTM-RNN. There are two LSTM-RNN layers which are capable of remembering values for either long or short durations of time. In Fig. 1, the LSTM-RNN layers on the left of this subnetwork which share weights are deemed as the first layer. The first layer of multi-layer LSTM-RNN has 1024 units. The second layer of the multi-layer LSTM-RNN has 2048 units. At each time step n, two 1024-dimensional hidden states of the first-layer LSTM-RNN are concatenated into a 2048-dimensional vector. The 2048-dimensional vector is then fed into the second layer of multi-layer LSTM-RNN with 2048 units. This multi-layer LSTM-RNN outputs the hidden state $\boldsymbol{h}_n \in \mathbb{R}^{2048}$.

Temporal Attention Module. The temporal attention module is implemented by a fully connected layer. At each time step n, given the $\boldsymbol{h}_n$ from multi-layer LSTM-RNN, it can calculate the temporal location of the next frame $f_{n+1} \in [0, 1]$ to be analyzed.

$$f_{n+1} = \mathbf{W}_{tem}\boldsymbol{h}_n + b_{tem} \tag{3}$$

Where $\mathbf{W}_{tem}$ and b_{tem} are the learnable weights matrixes and bias parameter of the fully connected layer respectively.

Prediction Module. The prediction module mainly consists of two fully connected layers. The first fully connected layer is followed by a ReLU nonlinearity. The second fully connected layer is followed by a softmax function. At the final time step N, given the hidden state $\boldsymbol{h}_N$, the prediction is formulated as $\boldsymbol{p} = (p_1, ..., p_C)^T$. The predicted probability of arousal or valence being the kth class is $p_k = p\left(C_k | \boldsymbol{h}_N\right)$ with $k = 1, ..., C$, which is calculated through this module. The C_k means that the prediction is belong to the C_k class. In our work, we divided the arousal and valence of emotions into nine classes respectively.

3.4 Training of Network

Due to the mutual effect among three subnetworks and the non-differentiability of f_{n+1}, it is challenging to train the whole network.

Loss Function. We train the prediction p with Back propagation through time (BPTT). Given a training sample, the network aims to minimize the following regularized loss function included cross-entropy function and regularized item. The regularized item is formulated to equally focus on three bands.

$$L = - \sum_{k=1}^{C} (y_k \log p_k + (1 - y_k) \log (1 - p_k)) + \gamma \sum_{j=1}^{3} \left(1 - \frac{\sum_{n=1}^{N} \theta_{en,j}}{N} \right)^2 \quad (4)$$

Where $\boldsymbol{y} = (y_1, ..., y_C)^T$ with $k = 1, ..., C$ denotes the ground truth label which is a one-hot encoding. p_k means the predicted probability being the kth class given the sample of sequential emotional data. γ is a balance factor. In this paper, we use $\gamma = 0.02$.

Reward Function. Due to non-differentiable output f_{n+1} which has to resort to some form of sampling during the training process, we introduce deep reinforcement learning which is based on Monte-Carlo policy gradient [4]. The policies aim to maximize the classification rate and F1-score. Therefore, we design a reward function that leads to overall maximization of the true positive while minimizing the false negative and false positive.

$$R = \lambda_{tp} TP + \lambda_{fp} FP + \lambda_{fn} FN \quad (5)$$

where TP, FP, FN are the number of true positive, false positive and false negative respectively. Additionally, we suppose $\lambda_{tp}(> 0)$, $\lambda_{fp}(< 0)$ and $\lambda_{fn}(< 0)$ as the weights for TP, FP and FN respectively. Throughout the paper, we use $\lambda_{tp} = 1$, $\lambda_{fp} = -0.5$ and $\lambda_{fn} = -5$.

Training Scheme. In order to efficiently train the overall network, we divided the process of training into three steps.

The first step is to pre-train the visual subnetwork. The VGG-16 network in this subnetwork has been fine-tuned on the MAHNOB-HCI dataset. All the VGG-16 parts in our work will be fixed after and just used for extracting FC-7 layer features. We train the visual subnetwork followed by an auxiliary network which has the same architecture with the LSTM-RNN subnetwork. In the auxiliary network, we set a multi-layer LSTM-RNN with 1024 units in each layer. The auxiliary network is mainly used for extracting the temporal features. In this case, there is no regularized item in loss function.

The second step is to pre-train the EEG signals subnetwork. The fine-tuned VGG-16 networks extract the FC7-layer features. An auxiliary network with the same architecture of the LSTM-RNN subnetwork is added on top of it. The multi-layer LSTM-RNN in the auxiliary network has 1024 units in each layer.

The third step is to train the LSTM-RNN subnetwork. We fix both visual and EEG signals subnetworks and delete two auxiliary networks. The LSTM-RNN takes the outputs from two pre-trained subnetworks as inputs. Finally, the whole network is obtained.

4 Experiment

4.1 Dataset

We conduct our experiments on the MAHNOB-HCI dataset [14] which contains 527 groups of completed, untrimmed video, audio and EEG signals collected from 27 participants watching 20 video clips. After watching each video, the participants used Self-Assessment Manikins (SAM) for reporting their arousal, valence, control on discrete label which is from 1 to 9. We focus on predicting the arousal and valence of emotions.

4.2 Implementation Details

For the training of network, we utilize Adam optimization [8] for 5 epochs over the train-set. We suppose the value of dropout as 0.5 to overcome overfitting and define the batch size as 12. Meanwhile, we fix the max time step as 30. To adapt the dataset to our model, the video is downsampled to 8 fps and processed in sequences of 300 frames. We crop faces in videos and resize these to size 256×256. The processing of EEG-signals is mentioned in Sect. 3.2. We randomly divided the dataset into three parts, the 20 participants for training, 4 participants for validation and 3 participants for testing.

4.3 Experimental Results

Representation of Two Attention Mechanisms. We visualize the learned band and temporal attention for intuitively demonstrating the performance of the introduction of two attention mechanisms. We just pick up four time steps to show the policy of temporal attention.

As shown in Fig. 2, our model can rapidly and precisely locate the start of "peak frames" after 10 time steps and frequently analyze peak frames. On the

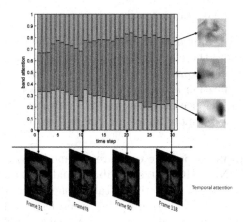

Fig. 2. Presentation of the band attention weights on EEG signals and the temporal attention policy for a "nervous" man with arousal = 7. (Color figure online)

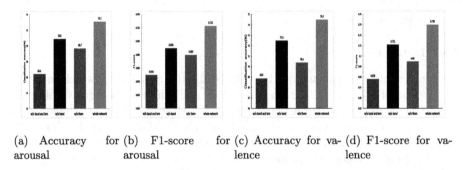

(a) Accuracy for arousal   (b) F1-score for arousal   (c) Accuracy for valence   (d) F1-score for valence

Fig. 3. Classification accuracy and F1-scores for arousal and valence.

right of Fig. 2, the three images are transformed from EEG signals on three frequency bands. On the top of Fig. 2, the green, red and blue bars at each time denotes the weights which are applied on α wave, β wave and θ wave respectively. There is an interesting phenomenon. It seems that as the man becomes more and more nervous, the weights on β wave is growing, which shows the β wave dominates the emotions if human beings is in mental stress with high arousal.

Ablation Studies. For the quantitative analysis of different components in our model, we conduct ablation experiments with different settings as follows.

- vis-EEG-LSTM(w/o band and temp): The visual subnetwork, the EEG signals subnetworks without band attention module and the LSTM-RNN subnetwork without temporal attention moudule.
- vis-EEG-LSTM(w/o band): The visual subnetwork, the EEG signals subnetworks without band attention module and the LSTM-RNN subnetwork.
- vis-EEG-LSTM(w/o temporal): The visual subnetwork, the EEG signals subnetworks and the LSTM-RNN subnetwork without temporal attention module.
- vis-EEG-LSTM: The overall network.

As shown in Fig. 3, comparing with the result of the network without band and temporal attention, the classification accuracy and F1-score of the overall network are respectively improved by 6.7% and 0.07 for arousal classification. Meanwhile, the classification accuracy and F1-score are respectively improved by 5.6% and 0.05 for valence classification. Furthermore, it is shows that the temporal attention plays a more important role for improving the performance.

Performance Comparisons. We compare our model with a state-of-the-art methods on the MAHNOB-HCI dataset. Tables 1 and 2 list the results in classification accuracy and F1-score respectively. Table 1 shows that our model achieves 73.1% and 74.5% classification accuracy for arousal and valence classification respectively. Table 2 illustrates that our model achieves 0.723 and 0.730 F1-score for arousal and valence classification respectively. Especially, the method of baseline employs eye gaze data in video with high performance for valence, but, is ineffective for arousal. In general, our model outperforms others in emotion recognition. Furthermore, it only runs over the 10% of the emotional data with higher efficiency.

Table 1. Comparison for classification accuracy(%)

Method	Arousal	Valence
Baseline [14]	67.7	76.1
Koelstra et al. [9]	72.5	73.0
Huang et al. [6]	63.2	66.3
Our model	73.1	74.5

Table 2. Comparison for F1-Score

Method	Arousal	Valence
Baseline [14]	0.620	0.740
Koelstra et al. [9]	0.709	0.718
Our model	0.723	0.730

5   Conclusion

We propose a multi-layer LSTM-RNN based model with two attention mechanisms for multi-modal emotion recognition, using the untrimmed videos and EEG-signals. To effectively utilize EEG signals, we transform the EEG time-series signals into the sequences of images and introduce the band attention mechanism for dynamically assigning the different attentions to different frequency bands of EEG signals. To boost the efficiency of our model, we introduce the temporal attention mechanism to automatically skip the redundant information of the emotional data. To fuse the information from two modalities in middle-level, we build our model based on a multi-layer LSTM-RNN. The experimental results show the high accuracy and efficiency of the proposed model.

Acknowledgements. This work has been funded by National Natural Science Foundation of China (Grant No. 91520301).

References

1. Atrey, P.K., Hossain, M.A., El Saddik, A., Kankanhalli, M.S.: Multimodal fusion for multimedia analysis: a survey. Multimed. Syst. **16**(6), 345–379 (2010)
2. Bashivan, P., Rish, I., Yeasin, M., Codella, N.: Learning representations from EEG with deep recurrent-convolutional neural networks. arXiv preprint arXiv:1511.06448 (2015)

3. Bradley, M.M., Lang, P.J.: Measuring emotion: the self-assessment manikin and the semantic differential. J. Behav. Ther. Exp. Psychiatry **25**(1), 49–59 (1994)
4. Deisenroth, M.P., Neumann, G., Peters, J.: A survey on policy search for robotics. Found. Trends Robot. **2**(1–2), 1–142 (2013)
5. He, L., Jiang, D., Yang, L., Pei, E., Wu, P., Sahli, H.: Multimodal affective dimension prediction using deep bidirectional long short-term memory recurrent neural networks. In: International Workshop on Audio/Visual Emotion Challenge, pp. 73–80 (2015)
6. Huang, X., Kortelainen, J., Zhao, G., Li, X., Moilanen, A., Seppänen, T., Pietikäinen, M.: Multi-modal emotion analysis from facial expressions and electroencephalogram. Comput. Vis. Image Underst. **147**, 114–124 (2016)
7. Kim, Y., Lee, H., Provost, E.M.: Deep learning for robust feature generation in audiovisual emotion recognition. In: IEEE International Conference on Acoustics, Speech and Signal Processing, pp. 3687–3691. IEEE (2013)
8. Kingma, D.P., Ba, J.: Adam: A method for stochastic optimization. arXiv preprint arXiv:1412.6980 (2014)
9. Koelstra, S., Patras, I.: Fusion of facial expressions and EEG for implicit affective tagging. Image Vis. Comput. **31**(2), 164–174 (2013)
10. Levenson, R.W.: The intrapersonal functions of emotion. Cogn. Emot. **13**(5), 481–504 (1999)
11. Liu, Y., Sourina, O., Nguyen, M.K.: Real-time EEG-based emotion recognition and its applications. In: Gavrilova, M.L., Tan, C.J.K., Sourin, A., Sourina, O. (eds.) Transactions on Computational Science XII. LNCS, vol. 6670, pp. 256–277. Springer, Heidelberg (2011). https://doi.org/10.1007/978-3-642-22336-5_13
12. Luong, M.T., Pham, H., Manning, C.D.: Effective approaches to attention-based neural machine translation. arXiv preprint arXiv:1508.04025 (2015)
13. Sharma, S., Kiros, R., Salakhutdinov, R.: Action recognition using visual attention. arXiv preprint arXiv:1511.04119 (2015)
14. Soleymani, M., Lichtenauer, J., Pun, T., Pantic, M.: A multi-modal affective database for affect recognition and implicit tagging. IEEE Trans. Affect. Comput. **3**, 42–55 (2012)
15. Song, S., Lan, C., Xing, J., Zeng, W., Liu, J.: An end-to-end spatio-temporal attention model for human action recognition from skeleton data. arXiv preprint arXiv:1611.06067 (2016)
16. Xu, K., Ba, J., Kiros, R., Cho, K., Courville, A., Salakhutdinov, R., Zemel, R., Bengio, Y.: Show, attend and tell: Neural image caption generation with visual attention. In: International Conference on Machine Learning, pp. 2048–2057 (2015)
17. Yin, Z., Zhao, M., Wang, Y., Yang, J., Zhang, J.: Recognition of emotions using multimodal physiological signals and an ensemble deep learning model. Comput. Methods Programs Biomed. **140**, 93–110 (2016)
18. Zhalehpour, S., Akhtar, Z., Erdem, C.E.: Multimodal emotion recognition with automatic peak frame selection. In: IEEE International Symposium on Innovations in Intelligent Systems and Applications, pp. 116–121 (2014)
19. Zheng, W.L., Zhu, J.Y., Peng, Y., Lu, B.L.: EEG-based emotion classification using deep belief networks. In: IEEE International Conference on Multimedia and Expo, pp. 1–6 (2014)

Multimodal Fusion of Spatial-Temporal Features for Emotion Recognition in the Wild

Zuchen Wang and Yuchun Fang[(⊠)] [iD]

School of Computer Engineering and Science,
Shanghai University, Shanghai, China
wzuchen@t.shu.edu.cn, ycfang@shu.edu.cn

Abstract. Making the machine understand human emotion is a challenge to realize artificial intelligence. Considering the temporal correlation widely exists in the video, we present a multimodal fusion of spatial-temporal features system to recognize emotion. For the visual modality, the spatial-temporal features are extracted to represent the dynamic emotional variance along with the facial action in the video. The audio modality is utilized to assist the visual modality. A decision-level fusion approach is presented to make full use of the complementarity between visual modality and audio modality to boost the performance of the emotion recognition system. The experiments on a challenging dataset AFEW4.0 show that the proposed system achieves better generalization performance compared with other state-of-the-art methods.

Keywords: Emotion recognition · Multimodal fusion
Spatial-temporal features

1 Introduction

Recently, emotion recognition is becoming a hot topic in computer vision and artificial intelligence. Recognizing emotion from the video in the wild remains an ongoing challenge due to two reasons. First, it is hard to capture critical and subtle detail from the expression variance. Second, the expression is easily disturbed by the head poses, accessories, etc.

Since 2D convolutional neural networks (Conv2DNets) has made a brilliant achievement in feature extraction. Compared with hand-designed features, CNN can learn an effective representation from data. Zhao et al. [5] proposed Peak-Piloted Deep Network (PPDN) to recognize emotion from image sequences. But Conv2DNets can't learn temporal information from videos.

Recurrent neural network (RNN) can learn context semantic information from time-related data. Khorrami et al. [13] proved that the architecture of Conv2DNets +RNN is able to learn the temporal and spatial information from the video. Fan et al. [19] incorporated Conv2DNets into LSTM to recognize the emotion from videos. The gated recurrent unit (GRU) [20] is a gating mechanism in the RNN, which is widely adopted to process sequences into a fixed length vector representation. It has comparable performance with LSTM but has less parameters. We combine Conv2DNets and GRU to extract spatial-temporal information from the video.

© Springer International Publishing AG, part of Springer Nature 2018
B. Zeng et al. (Eds.): PCM 2017, LNCS 10735, pp. 205–214, 2018.
https://doi.org/10.1007/978-3-319-77380-3_20

3D convolutional neural network (Conv3DNet) is a useful feature learning machine that models appearance and motion simultaneously. The convolution and pooling operations in Conv3DNets are performed spatial-temporally while they are done only spatially in Conv2DNets. Compared with Conv3DNets, Conv2DNets+RNN only attains the temporal information via modeling the outputs of Conv2DNets. In [7], the success of Conv3DNets in action recognition, scene classification and object recognition has proved that it can learn robust spatial-temporal features from videos.

Assuming the features are not independent, it is essential to learn the complementary relationship between them to boost the accuracy and robustness through fusion. The fusion method can be divided into two categories: feature-level fusion and decision-level fusion. In the feature-level fusion case, the features are combined most commonly by simply concatenating and using the output for estimation. However, in general, this approach has a tendency to create very high dimensional feature vectors and further cause overfitting. The fusion in decision level is to find an optimal combination of the outputs of all classifiers. And it can be achieved in many ways, like average and random search. But they can't take full advantage of the complementarity. We present a new feature fusion method which makes full use of the complementarity to improve the system's robustness.

In this paper, a multimodal spatial-temporal features fusion system is proposed to recognize emotion from videos in the wild. We extract different spatial-temporal features to represent the emotional variation in videos from a variety of perspectives for the visual modality. Meanwhile, the audio modality is used to assist the visual modality. Then, the audio modality and visual modality are fused at the decision level to utilize the complementarity to boost the system's robustness. We also analyze the difficulty of emotion recognition in the wild from the aspect of social psychology.

2 Multimodal Fusion of Spatial-Temporal Features

2.1 Overview

In this work, a multimodal spatial-temporal fusion system is proposed to recognize emotion in the wild. The system is illustrated in Fig. 1. It contains visual and audio modality. For the visual modality, we utilize four different models to recognize emotion from the video. Specifically, Conv3DNets is employed to learn spatial-temporal representation of the video directly. The GRU is utilized to explore the temporal relationship from a series of spatial features which are learned from Conv2DNets. The LBPTOP feature is extracted from the video to represent the variation of the texture in the time and space domain. A facial motion information model is proposed to model the variation of the emotions along with the facial components. In addition, the audio modality is used to assist the visual modality. All the scores are fused at the decision level to boost the recognition rate. We will describe each phase in detail separately.

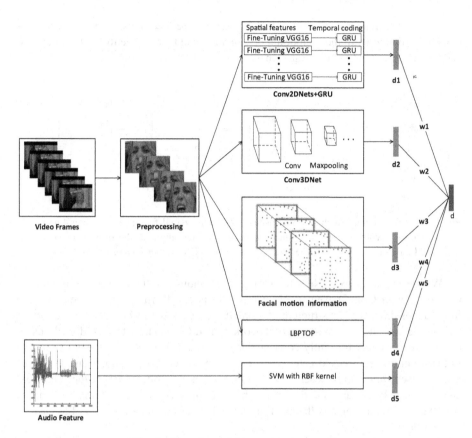

Fig. 1. Overview of the proposed approach

2.2 Visual Modality

We incorporate Conv2DNets into GRU to recognize emotion from the video. Specifically, we treat the Conv2DNets as the spatial feature extractor. And the GRU encodes the appearance features extracted by the Conv2DNets.

The architecture of the Conv2DNets+GRU is illustrated in Fig. 2. It is a challenge to train a complex Conv2DNets using a small amount of training data without over-fitting. Fortunately, Zhao et al. [5] showed that supervised fine-tuning with a relatively small dataset on a pre-trained network with a large image dataset of generic tasks can achieve a significant improvement in performance. Thus, we use auxiliary data to train our spatial feature extractor which is shown in the dashed box in Fig. 2. The VGG16 [14] serves as the base model of our spatial feature extractor. Owing to the limitation of the data amount, the last three fully-connected layers in VGG16 are replaced with two simple fully-connected layers. Based on the fact that the shallow layers learn the general features, while the deep layers learn the high-level semantic information. We fix the parameters of first three blocks and fine-tuning the rest. The output of the fc6 layer in spatial feature extractor is denoted as a spatial feature vector. As a result, a video can be represented by a set of feature vectors. We feed the spatial feature vectors to a GRU layer to learn the temporal representation and then utilize the softmax layer to classify the emotions, as illustrated in Fig. 2.

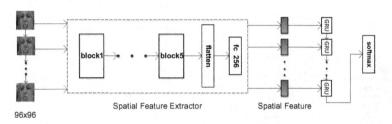

Fig. 2. The architecture of the Conv2DNets+GRU. The spatial feature extractor is fine-tuning on VGG16 [14] with the FER-2013 face database [6]. The output of the fully connected layer with 256 hidden units serves as the spatial feature. The GRU layer has 128 hidden units.

We design a Conv3DNets to learn the emotion-specific features from videos. Compared with Conv2DNets+GRU, Conv3DNets can learn spatial-temporal feature from videos directly. The structure of Conv3DNet is shown in Fig. 3. The network in the dashed box shows a pre-trained network named C3D [7]. Instead of directly using the feature extracted from fully-connected layer in the C3D to classify the emotions, we further train the features extracted from the conv5b layer. We do so because that there is a great semantic gap between action recognition and emotion recognition. Three 3D convolutional layers are added to learn the emotion-specific spatial-temporal feature. And then the feature map is flattened. In the end, a softmax layer is utilized to classify the emotions.

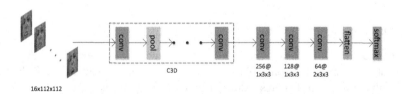

Fig. 3. The structure of Conv3DNets. The dashed box denotes a pre-trained model named C3D [7]. The symbol 256@1 × 3 × 3 denotes that a 3D convolutional layer which has 256 filters with the kernel size 1, 3, 3 on time, weight and height, respectively.

Local binary patterns from three orthogonal planes (LBPTOP) [8] is an extension of local binary patterns (LBP) in the temporal domain, generated by concatenating LBP on three orthogonal planes: XY, XT and YT. It is an efficient representation of dynamic texture and widely used in video analysis. In this work, the uniform LBP which is more robust and faster than LBP is used to encode a block to a vector to represent texture information. The video is divided into blocks on three orthogonal planes. And all the texture features extracted from each block volume are connected to one high dimensional vector to represent the dynamic texture features of a video.

Given a face image I, the facial shape s can be considered as a vector consists of x, y-coordinates of landmarks, i.e. $s = \{x_1, y_1, x_2, y_2, \ldots, x_n, y_n\}$, where n is the total number of landmark points in I. To capture accurate facial motion information, a facial landmark trajectory model is proposed to learn emotional variation along with the facial shape. 49 landmarks are provided by AFEW4.0 dataset and their locations are presented in Fig. 1. It is inappropriate to directly use the s as the shape feature because the landmarks in different images have different scales. Thus, the normalization method is performed according to Jung et al. [15]. Then, a Gradient Boosting Decision Tree (GBDT) is learned for emotion recognition.

2.3 Audio Modality

As well as facial expression, the auditory emotion recognition has become a hotspot in recent years. In this work, the audio modality is used to assist visual modality for emotion recognition. The audio feature is calculated using the OpenSmile toolkit [21]. The features include energy/spectral Low Level Descriptors (LLD) and voicing related LLD. More details about the features are described in [9, 10].

2.4 Decision-Level Fusion

A new decision-level fusion approach is proposed to make full use of the complementary information between visual and audio modality for achieving the optimal results. Assuming the output of the i-th decider is $d_i = [r_1, r_2, \ldots, r_N]^T$, where N is the number of samples. And r_j is the decision vector of the j-th sample, it can be formulated as $r_j = [p_1, p_2, \ldots, p_K]$, where p_k is the probability that a sample belongs to the k-th class. Then, the proposed fusion method can be achieved by optimizing the following function,

$$\text{argmax}_W \left(g \left(f \left(\sum\nolimits_{i=0}^{M} w_i d_i \right), L \right) \right) \text{ s.t. } \sum\nolimits_{i=0}^{N} w_i = 1, 0 < w_i < 1, \tag{1}$$

where M is the number of deciders, $W = [w_1, w_2, \ldots, w_M]$ is a weight vector and w_i controls the contribution of the i-th decider to the final result, $L = [l_1, l_2, \ldots, l_n]$ is the true label of all the samples, f is a function which map the probability to the related emotions and g is the cross-entropy cost function.

3 Experiments

3.1 AFEW4.0 Dataset

The Acted Facial Expression in The Wild (AFEW) 4.0 [11] dataset was established for the EmotiW2014. The AFEW4.0 dataset was collected from different movies showing close-to-real-world conditions [1]. It is divided into three subsets, Train, Validation and Test, and the number of three sets of emotion data are 578, 383 and 407, respectively. The task is to classify audio-video clip into one of seven emotion categories, i.e. angry, disgust, fear, happy, neutral, sad, and surprise. As the dataset is only available to the participants, we can only get the Train and Validation emotion data. Consequently, we report the recognition rate on Validation subset as our final emotion recognition result. And we also compare our results with some state-of-the-art approaches.

3.2 Implementation Details

The video can be viewed as a set of images and its frames are extracted by FFmpeg tools[1]. The histogram equalization is utilized to enhance the contrast of the frames. The face detector[2] is applied to filter the non-face images. 49 landmarks are labeled for the dataset as shown Fig. 1. We use a fixed length of frames to represent a video clip because the adjacent frames in a video clip have redundancy. A series of 16 frames is selected for each video clip by a stride which is decided by the total frames divided by 16. If a video clip does not have enough frames, we pad the last frame.

We use the FER-2013 face database [6] as auxiliary data to fine-tune the VGG16. The FER-2013 dataset contains 28709 training images, 3589 validate (public) images and 3589 test (private) images. The training images and validation images are used to fine-tune the VGG16 with verifying the performance on test images. We get 68.93% classification accuracy on test images of the FER-2013 dataset.

In the Conv2DNets+GRU, every frame is resized to 96×96. The 256 dimensional feature vector are extracted from the spatial feature extractor. Then a video clip can be represented by a 16×256 matrix. With the Conv2DNet+GRU, 45.01% classification accuracy is achieved on the validation set, and the confusion matrix is presented in Fig. 4a.

For the Conv3DNet, all face images are cropped to 112×112 followed [7]. The parameters of spatial feature extractor which is based on the C3D model can be seen from [7]. The feature map of the conv5b layer has a shape of $512 \times 2 \times 7 \times 7$. The feature maps are then further trained for attaining the emotion-specific features. We get 41.24% classification accuracy on validation set and draw confusion matrix in Fig. 4b.

Similar to the frames in the video, redundancies also exist in landmarks among the frames. Thus, we extract key landmarks in the same manner as the key frame extraction. After the normalization, a video clip can be represented by $16 \times 98 = 1568$ dimensions facial motion information. A Gradient Boosting Decision Tree (GBDT) is learned for emotion recognition. The facial motion information achieves 25.87% classification accuracy on validation set and the confusion matrix is drawn in Fig. 4c.

The LBPTOP feature we used is provided by the datasets. The 33.15% classification accuracy on the validation set are achieved in the baseline system [11] by performing SVM with RBF kernel on LBPTOP features. Ringeval et al. [12] improved the classification accuracy by tuning the parameters of SVM. Inspired by Ringeval et al. [12], the 39.35% classification accuracy is obtained by performing Logistic Regression on the LBPTOP features. The confusion matrix can be observed in Fig. 4d.

The 1582 dimensions of audio features are provided by the organizer of EmotiW2014. The baseline classification accuracy on validation is 26.10%.

---

[1] http://ffmpeg.org.

[2] https://github.com/ShiqiYu/libfacedetection.

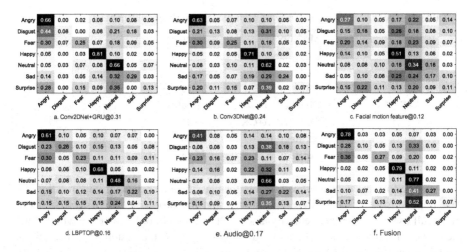

Fig. 4. The confusion matrix of each method on the validation set of AFEW4.0. And the decimal after @ is the contribution of each single model for the final fusion.

Comparing with the audio baseline, we get a little better classification accuracy 26.95%. The confusion matrix can be seen from Fig. 4e.

We apply the proposed decision-level fusion method on the decision level on the five models. The optimal classification accuracy on the validation set is 47.98% and the confusion matrix is shown in Fig. 4f.

3.3 Comparison Between Different Features

The classification accuracy of every feature is shown in Table 1. The classification accuracies of Conv3DNets and Conv2DNets+GRU are higher than that of LBPTOP, which indicates that the feature learned from the data are more robust than the hand-designed feature. It is surprising that the classification accuracy of the Conv2DNet+GRU is much higher than that of Conv3DNet. We think that although the Conv3DNet can learn the spatial-temporal feature directly, the Conv2DNet+GRU can also learn it in an indirect way. Moreover, the Conv3DNet needs more data to train. Both Conv3DNet and Conv2DNet+GRU utilize pre-trained model. The Conv2DNet +GRU exploits additional data to fine-tuning while the Conv3DNet does not. Besides, we also try to recognize emotion using Conv3DNet without pre-training, but achieve no effect.

It can be clearly seen that the classification accuracies of facial motion feature and audio feature are much lower than others. We think that the facial motion feature can only depicts the general variation of the facial shape due to the influence of the head poses, illumination, and occlusion. For the audio feature, it is easily distributed by noise for two reasons. First, most of the video clips have background noise. Second, the video clip contains a small quantity useful information as it is too short (maximum duration is the 5.4 s).

Table 1. The classification accuracy of each modality on the validation set of AFEW4.0

Modality	Accuracy
Facial motion features	25.87%
Audio	26.95%
LBPTOP	39.35%
Conv3DNet	41.24%
Conv2DNet+GRU	45.01%
Strategy 1	**46.36%**
Strategy 2	**47.98%**

After performing decision-level fusion, the classification accuracy improves by 3%. The improvement of accuracy demonstrates that the proposed fusion approach can make full use of the complementarity among all features. In order to verify whether the facial motion information and audio feature contribute to the system, we fuse all the modalities expect them (denotes as Strategy 1 in Table 1). Then we achieve 46.36% classification accuracy. On the one hand, it proves that the facial motion feature and audio modality are effective. On the other hand, it demonstrates that the proposed fusion method can utilize the complementarities among the modalities.

3.4   Comparison with the State-of-the-Art Methods

We also compare the classification accuracy with the some state-of-the-art methods and the results are shown in Table 2. Performance of various approaches on AFEW4.0. It can clearly see that the classification accuracy of our multimodal fusion of spatial-temporal feature system is better than those using multimodal fusion technology. It proves that our proposed decision-level fusion method can make full use of the complementarities of all the modalities. We find that the part fusion is also better than most of the works in this table. It also demonstrates that the spatial-temporal feature is more robust than the features based on the static image. The slightly lower classification accuracy than the Liu et al. [4] is more likely due to the fact that the proposed method needs a large amount of data to train while the dataset is not large enough.

Table 2. Performance of various approaches on AFEW4.0

Method	Accuracy
Baseline [11]	33.15%
Chen et al. [2]	40.21%
Sun et al. [3]	45.55%
Liu et al. [4]	48.52%
Kaya and Salah [16]	44.20%
Huang et al. [17]	45.82%
Yan et al. [18]	47.00%
Ringeval et al. [12]	36.97%
Strategy 1	**46.36%**
Strategy 2	**47.98%**

3.5 Reflection on Misclassification

We find that the classification accuracies of angry, happy and neutral are much higher than others from Fig. 4. We guess it is because that the emotional state of human being is neutral in most cases. Thus, the neutral emotional state is not difficult to recognize. Besides, it is easily to recognize angry and happy because people don't tend to cover up them.

Cognitive psychology points out that people tend to disguise negative emotions, especially people prefer to pretend as if nothing happens when they are sad and surprise. The phenomenon that the emotions which are misclassified are largely perceived as neutral by the emotion recognition system supports this perspective.

4 Conclusion

In this paper, we present a multimodal spatial-temporal features fusion system to recognize emotion from the video in the wild. We find that the spatial-temporal feature has more powerful representative ability than the static feature. The experiments show that the multi feature fusion is needed because it can take full advantage of the complementarity between the visual modality and the audio modality to boost the system's accuracy and generalization. Moreover, we verify that the pre-training can avoid overfitting, to an extent. Besides, we think it is worth exploring a better integration of visual modality and other modalities.

Acknowledgements. The work is funded by the National Natural Science Foundation of China (No. 61371149, No. 61170155), Shanghai Innovation Action Plan Project (No. 16511101200) and the Open Project Program of the National Laboratory of Pattern Recognition (No. 2016 00017).

References

1. Dhall, A., Goecke, R., Lucey, S., Gedeon, T.: Collecting large, richly annotated facial-expression databases from movies. IEEE Multimedia **19**, 34–41 (2012)
2. Chen, J., Chen, Z., Chi, Z., Fu, H.: Emotion recognition in the wild with feature fusion and multiple kernel learning. In: Proceedings of the 16th International Conference on Multimodal Interaction, pp. 508–513 (2014)
3. Sun, B., Li, L., Zuo, T., Chen, Y., Zhou, G., Wu, X.: Combining multimodal features with hierarchical classifier fusion for emotion recognition in the wild. In: Proceedings of the 16th International Conference on Multimodal Interaction, pp. 481–486 (2014)
4. Liu, M., Wang, R., Li, S., Shan, S., Huang, Z., Chen, X.: Combining multiple kernel methods on riemannian manifold for emotion recognition in the wild. In: Proceedings of the 16th International Conference on Multimodal Interaction, pp. 494–501 (2014)
5. Zhao, X., Liang, X., Liu, L., Li, T., Han, Y., Vasconcelos, N., Yan, S.: Peak-piloted deep network for facial expression recognition. In: Leibe, B., Matas, J., Sebe, N., Welling, M. (eds.) ECCV 2016. LNCS, vol. 9906, pp. 425–442. Springer, Cham (2016). https://doi.org/10.1007/978-3-319-46475-6_27

6. Carrier, P.L., Courville, A., Goodfellow, I.J., Mirza, M., Bengio, Y.: FER-2013 face database. Technical report (2013)
7. Tran, D., Bourdev, L., Fergus, R., Torresani, L., Paluri, M.: Learning spatiotemporal features with 3d convolutional networks. In: Proceedings of the IEEE International Conference on Computer Vision, pp. 4489–4497 (2015)
8. Zhao, G., Pietikainen, M.: Dynamic texture recognition using local binary patterns with an application to facial expressions. IEEE Trans. Pattern Anal. Mach. Intell. **29**, 915–928 (2007)
9. Schuller, B., Steidl, S., Batliner, A., et al.: The INTERSPEECH 2010 paralinguistic challenge. In: Conference of the International Speech Communication Association, INTERSPEECH 2010, pp. 2794–2797 (2010)
10. Schuller, B., Valstar, M., Eyben, F., McKeown, G., Cowie, R., Pantic, M.: AVEC 2011–the first international audio/visual emotion challenge. In: D'Mello, S., Graesser, A., Schuller, B., Martin, J.-C. (eds.) ACII 2011. LNCS, vol. 6975, pp. 415–424. Springer, Heidelberg (2011). https://doi.org/10.1007/978-3-642-24571-8_53
11. Dhall, A., Goecke, R., Joshi, J., Sikka, K., Gedeon, T.: Emotion recognition in the wild challenge 2014: baseline, data and protocol. In: Proceedings of the 16th International Conference on Multimodal Interaction, pp. 461–466 (2014)
12. Ringeval, F., Amiriparian, S., Eyben, F., Scherer, K., Schuller, B.: Emotion recognition in the wild: incorporating voice and lip activity in multimodal decision-level fusion. In: Proceedings of the 16th International Conference on Multimodal Interaction, pp. 473–480 (2014)
13. Khorrami, P., Le Paine, T., Brady, K., Dagli, C., Huang, T.: How deep neural networks can improve emotion recognition on video data. In: 2016 IEEE International Conference on Image Processing (ICIP), pp. 619–623 (2016)
14. Simonyan, K., Zisserman, A.: Very deep convolutional networks for large-scale image recognition. arXiv preprint arXiv:1409.1556 (2014)
15. Jung, H., Lee, S., Yim, J., Park, S., Kim, J.: Joint fine-tuning in deep neural networks for facial expression recognition. In: Proceedings of the IEEE International Conference on Computer Vision, pp. 2983–2991 (2015)
16. Kaya, H., Salah, A.: Combining modality-specific extreme learning machines for emotion recognition in the wild. J. Multimodal User Interfaces **10**, 139–149 (2016)
17. Huang, X., He, Q., Hong, X., Zhao, G., Pietikainen, M.: Improved spatiotemporal local monogenic binary pattern for emotion recognition in the wild. In: Proceedings of the 16th International Conference on Multimodal Interaction, pp. 514–520 (2014)
18. Yan, J., Zheng, W., Xu, Q., Lu, G., Li, H., Wang, B.: Sparse kernel reduced-rank regression for bimodal emotion recognition from facial expression and speech. IEEE Trans. Multimedia **18**, 1319–1329 (2016)
19. Fan, Y., Lu, X., Li, D., Liu, Y.: Video-based emotion recognition using CNN-RNN and C3D hybrid networks. In: Proceedings of the 18th ACM International Conference on Multimodal Interaction, pp. 445–450 (2016)
20. Cho, K., Van Merriënboer, B., Gulcehre, C., Bahdanau, D., Bougares, F., Schwenk, H., Bengio, Y.: Learning phrase representations using RNN encoder-decoder for statistical machine translation. arXiv preprint arXiv:1406.1078 (2014)
21. Eyben, F., Wöllmer, M., Schuller, B.: OpenSmile: the Munich versatile and fast open-source audio feature extractor. In: ACM International Conference on Multimedia, pp. 1459–1462 (2010)

A Fast and General Method for Partial Face Recognition

Qianhao Wu and Zechao Li[✉]

Nanjing University of Science and Technology, Nanjing, China
wqhIris@163.com, zechao.li@njust.edu.cn

Abstract. Recently, holistic face recognition technology has been increasingly mature. However, as for many unconstrained environments, the captured face image is more likely not holistic, but partial discriminative face area. To address this, we propose a fast and general method for partial face recognition. There, our method needn't alignment by fiducial points or cropping to the same size, for all facial images in the gallery set and probe set. In other words, we use the initial captured faces as input. Besides, our method can deal with single sample face recognition problem. For a pair of gallery image and probe image, firstly we detect key-points as well as extracting their local descriptors. Specially, in order to improve robustness of descriptors, we exploit gradient orientation modification and L2 normalization. Then, we use sparse representation based on multi-descriptors to recognize probe image. Experimental results on public face datasets demonstrate the effectiveness of the proposed method.

Keywords: Partial face recognition · Alignment free · L2 normalization
Gradient orientation modification · Sparse representation

1 Introduction

Face recognition technique has played an important role in finance, education, public security and other fields. So far, researchers have developed many algorithms [1–7], some of which achieved promising results on the LFW dataset [8]. While in the real-world scenarios, their performance degrades drastically. Because of the complex variations, it is a challenge to explore an approach which can recognize identities in the unconstrained environment effectively.

In unconstrained environments, it is frequent that the captured faces are not holistic. In this paper, such partial face is divided into two types. The first one is the occluded faces. It is a common phenomenon in the real-world. Glasses, wearable device, hair or other objects, can occludes some face components, as shown in Fig. 1a. The second type is called arbitrary face patches. It means that the face image only contains partial facial components, and may lost mouth, eye, nose or combination of above. Besides, the arbitrary face patches may even contain illumination or pose variations at the same time. Some examples are shown in Fig. 1b. Usually, the arbitrary face patches are produced due to the limit of capture window.

Recognizing partial faces is required urgently by some important applications in public security, the topical one is video surveillance. Surveillance devices cannot

© Springer International Publishing AG, part of Springer Nature 2018
B. Zeng et al. (Eds.): PCM 2017, LNCS 10735, pp. 215–224, 2018.
https://doi.org/10.1007/978-3-319-77380-3_21

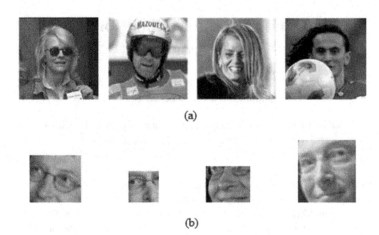

(a)

(b)

Fig. 1. Examples for two types of partial faces, which belong to the LFW dataset [8]. (a) Examples for the occluded faces. (b) Examples for arbitrary face patches.

guarantee to capture holistic faces that can be recognized conveniently. Furthermore, someone will take disguises to avoid being captured, which makes the recognition more difficult. In a word, the cost will be expensive if the whole task only relies on manual effort. Consequently, developing a model to recognize partial face automatically is desirable.

Face Forensics Company has developed a SDK that is able to recognize arbitrary face patches [9]. Although its performance is well, the drawback is the SDK needs to align the face patch manually with the 3D face model, which is inconvenient when the data is mass. In contrast, our method is fully automatic, needn't manual alignment.

In order to recognize partial faces, the first step is to localize facial key-points and extract descriptors. Several methods [10–12] will produce a large number of imposter facial landmarks when meeting occlusions or large pose variations. As for our method, the number of key-points is determined by the actual content of the image due to exploiting SIFT key-point detectors. After extracting descriptor, it is necessary to remove outliers, especially for the features extracted from occluded parts [13, 14]. While we find that the accuracy of Ma [13] degrades drastically if the size of two images differs much. In fact, arbitrary face patches have different size. As for Huo [14], it also needs face alignment. In opposite, our method needn't crop images to the same size or aligning faces by fiducial points, which is more convenient.

As for single sample face recognition, most methods are based on sparse representation. Lu [15] only learns information from its own data, which makes it cannot deal with many variations. To solve this limitation, Huang [16] and Yang [17] develop an external variation set, but its quality makes large influence to the final performance. However, in the real world, it is difficult to get suitable external variation set. As for occlusion or other facial variations, several methods get well results. However, Chen [18] needs normalizations before being input and it is sensitive to the pose variations. Zhang [19] also needs manual alignment as pre-process. Yang [20, 21] can't deal with single sample face recognition problem. As for partial face recognition, the research is developed just in recent years. Liao [22] is a really fast method, but it will get bad recognition accuracy when facing occlusions. Liu [23] can do well with arbitrary face patches recognition, but cannot deal with occlusions and single sample recognition. Weng [24] gets well recognition results but costs much time. And it easily recognizes wrongly if there are not enough matched point-pairs.

The above methods have various limitations, in order to alleviate them, we develop a fast and general method for partial face recognition. Given a pair of gallery image and probe image, firstly we detect key-points as well as extracting local descriptors of each key-point. In order to keep robustness and accuracy, we exploit gradient orientation modification and L2 normalization into the descriptors. Then, we concatenate all the gallery descriptors to construct a dictionary and filter out its outliers. Finally, to decrease time cost and avoid the effect of lacking matched point-pairs, we use SRC [25] for recognition. The experimental results show that the speed of our method has been raised considerably, and kept competitive accuracy among other methods at the same time. The contributions of our method are concluded as follow:

- Our method is a general method that needn't crop images to the same size or aligning faces by fiducial points. Besides, it can deal with single sample face recognition, pose variations, illumination variations and so on.
- Our method is a fast as well as keeping competitive accuracy method.
- The number of key-points detected by SIFT detector is determined by the actual content of the image. Therefore, our method can adaptively represent holistic or partial faces.
- In order to improve robustness, we exploit gradient orientation modification and L2 normalization into the descriptors, which outperforms the one of Weng [24]. Experimental results confirm this really improve our method's recognition performance.

The remainder of this paper is organized as follows: In Sect. 2, we describe the details of the proposed method. In Sect. 3, we demonstrate extensive experiments. In Sect. 4, we conclude the whole work.

2 Proposed Method

2.1 Feature Extraction

Weng [24] proposes a novel descriptor, it first extracts SIFT, SURF and LBP descriptors for each key-point, then concatenates these descriptors into a single one. However, based on the above descriptor, the number of imposter matches is still much, which decrease the recognition performance. Therefore, it is necessary to modify the descriptor.

Firstly, we replace SIFT by GOM-SIFT [26]. The GOM means gradient orientation modification. Yi [26] modifies gradient orientation of SIFT descriptor when samples around the key-point. The modification is defined as

$$\beta = \begin{cases} \alpha, & \alpha \in [0, \ 180°] \\ 360 - \alpha, & \alpha \in (180°, \ 360°) \end{cases} \quad (1)$$

where α is the original gradient orientation, and β is the modified one. GOM-SIFT can remove some imposter matches when the image is self-similitude. Considering face image is just self-similitude, so we try to apply it. Figure 2 illustrates that using GOM-SIFT produces less wrong matches, although it also produces some new imposter matches.

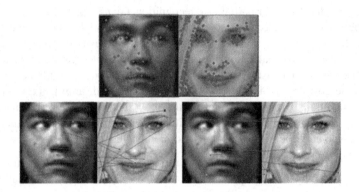

Fig. 2. The first row is key-points of two images, which are marked as green dots. The second row is matching results. And the left image belongs to SIFT, the right one belongs to GOM-SIFT. By the way, the yellow lines mean correct matches, the blue lines mean incorrect ones. (Color figure online)

Secondly, we apply L2 normalization to the descriptor. Because it projects all the value into the same range, which is able to avoid the impact of outliers. Let $\mathbf{x} = [x_1, x_2, \cdots, x_n]'$ be an original descriptor, and $\mathbf{y} = [y_1, y_2, \cdots, y_n]'$ be the normalized one. As for each element x_i, the L2 normalization is defined as

$$y_i = \frac{x_i}{\sqrt{\sum_{k=1}^{n} x_k^2}} \tag{2}$$

The experimental results show that, as for arbitrary face patches recognition, the L2 normalization can really improve the performance. However, it takes little effect on the occlusions problem. Therefore, in this paper, we define two versions of the proposed method, one without L2 normalization and the other with L2 normalization, denoted as "ours" and "ours-L2norm", respectively.

2.2 Gallery Dictionary Construction

After extracting the features, we concatenate the feature descriptors of gallery images to construct a overcomplete dictionary, in order to prepare for the following recognition. However, such dictionary has some noises. For instance, some descriptors are extracted from occluded areas or irrelative parts. These regions should be excluded when compute similarity score. Thus, we filter out the noises by matching the feature sets of each gallery image and a probe image as well as removing the unmatched features.

To achieve this, we also apply Lowe's matching scheme [27]. Given a point P in one image, and in another image, point M is the closest neighbor of P, point N is the second-closest one. Whether P and M is matched is determined by the value of the indicator function as follow

$$
Lowe(d_{first}, d_{second}) = \begin{cases} 1, & if\ d_{first}/d_{second} < \tau \\ 0, & others \end{cases}
\tag{3}
$$

where d_{first} is the distance between P and M, d_{second} is the distance between P and N, then τ is a pre-defined threshold. $Lowe(\cdot, \cdot) = 1$ means P and M is matched, otherwise they are unmatched.

2.3 Recognition

After constructing the sub-dictionary that is nearly filtered out noises, we represent the probe image's feature descriptors by a sparse linear combination of the sub-dictionary. Let $\mathbf{Z} = [z_1, z_2, \cdots, z_n]$ be a probe face image with n descriptors, $\mathbf{D}$ be the sub-dictionary. Inspired by SRC [25], as for each descriptor z_i, we can calculate its sparse coefficient $\hat{a}_i$ by solving

$$
\hat{a}_i = \arg\min_{a_i} \|z_i - \mathbf{D}a_i\|_2^2 + \lambda\|a_i\|_1
\tag{4}
$$

Then we can determine the label c of probe image $\mathbf{Z}$ by solving

$$
c = \arg\min_c \frac{1}{n} \sum_{i=1}^{n} \|z_i - \mathbf{D}_c \delta_c(\hat{a}_i)\|_2^2
\tag{5}
$$

where $\mathbf{D}_c$ is the subset which is belongs to class c, and $\delta_c(\cdot)$ is a function that selects coefficients only associated with class c. By the way, in order to become faster, we apply the fast filtering strategy in Liao [22] when recognizing.

3 Experiment

In this section, we first conduct experiment to confirm the effectiveness of the improvements in this work. Then we conduct a partial face verification experiment to evaluate the performances of our method. Finally, we conduct an occluded face recognition experiment to illustrate the performance and the time cost of our method.

We select RPSM [24] and MKD-SRC [22] as baseline algorithms. Specially, we define four versions of proposed method for comparing modifications' effectiveness. "ours" denotes our proposed method. "ours-srcDescr" is our method without gradient orientation modification. "ours-L2norm" is our method with L2 normalization. "ours-noDel" is our method without removing noises of dictionary.

3.1 Data Set

PubFig: This dataset [28] has 200 subjects, the photos of 140 are used for evaluation, and the rest are used as development set. All photos are obtained in the uncontrolled real scenarios. We choose evaluation set as samples. Manually select 5 images for each identity, and generate the face patches from the selected images by random transformations, such as randomly rotating, cropping, and scaling.

CASIA-WebFace: This dataset [29] has 313,162 facial images of 10,566 subjects. All images are obtained in the uncontrolled environment. In the same way, we generate the face patches by random transformations. Then remove the objects only have one image. In the following, we will call this sub-dataset as "CASIA".

10 k US Adult Faces Database: This dataset [30] only has one image per subject. We firstly use OpenCV implementation of the Viola-Jones face detector to crop out the facial regions. Then, manually remove bad results and undetected ones, leaving 8,802 images. Finally, we also take the random transformations above. In the following, we will call this sub-dataset as "10 k".

AR: This dataset [31] contains 126 subjects, each subject has 26 images in two different sessions. While in this work, we choose 100 subjects with 50 males and 50 females as samples. And we only use neutral image in first session, three images with sunglasses and three images with scarf both in two sessions.

3.2 Partial Face Recognition on PubFig

To confirm the effectiveness of the improvements, we exploit the 5-fold testing scheme: within each round, select one subset as gallery set, and the rest four as probe set. Besides, all the images in gallery set and probe set are partial faces. Table 1 shows the average rank-K recognition accuracy of methods. Comparing the results of "ours-srcDescr" and "ours", it shows that our improved descriptor is much better than the descriptor of RPSM [24]. The results between "ours-L2norm" and "ours" shows that L2 normalization can improve the performance. Comparing "ours-noDel" and "ours", it shows removing outliers is really necessary.

Table 1. Average recognition accuracy of the comparing methods at various ranks on PubFig

Method	Rank 1	Rank 10
ours	21.50%	45.89%
ours-srcDescr	12.79%	36.61%
ours-L2norm	23.04%	48.50%
ours-noDel	13.39%	37.75%

3.3 Open Set Partial Face Verification

We conduct a partial face verification experiment to evaluate the performances of our method. In order to make SRC-based method take face verification, we apply idea of MKD-SRC [22]. As for the images I and J, background sample B, firstly, we combine I and B as the gallery set, and regard J as probe. Secondly, we combine J and B while regarding I as probe. Finally, the average score of two times is the final score. As for genuine pairs, firstly, we randomly choose 2,000 subjects from 10,566 ones in CASIA. Then, we divide them into 5 subsets, and randomly choose 2 images for each subject. Finally, there are 5 subsets and 400 genuine pairs per subset. As for imposter pairs, we firstly randomly choose 4,000 subjects from 8,802 ones in 10 k. Secondly, divide them into 2 subjects and divide the resulting 2,000 pairs into 5 subsets. This results in 5 subsets and 400 imposter pairs per subset. As for background sample, we choose 100 undetected images of 10 k and manually crop out the faces regions. Then, we produce arbitrary face patches by taking random transformations.

As for testing, within each round, we choose one subset from genuine pairs, and another from imposter pairs. Figure 3 shows the ROC curves. Table 2 lists the accuracy (u) as well as its standard deviation (Std). This time, "ours-L2norm" gets the best result, but its standard deviation is also the highest. The second one is MKD-SRC [22]. The other versions of our method are all better than RPSM [24], which shows the success of our improvements. What's more, the results illustrate that the impact of no-filtering out outliers is more serious than no-using modified descriptor.

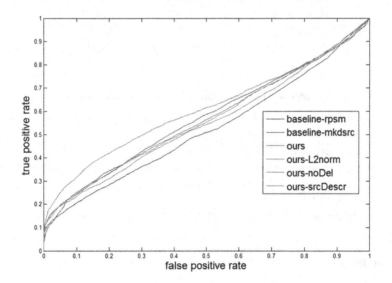

Fig. 3. The average ROC curves of the comparing methods.

3.4 Occluded Face Recognition on AR

We conduct a face recognition experiment for occluded holistic faces, in order to evaluate the performance and time cost of our method. As for gallery set, we select the neutral images in the first session of each subjects. As for the probe set, we produce four type probe sets. For example, S1-G contains all images with sunglasses in session 1. Similarly, S2-S represents all images with scarf in session 2. Table 3 shows, except "ours-srcDescr", the other versions of our method have competitive accuracy with

Table 2. Average verification accuracy (u) as well as corresponding standard deviations (Std) of the comparing methods

Method	u ± Std	Method	u ± Std
ours	0.533 ± 0.0285	ours-noDel	0.525 ± 0.0287
ours-srcDescr	0.532 ± 0.0282	RPSM [24]	0.511 ± 0.0267
ours-L2norm	0.553 ± 0.0453	MKD-SRC [22]	0.537 ± 0.0294

RPSM [24]. Besides, all of them takes much less time than RPSM [24] as in Table 4. While MKD-SRC [22] gets worst results despite with fastest speed.

Table 3. The recognition accuracy of the comparing methods

Method	S1-G	S1-S	S2-G	S2-S
ours	75.00%	94.00%	52.33%	89.33%
ours-srcDescr	68.00%	91.67%	44.67%	83.67%
ours-L2norm	72.00%	94.00%	49.33%	89.33%
ours–noDel	73.67%	92.67%	51.67%	87.67%
RPSM [24]	76.00%	96.00%	61.00%	88.33%
MKD-SRC [22]	41.67%	58.33%	23.33%	34.00%

Table 4. The computational time of each method

Method	S1-G	S1-S	S2-G	S2-S
ours	820.14 s	734.03 s	839.54 s	773.03 s
ours-srcDescr	775.22 s	705.30 s	781.33 s	709.12 s
ours-L2norm	809.67 s	764.92 s	865.39 s	778.18 s
ours–noDel	737.81 s	637.06 s	742.68 s	642.45 s
RPSM [24]	16236.39 s	17413.74 s	14476.01 s	20086.23 s
MKD-SRC [22]	242.12 s	247.42 s	240.96 s	241.54 s

4 Conclusion

In this paper, we propose a fast and general partial face recognition method for arbitrary face patches and occlusions. It needn't alignment or cropping into same size. We exploit gradient orientation modification and L2 normalization to improve the robustness of descriptors. Then use sparse representation to fast recognition. The several experimental results confirm that our method has the competitive recognition accuracy, while taking less time cost.

Acknowledgements. This work was partially supported by the 973 Program (Project No. 2014 CB347600), the National Natural Science Foundation of China (Grant No. 61672304 and 61672285) and the Natural Science Foundation of Jiangsu Province (Grant BK20140058 and BK20170033).

References

1. Turk, M., Pentland, A.: Eigenfaces for recognition. J. Cogn. Neurosci. **3**, 71–86 (1991)
2. Belhumeur, P., Hespanha, J., Kriegman, D.: Eigenfaces vs. Fisherfaces: recognition using class specific linear projection. IEEE Trans. Pattern Anal. Mach. Intell. **19**, 711–720 (1997)
3. Jain, A., Li, S.: Handbook of Face Recognition. Springer, London (2011)
4. Tai, Y., Yang, J., Zhang, Y., Luo, L., Qian, J., Chen, Y.: Face recognition with pose variations and misalignment via orthogonal procrustes regression. IEEE Trans. Image Process. **25**, 2673–2683 (2016)
5. Zhuang, L., Yang, A., Zhou, Z., Sastry, S., Ma, Y.: Single-sample face recognition with image corruption and misalignment via sparse illumination transfer. In: 2013 IEEE Conference on Computer Vision and Pattern Recognition, pp. 3546–3553 (2013)
6. Klum, S., Han, H., Jain, A., Klare, B.: Sketch based face recognition: Forensic vs. composite sketches. In: 2013 International Conference on Biometrics, pp. 1–8 (2013)
7. Sun, Y., Wang, X., Tang, X.: Deep learning face representation from predicting 10,000 classes. In: 2014 IEEE Conference on Computer Vision and Pattern Recognition, pp. 1891–1898 (2014)
8. Huang, G., Ramesh, M., Berg, T., Learned-Miller, E.: Labeled faces in the wild: a database for studying face recognition in unconstrained environments. Technical report 07-49, University of Massachusetts, Amherst (2007)
9. The Face Forensics SDK. Face Forensics. http://www.faceforensics.com/ (2010)
10. Cootes, T., Taylor, C., Cooper, D., Graham, J.: Active shape models-their training and application. Comput. Vis. Image Underst. **61**, 38–59 (1995)
11. Cootes, T., Edwards, G., Taylor, C.: Active appearance models. IEEE Trans. Pattern Anal. Mach. Intell. **23**, 681–685 (2001)
12. Xiong, X., De la Tore, F.: Supervised descent method and its applications to face alignment. In: 2013 IEEE Conference on Computer Vision and Pattern Recognition, pp. 532–539 (2013)
13. Ma, J., Zhou, H., Zhao, J., Gao, Y., Jiang, J., Tian, J.: Robust feature matching for remote sensing image registration via locally linear transforming. IEEE Trans. Geosci. Remote Sens. **53**, 6469–6481 (2015)
14. Huo, J., Gao, Y., Shi, Y., Yang, W., Yin, H.: Ensemble of sparse cross-modal metrics for heterogeneous face recognition. In: Proceedings of the 2016 ACM on Multimedia Conference, pp. 1405–1414 (2016)
15. Lu, J., Tan, Y., Wang, G.: Discriminative multi-manifold analysis for face recognition from a single training sample per person. In: 2011 IEEE International Conference on Computer Vision, pp. 1943–1950 (2011)
16. Huang, D., Wang, Y.: With one look: robust face recognition using single sample per person. In: Proceedings of the 2013 ACM on Multimedia Conference, pp. 601–604 (2013)
17. Yang, M., Van Gool, L., Zhang, L.: Sparse variation dictionary learning for face recognition with a single training sample per person. In: Proceedings of the 2013 IEEE International Conference on Computer Vision, pp. 689–696 (2013)
18. Chen, Weiping, Gao, Yongsheng: Recognizing partially occluded faces from a single sample per class using string-based matching. In: Daniilidis, K., Maragos, P., Paragios, N. (eds.) ECCV 2010. LNCS, vol. 6313, pp. 496–509. Springer, Heidelberg (2010). https://doi.org/10.1007/978-3-642-15558-1_36
19. Zhang, L., Yang, M., Feng, X.: Sparse representation or collaborative representation: which helps face recognition? In: 2011 IEEE International Conference on Computer Vision, pp. 471–478 (2011)

20. Yang, M., Zhang, L., Shiu, S., Zhang, D.: Robust kernel representation with statistical local features for face recognition. IEEE Trans. Neural Networks Learn. Syst. **24**, 900–912 (2013)
21. Yang, M., Zhang, L., Shiu, S., Zhang, D.: Gabor feature based robust representation and classification for face recognition with Gabor occlusion dictionary. Pattern Recogn. **46**, 1865–1878 (2013)
22. Liao, S., Jain, A., Li, S.: Partial face recognition: alignment-free approach. IEEE Trans. Pattern Anal. Mach. Intell. **35**, 1193–1205 (2013)
23. Liu, L., Tran, T., Chin, S.: Partial face recognition: a sparse representation-based approach Partial face recognition: A sparse representation-based approach. In: 2016 IEEE International Conference on Acoustics, Speech and Signal Processing, pp. 2389–2393 (2016)
24. Weng, R., Lu, J., Tan, Y.: Robust point set matching for partial face recognition. IEEE Trans. Image Process. **25**, 1163–1176 (2016)
25. Wright, J., Yang, A., Ganesh, A., Sastry, S., Ma, Y.: Robust face recognition via sparse representation. IEEE Trans. Pattern Anal. Mach. Intell. **31**, 210–227 (2009)
26. Yi, Z., Zhiguo, C., Yang, X.: Multi-spectral remote image registration based on SIFT. Electron. Lett. **44**, 107 (2008)
27. Lowe, D.: Distinctive image features from scale-invariant keypoints. Int. J. Comput. Vis. **60**, 91–110 (2004)
28. Kumar, N., Berg, A., Belhumeur, P., Nayar, S.: Attribute and simile classifiers for face verification. In: 2009 IEEE International Conference on Computer Vision, pp. 1–9 (2009)
29. Yi, D., Lei, Z., Liao, S., Li, S.: Learning face representation from scratch. arXiv preprint arXiv:1411.7923 (2014)
30. Bainbridge, W., Isola, P., Oliva, A.: The intrinsic memorability of face photographs. J. Exp. Psychol. Gen. **142**, 1323–1334 (2013)
31. Martinez, A., Benavente, R.: The AR face database. Technical report, CVC (1998)

Tracking and Action Recognition

Freedom and Legten Republican

Adaptive Correlation Filter Tracking with Weighted Foreground Representation

Chunguang Qie[1], Hanzi Wang[1(✉)], Yan Yan[1], Guanjun Guo[1], and Jin Zheng[2]

[1] Fujian Key laboratory of Sensing and Computing for Smart City,
School of Information Science and Engineering, Xiamen University,
Xiamen 361005, China
hanzi_wang@163.com
[2] Beijing Key Laboratory of Digital Media, School of Computer Science
and Engineering, Beihang University, Beijing 100191, China

Abstract. In recent years, the correlation filter based algorithms show impressive performance for visual tracking. However, the object representations (*i.e.*, feature descriptors) are still not robust. In addition, the models in existing correlation filter based algorithms may be updated by using corrupted samples when the tracking targets are occluded, thus leading to the drifting problem. In this paper, we present a weighted foreground appearance feature descriptor which effectively characterizes the appearance of objects. Moreover, we propose an adaptive model updating strategy to mitigate the problem that the models are updated by using corrupted samples. Our works are based on a recently proposed correlation filter based algorithm, *i.e.*, Staple. By effectively combining the proposed feature descriptor with the adaptively updated Staple framework, the proposed algorithm is highly robust and it can achieve promising performance under complex conditions, such as deformation, rotation and scale variation. Experimental results on the OTB-50 and OTB-100 datasets demonstrate the effectiveness of the proposed tracking algorithm, compared with several other state-of-the-art algorithms.

Keywords: Visual tracking · Correlation filter · Staple

1 Introduction

Visual tracking is one of the most fundamental and important research areas in computer vision, which can not only be used for video surveillance, but also be integrated into the different intelligent systems, such as robots and driverless cars. Regardless of the great success in visual tracking, there are still many problems unsolved.

In recent years, the correlation filter based tracking algorithms [1,2,5,6,9, 10,12,18] become popular due to their fast running speed and promising performance. These tracking algorithms employ the Ridge Regression technique and take advantage of discrete Fourier transform (DFT) to perform efficient training and detection. Besides, many of them improve the tracking performance

© Springer International Publishing AG, part of Springer Nature 2018
B. Zeng et al. (Eds.): PCM 2017, LNCS 10735, pp. 227–237, 2018.
https://doi.org/10.1007/978-3-319-77380-3_22

from different aspects, including designing different feature descriptors or using the kernel tricks (*e.g.*, [3,10]). Among these works, the KCF algorithm [10] is particularly representative, which demonstrates that the kernel tricks could be integrated into the correlation filter based algorithms to improve the tracking performance. But there are several problems in KCF. For example, the fixed learning rate will lead to the drifting problem when the model is incorrectly updated and the searching region used in KCF is too small. A recently proposed SRDCF algorithm [5] enhances the correlation filter algorithm by introducing the spatially regularization strategy to learn a better discriminative model. However, because of the iterative procedure used to solve the optimization problem in the SRDCF algorithm, its computational complexity is very high, which limits its application to real-time tracking. The recently proposed Staple algorithm [1] combines the response of correlation filter with the color response derived from color histograms. Although the response-fusion mechanism used in Staple is effective for improving the tracking performance, Staple has the same problems as KCF, *i.e.*, the models in Staple are updated with a fixed learning rate and the HOG feature descriptor employed in the algorithm is not robust to deal with the rotation and deformation of objects.

Besides the observation model (defined in [15]) used in a tracking system, the employed feature descriptor also has a significant influence on the final tracking performance. The HOG feature descriptor [4] is a popular feature descriptor used in visual tracking. Many state-of-the-art object tracking algorithms, such as Struck [8], KCF [10], SDRCF [5] and Staple [1], employ HOG as the feature descriptor. However, HOG mainly describes the edges of an object, and is not robust to the rotation and deformation of objects. In contrast, the color information is stable when the object undergoes deformation. Therefore, the color feature descriptor and the HOG feature descriptor are complementary to each other for describing the appearance of objects. However, because the color information in the surrounding background of the object is undesirable, the direct usage of the color information in a tracking algorithm will lead to inaccurate training and detection. Besides the feature descriptors mentioned above, the tracking algorithms based on deep learning (such as MDNet [14] and CF2 [13]) use the convolutional networks to extract features from each frame. The deep learning based algorithms achieve extremely high performance at the cost of tracking speed and more expensive hardwares, which limits their applications in real-time systems.

In this paper, we improve the Staple tracking algorithm in two aspects. We summarize our works as follows:

1. We propose a weighted foreground appearance (WFA) feature descriptor. The WFA is based on the HOG feature descriptor and RGB feature descriptor. The advantage of WFA is that it contains the foreground appearance information of the tracked object and removes the negative influence of the background.
2. We propose an approach to update the correlation filter and color histogram models in the Staple algorithm with an adaptive learning rate. As a result,

the updating strategy improves the discriminative ability of the model and protects the model from the contamination incurred by invalid samples, such as occluded samples.

After integrating the WFA feature descriptor into the adaptively updated Staple tracking framework, the proposed algorithm achieves promising tracking performance and outperforms several other state-of-the-art tracking algorithms on the OTB-50 and OTB-100 benchmarks. Besides, the proposed algorithm (implemented by Matlab) runs at more than 60 FPS on a desktop workstation equipped with a 3.60 GHz CPU and 16 GB memory.

2   The Proposed Algorithm

In this section, we present the details of the proposed algorithm. We begin with a brief review of the Staple algorithm. Readers can refer to [1] for more details of Staple.

2.1   Review of the Staple Algorithm

The Staple algorithm combines the responses of the two models (i.e., the correlation filter and the color histogram) to perform visual tracking. One response is calculated based on the correlation filter, while the other response is calculated by maintaining the two color histograms of the foreground region and the background region, respectively.

For the correlation filter model, the Staple first computes the prediction function $f(x)$. The target of $f(x)$ is to minimize the squared error over a set of samples $\{x_1, x_2, \ldots, x_n\}$ and the corresponding regression targets $\{y_1, y_2, \ldots, y_n\}$, i.e., $\min_\beta \sum_i^n (f(x_i) - y_i)^2 + \lambda ||\beta||^2$, where λ is a regularization parameter, i and n denote the index and the number of training samples, respectively. $f(x) = \beta^T x$, where β is the parameter of the prediction function.

Due to the important properties of circulant matrix [7], β can be solved efficiently by employing the discrete Fourier transform (DFT) and the inverse DFT:

$$\beta = F^{-1}\left(\frac{F(x)^* \odot F(y)}{F(x)^* \odot F(x) + \lambda}\right), \tag{1}$$

where F and F^{-1} respectively denote the DFT and the inverse DFT operator, $*$ denotes the complex-conjugate operator, and $\odot$ means the element-wise product.

Besides, the Staple algorithm computes the pixel-wise scores $P(x)$ (see Fig. 1(b) for an example) for the sample image, as follows,

$$P_{i,j}(x) = \frac{\delta_{i,j}^{\mathcal{F}}(x)}{\delta_{i,j}^{\mathcal{F}}(x) + \delta_{i,j}^{\mathcal{B}}(x)}. \tag{2}$$

Given a position (i, j) in the sample image, $P_{i,j}(x)$ is the corresponding pixel-wise score, and $\delta_{i,j}^{\mathcal{F}}(x)$ and $\delta_{i,j}^{\mathcal{B}}(x)$ are the numbers of pixels of the quantized bin

(a) sample   (b) scores   (c) WFA-RGB   (d) WFA-HOG   (e) HOG

Fig. 1. Visualization of a sample image, pixel-wise scores, the corresponding weighted foreground appearance feature descriptor (*i.e.,* WFA-RGB and WFA-HOG) and the corresponding HOG feature descriptor. (a) The sample image at the current frame. (b) The image derived from the pixel-wise scores of (a). (c) The visualization of WFA-RGB feature descriptor of (a). (d) The visualization of WFA-RGB feature descriptor of (a). (e) The visualization of the HOG feature descriptor of (a).

in the foreground color histogram and the background color histogram, respectively. Then, the Staple algorithm computes the integral image of the scores to generate the color response $C(x)$.

Finally, the responses from the correlation filter and the color histograms are fused to yield the final response,

$$f_{final}(x) = (1 - \gamma)f(x) + \gamma C(x), \tag{3}$$

where γ is the merge factor. And the position *pos* of the tracked target is chosen from a set of the possible positions in the searching area S by maximizing the final response score:

$$pos = \arg\max_{S} f_{final}(x). \tag{4}$$

2.2 The Weighted Foreground Appearance Feature Descriptor

To effectively overcome the influence of background, we propose a new weighted foreground appearance (WFA) feature descriptor, which contains two parts of feature descriptors. We first combines the pixel-wise scores with the raw pixels to obtain the first part of WFA, that is,

$$D_{WFA\text{-}RGB}(x) = P(x) \odot S(x), \tag{5}$$

where $P(x)$ is the pixel-wise scores obtained by using Eq. (2), and $S(x)$ denotes the sample image (shown in Fig. 1(a)). As shown in Fig. 1(c), WFA-RGB contains the RGB features of the foreground region and removes the disturbance of the background region.

The HOG feature descriptor extracts the edge information of the object, but it also contains the edge information of the background (as shown in Fig. 1(e)), which has the negative influence on the training and detection of the model. Thus, instead of extracting HOG feature descriptor from the original sample, we extract HOG feature descriptor from the WFA-RGB and obtain WFA-HOG (as shown in Fig. 1(d)). Then we concatenate them together as the final feature descriptor $\Gamma(\boldsymbol{x})$ for the sample image $\boldsymbol{x}$,

$$\Gamma(\boldsymbol{x}) = [D_{WFA\text{-}HOG}(\boldsymbol{x}), D_{WFA\text{-}RGB}(\boldsymbol{x})], \tag{6}$$

where $D_{WFA\text{-}HOG}(\boldsymbol{x})$ denotes the HOG feature descriptor extracted from $D_{WFA\text{-}RGB}(\boldsymbol{x})$. Thus, $\Gamma(\boldsymbol{x})$ contains both the shape information ($D_{WFA\text{-}HOG}(\boldsymbol{x})$) and the color information ($D_{WFA\text{-}RGB}(\boldsymbol{x})$) of the tracked object.

2.3   Staple Framework with Adaptive Learning Rate

In this section, we represent the details of the proposed adaptive learning rate strategy.

In the proposed algorithm, the final response is obtained by Eq. (3). But we replace $f(\boldsymbol{x})$ with $f(\Gamma(\boldsymbol{x}))$, which is computed by the correlation filter using the feature descriptor $\Gamma(\boldsymbol{x})$ proposed in Sect. 2.2. Then, the position of the tracked target is obtained by Eq. (4).

After the detection of current frame, both the correlation filter and the color histograms need to be updated. Ideally, we expect that the model is updated with a large learning rate for good samples, and with a small learning rate for corrupted samples, such as occluded samples or deformed samples. Since $P(\boldsymbol{x})$ denote the scores of pixels belonging to the foreground, the values of $P(\boldsymbol{x})$ are small when the sample is corrupted. Thus, we propose to calculate an adaptive learning rate based on $P(\boldsymbol{x})$ and the larger learning rate will be obtained for the samples which contain more foreground pixels. Specifically, let $P^{(t)}(\boldsymbol{x})$ denote $P(\boldsymbol{x})$ in the t-th frame, we firstly normalize $P^{(t)}(\boldsymbol{x})$, which is defined as

$$PN_{i,j}^{(t)}(\boldsymbol{x}) = \frac{P_{i,j}^{(t)}(\boldsymbol{x})}{\max\limits_{i,j}(P_{i,j}^{(t)}(\boldsymbol{x}))}, \tag{7}$$

where $PN^{(t)}(\boldsymbol{x})$ is the normalization of $P^{(t)}(\boldsymbol{x})$.

Then we binarize $PN^{(t)}(\boldsymbol{x})$ as $B^{(t)}(\boldsymbol{x})$, which is written as

$$B_{i,j}^{(t)}(\boldsymbol{x}) = \begin{cases} 1 & PN_{i,j}^{(t)}(\boldsymbol{x}) > \epsilon \\ 0 & \text{otherwise} \end{cases}, \tag{8}$$

where ϵ is a binarizing threshold.

Finally we use the proportion of ones in $B_{i,j}^{(t)}(\boldsymbol{x})$ as the learning rate factor $\rho^{(t)}$ in the t-th frame:

$$\rho^{(t)} = \frac{\sum_{i,j} B_{i,j}^{(t)}(\boldsymbol{x})}{|B^{(t)}(\boldsymbol{x})|}, \tag{9}$$

where $|B^{(t)}(\boldsymbol{x})|$ denotes the number of the elements in $B^{(t)}(\boldsymbol{x})$. $\rho^{(t)}$ can be treated as the proportion of the foreground pixels in the sample of the t-th frame. Therefore, we use $\rho^{(t)}$ to obtain $\eta_{cf}^{(t)}$ and $\eta_{col}^{(t)}$ as the learning rates for the correlation filter and the color histograms of the t-th frame by using the following equations:

$$\eta_{cf}^{(t)} = \rho^{(t)} \eta_{cf}, \tag{10}$$

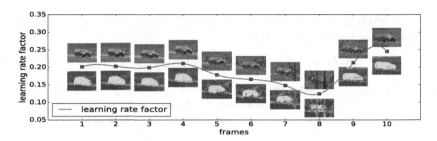

Fig. 2. The demonstration of the changes of the learning rate factor obtained on the *CarScale* sequence of OTB-100 dataset.

$$\eta_{col}^{(t)} = \rho^{(t)} \eta_{col}, \tag{11}$$

where η_{kcf} and η_{col} denote the base learning rates for the correlation filter and the color histograms, respectively.

Figure 2 shows the changes of the learning rate factor obtained on the *CarScale* sequence of the OTB-100 dataset. As shown in Fig. 2, when the object is occluded, the learning rate becomes small, by which the model avoids being updated by using corrupted samples.

After calculating $\beta^{(t)'}$ and $\eta_{cf}^{(t)}$ at the t-th frame by Eqs. (1) and (10). We can calculate $\beta^{(t)}$, which is used to detect the object in the next frame,

$$\beta^{(t)} = (1 - \eta_{kcf}^{(t)}) \beta^{(t-1)} + \eta_{kcf}^{(t)} \beta^{(t)'}. \tag{12}$$

For the color model, at the t-th frame, after calculating the histograms of the foreground region $\delta^{\mathcal{F}(t)'}$ and the background region $\delta^{\mathcal{B}(t)'}$, we respectively update the corresponding histograms $\delta^{\mathcal{F}(t)}$ and $\delta^{\mathcal{B}(t)}$ used in next frame by the following equations:

$$\delta^{\mathcal{F}(t)} = (1 - \eta_{col}^{(t)}) \delta^{\mathcal{F}(t)} + \eta_{col}^{(t)} \delta^{\mathcal{F}(t)'}, \tag{13}$$

$$\delta^{\mathcal{B}(t)} = (1 - \eta_{col}^{(t)}) \delta^{\mathcal{B}(t)} + \eta_{col}^{(t)} \delta^{\mathcal{B}(t)'}, \tag{14}$$

where $\eta_{col}^{(t)}$ denotes the learning rate for the color histograms.

3   Experiments

In this section we first analyse the components (*i.e.*, the WFA and adaptive learning rate) used in the proposed algorithm to demonstrate the effectiveness of each component. Then we demostrate that the proposed algorithm achieves state-of-the-art results by comparing with the several recently proposed state-of-the-art algorithms.

To demonstrate the effectiveness of the proposed WFA feature descriptor, the parameters of the WFA-HOG feature descriptor, the number of bins in the color histograms and the scale factor γ are set to be the same as [1]. We set the base learning rates $\eta_{col} = 0.20$ and $\eta_{col} = 0.025$ and set the binarizing threshold $\epsilon = 0.7$.

In the experiments, we use the OTB-50 [16] and OTB-100 [17] datasets to evaluate the proposed tracker and adopt precision and success rate as the evaluation metrics. The precision is measured as the intersection over union between the bounding box predicted by a tracking algorithm and the groundtruth bounding box. And the success is declared when the precision is above a threshold t_0.

3.1 Analysis of the Influence of Different Components

We evaluate 4 algorithms (*i.e.*, *Algor. 1–4*) which correspond to the different combinations of the components. The details of Algor. 1–4 are shown in Table 1.

Table 1. Details of the Algor. 1–4. T means the component is used in the algorithm and F means the component is not used.

Tracker	Adaptive learning rate	WFA	HOG	Raw pixels
Algor. 1	T	T	F	F
Algor. 2	F	T	F	F
Algor. 3	F	F	T	T
Algor. 4	F	F	T	F

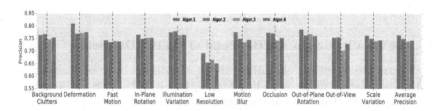

Fig. 3. Comparison of the four algorithms. Details of Algor. 1–4 can be found in Table 1. The comparisons in the first 11 columns starting from left respectively use the 11 challenging attributes given by the OTB-100 dataset, and the comparison in the last column reports the average precision on 100 test sequences of OTB-100 dataset.

The test sequences of the OTB-100 dataset are annotated by 11 different challenging attributes, such as background clusters, deformation and fast motion. All the attributes are shown in Fig. 3. For better evaluation and analysis of the strength and weakness of each component, we use the precision as the evaluation metric and compare Algor. 1–4 according to these 11 attributes, as shown in Fig. 3. Additionally, we also compare the average precision on the 100 test sequences of OTB-100 dataset in Fig. 3 for more intuitive comparison of performance. From Fig. 3, we have the following conclusions: (1) By comparing the precisions obtained by Algor. 1 and Algor. 2, it shows that the adaptive learning rate strategy effectively improves the average precision, and the precisions under 7 of 11 attributes, including deformation, fast motion, rotation and occlusion. This is mainly because that under these attributes, the models might be wrongly updated when the object is rotated or deformed, which may reduce the discriminative ability of the models. Based on the adaptive learning rate strategy, the models can preserve the discriminative ability even when the models are updated with rotated or occluded samples. However, there is slight precision decrease for the sequences with background clutters and illumination variation. This is because that the calculation of adaptive learning rate is based on the pixel scores obtained by the color histograms of Staple algorithm, which becomes less effective when the object undergoes background clutter and illumination variation. (2) Algor. 2 improves the average precision, and the precisions of 6 attributes compared with Algor. 3. This is because WFA focuses on the object other than the background, which alleviates the influence of background for online model training and detection. We also admit that WFA becomes ineffective for background clutters, deformation and low resolution attributes. This is because that the color histogram may not describe the foreground and the background accurately for these attributes. (3) The raw pixels feature descriptor used in Algor. 3 can not improve the average precision and the precisions under 7 attributes compared with Algor. 4. Furthermore, for the out-of-view and motion-blur attributes, Algor. 3 obtains worse performance than Algor. 4 because of the negative influence of the background pixels. (4) Algor. 1 achieves higher precision than Algor. 4, *i.e.*, the original Staple algorithm, which means our works are effective to improve the tracking performance of the Staple algorithm.

3.2   The Results on the OTB-50 and OTB-100 Datasets

We compare the proposed algorithm with 8 algorithms. Five of them are also based on correlation filter, including Staple [1], SRDCF [5], SAMF [18], KCF [10] and CSK [9]. And 2 algorithms are Struck [8] and TLD [11], which also use the tracking-by-detection framework. The last one is the recently proposed algorithm based on deep learning, *i.e.*, MDNet [14].

We firstly evaluate the proposed algorithm on the OTB-50 dataset and plot the results in Fig. 4. As shown in Fig. 4, the proposed algorithm achieves 63.94% and 79.35% in terms of the success rate and precision, respectively, outperforming 7 competing algorithms except for MDNet, which is based on the deep learning method. As an improved version, the proposed algorithm outperforms the Staple algorithm with a relative improvement of 2.99% on the success rate and 4.74% on the precision. This is because that the WFA feature descriptor used in the proposed algorithm focuses more on the foreground region, which can effectively eliminate the influence of the background. By introducing the adaptive learning rate to the Staple tracking framework, the proposed algorithm becomes more robust. Moreover, the proposed algorithm significantly outperforms the Struck algorithm by 15.54% and 15.80% on the success rate and

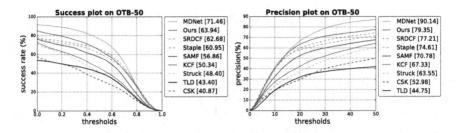

Fig. 4. Results on the OTB-50 dataset.

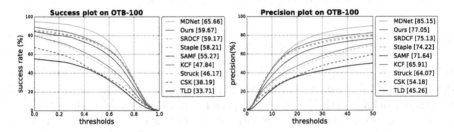

Fig. 5. Results on the OTB-100 dataset.

precision, respectively. Furthermore, the proposed algorithm outperforms the SRDCF algorithm by a slight margin, with 1.26% on the success rate and 2.14% on the precision, respectively. However, the proposed algorithm achieves both lower success rate and precision than MDNet because of the high robustness of deep features and the larger search area of MDNet.

In order to show the generalization ability of the proposed algorithm, we evaluate the proposed algorithm with the same parameter settings on the OTB-100 dataset, where the number of the test sequences is 100. As shown in Fig. 5, the proposed algorithm achieves 59.67% and 77.05% on the success rate and precision, respectively, which still outperforms the seven competing algorithms except for MDNet. More specifically, the proposed algorithm outperforms the Staple algorithm by a moderate margin, which is 1.46% on the success rate and 2.83% on the precision, respectively. Besides, the proposed algorithm also achieves better performance than SRDCF and the other four competing algorithms (*i.e.*, SAMF, KCF, Struck, and TLD). These results reflect that the WFA and the adaptive learning rate have a stable effectiveness for improving the tracking performance.

Table 2. Evaluation of tracking speed (**G** means evaluated on GPU)

Tracker	Ours	MDNet	SRDCF	Staple	SAMF	KCF	Struck	TLD	CSK
Speed	61.07	0.9 (**G**)	9.33	69.65	23.15	205.03	9.84	64.11	354.38

In terms of running speed (see Table 2), although the proposed algorithm runs slightly slower than the Staple algorithm due to the extra computation used to compute WFA and the adaptive learning rate, it still runs at 61.07 FPS which is applicable to the task of real-time tracking. Even when the MDNet is evaluated on GPU, the proposed algorithm is 60 times faster than MDNet. Besides, the proposed algorithm runs about 7 times faster than the SRDCF and Struck algorithms, 2.5 times faster than the SAMF algorithm, respectively. Except for Staple, there are other 3 algorithms faster than the proposed algorithm, *i.e.*, KCF, TLD and CSK. However, all of them have achieved much lower precision and success rate compared with the proposed algorithm.

4 Conclusion

In this paper, we have proposed a weighted foreground appearance feature descriptor (WFA), which effectively alleviates the disturbance of background in visual tracking. Then we have proposed a novel adaptive update strategy for updating the models in Staple with an adaptive learning rate, by which the discriminative ability of the models can be improved. By integrating the proposed WFA feature descriptor into the adaptively updated Staple algorithm, the proposed algorithm can achieve robust performance under several challenging attributes. Moreover, the proposed algorithm outperforms several state-of-the-art algorithms on the OTB-50 and OTB-100 datasets.

Acknowledgments. This work was supported by the National Natural Science Foundation of China under Grants U1605252, 61472334, 61571379 and 61370124, and by the Natural Science Foundation of Fujian Province of China under Grant 2017J01127.

References

1. Bertinetto, L., Valmadre, J., Golodetz, S., Miksik, O., Torr, P.H.S.: Staple: complementary learners for real-time tracking. In: CVPR, pp. 1401–1409 (2016)
2. Bolme, D.S., Beveridge, J.R., Draper, B.A., Lui, Y.M.: Visual object tracking using adaptive correlation filters. In: CVPR, pp. 2544–2550 (2010)
3. Casasent, D., Patnaik, R.: Analysis of kernel distortion-invariant filters. In: SPIE, p. 67640Y (2007)
4. Dalal, N., Triggs, B.: Histograms of oriented gradients for human detection. In: CVPR, pp. 886–893 (2005)
5. Danelljan, M., Häger, G., Khan, F.S., Felsberg, M.: Learning spatially regularized correlation filters for visual tracking. In: ICCV, pp. 4310–4318 (2015)
6. Danelljan, M., Häger, G., Shahbaz Khan, F., Felsberg, M.: Accurate scale estimation for robust visual tracking. In: BMVC (2014)
7. Gray, R.M.: Toeplitz and Circulant Matrices: A Review. Now Publishers Inc., Norwell (2006)
8. Hare, S., Saffari, A., Torr, P.H.: Struck: structured output tracking with kernels. In: ICCV, pp. 263–270 (2011)

9. Henriques, J.F., Caseiro, R., Martins, P., Batista, J.: Exploiting the circulant structure of tracking-by-detection with kernels. In: Fitzgibbon, A., Lazebnik, S., Perona, P., Sato, Y., Schmid, C. (eds.) ECCV 2012. LNCS, vol. 7575, pp. 702–715. Springer, Heidelberg (2012). https://doi.org/10.1007/978-3-642-33765-9_50

10. Henriques, J.F., Caseiro, R., Martins, P., Batista, J.: High-speed tracking with kernelized correlation filters. IEEE Trans. PAMI **37**(3), 583–596 (2014)

11. Kalal, Z., Mikolajczyk, K., Matas, J.: Tracking-learning-detection. IEEE Trans. PAMI **34**(7), 1409–1422 (2012)

12. Liu, S., Zhang, T., Cao, X., Xu, C.: Structural correlation filter for robust visual tracking. In: CVPR, pp. 4312–4320 (2016)

13. Ma, C., Huang, J.B., Yang, X., Yang, M.H.: Hierarchical convolutional features for visual tracking. In: ICCV, pp. 3074–3082 (2015)

14. Nam, H., Han, B.: Learning multi-domain convolutional neural networks for visual tracking. In: CVPR, pp. 4293–4302 (2016)

15. Wang, N., Shi, J., Yeung, D.Y., Jia, J.: Understanding and diagnosing visual tracking systems. In: ICCV, pp. 3101–3109 (2015)

16. Wu, Y., Lim, J., Yang, M.H.: Online object tracking: a benchmark. In: CVPR, pp. 2411–2418 (2013)

17. Wu, Y., Lim, J., Yang, M.H.: Object tracking benchmark. IEEE Trans. PAMI **37**(9), 1834–1848 (2015)

18. Li, Y., Zhu, J.: A scale adaptive kernel correlation filter tracker with feature integration. In: Agapito, L., Bronstein, M.M., Rother, C. (eds.) ECCV 2014. LNCS, vol. 8926, pp. 254–265. Springer, Cham (2015). https://doi.org/10.1007/978-3-319-16181-5_18

A Novel Method for Camera Pose Tracking Using Visual Complementary Filtering

Xiangkai Lin and Ronggang Wang[✉]

Shenzhen Graduate School, Peking University, Beijing, China
rgwang@pkusz.edu.cn

Abstract. Camera pose tracking is one of the major problems of Augmented Reality (AR) system. While tracking technologies based on fiducial markers have dominated the development of AR applications for almost a decade, various real-time approaches to Natural-Image-Marker tracking have recently been presented. However, most existing approaches do not yet achieve sufficient frame rates for AR on mobile phones or at least require an extensive training phase in advance. In this paper, we propose a novel method for fast camera pose tracking using visual complementary filtering. Compared with existing methods, our method improves the accuracy at the same time guarantee the running speed. Our method can be used in Augmented Reality System with a stored natural image. The implementation is very fast and robust, allowing running even on mobile phones at highly interactive rates and accuracy. Our implementation can immediately track features captured from a photo without any training.

Keywords: Augmented Reality (AR) · Camera pose tracking
Visual complementary filtering · Mobile computing

1 Introduction

In a typical AR game application scenarios, we demand that users can interact with a certain object, such as a marker of a nature image (c.f. Fig. 1(a)). The user can observe the marker through the camera, while AR algorithm will draw a virtual object on the corresponding marker position (c.f. Fig. 1(b)). To ensure that the virtual object remain stationary as the camera moves, we need to track the precise camera pose from the marker. Such camera pose tracking algorithms face great challenges in tracking accuracy and running speed.

Existing nature image marker tracking AR systems can be divided into two categories: the first kind of methods first detect the marker, then perform tracking based on its salient feature points (e.g. [1]). The second kind of methods perform detection and tracking simultaneously, then fuse their results using optimization (e.g. [2]). The former is easy to be lost due to its simplicity, while the latter is too complex to achieve real-time on mobile devices.

To deal with above problem, we employ visual complementary filtering to fuse the results of detection and tracking, avoiding complex optimizing process while significant reduce the running time and improve the robustness.

The main contributions of this paper are as follows.

© Springer International Publishing AG, part of Springer Nature 2018
B. Zeng et al. (Eds.): PCM 2017, LNCS 10735, pp. 238–246, 2018.
https://doi.org/10.1007/978-3-319-77380-3_23

(a)   (b)

Fig. 1. (a) Nature image marker. (b) Draw virtual objects on the marker.

- We propose a method based on visual complementary filtering to fuse the results of detection and tracking.
- We design a fast and robust camera pose tracking system, which can be used in Augmented Reality.

2   System Overview

Our system consists of four modules. A Rigid Detector which is used for initialize our system through a rigid marker detection. Then we use a Tracker to track significantly feature corners in main thread. At the same time a Fast Detector is running in the background thread preparing to update the Tracker. And we design a Fusion using a visual complementary filtering to fuse the results of detection and tracking. The framework is shown in Fig. 2.

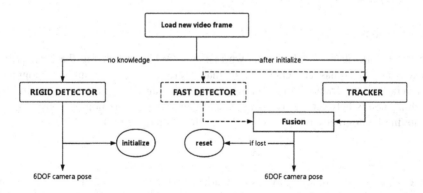

Fig. 2. Framework of our camera pose tracking system.

2.1 Rigid Detector

The framework of the Rigid Detector is shown in Fig. 3. The Rigid Detector is awakened only when the system starts for the first time or the Tracker has been interrupted in the previous frame, and it will sleep other time.

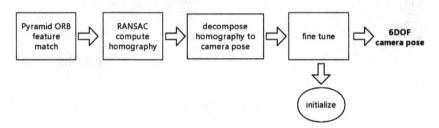

Fig. 3. Framework of the Rigid Detector.

The ORB features [3] are detected in the coming frame. Afterwards these features are matched against a reference feature map. This feature map is generated when given a new marker image, which detected features from the marker image in multiscale. Then, the 2D feature matches are taken to calculate the homography from marker image to the current frame by applying several RANSAC iterations [4]. Considering all the corresponding 3D features in the marker are on the same plane, we generate a truncated extrinsic matrix from homography [5], which can be taken to decompose the exact camera 6-DOF pose [5]. Followed by a pose refinement step with a non-linear-least-square algorithm [6], we can get the accurate 6-DOF camera pose.

If a sufficient number of feature correspondences have been detected and validated by RANSAC iterations, we initialize our Tracker and Fast detector. We use the camera pose to find the marker area in current frame and then update the homography from marker image to current frame.

2.2 Tracker

The framework of the Tracker is shown in Fig. 4. While initializing the Tracker, we detect some Shi-Tomasi corners [7] in the marker area and store the initial homography H_{lm}. When a new frame comes, we use the Lucas-Kanade algorithm [7] to find the matching points between the two frames and then compute the homography H_{cl}. We update the homography iteratively to get the final homography H_{cm} using:

$$H_{cm} = H_{cl} \times H_{lm} \tag{1}$$

where H_{cm} is the homography from marker image to current frame, H_{cl} is the homography from current frame to latest frame and H_{lm} is the homography from current frame to marker image.

After that, we decompose H_{cm} to get the camera pose from marker to current frame. Finally, we update the H_{lm} to H_{cm} and wait the next cycle.

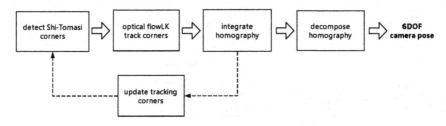

Fig. 4. Framework of the Tracker.

We can use the result to find the current marker area and update the tracking Shi-Tomasi corners. It's no need to run it every cycle, so we put it in background.

Once Tracker is initialized, it can run without detector. Since we only track very few corners, it can be very fast. However, the error may accumulate with the iteration, resulting in drift. If Tracker lost, we will reset our system and call the Rigid Detector.

2.3   Fast Detector

As we can see in Fig. 5, compared with the Rigid Detector, the Fast Detector only detect features in the marker area and relax the feature extracted parameters. In matching process, it takes into account the latest camera pose to speed up matching. And it won't do the time-consuming fine tune.

Fast Detector will only run in background thread. Once have a result, we use it to correct our Tracker's bias.

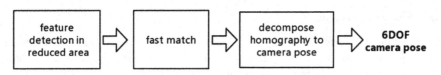

Fig. 5. Framework of the Fast Detector.

2.4   Fusion with Visual Complementary Filtering

The framework of the Fusion is shown in Fig. 6. The camera pose result of the Tracker T_t is accurate and smooth, but it will accumulate error and gradually leads to a drift. The Detector's result T_t has a high frequency error but the mean is stable. The two modules are complementary in frequency characteristic [8]. So, we use a low-pass filter F_l to filtering T_d, and a high-pass filter F_h to filtering T_t, and use the complementary filtering method to combine the two results and then get the accurate camera pose T_f.

$$T_f = F_l \times T_d + F_h \times T_t \qquad (2)$$

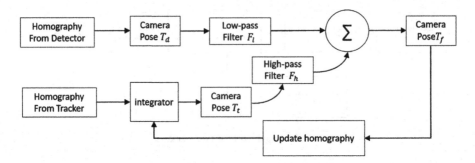

Fig. 6. Framework of the Fusion with Visual Complementary Filtering.

As in Eq. (2), $F_l = \frac{c}{s+c}$, $F_h = 1 - F_l$, where s is a constant number and c is an all-pass filter. In our method, we choose the parameter c as a constant number 9, while parameter s as 1.

We can directly use Eq. (2) to filter the translation. While dealing with rotation, we should firstly change it into quaternions and then filter with a SLERP interpolation. The final result T_f will be used to update the Tracker.

3 Experiments and Analysis

We test our system in terms of running speed and tracking accuracy. All the input frames are resized into size 640×480.

3.1 Tracking Precision Test

We compare the performance of our system with that of ARToolkit, which is the currently best open-source AR system. We use the same marker image as ARToolkit.

To evaluate the tracking accuracy of the camera pose, we use a ray tracer to generate images with known ground truth (c.f. Fig. 7). We can use a Rendering Engine like OPENGL to generate it.

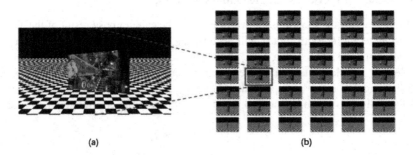

(a)   (b)

Fig. 7. (a) A synthetic image. (b) A small part of our synthetic image data set.

The first experiment measured the orientation accuracy of targets while fixing the distance. We measure rotation accuracy by term:

$$E_r = \sqrt{\left(g\left(f(R_t) - f(R_g)\right)\right)^2} \tag{3}$$

where R_t is the current rotation matrix and R_g is the ground-truth rotation matrix. The function f(.) is to changes the rotation matrix to a quaternion vector, and the function g(.) is to calculate inner product.

We set the marker on the screen as the initial pose, and rotate marker around an axis from degrees 0 to 90. At the same time, we generate the rotation-test data set.

Test result is shown in Fig. 8. We can see that error is increasing with the increase of rotation angle. The reason is through rotation, image will suffer a significant affine transformation, which will destroy the features in tracking. Compared with ARtookit, our system has smaller error while rotating. Besides, our system can work in a larger range of vision rotation.

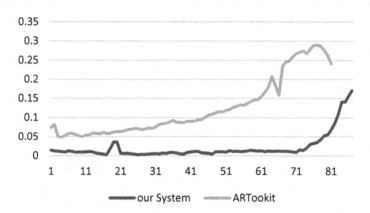

Fig. 8. Comparison of rotation accuracy. The abscissa is the rotation angle.

The complementary experiment is to hold angle and vary the distance. We move the marker away from the screen in a consistent distance and create our translation-test data set. We can measure translation accuracy by the translation data variance. Since different systems have different scale factors, we should firstly normalize their results.

Test result is shown in Fig. 9. When the marker is close, we can only see a part of it, so it is hard to initialize. Once initialized, a closer image will provide more clear features to track, which makes the result more accuracy. As distance increases, the accuracy will decrease. Compared with ARtookit, our system can be initialized in a closer distance. Besides, our system provides significantly more robust results.

We also compare the performance of our whole system with only use the Tracker and the Detector. We compare their rotation accuracy using the rotation-test data set.

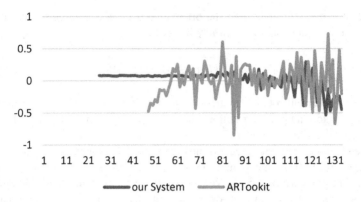

Fig. 9. Comparison of translation accuracy. The abscissa is normalized distance.

From Fig. 10, the Detector work in a smaller range of angle range with a larger deviation. The Tracker will accumulate error over time. Finally, through our method of visual complementary filtering, we can get the best results with least error.

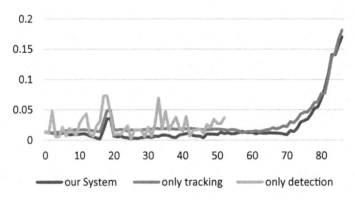

Fig. 10. Internal comparison results of rotation accuracy.

3.2 Running Speed Test

We test the running speed of our system both on desktop hardware and mobile phones. We calculate the time from the acquisition of a new frame to the calculation of a new camera pose result. All performance values are averaged over 30 iterations. And we separately test the Rigid Detector, the Fast Detector, the Tracker and the main thread.

As for desktop hardware, we use a Lenovo y720 with an Inter i5-6300HQ CPU@2.3 Ghz, an ASUS n56 with an Inter i5-3230M CPU@2.6 Ghz, and a Surface 3 with an Inter Atom x7-Z8700 CPU@1.6 Ghz. The testing results are shown in Table 1.

As for mobile phones, we choose Samsung s7, Xiaomi 5, and Meizu note3 as our test platform. The testing results are shown in Table 2.

Table 1. Average running time in desktop hardware. All values are given in milliseconds.

PC	Lenovo r720	ASUS n56	Surface 3
Rigid Detector	11.38	20.71	32.21
Fast Detector	8.14	18.49	28.45
Tracker	2.52	3.42	6.65
Main Thread	3.12	4.16	7.99

Table 2. Average running time on mobile phone. All values are given in milliseconds.

Phone	Samsung S7	Xiaomi 5	Meizu note3
Rigid Detector	22.47	25.21	57.13
Fast Detector	18.35	21.28	51.36
Tracker	6.36	8.57	18.92
Main Thread	7.39	9.56	19.18

As shown in Table 1 and Table 2, both on the desktop hardware and mobile phones, the most time-consuming part is the Rigid Detector. However, it is an one-time run only happen in initialization. The second time-consuming module is the Fast Detector, which runs in the background thread and won't block the main thread. Tracker is very fast, which make our system run in no more than 20 ms per frame even in low-end mobile phones.

4   Conclusion

In this paper, we present a novel camera pose tracking method using visual complementary filtering. Our system is broadly practical since it only needs a picture of nature image as the marker to track camera pose. The experiments show that our system can achieve higher speed and higher accuracy compared with other implementations. Our system can be easily applied to AR applications in mobile phones.

Acknowledge. Thanks to National Natural Science Foundation of China 61672063, 61370115, China 863 project of 2015AA015905, Shenzhen Peacock Plan, Shenzhen Research Projects of JCYJ20160506172227337 and GGFW2017041215130858, and Guangdong Province Projects of 2014B010117007 and 2014B090910001 for funding.

References

1. Wagner, D., Reitmayr, G., Mulloni, A., Drummond, T., Schmalstieg, D.: Pose tracking from natural features on mobile phones. In: Proceedings of the 7th IEEE/ACM International Symposium on Mixed and Augmented Reality, ISMAR 2008, pp. 125–134. IEEE/ACM (2008)
2. Engedal, T.: Camera pose estimation apparatus and method for augmented reality imaging: U.S. Patent 8,452,080, 28 May 2013

3. Rublee, E., Rabaud, V., Konolige, K., Bradski, G.: ORB: an efficient alternative to SIFT or SURF. In: IEEE International Conference on Computer Vision (ICCV), pp. 2564–2571. IEEE (2011)
4. Herling, J., Broll, W.: An adaptive training-free feature tracker for mobile phones. In: ACM Symposium on Virtual Reality Software and Technology, pp. 35–42. IEEE (2010)
5. Olson, E.: AprilTag: a robust and flexible visual fiducial system. In: 2011 IEEE International Conference on Robotics and Automation (ICRA), vol. 19, no. 6, pp. 3400–3407. IEEE (2011)
6. Hartley, R., Zisserman, A.: Multiple View Geometry in Computer Vision, 2nd edn. Cambridge University Press, New York (2004)
7. Lucas, B.D., Kanade, T.: An iterative image registration technique with an application to stereo vision. In: International Joint Conference on Artificial Intelligence, pp. 674–679. Morgan Kaufmann Publishers Inc (1981)
8. Chang-Siu, E., Tomizuka, M., Kong, K.: Time-varying complementary filtering for attitude estimation. In: International Conference on Intelligent Robots and Systems, pp. 2474–2480. IEEE (2011)

Trajectory-Pooled 3D Convolutional Descriptors for Action Recognition

Xiusheng Lu, Hongxun Yao$^{(\boxtimes)}$, Xiaoshuai Sun, Shengping Zhang,
and Yanhao Zhang

School of Computer Science and Technology, Harbin Institute of Technology,
Harbin, China
xiusheng.lu.cs@gmail.com, {h.yao,xiaoshuaisun,yhzhang}@hit.edu.cn,
shengping.zhang@gmail.com

Abstract. Hand-crafted and learning-based features are two main types of video representations in the field of video understanding. How to combine their merits to design good descriptors has been the research hotspot recently. Following the idea of TDD [1], in this paper, we investigate if the trajectory pooling method is suitable to 3D ConvNets [2]. Specifically, we calculate dense trajectories from the input video and perform trajectory pooling on feature maps of 3D CNN and present a novel trajectory-pooled 3D convolutional descriptor (TC3D) for action recognition. The proposed descriptor combines two advantages: 3D CNN has the ability to extract high-level semantic information from videos and trajectory pooling method utilizes the temporal information of videos subtly. The experiments on the datasets of HMDB51 and UCF101 demonstrate that the proposed descriptor achieves state-of-the-art results.

Keywords: Trajectory pooling · 3D ConvNets · Action recognition

1 Introduction

Action recognition [3–6] has attracted increasing attention in recent years, owing to its potential applications in different fields such as video surveillance, human-computer interaction and robot perception. Numerous researchers dedicate to this area to deal with the challenges like occlusions, low resolution, background clutter and camera motions.

Feature extraction is the fundamental and critical step in the framework of action recognition. There are two main types of features for video description: hand-crafted descriptors and learning-based descriptors. The hand-crafted descriptors contain Histograms of Optical Flows (HOF) [7], Motion Boundary Histograms (MBH) [8], HOG3D [9], 3D SIFT [10], and so on. The process of extracting hand-crafted descriptors mainly can be divided into two steps: the first to detect interest points using some interest-point detector [11] or in a dense way, and then the local information (e.g. pixel value, optical flow) or its gradient in the neighborhood of detected points is aggregated to construct a

© Springer International Publishing AG, part of Springer Nature 2018
B. Zeng et al. (Eds.): PCM 2017, LNCS 10735, pp. 247–257, 2018.
https://doi.org/10.1007/978-3-319-77380-3_24

histogram. The most successful hand-crafted descriptor for action recognition so far is Improved Dense Trajectories (iDT) [5]. In essence, it extracts special spatio-temporal interest areas using dense trajectories where HOG, HOF, and MBH descriptors are calculated. iDT outperforms other hand-crafted descriptors in almost all the public action datasets. These hand-crafted descriptors contain researchers' observation and experience and thus achieve great successes in this area.

For learning-based descriptors, a transformation from raw input to the representation is learned by machine learning methods. Convolutional neural networks (CNN) [12], inspired by the behavior of the animal visual cortex, is proved to be an effective feature learning technique in action recognition [6,13]. CNN can be used to process videos in an end-to-end way or provide deep features as the inputs of feature encoding approaches [14,15] and classifiers. Some deep descriptors (e.g. Deep ConvNets [6]) learn high-level features from raw videos directly by 2D convolutions. Convolutional 3D descriptors (C3D) [2] apply 3D convolution and 3D pooling operations to model the temporal information of the videos better and give superior results. Two-stream ConvNets [13] uses two networks to handle the spatial and temporal information separately and the inputs of its spatial and temporal stream ConvNets are RGB frames and optical flow fields. These deep descriptors work well due to the high discriminative capacity and good generalization ability of deep neural networks.

How to combine the benefits of these two kinds of features to design good descriptors has been an active research area. For instance, trajectory-pooled deep-convolutional descriptor (TDD) [1] unites dense trajectories of iDT descriptors with two-stream ConvNets [13] and achieves good performance. Motivated by TDD, in this paper we focus on integrating trajectory pooling method with C3D descriptors and present a novel trajectory-pooled 3D convolutional descriptor (TC3D) for action recognition, as shown in Fig. 1. Specifically, dense trajectories and the C3D features of *conv4b* and *conv5b* layers are first computed from the input videos. Then we conduct max pooling on *conv4b* and *conv5b* feature maps of C3D to shrink their temporal dimensions to one. In this way, a 16-frame-long trajectory is mapped to 16 points on one corresponding pooled feature map. After two types of normalization techniques, we perform trajectory pooling to the normalized feature maps and obtain the proposed TC3D descriptors.

The proposed descriptor combines the merits of C3D and trajectory pooling method: 3D ConvNets has the ability to extract discriminative and shift-invariant features from videos, while the trajectory pooling method captures the temporal information of videos contained in the trajectories of objects. We should note that our TC3D is different from the process of TDD. In TDD, the feature maps of two-stream ConvNets have the same number of frames to input videos and trajectory pooling method is conducted on different frames of feature maps, whereas we pool the points on the feature maps whose temporal dimensions are one in proposed TC3D. After TC3Ds are gained, we employ Fisher vector [15] to encode them and feed the encoding results to a linear SVM classifier. We evaluate the performance of TC3D on two challenging action datasets:

HMDB51 [16] and UCF101 [17]. The proposed TC3D alone achieves 55.5% and 86.5% on HMDB51 and UCF101. TC3D outperforms C3D (one net) by **4.2%** on UCF101 with the same pre-trained model. When combined with iDT, TC3D obtains accuracies of 64.5% and 90.1% on HMDB51 and UCF101.

The remainder of this paper is organized as follows: In Sect. 2, the proposed trajectory-pooled 3D convolutional descriptor is introduced in detail. We report the experimental results on HMDB51 and UCF101 datasets in Sect. 3. Finally, the whole paper is concluded in Sect. 4.

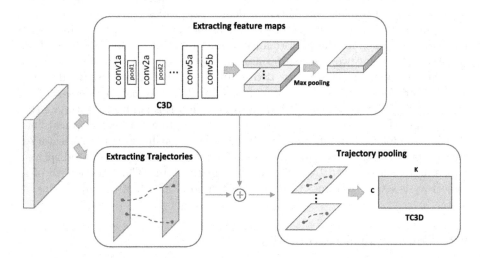

Fig. 1. The process of extracting TC3D. The TC3D framework contains three steps: extracting feature maps of C3D and dense trajectories from raw videos and conducting trajectory-constrained pooling on the extracted feature maps. Finally, TC3Ds that has $C \times K$ dimensions are obtained, where C is the number of channels of feature maps and K is the number of trajectories of the input video.

2 Trajectory-Pooled 3D Convolutional Descriptors

In this section, we elaborate a new trajectory-pooled 3D convolutional descriptor for video representation, as shown in Fig. 1. We first explain the extraction process of dense trajectories and 3D convolutional feature maps from the raw videos. Then, the feature map normalization and trajectory pooling steps are described in detail.

2.1 Dense Trajectories

We adopt improved trajectories [5], which is originally used to compute iDT descriptor, to extract dense trajectories due to its good performance. Improved trajectories is a modified version of dense trajectories [18]. In dense trajectories, feature points are first sampled on a grid spaced by 5 pixels on 8 spatial scales.

Then each point is tracked by median filtering in a dense optical flow field $w = (u_t, v_t)$.

$$P_{t+1} = (x_{t+1}, y_{t+1}) = (x_t, y_t) + (M * w)|_{(\overline{x}_t, \overline{y}_t)} \tag{1}$$

where $P_t = (x_t, y_t)$ represents the feature point at frame t, M is the kernel for median filtering, and $(\overline{x}_t, \overline{y}_t)$ is the rounded position of (x_t, y_t). After the dense optical flow field is calculated, points of adjacent frames are linked to get the trajectories. To avoid drifting problem, the length of a trajectory is limited to 15 frames in [5]. Static trajectories and trajectories with sudden large displacements are also removed to make the obtained dense trajectories more robust.

Compared with dense trajectories, camera motion is considered in improved trajectories to enhance the performance. Camera motion is calculated based on the assumption that two adjacent frames are associated by a homography [19]. To compute the homography matrix, two complementary methods, SURF descriptor [20] and dense optical flow, are combined to find the matches between two frames at first. Afterward, the RANSAC approach [21] is applied to estimate the homography. Eventually, camera motion is removed to get a better optical flow that is more focused on foreground moving objects. In this way, the trajectories generated by background camera motion are suppressed to get small displacements and then removed by a thresholding method. In TC3D, the length of a trajectory is set at 16 frames to match the temporal length of the input clips of C3D.

2.2   Convolutional Feature Maps

We employ 3D ConvNets to learning features from videos in TC3D. 3D convolution and 3D pooling operations are adopted in 3D ConvNets. 3D convolution is the natural extension of 2D convolution. Both 3D convolution and 2D convolution can have multi-dimensional inputs, and the differences exist in the outputs. The outputs of 2D convolution are two-dimensional feature maps, whether its output has two or more dimensions. In contrast, the output volumes of 3D convolution can have multiple dimensions. In other words, 3D convolution conserves the temporal information of the input videos. Hence, we can utilize multiple 3D convolutional layers to handle the spatial and temporal information of the inputs in a hierarchical way simultaneously.

The architecture of C3D is illustrated in Tables 1 and 2. 3D convolution and pooling kernels with a size of $S \times S \times T$ are used, where S and T represent the spatial and temporal size of the kernels. C3D net has 8 convolution layers, which have $3 \times 3 \times 3$ convolutional filters, with stride $1 \times 1 \times 1$. The kernel size of $pool1$ layer is $2 \times 2 \times 1$, with stride $2 \times 2 \times 1$. The other 4 max-pooling layers have $2 \times 2 \times 2$ pooling kernels, with stride $2 \times 2 \times 2$. In our experiments C3D net is used to cope with videos as convolutional feature extractors, not in an end-to-end way. Specifically, we compute feature maps of $conv4b$ and $conv5b$ layers from the input videos and the full-connected layers are abandoned.

We denote the size of the inputs or feature maps by $H \times W \times D \times C$, where H and W are the height and width in spatial dimension, D is the depth in temporal

Table 1. The convolutional layers of the C3D Architecture. C3D net has 8 convolution layers. The kernel sizes of all of the convolution layers are $3 \times 3 \times 3$, with stride $1 \times 1 \times 1$. Ratio represents the spatial map size ratio.

Layer	conv1a	conv2a	conv3a	conv3b	conv4a	conv4b	conv5a	conv5b
Size	$3 \times 3 \times 3$	$3 \times 3 \times 3$	$3 \times 3 \times 3$	$3 \times 3 \times 3$	$3 \times 3 \times 3$	$3 \times 3 \times 3$	$3 \times 3 \times 3$	$3 \times 3 \times 3$
Stride	$1 \times 1 \times 1$	$1 \times 1 \times 1$	$1 \times 1 \times 1$	$1 \times 1 \times 1$	$1 \times 1 \times 1$	$1 \times 1 \times 1$	$1 \times 1 \times 1$	$1 \times 1 \times 1$
Channel	64	128	256	256	512	512	512	512
Ratio	1	1/2	1/4	1/4	1/8	1/8	1/16	1/16

Table 2. The pooling layers of the C3D Architecture. C3D net has 5 pooling layers, which have $2 \times 2 \times 2$ pooling kernels, with stride $2 \times 2 \times 2$, except for *pool1* layer. Ratio represents the spatial map size ratio.

Layer	pool1	pool2	pool3	pool4	pool5
Size	$2 \times 2 \times 1$	$2 \times 2 \times 2$	$2 \times 2 \times 2$	$2 \times 2 \times 2$	$2 \times 2 \times 2$
Stride	$2 \times 2 \times 1$	$2 \times 2 \times 2$	$2 \times 2 \times 2$	$2 \times 2 \times 2$	$2 \times 2 \times 2$
Channel	64	128	256	512	512
Ratio	1/2	1/4	1/8	1/16	1/32

dimension, and C is the number of channels. Then the size of the input clips of C3D net is $112 \times 112 \times 16 \times 3$. The *conv4b* and *conv5b* feature maps has a size of $14 \times 14 \times 4 \times 512$ and $7 \times 7 \times 2 \times 512$ respectively. Whereafter, we conduct a max-pooling operation to reduce the temporal sizes of *conv4b* and *conv5b* feature maps be to one. Finally given a clip V, the representation $F_v \in \mathbb{R}^{H \times W \times C}$ are gained, where H and W are 7 or 14 and C is 512.

2.3   Feature Map Normalization and Trajectory Pooling

Given the representation F_v, two types of normalization approaches (not shown in Fig. 1) are adopted as in TDD. The first one is spatiotemporal normalization. The result of a convolutional layer for each channel can be viewed as a spatiotemporal block. Spatiotemporal normalization is conducted by dividing the feature map values by the maximum value of the spatiotemporal block for each channel.

$$\tilde{F}_{ch}(h, w, c) = F(h, w, c) / max_{h,w} F(h, w, c) \qquad (2)$$

The second normalization method is channel normalization, and the feature map values are divided by the maximum value in the same spatio-temporal position across different channels.

$$\tilde{F}_{st}(h, w, c) = F(h, w, c) / max_c F(h, w, c) \qquad (3)$$

After normalization, the values on the feature map are aligned into a same interval. In experiments, these two normalization approaches are used separately and their results $\tilde{F}_{st}(h, w, c)$ and $\tilde{F}_{ch}(h, w, c)$ are fused to further enhance the performance.

In C3D net, spatial and temporal padding are implemented on the convolutional layers to make its inputs and outputs have the same size. And the effect of the padding is that it create the mappings between the points in videos and those on feature maps. For example, the point with coordinate (h, w, d) in clip V corresponds to that with coordinate $(r \times h, r \times w)$ on the obtained representation F_v, where r is the spatial map size ratio calculated in advance, as shown in Tables 1 and 2. In this way, the points on the trajectories in original features are mapped to those on current representations directly when conducting trajectory pooling.

Given a normalized feature map $\tilde{F}$ and a trajectory T_k, trajectory pooling is carried out as follows:

$$V(T_k, \tilde{F}) = \max_p \tilde{F}(\overline{(r \times h_p^k)}, \overline{(r \times w_p^k)}, c) \qquad (4)$$

where r is the spatial map size ratio, $(r \times h_p^k, r \times w_p^k)$ is mapped from the corresponding p^{th} point (h_p^k, w_p^k, d_p^k) of original video in trajectory T_k, $\overline{(\cdot)}$ is the rounding operation. $V(T_k, \tilde{F}) \in \mathbb{R}^{C \times K}$ is the designed trajectory-pooled 3D convolutional descriptors, where C is the number of channels and K is the number of trajectories.

3   Experiments

In this section, we test the proposed feature on two public datasets: HMDB51 [16] and UCF101 [17]. We first describe the datasets and implementation details. Then the proposed descriptor is evaluated and compared with other methods.

3.1   Datasets and Implementation Details

The HMDB51 dataset has 6766 video clips taken from movies, YouTube, Google videos, etc. This dataset contains five types of actions from general facial actions to body movements for human interaction and covers 51 action categories. We employ three training/testing splits and report average accuracy over three splits as in [16]. The UCF101 dataset involves realistic videos collected from YouTube. It includes 13320 video sequences and has 101 action classes. Each class has 25 groups and the sequences in the same group may share some common characteristics (i.e. similar background). We use the three training/testing splits as in [17] and also report average accuracy.

In the experiments, feature maps of *conv4b* and *conv5b* layers of C3D net are extracted, whose sizes are $14 \times 14 \times 4 \times 512$ and $7 \times 7 \times 2 \times 512$. When computing features maps from the HMDB51 and UCF101 datasets, a C3D model that is pre-trained on Sports-1M and released by Tran et al. in [2] is employed. After max pooling operation in temporal dimension, a representation whose size is

$7 \times 7 \times 512$ or $14 \times 14 \times 512$ is acquired. We conduct spatiotemporal and channel normalization to the representation, and the two normalized representations and the original representation are utilized to compute different TC3Ds, which will be fused to boost the experimental results. The 16-frame-long dense trajectories from videos are extracted because the input of C3D net is 16-frame-long clip. Then we obtain TC3D with a size of $512 \times K$ by trajectory pooling, where K is the number of trajectories in this video. Next, PCA is used to reduce TC3Ds to 128 dimensions to cut down the time and space overhead. After we get TC3Ds from the videos, Fisher vector [15] is applied to encode them. We first build a dictionary of visual words by GMM with $G(G = 256)$ mixtures. Then we assign TC3D to their nearest visual words and gain a vector with $2 \times 128 \times 256$ dimensions. At last, linear SVM is employed as the classifier.

3.2 Experimental Results

We first evaluate the performance of sum pooling and methods in trajectory pooling step on three splits of HMDB51. TC3D with *conv5* feature maps and spatiotemporal normalization are used in the experiments and the results are summarized in Table 3. The average accuracy of max pooling is 0.4 higher than sum pooling. Therefore max trajectory pooling is chose in our TC3D pipeline. Table 4 reports the recognition results of TC3D with different convolutional layers. We see that the combination of *conv4* and *conv5* improves the average accuracy, which indicates that TC3Ds with different layers are complementary to each other.

We compare TC3D with other algorithms and summarize the action recognition accuracy in Table 5. The upper part shows the recognition methods whose inputs are only RGB videos. The lower part presents other algorithms that take

Table 3. The performance of different trajectory pooling methods (with *conv5* feature maps and spatiotemporal normalization) on three splits of HMDB51 dataset. Max pooling outperforms sum pooling by 0.4%.

HMDB51	Split1	Split2	Split3	Ave
Sum pooling	52.6	50.4	49.7	50.9
Max pooling	52.6	51.8	49.6	**51.3**

Table 4. The average accuracy of TC3D with different layers on HMDB51 and UCF101. The combination of *conv4* and *conv5* achieves better results.

Datasets	conv4	conv5	conv4 + conv5
HMDB51	49.7	54.2	**55.5**
UCF101	83.2	83.1	**86.5**

Table 5. Action recognition results on HMDB51 and UCF101. The upper part shows the recognition methods whose inputs are only RGB frames. The lower part presents the algorithms that takes both RGB frames and optical flow fields as inputs. TC3D outperforms C3D (1 net) by **4.2%** on UCF101 with the same pre-trained model.

Method	HMDB51	UCF101
HOG [5] + FV	40.2	72.4
Deep networks [6]	-	65.4
Spatial stream network [13]	39.0	72.6
LRCN [22]	-	71.1
LSTM composite model [23]	44.1	75.8
C3D (1 net) [2]	-	82.3
Spatial conv4 and conv5 of TDD [1] + FV	50.0	82.8
TC3D + FV	**55.5**	**86.5**
iDT [5] + FV	57.2	84.7
Two-stream networks [13]	59.4	88.0
LRCN [22]	-	82.9
LSTM composite model [23]	-	84.3
Conv. pooling on long clips [24]	-	88.2
LSTM on long clips [24]	-	88.6
TDD [1] + FV	63.2	**90.3**
TC3D and iDT + FV	**64.5**	90.1

both RGB frames and precomputed optical flow fields as inputs. We can see that TC3D combined with Fisher vector and linear SVM performs much better than HOG descriptor and other RGB videos based deep neural networks, containing Deep networks [6], Spatial stream network [13], LRCN [22] and LSTM composite model [23]. TC3D also outperforms C3D [2] and conv4 and conv5 spatial layers of TDD [1]. TC3D and C3D (1 net) use the same pre-trained model in the whole experiments and TC3D performs **4.2%** better than C3D (1 net) on UCF101. The results indicate that trajectory pooling method captures the inherent nature of temporal dimension and promotes the recognition accuracy. When united with iDT descriptors, TC3D performs better than other deep learning methods whose inputs are RGB frames and optical flow fields, except slightly worse than TDD on UCF101. One possible reason is that in TDD multi-scale pyramid representations of frames and optical flow fields (5 scales) are employed, while only one scale information is utilized in proposed TC3D. The confusion matrices of the recognition results using TC3D on Split1 of HMDB51 and UCF101 are illustrated to give an intuitive view in Fig. 2.

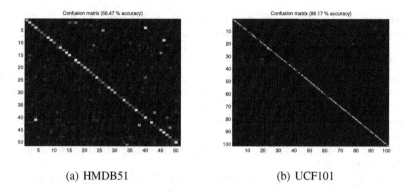

(a) HMDB51   (b) UCF101

Fig. 2. The confusion matrices of the recognition results of TC3D on Split1 of HMDB51 and UCF101 datasets.

4 Conclusion and Future Work

In this paper, we combine C3D with dense trajectories and present a new trajectory-pooled 3D convolutional descriptor for action recognition. We take advantage of both 3D ConvNets that extracts high-level features from videos and trajectory pooling strategy that utilizes important motion information. Experiments validate the superior performances of the proposed descriptor on two challenging datasets. However, the spatial size of $conv4b$ and $conv5b$ feature maps in C3D net is only 14×14 and 7×7, which limits the performance of TC3D. In future, we will imitate C3D net and train our own 3D ConvNets that is more suitable for trajectory pooling method.

Acknowledgements. This work was supported by the National Natural Science Foundation of China (No. 61472103).

References

1. Wang, L., Qiao, Y., Tang, X.: Action recognition with trajectory-pooled deep-convolutional descriptors. In: Proceedings of the IEEE Conference on Computer Vision and Pattern Recognition, pp. 4305–4314 (2015)
2. Tran, D., Bourdev, L., Fergus, R., Torresani, L., Paluri, M.: Learning spatiotemporal features with 3D convolutional networks. In: Proceedings of the IEEE International Conference on Computer Vision, pp. 4489–4497 (2015)
3. Aggarwal, J.K., Ryoo, M.S.: Human activity analysis: a review. ACM Comput. Surv. (CSUR) **43**(3), 16 (2011)
4. Poppe, R.: A survey on vision-based human action recognition. Image Vis. Comput. **28**(6), 976–990 (2010)
5. Wang, H., Schmid, C.: Action recognition with improved trajectories. In: Proceedings of the IEEE International Conference on Computer Vision, pp. 3551–3558 (2013)

6. Karpathy, A., Toderici, G., Shetty, S., Leung, T., Sukthankar, R., Fei-Fei, L.: Large-scale video classification with convolutional neural networks. In: Proceedings of the IEEE conference on Computer Vision and Pattern Recognition, pp. 1725–1732 (2014)

7. Laptev, I., Marszałek, M., Schmid, C., Rozenfeld, B.: Learning realistic human actions from movies. In: IEEE Conference on Computer Vision and Pattern Recognition, CVPR 2008, pp. 1–8. IEEE (2008)

8. Dalal, N., Triggs, B., Schmid, C.: Human detection using oriented histograms of flow and appearance. In: Leonardis, A., Bischof, H., Pinz, A. (eds.) ECCV 2006. LNCS, vol. 3952, pp. 428–441. Springer, Heidelberg (2006). https://doi.org/10.1007/11744047_33

9. Klaser, A., Marszałek, M., Schmid, C.: A spatio-temporal descriptor based on 3D-gradients. In: BMVC 2008–19th British Machine Vision Conference, p. 275-1. British Machine Vision Association (2008)

10. Scovanner, P., Ali, S., Shah, M.: A 3-dimensional sift descriptor and its application to action recognition. In: Proceedings of the 15th International Conference on Multimedia, pp. 357–360. ACM (2007)

11. Harris, C., Stephens, M.: A combined corner and edge detector. In: Alvey Vision Conference, vol. 15, p. 50. Citeseer (1988)

12. Krizhevsky, A., Sutskever, I., Hinton, G.E.: ImageNet classification with deep convolutional neural networks. In: Advances in Neural Information Processing Systems, pp. 1097–1105 (2012)

13. Simonyan, K., Zisserman, A.: Two-stream convolutional networks for action recognition in videos. In: Advances in Neural Information Processing Systems, pp. 568–576 (2014)

14. Fei-Fei, L., Perona, P.: A Bayesian hierarchical model for learning natural scene categories. In: IEEE Computer Society Conference on Computer Vision and Pattern Recognition, CVPR 2005, vol. 2, pp. 524–531. IEEE (2005)

15. Sánchez, J., Perronnin, F., Mensink, T., Verbeek, J.: Image classification with the fisher vector: theory and practice. Int. J. Comput. Vis. 105(3), 222–245 (2013)

16. Kuehne, H., Jhuang, H., Garrote, E., Poggio, T., Serre, T.: HMDB: a large video database for human motion recognition. In: 2011 IEEE International Conference on Computer Vision (ICCV), pp. 2556–2563. IEEE (2011)

17. Soomro, K., Zamir, A.R., Shah, M.: Ucf101: A dataset of 101 human actions classes from videos in the wild. arXiv preprint arXiv:1212.0402 (2012)

18. Wang, H., Kläser, A., Schmid, C., Liu, C.L.: Action recognition by dense trajectories. In: 2011 IEEE Conference on Computer Vision and Pattern Recognition (CVPR), pp. 3169–3176. IEEE (2011)

19. Szeliski, R.: Image alignment and stitching: a tutorial. Found. Trends® Comput. Graph. Vis. 2(1), 1–104 (2006)

20. Bay, H., Tuytelaars, T., Van Gool, L.: SURF: speeded up robust features. In: Leonardis, A., Bischof, H., Pinz, A. (eds.) ECCV 2006. LNCS, vol. 3951, pp. 404–417. Springer, Heidelberg (2006). https://doi.org/10.1007/11744023_32

21. Fischler, M.A., Bolles, R.C.: Random sample consensus: a paradigm for model fitting with applications to image analysis and automated cartography. Commun. ACM 24(6), 381–395 (1981)

22. Donahue, J., Anne Hendricks, L., Guadarrama, S., Rohrbach, M., Venugopalan, S., Saenko, K., Darrell, T.: Long-term recurrent convolutional networks for visual recognition and description. In: Proceedings of the IEEE Conference on Computer Vision and Pattern Recognition, pp. 2625–2634 (2015)

23. Srivastava, N., Mansimov, E., Salakhutdinov, R.: Unsupervised learning of video representations using LSTMs. In: ICML, pp. 843–852 (2015)
24. Ng, J.Y.-H., Hausknecht, M., Vijayanarasimhan, S., Vinyals, O., Monga, R., Toderici, G.: Beyond short snippets: deep networks for video classification. In: Proceedings of the IEEE Conference on Computer Vision and Pattern Recognition, pp. 4694–4702 (2015)

Temporal Interval Regression Network for Video Action Detection

Qing Wang[1,2], Laiyun Qing[1,2(✉)], Jun Miao[3], and Lijuan Duan[4]

[1] School of Computer and Control Engineering,
University of Chinese Academy of Sciences, Beijing 101400, China
lyqing@ucas.ac.cn
[2] Key Lab of Intelligent Information Processing of Chinese Academy of Sciences
(CAS), Institute of Computing Technology, CAS, Beijing 100190, China
qing.wang@vipl.ict.ac.cn
[3] Beijing Key Laboratory of Internet Culture and Digital Dissemination Research,
School of Computer Science, Beijing Information Science and Technology University,
Beijing 100101, China
jmiao@bistu.edu.cn
[4] Faculty of Information Technology, Beijing University of Technology,
Beijing 100124, China
ljduan@bjut.edu.cn

Abstract. Temporal action detection in untrimmed video is an important and challenging task in computer vision. In this paper, a straightforward and efficient regression model is proposed by us to detect action instance and refine action interval in long untrimmed videos. We train a single 3D Convolutional Networks (3D ConvNets) jointly with two sibling output layers: a classification layer to predict the class label and a temporal interval regression layer to modify the temporal localization of input proposal. We also introduce an effective method to sample negative and positive proposals which are discriminative to feature extractor and classifier during training. On THUMOS 2014 dataset, our method achieves competitive performance compared with recent state-of-the-art methods.

Keywords: Action detection · Temporal interval regression
3D ConvNets · Multi-task loss

1 Introduction

Video is the world's largest generator of data, captured by hundreds of millions of cameras in public places where the key information is mostly composed of human action. With the escalating demanding on safety surveillance and video content based retrieval, action recognition and detection task become significant in computer vision, which can turn anonymized video into valuable insights.

Boosting by the powerful image reasoning ability of Convolutional Neural Networks (CNNs), action recognition task has achieved impressive progress in

© Springer International Publishing AG, part of Springer Nature 2018
B. Zeng et al. (Eds.): PCM 2017, LNCS 10735, pp. 258–268, 2018.
https://doi.org/10.1007/978-3-319-77380-3_25

recent years [1,8,10,16,21]. However current action recognition task is limited by manually trimmed short videos in the training and testing sets, while videos captured in the wild are actually long and untrimmed. In order to design generalized model for realistic videos, a more challenging task was proposed by researchers – *temporal action detection task*: besides predicting the class label of the action in videos, the temporal interval (start and end time) of this action is also required [6].

Here we refer to surveys [10,21] to retrospect the history of temporal action detection. CNN-based algorithms remain a popular choice in action detection [12, 13,15,17,24]. Most recent research localizes actions temporally by two strategies: (1) sliding a temporal window to determine the action location and class [3,15, 18], (2) using LSTM-RNNs [12,13].

Classic sequential pipeline approach [4,5,14] in object detection task is profound to action detection. R-CNN [5] consists of selective search, CNN feature extraction, SVM Classification, and bounding box regression. Fast R-CNN [4] improves R-CNN into a single stage with the multi-task loss and the RoI pooling enables proposals to share the feature within one image feature map. Similarly to [5], most of the methods in temporal action detection task consists of the following three parts. The first part is proposal generation. It either uses sliding window approach [15,23] or learns a sparse action proposal dictionary [2] to generate a large amount of video segment candidates. Second, improved Dense Trajectory [20] encoded with Fisher Vector [7] feature or C3D features [19] are extracted by traditional local feature method or Deep ConvNet method. Third, a one-vs-rest SVM classifier or softmax classifier is applied to the third part to give the final decision. Although encouraging performance has been achieved, this sequential pipeline method still remains several problems:

(1) Feature extraction might execute in both proposal generation stage and classification stage. In order to handle the sample skewed problem caused by large background data, some methods facilitate multiple networks to extract feature, which will cause feature redundancy.
(2) Current methods are also constrained by the quality of initial proposals, which defines the upper bound of the model's ability. Once sliding window proposals are determined, temporal intervals of those proposals are fixed and won't be changed in the following progress.

In order to address above problems, we propose a straightforward multi-task learning framework to learn classification and regression tasks jointly as illustrated in Fig. 1. After the proposal generating, we adopt a single 3D ConvNets as feature extractor with two outputs to predict the class label and refine temporal localization respectively. Inspired by bounding box regression task in R-CNN [5], we design a temporal interval regression network to refine the final detected action region, which can break the constraint caused by initial proposal generating method. We conduct experiments on untrimmed video dataset THUMOS 2014 [9] and demonstrate our competitive performance in this dataset.

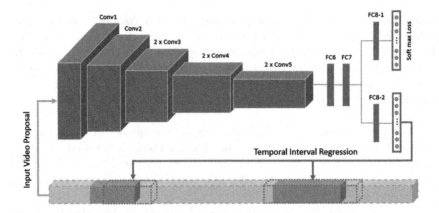

Fig. 1. Overview of our proposed Temporal Interval Regression Network (TIRN). A set of uniformly sampled video proposals are fed into single 3D ConvNets with a softmax layer to output classification scores and a temporal interval regression layer to refine the proposal temporal location. The refined proposal temporal location is regarded as the final predicted result.

2   The Proposed Temporal Interval Regression Network

In this section, we firstly introduce our temporal interval regression network architecture. Second, we describe the training procedure of our model and training proposal sampling method. In the end, we provide details about post-processing with the window length restraint and non-maximum suppression.

2.1   Network Architecture

The main framework we proposed is illustrated in Fig. 1. The input of our Temporal Interval Regression Network (TIRN) is a set of video segment proposals $\{P^i\}_{i=1,\cdots,N}$ generated by video V. Each proposal P^i is fed into a single 3D ConvNets to model its spatio-temporal features. Our goal is to predict each input proposal P^i's class label u^i and refine the start time s^i and end time e^i of the current proposal P^i through our temporal interval regression to make a more precise temporal detection with modified start time s_m^i and end time e_m^i.

3D Convolutional Networks. We adopt 3D Convolutional Networks (3D ConvNets) [19] as our basic feature extractor, since it can efficiently and effectively capture interpretable spatial and temporal information of videos through 3-dimensional convolution and pooling. Refer to the standard C3D (Convolutional 3D) architecture, our network has 8 convolution, 5 max-pooling, and 2 fully convolutional layers, followed by two output layers: a softmax classification layer and a temporal interval regression layer which we will refer in next subsection. The input of 3D ConvNets is 16-frames video clip, the input dimensions are $3 \times 16 \times 128 \times 171 \times 3$. To elucidate the details in network, the number of filters for 8 convolution layers from 1 to 8 are 64, 128, 256, 256, 512, 512, 512, 512, respectively. All convolution kernels are in size of $3 \times 3 \times 3$ with appropriate padding and stride 1. Except for the first and second convolution layers, every two layers are followed by a max-pooling of kernel size $2 \times 2 \times 2$ with stride 1.

Temporal Interval Regression. In analogy to spatial bounding box regression [4,5] in object detection task for images, we extend this notion to action detection task for video, namely *temporal interval regression*, to regress the start time and end time transformation of a video proposal. In Sect. 1 we mentioned that the quality of proposals we generate actually defines the upper bound of detection performance. Here we intend to break this restriction, so that no matter what kind of proposal generating method is used we still can refine the region of temporal interval to achieve further improvement. To this end, we propose temporal interval regression method to regress the transformation of the start time and end time positions. Each input proposal P^i with its temporal location ground-truth G^i is a set of N training pairs $\{(P^i, G^i)\}_{i=1,...,N}$, where $P^i = (P_c^i, P_l^i)$ specifies the center time position and interval length of proposal P^i. Each ground-truth temporal interval is specified in the same way: $G^i = (G_c^i, G_l^i)$. Our goal is to learn a transformation that maps a proposal interval (s^i, e^i) to a ground-truth interval (s_{gt}^i, e_{gt}^i). For convenience, we omit the superscript i in the following description.

We design a pair of transformations (t_c, t_l) as our regression targets, where t_c represents a scale-invariant translation between P_c and G_c, and t_l specifies the log translation of the length between P_l and G_l. For the training pair (P, G), regression targets are defined as

$$t_c = (G_c - P_c)/P_l \tag{1}$$

$$t_l = \log (G_l/P_l). \tag{2}$$

After learning above targets, we can transform an input proposal P into a predicted temporal interval $\widehat{G}$ by applying the transformation

$$\widehat{G}_c = P_l t_c + Pc \tag{3}$$

$$\widehat{G}_l = P_l \exp(t_l). \tag{4}$$

2.2 Training Procedure

Video Proposal Sampling. The training set Φ consists of trimmed videos $\{V_t^i\}_{i=1,...,N_t}$ and untrimmed videos $\{V_u^i\}_{i=1,...,N_u}$. Frame images are extracted from each video with frame rate 25 fps. In order to generate multi-scale video proposals, we implement 6 types of window size at 16, 32, 64, 128, 256, 512 frames to sample uniformly with overlap 0.75 through each video. For the untrimmed video, action instances would be only a small portion of total video while others are non-action backgrounds. In this case, the ratio of positive and negative examples is an important hyper-parameter for our network training procedure.

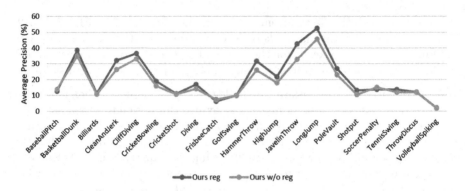

Fig. 2. Impact of the temporal interval regression for per-class breakdown at THUMOS 2014. y-axis is the average precision for each class.

All of the trimmed videos are regarded as positive proposals. As for untrimmed videos, we sample them with Intersection over Union (IoU) at threshold α. We measure IoU of proposal P^i with its nearest ground truth G^i in the video. Therefore positive examples are those proposals with $\alpha > 0.5$ and negative examples are those proposals with $\alpha < 0.3$.

However, we notice that negative examples sampled by IoU threshold are probably not the real background, since the low IoU value might indicate short proposals which actually contain a small portion of action instance. This condition could substantially confuse the classifier and degrade the network performance. In order to prevent the confusion of positive/negative examples in the training set, we re-sample negative examples with temporal actionness threshold [25] β which indicates the temporal proportion of action instance in the current proposal. We randomly sample proposals with $0.01 < \beta < 0.5$ to specifically ensure the ability of our network to distinguish full action contained proposals and partial action contained proposals.

Multi-task Loss. Our Temporal Interval Regression Network has two output layers to implement action classification and temporal interval refinement. For each proposal P^i, we annotate it with a class label $u = \{0, 1, ..., 20\}$ and an interval regression target (g_c, g_l). We adopt a softmax loss L_{cls} to learn the probability distribution $P_{\text{prob}} = (p_0^i, ..., p_k^i)$ over $K + 1$ (background) categories. For the temporal interval regression, we apply smooth $L1$ loss to learn the interval regression target $P_{t^k} = (t_c^k, t_l^k)$ for K classes with its corresponding ground truth target (g_c^k, g_l^k). The regression target for trimmed video proposal is the zero-mean of untrimmed video's regression target. We use a multi-task loss L to train two losses jointly by the end-to-end strategy:

$$L = L_{\text{cls}}(p, u) + \lambda L_{\text{reg}}(t, g). \tag{5}$$

The hyper-parameter λ in Eq. (5) balances the two tasks' loss value. All experiments use $\lambda = 1$. For temporal interval regression, we use the smooth $L1$ loss

$$L_{\text{reg}}(t, g) = \sum_{q \in \{c,l\}} \text{smooth}_{L_1}(t_q - g_q), \qquad (6)$$

in which

$$\text{smooth}_{L_1}(x) = \begin{cases} 0.5x^2 & \text{if} |x| < 1 \\ |x| - 0.5 & \text{otherwise.} \end{cases} \qquad (7)$$

2.3 Post-processing

For test procedure, we adopt the same sliding window sampling strategy with the training set. Among all the test proposals, we uniformly sample 16 frames of each proposal and feed them into our network. For class prediction, we only keep proposals with $u \neq 0$, namely discarding predicted background proposals. Then we transform the original interval of proposal to the refined temporal interval with regression output. We apply the same window length restraint method in Shou et al. [15] to the final refined temporal interval and conduct NMS with the threshold 0.4.

3   Experiments

In this section, we show experimental results of our temporal interval regression network. Firstly, we provide the implementation details of our network and introduce the THUMOS 2014 dataset we used to evaluate our model. Then we analyze the impact of our proposed temporal interval regression task.

Table 1. Temporal action detection results on THUMOS 2014 dataset. The first 3 methods are top 3 performance on the THUMOS 2014 challenge leaderboard. The next 3 methods in the middle section are recent state-of-the-art approaches. The last two are our approaches. The results show that the performance of our approach is competitive. mAP is reported for different Intersection-over-Union (IoU) threshold α.

Method	$\alpha = 0.1$	$\alpha = 0.2$	$\alpha = 0.3$	$\alpha = 0.4$	$\alpha = 0.5$
Svebor et al. [18]	4.6	3.4	2.1	1.4	0.9
Limin et al. [11]	18.2	17.0	14.0	11.7	8.3
Dan et al. [3]	36.6	33.6	27.0	20.8	14.4
Yeung et al. [22]	**48.9**	**44.0**	36.0	26.4	17.1
Shou et al. [15]	47.7	43.5	36.3	28.7	19.0
Zhu et al. [25]	47.7	43.6	36.2	28.9	19.0
Ours w/o interv. reg.	45.8	43.3	35.1	27.3	18.7
Ours intev. reg.	47.2	43.6	**36.6**	**29.4**	**21.2**

3.1 Implementation Details

We fine-tune our temporal regression network with the Sports-1M pre-trained 3D ConvNet model [19]. To set up training, we use a learning rate of 0.0001, with the exception of 0.01 for fc8-1 and fc8-2. The momentum is set to 0.9 and weight decay factor is 0.0005. We drop the learning rate by a factor of 0.1 for every 10 K iterations.

3.2 THUMOS Challenge 2014

Temporal action detection task in THUMOS Challenge 2014 is dedicated to localize action instances in long untrimmed videos. The detection task involves 20 categories. We deploy 2,755 trimmed videos in UCF101 and 200 untrimmed videos in validation set as our training set, both of which contain only 20 actions of detection. The test set contains 3,358 action instances from 1574 untrimmed videos, whereas only 213 of them contain action instances of interest. We exclude remaining 1361 background videos in the test set.

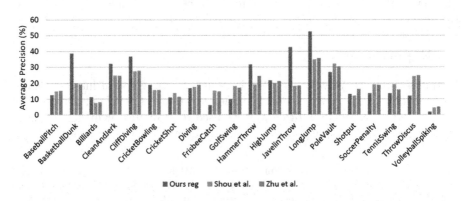

Fig. 3. Histogram of average precision (%) for each class on THUMOS 2014 at IoU of α = 0.5, compared with Shou et al. [15] and Zhu et al. [25] approaches.

Table 1 shows results on this dataset. We report mAPs for different IoU threshold α, and compare our methods with the top 3 methods on the THUMOS 2014 challenge leaderboard and recent state-of-the-art methods. The first 3 rows of method in Table 1 either use Dense Trajectory features [20] or CNN features with the sliding window approach to produce detection predictions. Method [22] leverages CNN as the observation network to find possible action instance frame-wisely and feeds those CNN feature into REINFORCE-based agent to emit the prediction of temporal action location. [22] has the best performance at the lower IoU threshold. This is probably due to its fine-grained frame level features. Method [15] adopt multi-stage 3D ConvNets to eliminate the number of background video segments via the proposal network. Then, [15] uses a localization network to further refine the classification score of testing examples. Although method [15] shows its effectiveness in proposal filtering, training and testing with multiple networks consume a substantial computation time and storage. Method [25] uses the multi-task learning to combine the proposal generation, classification, and localization tasks into a single 3D ConvNets which further improves the efficiency compared with [15]. However, using three softmax layers with conv5, fc6, and fc8 features to enhance the classification score and in all fusing five losses to predict the final results remain [25] redundant. And extra efforts are needed to balance those losses. As for our straightforward method, a single 3D ConvNets with two losses is easier to train with the end-to-end strategy and perform more efficient during training and testing procedures.

Fig. 4. Two examples from test set illustrate the predicted results of our Temporal Interval Regression Network.

Ablation Study. Table 1 also shows results for the ablation study results for temporal interval regression at the last two rows. For *ours w/o interv. reg.* method, we apply the same post-processing method on the ith proposal's original temporal interval (s^i, e^i) without regression refinement. We find that the higher evaluation IoU threshold will lead to a more severe performance degradation. In Fig. 2, we further illustrate impacts of temporal interval regression on 20 action categories respectively. It can be seen that interval refinement has positive effects on most of action categories, except for baseball pitch, frisbee catch, and soccer penalty, where their APs are a little lower with interval refinement. This is probably because the boundaries of these actions are ambiguous and hard to define for the detection task.

Per-class Breakdown. We show the performance of our network on each class compared with method [15,25] in Fig. 3. Our model outperforms the two methods on 9 out of 20 classes. Specifically, our method improved significantly in some challenging class: basketball dunk, javelin throw and long jump. In Fig. 4, we illustrate two examples of our prediction results for temporal interval regression. The upper one is an example of javelin throw showing that the temporal interval regression shift the original proposal ahead of the time to get closer to ground truth. The bottom one is an example of cliff diving showing that the length of origin proposal is rescale to further match the ground truth. Notably, form this example we find that our model is also robust to shot change.

Efficiency Analysis. We measure the processing speed of our method and compare it against approach [15] on the THUMOS 14 dataset as shown in Table 2. The reported time is the average time needed to process the sliding window approach generating proposals from a single 2-minute video. We can tell from the results that our method speeds up the computational time of detection, since we only use a single 3D ConvNets to extract C3D features. For the fair evaluation, we adopt the same proposal generating strategy and test both methods under one testing environment with a single Nvidia GTX Titan X GPU.

Table 2. Time comparison between our approach with [15]. Reported times correspond to the average processing time for a single 2-minute video from the THUMOS 2014 test set.

Method	Time(seconds)	Num. of proposals	FPS
Shou et al. [15]	64.4	1588	50.7
Ours intev. reg.	47.3	1588	**69.1**

4   Conclusions

In this paper, we propose Temporal Interval Regression Network (TIRN) to detect action instances in videos. Our network is implemented with a single 3D ConvNets followed by two sibling losses to conduct classification and regression tasks. This simple but effective framework enables our network to modify the start time and end time of input proposals adaptively. We also introduce a valid training proposal sampling approach which leverages the actionness threshold to prevent the confusion of full action contained proposals and partial action contained proposals. By training our network end-to-end with the multi-task loss, our method achieves competitive results compared with recent state-of-art works in THUMOS 2014 dataset.

Acknowledgments. This research is partially sponsored by Natural Science Foundation of China (Nos. 61472387, 61650201 and 61370113), Beijing Natural Science Foundation (Nos. 4152005 and 4162058), the Science and Technology Program of Tianjin (15YFXQGX0050), and the Qinghai Natural Science Foundation (2016-ZJ-Y04).

References

1. Bilen, H., Fernando, B., Gavves, E., Vedaldi, A., Gould, S.: Dynamic image networks for action recognition. In: Proceedings of the IEEE Conference on Computer Vision and Pattern Recognition, pp. 3034–3042 (2016)
2. Caba Heilbron, F., Carlos Niebles, J., Ghanem, B.: Fast temporal activity proposals for efficient detection of human actions in untrimmed videos. In: Proceedings of the IEEE Conference on Computer Vision and Pattern Recognition, pp. 1914–1923 (2016)

3. Dan, O., Jakob, V., Cordelia, S.: The LEAR submission at Thumos 2014 (2014)
4. Girshick, R.: Fast R-CNN. In: Proceedings of the IEEE International Conference on Computer Vision, pp. 1440–1448 (2015)
5. Girshick, R., Donahue, J., Darrell, T., Malik, J.: Rich feature hierarchies for accurate object detection and semantic segmentation. In: Proceedings of the IEEE Conference on Computer Vision and Pattern Recognition, pp. 580–587 (2014)
6. Idrees, H., Zamir, A.R., Jiang, Y.G., Gorban, A., Laptev, I., Sukthankar, R., Shah, M.: The Thumos challenge on action recognition for videos "in the wild". Comput. Vis. Image Underst. **155**, 1–23 (2017)
7. Jaakkola, T.S., Haussler, D., et al.: Exploiting generative models in discriminative classifiers. In: Advances in Neural Information Processing Systems, pp. 487–493 (1999)
8. Ji, S., Xu, W., Yang, M., Yu, K.: 3D convolutional neural networks for human action recognition. IEEE Trans. Pattern Anal. Mach. Intell. **35**(1), 221–231 (2013)
9. Jiang, Y., Liu, J., Zamir, A.R., Toderici, G., Laptev, I., Shah, M., Sukthankar, R.: Thumos challenge: action recognition with a large number of classes (2014)
10. Kang, S., Wildes, R.P.: Review of action recognition and detection methods (2016). http://arxiv.org/abs/1610.06906
11. Limin, W., Yu, Q., Xiaoou, T.: Action recognition and detection by combining motion and appearance features (2014)
12. Ma, S., Sigal, L., Sclaroff, S.: Learning activity progression in LSTMs for activity detection and early detection. In: Proceedings of the IEEE Conference on Computer Vision and Pattern Recognition, pp. 1942–1950 (2016)
13. Ni, B., Yang, X., Gao, S.: Progressively parsing interactional objects for fine grained action detection. In: Proceedings of the IEEE Conference on Computer Vision and Pattern Recognition, pp. 1020–1028 (2016)
14. Ren, S., He, K., Girshick, R., Sun, J.: Faster R-CNN: towards real-time object detection with region proposal networks. In: Advances in Neural Information Processing Systems, pp. 91–99 (2015)
15. Shou, Z., Wang, D., Chang, S.F.: Temporal action localization in untrimmed videos via multi-stage CNNs. In: Proceedings of the IEEE Conference on Computer Vision and Pattern Recognition, pp. 1049–1058 (2016)
16. Simonyan, K., Zisserman, A.: Two-stream convolutional networks for action recognition in videos, pp. 568–576 (2014)
17. Singh, B., Marks, T.K., Jones, M., Tuzel, O., Shao, M.: A multi-stream Bidirectional recurrent neural network for fine-grained action detection. In: Proceedings of the IEEE Conference on Computer Vision and Pattern Recognition, pp. 1961–1970 (2016)
18. Svebor, K., Lorenzo, S., Alberto, Del, B.: Fast saliency based pooling of fisher encoded dense trajectories (2014)
19. Tran, D., Bourdev, L., Fergus, R., Torresani, L., Paluri, M.: Learning spatiotemporal features with 3D convolutional networks. In: Proceedings of the IEEE International Conference on Computer Vision, pp. 4489–4497 (2015)
20. Wang, H., Schmid, C.: Action recognition with improved trajectories. In: Proceedings of the IEEE International Conference on Computer Vision, pp. 3551–3558 (2013)
21. Weinland, D., Ronfard, R., Boyer, E.: A survey of vision-based methods for action representation, segmentation and recognition. Comput. Vis. Image Underst. **115**(2), 224–241 (2011)

22. Yeung, S., Russakovsky, O., Mori, G., Fei-Fei, L.: End-to-end learning of action detection from frame glimpses in videos. In: Proceedings of the IEEE Conference on Computer Vision and Pattern Recognition, pp. 2678–2687 (2016)

23. Yu, G., Yuan, J.: Fast action proposals for human action detection and search. In: Proceedings of the IEEE Conference on Computer Vision and Pattern Recognition, pp. 1302–1311 (2015)

24. Ng, J.Y.-H., Hausknecht, M., Vijayanarasimhan, S., Vinyals, O., Monga, R., Toderici, G.: Beyond short snippets: deep networks for video classification. In: Proceedings of the IEEE Conference on Computer Vision and Pattern Recognition, pp. 4694–4702 (2015)

25. Zhu, Y., Newsam, S.: Efficient action detection in untrimmed videos via multi-task learning. In: 2017 IEEE Winter Conference on Applications of Computer Vision (WACV), pp. 197–206. IEEE (2017)

Semantic Sequence Analysis for Human Activity Prediction

Guolong Wang, Zheng Qin$^{(\boxtimes)}$, and Kaiping Xu

School of Software, Tsinghua University, Beijing, China
{wanggl16,xkp13}@mails.tsinghua.edu.cn, qingzh@tsinghua.edu.cn

Abstract. The task of long video analysis is challenging, and it is often the case that many human actions occur but only a few contribute to the semantic topic of the video. However, compared with short video human activity studies, long video analysis has its practical utility especially considering the effort of watching a long video for human. In this paper, we propose to learn semantic symbol sequence patterns of complex videos for activity prediction. The prefix method of semantic stream is designed based on the semantic symbol sequence and their time marks. The prediction phase is implemented via matching semantic sequence of incomplete videos and sequence patterns of different activities. We evaluate various prediction methods depending on low-level features or high-level descriptions. The empirical result suggests that when applied to activity prediction, sequence pattern mining can effectively reduce its reliance upon the low level features and improve predicting performance.

1 Introduction

In recent years, most of the media resources on the Internet are videos containing more information than characters and images. Videos become also easy to be stored and transmitted due to the improved transmission condition and reduced cost of the hardware storage. Therefore, the video-based human activity analysis research has become a hot topic in the computer vision field [1–4]. The solutions to this topic mainly focus on human activity recognition and prediction. When observed videos contain completed activities, the research have produced many application systems which are already used in surveillance system, medical monitor system and human-computer interactive system [6–8].

When observed videos contain only unfinished ongoing activities, we need a system to predict the state at the end of the activity. Ryoo and Aggarwal [9,11] defined human activity prediction as recognizing unfinished activity and solved this problem by Dynamic BoW and Integral BoW. Kitani et al. [12] then defined it as a decision progress using semantic scene annotation and inverse optimal control and can be applied to predict human walking routine by analyzing training data. Li and Fu [13] proposed complicated activity prediction in long-time videos on semantic level with causality, context and predictability. Cheng et al. [14] proposed a sub-event coding method using Sequence Data

© Springer International Publishing AG, part of Springer Nature 2018
B. Zeng et al. (Eds.): PCM 2017, LNCS 10735, pp. 269–279, 2018.
https://doi.org/10.1007/978-3-319-77380-3_26

Memoizer to capture temporal context features from visual word sequences and is more adaptable to small training dataset compared to the method in [13]. Xu et al. [15] formulated activity prediction as a query auto-completion (QAC) problem. Hu et al. [16] proposed a new RGB-D feature called local accumulative frame feature (LAFF) and can improve the computing efficiency.

Though research on human activity prediction has been carried out, that is not an easy task. The videos observed by different devices would be noisy and incomplete during their transmission and integration. In addition, many object classification and optimal regression models for 2D image processing are not easy to be transformed to 3D algorithms for videos. The traditional data prediction methods are hard to design for event prediction in human activities from videos. The lack of labeled datasets which are suitable for scene understanding through incomplete videos is another problem. Moreover, low-level features are not effective enough to support high-level analysis of the result of human activity. Especially when long videos which contain complicated activities such as playing tennis, attacking with a weapon or cooking are observed, the results of the activities are hard to tell and still need further research.

In this paper, a probabilistic model of human activity is designed and a framework to semantically analyze and predict human activities in long videos is proposed. For long-time videos with a complex activity, the semantic stream prefix method is designed with the combination of semantic symbol sequence and time marks. The prediction phase is implemented through matching semantic sequences of incomplete videos with sequence patterns of different activities. The computational cost is reduced because of the key element extraction based on the fundamental kinematics regularity and sequence alignment. The result shows that sequence pattern mining can effectively reduce its reliance upon the low level features when applied to activity prediction.

2   Proposed Approach

To ensure the accuracy and representativeness of human activity prediction results, we propose a hierarchical framework that considers both sparsity and relativity and take advantage of both low-level space-time features and high-level semantic descriptions in a unified approach as illustrated in Fig. 1. It involves the following steps:

1. Key unit extraction: Videos viewed as a complicated activity are segmented into multiple action units according to local space-time features and then keyframes are extracted. Action units in which some keyframes occur are selected as key units;

2. Action recognition: The human activity in the video can be described as a time series of action units. In this phase, we build a symbol-feature map in which each action symbol is corresponding to a template of features. The sequence of key units can be turned into sequence of action symbols;

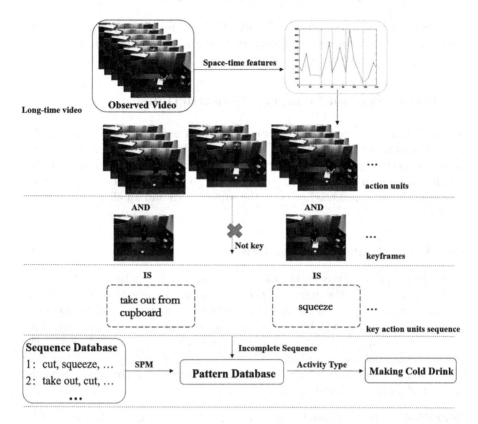

Fig. 1. The unified approach: (1) a long video is described as a key unit sequence after segmentation and keyframe extraction; (2) a semantic symbol sequence is generated after action annotation; (3) pattern database is constructed by sequence pattern mining for template matching in prediction phase.

3. Acitivity prediction: To cope with incomplete videos with unfinished activities, we design a sequence database and adapted PrefixSpan algorithm to match incomplete sequence in database. The final objective is to summarize the activity in the video with incomplete action symbol sequence.

We identify the following contributions of this paper:

- *Semantic understanding of human activity:* we provide a semantic prediction of unfinished human activity instead of some methods depending on feature descriptors only and experimentally assess the reliability of the human activity prediction on semantic level.
- *Hierarchical framework:* we observe the perspective as well the efficiency of including human annotation and key unit extraction in the computational chain by proposing a unified framework where sequence pattern mining plays the estimation of human activity and key unit extraction with human annotation plays the role of reducing the time and resource consumption.

– *Reduced reliance upon low-level features:* we introduce key unit extraction based on the fundamental kinematics regularity and can estimate ongoing activity with high-level understanding.

3   Action Symbol Sequence Construction

In this section, a semantic description structure is defined to represent activity in the videos with a series of action units. Then a key unit extraction method is proposed according to video segmentation based on space-time features and the length of the semantic sequence is compressed. To build the illustrated sequence database, the sequence need to be in the same length and an alignment method is used.

3.1   Action Symbol Sequence Definition

To describe a human activity, the hierarchical semantic structure should be analyzed. In our method, the high-level activity is activity suggesting the result and the action unit is action with simple task finished. The action units consist of some action elements which are the smallest unit of semantic integrity. Take 'making fruit salad' as a high level activity, then the action unit is 'opening the fridge', 'taking out fruits' and other relative actions. As for action unit 'opening the fridge', it is composed of action elements like 'stretching the hand', 'turning' and 'withdrawing the hand'.

Definition 1. *We shall say that an action unit is written as $S = (s, [l, r])$, which is composed of sequence symbol s and non-null frame pair $[l, r]$, $l, r \in R, l < r$.*

Definition 2. *We shall say that an action unit sequence A is set of action units*

$$A = \{(a_i, [l_i, r_i])\}_{i \in N_n} \tag{1}$$

which $\forall i, j \in N, 0 \leq i < j \leq n, l_i < l_j \vee (l_i = l_j \wedge (a_i < a_j \vee (a_i = a_j \wedge r_i < r_j)))$. The length of an action unit sequence is the number of the action unit, that is $|A| = n$. l_i (resp. r_i) is the beginning (resp. end) occurrence frame number of the action unit. Action units are strictly ordered by beginning frame number. End frame number denote the length of the action which is also an basis for recognition.

Definition 3. *Given an action unit sequence A, the sequence of its symbols: $\underline{A} = \{a_i\}_{i \in N_n}$. The order of symbols in the symbolic sequence is the same as the one in the action unit sequence.*

The operations of the sequences (e.g. δ, π) refer to [17] and two of them is updated as follows.

Definition 4. *Let A^1 and A^2 be two action unit sequences. The dissimilarity between A^1 and A^2, $d(A^1, A^2)$, is defined as:*

$$d(A^1, A^2) = \begin{cases} \infty & A^1 \notin A^2 \cap A^2 \notin A^1 \\ \delta(\pi(A^1), \pi(A^2)) \end{cases} \tag{2}$$

Definition 5. *Let $S_1 = (s_1, [l_1, r_1])$ and $S_2 = (s_2, [l_2, r_2])$ be two action units. The difference operation $S_1 - S_2$ is defined as:*

$$S_1 - S_2 = \begin{cases} \infty & s_1 \neq s_2 \\ mid[l_1, r_1] - mid[l_2, r_2] & s_1 = s_2 \end{cases} \tag{3}$$

The mid operation refers to [18].

3.2 Key Unit Extraction

In this subsection, video segmentation and keyframe extraction will be analyzed. As for video segmentation, we propose global shift series based on the kinematics characteristics. When an action is over, the positions of space-time interest points between two adjacent frames are nearly the same, which can be applied in movie clips, news clips and sports clips. D_t denotes the global shift series.

$$D_t = \prod_{p(x_{i,t}, y_{i,t})}^{n} ((x_{i,t} - x_{i,t-1})^2, (y_{i,t} - y_{i,t-1})^2) \tag{4}$$

t denotes frame F_t. p_i is the ith interest point on frame F_t and its position is $(x_{i,t}, y_{i,t})$. The troughs of the D_t curve are the segmentation points.

In keyframe extraction, the algorithm is illustrated in Algorithm 1. The segmentation points are used as the initial endpoints and the D_t curve is projected on high dimension space. For one part of the video (i.e. action unit), $findEnd$ is used to locate the frame number of its endpoints and $CalculateDistance$ is used to calculate the distance between D_t curve and the line connecting two endpoints of each frame (line 4–5). The frame in this part with largest distance is selected as keyframe (line 6–14). The new keyframe is added to the set of endpoints for the next iteration until the number of keyframes reaches $keyNum$.

The action units with keyframe are key action units. As in Algorithm 1, more than one keyframes may occur in one action unit, then the action unit sequences may be hard to comparison and classification in data training phase. The available alignment methods are dynamic time warping (DTW) and canonical time warping (CTW). These two still rely on basic linear cost models and cost too much machine resources. To solve the problems, we use the hidden Markov model (HMM) for the alignment of symbol sequences of action units.

Algorithm 1. Key Frame Extraction.

Input: $Keyframes, keyNum, D_t$
Output: $Keyframes$
1: **Initialize** $Keyframes, curPos = 1, maxDis = 0$;
2: **while** $length(keyframes) < keyNum$ **do**
3:     **for all** $frame$ **do**
4:         $line \leftarrow$ **findEnd**$(Keyframes, frame)$
5:         $dis \leftarrow$ **Calculate distance**$(line, frame)$
6:         **if** $dis > maxDis$ **then**
7:             $maxDis \leftarrow dis$
8:             $Keyframe \leftarrow frame$
9:         **end if**
10:     **end for**
11:     $Keyframes \leftarrow$ **cat**$(Keyframes, Keyframe)$
12:     **sort**$(Keyframes)$
13: **end while**

---

4   Activity Prediction

In activity prediction phase, the modified PrefixSpan is used for sequence pattern mining to build a map between sequence pattern and activity type. In the Section *Action Symbol Sequence Construction*, the database of sequences DS is constructed. To extract sequence patterns of each activity, all symbols are extracted from DS and constructed to a symbol set S. The request parameters $f_{min} \in [0,1]$, $\epsilon \in R^+$ for PrefixSpan will be confirmed by experiment. The prefix pattern P is initialized with empty set and the output is frequent pattern set FP. For each symbol e in S, the projection of DS on the $NP = P \oplus e$ is computed and the supporting set $L(NP)$ is constructed. Then for building a sequence pattern, we set Mr with the same symbols as NP. Each frequent pattern $q \in Mr$ is added to the list of explored patterns after the previous steps and PrefixSpan is called recursively with another symbol e. The pattern construction algorithm based on clustering and extending of Mr. As two sequences with large distance may in the same activity type, DBSCAN is used as the cluster method instead of K-means.

To adapt the PrefixSpan to activity prediction task, we note that some action unit sequence like ['open drawer', 'take out from drawer', 'close drawer'] nearly appears in all activities and can contribute little to the prediction. Consequently, we introduce a weight threshold w_{max} in PrefixSpan. If a sequence with cumulative weight $w = \sum_i^n w_i$ greater than w_{max}, it can not be added into the supporting set $L(NP)$. The modified PrefixSpan can be illustrated in Algorithm 2. sp denotes a sequence in $L(NP)$, $sp.id$ denotes the rank of sp in DS, $sp.pos$ denotes the position of first action unit in the sequence, $sp.tuples$ denotes the list of tuples corresponding to sp and $sp.w$ is the cumulative weight of the whole sequence.

For each activity type A_p, the training sampling sequences are made as database DS_p with the same procedure as before. For each DS_p, the frequent sequence pattern set FP_p is computed. Given a test video O with an unfinished complicated high-level activity, the action unit sequence $A_O = a_i, i = 1, \ldots, m$ and the corresponding activity type is $A_p = a_i, i = 1, \ldots, n$. Then $A_O \subseteq A_p$ and

Algorithm 2. Modified PrefixSpan.

Input: f_{min}, ϵ, DS, P
Output: FP
1: **Construction Symbol Set** S in DS
2: **for all** e in S **do**
3:     $NP \leftarrow P \oplus e$
4:     $L(NP) \leftarrow \emptyset$
5:     **for all** sp in L(P) **do**
6:         $A \leftarrow DS(sp.id)$
7:         **for all** $i : i < sp.pos + 1 \wedge a_i = e$ **do**
8:             $ComputeWeight(sp.tuples)$
9:             **if** $sp.w < w_{max}$ **then**
10:                 $L(NP) \leftarrow ProjectionCompute(sp)$
11:             **end if**
12:         **end for**
13:     **end for**
14:     $Mr \leftarrow PatternConstruction(NP)$
15:     **for all** q in Mr **do**
16:         **if** $q \notin Explored$ **then**
17:             $Explored \leftarrow Explored \cup q$
18:             **if** $|L(q)| > f_{min} * |DS|$ **then**
19:                 $Pats \leftarrow PrefixSpan(f_{min}, \epsilon, DS, q)$
20:                 $FP \leftarrow FP \cup Pats$
21:             **end if**
22:         **end if**
23:     **end for**
24: **end for**

$m \leq n$. The symbol set of FP_p is $\overline{FP_p}$, the dissimilarity between observed action unit sequence A_O and FP_p , $d(A_O, FP_p)$, is defined as:

$$d(A_O, FP_p) = \begin{cases} \infty & \overline{A_O} \not\subset \overline{FP_p} \\ \sum_{i=1}^{|FP_p|} \delta(\pi(P_i), \pi(A_O))) & \overline{A_O} \subseteq \overline{FP_p} \end{cases} \tag{5}$$

The activity type of the observed video O is defined as:

$$p^* = \min_p d(A_O, FP_p) \tag{6}$$

5 Experiment

In this section, we select two datasets for the tests: one is Drinking & Smoking [19] dataset and the other is MPII-cooking [20] dataset. The former is used to test our key units construction for two reasons. One reason is that for each activity in this dataset, the videos are captured from two views: the frontal and the lateral side. The other is that enough training samples with keyframe number annotations can be found in this dataset. The latter dataset is composed of 44 videos classified into 14 activities (dishes). Videos are already segmented into action units in this dataset and we can use it to test our semantic sequence construction and human activity prediction method. In the experiment, we only select 10 activities from MPII-cooking: 'pizza', 'mashed potato', 'fruit salad', 'cold drink', 'salad', 'sandwich', 'hot drink', 'soup', 'snack plate' and 'casserole'. The others are in short of training samples with only one or two videos in this activity (i.e. 'fried potatoes', 'pancake potato', 'omelet' and 'cake').

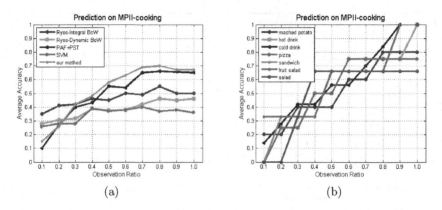

Fig. 2. (a) Performance on MPII-cooking dataset. Our method performs best when more than 30% frames are observed, and outperforms PAF+PST which also uses semantic analysis. (b) Performance on different *dishes* in MPII-cooking dataset [20].

5.1 Evaluation on Semantic Sequence Construction

The reliability of spatio-temporal interesting points is vital for following steps. In MPII-cooking dataset, gesture data in all frames are extracted for recognizing six different parts of human body: torso, head, right arm, left arm, right front arm and left front arm. The average recognition rate of all body parts is about 68%. The rate of the head and the torso could reach as high as 80%, while those of the other four parts are between 60% and 70%.

In the test of action symbol sequence construction, the results are compared to annotations in Drinking & Smoking dataset. Because annotations cannot be accessed in MPII-cooking dataset, user study would be the only way to evaluate the performance of keyframe extraction in that case. User study is involved with human judgments which are not corresponding to the automatic analysis task and the judgments are subjective which have impact on the results. At the same time, the efficiency is evaluated on both datasets. The average duration of videos in MPII-cooking is 403 s with 29.4 fps. When the extraction of the keyframes is set at the ratio of 3%, the average time lasts for 1117 s. In Drinking & Smoking dataset, each video is strictly sampled with 25 fps and 275 frames. When the ratio is set as 3%, the average time lasts for 3 s.

5.2 Evaluation on Activity Prediction

In the phase of prediction, our method is used to expect the result of ongoing human activities. Since there are only 38 videos in 10 activities we select on MPII-cooking and video numbers in each activity are not equal, we concatenate and segment the videos as follows with video number is set to 7. For example, there are only 3 videos for 'salad'. To make another 4 videos, we first concatenate the three videos into a long video and then split it to 4 short ones. At last, 70 videos and 7-fold leave-one-sequence-out cross validation can be used to measure performance. For each round, 10 videos are selected and each is from a distinct activity, and other 60 videos are used for training. We use *Observation Ratio* to represent the observed rate of input video of which the range is set to $[0.1, 1]$ and the step length is set to 0.1. The minimum frequency threshold f_{min} is set to 0.65 and the maximal dissimilarity ϵ is set to 6. We choose the method of Li Kang [13] which also contributes to semantic analysis based on PAF (Predictive Accumulative Function) and PST (Probabilistic Suffix Tree) as the first comparison. Besides, the Ryoo's methods (i.e. Dynamic BoW and Integral BoW) are also selected to be compared with our method. To implement Ryoo's methods, Dynamic histograms and Integral histograms are extracted for description and linear kernel SVM classifiers are constructed for classification in each step. If *Observation Ratio* $= 0.1$, both the input of the SVM classifier and the training set of the Bag-of-visual words are the first 10% image sequence of videos. According to the rate, PAF+PST and our method both symbolize the first 10% image sequence and generate activities consist of action units.

As shown in Fig. 2(a), our method outperforms Dynamic BoW, Integral BoW, SVM, PAF+PST except when the observation ratio is below 30%. The reason is that key unit extraction's contribution is much more obvious in that situation which means after sequence compression the size of available samples in our method is smaller than that in the other methods. Besides, the methods based on semantic analysis i.e. PAF+PST and our method perform better than those based on low-level features when the observation ratio is over 40%.

As shown in Fig. 2(b), the performance on the seven types of activity on MPII-cooking is illustrated. The prediction precision is calculated based on binary classification. The prediction performance on 'cold drink' is better than the other types in that the construction of the activity is simple to understand and actions in this type are easy to recognize. For some specific activities, the constructed symbol sequences have same prefix. 'take out from cabinet', 'take out from drawer' always occur at the beginning of activities such as 'mashed potato', 'hot drink', and 'cold drink'. Therefore the prediction based on the videos is faulty as those videos contain only the beginning part. In 'mashed potato', the prefix is followed by 'peel' and in 'hot drink' the prefix is followed by 'unpack'. Those two actions are totally different in spatio-temporal description and the dissimilarity between two sequences becomes easy to discover. That is why the performance is going better as the observation ratio is becoming higher.

6   Conclusion

In this paper, we introduce a novel framework for predicting unfinished human activities from long videos. We segment the input videos and label semantic symbols on those parts in which keyframes can be extracted. The so called 'key units' are selected and the spatio-temporal features analysis task is reduced into sequence pattern mining task by modified prefixSpan. We evaluate the proposed method on human activity prediction from long videos with complex activities consisting of many actions. The experimental results confirm that the proposed methods is able to produce better performance on predicting human activities from long videos than the state-of-the-art methods.

For future work, it involves further study to verify if our method can be transferred to a general situation because the current training dataset contains only 44 videos in total which is still limited. We will also pursue the state-of-the-art methods by establishing a dataset with videos labeled complicated activities. Saliency detection e.g. [5, 10] can also be a potential topic for unsupervised video learning as an extension to the present work.

References

1. Yuan, C., Li, X., Hu, W.M., et al.: 3D R transform on spatio-temporal interest points for action recognition. In: CVPR, pp. 724–730 (2013)
2. Soomro, K., Idrees, H., Shah, M.: Predicting the where and what of actors and actions through online action localization. In: CVPR, pp. 2648–2657 (2016)
3. Wang, L., Zhao, X., Cao, L., et al.: Context-associative hierarchical memory model for human activity recognition and prediction. IEEE Trans. Multimedia **19**(3), 646–659 (2017)
4. Seo, H.J., Milanfar, P.: Action recognition from one example. IEEE Trans. Pattern Anal. Mach. Intell. **33**(5), 867–882 (2011)
5. Yan, J., Zhu, M., Liu, H., et al.: Visual saliency detection via sparsity pursuit. IEEE Signal Process. Lett. **17**(8), 739–742 (2010)
6. Gan, C., et al.: DevNet: a deep event network for multimedia event detection and evidence recounting. In: CVPR, pp. 2568–2577 (2015)
7. Liu, W,. Mei, T., Zhang, Y., et al.: Multi-task deep visual-semantic embedding for video thumbnail selection. In: CVPR, pp. 3707–3715 (2015)
8. Kitani, K.M., Okabe, T., Sato, Y., et al.: Fast unsupervised ego-action learning for first-person sports videos. In: CVPR, pp. 3241–3248 (2011)
9. Ryoo, M.S., Aggarwal, J.K.: Observe-and-explain: a new approach for multiple hypotheses tracking of humans and objects. In: CVPR, pp. 1–8 (2008)
10. Li, Y., Zhou, Y., Yan, J., Niu, Z., Yang, J.: Visual saliency based on conditional entropy. In: Zha, H., Taniguchi, R., Maybank, S. (eds.) ACCV 2009. LNCS, vol. 5994, pp. 246–257. Springer, Heidelberg (2010). https://doi.org/10.1007/978-3-642-12307-8_23
11. Ryoo, M.S.: Human activity prediction: early recognition of ongoing activities from streaming videos. In: Proceedings, vol. 24(4), pp. 1036–1043 (2011)
12. Kitani, K.M., Ziebart, B.D., Bagnell, J.A., Hebert, M.: Activity forecasting. In: Fitzgibbon, A., Lazebnik, S., Perona, P., Sato, Y., Schmid, C. (eds.) ECCV 2012. LNCS, vol. 7575, pp. 201–214. Springer, Heidelberg (2012). https://doi.org/10.1007/978-3-642-33765-9_15
13. Li, K., Fu, Y.: Prediction of human activity by discovering temporal sequence patterns. IEEE Trans. Pattern Anal. Mach. Intell. **36**(8), 1644–1657 (2014)
14. Cheng, Y., Fan, Q., Pankanti, S., et al.: Temporal sequence modeling for video event detection. In: CVPR, pp. 2235–2242 (2014)
15. Xu, Z., Qing, L., Miao, J.: Activity auto-completion: predicting human activities from partial videos. In: ICCV, pp. 3191–3199 (2015)
16. Hu, J.-F., Zheng, W.-S., Ma, L., Wang, G., Lai, J.: Real-time RGB-D activity prediction by soft regression. In: Leibe, B., Matas, J., Sebe, N., Welling, M. (eds.) ECCV 2016. LNCS, vol. 9905, pp. 280–296. Springer, Cham (2016). https://doi.org/10.1007/978-3-319-46448-0_17

17. Guyet, T., Quiniou, R.: Extracting temporal patterns from interval-based sequences. In: IJCAI, pp. 1306–1311 (2014)
18. Aggarwal, C.C., Han, J.W.: Frequent Pattern Mining. Springer, New York (2014). https://doi.org/10.1007/978-3-319-07821-2
19. Laptev, I., Perez, P.: Retrieving actions in movies. In: ICCV, pp. 1–8 (2007)
20. Schiele, B., Andriluka, M., Amin, S., et al.: A database for fine grained activity detection of cooking activities. In: CVPR, pp. 1194–1201 (2012)

Motion State Detection Based Prediction Model for Body Parts Tracking of Volleyball Players

Fanglu Xie$^{(\boxtimes)}$, Xina Cheng, and Takeshi Ikenaga

Graduate School of Information, Production and Systems,
Waseda University, Kitakyushu, Japan
waseda-xiefl@fuji.waseda.jp

Abstract. Among sports analysis, tracking of athletes' body parts becomes a popular theme. Marking positions of body parts on the videos which contributes to TV contents and concrete motion capture of athletes which helps promotion of sports technology make sports analysis a commercially-viable research theme. This paper proposes motion state detection based prediction model to predict the near future motions of players' arms, band-width sobel likelihood model to observe the shape of human body parts and cluster scoring based estimation to avoid huge error. The motion state detection based prediction model can realize the tracking of players' high-speed and random motions without templates. The band-width sobel likelihood model can fully express unique shape features of target player's body parts. And the cluster scoring based estimation utilizes k-means cluster method to divide particle into 3 clusters and evaluate each cluster by scoring in order to prevent huge error from similar noises. The experiments are based on videos of the Final Game of 2014 Japan Inter High School Games of Men's Volleyball in Tokyo. The tracking success rate reached over 97% for lower body and over 80% for upper body, achieving average 64% improvement of hands compared to conventional work [1].

Keywords: Body parts tracking · Particle filter · Motion state detection
Prediction model · Likelihood model · K-means cluster

1 Introduction

Nowadays sports analysis of players becomes an urgent task due to the popularity of sports and audiences' need for new sports experiences. Sports data got from body parts tracking can be really useful for player evaluation, tactics analysis, motion capture and TV contents which make sports analysis not only an interesting research topic but also a valuable commercial opportunity. For example, marking the block and jump height on the video can enrich the TV contents. Meanwhile, precise motions models of athletes and accurate 3D distance between athletes are useful for athlete training and tactics analysis. To meet the requirements of TV contents, tracking players' body parts and getting the trajectories of hands or feet are the prerequisites to calculate the height, speed and other data of players' motions. Our research target is utilizing 3D articulated model through tracking players' body parts to get 3D positions of hands, elbows, head,

© Springer International Publishing AG, part of Springer Nature 2018
B. Zeng et al. (Eds.): PCM 2017, LNCS 10735, pp. 280–289, 2018.
https://doi.org/10.1007/978-3-319-77380-3_27

shoulders, hips, knees and feet based on videos from 3 views and 3D positions of players' bodies [2]. The target motion of volleyball player is blocking.

There are several conventional methods for body parts tracking of people. We transit the framework of multiple particle filters [1] tracking for lower body to track the upper body. However, the motion range of legs is smaller than arms, so the platform-shaped prediction model is hard to catch the motion of arms. As for catching the motion of human, many tracking system [3–5] utilizing accurate silhouette got from background subtraction method based on video with simple background to predict the motion of people. Lee [3] gets referential position of head and hands based on a head-shoulder contour and peaks of convex curvature along the silhouette boundary which means that the detection accuracy is dependent on an accurate shape of the silhouette. However, in our research, other moving players' behaviors can also be detected as foreground, which results in inaccurate silhouette of target player. It is very hard to build correct articulated human models related to inaccurate silhouette to match the motion of athlete. Moreover, many motion tracking systems [5, 6] only can be utilized on people who are doing some regular motion such as walking or running. Zhao and Nevatia [5] use predicted leg motion templates with 16 phases to predict the motion of walking people which is not suitable for tracking of random athlete motions. Ramanan and Forsyth [6] limit the predicted angle of arms to predict the arm motion while people are walking or running which is not suitable for predicting the motion like blocking because the movement range of arm is very large.

In our research, there are mainly three problems should be solved. Firstly, the high speed and random motion of each body part make the prediction of the near future motions of athletes really difficult. Because of random motions, there is no template used as referential data for prediction of players' motions. In addition, background subtraction based motion detection also are not suitable for our research due to the heavy noises caused by other moving players. Secondly, body parts are really small and consist of few pixels which results in a lack of feature which makes body parts hard to be distinguished. Thirdly, the high similarity between body parts of multiple athletes leads to difficult judgment between body parts of target athlete and interferential body parts. Furthermore, the tracking results of right limb and left limb are also easy to be confused by each other which resulting in huge error.

To solve these problems, we propose multiple particle filters (PF) [7] with 3D articulated model with proposed prediction model and proposed likelihood model to track 7 types of body parts of volleyball players. In order to track fast and random arm motion of players without fixed template, the motion state detection based prediction model is proposed. And in order to extend the amount of body parts' features, we propose the band-width sobel likelihood mode fully utilizing the irregular shape features of body parts. Furthermore, to avoid huge tracking error, cluster scoring based estimation is proposed to select the most probable particle within high-scored cluster.

The remainder of this paper is organized as follows. Section 2 describes our 3D tracking system and describes details of proposals. Experimental results and analysis are given in Sect. 3, and Sect. 4 concludes the whole paper.

2   Proposal

The tracking framework and the flowchart of our proposals based on particle filter is shown in Fig. 1. Since there are many tracking targets of our work, we divide the tracking of body parts into two paralleled processes: upper body and lower body. Within each process, the tracking order of body parts is set sequential to reduce the computational complexity. And we repeat 7 types of particle filters to track 7 types of body parts. The tracking order is showed as Fig. 1(a). The referential 3D position of torso [2] is got in advance as input. Based on tracking result of previous body parts, the following body parts are tracked by particle filters showed as Fig. 1(b).

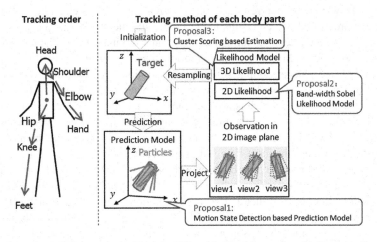

Fig. 1. Overview of Proposals in Particle Filter (a) Tracking order (b) Particle filter based tracking of each body part

For tracking method of each body part, stick-shaped particle which consists of two points: P_{start}, P_{end} are used to fit the real shape of shoulders, upper/lower arm or upper/lower leg in 3D space. One point based particle is only used for tracking of head. Each point consists of three dimensional factors in 3D space. State vector $X_{head,k}$ of particle filter (tracking for head) consists of 3 factors, while state vector $X_{\xi,k}$ of other particle filters (tracking for arms, legs and shoulders) consisting of 6 factors showed as Eq. (1). And k stands for time.

$$X_{\xi,k} = \begin{cases} \left[x_{\xi,k}, y_{\xi,k}, z_{\xi,k}\right]^T & \xi = head \\ \left[x_{\xi,k}^{start}, y_{\xi,k}^{start}, z_{\xi,k}^{start}, x_{\xi,k}^{end}, y_{\xi,k}^{end}, z_{\xi,k}^{end}\right]^T, & \xi = shoudler, upper\,arm, lower\,arm, thigh, shank \end{cases} \quad (1)$$

The tracking method, particle filter, of each body part is showed as Fig. 1(b). At initialization step, the initial positions of target are got manually. Then, at the prediction step, plenty of particles are set to estimate the position of target in 3D space. Proposal 1 (motion state detection based prediction model) modifies the prediction model to be adaptive to the movement of players which is introduced in Sect. 2.1. Then each particle is projected in 2D planes of 3 views to execute the likelihood calculation. Through the estimation step, probable particle with higher likelihood is selected as tracking result. Proposal 2 (band-width sobel likelihood model) is used for modification of 2D likelihood which is introduced in Sect. 2.2. Proposal 3 (cluster scoring based estimation) which is used to modify the estimation step introduced in Sect. 2.3.

2.1 Motion State Detection Based Prediction Model

The prediction model is used to predict the motion of players while jumping. When track the motions of players, high speed and random motion of athletes make the Gaussian model based prediction model hard to predict the near future motions. To ensure high tracking accuracy, our proposal predicts a predicted position based on motion rules of blocking related to different motion states in advance to pull the predicted particles near to the real body parts' positions.

About the motion rules of blocking, as Fig. 2 shows, the process of blocking can be divided into 4 states by 3 key points. State0 is the situation when player is moving on the floor. At state0, the motion of arm is really small and random. State1 is the situation that the player is jumping up. When the athlete is jumping up, the arms are getting higher and higher within a large range from. State2 is the situation when the player stops for a few frames when the player reaches the highest point. At this state, the angle change of arm is also very small. State3 stands for player falling down. And players' arms are getting slower and slower. Key points showed in Fig. 2 can be detected by analysis from torso trajectory.

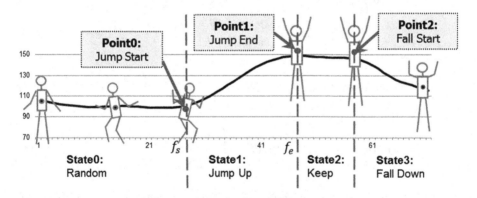

Fig. 2. Motion states of block motion

There are three steps to realize the proposal. The first step of our proposal is getting key points from trajectory analysis. The second step is generating the predicted positions based on motion rules. The third step is searching the real positions of body parts by creating particles based on adaptive Gaussian model.

As for the first step, the trajectory of torso's positions in 3D space is smoothed by quadratic Bézier spline interpolation method [8]. The accurate highest point and the lowest point of this trajectory can be got as candidates of key points. And the highest

284 F. Xie et al.

point is set as the end point of state1 (point1). Then based on the smoothed curve, the turning point of this trajectory can be got by two derivatives. In theory, the turning point stands for the time when the feet of players leaves the floor which should be set as start point of blocking (point0). However, sometimes, the result of turning point is inaccurate even based on highly-smoothed trajectory because the noises of the trajectory can't be removed totally. In this situation, the lowest point is set as the start point of jumping (point0) instead of turning point when wrong turning point is detected. At last, the end point of jumping (point2) is set based on a fixed number of frames to point1. In this way, the boundary lines between the motion states can be detected based on these 3 key points.

For the second step, the generation method of the predicted positions is dependent on the motion regulation of blocking. When the athlete starts jumping up (point0), the angle between his upper arm and torso is always 90°. And the angle between upper arm and lower arm is always 90°. When the athlete is at the highest point, the angle between his upper arm and torso is always 180°. At the same time, the angle between upper arm and lower arm is also always 180°. So our proposal pulls the value of predicted angle closer to each regular value at each key point by changing the value of $\Delta\theta_z$ and $\Delta\theta_{xy}$ showed as Eq. (2) frame by frame. L is the fixed length of upper arm or lower arm calculated at the first frame. The value of θ_z and $\Delta\theta_z$ for upper/lower arms are showed as Eq. (3)/Eq. (4). In addition, the value of $\Delta\theta_{xy}$ is random based on Gaussian distribution. Because the angle change can't be observed by prospective trajectory and the angle change of lower arm is smaller than upper arm when falling down, the fixed value of angle change of lower arm is set smaller than upper arm at state3.

$$\begin{cases} x^{end} = x^{start} + L \cdot sin(\theta_z + \Delta\theta_z) \cdot cos(\theta_{xy} + \Delta\theta_{xy}) \\ y^{end} = y^{start} + L \cdot sin(\theta_z + \Delta\theta_z) \cdot sin(\theta_{xy} + \Delta\theta_{xy}) \\ z^{end} = z^{start} - L \cdot cos(\theta_z + \Delta\theta_z) \end{cases} \qquad (2)$$

$$upper\,arm: \quad \theta_z = \theta_z^u; \quad \Delta\theta_z = \begin{cases} \frac{180 - \theta_{z_{f=fs}}^u}{f_e - f_s} & f_s \le f < f_e \\ -2.0 & f \ge f_e \end{cases} \qquad (3)$$

$$lower\,arm: \quad \theta_z = \theta_z^l = \theta_z^u; \Delta\theta_z = \begin{cases} \frac{180 - |\theta_z^l - \theta_z^u|_{f=fs}}{f_e - f_s} & f_s \le f < f_e \\ -1.5 & f \ge f_e \end{cases} \qquad (4)$$

At final step, generation of system noises, fewer particles as system noises are adaptive to the motion states. For example, when the player is jumping up (state1), more particles are set above the arms, because the possibility of the situation that the arm is at the higher position is much higher than other situations. Whereas, if the player is falling down (state3), the number of particles which are below the predicted position is set higher which can contribute to higher tracking accuracy. Meanwhile, system noises are created at other motion states (state0, state2) is based on Gaussian model within a small range. In this way, this proposal can track random and fast motions without fixed templates or limit of motion range with fewer particles.

2.2 Band-Width Sobel Likelihood Model

During likelihood evaluation step, each particle executes likelihood calculation step based on observation ranges related to 2D image planes of 3 views. As the Fig. 3 shows, from the sobel image, the edge of head is not circle. And the edge of arms, legs are not straight line. So the conventional line-shaped observation range [9] can't fit to the shape of body parts correctly. So, our proposal changes the observation range from line to band width as Fig. 3 shows. Besides, this proposal can be implemented to both the upper body and the lower body.

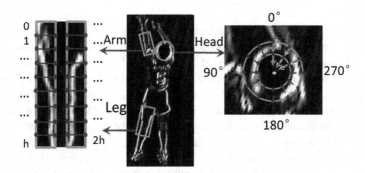

Fig. 3. Band-width observation range

Based on each particle, one sobel gradient histogram is got from one 2D image plane. The horizontal ordinate of the histogram is from $0°$ to $360°$ for head. And 0 to $2*h$ for arms or legs. The value of vertical coordinates is the average value of sobel gradient within the band-width observation range showed as Eq. (5) which can increase the possibility for catching the edge of body parts. The referential histogram is updated during the tracking process by each frame. During the tracking process, the distance between referential histogram and current histogram of each particle is calculated based on Bhattacharyya distance.

$$f(x) = \sum_{i=0}^{i=band\_width} g_i/band\_width, \begin{cases} head : x \in (0, 360°) \\ arm, leg : x \in (0, 2*h) \end{cases} \quad (5)$$

As the shape of human body, for example, because the head is not a standard circle, at some degrees, the circle-shaped observation range has a certain deviation to the real shape of head. So, sometimes, useful data is lost. But for our proposal, band-width observation range, the value in 360° can be used totally. In this way, the irregular shape feature can be fully utilized by more pixels calculated within the enlarged range.

2.3 Cluster Scoring Based Estimation

The motion of player is random and the large ranged particles are really easy to be located on other players or some similar noises. Therefore, an efficient estimation method should be proposed to evaluate the particle with not only visual features but also 3D position information which contributes to a higher tracking accuracy.

Cluster scoring based estimation consists of two steps, k-means cluster step and scoring step. First, particles used for prediction of lower arm with 6 factors by two points in 3D space (e.g. P_{elbow} and P_{hand}) are clustered into 3 groups by k-means method. Then we sort particles based on likelihood within each group and record the highest value of likelihood as L_δ showed in Eq. (6). δ stands for the serial number of cluster.

$$Score_\delta = L_\delta \times \sum_{n=0}^{M_\delta} \frac{N_f}{wh} \times \sum_{n=0}^{M_\delta} \frac{N_{skin}}{h} \times MS, \qquad \delta = 1, 2, 3 \qquad (6)$$

M_δ is the number of particle of each cluster. w and h are the width and height of the search window of each body part. For scoring step, ratio of foreground pixel by each search window of particle is calculated based on background subtraction. N_f is the number of foreground pixel within the search window. Besides, ratio of skin color pixel by each cluster is also calculated in HSV color space. N_{skin} is the number of skin-colored pixel at the middle axis of each search window. Besides, MS stands for the weight adaptive to different motion state. For example, when the player is jumping up, MS of the cluster who locates at higher place is set higher than normal cases. At last, the cluster with the highest score is selected. Furthermore, particle with highest likelihood within selected cluster is set as tracking result, resulting in higher tracking accuracy.

3 Experiment

3.1 Evaluation Method

Volleyball videos used in our experiment are the Final Game of 2014 Japan Inter High School Games of Men's Volleyball in Tokyo Metropolitan Gymnasium. We use three cameras located at the left corner, right corner and middle behind the target team to realize the requirement of 3D tracking. We randomly select 23 sequences to test the tracking algorithm. And total sequences contain 1611 frames in all. One sequence stands for one flow of blocking motion. The final resolution of the videos is 1920×1080 and the frame rate is 60 frames per second. We set the shutter speed as 1000/s to avoid the motion blurs. Our proposal is implemented using C++ and OpenCV 2.4.10.

To make the tracking result be observed visually, we draw the projected 2D tracking results using eight green rectangles to cover arms and legs in each directional video sequence. And we draw green circle covering head, triangle covering shoulders showed as Fig. 4. We define the evaluation methods divided by 10 parts: head, shoulders, left upper arm, right upper arm, left lower arm, right lower arm, left thigh, right thigh, left shank and right shank. If the projected search window exactly covers or covers part of the tracking target within a certain error range, this frame is set as a successful frame.

Fig. 4. Projected 2D tracking windows (Color figure online)

$$success\ rate = \frac{\sum success\ frame}{\sum frame} \times 100\% \tag{7}$$

3.2 Result and Analysis

In order to show the contribution of each proposal, we evaluated the proposals step by step. The main target of our work is to get higher tracking result of upper body. And based on the proposed algorithm, the tracking results of lower body are also be improved.

First, we test the conventional work tracking for [1] upper body evaluated the conventional work with mixture particle filters. And we found that the conventional mixture particle filters [1] are not suitable for tracking of upper body because the lower arm is very thin and has very few features. So we changed the structure of tracking frame-work from two paralleled particle filters to sequential particle filters to track arms in order and the results are showed as the first line of Table 1. Then, we evaluated the experimental results of tracking of upper body parts with motion state detection based prediction model. We also test the tracking algorithm for the upper body parts with band-with sobel likelihood model and cluster scoring based estimation whose result are showed as Table 1. In addition, we test the tracking results of lower body with band-with sobel likelihood model and cluster scoring based estimation and the results are showed as Table 2.

The method described in this paper can't achieve perfect tracking accuracy because of several factors. Opposite players' body parts influence the tracking system a lot. The color of player's shadow, which is similar to skin color, and the color of the clothes, which is same as the sleeves, influence the tracking result a lot.

For future, we plan to improve the tracking accuracy by utilizing the direction of optical flow calculated by each body part comparing to the moving direction of torso.

Table 1. Evaluation result of upper body

Success rate (%)	Head	Shoulders		Elbows		Hands	
		Left	Right	Left	Right	Left	Right
Conventional work [1]	77.1	91.9	92.3	38.7	37.1	16.8	15.5
P1	89.9	96.2	96.0	71.8	72.4	63.1	66.5
P1&P2	92.6	96.4	96.3	80.0	81.4	77.3	75.4
P1&P2&P3	92.6	96.4	96.3	88.1	89.1	80.0	80.3

Table 2. Evaluation result of lower body

Success rate (%)	Hips		Knees		Feet	
	Left	Right	Left	Right	Left	Right
Conventional work [1]	97.7	98.5	91.4	92.2	93.9	93.8
P2	98.3	98.8	97.5	95.3	97.8	95.0
P2&P3	98.3	98.8	98.1	97.1	98.2	97.0

P1: Motion State Detection based Prediction Model;
P2: Band-width Sobel Likelihood Model;
P3: Cluster Scoring based Estimation

4 Conclusion

In this paper, aiming at achieving high success rate of tracking player's body parts in 3D space, we propose a motion state detection based prediction model to predict the near future motions of arms based on motion rule related to different motion state. Motion state detection based prediction model contributes to track the upper body without fixed templates and creating more accurate models located on arms. Band-width sobel likelihood model fully express unique shape features of target player's body parts by calculating all the pixels within the band-width search window. Cluster scoring based estimation selects the particle based on not only visual features buy also 3D position information which can avoid huge error caused from similar noises. The tracking success rate reaches over 97% for lower body and over 80% for upper body.

For future work, the current tracking system can be applied to other actions such as spike, and serve, which is very useful for enriching the TV contents. Furthermore, hardware based acceleration is also an important research theme.

Acknowledgments. This work was supported by KAKENHI (16K 13006) and Waseda University Grant for Special Research Projects (2017K-263).

References

1. Xie, F., Cheng X., Ikenaga T.: Mixture particle filter with block jump biomechanics constraint for volleyball players lower body parts tracking. In: IAPR International Conference on Machine Vision Applications (MVA 2017) (2017)
2. Huang, S., Zhuang, X., Ikoma, N., Honda, M., Ikenaga, T.: Particle filter with least square fitting prediction and spatial relationship based multi-view elimination for 3D Volleyball players tracking. In: 2016 IEEE 12th International Colloquium on Signal Processing & Its Applications (CSPA), pp. 28–31. IEEE (2016)
3. Lee, M.W., Cohen, I., Jung, S.K.: Particle filter with analytical inference for human body tracking. In: Proceedings of the Workshop on Motion and Video Computing, pp. 159–165. IEEE (2002)
4. Delamarre, Q., Faugeras, O.: 3D articulated models and multiview tracking with physical forces. Comput. Vis. Image Underst. **81**(3), 328–357 (2001)
5. Zhao, T., Nevatia, R.: Tracking multiple humans in complex situations. IEEE Trans. Pattern Anal. Mach. Intell. **26**(9), 1208–1221 (2004)
6. Ramanan, D., Forsyth, D.A., Zisserman, A.: Strike a pose: tracking people by finding stylized poses. In: IEEE Computer Society Conference on Computer Vision and Pattern Recognition, CVPR 2005, pp. 271–278 (2005)
7. Galata, A., Johnson, N., Hogg, D.: Learning variable-length Markov models of behavior. Comput. Vis. Image Underst. **81**(3), 398–413 (2001)
8. Prautzsch, H., Boehm, W., Paluszny, M.: Bézier and B-spline techniques. Springer Science & Business Media (2013)
9. Cheng, X., Zhuang, X., Wang, Y., Honda, M., Ikenaga, T.: Particle filter with ball size adaptive tracking window and ball feature likelihood model for ball's 3D position tracking in volleyball analysis. In: Ho, Y.-S., Sang, J., Ro, Y.M., Kim, J., Wu, F. (eds.) PCM 2015. LNCS, vol. 9314, pp. 203–211. Springer, Cham (2015). https://doi.org/10.1007/978-3-319-24075-6_20

Detection and Classification

Adapting Generic Detector
for Semi-Supervised Pedestrian Detection

Shiyao Lei, Qiujia Ji, Shufeng Wang, and Si Wu[✉]

School of Computer Science and Engineering, South China University of Technology,
Guangzhou 510006, Guangdong, People's Republic of China
shiyao.lei@foxmail.com, {ji.qiujia,w.shufeng}@mail.scut.edu.cn,
cswusi@scut.edu.cn

Abstract. This paper presents a pedestrian detector adaptation approach that aims at adapting a generic detector pre-trained on a public dataset to a specific scene. We hypothesize that the components of the generic detector are useful for constructing a scene-specific detector. For this purpose, our proposed approach is applied to determine the appropriate weights for recombining the components, such that the new detector is expected to perform better in the target scene. Next, the new detector is used to collect new training samples from unlabeled target data. Finally, a weighted CNN is fine-tuned on the extended training set. The experiments demonstrate that the improvements due to the strategies adopted in the proposed approach are significant.

Keywords: Pedestrian detection · Domain adaptation
Weighted CNN

1 Introduction

The problem of adapting a generic detector to a scene-specific context is often refer to as domain adaptation. The source datasets usually include lots of annotated data, while there are a limited number of labeled samples from the target scene. A widely used solution is to perform feature projection. For instance, the extracted features were projected on manifolds in [4]. Since different feature representations lead to different errors, a co-training framework was used by training two detectors with different features iteratively in [5]. In addition, transfer learning methods were applied to domain adaptation problem, such as Cross-domain SVM [6] and TrAdaBoost [1].

The sample distributions of the source and target domains might differ significantly. In order to avoid a labour-intensive task of manual annotations on the target data, a widely used strategy is to employ generic detectors trained on the source datasets to automatically extract new samples from the target domain. In [9], a self-training scheme was proposed to retrain a detector on the updated training set in which the samples were confidently distinguished by the current detector. Another strategy is to employ tracking methods for collecting

© Springer International Publishing AG, part of Springer Nature 2018
B. Zeng et al. (Eds.): PCM 2017, LNCS 10735, pp. 293–302, 2018.
https://doi.org/10.1007/978-3-319-77380-3_28

new samples. In [10], the detection results were tracked on the target data without any annotation. However the simple combination of detection and tracking might lead to that the errors from both detection and tracking were amplified. To obtain reliable samples from the target domain, the prior knowledge about locations, sizes and paths of objects in the target scene was used to filtering the detections of a generic detector. More recently, deep networks have been used for the problem of domain adaptation. Zeng et al. [15] proposed a deep model serving both classification and reconstruction tasks to learn scene-specific feature representation and target sample distribution. Different to the above work, we found that incorporating a few manually labeled samples and a large number of unlabeled samples with the specified weights leads to a significant performance gain.

In this paper, we present a detector adaptation approach for improving scene-specific pedestrian detection. Although a generic detector is considered empirically to be inapplicable to specific scenes, we consider that its components are useful for constructing a new detector. Based on this hypothesis, we propose a recombination approach to determine the relevant components and the corresponding weights. The new detector outperforms the generic detector, and is used to scan unannotated target images for collecting new training samples. A deep model is trained on the extended training set. Since there are errors in labeling, we assign different weights to the manually labeled samples and the newly obtained samples, resulting into a 'Weighted CNN' model. The training process of the proposed framework is illustrated in Fig. 1. The effectiveness of the

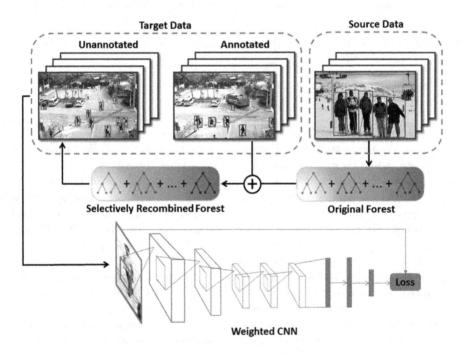

Fig. 1. The training pipeline of the proposed pedestrian detection approach.

proposed approach in improving scene-specific pedestrian detection is verified in the extensive experiments.

The contributions of this paper are threefold. First, we adapt a generic detector pre-trained on a source dataset to a specific scene by recombining its components. The new detector performs much better than the generic detector in collecting new training samples from the target scene. Second, a weighted CNN trained on the extended training set achieves satisfactory performances on challenging datasets. Third, the improvements due to the strategies adopted in the proposed approach are significant.

2 Learning Scene-Specific Detection Model

Since a limited number of labeled samples are insufficient for training a robust detector, a possible solution is to train a genetic detector on a public dataset first, and then adapt it to the target scene. Although the performance of the generic detector may be unsatisfactory in the target scene, we observe that some useful components associated with local region features could be exploited in building a scene-specific detector.

2.1 Generic Detector

The 'Checkerboards' detector [16] has shown excellent performance in pedestrian detection. Each 'Checkerboards' filter can be defined by a combination of two kinds of uniform squares to measure horizontal or vertical gradients. There are a total of 25 filters from 1×1 to 3×3 cells, and each cell is a rectangular region taking a value in the set $\{-1, +1\}$. We use the oriented gradient magnitude and color feature channels. In our case, the input image is represented by total 10 'HOG+LUV' feature channels. We apply all the filters over each channel, and the feature vector is generated by sum-pooling over the set of cells. The AdaBoost algorithm is used to build a decision forest. For each node of the decision trees, an exhaustive search strategy is performed. Although the designed features are high-dimensional, only a subset of the elements are selected for prediction.

2.2 Decision Tree Recombination

Each decision tree of the generic detector is associated with several features extracted from local regions that capture local structures of human body. Given target samples, it is possible to recombine these decision trees to build a new detector, which performs better in the target scene. Our object is to determine the corresponding weights for recombination. In our case, we consider the decision trees of the generic detector as a set of mappings, and each labeled sample can be projected to a new feature vector. We formulate our problem as follows.

Given a set of labeled data $\{x_i, y_i\}_{i=1}^{N}$, we denote x_i as the feature vector and y_i as the corresponding label. When using the decision trees as mapping functions $\{\phi_j\}_{j=1}^{M}$, x_i is projected to $\phi_i \equiv [\phi_1(x_i), \ldots, \phi_M(x_i)]$. We introduce a vector $s = [s_1, \ldots, s_M] \in S$ to indicate the sparsity of the recombination solution, where $s_j \in \{0, 1\}, j = 1, \ldots, M$, $S = \{s | \sum_{j=1}^{M} s_j \leq B\}$ is the domain of s, and B controls the sparsity of s. As a result, a discrimination function can be represented as $f(\phi) = (\omega \odot s)'\phi$, where ω denotes the weight vector, and $\odot$ denotes the element-wise product. We aim at finding a sparse solution with respect to the mapping functions to a linear SVM, and the corresponding problem can be stated by the following representation form:

$$\min_{s \in S} \min_{\omega, \xi, \rho} \frac{1}{2}\|\omega\|^2 + \frac{\lambda}{2}\sum_{i=1}^{N} \xi_i^2 - \rho \tag{1}$$
$$s.t. \quad y_i \omega'(\phi_i \odot s) \geq \rho - \xi_i, \ i = 1, \ldots, N,$$

where ξ_i is the positive constraint, and the coefficient λ keeps the balance between the model complexity and classification accuracy. Tan et al. [11] designed a cutting plane algorithm to efficiently find a sparse solution for this mixed-integer programming problem. Based on the solution of Eq. (1), the new detector can be built by the weighted combination of the decision trees as follows:

$$\Psi(x) = \sum_{k=1}^{K} \omega_{a_k} \phi_{a_k}(x), \tag{2}$$
$$s.t. \quad s_{a_k} = 1, \ a_k \in \{1, \ldots, M\}, \ k = 1, \ldots, K,$$

where K is the number of the selected decision trees. The value of K is usually much smaller than the value of M.

2.3   Weighted CNN

Since only a limited number of annotated data from the application domain is considered to be available, the positive training sample set will lack of representativeness. Therefore it is necessary to extract more training samples from the target domain. Specifically, we use the new detector to scan unannotated target images, and collect new samples to enlarge the training set. Since the newly obtained samples are not as reliable as the labeled samples, a weighted CNN is proposed and trained on the extended training set. Instead of directly using labeled samples combined with newly obtained samples for training, we treated the two kinds of samples differently by assigning them different weights. Our deep model is based on the AlexNet [7]. The loss function is usually in form of a combination of multinomial logistic loss and softmax. In order to handle the two kinds of training samples, we assign weights to the samples inside the softmax loss in order to avoid having a large number of newly obtained samples dominating the training process. For this purpose, the weighted softmax loss is defined as follows:

$$\mathcal{L} = -\frac{1}{|A|} \sum_{x_i \in A} \sum_{c=0}^{1} \mathbf{1}\{y_i = c\} \log p(x_i|c)$$
$$-\frac{\mu}{|U|} \sum_{x_j \in U} \sum_{c=0}^{1} w_j \mathbf{1}\{y_j = c\} \log p(x_j|c), \tag{3}$$

where A denotes the labeled sample set, U denotes the newly obtained sample set, y is the class label of the input region proposal x, and w denotes its weight. The constant μ is used to keep the balance between the labeled samples and newly obtained samples. The probabilistic prediction $p(x|c)$ is computed via a softmax function transforming the predictions into normalized non-negative values. The weights of the labeled samples are set to be larger than those of newly obtained samples. The weights w_j should be within the range $[0, 1]$. Specifically, the weight of a newly obtained sample is defined as the ratio of the similarity between the sample and A and the similarity between A and U as follows:

$$w_j = \frac{\max_{x_i \in A} S_{ij}}{\max_{x_i \in A, x_j \in U} S_{ij}}, \tag{4}$$

where

$$S_{i,j} = \frac{1}{\|\Psi(x_i) - \Psi(x_j)\|}, \tag{5}$$

$S_{i,j}$ denotes the similarity between the labeled sample x_i and the newly obtained sample x_j. Since the defined softmax loss is continuous, stochastic gradient descent can be used to update the parameters of our weighted CNN.

3 Experiments

In this section, we first investigate the effectiveness of each stage of the proposed framework, and then evaluate the performance of the proposed scene-specific detection model. The evaluation is performed on the CUHK-Square dataset [12] and MIT-Traffic dataset [13] which are used in many studies on scene-specific human detection. Compared to the INRIA dataset, the videos are taken from significantly different viewpoints in these two datasets. Since the typical human sizes in these two datasets are too small (38×76 pixels and 18×36 pixels), the raw frames are usually resized by 2 and 4 times, and therefore the test image sizes become into 1440×1152 pixels and 2280×1920 pixels respectively. We follow the evaluation protocol as described in [3]. The detection criterion is that the ratio of the intersection region compared to the union (IoU) should be greater than 0.5. The performance is evaluated in terms of detection-error-tradeoff curves: the recall rate versus false positive per image (FPPI).

3.1   Experimental Setting

We trained our model using the following experimental configuration. To obtain a generic detector, we chose the 'Checkerboards' filters to extract the Haar-like features from each region proposal. The size of detection window is 60×120 pixels, and the sliding window stride is set to 8×8 pixels. We used a cell size of 6×6 pixels and a template size ranging from 1×1 to 3×3 cells. As a result, a total of 2798 filters were generated by shifting with a step size of one cell. We extract 10 'HOG+LUV' feature channels to represent each image patch, the final feature vector has 27980 dimensions when applying all the filters over each channel. We selected the INRIA dataset as the source dataset in our experiment, and trained a decision forest composed of 1024 decision trees with a maximum depth equal to 3.

In the semi-supervised setting, a limited number of labeled samples are usually available in specific scenes. In our case, we use only 5% of the training frames in all the experiments. We first recombine the decision trees of the generic detector which are already trained on the INRIA dataset. We then use the new detector to scan the other 95% training frames without any annotation for new sample collection. The new detector is also used to provide 1000 region proposals per image. Both the manually labeled samples and newly obtained samples are used to fine-tune a weighted CNN, which is pre-trained on the ILSVRC2012 dataset [2]. We frozen the convolutional layers and only update parameters in fully connected layers. The initial learning rate for fine-tuning is set to 0.001, and we decrease the learning rate by a factor 0.1 every 2000 iterations.

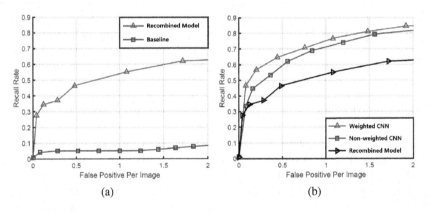

Fig. 2. Detection results of the proposed (a) recombined model and (b) weighted CNN on the MIT-Traffic dataset.

3.2   MIT-Traffic

The MIT-Traffic dataset describes pedestrians crossing an intersection. There are 420 training frames and 100 test frames, which are sampled uniformly from a 90-min long video. We evaluate and analyze the contribution of each stage of our framework. Specifically, the generic detector 'Baseline' is compared with the new detector 'Recombined Forest' built by recombining the decision trees of the generic detector. The results are shown in Fig. 2(a). As mentioned above, there are significantly differences between the INRIA dataset and MIT-Traffic dataset, and thus the generic detector underperforms the new detector because no adaptation is performed. As expected, by using the recombination approach described in Sect. 2.2, 'Recombined Forest' achieves much better performance by 46% points as it exploits the relevant features captured by the generic detector. Furthermore, we compare 'Recombined Forest' with the weighted CNN. We investigate the effect of two strategies of combining labeled samples and newly obtained samples. One is to directly combine the two kinds of training sample without weighting 'Non-weighted CNN', and the other is to assign the weights according to Eq. (4) 'Weighted CNN'. As shown in Fig. 2(b), both strategies improve the detection performance up to 15 and 20% points respectively. However, the second strategy performs the best and the detection rate reaches 0.75. Some representative detection results of the proposed approach are shown in Fig. 3(a). We also compare our approach with the scene-specific human detection methods: 'Scene Structure-Based Detector' [13], 'Transferring Boosted Detector' [8], 'Confidence-Encoded SVM' [14] and 'Data-Reconstructed CNN' [15]. The detection rates are shown in Table 1. The proposed approach performs better than the other methods mainly due to the new detector providing better high-confidence samples. The detection rate of the proposed approach is higher than that of 'Data-Reconstructed CNN' by 10% points.

(a)   (b)

Fig. 3. Representative results of the generic detector (top), recombined model (middle), weighted CNN (bottom) on the (a) MIT-Traffic and (b) CUHK-Square datasets.

Table 1. Comparison of detection rate on the MIT-Traffic dataset (FPPI=1).

Method	Detection rate
Scene Structure-Based Detector	0.30
Confidence-Encoded SVM	0.50
Transferring Boosted Detector	0.53
Data-Reconstructed CNN	0.65
Our Model	**0.75**

3.3   CUHK-Square

The CUHK-Square dataset describes pedestrians walking in a square. This dataset contains 352 training frames and 100 test frames by uniformly sampling from a 60-min long video. Similar to Sect. 3.2, we first investigate the contribution of each stage of our framework on the CUHK-Square dataset. As shown in Fig. 4, 'Recombined Forest' outperforms the generic detector by about 27% points. Furthermore, our weighted CNN improves the detection rate to 0.7 higher than 'Recombined Forest' by about 20% points. In addition, we compare our approach with 'Scene Structure-Based Detector', 'Transferring Boosted Detector', 'Confidence-Encoded SVM', 'Data-Reconstructed CNN', and 'Transfer Sparse Coding' [17]. Similar conclusions can be obtained as those from the above experiments, and our approach achieves a higher detection rate than the other methods. The results shown in Table 2 demonstrate that our approach outperforms the second best method 'Data-Reconstructed CNN' by 8% points.

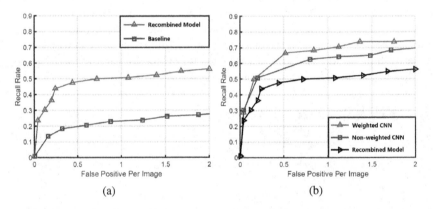

(a)   (b)

Fig. 4. Detection results of the proposed (a) recombined model and (b) weighted CNN on the CUHK-Square dataset.

Table 2. Comparison of detection rate on the CUHK-Square dataset (FPPI = 1).

Method	Detection rate
Scene Structure-Based Detector	0.24
Transferring Boosted Detector	0.43
Confidence-Encoded SVM	0.51
Transfer Sparse Coding	0.57
Data-Reconstructed CNN	0.62
Our Model	**0.70**

4 Conclusion

In this paper, we proposed a semi-supervised scene-specific pedestrian detection approach by adapting a generic detector and learning a weight CNN. When only a limited number of labeled samples are available, we propose a recombination algorithm to adapt a generic detector trained on a public dataset to the specific scene by recombining its components. The new detector is applied for extracting new training samples, and a weighted convolutional network is deployed on the extended training set. Instead of equally treating the manually labeled samples and newly obtained samples, we adopt a weighting strategy to boost the performance of our network. The effectiveness of the strategies used and the superiority of the proposed approach are verified in the experiment.

Acknowledgments. This work was supported in part by the National Natural Science Foundation of China (Project No. 61502173), and in part by the Natural Science Foundation of Guangdong Province (Project No. 2016A030310422).

References

1. Dai, W., Yang, Q., Xue, G.R., Yu, Y.: Boosting for transfer learning. In: ICML, pp. 193–200 (2007)
2. Deng, J., Berg, A., Satheesh, S., Su, H., Khosla, A., Fei-Fei, L.: Imagenet large scale visual recognition competition (2012). http://www.image-net.org/challenges/LSVRC/2012/
3. Dollar, P., Wojek, C., Schiele, B., Perona, P.: Pedestrian detection: an evaluation of the state of the art. IEEE TPAMI **34**(4), 743–761 (2012)
4. Gong, B., Shi, Y., Sha, F., Grauman, K.: Geodesic flow kernel for unsupervised domain adaptation. In: CVPR, pp. 2066–2073 (2012)
5. Javed, O., Ali, S., Shah, M.: Online detection and classification of moving objects using progressively improving detectors. In: CVPR, pp. 696–701 (2005)
6. Jiang, W., Zavesky, E., Chang, S., Loui, A.: Cross-domain learning methods for high-level visual concept classification. In: ICIP, pp. 161–164 (2008)
7. Krizhevsky, A., Sutskever, I., Hinton, G.E.: Imagenet classification with deep convolutional neural networks. In: NIPS, pp. 1106–1114 (2014)
8. Pang, J., Huang, Q., Yan, S., Jiang, S., Qin, L.: Transferring boosted detectors towards viewpoint and scene adaptiveness. IEEE TIP **20**(5), 1388–1400 (2011)
9. Rosenberg, C., Hebert, M., Freund, Y.: Semi-supervised self-training of object detection models. In: IEEE Workshop Application of Computer Vision, pp. 29–36 (2005)
10. Stalder, S., Grabner, H., Van Gool, L.: Cascaded confidence filtering for improved tracking-by-detection. In: Daniilidis, K., Maragos, P., Paragios, N. (eds.) ECCV 2010. LNCS, vol. 6311, pp. 369–382. Springer, Heidelberg (2010). https://doi.org/10.1007/978-3-642-15549-9_27
11. Tan, M., Wang, L., Tsang, I.W.: Learning sparse SVM for feature selection on very high dimensional datasets. In: ICML, pp. 1047–1054 (2010)
12. Wang, M., Li, W., Wang, X.: Transferring a generic pedestrian detector towards specific scenes. In: CVPR, pp. 3274–3281 (2012)

13. Wang, M., Wang, X.: Automatic adaptation of a generic pedestrian detector to a specific traffic scene. In: CVPR, pp. 3401–3408 (2011)
14. Wang, X., Wang, M., Li, W.: Scene-specific pedestrian detection for static video surveillance. IEEE TPAMI **36**(2), 361–374 (2014)
15. Zeng, X., Ouyang, W., Wang, M., Wang, X.: Deep learning of scene-specific classifier for pedestrian detection. In: Fleet, D., Pajdla, T., Schiele, B., Tuytelaars, T. (eds.) ECCV 2014. LNCS, vol. 8691, pp. 472–487. Springer, Cham (2014). https://doi.org/10.1007/978-3-319-10578-9_31
16. Zhang, S., Benenson, R., Schiele, B.: Filtered channels features for pedestrian detection. In: CVPR, pp. 1751–1760 (2015)
17. Zhang, X., He, F., Tian, L., Wang, S.: Cognitive pedestrian detector: adapting detector to specific scene by transferring attributes. Neurocomputing **149**, 800–810 (2015)

StairsNet: Mixed Multi-scale Network for Object Detection

Weiyi Gao[1,2]([⊠]), Wenlong Cao[1,2], Jian Zhai[2], and Jianwu Rui[2]

[1] University of Chinese Academy of Sciences, Beijing, China
{weiyi,wenlong}@nfs.iscas.ac.cn
[2] Institute of Software, Chinese Academy of Sciences,
National Engineering Research Center of Fundamental Software, Beijing, China

Abstract. It is common to choose image classification network as backbone in the object detector. The art-of-the-state image classification network exhibits excellent performance on image classification, but that network hurts the detection efficiency, mainly due to the coarseness of features from several convolution and pooling layers. In this paper, we present a single deep neural network with inceptions, called *StairsNet*, to take advantage of the art-of-the-state image classification network in object detection. In contrast to previous single network SSD [13] which uses VGG-16 as a feature to extract network, our approach applies recently state-of-the-art classification network Residual Network (ResNets [5]). Meanwhile, to avoid coarseness of the last CNN feature, StairsNet not only utilizes various of scale features, but also mixes different scale features to predict. To this end, we insert two stairs-like architectures into the network: top stairway network that mixes multi-scale feature maps as input to predict bounding boxes and bottom stairway network that turns into two different scale feature branches. Our StairsNet significantly increases the PASCAL-style mean Average Precision (mAP) from 75.0% (SSD + ResNet-101) to 77.7%. Code is available at https://github.com/gwyve/caffe/tree/StairsNet.

Keywords: StairsNet · Object detection · ResNet · Inception

1 Introduction

With the recent advance of convolution neural networks (CNNs) [6], a great progress has been made these years on image classification [5,9,20,22] and object detection [4,13,17,24]. Since R-CNN [4] was established by Girshick *et al.*, many recent detectors followed this paradigm: firstly, a object proposal algorithm [26] generates candidate regions; secondly, the CNNs classify every proposed region. Faster R-CNN [17] replaces conventional object proposal algorithm with a new CNN RPN (Region Proposal Networks). On the other hand, following Multi-Box [3,23], a much faster detector, SSD [13], utilizes a single network to predict bounding box.

© Springer International Publishing AG, part of Springer Nature 2018
B. Zeng et al. (Eds.): PCM 2017, LNCS 10735, pp. 303–314, 2018.
https://doi.org/10.1007/978-3-319-77380-3_29

Recently, many modern object detectors are changing the extract feature layers with the change of state-of-the-art image classification networks. It is tempting to focus on adding recent state-of-the-art image classification networks such as Residual Network (ResNets [5]) and GoogLeNet [22] into the object detection architecture. However, the combination of a state-of-the-art classifier (ResNet-101 [5]) and SSD doesn't show dramatic performance in improving accuracy, as the phenomenon that inferior detection accuracy doesn't match the network's superior classification accuracy. Dai et al. [10] argued that the issue is caused by lack of respecting variance for object detection and inserted position-sensitive score maps into the framework to remedy that issue. However, it applies the expensive RPN to generate proposal regions in R-FCN [10], as in Faster R-CNN [17].

To make SSD with ResNet-101 more excellent detector, we not only append ResNet block to the extract feature layers, but also insert Inception-style architecture [7,11,21,22] into the network to predict the bounding boxes and classify the object. Inspired by Inception [21,22,25], we use inception to capture the nonlinear concepts from CNN feature map. Meanwhile, the last CNN feature map is too coarse to detect some small-size objects. Although SSD uses six scales to detect the object, we support the method that combining multi-scale features before predicting networks can improve ability to detect small-size objects [12]. Motivated by that fact, we mix multi-scale features to predict. Each inception located at each scale pipeline captures the nonlinear concepts from single scale CNN feature map before combination.

In this paper, we develop a object detection framework called **StairsNet**. Our network consists of the 101-layer Residual Net (ResNet-101) as the backbone and several stair modules. The stairs networks are divided into two stairways: top stairway network that mixes multi-scale feature maps as input to predict bounding boxes and bottom stairway network that turns into two different scale feature branches. When being evaluated, our StairsNet significantly increases the PASCAL-style mean Average Precision (mAP) from 75.0% (SSD + ResNet-101) to 77.7%. Code is available at https://github.com/gwyve/caffe/tree/StairsNet.

2   Related Work

Object detection is one of the fundamental tasks in computer vision and rapid progress recently. Many researches follow R-CNN, a two-stage detection paradigm: Firstly, an object algorithm generates candidate regions that may contain an object; Secondly, the CNNs classify each proposed region. Before using deep networks, the majority of proposal algorithms include those based on grouping super-pixels (e.g. MCG [14], CPMC [2], Selective Search [26]) and those based on sliding windows (e.g. EdgeBoxes [27], objectness in windows [1]). In the Faster R-CNN paper, the Selective Search region proposals, which are based on low-level image features, are replaced by the ones learned from a region proposal network (RPN). The YOLO approach by Redmon et al. [15] uses a single network to predict bounding boxes and class probabilities, in an end to end network. It divides the input image into a grid of cells and predicts the coordinates and confidences of objects contained in the cells. Adopting one-stage detection, the YOLO is much faster than Faster R-CNN. Similar with YOLO, SSD also adopts a single network in that. The difference is that SSD uses a fixed set of default boxes for prediction, which is like the anchor in RPN.

Multi-scale: Overfeat [19] classifies different scale boxes. In recent MultiBox works [3,23], there are multi-scale features from different convolution layers to be used as input. The SSD adopts six scale features to predict, in which progress we use the combination of two of those scale features. Additionally, HyperNet [8] combines all the feature of different scales with deconvolution, different from the method we only combine two scale feature.

Inception-Style Network: Following the Network in Network (NIN) [11], Szegedy et al. [22] inserted inception in pipeline. They verified that approximating the expected sparse structure-Inception by readily available dense building blocks is a viable method for improving neural networks for detection. Szegedy et al. [25] provides several design principles in the context of the Inception. Based on the principles, various types of Inception architecture have been presented. As the introduction of residual connection [21], training with residual connection accelerates the training of Inception networks significantly.

3   Model

Our object detection system is named as **StairsNet**, a stairs-like architecture. The entire system is a single, unified network for object detection, which use ResNet-101 as backbone. StairsNet is divided into two flights of stairs (Top-Stairs and Bottom-Stairs) by landing. Each stair tread of Top-Stairs has two inceptions (Up-Inception and Down-Inception) and features-combined module in StairsNet. Figure 1 is an overview of the system. In Sect. 3.1 we illustrate the details about using Residual-101 as backbone. In Sect. 3.2 we introduce the two modules of StairsNet and we demonstrate different inception-style architecture in Sect. 3.3. In Sect. 3.4 we show the details about training strategy for StairsNet. In Sect. 3.5 we show some training details.

3.1   Using Residual-101 as Backbone

Single Shot MultiBox Detector (SSD [13]) chooses truncated VGG-16 [20] as base network, and appends extra convolution layers to base network. Each of the added layers is used to predict scores and offsets for some predefined default bounding boxes. With dramatic success of ResNet in image classification, using ResNet as backbone in the object detector becomes a prevalent method. To use the advantage of ResNet, we replace VGG-16 with Residual-101. Additionally, we append additional four residual blocks (Res6_x, Res7_x, Res8_x, Res9_x) after Res5_x block which is the end of Residual-101's full-convolution layers as Table 1 shows. Because of the mismatch of residual block and the input size in original SSD paper, we change the input size to 321×321. Simply doing those doesn't improve accuracy and therefore we present StairsNet modules in our framework.

Table 1. Architectures ResNet-101 vs. StairsNet. We replace VGG-16 with Residual-101. Additionally, we append additional four residual blocks (Res6_x, Res7_x, Res8_x, Res9_x) after Res5_x which is the end of Residual-101's full-convolution layers.

SSD layer	ResNet 101	StairsNet	StairsNet layer	Output size
conv1	7 × 7, 64, stride 2	7 × 7, 64, stride 2	Res1_x	161 × 161
conv2_x	3 × 3 max pool, stride 2	3 × 3 max pool, stride 2	Res2_x	80 × 80
	$\begin{bmatrix} 1\times1, 64 \\ 3\times3, 64 \\ 1\times1, 256 \end{bmatrix}$ ×3	$\begin{bmatrix} 1\times1, 64 \\ 3\times3, 64 \\ 1\times1, 256 \end{bmatrix}$ ×3		
conv3_x	$\begin{bmatrix} 1\times1, 128 \\ 3\times3, 128 \\ 1\times1, 512 \end{bmatrix}$ ×4	$\begin{bmatrix} 1\times1, 128 \\ 3\times3, 128 \\ 1\times1, 512 \end{bmatrix}$ ×4	**Res3_x**	40 × 40
conv4_x	$\begin{bmatrix} 1\times1, 256 \\ 3\times3, 256 \\ 1\times1, 1024 \end{bmatrix}$ ×23	$\begin{bmatrix} 1\times1, 256 \\ 3\times3, 256 \\ 1\times1, 1024 \end{bmatrix}$ ×23	Res4_x	20 × 20
conv5_x	$\begin{bmatrix} 1\times1, 512 \\ 3\times3, 512 \\ 1\times1, 2048 \end{bmatrix}$ ×3	$\begin{bmatrix} 1\times1, 512 \\ 3\times3, 512 \\ 1\times1, 2048 \end{bmatrix}$ ×3	**Res5_x**	20 × 20
conv6_x		$\begin{bmatrix} 1\times1, 256 \\ 3\times3, 256 \\ 1\times1, 512 \end{bmatrix}$ ×1	**Res6_x**	10 × 10
conv7_x		$\begin{bmatrix} 1\times1, 256 \\ 3\times3, 256 \\ 1\times1, 512 \end{bmatrix}$ ×1	**Res7_x**	5× 5
conv8_x		$\begin{bmatrix} 1\times1, 256 \\ 3\times3, 256 \\ 1\times1, 512 \end{bmatrix}$ ×1	**Res8_x**	3 × 3
conv9_x		$\begin{bmatrix} 1\times1, 256 \\ 3\times3, 256 \\ 1\times1, 512 \end{bmatrix}$ ×1	**Res9_x**	1 × 1

3.2   StairsNet

Similar with U-shaped stairs, StairsNet is divided into two *flights* of stairs by *landing* .The first module is set of Inception-Style networks named **Top-Stairs**. The second module named **Bottom-Stairs** is one-by-one corresponded by *newel* with the first module every stairstep.

Bottom-Stairs includes 5 stairsteps as the color pink block showed in Fig. 1. We use state-of-the-art classification model ResNet-101 neural network in place of VGG-16 in SSD to get the more discriminable image feature. The *tread* of upstairs is the different residual layers of ResNet-101. More details are showed in Sect. 3.1.

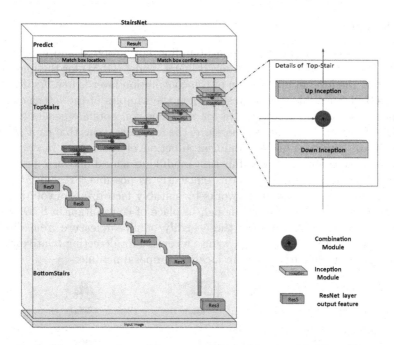

Fig. 1. StairsNet network architecture. The red layers of Bottom-Stairs are Res-block as extra layers. Each stair tread of Top-Stairs has two inceptions and combination module. The *newel* connected Top-Stairs and Bottom-Stairs one-by-one is the residual layer feature for predictor. (Color figure online)

Landing is where a 180° change in direction is made. In our system, the *landing* is where the feature transform direction changes, *e.g.* Res9_x in Fig. 1. After the *Landing*, the input data not only comes from the previous layers, but also combines the deconv information from the successor. In Fig. 1 red circle is combination mixing different scale features.

(**Top-Stairs**) module of StairsNet is used to get location proposals and to match bounding boxes. One stairstep has two inception blocks and a features-combined module. The inception of each stairsteps changes depending on the difference of feature scale. Top-stairs uses three different inceptions which are showed in Fig. 2. In Fig. 1, downwards, the first two represents Inception-A, the middle of inceptions represents Inception-B, and the last two represents Inception-C. More details about inceptions we use is showed in next section. The combination module changes the large scale to small scale by deconvolution, and then uses Eltwise layer to mix the two feature maps. As is shown in color green block in Fig. 1, some *newel* connects Bottom-Stairs and Top-Stairs one-by-one is the residual layer feature for predictor, and the stairstep's input is the combination of different scale features.

3.3   Inception

SSD [13] uses convolution filter as a bounding box proposal and classification module. We argue that, as a generalized linear model (GLM) for the underlying data patch, the level of abstraction of the convolution layer is low. As described in [11], GLM can achieve great result when the samples of the latent concepts are linearly separable, and the data for the same concepts are generally highly nonlinear function of the input. Therefore, the representations that capture these concepts are generally highly nonlinear function of the input. Inception [11] has been a successful nonlinear function module in neural network design [22]. To utilize the added computation as efficiently as possible, Szegedy *et al.* [25] explored methods to scale up networks by suitably factorized convolutions and aggressive regularization. In our model, in place of convolution in SSD, we use Fig. 2(a), (b) and (c) to capture these highly nonlinear feature from different scales for next stage. Additionally, we use inception for detecting relatively small and large objects simultaneously in location proposal module.

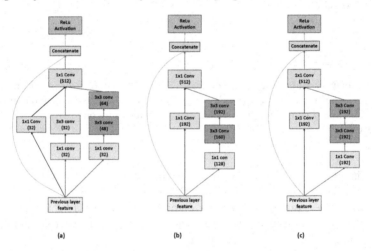

Fig. 2. Inception Module. (a) is Inception-A used for Res3_x's and Res5_x's Top-Stairs. (b) is Inception-B used for Res6_x's Top-Stairs and (c) is Inception-C used for Res7_x's and Res8_x's Top-Stairs.

3.4   Optimizing Strategy

Similar to SSD, the StairsNet objective is extending MultiBox objective [3,23] to handle multiple object categories. During training, we are selecting from default boxes of different location at each location in several feature maps with different scales, with using matching strategy in SSD which is for each groundtruth box. For the i-th default bounding box($d_i = (d_i^{cx}, d_i^{cy}, d_i^w, d_i^h)$), we predict the offsets to the j-th groundtruth box($g_j = (g_j^{cx}, g_j^{cy}, g_j^w, g_j^h)$),

$$\hat{g}_j^{cx} = \frac{(g_j^{cx} - d_i^{cx})}{d_i^w} \qquad\qquad \hat{g}_j^{cy} = \frac{(g_j^{cy} - d_i^{cy})}{d_i^h} \qquad (1)$$

$$\hat{g}_j^w = \log(\frac{g_j^w}{d_i^w}) \qquad\qquad \hat{g}_j^h = \log(\frac{g_j^h}{d_i^h}) \qquad (2)$$

and the predict location (l_i) will be get the confidences for all object categories. The overall model loss is a weighted (λ) sum of the localization loss (loc) and the confidence loss $(conf)$.

$$L(x, c, l, g) = \frac{1}{N}(L_{conf}(x, c) + \lambda L_{loc}(x, l, g)) \qquad (3)$$

where N is the number of matched default boxes, $x_{ij}^p = \{0, 1\}$ be an indicator for matching the i-th default box to the j-th groundtruth box of category p.

$$L_{loc}(x, l, g) = \sum_{i \in Positive}^{N} \sum_{m \in \{cx, cy, w, h\}} x_{ij}^k Smooth\_L_1(l_i^m - \hat{g}_j^m) \qquad (4)$$

$$L_{conf}(x, c) = - \sum_{i \in Positive}^{N} x_{ij}^p \log(\hat{c}_i^p) - \sum_{i \in Negative} \log(\hat{c}_i^0) \qquad (5)$$

where $\hat{c}_i^p = \frac{\exp(c_i^p)}{\sum_p \exp(c_i^p)}$, and the λ is set to 1 and the positive default bounding box is matched with groundtruth box object and the rest as negatives.

3.5 Training

In contrast to SSD, StairsNet has a small change in the prior box aspect ratio setting. The original SSD model, boxes with aspect ratios of 2 and 3 were proven useful from the experiments. Similar with [16], we run k-means clustering on the training boxes with square root of box area as the feature. Results show that most of boxes ratios fall within a range of 1–3. Therefore, we add 1.6 to the aspect radios, and use total three aspect radios at each prediction layer.

The key difference between training SSD is that we train the model including separated 2 steps. Firstly, we build and train base network using Residual-101 classification model, which is pre-trained on the ILSVRC CLS-LOC dataset [18], as backbone instead of VGG-16. Secondly, frozing the the backbone network (Residual-101) parameter, we add the Bottom-stairs and Top-stairs into the architecture and train the entire StairsNet. We apply the same network architecture we used for VOC2007 + 2012 dataset. When training the base network, we first train the model with 10^{-3} learning rate for 40k iterations, and then continue training for 20k iterations with 10^{-4} and 10^{-5}. Lastly, we continue training our model StairsNet for 20k iterations with learning rating 10^{-3}, 10^{-4} and 10^{-5}, with utilizing the trained base network model. We can achieve 77.7% mAP on the VOC2007 test set.

4 Experiments

4.1 Model Result on VOC2007

We compare against Faster R-CNN, SSD, StairsNet on VOC2007 `test` (4950 images). All methods are trained on VOC2007 + 2012 `train`. Figure 1 shows the architecture details of the StairsNet321 model. The results show StairsNet have better effect on object detection and large size input will increase result (Table 2).

Table 2. Pascal VOC2007 `test` detection result. Faster R-CNN use input images whose minimum dimension is 600. The SSD models have exactly the same settings except different input sizes (300 × 300 vs. 512 × 512). SSD+ResNet321 is that ResNet-101 instead of VGG-16 of SSD and input size is 321 × 321. The two StairsNet models have same settings except that they have different input sizes (321 × 321 vs. 513 × 513).

Method	Dataset	Base network	Using inception	mAP
Faster R-CNN	VOC2007	VGG-16	N	73.2%
SSD300	VOC2007	VGG-16	N	77.2%
SSD512	VOC2007	VGG-16	N	79.8%
SSD+ResNet321	VOC2007	ResNet-101	N	**75.0%**
StairsNet321	VOC2007	ResNet-101	Y	**77.7%**
StairsNet513	VOC2007	ResNet-101	Y	80.1%

4.2 Inference Time

We measure the speed with batch size 1 using NVIDIA GTX 1080Ti and cuDNN v5 with Intel(R) Core(TM) i7-6700K CPU@4.00GHz. Table 3 shows the comparison between StairsNet, Faster R-CNN [17], SSD [13]. Our proposed model is not fast as the SSD for two reasons. Firstly, the ResNet-101 is slower than VGGNet. Secondly, the extra layers we added to the model introduce extra overhead. Both our StairsNet321 and StairsNet513 method outperforms Faster R-CNN in both speed and accuracy. Our StairsNet513 model has better accuracy, but is slightly slower. Therefore, using a faster base network could even further improve the speed, which can possibly make the StairsNet513 model real-time as well.

4.3 Model Analysis

To understand the affects of each component in StairsNet, we carry out controlled experiments. In all the experiments, we use the same settings and input size (321 × 321) in specified changes to the settings or component(s).

Do Inceptions Help?
Each Top-Stairs module has two inceptions at the both sides of the deconvolution. Closer to the output, the Up-Inception can capture highly nonlinear features after being mixed by deconvolution. As Table 4 shows, the model can't

Table 3. Pascal VOC2007 test detection results. StairsNet321 is real-time detection method that can achieve above 77.7% mAP. By using a larger input image, Stairs513 outperforms all methods on accuracy.

Method	mAP	FPS	Batch size	#Boxes	Input resolution
Faster R-CNN (VGG16)	73.2	14	1	~ 6000	~ 1000 × 600
SSD300	77.2	92	1	8732	300 × 300
SSD512	79.8	38	1	24564	512 × 512
StairsNet321	77.7	20	1	17080	321 × 321
StairsNet513	80.1	13	1	43936	513 × 513

find any detection unless using Up Inception. This fact shows Up-Inception has a tremendous effect on mixed feature to predict. In Table 4, the low result when not using Down-Inception shows the function of Down-Inception in StairsNet.

Table 4. Effects of various design choices and components on StairsNet performance. ✱ represents that the model couldn't find any detection when evaluated.

Component name	StairsNet321				
Deconvolution		✓	✓	✓	✓
Up-Inception			✓		✓
Down-Inception				✓	✓
VOC2007 test mAP	75.0%	✱	77.2%	✱	**77.7%**

Can We Utilize the Same Inceptions?
In StairsNet, depending on the different scales, we utilize the three kinds of inceptions to handle different scale nonlinear features. Is it necessary to build different inceptions? Will all the same inceptions with more parameters helps? To this end, we replace all inceptions in StairsNet with the Inception-C. The mAP of the StairsNet with the same inceptions is 70.0%. The result shows that it is better to use various of inceptions depending on the different scales.

Large Size Image will Help Result?
Although increasing the size of input will spend more time to train and test, Similar with SSD, using large size image as input will increase mAP. By increasing the training and testing image size 513 × 513, we are 0.3% more accurate than using SSD 512 × 512 model.

4.4 Visualization Our Result

In Fig. 3, we show some detection examples on VOC2007 test with SSD300 and StairsNet321 models. Compared to SSD, the small size objects and certain classes that have distinct context have been improved.

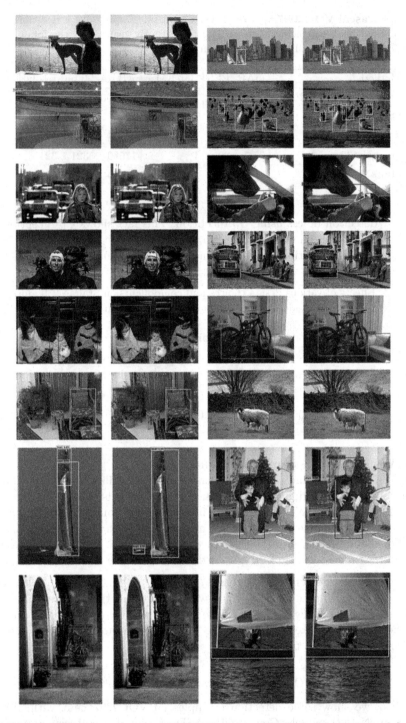

Fig. 3. Detection examples on VOC2007 test with StairsNet321 model. For each pair, the left side is the result of **SSD** and right side is the result of **StairsNet**. We show detection result with scores higher than 0.6. Each color corresponds to an object category.

5 Conclusions

We have presented StairsNet, a single deep neural network for object detection in images. StairsNet provides with an effective features-combined method to utilize the mixed multi-scale features to predict. Meanwhile, inceptions added not only captures the nonlinear concepts from different scale features, but also decides the effect of mixed features. We demonstrate its effectiveness on benchmark datasets by the experiments in this paper. Using ResNet and mixing multi-scale feature, StairsNet has the better effect in object detection.

Acknowledgments. This work is supported by the National Natural Science Foundation of China under Grant No. 61432001, the National Science and Technology Major Project under Grant No. 2014ZX01029101-002, the Youth Innovation Promotion Association CAS under Grant No. 2016105, and the National High-tech R&D Program (863 Program) under Grant No. 2013AA01A603.

References

1. Alexe, B., Deselaers, T., Ferrari, V.: Measuring the objectness of image windows. IEEE Trans. Pattern Anal. Mach. Intell. **34**(11), 2189–202 (2012)
2. Carreira, J., Sminchisescu, C.: CPMC: automatic object segmentation using constrained parametric min-cuts. IEEE Trans. Pattern Anal. Mach. Intell. **34**(7), 1312–1328 (2012)
3. Erhan, D., Szegedy, C., Toshev, A., Anguelov, D.: Scalable object detection using deep neural networks. In: Proceedings of the IEEE Conference on Computer Vision and Pattern Recognition, pp. 2147–2154 (2014)
4. Girshick, R., Donahue, J., Darrell, T., Malik, J.: Rich feature hierarchies for accurate object detection and semantic segmentation. In: Proceedings of the IEEE Conference on Computer Vision and Pattern Recognition, pp. 580–587 (2014)
5. He, K., Zhang, X., Ren, S., Sun, J.: Deep residual learning for image recognition. In: Proceedings of the IEEE Conference on Computer Vision and Pattern Recognition, pp. 770–778 (2016)
6. Hinton, G.E., Salakhutdinov, R.R.: Reducing the dimensionality of data with neural networks. science **313**(5786), 504–507 (2006)
7. Ioffe, S., Szegedy, C.: Batch normalization: Accelerating deep network training by reducing internal covariate shift (2015) arXiv preprint arXiv:1502.03167
8. Kong, T., Yao, A., Chen, Y., Sun, F.: HyperNet: towards accurate region proposal generation and joint object detection. In: Proceedings of the IEEE Conference on Computer Vision and Pattern Recognition, pp. 845–853 (2016)
9. Krizhevsky, A., Sutskever, I., Hinton, G.E.: ImageNet classification with deep convolutional neural networks. In: Advances in neural information processing systems, pp. 1097–1105 (2012)
10. Li, Y., He, K., Sun, J., et al.: R-FCN: Object detection via region-based fully convolutional networks. In: Advances in Neural Information Processing Systems, pp. 379–387 (2016)
11. Lin, M., Chen, Q., Yan, S.: Network in network (2013). arXiv preprint arXiv:1312.4400
12. Lin, T.Y., Dollár, P., Girshick, R., He, K., Hariharan, B., Belongie, S.: Feature Pyramid Networks for Object Detection (2016)

13. Liu, W., Anguelov, D., Erhan, D., Szegedy, C., Reed, S., Fu, C.-Y., Berg, A.C.: SSD: single shot multibox detector. In: Leibe, B., Matas, J., Sebe, N., Welling, M. (eds.) ECCV 2016. LNCS, vol. 9905, pp. 21–37. Springer, Cham (2016). https:// doi.org/10.1007/978-3-319-46448-0_2

14. Pont-Tuset, J., Arbelaez, P., Barron, J.T., Marques, F., Malik, J.: Multiscale combinatorial grouping for image segmentation and object proposal generation. IEEE Trans. Pattern Anal. Mach. Intell. **39**(1), 128–140 (2017)

15. Redmon, J., Divvala, S., Girshick, R., Farhadi, A.: You only look once: Unified, real-time object detection. In: Proceedings of the IEEE Conference on Computer Vision and Pattern Recognition, pp. 779–788 (2016)

16. Redmon, J., Farhadi, A.: Yolo9000: Better, Faster, Stronger (2016). arXiv preprint arXiv:1612.08242

17. Ren, S., He, K., Girshick, R., Sun, J.: Faster R-CNN: Towards real-time object detection with region proposal networks. In: Advances in neural information processing systems, pp. 91–99 (2015)

18. Russakovsky, O., Deng, J., Su, H., Krause, J., Satheesh, S., Ma, S., Huang, Z., Karpathy, A., Khosla, A., Bernstein, M.: Imagenet large scale visual recognition challenge. Int. J. Comput. Vision **115**(3), 211–252 (2015)

19. Sermanet, P., Eigen, D., Zhang, X., Mathieu, M., Fergus, R., LeCun, Y.: OverFeat: Integrated recognition, localization and detection using convolutional networks (2013). arXiv preprint arXiv:1312.6229

20. Simonyan, K., Zisserman, A.: Very deep convolutional networks for large-scale image recognition (2014). arXiv preprint arXiv:1409.1556

21. Szegedy, C., Ioffe, S., Vanhoucke, V., Alemi, A.: Inception-v4, Inception-Resnet and the impact of residual connections on learning (2016). arXiv preprint arXiv:1602.07261

22. Szegedy, C., Liu, W., Jia, Y., Sermanet, P., Reed, S., Anguelov, D., Erhan, D., Vanhoucke, V., Rabinovich, A.: going deeper with convolutions. In: Proceedings of the IEEE Conference on Computer Vision and Pattern Recognition, pp. 1–9 (2015)

23. Szegedy, C., Reed, S., Erhan, D., Anguelov, D., Ioffe, S.: Scalable, high-quality object detection. Computer Science (2014)

24. Szegedy, C., Toshev, A., Erhan, D.: Deep neural networks for object detection. In: Advances in Neural Information Processing Systems, pp. 2553–2561 (2013)

25. Szegedy, C., Vanhoucke, V., Ioffe, S., Shlens, J., Wojna, Z.: Rethinking the inception architecture for computer vision. In: Proceedings of the IEEE Conference on Computer Vision and Pattern Recognition, pp. 2818–2826 (2016)

26. Uijlings, J.R., Van De Sande, K.E., Gevers, T., Smeulders, A.W.: Selective search for object recognition. Int. J. Comput. Vision **104**(2), 154–171 (2013)

27. Zitnick, C.L., Dollár, P.: Edge Boxes: locating object proposals from edges. In: Fleet, D., Pajdla, T., Schiele, B., Tuytelaars, T. (eds.) ECCV 2014. LNCS, vol. 8693, pp. 391–405. Springer, Cham (2014). https://doi.org/10.1007/978-3-319-10602-1_26

A Dual-CNN Model for Multi-label Classification by Leveraging Co-occurrence Dependencies Between Labels

Peng-Fei Zhang[1], Hao-Yi Wu[2], and Xin-Shun Xu[1(✉)]

[1] School of Computer Science and Technology, Shandong University, Jinan, China
xuxinshun@sdu.edu.cn
[2] Faculty of Science, Engineering and Technology,
University of Tasmania, Hobart, Australia

Abstract. In recent years, deep convolutional neural network (CNN) has demonstrated its great power in image classification. In real world, there are many images contain abundant contents so that they have multiple labels. Moreover, there are correlations between labels. Traditional deep methods for such data rarely take into account such correlations. In this paper, we propose a dual-CNN model, i.e., Dual-CNN model for Multi-Label classification (Dual-CNN-ML), which can make full use of the dependencies of labels to enhance classification performance. Specifically, we first obtain co-occurrence dependency matrix from training datasets; then, we merge the co-occurrence dependency matrix and image representation together; finally, we use the new representation to predict labels of samples. Extensive experiments on public benchmark datasets demonstrate that the proposed method obtains satisfying results and outperforms several state-of-the-art methods.

Keywords: CNN · Multi-label · Classification
Label co-occurrence dependencies

1 Introduction

The past few years have witnessed the great success of Deep Neural Network (DNN) in computer vision, e.g., recognition [15,16] and classification [1,19,21], etc. Many works have demonstrated that, given sufficient training data, CNN can achieve great performance in vision tasks [4,8,12]. For example, for image classification task, DNN models can obtain much better results than non-deep models. In early years, most deep models only consider the scenario that each sample contains one label [9,16,25]. However, as shown in Fig. 1, in real world, one image may be associated with multiple semantic labels, because an image normally abounds with rich semantic information, such as objects, parts, scenes, actions, and their interactions or attributes [19]. Thus, multi-label image classification is a more general and practical problem compared to single-label image

© Springer International Publishing AG, part of Springer Nature 2018
B. Zeng et al. (Eds.): PCM 2017, LNCS 10735, pp. 315–324, 2018.
https://doi.org/10.1007/978-3-319-77380-3_30

(a) keyboard, mouse, monitor   (b) car, person

Fig. 1. Samples with multiple labels.

classification. As a result, multi-label problem has attracted much attention in machine learning and other communities. Correspondingly, many methods have been proposed to address this challenging problem [5,13,20]. In addition, there are correlations between labels. For example, as shown in Fig. 1(a), the mouse is very small and hard to be recognized. However, if a model could consider that mouse and keyboard often appear together, it could predict the mouse label with high probability. Similarly, the sample problem exists in Fig. 1(b).

Many works have shown that exploiting label correlations is helpful for multi-label image classification [6,11,17,18,22–24]. For example, in [6], the authors use Markov random fields to capture the correlations between labels. The method in [24] constructs co-occurrence matrix by means of harmonic mean on empirical conditional probabilities. The method in [14] trains a set of classifier to predict a label based on previous predicted labels and image representation. These method try to make full use of the correlations in labels; however, they only consider pairwise labels and ignore the complex structure of labels. That is to say, they cannot model complex high-order correlations between labels.

To deal with multi-label image classification, a typical approach in deep neural network is to convert multi-label image classification into multiple single-label image classification problems, so that this problem can be easily handled with existing single-label image classification methods. For example, Hypotheses-CNN-Pooling (HCP) [20] deep network extracts and selects a set of candidate object windows and then feeds them into CNN. Finally, it combines the representations as the final representation. Apparently, such work treats labels independently, and ignores the correlations in labels as shown in Fig. 1.

In order to model high-order label co-occurrence dependencies, in this paper, we utilize CNN to model label co-occurrence dependencies. The framework of the proposed model is shown in Fig. 2, which mainly contains two sub-networks: The image CNN accepts images as input to generate image embeddings; the matrix CNN takes label co-occurrence matrix as input to get matrix embedding. Then the two embeddings are imported into fusion layer to get the joint embedding. At last, by dealing with the joint embedding, we can predict labels for multi-label images. The matrix CNN can not only capture local feature which is the relation between labels, but also obtain global feature (correlations in all labels).

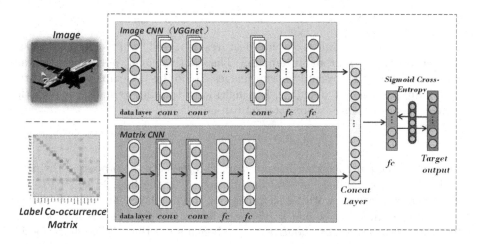

Fig. 2. Overview of the proposed model for multi-label classification task.

By this way, the proposed method can model the high-order label co-occurrence dependency. Moreover, the proposed model can be trained in end-to-end way.

Compared to previous methods, our main contributions are as follows:

- We propose an efficient end-to-end CNN framework to tackle multi-label image classification problem, and experiments on public datasets prove that our model can achieve better performance than previous works.
- By applying CNN on label co-occurrence matrix, our framework can efficiently model the high-order label co-occurrence dependencies and the complex relevance with images, which will be jointly learned to generate labels.
- We conduct extensive experiments on two benchmark multi-label datasets, e.g., Pascal VOC 2007 and VOC 2012. The results demonstrate that the proposed method can achieve competitive results compared with several state-of-the-art methods.

2   Proposed Model

The framework of our proposed model for multi-label image classification is shown in Fig. 2. The architecture contains three components: image CNN, matrix CNN and the convolution fusion and prediction layers. Specifically, the image CNN takes image as input and then extracts the image representation; the matrix CNN models label co-occurrence dependencies; at last the convolution fusion layers fuse the image and co-occurrence matrix representations together and obtain the new representation. At the same time, the joint representation is input to prediction layer to generate the labels. These three parts are connected tightly and trained together. The details of each part are given in the following subsections.

2.1   Image CNN

Compared with hand-crafted features, features extracted from the deep networks are more abstract, exact and meaningful. Thus, in this paper, we use deep neural network to extract representations for images. To do this, we employ the network in [16]. Suppose that $\mathcal{X} = \{x_i\}_{i=1}^n$ is a multi-label training set and x_i is the i-th sample, them the image representation can be denoted as:

$$u_i = \phi\left(w_t\left(F\left(x_i\right)\right) + b_t\right), \tag{1}$$

where w_t is the parameter for feature map, F represents the process of the network [16], ϕ is a nonlinear activation function, b_t is the bias. In this part, we slightly modify the network by chopping out the last layer, and add a nonlinear activation function behind it. For each image, the final representation is a 1000-dimension vector. By doing this, the benefits are that the nonlinear activation function can enhance the nonlinear property of model, on the other hand lower dimension representation can reduce the number of parameters that will be trained in fusion layer.

2.2   Matrix CNN

In CNN, the local receptive field of the convolution unit can perceive local information of the input and transport information to higher layers; then, higher layers further process these feature maps and obtain the global representation. Correspondingly, by means of these stacked convolution layers, we can capture the complex structure and content contained in an input. To model the high-order label co-occurrence dependencies, here we introduce a CNN into our framework to process the label co-occurrence matrix. By doing this, CNN can capture the local feature and the global feature of the input so that we could obtain the abundant contents about label co-occurrence dependencies. This process is shown in Fig. 3(a). Note that, in Fig. 3(a), C is the convolutional layer, P is the pooling layer, FC is the fully connected layer. Totally, it contain four layers: two convolutional layers and two fully connected layers. For a label co-occurrence matrix M, the convolutional process for nonlinear feature map of the l-th layer is:

$$T^l = \phi\left(w_m^l T^{l-1} + b_m^l\right), \tag{2}$$

where w_m^l denotes the parameters of feature map of the l-th layer, ϕ is the nonlinear activation function, T^{l-1} is the output of the $(l-1)$-th layer, b_m^l is the corresponding bias.

Note that our model is not the first work that use the label co-occurrence matrix. The method in [24] constructs co-occurrence matrix by means of harmonic mean on empirical conditional probabilities. Different from that in [24], our label co-occurrence matrix records the times of label co-occurrence. The reason is that we want to maintain the original information in labels so that CNN can capture such original information. For a training set, we count the times of

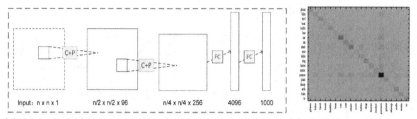

(a) Matrix CNN learning label co-occurrence depen-(b) Label co-occurrence
dencies.   matrix.

Fig. 3. Matrix CNN learning label co-occurrence dependencies and corresponding label
co-occurrence matrix extracted from Pascal VOC 2007.

appearance of pairwise labels as the elements of the label co-occurrence matrix,
if the value of a element is too big, we divide matrix by a certain definite value.

To show that the above method can obtain the co-occurrence dependencies,
we show the label co-occurrence matrix extracted from Pascal VOC 2017 by
using the process above, which is shown in Fig. 3(b). In this figure, the color is
deeper, the labels appear together more frequently.

2.3   Fusion and Prediction Layer

After obtaining the image and co-occurrence matrix presentations, we concatenate these two representations and use the fully connected layer to produce
the new representation. We denote the new representation as $\mathcal{V} = \{v_i\}_{i=1}^n$,
$v_i = \{v_i^k\}_{k=1}^K$, K is the number of category.

$$c_i = u_i \parallel \mathcal{T}, \tag{3}$$

$$v_i = w_f * c_i + b_f, \tag{4}$$

where u_i is the i-th image representation and $\mathcal{T}$ is the matrix representation, w_f
and b_f are the parameters of feature map, c_i is the input of the fully connected
layer.

Thereafter, we use the sigmoid cross entropy loss as the loss function for our
multi-label classification task, which is formulated as:

$$\mathcal{E}_i = \sum_{k=1}^K \left[p_i^k \log \hat{p}_i^k + \left(1 - p_i^k\right) \log \left(1 - \hat{p}_i^k\right) \right], \tag{5}$$

where

$$\hat{p}_i^k = 1/ \left(1 + exp\left(-v_i^k\right)\right), p_i^k \in [0,1], \tag{6}$$

where $\mathcal{E}_i$ is the loss for i-th sample, $\hat{p}_i^k$ is the probability of that v_i belongs to
the k-th category, p_i^k is the target probability.

Table 1. Results on Pascal VOC 2007

	Plane	Bike	Bird	Boat	Bottle	Bus	Car	Cat	Chair	Cow	Table
INRIA [7]	77.2	69.3	56.2	66.6	45.5	68.1	83.4	53.6	58.3	51.1	62.2
NUS [1]	82.5	79.6	64.8	73.4	54.2	75.0	77.5	79.2	46.2	62.7	41.4
AGS [2]	82.2	83.0	58.4	76.1	56.4	77.5	88.8	69.1	62.2	61.8	64.2
CNN-SVM [15]	88.5	81.0	83.5	82.0	42.0	72.5	85.3	81.6	59.9	58.5	66.5
I-FT [20]	91.4	84.7	87.5	81.8	40.2	73.0	86.4	84.8	51.8	63.9	67.9
HCP-1000C [20]	95.1	90.1	92.8	89.9	51.5	80.0	**91.7**	91.6	57.7	77.8	70.9
CNN-RNN [19]	96.7	83.1	94.2	**92.8**	61.2	82.1	89.1	94.2	**64.2**	83.6	70.0
Dual-CNN-ML	**96.9**	**94.1**	**96.5**	90.4	**71.7**	**90.1**	79.4	**96.1**	59.1	**84.4**	**73.4**
	Dog	Horse	Motor	Person	Plant	Sheep	Sofa	Train	Tv	MAP	
INRIA[7]	45.2	78.4	69.7	86.1	52.4	54.4	54.3	75.8	62.1	63.5	
NUS[1]	74.6	85.0	76.8	91.1	53.9	61.0	67.5	83.6	70.6	70.5	
AGS[2]	51.3	85.4	80.2	91.1	48.1	61.7	67.7	86.3	70.9	71.1	
CNN-SVM[15]	77.8	81.8	78.8	90.2	54.8	71.1	62.6	87.4	71.8	73.9	
I-FT [20]	82.7	84.0	76.9	90.4	51.5	79.9	54.1	89.5	65.8	74.4	
HCP-1000C[20]	89.3	89.3	85.2	93.0	64.0	85.7	62.7	94.4	78.3	81.5	
CNN-RNN [19]	**92.4**	**91.7**	84.2	**93.7**	59.8	**93.2**	75.3	**99.7**	78.6	84.0	
Dual-CNN-ML	84.3	89.7	**91.5**	90.6	**81.6**	89.2	**78.5**	82.6	**83.8**	**85.2**	

3 Experiments

In this section, we test our proposed method on two benchmark multi-label image datasets, e.g., Pascal VOC 2007 and VOC 2012 [3]. We employ the VGG-16 [16] network pretrained on ImageNet dataset as the image CNN. The dimension of image and matrix representations is set to 1000. The evaluation metric is the mean average precision (mAP).

On VOC 2007, we compare the proposed model with seven state-of-the-art methods including INRIA [7], NUS [1], AGS [2], CNN-SVM [15], I-FT [20], HCP-1000C [20], and CNN-RNN [19]. INRIA [7] employs the traditional feature extraction-coding-pooling pipeline. NUS [1] trains a codebook for descriptors from VOC. AGS [2] learns a layered representation by transferring VOC data to subcategories. CNN-SVM [15] is based on the OverFeat features and applies SVM as the classifier. I-FT [20] applies the squared loss function for multi-label classification. HCP-1000C [20] employs hypotheses extraction approach to get input hypotheses of the given images and then utilizes the cross-hypothesis max-pooling operation to produce the final prediction. In [19], the authors propose a unified CNN-RNN model which uses the RNN to model the label co-occurrence dependencies by learning the joint image-label embedding.

On VOC 2012, the proposed model is compared with six models including I-FT [20], PRE-1000C and PRE-1512 [13], HCP-1000C [20], LeCun et al. [10], and NUS-PSL [20]. NUS-PSL [20] combines the ambiguity-guided Mixture Model(AMM)[1] and the ambiguity Guided Subcategory (AGS [2]) mining approach. PRE-1000C and PRE-1512 [13] transfer CNN parameters pre-trained on

Table 2. Image classification result on pascal VOC 2012

	Plane	Bike	Bird	Boat	Bottle	Bus	Car	Cat	Chair	Cow	Table
I-FT [20]	94.6	74.3	87.8	80.2	50.1	82.0	73.7	90.1	60.6	69.9	62.7
PRE-1000C [13]	93.5	78.4	87.7	80.9	57.3	85.0	81.6	89.4	66.9	73.8	62.0
LeCun-ICML [10]	96.0	77.1	88.4	85.5	55.8	85.8	78.6	91.2	65.0	74.4	67.7
HCP-1000C [20]	**97.7**	83.0	93.2	**87.2**	59.6	88.2	81.9	**94.7**	66.9	81.6	68.0
NUS-PSL [20]	97.3	84.2	80.8	85.3	60.8	89.9	**86.8**	89.3	**75.4**	77.8	75.1
PRE-1512 [13]	94.6	82.9	88.2	84.1	60.3	89.0	84.4	90.7	72.1	**86.8**	69.0
Dual-CNN-ML	92.2	**91.1**	**94.0**	**87.2**	**79.7**	**96.0**	80.7	90.9	68.8	72.9	**69.1**
	Dog	Horse	Motor	Person	Plant	Sheep	Sofa	Train	Tv	MAP	
I-FT [20]	86.9	78.7	81.4	90.5	45.9	77.5	49.3	88.5	69.2	74.7	
PRE-1000C [13]	89.5	83.2	87.6	95.8	61.4	79.0	54.3	88.0	78.3	78.7	
LeCun-ICML [10]	87.8	86.0	85.1	90.9	52.2	83.6	61.1	91.8	76.1	79.0	
HCP-1000C [20]	**93.0**	88.2	87.7	92.7	59.0	85.1	55.4	93.0	77.2	81.7	
NUS-PSL [20]	83.0	87.5	**90.1**	95.0	57.8	79.2	**73.4**	94.5	80.7	82.2	
PRE-1512 [13]	92.1	**93.4**	88.6	**96.1**	64.3	86.6	62.3	91.1	79.8	82.8	
Dual-CNN-ML	92.8	73.3	83.3	91.9	**90.3**	**91.4**	73.0	**95.0**	**85.9**	**85.0**	

the ImageNet dataset with 1000 categories and the augmented one with 1512 categories to other visual recognition tasks with limited training data, respectively.

The results on VOC 2007 are shown in Table 1. From this table, we can see that when taking the label co-occurrence dependencies into consideration, CNN-RNN [19] and Dual-CNN-ML can achieve better performance on most cases than other approaches that do not consider the label co-occurrence dependencies. This confirms that the label co-occurrence dependencies are helpful for multi-label classification. In addition, Dual-CNN-ML obtains better performance than CNN-RNN. It is worthy to note that Dual-CNN-ML performs poorly on some labels. The possible reason is that Dual-CNN-ML pays more attention to some labels with high dependencies, such as "bottle" and "table"; therefore, it may ignore some labels that have little dependencies with other labels, e.g., "train".

The results on VOC 2012 are shown in Table 2. From this table, we can observe that Dual-CNN-ML obtains better results on ten labels than other methods. Moreover, it has the best overall performance, i.e., the best MAP. Note that PRE-1000C [13], PRE-1512 [13] and HCP-1000C [20] obtain the best results on several labels. The main reason is that they use additional samples for training, from which they learn more information.

From Tables 1 and 2, we can find that our proposed method–Dual-CNN-ML can work well for the multi-label classification task.

In addition, to get an intuitive observation of the results of Dual-CNN-ML, we further show some image classification results and its ground-truth in Fig. 4. From this figure, we can observe that Dual-CNN-ML can correctly predict most labels of these instances.

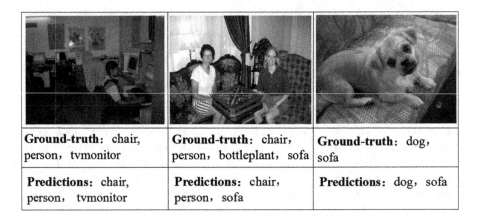

Ground-truth: chair, person, tvmonitor	Ground-truth: chair, person, bottleplant, sofa	Ground-truth: dog, sofa
Predictions: chair, person, tvmonitor	Predictions: chair, person, sofa	Predictions: dog, sofa

Fig. 4. Example prediction results and ground-truth on Pascal VOC datasets.

4   Conclusion

In this paper, we propose a novel CNN based model for multi-label image classification task, i.e., Dual-CNN-ML, which makes use of two CNN models (image CNN and matrix CNN) to extract features and label co-occurrence dependencies, respectively. Specifically, the image CNN takes image as input and then extracts the image representation; the matrix CNN models label co-occurrence dependencies. In addition, the convolution fusion layers fuse the image and co-occurrence matrix representations together and obtain the new representation. Finally, the joint representation is input to prediction layer to generate the labels. Extensive experiments on benchmark datasets demonstrate that our method can achieve competitive results compared with several state-of-the-art approaches.

Acknowledgement. This work was partially supported by National Natural Science Foundation of China (61173068, 61573212), Program for New Century Excellent Talents in University of the Ministry of Education, Key Research and Development Program of Shandong Province (2016GGX101044).

References

1. Chen, Q., Song, Z., Dong, J., Huang, Z., Hua, Y., Yan, S.: Contextualizing object detection and classification. IEEE Trans. Pattern Anal. Mach. Intell. **37**(1), 13–27 (2015)
2. Dong, J., Xia, W., Chen, Q.. Feng, J., Huang, Z., Yan, S.: Subcategory-aware object classification. In: Proceedings of IEEE Conference on Computer Vision and Pattern Recognition, pp. 827–834 (2013)
3. Everingham, M., Van Gool, L., Williams, C.K., Winn, J., Zisserman, A.: The pascal visual object classes (VOC) challenge. Int. J. Comput. Vis. **111**(1), 117–176 (2010)
4. Gong, Y., Jia, Y., Leung, T., Toshev, A., Ioffe, S.: Deep convolutional ranking for multilabel image annotation. arXiv (2013)

5. Guillaumin, M., Mensink, T., Verbeek, J., Schmid, C.: Tagprop: Discriminative metric learning in nearest neighbor models for image auto-annotation. In: Proceedings of IEEE International Conference on Computer Vision, pp. 309–316 (2009)
6. Guo, Y., Gu, S.: Multi-label classification using conditional dependency networks. In: Proceedings of International Joint Conference on Artificial Intelligence, pp. 1300–1305 (2011)
7. Harzallah, H., Jurie, F., Schmid, C.: Combining efficient object localization and image classification. In: Proceedings of IEEE International Conference on Computer Vision, pp. 237–244 (2009)
8. Kan, M., Shan, S., Chen, X.: Multi-view deep network for cross-view classification. In: Proceedings of IEEE Conference on Computer Vision and Pattern Recognition, pp. 4847–4855 (2016)
9. Krizhevsky, A., Sutskever, I., Hinton, G.E.: Imagenet classification with deep convolutional neural networks. In: Proceedings of Advances in Neural Information Processing Systems, pp. 1097–1105 (2012)
10. LeCun, Y., Ranzato, M.: Deep learning tutorial. In: Proceedings of International Conference on Machine Learning (2013)
11. Li, X., Zhao, F., Guo, Y.: Multi-label image classification with a probabilistic label enhancement model. In: Proceedings of International Conference on Uncertainty in Artificial Intelligence, pp. 430–439 (2014)
12. Murthy, V.N., Singh, V., Chen, T., Manmatha, R., Comaniciu, D.: Deep decision network for multi-class image classification. In: Proceedings of IEEE Conference on Computer Vision and Pattern Recognition, pp. 2240–2248 (2016)
13. Oquab, M., Bottou, L., Laptev, I., Sivic, J.: Learning and transferring mid-level image representations using convolutional neural networks. In: Proceedings of IEEE Conference on Computer Vision and Pattern Recognition, pp. 1717–1724 (2014)
14. Read, J., Pfahringer, B., Holmes, G., Frank, E.: Classifier chains for multi-label classification. Mach. Learn. **85**, 333–359 (2011)
15. Sermanet, P., Eigen, D., Zhang, X., Mathieu, M., Fergus, R., LeCun, Y.: Overfeat: Integrated recognition, localization and detection using convolutional networks. arXiv (2013)
16. Simonyan, K., Zisserman, A.: Very deep convolutional networks for large-scale image recognition. arXiv (2014)
17. Song, X., Jiang, S., Herranz, L.: Multi-scale multi-feature context modeling for scene recognition in the semantic manifold. IEEE Trans. Image Process. **26**(6), 2721–2735 (2017)
18. Song, X., Jiang, S., Herranz, L., Kong, Y., Zheng, K.: Category co-occurrence modeling for large scale scene recognition. Pattern Recogn. **59**, 98–111 (2016)
19. Wang, J., Yang, Y., Mao, J., Huang, Z., Huang, C., Xu, W.: CNN-RNN: A unified framework for multi-label image classification. In: Proceedings of IEEE Conference on Computer Vision and Pattern Recognition, pp. 2285–2294 (2016)
20. Wei, Y., Xia, W., Huang, J., Ni, B., Dong, J., Zhao, Y., Yan, S.: CNN: Single-label to multi-label. arXiv (2014)
21. Wu, J., Yu, Y., Huang, C., Yu, K.: Deep multiple instance learning for image classification and auto-annotation. In: Proceedings of IEEE Conference on Computer Vision and Pattern Recognition, pp. 3460–3469 (2015)
22. Xu, X.-S., Jiang, Y., Peng, L., Xue, X., Zhou, Z.-H.: Ensemble approach based on conditional random field for multi-label image and video annotation. In: Proceedings of ACM International Conference on Multimedia, pp. 1377–1380 (2011)

23. Xu, X.-S., Jiang, Y., Xue, X., Zhou, Z.-H.: Semi-supervised multi-instance multi-label learning approach for video annotation task. In: Proceedings of ACM International Conference on Multimedia, pp. 737–740 (2012)
24. Xue, X., Zhang, W., Zhang, J., Wu, B., Fan, J., Lu, Y.: Correlative multi-label multi-instance image annotation. In: Proceedings of IEEE International Conference on Computer Vision, pp. 651–658 (2011)
25. Zhou, F., Lin, Y.: Fine-grained image classification by exploring bipartite-graph labels. In: Proceedings of IEEE Conference on Computer Vision and Pattern Recognition, pp. 1124–1133 (2016)

Multi-level Semantic Representation for Flower Classification

Chuang Lin, Hongxun Yao[(⊠)], Wei Yu, and Wenbo Tang

School of Computer Science and Technology,
Harbin Institute of Technology, Harbin, China
linchuang1994@126.com, {h.yao,w.yu}@hit.edu.cn,
wenbotang@stu.hit.edu.cn

Abstract. Fine-grained classification is challenging since sub-categories have little intra-class variances and large intra-class variations. The task of flower classification can be achieved through highlighting the discriminative parts. Most traditional methods trained Convolutional Neural Networks (CNN) to handle the variations of pose, color and rotation, which only utilize single-level semantic information. In this paper, we propose a fine-grained classification approach with multi-level semantic representation. With the complementary strengths of multi-level semantic representation, we attempt to capture the subtle differences between sub-categories. One object-level model and multiple part-level model are trained as a multi-scale classifier. We test our method on the Oxford Flower dataset with 102 categories, and our result achieves the best performance over other state-of-the-art approaches.

Keywords: Fine-grained classification · CNN · Multi-level representation

1 Introduction

Basic-level image classification is to recognize objects that have large differences, e.g., predicting dogs and birds are different classes. However, basic-level image classification is not powerful to distinguish different sub-categories, such as the different breeds of birds [1]. Thus, fine-grained classification is an important and challenging research topic.

The fine-grained flower classification has three challenges: (1) we can not collect enough training samples for some endangered flower breeds, (2) it needs to distinguish subtle differences in part locations (e.g. the shape of the stamens), (3) fine-grained sub-categories often share same parts which leads to little inter-class variances. Meanwhile, it has large intra-class variations due to poses, instance, scale, view and so on, as shown in Fig. 1. Hence, there are two key-points to solve fine-grained flower classification. One is extracting powerful features to represent image, the other is finding discriminative part localization to distinguish similar classes.

Many existing fine-grained classification methods use the one-vs-all strategy [2, 3], which can only learn a single classifier for each breed. Apparently, it's an easy way to handle large intra-class variation, but it is not powerful enough to solve too many breeds. In order to highlight the effects of foreground region, most existing works

© Springer International Publishing AG, part of Springer Nature 2018
B. Zeng et al. (Eds.): PCM 2017, LNCS 10735, pp. 325–335, 2018.
https://doi.org/10.1007/978-3-319-77380-3_31

Fig. 1. The different instances with same flower class label.

explicitly require annotations at training and testing stages. However, it is especially hard for annotations which is expensive and non-scalable in practical applications. Our design only use the image label to solve intra-class variation.

LLC features [2], Fisher vectors [4] may be more popular in the early time. A recent trend of research are training CNN model [5] since its excellent performance. CNN models have been proven to be effective for many vision recognition tasks, such as image classification [6], digit recognition [7], and pedestrian detection [8]. It is noted that most of fine-grained classification datasets are too small, many study focus on pre-training CNN on a large-scale dataset (e.g., the Image Net [9]) and extracting features from the pre-trained model.

Some recent researches shows the superior performances of CNN as the feature extractors [10, 11]. We can capture object-level semantic representation through training CNN on whole flower images. Meanwhile, the key of fine-grained classification is to discover the discriminative part of object. Considering the feature extractors of CNN, we can capture a part-level model based on the discriminative parts using the mid-level semantic representation. We employ two separate pipelines to implement object-level and part-level semantic representations. Here is a high level summary of our method:

1. We fine-tune the pre-trained CNN as an object-level model.
2. We capture the saliency map based on the activation map.
3. With the receptive field, the discriminative parts are cropped and are used to train part-level model as mid-level semantic representations.
4. The object-level model and part-level models are combined as the final fine-grained classifier.

2 Related Work

2.1 Flower Classification

Fine-grained classification has been extensively studied recently [12–14]. Most flower categories share similar components with small variations, which makes fine-grained flower classification being a challenging task. Sparse Representation-based Classification method [15] applies sparse representation to predict flower label. Yang et al. [16] train the Fisher Discrimination Dictionary Learning model to learn structured dictionaries, which yields impressive performance on flower classification. Recently, Qian and Jin [17] proposes to explicitly address the flower classification via distance metric learning, which keeps small intra-class distance and enlarges the inter-class distance. Since the small size of flower dataset, Lin et al. [29] propose the idea to recall similar patterns from the pre-trained model and include these recalled images in retraining the network.

2.2 Part Localization

As the key of fine-grained classification is discovering the discriminative parts, most works rely on the annotations which contain bounding box and part landmarks more or less. The strongest supervised setting is that annotations are available at both training and testing stages [18–20], but it suffer from high cost. Later, some works consider a more reasonable setting, object/part level annotations at only training stage. Donahue et al. [21] introduce regions with CNN features(R-CNN). Based on R-CNN, Zhang et al. propose Part-based R-CNN [22] to detect part.

To be suitable to a wide deployment, a recent research trend considers the condition without bounding annotation at both training and testing stages. Wah et al. [20] propose to localize parts with constellation model, which incorporates CNN into deformable part model [23]. In the recent progress of scene recognition, Song et al. [30] proposed discriminative patch representations using neural networks and further proposed a hybrid architecture in which the semantic manifold is built on top of multiscale CNNs, which can significantly improve the recognition performance of the previous semantic manifold approach and its variants.

2.3 Multi-level Feature

Comparing with the handcrafted descriptors [24, 25], CNN model are able to extract multi-scale features in an end-to-end manner. Since Krizhevsky et al. [6] demonstrated the outstanding performance of CNN trained on ImageNet, more works focus on transferring pre-trained CNN features to other smaller datasets. For example, Zhang et al. further improved the performance of CNN feature extractors by fine-tuning on fine-grained dataset [22]. Some recent works also attempt to avoid deeper layers, which are more domain specific. Cimpoi et al. [26] achieve considerable improvements for texture recognition using the features of convolutional layers.

Our method adopts the same general principle. We utilize the receptive fields with high activations and train the part-level model using the flower parts. Comparing with traditional methods, we exploit the complementary strengths of different layers, rather than only fully-connected layers. The multi-scale models show more powerful semantic representation for flower classification.

3   Methods

We attempt to use the multi-level semantic representations to improve flower classification. Figure 2 shows the workflow of our method. There are three main components
at training stage. Firstly, we fine-tune the pre-trained CNN model (VGG-16) as
high-level model (object-level model). Secondly, we capture the multiple saliency
maps based on the activation maps of different layers. With the receptive field, the
discriminative parts with high salience value are cropped and are used to train
mid-level models (part-level model). Thirdly, the object-level model and part-level
models are combined as the final fine-grained classifier.

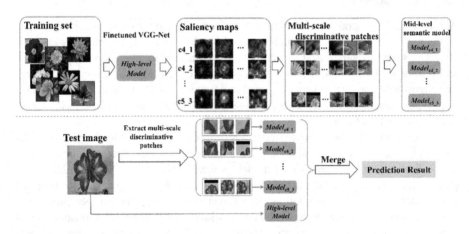

Fig. 2. The complete classification pipeline of our method.

At testing stage, multi-scale discriminative patches are extracted based on the
saliency maps of different layers, which are used to capture the mid-level semantic
representation through corresponding mid-level model. The prediction of whole image
is regarded as high-level semantic representation. The high- and mid-level semantic
representations are merged as final prediction.

3.1   High-Level Semantic Representation

The object-level model is trained firstly to recognize the object. We use the VGG-16
architecture [27] and fine-tune the fully-connected layers for our task. Without
re-training the model, we can get a considerable results through a relatively small
number of iterations which greatly improving the efficiency. We use the stochastic
gradient descent to train the network, maximizing the multinomial logistic regression
objective. Training object-level model has two benefits. First, the model itself is a good
fine-grained classifier. What's more, its internal features now allow us to build other
scale semantic model, we will explain this in next section.

3.2   Mid-Level Semantic Representation

With the object-level model, we can classify the flower images by high-level semantic representation. However, the key of fine-grained flower classification is the discriminative parts, such as the color of the petals, the shape of the petals or the stamens. According to DPD [28] and Part-RCNN [22], certain discriminative local features are critical to fine-grained classification. For this reason, we introduce the local regions based on mid-level semantic representation to improve the fine-grained classification. We can get discriminative localized regions of similar but different classes of flowers, as shown in Fig. 3.

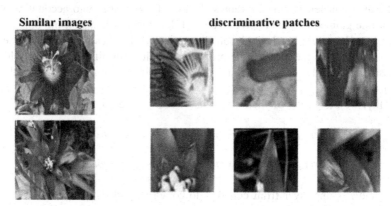

Fig. 3. The discriminative parts between similar images.

We introduce saliency map based on activation map. On one hand, the high-level semantic representation completes the "coarse" classification of the images and builds the basic model. On the other hand, the mid-level semantic information avoiding the requirement for costly manual annotations, which focuses on completes the "fine" classification of part localizations. Some detection results are shown on Fig. 4.

Fig. 4. Some detection results of the flowers. The detection results are focus on the color of the petals, the shape of the petals or the stamens.

Instead of using the strong labels on parts and key points [18, 22, 28], we pick the receptive fields which are responded actively by the neurons in hidden layers. The activation map is denoted as M, where $|M| = (h, w, c)$. The saliency map S is taken the maximum magnitude across all channels $S = \max_c M$. With receptive field, the discriminative parts are cropped from input image based on the salience value. In particular, we capture discriminative parts from different convolutional layers. The training dataset and the test dataset use the same strategy to get the patches.

3.3 Multi-scale Model

We take the multi-level semantic representation of the images into account, and train different fine-grained classifiers. We hope high-level model focus on the object, while mid-level model works exclusively on discriminative patches. Considering the final prediction result, we merge multiple prediction result form different scales. Although all classifiers have the same structure, they have different representation with complementary strengths.

Finally, we merge the prediction results of multi-scale models:

$$score_{final} = \alpha \times score_{high-level} + (1 - \alpha) \times score_{mid-level} \tag{1}$$

$$score_{mid-level} = \beta * score_{model_i} + (1 - \beta) * score_{model_j} \tag{2}$$

where i and j is one layer from conv4_1 to conv5_3, and α, β is selected using the validation method.

4   Experiments

4.1   Datasets

The empirical evaluation is performed on the Oxford 102 Category Flower Dataset, which contains a total of 8,189 images. There are 102 categories flower and 40 – 258 images per class. Although the dataset is predefined into different sets, we use only the training (a total of 6,149 images) and test (10 images per class) sets. The dataset ensure large variations within the class and small variations with some classes, which contains multiple variations, such as scale, pose, and light. In this task, only image-level class labels are available. It is noted that there are pre-segmentations for datasets, but we just use the raw images for making our approach more suitable for practical applications.

4.2   Implementation Details

Our CNN architecture is essentially same with the popular VGG-16 [27], except the number of neurons of the output layer is set as number of categories. As our methods is the weakest supervision, we only resize the input image and subtract image mean. Besides, we speed up this layer of learning rate to achieve the purpose of rapid convergence. We fixed the weight of layer before conv5_3 when fine-tuning the VGG-Net model. In addition, we adjusted the parameter *base_lr* to 0.001, avoiding the learning rate is too large to converge. The other parameters remain the same as the original VGG-Net network structure parameters.

After fine-tuning, we get a high-level model achieves an accuracy of 92.3% after 4000 iterations. It is a better feature extractor for flower classification, which helps for finding part localization. We extract descriptors from conv4_1 to conv5_3 layers and find the top 6 salience values of each image. According to extracting the receptive fields, we get the mid-level semantic patches and rescale them to the target size 224 × 224 pixels. For every mid-level model, there are 36894 images in training set and 6120 images in test set.

4.3   Results and Comparisons

We compare the results of different convolutional layers from three perspectives: mid-level model or high-level model only, the combination of both, and multi-scale semantic representation.

Single Semantic Representation. We compare the results of the three groups: the first set is single mid-level models, the second uses the high-level model, and the third set includes the state-of-the-art results from recent literatures [17, 30].

As shown in Fig. 5, the higher layer, the better classification performance. The result of using mid-level model alone is not as good as high-level model, as there are still more ambiguities in mid-level semantic representation. This demonstrates that the higher layer can represent more complete semantic which is an important condition for CNN to achieve higher accuracy.

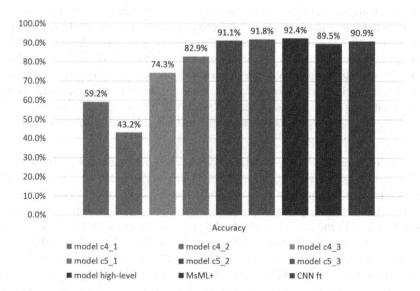

Fig. 5. Comparison of mid-level models, high-level models and recent works. The accuracy of high-level model have surpassed the state-of-the-art results of prior work.

Two-level Semantic Representation. In order to prove the guess that the combination of mid-level semantics and high-level semantics can achieve better results, we first try merge two-level model using the Eq. (1). Figure 6 shows the classification accuracy of different level combinations models with *a* change.

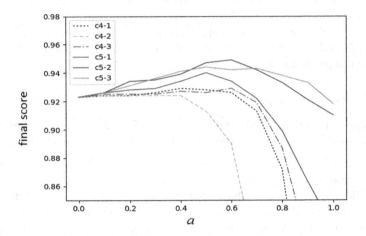

Fig. 6. Two-level models results with *a* change. The result shows that the combination of mid-level semantics and high-level semantics can achieve better results.

Obviously, the combination of c5_2 model and high-level model increase the accuracy rate by 94.9%. Although the c5_3 model has the highest accuracy rate in the single middle model, the receptive fields of convolution layers conv5_3 is 196×196, which is similar to the input image size 224×224. It may fail to distinguish the flowers better since patches selected by convolution layers conv5_3 are not distinguishing enough. The result of high-level model is higher than all of the mid-level models, but the result of two-level models is better than high-level model and mid-level model. This further demonstrates the effectiveness of distinguishing part localization in the fine-grained classification of flowers. Combining mid-level semantic representation, the error rate drops, which is significantly better than the single. From another point of view, by selecting the part localization, this method achieves pose normalization to resist large pose variations.

Multi-scale Semantic Representation. We have shown that classification models trained with two-level semantic representation delivers superior classification performance. Further, we attempt to merge multiple part-level models.

Table 1 shows the comparison results using different multiple layer combinations. Using the Eqs. (1) and (2), our method achieves an accuracy of 95.2% in the fusion of c5_1, c5_2 and high-level models, when a, β is set 0.4 and 0.1. This indicates that multi-scale semantic representation may have a stronger effect in the fine-grained classification. Few works report results on this dataset, since there are not too many fine-grained classification study in flowers. The most comparable result with our method is [29], which trains AlexNet model and obtain an accuracy of 90.9%. Our method improves it by over 4.3%.

Table 1. Result comparing on different layer combinations

Model combination	a	β	Top1 precision
conv4_1,conv5_2	0.5	0.1	94.3%
conv4_1,conv5_2	0.4	0.1	95.0%
conv5_1,conv5_2	0.4	0.1	95.2%

In this section, we compare the different layer combinations. It is no doubt that multi-scale semantic representation has the best performance.

5 Conclusions

In this paper, we propose a fine-grained classification pipeline based on multi-level semantic representation with the weakest supervision. The high-level model can classify the flowers from an overall point of view and serve as a feature extractor for mid-level models. The mid-level models focus on local discriminate patterns which are more important in flower classification. The advantage of our methods is that we get the local discriminate patterns without any manual annotations and train a set of models based on these picked patterns iteratively.

We find two directions that can be solved in the future. On one hand, current dataset is small for CNN training, the size of dataset is an important research direction for CNN-based method. On the other hand, our method focuses on the saliency map based on activation map. The trained filters of different layers also can be considered as mid-level semantic.

Acknowledgements. This work was supported by the National Natural Science Foundation of China (No. 61472103).

References

1. Welinder, P., Branson, S., Mita, T., Wah, C., Schroff, F., Belongie, S., Perona, P.: Caltech-UCSD birds 200. 2010. In: Chen, W.-K. (ed.) Linear Networks and Systems, Wadsworth, Belmont, pp. 123–135 (1993)
2. Angelova, A., Zhu, S.: Efficient object detection and segmentation for fine-grained recognition. In: CVPR (2013)
3. Chai, Y., Rahtu, E., Lempitsky, V., Van Gool, L., Zisserman, A.: TriCoS: a tri-level class-discriminative co-segmentation method for image classification. In: Fitzgibbon, A., Lazebnik, S., Perona, P., Sato, Y., Schmid, C. (eds.) ECCV 2012. LNCS, vol. 7572, pp. 794–807. Springer, Heidelberg (2012). https://doi.org/10.1007/978-3-642-33718-5_57
4. Gavves, E., Fernando, B., Snoek, C.G.M., Smeulders, A.W.M., Tuytelaars, T.: Fine-grained categorization by alignments. In: ICCV, pp. 1713–1720 (2013)
5. LeCun, Y., Bottou, L., Bengio, Y., Haffner, P.: Gradient-based learning applied to document recognition. Proc. IEEE **86**(11), 2278–2324 (1998)
6. Krizhevsky, A., Sutskever, I., Hinton, G.E.: ImageNet classification with deep convolutional neural networks. In: Proceedings of NIPS, pp. 1106–1114 (2012)

7. Ciresan, D.C., Meier, U., Schmidhuber, J.: Multi-column deep neural networks for image classification. In: Proceedings of CVPR, pp. 3642–3649 (2012)
8. Sermanet, P., Kavukcuoglu, K., Chintala, S., LeCun, Y.: Pedestrian detection with unsupervised multi-stage feature learning. In: Proceedings CVPR, pp. 3626–3633 (2013)
9. Deng, J., Dong, W., Socher, R., Li, L.-J., Li, K., Fei-Fei, L.: ImageNet: a large-scale hierarchical image database. In: Proceedings of CVPR, pp. 248–255 (2009)
10. Zeiler, M.D., Fergus, R.: Visualizing and understanding convolutional neural networks. arXiv preprint arXiv:1311.2901 (2013)
11. Razavian, A.S., Azizpour, H., Sullivan, J., Carlsson, S.: CNN Features off-the-shelf: an Astounding Baseline for Recognition. arXiv preprint arXiv:1403.6382 (2014)
12. Wah, C., Branson, S., Welinder, P., Belongie, S.: The Caltech-UCSD Birds-200-2011 dataset (2011)
13. Welinder, P., Branson, S., Mita, T., Wah, C., Schroff, F., Perona, P.: Caltech-UCSD birds 200 (2010)
14. Khosla, A., Jayadevaprakash, N., Yao, B., Li, F.-F.: Dataset for fine-grained image categorization. In: First Workshop on Fine-Grained Visual Categorization, CVPR (2011)
15. Wright, J., Yang, A.Y., Ganesh, A., Sastry, S.S., Ma, Y.: Robust face recognition via sparse representation. IEEE Trans. Pattern Anal. Mach. Intell. 31(2), 210–227 (2009)
16. Yang, M., Zhang, L., Feng, X., Zhang, D.: Sparse representation based fisher discrimination dictionary learning for image classification. Int. J. Comput. Vis. 109(3), 209–232 (2014)
17. Qian, Q., Jin, R.: Fine-grained visual categorization via multi-stage metric learning. In: CVPR (2015)
18. Parkhi, O.M., Vedaldi, A., Jawahar, C., Zisserman, A.: The truth about cats and dogs. In: ICCV, pp. 1427–1434. IEEE (2011)
19. Parkhi, O.M., Vedaldi, A., Zisserman, A., Jawahar, C.: Cats and dogs. In: CVPR (2012)
20. Wah, C., Branson, S., Welinder, P., Perona, P., Belongie, S.: The Caltech-UCSD Birds-200-2011 Dataset. Technical report CNS-TR-2011-001, California Institute of Technology (2011)
21. Donahue, J., Jia, Y., Vinyals, O., Hoffman, J., Zhang, N., Tzeng, E., Darrell, T.: DeCAF: a deep convolutional activation feature for generic visual recognition. In: Proceedings of the 31st International Conference on Machine Learning, pp. 647–655. ACM, Beijing (2014)
22. Zhang, N., Donahue, J., Girshick, R., Darrell, T.: Part-Based R-CNNs for fine-grained category detection. In: Fleet, D., Pajdla, T., Schiele, B., Tuytelaars, T. (eds.) ECCV 2014. LNCS, vol. 8689, pp. 834–849. Springer, Cham (2014). https://doi.org/10.1007/978-3-319-10590-1_54
23. Simon, M., Rodner, E.: Neural activation constellations: unsupervised part model discovery with convolutional networks. In: ICCV (2015)
24. Lowe, D.G.: Distinctive image features from scale-invariant keypoints. Int. J. Comput. Vis. 60(2), 91–110 (2004)
25. Perronnin, F., Sánchez, J., Mensink, T.: Improving the Fisher Kernel for large-scale image classification. In: Proceedings ECCV, pp. 143–156 (2010)
26. Cimpoi, M., Maji, S., Vedaldi, A.: Deep filter banks for texture recognition and segmentation. In: CVPR (2015)
27. Simonyan, K., Zisserman, A.: Very deep convolutional networks for large-scale image recognition. CoRR (2014)
28. Perronnin, F., Sánchez, J., Mensink, T.: Improving the Fisher Kernel for large-scale image classification. In: Daniilidis, K., Maragos, P., Paragios, N. (eds.) ECCV 2010. LNCS, vol. 6314, pp. 143–156. Springer, Heidelberg (2010). https://doi.org/10.1007/978-3-642-15561-1_11

29. Lin, K., Yang, H.-F., Chen, C.-S.: Flower classification with few training examples via recalling visual patterns from deep CNN. In: IPPR Conference on Computer Vision, Graphics, and Image Processing (CVGIP) (2015)
30. Song, X., Jiang, S., Herranz, L.: Multi-scale multi-feature context modeling for scene recognition in the semantic manifold. IEEE Trans. Image Process. **26**(6), 2721–2735 (2017)

Multi-view Multi-label Learning via Optimal Classifier Chain

Yiming Liu$^{(\boxtimes)}$ and Xingwei Hao

Geometric Design and Information Visualization Laboratory,
Shandong University, Jinan, China
yiming0704@126.com

Abstract. Multiple feature views arise in the multimedia classification task, where one object usually has different representations from multiple views. Multi-label classification with multiple views is an emerging challenge. In this paper, we propose a new classification framework, named Multi-view Multi-label via Optimal Classifier Chain (MVM-LOCC), which establishes an optimal classifier chain for each view of the data sets. Thus, these generated multiple classifiers will be diverse and complementary. Furthermore, considering the different performance of these classifiers, we adjust the weights of the chained learners to predict the unknown instances. The proposed method makes full use of the multi-label correlation information as well as the consistency information from multiple views. Experiments on three challenging real-world multi-label learning datasets (**Corel5k**, **EspGame**, as well as **PASCAL VOC**), show that the proposed method achieves superior performance to some state-of-the-art methods.

Keywords: Multi-view · Multi-label · Classification
Weight adjustment

1 Introduction

Multi-label classification, where each instance is associated with multiple labels simultaneously, has received an increasing attention. For example, in the multimedia classification, a movie may be tagged with the action, family and many other topics; a landscape image may have both seagulls and ship semantic markers [1]. The classification on these multiple labeled data is the task of multi-label classification.

Since each instance in multi-labeled data could belong to multiple classes, one popular strategy is to transform the original problem into a series of binary classification problem [2]. Binary Relevance is a simple and classic model, which trains a binary classifier for each label. However, class concepts are interdependent on each other in multi-label classification area. According to this rule, modeling the label dependency becomes an emerging strategy soon, which is proved to achieve

© Springer International Publishing AG, part of Springer Nature 2018
B. Zeng et al. (Eds.): PCM 2017, LNCS 10735, pp. 336–345, 2018.
https://doi.org/10.1007/978-3-319-77380-3_32

better performance [3–5]. But, there are still lots of difficulties, such as the high dimensionality of the output space [6] and the high-dimensional computation.

Meanwhile, one object with multiple labels usually has different representations from different views as with the development of computer science and technology. For example, a landscape image can be associated with sea and seagulls, it can also be described by multiple feature sets, such as shape cue (SIFT) [7], color information (HSV) [8], global structure (GIST) [9]. It is proved that the different sets of features from different views can provide complementary information with each other. The goal of multi-view learning is to learn models combining the consistency information among the views [10] so as to achieve better performance than those models learned from independent view data.

Based on the above considerations, we propose a new multi label learning strategy: multi view multi label optimal classifier chain learning model. The basic ideas are as follows: taken the label dependency into account, we adopt the multi label optimal chain classifier model [11] as the base classifier. Firstly, we train a base classifier for each view of the data set. Then, we synthesize the optimal chain learning from all angles to generate a final classifier to predict unknown samples. As the fact that training data from each view could bring different information, which leads to different learn performance, we put forward a resolution that we assign different weights due to different contribution to better performance. To summarize, the main contributions of this paper are as follows:

(1) We propose a novel multi-label method combined multiple views, which can dynamically adjust the weight of each view.
(2) Different from the traditional multi label learning, our method combines the multiple label correlations with the complementary information and integrity of the multiple views.
(3) The proposed method achieves better performance compared with some state-of-the-art methods under five different evaluation metrics. In addition, the proposed method has good generalization ability compared with the existing methods.

In the remainder of this paper is organized as follows. In Sect. 2, we briefly review the related works about BR method and CC method. In Sect. 3, we describe the $MVMLOCC$ method in detail. In Sect. 4, we discuss the corresponding experiments and some metrics to evaluate our method and other multi-label classification methods. Section 5 concludes our work and introduces future work.

2   Related Work

In this section, we first introduce the formal definition of multi-view multi-label classification, then briefly review the BR method and CC method. The following notion is used throughout this paper. In the $MVML$ classification task, we are given n data instances tagged with L labels from M independent views, for each view, there will be an output space with n labels. we denote the matrix $\{(X_1^m, y_1^m), \cdots, (X_n^m, y_n^m)\}$, $X_i^m \in R^{d_m}$ as the input data, with the detailed definition as follows: $i \in \{1, 2, \cdots, n\}$, $m \in \{1, 2, \cdots, M\}$. We denote $y_i^m \in \{-1, +1\}^L$ as output label space of L possible labels, $y_i^m(l) = \{+1\}$ means the instance x_i^m is associated with the lth label, otherwise it is not.

2.1   The Binary Relevance Method (BR)

Binary Relevance (BR) method directly decomposes the multi-label classification problems into L independent binary classification problems, which is similar to the One-versus-All approach employed in the multiclass problems. After BR's L binary problems are separated, we could run each label problem separately, in either parallel or serial ways [6]. BR strategy is a simple method which helps build multiple state-of-the-art multi-label learning techniques. But it ignores the correlations and interdependencies between multiple labels.

Nevertheless, it is clear that modeling label correlations may increase the predictive performance. In the next, we present a novel binary relevance method, CC, which can model label correlations, while maintaining acceptable complexity similar to BR.

2.2   The Classifier Chain Method (CC)

Modeling the label dependency is one of the major challenges in multi-label classification problems. Amongst models have been established, Classifier Chains model (CC) is one of the most popular methods which simply transforms multi-label classification problem into a chain of binary classification problems. The CC method builds subsequent binary classifiers in a chain upon the predictions of the preceding ones [12]. One classifier is trained for each label, which means CC is also a binary relevance method. However it takes the label correlations into account which could make a promising experimental results. Given an unknown instance x, its associated label set Y is predicted by traversing the classifier chain iteratively, CC firstly predicts the value of the first label, then takes this instance together with the predicted value as the input to predict the value of the next label.

However, it will seriously affect the predict value of the next label if one or two labels are predicted the wrong value, especially when the label order of the chain is randomly organized. In the next, we propose a newly method combining the multi-view consistency information and multi-label correlation, which could help decrease the effect the error made mentioned above.

3   The MVMLOCC Method

The basic idea of this method is inspired by the CC method. However, in the CC method, the label order in the chain is randomly selected, which may lead to poor performance when labels in procedure are wrongly predicted. In addition, as the multimedia technology updates continuously, one object usually has different representations consistent of multiple views. Here, we propose a multi view multi label learning optimal classifier chain model ($MVMLOCC$). Suppose that each instance could be represented by a set of features from M views. For each view, we train an optimal chain classifier based on Support Vector Machine (SVM) [13] as the base classifier. Each chain may bring different predictive performance because of the complementary information from these single views. At the same time, in order to avoid the performance loss caused by wrongly predictive label value during the chain traverses, we assign each classifier chain a weight ($\alpha = [\alpha_1, \cdots, \alpha_m]$) according to their predictive performance, and when an unknown instance is input, the final prediction is obtained by the outputs multiply their weight.

The model proposed in this paper for multi-label classification can be written as the following form:

$$H(x) = \sum_{m=1}^{M} \alpha_m h_m(x). \tag{1}$$

where each basic function h_m is an optimal classifier chain trained on each single view of the multi-label training data. The weight coefficient α_m represents the predictive weight vector of the m-th classifier chain, where $\alpha_m(l)$ is the predictive weight of l-th label.

3.1   Label Order Based on the Label Correlations

The Classifier Chains model (CC) builds subsequence binary classifiers in a chain according to randomly selected label order, which may lead to poor prediction accuracy. In this paper, we design a label order based on the label correlations, through which, we could improve the performance. Since label correlation exists among the multi-label data, we describe the label correlations as a network structure, which is defined as a weighted network $G = (V, E, W)$. V is the nodes set (label set), E represents the edge collection, and W is the weight set, the weight of an edge represents the correlation between two labels.

Given N data instances tagged with L labels, we first define a $L \times N$ label matrix $T = (t_{ij})$, $t_{ij} = 1$ indicates the instance j has label i, otherwise it does not have. Referencing the idea of $TF - IDF$ (term frequencyCinverse document frequency [14]), which uses an incidence matrix to enhance the representation of each single word's information, here we define a $L \times N$ incidence matrix $A = (a_{ij})$, where a_{ij} is calculated as below:

$$a_{ij} = t_{ij} \times log\frac{N}{I_i}. \tag{2}$$

I_i represents the number of instances labeled by i. Here, each label's information is represented as a row vector A_i in the incidence matrix A. As the correlation between labels can be calculated by the label's row vector distance in space, we use cosine similarity to calculate the correlation values between two vectors.

The smaller the value, the more relevant the two vectors are. The label correlation matrix is defined as below:

$$sim\left(A_i, A_j\right) = cos\left(\Theta_{ij}\right) = \frac{\sum_{n=1}^{N} a_{in} a_{jn}}{\sqrt{\sum_{n=1}^{N} a_{in}^2 \sum_{n=1}^{N} a_{jn}^2}}. \tag{3}$$

Notice that we are given data sets labeled $\{-1, +1\}$, we change all the -1 into 0, in order to enhance the calculation about the two correlation vectors. Here, we get the W value of label correlation network structure $G = (V, E, W)$. To save time, we use Label Sequence-Greedy Algorithm to construct one label sequence based on their relevance (weights) in the network structure. Algorithm 1 describes the processes in detail.

Algorithm 1. The Label Sequence-Greedy Algorithm

Input:
  Training data matrix $\mathbf{X} \in \mathbb{R}^{n \times d}$, $\mathbf{Y} \in \mathbb{R}^{n \times m}$ and the number of classifier chain M;
Output:
  The label sequence including the total M labels
1: **Initialize** incidence matrix $A_{m \times m}$.
2: Transform the Label Matrix into its incidence matrix A, according to function (2);
3: Calculate the relevance between any two vector A_i and A_j as the weight between the two labels using the function (3);
4: Build the correlation network $G = (V, E, W)$ using the weights calculated.
5: Build the minimum spanning tree T using Kruskal Algorithm;
6: Traverse the minimum spanning tree T, and Save the vertex(label) sequence.

After that, we use the Kruskal Algorithm simply to obtain label order based on the label correlations, since we always find the most relevant label to predict.

Algorithm 2. Multi-View Multi-Label Learning via Optimal Classifier Chain

---

Input:
  Training data matrix $\mathbf{X} \in \mathbb{R}^{n \times d}$, $\mathbf{Y} \in \mathbb{R}^{n \times m}$ and the number of classifier chain M, learning parameter r;
Output:
  The model framework including m classifier chains, the weight vector $\boldsymbol{\alpha}_m$.
1: **Initialize** $\{\alpha_m = 1\}_{m=1}^{M}$.
2: **repeat**
3:   For each $m \in [1,M]$ **do:**
       $\Longrightarrow$ Build the corresponding label order via the Label Sequence-Greedy Algorithm 1(each for a view dataset);
       $\Longrightarrow$ Using the corresponding view data set, train the Classifier Chain according to the corresponding initialized label order;
4:   Learn α_m by minimizing object function (4);
5: **until** the object function's minimization satisfied.

3.2 Weight Vector Calculation for the Framework

In the model framework, we need to train M optimal classifier chain using the given training set. Considering different influence of label correlations on different instances, different classifier chain would make different predictive performance. As mentioned above, we assign different weight vector α_m to the M optimal classifier chain according to the their performance. In the experiment, in order to obtain the value of the weight vectors, we learn a loss function for multiple labels as $l(x, y)$ which measures the loss of assigning label vector y to the instance x. Assume that we have M base optimal classifier chain, the weight vectors is learned by minimizing objective function as follows:

$$Q(\alpha) = \sum_{m=1}^{M} \frac{1}{2} \left\{ \alpha_m^r \left\| \tilde{Y} - Y \right\|_F^2 \right\} s.t \sum_{m=1}^{M} \alpha_m^r = 1, \alpha \geq 0. \tag{4}$$

We adopt weighting the multiple optimal classifier chain according to the training error, which is inspired by the paper [15]. Here we set $r > 1$ to avoid trivial solution which makes the final prediction result considers only one of the classifier, thus our model can adjust the complementarity of the multiple optimal classifier chains.

The detail of our algorithm is summarized on the Algorithm 2. After obtaining the weight vector α_m, we can predict new instances by using the model $H(x) = \sum_{m=1}^{M} \alpha_m h_m(x)$ mentioned in the last section.

4 Experiment

In this section, we describe our experiment to evaluate the performance of $MVMLOCC$ method, include the experimental framework as well as the data sets used and evaluation metrics.

4.1 Experimental Datasets

To evaluate the performance of $MVMLOCC$ model, we conduct our experiments on 3 benchmark multi-label datasets, **Corel5k**, **ESP Game** and **PASCAL VOC**. Each instance in the data set is an image, which is associated with multiple labels.

Table 1. The basic statistic information of data sets

Dataset	Total instance	Training instance	Test instance	Total label
Corel5k	4999	4500	499	266
ESP Game	20770	18689	2081	268
PASCAL VOC	10000	5011	4952	20

The basic statistic information is shown in Table 1. All these datasets are from the Mulan website[1] where you can find more details about these data sets.

4.2 Evaluation Measures

In multi-label classification tasks, a number of evaluation metrics are proposed, which can be generally categorized into two groups, example-based metrics and label-based metrics [16]. In this paper, we select five common multi-label classification evaluation measures summarized in [1]: hamming loss, ranking loss, One-error, Coverage, and Average precision to evaluate the performance of the compared methods.

4.3 Baseline Methods

We compare our model framework with four peer algorithms: MLkNN, BP-MLL, ML-RBF and a newly multi-view multi-label algorithm MV3LapRLS. Among the four algorithms, the core idea of the ML-KNN is to adapt k-nearest neighbor techniques to deal with multi-label data, where maximum a posteriori (MAP) rule is utilized to make predictions by reasoning with the labeling information embodied in the neighbors [17]; the BP-MLL method which is adapted from traditional Back Propagation (BP) algorithm, adjusts the traditional multi-layer forward neural network to learn multi-label problem [18]; the ML-RBF algorithm is also adapted from Radial Basis Function (RBF) Neural Network [19], which can solve linear indivisible classification problem. Meanwhile, the MV3LapRLS algorithm uses both the label dependency as well as the consistency information among the views [20]. For all these algorithms, the regularization parameters are all tuned to the best performance using a five-fold cross-validation.

4.4 Experiment Setup and Performance Analysis

Now that one object usually has different representations from different views, we select the data set from four common views (Gist [9], DenseHue [21], DenseSift [7], and Hsv [8]) to simplify the experiment. Firstly, we train a classifier chain for each data set from the views selected. Then we select one classifier chain with the best test performance. To highlight the advantages of multi-view learning, we merge the four sets of features as a whole, with which we could train and test these multi-label models based on all the algorithms including the $MVMLOCC$ model we proposed. To ensure the accuracy of the experimental data, in the experiment, we randomly sample some of the training data (calculated at 0.6 of the total) from the training set, and report the mean and the standard deviation of the results on the data sets mentioned above.

Table 2 documents the performance results of the different methods on the benchmark datasets. For the classification experiments on each data set, the average performance of the corresponding algorithm under the evaluation metrics

---

[1] http://mulan.sourceforge.net/datasets-mlc.html.

Table 2. The performance results of the different methods on the benchmark datasets

Data	Metrics	MLkNN		BP-MLL		MV3LapRLS		ML-RBF		MVMLCC	
		BestSV	ConV	BestSV	ConV	-	ConV	BestSV	ConV	BestSV	ConV
PASCAL VOC	Ranking loss	.191±.013	.246±.009	.297±.016	.201±.014	-	.177±.019	.164±.018	.132±.015	.091±.008	**.082±.011**
	Hamming loss	.064±.025	.068±.016	.235±.019	.147±.021	-	.070±.011	.063±.015	.058±.012	.051±.021	**.039±.013**
	One-error	.529±.021	.586±.028	.594±.022	.557±.013	-	.523±.017	.575±.021	.458±.018	.476±.021	**.342±.019**
	Coverage	.308±.011	.301±.016	.499±.009	.358±.012	-	.231±.012	.273±.014	.240±.018	.243±.021	.235±.017
	Average precision	.414±.014	.471±.021	.341±.016	.479±.013	-	.573±.014	.361±.016	.495±.019	.571±.017	**.653±.012**
ESP Game	Ranking loss	.266±.013	.241±.016	.329±.015	.305±.026	-	.294±.016	.317±.014	.296±.018	.249±.018	**.228±.016**
	Hamming loss	.017±.004	.017±.008	.037±.012	.026±.007	-	.018±.004	.026±.002	.021±.003	.024±.001	.019±.002
	One-error	.605±.017	.588±.021	.698±.019	.649±.020	-	.513±.016	.549±.017	.485±.017	.510±.013	**.457±.015**
	Coverage	.641±.015	.639±.023	.768±.014	.722±.021	-	.614±.031	.750±.004	.707±.017	.713±.014	.616±.011
	Average precision	.120±.007	.157±.011	.101±.009	.110±.014	-	.183±.016	.102±.009	.113±.012	.128±.017	**.214±.013**
Corel5k	Ranking loss	.136±.013	.140±.018	.215±.015	.201±.012	-	.135±.014	.185±.011	.154±.009	.146±.018	**.129±.015**
	Hamming loss	.021±.004	.018±.002	.047±.001	.031±.001	-	.015±.002	.041±.021	.029±.017	.018±.003	.013±.002
	One-error	.539±.014	.603±.012	.487±.016	.477±.019	-	.472±.012	.568±.012	.493±.019	.465±.018	**.387±.013**
	Coverage	.357±.011	.327±.013	.451±.018	.438±.013	-	.317±.014	.359±.014	.297±.016	.387±.012	.319±.016
	Average precision	.298±.012	.317±.011	.206±.017	.271±.013	-	.425±.018	.214±.015	.348±.011	.368±.019	**.482±.014**

is filled in the corresponding position of the table, where the BestSV column indicates that the corresponding algorithm best model within the four views, the ConV column shows the results of the model trained by the corresponding algorithm under the merged data sets from the four single views. From the table we can observe: (1) for multi-label classification algorithm, models trained under the multiple views achieve superior performance than those under any single view. (2) Compared to other methods, our model can achieve more advantageous performance on three data sets, especially on the Corel5k dataset, which proves the efficiency of our method. (3) Our model shows more robust under different data sets. Although MV3LapRLS is a new multi-angle multi-tag classification algorithm, our method could achieve the same performance, even could be better in some metrics. Obviously, the experimental results can prove the effectiveness of our method.

5   Conclusion and Future Work

This paper proposes a new multi-label classification method, named MVM-LOCC, which combines label dependency and the consistency information from different views. The basic idea of this method is inspired by the CC method which create a classifier chain with a random label order. However random label order may lead to less robust, and CC can not make full use of label correlations. MVMLOCC has the advantage of combining label correlations and the consistency information from multiple views into a unified framework. Experimental results show that our method has competitive performance against state-of-the-art multi-label classification methods. In the future, it is possible to develop other approaches to combine the multi-label with multi-view to make better performance. In addition, we will also look for new data sets from different areas to validate our method.

Acknowledgments. This work was supported by Natural Science Foundation of China (U1609218) and Union Foundation (61572292).

References

1. Boutell, M.R., Luo, J., Shen, X., Brown, C.M.: Learning multi-label scene classification. Pattern Recogn. **37**(9), 1757–1771 (2004)
2. Zhang, M.-L., Zhou, Z.-H.: A k-nearest neighbor based algorithm for multi-label classification. In: 2005 IEEE International Conference on Granular Computing, vol. 2, pp. 718–721. IEEE (2005)
3. Jin, B., Muller, B., Zhai, C., Xinghua, L.: Multi-label literature classification based on the gene ontology graph. BMC Bioinform. **9**(1), 525 (2008)
4. Tsoumakas, G., Dimou, A., Spyromitros, E., Mezaris, V., Kompatsiaris, I., Vlahavas, I.: Correlation-based pruning of stacked binary relevance models for multi-label learning. In: Proceedings of the 1st International Workshop on Learning from Multi-label Data, pp. 101–116 (2009)

5. Dharmadhikari, S.C., Ingle, M., Kulkarni, P.: Multi label text classification through label propagation. Int. J. Eng. **1**(9), 09–14 (2012)

6. Zhang, M.-L., Zhou, Z.-H.: A review on multi-label learning algorithms. IEEE Trans. Knowl. Data Eng. **26**(8), 1819–1837 (2014)

7. Lowe, D.G.: Distinctive image features from scale-invariant keypoints. Int. J. Comput. Vis. **60**(2), 91–110 (2004)

8. Qian, B., Wang, X., Ye, J., Davidson, I.: A reconstruction error based framework for multi-label and multi-view learning. IEEE Trans. Knowl. Data Eng. **27**(3), 594–607 (2015)

9. Luo, Y., Tao, D., Chang, X., Chao, X., Liu, H., Wen, Y.: Multiview vector-valued manifold regularization for multilabel image classification. IEEE Trans. Neural Netw. Learn. Syst. **24**(5), 709–722 (2013)

10. Gibaja, E.L., Moyano, J.M., Ventura, S.: An ensemble-based approach for multi-view multi-label classification. Prog. Artif. Intell. **5**(4), 251–259 (2016)

11. Liu, W., Tsang, I.: On the optimality of classifier chain for multi-label classification. In: Advances in Neural Information Processing Systems, pp. 712–720 (2015)

12. Read, J., Pfahringer, B., Holmes, G., Frank, E.: Classifier chains for multi-label classification. Mach. Learn. **85**(3), 333–359 (2011)

13. Bartlett, P., Shawe-Taylor, J.: Generalization performance of support vector machines and other pattern classifiers. In: Advances in Kernel Methods-Support Vector Learning, pp. 43–54 (1999)

14. Aizawa, A.: An information-theoretic perspective of TF-IDF measures. Inf. Process. Manag. **39**(1), 45–65 (2003)

15. Wang, M., Hua, X.-S., Yuan, X., Song, Y., Dai, L.-R.: Optimizing multi-graph learning: towards a unified video annotation scheme. In: Proceedings of the 15th ACM International Conference on Multimedia, pp. 862–871. ACM (2007)

16. Tsoumakas, G., Vlahavas, I.: Random k-labelsets: an ensemble method for multilabel classification. In: Kok, J.N., Koronacki, J., Mantaras, R.L., Matwin, S., Mladenič, D., Skowron, A. (eds.) ECML 2007. LNCS (LNAI), vol. 4701, pp. 406–417. Springer, Heidelberg (2007). https://doi.org/10.1007/978-3-540-74958-5_38

17. Zhang, M.-L., Zhou, Z.-H.: ML-KNN: a lazy learning approach to multi-label learning. Pattern Recogn. **40**(7), 2038–2048 (2007)

18. Zhang, M.-L., Zhou, Z.-H.: Multilabel neural networks with applications to functional genomics and text categorization. IEEE Trans. Knowl. Data Eng. **18**(10), 1338–1351 (2006)

19. Zhang, M.-L.: ML-RBF: RBF neural networks for multi-label learning. Neural Process. Lett. **29**(2), 61–74 (2009)

20. Luo, Y., Tao, D., Xu, C., Li, D., Xu, C.: Vector-valued multi-view semi-supervised learning for multi-label image classification. In: AAAI, pp. 647–653 (2013)

21. van de Weijer, J., Schmid, C.: Coloring local feature extraction. In: Leonardis, A., Bischof, H., Pinz, A. (eds.) ECCV 2006. LNCS, vol. 3952, pp. 334–348. Springer, Heidelberg (2006). https://doi.org/10.1007/11744047_26

Tire X-ray Image Impurity Detection Based on Multiple Kernel Learning

Shuai Zhao[1,2], Zhineng Chen[2(✉)], Baokui Li[1], and Bin Zhang[3]

[1] School of Automation, Beijing Institute of Technology, Bejing 100081, China
zshuaibit@163.com, libaokui@bit.edu.cn
[2] Institute of Automation, Chinese Academy of Sciences, Bejing 100190, China
zhineng.chen@ia.ac.cn
[3] MESNAC Co., Ltd., Shandong 266042, China
zhangb1@mesnac.com

Abstract. Impurity detection on tire X-ray image is an indispensable phase in tire quality control and the widely adopted manual inspection could not attain satisfactory performance. In this work we propose an idMKL method to automatically detect impurities by leveraging multiple kernel learning (MKL). idMKL first applies image processing techniques to separate different regions of a tire image and suppress their normal texture characteristics. As a result, candidate blobs containing both true impurities and false alarms are obtained. We extract different features from the blobs and evaluate their effectiveness in impurity detection. MKL is then employed to adaptively combine the features to maximize the detection performance. Experiments on thousands of images show that idMKL can well separate the blobs and achieves promising results in tire impurity detection. Moreover, idMKL has been adopted as a mean complementary to the manual inspection by tire factories and shown to be effective.

Keywords: Tire X-ray image · Multiple kernel learning
Defect detection

1 Introduction

Tire is a basic equipment in vehicles. However, it is not rare that improper handles and unclean materials are involved in the tire manufacturing. As a result, tires may be contaminated by various defects, such as metallic and non metallic impurities (e.g., steel threads, screws, and plastic fragments), bubbles, etc. Statistics indicates that 40% of traffic accidents are relevant to tire quality [1]. Inspection based on the tire X-ray image is an important means for tire quality control, especially for defects inside rubbers. Currently, the inspection is performed manually in most tire factories. Nevertheless, a number of practices show that the human inspection, not only with high labor costs, still let many defects undetected because of not being easy to be observed, visual fatigue [2], etc. Automatic defect detection systems are highly demanded.

© Springer International Publishing AG, part of Springer Nature 2018
B. Zeng et al. (Eds.): PCM 2017, LNCS 10735, pp. 346–355, 2018.
https://doi.org/10.1007/978-3-319-77380-3_33

This work discusses detecting impurities, one major kind of defects on the tire. Impurity detection is a difficult task whose challenges mainly come from three aspects. First, a tire X-ray image is often with resolution of no less than 2200*10000 while many impurities occupy less than 100 pixels and with various shapes and intensities. Even skillful workers could not discover them well. Second, due to the complicated manufacturing process, the image exhibits many irregular and cluttered texture similar to impurities such that false alarms are easily reported. Third, there are hundreds of tire models. It is not easy to develop a generic algorithm that is capable of suppressing normal texture characteristics across the models.

In the literature, there are some research efforts dedicated to this task. Zhang et al. [3] propose an improved Canny edge detection scheme to detect impurities in tire X-ray image based on curvelet and the multiscale geometric transform. While later in [4], they proposed a method for detecting tire defects based on wavelet multiscale analysis. In [5], Xiang et al. present a dictionary based detection method by analyzing the distribution of representative coefficients. However, its performance heavily relies on parameters. Tajeripour et al. [6] and Kumar et al. [7] also propose detection methods which employ local binary pattern (LBP) to extract texture features. Despite progresses made, these efforts are somehow heuristic, especially at the level of handling candidate impurity blobs, i.e., determining which suspected blobs are impurities and which ones are false alarms. Moreover, They are only evaluated on dozens of to a few hundred tire images while no message shows these methods have been applied to the industrial, e.g., tire factories. We argue that the complex blob patterns (See Fig. 3) are difficult to describe by heuristics. It is advantageous to use machine learning techniques to distinguish them. However, they are totally ignored except for [8]. In this work, Xue et al. propose a topographic independent component analysis based method to extract discriminative features based on tire X-ray image, and then implement the defect detection by using support vector machine (SVM).

In this work we propose a novel idMKL method to detect impurities based on the tire X-ray image by leveraging multiple kernel learning (MKL) [9]. Specifically, given a tire image (Fig. 2(a) shows a fraction of an image), image processing techniques are applied first to segment the image to different functional regions from left to right. Since the regions are with quite different appearance, different strategies are applied to them separately to remove their normal texture for the sake of highlighting possible impurities, as shown in Fig. 2. As a result, candidate blobs containing both true impurities and false alarms are obtained. These blobs differ in location, size, sharp, intensity, etc. It is difficult to describe them by simple heuristics or features. To this end for each blob, we propose to extract multiple features from different image domains to acquire a complete but redundant description. Then, MKL is employed to distinguish these features and combine them in a weighted manner, where large weights are adaptively allocated to discriminative features while the weights for useless features are negligible. Experiments on thousands of images obtained from tire factories show that idMKL well separate the candidate blobs and achieves promising results in detecting impurities from the whole tire X-ray image. Moreover, due to its superiority, idMKL has been equipped by tire factories to double inspect tire images passed the human inspection. It is shown that this novel tire quality control pipeline has played a more prominent role than human in tire inspection.

Contribution of this work is threefold: first, we propose to use MKL to model complex impurity patterns, where multiple useful features are appropriately combined and a powerful description is generated accordingly. To our knowledge, it is the first attempt that using MKL to detect tire impurities. Second, image processing and machine learning are appropriately integrated in the proposed idMKL. It forces machine learning to focus on distinguishing those small and hard-to-described blobs rather than the whole image thus leverages its merit. Third, comprehensive and rigorous evaluations are carried out on thousands of images, from which effectiveness of the proposed idMKL is verified by both large-scale data and the industrial.

2 The idMKL Method

2.1 Candidate Impurity Extraction

A tire is primarily composed of five functional regions including two tire beads, two sidewalls and a tread from left to right and from right to left [1]. Since different materials and processes are applied, these regions exhibit quite differently in the X-ray image, as shown in Fig. 2(a). Impurities may be contained in every part of the tire with diverse appearance. Typical examples are given by Fig. 1(a)–(f), where metallic, non metallic and overlap impurities on the three kinds of regions are depicted. By zooming in the image, it is also seen that some normal texture looks similar to impurities. Even human can not distinguish them well regardless of their spatial layouts, surrounding texture, etc.

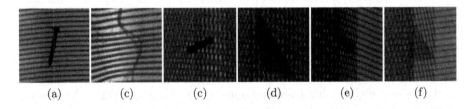

(a)   (c)   (c)   (d)   (e)   (f)

Fig. 1. Typical X-ray image impurities (a)–(f)

Since textual characteristics are similar for the same kind of region but different for different regions, we propose a two-step pipeline to identify the possible impurities. First, the functional regions are segmented. Then, different textual removal strategies are separately applied to these regions, with the same purpose of highlighting possible impurities. In region segmentation, note that both bead and tread regions exhibit certain mash-like structures while the main pattern in sidewall is horizontal steel cords. Morphological filtering method is applied at first to remove the steel cords as much as possible and histogram equalization column-by-column is also adopted meanwhile to highlight impurity areas as shown in Fig. 2(b). Then, local pixel scanning is carried out column-by-column at multiple scales, to find the appropriate local high pixel areas, as shown in Fig. 2(c) (the areas are marked by white). Since mash-like structures always correspond to many such small areas, and moreover, both bead and tread regions are darker than the sidewall, the region boundaries can be derived by jointly analyzing the distribution of small areas and column-projected pixel values. With regions segmented by the boundaries, classic image processing techniques including several kinds of filtering, connectivity analysis, binarization, etc., are appropriately assembled for every functional region to remove the normal texture and highlight possible impurity blobs, as shown in Fig. 2(d). Note that we only give a quite brief description of this part, as it is not the major contribution of this work.

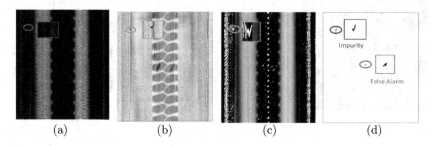

(a)   (b)   (c)   (d)

Fig. 2. Candidate impurity extraction pipeline. (a) Source image, (b) column-equalized image, (c) image with marked areas, (d) binary image with suspected impurities.

Since the extraction above is rather challenging, it is not surprise the generated blobs are composed of impurities, normal texture and small flaws that not affect the tire quality. It is difficult to distinguish them by simple features or heuristics, as no significant pattern can be observed from different kinds of blobs. The fact motivates us to employ machine learning techniques described below to address the problem.

2.2 Candidate Impurity Representation

By leveraging machine learning, a straightforward idea is to extract features from the blobs and then using SVM classification to distinguish impurities and false alarms including normal texture and small flaws. Typically, SVM use a kernel function to map the feature vector from low dimensional to high dimensional space, from which the classification boundary can be determined easier [10].

Choosing what features to represent the blobs is a critical issue. Intuitively, the blobs differ in size, sharp, intensity, etc. Typical color, geometric and texture features are all useful in representing them. However, it is insufficient to describe them by using any of the features individually, as other kinds of features are also helpful apparently but missed. Moreover, we observe that there are many normal texture also looked similar to some impurities from the source tire image. It would be beneficial to extract features from other domains.

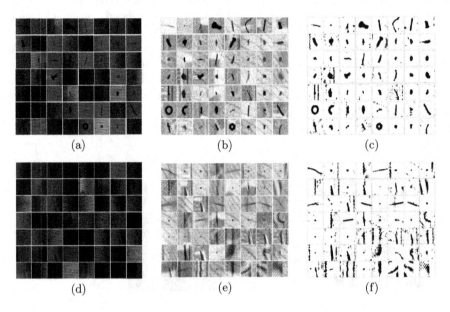

Fig. 3. Positive impurity samples (a–c) and negative impurity samples (d–f). (a, d) in source image, (b, e) in column-equalized image, (c, f) in binary image.

Based on these observations, we propose to extract five kinds of features from three domains as follows. The three domains are: (1) the source tire image, (2) the column-equalized image, where histogram equalization is carried out column-by-column on the source image, and (3) the binary image obtained from Sect. 2.1. Blobs are simultaneously extracted from all the three domains and normalized to the same resolution of 120 × 120, as depicted in Fig. 3. As for the five kinds of features, they are: (1) a 256-d color histogram to represent the blob's statistical information in the HSI space; (2) a 360-d gabor wavelet feature that is invariant to affine transformations and high resistance to noise [11]; (3) a 576-d histogram of oriented gradient (HOG) feature that efficiently captures the local shape statistics [12]; (4) a 52-d LBP feature and (5) a 8-d gray level co-occurrence matrix (GLCM) feature to express the blob texture [13]. By extracting the five kinds of features on the three domains, we obtain 15 groups of feature vectors describing the blobs from different aspects. These feature vectors constitute a complete but redundant representation for the candidate blobs.

2.3   Multiple Kernel Learning Module

The traditional support vector machine (SVM) is a discriminative classifier proposed for binary classification problems. Let $\{(\mathbf{x}_i, y_i)\}_i^N$ denotes a sample of N independent and identically distributed training instances. $\mathbf{x}_i$ is the D-dimensional vector and $y_i \in \{-1, +1\}$ is its class label. Let assume the mapping function $\boldsymbol{\Phi} : \mathbb{R}^D \to \mathbb{R}^S$. The discriminating hyperplane can be represent as formulation (1). So the classifier can be trained by solving the quadratic optimization problem function (2):

$$\langle \mathbf{w}, \varPhi(\mathbf{x}_i) \rangle + b = 0 \tag{1}$$

$$\min \quad \frac{1}{2} \|\mathbf{w}\|_2^2 + C \sum_{i=1}^{N} \xi_i$$
$$s.t. \quad y_i \left(\langle \mathbf{w}, \varPhi(x_i) \rangle + b \right) \geqslant 1 - \xi_i$$
$$\xi_i \geqslant 0, \ \forall i = 1, ..., N \tag{2}$$

While $\mathbf{w}$ is the vector of weight coefficients, C is given misclassification penalty which maximises the margin while minimising the hinge loss on training set $\{(\mathbf{x}_i, y_i)\}$. ξ is the vector of slack variables, and b is the bias term of the separate hyperplane. However, we always employ the Lagrangian dual function to solve this problem indirectly since it will turn the tough problem to be much easier.

$$\max \quad \sum_{i=1}^{N} \alpha_i - \frac{1}{2} \sum_{i=1}^{N} \sum_{j=1}^{N} \alpha_i \alpha_j y_i y_j \underbrace{\langle \boldsymbol{\Phi}(\mathbf{x_i}), \boldsymbol{\Phi}(\mathbf{x_j}) \rangle}_{k(\mathbf{x}_i, \mathbf{x}_j)}$$
$$s.t. \quad \sum_{i=1}^{N} \alpha_i y_i = 0, \ C \geqslant \alpha_i \geqslant 0 \ \ \forall i = 1, ...N \tag{3}$$

Where $k : \mathbb{R}_D \times \mathbb{R}_D \to \mathbb{R}$ is called the *kernel function* and $\boldsymbol{\alpha}_i$ and $\boldsymbol{\alpha}_j$ are the vectors of dual variables respectively corresponding to each separation constraint. Then we can get $\mathbf{w} = \sum_{i=1}^{N} \alpha_i y_i \boldsymbol{\Phi}(\boldsymbol{x_i})$ after solving formulation (3) above. So, the new discriminant function can be rewritten as following:

$$f(\mathbf{x}) = \sum_{i=1}^{N} \alpha_i y_i k(\boldsymbol{x}_i, \boldsymbol{x}_j) + b \tag{4}$$

Unlike SVM classification that performs learning based on a single kernel, MKL uses multiple kernels to perform the learning. Mathematically, assume $\mathbf{X}_i = \{\mathbf{x}_i^m\}_{m=1}^{P}$ the feature matrix of the ith instance with P kinds of feature descriptors. So, we train distance functions $f_1, ..., f_P$ at first, the descriptors and distance functions are then "kernelised" to yield base kernels matrices $\boldsymbol{K}_1, ..., \boldsymbol{K}_P$. Then the optimal kernel combination is approximated by

$K_{opt} = \sum_{m=1}^{P} \eta_m K_m$, where parameters $\boldsymbol{\eta}$ adjust the weights of different features. Similar to SVM, the optimization objective is to achieve the best classification performance. The objective function can be written as:

$$J(\boldsymbol{\eta}) = min \quad \frac{1}{2} \|W_\eta\|_2^2 + C \sum_{i=1}^{N} \xi_i + \sum_{m=1}^{P} \delta_m \eta_m$$

$$s.t. \quad y_i (\langle \mathbf{w}_\eta, \Phi_e ta(x_i) \rangle + b) \geqslant 1 - \xi_i \qquad (5)$$

$$\boldsymbol{\xi} \geqslant 0, \boldsymbol{\eta} \geqslant 0, \quad \forall i = 1, ..., N$$

$$\boldsymbol{W_\eta} \in \boldsymbol{R}^{S_\eta}, \boldsymbol{\xi} \in \boldsymbol{R}_+^N, b \in \boldsymbol{R}, \delta \in \boldsymbol{R}_+^P$$

To tackle this optimization problem, we adopt the minimax optimization strategy of [14]. In the method, the primal strategy is to minimise $J(\eta)$ through the iteration $\boldsymbol{\eta}^{n+1} = \boldsymbol{\eta}^n - \varepsilon^n \nabla J$ under the constraints $\boldsymbol{\eta} \geqslant 0$. The minimax algorithm consists of two iterative stages. First, let η fixed and therefore $\boldsymbol{K} = \sum_{m=1}^{P} \eta_m K_m$ are also fixed. $\boldsymbol{W}$ is a standard SVM dual with kernel matrix $\boldsymbol{K}$ as $\sum_{m=1}^{P} \delta \eta_m$ is a constant. Second, minimise J by projected gradient descent algorithm and get the optimal weight parameters. The two steps are repeated iteratively until it is convergenced or a fixed number of iterations is reached. With the learned weights and parameters, a new sample $\boldsymbol{X}$ can be classified by the decision function $sign \left(\sum_{i=1}^{N} \alpha_i y_i K_i (\boldsymbol{X}, \boldsymbol{X}_i) + b \right)$.

3   Experiments

To evaluate the effectiveness of the proposed idMKL method, we collect a dataset containing over 5000 tire X-ray images from a large tire factory. In the dataset, there are 550 images containing different impurities, while the rest 4500 ones are images without impurity defect. The width of the images ranges from 2200 to 2700, while their height ranges from 10800 to 12400. All pixels are with 256 gray levels. The images cover dozens of major tire models. We take *Detected Rate* (DR) and *Error Rate* (ER) as the evaluation metrics [3]. Assume P_c and P_m are the number of impurity images that are detected and missed by the algorithm, respectively, while N_a and N_e are the number of normal images that are detected as normal and impurity images respectively, the two metrics are defined as:

$$DR = \frac{P_c}{P_c + P_m}, ER = \frac{N_e}{N_a + N_e} \qquad (6)$$

Obviously, higher DR indicates the algorithm is less likely to miss true impurities, while lower ER implies less efforts are required to double check the reported tires. We first evaluate effectiveness of the 15 features individually. By merely using image processing techniques described in Sect. 2.1 to the 4500 impurity-free images, 580 false alarm blobs are collected. We also crop 566 impurity blobs from the 550 impurity images. The two sets of blobs are first randomly split following the fixed ratios of 7:3. They are then mixed accordingly to constitute the training

Table 1. SVM classification result on the collected dataset.

(a) Source image results

SourIm	GLCM	LBP	HOG	HSI	Gabor
DR	0.834	0.72	0.55	0.705	0.808
ER	0.008	0.012	0.025	0.015	0.012

(b) Column-equalized image results

ColeIm	GLCM	LBP	HOG	HSI	Gabor
DR	0.852	0.745	0.502	0.725	0.832
ER	0.005	0.016	0.02	0.012	0.01

(c) Binary image results

BinaIm	GLCM	LBP	HOG	HSI	Gabor
DR	0.738	0.746	0.570	0.550	0.788
ER	0.005	0.015	0.02	0.01	0.018

Table 2. The performance of impurity detection.

Data	IP		bSVM		aSVM		idMKL	
	DR	ER	DR	ER	DR	ER	DR	ER
D550	0.973	0.091	0.955	0.044	0.960	0.040	0.964	0.033
D4500	NA	0.093	NA	0.055	NA	0.055	NA	0.044

and testing sets. Table 1 gives the experimental results. In the table, SourIm, ColeIm and BinaIm denote the source tire image, column-equalized image and the binary image, respectively.

From the table we can see that all the 15 features can distinguish the impurity to some extent, not only correctly classifying non-impurities, but also classifying a few impurities as non-impurities. Since GLCM on ColeIm achieves the highest DR and lowest ER, we fix the setting as the bSVM and will further analyze it in the following experiments.

We then evaluate different methods on the image-level impurity detection. Specifically, four groups of evaluations are carried out. (1) IP: using image processing techniques purely to get the result, i.e., all candidate blobs obtained from Sect. 2.1 are regarded as impurities; (2) bSVM: the setting achieves the best performance when evaluating the 15 features individually; (3) aSVM: all the 15 features are concatenated to form a single feature vector. SVM classification is then applied to get the result; (4) the proposed idMKL method. Impurity detection results of the four methods are given by Table 2. In the table, for the sake of better explaining the methods, we show the results on impurity and non-impurity images separately, i.e., D550 and D4500 are the collection of impurity images and impurity-free images, respectively. Moreover, since DR is meaningless for impurity-free images, we place "NA" in the corresponding position.

As can be seen, compared with the IP baseline, bSVM reduces ER but its DR is also reduced. aSVM get slightly better performance than bSVM. idMKL get better results than aSVM and bSVM on both DR and ER, which clear validate the superior of leveraging MKL. Interestingly, only a marginal improvement is observed when comparing aSVM with bSVM. This can be explained as the concatenated vector, despite more complete, also contains many redundant information that is not helpful to the SVM learning. It is observed that 3.6% of impurities are missed by idMKL, from which 75% are missed by the IP process while the rest 25% are wrongly classified by MKL. This prohibits idMKL to be a fully automatic system currently, as the objective of quality inspection is to discover the impurity such that ideally, DR should approach 100%. On the other hand, since idMKL already achieves promising results. It has been adopted as a complementary way to the manual inspection by tire factories, i.e., tires images passed the human inspection are double checked by our idMKL method, workers are asked to check again when there are impurities reported. Encouraging feedbacks are reported: Human inspection only discover 0.9% defect tires, while the ratio reported by idMKL and further confirmed by workers are 1.5%. That is to say. idMKL is a complementary or even more reliable method than humans in impurity defect detection.

In Fig. 4, we also sort the weights of different features learned by idMKL. Similar to previous observations, GLCM and Gabor on ColeIm are ranked at the top. On the contrary, the weights for LBP, HIS, HOG on BinaIm are negligible. Their classification ability is well covered and replaced by other features. This also explains the redundant nature of the extracted features.

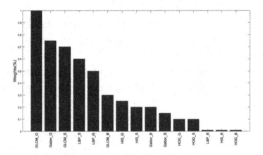

Fig. 4. The kernel weights rank of different features.

4   Conclusion

Automatic tire quality inspection is strongly demanded by tire industry to replace the manual inspection. In this paper, we propose an efficient tire impurity detection method named idMKL to approach this goal. idMKL is featured by leveraging MKL to adaptively combine the discriminative features from a complete but noisy feature pool. Experimental results on thousands of tire images basically validate that idMKL can effectively classify impurity and non impurity blobs. idMKL is also shown to be more useful than human in inspecting tire impurities. However, idMKL is limited by the fact that its DR is still not perfect. Thus, future work includes studies on further enhancing DR. Besides, we are also interested in developing methods towards automatically detect more kinds of defects such as bubbles, and investigating schemes that are more suitable for industrial environments [15,16] in the near future.

References

1. Guo, Q., Wei, Z.: Tire defect detection using image component decomposition. Res. J. Appl. Sci. Eng. Technol. **4**(1), 41–44 (2012)
2. Zhang, Y., Li, T., Li, Q.: Defect detection for tire laser shearography image using curvelet transform based edge detector. Opt. Laser Technol. **47**(4), 64–71 (2013)
3. Zhang, Y.: Research on nondestructive tire defect detection using computer vision methods. Ph.D. thesis, Qingdao University of Science and Technology (2014). (in Chinese)
4. Zhang, Y., Dimitr, L., Li, Q.L.: Automatic detection of defects in tire radiographic image. IEEE Trans. Autom. Sci. Eng. 1–9 (2017, accepted)
5. Xiang, Y., Zhang, C., Guo, Q.: A dictionary-based method for tire defect detection. In: IEEE International Conference on Information and Automation, pp. 519–523 (2014)
6. Tajeripour, F., Kabir, E., Sheikhi, A.: Fabric defect detection using modified local binary patterns. EURASIP J. Adv. Sign. Process. **2008**(1), 1–12 (2007)
7. Kumar, A.: Computer-vision-based fabric defect detection: a survey. IEEE Trans. Indus. Electron. **55**(1), 348–363 (2008)
8. Cui, X., Liu, Y., Wang, C., Li, H.: A novel method for feature extraction and automatic recognition of tire defects. In: ICIMM International Conference on Intelligent Manufacturing and Materials, pp. 1–9 (2016)
9. Qiu, S., Lane, T.: A framework for multiple kernel support vector regression and its applications to sIRNA efficacy prediction. IEEE/ACM Trans. Comput. Biol. Bioinform. **6**(2), 190–199 (2009)
10. Kumar, A., Sminchisescu, C.: Support kernel machines for object recognition. In: IEEE International Conference on Computer Vision, pp. 1–8 (2007)
11. Ke, Y., Youbin, C., David, Z.: Gabor surface feature for face recognition. In: Pattern Recognition, pp. 288–292 (2011)
12. Dalal, N., Triggs, B.: Histograms of oriented gradients for human detection. In: IEEE Computer Society Conference on Computer Vision and Pattern Recognition, pp. 886–893 (2005)
13. Crosier, M., Griffin, L.D.: Using basic image features for texture classification. Int. J. Comput. Vis. **88**(3), 447–460 (2010)
14. Varma, M., Ray, D.: Learning the discriminative power-invariance trade-off. In: IEEE International Conference on Computer Vision, pp. 1–8 (2007)
15. Gao, X., Gu, Z., et al.: ContainerLeaks: emerging security threats of information leakages in container clouds. In: IEEE International Conference on Dependable Systems and Networks, pp. 1–12 (2017)
16. Gao, X., Liu D., et al.: E-Android: a new energy profiling tool for smartphones. In: 37th IEEE International Conference on Distributed Computing Systems, pp. 492–502 (2017)

Multimedia Signal Reconstruction and Recovery

CRF-Based Reconstruction from Narrow-Baseline Image Sequences

Yue Xu[1,2], Qiuyan Tao[1,2], Lianghao Wang[1,2,3(✉)], Dongxiao Li[1,2], and Ming Zhang[1,2]

[1] College of Information Science and Electronic Engineering,
Zhejiang University, Hangzhou, People's Republic of China
wanglianghao@zju.edu.cn
[2] Zhejiang Provincial Key Laboratory of Information Processing,
Communication and Networking, Hangzhou, People's Republic of China
[3] State Key Laboratory for Novel Software Technology, Nanjing University,
Nanjing, People's Republic of China

Abstract. Given an image sequence of a scene it is possible to recover a depth map. Though multiview stereo algorithms are well-studied, rarely are those algorithms considered in the context of narrow baseline. In this paper, a practical method is proposed to generate dense depth map using a narrow-baseline image sequence. We introduce a new structure from small motion method tailored for narrow baseline which allows us to recover sparse scene structure and camera poses. In the dense reconstruction, we adopt a space-sweeping method for dense matching and a fully connected conditional random field model for depth refinement. As opposed to prior methods that guide CRF with color information alone, we creatively add depth information guidance which effectively avoids over-smoothing and bad impact from error color information. Our approach produces higher-quality dense depth results than state-of-the-art algorithms under the same baseline configuration.

Keywords: Dense reconstruction · Structure from small motion
Conditional random field · Narrow baseline

1 Introduction

When people take still photos by smartphones or hand-held cameras, the photographer always spends several seconds before pressing the button and tiny vibrations are inevitable. If we save the short videos before freeze-frame, we will find them useful for a variety of applications, such as synthetic refocusing and view synthesis. These applications are based on the technology of 3D reconstruction.

Structure from motion (SfM) in [1–3] can be widely used to recover the sparse 3D geometry and camera poses from wide-baseline images. Based on the sparse result, several multiview stereo (MVS) algorithms [4, 5] can be applied to do depth propagation from sparse to dense. Traditional SfM algorithms generate 3D locations of feature points from two-view reconstruction as initialization and then add more frames to estimate camera pose of each frame. Based on the estimated camera poses, bundle

© Springer International Publishing AG, part of Springer Nature 2018
B. Zeng et al. (Eds.): PCM 2017, LNCS 10735, pp. 359–369, 2018.
https://doi.org/10.1007/978-3-319-77380-3_34

adjustment is carried out to optimize parameters globally. However, under the circumstance of small motion, the baseline between input pairs is too narrow to make the two-view reconstruction work and it will lead to the failure of structure from motion. Several researches have studied the 3D reconstruction from small motion. Yu and Gallup [6] propose a novel method that estimates camera poses from a clip of small motion. Unfortunately, it is indispensable for them to adopt calibrated and rectified inputs. Im et al. [7] present a model for rolling shutter (RS) to improve the geometric model of [6]. Instead of performing dense matching, they present a geometric guidance model to do depth propagation. Ha et al. [8] analyze the effect of radial distortion in projection model and utility the minimum spanning tree structure to do dense matching. However, their results are not good enough with error depth values and holes.

Since our image sequences are of small motion, the dense results generated by multiview stereo methods are noisy and of high uncertainty. Therefore, it is necessary to do the refinement. The Conditional Random Field (CRF) [5, 9] and Markov Random Field (MRF) [10, 11] framework are proposed to smooth the raw depth results. As a matter of fact, low order conditional random field methods not only cannot regularize the depth effectively but also smooth out the details.

In order to obtain dense depth map from image sequences with narrow baseline, a method has been proposed in this paper. We present a structure from small motion method tailored for narrow baseline to obtain camera parameters and generate sparse 3D points. Instead of using the result of two-view reconstruction as the initialization of bundle adjustment, we roughly initialize all the camera poses with zero rotation and translation to carry out bundle adjustment directly. Thanks to the narrow baseline, the crude way works quite effectively. We parameterize the 3D position of a point as the depth relative to the reference view because the viewpoints of all frames are similar. Our bundle adjustment optimizes the intrinsic parameters and extrinsic parameters jointly. On the basis of the camera poses and sparse depth results, we utilize a space-sweep method to generate a dense depth result. At last, under the guidance of both raw depth information and color information, we propose a novel full-connected CRF framework to refine the depth map. Different from the first-order CRF framework, our CRF method establishes pairwise potential on all pairs of pixels in the images, containing their positions, colors vectors as well as the raw depth values estimated by plane sweeping. We test our system on both synthetic and real-world data. Experimental results show that we have improved the quality of depth map in terms of accuracy and precision.

2 Raw Depth Generation

In this section, we introduce our structure from small motion method tailored for narrow baseline to recover sparse structure and camera parameters. Based on these estimated parameters, a space-sweep based multiview stereo method is proposed for dense matching.

2.1 Self-calibrating Structure from Small Motion

Feature Extraction. Since the baseline is narrow, the accurate extraction of features and correspondences are crucial for the whole reconstruction. We utilize the Harris corner detector [12] and Kanade-Lucas-Tomasi (KLT) tracker [13] to extract sub-pixel features in reference frame and then track them in other frames. KLT is based on the assumption of brightness constancy and small motion, which perfectly meets our requirements. Instead of using all the tracking features for bundle adjustment, we use RANSAC [14] to remove features on moving objects which guarantees that all the features can be tracked in all the frames.

Bundle Adjustment. Two-view reconstruction is always used as the initialization of bundle adjustment in traditional SfM methods. However, the baseline of our inputs is too narrow to make the two-view reconstruction work. Surprisingly, thanks to the narrow baseline, we can simply initialize all the camera poses as zero rotation and translation camera matrix to carry out the bundle adjustment directly. We regard the L2 norm [15] of reprojection error as the cost function of bundle adjustment:

$$\arg \min E_{K,R,t,z} = \sum_{i=1}^{N-1} \sum_{j=1}^{M} \left\| c_{ij}x_{ij} - \pi(X_j, R_i, t_i) \right\|^2 \tag{1}$$

where N and M are the number of images and features. R_i and t_i are translation and rotation matrix for each frame. x_{ij} is the coordinate of the j-th feature in the i-th frame. c_{ij} is the distortion correct coefficient for pixel x_{ij}. We take radial distortion [16] caused by lenses into consideration. We modify the 2D coordinates before applying it into the bundle adjustment model to reduce deviation. c_{ij} is defined as:

$$c_{ij} = 1 + k_1 \left\| \frac{x_{ij}}{f} \right\|^2 + k_2 \left\| \frac{x_{ij}}{f} \right\|^4 \tag{2}$$

$\pi(\cdot)$ is the projection function from 3D to 2D. Regard the first frame as the reference frame I_0. The 3D coordinates X_j of the back-projection of the feature x_{0j} from reference frame can be parameterized using its depth z_j. The function defines the projection of X_j onto the i-th viewpoint can be described as follows:

$$\pi(X_j, R_i, t_i) = <R_iX_j + t_i> = <R_i \begin{bmatrix} c_{0j}\frac{x_{0j}z_j}{f} \\ z_j \end{bmatrix} + t_i > \tag{3}$$

where $<[x,y,z]> = [x/z, y/z]$. When dealing with the condition of small motion, it is noticeable that small angle approximation of the camera rotation matrix R_i is able to reduce the complexity of the cost function. The rotation angle θ is so narrow that $\sin\theta$ can be approximated as zero and $\cos\theta$ as one. R_i can be expressed as:

$$R_i = \begin{bmatrix} 1 & -r_i^z & r_i^y \\ r_i^z & 1 & -r_i^x \\ -r_i^y & r_i^x & 1 \end{bmatrix} \tag{4}$$

In order to optimize the extrinsic and intrinsic camera matrix as well as the depth of feature points globally, we minimize the reprojection error in Eq. (1) with Ceres Solver [17]. We initialize all the camera poses with zero rotation and translation and utility the depth relative to the reference view to parameterize the 3D position of a point. To verify the estimation of intrinsic camera matrix, we test on the inputs with known focal length and compare our estimated values with the ground truth. Figure 1 shows that our estimated parameters are close to the ground truth even when the initial value is far away from the ground truth.

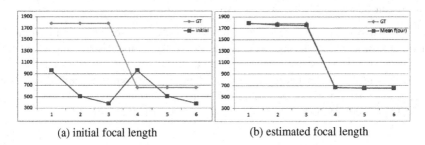

(a) initial focal length   (b) estimated focal length

Fig. 1. Our estimated focal length by structure from small motion. We test on six datasets with two different ground truth f. For each dataset, 30 experiments are carried out and mean values are calculated as the result. The left image is the initial focal length compared with the ground truth. The right image is our estimated results compared with the ground truth.

2.2 Space-Sweep Based Multiview Stereo

After obtaining the intrinsic and extrinsic camera parameters from structure from small motion, we propose a multiview stereo algorithm which concentrated on space-sweep method to generate dense depth map. Since the viewpoints of different frames are similar, we are supposed to regard the dense depth result relative to the reference view as the dense reconstruction result of the scene.

Traditional space-sweep approach [18] back-projects features onto virtual planes of different depths. When feature points back-projected from different frames gather in an acceptable small region, we can regard the corresponding virtual plane depth as the depth of the feature point. Otherwise, traverse other virtual planes. This space-sweep method sweeps between virtual planes and calculates photo consistency of the warped images. Inspired by the method, we take all pixels into consideration. Instead of calculating photo consistency, we measure the consistency of the intensity profile. Intensity profile is defined as the intensity distribution of the pixels in the warped images and these pixels correspond to the same point on the virtual plane. When the pixels are projected from the correct depth, the intensities acquired from pixels of the warped images tend to be similar. Hence, for each pixel, uniform intensity profile indicates correct depth of sweeping plane.

We sweep the plane along the Z-axis of the scene. Assume Z-axis is divided into K depth labels and the depth of the k-th virtual plane is z_k. The reference frame is back-projected onto a virtual plane of depth z_k and then projected onto the i-th non-reference viewpoint. The transformation can be expressed by the homography matrix $H_{i,k}$ as:

$$H_{i,k} = K \begin{bmatrix} 1 & -r_i^z & r_i^y + z_k^{-1}t_x \\ r_i^z & 1 & -r_i^x + z_k^{-1}t_y \\ -r_i^y & r_i^x & 1 + z_k^{-1}t_z \end{bmatrix} K^{-1} \tag{5}$$

where K is intrinsic camera matrix. (r_i^x, r_i^y, r_i^z) are parameters of rotation matrix in Eq. (4) and (t_x, t_y, t_x) are translation matrix. After the transformation, pixel j in the reference image can be warped to the i-th frame viewpoint by $H_{i,k}p_j$ and its intensity $IN_{ik}(p_j)$ is defined as the intensity of pixel $H_{i,k}p_j$ in the i-th frame. The intensity profile of pixel j which is warped onto all non-reference frames through depth z_k is defined as: $IP(p_j, z_k) = [IN_{1k}(p_j), \cdots, IN_{(N-1)k}(p_j)]$. [·] here means a set. For each pixel p_j, the consistency measurement of the intensity profile is defined as:

$$E(p_j, z_k) = var\, IP(p_j, z_k) + var\frac{\partial IP(p_j, z_k)}{\partial p_j^x} + var\frac{\partial IP(p_j, z_k)}{\partial p_j^y} \tag{6}$$

where var[·] means the variance of a set. Considering the importance of image edges, the horizontal and vertical gradients of the intensity profile are added into the cost function. We select $z_k = \arg\min E(p_j, z_k)$ as the depth of pixel p_j which indicates the intensity distribution acquired from depth z_k is the most uniform. By assigning a depth to each pixel, a dense depth map is generated. Figure 2 shows the dense results generated by space-sweeping based multiview stereo.

Fig. 2. Our dense depth map generated by space-sweeping stereo method. For each dataset, the left image are average images which proves our image sequences are of narrow baseline. The right image shows the estimated dense depth map before refinement. We declare that the depth value of each pixel corresponds to pixel in the reference frame.

3 Depth Refinement

After applying the space-sweep based multiview stereo, we can obtain a dense depth estimation. Although the estimation is generally reliable, depth values of several pixels may be noisy. Hence, depth refinement is essential.

Basic CRF models are composed of unary potentials on individual pixels/patches and pairwise potentials on neighboring pixels/patches [5, 9]. However, under the circumstance of narrow baseline, the confidence of the depth minima is low not only in texture-less areas but also in richly-textured areas. Traditional CRF models always smooth out the details. To solve the problem, we come up with a fully connected CRF model which establishes pairwise potentials on all pairs of pixels. Different from [6] who estimate the depth assignment based on the color intensities and locations in reference frame, we add the depth guidance into the CRF model. Although depth result generated by the space-sweeping method is noisy, we find experimentally that it can provide reliable constraint in the CRF model. Thanks to the modification, our results are accurate while the results of [6] have error depth values caused by wrong color information, such as shadows.

The reference frame and the raw depth generation are considered as the input color image I and depth image D of the model. Assume I and D are of size N and the number of targeted depth label is K. The random depth label field X is defined over $\{X_1, \ldots, X_N\}$. X_i is the corresponding depth label of pixel i. The domain of each variable X_i is a set of labels $L = \{l_1, l_2, \ldots, l_k\}$. We aim at generating the best distribution of X based on the guidance of I and D. The Gibbs distribution of the conditional random field is as follow:

$$P(X|I, D) = \frac{1}{Z(I, D)} exp\left(-\sum_{c \in C_g} \emptyset_c(X_c|I, D)\right) \tag{7}$$

where $g = (V, E)$ is a graph on **X**. According to the maximum a posteriori (MAP), the purpose is to find $X' = \arg\max P(X|I, D)$. In other words, minimize the Gibbs energy $\sum_c \emptyset_c(X_c|I, D)$. For convenience, $\emptyset_c(X_c|I, D)$ is denoted as $\varphi_c(X_c)$. The Gibbs energy function composed of unary potential and pairwise potentials is defined as:

$$\arg\min E(x) = \sum_{i \in 1 \sim N} \varphi_u(x_i) + \sum_{\substack{i,j \in 1 \sim N \\ i<j}} \varphi_p(x_i, x_j) \tag{8}$$

The unary potential $\varphi_u(x_i)$ constructs the distribution of labels based on the initial depth value. The initial depth label of pixel i is $d_i \in L$ in D which is true with α probability. Assume the probability of the rest labels for the pixel i as the normalized Gaussian distribution. $\varphi_u(x_i)$ is defined as:

$$\varphi_u(x_i) = \begin{cases} -log(\alpha) & x_i = d_i \\ -log\left(\frac{1-\alpha}{z} exp\left(\frac{(x_i - d_i)^2}{2\theta_u^2}\right)\right) & x_i \neq d_i \end{cases} \tag{9}$$

where θ_u is the standard deviation and z is the normalizer of Gaussian distribution.

The pairwise potential is a combination of Gaussian potentials. Instead of guiding with color image alone [6], we creatively utilize the raw depth result together to restrain the final result. The feature f_i includes information concerning position in reference frame $P_i = [x_i, y_i]$, color vector $I_i = [r_i, g_i, b_i]$ and the initial depth value d_i. The concrete form of pairwise potential is as follow:

$$\varphi_p(x_i, x_j) = \mu_c(x_i, x_j)\left[k_a(f_i, f_j) + k_s(f_i, f_j)\right] \tag{10}$$

Label compatibility function μ_c in Eq. (11) represents the penalty for different labels. With the assumption that pixel pairs with similar features are likely to have similar depth labels, the appearance kernel in Eq. (12) means that adjacent pixels with similar color information or similar initial depth value tend to have similar depth. The smoothness kernel in Eq. (13) removes the small isolated regions. Gaussian potentials are defined as:

$$\mu_c(x_i, x_j) = \begin{cases} |x_i - x_j| & |x_i - x_j| < t \\ t & |x_i - x_j| \geq t \end{cases} \tag{11}$$

$$k_a(f_i, f_j) = w_a exp\left(-\frac{|P_i - P_j|^2}{2\theta_P^2} - \frac{|I_i - I_j|^2}{2\theta_I^2}\right) + w_d exp\left(-\frac{|d_i - d_j|^2}{2\theta_d^2}\right) \tag{12}$$

$$k_s(f_i, f_j) = w_s exp\left(-\frac{|P_i - P_j|^2}{2\theta_s^2}\right) \tag{13}$$

where f_i and f_j are feature vectors of pixel pairs. θ_p, θ_I and θ_d are parameters which control the degrees of nearness and similarity. Instead of optimizing directly, we apply the efficient inference algorithm [19, 20] which is based on a mean field approximation to the CRF distribution for acceleration. This approximation yields an iterative message passing algorithm for approximate inference.

4   Experiment

In this part, the experimental results of dense depth reconstruction will be shown. We apply our method to two datasets. One is the real world scene of narrow baseline provided by Yu and Gallup [6] with 100 frames in each dataset. The other is the HCI datasets [21] including synthetic and real scenes with 81 frames in each dataset. The HCI datasets contain the ground truth of the depth map and we can objectively evaluate the quality of our results.

Our proposed algorithm is carried out with the parameters as follows. For each dataset, we utilize all the frames of the image sequence and all the frames are of full resolution, which ensures that we can preserve as much information as possible. The connection threshold t in label compatibility function μ_c in Eq. (11) is chosen to be 15% of the total label number. The coefficients θ_p, θ_I and θ_s in Eqs. (12) and (13) are adjusted to the size of the color images. Especially, θ_d for depth information guidance is changed with the quality of the initial depth result. Figure 3 shows high-quality depth maps generated by our reconstruction method.

Fig. 3. Depth maps acquired by our method. The first and the third row are the average image of each dataset, which proves that our image sequences are of small motion. The second and the forth row are the dense depth result generated by our 3D reconstruction method. Since the viewpoints of different frames are similar, we can regard the dense depth map relative to the reference frame as the dense reconstruction result of the scene.

4.1   Comparison with [6–8]

The dense depth results generated by Yu and Gallup [6], Im et al. [7], Ha et al. [8] and our approach are compared in the Fig. 4. Our improvements are marked with red rectangles. The results of [6] have inaccurate depth values since their CRF model is guided by color images alone which simply regards pixels with similar colors as consistent depth. However, wrong color information such as shadow leads to a wrong depth result in depth refinement. Note that our approach performs a self-calibration of intrinsic camera parameters in structure from small motion, while [6] owns known focal length and ignores the lens distortion. The depth discontinuity of [7] is too smooth. Our results share similar depth values with [8], however, they have errors which are marked in red rectangle 2 and 4.

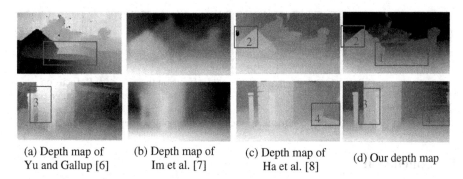

(a) Depth map of Yu and Gallup [6]   (b) Depth map of Im et al. [7]   (c) Depth map of Ha et al. [8]   (d) Our depth map

Fig. 4. 3D reconstruction results of our proposed system, compared with the dense depth result generated by Yu and Gallup [6], Im et al. [7] and Ha et al. [8]. Improvements are marked with red rectangles. Please note that our method needs inputs neither with camera calibration nor the image rectification. (Color figure online)

In order to verify the effectiveness of our method more objectively and numerically, we apply the system to the HCI datasets with ground truth depth values. Each HCI datasets has 81 images with narrow baseline. We take RMSE between the ground truth depth map and the depth results generated by different algorithms as the criteria for evaluation. The results are shown in Table 1. Our method gets the best performance in general. It seems that our depth map fits the ground truth better which means our depth results are the most accurate.

Table 1. Quantitative evaluation. RMSE results of depth map generated by [6–8] and our method are compared with the ground truth depth map provided by HCI datasets. The best result is highlighted in bold and the second best is underlined.

Datasets	Buddha	Horses	Monas	Medieval	Stilllife
[6]	6.8864	8.7577	7.2983	7.0105	7.6475
[7]	20.1381	26.7625	25.0199	18.6259	21.3907
[8]	1.2490	**2.2173**	2.0943	1.9325	2.0532
Ours	**0.7844**	2.4216	**1.8211**	**1.3352**	**2.0345**

4.2 Refocusing Application

As mentioned above, the depth map reconstructed from small motion image sequences can be used i n various fields. We have applied our depth result for the application of synthetic refocusing which means that the accuracy of depth edge is of the most importance. Figure 5 shows that our focused image gives realistic defocus blurs. We focus on two objects separately in Fig. 5(c) and (d).

(a)Reference frame   (b)Our depth map   (c) Refocus on the   (d) Refocus on
                                           black stone   the green tree

Fig. 5. Synthetic refocusing focuses on two objects separately.

5 Conclusion

In this paper, a practical pipeline is put forward to generate high-quality depth map from uncalibrated image sequence with narrow baseline. Three major contributions have been introduced: structure from small motion method with self-calibrating bundle adjustment, space-sweeping based multiview stereo for dense reconstruction and a fully connected CRF model guided by both depth and color information for depth refinement. According to the experimental results, our depth results are accurate without missing values, which outperforms other methods qualitatively and quantitatively. In the future, we will try to improve the time efficiency of the method and make it be real-time.

Acknowledgements. This work was supported in part by the National Natural Science Foundation of China (Grant No. 61401390).

References

1. Hartley, R., Zisserman, A.: Multiple View Geometry in Computer Vision, pp. 1865–1872. Cambridge University Press, New York (2000)
2. Snavely, N., Seitz, S.M., Szeliski, R.: Photo tourism: exploring photo collections in 3D. ACM Trans. Graph. **25**, 835–846 (2006)
3. Häming, K., et al.: The structure-from-motion reconstruction pipeline - a survey with focus on short image sequences. Kybernetika **46**(5), 926–937 (2010). Praha
4. Okutomi, M., Kanade, T.: A multiple-baseline stereo. IEEE Trans. Pattern Anal. Mach. Intell. (PAMI) **15**(4), 353–363 (1993)
5. Hernndez, C., Vogiatzis, G.: Shape from photographs: a multi-view stereo pipeline. In: Cipolla, R., Battiato, S., Farinella, G.M. (eds.) Computer Vision. Studies in Computational Intelligence, vol. 285, pp. 281–311. Springer, Heidelberg (2010). https://doi.org/10.1007/978-3-642-12848-6_11
6. Yu, F., Gallup, D.: 3D reconstruction from accidental motion. In: IEEE Conference on Computer Vision and Pattern Recognition, pp. 3986–3993. IEEE (2014)
7. Im, S., et al.: High quality structure from small motion for rolling shutter cameras. In: IEEE International Conference on Computer Vision IEEE, pp. 837–845 (2015)
8. Ha, H., et al.: High-quality depth from uncalibrated small motion clip. In: IEEE Conference on Computer Vision and Pattern Recognition. IEEE (2016)

9. Campbell, N.D.F., et al.: Using multiple hypotheses to improve depth-maps for multi-view stereo. In: European Conference on Computer Vision, Marseille, France, 12–18 October 2008, pp. 766–779

10. Woodford, O., et al.: Global stereo reconstruction under second-order smoothness priors. IEEE Trans. Pattern Anal. Mach. Intell. **31**(12), 2115–2118 (2009)

11. Komodakis, N., Paragios, N.: Beyond pairwise energies: efficient optimization for higher-order MRFs. In: IEEE Conference on IEEE Xplore Computer Vision and Pattern Recognition, pp. 2985–2992 (2009)

12. Shi, J., Tomasi, C.: Good features to track. In: CVPR, pp. 593–600 (1994)

13. Tomasi, C.: Detection and tracking of point features. Technical report 91.21(1991), pp. 9795–9802 (1991)

14. Fischler, M.A., Bolles, R.C.: Random sample consensus: a paradigm for model fitting with applications to image analysis and automated cartography. Commun. ACM **24**, 381–395 (1981)

15. Hartley, R., et al.: Verifying global minima for L2 minimization problems in multiple view geometry. Int. J. Comput. Vis. **101**, 288–304 (2013)

16. Ma, L., Chen, Y., Moore, K.L.: Rational radial distortion models of camera lenses with analytical solution for distortion correction. Int. J. Inf. Acquis. **1**, 135–147 (2012)

17. Agarwal, S., Mierle, K.: Ceres Solver: Tutorial & Reference. Google Inc. (2012)

18. Collins, R.T.: A space-sweep approach to true multi-image matching. In: Conference on Computer Vision and Pattern Recognition IEEE Computer Society, pp. 358–363. IEEE (1996)

19. Krähenbühl, P., Koltun, V.: Efficient inference in fully connected CRFs with Gaussian edge potentials. In: Advances in Neural Information Processing Systems, pp. 109–117 (2011)

20. Krähenbühl, P., Koltun, V.: Parameter learning and convergent inference for dense random fields. In: International Conference on Machine Learning, Atlanta, USA, vol. 46, pp. 346–350 (2013)

21. Wanner, S.: Datasets and Benchmarks for Densely Sampled 4D Light Fields. The Eurographics Association (2013)

Better and Faster, when ADMM Meets CNN: Compressive-Sensed Image Reconstruction

Chen Zhao$^{(\boxtimes)}$, Ronggang Wang, and Wen Gao

Peking University Shenzhen Graduate School, Shenzhen 518055, China
{zhaochen,rgwang}@pkusz.edu.cn, wgao@pku.edu.cn

Abstract. Compressive sensing (CS) has drawn enormous amount of attention in recent years owing to its sub-Nyquist sampling rate and low-complexity requirement at the encoder. However, it turns out that the decoder in lieu of the encoder suffers from heavy computation in order to decently recover the signal from its CS measurements. Inspired by the recent success of deep learning in low-level computer vision problems, in this paper, we propose a solution that utilizes deep convolutional neural network (CNN) to recover image signals from CS measurements effectively and efficiently. Rather than training a neural network from scratch that inputs CS measurements and outputs images, we incorporate an off-the-shelf CNN model into the CS reconstruction framework even without the effort of finetuning. To this end, we formulate the CS recovery problem into two subproblems via the alternate direction method of multiplers (ADMM): a convex quadratic problem and an image denoising problem, in which CNN has exhibited its desirable reconstruction performance and low computational complexity. Hereby, powerful GPU could be utilized to speed up the reconstruction. Experiments demonstrate that our proposed CS image reconstruction solution surpasses state-of-the-art CS models by a significant margin in speed and performance.

Keywords: Compressive sensing · Deep learning · Image denoising
Alternate direction method of multiplers (ADMM)
Convolutional neural network (CNN)

1 Introduction

Nowadays has seen tremendous interest in compressive sensing (CS), which provides the possibility to sample a signal at a sub-Nyquist rate and still be able to reconstruct the original signal [1]. What it differs from traditional sampling method lies in that it acquires digital measurements by linearly projecting the

This work is supported by National Postdoctoral Program for Innovative Talents (BX201600006), National Natural Science Foundation of China (61672063, 61370115), China 863 project (2015AA015905), which are gratefully acknowledged.

© Springer International Publishing AG, part of Springer Nature 2018
B. Zeng et al. (Eds.): PCM 2017, LNCS 10735, pp. 370–379, 2018.
https://doi.org/10.1007/978-3-319-77380-3_35

original signal onto a lower-dimensional space. From these fairly few measurements, the original signal can be robustly reconstructed if it exhibits sparsity in some domain, according to the CS theory. CS opens up a new paradigm for signal processing, making it unnecessary to perform the intricate and time-consuming signal compression at the encoder.

To convert the measurements back into the higher-dimensional original signal space, an effective signal model is desirable in the decoder side. This model, to suit to various signal characteristics, is generally computation-intensive and domain-knowledge dependent. It is generally handcrafted and how it is design largely determines the reconstruction performance. Letting alone the human efforts involved in this model crafting, high computational complexity for solving a model-driven optimization problem with respect to each signal is typically inevitable. This becomes one critical issue that hampers CS from extensive application.

Another emerging technology — deep learning (DL) [2], which came to light almost at the same time as CS, has demonstrated its pervasive influence in academia and industry in recent years. Owing to its superior performance and high inference efficiency, DL is welcomed by researchers in a variety of fields and is continuously demonstrating its alchemy.

One recent success of DL in computer vision is that deep neural network can achieve comparable or even superior results to traditional image denoising methods in terms of reconstruction performance as well as processing time [3, 4]. Moreover, owing to its 'one-size-fits-all' nature, the deep learning denoising models can be directly utilized elsewhere once the training phase is completed.

Building on this sucess, in this paper, we propose an effective and efficient CS image reconstruction method. It utilizes the alternate direction method of multiplers (ADMM) and convolutional neural network (CNN), hence called ADMM-CNN-propelled CS image reconstruction (ACIR). Rather than modelling an image explicitly as traditional methods do, we mathematically transform the CS image reconstruction problem into alternate steps of a quadratic programming problem and an image denoising problem on the basis of ADMM. By this means, an off-the-shelf CNN model can be directly utilized to produce a solution to the denoising problem. In addition, we explore the connection between the CNN model and the CS problem with respect to the noise levels to optimize the model selection.

ACIR features three advantages over traditional CS image reconstruction methods. Firstly, it requires no handcrafted image model and has only one argument[1] to tune, which greatly relieves human labor. Secondly, by transforming into an image denoising problem, it skips the time-consuming training phase of deep learning and simply goes through an off-the-shelf feed-forward network. Thirdly, it resorts to the powerful GPU for running CNN, further speeding up

---

[1] To avoid confusion, we use the word 'parameter' specially for the weights and biases in the deep neural network, and use 'argument' instead for the factors that possibly affect the algorithm and need to be manually set.

the entire computation. Experiments demonstrate that the proposed ACIR not only yields *better* reconstruction results, but also runs *faster* than traditional methods.

The remainder of this paper is organized as follows. Section 2 introduces the general framework of compressive sensing, briefly overviews CS image reconstruction methods in the literature and provides a basic concept of CNN. In Sect. 3, we present the proposed ACIR in detail. Section 4 describes our experimental results and Sect. 5 concludes this paper.

2   Background

2.1   Compressive Sensing

In this subsection, we mathematically formulate the procedures of CS acquisition and reconstruction. Denote the original signal by $\mathbf{x} \in \mathbb{R}^N$, and its measurements by $\mathbf{y} \in \mathbb{R}^M$, $M < N$ (the ratio M/N is called sampling rate or subrate). Then signal acquisition process is formulated as the linear projection as follows

$$\mathbf{y} = \Phi\mathbf{x}, \tag{1}$$

where $\Phi \in \mathbb{R}^{M \times N}$ is a projection matrix with random-valued elements. According to the CS theroy, if the signal $\mathbf{x}$ meets the sparsity requirement, it can be robustly reconstructed from the measurements. Directly computing $\mathbf{x}$ from Eq. (1) is an under-determined problem due to the lowered dimension of the measurements $\mathbf{y}$. Therefore, in order to obtain a unique solution, a signal prior model is required and hereby leads to the following optimization problem

$$\hat{\mathbf{x}} = \arg\min_{\mathbf{x}} f(\mathbf{x}), \text{ s.t. } \mathbf{y} = \Phi\mathbf{x}. \tag{2}$$

In Eq. 2, $f(\mathbf{x})$ represents a prior model, which usually depicts some intrinsic characteristic of the original signal. It is the prominent factor that determines the reconstruction efficacy and efficiency. In the next subsection, the prior model for CS image reconstruction is briefly reviewed.

2.2   CS Image Reconstruction Methods

Traditionally, in order to reconstruct the original image from its CS measurements, an explicit image model, i.e., a specific form for $f(\mathbf{x})$, is required. In this subsection, we review different image models for the CS reconstruction problem in the literature and provide a concept of their efficacy and efficiency.

A straightforward way to model image signals is to characterize its sparsity in a generic domain, e.g., TV [5], DCT [6], and DWT [6]. This category of image models is universally applicable to any natural image, regardless of its texture or structure. However, due to the model's signal-independent nature, its reconstruction performance is far from satisfactory [7,8].

To rectify the problem, Wu et al. [9] propose a model-guided adaptive recovery of compressed sensing (MARX) via a piecewise autoregressive model that adapts to the changing second order statistics of natural images. Other works incorporate knowledge about transform coefficients (statistical dependencies, structure, etc.) into the CS recovery framework, such as Gaussian scale mixtures (GSM) models [10], tree-structured wavelet [11], and collaborative sparsity [12]. There are also works that build an adaptive image dictionary [13–15], based on which coefficient sparsity is enforced as the prior model.

These adaptive methods take different features of various images into account and seek to build an image-dependent model. They generally lead to sparser representation and hence better reconstruction efficacy. However, an arising issue is that they require time-consuming patch-searching or large-matrix inversion operations. Consequently, computation time is evidently increased and algorithm efficiency is tremendously impaired.

2.3 Convolutional Neural Network

Convolutional neural network (CNN) is nowadays becoming more and more popular for its easy training and high performance compared to other deep neural networks. It is designed to take advantage of the 2D structure of an input image (or other 2D input such as a speech signal), featuring shared-weights architecture and translation-invariance characteristics. One benefit of CNNs is that it has fewer parameters than fully connected networks with the same number of hidden units. It has been widely applied in computer vision, natural language processing, etc.

3 Method

Unlike traditional CS image reconstruction methods, we do not explicitly model an image. Rather, we take a mathematical perspective and start from dissecting the optimization problem (Eq. (2)) into two subproblems via ADMM, which is detailed in the first subsection. Then we tackle each subproblem respectively in the following subsections.

3.1 Problem Dissection Based on ADMM

Equation (2) is a constrained minimization problem, and for the sake of convenience, we first rewrite it in an equivalent unconstrained form as follows:

$$\hat{\mathbf{x}} = \arg\min_{\mathbf{x}} f(\mathbf{x}) + \mathbb{1}(\mathbf{x}), \tag{3}$$

where

$$\mathbb{1}(\mathbf{x}) = \begin{cases} 0, & \text{if } \mathbf{y} = \Phi\mathbf{x}, \\ \infty, & \text{otherwise.} \end{cases} \tag{4}$$

For now, neither the specific form of the first term $f(\mathbf{x})$ nor its properties are known, therefore simultaneously optimizing the two terms is inoperable. Resorting to ADMM, which becomes an increasingly popular method owing to its fast convergence and low memory-footprint, we introduce an auxiliary variable $\mathbf{z}$ to decouple the two terms in Eq. (3) and arrive at the following equivalent problem

$$\hat{\mathbf{x}}, \hat{\mathbf{z}} = \arg\min_{\mathbf{x}, \mathbf{z}} f(\mathbf{x}) + \mathbb{1}(\mathbf{z}), \quad \text{s.t. } \mathbf{x} = \mathbf{z}. \tag{5}$$

Then we transform Eq. (5) into three iterative steps via alternating optimization as follows

$$\hat{\mathbf{x}}^{(j+1)} = \arg\min_{\mathbf{x}} f(\mathbf{x}) + \frac{\rho}{2} \left\| \mathbf{x} - \mathbf{z}^{(j)} + \mathbf{b}^{(j)} \right\|_2^2, \tag{6}$$

$$\hat{\mathbf{z}}^{(j+1)} = \arg\min_{\mathbf{z}} \mathbb{1}(\mathbf{z}) + \frac{\rho}{2} \left\| \mathbf{x}^{(j+1)} - \mathbf{z} + \mathbf{b}^{(j)} \right\|_2^2, \tag{7}$$

$$\mathbf{b}^{(j+1)} = \mathbf{b}^{(j)} + \left(\mathbf{x}^{(j+1)} - \mathbf{z}^{(j+1)} \right), \tag{8}$$

where the superscript (j) denotes the j-th iteration and $\mathbf{b}$ is the dual variable. ρ is a positive argument, which will be seen fade out in the following process. We can see that Eq. (8) is a simple update step and straightforward to compute. Equations (6) and (7) are subproblems with respect of $\mathbf{x}$ and $\mathbf{z}$, respectively. We will focus on solving these two problems in the following subsections.

3.2   The x Subproblem: CNN for Image Denoising Problem

Let's observe Eq. (6) more closely. By making $\mathbf{r} = \mathbf{z}^{(j)} - \mathbf{b}^{(j)}$, we rewrite Eq. (6) in the following form

$$\hat{\mathbf{x}}^{(j+1)} = \arg\min_{\mathbf{x}} f(\mathbf{x}) + \frac{\rho}{2} \|\mathbf{x} - \mathbf{r}\|_2^2, \tag{9}$$

which is literally an image denoising model. $\mathbf{r}$ is deemed as a noisy image, $\mathbf{x}$ is the original clean image, $\hat{\mathbf{x}}^{(j+1)}$ is the corresponding de-noised image, and $f(\mathbf{x})$ is a mathematical model that characterizes the image property.

In contrast to explicitly modelling $f(\mathbf{x})$, we use a deep convolutional neural network (CNN) to learn the relationship between the input noisy image and the output de-noised image. Specifically, we adopt the CNN architecture proposed in [4] (any other CNN architecture for image denoising is also applicable), which is illustrated in Fig. 1. The kernal size of all convolutional layers is set to $3 \times 3 \times 64$; the stride size of all layers is set to 1 and no pooling layers are placed in order to keep the image spatial resolution.

A design worth noticing in this network is the output being the image of noise, i.e., the residual between the original clean image and the input noisy image. Therefore, the objective function for training the CNN is to minimize the error between the trained residual and the actual residual, formulated as follows

$$\hat{\Theta} = \arg\min_{\Theta} \frac{1}{2N} \sum_{i}^{N} \|g(\mathbf{r}_i; \Theta) - (\mathbf{x}_i - \mathbf{r}_i)\|_2^2, \tag{10}$$

Noisy Image   Residual Image

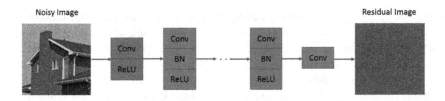

Fig. 1. The architecture of the CNN for image denoising

where $\mathbf{x}_i$ and $\mathbf{r}_i$ are respectively the clean image and the noisy image of the i-th training sample, and $\mathbf{x}_i - \mathbf{r}_i$ represents the actual residual. $g(\mathbf{r}_i; \Theta)$, calculating the trained residual, represents the CNN feed-forward computation (as shown in Fig. 1), $\mathbf{r}_i$ as input and Θ as parameters. Please note that all superscripts are omitted in this subsection for the sake of conciseness.

Equation (10) is solved via a gradient descent method, in which the gradient of all parameters are computed through back propagation. Though computation-intensive, this training process is completely off-line, meaning once it is completed, the only computation for each image-to-process is to go through the feed-forward network merely once. Concretely, using off-the-shelf values of Θ, we generate the de-noised image $\hat{\mathbf{x}}^{(j+1)}$ from the noisy image $\mathbf{r}$ with the following one-step computation

$$\hat{\mathbf{x}}^{(j+1)} = g(\mathbf{r}; \Theta) + \mathbf{r}. \tag{11}$$

Generally, a deep neural network as in Fig. 1 is trained under a specific noise level. At different noise levels, different models are separately trained and different parameter values are obtained. Thus, in our problem, we need to evaluate the noise level of the noisy image $\mathbf{r}$ to choose the best-matched CNN model. The noisy image $\mathbf{r}$ is essentially determined by the CS subrate, the larger the subrate is, the less noisy the image $\mathbf{r}$ will be. We will provide our observation of how the noise level relates to the subrate in the experiment section. Once a suitable noise level is selected, the corresponding well-trained CNN is directly utilized to solve our $\mathbf{x}$ problem, even without any finetuning operation. Actually, this noise level is the only argument that needs to be manually set in our algorithm.

3.3 The z Subproblem: Quadratic Programming

For the $\mathbf{z}$ subproblem in Eq. (7), we first plug Eq. (4) back into it and get the following constrained form

$$\hat{\mathbf{z}}^{(j+1)} = \arg\min_{\mathbf{z}} \frac{\rho}{2} \|\mathbf{z} - \mathbf{u}\|_2^2, \text{ s.t. } \mathbf{y} = \Phi\mathbf{z}, \tag{12}$$

where $\mathbf{u} = \mathbf{x}^{(j+1)} + \mathbf{b}^{(j)}$.

Obviously, this is a convex quadratic programming problem, which can be solved based on the Karush–Kuhn–Tucker (K.K.T.) conditions. Hereby, we arrive at its solution as follows

$$\mathbf{z}^* = \Phi^T \left(\Phi\Phi^T\right)^{-1} (\mathbf{y} - \Phi\mathbf{u}) + \mathbf{u}. \tag{13}$$

Note that $\Phi\Phi^T$ is an invertible matrix owing to the fact that the matrix $\Phi \in \mathbb{R}^{M \times N}, M < N$ is flat. Also note that the inverse operation on $\Phi\Phi^T$ is only calculated once before all the iterative steps of ADMM, given the matrix Φ. In addition, be aware that the argument ρ is cancelled out during derivation and therefore, no arguments need to be manually set anymore in Eq. (13). This happens to be one benefit of formulating CS reconstruction in a constrained way compared to the unconstrained formulation in [13].

4   Experiments

In this section, we present the experimental results to demonstrate the performance of the proposed ACIR. We adopt 12 widely used testing images, which are shown in Fig. 2. We compare ACIR to four representative CS image reconstruction methods in the literature: TV [5], DWT [6], MH [16], GSR [13]. For all methods, the CS measurements are obtained by projecting the original image onto a Gaussian random matrix under various sampling rates, i.e., $0.1, 0.2, 0.3, 0.4$. For memory efficiency, we apply block-based compressive sensing for all the methods, with a block size of 32×32.

Fig. 2. Testing images. From left to right: C. man, House, Peppers, Starfish, Monar., Airplane, Parrot, Lena, Barbara, Boat, Man, Couple. The first seven images are of size 256×256 and the rest are of size 512×512.

For ACIR, there is only one argument to be considered, i.e., the noise level that determines which CNN model to choose for solving the $\mathbf{x}$ problem. Having extensively tested the algorithm performance with CNN models at different noise levels, we find that at a lower sampling rate, the CNN model at a larger noise level leads to better performance; and at a higher sampling rate, the CNN model at a smaller noise level is better. This observation is in line with the intuition that the lower the sampling rate is, the noisier the initial reconstruction should be, which accordingly influences the noisy level of $\mathbf{r}$ in the $\mathbf{x}$ subproblem. Specifically, the optimal noise levels corresponding to the sample rates 0.1, 0.2, 0.3, 0.4 are 25, 15, 15, 10. It is worthwhile to emphasize that compared to methods like SGR, which require such arguments as reconstruction patch size, regularization strength, the weight for ℓ_2 term in ADMM, etc., our algorithm is much easier to operate and human-friendly.

Table 1 shows the PSNR scores of the reconstructed images for all the methods at various subrates. We can see that ACIR evidently outperforms the other methods in most cases and on average. We need to mention that there are two exceptional cases — the testing images 'House' and 'Barbara', where GSR works the best. This is because these two images have rich repetitive patterns to which the non-local searching strategy of GSR is specially geared.

Table 1. The PSNR (dB) results of different CS image reconstruction methods

Subrate	Methods	C. man	House	Peppers	Starfish	Monar.	Airplane	Parrot	Lena	Barbara	Boat	Man	Couple	**Average PSNR**
	TV	22.40	27.90	23.64	22.30	22.7	22.05	21.45	28.07	22.50	25.18	26.4	25.02	24.13
	DWT	21.72	28.07	25.70	23.10	22.50	21.93	20.89	28.08	21.25	25.25	25.96	24.69	24.10
0.1	MH	22.13	30.28	26.00	22.54	23.19	22.15	22.16	29.61	27.31	25.81	26.44	25.55	25.26
	GSR	22.90	**33.75**	28.71	23.60	25.29	22.66	22.90	**30.80**	**30.68**	27.31	27.38	26.87	26.90
	ACIR	**25.02**	32.67	**29.06**	**25.25**	**28.06**	**23.53**	**23.42**	30.65	26.34	**27.60**	**27.51**	**27.37**	**27.21**
	TV	25.15	31.54	28.48	25.15	26.77	25.06	24.60	30.61	23.57	27.92	28.88	27.59	27.11
	DWT	25.56	32.97	29.53	25.93	26.68	25.24	25.52	32.62	23.97	28.45	29.05	27.73	27.77
0.2	MH	25.88	33.84	29.78	25.93	27.10	25.08	25.76	32.95	31.35	29.32	29.35	28.87	28.77
	GSR	26.76	**37.31**	32.43	29.42	30.77	25.88	26.30	34.38	**34.44**	31.29	30.42	30.62	30.84
	ACIR	**28.88**	36.18	**33.94**	**31.92**	**33.87**	27.34	**27.62**	**34.72**	31.00	**31.81**	**31.29**	**31.39**	**31.66**
	TV	27.47	33.76	31.67	27.47	29.94	27.58	26.80	32.54	24.50	29.94	30.71	29.64	29.34
	DWT	27.93	35.21	31.27	27.90	28.88	27.38	27.84	34.66	26.50	30.21	30.67	29.36	29.82
0.3	MH	28.08	35.69	31.35	27.90	29.20	27.10	27.56	34.85	33.60	31.18	31.02	30.73	30.69
	GSR	29.04	**39.26**	35.11	33.00	34.24	28.40	28.76	36.48	**36.66**	33.66	32.76	32.94	33.36
	ACIR	**31.40**	38.06	**35.91**	**35.24**	**37.10**	**30.43**	**30.07**	**36.76**	33.58	**33.84**	**33.61**	**33.80**	**34.15**
	TV	29.51	35.41	34.05	29.61	32.69	29.87	28.73	34.2	25.54	31.74	32.35	31.54	31.27
	DWT	29.81	36.65	32.96	29.62	30.80	29.06	29.65	36.17	28.67	31.63	32.06	30.78	31.49
0.4	MH	29.88	36.65	32.96	29.62	31.13	29.06	29.09	36.41	35.28	32.79	32.48	32.19	32.30
	GSR	31.25	**40.90**	37.02	35.63	36.86	30.93	30.67	38.14	**38.38**	**35.55**	34.83	34.92	35.42
	ACIR	**33.27**	39.84	**37.72**	**37.78**	**39.76**	**32.60**	**31.96**	**38.34**	35.42	35.36	**35.65**	**35.55**	**36.10**

(a) Original image   (b) TV (22.40 dB)   (c) DWT (21.72 dB)

(d) MH (22.13 dB)   (e) GSR (22.90 dB)   (f) ACIR (25.02 dB)

Fig. 3. Visual comparison of the reconstructed 'C. man' by different methods (subrate = 0.1). Corresponding PSNR scores are shown in the brackets.

Table 2. Average execution time for each method

	TV	DWT	MH	GSR	Proposed
Average time (sec)	5.24	7.15	13.03	1015.8	6.75

Figures 3 and 4 demonstrate two of the reconstructed images by these methods at the subrate 0.1 and 0.2, respectively. We can see that at such low subrates,

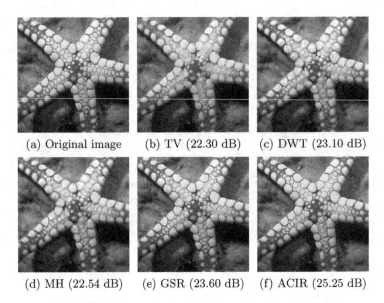

(a) Original image   (b) TV (22.30 dB)   (c) DWT (23.10 dB)

(d) MH (22.54 dB)   (e) GSR (23.60 dB)   (f) ACIR (25.25 dB)

Fig. 4. Visual comparison of the reconstructed 'Starfish' by different methods (subrate = 0.2). Corresponding PSNR scores are shown in the brackets.

ACIR can still reconstruct the object boundaries clearly and even show visible texture details, without obviously noticeable distortion or artifacts. In contrast, other comparative methods lead to distorted information in one way or another.

In Table 2, we list the average running time to reconstruct one image for each method. It is shown that the running time for ACIR is on par with TV and DWT, and much less than the more sophisticated GSR. This comparison clearly verifies the efficiency of ACIR apart from its efficacy.

5 Conclusions

In this paper, we propose to incorporate deep neural network into the CS image reconstruction framework via a mathematical derivation and arrive at a high-efficacy-and-efficiency and argument-economic algorithm. This algorithm does not need any training effort by resorting to off-the-shelf CNN denoising models and takes advantage of efficient GPU computation for running the feed-forward network.

The essence of this work is to make ample use of existing valuable achievement of scholars to save humans from trivial or redundant work. The creativity lies in how to bridge the previous knowledge and the current problem to produce a better outcome. Further thought on this work includes mathematically formulating the relationship between subrate and noise level, automatically determining the optimal CNN model in each iteration, etc.

References

1. Donoho, D.L.: Compressed sensing. IEEE Trans. Inf. Theor. **52**(4), 1289–1306 (2006)
2. LeCun, Y., Bengio, Y., Hinton, G.: Deep learning. Nature **521**(7553), 436–444 (2015)
3. Burger, H.C., Schuler, C.J., Harmeling, S.: Image denoising: can plain neural networks compete with BM3D? In: Proceedings of IEEE Conference on Computer Vision Pattern Recognition, pp. 2392–2399 (2012)
4. Zhang, K., Zuo, W., Chen, Y., Meng, D., Zhang, L.: Beyond a Gaussian denoiser: residual learning of deep CNN for image denoising. IEEE Trans. Image Process. **26**, 3142–3155 (2017)
5. Li, C., Yin, W., Zhang, Y.: Users guide for TVAL3: TV minimization by augmented lagrangian and alternating direction algorithms. CAAM report (2009)
6. Mun, S., Fowler, J.E.: Block compressed sensing of images using directional transforms. In: IEEE International Conference on Image Processing (ICIP), pp. 3021–3024 (2009)
7. Zhao, C., Ma, S., Gao, W.: Image compressive-sensing recovery using structured laplacian sparsity in DCT domain and multi-hypothesis prediction. In: IEEE International Conference on Multimedia and Expo (ICME), pp. 1–6 (2014)
8. Zhao, C., Ma, S., Zhang, J., Xiong, R., Gao, W.: Video compressive sensing reconstruction via reweighted residual sparsity. IEEE Trans. Circuits Syst. Video Technol. **27**, 1182–1195 (2016)
9. Wu, X., Zhang, X., Wang, J.: Model-guided adaptive recovery of compressive sensing. In: Proceedings of IEEE Data Compression Conference, pp. 123–132 (2009)
10. Kim, Y., Nadar, M.S., Bilgin, A.: Compressed sensing using a Gaussian scale mixtures model in wavelet domain. In: Proceedings of IEEE International Conference on Image Processing, pp. 3365–3368 (2010)
11. He, L., Carin, L.: Exploiting structure in wavelet-based Bayesian compressive sensing. IEEE Trans. Signal Process. **57**(9), 3488–3497 (2009)
12. Zhang, J., Zhao, D., Zhao, C., Xiong, R., Ma, S., Gao, W.: Image compressive sensing recovery via collaborative sparsity. IEEE J. Emerg. Selec. Topics Circuits Syst. **2**(3), 380–391 (2012)
13. Zhang, J., Zhao, D., Gao, W.: Group-based sparse representation for image restoration. IEEE Trans. Image Process. **23**(8), 3336–3351 (2014)
14. Zhang, J., Zhao, D., Jiang, F., Gao, W.: Structural group sparse representation for image compressive sensing recovery. In: IEEE Data Compression Conference (DCC), pp. 331–340 (2013)
15. Zhang, J., Zhao, C., Zhao, D., Gao, W.: Image compressive sensing recovery using adaptively learned sparsifying basis via L0 minimization. Sig. Process. **103**, 114–126 (2014)
16. Chen, C., Tramel, E.W., Fowler, J.E.: Compressed-sensing recovery of images and video using multihypothesis predictions. In: Asilomar Conference on Signals, Systems and Computers, pp. 1193–1198 (2011)

Sparsity-Promoting Adaptive Coding with Robust Empirical Mode Decomposition for Image Restoration

Rui Chen$^{(\boxtimes)}$, Huizhu Jia, Xiaodong Xie, and Gao Wen

National Engineering Laboratory for Video Technology,
Peking University, Beijing, China
{rchen,hzjia,xdxie,wgao}@jdl.ac.cn

Abstract. In this paper, a novel data-driven sparse coding framework is proposed to solve image restoration problem based on a robust empirical mode decomposition. This powerful analysis tool for multi-dimensional signals can adaptively decompose images into multiscale oscillating components according to intrinsic modes of data self. This treatment can obtain very effective sparse representation, and meanwhile generates a dictionary at multiple geometric scales and frequency bands. The distribution of sparse coefficients is reliably approximated by generalized Gaussian model. Moreover, a sparse approximation of blur kernel is also obtained as a strong prior. Finally, latent image and blur kernel can be jointly estimated via alternating optimization scheme. The extensive experiments show that our approach can effectively and efficiently recover the sharpness of local structures and suppress undesirable artifacts.

Keywords: AM-FM signal · Empirical mode decomposition
Generalized Gaussian model · Image restoration · Sparse coding

1 Introduction

The image restoration aims at recovering the high-quality clear image from its blurred and noisy measurement [1]. This process can be modeled by a linear operator $\mathcal{A}$ applied to the input degraded image $\mathbf{I}_d$:

$$\mathbf{I}_d = \mathcal{A}\mathbf{I}_0 + n \tag{1}$$

where $\mathbf{I}_0$ is the latent image and n denotes Gaussian noise with variance σ^2. The operator $\mathcal{A}$ is a convolution process of the blur kernel which is determined by the imaging process. The estimates for the latent image and kernel are ill-posed inverse linear problem due to the inadequate constraints. To derive the closed-form solutions, certain prior information of original image and kernel need be introduced to regularize the recovery process [2].

The sparsity-based priors have been playing a very important role in recent developments of image restoration approaches [3, 4]. Most of important information in images are preserved in multi-bands or transform coefficients by using suitable signal analysis tools [5]. Thus, the recovery process for the degraded image is regularized by

© Springer International Publishing AG, part of Springer Nature 2018
B. Zeng et al. (Eds.): PCM 2017, LNCS 10735, pp. 380–389, 2018.
https://doi.org/10.1007/978-3-319-77380-3_36

minimizing energy function that promotes the sparsity of the solutions in transform domain. The effectiveness of the sparsity-based methods is highly dependent on how efficiently the chosen transforms sparsify images of interest [6]. Many types of multiscale decomposition transforms such as the curvelet [7], framelet [8] and other frame wavelets [9–11] have been developed to apply in image restoration tasks. Nevertheless, these techniques fail to optimally self-adjust according to the characteristics of signal itself. To adaptively handle the non-stationary and non-linear signals, Huang et al. [12] introduced empirical mode decomposition (EMD) technique, which can decompose the signal into a collection of intrinsic mode functions (IMFs) without any pre-determined basis function. Essentially, each IMF can be seen as an amplitude modulated (AM)-frequency modulated (FM) oscillatory function in sense of compressive sensing theory [13, 14]. By advantage of the EMD properties, many EMD-based methods have been proposed and developed for image analysis [15–19]. Since sparse coefficients of images are easier to model, statistical priors also have been extensively studied in recent restoration methods [4, 5].

In this work, we propose a robust EMD to construct an adaptive sparse coding framework. In our EMD algorithm, the envelopes are estimated by optimizing a smoothness functional, and the mode mixing in sifting process is resolved with adaptive masking. Due to the fact that this improved EMD is robust to noisy and intermitted signal, natural images are reliably represented. At decomposition stage, the generated AM-FM atoms are used to construct an IMF dictionary. Due to the fact that the EMD is robust to noisy and intermitted signal, natural image can be reliably sparse coding. By characterizing sparse coefficients with generalized Gaussian model (GGM), we can effectively exploit the local dependencies among image structures. The experimental results have shown the superiority of our restoration method.

2 Sparse Representation via Robust EMD

In this section, we specifically design a robust EMD method to overcome some drawbacks of the standard EMD such as the sensitivity to noised data, intermittences and mode mixing [20–22].

2.1 Mean Envelope Construction Using Bilateral Filter

In iterative decomposition procedure, mean envelope is defined as the average of the upper and lower envelopes, which are generated by interpolating extracted local maxima and minima points in the signals [12]. Because main oscillatory patterns of a signal are confined between upper and lower envelopes, computing a good mean envelope is crucial to the success of EMD-type algorithms [21]. All the extrema are identified by comparing all noisy data in segment lines. The extrema extraction is usually to perform using the morphological filter [15]. Due to instabilities to the noise and outliers, standard method is difficult to obtain the mean envelope accurately. This result will cause the deviation of tendency estimation for an AM-FM image and the wrong separation of its components [22]. Our EMD method can alleviate the limitation and extended to apply in image analysis.

The key stage in our EMD procedure is first to smooth fine-scale oscillating components while retaining the IMF information in the image **I**. The bilateral filter is a well-known technique to remove noises and smooth an image while preserving fine features [23]. It is a 2D weighted averaging filter with the closeness smoothing function in terms of spatial distance and the similarity weight function in terms of intensity difference. We adapt this filter to process image data while well balancing between the smoothing mechanism and the preserving capability. Each point in expected envelope **E** is smoothed by an implicit filtering process. The estimated output value $\widehat{\mathbf{E}}[k,j]$ at every position is evaluated by

$$\widehat{\mathbf{E}}[k,j] = \sum_{m=-H}^{H} \sum_{n=-H}^{H} w_{\{m,n\}}[k,j]\mathbf{E}[k-m, j-n] \tag{2}$$

where H dictates the neighboring range between the center pixel (k, j) and its neighbors $\{(k-m, j-n); m, n \neq 0\}$. The weights are computed by

$$w_{\{m,n\}}[k,j] \propto \exp\left(-\frac{\Delta\mathbf{I}[m,n;k,j]^2}{2\sigma_r^2} - \frac{m^2+n^2}{2\sigma_s^2}\right) \tag{3}$$

The function $\Delta\mathbf{I}[m,n;k,j]$ denotes the difference between the intensities of pixel pairs. Considering for the smoothing effect, H is set to be small value. In addition, important parameters of this filter are adaptively tuned rather not pre-determined. The parameters, σ_r and σ_s, are locally adaptive to the noise and image content. In detail, σ_r is set to the same value of patch size, and σ_s is set as the value close to the standard deviation of noise present in the image.

The local extrema are used to detect the oscillations at different scales. By interpolating a set of extremal points $\mathcal{E}$, the maxima and minima envelopes can be constructed. And then the mean envelope is also obtained by averaging them. The correlation and local smoothness constraints are added in objective function. We seek the envelope by optimizing the following functional

$$\arg\min_{\mathbf{E}} \left\{ \|\mathbf{P}_e(\mathbf{E} - \mathbf{I})\|_2^2 + \lambda \left\|\mathbf{E} - \widehat{\mathbf{E}}\right\|_2^2 \right\} \tag{4}$$

where the matrix $\mathbf{P}_e$ depends on the locations of local extrema and it imposes on the mode $\mathbf{E}[k_e, j_e] = \mathbf{I}[k_e, j_e]$ at each extrema $(k_e, j_e) \in \mathcal{E}$. The regularization parameter $\lambda > 0$ is used to control the trade-off between the smoothness and IMF-like mode. The quadratic functional (4) is reduced to solving a sparse linear system. This convex optimization problem has a unique solution:

$$\mathbf{E}^* = [\mathbf{P}_e^T\mathbf{P}_e + \lambda(\mathbf{D} - \mathbf{W})^T(\mathbf{D} - \mathbf{W})]^{-1}\mathbf{P}_e^T\mathbf{P}_e\mathbf{I} \tag{5}$$

Here, **D** is diagonal matrix and its diagonal elements are 1. The matrix **W** has the entries computed by the Eqs. (2) and (3). When its entries are out of the border, we simply set their values to zero.

2.2 Sifting Process Based on Adaptive Masks

The sifting process is to iteratively identify IMFs from the initial image. An IMF must satisfy two conditions: (1) In the whole data set, the number of extreme points (local maxima and minima) and the number of zero-crossing points must be equal to each other or differ by one at most; (2) At any point of the image, the mean value of the envelope defined by local maxima and the envelope defined by the local minima must be equal to zero. If the image contains the intermittencies, the generated i-th IMF h_i will introduce the mode mixing which has the components of different frequencies and cause artifact effects [19]. Based on the sampling theory, we identify the mode mixing in h_i by using the following criteria:

$$0.5\ell_{\min} < \bar{\ell} < 2\ell_{\max} \tag{6}$$

where $\ell_{\min}$ and $\ell_{\max}$ denote the minima and maxima values in the distance set $\mathcal{L}$, respectively. $\bar{\ell}$ is the median value in this set. If this condition is satisfied, it manifests that the mode mixing exists in the candidate IMF h_i^c.

The masking signal technique is adopted to solve the mode mixing problem of an IMF [20]. Based on this technique, a cosine signal is selected as the mask $\mathbf{M}_{cos}$ and then added to input image $\mathbf{I}$, which can prevent lower frequency components included in the candidate IMF. By choosing a masking frequency higher than the median frequency component determined by $\bar{\ell}$, the modulated frequencies can be effectively separated. The mask is formulated as

$$\mathbf{M}_{cos}[k, j] = A \cos \frac{2\pi}{\bar{\ell}} k \, \cos \frac{2\pi}{\bar{\ell}} j \tag{7}$$

where the amplitude A is computed by the average of the maximum and minimum amplitudes of h_i^c. Auxiliary IMFs h_i^+ and h_i^- can be obtained by sifting operation on $\mathbf{I} + \mathbf{M}_{cos}$ and $\mathbf{I} - \mathbf{M}_{cos}$. The IMF h_k is generated by averaging h_i^+ and h_i^-.

2.3 Sparse Representation for Natural Images

Based on the improvements for the EMD method, the steps for the implementation are described in Algorithm 1. By means of robust EMD method, the IMFs can adaptively form a complete and nearly orthogonal basis for 2D signal. The image $\mathbf{I}$ can be decomposed with the following formulation:

$$\mathbf{I}[j, k] = \sum_{i=1}^{Q} h_i[j, k] + \mathbf{R}_{es} \tag{8}$$

where the superscript Q is the total number of 2D IMFs and it represents the scale level for image decomposition. $\mathbf{R}_{es}$ denotes the residue of the image decomposition and is generally a small monotonic or constant component. The IMFs with lower indices contain the faster oscillations presented in the image, whereas IMFs with higher indices contain the slower oscillations. Typically, each IMF can be approximated as the

AM-FM function of form $A_i(j,k)\cos\varphi_i(j,k)$. Thus, the image is sparsely represented by the combination of an overcomplete dictionary **D**:

$$\mathbf{I} = \mathbf{D}\alpha, \quad d_i = A_i(j,k)\cos\varphi_i(j,k) \quad \forall i. \tag{9}$$

where d_i is the i-th atom. The coefficient vector α can essentially affect the reconstruction quality of image structures. In this coding paradigm, the sparsest approximation is adaptively found while preserving multi-scale image features.

Algorithm 1: Robust EMD for image representation

1: **Input** the image $\mathbf{I}_{(i)}[j,k]$ with size of M× N , and set
   $\sigma_r = 3$, $\sigma_s = 100$, $H = 4$, $\lambda = 0.8$, $i = 1$.
2: **Identify** all points of 2D local maxima and all points of 2D
   local minima of 3×3 image patches.
3: **Smooth** the estimated envelope by using the Eq. (3) to com
   pute the weights at every point.
4: **Create** the maxima envelope $E_{\max}$ and the minima envelope
   $E_{\min}$ by solving the Eq. (5).
5: **Compute** the mean envelope $\overline{E}_{(i)} = (E_{\max} + E_{\min})/2$.
6: **Extract** the candidate IMF function $h_i^c = I_{(i)} - \overline{E}_{(i)}$.
7: **Repeat** the steps 3 to 6 until it can satisfy two IMF conditions,
   and then set IMF $h_i = h_i^c$.
8: **Detect** mode-mixing problem for h_i using the Eq. (6). If exists,
   the masking signal $\mathbf{M}_{cos}$ is constructed using the Eq. (7). Then
   compute h_i^+ and h_i^- to update the obtained IMF as
   $h_i = (h_i^+ + h_i^-)/2$.
9: **Estimate** the residual component $\mathbf{R}_{es} = \mathbf{I}_{(i)} - h_i$; If it does not
   contain any more points, the EMD process is stopped; Otherwise,
   update $i = i + 1$ and $\mathbf{I}_{(i)} = \mathbf{R}_{es}$, and then go to step 2.
10: **Output**: the final IMFs $\{h_i\}$ and the residue $\mathbf{R}_{es}$.

---

3   Proposed Restoration Algorithm

In our framework, unknown kernel function and original image can be estimated simultaneously. Different from the simple use of nonnegative and normalization constraints, the kernel is regularized through good sparsity patterns. In order to obtain an effective regularizer, the sparse coefficients of the image need be further modeled based on the statistical distributions.

3.1   Distribution Modeling of Sparse Coefficients

If the sparse coefficients of the expected image are directly constrained in a regularization term, it may not be accurate. The sparse representations of natural images are usually regarded as the heavy-tailed densities. Following the work in sparse coding [4], the distribution of coefficients is fit by general exponential family distributions. Here, GGM is used as a fitting model and its probability density is defined as

$$P(x; \beta) = \frac{1}{2\Gamma(1/\beta + 1)} \exp(-|x|^{\beta}) \tag{10}$$

where Γ is the gamma function, and β is the shape parameter which controls the overall shape of the distribution. The sparse coefficients are centralized and normalized by using its mean value and standard deviation. To find the shape parameter that can best fit the distribution of coefficients, we employ Kullback-Leibler (KL) divergence to measure fitting errors of GGM. The optimal β falls near 1.1. For the convenience of computation, β is set as 1.

3.2 Restoration Formulation

To overcome inherent ill-posedness in Eq. (1), two sparsity priors are derived and added as the regularization terms. Based on the robust EMD, blur function $\mathcal{A}$ is represented by the dictionary $\mathbf{B}$ and the coefficient vector θ; true sharp image $\mathbf{I}_0$ is represented by the formulation in Eq. (9). The L_1-norms of θ and α put the more weights on small coefficients and the less weights on large coefficients. By using the analysis-based regularizers, the energy function has the following formulation:

$$E(\alpha, \theta) = \frac{1}{2} \|\mathbf{I}_d - \mathcal{A}\mathbf{I}_0\|_2^2 + \lambda_1 \|\theta\|_1 + \lambda_2 \sum_{i=1}^{N} \left\| \frac{\alpha_i - \mu_i}{\sigma_i^2} \right\|_1 \tag{11}$$

where λ_1 and λ_2 are regularization parameters. The third term favors the energy mostly concentrated in a few large coefficients, which conform to sparsity property of clear image. The expectation μ_i is estimated as the median value of the coefficients. The stand deviation σi is estimated by using GGM for the observed image.

By globally minimizing the energy function in (11), the meaningful solutions to unknown $\mathcal{A}$ and $\mathbf{I}_0$ can be reliably found. This optimization procedure is performed by alternately iterating until convergence. The initial solution for $\mathbf{I}_0$ can be simply chosen as $\mathbf{I}_d$. While fixing $\mathcal{A}$, α is updated by solving the following subproblem:

$$\hat{\alpha} = \arg \min_{\alpha} \frac{1}{2} \|\mathbf{I}_d - \mathcal{A}\mathbf{D}\alpha\|_2^2 + \lambda_2 \sum_{i=1}^{N} \left\| \frac{\alpha_i - \mu_i}{\sigma_i^2} \right\|_1 \tag{12}$$

Since the most blurring operators can be modeled by 2D Gaussian function, the initial kernel function is selected as a normalized Gaussian template for a correct start [24]. While holding $\mathbf{I}_0$ fixed, the estimate of $\mathcal{A}$ is solved by updating the following form:

$$\hat{\theta} = \arg \min_{\theta} \frac{1}{2} \|\mathbf{I}_d - \mathbf{B}\theta\mathbf{I}_0\|_2^2 + \lambda_1 \|\theta\|_1 \tag{13}$$

Herein, the detailed numerical scheme for (12) and (13) solver adopts the split Bregman iteration method proposed in [8]. By solving two subproblems to estimate α and θ, the clean and sharp image can be reconstructed.

4   Experimental Results

In this section, we conduct a series of experiments to illustrate the performance of our approach and compare it with three state-of-the-art methods including FrameDB [8], HLSP [11] and MultiVB [24]. All experiments were carried out using a workstation with Intel CORE i7 CPU and 64 GB memory, and our algorithm was implemented in Matlab 2010. In our EMD procedure, σ_r is equal to the standard variance σ of Gaussian noise, and σ_s is set to 2. λ_1 can affect estimated accuracy of the kernel and is empirically set to 0.01; λ_2 plays the role of reducing the possible artifacts and suppressing the noise, and is set to 0.12 uniformly for all experiments. The maximum iteration threshold is set to 200 when solving for numerical solutions.

To evaluate the restoration capability for various blurs, a standard test image is degraded by motion-blur kernel with the length 20 pixels and the orientation 40°. The blurred image is further corrupted by additive white Gaussian noise with low level ($\sigma = 3$). It can be observed from Fig. 1 that our restoration approach significantly outperforms other three methods with the better visual quality and less artifacts. Moreover, the estimated kernel is more accurate in our result, by which more sharp and clear edges or textures can be recovered. One explanation for the deblurring results is that our sparse coding paradigm is very effective and adaptive for natural edges or textures by using the robust EMD. In similar way, this method can be adopted to handle the defocus blur and Gaussian blur.

(a) Ground truth   (b) Degraded image   (c) FrameDB

(d) HLSP   (e) MultiVB   (f) Proposed

Fig. 1. Restoration results for image *Cameraman*

The robustness of our restoration methods is evaluated on the noisy and blurry image. The test image in Fig. 2(a) is taken from Zhong's dataset [25]. The degraded image in Fig. 2(b) is blurred using the blur kernel in Levin's dataset. Then the noise with high level ($\sigma = 10$) is added into the image. In this situation, the heavy noise can degrade the quality of blur kernel estimation dramatically. As shown in Fig. 2, the proposed method has recovered many details while other methods have slightly sharper than input image. The results suggest that the sparsity constraint modeled by AM-FM signals is a stronger prior for blur kernel. It also can be seen from Fig. 2 that the denoising performance of our method is comparable to other methods because GGM is suitable for approximating the coefficient distribution. We also evaluate the results quantitatively by computing the Peak Signal-to-Noise Ratio (PSNR). From results in Table 1, our method has obtained the highest PSNRs on several typical datasets. The comparison shows our estimated blur kernels are closer to the ground truth. All the parameters in the experiments are determined by the trial-and-error method and their values are the same for natural degraded images. The average computational time of FrameDB, HLSP, MultiVB and our method are 131 s, 98 s, 278 s and 204 s.

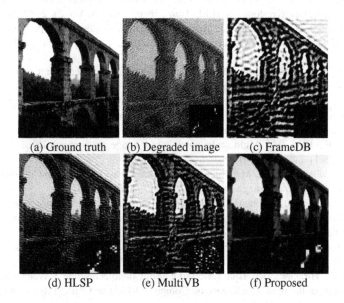

(a) Ground truth	(b) Degraded image	(c) FrameDB
(d) HLSP	(e) MultiVB	(f) Proposed

Fig. 2. Restoration results for image *Aque*

Table 1. The comparisons of PSNR (dB)

Image set	DS-MAP	FrameDB	HLSP	Proposed
Cameraman (326 × 340)	30.81	31.23	33.69	**34.35**
Aque (360 × 270)	27.19	25.93	29.26	**31.06**
Levin's (255 × 255)	28.74	29.11	31.55	**32.64**
Zhong's (350 × 256)	27.37	26.92	28.89	**30.27**

5 Conclusions

In this paper, we proposed a new multi-scale decomposition method named robust EMD and explored its applications on image restoration problem. Through this fully-adaptive data-driven analysis tool, images are optimally represented and sparsely coded. Then two sparsity priors are introduced to capture the spatial, scale and directional characteristics of images. In addition, to accurately characterize the prior information, GGM is used to model the distribution of coefficients. The latent sharp image and blur kernel can be obtained by minimizing derived energy function. Extensive experimental results have shown that our algorithm can both produce clear restoration images and suppress undesirable artifacts more effectively than other competing approaches. The performance improvements are mainly attributed to the better preservation and estimate of edge sharpness in the restored images.

References

1. Figueiredo, M., Bioucas-Dias, J., Nowak, R.: Majorization-minimization algorithms for wavelet-based image restoration. IEEE Trans. Image Process. **16**(12), 2980–2991 (2007)
2. Dong, W., Shi, G., Ma, Y., Li, X.: Image restoration via simultaneous sparse coding: where structured sparsity meets Gaussian scale mixture. Int. J. Comput. Vis. **114**(2), 217–232 (2015)
3. Elad, M., Figueiredo, M., Ma, Y.: On the role of sparse and redundant representations in image processing. Proc. IEEE **98**, 972–982 (2010)
4. Levin, A., Weiss, Y., Durand, F., Freeman, T.: Efficient marginal likelihood optimization in blind deconvolution. In: Proceedings of the IEEE Conference on Computer Vision and Pattern Recognition (CVPR), pp. 2657–2664 (2011)
5. Papyan, V., Elad, M.: Multi-scale patch-based image restoration. IEEE Trans. Image Process. **25**(1), 249–261 (2016)
6. Ram, I., Cohen, I., Elad, M.: Patch-ordering-based wavelet frame and its use in inverse problems. IEEE Trans. Image Process. **23**(7), 2779–2792 (2014)
7. Cai, J., Ji, H., Liu, C., Shen, Z.: High-quality curvelet-based motion deblurring from an image pair. In: Proceedings of the IEEE Conference on Computer Vision and Pattern Recognition (CVPR), pp. 1566–1573 (2009)
8. Cai, J., Ji, H., Liu, C., Shen, Z.: Framelet-based blind motion deblurring from a single image. IEEE Trans. Image Process. **21**(2), 562–572 (2012)
9. Zhang, Y., Hirakawa, K.: Blur processing using double discrete wavelet transform. In: Proceedings of the IEEE Conference on Computer Vision and Pattern Recognition (CVPR), pp. 1091–1098 (2013)
10. Quan, Y., Ji, H., Shen, Z.: Data-driven multi-scale non-local wavelet frame construction and image recovery. J. Sci. Comput. **63**(2), 307–329 (2015)
11. Chen, R., Jia, Z., Xie, X., Gao, W.: A structure-preserving image restoration method with high-level ensemble constraints. In: Proceedings of the IEEE Conference on Visual Communications and Image Processing (VCIP), pp. 1–4 (2016)
12. Huang, N., Shen, Z., Long, S., et al.: The empirical model decomposition and Hilbert spectrum for nonlinear and nonstationary time series analysis. Proc. R. Soc. A **454**(1971), 903–995 (1998)

13. Hou, T., Shi, Z.: Data-driven time-frequency analysis. Appl. Comput. Harmon. Anal. **35**(2), 284–308 (2013)
14. Pattichis, M., Bovik, A.: Analyzing image structure by multidimensional frequency modulation. IEEE Trans. Patt. Anal. Mach. Intell. **29**(5), 753–766 (2007)
15. Wu, Z., Huang, N., Chen, X.: The multi-dimensional ensemble empirical mode decomposition method. Adv. Adapt. Data Anal. **1**(3), 339–372 (2009)
16. Bhuiyan, S., Atton-Okine, N., Barner, K., Ayenu-Prah, A., Adhami, R.: Bidimensional empirical mode decomposition using various interpolation techniques. Adv. Adapt. Data Anal. **1**(2), 309–338 (2009)
17. Daubechies, I., Lu, J., Wu, H.: Synchrosqueezed wavelet transforms: an empirical mode decomposition-like tool. Appl. Comput. Harmon. Anal. **30**(2), 243–261 (2011)
18. Diop, E., Alexandre, R., Moisan, L.: Intrinsic nonlinear multiscale image decomposition: a 2D empirical mode decomposition-like tool. Comput. Vis. Image Und. **116**(1), 102–119 (2012)
19. Gilles, J., Tran, G., Osher, S.: 2D empirical transform. wavelets, ridgelets, and curvelets revisited. SIAM J. Imaging Sci. **7**(1), 157–186 (2014)
20. Hu, X., Peng, S., Hwang, W.: EMD revisited: a new understanding of the envelope and resolving the mode-mixing problem in AM-FM signals. IEEE Trans. Signal Process. **60**(3), 1075–1086 (2012)
21. Park, M., Kim, D., Oh, H.: Quantile-based empirical mode decomposition: an efficient way to decompose noisy signals. IEEE Trans. Instrum. Meas. **64**(7), 1802–1813 (2015)
22. Oberlin, T., Meignen, S., Perrier, V.: An alternative formulation for the empirical mode decomposition. IEEE Trans. Signal Process. **60**(5), 2236–2246 (2012)
23. Subr, K., Soler, C., Durand, F.: Edge-preserving multiscale image decomposition based on local extrema. ACM Trans. Graph. **28**(5), 1472–1479 (2009)
24. Sonogashira, M., Funatomi, T., Liyama, M., Minoh, M.: Variational Bayesian approach to multiframe image restoration. IEEE Trans. Image Process. **26**(5), 2163–2178 (2017)
25. Zhong, L., Cho, S., Metaxas, D., Paris, S., Wang, J.: Handling noise in single image deblurring using directional filters. In: Proceedings of the IEEE Conference on Computer Vision and Pattern Recognition (CVPR), pp. 612–619 (2013)

A Splicing Interpolation Method for Head-Related Transfer Function

Chunling Ai[1,2], Xiaochen Wang[1,2,3]($\boxtimes$), Yafei Wu[1,2,3], and Cheng Yang[1,4]

[1] National Engineering Research Center for Multimedia Software,
School of Computer Science, Wuhan University, Wuhan, China
chunling@whu.edu.cn, clowang@163.com, yafee_wu@163.com,
yangcheng41506@126.com
[2] Hubei Key Laboratory of Multimedia and Network Communication Engineering,
Wuhan University, Wuhan, China
[3] Research Institute of Wuhan University in Shenzhen, Shenzhen, China
[4] School of Physics and Electronic Science,
Guizhou Normal University, Guiyang 550001, China

Abstract. We proposed a new head-related transfer function (HRTF) interpolation method based on splicing. The sound spreads from sound source to listener's ears, the wave of head-related impulse response (HRIR) clearly indicates time delay which can be symbolized by the sample number of the first obvious peak and the signal filtered by the diffraction and reflection properties of the torso, head, and pinna. Based on this feature and the importance of the time delay in interpolation, we split the measured HRIR into three parts according to the first obvious peak of the wave and the length of the useful signal. First, we used radial basis function neural network to construct regression forecast models using spatial parameters (i.e., azimuth, elevation, and distance) and the HRIRs sample number of the first obvious peak. Then, we used the tetrahedral interpolation with barycentric weights to calculate the second part of the HRIR. Finally, we spliced the forecast information and the useful signal in terms of the sample number of the first obvious peak. For an unknown position in three-dimensional space of near-field, we interpolated its HRIR by the proposed method. The Signal-to-Deviation ratio (SDR) increased 5 dB compared with the tetrahedron interpolation in the time domain.

Keywords: HRTF interpolation · RBF neural network
Splicing interpolation · Tetrahedron interpolation

The research was supported by National High Technology Research and Development Program of China (863 Program) (No. 2015AA016306); Hubei Province Technological Innovation Major Project (No. 2016AAA015); National Nature Science Foundation of China (No. 61231015, 61671335, 61662010).

© Springer International Publishing AG, part of Springer Nature 2018
B. Zeng et al. (Eds.): PCM 2017, LNCS 10735, pp. 390–399, 2018.
https://doi.org/10.1007/978-3-319-77380-3_37

1 Introduction

A head-related impulse response (HRIR) is a measurement of sound localization, it records the transfer of the sound from a source to the listener's ears in space [1,2]. It differs due to the space parameters (i.e., azimuth, elevation, and distance) and the listener's anthropometry parameters [1,2]. HRTFs (the Fourier transform of the HRIR) are a function of the sound source's azimuth, elevation and distance with respect to the listener's head. For the localization of sound in near-field (the region within 1 m away from the center of the head) virtual auditory space, the interaural time difference (ITD) and the interaural level difference (ILD) can help listener deal with lateral localizing problems, the HRTFs deal with the problem complementally, especially in the median plane [2,3].

With the development of the 3D audio, the HRTF has been active among researchers. In the virtual auditory space, the sound revealed in the headphones can be spatially positioned by filtering its sound signal with a measured HRIR [2,3]. To get a spatially located virtual sound, the HRIR of the position is prerequisite. Although there are several HRTF databases by measurement (i.e., the CIPIC HRTF database, the PKU&IOA HRTF database [1] and the MIT HRTF database and so on) available, the resolutions of these HRTF databases are not high enough. On the one hand, the positions in the databases measured with at best 5° spatial resolution cannot cover the whole sphere, because of the equipment size and the measurement accuracy. This can be problematic when the sound source in the right of the listener's head, because humans have a good perception at there with as low as 0.97° accuracy [4,5]. The other hand, the measurement process requires much time and effort. If HRIR measurement is not available for the desired sourced position, interpolation can be used to obtain an HRIR estimate with HRIRs measured nearby.

For the HRTF interpolation technology, it can be classified into two categories. One is the most straightforward interpolation methods estimating an HRTF at an unknown position combining nearby measured HRTFs with weights [6–8]. Most linear combinations of these methods didn't take the time delay of the wave into account. The other is novel interpolation means calculating the data from low-order representations of all the HRTFs got by dimensionality reduction technique like Isomap [8], locally linear embedding (LLE) [9], principal component analysis (PCA) [10]. But, these data dimension reduction processes always done in frequency domain, could not focus on the time delay of the wave in time domain. Actually, scholars have noticed this problem, and pointed that the time delay difference should be eliminated before interpolation [6,11,12]. One method is aligning HRTFs based on phase [11] or correlation [6], due to the phase's periodicity and the relevant standards of the correlation, the result is not good enough. The other is detecting the time delay difference [12], but as the time delay difference is microsecond level, it is hard to detect. We change the mind of eliminating the time delay difference, keep it through the sample number of the first obvious peak in the HRIR wave, and forecast it before interpolation in the time domain [6,12].

Here, a new HRIR interpolation method based on splicing called splicing interpolation is proposed. In order to test the feasibility in 3D space, we select the PKU&IOA HRTF database which has measured different distances from 20 cm to 160 cm, and the total measurement locations are 6344, the used impulse signal is about 0.5 ms [1]. The HRIR data of a position can be divided into three parts, the initial time delay, the response that lasts for 2 ms since the arrival of direct pulse as depict in Fig. 2 and the rest of the weak signal due to reflection, diffraction or the recording of the equipment. In the near-field virtual acoustic space, for an unknown HRIR of a point, we (i) forecast the sample number of the first obvious peak with the radial basis function (RBF) neural network using some measured HRIRs, (ii) calculate the response that lasts for 2 ms with tetrahedron interpolation in the time domain using some training data, (iii) combine the time delay to the response. The contribution of this article lie in the splicing of the HRIR and predicting the time delay which is symbolized by the sample number of the first obvious peak before interpolation. The performance of the proposed method is shown in Sect. 3.

2   Proposed Method

In this section, the proposed method is illuminated carefully. The flow chart of the method is shown in Fig. 1.

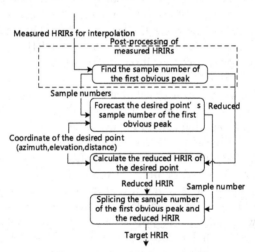

Fig. 1. The flow chart of the proposed method.

2.1   Post-processing of HRIRs

For the measurement of the HRIR, different impulses and different record equipment can choose different sample rate and sample time. We use the sample number of the first obvious peak to symbolize the initial time delay, for the sound firstly strikes the listener with the biggest wave. Once the initial time delay was symbolized, the samples before it should be removed.

As the previous statement, the HRIR can be truncated into 128 points, corresponding to a duration of 2 ms given a sample rate of 65536 Hz [1] in the PKU&IOA HRTF database. The specific truncated signal is determined as follows. First, the sample number of the first obvious peak in the recorded signal HRIR(θ, φ, γ) is found and taken as the reference sample point; then the 5th sample point before the reference point is taken as the start point, and the 122th sample point after the reference point is taken as the end point. The post-processing HRIR(θ, φ, γ) is constructed from the start point to the end point like Fig. 2.

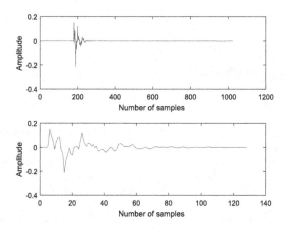

Fig. 2. Measured HRIR (top) and its post-processing HRIR (bottom) at position $(0°, -10°, 100\,\mathrm{cm})$.

We can calculate the power of the truncated signal by

$$power = \sum_{i=1}^{N} HRIR(i). \tag{1}$$

in which N = 128 is the number of samples, and HRIR(i) is the ith sample of the post-processing HRIR for a measured position. The power of the post-processing HRIR accounts averagely for 99.34% of the power of the measured left HRIR (N = 1024), and 99.50% of the right HRIR (N = 1024).

2.2 Forecast with RBF Neural Network

Actually, the sample number of the first obvious peak in the HRIR which indicates the initial time delay is closely related to the spatial parameters (i.e., azimuth, elevation, and distance), as shown in Fig. 3(a). We noticed the data, analyzed it with the transfer distance (see Fig. 3(b)), and imaged the relationship between the sample number of the first obvious peak and the spatial parameters.

The RBF neural network is always used to find the mapping relation of two sets of data. For actual use, the RBF neural network has a fast convergence speed and nonlinear fitting ability, and compared with BP neural network, there is no local minimum problem. So, we trained the RBF neural network with the spatial parameters (input layer) and the sample numbers of the first obvious peak (output layer). There are newrb, newrbe and newgrnn in MATLAB. After the comparison in experiments, we found that newgrnn has a shorter time for training and smaller prediction error.

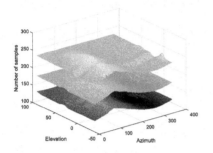

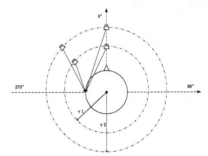

(a) The mesh of the first obvious peak sample number of the left HRIR$(\theta, \varphi, \gamma)$, $(\gamma=75\text{cm})$ and $(\gamma=100\text{cm})$ and $(\gamma=130\text{cm})$ from PKU&IOA HRTF database.

(b) Distance from source to left ear. When the source $(\theta, \varphi, \gamma)$ is at the position that γ is smaller, as well as θ is near 270°, and φ is near 0°, the distance is much shorter.

Fig. 3. The sample number of the first obvious peak in the HRIR is closely related to the spatial parameters (i.e., azimuth, elevation, and distance).

To verify the performance of the RBF neural network, the aligning method based on correlation (AMBC) method [6] are experimented with the same testing data. And the result of the comparison is shown in Fig. 4.

2.3   Calculate with Tetrahedron Interpolation

We have reduced the HRIR of 1024 points into 128 points, and the power maintains about 99% of the whole signal. For the reduced 128 points post-processing HRIR, we use the tetrahedron interpolation to calculate the unknown HRIR. In the PKU&IOA HRTF database, the interval of different elevation angle is diverse due to the characteristics of a sphere. That is shown in the Table 1. The linear interpolation and the bilinear interpolation are depending on the related spatial position relationship of the desired point, and the interpolation precision is limited to this relationship [6]. So, they cannot be used advantageously in three-dimension space interpolation.

The tetrahedron interpolation uses Delaunay triangulation to generate a tetrahedron mesh of a set of measured points. The Delaunay triangulations maximize the minimum angle of all the angles of the triangles in the triangulation.

Table 1. The measurement interval of different elevations in the PKU&IOA HRTF database.

Elevation:°	Interval of Azimuth:°
$-40, -30, \cdots, 40, 50$	5
60	10
70	15
80	30
90	360

Any point in the measurement grid is contained by exactly one tetrahedron, except if the point lies on a vertex, edge, or facet. Theoretically, the tetrahedron interpolation is a flexible form of the linear interpolation and trigonometric interpolation. After a tetrahedron mesh of the set of measured points were generated by Delaunay triangulation, an unknown point $X(\theta, \varphi, \gamma)$ can be obtained by interpolating the vertices of the tetrahedron containing X. If the point X within the tetrahedron, that is, the HRIR of point X can be represented as a linear combination of the vertices $A(\theta_1, \varphi_1, \gamma_1)$, $B(\theta_2, \varphi_2, \gamma_2)$, $C(\theta_3, \varphi_3, \gamma_3)$ and $D(\theta_4, \varphi_4, \gamma_4)$ like this:

$$HRIR(\theta, \varphi, \gamma) = \alpha_1 * HRIR(\theta_1, \varphi_1, \gamma_1) + \alpha_2 * HRIR(\theta_2, \varphi_2, \gamma_2)$$
$$+\alpha_3 * HRIR(\theta_3, \varphi_3, \gamma_3) + \alpha_4 * HRIR(\theta_4, \varphi_4, \gamma_4). \quad (2)$$

Where the α_i is the scalar weight calculated by the way proposed by Hannes Gamper in [7]. With the additional constraint.

$$\sum_{i=1}^{4} \alpha_i = 1. \quad (3)$$

There are four sorts regarding to the position of the point X,

  (i) the point X is the vertex of the tetrahedron, there is no need to interpolate;
 (ii) the point X is on the edge of the tetrahedron, it is equivalent to the linear interpolation of one choice;
(iii) the point X is on the surface of the tetrahedron, it is like the trigonometric interpolation;
(iv) the point X is inside the tetrahedron;

We use the tetrahedron interpolation in the time domain to obtain the unknown 128 samples HRIR of the position $(\theta, \varphi, \gamma)$. In the Hannes experiment [7], the HRIR is transformed into HRTF, and all operations are based on HRTFs, but they neglected the time delay difference between HRTFs, even the HRTF without aligning the time delay has the same magnitude spectrum, the phase spectrum can be very different. So, the HRIR interpolation can retain more information. The linear combination is more flexible with the tetrahedron interpolation in three dimension space.

2.4   Splicing the HRIR

After we use the RBF neural network to simulate the relationship between the spatial parameters (i.e., azimuth, elevation, and distance) and the sample number of the first obvious peak of the HRIR. For a desired position $(\theta, \varphi, \gamma)$, we can forecast its first obvious peak sample number of the left wave under the sample rate of 65536 Hz, which represents the sound transferring from the sound source to the left ear canal. And then calculate the 128 samples signal by the linear combination with different weights of the vertex of the tetrahedron. We splice the HRIR of the desired position by moving the 128 samples to the right sample number indicated the initial time delay.

3   Evaluation

In this section, we carry out two experiments to verify the performance of our work. First experiment verifies the accuracy of finding the sample number of the first obvious peak by the forecast with RBF neural network, compared with the AMBC method [6], which combined the linear interpolation and the bilinear interpolation.

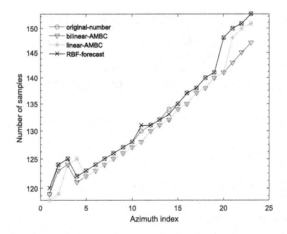

Fig. 4. The sample number of the first obvious peak of HRIR where θ from 305° to 55°, $\varphi = 0°$ and $\gamma = 75$ cm got from two methods.

And the second experiment proves the tetrahedron interpolation with the right initial time delay can have a good performance in three dimension space. For one location, there are two HRIRs for the right and left ear, and for all the experiments, we just use the left HRIR.

The first experiment is carried out to verify the effectiveness of the forecast with RBF neural network, for the convenience of the comparison with the AMBC method, the chosen test data to be experienced is the data mentioned in [6].

From the comparison diagram Fig. 4, the forecast with the RBF neural network under the training data nearly 100% (remove the test data only) of the database and the spread of radial basis functions is about 0.001, we get better performance than the AMBC method with linear interpolation or the bilinear interpolation. The average deviation of the AMBC method with linear interpolation is 1.783, and the bilinear interpolation is about 2.087, while the forecast answer is almost right.

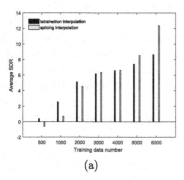
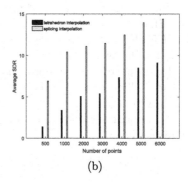

(a)   (b)

Fig. 5. The average SDR as a function of the different number of points for interpolation, (a) forecast with the same points (compared with tetrahedron interpolation) in splicing interpolation; (b) forecast with nearly 100% (remove the test data only) of the database in splicing interpolation.

Now that we have forecasted the initial time delay for the desired position with a satisfactory accuracy rate, the interpolation can move on. As mentioned in the Sect. 2.3, for the desired position, to get its own HRIR, we use the measured position to build a tetrahedron mesh, search the tetrahedron which the desired position belongs to, judge the relative position with the tetrahedron, calculate the weights with the points, finally, get a linear combination of the chosen positions post-processing HRIRs. Unlike the linear interpolation or the bilinear interpolation, the tetrahedron interpolation can get more flexibility for a linear combination within a tetrahedron. In the experiment, we choosed 100 desired points as the test data randomly from the PKU&IOA HRTF database to interpolate with two methods, one is splicing interpolation, the other is tetrahedron interpolation in the time domain. There were two training data sets for the forecast in splicing interpolation, one was the same data set in tetrahedron interpolation, two was nearly 100% (remove the test data only) of the database. The data set of the hetrahedron interpolation was 500, 1000, ···, 6000 in the database. Then spliced the HRIR based on the forecast answer. We use the parameter Signal-to-Deviation ratio (SDR) to evaluate the accuracy of the proposed interpolation method. The SDR can be derived by:

$$SDR = 10 * lg \frac{\sum\limits_{n=1}^{N}[h_r(n)]^2}{\sum\limits_{n=1}^{N}[h_r(n) - h_i(n)]^2}. \tag{4}$$

Where N = 1024, for the proposed method, $h_r(n)$ is the measured HRIR for the unknown position, while $h_i(n)$ is the splicing interpolation or tetrahedron interpolation result. With two data set in the forecast, the answer can be convincing in Fig. 5. As the randomness of the test and training data, from the average SDR shown in Fig. 5, we can say that the method we proposed increases the SDR 5 dB on average with the forecast error under 1. There is a intuitive example for the two interpolation method, like Fig. 6. We can say the splicing interpolation have a better performance. But when the training data is below 30% of the whole measured data, we may get a worse answer than the tetrahedron interpolation on average. This limits the condition of the method we proposed, for training data, the data size is required to greater than 30% of the whole measured data.

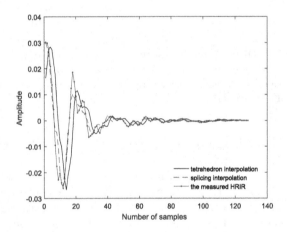

Fig. 6. The measured HRIR ($80°$, $-10°$, $100°$) and the part of interpolated HRIR by the splicing interpolation and tetrahedron interpolation. The SDR increased 8.9 dB with our method.

4   Conclusion

The method we proposed emphasized the initial time delay in the HRIR, and symbolized it with the first obvious peak sample number. Unlike the methods limited by the space position relationship, this framework for three-dimension space at various distance was proposed and worked well. An objective evaluation shows the good performance between the interpolated and the measured HRIRs. Compared with tetrahedron interpolation, this splicing interpolation did better in the time domain as long as the training data number was higher than 30% of the whole data. This interpolation pays much attention to the integrity of the information, and it is important to the further research in HRTF personalization and the perception of 3D audio.

References

1. Qu, T., Xiao, Z., Gong, M., et al.: Distance-dependent head-related transfer functions measured with high spatial resolution using a spark gap. IEEE Trans. Audio Speech Lang. Process. **17**(6), 1124–1132 (2009)
2. Begault, D.R.: 3-D Sound for Virtual Reality and Multimedia. Academic Press Professional Inc., San Diego (1994)
3. Sodnik, J., Sušnik, R., Štular, M., et al.: Spatial sound resolution of an interpolated HRIR library. Appl. Acoust. **66**(11), 1219–1234 (2005)
4. Perrott, D.R., Saberi, K.: Minimum audible angle thresholds for sources varying in both elevation and azimuth. J. Acoust. Soc. Am. **87**(4), 1728–1731 (1990)
5. Mills, A.W.: On the minimum audible angle. J. Acoust. Soc. Am. **30**(4), 237–246 (1958)
6. Wu, T., Hu, R., Wang, X., Gao, L., Ke, S.: Head related transfer function interpolation based on aligning operation. In: Chen, E., Gong, Y., Tie, Y. (eds.) PCM 2016. LNCS, vol. 9916, pp. 418–427. Springer, Cham (2016). https://doi.org/10.1007/978-3-319-48890-5_41
7. Gamper, H.: Head-related transfer function interpolation in azimuth, elevation, and distance. J. Acoust. Soc. Am. **134**(6), EL547 (2013)
8. Grijalva, F., Martini, L.C., Florencio, D., et al.: Interpolation of head-related transfer functions using manifold learning. IEEE Sig. Process. Lett. **24**(2), 221–225 (2017)
9. Duraiswami, R., Raykar, V.C.: The manifolds of spatial hearing. In: Proceedings of the IEEE International Conference on Acoustics, Speech, and Signal Processing (ICASSP 2005), vol. 3, pp. iii/285–iii/288. IEEE (2005)
10. Wang, L., Yin, F., Chen, Z.: Head-related transfer function interpolation through multivariate polynomial fitting of principal component weights. Acoust. Sci. Technol. **30**(6), 395–403 (2009)
11. Kulkarni, A., Isabelle, S.K., Colburn, H.S.: On the minimum-phase approximation of head-related transfer functions. In: IEEE ASSP Workshop on Applications of Signal Processing to Audio and Acoustics, pp. 84–87. IEEE (1995)
12. Matsumoto, M., Yamanaka, S., Toyama, M., et al.: Effect of arrival time correction on the accuracy of binaural impulse response interpolation-interpolation methods of binaural response. J. Audio Eng. Soc. **52**(1/2), 56–61 (2004)

Structured Convolutional Compressed Sensing Based on Deterministic Subsamplers

Shu Wang[1](✉), Zhongyuan Wang[2,3], and Yimin Luo[4]

[1] Department of Electrical Engineering, Imperial College London, London, UK
shu.wang15@imperial.ac.uk
[2] Computer School of Wuhan University, Wuhan, China
[3] Research Institute of Wuhan University in Shenzhen, Wuhan, China
[4] School of Wuhan University, Remote Sensing Information Engineering, Wuhan, China

Abstract. As a novel method to process sparse signals, compressed sensing (CS) attracts huge attention in recent years. The sensing matrix in traditional CS is completely Gaussian random, resulting in high complexity and expensive implementation cost. To solve the problem of randomness reduction, this paper investigates and applies some partially deterministic sensing matrices like Golay families, and realizes them based on several different recovery algorithms. The core procedure of structured convolutional CS is orderly selecting sparsified samples, usually in various frequency domains, then reconstructing using the same deterministic sensing matrices based on several popular recovery algorithms. Conclusions can be drawn that with these structured sensing matrices, we can get better reconstruction quality and more stable performance with less time cost.

Keywords: Compressed Sensing (CS) · Structured Random Matrix
Random Convolution (RC) · Golay sequence
Frank Zad-off-Chu (FZC) sequence

1 Introduction

COMPRESSED Sensing (CS), a recently proposed reconstruction technique, can sense the useful information from K-sparse vectors and reconstruct it from the sensing results in an inverse way [1, 2]. As this technique can be applied to save the bandwidth significantly, it trigs booming researches in the past few years.

Let A^{CS} represent the sensor in CS, usually, to satisfy RIP rules [1], its arbitrary $2K$ columns should be linear independent, the former popular method is to make sparsifying transform Ψ fixed and then if the pre-randomizer Φ is a Gaussian random

---

Supported by: National Natural Science Foundation of China (61671332); Applied Basic Research Program of Wuhan City (2016010101010025); Basic Research Program of Shenzhen City (JCYJ20170306171431656); Fundamental Research Funds for the Central Universities (2042016gf0033); National Key Research and Development Program of China (2016YFB0100901).

© Springer International Publishing AG, part of Springer Nature 2018
B. Zeng et al. (Eds.): PCM 2017, LNCS 10735, pp. 400–410, 2018.
https://doi.org/10.1007/978-3-319-77380-3_38

matrix, the sensor A^{CS} will satisfy RIP rules in a high probability. However, to signals in high dimensions, using Gaussian matrix may sustain high complexity; besides, fixed Ψ cannot guarantee enough sparsity.

Previous works mainly focus on how to modify the reconstruction algorithms, which we have Bayesian sparse reconstruction algorithm [3] like FOCUSS [4], IRLS [5], BEPA [6] and BCS [7]; greedy algorithms [8] like OMP [9], and CoSaMP [10]; recursive thresholds algorithms [11]; convex relaxation algorithms [12]. But all of them are using complete random subsamplers and ignore the construction of deterministic ones for optimization.

Motivated by reducing the randomness in CS, the method used in this paper reconstructs several subsamplers with certain structures like Golay sequences [13], Frank Zad-off-Chu (FZC) sequences [14] and Toeplitz matrix [15] to replace Gaussian random matrix, as well as try to recover images on other sparsifying transform like wavelet basis and Discrete Cosine Transformation (DCT) basis. Basically, the whole working procedure is similar to traditional compressed sensing. The word "structured" mainly refers to the Structured Random Matrix (SRM) Φ. These newly proposed SRMs are proved to satisfy RIP rules like traditional sensing matrices. Results show the use of these deterministic subsamplers can guarantee less time cost and complexity without worsening reconstruction quality, making it more realistic to apply CS method in hardware implementation.

Figure 1 illustrates the general framework of structured convolutional compressed sensing, and this paper's main contribution, which is displayed in red box, is the construction of structured random matrices and its successful sensing application in CS, reducing the randomness as well as lowering relevant time cost.

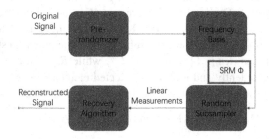

Fig. 1. The architecture of structured convolutional compressed sensing

2   Backgrounds of Compressed Sensing

2.1   Classic Compressed Sensing Working Procedure

General encoding equation [1] to express how CS works can be described by (1):

$$\vec{y} = \Phi * \Psi * \vec{s} = A^{CS} * \vec{s} = \Phi * \vec{x} \tag{1}$$

Where $\vec{s}$ is the representation of original signal $\vec{x}$ in some transform domains. It is a K-sparse column vector with the length of N; Ψ is a $N \times N$ sparsifying transform with full rank, Φ is a $M \times N$ sensing matrix which is non-invertible because it is not full rank and it is extremely different to Ψ; $\vec{y}$ is the linear measurement with the length of M, and M is much smaller than N, usually $M = 4K$ or $M = K\ ln(N/K)$. We can define A^{CS} as the compressed sensor.

Correspondingly, the decoding procedure can be described by (2) and (3):

$$\vec{s} = \Psi^H * \vec{x} \tag{2}$$

$$\vec{y} = \Phi * \vec{x} = A^{CS} * \vec{s} \tag{3}$$

Where $\vec{y}$ is the incomplete signal we get, Ψ^H is sparsifying transform's inverse, and we can reconstruct $\vec{s}$ from $\vec{y}$ reversely. However, as above equations are just general explanations of CS, they cannot be applied in specific simulation, detailed methodology will be demonstrated in Sect. 4.

2.2   Mathematical Tools, Notations, and Preliminaries

Generally, in CS, a_i represents the i-th element of a vector $\vec{a}$, where $i \in \{0, 1 \ldots, n - 1\}$, $\vec{a}_0, \ldots, \vec{a}_{n-1}$ represent a sequence of vectors; $\vec{1}_q$ represents a vector with all ones; A is a matrix, and A_{jk} denotes the element from the j-th row and k-th column; similarly, $A_0, \ldots, A_{n-1}$ represent a sequence of matrices. A^{-1} is A's inverse form while A^* is its Hermitian transpose. $A \otimes B$ is their Kronecker product, $A \odot B$ is their Hadamard product. A's Frobenius norm is defined by $||A||_F = \sqrt{tr(A^*A)}$. Besides, F^* is the normalized inverse Discrete Fourier Transform matrix (F is the Fourier Transform), I_l is an $l \times l$ identity matrix. Let $\Omega \subset \{0, \ldots, n - 1\}$ be an arbitrary or deterministic set of cardinality m, then R_Ω is the deterministic subsampling operator with strictly selecting a vector $\vec{x} \in C^n$ as its entries in Ω from $C^n \subset C^m$, while $R_{\Omega'}$ is a random subsampling operator with independently and uniformly selected elements in Ω'.

To construct these deterministic subsamplers, some structured sequence families have been applied. The first one is Hadamard matrix: let $H_N = \begin{bmatrix} 1 & 1 \\ 1 & -1 \end{bmatrix}$, then $H_{2N} = \begin{bmatrix} H_N & H_N \\ H_N & H_{-N} \end{bmatrix}$ can form the $2N \times 2N$ Hadamard matrix. The next is Rademacher matrix, it is a matrix with entries selected randomly from $[+1, -1]$ with equal probability. So does the Rademacher vector. Then, we can form a Toeplitz matrix (diagonal-constant matrix) with its diagonal kernel is Rademacher vector. Then the famous Golay sequence family has been investigated and applied, by initializing the start with $\vec{a}_0 = [+1, +1]$, $\vec{b}_0 = [+1, -1]$, after iterated by $\vec{a}_{i+1} = [\vec{a}_i, \vec{b}_i]$, $\vec{b}_{i+1} = [\vec{a}_i, -\vec{b}_i]$, we can have the original Golay sequence, the needed output is usually $\vec{a}_{i+1}$; then we can generate the extended Golay sequence by assembling the original one and its flip-flop version. Except for Golay sequence family, the Frank

Zad-Off-Chu family can also satisfy both the polyphase and 2^N length conditions, and the γ-th sequence within FZC family is formed by formula (4):

$$\vec{\sigma}_k = \begin{cases} e^{-\frac{j\pi\gamma k^2}{N}} \textit{ for even } N \\ e^{-\frac{j\pi\gamma k(k+1)}{N}} \textit{ for odd } N \end{cases} \tag{4}$$

Where γ should be some integer coprime with N, and the used value in experiments is 1.

The measurement of reconstruction quality in this paper is Signal-to Noise ratio (abbreviation is SNR or S/N). It is defined by the ratio of signal power (variance) to the noise power (variance), often expressed in decibels.

3 Theoretical Feasibility Analysis of Proposed Deterministic Subsamplers

In [1], Candes and Tao prove that the sensor A^{CS} should satisfy RIP rules for the sake of a successful reconstruction. Thus, [16] gives Proposition 1 and Theorem 3 to clarify the theoretical construction and feasibility of deterministic subsamplers.

Proposition 1: We can form a $M \times N$ matrix with frame vectors as its columns $A = [\vec{a}_0, \ldots, \vec{a}_{N-1}]$, and the M nonzero singular values of A equal $\sqrt{N/M}$, the rows of $\left\{ \left(\sqrt{N/M} \right) A \right\}$ form an orthogonal base. Then it is easily verified that the following two matrices are UTFs [16].

$$P_1 = \vec{1}_L^T \otimes F^* = [F^* F^*, \ldots, F^*] \tag{5}$$

$$P_2 = \vec{1}_L^T \otimes I_m = [II, \ldots, I] \tag{6}$$

Theorem 3: Introduce a framework consisting of 3 parts $A^{CS} = UDB$, where $U \in C^{M \times N}$ is a UTF, $D = diag\left(\vec{\xi} \right)$ ($\vec{\xi}$ is a length N random vector with independent, zero-mean, unit-variance, and r-sub Gaussian entries), $B \in C^{N \times N}$ is a column-wise orthogonal matrix ($B \times B^* = I$), then when $\delta \in (0, 1)$, $M \geq c_1 \delta^{-2} KN\mu^2(B(ln^2 K ln^2 N))$, where c_1 is a positive constant, μ stands for mutual coherence [17]. The recovery probability under this circumstance will exceed $1 - N^{-(lnN)(lnK)^2}$, and the RIP rule holds for $\delta_K < \delta$. If we combine UD as a randomly modulated UTF, the theorem still holds when B is a unitary matrix, and when we choose bounded column-wise orthogonal B, $\mu(B) = O(1/\sqrt{N})$. Set another constant $c_2 > 0, N' = c_2 N$, then the number of measurements can be reduced to $M = c_3 \delta^{-2} K ln^2 K ln^2 N$, $c_3 > 0$.

It is also mentioned in [1], if $M \geq c\delta^{-2} KN\mu^2(\Psi)ln^4 N$, $A^{CS} = \sqrt{N/M}R_\Omega\Psi$ will satisfy RIP rule in a high probability.

Similarly, constructing Φ with Golay sequence stated as before, we can get its coherence $\mu(\Phi) = 2/\sqrt{N}$, which is small enough for guaranteeing successful recovery. The proof is below:

By adding Golay sequence family before the Partially Random Circulant (PRC) matrix, and denoting $\Lambda = diag\left(\vec{\lambda}\right)$, where $\vec{\lambda}$ is the Golay sequence or extended Golay sequence, then Λ is a $N \times N$ unitary diagonal matrix [16]. The proposed sensing model then can be expressed as (7):

$$\Phi = \frac{1}{\sqrt{M}} R_\Omega H_r \Lambda \tag{7}$$

Suppose $\vec{r} = F^*\vec{\xi}$, $D = diag\left(\vec{\xi}\right)$, then $H_r = F^*D\,F$.
After that, Φ can be re-written as Eq. (8).

$$\Phi = \sqrt{\frac{N}{M}} R_\Omega F^* D F \Lambda \tag{8}$$

For $A^{CS} = \Phi * \Psi = \sqrt{N/M} R_\Omega F^* D F \Lambda \Psi$, it can be observed that $U = \sqrt{N/M} R_\Omega F^*$ is a UTF, and the rest $B = F\Lambda\Psi$ is a unitary matrix. Through *Theorem* 3, A^{CS} satisfies RIP rule with high probability if the number of linear measurements $M \geq \mu^2 (Bln^2Kln^2N)c_4\delta^{-2}KN$.

The above proof holds for any sampling model that employs a partial random circulant matrix with a deterministic phase modulation on any orthonormal sparsifying basis.

Then we do coherence analysis for FZC sequence: In [18], it is stated that the Fourier transform of an FZC sequence is another FZC sequence, implying both time and frequency domain can be applied in practice and that the sensing matrices also satisfy the conjugate symmetric condition. Under these conditions, the sensing matrix Φ is a unitary circulant matrix with ideal coherence parameter $\mu(\Phi) = 1/\sqrt{N}$.

And for scheme Orthogonal Symmetric Toeplitz Matrix (OSTM) [18], it can be treated as a special case of convolutional compressed sensing with the following sequence (9):

$$\vec{\sigma} \in \{-1, +1\}^{N/2}\{(-1, -1, \ldots, -1), (+1, +1, \ldots, +1)\} \tag{9}$$

[18] proves its feasibility of fast reconstruction with isotropic TV l_1–l_2 minimization algorithm, thus, it is used to complete the experiment in Sect. 4.3.

4   Experiments and Results

Figure 2 above depicts the whole working procedure of CS, the right one and the left one are data preparations while the middle one represents the step-by-step flowchart, and the optimization in this paper mainly lies within the red rectangle. The testing data is from classic MATLAB image set, like Lena image. To construct these deterministic subsamplers Φ, several SRMs have been applied to replace traditional Random Convolution (RC) matrix and Partial Random Circulant (PRC) matrix, like Hadamard matrix, Golay family based matrix, as well as Toeplitz matrix. Besides, the sparsifying transform Ψ is also replaced by other frequency bases except for traditional FFT and identity matrix.

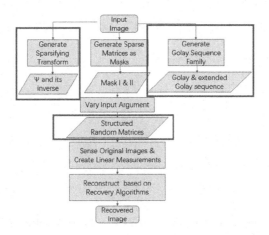

Fig. 2. The flow chart of general compressed sensing's working procedure

4.1 Compressed Sensing with Proposed Hadamard Matrix Based Subsamplers

The first model samples Hadamard matrix in both random and ordered way and applies it as the sensing matrix Φ in CS, then compares its effect to traditional i.i.d Gaussian sensing matrix.

After sparsifying and subsampling as above, we have M linear measurements. Then we generate an identity matrix I and randomly select its K elements to get the sparse vector $\vec{x}$, (we say $\vec{x}$ is sparse over Ψ with K nonzero elements at fixed location), and recovered using Eq. (3). As $\Psi = I$, its inverse $\Psi^H = I$. The last step is to recover the input signals by modified version of FPC-AS algorithm [19].

Figure 3 shows the superiority of the two Hadamard-matrix based deterministic subsamplers to random Gaussian matrix–significantly reducing the time cost during recovery procedure. The trial number to generate one point is 500, so the randomness of the results can be ignored. With traditional random i.i.d Gaussian subsampler, it takes nearly 250 s to complete the loop when sparsity, $K \geq 20$, while for Random Hadamard & deterministic Hadamard subsampler, it only takes less than 50 s. The explanation of above phenomenon can be simple: A successful estimation from randomly sampled linear measurements can be hard, consequently, more iterations are needed to control the relative error under acceptable level; and from the construction method of Hadamard matrix, there is no randomness existing, so the randomness only exists in the subsampling position or the diagonal mask, reducing the recovery difficulty level. There is extra advantage of using deterministic sensing matrices: In fixed entries scheme, there is no randomness in sensing matrix construction, in this situation, deterministic matrices with strict size constraints from coding theory will be the only candidates [17].

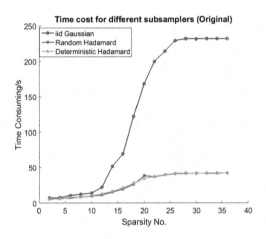

Fig. 3. Time cost comparison between random Gaussian subsamplers and proposed partially deterministic subsamplers along sparsity

Besides, it can also be concluded that the time cost for i.i.d Gaussian subsampler is nearly exponentially rising as the increase of sparsity number when $K \in [3, 21]$, and remains stable when $K > 21$; however, the rising speed is much less significant for deterministic ones. The performance coincides with the fact that with more K non-zeros we need to recover, the reconstruction complexity will grow, resulting in an ascending time cost curve. But it is worth pointing out CS using deterministic subsamplers might need more linear measurements as a compromise comparing with that of random one [17]. Generally, we should consider the trade-off between quantity of measurements and randomness.

4.2 Convolutional Compressed Sensing with Golay Sequence Based Phase Modulation

This model utilizes Golay sequence family during phase modulation to revise the previous PRC matrix.

Before generating those SRMs, we need to prepare two sparse matrices as masks: one is a sparse matrix with just one nonzero vector–column mask; the other is an identity sparse matrix with nonzero diagonal line–identity mask. The sparsity in both mask is approximately equal to the subsampling ratio M/N.

With those masks, we can then generate the structured random matrices defined in Eq. (8), as well as their corresponding adjoint matrices for the use of recovery reversely. The proposed sensing model recovers signal with BPDN algorithm [20].

In Figs. 4 and 5, we can see clearly that the previous PRC sensing matrix has the worst performance w.r.t. SNR, and less robust to outside changes. By adding the Golay sequence or the extended Golay sequence before phase modulation, the performance is improved to be the same with traditional RC matrix while the randomness of sensing model declines.

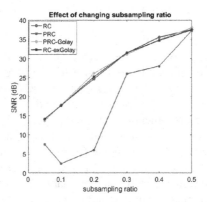

Fig. 4. Comparison between RC, PRC and Golay sequence-based sensing matrices along subsampling ratio M/N w.r.t. SNR

Besides, by varying the subsampling ratio, Fig. 4 dovetails the fact that more samples give better recovery results; while it is interesting that in Fig. 5, higher wavelet decomposition level of Ψ does not necessarily guarantee higher recovery SNR, but it does take longer time to complete the whole CS process. This phenomenon can be explained by the following wavelet property: from the decomposition and reconstruction procedure described in [21], higher decomposition level provides you more information about original images' frequency components; but when the decomposition goes up to certain level, there might be some discontinuities or shifts occurring.

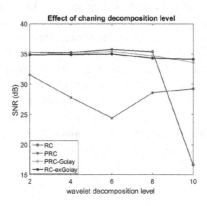

Fig. 5. Comparison between RC, PRC and Golay sequence-based sensing matrices along wavelet decomposition level of Ψ w.r.t. SNR

Table 1. Comparison between traditional RC & PRC matrix and proposed Golay sequence based sensing model w.r.t. SNR

Base	SNR (dB)	RC	PRC	PRC-Golay (ours)	RC-exGolay (ours)
FFT	Mean	35.30	26.12	35.12	34.87
	Variance	0.10	**26.64**	0.14	0.06
DCT	Mean	25.21	3.38	25.66	25.59
	Variance	0.16	**0.42**	0.43	0.29

Table 1 gives the recovery results between traditional subsamplers and proposed subsamplers w.r.t. SNR in different bases, trials tested are 5000 times. In terms of mean SNR, PRC has the worst performance, especially in DCT base, after adding Golay sequence before modulation by proposed sensing model, two bases both show significant improvement of reconstruction quality.

Generally, previous models are sparsified in FFT base, inspired by DCT's better condensed property, a comparison experiment is performed in these two bases. Table 1 shows that DCT base helps to reduce the SNR's variance of recovery, especially for PRC sensing model, which means DCT is a more stable choice for realistic application, while FFT can guarantee better result in singe trial.

4.3 Reconstruction from Partial Fourier Data (RecPF) Modified Based on FZC Sequence and OSTM

RecPF is first proposed in [22] *Algorithm* 2 for simplicity. The experiment procedure is similar to B model's procedure with replacing Golay sequence family with FZC sequence family and OSTM, then recovered by the TV $l_1 - l_2$ minimization algorithm also in [22].

Figure 6 shows that the sensing matrix based on FZC sequence has slightly worse performance at the beginning compared with the other three, while the OSTM based sensing model can achieve the same SNR as the former proposed SRMs.

In terms of the good performance on OSTM, it can be explained by the equivalency between Toeplitz matrix and the convolution process in communication system, as Toeplitz matrix consists of transmitted signals multiplied by the impulse response of a system, there is randomness in every row but strong structure exists between each row, making OSTM significant in practical application.

From the above results and analysis, we can see compared to traditional CS, structured CS with these proposed deterministic subsamplers can also guarantee successful recoveries. To be more specific, the Hadamard based sensing model can give even better performance in terms of time cost, Golay sequence based sensing model is more robust, and all the proposed sensing models lead to a result of reduction in randomness, helping the future corresponding hardware implementation less expensive.

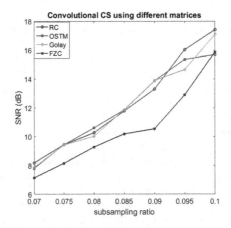

Fig. 6. Comparison between traditional RC and revised SRMs based on Golay, OSTM and FZC sequence along subsampling ratio M/N w.r.t. SNR

5   Conclusion and Future Works

The contribution of this paper mainly consists of reducing the randomness of existing sensing matrices in CS, while maintaining the performance, the time cost is reduced in a certain level, meanwhile, other deterministic subsamplers are tested through feasibility proofs. And all the experiment results are given through various recovery algorithms like [19, 20, 22], which helps to testify the robustness of proposed SRMs.

However, the design of these SRMs are rather complicated, resulting in the difficulty of engineering realization. The lack of PRC-exGolay and RC-Golay is because of the duplication and similarity with existing ones, proposed SRMs have already shown the feasibility and superiority, but deeper research will be added to enhance persuasiveness in the future.

At the same time, big data becomes the hottest topic in signal processing field, easier models about structured CS are needed for the application in relevant fields like dealing with streaming signals.

References

1. Candès, E.J., Tao, T., Romberg, J.: Robust uncertainty principles: Exact signal reconstruction from highly incomplete frequency information. IEEE Trans. Inf. Theory **52**, 489–509 (2006)
2. Donoho, D.L.: Compressed sensing. IEEE Trans. Inf. Theory **52**, 1289–1306 (2006)
3. Saab, R., Chartrand, R., Yilmaz, Ä.O.: Stable sparse approximations via non-convex optimization. In: IEEE International Conference on Acoustics, Speech and Signal Processing, pp. 3885–3888 (2008)
4. Gorodnitsky, I.F., Rao, B.D.: Sparse signal reconstruction from limited data using FOCUSS: a re-weighted minimum norm algorithm. IEEE Trans. Signal Process. **45**(3), 600–616 (1997)

5. Chartrand, R., Yin, W.T.: Iteratively reweighted algorithms for compressive sensing. In: IEEE International Conference on Acoustics, Speech and Signal Processing, pp. 3869–3872 (2008)
6. Wu, J., Liu, F., Jiao, L.C., Wang, X.D.: Compressive sensing SAR image reconstruction based on Bayesian framework and evolutionary computation. IEEE Trans. Image Process. **20**(7), 1904–1911 (2011)
7. Ji, S.H., Xue, Y., Carin, L.: Bayesian compressive sensing. IEEE Trans. Signal Process. **56** (6), 2346–2356 (2008)
8. Eldar, Y.C., Kutyniok, G.: Compressed Sensing: Theory and Applications, pp. 348–393. Cambridge University Press, Cambridge (2012)
9. Pati, Y., Rezaiifar, R., Krishnaprasad, P.: Orthogonal matching pursuit: recursive function approximation with application to wavelet decomposition. In: Asilomar Conference on Signals, Systems and Computers (1993)
10. Needell, D., Tropp, J.A.: CoSaMP: iterative signal recovery from incomplete and inaccurate samples. Appl. Comput. Harmon. Anal. **26**, 301–321 (2009)
11. Eldar, Y.C., Kutyniok, G.: Compressed Sensing: Theory and Applications, pp. 305–347. Cambridge University Press, Cambridge (2012)
12. Tropp, J.A.: Algorithms for simultaneous sparse approximation. Part II: convex relaxation. IEEE Trans. Signal Process. **86**(3), 589–602 (2006)
13. Ferguson, R.A., Borwein, P.B.: A complete description of Golay pairs for lengths up to 100. Math. Comput. **73**, 967–985 (2003)
14. Frank, R.L.: Polyphase codes for good periodic correlation properties. IEEE Trans. Inf. Theory **9**(1), 43–45 (1963)
15. Bareiss, E.H.: Numerical solution of linear equations with Toeplitz and vector Toeplitz matrices. Numer. Math. **9**(1), 404–424 (1969)
16. Zhang, P., Gan, L., Sun, S., Ling, C.: Modulated unit-norm tight frames for compressed sensing. IEEE Trans. Signal Process. **63**(15), 3974–3985 (2015)
17. Li, K., Cong, S.: State of the art and prospects of structured sensing matrices in compressed sensing. Front. Comput. Sci. **9**(5), 665–677 (2015)
18. Li, K., Gan, L., Ling, C.: Convolutional compressed sensing using deterministic sequences. IEEE Trans. Signal Process. **61**(3), 740–752 (2013)
19. Wen, Z., Yin, W.: User Manual FPC-AS, A MATLAB solver for l_1 regularized least squares problems. Version 1.0 (2008)
20. Combettes, P.L., Pesquet, J.-C.: A Douglas-Rachford splitting approach to non-smooth convex variational signal recovery. IEEE J. Sel. Top. Signal Process. **1**(4), 564–574 (2007)
21. Mallat, S.: A Wavelet Tour of Signal Processing (The Sparse Way), pp. 298–307. Elsevier Academic Press, Amsterdam (2009)
22. Yang, J., Zhang, Y., Yin, W.: A fast TV l_1–l_2 minimization algorithm for signal reconstruction from partial Fourier data. IEEE Signal Process. **4**(2), 288–297 (2010)

Blind Speech Deconvolution via Pretrained Polynomial Dictionary and Sparse Representation

Jian Guan[1], Xuan Wang[1(✉)], Shuhan Qi[1], Jing Dong[2], and Wenwu Wang[3]

[1] Computer Application Research Center, Shenzhen Graduate School,
Harbin Institute of Technology, Shenzhen 518055, China
{j.guan,wangxuan,shuhanqi}@cs.hitsz.edu.cn
[2] College of Electrical Engineering and Control Science,
Nanjing Tech University, Nanjing 211800, China
jingdong@njtech.edu.cn
[3] Centre for Vision, Speech and Signal Processing,
University of Surrey, Guildford GU2 7XH, UK
w.wang@surrey.ac.uk

Abstract. Blind speech deconvolution aims to estimate both the source speech and acoustic channel from a reverberant speech signal. The problem is ill-posed and underdetermined, which often requires prior knowledge for the estimation of the source and channel. In this paper, we propose a blind speech deconvolution method via a pretrained polynomial dictionary and sparse representation. A polynomial dictionary learning technique is employed to train the dictionary from room impulse responses, which is then used as prior information to estimate the source and the acoustic impulse responses via an alternating optimization strategy. Simulations are provided to demonstrate the performance of the proposed method.

Keywords: Blind deconvolution · Speech dereverberation
Polynomial dictionary learning · Acoustic channel estimation

1 Introduction

Blind speech deconvolution aims to estimate the source speech and acoustic room impulse responses (RIRs) from the observed reverberant speech. This is a common problem which can be benificial for several applications, such as automatic speech recognition (ASR) [17], sound reproduction [3], hearing aids [10], and multimedia affective computing [14,18].

The reverberant speech $\mathbf{y} \in \mathbb{R}^L$ of a single-input and single-output (SISO) acoustic system is generated by the linear convolution of the source speech $\mathbf{s} \in \mathbb{R}^M$ and the acoustic RIR $\mathbf{h} \in \mathbb{R}^N$, which can be expressed as follows

$$\mathbf{y} = \mathbf{s} * \mathbf{h} + \mathbf{w}, \tag{1}$$

© Springer International Publishing AG, part of Springer Nature 2018
B. Zeng et al. (Eds.): PCM 2017, LNCS 10735, pp. 411–420, 2018.
https://doi.org/10.1007/978-3-319-77380-3_39

where $*$ denotes the convolution operation, $\mathbf{w}$ is the system noise, and $L = M + N - 1$. In matrix form, (1) can be written as

$$\mathbf{y} = \mathcal{S}\mathbf{h} = \mathcal{H}\mathbf{s} + \mathbf{w}, \tag{2}$$

where $\mathcal{S} \in \mathbb{R}^{L \times N}$ and $\mathcal{H} \in \mathbb{R}^{L \times M}$ are the linear convolution matrices constructed from $\mathbf{s}$ and $\mathbf{h}$, respectively. Assuming both $\mathbf{s}$ and $\mathbf{h}$ are unknown, given only the observation $\mathbf{y}$, the estimation of $\mathbf{s}$ and $\mathbf{h}$ becomes blind, which is an ill-posed and undetermined inverse problem [2]. There are unlimited possible combinations of $\mathbf{s}$ and $\mathbf{h}$ which satisfy (1). To address this problem, prior information (such as sparsity of signals [13,15,16] or acoustic impulse responses [7]) is usually exploited to reduce the solution space for the estimation of $\mathbf{s}$ and $\mathbf{h}$.

In our previous work [7], we take into account the sparsity of a sparse SISO acoustic system as the prior knowledge to solve the blind speech deconvolution problem. The RIR of an acoustic system usually consists of three parts: direct signal, early reflections and late reverberation. In [7], we assume the acoustic system has a very low reverberation level, so that the late reflection is negligible, and the RIR $\mathbf{h}$ of such an acoustic system can be seen as sparse. However, the proposed method in [7] cannot be used to fully recover the RIR of an acoustic system with a higher level of reverberation, as the sparse prior knowledge is not applicable for such an acoustic system. In some recent works, the pretrained dictionaries have been used to exploit the sparsity property of signals in blind deconvolution. For example, in [9], a learned dictionary is employed in blind deconvolution for infrared spectrum restoration, where each spectrum can be sparsely represented by the overcomplete dictionary. In [8], adaptive dictionary learning is applied for single image deblurring, where each image patch is encoded by the sparse representation of an overcomplete dictionary.

In this paper, we focus on blind speech deconvolution for an SISO acoustic system with a high level of reverbertion, and propose a blind speech deconvolution method by utilizing a dictionary learned from the acoustic RIRs. However, it is challenging to learn the dictionary from the signals with time delays (e.g. acoustic RIRs), as conventional dictionary learning methods cannot be applied directly to process the signals with time delays. In order to address this problem, we use a polynomial dictionary learning method [6] to learn the dictionary for blind speech deconvolution. In [6], we developed a polynomial dictionary learning technique to deal with the signals with time lags, by using polynomial matrices for acoustic RIRs modeling, where each RIR is split into several segments, and each segment can be seen as a FIR filter and modeled by a polynomial. Therefore, a polynomial dictionary can be learned, and the acoustic RIRs can then be sparsely represented by the learned polynomial dictionary. Here, such a polynomial dictionary is trained to provide the prior information for sparsely representing the acoustic RIR which needs to be estimated for blind speech deconvolution. By using the polynomial dictionary, we introduce a blind speech deconvolution model with polynomial sparse representation, and propose an alternating optimization method to estimate the source speech and acoustic RIR in two steps, by fixing one and updating the other iteratively. To the best of our knowledge, we are the first to introduce and apply the polynomial dictionary technique for blind speech deconvolution.

The rest of the paper is organized as follows: Sect. 2 briefly reviews the previous work about blind speech deconvolution and introduces polynomial sparse representation. Section 3 presents the proposed model and method in detail. Section 4 shows the simulation results; Sect. 5 concludes the paper and discusses the potential future work.

2   Preliminaries

2.1   Sparse Blind Speech Deconvolution

In [7], assuming an acoustic system is sparse, and taking into account the sparsity of RIR $\mathbf{h}$, a sparse blind speech deconvolution model is proposed as follows

$$F(\mathbf{s}, \mathbf{h}) = \|\mathbf{s} * \mathbf{h} - \mathbf{y}\|_2^2 + \lambda \|\mathbf{h}\|_1 + r(\mathbf{s}), \tag{3}$$

where the L2-norm is the data fidelity term, the regularization $r(\mathbf{s})$ is an indicator function [11] which accounts for the dynamic range of $\mathbf{s}$, and the L1-regularization takes into account the sparsity of $\mathbf{h}$, where λ is the penalty parameter. Using (2), the model (3) can be reformulated as

$$\begin{aligned} F(\mathbf{s}, \mathbf{h}) &= \|\mathcal{S}\mathbf{h} - \mathbf{y}\|_2^2 + \lambda \|\mathbf{h}\|_1 + r(\mathbf{s}) \\ &= \|\mathcal{H}\mathbf{s} - \mathbf{y}\|_2^2 + \lambda \|\mathbf{h}\|_1 + r(\mathbf{s}). \end{aligned} \tag{4}$$

An alternating optimization method is used in [7] to address the sparse blind speech deconvolution problem (3).

2.2   Polynomial Sparse Representation

In [6], we have developed a polynomial dictionary learning technique to process the acoustic signals with time delays, where the signals can be sparsely represented by a pretrained polynomial dictionary. First, the training signals are modeled by a polynomial matrix, and the polynomial dictionary is learned by using the method in [6]. Then, the learned polynomial dictionary is used to approximate the test acoustic signals.

Assuming $\mathbf{D}(z)$ is the learned polynomial dictionary, and $\mathbf{h}$ is the acoustic signal that needs to be sparsely represented, then $\mathbf{h}$ can be modeled by a polynomial matrix $\mathbf{H}(z)$. Here, $\mathbf{H}(z)$ can be sparsely approximated as follows

$$\mathbf{H}(z) = \mathbf{D}(z)\mathbf{X}, \tag{5}$$

where $\mathbf{X}$ is the sparse representation matrix. (5) can be reformulated to the following equation

$$\underline{\mathbf{H}} = \underline{\mathbf{D}}\mathbf{X}, \tag{6}$$

where $\underline{\mathbf{H}}$ and $\underline{\mathbf{D}}$ denote the concatenated coefficient matrices of $\mathbf{H}(z)$ and $\mathbf{D}(z)$, respectively, defined as

$$\underline{\mathbf{H}} = [\mathbf{H}(0); \ldots; \mathbf{H}(\ell); \ldots; \mathbf{H}(\mathcal{L} - 1)], \tag{7}$$

$$\underline{\mathbf{D}} = [\mathbf{D}(0); \ldots; \mathbf{D}(\ell); \ldots; \mathbf{D}(\mathcal{L} - 1)], \tag{8}$$

where $\mathbf{H}(\ell)$ and $\mathbf{D}(\ell)$ are the coefficient matrices of $\mathbf{H}(z)$ and $\mathbf{D}(z)$ at lag ℓ, respectively. $\mathcal{L}$ denotes the maximum time lags of each polynomial element of the polynomial matrix.

In this paper, the polynomial dictionary $\mathbf{D}(z)$ is learned from the training acoustic RIRs, and the desired RIR $\mathbf{h}$ can be sparsely approximated by the pretrained dictionary $\mathbf{D}(z)$.

First, $\mathbf{h}$ is modeled by $\mathbf{H}(z)$, and reformulated as $\underline{\mathbf{H}}$. Then, $\underline{\mathbf{H}}$ can be sparsely represented by the linear combination of atoms in the new dictionary $\underline{\mathbf{D}}$ weighted by $\mathbf{X}$, where $\mathbf{X}$ can be calculated by optimizing the following loss

$$\min_{\mathbf{X}} \|\underline{\mathbf{H}} - \underline{\mathbf{D}}\mathbf{X}\|_F^2$$
$$\text{subject to } \forall i, \ \|\mathbf{x}_i\|_0 \leq \kappa, \tag{9}$$

where $\mathbf{x}_i$ is the ith column from $\mathbf{X}$, and κ is sparsity which accounts for the number of nonzero entries. Here, the orthogonal matching pursuit (OMP) algorithm [12] can be used to solve (9).

Once $\mathbf{X}$ is obtained, $\underline{\mathbf{H}}$ can be sparsely represented by using (6), so that the desired RIR $\mathbf{h}$ can be reconstructed by a "vectorization" operation, which aims to recover $\mathbf{h}$ from $\mathbf{H}(z)$ or $\underline{\mathbf{H}}$. The vectorization operation is defined as

$$\mathbf{h} = vec(\mathbf{H}(z)) = vec(\underline{\mathbf{H}}) = vec(\underline{\mathbf{D}}\mathbf{X}), \tag{10}$$

where vec is the vectorization operator.

3   Blind Speech Deconvolution with Polynomial Sparse Representation

3.1   Proposed Model

By employing the polynomial dictionary to approximate the RIR $\mathbf{h}$, we propose the blind speech deconvolution model as follows

$$F(\mathbf{s}, \mathbf{h}) = \|\mathbf{s} * \mathbf{h} - \mathbf{y}\|_2^2 + \gamma \|\mathbf{H}(z) - \mathbf{D}(z)\mathbf{X}\|_2^2 + \beta \sum \|\mathbf{x}_i\|_0 + r(\mathbf{s}), \tag{11}$$

where $\|\mathbf{s} * \mathbf{h} - \mathbf{y}\|_2^2$ represents the data fidelity term, and $*$ is the convolution operator. $\mathbf{H}(z)$ is the polynomial matrix used to model the RIR $\mathbf{h}$, and $\mathbf{D}(z)$ is the pretrained polynomial dictionary. Here, $\|\mathbf{H}(z) - \mathbf{D}(z)\mathbf{X}\|_2^2$ denotes the sparse representation of RIR $\mathbf{h}$ with $\mathbf{D}(z)$, and $\mathbf{X}$ is the representation coefficient matrix which is also unknown. γ and β are the penalty parameters. $r(\mathbf{s})$ is the regularization on $\mathbf{s}$, which is an indicator function that accounts for the dynamic range of the source speech. It is used to reduce the solution space for the estimation of $\mathbf{s}$. Note that, $r(\mathbf{s})$ is defined in our previous work [7].

According to (5) and (6), the proposed model (11) can be recast as

$$F(\mathbf{s}, \mathbf{h}) = \|\mathbf{s} * \mathbf{h} - \mathbf{y}\|_2^2 + \gamma \|\underline{\mathbf{H}} - \underline{\mathbf{D}}\mathbf{X}\|_2^2 + \beta \sum \|\mathbf{x}_i\|_0 + r(\mathbf{s}). \qquad (12)$$

In addition, (12) can be further reformulated as

$$\begin{aligned} F(\mathbf{s}, \mathbf{h}) &= \|\mathcal{S}\mathbf{h} - \mathbf{y}\|_2^2 + \gamma \|\underline{\mathbf{H}} - \underline{\mathbf{D}}\mathbf{X}\|_2^2 + \beta \sum \|\mathbf{x}_i\|_0 + r(\mathbf{s}) \\ &= \|\mathcal{H}\mathbf{s} - \mathbf{y}\|_2^2 + \gamma \|\underline{\mathbf{H}} - \underline{\mathbf{D}}\mathbf{X}\|_2^2 + \beta \sum \|\mathbf{x}_i\|_0 + r(\mathbf{s}). \end{aligned} \qquad (13)$$

An alternating optimization strategy is employed to solve (13), by fixing one and updating the other iteratively, and the proposed method includes two steps: **RIR h Estimation** and **Signal s Estimation**, as described next.

3.2   Proposed Alternating Optimization Method

RIR h Estimation. In this step, by fixing signal $\mathbf{s}$, the optimization of the cost function (13) is reduced to

$$\mathbf{h}^{(k+1)} = \underset{\mathbf{h}}{\operatorname{argmin}} \|\mathcal{S}^{(k)}\mathbf{h} - \mathbf{y}\|_2^2 + \gamma \|\underline{\mathbf{H}} - \underline{\mathbf{D}}\mathbf{X}\|_2^2 + \beta \sum \|\mathbf{x}_i\|_0, \qquad (14)$$

where $\mathcal{S}^{(k)}$ is the linear convolution matrix constructed from $\mathbf{s}^{(k)}$ at the kth iteration. Note that, $\mathbf{s}^{(0)}$ is initialized by using the observation $\mathbf{y}$. In order to optimize (14), we split (14) into two sub-optimization problems.

First, we start by initializing $\mathbf{h}$ with $\mathbf{h}_0$, as $\mathbf{h}^{(0)} = \mathbf{h}_0$. Here, $\mathbf{h}_0$ is a randomly generated Gaussian vector with zero mean and unit variance. Therefore, (14) can be reduced to the following sub-optimization problem

$$\mathbf{X}^{(k+1)} = \underset{\mathbf{X}}{\operatorname{argmin}} \|\underline{\mathbf{H}}^{(k)} - \underline{\mathbf{D}}\mathbf{X}\|_2^2 + \beta \sum \|\mathbf{x}_i\|_0, \qquad (15)$$

where $\underline{\mathbf{H}}^{(k)}$ is the concatenated coefficient matrix of $\mathbf{H}^{(k)}(z)$ used to model $\mathbf{h}^{(k)}$ at the kth iteration. Here, the sparse representation $\mathbf{X}$ can be calculated by optimizing (15), using the OMP algorithm.

Then, once $\mathbf{X}^{(k+1)}$ is obtained, (14) can be reduced to another sub-optimization problem, which is

$$\mathbf{h}^{(k+1)} = \underset{\mathbf{h}}{\operatorname{argmin}} \|\mathcal{S}^{(k)}\mathbf{h} - \mathbf{y}\|_2^2 + \gamma \|\underline{\mathbf{H}} - \underline{\mathbf{D}}\mathbf{X}^{(k+1)}\|_2^2. \qquad (16)$$

With a vectorization operation, (16) can be further rewritten as

$$\mathbf{h}^{(k+1)} = \underset{\mathbf{h}}{\operatorname{argmin}} \|\mathcal{S}^{(k)}\mathbf{h} - \mathbf{y}\|_2^2 + \gamma \|\mathbf{h} - vec(\underline{\mathbf{D}}\mathbf{X}^{(k+1)})\|_2^2. \qquad (17)$$

Here, the CVX toolbox [5] is used to optimize (17) for $\mathbf{h}$ estimation. After obtaining $\mathbf{h}^{(k+1)}$, we can update $\mathcal{H}^{(k+1)}$ for $\mathbf{s}$ estimation at the current iteration.

Signal s Estimation. In this step, by fixing RIR **h**, the optimization of (13) is reduced to the following form

$$s^{(k+1)} = \underset{s}{\mathrm{argmin}} \|\mathcal{H}^{(k+1)}s - y\|_2^2 + r(s). \tag{18}$$

Here, we use a variable metric forward-backward method (VMFB) [4] to minimize (18).

Once **s** is updated, then $\mathcal{S}^{(k+1)}$ can be constructed by using $s^{(k+1)}$ for updating **h** at the next iteration until the stopping criterion is met. Here, the stopping criterion is defined as $\|s^{(k+1)} - s^{(k)}\|_2^2 \leq \epsilon$, where ϵ is set typically as 10^{-6}. The proposed method is given in Algorithm 1.

Algorithm 1.

Input: observation **y**, polynomial dictionary $\mathbf{D}(z)$
Output: s_{opt}, h_{opt}
    Initialization: $s^{(0)} = y$, construct $\mathbf{S}^{(0)}$ from $s^{(0)}$, $h^{(0)} = h_0$, model $h^{(0)}$ by $\mathbf{H}^0(z)$ and reformulate it as $\underline{\mathbf{H}}^0$, reformulate $\mathbf{D}(z)$ as $\underline{\mathbf{D}}$, $\gamma = 0.001$, $I_k = 1200$, $\epsilon = 10^{-6}$.
    Iterations:
    for $k = 1, \ldots, I_k$ do
      RIR h Estimation:
      Update $\mathbf{X}^{(k+1)}$ by solving (15), using OMP algorithm.
      Sparsely approximate $\underline{\mathbf{H}}$ as $\underline{\mathbf{D}}\mathbf{X}^{(k+1)}$, and conduct vectorization operation as $vec(\underline{\mathbf{D}}\mathbf{X}^{(k+1)})$.
      Update $h^{(k+1)}$ by optimizing (17), using CVX toolbox.
      Construct $\mathcal{H}^{(k+1)}$ from $h^{(k+1)}$.
      Signal s Estimation:
      Update $s^{(k+1)}$ by minimizing (18), using VMFB as in [7].
      Construct $\mathcal{S}^{(k+1)}$ from $s^{(k+1)}$.
      Stopping criterion: If $\|s^{(k+1)} - s^{(k)}\|_2^2 <= \epsilon$, then $s_{opt} = s^{(k+1)}$, $h_{opt} = h^{(k+1)}$, and break, else continue.
    end for

---

4 Simulations and Results

In this section, we carry out several experiments by using the proposed method for blind speech deconvolution. The polynomial dictionary used is pretrained from simulated acoustic RIRs, and the proposed method is applied to deconvolve the reverberant speech with different levels of noise. Here, reconstruction error is used to evaluate the performance for the signal and RIR estimation, defined as

$$R_{err} = \frac{1}{n} \sum_{i=1}^{n} (a_i - \hat{a}_i)^2, \tag{19}$$

where n is the length of **a**, with a_i representing the ith element of **a**, **a** and $\hat{a}$ represent the original signal and estimated signal respectively, both normalized as $a = \frac{a}{max(|a|)}$. Note that, **a** can denote either signal **s** or RIR **h**.

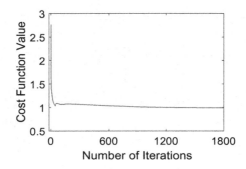

Fig. 1. Convergence of the proposed method.

4.1 Experimental Setup

The polynomial dictionary is learned from 1200 acoustic RIRs, which are simulated in a small room of size $8 \times 10 \times 3\,\mathrm{m}^3$ by the room image model [1]. The reverberation time is 900 ms, and the sampling frequency is 16 kHz. The length of the simulated RIRs is 1200 samples, which includes the first 480 samples from the early reflections and the last 720 samples from the late reflections. 5 speech signals are selected from TIMIT database as source signals, where the length of each signal is 500 samples. The first 500 samples from the observation **y** (discounting the silence part) are used to initialize the signal **s**.

4.2 Results and Analysis

First, we conduct experiments to illustrate the performance of the proposed method for blind speech deconvolution, and compared it with the method in [7]. Here, no noise is added to the observation **y**.

Figure 1 shows the change of cost function value with iterations. We can see that the proposed method can converge within 1800 iterations. Note that, the value becomes stable after 1200 iterations, so that the number of iterations is set to be 1200 in the following experiments. Figure 2 illustrates the deconvolution performance of the proposed method, as compared with the method in [7]. As can be seen from Fig. 2, both methods can resemble the source signal very well, as shown in the subplots (c) and (e). However, the RIR estimated by the method in [7] is more sparse, where the late part is almost smoothed, as shown in the subplot (f). This is reasonable, as the method in [7] only considers the sparsity of an acoustic system, and imposes an L1-norm constraint on the RIR for **h** estimation. In contrast, the proposed method can achieve a better performance for RIR estimation, which can fully recover the RIR including the late reflections, as shown in the subplot (d). This is because the polynomial dictionary used to approximate the RIR can provide useful prior information for the RIR estimation.

Then, another experiment is carried out to further evaluate the performance of the proposed method, where white Gaussian noise with zero mean and

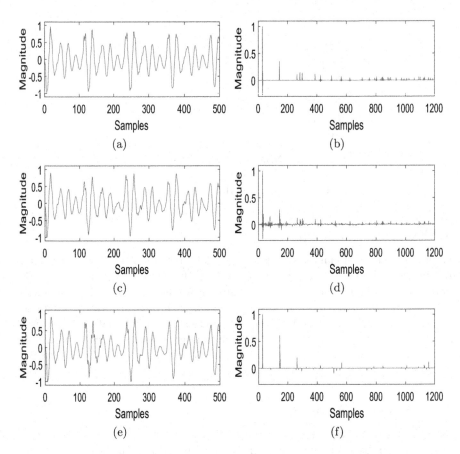

Fig. 2. Illustration of blind speech deconvolution by using the proposed method, and the method in [7]: (a) and (b) are the original source signal and RIR respectively; (c) and (d) are the estimated source and RIR respectively, by the proposed method; (e) and (f) are the estimated source and RIR respectively, by the method in [7].

variance chosen to achieve different signal-to-noise ratios (SNRs) is added to the observation **y**, i.e., for SNR at 10 dB, 20 dB and 30 dB. In addition, we also test the observation **y** without noise interference. 5 speech signals and one RIR are tested, and 20 realizations are conducted for each noise level. Table 1 shows the average reconstruction errors.

From Table 1, we can see that the proposed method can provide better performance for signal and RIR estimation with low levels of noise (e.g., for SNR at 20 dB and 30 dB), as well as without noise interference. However, the method in [7] obtains a better estimation result for a high level of noise (e.g., for SNR at 10 dB).

Table 1. Performance comparison in terms of reconstruction error for signal and RIR estimation at different noise levels (SNRs). Note that, ∞ denotes no noise is added to the observation **y**.

Noise levels (dB)		10	20	30	∞
Proposed method	Signal error	0.2840	**0.1628**	**0.1456**	**0.1302**
	RIR error	0.0588	**0.0306**	**0.0256**	**0.0139**
Method in [7]	Signal error	0.1838	0.1685	0.1662	0.1621
	RIR error	0.0346	0.0351	0.0353	0.0365

5 Conclusions and Future Work

In this paper, we introduced a blind speech deconvolution model with polynomial sparse representation term, where a polynomial dictionary was used to provide the prior information for blind speech deconvolution. A polynomial dictionary learning technique was employed to train the polynomial dictionary and sparsely approximate the acoustic RIR for blind speech deconvolution. In order to estimate both the signal and RIR, an alternating optimization method was then proposed to address the blind speech deconvolution problem. The proposed method was applicable for the acoustic system with different levels of reverberation and can be used to fully recover the RIR with late reflections, as the pretrained polynomial dictionary can better fit with the representation of the RIRs. Simulations demonstrated the validity of the proposed method, and the results have shown that the proposed method can provide better performance for blind speech deconvolution, especially, for the RIR estimation. In our future work, we will learn polynomial dictionary from real acoustic RIRs, and apply the proposed method for real acoustic systems.

Acknowledgements. The work was initially conducted when J. Guan was visiting the Centre for Vision, Speech and Signal Processing (CVSSP), the University of Surrey. This work was supported in part by International Exchange and Cooperation Foundation of Shenzhen City, China (No. GJHZ20150312114149569).

References

1. Allen, J.B., Berkley, D.A.: Image method for efficiently simulating small-room acoustics. J. Acoust. Soc. Am. **65**(4), 943–950 (1979)
2. Benichoux, A., Vincent, E., Gribonval, R.: A fundamental pitfall in blind deconvolution with sparse and shift-invariant priors. In: Proceedings of International Conference on Acoustics, Speech, and Signal Processing (ICASSP), pp. 6108–6112. IEEE (2013)
3. Betlehem, T., Abhayapala, T.D.: A modal approach to soundfield reproduction in reverberant rooms. In: Proceedings of International Conference on Acoustics, Speech, and Signal Processing (ICASSP), vol. 3, pp. 289–292. IEEE (2005)

4. Chouzenoux, E., Pesquet, J.C., Repetti, A.: A block coordinate variable metric forward-backward algorithm. J. Glob. Optim. **66**, 1–29 (2016)
5. Grant, M., Boyd, S., Grant, M., Boyd, S., Blondel, V., Boyd, S., Kimura, H.: CVX: matlab software for disciplined convex programming, version 2.1. In: Recent Advances in Learning and Control, pp. 95–110 (2014)
6. Guan, J., Dong, J., Wang, X., Wang, W.: A polynomial dictionary learning method for acoustic impulse response modeling. In: Vincent, E., Yeredor, A., Koldovský, Z., Tichavský, P. (eds.) LVA/ICA 2015. LNCS, vol. 9237, pp. 211–218. Springer, Cham (2015). https://doi.org/10.1007/978-3-319-22482-4_24
7. Guan, J., Wang, X., Wang, W., Huang, L.: Sparse blind speech deconvolution with dynamic range regularization and indicator function. Circ. Syst. Sig. Process. **36**(10), 4145–4160 (2017)
8. Hu, Z., Huang, J.B., Yang, M.H.: Single image deblurring with adaptive dictionary learning. In: Proceeding of International Conference on Image Processing (ICIP), pp. 1169–1172. IEEE (2010)
9. Liu, H., Liu, S., Huang, T., Zhang, Z., Hu, Y., Zhang, T.: Infrared spectrum blind deconvolution algorithm via learned dictionaries and sparse representation. Appl. Opt. **55**(10), 2813–2818 (2016)
10. Löllmann, H.W., Vary, P.: Low delay noise reduction and dereverberation for hearing aids. EURASIP J. Adv. Sig. Process. **2009**(1), 437–807 (2009)
11. Parikh, N., Boyd, S.: Proximal algorithms. Found. Trends Optim. **1**(3), 127–239 (2014)
12. Pati, Y.C., Rezaiifar, R., Krishnaprasad, P.: Orthogonal matching pursuit: recursive function approximation with applications to wavelet decomposition. In: Proceedings of the 27th Asilomar Conference on Signals, Systems and Computers, pp. 40–44. IEEE (1993)
13. Repetti, A., Pham, M.Q., Duval, L., Chouzenoux, E., Pesquet, J.C.: Euclid in a taxicab: sparse blind deconvolution with smoothed regularization. IEEE Sig. Process. Lett. **22**(5), 539–543 (2015)
14. Schuller, B.: Affective speaker state analysis in the presence of reverberation. Int. J. Speech Technol. **14**(2), 77–87 (2011)
15. Selesnick, I.: Sparse deconvolution (an MM algorithm) (2012). http://cnx.org/content/m44991/
16. Wang, L., Chi, Y.: Blind deconvolution from multiple sparse inputs. IEEE Sig. Process. Lett. **23**(10), 1384–1388 (2016)
17. Wang, L., Nakagawa, S., Kitaoka, N.: Blind dereverberation based on CMN and spectral subtraction by multi-channel LMS algorithm. In: Proceedings of INTERSPEECH 2008, pp. 1032–1035 (2008)
18. Zhao, S., Yao, H., Gao, Y., Ji, R., Ding, G.: Continuous probability distribution prediction of image emotions via multitask shared sparse regression. IEEE Trans. Multimed. **19**(3), 632–645 (2017)

Text and Line Detection/Recognition

Multi-lingual Scene Text Detection Based on Fully Convolutional Networks

Shaohua Liu[1], Yan Shang[1,2], Jizhong Han[2], Xi Wang[2(✉)], Hongchao Gao[2], and Dongqin Liu[2]

[1] Laboratory of Cyber-Physical Systems, Beijing University of Posts and Telecommunications, Beijing, China
{liushaohua,shangyan}@bupt.edu.cn
[2] Laboratory for Cyberspace Technologies, Institute of Information Engineering, Chinese Academy of Sciences, Beijing, China
{hanjizhong,wangxi1,gaohongchao,liudongqin}@iie.ac.cn

Abstract. In the paper, we propose a method based on transfer learning to detect multi-lingual text in natural scenes. First, a semantic segmentation map of the input image is obtained through a fully convolution network (FCN). In this map, each pixel is classified to text or none-text. And then, the candidate boxes of text regions are computed based on the map. In this procedure, VGG network is trained to obtain a basic character classifier of single language. Based on this VGG model, FCN has the ability to classify each pixel to text or none-text for multi-lingual with doing transfer learning. Finally, the bounding boxes of text are carry out by filtering the unsatisfied candidates with some rules. The experimental results show that our method achieves good performance on the task of multi-lingual text detection. And compared with other advanced method, the time cost of our method is shortest.

Keywords: Sence text detection · Multi-language · Transfer learning
Fully convolution networks

1 Introduction

Text, as a human-specific means of communication, can be embedded in the document or scene, as a means of communicating information. Especially, with the emergence of applications on mobile devices [1], How to translate text into other languages having inspired the re-interest in these issues . As a result, the problem of text detection and identification in images or videos in real time has received increasing attention in recent years [1,2,8,9,11,12].

Text detection involves generating candidate character or word region detections. The text that appears in the natural scene images is a huge change in appearance and layout, extracted from variation of text contents and styles, subject to inconsistent lighting, occlusion, orientation, noise, and the presence of background objects can lead to false positive detection [2,3]. Previous works

© Springer International Publishing AG, part of Springer Nature 2018
B. Zeng et al. (Eds.): PCM 2017, LNCS 10735, pp. 423–432, 2018.
https://doi.org/10.1007/978-3-319-77380-3_40

for scene text detection have utilized the sliding window method [3, 6, 7] and connected component analysis [8–10]. The first type of methods detect text regions of a given image by shifting a window onto all proposes in multiple scales. By using exhaustive search, these methods can achieve high recall rates, while, heavy computations are unavoidable. To make thing worse, a huge number of region proposes can lead to a lot of false positives [2, 5].

On the other hand, connected component based methods first extract character region proposes from an given image, and then by using a candidates classifier to filter non-text candidates. There are two representative techniques for this type of methods: mximally stable extremal region (MSER) [7, 10, 14] and Stroke width transform (SWT) [12, 13]. These methods as well as variants have achieved outstanding performance in text detection task. But, common constraints or region classifier used for refining candidates are considered to preserve various true characters, leading to low recall rate in practice.

In recent years, deep convolutional neural network has been widely used in both image classification and speech recognition [3, 4]. The successful application of deep convolutional neural network on images: object detection and semantic segmentation has made great progress [16, 18]. Text, which can be treated as objects with unconstrained lengths, possesses very distinctive appearance and shape compared to generic objects [4]. Therefore, these efficient methods can be used for text region detection. Howerver, some methods, such as TextBoxes [16], SSD [18], adopted the deep neural network which designed for object detection to text detection. In these methods, the input image must be scaled to a fixed size (e.g. 300×300) firstly. It may causes some image distortion of the text regions. On the other hand, no matter how many text regions are actually included in the image, a fixed number of proposals is required.

In this paper, fully convolutional network(FCN) [15], that is trained end-to-end, pixels-to-pixels on semantic segmentation, is used to detecte text regions in given images. By using FCN, the model can accept a more flexible input image size, to avoid the distortion caused by the size of the transformation and a pixel-wise text or none-text salient map is efficiently generated. Further more, through transfer learning of this model [19, 20], the detection freamwork can also be applied to multilingual text detection tasks. Experiments results show that our detection freamwork has good results in nine languages.

The remainder of this paper is organized as follows: The details of proposed method are introduced in Sect. 2. In Sect. 3, the experimental results are described. Finally, the conclusion is showed in Sect. 4.

2   The Proposed Method

The FCN [15] is proposed to solve the problem of image semantic segmentation, and it has achieved the classification at the pixel level. By transferring the fully connected layer of the traditional neural network into convolution layer, it makes the model get rid of the fixed size of the input images and preserves the spatial information of the original image. And VGGNet [21] is choosed as our base model in our method, VGGNet is mainly used for image classification task, its mainly proves that the deepening of the network can have the impact of network performance to some extent, the deepening of the network layer can improve the performance of the network. In our detection task in complex scene, since the VGG-19 [21] network is too complex, the training time cost and data volume requirements are relatively high, not within the scope of our choice, and ultimately VGG-16 [21] network was choosed as FCN candidate feature extractor.

There are two outstanding advantages to the text detection in the complex scene by using FCN. Compared with the other target detection algorithms, One advantage is that FCN does not need to select the candidate boxes, so there is no trouble to classify secondary discrimination of the candidate boxes. The other one is FCN output is a up sampled feature map, all the candidate boxes will be output at a time, belonging to the pixel level detection, while ensuring the input image in the text region of the spatial scale characteristics. To some extent, it is still effective for the case of extreme text region ratios, and candidate boxes selected by FCN are robust to the spatial scale of the text region compared with other method.

2.1   Feature Extractor of Characters with VGG-16

Using VGG-16 to train a character classifier, the Arabic language was selected as our training language, first of all Arabic is the character of the word formation method, so that in the space scale can guarantee continuity, followed by the arabic character form varied. 110 characters were parsed form the font file and 20000 single character images were generated by our system. All generated images were same size. With the training of these images, it made the VGG-16 model has the ability to extract character features.

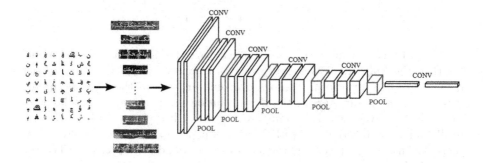

Fig. 1. The architecture of training feature extractor of Arabic characters.

As shown in the Fig. 1, Arabic was choosed as training language, and then we extract all the glyphs of different fonts from the ttf font file to construct a complete set of characters. Finally, random characters are combined and complex backgrounds are added based on the baseline of the Arabic language feature.

In order to generate a variety of training data, 75 kinds of fonts were selected as a complete set of characters, and each font has 110 Arabic characters graphs, the character set a total of 8250 single alternative characters. Using the constructed training dataset, FCN model can be trained to detect a single language, and then we can use transfer learning to do text detection in other languages.

2.2   Transfer VGG-16 Classifier to FCN

The FCN detection model is fine-tuned based on the parameters that have been trained by the VGG-16 classification model, thus realizing the task of classification into the semantic segmentation through the transfer learning. As we can see in the Table 1, this is VGG-FCN architecture employed by multi-lingual scene text detection network.

Table 1. The VGG-FCN architecture employed by our multi-lingual scene text detection network

Layer	Kernel	Stride	Pad	Outputs	Layer	Kernel	Stride	Pad	Outputs
conv1_1	3 × 3	1 × 1	100	64	conv4_2	3 × 3	1 × 1	1	512
conv1_2	3 × 3	1 × 1	1	64	conv4_3	3 × 3	1 × 1	1	512
pool1	2 × 2	2 × 2	0	-	pool4	2 × 2	2 × 2	0	-
conv2_1	3 × 3	1 × 1	1	128	conv5_1	3 × 3	1 × 1	1	512
conv2_2	3 × 3	1 × 1	1	128	conv5_2	3 × 3	1 × 1	1	512
pool2	2 × 2	2 × 2	0	-	conv5_3	3 × 3	1 × 1	1	512
conv3_1	3 × 3	1 × 1	1	256	pool5	2 × 2	2 × 2	0	-
conv3_2	3 × 3	1 × 1	1	256	fc6_conv	7 × 7	1 × 1	0	4096
conv3_3	3 × 3	1 × 1	1	256	fc7_conv	1 × 1	1 × 1	0	4096
pool3	2 × 2	2 × 2	0	-	score_fr	1 × 1	1 × 1	0	2
conv4_1	3 × 3	1 × 1	1	512	upscore	4 × 4	2 × 2	0	2

VGG-16 networks has been trained into a basic character classification model and then the fully connected layer, such as fc6_conv layer and fc7_conv layer in the Table 1, is transformed into a convolution layer in the VGG networks. In terms of the parameters of the deconvolution layer, there are two kinds of deconvolution layers which is configured as 4 × 4 kernel size with 2 stride, 0 padding or 16 × 16 kernel size with 8 stride, 0 padding, these two deconvolution layers are linearly sampled from the feature map from different scales. When the deconvolution layer was trained such as upscore layer in the Table 1, the learning rate of the layer is usually set to 0. In other words, the deconvolution layer does not participate in the model optimization.

2.3   Bounding Box Selection

For the FCN output picture which still contains some noise, and a algorithm has been proposed in order to increases the value of IoU and improves the accuracy of the test results. In this selection algorithm, we use some advanced morphological processing techniques including threshold segmentation, closed operation, etc. First, we cut the output prediction threshold so that each piece of text region is more consistent with the attributes and then through the closed operation, including the expansion of the detected text region to fill small holes and connect the adjacent text region, closed operation in the smooth text region at the same time and will not significantly change its size. Finally, we get the text regions by locating the connected area, and then you can obtain the text region of the external rectangle.

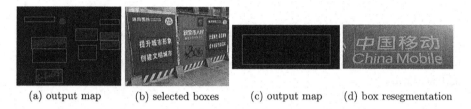

(a) output map   (b) selected boxes   (c) output map   (d) box resegmentation

Fig. 2. The results of bounding box selection. (a) Output map by VGG16-FCN. (b) Boxes by selection algorithm. (c) Output map overlapped. (d) Resegmentation of overlapped map.

As shown in the Fig. 2, (a) and (b) shows the final result of the text region selection algorithm, even if there are some text region is filtered out, but most of the text is selected by the correct region out. Figure 2(c) shows that the text box determined by the text region selection algorithm still has multiple text region divided into the same text region. According to the characteristics of this situation, a statistical histogram for the horizontal and vertical directions is made for the output prediction map, and it is judged by the mean truncation whether or not there is a plurality of text region in a bounding box. And Fig. 2(d) shows that if there are multiple text region, the text region is separated by a middle index horizontally or vertically which makes the predicted bounding box much more accurate there now.

2.4   Transfer to Multi-lingual Detection Task

Our ultimate goal is to detect the text region, not the text regions of a specific language, that is to say we want to detect the text regions which is not limited a specific language. Meanwhile, it will bring about a very challenging problem is that the generalization ability of the model is highly required. We use transfer learning to solve multi-lingual scene text detection, transfer learning is to migrate well-trained model parameters to new similar tasks to help the new task training model. On the one hand, it saves time and cost of training which for not have to retrain a new model. On the other hand, it solves the problem of missing large amounts of annotation data. We can still apply the model in other complex fonts characters such as Vietnam, Cambodia, Thailand, Myanmar, Malaysia, Indonesia in the Southeast Asia.

3   Experimental Results

3.1   Performance on ICDAR2017-MLT Dataset

Our test dataset comes from ICDAR2017 Competition on Multi-lingual scene text detection and script identification and it has 7200 multi-lingual images in total, including Arabic, Latin, Chinese, Japanese, Korean, Bangla and some special symbols. Since this competition hasn't started yet, and just released the training set. In our experiments, we try two way to test the performance on ICDAR2017-MLT.

Finetuned Model. Fine-tuning the FCN model with a small amount of multi-lingual scene images. In this way, 1000 images from ICDAR2017-MLT dataset is used to fine-tune the Arabic detection model and the rest 6200 images is used as test data.

No-Finetuned Model. The original FCN model without fine-tuning is directly used to test the model performance. In this way, all 7200 images are set to the test data.

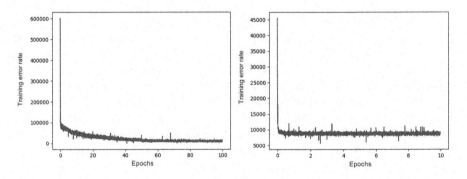

Fig. 3. The process of model optimization

IoU (Intersection over Union) refers to the intersection of the predicted bounding box of the model prediction and the groud truth bounding box. In our evaluation protocol, a detected bounding box will be marked as true positive if IoU is over the threshold. In order to compare the models, we set different IoU thresholds to test the performance between Finetuned model and No-Finetuned model.

The process of model optimization is showed in the Fig. 3, the left figure is an optimization process that training the Arabic detection model with FCN, and the right figure is an optimization process that using 1000 multi-language natural scene text images to fine-tune the Arabic detection FCN model. There are 2000 iterations per epoch, and this training process takes more than seven hours with single Tesla M40 GPU device, because the input of FCN model must

Table 2. The result of Finetuned model and No-Finetuned model

Models	Finetuned model			No-Finetuned model		
Threshold	Precision(%)	Recall(%)	F1-score	Precision(%)	Recall(%)	F1-score
0.1	88.80	47.03	0.61	83.88	45.61	0.59
0.2	72.57	42.05	0.53	68.51	40.65	0.51
0.3	63.05	38.67	0.48	59.74	37.40	0.46
0.4	53.65	34.92	0.42	51.89	34.16	0.41
0.5	43.04	30.09	0.35	42.53	29.84	0.35
0.6	32.38	24.46	0.28	32.87	24.74	0.28
0.7	23.33	18.92	0.21	24.05	19.38	0.21
0.8	16.16	13.91	0.15	17.04	14.56	0.16
0.9	11.12	10.01	0.10	11.20	10.08	0.11

be one by one, it makes the training process takes a long time, but it has no limit with the image size of training data.

Using precision rate, recall rate, and F1-score as three indicators to compare performance between the modle transfered directly without fine-tuning and the model after fine-tuning. The results of the two sets of experiments are in the Table 2.

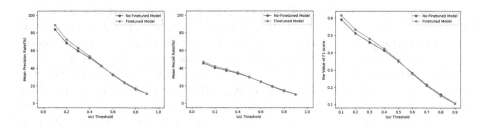

Fig. 4. The comparison between Finetuned model and No-Finetuned model

In contrast to the experimental results, when the IoU threshold is less than 0.6, the performance of the trimmed model is better than the model that has not been fine-tuned with the average recall rate is 2.91% and the recall rate is 1.01% higher on average. This shows that the fine-tuning model has a certain effect on the performance of the model, although the effect is not particularly large. When the threshold is greater than 0.6, The performance of the two models is less than 1%, which shows that fine-tuning model does not improve the performance of the model too much. In order to better compare the experimental results, we visualized the results of the two groups of experiments by plotting the graphs, the result is showed in Fig. 4. And the final bounding boxes are shown in Fig. 5. We can observe that our method has a good effect for multi-lingual text detection.

The experimental results show that the bounding boxes accurately surround the text regions but no the text lines, since FCN is not good at dealing with the blank between different lines. Therefore, using current general evaluation system based on text lines, the score of our method is not high enough.

However, in order to accurately get each character area, the background segmentation and other processing is usually carried out in the recognition stage and our results can be satisfactory the requirements completely in the next recognition task.

Fig. 5. The examples of multi-lingual scene text detection

3.2   Performance on MSRA-TD500 Dataset

In terms of the performance of time cost, we evaluate the performance of our proposed method with MSRA-TD500 data set. As shown in Table 3, detection speed of our proposed method is the fastest on MSRA-TD500 and the proposed method achieves precision 0.69, recall 0.51 and f-measure 0.59. In terms of time cost, our method takes 0.58 s for each image in average on MSRA-TD500 with a acceptable precision and recall, faster 0.22 s than the current fastest detection algorithm from Yin et al. Compared with best algorithm on precision and recall from Bai et al., each image takes 2.1 s which means that the method is 3.62 times faster, however, some limit of recall should be acceptant.

Table 3. Performance comparisons on the MSRA-TD500 dataset.

Algorithm	Precision	Recall	F-measure	Time cost
Bai et al. [4]	0.83	0.67	0.74	2.1 s
Yin et al. [3]	0.81	0.63	0.71	1.4 s
Kang et al. [6]	0.71	0.62	0.66	-
Yin et al. [7]	0.71	0.61	0.65	0.8 s
Proposed	0.69	0.51	0.59	**0.58 s**
Yao et al. [8]	0.63	0.63	0.60	7.2 s

4 Conclusion

This paper proved that for a single language detection model can be transfered directly to the task of multi-lingual scene text detection without fine-tuning. The experimental results also prove our conclusion, in the lower IoU threshold, the performance of finetuned model is better than the model without finetuning. However, the performance is not significantly improved. In the case of a higher IoU threshold, there is no difference in terms of performance of model with or without finetuning. Therefore, the conclusion is that the practice of applying a single language text detection model directly through transfer learning to multi-lingual text detection is feasible and does not require any model fine-tuning. To some extent, the conclusion can be interpreted in such a way, the model has learned the abstract concept of "character", rather than a specific definition of a character pattern, as human beings see unfamiliar language characters, but still can determine that is the character and not something else. From the perspective of models, the detection task is essentially a two classification task, but VGG-16 is a very complex model with a huge training dataset which makes the model abstract out the "character" concept instead of a special language character. Good generalisation is always difficult with maximum likelihood training, but it has been proved to be feasible on multi-lingual scene text detection. In the future, we will continue to explore methods to improve precision and recall, and prove the same generalization performance in the recognition task.

Acknowledgments. This research is partly supported by the National Defense Equipment Advance Research Key Program of China (Grant No. 9140A15030115DZ0 8042), the Equipment Technology Foundation of China (Grant No. YXBYD20162 QB01, YXBYD20162QB02) and the National Natural Science Foundation of China (Grand No. 61702502).

References

1. Liu, C., Wang, C., Dai, R.: Text detection in images based on unsupervised classification of edge-based features. In: 2005 Proceedings of the Eighth International Conference on Document Analysis and Recognition, pp. 610–614. IEEE (2005)
2. Ye, Q., Doermann, D.: Text detection and recognition in imagery: a survey. IEEE Trans. Pattern Anal. Mach. Intell. **37**(7), 1480–1500 (2015)
3. Yin, X.C., Pei, W.Y., Zhang, J., et al.: Multi-orientation scene text detection with adaptive clustering. IEEE Trans. Pattern Anal. Mach. Intell. **37**(9), 1930–1937 (2015)
4. Zhang, Z., Zhang, C., Shen, W., et al.: Multi-oriented text detection with fully convolutional networks. In: Proceedings of the IEEE Conference on Computer Vision and Pattern Recognition, pp. 4159–4167 (2016)
5. Cho, H., Sung, M., Jun, B.: Canny text detector: fast and robust scene text localization algorithm. In: Proceedings of the IEEE Conference on Computer Vision and Pattern Recognition, pp. 3566–3573 (2016)
6. Kang, L., Li, Y., Doermann, D.: Orientation robust text line detection in natural images. In: Proceedings of the IEEE Conference on Computer Vision and Pattern Recognition, pp. 4034–4041 (2014)

7. Yin, X.C., Yin, X., Huang, K., et al.: Robust text detection in natural scene images. IEEE Trans. Pattern Anal. Mach. Intell. **36**(5), 970–983 (2014)

8. Yao, C., Bai, X., Liu, W., et al.: Detecting texts of arbitrary orientations in natural images. In: 2012 IEEE Conference on Computer Vision and Pattern Recognition (CVPR), pp. 1083–1090. IEEE (2012)

9. Yi, C., Tian, Y.: Localizing text in scene images by boundary clustering, stroke segmentation, and string fragment classification. IEEE Trans. Image Process. **21**(9), 4256–4268 (2012)

10. Neumann, L., Matas, J.: Real-time scene text localization and recognition. In: 2012 IEEE Conference on Computer Vision and Pattern Recognition (CVPR), pp. 3538–3545. IEEE (2012)

11. Epshtein, B., Ofek, E., Wexler, Y.: Detecting text in natural scenes with stroke width transform. In: 2010 IEEE Conference on Computer Vision and Pattern Recognition (CVPR), pp. 2963–2970. IEEE (2010)

12. Huang, W., Lin, Z., Yang, J., et al.: Text localization in natural images using stroke feature transform and text covariance descriptors. In: Proceedings of the IEEE International Conference on Computer Vision, pp. 1241–1248 (2013)

13. Matas, J., Chum, O., Urban, M., et al.: Robust wide-baseline stereo from maximally stable extremal regions. Image Vis. Comput. **22**(10), 761–767 (2004)

14. Neumann, L., Matas, J.: A method for text localization and recognition in real-world images. In: Kimmel, R., Klette, R., Sugimoto, A. (eds.) ACCV 2010. LNCS, vol. 6494, pp. 770–783. Springer, Heidelberg (2011). https://doi.org/10.1007/978-3-642-19318-7_60

15. Long, J., Shelhamer, E., Darrell, T.: Fully convolutional networks for semantic segmentation. In: Proceedings of the IEEE Conference on Computer Vision and Pattern Recognition, pp. 3431–3440 (2015)

16. Liao, M., Shi, B., Bai, X., et al.: TextBoxes: a fast text detector with a single deep neural network. arXiv preprint arXiv:1611.06779 (2016)

17. Girshick, R., Donahue, J., Darrell, T., et al.: Rich feature hierarchies for accurate object detection and semantic segmentation. In: Proceedings of the IEEE Conference on Computer Vision and Pattern Recognition, pp. 580–587 (2014)

18. Liu, W., Anguelov, D., Erhan, D., Szegedy, C., Reed, S., Fu, C.-Y., Berg, A.C.: SSD: single shot multibox detector. In: Leibe, B., Matas, J., Sebe, N., Welling, M. (eds.) ECCV 2016. LNCS, vol. 9905, pp. 21–37. Springer, Cham (2016). https://doi.org/10.1007/978-3-319-46448-0_2

19. Do, C., Ng, A.Y.: Transfer learning for text classification. In: NIPS, pp. 299–306 (2005)

20. Pan, S.J., Yang, Q.: A survey on transfer learning. IEEE Trans. Knowl. Data Eng. **22**(10), 1345–1359 (2010)

21. Simonyan, K., Zisserman, A.: Very deep convolutional networks for large-scale image recognition. arXiv preprint arXiv:1409.1556 (2014)

Cloud of Line Distribution for Arbitrary Text Detection in Scene/Video/License Plate Images

Wenhai Wang[1], Yirui Wu[1,2], Shivakumara Palaiahnakote[3], Tong Lu[1(✉)], and Jun Liu[4]

[1] National Key Lab for Novel Software Technology,
Nanjing University, Nanjing, China
wangwenhai362@163.com, wuyirui@hhu.edu.cn, lutong@nju.edu.cn
[2] College of Computer and Information, Hohai University, Nanjing, China
[3] Department of Computer System and Information Technology,
University of Malaya, Kuala Lumpur, Malaysia
shiva@um.edu.my
[4] School of Electrical and Electronic Engineering,
Nanyang Technological University, Singapore, Singapore
jliu029@ntu.edu.sg

Abstract. Detecting arbitrary oriented text in scene and license plate images is challenging due to multiple adverse factors caused by images of diversified applications. This paper proposes a novel idea of extracting Cloud of Line Distribution (COLD) for the text candidates given by Extremal regions (ER). The features extracted by COLD are fed to Random forest to label character components. The character components are grouped according to probability distribution of nearest neighbor components. This results in text line. The proposed method is demonstrated on standard database of natural scene images, namely ICDAR 2015, video images, namely ICDAR 2015 and license plate databases. Experimental results and comparative study show that the proposed method outperforms the existing methods in terms of invariant to rotations, scripts and applications.

Keywords: Extremal regions · Text candidates · COLD
Text detection · License plate detection

1 Introduction

As technology grows, flexibility in capturing images and videos increases. This leads to have data of diversified images, such as scene images captured by high resolution camera, video images captured by low resolution camera and license plate images captured when vehicle is moving fast [1–3]. As results, one can

---

W. Wang and Y. Wu indicates equal contribution.

© Springer International Publishing AG, part of Springer Nature 2018
B. Zeng et al. (Eds.): PCM 2017, LNCS 10735, pp. 433–443, 2018.
https://doi.org/10.1007/978-3-319-77380-3_41

expect images affected by multiple diverse factors, such as low contrast, complex background, illumination effect, blur, occlusion etc. Therefore, there is tremendous scope for developing a method which can withstand the above multiple diverse factors. There are methods in literature, most methods focus on particular data with limited causes to achieve better results [1,2,4]. For example, Shivakumara et al. [5] proposed a new multi-modal approach to bib number/text detection and recognition in Marathon images. It combines biometric features with text feature to detect text in Marathon images. Recently, the methods are explored deep learning for text detection in natural scene images [6]. However, these methods require large number of labeled data and it is hard to optimize the parameters for different application and dataset [7]. Similarly, we can find many methods for text detection in video images. For example, Shivakumara et al. [8] proposed optical flow based dynamic curved video text detection. The method explores constant velocity and uniform magnitude properties of text components for text detection.

In the same way, there are methods for license plate detection in the images. In this work, we consider license plate detection is also text detection task because license plate is nothing but text with numerals. Moreover, it is challenging compared to scene and video data due to sever illumination effect, blur, contrast variations and distortions due to vehicle movements. Panahi and Gholampour [9] proposed accurate detection and recognition of dirty vehicle plate numbers for high speed applications. However, this method adapts specific language features for achieving results. In summary, it is noted that there are sophisticated methods for text detection in natural scene images, videos and license plate images. However, these methods focus on particular dataset with specific cause but not the images affected by multiple causes. Motivated by the work proposed in [10] for text spotting in natural scene images and license plate images, we propose a new method for text detection in all three types of images. The method used in [10] works well for high contrast images but not video images captured low resolution camera. Our aim is to address the challenges posed by natural scene images, video images as well as license plate images.

2   The Proposed Method

It is fact that text components in image of different types have characteristics which play a prominent role in representing character components, namely, shape, contrast, stroke information, uniform spacing between the characters. These characteristics are invariant to rotation, scaling, to some extent to distortions, illumination effects. To exploit such features, we propose Extremal Regions (ER) to detect text candidates which represent text. Due to background and foreground variations, ER couldn't detect text candidates accurately. Therefore, we propose filters to eliminate false text candidates. Then the proposed method uses polygonal approximation to detect dominant points on contour of the text candidates. The shape of the text candidates is studied by applying new concept called Cloud of Line Distribution (COLD) which finds unique property based

Fig. 1. Text candidates detection results, where (a) is the input image, (b) is the ER detection result and (c) represents the result of text candidate detection.

on angle information between dominant points. This results in character components. The character components are used to form text lines based alignment and spacing between character components.

2.1 Text Candidate Detection

For an input image, we generate text candidates, say $\{e_i\}$ of the input image I by detecting ER in multi-channels $\{C_l | l = 1...3\}$, namely, RGB channels [11]. Since the problem is complex, we propose the following filters for the output of ER.

(1) Filter using geometric properties: Since characters usually have similar geometric appearance, we estimate the ratio between the area and diameter of ER. In addition, this filter also used Euler number for eliminating false text candidates.

(2) Filter using intensity distribution: Inspired by the fact that characters have uniform color values. The proposed method discards the text candidates, which have high variation in intensity values. We first perform histogram operation on intensity values and adopt mean of the maximal and second-maximal value of the histogram as the split value. Then the proposed method calculates the intensity variance H_i of ER by

$$H_i = \frac{n_f \cdot \sum_{x \in e_{i,f}} (I_x - A_{e_{i,t}})^2 + n_b \cdot \sum_{x \in e_{i,b}} (I_x - A_{e_{i,b}})^2}{n_t + n_b} \tag{1}$$

where $e_{i,f}$ and $e_{i,b}$ represent the text and non-text of e_i respectively, n refers to the number of pixels and A represents the mean value. The effect of ER and Filtering is illustrated in Fig. 1 where (a) is the input image with arbitrary oriented text, (b) is the result of ER and (c) is the result of filtering. It is noticed from Fig. 1(c) that the above filtering classifies non-text candidates as text candidates. This is due to components in the background share filtering properties.

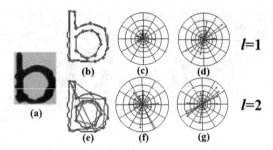

Fig. 2. Illustration of the process of the dominate points detection and COLD feature construction, where (a) is the example text ER, (b) and (e) define dominate point pairs with $l = 1$ and $l = 2$, (c), (f) and (d), (g) are the result distributions in Euclidean space and Tangent space, respectively.

2.2   Polygonal Approximation for Contour Points Detection

For each text candidate, the proposed method obtains Canny edges. The reason to choose Canny edge operator for edge contour detection is that Canny gives fine contours irrespective of contrast compared to Sobel and Prewitt which are sensitive to contrast variations. The dominant points p_k for each edge image of the text candidate are defined as

$$\begin{cases} \{c_j | j = 1...m\} = f_{cc}(Edge(e_i)) \\ \{p_{j,k} | j = 1...m, k = 1...n\} = f_\varphi(c_j) \end{cases} \tag{2}$$

where m and n refer to the number of connected components and dominant points, function $Egde()$ represents the Canny edge operator, function $f_{cc}()$ represents the operation of labeling connected components $\{c_j\}$ based on Canny edge image, function $f_\varphi()$ means the operation of detecting dominant points for each connected component c_j. The process of finding dominant points for the contour is known as polygonal approximation which is widely used in handwriting recognition [12] and shape classification [13]. Formally, we use the classical Ramer-Douglas-Peucker algorithm [14,15] as $f_\varphi()$ to detect dominant points, since it gives robust approximation results for complex contours and supports fast computing.

When we observe the output of polygonal approximation of the text candidates, text candidates representing actual characters have more straight lines while the text candidate representing false characters have more irregular lines. This observation motivates us to introduce shape descriptor called Cloud of Line Distribution (COLD) which extracts such observations in the form of distributions in angular space. This will be discussed in detail in subsequent section.

2.3   Cloud of Line Distribution for Character Component Detection

This section presents COLD feature extraction based on detected dominant points $\{p_{j,k}\}$, which describes shape of contours in multiple levels and space.

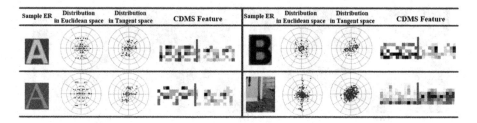

Fig. 3. The result cloud of point distributions and log-polar histograms based feature for different kinds of ER. Note that the red line is set to split feature into Euclidean-based and Tangent-based feature. (Color figure online)

Given an input image I and the ordered dominant points $\{p_{j,k}\}$, we aim to model the relation between pairs of dominant points in both Euclidean space $\mathcal{E}$ and Tangent space $\mathcal{T}$. Note that dominant points in $\mathcal{T}$ could be represented as $p_{\mathcal{T}} = (x, y, \rho)$, where we use Principle Components Analysis (PCA) to calculate tangent vector ρ and ρ is regarded as the orientation of this dominant point. In other words, ρ gives the direction based on neighbor information. We choose PCA and neighbor pixel information to find the orientation rather than choosing the gradient direction as used in the past for skeleton extraction [16] to focus on shape representation of contours and save the number of computations. The relation of dominant point pair $(p_{j,a}, p_{j,b})$ is thus measured as differences of orientation and distance, i.e. $\{\theta, d\}$, which could be represented as follows:

$$(p_{j,a}, p_{j,b}) = \begin{cases} d_{\mathcal{E}} = \sqrt{(x_b - x_a)^2 + (y_b - y_a)^2} \\ \theta_{\mathcal{E}} = \arctan(\frac{y_b - y_a}{x_b - x_a}) \\ d_{\mathcal{T}} = |\rho_a - \rho_b| \\ \theta_{\mathcal{T}} = f_\varphi(\rho_a - \rho_b) \end{cases} \quad (3)$$

where (x_a, y_a) and (x_b, y_b) are the coordinates of $p_{j,a}$ and $p_{j,b}$ respectively, ρ_a and ρ_b are the tangent vectors for $p_{j,a}$ and $p_{j,b}$ respectively and function $f_\varphi()$ computes the angle between a vector and horizontal line. Inspired by the Shape Context [17], we transform the $(\theta_{\mathcal{E}}, d_{\mathcal{E}})$ and $(\theta_{\mathcal{T}}, d_{\mathcal{T}})$ into log-polar space, which generates cloud of point distributions in multiple space. The two normalized log-polar histograms thus form the final feature vector $F_j(e_i) = [F_{j,e}, F_{j,t}]$ for the jth connected component, which is the proposed COLD feature and could be adopted as shape descriptors to classify text candidates as text or non-text. To describe relation between points in far distance, we define pairs every l points. In other words, we represent $p_{j,k}$ and $p_{j,k+l}$ as dominant point pair. Figure 2(b) and (e) show the process of defining pairs with $l = 1$ and $l = 2$ respectively and the corresponding result distributions with log-polar space are shown in Fig. 2(c), (f), (d) and (g). With variant values of l, we successfully capture properties of shape of contours in different levels. In other words, we describe shape of contours in local manner when l is small. When l is a larger value, we intend to construct a more global shape descriptors.

Fig. 4. The result of text line formation: (a) text candidates detection result, (b) text components after removing non-text components, (c) text line detection result.

We thus concatenate the COLD features with different l and different j together to form the final feature vector $F = [F_{j,k}(e_i)|j = 1...m, k = 1...l]$ for ith ER region. To present the description ability for shape of contours by our proposed COLD feature, we show the cloud of line distributions and log-polar histograms based feature F for different kinds of ER in Fig. 3. It is observed from Fig. 3 that the same character (Two A) tends to own the similar distributions and features, while different characters(A and B) or characters and background have different distributions and features. Finally, we apply COLD feature F in a random forest model to achieve the label for ith ER as $L = f_\tau(F(e_i))$. The final result of COLD is shown in Fig. 4, where (a) is text candidate image and (b) is the result of applying COLD. It is noted from Fig. 4(b) that all non-text candidates are removed.

2.4   Text Line Formation

Let text candidate be S which provides coarse locations of character components. To draw bounding box for the extracted text line, the proposed method groups the character components that share the common properties such as scale, orientation and color contrast. Inspired by [18], we find the color of character components which has uniform values compared to it background. Thus, we propose perceptual divergence to measure the perceptual divergence of a region against its surroundings as $PD(s) = \sum_{R,G,B} \sum_{\delta=1}^{w} h_\delta(s) \log \frac{h_\delta(s)}{h_\delta(\tilde{s})}$, where the term the Kullback-Leibler divergence (KLD) measuring the dissimilarity of two probability distributions, $h_\delta(s)$ and $h_\delta(\tilde{s})$ represent the histograms of text candidate and its surroundings. In this way, the proposed method groups the text candidates into text lines with the following conditions:

$$
\begin{cases}
2/3 \leq |H_p/H_q| \leq 3/2 \\
|\theta_p - \theta_q| \leq \pi/8 \\
|f_d(p,q) - (W_p + W_q)/2| \leq H_p + H_q \\
|PD(p) - PD(q)| \leq 7
\end{cases}
\tag{4}
$$

where H, W and θ represent the height, width and orientation of text region respectively, and $f_d(p,q)$ refers to the distance between center of p and q.

Note that all the parameters in Eq. (4) are determined experimentally. If character components satisfy this property, the proposed method considers the character components for grouping as shown in Fig. 4(c), where one can see how the proposed method fixes bounding boxes for different oriented text lines.

3   Experiments

To evaluate the robustness of the proposed method, we consider three benchmark databases, namely, ICDAR 2015 scene [24], ICDAR2015 video [24] and Medialab License Plate database [22]. We select 10 videos from ICDAR2015 video dataset for our experiments. Medialab LPR is designed for license plate recognition and complex due to the images affected by severe illumination, touching characters, blur effect and perspective distortion effect. The evaluation scheme and instructions given in [24] are used for calculating standard measures, namely, Recall, Precision, F-measure and time cost per image. Note that the results of Table 1 are directly sampling from website of ICDAR 2015 scene competition [25]. In order to show effectiveness of the proposed method for video images, we implement Wu et al. [20] which explore character shape restoration for text detection in both natural and video images, Huang et al. [21] which uses the concepts of MSER and convolutional neural networks for text detection in natural scene images. In the same way, we use available code of the Yin et al. [19] and Neumann and Mattas [11] which use MSER concept for text detection in natural scene images. We also implement Anagnostopoulos et al. [22], Zhu et al. [23] and Zambeerletti et al. [10] to compare the effectiveness for text detection on licence plate images.

Table 1. Performance of text detection on ICDAR 2015 scene

Method	Precision	Recall	F-measure	Time-cost
Proposed	0.72	0.55	0.62	3.44
Only Euclidean space	0.70	0.51	0.59	3.42
Only Tangent space	0.69	0.52	0.59	3.43
CTPN	**0.74**	0.52	0.61	**1.40**
CNN Pro	0.35	0.34	0.35	–
HUST	0.44	0.38	0.41	–
NJU-Text	0.70	0.36	0.47	–
MSRA-v1	0.74	0.85	**0.79**	–

Quantitative results of the proposed and existing method are reported in Tables 1, 2 and 3 for the ICDAR 2015 scene data, ICDAR 2015 video data and License Plate data, respectively. Note that we achieve our results on a Laptop with 2.2 GHz Core2 i7, 6 GB RAM and Nvidia GTX 960M. Table 1 shows that

Table 2. Performance of text detection on subset of ICDAR 2015 video

Method	Precision	Recall	F-measure	Time-cost
Proposed	0.73	**0.65**	**0.69**	1.74
Only Euclidean space	0.72	0.60	0.65	1.72
Only Tangent space	0.70	0.62	0.66	1.72
Yin et al. [19]	0.64	0.57	0.60	**1.54**
Neumann et al. [11]	0.48	0.58	0.53	1.78
Wu et al. [20]	0.51	0.61	0.55	1.77
Huang et al. [21]	**0.79**	0.60	0.68	3.91

Table 3. Performance of text detection on Medialab LPR

Method	Precision	Recall	F-measure	Time-cost
Proposed	**0.90**	**0.81**	**0.85**	1.23
Only Euclidean space	0.85	0.78	0.81	1.02
Only Tangent space	0.85	0.73	0.78	1.03
Anagnostopoulos et al. [22]	0.81	0.63	0.71	0.87
Zhu et al. [23]	0.82	0.73	0.77	0.70
Zambeerletti et al. [10]	0.83	0.76	0.79	**0.61**

the proposed method is the second best at F-measure and Recall and third best at Precision for the ICDAR 2015 scene database. Focusing on shape information of text, the proposed method even outperforms MSER+CNN method, i.e. CNN Pro and NJUText, in f-measure. These facts show the importance of shape information for text detection task. Meanwhile, the proposed method would fail with cases where text appear with broken shape. Considering that most of the characters in ICDAR 2015 scene own solid shape, the proposed method thus achieves a good precision and recall performance. Several CNN-based methods, i.e. CTPN and MSRA-v1, score higher than our method in ICDAR 2015 scene. However, the proposed method achieves detection results with much lower time, computation and hardware cost. From Table 2, the proposed method scores the best results at Recall and F-measure and second best at Precision for subset of ICDAR 2015 video database compared to existing methods. Based on detection results of ICDAR 2015 scene and video, we could conclude the proposed method remain consistent in performance for various scenarios. Table 3 shows the proposed method score best in precision, recognition and F-measure but the last in time cost. The listed three methods are designed especially for car plate detection task. In that case, they try to get balance between computation cost and performance. Meanwhile, our method could handle with various situations, such as scene, video and car plate text. Qualitative results of the proposed method for the different database are shown in Fig. 5 where we can notice that the proposed method detects text well regardless of database, orientation, background

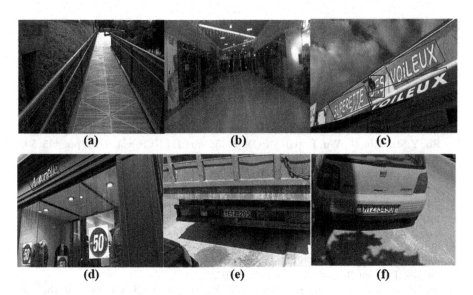

Fig. 5. Detection examples of the proposed method on ICDAR 2015 scene, ICDAR 2015 video and Medialab LPR.

complexity, font size and font variations. In summary, we can conclude that the proposed method is robust and generic as it gives consistent results for the different databases and outperforms the existing methods.

4   Conclusion

We have proposed a new method for arbitrary text detection in natural scene, video and license plate images. The proposed method explores ER for detecting text candidates. For text candidates, the proposed method uses polygonal approximation for dominant point detection over contour of text candidates. To eliminate false text candidates, we have introduced Cloud of Line Distribution which results in character components. Experimental results show the proposed method outperforms the existing methods for three different databases.

Acknowledgements. This work was supported by the Natural Science Foundation of China under Grant 61672273, Grant 61272218, and Grant 61321491, by the Science Foundation for Distinguished Young Scholars of Jiangsu under Grant BK20160021, by the Science Foundation of Jiangsu under Grant BK20170892, by the Fundamental Research Funds for the Central Universities under Grant 2013/B16020141 and by the open Project of the National Key Lab for Novel Software Technology in NJU under Grant KFKT2017B05.

References

1. Ye, Q., Doermann, D.S.: Text detection and recognition in imagery: a survey. IEEE Trans. PAMI **37**(7), 1480–1500 (2015)
2. Yin, X., Zuo, Z., Tian, S., Liu, C.: Text detection, tracking and recognition in video: a comprehensive survey. IEEE Trans. IP **25**(6), 2752–2773 (2016)
3. Weng, Y., Shivakumara, P., Lu, T., Meng, L.K., Woon, H.H.: A new multi-spectral fusion method for degraded video text frame enhancement. In: Ho, Y.-S., Sang, J., Ro, Y.M., Kim, J., Wu, F. (eds.) PCM 2015, Part I. LNCS, vol. 9314, pp. 495–506. Springer, Cham (2015). https://doi.org/10.1007/978-3-319-24075-6_48
4. Roy, S., Shivakumara, P., Mondal, P., Raghavendra, R., Pal, U., Lu, T.: A new multi-modal technique for bib number/text detection in natural images. In: Ho, Y.-S., Sang, J., Ro, Y.M., Kim, J., Wu, F. (eds.) PCM 2015, Part I. LNCS, vol. 9314, pp. 483–494. Springer, Cham (2015). https://doi.org/10.1007/978-3-319-24075-6_47
5. Shivakumara, P., Raghavendra, R., Qin, L., Raja, K.B., Lu, T., Pal, U.: A new multi-modal approach to bib number/text detection and recognition in marathon images. Pattern Recogn. **61**, 479–491 (2017)
6. Jaderberg, M., Simonyan, K., Vedaldi, A., Zisserman, A.: Reading text in the wild with convolutional neural networks. IJCV **116**(1), 1–20 (2016)
7. Liu, W., Wang, Z., Liu, X., Zeng, N., Liu, Y., Alsaadi, F.E.: A survey of deep neural network architecture and their applications. Neurocomputing **234**, 11–26 (2017)
8. Shivakumara, P., Lubani, M., Wong, K., Lu, T.: Optical flow based dynamic curved video text detection. In: Proceedings of ICIP, pp. 1668–1672 (2014)
9. Panahi, R., Gholampour, I.: Accurate detection and recognition of dirty vehicle plate numbers for high-speed applications. IEEE Trans. Intell. Transp. Syst. **18**, 767–779 (2016)
10. Zamberletti, A., Gallo, I., Noce, L.: Augmented text character proposals and convolutional neural networks for text spotting from scene images. In: Proceedings of ACPR, pp. 196–200 (2015)
11. Neumann, L., Matas, J.: Real-time scene text localization and recognition. In: Proceedings of CVPR, pp. 3538–3545 (2012)
12. He, S., Schomaker, L.: Writer identification using curvature-free features. Pattern Recogn. **63**, 451–464 (2017)
13. Wang, X., Feng, B., Bai, X., Liu, W., Latecki, L.J.: Bag of contour fragments for robust shape classification. Pattern Recogn. **47**(6), 2116–2125 (2014)
14. Ramer, U.: An iterative procedure for the polygonal approximation of plane curves. Comput. Graph. Image Process. **1**(3), 244–256 (1972)
15. Prasad, D.K., Leung, M.K.H., Quek, C., Cho, S.: A novel framework for making dominant point detection methods non-parametric. Image Vis. Comput. **30**(11), 843–859 (2012)
16. Wu, Y., Shivakumara, P., Wei, W., Lu, T., Pal, U.: A new ring radius transform-based thinning method for multi-oriented video characters. IJDAR **18**(2), 137–151 (2015)
17. Belongie, S.J., Malik, J., Puzicha, J.: Shape matching and object recognition using shape contexts. IEEE Trans. PAMI **24**(4), 509–522 (2002)
18. Li, Y., Jia, W., Shen, C., van den Hengel, A.: Characterness: an indicator of text in the wild. IEEE Trans. IP **23**(4), 1666–1677 (2014)

19. Yin, X., Yin, X., Huang, K., Hao, H.: Robust text detection in natural scene images. IEEE Trans. PAMI **36**(5), 970–983 (2014)
20. Wu, Y., Shivakumara, P., Lu, T., Lim Tan, C., Blumenstein, M., Kumar, G.H.: Contour restoration of text components for recognition in video/scene images. IEEE Trans. IP **25**(12), 5622–5634 (2016)
21. Huang, W., Qiao, Y., Tang, X.: Robust scene text detection with convolution neural network induced MSER trees. In: Fleet, D., Pajdla, T., Schiele, B., Tuytelaars, T. (eds.) ECCV 2014, Part IV. LNCS, vol. 8692, pp. 497–511. Springer, Cham (2014). https://doi.org/10.1007/978-3-319-10593-2_33
22. Anagnostopoulos, C., Anagnostopoulos, I., Loumos, V., Kayafas, E.: A license plate-recognition algorithm for intelligent transportation system applications. IEEE Trans. Intell. Transp. Syst. **7**(3), 377–392 (2006)
23. Zhu, S., Dianat, S.A., Mestha, L.K.: End-to-end system of license plate localization and recognition. J. Electron. Imaging **24**(2), 023020 (2015)
24. Karatzas, D., Gomez-Bigorda, L., Nicolaou, A., Ghosh, S., Bagdanow, A., Iwamura, M., Matas, J., Neumann, L., Chandrsekha, V.R.: ICDAR 2015 competition on robust reading. In: Proceedings of ICDAR, pp. 1156–1160 (2015)
25. ICDAR 2015 robust reading competition. http://rrc.cvc.uab.es/?ch=4&com=evaluation&task=1&gtv=1

Affine Collaborative Representation Based Classification for In-Air Handwritten Chinese Character Recognition

Jianshe Zhou[1(✉)], Zhaochun Xu[2], Jie Liu[1], Weiqiang Wang[2], and Ke Lu[2]

[1] Beijing Advanced Innovation Center for Imaging Technology,
Capital Normal University, Beijing, China
zhoujianshe@solcun.net, liujie@cnu.edu.cn
[2] School of Computer and Control Engineering,
University of Chinese Academy of Sciences, Beijing, China
xuzhaochun14@mails.ucas.ac.cn, {wqwang,luk}@ucas.ac.cn

Abstract. This paper presents a study of using affine collaborative representation based classification (ACRC) for recognizing the in-air handwritten Chinese characters, which is collected by Leap Motion, one kind of 3-dimensional sensing device. This classifier uses the form of collaborative representation based classification (CRC), namely it also use the l_2-norm for sparse coding. But there exists differences between them. Firstly, the atoms of ACRC's dictionary comes from the eigenvectors of each class's covariance matrix, which is easy to obtain in the dictionary learning stage and the size can be much smaller than CRC. Secondly, we compute the coefficients of each class separately on each class's dictionary atoms, instead of computing on the total atoms of the whole classes. For evaluating this classifier's performance, we conduct a series of experiments on the in-air handwritten Chinese character dataset, IAHCC-UCAS2016. And supplementally, we also do the experiments on the online handwritten Chinese character dataset, SCUT-2009. The results are satisfying for the sufficiently high recognition accuracy and the high speed of computation.

Keywords: In-air handwritten Chinese character recognition
Collaborative representation based classification · Sparse coding

1 Introduction

During last several decades, the problem of online handwritten Chinese character recognition (OLHCCR) has been studied by many researchers [1,2]. The related works make tremendous improvement on the recognition accuracy, computation efficiency and storage cost [3]. Nowadays, the related techniques have created many popular applications in our daily lives. With the development of

© Springer International Publishing AG, part of Springer Nature 2018
B. Zeng et al. (Eds.): PCM 2017, LNCS 10735, pp. 444–452, 2018.
https://doi.org/10.1007/978-3-319-77380-3_42

(a) general handwritten samples   (b) in-air handwritten samples

Fig. 1. Samples of general and in-air handwritten Chinese characters " 的 " , " 最 "

3-dimensional sensing devices, a new form of OLHCCR called in-air handwritten Chinese character recognition (IAHCCR) is becoming a new research topic in OLHCCR community [4,5]. Compared with the general OLHCCR, writing in the air by only using the 3D sensing devices is more natural and convenient. Some examples of general and in-air handwritten Chinese characters are shown in Fig. 1. We can see that because when in-air handwriting there's no pen-up and pen-down action, the variation of the in-air handwritten Chinese characters' structure is richer, which makes IAHCCR more challenging.

Sparse representation as a key technique has been successfully applied to solve the problems in computer vision and image processing in recent years [6–8]. It provides a compact description of natural signals by linear combination of the basic signals. To extend its power, sparse representation based classification (SRC) was proposed by Wright et al. [9]. This classifier first encodes a given input with l_1-norm sparsity constraint to guarantee the coefficients's sparsity, then uses the atoms of each class to reconstruct the input signal and determine its class label by the reconstruction error. Though it is widely believed that the success of SRC is mostly depended on the l_1-norm sparsity constraint, Zhang et al. [10] show that collaborative representation mechanism plays a more significant role than the sparsity constraint in classification and they presented the collaborative based classification (CRC) with l_2-norm sparsity constraint to make the computation of coding coefficients more efficient.

In this paper, we utilize the framework of SRC and CRC to solving the problem of IAHCCR by following [11]'s idea. To efficiently obtain the dictionary of each class in the training stage, inspired by [12,13] we use the PCA method to compute the PCA-patch vectors as the atoms of each class' dictionary, which consists of the most discriminative basis vectors. By this method, we dramatically reduce the size of dictionary, in comparison to the SRC or CRC which directly use the training sample as the dictionary. At the recognition stage, we first move the test input into each class' affine subspace, then encode it by solving the collaborative representation problem via l_2-norm minimization. Finally we classify the input by the minimum construction error criterion. Through the process above, this paper easily solved the problem of hardly applying the general SRC and CRC on IAHCCR and achieve a satisfying result both on recognition accuracy and computational efficiency.

2   Related Works

Given an input vector $x \in R^d$ and to get a compact description based on an over-complete dictionary $D \in R^{d \times K}$, sparse representation sum up this problem as the following minimization problem,

$$\min_{\alpha} \|\alpha\|_0 \quad s.t. \quad x = D\alpha \tag{1}$$

where $\alpha \in R^K$ is the coding coefficients on the dictionary D and the symbol $\|\alpha\|_0$ means the l_0-norm, namely the counts of nonzero numbers in α. Though this is the most strict expression for sparsity constraint, we cannot directly solve it for it is an NP-hard problem. But related researches show that we can use the l_1-norm minimization to approach the l_0-norm minimization, for that the l_1-norm minimization is a convex optimization problem. In fact, due to the noises, we always get an approximate representation by linear combination of the atoms in D for x. So we rewrite this problem as

$$\min_{\alpha} \|\alpha\|_1 \quad s.t. \quad \|x - D\alpha\|_2^2 \leq \varepsilon \tag{2}$$

where ε is a small constant. To solve this optimization problem, Eq. (2) can be converted by Lagrange formula into

$$\min_{\alpha} \|x - D\alpha\|_2^2 + \lambda \|\alpha\|_1 \tag{3}$$

where λ is the regularization parameter which controls the sparsity. To solve the l_1-norm minimization in Eq. (3), many algorithms were proposed like Gradient Projection and Augmented Lagrange Multiplier (ALM) [14], and a related review can be found in literature [15].

To extend sparse representation's power, Wright et al. proposed the sparse representation based classification (SRC) for robust face recognition [9]. SRC uses all the training data $[X_1, X_2, ...X_C] \in R^{d \times N}$ as the dictionary D, where $X_c \in R^{d \times N_c}$ is composed by the cth class's training images as its columns and each column's l_2-norm is normalized to 1.

When given a test input y, we encode it on the whole dictionary D by Eq. (3) to get the coefficients $\alpha \in R^N$, where $\alpha = [\alpha_1; \alpha_2; ...\alpha_C]$ and $\alpha_c \in R^{N_c}$ are the coefficients corresponding to the cth class's training data X_c. So we can easily get y's reconstruction on each class by $X_c \alpha_c$ and the classification will be done based on the minimum reconstruction error criterion, namely we classify y's class by the following rule,

$$c^* = arg \min_c \|y - X_c \alpha_c\|_2^2. \tag{4}$$

SRC is an efficient classifier for face recognition, but the computation for l_1-norm minimization to get the coefficients is complex and time-consuming though researchers are devoted to speed up the l_1-minimization process [15]. Zhang et al. [10] analyzed the working mechanism of SRC and found that it is the collaborative representation (CR) that plays a crucial role in classification rather than the l_1-norm sparsity. To reduce the computation burden, collaborative representation based classification (CRC) chooses the l_2-norm, so the corresponding minimization problem can be rewritten as

$$\min_{\alpha} \|x - D\alpha\|_2^2 + \lambda\|\alpha\|_2. \tag{5}$$

The solution of Eq. (5) can be easily derived by the regularized least square method, i.e.

$$\hat{\alpha} = (D^T D + \lambda I)^{-1} D^T x. \tag{6}$$

Notice that $P = (D^T D + \lambda I)^{-1} D^T$ is independent of the test input x, so when the dictionary D is settled, we can pre-compute it and $\hat{\alpha}$ can be fast computed out by $\hat{\alpha} = Px$.

For classification, it's same as SRC by using Eq. (4) to determine x's class. What's more, the l_2-norm $\|\hat{\alpha}_c\|_2^2$ also has some discrimination information, so it can be used to improve the classification accuracy by

$$c^* = arg \min_{c} \|y - X_c\hat{\alpha}_c\|_2 / \|\hat{\alpha}_c\|_2. \tag{7}$$

In [10], it does slightly improve the classification accuracy over the general one.

3   Affine Collaborative Representation Based Classification

In this section, we will detailly study the affine collaborative representation based classification (ACRC). ACRC consists of two parts, namely the dictionary learning stage and the classification stage. We will first present how we obtain the dictionary of ACRC separated for each class, and then furtherly explain how to use ACRC for classification.

3.1   The Dictionary Learning Stage

Inspired by [13], here we also describe the geometry of feature space by an ensemble of all classes' affine subspaces which are attached to their respectively original points subspaces:

$$S_c = \{\mu_c + D_c\alpha, \alpha \in R^k\}, c = 1, 2...C \tag{8}$$

where $\mu_c \in R^d$ denotes the cth class' original point, $D_c \in R^{d \times k}$ denotes the cth class' basis vectors and $\alpha \in R^k$ denotes the coordinates, by which we can represent the cth class' affine subspace. And when given cth class' point y, we can compute its coordinates as long as we have the μ_c and D_c, which can be seen as an encoding process.

To gain the basis vectors of each class, we use the PCA method on each class' samples. Principal component analysis(PCA) [16] is well known as an effective dimensionality reduction method. Its basic idea is that the features with larger variance are more important while the features with small variances are redundant. To reduce the dimensionality of original vectors, PCA needs to seek the orthogonal basis vectors to span the given samples' space. These basis vectors $[\boldsymbol{u}_1, \boldsymbol{u}_2, ... \boldsymbol{u}_d]$ can be obtained via calculating the eigenvectors of the given samples' covariance matrix $\boldsymbol{\Sigma}$. Then for the feature vector $\boldsymbol{x}$ among the given samples, its coordinate $\boldsymbol{\alpha}^{(i)}$ on $\boldsymbol{u}_i$ can be computed out by $\boldsymbol{\alpha}^{(i)} = \boldsymbol{x}^T \boldsymbol{u}_i$.

For ACRC, the dictionary of each class comes from the basis vectors of the corresponding class' subspace, in other words, comes from the eigenvectors of the corresponding class' covariance matrix. Due to the same reason of PCA dimensional reduction that the eigenvectors with larger eigenvalues are more significant directions and robust to the noise, we employ the eigenvectors with larger eigenvalues as the corresponding class' dictionary. The appropriate number of atoms for each class' dictionary are determined by the experimental results.

So given the data matrix $\boldsymbol{X}_c = [\boldsymbol{x}_1, \boldsymbol{x}_2, ... \boldsymbol{x}_{N_c}]$ for the cth class, we first compute its mean vector $\boldsymbol{\mu}_c$, then we calculate the covariance matrix $\boldsymbol{\Sigma}_c$ by

$$\boldsymbol{\Sigma}_c = \frac{1}{N_c - 1} \sum_{i=1}^{N_c} (\boldsymbol{x}_i - \boldsymbol{\mu}_c)(\boldsymbol{x}_i - \boldsymbol{\mu}_c)^T. \tag{9}$$

Finally, we calculate $\boldsymbol{\Sigma}_c$'s eigenvectors and choose the most significant eigenvectors to form the cth class's dictionary $\boldsymbol{D}_c = [\boldsymbol{u}_{c1}, \boldsymbol{u}_{c2}, ... \boldsymbol{u}_{ck}]$.

3.2   The Classification Stage

After obtaining the dictionary of each class, we will do the classification for the test input vector $\boldsymbol{y}$. But firstly, the number of Chinese characters is very large (about 3755), this makes the whole dictionary too big to compute the coding coefficients of all classes once like the general SRC and CRC; secondly, the atoms of each class's dictionary are the eigenvectors which build the corresponding class's subspace as presented in Eq. (8), we should not encode $\boldsymbol{y}$ directly but should move it into the subspace at first.

In ACRC we also determine the test input vector $\boldsymbol{y}$'s class according to the minimum reconstruction error criterion like in SRC or CRC. To compute the reconstruction error $\boldsymbol{r}_c$ of $\boldsymbol{y}$ on the cth class, we first move $\boldsymbol{y}$ to cth class's space by subtracting cth class's mean vector $\boldsymbol{\mu}_c$ which is used to estimated the original point, then the new vector is encoded to obtain the coefficients $\boldsymbol{\alpha}_c$, these processes can be presented by the following objective function

$$\min_{\boldsymbol{\alpha}_c} \| (\boldsymbol{y} - \boldsymbol{\mu}_c) - \boldsymbol{D}_c \boldsymbol{\alpha}_c \|_2^2 + \lambda \| \boldsymbol{\alpha}_c \|_2^2, \tag{10}$$

which is very similar to Eq. (5) in CRC, so the solution for $\hat{\boldsymbol{\alpha}}_c$ derived by the regularized least square method will be

$$\hat{\boldsymbol{\alpha}}_c = (\boldsymbol{D}_c^T \boldsymbol{D}_c + \lambda \boldsymbol{I})^{-1} \boldsymbol{D}_c^T (\boldsymbol{y} - \boldsymbol{\mu}_c). \tag{11}$$

Notice that D_c is composed by the unit orthogonal eigenvectors, so Eq. (10) can be simplified as

$$\hat{\alpha}_c = (1 + \lambda)^{-1} D_c^T (y - \mu_c). \tag{12}$$

Then y's reconstruction error on cth class is computed out by $r^{(c)} = \|y - \mu_c - D_c \alpha_c\|_2^2$. Finally using $c^* = \arg\min_c r^{(c)}$, we determine y's class.

4   Experimental Results

In this section, we evaluate the proposed method by comparing it with the modified quadratic discriminant function (MQDF) which is a common classifier for OLHCCR [17] and one variant of SRC, the locality-constrained SRC (LSRC) [11] which also train the dictionary and encode the coefficients separated on each class mentioned above. Before the experiments, the related preprocessing of OLHCCR. Then for each sample, the 512-dimensional 8-directional feature vector [18] is extracted and we reduce its dimension by PCA and LDA to 160 dimension.

We employ two challenging HCCR datasets for performance evaluation, which both contains 3755 Chinese characters. One is the public OLHCCR dataset SCUT-COUCH2009 [19]. In this dataset, each character has 188 samples, from which 150 samples are randomly chosen for training. The other one is a Chinese in-air handwriting dataset IAHCCR-UCAS2016. In this dataset, each character has 115 samples, from which 92 samples are randomly chosen for training. The following experiments are carried out on an Intel Quad Core PC with 2.83 GHz processors and 4 GB RAM.

4.1   Experiments

As mentioned above, each feature vector is 160-dimensional, so for each class there are at most 160 eigenvectors as atoms to form the current class's dictionary, and the eigenvector with larger eigenvalue will be chosen preferentially. But just like the dimensionality reduction, the more atoms does not mean the higher recognition accuracy. So we randomly choose 500 classes in IAHCCR and then implement a series of experiments by changing the number of atoms in each class to investigate how many atoms per class are suitable to have the highest recognition accuracy. The related experimental results are depicted in Fig. 2. We can see that when we assign the 15 atoms for each class, we can obtain the highest recognition rate.

To evaluate the performance of ACRC compared with MQDF and LSRC, we conduct another group of experiments. For MQDF, empirically we choose 40 for the number of the dominant eigenvectors. For LSRC, we choose 6 for the number of atoms per class and $\lambda = 0.01$ by which we can achieve best performance of LSRC. For ACRC, the number of atoms is 15 and $\lambda = 1$. Besides comparing the recognition rate shown in Tables 1 and 2, we also compare the consuming time for every recognition and the storage space which is shown in Table 3.

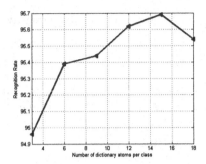

Fig. 2. Recognition rate using ACRC versus different number of atoms per class

Table 1. Recognition accuracy (%) of MQDF, LSRC and ACRC on IAHCCR-UCAS2016

Methods	Top 1	Top 5	Top 10
MQDF	88.17	96.80	97.89
LSRC	86.46	96.31	97.54
ACRC	**88.53**	**96.95**	**97.99**

Table 2. Recognition accuracy (%) of MQDF, LSRC and ACRC on SCUT-COUCH2009

Methods	Top 1	Top 5	Top 10
MQDF	**95.34**	**99.11**	99.42
LSRC	94.06	98.83	99.30
ACRC	94.99	99.06	**99.43**

Table 3. The total storage space and the average computation time of for each sample in seconds for MQDF, LSRC and ACRC on IAHCCR-UCAS2016

Comparison item	MQDF	LSRC	ACRC
Testing(s)	0.395	0.381	**0.150**
Space(MB)	712.73	**26.41**	70.40

In Tables 1 and 2 we can see that on the IAHCCR-UCAS dataset, ACRC achieves the highest recognition rate, however on the SCUT-COUCH2009 MQDF achieves the highest rate. In Table 3, we can see that ACRC runs fastest and its space consumption is in the acceptable scope.

5   Conclusions

In this paper, we study the affine collaborative representation based classification (ACRC) for in-air handwritten Chinese character recognition (IAHCCR). We can obtain ACRC's dictionary easily by choosing the principal eigenvectors of each class and its classifier is similar to CRC. Compared with MQDF, it achieves the comparable recognition rate but runs much faster and consumes much less storage cost.

Acknowledgments. The work is supported by the National Natural Science Foundation of China under Grant No. 61271434, No. 61232013, and by Beijing Advanced Innovation Center for Imaging Technology under Grant No. BAICIT-2016009.

References

1. Liu, C.L., Jaeger, S., Nakagawa, M.: Online recognition of Chinese characters: the state-of-the-art. IEEE Trans. Pattern Anal. Mach. Intell. **26**(2), 198–213 (2004)
2. Liu, C.L., Yin, F., Wang, D.H.: Online and offline handwritten Chinese character recognition: benchmarking on new databases. Pattern Recognit. **46**(1), 155–162 (2013)
3. Long, T., Jin, L.W.: Building compact MQDF classifier for large character set recognition by subspace distribution sharing. Pattern Recognit. **41**(9), 2916–2925 (2008)
4. Xu, N., Wang, W.Q., Qu, X.W.: Recognition of in-air handwritten Chinese character based on leap motion controller. In: Proceedings of the IEEE International Conference on Image and Graphics (ICIG), pp. 160–168 (2015)
5. Tang, J., Cheng, H., Yang, L.: Recognizing 3D continuous letter trajectory gesture using dynamic time warping. In: Ho, Y.-S., Sang, J., Ro, Y.M., Kim, J., Wu, F. (eds.) PCM 2015. LNCS, vol. 9315, pp. 191–200. Springer, Cham (2015). https://doi.org/10.1007/978-3-319-24078-7_19
6. Elad, M., Figueiredo, M., Ma, Y.: On the role of sparse and redundant representations in image processing. Proc. IEEE **98**(6), 972–982 (2010)
7. Wright, J., Ma, Y., Mairal, J., Sapiro, G., Huang, T., Yan, S.C.: Sparse representation for computer vision and pattern recognition. Proc. IEEE **98**(6), 1031–1044 (2010)
8. Toić, I., Frossard, P.: Dictionary learning: what is the right representation for my signal? IEEE Signal Process. Mag. **28**(2), 27–38 (2011)
9. Wright, J., Yang, A., Ganesh, A., Sastry, S., Ma, Y.: Robust face recognition via sparse representation. IEEE Trans. Pattern Anal. Mach. Intell. **31**(2), 210–227 (2009)
10. Zhang, L., Yang, M., Feng, X.C.: Sparse representation or collaborative representation: which helps face recognition. In: Proceedings of the IEEE International Conference on Computer Vision (ICCV), pp. 471–478 (2011)
11. Wei, C.P., Chao, Y.W., Yeh, Y.R., Wang, Y.F.: Locality-sensitive dictionary learning for sparse representation based classification. Pattern Recognit. **46**(5), 1277–1287 (2013)
12. Wang, Z., Fan, B., Wu, F.: Affine subspace representation for feature description. In: Fleet, D., Pajdla, T., Schiele, B., Tuytelaars, T. (eds.) ECCV 2014. LNCS, vol. 8695, pp. 94–108. Springer, Cham (2014). https://doi.org/10.1007/978-3-319-10584-0_7

13. Li, P.H., Lu, X.X., Wang, Q.L.: From dictionary of visual words to subspaces: locality-constrained affine subspace coding. In: Proceedings of the IEEE International Conference on Computer Vision and Pattern Recognition (CVPR), pp. 2348–2357 (2015)
14. Yang, J.F., Zhang, Y.: Alternating direction algorithms for l_1-problems in compressive sensing. SIAM J. Sci. Comput. **33**(1), 250–278 (2011)
15. Yang, A.Y., Ganesh, A., Zhou, Z.H., Sastry, S.S., Ma, Y.: Fast l_1-minimization algorithms and application in robust face recognition. UC Berkeley, Technical report
16. Wold, S., Esbensen, K., Geladi, P.: Principal component analysis. Chemom. Intell. Lab. Syst. **2**(1–3), 37–52 (1987)
17. Kimura, F., Takashina, K., Tsuruoka, S., et al.: Modified quadratic discriminant function and its application to Chinese character recognition. IEEE Trans. Pattern Anal. Mach. Intell. **9**(1), 149–153 (1987)
18. Bai. Z.L., Huo, Q.: A study on the use of 8-directional features for online handwritten Chinese character recognition. In: Proceedings of the IEEE International Conference on Document Analysis and Recognition, pp. 232–236 (2005)
19. Jin, L.W., Gao, Y., Liu, G., Li, Y.Y., Ding, K.: SCUT-COUCH2009 a comprehensive online unconstrained Chinese handwriting database and benchmark evaluation. Int. J. Doc. Anal. Recognit. **14**(1), 53–64 (2010)

Overlaid Chinese Character Recognition
via a Compact CNN

Hongzhu Li[✉] and Weiqiang Wang

University of Chinese Academy of Sciences, Beijing, China
lihongzu14@mails.ucas.ac.cn

Abstract. Great successes have been enjoyed in the previous work for Chinese character recognition (CCR), however, few impressive works have been done about the recognition of Chinese characters with complex backgrounds. This paper focuses on the recognition of overlaid Chinese characters - the Chinese characters embedded in images or videos - which are often with complex backgrounds and of diverse typefaces and styles. In this paper, we present a high-performance recognizer based on the deep convolutional neural network (CNN). To train the CNN, a large number of character images are first collected by the synthetic way. By fully considering the input size, depth, width, and filter sizes of a network, we present multiple candidate models with compact network architectures. Comprehensive comparison experiments are carried out to help us select the model, which requires only 13.6M for storage (3.6M parameters) and takes only 0.038 s for recognizing 3755 character images on a GPU. The experimental results shows that the model achieves the recognition rate of 99.77% on the test set, and a good generalization performance is also validated on the dataset of typefaces not included in the training set. Besides, the extensive comparison experiments presented in this paper might give lights into the formation of deep CNN.

Keywords: Overlaid Chinese character recognition
Character recognition · Convolutional Neural Network

1 Introduction

Overlaid text generally refers to the embedded text in images or videos added by synthetic technology in the postproduction phase. As a kind of high-level semantic content, overlaid text plays a significant role in conveying information; furthermore, text is much easier to recognize compared with other semantic cues. In this paper, we focus on the recognition of overlaid Chinese characters for its strong practical value as well as the shortage of corresponding researches.

Nowadays, convolutional neural networks (CNNs) have been widely adopted to handle CCR and result in state-of-art performances. For instance, the results in [5,10] have surpass human performance and set new benchmarks in handwritten CCR. However, the input data of HCCR are generally gray-scale images with

© Springer International Publishing AG, part of Springer Nature 2018
B. Zeng et al. (Eds.): PCM 2017, LNCS 10735, pp. 453–463, 2018.
https://doi.org/10.1007/978-3-319-77380-3_43

constant character stroke width and clean backgrounds. The multi-font printed CCR in [11] deals with 280 distinct typefaces which have various outlines, yet still being performed on binary images.

For recognition of texts with complex backgrounds, the studies mainly focus on scene English text [7,8]. Though some researches have been done dealing with scene Chinese characters [1,12], the results are not very satisfying. As overlaid text has similar property compared with scene text, meanwhile relatively standard outline without occlusion or perspective distortion, we currently fix our attention on overlaid Chinese character recognition, and consider it the fundamental basis of scene Chinese character recognition.

In the previous work of overlaid Chinese text recognition, the segmentation is often carried out on the raw pixels to obtain the binary image of the characters, which is then fed into an optical character recognizer [3]. The process of binaryzation not only costs additional processing time, but also might reduce the recognition accuracy due to poor segmentation results. Therefore, the recognition methods directly work on raw text images may help increase the efficiency and accuracy of the recognition. Though there are some similar researches about the recognition of overlaid Chinese text that being called as Chinese image text in [1,9], these works treat a text line as a whole and pay little attention on single character recognition. We argue that single character recognition plays an important role in text line recognition and researches on single character recognition would benefit further studies of text line recognition.

In this paper, we present a deep CNN-based recognizer of overlaid Chinese characters. To train the CNN, a large amount of character images are first created in the synthetic way. Then, a suitably small input size is chosen as long as the topological information of Chinese characters is sufficiently retained. We propose a streamline version of the VGG network [4] as our baseline network - a more compact network architecture with less and thinner layers depending on the analysis of the size of receptive field. In addition, taking the width of a network and filter sizes into account, we present multiple candidate models with different modification on the architectures. Then, comprehensive comparison experiments are carried out to select the best model according to three aspects, i.e., recognition accuracy on the testing dataset, generalization and model storage size. A very satisfying performance have been achieved in the experiments. Besides, the extensive experiments also provide some useful experiences and give lights into the formation of deep CNN for further researches.

The remaining parts of this paper are organized as follows. Section 2 introduces the synthetic dataset. Section 3 formulates the receptive field and related concepts. We describe the whole process in designing the network architectures in Sect. 4. Section 5 presents the implementation details. Section 6 reports the comprehensive experimental results and gives the related analysis. Section 7 concludes the paper.

2 Synthetic Dataset

To achieve a good performance, it is necessary to train the deep neural network with sufficient samples. However, collecting data from real world takes a lot of time and energy meanwhile cannot ensure the diversity or quantity of samples. Therefore, we create a synthetic dataset of overlaid Chinese characters for training our recognizer in the experiments.

There are 3755 classes in this dataset corresponding to Chinese characters in GB2312-80 level-1 standard. Each class contains 20 typefaces, which are commonly used as overlaid text typefaces. We adopt many different videos to generate the backgrounds of overlaid characters by randomly cutting patches from different positions on the video frames. Then characters are overlaid on background images to generate samples, the styles of which are randomly chosen from the predefined styles of different colors, sizes, etc. We create 125 samples for every typeface of each character, i.e., each character class contains $125 \times 20 = 2500$ samples. We name the synthetic dataset VOT2016-UCAS, where VOT stands for video overlaid text. Some samples in the dataset are shown in Fig. 1.

Fig. 1. Samples from the synthetic dataset.

3 Related Concepts

The CNN is a hierarchical neural network that extracts topological information by convolving the input with a series of filters. Some basic parameters are used to define the convolution/pooling operation in CNN, such as the size of filter kernels, strides, padding size.

3.1 Feature Map Size

The output images of each layer in a CNN are called feature maps, The spatial resolution of which is gradually decreasing in successive convolutional and pooling layers until a reasonable resolution is obtained, before fully connected layers. Let f_l denote the size of feature maps of the lth layer, as well as the input size of the $(l+1)^{th}$ layer. Let k_l, s_l and p_l denote the kernel size, the stride and the padding size of the lth layer respectively. The size of feature maps f_l can be calculated layer-wise by

$$f_l = (f_{l-1} + 2p_l - k_l)/s_l + 1. \tag{1}$$

3.2 Receptive Field

The value of each pixel in l^{th} layer's feature maps is determined by pixels in a corresponding region of the input image. This region is called the receptive field of the pixel. If we consider filtering and sub-sampling the input image layer by layer as directly applying more complex filters on the original image, the imaginary complex filters for l^{th} layers can be described with stacked kernel size, stacked stride and stacked padding, donated by K_l, S_l, P_l. It is clear that the receptive field of lth layer has the same size as the imaginary filters, i.e., $K_l \times K_l$. And the size of feature maps f_l can be directly calculated by the parameters of imaginary filters for layer l, i.e.,

$$f_l = (f_0 + 2P_l - K_l)/S_l + 1, \tag{2}$$

where f_0 denotes the input size of the first layer, i.e., the size of the original image. It is easy to know that the receptive field of the first layer is the filter size, i.e., $K_1 = k_1$, $S_1 = s_1$, $P_1 = p_1$. By directly substituting Eq. (2) into Eq. (1) for f_{l-1}, we can get the layer-wise calculation way for K_l, S_l, P_l as follows,

$$K_l = (k_l - 1) \cdot S_{l-1} + K_{l-1}, \tag{3}$$

$$S_l = s_l \cdot S_{l-1}, \tag{4}$$

$$P_l = p_l \cdot S_{l-1} + P_{l-1}. \tag{5}$$

Fully connected layers can be thought as some kind of convolutional layers and the sizes of feature maps in fully connected layer are always 1×1. Let $f_l = 1$ in Eq. (2), we can get the size of receptive field size K_F for fully connected layers by

$$K_F = f_0 + 2P_F, \tag{6}$$

where P_F denotes the stacked padding of fully connected layers which does not change because there is no padding in fully connected layers.

4   Architectures

We design the architecture of our recognizer for overlaid Chinese character on the basis of the VGG network [4] for its outstanding performance in the ILSVRC-2014 contest, as well as its neat structure that is easy to modify. In this section, we first propose a VGG-based architecture as the baseline network. Then, we cut off the depth of the baseline network depending on the receptive field size. Besides that, several groups of candidate models with control-architectures are proposed to explore the most suitable one for the recognizer of overlaid Chinese characters.

4.1   Input Size

If an image can be correctly recognized by human eyes, it must contain enough information for computers to perform the same task. This is how we choose the smallest input size possible for our recognition task. After visual inspection of a large number of characters rescaled to various sizes, we finally determine to use 32×32 pixels as the input size, since even complicated Chinese characters can be clearly recognized by human eyes under this size.

Table 1. Network architectures. $32 \times 32 \times 3$ denotes the width, height and channels of the input layer, xCyPz denotes a convolutional layer with x channels and the filers of $y \times y$ units and the padding of z pixels (default to zero), MPy denotes a max-pooling layer with the pooling size of $y \times y$ without overlap, xN denotes a fully connected layer with x neurons.

#	Architecture
0	$32 \times 32 \times 3$ - 64C3P1-64C3P1-MP2-128C3P1-128C3P1-MP2-256C3P1-256C3P1-256C3P1-MP2-512C3P1-512C3P1-512C3P1-MP2-4096N-4096N-3755N
1	$32 \times 32 \times 3$ - 64C3P1-64C3P1-MP2-128C3-128C3-MP2-256C3-256C3-512N-512N-3755N
2	$32 \times 32 \times 3$ - 64C3P1-64C3P1-MP2-128C3-128C3-MP2-256C3-256C3-512N-3755N
3	$32 \times 32 \times 3$ - 64C3P1-64C3P1-MP2-128C3-128C3-MP2-256C3-256C3-3755N
4	$32 \times 32 \times 3$ - 64C3P1-64C3P1-MP2-128C3-128C3-MP2-256C3-256C3-256N-3755N
5	$32 \times 32 \times 3$ - 64C3P1-64C3P1-MP2-128C3-128C3-MP2-256C3-256C3-1024N-3755N
6	$32 \times 32 \times 3$ - 64C5P2-MP2-128C5-MP2-256C5-512N-3755N
7	$32 \times 32 \times 3$ - 64C5P2-MP2-128C3-128C3-MP2-256C3-256C3-512N-3755N
8	$32 \times 32 \times 3$ - 64C3P1-64C2-64C2P1-MP2-128C2-128C2-128C2-128C2-MP2-256C2-256C2-256C2-256C2-512N-3755N

4.2   Baseline Network

Since we have a much smaller input size, the feature map size will decrease to 2×2 after the fourth sub-sample layer. So we remove the last three convolutional layers and one max pooling layer of the VGG-16 network, and keep the remaining architecture as our baseline network. The details of the architecture is described in Table 1 as model#0.

4.3   More Compact Architecture

The spatial padding preserving the resolution after convolution makes it possible for us to stack as many layers as we like, but stacking too many layers can result in an oversize receptive field. For the baseline network, the receptive field of each layer and related informations are summarized in Table 2.

The receptive field of the fully connected layers is 116×116, which is much larger than the input size 32×32. In this case, most area of the receptive field is filled with padding pixels, and the information carried by the feature maps must involve great redundance. In order to get a reasonable receptive field size in the

Table 2. Layer-wise receptive field of model#0.

#0	Input	C3P1	C3P1	MP2	C3P1	C3P1	MP2	C3P1	C3P1	C3P1	MP2	C3P1	C3P1	C3P1	MP2	FC
f_l	32	32	32	16	16	16	8	8	8	8	4	4	4	4	2	1
k_l	-	3	3	2	3	3	2	3	3	3	2	3	3	3	2	2
s_l	-	1	1	2	1	1	2	1	1	1	2	1	1	1	2	-
p_l	-	1	1	0	1	1	0	1	1	1	0	1	1	1	0	0
K_l	-	3	5	6	10	14	16	24	32	40	44	60	76	92	100	116
S_l	-	1	1	2	2	2	4	4	4	4	8	8	8	8	16	16
P_l	-	1	2	2	4	6	6	19	14	18	18	26	34	42	42	42

fully connected layers, we set padding to zero in each convolutional layer despite the first two. Then we will get a much smaller $P_F = 2$, which results in a smaller $K_F = 32 + 2 \times 2 = 36$ referring to Eq. (6). Without as many padding pixels, the size of feature maps decreases to 2×2 at the eighth layer. So we remove the convolutional/pooling layers after the eighth one from the baseline.

Besides that, since the input channel of the first fully connected layer is now 1024 ($= 256 \times 2^2$), we consider 512 more reasonable than 4096 to be the width of the fully connected layers. The more compact architecture after these two modifications is described in Table 1 as model#1.

4.4 Fully Connected Layers

To explore the effects of fully connected layers, we conduct two groups of control experiments on the number and width (output channels) of layers. The architectures of these models are exactly the same except for fully connected layers.

In the first group of experiments, we investigate three architectures corresponding to model#1, model#2, model#3 in Table 1, which have three, two, one fully connected layer(s) respectively. It is noteworthy that more layers does not necessarily mean more parameters.

In the second group of experiments, we investigate another two models, i.e., model#4 and model#5, plus the model#2, to show the influence of layer width on the performance of the proposed recognizer. The numbers of neurons in the first fully connected layers for model#4, model#2 and model#5 are 256, 512 and 1024 respectively.

4.5 Filter Sizes

It is easy to know, without changing the size of receptive field, the smaller filter sizes allow for a deeper network. The previous research [2] investigated the trade-offs between network depth and filter sizes. In their experiments, although the deeper networks with smaller filter sizes show better results than the shallower networks with the filters of larger size, it is also verified that overly increasing depth can harm the accuracy. For different kinds of tasks, the needs of network depth may be different, and deeper network can not guarantee to perform better in the task of overlaid Chinese character recognition.

To explore the proper filter sizes and depth of the network, we propose model#7 which replaces the first two convolutional layers with 3×3 filters in model#2 by a single convolutional layer with 5×5 filters, model#6 which replaces every two convolutional layers with 3×3 filters by one with 5×5 filters, and model#8 which replaces each convolutional layer with 3×3 filters by two layers with 2×2 filters.

5   Implementation Details

We use the synthetic dataset VOT2016-UCAS mentioned in Sect. 2 to train our recognizer in the experiments, which contains 3755 classes, 20 typefaces in each class, and 125 samples for each typeface. We randomly choose 100 samples from the 125 ones of each typeface in each class as training data, and the rest as testing data.

The character images are first resized to 36×36 regardless of their aspect ratios, and converted into data with the format LMDB (Lightning Memory-Mapped Database Manager). From the 36×36 pixels, a 32×32 patch is crop at random positions in training phase, while at the centre in testing phase, then fed into the network.

Stochastic gradient descent with a mini-batch size of 256 is used for optimization. The decay rate of weights is 0.0005, and the momentum is 0.9. The learning rate is initially set to 0.001, and manually decreased by a factor of 0.1 when the validation error drops no more. Rectified linear unit (ReLU) is used as the activation function. Dropout is adopted after each fully connected layer with the ratio 0.5 except for the output layer.

All the experiments are conducted on the open platform Caffe [6] using a Quadro M4000 GPU card.

6   Experiments

On the self-established dataset VOT2016-UCAS, we train the multiple CNN-based recognizers with proposed architectures. The experimental results are summarized in Table 3.

In addition, six different typefaces not included in our dataset are used to evaluate the generalization the candidate models for new typefaces. To concentrate on the impact of typefaces, we adopt binary character images in the experiment to suppress the interference from background. Some examples of character images can be viewed in Fig. 2, and the recognition accuracies are shown in Table 4.

6.1   Compactness of Models

By narrowing the fully connected layers and cutting off network depth, we have gained a considerable decrease in the model size and running time. As listed in

Table 3. Performance of models. Mod.Size: the storage size of a caffe model file, which would be generated by Caffe [6] to save parameters of each model; Trn.Time: the seconds consumed to perform one batch of size 256 during training; Tst.Time: the seconds consumed to perform one batch of size 3755 during testing; Accuracy: recognition accuracy on test set.

#	0	1	2	3	4	5	6	7	8
Mod.size(KB)	188,259	15,077	14,051	19,511	9,271	23,611	13,597	13,919	14,199
Trn.time(s/b-256)	0.319	0.104	0.103	0.104	0.101	0.106	0.070	0.067	0.131
Tst.time(s/b-3755)	2.087	0.550	0.546	0.556	0.539	0.546	0.320	0.380	0.661
Accuracy(%)	99.78	99.75	99.79	97.40	99.79	99.79	99.77	99.77	99.76

(a) KangTi   (b) BaoSong   (c) QingKe   (d) ShouJin   (e) CuQian   (f) CuSong

Fig. 2. Six new typefaces used for model robustness testing.

Table 4. Recognition accuracies (%) on the six new typefaces. The last two columns correspond to the average and standard deviation of the accuracies for each typeface.

#	0	1	2	3	4	5	6	7	8
KangTi	78.0	87.2	91.3	79.8	90.6	91.1	76.4	90.5	91.8
BaoSong	87.3	95.0	98.4	90.6	97.5	98.3	94.5	97.9	84.8
QingKe	88.6	97.7	98.7	94.1	98.5	98.9	97.4	98.4	93.2
ShouJin	64.6	60.4	82.6	67.5	77.2	84.7	50.4	84.5	69.5
CuQian	73.3	83.6	86.8	74.3	85.9	86.1	85.3	87.5	72.8
CuSong	95.2	97.9	98.5	94.5	98.1	98.7	98.9	99.1	94.1
Average	81.2	87.0	92.7	83.5	91.3	93.0	83.8	93.0	84.4
Std.dev	10.3	13.0	6.3	10.3	7.8	6.0	16.9	5.8	9.9

Table 3, the model sizes for the modified architectures are about 1/20 to 1/8 of that of the baseline network (model#0), and about two to five times faster than the baseline in training and testing. Meanwhile, the compact networks achieve quite good performance for our task, i.e., overlaid Chinese character recognition.

6.2   How Many Fully Connected Layers

As can be seen in Tables 3 and 4, model#2 has a smaller size but better performance compared with model#1 and model#3. We believe that model#1 with more layers should have better capacity, however, deeper architecture makes it harder to converge to a good solution. As explained in Sect. 4.4, model#3 has the most parameters among the three, however, the worst recognition accuracy is obtained on the both dataset. This shows that an intermediate fully connected layer used for dimension reduction can help decrease the number of parameters and at the same time increase the recognition accuracy.

6.3 Width of Fully Connected Layer

In the performance comparison among model#4, model#2 and model#5 in Table 4, we can find the generalization of network recognizer slightly increases with its width. The increase in accuracy is not so obvious as the parameter quantity grows, though. While taking the spatial and temporal efficiency into consideration, the model#2 with the 512 neurons in the first fully connected layer is a good selection of models in this task.

6.4 Filter Sizes and Network Depth

For model#2, model#6, model#7 and model#8, as shown in Table 3, the models with shallower network architectures runs faster. The model#2 performs a little better than the other three on the testing set. At the same time, model#7 has the best generalization for typefaces among the four models.

6.5 Comparisons of All the Models

We compare the performance of all the models in three ways: recognition accuracy on the testing dataset, generalization on new typefaces and model storage size. These factors can be intuitively compared in Fig. 3.

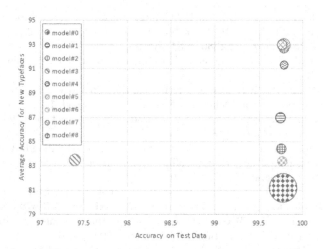

Fig. 3. Bubble chart of models' performance. Area of bubble represents the model size.

According to the recognition accuracy on the testing set, all the models have similar accuracies except for model#3 which performs poorer. When it comes to generalization for new typefaces, model#2, model#5 and model#7 achieve higher accuracy than others. We pick model#7 as our final recognizer for overlaid Chinese characters for its high recognition accuracies and fairly small model size.

7   Conclusion

To address the recognition problem of overlaid Chinese characters, we present a deep CNN-based recognizer which directly works on the character images with complex backgrounds. In the construction of the recognizer, a huge volume of synthetic data are used and the VGG network architecture is referred to. By fully considering various factors on the recognition performance, including the input size, the depth, width of a network and filter sizes, we present multiple models with compact network architectures. Comprehensive comparison experiments are carried out and help us select a suitable model, i.e., the model#7. The proposed model#7 requires only 13.6M for storage and can deal with $9882(\approx 3755/0.038)$ character images per second on a GPU, meantime achieves the recognition rate of 99.77% on the testing set, and a good generalization performance as well. Besides, the extensive comparison experiments offer some useful experience in the formation of deep CNN, which may help in further studies.

Acknowledgments. The work is supported by the National Natural Science Foundation of China under Grant No. 61271434, No. 61232013, and by Beijing Advanced Innovation Center for Imaging Technology under Grant No. BAICIT-2016009.

References

1. Bai, J., Chen, Z., Feng, B., Xu, B.: Chinese image text recognition on grayscale pixels. In: ICASSP 2014–2014 IEEE International Conference on Acoustics, Speech and Signal Processing, pp. 1380–1384 (2014)
2. He, K., Sun, J.: Convolutional neural networks at constrained time cost, pp. 5353–5360 (2014)
3. Liu, X., Wang, W.: Robustly extracting captions in videos based on stroke-like edges and spatio-temporal analysis. IEEE Trans. Multimed. **14**(2), 482–489 (2012)
4. Simonyan, K., Zisserman, A.: Very deep convolutional networks for large-scale image recognition. Comput. Sci. (2014)
5. Xiao, X., Jin, L., Yang, Y., Yang, W., Sun, J., Chang, T.: Building fast and compact convolutional neural networks for offline handwritten Chinese character recognition. Pattern Recognit. **72**, 72–81 (2017)
6. Yangqing, J., Evan, S., Jeff, D., Sergey, K., Jonathan, L.: Caffe: Convolutional architecture for fast feature embedding. Eprint Arxiv, pp. 675–678 (2014)
7. Ye, Q., Doermann, D.: Text detection and recognition in imagery: a survey. IEEE Trans. Pattern Anal. Mach. Intell. **37**(7), 1480–1500 (2015)
8. Yin, X.C., Zuo, Z.Y., Tian, S., Liu, C.L.: Text detection, tracking and recognition in video: a comprehensive survey. IEEE Trans. Image Process. **25**(6), 1 (2016)

9. Zhai, C., Chen, Z., Li, J., Xu, B.: Chinese image text recognition with BLSTM-CTC: a segmentation-free method. In: Tan, T., Li, X., Chen, X., Zhou, J., Yang, J., Cheng, H. (eds.) CCPR 2016. CCIS, vol. 663, pp. 525–536. Springer, Singapore (2016). https://doi.org/10.1007/978-981-10-3005-5_43

10. Zhang, X.Y., Bengio, Y., Liu, C.L.: Online and offline handwritten chinese character recognition: a comprehensive study and new benchmark. Pattern Recognit. **61**, 348–360 (2016)

11. Zhong, Z., Jin, L., Feng, Z.: Multi-font printed Chinese character recognition using multi-pooling convolutional neural network. In: International Conference on Document Analysis and Recognition, pp. 96–100 (2015)

12. Zhou, X., Zhou, S., Yao, C., Cao, Z., Yin, Q.: ICDAR 2015 text reading in the wild competition. Comput. Sci. (2015)

Efficient and Robust Lane Detection Using Three-Stage Feature Extraction with Line Fitting

Aming Wu and Yahong Han[(✉)]

School of Computer Science and Technology, Tianjin University, Tianjin, China
{tjwam,yahong}@tju.edu.cn

Abstract. Lane detection plays an important role in advanced driver assistance system. The objective of lane detection is to separate lane markings from background and to locate their positions. Challenges of lane detection mainly lie in large appearance variations. These variations mainly include shadows, occlusion, variable lighting conditions, and different weather conditions, e.g., sunny or rainy days. In this paper, we propose a method named Lane Detection with Three-stage Feature Extraction to detect lane proposals. The three-stage features include contrast feature, line structure feature, and convex signal feature. Three feature extraction methods are devised for each of the three-stage respectively. After getting lane proposals through the processing of the three methods, we use straight line model to fit these proposals based on RANSAC method. Extensive experiments demonstrate that our method is stable and can find lane proposals exactly given the lane in the scene.

Keywords: Lane detection · Three-stage feature extraction
RANSAC

1 Introduction

Within recent years, more and more researches about advanced driver assistance systems [1] have been developed to ensure road safety. There are many components in advanced driver assistance system such as vehicle recognition and pedestrian recognition etc. Lane Departure Warning [2] is an important module in advanced driver assistance system. The module could reduce some accidents which are caused by driver error and distractions. And Lane detection is an important step of lane departure warning system.

The objective of lane detection is to separate lane markings from background clutter and to locate their exact positions [3]. In this work, we focus on vision-based approaches. As images contain rich scene information, we can get useful information from them. However, there still lies lots of challenges for the vision-based methods. Firstly, because realistic road scene is more complex, the captured scene images always contain noises, such as shadows, variable lighting

© Springer International Publishing AG, part of Springer Nature 2018
B. Zeng et al. (Eds.): PCM 2017, LNCS 10735, pp. 464–473, 2018.
https://doi.org/10.1007/978-3-319-77380-3_44

Fig. 1. Images of advanced driver assistance system. In (a), road is full of noises. In (b), in the rainy day, the lane is very blurry. In (c), the lane is worn. In (d), there are variant lighting conditions.

conditions, and variable weather conditions etc. Secondly, images captured by the advanced driver assistance system are often blurred by the windshield. In Fig. 1, we show some examples. Thus, how to extract robust lane features turns out to be a challenge.

Many algorithms for lane detection have been proposed recently. In [4,5], authors extract ridges as lane feature and implement RANSAC [6] to fit models. This method could find lane feature exactly, but extracting ridge is very complex and needs large computation. In [7], the author proposed a method which is based on Inverse Perspective Mapping (IPM) of road. He first gets the IPM of road and then filters with selective oriented gaussian filters and uses RANSAC algorithm to fit lines. However, the computation of IPM and the gaussian filters makes this method heavy in computation cost. In [8,9], authors proposed methods which are based on spine model and B-Snake model. But if we use these methods, we should firstly determine a set of control points exactly. In [10], authors first extend a road segmentation method [11] in an illumination-invariant color image and use a ridge operator to detect lane markings. Then they use RANSAC to estimate road geometry. As this method is segmentation depended, the performance is easily affected by noises. Thus, for all these methods, the common practice is firstly searching for lane features and then using a model to fit these extracted features.

Recently, learning-based methods have also shown their promising performance. In [12], the author proposed the support vector machine (SVM) based lane detection algorithm. However, learning based methods require lots of well-labeled training data to ensure the good performance. And it is hard and expensive to collect these well-labeled training data.

In this work, we propose a method of using three-stage feature extraction to locate the lane positions. The three-stage features include contrast feature, line structure feature, and convex signal feature. First, we use the three-stage method to get lane proposals and then use RANSAC to fit these proposals. Experiments show that our method could efficiently extract lane proposals.

2   Three-Stage Feature Extraction

Let $f(x, y)$ be gray value of a pixel of the lane image. Here x and y are the coordinates of the pixel. To a real image, we first compute image gradient.

$$G_x = f(x, y) - f(x - 1, y) \tag{1}$$

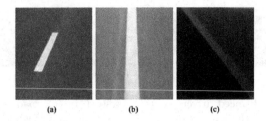

(a) (b) (c)

Fig. 2. Obvious contrast of lane. Along the edge of lane, the sum of lane region is higher than the sides of lane.

$$G_y = f(x,y) - f(x, y - 1) \tag{2}$$

where G_x is the gradient of horizontal direction and G_y is the gradient of vertical direction. After this processing, a gray image turns into a vector map. Every pixel is represented by a three-dimension vector. Elements of the vector are gray value, vector direction, and vector length. We use the slope to represent the vector direction.

$$k = -1.0/Gd, \tag{3}$$

where

$$Gd = G_y/G_x, \tag{4}$$

where k is the vector direction which is perpendicular to the gradient direction, Gd is the gradient direction.

In the following, we will introduce extraction of the three-stage features in detail. And we only take the left side of lane for example to introduce our methods. We can use the same method to detect the right side of lane.

2.1 Obvious Contrast Feature

Obvious contrast is an important attribute of lane. In Fig. 2, along the left edge of lane, the sum of gray in the right region of left edge is bigger than the sum of gray in the left region of left edge. So if we find a pixel which has the attribute, we save it as a contrast proposal. Our contrast proposal detection procedure works as follows. We first use vector map which is computed using Eqs. (1)–(4) to compute slope and intercept of every pixel. Then we take the pixel as the center and in a small range, we calculate the gray sum in right range and the gray sum in left range. If the sum of right is bigger than the sum of left, we take the pixel as a contrast proposal. The method is detailed in Algorithm 1.

In Fig. 3, we show an example of the Algorithm 1. In (a), we show the source image which is got in rainy day and we only process the region under the red line. In (b), we show the result of Algorithm 1. We can see that lane proposals have been appeared on the result. But because we do not use the structure information, the result is not clear and exact and full of noises.

Algorithm 1. Contrast Proposal Detection

Require:

  Obtain vector map using Eq. 1−4

  Set threshold of gradient of horizontal direction T_{min}

  Set search range of vertical direction H_{range}

  Set sum length of horizontal direction $Length$

Ensure:

  Set of contrast proposal $S_{contrast}$

  for each pixel(x, y) in vector map **do**

    if $G_x > T_{min}$ **then**

      Get the slope k using Eq. 3 and compute the intercept $b = y - k * x$

      Set $Sum_L = 0$ and $Sum_R = 0$

      for each $i \in [y - H_{range}, y + H_{range}]$ **do**

        $t_y = i$ and $t_x = (t_y - b)/km$

        for each $n \in [t_x + 1, t_x + Length]$ **do**

          $Sum_R = Sum_R + gray(n)$

        end for

        for each $n \in [t_x - Length, t_x - 1]$ **do**

          $Sum_L = Sum_L + gray(n)$

        end for

        if $Sum_R > Sum_L$ **then**

          Save the pixel to the set $S_{contrast}$

        end if

      end for

    end if

  end for

2.2 Linear Structure Feature

After contrast detection, we obtain the contrast proposal set. Now we need structure information to locate the lane exactly. Based on human impression of lane, the lane should have linear structure. The linear structure is that lane proposals should be on many same lines. So if we can find linear structure, we could find lane proposals much more exactly.

Our linear structure detection procedure now works as follows. We first use the contrast set which is got from Algorithm 1 to compute its corresponding slope and intercept. So the pixel of the contrast set gives a straight line equation. Then to each pixel in the set, we calculate the distance of the pixel to the straight line. If this distance is smaller than our threshold, we think it belongs to the straight line and save it. Because of the curve can be partial linearization, our method also applies to curve lane. The general method is detailed in Algorithm 2.

In Fig. 4(b), we show the result of Algorithm 2. In contrast to (a), we can see that the noise is reduced.

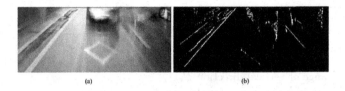

Fig. 3. Result of Algorithm 1. (a) is the source image under the rain. (b) is the result of Algorithm 1. We can find lane structure from (b).

Fig. 4. Result of Algorithm 2. (a) is the result of Algorithm 1. (b) is the result of Algorithm 2. We can see that noise getting less.

2.3   Convex Signal Feature

After processing of the above two steps, we can get lane proposals exactly. However, if we add the constraint of convex signal, the result could get much better. The constraint of convex signal is that the gray sum of lane is much bigger than the sum of both sides of lane. Obviously, this constraint holds in most cases. In practice, the lane is often full of noises and often blurry. In Fig. 5, we show some signal analysis of middle row of lane images in many situations. In (a), (b) and (c), the lane is blurry and full of noise. But all signal structures of these lane image are all convex. So the convex constraint can apply to a number of situations and help to get much more robust lane proposals.

Our convex signal structure detection procedure now works as follows. We first get line structure set which is got from Algorithm 2 and to every pixel of line set, we get its neighbourhood and count the number of pixel which belongs to the contrast set. If the number is smaller than threshold, we throw away the pixel. Then we get gray sum of left region, gray sum of middle region, and gray sum of right region. If sum of middle region is the biggest among these three sum of region, we save corresponding pixel to the ultimate set. The proposed method is detailed in Algorithm 3.

In Fig. 5(b), we show the result of Algorithm 3. In contrast to the result of Algorithm 2, we can see that the noises is reduced. After processing of the above three steps, we can get the final result. Although there may be some noises left in the results, these noises have little impact on the detected lane.

2.4   Vanishing Point Detection

With vanishing point, we can only process the image region under the vanishing point and reduce the amount of computation. In graphical perspective,

---

Algorithm 2. Linear Structure Detection

Require:

  Obtain vector map using Eq. 1–4

  Obtain contrast set $S_{contrast}$ using Algorithm 1

  Set search range of vertical direction H

  Set distance threshold $DistThresh$ and threshold N_{thresh}

Ensure:

  Linear structure set S_{line}

  for each pixel(x, y) in $S_{contrast}$ **do**

    Get the slope k using Eq. 3 and compute the intercept $b = y - k*x$ Set $Number = 0$

    for each $i \in [y - H, y + H]$ **do**

      $t_y = i$ and $t_x = (t_y - b)/k$

      if the pixel belongs to $S_{contrast}$ **then**

        Calculate the distance of pixel to the straight line. The distance is computed

        as follows: $d = |k * t_x - t_y + b|/\sqrt{k * k + 1}$

        if $d < DistThresh$ **then**

          $Number = Number + 1$

        end if

        if $Number > N_{thresh}$ **then**

          save these pixels to the set S_{line}

        end if

      end if

    end for

  end for

---

a vanishing point is a point in the picture plane that is the intersection of the projections (or drawings) of a set of parallel lines in space on to the picture plane. There are many methods for vanishing point detection [13]. Some methods make use of line segments detected in images.

There are significantly large numbers of vanishing points present in an image. Therefore, the aim is to detect the vanishing point that correspond to the principal direction of a scene. In this paper, we can use the detected lane to find the vanishing point. In real scene, the left and right lane lines are parallel expect the curve lane. So we can use the detected lane to find the principal direction and the vanishing point. The intersection of left and right lane lines is the vanishing point.

3 Lane Detection Using Three-Stage Feature Extraction and RANSAC

This paper uses the lane proposals generated by three-stage feature extraction. This section details our whole framework for lane detection.

Learning or fitting based approach is the main method used for lane detection. In [12], the author has proposed the SVM based lane detection algorithm. In [14], authors have proposed the boosting algorithm to select relevant features

---

Algorithm 3. Convex Signal Detection

Require:
    Obtain contrast sequence $S_{contrast}$ using Algorithm 1
    Obtain line set S_{line} using Algorithm 2
    Set threshold N_{thresh}, and sum range LEN
Ensure:
    Ultimate set $S_{proposal}$

    for each pixel(x,y) in S_{line} **do**
      Get the neighbourhood S_n of the pixel and set $Count = 0$
      for each pixel in S_n **do**
        if the pixel belongs to $S_{contrast}$ **then**
          $Count = Count + 1$
        end if
        if $Count > N_{thresh}$ **then**
          set $sum_L = 0$, $sum_M = 0$, and $sum_R = 0$
          for $c \in [1, LEN]$ **do**
            $Lp = (x - c, y)$ and $sum_L = sum_L + gray(Lp)$
            $Mp = (x + c - 1, y)$ and $sum_M = sum_M + gray(Mp)$
            $Rp = (x + LEN + c - 1, y)$ and $sum_R = sum_R + gray(Rp)$
          end for
          if $sum_M > sum_L$ and $sum_M > sum_R$ **then**
            save the pixel to the ultimate set $S_{proposal}$
          end if
        end if
      end for
    end for

---

used for lane detection. However, learning based methods require lots of well-labeled training data to ensure the good performance, which is hard or expensive to be collected. In this paper, we use the random sample consensus (RANSAC) method to fit straight lines. RANSAC is an iterative method to estimate parameters of a mathematical model from a set of observed data that contains outliers, which is much more stable than hough transform.

We first use the above method to extract lane feature proposals and then use RANSAC method to fit lines. At last, we find that we can make use of slope and intercept to make tracking and lane departure warning (LDW). In Fig. 6, we show an example result of lane detection.

4   Experimental Results

We have tested the proposed method in sequences which got in vehicle by different CMOS based cameras. In all cases the images are 640×480. We only process the region below the red line in order to reduce computation amount. In all sequences, we set those parameters of algorithms with same value. In Algorithm 1, we set $T_{min} = 3$, $H_{range} = 15$, and $Length = 15$. In Algorithm 2, we set

Fig. 5. Result of Algorithm 3. (a) is the result of Algorithm 2. (b) is the result of Algorithm 3.

Fig. 6. Lane detection results. The blue line is the detected lane. (Color figure online)

$H = 5$, $DistThresh = 5$, and $N_{thresh} = 5$. In Algorithm 3, we set $N_{thresh} = 8$ and $LEN = 15$. And we mainly evaluate the proposed detection algorithm on daylight and rainy day.

A major problem in acquiring quantitative results is the lacking of ground truth in real scene. Thus we only show examples of challenging situations involving lanes in rainy day, shadows, and different lighting conditions etc.

In Fig. 7, we give some results of lane proposals detection. In these experiments, we respectively apply our algorithm to detect the left side proposals and the right side proposals. In (a), (b), (d) and (e), even in the presence of variant lighting conditions, the proposed method is able to find lane proposals exactly. However, we can see that some noise results also appear because of the interference of the windshield. In (c), we can see that the method is able to find lane proposals in the presence of curve lane. In (f)−(i) and (l), in the rainy day, lanes are very blurry. The method also can find lane proposals exactly though there exits some noise in the results. In (j) and (k), the road is full of noises and the lanes are also very blurry. We can see that this method also can find lane proposals exactly. If we use learning based lane detection, these proposals could reduce search range and accelerate feature extraction. In practice, we have tested this method in lots of scenes and found that if there exits lane in scene, our method can find lane proposals exactly.

In Fig. 8, we show some results of lane detection with the method of RANSAC based on the results of Fig. 8. Note that, in these experiments, we only fit the left side proposals. In (a), (b), (d) and (e), even in the presence of noise, the method could fit line exactly. In (g)−(i) and (l), in the rainy day, the lane is very blurry and this method could also fit it very exactly. In (j) and (k), the results are also very exactly. We find that if the lane proposals are detected exactly, we can fit the lane exactly. What's more, we add some strategies based on slope and intercept for tracking and lane departure warning.

Fig. 7. Lane proposals detection. There are many scenes in the figure such sunny day, rainy day etc.

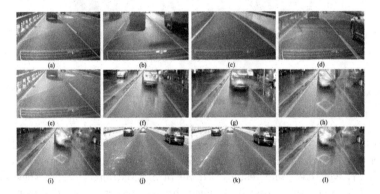

Fig. 8. Lane detection results under some challenge scenarios.

Since the proposed method does not have very complex operations, we can easily transplant the algorithm to the embedded platform, and require a small amount of computing resources.

5   Conclusion

A novel framework for detecting lane proposals from one single image is proposed, which is based on three-stage feature extraction. With the processing of this method, we can get lane proposals. Then we use these proposals to fit lines with RANSAC.

We have made extensive experiments and found this method is very stable. If there exits lane in a scene, the method can find lane proposals.

Acknowledgments. This work was supported by the NSFC (under Grant U1509206, 61472276).

References

1. Gujanatti, R., Tigadi, A., Gonchi, A.: Advanced driver assistance systems. Int. J. Eng. Res. Gen. Sci. **4**, 151–158 (2016)
2. Kumar, A.M., Simon, P.: Review of lane detection and tracking algorithms in advanced driver assistance system. Int. J. Comput. Sci. Inf. Technol. **7**, 65–78 (2015)
3. Mingliang, X., Lv, P., Niu, J., Lu, J., Zhao, X.: Robust lane detection using two-stage feature extraction with curve fitting. Pattern Recognit. **59**, 225–233 (2016)
4. Canero, C., Lopez, A., Serral, J., et al.: Detection of lane markings based on ridgeness and RANSAC. In: IEEE Conference on Intelligent Transportation Systems, pp. 13–16 (2005)
5. Canero, C., Lopez, A., Serral, J., et al.: Robust lane markings detection and road geometry computation. Int. J. Automot. Technol. **11**, 395–407 (2009)
6. Fischler, M.A., Bolles, R.C.: Random sample consensus: a paradigm for model fitting with applications to image analysis and automated cartography. In: ACM, vol. 6, pp. 381–395 (1981)
7. Aly, M.: Real time detection of lane markers in urban streets. In: Intelligent Vehicles Symposium (2008)
8. Teoh, E.K., Wang, Y., Shen, D.: Lane detection using spline model. In: Image and Vision Computing, pp. 677–689 (2000)
9. Teoh, E.K., Wang, Y., Shen, D.: Lane detection and tracking using B-snake. In: Image and Vision Computing, pp. 269–280 (2003)
10. Verl, A., Beyeler, M., Mirus, F.: Vision-based robust road lane detection in urban environments. In: ICRA (2014)
11. Alvarez, J.M.A., Lopez, A.M.: Road detection based on illuminant invariance. In: IEEE Conference on Intelligent Transportation Systems, vol. 12, pp. 184–193 (2008)
12. Kim, Z.: Robust lane detection and tracking in challenging scenarios. In: IEEE Conference on Intelligent Transportation Systems, vol. 9, pp. 16–26 (2008)
13. Audibert, J., Ponce, J., Kong, H.: Vanishing point detection for road detection. In: CVPR, pp. 96–103 (2009)
14. Shneier, M., Gopalan, R., Hong, T., Chellappa, R.: A learning approach towards detection and tracking of lane markings. In: IEEE Conference on Intelligent Transportation Systems, vol. 13 (2012)

Social Media

Saliency-GD: A TF-IDF Analogy for Landmark Image Mining

Wei Li, Jianmin Li$^{(\boxtimes)}$, and Bo Zhang

State Key Laboratory of Intelligent Technology and Systems, TNList,
Department of Computer Science and Technology, Tsinghua University,
Beijing, China
lijianmin@mail.tsinghua.edu.cn

Abstract. In this paper we address the problem of unsupervised land-mark mining, which is to automatically discover frequently appearing landmarks from an unstructured image dataset. Landmark mining often suffers from false matches resulted from cluttered backgrounds and fore-grounds, inter-class similarities, and so on. Analogous to TF-IDF in image retrieval, we propose the Saliency-GD weighting scheme of visual words, which can be easily integrated into state-of-the-art local-feature-based visual instance mining frameworks. Saliency detection provides feature weighting in image space from the attention perspective, and in feature space, the knowledge of geographic density (GD) transferred from a separate training dataset gives a multimodal selection of mean-ingful visual words. Experiments on public landmark datasets show that Saliency-GD weighting scheme greatly improves the landmark mining performance with increasing discrimination power of visual features.

Keywords: Landmark mining · Saliency · Geographic Density
Weighting scheme

1 Introduction

This paper addresses the problem of unsupervised landmark image mining. Its goal is to automatically discover all frequently appearing landmarks from an unstructured image dataset. The mining problem differs from image retrieval [15] and duplicate image detection [21], since the latter two problems have a query as entry point and output only one cluster. It is also different from [10,11,23], as there is no additional information (such as annotations or captions) available in the mining dataset. Figure 1 illustrates some landmark images.

Landmark mining often suffers from false matches resulted from cluttered backgrounds/foregrounds, inter-class similarities, and so on. Appropriate weighting strategy can be effective in selecting discriminative local features. However, related works [2,3,12,22] usually use simple TF-IDF or ignore this issue. TF-IDF can be viewed as a weighting scheme of visual words in two dimensions, the image space and the feature space. However, in image space, we find that

© Springer International Publishing AG, part of Springer Nature 2018
B. Zeng et al. (Eds.): PCM 2017, LNCS 10735, pp. 477–486, 2018.
https://doi.org/10.1007/978-3-319-77380-3_45

Fig. 1. Example images of the landmarks in Oxford [15] (first row) and Paris [16] (second row) datasets

most visual words only appear once in each image. Moreover, those visual words which do appear multiple times in an image often represent meaningless repetitive shapes. These facts restrict the usefulness of TF in landmark mining. In feature space, although document frequency proved to be a good feature selection strategy, we ask a more interesting question: is it possible to learn better weighting from another image dataset with multimodal information?

In this work we propose Saliency-GD weighting scheme, a TF-IDF analogy for landmark image mining. In image space we leverage saliency detection to estimate the importance of each local feature from the attention perspective, while in feature space we train a novel geographic density (GD) measure to select meaningful visual words in a multimodal way, on an Internet image dataset which contains both visual and geographic information. In the literature saliency detection is mostly used in image manipulation [6], image retrieval [8], and image segmentation [18], and is rarely applied to unsupervised settings. Geographic information, on the contrary, has shown its effectiveness in some mining problems such as [4,5,17]. But our formulation differs from all these works: we do not require the *mining* dataset to contain geographic data. Instead we transfer the geographic knowledge from another separate *training* dataset.

With our elegantly designed parameterless weight mapping, the Saliency-GD weighting scheme can be seamlessly integrated into existing local-feature-based mining frameworks. Taking the state-of-the-art instance graph (IG) framework [12] as an example, experiments on two public landmark datasets show that our novel weighting scheme brings superior mining performance with increasing discrimination power of visual features.

The rest of the paper is organized as follows. Section 2 introduces the Saliency-GD weighting scheme in detail. The integration into the instance graph framework is discussed in Sect. 3. Section 4 presents the experimental results, followed by conclusions and future work in Sect. 5.

2   The Saliency-GD Weighting Scheme

Similar to TF-IDF, our scheme gives weights to visual words in two dimensions. Saliency and geographic density (GD) correspond to image space and feature space, respectively.

2.1   The Image Space: Saliency

One source of false matches in landmark mining is the cluttered environment, in which lies many irrelevant visual elements, such as trees, roads, and pedestrains. We observe that for most landmark images, the most salient object is the main body of the landmark. Therefore we leverage saliency detection algorithm to effectively differ the landmark from distracting environment elements.

We adopt the state-of-the-art salient object detection algorithm [1] to compute saliency map for each image in the mining dataset. In order to convert the pixel-level saliency given by the algorithm to feature-level saliency, we compute the weighted average of all saliency values in the local feature region. Specifically, the saliency S_f of a local feature f at location (x, y) with radius r is defined as

$$S_f = \frac{\sum_{(x',y')\in N(x,y)} e^{-\frac{2\sqrt{(x'-x)^2+(y'-y)^2}}{r}} S(x', y')}{\sum_{(x',y')\in N(x,y)} e^{-\frac{2\sqrt{(x'-x)^2+(y'-y)^2}}{r}}}, \tag{1}$$

where $N(x, y) = \{(x', y')|(x' - x)^2 + (y' - y)^2 \leq r^2\}$ is the set of points that covered by the local feature and $S(x', y')$ is the saliency value at coordinate (x', y').

In practice this computation could be slow. Instead we use a sample of points in $N(x, y)$ to approximate the above computation. In the experiments we select the central point (x, y), the four points in each direction with distance $r/2$ to the central point, and the four points in each direction with distance r to the central point.

2.2   The Feature Space: Geographic Density

In feature space, our preliminary experiments find that there are similar patterns between document frequencies trained on the mining dataset and those trained a separate Internet image dataset, and they have similar contributions to the improvement of landmark mining performance. This shows that knowledge of local features can be transferred across datasets. We are interested in whether we can transfer more knowledge about visual words if more information is available in the training dataset. In this work we answer this question with the usage of geographic information. Among the multimodal information available for Internet images, we select geographic information because it is widely available and relatively accurate compared to other forms of data such as tags, as new smart phones and cameras are mostly equipped with GPS modules. We argue that for unsupervised or weakly-supervised tasks, the availability and accuracy of these data matter the most.

Given a training dataset with geographic data, we design a novel measure to combine the document frequency and the geographic information, called geographic density (GD), that gives each visual word a weight. We first compute two simpler measures: the traditional document frequency (DF) and our proposed geographic frequency (GF). DF, as in TF-IDF, is the number of images where the visual word appears. To compute GF, we partition the latitude-longitude coordinate system of earth surface by a 5-degree-by-5-degree grid, and count the number of cells where the visual word appears. The intuition is that the less cells a visual word appears in, the more geographically discriminative it is. GD is then defined as DF divided by GF, thus captures both information. We call it *density* because this value represents the average number of visual word occurrences in geographic cells (ignoring cells with no occurrence of the specific word). In Sect. 4 we compare all three measures (DF, GF, and GD) and verify the effectiveness of this combination. Details of the training dataset are also discussed in Sect. 4.

3   Integration into the IG Framework

We first have a brief review of the instance graph framework. It first extracts local SIFT [13] features on detected Hessian-Affine regions [14], quantizes them [19], and augments each local feature with Hamming Embedding (HE) [9] and its neighboring features. Then it builds a weighted undirected graph with images as vertices. The matching scores between augmented local features, which combine the HE similarity [9] and the Jaccard similarity of neighboring visual word sets, contribute to the weights of edges. Finally instance clusters are efficiently discovered by a greedy breadth-first search algorithm on the sparse graph.

We focus on its computation of similarity score s_{ij} between two augmented local features f_i and f_j. In IG framework, it only reflects the *matching* score, but ignores the *discrimination* score. Our Saliency-GD weighting scheme can introduce the latter by replacing the similarity measure s_{ij} with $s'_{ij} = s_{ij} d_{ij}$, where d_{ij} represents the discrimination power of the two corresponding central features.

The remaining problem is how to compute d_{ij}. A good weighting scheme should have the following properties: (a) it does not bring large impact to the parameters of the existing framework; (b) it does not introduce any new parameters; and (c) it can effectively filter out very indiscriminative features while does not weigh too much on top discriminative ones. As the raw weights computed in Sect. 2 have different ranges of possible values, we propose a unified parameterless weight mapping which have all above properties. In general, for a feature f_k, there will be a mapped image space weight u_k and a mapped feature space weight v_k, both in the range $[0, 2)$. More specifically, in image space, the saliency map value (ranging from 0 to 255) is linearly mapped to $[0, 2)$. In feature space, we first sort the original weights of all visual words and take their rankings as an intermediate measure, then we map this ranking, also linearly, to $[0, 2)$. Note that there may be multiple visual words having the same original weight, and in this case we set their rankings to the same value, i.e., the average of their rankings. Finally the discrimination score is computed by $d_{ij} = u_i u_j v_i v_j$, taking both features and both spaces into consideration.

Note that although in this work we take the IG framework as an example to illustrate our weighting scheme, with the above weight mapping, Saliency-GD can also work in other frameworks, for example thread of features [22].

4   Experiments

In this section we present our experimental results to demonstrate the effectiveness of the Saliency-GD weighting scheme.

4.1   Datasets and Evaluation Measures

We evaluate our proposal by mining on two public landmark datasets, Oxford [15] and Paris [16], both with ground truth for image retrieval tasks. Similar to [22], for each landmark, we take the union of all query images and result lists as a ground truth cluster for our mining problem. Statistics of these two datasets are shown in Table 1 and example landmark images are demonstrated in Fig. 1.

Table 1. Statistics on the two landmark datasets

Dataset	# images	# clusters	# images per cluster
Oxford	5062	11	78.8 ± 95.2
Paris	6392	11	312.7 ± 170.2

For the GD training dataset, we choose MediaEval13 [7], which contains a large number of Flickr images and their high-accuracy GPS locations and user tags. However, we discover that in the original dataset there are many images irrelevant to landmark mining, for example selfies and indoor activity images. Therefore we propose two steps to filter this dataset to make it more appropriate for our landmark mining task. First we adopt the Haar cascade face detection algorithm [20] to filter out those images that have faces in them. Second we filter out images with tags that describe certain indoor activities, such as birthday, party, wedding, etc. For fair comparison in the experiments, we also remove images taken in the areas of Oxford and Paris, to avoid possible duplicate images or appearance of the same landmark. After filtering we randomly sample 60k images to form our final training dataset. The size of the dataset is set empirically, as we observe that a larger value will not bring further improvement to the result.

Same as [12,22], we adopt pair measures (P_{pr}, R_{pr}, and F_{pr}) for quantitative evaluation. However, there are a number of other visual instances existing in

Oxford and Paris datasets, and most of them are not landmarks. To focus our evaluation on landmark mining, instead of using existing fully-annotated ground truth [22], we simply ignore image pairs consisting of two out-of-ground-truth images. This can be viewed as a sampling of the result. We conducted separate experiments to compare this sampling strategy with the use of full ground truth on Oxford dataset, and validated that the sampling can give a reasonable evaluation for landmark mining. To differ between fragmented clusters and a single big cluster in the results, we also compute the cluster measures (P_{cr}, R_{cr}, and F_{cr}) proposed in [12].

4.2   Quantitative Comparison

We take the original instance graph framework as the baseline (Baseline) and compare some variants of our weighting scheme with it, including image space saliency (Saliency), feature space document frequency (DF), geographic frequency (GF), and geographic density (GD), and also the full weighting scheme (Saliency-GD). Quantitative comparison of all these methods is summarized in Table 2.

Table 2. Quantitative comparison of different methods with best parameters. The best results are marked with bold font

Dataset	Method	P_{pr}	R_{pr}	F_{pr}	P_{cr}	R_{cr}	F_{cr}	# search hits
Oxford	Baseline	0.393	0.358	0.374	0.866	0.384	0.533	49144
Oxford	Saliency	0.458	0.381	0.416	0.959	0.392	0.556	51762
Oxford	DF	0.451	0.416	0.433	0.906	0.395	0.550	49819
Oxford	GF	0.427	0.418	0.422	0.881	0.399	0.549	53709
Oxford	GD	0.450	0.448	0.449	0.902	0.420	**0.574**	54950
Oxford	Saliency-GD	0.560	0.417	**0.478**	0.910	0.384	0.540	**42559**
Paris	Baseline	0.367	0.199	0.258	0.905	0.295	0.445	196087
Paris	Saliency	0.373	0.226	0.281	0.896	0.304	0.454	154732
Paris	DF	0.435	0.203	0.277	0.904	0.297	0.447	154924
Paris	GF	0.388	0.210	0.273	0.853	0.311	0.456	168156
Paris	GD	0.426	0.215	0.286	0.891	0.318	**0.469**	175394
Paris	Saliency-GD	0.483	0.210	**0.293**	0.905	0.314	0.467	**126641**

It is obvious that all weighting schemes, even the simplest ones, result in improvement of landmark mining performance in both datasets. For the pair measures, we observe that GD usually have a better effect than saliency, and the combination of them achieves the best result of all. This proves that knowledge from image space and feature space is complementary. Furthermore, in feature space, we find that GD has superior performance over the simpler DF and GF, showing the power of multimodal information. Note that, because the IG framework naturally considers TF during local region matching, the results of DF in the table are actually those of the TF-IDF weighting scheme, which proved the superiority of Saliency-GD over TF-IDF. Another observation is that the Saliency-GD weighting scheme brings a larger performance boost in Oxford dataset than in Paris dataset (27.8% versus 13.6% relative improvement, respectively). This is because that Oxford dataset contains similar buildings and false match is a key reason to its low precision, which is addressed well by our weighting scheme. However, for Paris dataset, most landmarks have unique appearance, and a more dominant factor is its large cluster size, causing low recall and preventing further performance gain. For the cluster measures, GD gives the best result. This is likely due to the fact that saliency filters a large number of less informative features, leading to a high precision but having negative impact on recall, which results in more fragmented clusters.

The last column of Table 2 shows the number of search hits during the GBFS instance clustering step, a measure of redundancy in result clusters. It is clear that besides superior performance, the Saliency-GD weighting scheme also successfully reduces the redundancy, which is crucial to real-life applications.

Figure 2 plots the Pair F-Measure curves of the two datasets with varying Hamming threshold, the most sensitive parameter in the original framework. For most cases, the adoption of a weighting scheme requires a less strict Hamming threshold to achieve its best performance. This is consistent with our expectation, as a larger threshold allows more candidates to be inspected, while the precision is ensured by the weighting scheme. For Oxford dataset, due to its moderate cluster sizes and large number of false matches, weighting schemes can also reduce its parameter sensitivity, especially for large Hamming thresholds.

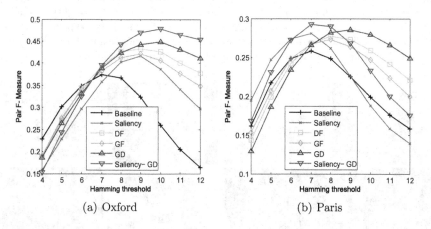

(a) Oxford   (b) Paris

Fig. 2. The Pair F-Measure curves of (a) Oxford and (b) Paris datasets with varying Hamming threshold

4.3   Qualitative Evaluation

Figure 3 visualizes different weighting schemes. From the examples we can see that saliency effectively differs the landmarks from the cluttered environments, and GD selects meaningful regions, usually complex structures. Full Saliency-GD

Fig. 3. Visualization of different weighting schemes on two example images. From left to right, the four columns show the original image, saliency only weighting scheme, GD only weighting scheme, and full Saliency-GD weighting scheme, respectively. Each marker shows a local feature and its color demonstrates the weight (red represents a large weight while green means a small one) (Color figure online)

Fig. 4. Example false matches in the baseline. The similarity scores corresponding to these image pairs are all reduced to less than 0.01 with our weighting scheme

weighting scheme combines the advantages of both: low weights are assigned to trees, windows, and other common components of landmarks, while discriminative local features are given more importance during matching.

Figure 4 demonstrates the elimination of false matches, including similar components of landmarks (for example, windows), similar low-level patterns and structures, and texts. For each image pair, the baseline gives a high matching score, but with the Saliency-GD weighting scheme, these false matches are effectively filtered. All shown image pairs receive weighted similarity scores below 0.01.

5 Conclusions

This work proposes the Saliency-GD weighting scheme of visual words for unsupervised landmark mining, in order to cope with the challenges of false matches resulted from cluttered backgrounds/foregrounds, inter-class similarities, as well as other reasons. Analogous to TF-IDF, our weighting scheme works in both image and feature space. In image space saliency provides feature selection from the attention perspective, and in feature space geographic density (GD) gives a multimodal filtering of meaningful visual words by transferring knowledge from a separate training dataset. This scheme can be easily integrated into existing local-feature-based visual instance mining frameworks. Experiments on two landmark datasets show that it brings superior landmark mining performance with increasing discrimination power of visual features.

Besides geographic information, the integration of more multimodal data, such as tags and user profiles, is a promising direction for future works. Some other possible extensions of this work include the construction of a high-quality training dataset, weighting in a higher-level (for example feature group or image patch level), and adaption of the weighting scheme to deep features.

Acknowledgment. This work was supported by the National Basic Research Program (973 Program) of China (No. 2013CB329403), and the National Natural Science Foundation of China (Nos. 61332007, 91420201 and 61620106010).

References

1. Cheng, M.M., Mitra, N., Huang, X., Torr, P., Hu, S.M.: Global contrast based salient region detection. IEEE Trans. Pattern Anal. Mach. Intell. **37**(3), 569–582 (2015)
2. Chum, O., Matas, J.: Large scale discovery of spatially related images. IEEE Trans. Pattern Anal. Mach. Intell. **32**(2), 371–377 (2010)
3. Chum, O., Perdoch, M., Matas, J.: Geometric min-hashing: finding a (thick) needle in a haystack. In: IEEE Conference on Computer Vision and Pattern Recognition (CVPR), pp. 17–24 (2009)
4. Crandall, D., Backstrom, L., Huttenlocher, D., Kleinberg, J.: Mapping the world's photos. In: World Wide Web Conference (WWW), pp. 761–770 (2009)

5. Doersch, C., Singh, S., Gupta, A., Sivic, J., Efros, A.: What makes Paris look like Paris. ACM Trans. Graph. **31**(4), 101:1–101:9 (2012)
6. Goldberg, C., Chen, T., Zhang, F.L., Shamir, A., Hu, S.M.: Data-driven object manipulation in images. Comput. Graph. Forum **31**(2), 265–274 (2012)
7. Hauff, C., Thomee, B., Trevisiol, M.: Working notes for the placing task at MediaEval 2013. In: MediaEval Workshop (2013)
8. He, J., Feng, J., Liu, X., Cheng, T., Lin, T.H., Chung, H., Chang, S.F.: Mobile product search with bag of hash bits and boundary reranking. In: IEEE Conference on Computer Vision and Pattern Recognition (CVPR), pp. 3005–3012 (2012)
9. Jegou, H., Douze, M., Schmid, C.: Improving bag-of-features for large scale image search. Int. J. Comput. Vis. **87**(3), 316–336 (2010)
10. Li, H.: Multimodal visual pattern mining with convolutional neural networks. In: ACM International Conference on Multimedia Retrieval (ICMR), pp. 427–430 (2016)
11. Li, H., Ellis, J., Ji, H., Chang, S.F.: Event specific multimodal pattern mining for knowledge base construction. In: ACM International Conference on Multimedia, pp. 821–830 (2016)
12. Li, W., Wang, C., Zhang, L., Rui, Y., Zhang, B.: Scalable visual instance mining with instance graph. In: British Machine Vision Conference (BMVC), pp. 98:1–98:11 (2015)
13. Lowe, D.: Distinctive image features from scale-invariant keypoints. Int. J. Comput. Vis. **60**(2), 91–110 (2004)
14. Mikolajczyk, K., Schmid, C.: Scale and affine invariant interest point detectors. Int. J. Comput. Vis. **60**(1), 63–86 (2004)
15. Philbin, J., Chum, O., Isard, M., Sivic, J., Zisserman, A.: Object retrieval with large vocabularies and fast spatial matching. In: IEEE Conference on Computer Vision and Pattern Recognition (CVPR), pp. 1–8 (2007)
16. Philbin, J., Chum, O., Isard, M., Sivic, J., Zisserman, A.: Lost in quantization: improving particular object retrieval in large scale image databases. In: IEEE Conference on Computer Vision and Pattern Recognition (CVPR), pp. 1–8 (2008)
17. Quack, T., Leibe, B., Van Gool, L.: World-scale mining of objects and events from community photo collections. In: ACM International Conference on Image and Video Retrieval (CIVR), pp. 47–56 (2008)
18. Rubinstein, M., Joulin, A., Kopf, J., Liu, C.: Unsupervised joint object discovery and segmentation in internet images. In: IEEE Conference on Computer Vision and Pattern Recognition (CVPR), pp. 1939–1946 (2013)
19. Sivic, J., Zisserman, A.: Video Google: a text retrieval approach to object matching in videos. In: IEEE International Conference on Computer Vision (ICCV), pp. 1470–1477 (2003)
20. Viola, P., Jones, M.: Rapid object detection using a boosted cascade of simple features. In: IEEE Conference on Computer Vision and Pattern Recognition (CVPR), pp. 1–9 (2001)
21. Wu, Z., Ke, Q., Isard, M., Sun, J.: Bundling features for large scale partial-duplicate web image search. In: IEEE Conference on Computer Vision and Pattern Recognition (CVPR), pp. 25–32 (2009)
22. Zhang, W., Li, H., Ngo, C.W., Chang, S.F.: Scalable visual instance mining with threads of features. In: ACM International Conference on Multimedia, pp. 297–306 (2014)
23. Zhu, Z., Xu, C.: Organizing photographs with geospatial and image semantics. Multimed. Syst., 1–9 (2016)

An Improved Clothing Parsing Method Emphasizing the Clothing with Complex Texture

Juan Ji and Ruoyu Yang$^{(\boxtimes)}$

State Key Laboratory for Novel Software Technology,
Nanjing University, Nanjing, China
jij_cheerup@163.com, yangry@nju.edu.cn

Abstract. Recently, researches on clothing segmentation and style recognition in still images have made a big breakthrough. Clothing parsing, as the basis of the above researches, has also made great progress. Unfortunately, it still tends to over-segmentation and poor accuracy when parsing the clothing with complex texture. To address this issue, we consider improving both graph-based image segmentation method and pixel labeling method. For image segmentation, we attempt to reduce the over-segmentation by taking image cells instead of pixels as vertices of the graph, and expanding the range for finding out adjacent vertices. Furthermore, we calculate the weight of edges using different features such as color and texture. For pixel labeling, we train a pairwise CRF model based on multi-level features of the pixel and the region, rather than relying on the human pose. We demonstrate the effectiveness of our approach on Fashionista dataset, which greatly reduce the over-segmentation and scattered pixel labeling of the clothing with complex texture.

Keywords: Clothing parsing · Complex texture · Image segmentation
CRF model

1 Introduction

Fashion and clothing play an important role in our life, and with the rapid development of electronic commerce and computer technology, clothing retrieval, clothing collocation and virtual try-on arise widespread concern, which also lead to more researches on clothing segmentation and style recognition. Clothing parsing, assigning a semantic label of clothing items or background to each pixel in the image, is one of the key resources for the above researches.

Despite a large quantity of researches on clothing, relatively few researchers pay attention to clothing details or variety of garment types, most of them focus on the overall garment [1, 2], or distinguish only a small number of garment types [3, 4]. Because of the inherent variability of pose and clothing appearance as well as the presence of self-occlusions, clothing parsing faces many difficulties. Besides, most researches cannot achieve desired results when dealing with the clothing with complex texture, as shown in Fig. 1. Due to the high variability of colors and rich edge information, it is prone to over-segmentation.

© Springer International Publishing AG, part of Springer Nature 2018
B. Zeng et al. (Eds.): PCM 2017, LNCS 10735, pp. 487–496, 2018.
https://doi.org/10.1007/978-3-319-77380-3_46

Fig. 1. The clothing with complex texture.

In this paper, we consider 21 kinds of different garment types (e.g. hat, coat, pants, socks), and focus on the clothing with complex texture. For this reason, we improve the graph-based image segmentation method and pixel labeling method. Our approach consists of two main stages: First, in the phase of producing coarse segmentation, we improve the traditional graph-based image segmentation method [5] from the graph model and image features, mainly to avoid the over-segmentation of the clothing with complex texture. The segmentation can provide region features for the following stage. Second, we train a pairwise Conditional Random Field (CRF) model and formulate the clothing parsing as one inference in it. Different from some researches which take into account the complex dependencies between clothing and the human pose [6–8], we extract multi-level features of the pixel and the region, not only to avoid the pixel labeling failure caused by the inaccurate pose estimation (see Fig. 2), but also to reduce scattered pixel labeling of the clothing with complex texture.

Fig. 2. Pixel labeling failure cases caused by inaccurate pose estimation.

The experimental results on Fashionista dataset [6] are promising and show that our approach significantly outperforms the state-of-the-art when parsing the clothing with complex texture like stripes and checks. The example of our results can be seen in Fig. 3.

The paper is organized as follows: In the next section we describe the previous work of clothing parsing, image segmentation and conditional random field model. Section 3 introduces the traditional graph-based image segmentation method and our improvement, while Sect. 4 presents the pairwise CRF model based on the multi-level features for pixel labeling. Finally, performance evaluation and conclusions are given in the final two sections.

Input   Truth   [6]   [7]   [8]   Ours

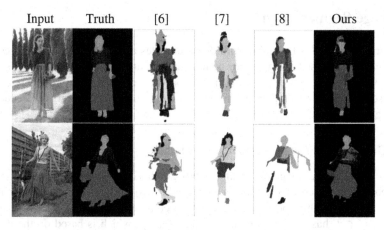

Fig. 3. Example of our result. We compare against the state-of-the-art. Despite some mistakes, our approach is more effective when parsing the clothing with complex texture.

2 Related Work

Clothing Parsing: Early clothing parsing only focused on the recognition of the upper body clothing in very limited situations [9]. Later Yamaguchi et al. [6] associate clothing parsing with pose estimation, great performance is obtained when garment types are given at test time. But the performance is rather poor when this kind of information is not provided. The approach proposed in [7] uses over 300000 weakly labeled training images and a small set of fully labeled examples in order to enrich the model of [6]. Simo-Serra et al. [8] construct a pose-aware CRF and develop a rich set of potentials which exploit the person's global appearance, figure/ground segmentation, shape and location priors for each garment.

Image Segmentation: The graph-based image segmentation method, firstly proposed by Felzenszwalb et al. [5], is a Minimum Spanning Tree-based algorithm, which increases the amount of data to be handled because of its efficiency with satisfactory segmentation results. However, this method uses a global threshold and ignores the local details so that the segmentation is very sensitive to noises. Besides, when segmenting the image with complex texture or mutation edges, the result is far from satisfactory. Many researchers attempt to make different improvements on this method, making it suitable for various images [10, 11].

Conditional Random Field: CRF model has been very successful in semantic segmentation tasks. Many researches develop different unary and pairwise potentials which exploit the detailed features such as edge, color and texture for semantic segmentation of urban and rural scene images [12, 13]. Moreover, higher-order potentials can capture long-range mutual interaction and enforce label consistency over regions [14, 15]. But parameter estimation and inference are relatively inefficient due to the complexity of the model.

3   Image Segmentation

There are many kinds of clothing with different styles and textures in still images. The traditional graph-based image segmentation method always gives poor results when dealing with the complex texture. In this section we focus on improving the traditional image segmentation method from the graph model and image features to reduce the over-segmentation.

3.1   Graph-Based Image Segmentation Method

Initially we treat the image as an undirected graph $G = (V, E)$ with vertices $v_i \in V$, corresponding to each of the pixel, and edges $(v_i, v_j) \in E$ corresponding to pairs of vertices that are within local 8-connected or 4-connected pixel neighborhoods. Each edge $(v_i, v_j) \in E$ has a corresponding weight $w(v_i, v_j)$, which is based on the dissimilarity between neighboring vertices v_i and v_j such as the difference in image color. We usually use the Euclidean distance between neighboring vertices as the edge weights.

In the method, we divide V into several connected components in the graph, and in general we hope to increase the similarity of the elements in the same component and reduce that in different components. The method starts with a trivial segmentation, with each component containing one pixel, and repeatedly merges pairs of components based on the following merge condition:

$$diff(C_1, C_2) \leq Int(C_1) + T(C_1) \ \&\& \ diff(C_1, C_2) \leq Int(C_2) + T(C_2) \qquad (1)$$

where $diff(C_1, C_2)$ is the difference between two components C_1 and C_2, which is defined to be the minimum edge weight between them; $Int(C_1)$ and $Int(C_2)$ are the internal difference of C_1 and C_2 respectively, which is defined to be the largest weight in the minimum spanning tree of the component; $T(C) = k/|C|$ is the threshold function based on the size of the component. Parameter k controls the size of the components in the segmentation, and a larger k causes a preference for larger components.

3.2   The Improvement and the Procedure

Improvement: We capture $h * h$ image cells by moving down one row or moving right one column at each turn. Assuming the image width is D and the image height is H, thus there are totally $(D + 1 - h) * (H + 1 - h)$ image cells and these image cells are mapped to the vertices V. We extract different features of the image cell such as Lab color, LBP and location feature. Besides, we use the Euclidean distance between vertices as the dissimilarity. In the $m * m$ neighborhood which is centered on each image cell, we pick up the l most similar (i.e., the smallest difference) image cells as adjacent vertices. This process is illustrated in Fig. 4.

Different from the traditional graph-based image segmentation method, we use $h * h$ image cells instead of pixels as vertices, not only extract color and location features, but also extract texture features. In addition, we select adjacent vertices from

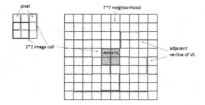

Fig. 4. The diagram of creating the graph. Taking the 2 * 2 image cell as an example, the top left illustrates the way to capture image cells which are mapped to the vertices. The middle figure shows that in the 7 * 7 neighborhood which is centered on vertex V1 (the red box), we pick up the four most similar image cells (the blue boxes) as adjacent vertices. (Color figure online)

$m * m$ neighborhood, rather than within local 8-connected or 4-connected pixel neighborhoods, with the benefit of finding out similar regions in local space and merging them, so as to avoid over-segmentation.

Procedure

1. Creating a graph model $G = (V, E)$ with vertices V and edges E, as well as edge weight W. Then sorting E by non-decreasing edge weight.
2. Starting with a trivial segmentation with each component containing one image cell.
3. Let C_1 and C_2 denote the vertices connected by a certain edge in the ordering, and repeatedly merging pairs of components based on the above merge condition (1).
4. Merging the regions with the size smaller than *min*.

4   The CRF Model for Pixel Labeling

In this section, we consider training a pairwise CRF model for pixel labeling. To avoid labeling failure caused by inaccurate pose estimation, we decide not to use human pose. Besides, we extract not only pixel features but also region features, so that spatial information can be fully used. Finally, we pose the clothing parsing problem as one inference in the model.

4.1   The CRF Model

Let x be the image features, $y = <y_1, \ldots y_n >$ consists of the semantic label of each pixel from a finite label set L (e.g. background, hat, coat, pants, socks), where n is the total number of image pixels. The conditional distribution for a pixel labeling y given image features x is formulated as:

$$p(y|x) = \frac{1}{Z(x)} exp \left\{ -\left[\sum_{i \in V} \sigma_i(y_i, x_i) + \beta \sum_{(i,j) \in E} \varphi_{ij}(y_i, y_j, x_i, x_j) \right] \right\} \quad (2)$$

where Z(x) is a partition function and takes the form:

$$Z(x) = \sum_{y_i \in y} exp\left\{ -\left[\sum_{i \in V} \sigma_i(y_i, x_i) + \beta \sum_{(i,j) \in E} \varphi_{ij}(y_i, y_j, x_i, x_j) \right] \right\} \tag{3}$$

The conditional distribution is defined over unary and pairwise potentials where σ_i is the unary potential for assigning label y_i to pixel i and φ_{ij} is a contrast-dependent smoothing prior that penalizes adjacent pixels i and j for taking different labels. The non-negative constant β trades-off the strength of the smoothness prior against the unary potential.

The unary potential is learned in two stages. In the first stage we learn a one-versus-all boosted decision tree classifier for each label in label set L. In the second stage we calibrate the output of the boosted decision tree classifiers via a multi-class logistic regression. The formula is defined as:

$$p(Y = y | X = x) = \begin{cases} \frac{exp(\theta_y^T x)}{1 + \sum_{i=1}^{L-1} exp(\theta_i^T x)}, & 1 \le y < L \\ \frac{1}{1 + \sum_{i=1}^{L-1} exp(\theta_i^T x)}, & y = L \end{cases} \tag{4}$$

where x is the output of the boosted decision tree classifiers.

The key features used for training boosted decision tree classifiers are as follows:

- Color feature: RGB color of the pixel (pixel feature).
- Texture feature: a 17-dimensional filter bank, including scaled Gaussians, Laplacians of Gaussians and Derivatives of Gaussians (pixel feature).
- Mask feature: different from using CPMC approach [8], we use the convolutional neural networks (CNN) method [16] to do human body segmentation. Pixels of the background are set to 0 and the others are set to 1 (pixel feature).
- Location feature: the location features of each segmented region produced in Sect. 3.2, including the starting location relative to the human body, the height ratio of the human body and the location in width relative to the human body (left, middle and right). Here we do not use human pose to extract location features, but respectively locate each segmented region and human body produced in previous section, then we extract location features according to the relative relationship between them (region feature).
- Shape feature: Hu moments of each segmented region produced in Sect. 3.2 (region feature).

In addition, we use the standard contrast sensitive Potts model as the pairwise potential, φ_{ij} takes the form:

$$\varphi_{ij}(y_i, y_j, x_i, x_j) = \begin{cases} exp\left(-\frac{\|x_i - x_j\|^2}{2\gamma} \right) & if \ y_i \ne y_j \\ 0 & otherwise \end{cases} \tag{5}$$

where x_i and x_j are the RGB color vectors for pixels i and j respectively, and γ is the mean square-difference between color vectors over all adjacent pixels in the image.

4.2   Learning and Inference

Learning: We use piecewise training method to learn the model parameters. Firstly, each potential function is trained separately. Here we use LBFGS algorithm to learn logistic regression parameter θ in the unary potential. Then we use space search method to learn the weight β of the formula (2).

Inference: Given the image features x and parameter δ, we wish to find out the pixel labeling that maximizes the conditional probability:

$$y^* = \arg max_y p(y|x, \delta) \qquad (6)$$

We use the α-expansion graph-cut algorithm to find out the optimal pixel labeling.

5   Experimental Results

5.1   Image Dataset

We evaluate our approach on Fashionista dataset provided in [6]. The dataset, in which a single person wears a diverse set of garments, has totally 685 images. Besides, the dataset provides annotated superpixels but annotations of the boundary are not completely accurate, and many classes have very few occurrences. Thus we compress the original 29 classes into 21 and modify the Fashionista dataset. According to the methodology in [7], we randomly select 456 images for training and 229 images for testing.

5.2   Graph-Based Image Segmentation

In this paper, we do not directly segment the image from Fashionista dataset, but the one based on human body segmentation with CNN method [16], where the background is set to black, as shown in Fig. 5(b). Besides, we set $h = 8$, $m = 5$, $l = 18$, and $min = 30$. Figure 5 shows some qualitative comparison results. It can be seen that more coherent regions are generated by our approach and our result looks visually much more natural.

5.3   Pixel Labeling

We train a pairwise CRF model and extract multi-level features of the pixel and the region, without the human pose, in order to avoid the pixel labeling failure caused by inaccurate pose estimation and reduce scattered pixel labeling of the clothing with complex texture. Due to few relevant results showed in [6, 8], we can only compare our results with their results on two images (see Fig. 3). Luckily, [7] provides lots of

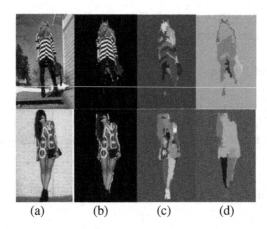

Fig. 5. Comparison of image segmentation results. (a) input image, (b) result of human body segmentation, (c) result of the traditional method and (d) our result.

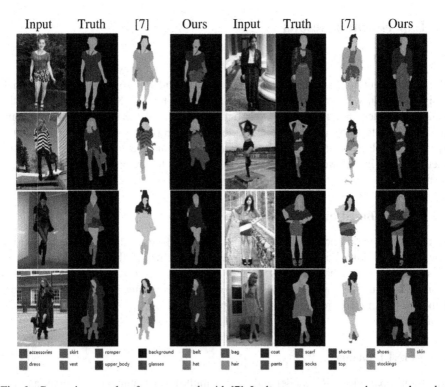

Fig. 6. Comparison results of our approach with [7]. In the top two rows we show good results obtained by our approach. In the bottom two rows we show failure cases that are in general caused by similar color, skin-like color or irregular complex texture. (Color figure online)

parsing results and the qualitative comparison of parsing results is visualized in Fig. 6. We can see a visible improvement over the clothing with complex texture. There are also several failure cases caused by skin-like color or irregular complex texture (Fig. 6-bottom). Besides, the pixel accuracy of our approach is up to 85.69%, and achieves a 1% over [8] and 8% over [6]. The quantitative comparison is shown in Table 1.

Table 1. Comparsion of pixel accuracy between different methods.

Method	[6]	[7]	[8]	Ours
Pixel accuracy	77.45%	84.68%	84.88%	85.69%

6 Conclusions

In this paper, we propose an improved clothing parsing method emphasizing the clothing with complex texture. We improve the traditional graph-based image segmentation method from the graph model and image features. And we train a pairwise CRF model based on multi-level features of the pixel and the region, without human pose. Experimental evaluation shows successful results. Despite these promising results, there are also several failure cases caused by similar color or ambiguous boundaries. In the future, we plan to improve image segmentation results to extract more accurate region features and further explore how to incorporate higher-order potentials for handling the diversity of garment classes.

Acknowledgement. This work was supported in part by the National Natural Science Foundation of China under Grant Nos. 61672273.

References

1. Sun, G.L., Wu, X., Chen, H.H., et al.: Clothing style recognition using fashion attribute detection. In: International Conference on Mobile Multimedia Communications. ICST (Institute for Computer Sciences, Social-Informatics and Telecommunications Engineering), pp. 145–148 (2015)
2. Surakarin, W., Chongstitvatana, P.: Classification of clothing with weighted SURF and local binary patterns. In: Computer Science and Engineering Conference, pp. 1–4. IEEE (2015)
3. Bourdev, L., Maji, S., Malik, J.: Describing people: a poselet-based approach to attribute classification. In: IEEE International Conference on Computer Vision, ICCV 2011, Barcelona, Spain, November, pp. 1543–1550. DBLP (2011)
4. Guan, P., Freifeld, O., Black, M.J.: A 2D human body model dressed in Eigen clothing. In: Proceedings of the European Conference on Computer Vision, ECCV 2010, Heraklion, Crete, Greece, 5–11 September 2010, pp. 285–298. DBLP (2010)
5. Felzenszwalb, P.F., Huttenlocher, D.P.: Efficient graph-based image segmentation. Int. J. Comput. Vis. **59**(2), 167–181 (2004)
6. Yamaguchi, K., Kiapour, M.H., Ortiz, L.E., et al.: Parsing clothing in fashion photographs. In: IEEE Conference on Computer Vision and Pattern Recognition, pp. 3570–3577. IEEE (2012)

7. Yamaguchi, K., Kiapour, M.H., Berg, T.L.: Paper Doll Parsing: retrieving similar styles to parse clothing items. In: IEEE International Conference on Computer Vision, pp. 3519–3526. IEEE Computer Society (2013)

8. Simo-Serra, E., Fidler, S., Moreno-Noguer, F., Urtasun, R.: A high performance CRF model for clothes parsing. In: Cremers, D., Reid, I., Saito, H., Yang, M.-H. (eds.) ACCV 2014. LNCS, vol. 9005, pp. 64–81. Springer, Cham (2015). https://doi.org/10.1007/978-3-319-16811-1_5

9. Borràs, A., Tous, F., Lladós, J., et al.: High-level clothes description based on colour-texture and structural features. In: Proceedings of the First Iberian Conference on Pattern Recognition and Image Analysis, IbPRIA 2003, Puerto de Andratx, Mallorca, Spain, 4–6 June 2003, pp. 108–116. DBLP (2003)

10. Zhang, M., Alhajj, R.: Improving the graph-based image segmentation method. In: IEEE International Conference on TOOLS with Artificial Intelligence, pp. 617–624. IEEE (2006)

11. Liu, Z., Hu, D.W., Shen, H., et al.: Graph-based image segmentation using directional nearest neighbor graph. Sci. China Inf. Sci. 56(11), 1–10 (2013)

12. He, X., Zemel, R.S.: Multiscale conditional random fields for image labeling. In: Proceedings of the 2004 IEEE Computer Society Conference on Computer Vision and Pattern Recognition, CVPR 2004, vol. 2, pp. II-695–II-702. IEEE (2004)

13. Gould, S., Rodgers, J., Cohen, D., et al.: Multi-class segmentation with relative location prior. Int. J. Comput. Vis. 80(3), 300–316 (2008)

14. Kohli, P., Ladický, L., Torr, P.H.S.: Robust higher order potentials for enforcing label consistency. Int. J. Comput. Vis. 82(3), 302–324 (2009)

15. Delong, A., Osokin, A., Isack, H.N., et al.: Fast approximate energy minimization with label costs. Comput. Vis. Patt. Recogn. 96, 2173–2180 (2012). IEEE

16. Wang, X., Zhang, L., Lin, L., et al.: Deep joint task learning for generic object extraction. Comput. Sci., 523–531 (2015)

Detection of Similar Geo-Regions Based on Visual Concepts in Social Photos

Hiroki Takimoto[1(✉)], Magali Philippe[2], Yasutomo Kawanishi[3], Ichiro Ide[3],
Takatsugu Hirayama[3], Keisuke Doman[4], Daisuke Deguchi[3],
and Hiroshi Murase[3]

[1] Graduate School of Information Science, Nagoya University, Nagoya, Japan
`takimotoh@murase.m.is.nagoya-u.ac.jp`
[2] ENSEEIHT, Toulouse, France
[3] Graduate School of Informatics, Nagoya University, Nagoya, Japan
[4] School of Engineering, Chukyo University, Nagoya, Japan

Abstract. Travel destination recommendation is useful to support travel. Considering the recommendation of regions within the destination area to visit, it could be difficult for the users to explicitly indicate their preference. Therefore, we considered that it would be more intuitive to recommend regions in the destination area that are similar to a region already well-known to the user. Thus, in this paper, we propose a method for the detection of similar geo-regions based on Visual Concepts in social photos. We report experimental results and analyses by applying the proposed method to the YFCC100M dataset.

Keywords: Travel · Support · Recommendation · Photo

1 Introduction

According to WTTC, the contribution of Travel and Tourism to world GDP rises to a total of 9.8% and the sector supports 284 million people in employment [1]. Because of such large effects on World economy and employment, promotion of the sector is very important. As one type of promotion, travel destination recommendation systems have been studied. Examples of these are systems which recommend travel routes, and those which detect and recommend landmarks to visit. We considered that it would be useful to recommend regions within the destination area to visit. However, in some cases it could be difficult for the users to explicitly indicate their preference. In order to handle such cases, we considered that it would be easier to recommend regions in the destination area that are similar to a region already well-known to the user. Thus, in this paper, we propose a method to detect similar regions (hereafter referred to as "geo-regions").

M. Philippe—Currently at SONY Electronics.

© Springer International Publishing AG, part of Springer Nature 2018
B. Zeng et al. (Eds.): PCM 2017, LNCS 10735, pp. 497–504, 2018.
https://doi.org/10.1007/978-3-319-77380-3_47

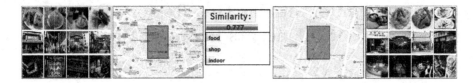

Fig. 1. Example of a detected similar geo-region pair. Both are geo-regions where people focus on Chinese-style streetscapes and Chinese foods; Chinatowns in Yokohama, Japan, and Los Angeles, USA.

To do this, we have to define "geo-regions" and somehow describe each geo-region's feature, and then calculate the similarity between a pair of geo-regions. Here, we focused on the recent trend of the diffusion of Social Network Services (SNS). When people travel, many of them take photos depending on their interests and post them to SNS. These photos contain rich information on the objects and activities that take place in the regions that they were taken. In order to extract the targets-of-interest from them, we decided to use Visual Concepts to represent the features of a geo-region. Focusing on the interests of the crowd instead of objective information such as that observed from a map or a satellite image, we expect to obtain more intuitive similarities.

The main contribution of this paper is the proposal of a method for the detection of similar geo-regions based on Visual Concepts in social photos. By applying the method to the YFCC100M dataset [8], we could detect similar geo-regions anywhere around the World (Fig. 1).

The remainder of this paper is organized as follows: Sect. 2 introduces related work. Section 3 introduces the proposed method for detecting similar geo-regions based on Visual Concepts detected from social photos. Section 4 reports and analyzes the results of the detected similar geo-regions, and finally Sect. 5 concludes the paper.

2   Related Work

As examples of travel recommendation systems, there are route recommendation systems, and landmark detection and recommendation systems.

As a route recommendation system, Kurashima et al. [3] proposed a method that makes use of the photographers' action history from geo-tagged photos on Flickr. Although they used geo-tagged photos to construct the photographer's behavior model, they focused especially on location information and the movement of each photographer, but not on detailed visual information in the photos. As a landmark detection and recommendation system, Shi et al. [6] proposed a personalized system. They used category information extracted from Wikipedia and recommended landmarks to users. They focused on landmarks and their predefined categories, whereas our method focuses on geo-regions and do not predefine categories.

Min et al. [4] proposed a probabilistic topic model called Multimodal Spatio-Temporal Theme Modeling (mmSTTM) and analyzed themes discovered from twenty popular landmarks around the World. They focused only on popular landmarks and also did not consider similarities between themes, whereas our method focuses on similarities of pairs of arbitrary geo-regions.

As for work which focuses on the similarity between geo-regions, there are two major approaches: Those that refer to texts and those that refer to images.

As work that refers to texts, Shimada et al. [7] proposed a sightseeing spot recommendation system based on text information on the Web. It detects similar geo-regions (locations) by calculating similarities between an user-selected favorite geo-region (location) and each sightseeing spot in their database. In this system, however, similarities cannot be calculated across different linguistic areas because they cannot directly compare keywords extracted from Web sites written in different languages. Considering globalization in the travel sector, for this reason, we decided not to rely on text, but rather make good use of non-linguistic information that can be extracted from image.

As work that refers to images, Pongpaichet et al. [5] implemented a visual analytics system of social photos and made event models to detect similar events. Each model is described by Bag-of-Visual Concepts that co-occur in a pre-defined event. They focusd on the similarity between a geo-region and a pre-defined model in order to detect photos on a certain event, whereas our method focuses on the similarity between geo-regions based on arbitrary events.

Ide et al. [2] proposed a method that automatically detects people's common attention in a geo-region from a large number of geo-tagged photos, and its visualization on a map. By classifying each local area into five scene categories based on global image features extracted from social photos, they classified a geo-region into one of the five categories. In their method, however, since the category of a geo-region was decided according to the majority of photos that belonged to the scene category, other photos that did not belong to the category were ignored and visual information in them were not used to describe the geo-region. Instead, our method makes use of the information in all the photos available and describes a geo-region with combination (distribution) of objects or activities detected from them.

3   Detection of Similar Geo-Regions Based on Visual Concepts in Social Photos

We propose a method for the detection of similar geo-regions based on Visual Concepts in social photos. First, geo-regions are fixed by spatially clustering a large number of geo-tagged photos. Next, for each geo-region, their features are described based on Visual Concepts detected from social photos taken there. Finally, the similarity between a pair of geo-regions is calculated and those with high similarity are output as similar geo-regions. Details of the three steps are described below.

3.1   Definition and Decision of Geo-Region

In general, a geo-region is defined as an area demarcated according to certain criteria: administrative division, climatic zone, and so on. However, since we aim to support travel, such objectively-defined areas do not necessarily satisfy the users' purposes. Instead, we subjectively define geo-regions based on the interests of the crowd.

For the decision of geo-regions, we focus on geo-tagged photos. With the diffusion of mobile devices equipped with a GPS function, more and more geo-tagged photos are posted to SNS. Since these photos directly reflect people's interests, we apply mean-shift clustering to locations where the photos were taken to decide geo-regions. Since some clusters (geo-regions) contain few photos, only those that contain sufficient numbers of photos (θ_p) to describe the geo-regions, are used.

3.2   Definition of Similarity

When a pair of geo-regions are similar, they should share something in common. Since our purpose is travel support, it should be based on subjective information in view of travelers. Therefore, as a criterion for measuring the similarity, we focus on the existence of similar objects or activities.

3.3   Description of Geo-Region's Feature

Since Visual Concepts detected from social photos indicate objects and activities that appear in photos taken by people at geo-tagged locations, they are used as a feature to describe the interests of the crowd in a geo-region. Visual Concepts are extracted and used as features to describe geo-regions as follows.

Extraction of Visual Concepts in Social Photos. Recently, more and more people use SNS. They often take photos of objects and activities which aroused their interests and post to SNS. Different people have different interests: One may be interested in the landscape, but others may be interested in a landmark or food. We considered that Visual Concepts could be used to describe such diverse interests. Recent advance in deep learning methods has allowed the robust and accurate detection of Visual Concepts. Therefore, in the proposed method, we describe image contents of social photos by combinations (distributions) of Visual Concepts detected in photos.

Let the number of categories of Visual Concepts that can be detected by a detector be N, for an input image, the probability of each Visual Concept is calculated and described as an N-dimensional vector $\mathbf{v}_l$.

Description of Geo-Region's Features. A geo-region's feature is described as follows. Let P_l be a set of photos taken in a geo-region c_l. For each photo

$p_{l,i} \in P_l$, the feature vector of $p_{l,i}$ is described as $\mathbf{v}_{l,i}$. The feature vector of a geo-region c_l is described as $\mathbf{V}_l = \sum_i \mathbf{v}_{l,i}$.

We should notice that some visual concepts are general and detected from many photos. Thus, we apply a TF-IDF-like approach to each component of $\mathbf{v}_l$. TF and IDF are calculated as follows. Let the n-th component of $\mathbf{V}_l$ and $\mathbf{v}_{l,i}$ be $V_l(n)$ and $v_{l,i}(n)$, respectively ($n = 1, 2, ..., N$), then,

$$\mathrm{TF}_{l,i}(n) = \frac{v_{l,i}(n)}{\sum_{m=1}^{N} v_{l,i}(m)}. \tag{1}$$

Let P be all the photos in the dataset, then,

$$\mathrm{IDF}(n) = \log \frac{|P|}{|\{p_j \mid v_j(n) > \theta_{\mathrm{vc}}, p_j \in P\}|}. \tag{2}$$

Here, θ_{vc} is a threshold for judging whether we should consider a Visual Concept exists in a photo or not. Finally, by calculating the following equation, we obtain the geo-region's feature vector $\mathbf{V}_l' = (V_l'(1), V_l'(2), ..., V_l'(N))$, where

$$V_l'(n) = \sum_{i=1}^{|P_l|} \mathrm{TF}_{l,i}(n) \cdot \mathrm{IDF}(n). \tag{3}$$

3.4 Similarity Calculation

Once the geo-regions are described by feature vectors, we calculate the similarity between a pair of them. For a given pair of geo-regions c_i, c_j, their similarity is calculated by Zero-mean Normalized Cross Correlation (ZNCC) as,

$$S_{i,j} = \frac{\sum_{n=1}^{N}(V_i'(n) - \overline{\mathbf{V}_i'})(V_j'(n) - \overline{\mathbf{V}_j'})}{\sqrt{\sum_{n=1}^{N}(V_i'(n) - \overline{\mathbf{V}_i'})^2 \cdot \sum_{n=1}^{N}(V_j'(n) - \overline{\mathbf{V}_j'})^2}}. \tag{4}$$

$$\overline{\mathbf{V}_l'} = \tfrac{1}{N} \sum_{n=1}^{N} V_l'(n). \tag{5}$$

Finally, pairs with similarities higher than a threshold θ_s are detected as similar geo-regions.

4 Experiment

In this section, we report and analyze experimental results by showing examples of the pairs of similar geo-regions detected by actual social photos.

4.1 Dataset

We used YFCC100M (Yahoo! Flickr Creative Commons 100 Million) dataset [8], which contains 100 million photos and videos from Flickr taken all over the World. Each photo in the dataset is accompanied with metadata (tags, timespan, location and so on). Since the proposed method needs location information of photos, we only used geo-tagged photos in the dataset. In addition to metadata, each photo is annotated with visual information detected by $N = 1,570$. Visual Concept classifiers using CNN. We used them to describe the Visual Concepts in each photo.

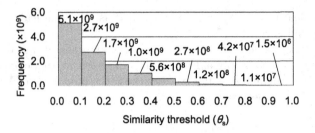

Fig. 2. Frequency of geo-regions according to their similarities.

4.2 Parameters

To decide geo-regions, we need to set the bandwidth for mean-shift clustering and the threshold θ_p for obtaining geo-regions which contain sufficient number of photos. We empirically decided bandwidth = 0.001 and $\theta_p = 50$.

To describe a geo-region's feature, parameters N and θ_{vc} need to be set. In the YFCC100M dataset, $N = 1,570$ and since each photo is already annotated with Visual Concepts (and their probabilities), we did not set a specific value for θ_{vc} in this experiment. For the threshold to detect similar geo-regions, we set $\theta_s = 0.7$.

4.3 Result

By applying the proposed method with the above parameters to the YFCC100M dataset, $152,409$ geo-regions and $54,834,813$ pairs of similar geo-regions out of $_{152,409}C_2 = 11,606,099,193$ pairs of geo-regions were yielded. The frequency of geo-regions according to their similarities is shown in Fig. 2.

4.4 Analysis

In this section, we analyze the pairs of similar geo-regions detected in Sect. 4.3. For this, we analyzed the results using an interface that visualizes them as shown in Fig. 1. With the interface, we can see the range of each geo-region on a map, Visual Concepts that highly contributed to the similarity, and photos that contained the highly-contributed Visual Concepts. The contribution of Visual Concept vc_k to the similarity is calculated as,

$$C_{vc_k,i,j} = \frac{(V_i'(k) - \overline{V_i'})(V_j'(k) - \overline{V_j'})}{\sqrt{\sum_{n=1}^{N}(V_i'(n) - \overline{V_i'})^2 \cdot \sum_{n=1}^{N}(V_j'(n) - \overline{V_j'})^2}}. \tag{6}$$

The detected similar geo-regions can be divided into two types; One which people focused on certain objects, and one which they focused on certain activities.

For geo-regions where people focused on objects, we found examples where people focused on "towers", "trains", "airport", "mountains", and so on.

Table 1. Top five contributed Visual Concepts for "Tokyo Tower" and "Eiffel Tower"

Rank	Visual Concept	Contribution
1	tower	0.182
2	architecture	0.104
3	building	0.048
4	steeple	0.038
5	skyline	0.003

Table 2. Top five contributed Visual Concepts for "Bali" and "Coolangatta"

Rank	Visual Concept	Contribution
1	surfing	0.175
2	water skiing	0.142
3	water sport	0.126
4	wave	0.120
5	water ski	0.117

Here, we introduce an example of similar geo-regions where people focused on a tower; "Tokyo Tower" in Tokyo, Japan and "Eiffel Tower" in Paris, France with a similarity of 0.719. From the top five contributed Visual Concepts shown in Table 1, we can see that people focused on "tower" in both geo-regions.

In addition, we found a geo-region which contained "Tokyo Skytree" in Tokyo, Japan which was similar to both of the above two geo-regions. In this case, although "Tokyo Skytree" appears visually different from them as a tower, by using Visual Concepts, we could still detect it as a similar geo-region that contains sceneries with a tower.

Meanwhile, for geo-regions where people focused on activities, we found two types; "eating" and "water sporting". As examples of the eating activities, we found pairs from Chinatowns in Yokohama, Japan and Los Angeles, USA as shown in Fig. 1. In addition, we found other pairs of Chinatowns as similar geo-regions: Nagasaki and Kobe, in Japan, and San Francisco, New York, and Chicago in USA, and so on. Highly contributed Visual Concepts common in these geo-regions were "food", "shop", "indoor", "text", "meal", and "architecture". We consider that in Chinatown, people focus not only on Chinese food detected as Visual Concepts "food" and "meal", but also on Chinese-style streetscapes detected as "shop" and "architecture". It seems that combinations of these Visual Concepts indicate activities in Chinatown. However, since these Visual Concepts do not directly indicate Chinese food or streetscapes, some geo-regions which are actually not Chinatown were also detected as similar geo-regions. Although it is still fine to detect them as geo-regions with eating activities, if we can detect more detailed Visual Concepts such as oriental architecture, we could detect more specific activities, precisely.

As examples of the water sporting activities, we found pairs from Bali, Indonesia and Coolangatta, Australia with a similarity of 0.905. From the top five contributed Visual Concepts shown in Table 2, we can see that people focused on water sporting. Although various activities can take place on a seashore; sightseeing, whale watching, beach volleyball, water sports, and so on, for travel recommendation, it is important to find those where specific activities take place.

5 Conclusions

We proposed a method for the detection of similar geo-regions based on Visual Concepts in social photos. From experimental results and their analyses, we confirmed the usefulness of the proposed method. Future work includes modelling of similar geo-regions based on common Visual Concepts in them, and also temporal analysis of the similar geo-regions.

Acknowledgment. Parts of this work were supported by Grant-in-aid for Scientific Research from MEXT/JSPS.

References

1. Travel & tourism economic impact 2016 annual update summary. http://www.wttc. org/-/media/files/reports/economic-impact-research/2016-documents/economic-impact-summary-2016_a4-web.pdf. Accessed 15 May 2017
2. Ide, I., Wang, J., Noda, M., Takahashi, T., Deguchi, D., Murase, H.: Construction of a local attraction map according to social visual attention. In: Watanabe, T., Watada, J., Takahashi, N., Howlett, R., Jain, L. (eds.) Intelligent Interactive Multimedia: Systems and Services, pp. 153–162. Springer, Heidelberg (2012). https://doi.org/10.1007/978-3-642-29934-6_15
3. Kurashima, T., Iwata, T., Irie, G., Fujimura, K.: Travel route recommendation using geotags in photo sharing sites. In: Proceedings of the 19th ACM International Conference on Information and Knowledge Management, pp. 579–588 (2010)
4. Min, W., Bao, B.K., Xu, C.: Multimodal spatio-temporal theme modeling for landmark analysis. IEEE Multimed. **21**(3), 20–29 (2014)
5. Pongpaichet, S., Tang, M., Jalali, L., Jain, R.: Using photos as micro-reports of events. In: Proceedings of the 2016 ACM International Conference on Multimedia Retrieval, pp. 87–94 (2016)
6. Shi, Y., Serdyukov, P., Hanjalic, A., Larson, M.: Nontrivial landmark recommendation using geotagged photos. ACM Trans. Intell. Syst. Technol. **4**(3), 17–37 (2013)
7. Shimada, K., Uehara, H., Endo, T.: A comparative study of potential-of-interest days on a sightseeing spot recommender. In: Proceedings of the 3rd IIAI International Conference on Advanced Applied Information, pp. 555–560 (2014)
8. Thomee, B., Shamma, D.A., Friedland, G., Elizalde, B., Ni, K., Poland, D., Borth, D., Li, L.J.: YFCC100M: the new data in multimedia research. Comm. ACM **59**(2), 64–73 (2016)

Unsupervised Concept Learning in Text Subspace for Cross-Media Retrieval

Mengdi Fan, Wenmin Wang$^{(\boxtimes)}$, Peilei Dong, Ronggang Wang, and Ge Li

School of Electronic and Computer Engineering, Peking University,
Lishui Road 2199, Nanshan District, Shenzhen 518055, China
fanmengdi@sz.pku.edu.cn, {wangwm,rgwang}@ece.pku.edu.cn,
pldong@pku.edu.cn, gli@pkusz.edu.cn

Abstract. Subspace (i.e. image, text or latent subspace) learning is one of the essential parts in cross-media retrieval. And most of the existing methods deal with mapping different modalities to the latent subspace pre-defined by category labels. However, the labels need a lot of manual annotation, and the label concerned subspace may not be exact enough to represent the semantic information. In this paper, we propose a novel unsupervised concept learning approach in text subspace for cross-media retrieval, which can map images and texts to a conceptual text subspace via the neural networks trained by self-learned concept labels, therefore the well-established text subspace is more reasonable and practicable than pre-defined latent subspace. Experiments demonstrate that our proposed method not only outperforms the state-of-the-art unsupervised methods but achieves better performance than several supervised methods on two benchmark datasets.

Keywords: Unsupervised · Concept learning · Text subspace
Cross-media retrieval · Neural networks

1 Introduction

With the expansion of multimedia data on the Internet, cross-media retrieval, which focuses on mining the correlations between different modalities, is becoming increasingly important. It aims to align the feature spaces to bridge the heterogeneity gap across modalities. As a solution, a majority of the existing predominant methods utilize the pre-defined category information to explore the semantic correlation particularly on image-text mixed multimedia data. However, this practice may be problematic in two aspects: Firstly, it strongly bases a possibly invalid hypothesis that a query will fall into a pre-defined category in the process of retrieval; Secondly, it might well be the case that labeled data is not available due to the expensive annotation process. Thus the primary challenge of cross-media retrieval in practice consists in finding a common semantic subspace to eliminate the heterogeneity as well as getting rid of the dependency on pre-defined category information. From the above point of view, the recent

© Springer International Publishing AG, part of Springer Nature 2018
B. Zeng et al. (Eds.): PCM 2017, LNCS 10735, pp. 505–514, 2018.
https://doi.org/10.1007/978-3-319-77380-3_48

progresses of cross-media retrieval can be categorized by two perspectives: (1) the works mapping into one of three subspaces, i.e. image subspace, text subspace and latent subspace; (2) the works using class labels or not, i.e. the supervised methods[1] which provide class labels for each modality, and the unsupervised methods[2] where only image-text pairs are used without class labels.

Many supervised methods for cross-media retrieval have been proposed in recent years. Wang *et al.* [22] unified coupled linear regression, L_{21} norm and trace norm regularization terms into a generic framework to jointly perform common subspace learning and coupled feature selection. Several years later, they have proposed a joint learning framework [21] which consists of subspace learning for different modalities, the L_{21} norm for coupled feature selection, and the multimodal graph regularization for preserving the inter-modality and intra-modality similarity. On the basis of [13], Wei *et al.* [23] proposed a deep semantic matching method to address the cross-modal retrieval problem with respect to samples annotated with one or multiple labels. Wang *et al.* [20] proposed a regularized deep neural network (RE-DNN) for semantic mapping across modalities and learned a joint model which can capture both intra-modal and inter-modal relationships. Peng *et al.* [11] proposed a cross-media multiple deep network (CMDN) to exploit the complex cross-media correlation by hierarchical learning. However, it is usually time-consuming and requires a lot of human annotation effort to manually label large-scale datasets.

Besides, a few unsupervised methods without using class labels are proposed. Canonical correlation analysis (CCA) [13] can learn a common latent subspace for different media types, which is able to maximize the correlation of them. Yan *et al.* [24] addressed the problem of matching images and captions in a joint latent space learnt with deep canonical correlation analysis (DCCA). The bilinear model (BLM) [19] can separate style and content by using singular value decomposition (SVD). It learns a shared subspace in which data of the same content and different modality is projected to the same coordinates. Partial least square (PLS) [14] uses the least square method to correlate the subspaces of CCA in order to avoid information dissipation in the process of different modal correlations. Corr-AE [5] is constructed by correlating hidden representations of two uni-modal autoencoders. Multimodal DBN [16] learns a joint representation of multimodal data, which models each media type with a separate two-layer DBN, and combines two networks by learning a joint RBM on top of them. Sun *et al.* [17] proposed an automatic visual concept discovery algorithm for image-sentence bi-directional retrieval. Liang *et al.* [8] proposed a self-paced cross-modal subspace matching method, where a joint feature learning and data grouping formulation has been developed.

In general, from the perspective of three subspaces, most of the cross-media retrieval methods are based on latent subspace. Some of them aim to align the images and texts directly from the low-level features in the latent subspace, such as CCA [13], KCCA [2], BLM [19] and PLS [14], but it's not the most

---

[1] https://en.wikipedia.org/wiki/Supervised_learning.
[2] https://en.wikipedia.org/wiki/Unsupervised_learning.

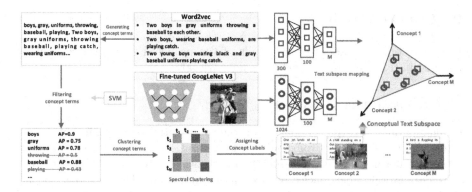

Fig. 1. Overview of our approach. The framework consists of four procedures: firstly generating concept terms, then filtering the terms without visual discrimination, thirdly clustering the terms into several compact concepts and lastly constructing two neural networks to map all texts and images into the self-learned conceptual text subspace.

effective place to find correlations, as the semantic gap is maximized [6]. Some of them first extract low-level features from each modality then the alignment is learned jointly by Corr-AE [5], Multimodal DBN [16] or CMDN [11]. However, when there is not enough labeled training data available, the deep networks might be overfitted due to their large number of parameters. Others explore the latent subspace with semantic associations heavily depending on pre-defined class labels, such as LCFS [22], JFSSL [21], CFMCM [4] and so on. More rarely, Dong et al. [3] proposed to embed the text into a visual feature space (image subspace) to capture both semantic and visual similarities.

Different from the above methods, we introduce a novel unsupervised concept learning approach in text subspace for cross-media retrieval, shown in Fig. 1, which can pretrain the text set to get the semantic concepts of texts without using class labels, then cast all modalities into a conceptual text subspace trained by neural networks based on the aggregated concept labels. The contributions of this paper are as follows:

- We introduce the idea of unsupervised concept learning for cross-media retrieval, which can automatically generate the concept labels to cope with the problem of missing class labels in practical applications.
- According to the self-learned concept labels, we propose two 3-layer neural networks to map all images and texts respectively into an isomorphic text subspace, which is more reasonable and interpretable than other subspaces.
- The retrieval results on Pascal Sentence dataset outperform all of the unsupervised and supervised methods we compare, and better results are also obtained for Wikipedia dataset.

2 Our Approach

In this section, we describe the details of the proposed unsupervised concept learning in text subspace for cross-media retrieval.

2.1 Concept Terms Generating

Given a paralleled corpus of images and their descriptive texts, we firstly extract the semantic information from the text data. Considering a sentence "Two boys in gray uniforms throwing a baseball to each other", we can extract some key words or several dependencies between individual words. For example, "boys", "uniforms" and "baseball" belong to nouns, "throwing" belongs to verb, and "grey" belongs to adjective. "Grey uniforms" is an adjective modifier dependency, and "throwing baseball" is the direct objective dependency.

To collect the above candidate concepts, we use Stanford CoreNLP Parser [9] to extract the unigrams and dependencies of interest, shown in Table 1. After parsing the whole corpus, we count the number of occurrences of the entire terms, including unigrams and dependencies. In order to eliminate the influence of very rare terms, we remove the terms which occur fewer than k times.

Table 1. Unigrams and dependencies of interest

Unigrams	Dependencies
Noun: NN, NNS, NNP, NNPS	acomp, agent, amod
Verb: VB, VBD, VBG, VBN, VBP, VBZ	dboj, iobj, nsubj
Adjective: JJ, JJR, JJS, ADJP	nsubjpass, nummod
Adverb: RB, RBR, RBS	prt, vmod

2.2 Concept Terms Filtering

In order to guarantee the semantic consistency of images and texts, the concept terms have to be associated with visual features as much as possible. But the terms generated in Sect. 2.1 may not have visual discrimination or may not be distinguished by visual features easily, we decide to filter the terms with the help of corresponding image features pretrained on deep convolutional neural networks (CNN).

For the images associated with a certain term, we do a 2-fold cross validation with LIBSVM [1], and the negative samples of which are randomly selected from training set. We can get the average precision (AP) for each term, and remove the terms with AP lower than a threshold. The filtered and preserved terms are partially listed in Table 2.

From Table 2, we can see that a term may be filtered if it's not visually discriminative (the first line), not detailed enough (the second line) or too complicated (the third line). And some terms beginning with capital letters are also filtered out (the last line).

Table 2. The filtered and preserved terms from Pascal Sentence dataset

Filtered terms	Preserved terms
facing, group, several	glasses, flowers
yellow, brown	yellow bus, brown horse
jet, airport	plane, air
People, Woman	people, woman

2.3 Concept Clustering

Many of the remaining concept terms are synonyms or belong to various transformations. If they serve as different concepts, the classifier in concept space will
be confused in the training process. Thus, it's important to cluster the terms
with the same semantics. Word2vec [10] is a recently developed technique for
building a neural network (NN) that maps words to real-number vectors, with
the desideratum that words with similar meanings will map to similar vectors.
The pre-trained 300-dimensional Word2vec vectors used to represent texts are
obtained from code.google.com/p/word2vec/. We take the average of the word
vectors from each word of the concept term, and $L2$-normalize the average vector. For each two concept terms t_i and t_j, the similarity can be computed by the
cosine distance of their word embeddings:

$$S(i, j) = cosine(t_i, t_j) \tag{1}$$

For N concept terms $T = \{t_1, t_2, \cdots, t_N\}$, we use Spectral Clustering [25]
to cluster the similarity matrix $S \in \mathbb{R}^{N \times N}$ into M concept groups $C = \{c_1, c_2, \cdots, c_M\}$. Each group is represented as a set of terms. Table 3 shows
some of the clustered concepts discovered by our framework. We can find that
the objects or scenes which often co-occur have been gathered together. Different transformations or patterns (the third line) are also merged. Besides, it can
automatically generate the concepts related to positions, activities, colors and
synonyms. We observe that there are some mixed type concepts (the last line)
of activities (*plant*) and objects (*trees*). It's possibly because they often appear
in one sentence.

Table 3. The clustered concepts from Pascal Sentence dataset

Type	Concept
Object	{bed, chair, coach, sofa}
Scene	{city, sidewalk, street}
Transform	{black cat, white cat, cats}
Position	{behind, back, up, down}
Activity	{laying, looking, running}
Color	{blue, green, orange, red}
Synonyms	{bicycle, bike}, {motorbike, motorcycle}
Mixed	{plant, trees, flowers, grass, wood}

2.4   Text Subspace Mapping

Each clustered concept is served as one dimension in text subspace. And what we need to solve is how to map all the images and texts into this subspace under the circumstances of preserving the isomorphic semantic information as much as possible.

The previous work of [7] shows the efficiency of "Semantic Matching", which tried to learn a shallow linear classifier with a probabilistic interpretation to produce a probability distribution over classes. Differently, we learns the 3-layer neural networks of several non-linear transformations to produce a probability distribution over our pre-defined concept labels as the semantic embedding.

For the ith pair of image and text, the most relevant concept $l_i \in \mathbb{R}^M$ is defined as:

$$l_i = \underset{j}{\mathrm{argmax}} \ \underset{c_j \in C}{cosine(w_i, c_j)} \tag{2}$$

where w_i is the average Word2vec vectors of the words in the ith text.

According to the self-learned concept label l, we can train a 3-layer fully-connected neural networks for images and texts separately. We take the image input as an example. $x_i^I \in \mathbb{R}^{D_I}$ represents the deep CNN features of the ith image, which is the input to the network. The output y_i, also called semantic embedding, is calculated as:

$$y_i = Softmax(W_2 \cdot \sigma(W_1 x_i^I + b_1) + b_2) \tag{3}$$

where $\sigma(\cdot)$ is the sigmoid function, W_1 and W_2 are the weights to be learned. Actually, the output of $Softmax$ produces a probability distribution over M concepts, the meaning of which is essentially the same as Semantic Matching but with more non-linear deep correlation.

We define the cost function as:

$$loss = \frac{1}{2n} \sum_{i=1}^{n} \|y_i - l_i\|^2 + \frac{\lambda}{2}(\|W_1\|^2 + \|W_2\|^2) \tag{4}$$

where n is the training number, and λ is the regularizer penalty parameter. Equation 4 is minimized by using stochastic gradient descent (SGD).

We can train a neural network similarly for texts given a fixed training set $\{(x_1^T, l_1), \cdots, (x_n^T, l_n)\}$, where $x_i^T \in \mathbb{R}^{D_T}$ equals to w_i of the ith text features. After casting all of the heterogeneous image and text features into this conceptual text subspace, we can easily perform *Img2Text* and *Text2Img* evaluated by the traditional similarity measurement, such as Centered Correlation (CC).

3   Experiments

In this section, we evaluate the performance of our method by conducting extensive experiments and compare with the existing unsupervised and supervised approaches on two benchmark datasets.

3.1   Datasets

(1) *Pascal Sentence dataset*[3] [12]: Pascal Sentence dataset is a subset of Pascal VOC, which contains 1,000 pairs of an image along with several sentences from 20 categories. The whole dataset is randomly split into a training set and a testing set with 600 and 400 pairs.

(2) *Wikipedia dataset*[4] [13]: Wikipedia dataset, generated from Wikipedia featured articles, is composed of 2,866 image-text pairs from 10 semantic classes. A random split was used to produce a training set of 2,173 documents, and a testing set of 693 documents.

3.2   Evaluation Scheme and Baseline Methods

We use mean average precision (mAP) as the performance measurement. For a query q and a set of R retrieved target documents, the average precision (AP) is defined as:

$$AP(q) = \frac{1}{L_q} \sum_{j=1}^{R} P_q(j)\delta_q(j) \qquad (5)$$

where L_q is the number of ground truth neighbors in the retrieved set, $P_q(j)$ is the precision of the top j retrieved results and $\delta_q(j)$ is an indicator function equaling 1 if the item at rank j is relevant, 0 otherwise.

With regards to baseline methods, CCA [13], Multimodal DBN [16], Corr-AE [5], SCSM [8] are four unsupervised methods, which merely use the pair-wised multimedia information to learn a common latent subspace. On the contrary, supervised methods such as LCFS [22], Deep-SM [23], JFSSL [21], CMDN [11] all take the category information into account, and they are also compared here.

3.3   Experimental Results

The parameter k in Sect. 2.1 is set to 15 for Pascal Sentence dataset and 20 for Wikipedia dataset. The threshold of AP in Sect. 2.2 is set to 0.7 for Pascal Sentence dataset and 0.6 for Wikipedia dataset. Figure 2 shows the curves of mAP when selecting different numbers of concept groups. We fix M to 100 for Pascal Sentence dataset and 20 for Wikipedia dataset to achieve the best results in our experiments. In view of [23], the visual features obtained from the pretrained or fine-tuned CNN model should be the primary candidate for cross-media retrieval. So our deep CNN features extracted from the 1024×1 final layer of Inception-v3 model [18] are fined-tuned by the images from two target datasets in our experiments. For the 3-layer fully-connected image and text neural networks in Sect. 2.4, the node number of hidden layer is set to 100, the learning rate is set as 0.01, the momentum equals to 0.9 and the epoch number is fixed at 2,000. We have attempted to change the layer number or node number but perform not as good as these two 3-layer networks.

---

[3] http://vision.cs.uiuc.edu/pascal-sentences/.
[4] http://www.svcl.ucsd.edu/projects/crossmodal/.

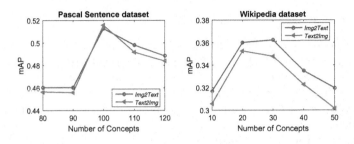

Fig. 2. Curves of the mAP values under different clustering numbers of semantic concept.

Table 4. The mAP scores on Pascal Sentence dataset and Wikipedia dataset

Methods	Pascal sentence dataset			Wikipedia dataset		
	Img2Text	*Text2Img*	*Average*	*Img2Text*	*Text2Img*	*Average*
CCA [13, 23]	0.364	0.387	0.376	0.251	0.199	0.225
Corr-AE [5]	0.290	0.279	0.285	0.335	0.368	0.352
Multimodal DBN [11, 16]	0.149	0.150	0.150	0.197	0.183	0.190
SCSM [8]	–	–	–	0.274	0.217	0.245
LCFS [22]	0.497	0.488	0.493	0.280	0.214	0.247
Deep-SM [23]	0.446	0.478	0.462	0.398	0.354	**0.376**
JFSSL [21]	–	–	–	0.306	0.228	0.267
CMDN [11]	0.334	0.333	0.334	0.393	0.325	0.359
Ours	**0.513**	**0.516**	**0.515**	**0.362**	**0.353**	**0.359**

Table 4 shows the mAP scores of different approaches on Pascal Sentence and Wikipedia dataset. On the whole, the supervised methods achieve higher scores than unsupervised methods. This is because supervised methods rely on semantic labels to reduce the semantic gap of different modalities, but unsupervised methods only use pair-wised information. For Pascal Sentence dataset, we can observe that the proposed method achieves the best performance with average mAP 0.515 among unsupervised methods even supervised methods. For Wikipedia dataset, our method obtains the best scores among unsupervised methods. Even though our method performs a little lower than Deep-SM [23], it still can beat other supervised methods, such as LCFS [22] and JFSSL [21].

Figure 3 shows two examples of *Text2Img* by our proposed approach. Row 1 and 2 correspond to the samples from Pascal Sentence dataset and Wikipedia dataset respectively. The first column contains the text queries and the second represents the paired images of the text queries. Column 3–7 are the top 5 retrieved images.

The excellent performance of Pascal Sentence dataset may derive from two aspects: Firstly, the concepts of the sentences are relatively simple, and from which we can exploit rich semantic information. Secondly, the 20 classes are all included in ImageNet and the images of Pascal Sentence dataset are very similar

Fig. 3. Two examples of *Text2Img* by our method for Pascal Sentence dataset and Wikipedia dataset respectively.

as those from ILSVRC 2012 [15]. In contrast, the texts in Wikipedia dataset are hard to parse and there are huge gaps between the latent meaning of the texts and the visual perception of the images. Despite the improved performance of some supervised methods, semantic labels are usually too expensive and time-consuming to obtain. Thus, it's of great significance to improve the effectiveness of unsupervised approaches for cross-media retrieval.

4   Conclusion

In this paper, we innovatively conduct cross-media retrieval through unsupervised concept learning in text subspace. The procedures of concept terms generating, filtering and clustering aim to automatically obtain concept labels, which lay a good foundation for text subspace mapping. And then, the isomorphic text subspace is trained by two well-designed 3-layer fully-connected neural networks individually for images and texts. Our method can successfully cope with the problem of missing class labels in practical applications. The retrieval results show that the proposed approach not only surpasses the unsupervised methods, but outperforms several supervised methods, achieving the state-of-the-art performance. In the future work, we will further explore the semantic correlation between the images and texts by unsupervised learning.

Acknowledgement. This project was supported by Shenzhen Peacock Plan (20130408-183003656), Shenzhen Key Laboratory for Intelligent Multimedia and Virtual Reality (ZDSYS201703031405467), and Guangdong Science and Technology Project (2014B010117007).

References

1. Chang, C.C., Lin, C.J.: LIBSVM: A library for support vector machines. ACM Transactions on Intelligent Systems and Technology (2007)
2. Costa, P.J., Coviello, E., Doyle, G., Rasiwasia, N., Lanckriet, G.R., Levy, R., Vasconcelos, N.: On the role of correlation and abstraction in cross-modal multimedia retrieval. IEEE Trans. Pattern Anal. Mach. Intell. **36**(3), 521–535 (2014)
3. Dong, J., Li, X., Snoek, C.G.M.: Word2VisualVec: Cross-media retrieval by visual feature prediction. arXiv (2016)
4. Fan, M., Wang, W., Wang, R.: Coupled feature mapping and correlation mining for cross-media retrieval. In: ICME Workshop (2016)

5. Feng, F., Wang, X., Li, R.: Cross-modal retrieval with correspondence Autoencoder. In: ACM MM, pp. 7–16 (2014)
6. Habibian, A., Mensink, T., Snoek, C.G.M.: Discovering semantic vocabularies for cross-media retrieval. In: ACM ICMR, pp. 131–138 (2015)
7. Han, L., Wang, W., Fan, M., Wang, R.: Cross-modality matching based on Fisher Vector with neural word embeddings and deep image features. In: ICASSP (2017)
8. Liang, J., Li, Z., Cao, D., He, R.: Self-paced cross-modal subspace matching. In: ACM SIGIR, pp. 569–578 (2016)
9. Marneffe, M.C.D., Maccartney, B., Manning, C.D.: Generating typed dependency parses from phrase structure parses. In: LREC (2006)
10. Mikolov, T., Chen, K., Corrado, G., Dean, J.: Efficient estimation of word representations in vector space. In: CoRR (2013)
11. Peng, Y., Huang, X., Qi, J.: Cross-media shared representation by hierarchical learning with multiple deep networks. In: IJCAI (2016)
12. Rashtchian, C., Young, P., Hodosh, M., Hockenmaier, J.: Collecting image annotations using Amazon's mechanical Turk. In: NAACL Workshop (2010)
13. Rasiwasia, N., Costa Pereira, J., Coviello, E., et al.: A new approach to cross-modal multimedia retrieval. In: ACM MM (2010)
14. Rosipal, R., Krämer, N.: Overview and recent advances in partial least squares. In: Saunders, C., Grobelnik, M., Gunn, S., Shawe-Taylor, J. (eds.) SLSFS 2005. LNCS, vol. 3940, pp. 34–51. Springer, Heidelberg (2006). https://doi.org/10.1007/11752790_2
15. Russakovsky, O., et al.: ImageNet Large scale visual recognition challenge. Int. J. Comput. Vision **115**(3), 211–252 (2015)
16. Srivastava, N., Salakhutdinov, R.: Learning representations for multimodal data with deep belief nets. In: ICML Workshop (2012)
17. Sun, C., Gan, C., Nevatia, R.: Automatic concept discovery from parallel text and visual corpora. In: IEEE International Conference on Computer Vision ICCV (2015)
18. Szegedy, C., Vanhoucke, V., Ioffe, S., Shlens, J., Wojna, Z.: Rethinking the inception architecture for computer vision. In: Computer Vision and Pattern Recognition CVPR (2015)
19. Tenenbaum, J.B., Freeman, W.T.: Separating style and content with bilinear models. Neural Comput. **12**(6), 1247–1283 (2000)
20. Wang, C., Yang, H., Meinel, C.: Deep semantic mapping for cross-modal retrieval. In: IEEE 27th International Conference on Tools with Artificial Intelligence ICTAI, pp. 1082–3409 (2015)
21. Wang, K., He, R., Wang, L., Wang, W., Tan, T.: Joint feature selection and subspace learning for cross-modal retrieval. IEEE Trans. Pattern Anal. Mach. Intell. **38**(10), 2010–2023 (2016)
22. Wang, K., He, R., Wang, W., Wang, L., Tan, T.: Learning coupled feature spaces for cross-modal matching. In: IEEE International Conference on Computer Vision ICCV (2013)
23. Wei, Y., Zhao, Y., Lu, C., Wei, S.: Cross-modal retrieval with CNN visual features: a new baseline. IEEE Trans. Cybern. **47**(2), 449–460 (2016)
24. Yan, F., Mikolajczyk, K.: Deep correlation for matching images and text. In: 2015 IEEE Conference on Computer Vision and Pattern Recognition CVPR (2015)
25. Zelnik-Manor, L., Perona, P.: Self-tuning spectral clustering. In: Proceedings of the 17th International Conference on Neural Information Processing Systems NIPS, pp. 1601–1608 (2004)

Image Stylization for Thread Art via Color Quantization and Sparse Modeling

Kewei Yang[1], Zhengxing Sun[1(✉)] ⓘ, Shuang Wang[1,2],
and Hui-Hsia Chen[3]

[1] State Key Laboratory for Novel Software Technology,
Nanjing University, Nanjing, China
szx@nju.edu.cn
[2] Jiangsu Vocational Institute of Commerce, Nanjing, China
[3] Asia University, Taiwan, China

Abstract. We present an image stylization method to simulate a graceful Chinese art—Random-needle Embroidery designated as Intangible Cultural Heritage. We first develop an effective way to simulate a single thread, and define rendering primitive called stitch which is a collection of threads arranged in a certain pattern. Then, we segment the input image and partition each region into non-uniform sub-regions, from which a color quantization method is proposed to select colors used in the rendering process for each sub-region from a specific color library. During runtime, new stitches can be synthesized for each sub-region via sparse modeling based on the pre-defined stitches. Smoothness constraints are added to this process to avoid local distortions. Finally, rendering image is generated by placing stitches with different attributes on the canvas. Experiments show that our method can perform fine images with the style of random-needle.

Keywords: Image-based artistic rendering · Random-needle Embroidery
Color quantization · Stitch selection · Sparse modeling

1 Introduction

Image-based artistic rendering (IB-AR) received significant attention in the past decades which covers a broad range of techniques to render different artistic styles [6]. However, because of their diversity and specificity, the creation of entirely new and original forms of arts is still one of the toughest challenges in IB-AR. So in this paper, we focus on random-needle rendering [10, 12] which attempts to emulate a new form of Chinese Embroidery art: Random-needle Embroidery (RNE). In brief, RNE utilizes thousands of intersecting threads to translate the source image into the art image with the style of random-needles based on the preservation of original main contents. The corresponding stylization process can be viewed as a recording process of the source image [6] which contains two problems: style definition and style rendering.

For the first problem, the differences among various artistic styles are mainly reflected in the rendering primitives. Since no single thread is of critical importance and threads must work together to express certain artistic style in RNE. Inspired by tonal art

© Springer International Publishing AG, part of Springer Nature 2018
B. Zeng et al. (Eds.): PCM 2017, LNCS 10735, pp. 515–525, 2018.
https://doi.org/10.1007/978-3-319-77380-3_49

map [8], we define stitches, i.e., collections of threads arranged in different patterns as the basic rendering primitives. We extend the work [10] by giving more comprehensive descriptions of the thread distributions and presenting an effective way to render each thread in the stitch with texture information. For the second problem, the style transfer process aims to extract the image contents which need to be expressed and construct the mapping relations between image contents and rendering primitives. The previous work of random-needle rendering [10, 12] directly use the source image color when parsing the input image. However, the RNE artists usually choose colors within a specific color library and create artworks with a limited number of thread colors. So it is necessary to approximate an image with a relatively small number of colors while minimizing color abbreviations. For mapping relation construction, existing works address this problem by seriatim matching each primitive with the image according to tone [8] and texture [9] similarity. This means only the existing primitives can be selected when rendering image. However, since random-needle rendering requires a relatively high degree of image content reproduction and it is hard to pre-define a complete stitch library to fit continuous image contents, selecting appropriate stitch by existing methods is inaccurate and may affect the rendering quality when no suitable stitch is found. Furthermore, stitch selection should pay additional attention to the smoothness of the selected stitch with its adjacent stitches so as to alleviate local distortions.

Accordingly, we present a new image stylization method for thread art via color quantization and sparse modeling which includes three main contributions: (1) We generate stitches with various styles to feed the sparse modeling system. Different thread distributions in stitches are first designed, and then stitches are generated on 2D pixel arrays by rendering each thread in the stitch. (2) We present a color quantization method to select dominant colors of the input image from a specific thread color library. (3) After generating a dictionary to represent the generated stitches, we propose a smoothness-constrained sparse representation method to adaptively select the most relevant dictionary atoms, so that new stitches can be synthesized to convey the image content.

2   The Proposed Method

Figure 1 shows the workflow of our method which incorporates three main modules. *Stitch definition and representation* defines our rendering primitive, namely, stitch. Since the style of RNE is based on free-form threads, we first design different thread distributions in stitches. Because the stylization is carried out in 2D pixel space, we also rasterize stitches on pixel arrays. Finally, we organize the stitches into groups, from which a series of sub-dictionaries are generated by sparse coding to give a compact representation of each stitch group. Together, these sub-dictionaries form our stitch dictionary. For *image parsing*, the input image is first segmented into object regions. Then, each region is further partitioned into sub-regions, from which we extract a color palette from a specific color library by color quantization. Corresponding attributes are also extracted for each sub-region. During *stitch selection and rendering*, for each sub-region, we synthesize a new stitch to express the sub-region's contents by optimizing a linear combination of the stitch dictionary atoms. Specifically, proper sub-dictionary is first selected according to the sub-region features. Next, the combination coefficients optimization of the sub-region atoms is modeled as minimization of an energy function by sparse representation. We also incorporate image feature and smoothness constraints into this optimization process to make the synthesized stitch conform to the convention of RNE and alleviate local distortions. Then, the synthesized stitch is placed on the canvas and connected to the adjacent stitches along a minimum error boundary (called stitch quilting). This process is repeated until all the sub-regions are processed.

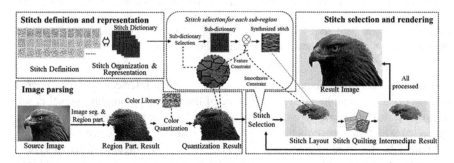

Fig. 1. The flowchart of our method. Note: seg. = segmentation, Part. = Partition

2.1   Stitch Definition

Similar to Yang et al. [10], the stitches are defined in two spaces: vector and pixel space. In vector space, we aim to design different thread distributions in stitches. In pixel space, we rasterize the stitches on 2D pixel arrays.

Vector Space Stitch Definition. Similar to Yang et al. [10], we choose to use two intersecting threads as the basic element (called intersecting-thread) to construct stitches. Figure 2(a) shows the intersecting-thread and its attributes. Different from traditional embroidery artworks which only use coarse and long interlacing knits of weft and warp, in RNE, the orientations, intersection angles, lengths and widths of intersecting-threads can vary with stitches. To design such complex distributions, we first design the single-layer stitch, meaning all intersection-threads in them have the same thread width. Then, the multi-layer stitch can be constructed by several stitch layers with each layer using a different thread width.

Single-Layer Stitch: There are two major stitch categories in RNE: *regular stitch* and *stochastic stitch*. The threads of regular stitch usually have a fixed orientation and threads of stochastic stitch are usually in a mess. In our current implement, we set all the orientations of intersecting-threads along the horizontal direction, and set orientations randomly for stochastic stitch. Then, for regular stitch, we use *directionality* calculated by the standard deviation of the thread directions α_i to distinguish different types of regular stitches, as shown in Fig. 2(b). High directionality stitch can create image style with a high texture directionality in pixel space which can be measured by orientation dominance [11]. To generate stitches with different directionalities, we first randomly choose the locations of the intersecting-threads within a unit square by

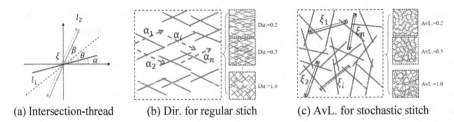

(a) Intersection-thread   (b) Dir. for regular stich   (c) AvL. for stochastic stitch

Fig. 2. Stitch design in vector space. (a) l_1 and l_2 represent two threads. Each thread has a specific length ξ and direction α. θ and β represent the intersection orientation and angle, respectively. (b) $\alpha_1 - \alpha_n$ represent the thread directions in the stitch. (c) $\xi_1 - \xi_n$ represent the thread lengths in the stitch. Note: Dir. = Directionality, AvL. = Average-length.

poisson disc sampling. Then, intersection angle for each intersecting-thread is generated by Gaussian sampling. The mean value of the Gaussian sampling kernel is set to be proportional to the measure of directionality so that small intersection angles can be generated when the directionality is high. For stochastic stitch, we use *average-length* calculated by the mean value of thread lengths ξ_i to distinguish different types of stochastic stitches, as shown in Fig. 2(c). Small average-length stitch can create image style with high contrast in pixel space. We use a similar method as before to generate such stitch, only that the Gaussian sampling is used to get the length of each intersecting-thread based on the average-length.

Multi-layer Stitch: In RNE, stitches constructed by multiple thread widths have stronger detail expression ability than those constructed by single thread width. Thus, besides single-layer stitch, we also design two-layer stitch and three-layer stitch, and the intersecting-threads of each layer can be generated by the above method.

Pixel Space Stitch Generation. An easy way to rasterize stitch on pixel space is to use line rasterization techniques [2] to pixelate each thread in the stitch. However, these techniques do not consider the characteristics of thread. According to Yang et al. [10], end points of a thread exit and enter the basic fabric, which generates a curve and modifies the tangent of the thread and in turn affects the lightness of the thread.

Thus, we propose a strategy to simulate texture and lightness of a thread. The algorithm is as follows: (1) Mapping current thread into the pixel space by the ratio of its coordinate and the stitch image size; (2) Interpolating all pixels of a thread using the Bresenham algorithm and extending this one pixel width line to d pixels (d represents the thread width); (3) Setting the lightness of the thread pixels to a random lightness in the range $[0.8, 1.0]$ and weakening the lightness at the endpoints of the thread by the formula:

$$L(x,y) = (0.75 + 0.25 \times l/l_0) \times L(x,y) \tag{1}$$

where $L(x,y)$ denotes the pixel lightness of the thread, l is the distance of the current pixel to the endpoint of the thread, l_0 is the threshold and is set to 35% of the thread length.

Stitch Organization and Representation. After generating the stitches, we aim to give a compact representation of them, which can reduce the searching space during stitch selection process. We choose sparse coding because it can generate dictionary effectively representing the input examples [7, 11]. Since the stitch styles and the image contents which the stitches are suitable for are very different, learning a global dictionary is inappropriate. Inspired by Yang et al. [11], we divided the dictionary generation task into several subtasks, and each subtask is defined as learning a sub-dictionary from some type of the stitches. To this end, we first organize the stitches according to their artistic styles; then for each stitch group, a sub-dictionary is generated.

We use a four-level tree structure to organize the generated stitch images. Level one distinguishes the regular stitch and stochastic stitch for different objects rendering. Recall that each stitch can be constructed using threads with various widths to express image contents with different levels of details. Thus at level two, regular stitch and stochastic stitch are further classified into single-layer stitch, two-layer stitch and three-layer stitch. Level three organizes stitches according to their sizes, we use stitches of seven sizes (from 200 * 200 – 50 * 50, interval 25) to express image contents with different saliences. Level four contains stitches with different directionalities/average-lengths which are used to reflect different style appearances. Together, we have $K(K = 2 \times 3 \times 7)$ groups of stitches. In this paper, we adopted the online learning for matrix factorization method [7] to determine the sub-dictionary $\{D^{(1)}, D^{(2)}, \ldots, D^{(K)}\}$ under which the stitches in each group can be sparsely coded, respectively.

2.2 Image Parse

Image Segmentation and Region Partition: Given an image, we first adopt the image segmentation method to paint the objects using different stitch styles. The mapping relations between stitch categories and objects are hard-coded. Regular stitch is assigned for objects such as petal, hair, water surface etc., and stochastic stitch is assigned for objects such as grass, rock, background, etc. We also generate an importance map E using Sobel operator and a vector field Θ by ETF [3] to guide the stitch sizes and orientations assignment for different parts of the image. Then, we integrate these image features and further partition each region into sub-regions. This is done by first generating stitch positions p_i through wang tiles [4] by taking the importance map as a density map. Based on the positions, we partition each region into non-uniform connected convex polygons using voronoi diagram. By distributing stitches according to the size of each sub-region, we are able to use smaller stitches in areas containing fine details.

Color Quantization: Our approach computes a color palette $\mathbb{C}$ on the basis of our image partition result. Common color quantization approaches use global optimization schemes that cluster similar colors and determine the base colors from the largest clusters [1]. These approaches, however, may absorb colors in the detail areas of the image. Furthermore, the base colors must be selected from a specific color library in RNE (we use the DMC thread color library). Thus in this paper, a scoring system is applied to classify sub-regions according to their normalized entropy. The color extraction is performed incrementally, starting with an empty palette. Extracted colors are inserted after each iteration. To find a new color for a given color palette $\mathbb{C}$, we seek for a sub-region Q_i of minimal score $\mathcal{H}(Q_i)$:

$$\mathcal{H}(Q_i) = \frac{\eta(Q_i)/|Q_i|}{\bar{\sigma}_i/|Q_i| \cdot \bar{L}_i/|Q_i|} = \frac{\eta(Q_i)}{\bar{\sigma}_i \cdot \bar{L}_i} \cdot |Q_i| \qquad (2)$$

where $|Q_i|$ denotes the area of the sub-region and is used to normalize the weights: image entropy $\eta(Q_i)$, lightness $\bar{L}$, and color distance $\bar{\sigma}$. The entropy of the image is computed from the probabilities $p_{Q_i}(c)$ that a binned color c appears in the sub-region Q_i: $\eta(Q_i) = -\sum_{c \epsilon Q_i} p_{Q_i}(c)\log_2 p_{Q_i}(c)$. To favor vivid colors, the sub-region score is weighted according to the lightness $\bar{L}_i = \sum_{p \in Q_i} L(p)$. Finally, to favor colors not yet present, the score is weighted according to the minimum color distance to colors of the current palette $\mathbb{C}$: $\bar{\sigma}_i = \sum_{p \epsilon Q_i} \sigma(p)^2$ with $\sigma(p) = \min_{c \epsilon \mathbb{C}}\|I(p) - c\|$. $I(p)$ denotes the source image color of point p, and $\|\cdot\|$ denotes the Euclidean distance. This way, more priority is given to extracting palettes with diverging color tones. Finally, the respective weights are divided by $|Q_i|$ to ensure that colors of the image detail areas can also be selected.

To find a color palette $\mathbb{C}$, the following steps are performed iteratively in CIE-Lab color space, n-times in total for a target palette size of n (Fig. 3): (1) To avoid re-computation in the sub-sequence steps, $\eta(Q_i)$ and $\bar{L}_i$ are precomputed for each sub-region; (2) Computing $\bar{\sigma}_i$ based on the current $\mathbb{C}$ and searching the sub-regions with the minim-um score; (3) Once a sub-region has been identified, we discretized its colors using the DMC color library as bins. The color of the highest bin is selected and inserted in $\mathbb{C}$; (4) Updating the minimal color distance $\sigma(p)$ for pixels in I to $\{c \epsilon \mathbb{C}\}$, and the results are buffered in a color difference mask (Fig. 3(d)–(i)).

Finally, for each sub-region Q_i, following attributes are calculated to guide the rendering process which including: orientation $\Theta(p_i)$, adjacent sub-regions $N(i)$, average importance E_i, orientation dominance R_i, image contrast T_i and color C_i. R_i is calculated by orientation dominance [11] which measures the texture directionality of Q_i. T_i is calculated by the standard deviation of the pixel lightness in Q_i. R_i and T_i are used to guide stitch selection in Sect. 2.3. C_i is calculated by first computing the average color $\bar{C}$ of Q_i, then, C_i is set to the color in $\mathbb{C}$ who has the minimal distance with $\bar{C}$.

2.3 Stitch Selection and Rendering

Based on the stitch dictionary and image parsing result, we aim to select appropriate stitch and place it on the canvas sub-region-by-sub-region. Since it is hard to pre-define a complete stitch library to fit continuous image contents. Thus, utilizing limited pre-defined stitches to express continuous image contents is a key problem for stitch selection. Our basic idea of stitch selection is inspired by recent methods for image reconstruction [7, 11] which suggest the input image signal can be coded by a linear combination of samples. In this paper, we adopt the theory of sparse representation to find the optimal linear combination since sparseness can adaptively select the most

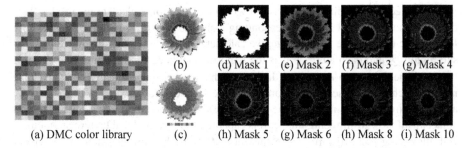

(a) DMC color library   (b)   (c)   (d) Mask 1   (e) Mask 2   (f) Mask 3   (g) Mask 4

(h) Mask 5   (g) Mask 6   (h) Mask 8   (i) Mask 10

Fig. 3. Color difference masks computed for an image with 10 colors. (b) is the source image. (c) is the color quantization result. The overlaid rectangles in (d)–(i) indicate the respective sub-regions with minimum score used for the color extraction.

relevant dictionary atoms which best represent the image contents. In this paper, the rendering process is achieved via three steps: (1) Recall that our stitch dictionary is composed of a set of sub-dictionaries, thus, we first select an appropriate sub-dictionary for the given sub-region Q_i; (2) Optimizing a sparse linear combination of the sub-dictionary atoms to code Q_i; (3) Assigning attributes to the synthesized stitch and placing it on the canvas; (4) Repeating step 1–3 until all the sub-regions are processed.

Sub-dictionary Selection. According to the mapping relations defined in Sect. 2.1, regular or stochastic stitch is assigned to each Q_i depending on its object category (level one). Then, we use E_i of each sub-region to choose the number of stitch layers at level two. Three-layer stitch is used for sub-region containing high frequency information, two-layer stitch is used for medium E_i and single-layer stitches are used for flat parts of the image. Finally, stitch size which has the minimum difference with the sub-region size S_i is selected (level three).

Linear Combination Optimization. After we determine the sub-dictionary $D^i \in \mathbb{R}^{e \times M}$ (e and M denotes the size and number of the atoms, respectively) for each Q_i, we minimize an energy function E to optimize the combinations of the atoms:

$$E = \frac{1}{2}\left\|I_i - D^i \gamma^i\right\|_2^2 + \lambda \left\|diag(\omega)\gamma^i\right\|_1 + \kappa^2 \sum_{j \in N(i)} \left\|D^j \gamma^j - D^i \gamma^i\right\|_2^2 \qquad (3)$$

The first term measures the difference between the synthesized stitch and the input image signal. For each sub-region Q_i, I_i is an image patch sampled at location p_i with length of side $\sqrt{e}$ and orientation $\Theta(p_i)$. $\gamma^i \in \mathbb{R}^M$ represents the coding coefficient of I_i under D^i. The second term is a l_1-norm regularization term to enforce the sparse representation. We also add some image feature constraints when optimizing the coefficients. In RNE, artists usually adopt strong directional stitches for areas with strong orientation dominances, and high contrast stitches for areas with high image contrasts (calculated in Sect. 2.2 and denoted as R_i and T_i). To incorporate the image feature constraints, we add a weight factor $\omega \in \mathbb{R}^M$ to each sub-dictionary atom.

$diag(\omega) \in \mathbb{R}^{M \times M}$ is a diagonal matrix in which each diagonal element $\omega_j, j \in 1 - M$ is the combination weight of the corresponding atom. To give priority to the atoms whose features are close to the input image, we calculate ω_j as the feature difference between sub-region Q_i and each atom. $\|\cdot\|_1$ is the l_1-norm calculated by the sum of the absolute value of coefficients in $diag(\omega)\gamma^i$. In reality, the source image usually contains some noises which may cause local distortions of the synthesized stitches. In this paper, we add the third term to measure the smoothness of the synthesized stitches with its adjacent stitches. Minimizing this term is capable of enforcing local texture smoothness and alleviating local distortions. In this term, $D^j\gamma^j$ is the current stitch to be synthesized, and $D^j\gamma^j$ is the synthesized stitches of its neighboring sub-regions $N(i)$. To solve Eq. 3, we denote $\tilde{D} = \left[(D^i)^T, \left(\kappa (D^j)^T, j \in N(i) \right) \right]^T$, and $\tilde{X} = \left[\frac{1}{2}I_i^T, \left(\kappa (\gamma^j D^j)^T, j \in N(i) \right) \right]^T$. Then, Eq. 3 can be transformed into a standard sparse representation formula:

$$\min_{\gamma^i} \frac{1}{2} \left\| \tilde{X} - \gamma^i \tilde{D} \right\|_2^2 + \lambda \left\| diag(\omega)\gamma^i \right\|_1 \tag{4}$$

Equation 4 can be solve interactively, within each iteration t, the $\gamma^i_{(t)}$ is updated by Lasso [7]. The iteration process continues when it exceeds the predefined maximum iteration number. We set weight factor $\lambda = 0.15$ and $\kappa = 0.7$ in our current implementation.

Stitch Layout and Rendering. After synthesizing the stitch for sub-region Q_i, we place the synthesized stitch on the canvas by rotating it towards orientation $\Theta(p_i)$, resizing it to size $|Q_i|$ (area of Q_i), and set its color to C_i. In order to achieve a smooth transition between stitches, alpha blending is an easy way to implement but can result in artifacts such as ghosting and blurring. In both cases, graph cuts can be used to find an optimal seam between patches [5]. Thus, once a new stitch is placed, we connect it to the adjacent stitches along a minimum error boundary which is calculated by [5].

3   Results and Experiments

Experiments are carried out to examine our method. In the reminder of this section, if without specification, we set the size of the palette to 20 for each region.

Evaluation of our Method. To evaluate our image quantization method, our algorithm is compare to the k-means algorithm in Fig. 4. There are three main benefits of our method: Firstly, notice how colors of the detail areas are accurately represented and not merged with colors of other area (e.g., the pistil of the flower, the eagle's beak and eyes of the animal). Secondly, our algorithm is deterministic unlike the k-means algorithm which the convergence is sensitive to the initialization. Thirdly, other color quantization methods cannot guarantee that the extracted colors are within the color library.

In order to evaluate the effectiveness of our stitch selection method, we use same stitches as input, and compare our default method (*M0*) with three downgraded

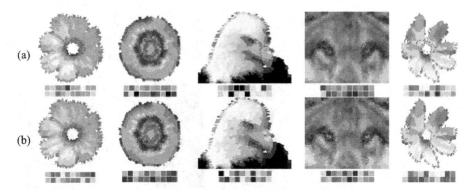

Fig. 4. Comparison of the median-cut algorithm to our approach for dominant color extraction. (a) shows the results of k-means algorithm, and (b) shows the results of our algorithm.

versions: *M1*, not using sparse coding for stitch selection, only using the stitch images generated in Sect. 2.1; *M2*, not adding weight ω in Eq. 3; *M3*, not adding smoothness constraint in Eq. 3. To give a clear comparison between *M0* and *M1*, we design an experiment which the original orientation dominance of the ramp increases from left to right, and stitches are selected only by orientation dominance similarity in *M1*. The stitch colors of Fig. 5(a) indicate the orientation dominance of the rendering result. Significant discontinuity artifacts can be found in *M1* because the stitch library does not contain suitable stitches. On the other hand, new stitches can be synthesized by sparse representation, which gives a more continuous effect. When comparing with *M2* (Fig. 5 (c)), by taking the stitch style appearance into consideration, our results can use stitches with strong texture directionality to portray the objects such as the growth direction of the petal. Finally, the results without the smoothness constraint (*M3*, Fig. 5(d)) are noisy and have local distortions. The results are cleaner and have much less mosaic effects for *M0*.

Comparison with the State-of-the-art Methods and the Real Artwork. Fig. 6(a)–(c) shows the rendering results generated respectively by the proposed method and two other state-of-the-art methods. From the results, it is clear that our method produces a better rendering quality. Zhou et al. [12] adopted a fixed thread width and size for the entire canvas. Thus, some local features such as the braids are rendered crudely. Com-paring to Yang et al. [10], by using sparse modeling, we can increase the diversity of stitches and make the results more visual-rich. Furthermore, by using our color quantization method, we eliminate the color absorption phenomenon in k-means, and the colors of the detail areas can be captured (red box). Figure 6(d) shows the comparison results with real artworks. From the figure, we can see that our method can generate rendering results which have comparable quality to those artworks produced by professional artists. Figure 7 gives more rendering images of our method.

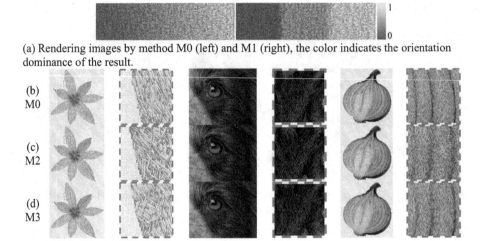

(a) Rendering images by method M0 (left) and M1 (right), the color indicates the orientation dominance of the result.

(b) M0

(c) M2

(d) M3

Fig. 5. Comparison among rendering images generated by method M0, M1, M2 and M3 respectively. Zoom 400% to view details

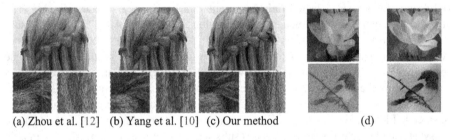

(a) Zhou et al. [12]   (b) Yang et al. [10]   (c) Our method   (d)

Fig. 6. (a), (b) and (c) compare images generated by Zhou et al. [12] and Yang et al. [10]. The image color of (a) and (b) is quantized using *k*-means algorithm. (d) compares images generated by our method (left) and artists (right). Zoom 400% to view details. (Color figure online)

Fig. 7. More rendering results (40 colors are used for the left top bird, the rest images are generated using 20 colors for each region). Zoom 400% to view details.

4   Conclusion

In this paper, we proposed an image stylization method via color quantization and sparse modeling which can translate an input image into the style of random-needle. We first defined the primitive called "stitch". Then, the input image is parsed, in which a color quantization scheme is proposed to determine the colors used in the rendering process. During runtime, we use sparse modeling to sparsely code the image contents. Experiments shows that random-needle rendering can be effectively achieved via our process and this framework can also be applied to hatching and stippling. Our further work will be focus on maintaining color smoothness in the color quantization process.

Acknowledgement. This work was supported by National High Technology Research and Development Program of China (No. 2007AA01Z334), National Natural Science Foundation of China (Nos. 61321491 and 61272219), Innovation Fund of State Key Laboratory for Novel Software Technology (Nos. ZZKT2013A12 and ZZKT2016A11), and Program for New Century Excellent Talents in University of China (NCET-04-04605).

References

1. Chang, H., Fried, O., Liu, Y., DiVerdi, S., Finkelstein, A.: Palette-based photo recoloring. TOG **34**(4), 139:1–139:11 (2015)
2. Inglis, T.C., Vogel, D., Kaplan, C.S.: Rasterizing and antialiasing vector line art in the pixel art style. In: NPAR 2013, pp. 25–32 (2013)
3. Kang, H., Lee, S., Chui, C.K.: Coherent line drawing. In: NPAR, pp. 43–50 (2007)
4. Kopf, J., Cohen-Or, D., Deussen, O., Lischinski, D.: Recursive Wang tiles for real-time blue noise. TOG **25**(3), 509–518 (2006)
5. Kwatra, V., Schödl, A., Essa, I., Turk, G., Bobick, A.: Graphcut textures: image and video synthesis using graph cuts. TOG **22**(3), 277–286 (2003)
6. Kyprianidis, J.E., Collomosse, J., Wang, T., Isenberg, T.: State of the "art": a taxonomy of artistic stylization techniques for images and video. TVCG **19**(5), 866–885 (2013)
7. Mairal, J., Bach, F., Ponce, J., Sapiro, G.: Online learning for matrix factorization and sparse coding. J. Mach. Learn. Res. **11**, 19–60 (2010)
8. Praun, E., Hoppe, H., Webb, M., Finkelstein, A.: Real-time hatching. In: SIGGRAPH 2001, pp. 581–586 (2001)
9. Qu, Y., Pang, W.M., Wong, T.T., Heng, P.A.: Richness-preserving manga screening. TOG **27**(5), 155:1–155:8 (2008)
10. Yang, K., Sun, Z., Ma, C., Yang, W.: Paint with stitches: a random-needle embroidery rendering method. In: CGI 2016, pp. 9–12 (2016)
11. Yang, S., Wang, M., Chen, Y., Sun, Y.: Single-image super-resolution reconstruction via learned geometric dictionaries and clustered sparse coding. TIP **21**(9), 4016–4028 (2012)
12. Zhou, J., Sun, Z., Yang, K.: A controllable stitch layout strategy for random needle embroidery. J. Zhejiang University SCIENCE C **15**(9), 729–743 (2014)

Least-Squares Regulation Based Graph Embedding

Si-Xing Liu[1(✉)], Timothy Apasiba Abeo[1,2], and Xiang-Jun Shen[1]

[1] School of Computer Science and Telecommunication Engineering,
Jiangsu University, Zhenjiang, China
lsx13794600090163.com
[2] Tamale Technical University, Box 3ER, Tamale, Ghana

Abstract. A large family of algorithms named graph embedding is widely accepted as an effective technique designed to provide better solutions to the problem of dimensionality reduction. Existing graph embedding algorithms mainly consider obtaining projection directions through preserving local geometrical structure of data. In this paper, a regulation formulation known as Least-Squares Reconstruction Errors, to unify various graph embedding methods within a common regulation framework for preserving both local and global structures, is proposed. With its properties of Least-Squares regulation, orthogonality constraint to data distributions and tensor extensions of supervised or semi-supervised scenarios, this common regulation framework makes a tradeoff between intrinsic geometrical structure and the global structure. Our experiments demonstrated that, our proposed method have better performances in keeping lower dimensional subspaces and higher classification results.

Keywords: Dimensionality reduction · Graph embedding
Subspace learning · Least-squares regulation

1 Introduction

In many machine learning and pattern recognition tasks, the data are usually provided in high-dimensional form in many application domains, bringing about the so called "curse of dimensionality" [1]. Dimensionality reduction (DR) is an effective approach to mitigate such problem by mapping the high dimensional data to a compact low-dimensional subspace. The typical linear algorithms include Principal Component Analysis (PCA) [2], Linear Discriminant Analysis (LDA) [3,4], Locality Preserving Projections (LPP) [5,6], Neighborhood Preserving Embedding (NPE) [7] and the Sparsity Preserving Projection (SPP) [8].

PCA seems to be the most famous technique that has been widely applied in the areas of science and engineering, in the quest to maximize the variance of projected data. It seeks a global low dimensionality subspace of data by minimizing the reconstruction error using the optimal orthogonal projections under the least-squares framework. Unlike PCA which is unsupervised, LDA is supervised,

© Springer International Publishing AG, part of Springer Nature 2018
B. Zeng et al. (Eds.): PCM 2017, LNCS 10735, pp. 526–533, 2018.
https://doi.org/10.1007/978-3-319-77380-3_50

where class information is employed in learning the embedding functions. PCA is optimal in representation, while LDA is optimal in discrimination. But both PCA and LDA try to estimate the global statistics, i.e. mean and covariance [4]. LPP is an unsupervised manifold learning method; it builds a graph model which reflects the intrinsic geometry by reconstructing each data point from its neighbors or by choosing data points within some fixed radius. Different from LPP, the affinity matrix in NPE is computed through a local least-square problem instead of defining it directly, while they have the same purpose at preserving the neighborhood structure of the data. SPP is another local structure preserving method by constructing an adjacent weight matrix [8] to preserve sparse reconstructive relationship of data. Although these graph embedding methods achieved so much progress in dimensionality reduction, there still exists a number of concerns on improvement: One is on how to add orthogonality constraints to graph embedding methods which can obtain more effective projection directions for preserving the intrinsic geometrical structure of data. Another is about achieving a balance between keeping local and global structures. Graph embedding methods construct graphs by local patches and rely on pair-wise distances leading them to be sensitive to noises in data, while by estimation global statistics may fail to discover the underlying structure, if the data lives on or close to a sub manifold of the ambient space [4].

It is worth noting that, all the aforementioned linear DR algorithms working with the spectral decomposition (or eigen decomposition) of the adjacency matrix [9] can be unified to a graph embedding framework [10] or to a patch alignment framework [11]. In this paper, we developed a different method, which can keep global and local structures of data, as well as making use of an orthogonality constraint to keep power of discrimination in low-dimensional subspace by utilizing PCA-Like idea of least-squares reconstruction error [12]. This PCA-Like idea in graph embedding makes the orthogonality constraint that, projections must be orthogonal to data, with consideration to distributions and local structures of data. Thus, a least-squares regulation based graph embedding is proposed for dimension reduction. And we mainly focused on linear approaches though similar to applying kernelization to the existing linear methods such as Kernel PCA (KPCA) [13,14], Kernel LDA (KLDA) [15,16], Kernel LPP (KLPP) [17], and Kernel NPE (KNPE) [18], our method can be easily kernelized as a nonlinear one [6,11]. We outlined here, the main characteristics of our proposed framework.

(1) The proposed least-squares regulation framework shares both advantages of Dimensionality Reduction (DR) and PCA-like least-squares reconstruction error. By adding such a regulation factor of reconstruction error in graph embedding methods, the "out-of-sample" problem [19] in graph embedding is naturally resolved.
(2) The technique proposed in this paper seeks orthogonality constraint while considering distributions and local structures of data. It is more effective than other traditional DR methods on the projection directions by preserving both the intrinsic geometrical and global structure of data.
(3) Our proposed framework can easily be extended to supervised and semi-supervised scenarios, on the existing DR framework.

(4) Extensive experiments were carried out on two handwritten digit recognition collections, where our proposed framework exhibited more advantages of superior performances than the other DR methods, such as LPP, LSDA (Locality Sensitive Discriminant Analysis) [4], NPE and SPP.

This paper is structured as follows. Section 2 contains a formulation of our proposed methodology, followed immediately with experimental results presented in Sect. 3. Finally, we drew conclusions in Sect. 4.

2 Proposed Method

In this section, we introduce our Least-Squares Regulation based Graph Embedding method, for simplicity we shall refer to it as LSRGE, which achieves a trade-off between keeping global and local structures of data. The main features of LSRGE can be described as least-squares regulation, orthogonality constraint to data distributions and tensor extensions of supervised and semi-supervised scenarios on the existing DR framework.

The generic problem of linear dimensionality reduction is the following; Given a matrix $\mathbf{X}$ consisting of a set $(\mathbf{x}_1, \mathbf{x}_2, \ldots, \mathbf{x}_m)$ in $\Re^n$, find a transformation matrix $\mathbf{W} = (\mathbf{w}_1, \mathbf{w}_2, \ldots, \mathbf{w}_d) \in \Re^{n \times d}$ that maps these m points to a low-dimensional subspace in $\Re^d$ $(d << n)$, which can represent $\mathbf{X}$. Inspired by the original idea of PCA, which uses the idea of least-squares reconstruction error [12] to keep global structure of data, we applied this idea to graph embedding. The method is formulated as follows.

$$\min_{\mathbf{w}} \quad \mathbf{w}^T \mathbf{X} \mathbf{G} \mathbf{X}^T \mathbf{w} + \alpha \left\| \mathbf{X} - \mathbf{w}\mathbf{w}^T \mathbf{X} \right\|_F^2 \tag{1}$$
$$s.t. \quad \mathbf{w}^T \mathbf{w} = 1$$

where matrix $\mathbf{G}$ represents the various local structures of graph embedding methods such as; LPP, LSDA, NPE, SPP and many others. In our proposed model, a global least-squares regulation is added to graph embedding methods, with an orthogonality constraint $\mathbf{w}^T\mathbf{w} = 1$. A balance between keeping global and local structures of data can be achieved by these properties, in which the former mitigates the sensitivity to noises, while the latter seeks the underlying structure on ambient space.

We further develop this model by making another orthogonality constraint that, projections can be orthogonal to each other with consideration to data distributions.

$$\min_{\mathbf{p}} \quad \mathbf{p}^T \mathbf{G} \mathbf{p} + \alpha \left\| \mathbf{X} - \mathbf{C}^{\frac{1}{2}} \mathbf{p}\mathbf{p}^T \mathbf{C}^{\frac{1}{2}} \mathbf{X} \right\|_F^2 \tag{2}$$
$$s.t. \quad \mathbf{p}^T \mathbf{C} \mathbf{p} = 1$$

Where $\mathbf{p} = \mathbf{X}^T\mathbf{w}$. In this generalized form, the orthogonality constraint is changed to $(\mathbf{C}^{\frac{1}{2}}\mathbf{p})^T \mathbf{C}^{\frac{1}{2}}\mathbf{p} = 1$, with consideration to distributions and local structures of data, where $\mathbf{C}$ is a diagonal matrix. In a special form, when $\mathbf{C}$ is an identity matrix, our proposed model is represented in the following form.

$$\min_{\mathbf{p}} \quad \mathbf{p}^T \mathbf{G} \mathbf{p} + \alpha \left\| \mathbf{X} - \mathbf{p}\mathbf{p}^T \mathbf{X} \right\|_F^2$$

$$s.t. \quad \mathbf{p}^T \mathbf{p} = 1 \tag{3}$$

The constraint is just the orthogonality projection vector on data, and does not consider applying any local structures of data in least squares reconstruction regulations. i.e. $\left\| \mathbf{X} - \mathbf{p}\mathbf{p}^T \mathbf{X} \right\|_F^2$, the same form in some graph embedding methods, e.g., NPE and SPP. Meanwhile, we can apply some definitions of local structures of data to construct $\mathbf{C}$ matrix, which can be seen to be added to constraints in both unsupervised (e.g. LPP) and supervised (e.g. LSDA) forms. This local structure is then used in global least squares reconstruction regulations i.e. $\left\| \mathbf{X} - \mathbf{C}^{\frac{1}{2}} \mathbf{p}\mathbf{p}^T \mathbf{C}^{\frac{1}{2}} \mathbf{X} \right\|_F^2$. This allows any graph embedding submitted to this framework to adjust itself to the requirement between preserving global and local structures.

By this least-squares regulation based graph embedding, we incorporate various graph embedding methods into a generalized form. By formulating the Lagrangian of the above problem, it leads to the following generalized eigenproblems on $\mathbf{p}$:

$$(\mathbf{G} - \alpha \mathbf{C} \mathbf{X} \mathbf{X}^T)\mathbf{p} = \lambda \mathbf{C} \mathbf{p} \tag{4}$$

And finally we can obtain the projection vector $\mathbf{w}$ with least squares regression solutions.

In the next section, extensive experiments are carried out on hand-written digit recognition to verify the classification performances in keeping lower dimensional subspaces, with other state-of-the-art DR methods, such as LPP, LSDA, NPE and SPP.

3 Experiments

In this section, we present experimental datasets, parameter setting and result analysis.

3.1 Experimental Setup

Datasets: We evaluated the proposed methods on two well-known public hand-written digit recognition datasets: MNIST[1] and USPS[2]. (i) MNIST: This database contains 28×28 grayscale images of 10 hand-written digits from 0 to 9. We used the subset of MNIST database with 4,000 samples, which are randomly and uniformly selected from the 70,000 samples in the original MNIST database. (ii) USPS: The USPS database contains 11,000 hand-written digit images, composed of 10 categories from 0 to 9 with size of 16×16.

---

[1] http://www.cad.zju.edu.cn/home/dengcai/Data/MLData.html.
[2] http://www.cs.nyu.edu/~roweis/data.html.

Table 1. Classification accuracy (%) on MNIST dataset (unsupervised LSRGE: LSRGE1, supervised LSRGE: LSRGE2).

		SPP construct			LPP construct			NPE construct			LSDA construct		
		SPP	Our method		LPP	Our method		NPE	Our method		LSDA	Our method	
			LSRGE1	LSRGE2		LSRGE1	LSRGE2		LSRGE1	LSRGE2		LSRGE1	LSRGE2
	α		−0.8	−0.8		−0.8	−0.8		−0.9	−0.9		−0.9	−0.9
60%	Accuracy	84.70	**91.30**	90.65	88.78	**91.19**	90.76	84.65	**91.19**	90.65	89.35	**91.35**	90.54
	Dimension	49	50	49	45	46	49	243	51	49	39	49	35
70%	Accuracy	86.75	**92.15**	91.61	89.66	**92.08**	91.54	86.38	**92.28**	91.61	90.81	**92.21**	91.54
	Dimension	74	61	69	50	48	49	246	75	61	31	59	33
80%	Accuracy	88.67	**94.25**	94.16	92.62	**94.42**	94.25	89.20	**94.34**	94.34	93.36	93.72	**94.34**
	Dimension	59	35	36	36	35	36	247	35	35	33	35	36

Evaluation Measure: Each dataset was divided into two parts: training and testing. The training data was randomly selected from each class as an incremental classification rate of 60%, 70% and 80%. The remaining percentages were used as testing data. For each configuration, we repeated this process 20 times independently using Simplest Nearest Neighbor (1-NN) classifier for classification. Four widely used graph embedding methods, i.e. SPP, LPP, NPE and LSDA were used for comparison.

Parameter Setting: In setting parameters for each algorithm, we shall highlight two portions in Least-Squares regulation based Graph Embedding, the graph construction models and the Least-Squares regulation.

Parameter setting on graph construction models specifically refers to the four types of graph and their parameter settings, which are as follows: (i) KNN-graph (LPP, NPE, LSDA): Their samples $\mathbf{x}_i$ and $\mathbf{x}_j$ are considered neighbors if $\mathbf{x}_j$ is among the k nearest neighbors of $\mathbf{x}_i$ or vice versa. In our experiments, in order to fairly compare the performance among the KNN-graph models, we set a uniform parameter of 5 as number of nearest neighbor in each dataset. The distance was measured by Heat Kernel and the kernel parameter is the average of the squared Euclidean distances for all edged pairs on the graph. (ii) SPP-graph: For constructing the adjacency weight matrix, we employed the idea of linear label propagation in [8]. The strategy we used is MSR, which is parameter-free.

There are two main parameters in LSRGE: (i) $\mathbf{C}$ corresponds to the type of Least-Squares regulation which can be constructed in two kinds, unsupervised and supervised. In our experiment, we selected LPP constraint model as unsupervised regulation and LSDA constraint model as supervised regulation. The strategy for the parameter selection is similar to KNN-graph mentioned above. (ii) α was selected for each dataset through an incremental iterative process. It is concretely listed in the table as parameter description of each dataset.

3.2 Experimental Results

As presented in Table 1 on MNIST dataset, unsupervised regulations significantly outperforms within any type of graph model. The accuracies of

Table 2. Classification accuracy (%) on USPS dataset (unsupervised LSRGE: LSRGE1, supervised LSRGE: LSRGE2).

		SPP construct			LPP construct			NPE construct			LSDA construct		
		SPP	Our method		LPP	Our method		NPE	Our method		LSDA	Our method	
			LSRGE1	LSRGE2		LSRGE1	LSRGE2		LSRGE1	LSRGE2		LSRGE1	LSRGE2
	α		0.1	0.1		−0.4	−0.4		0.9	0.9		40	40
60%	Accuracy	95.84	**96.73**	96.63	96.69	**96.75**	96.75	**96.69**	96.67	96.63	**96.79**	96.69	96.63
	Dimension	49	51	51	51	51	51	52	51	51	48	51	51
70%	Accuracy	96.54	**97.28**	97.26	97.14	97.23	**97.25**	96.82	97.21	**97.28**	97.28	97.28	**97.30**
	Dimension	46	50	50	40	50	45	51	50	49	38	40	40
80%	Accuracy	97.00	97.66	**97.69**	**97.31**	97.28	97.26	97.14	97.25	**97.28**	**97.53**	97.25	97.25
	Dimension	52	52	51	52	50	52	52	52	51	50	50	52

unsupervised regulations in each classification rate are about 4~5% higher than the original, while 1% higher than the supervised regulations throughout all classification rates. And Fig. 1 shows the classification results of MNIST dataset obtained from competing graph construction methods in four graphs construction model. It also illustrates that LSRGE can adequately utilize global and local structure information for classification in MNIST dataset.

From Table 2, there is another interesting observation. When the training sample size is large enough to sufficiently characterize the data distribution as in

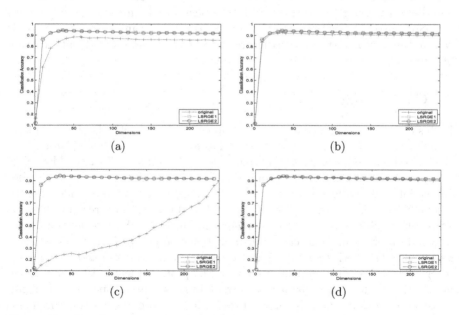

Fig. 1. The classification results obtained from competing graph construction methods on MNIST. (a) SPP construction model. (b) LPP construction model. (c) NPE construction model. (d) LSDA construction model.

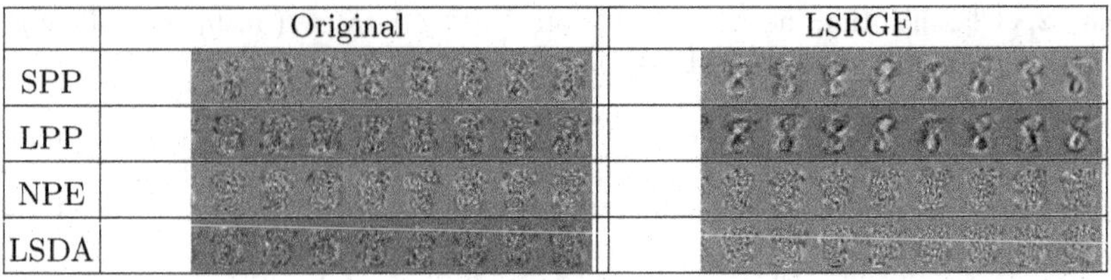

	Original	LSRGE
SPP		
LPP		
NPE		
LSDA		

Fig. 2. Ten basis vectors of graph construction calculated from the training set of USPS database.

the case of USPS dataset, all the methods conducted in the experiment showed an approximate effectiveness on classification accuracy. Especially, at 70% of classification rate, LSRGE had little improvement over the original, while accuracies of all the methods are very close, with a difference of about 2%. But this disparity reduced to less than 1% of accuracy when the classification rate increases to 80%, even the original obtained a higher accuracy in LPP and NPE models. This is because the accuracies of LSRGE are closed at a relatively low classification rate, and almost unvaried in accuracy from 70% to 80%, while the original rose slightly. This characteristic is a double-edged advantage to LSRGE, obtaining higher accuracies with limited training samples.

In Fig. 2, we illustrate the first 10 eigenvectors (or, eigen-pictures) of number 8 in USPS dataset. Those eigenvectors are obtained by both the original method and the supervised regulations of LSRGE. The eigen-pictures were reshaped into a square matrix just as the original object image size. It can be seen that LSRGE can capture not only the local structure of the data, but also the global structure of the data.

4 Conclusions

In this paper, we developed a different graph embedding method, which can keep global and local structures of data, as well as makes use of an orthogonality constraint to keep power of discrimination in low-dimensional subspace. The PCA-Like idea in graph embedding is applied in our work by making the orthogonality constraint that, projections must be orthogonal to data, with consideration to distributions and local structures of data. Thus, a least-squares regulation based graph embedding is proposed for dimension reduction.   Supervised and unsupervised graph embedding can both be adopted in our proposed least-squares regulation framework. Our experimental results on a variety of handwritten digit recognition collections demonstrated that, the proposed method has advantage of superior performances in keeping lower dimensional subspaces and higher classification results than the other state-of-the-art graph embedding methods.

Acknowledgments. This work was funded in part by the National Natural Science Foundation of China (No. 61572240), and the Open Project Program of the National Laboratory of Pattern Recognition (NLPR) (No. 201600005).

References

1. Jain, A., Duin, R., Mao, J.: Statistical pattern recognition: a review. IEEE Trans. Pattern Anal. Mach. Intell. **22**(1), 4–37 (2000)
2. Yang, J., Zhang, D., Yang, J.Y.: Constructing PCA baseline algorithms to reevaluate ICA-based face-recognition performance. IEEE Trans. Syst. Man Cybern. Part B (Cybernatics) **37**(4), 1015–1021 (2007)
3. Zuo, W., Zhang, D., Yang, J., Wang, K.: BDPCA plus LDA: a novel fast feature extraction technique for face recognition. IEEE Trans. Syst. Man Cybern. Part B (Cybernatics) **36**(4), 946–953 (2006)
4. Cai, D., He, X., Zhou, K., Han, J., Bao, H.: Locality sensitive discriminant analysis. IJCAI **2007**, 1713–1726 (2007)
5. He, X., Yan, S., Hu, Y., Niyogi, P., Zhang, H.J.: Face recognition using Laplacianfaces. IEEE Trans. Pattern Anal. Mach. Intell. **27**(3), 328–340 (2005)
6. Lu, J., Tan, Y.P.: Regularized locality preserving projections and its extensions for face recognition. IEEE Trans. Syst. Man Cybern. Part B (Cybernetics) **40**(3), 958–963 (2010)
7. He, X., Cai, D., Yan, S., Zhang, H.: Neighborhood preserving embedding. In: ICCV, pp. 1208–1213 (2005)
8. Qiao, L., Chen, S., Tan, X.: Sparsity preserving projections with applications to face recognition. Pattern Recogn. **43**(1), 331–341 (2010)
9. Luo, B., Wilson, R.C., Hancock, E.R.: Spectral embedding of graphs. Pattern Recogn. **36**(10), 2213–2230 (2003)
10. Tao, L., Ip, H.H., Wang, Y., Shu, X.: Low rank approximation with sparse integration of multiple manifolds for data representation. Appl. Intell. **42**(3), 430–446 (2015)
11. Zhang, T., Tao, D., Li, X., Yang, J.: Patch alignment for dimensionality reduction. IEEE Trans. Knowl. Data Eng. **21**(9), 1299–1313 (2009)
12. la Torre, F.D.: A least-squares framework for component analysis. IEEE Trans. Pattern Anal. Mach. Intell. **34**(6), 1041–1055 (2012)
13. Schölkopf, B., Burges, C.J.: Advances in Kernel Methods: Support Vector Learning. MIT press, Cambridge (1999)
14. Li, J.B., Gao, H.: Sparse data-dependent kernel principal component analysis based on least squares support vector machine for feature extraction and recognition. Neural Comput. Appl. **21**(8), 1971–1980 (2012)
15. Mika, S., Ratsch, G., Weston, J., Scholkopf, B., Mullers, K.R.: Fisher discriminant analysis with kernels. In: Neural Networks for Signal Processing IX, pp. 41–48 (1999)
16. Zhang, B., Qiao, Y.: Face recognition based on gradient gabor feature and efficient kernel fisher analysis. Neural Comput. Appl. **19**(4), 617–623 (2010)
17. Li, J.B., Pan, J.S., Chu, S.C.: Kernel class-wise locality preserving projection. Inf. Sci. **178**(7), 1825–1835 (2008)
18. Wang, Z., Sun, X.: Face recognition using kernel-based NPE. In: 2008 International Conference on Computer Science and Software Engineering, pp. 802–805 (2008)
19. Bengio, Y., Paiement, J.F., Vincent, P., Delalleau, O., Roux, N.L., Ouimet, M.: Out-of-sample extensions for LLE, Isomap, MDS, Eigenmaps, and spectral clustering. Adv. Neural Inf. Process. Syst. **16**, 177–184 (2004)

SSGAN: Secure Steganography Based on Generative Adversarial Networks

Haichao Shi[1,2], Jing Dong[3], Wei Wang[3], Yinlong Qian[3],
and Xiaoyu Zhang[1(✉)]

[1] Institute of Information Engineering,
Chinese Academy of Sciences, Beijing, China
zhangxiaoyu@iie.ac.cn
[2] School of Cyber Security, University of Chinese Academy
of Sciences, Beijing, China
[3] National Laboratory of Pattern Recognition, Institute of Automation,
Center for Research on Intelligent Perception and Computing,
Chinese Academy of Sciences, Beijing, China

Abstract. In this paper, a novel strategy of Secure Steganography based on Generative Adversarial Networks is proposed to generate suitable and secure covers for steganography. The proposed architecture has one generative network, and two discriminative networks. The generative network mainly evaluates the visual quality of the generated images for steganography, and the discriminative networks are utilized to assess their suitableness for information hiding. Different from the existing work which adopts Deep Convolutional Generative Adversarial Networks, we utilize another form of generative adversarial networks. By using this new form of generative adversarial networks, significant improvements are made on the convergence speed, the training stability and the image quality. Furthermore, a sophisticated steganalysis network is reconstructed for the discriminative network, and the network can better evaluate the performance of the generated images. Numerous experiments are conducted on the publicly available datasets to demonstrate the effectiveness and robustness of the proposed method.

Keywords: Steganography · Steganalysis · Generative adversarial networks

1 Introduction

Steganography is the task of concealing a message within a medium such that the presence of the hidden message cannot be detected. It is one of the hot topics in information security and has drawn lots of attention in recent years. Steganography is often used in secret communications. Especially in the fast-growing social networks, there are an abundance of images and videos, which provide more opportunities and challenges for steganography. Therefore, the design of a secure steganography scheme is of critical importance.

How to design a secure steganography method is the problem that researchers have always been concerned about. Existing steganographic schemes usually require the

© Springer International Publishing AG, part of Springer Nature 2018
B. Zeng et al. (Eds.): PCM 2017, LNCS 10735, pp. 534–544, 2018.
https://doi.org/10.1007/978-3-319-77380-3_51

prior of probability distribution on cover objects which is difficult to obtain in practice. Conventionally, the steganography method is designed in a heuristic way which does not take the steganalysis into account fully and automatically. For the sake of the steganography safety, we consider the steganalysis into the design of steganography.

At present, the image-based steganography algorithm is mainly divided into two categories. The one is based on the spatial domain, the other is based on the DCT domain. In our work, we focus on the spatial domain steganography.

Least Significant Bit (LSB) [11] is one of the most popular embedding methods in spatial domain steganography. If LSB is adopted as the steganography method, the statistical features of the image are destroyed. And it is easy to detect by the steganalyzer. For convenience and simple implementation, the LSB algorithm hides the secret to the least significant bits in the given image's channel of each pixel. Mostly, the modification of the LSB algorithm is called ±1-embedding [2]. It randomly adds or subtracts 1 from the channel pixel, so the last bits would match the ones needed. So we consider the ±1-embedding algorithm in this paper.

Besides the LSB algorithm, some sophisticated steganographic schemes use a distortion function which is used for selecting the embedding localization of the image. We called them the image content-adaptive steganography. These algorithms are the most popular and the most secure image steganography in spatial domain, such as HUGO (Highly Undetectable steGO), WOW (Wavelet Obtained Weights), S-UNIWARD, etc.

HUGO [12] is a steganographic scheme that defines a distortion function domain by assigning costs to pixels based on the effect of embedding some information within a pixel. It uses a weighted norm function to represent the feature space. HUGO is considered to be one of the most secure steganographic techniques, which we will use in this paper to demonstrate our method's security. WOW (Wavelet Obtained Weights) [8] is another content-adaptive steganographic method that embeds information into a cover image according to textural complexity of regions. In WOW shows that the more complex the image region is, the more pixel values will be modified in this region. S-UNIWARD [9] introduces a universal distortion function that is independent of the embedded domain. Despite the diverse implementation details, the ultimate goals are identical, i.e. they are all devoted to minimize this distortion function, to embed the information into the noise area or complex texture, and to avoid the smooth image coverage area.

So far as we know, when people design steganography algorithm, they usually heuristically consider the steganalysis side. For example, the message should embed into the noise and texture region of image which is more secure. In this paper, we propose a novel SSGAN algorithm, which implements secure steganography based on the generative adversarial networks. We consider it under adversarial learning framework, inspired by the work of Denis and Burnaev [5]. We use WGAN [3] to improve the security of steganography by generating more suitable covers. In the proposed SSGAN, covers are generated firstly using the generative network. Then we adapt the state-of-the-art embedding algorithm, like HUGO, to embed message into the generated image. Finally, we use the GNCNN [17] to detect on images whether there is a steganographic operation.

The contributions of our work can be concluded as follows:

Perceptibility. In this paper, we use WGAN instead of DCGAN to generate cover images to achieve generative images with higher visual quality and ensure faster training process.

Security. We use a more sophisticated network called GNCNN to assess the suitableness of the generated images instead of the steganalysis network proposed by [5].

Diversity. We also use GNCNN to compete against the generative network, which can make the generated images more suitable for embedding.

The rest of the paper is structured as follows: In Sect. 2, we discuss the related work of adversarial learning and elaborate the proposed method. In Sect. 3, experiments are conducted to demonstrate the effectiveness and security of the proposed method. In Sect. 4, we draw conclusions.

2 Secure Steganography Based on Generative Adversarial Networks

2.1 Adversarial Learning

Adversarial learning using game theory, and is combined with unsupervised way to jointly train the model. The independent model is trained to compete with each other, iteratively improving the output of each model. In Generative Adversarial Networks, the generative model G tries to train the noise to samples, while the discriminative model D tries to distinguish between the samples output by G and the real samples. Based on fooling the D, the weight of G is updated, and at the same time, the D's weight is updated by distinguishing between the fake and real samples.

Recent years, GANs have been successfully applied to image generation tasks [14] using convolutional neural networks (CNNs) for both G and D. But in traditional GANs, they are considered difficult to train. Because there is no obvious relationship between the convergence of the loss function and the sample quality. Typically, people choose to stop the training by visually checking the generated samples. So, a design arises recently, WGAN [3], using the Wasserstein distance instead of the Jensen-Shannon divergence, to make the data set distribution compared with the learning distribution from G. Obviously, they show that the sample quality is closely related with the network's convergence and the training rate is really improved.

Adversarial training has also been applied to steganography. The adversarial training process can be described as a minimax game:

$$\min_{G} \max_{D} J(D, G) = E_{x \sim p_{data}(x)} \log(D(x)) + E_{z \sim p_{noise}(z)} \log(1 - D(G(z))) \qquad (1)$$

where $D(x)$ represents the probability that x is a real image rather than synthetic, and G (z) is a synthetic image for input noise z. In this process, there are two networks, the G and the D, trained simultaneously:

- Generative Network, its input is a noise z from the prior distribution $p_{noise}(z)$, and transform it from the data distribution $p_{data}(x)$, to generate a data sample which is similar to $p_{data}(x)$.
- Discriminative Network, its input are the real data and the fake data generated from the Generative Network, and determine the difference between the real and fake data samples.

To solve the minimax problem, in each iteration of the mini-batch stochastic gradient optimization, we first perform the gradient ascent step on D and then perform the gradient descent step on G. So we let ω_N represents the neural network N, then we can see the optimization step:

- We let the D fixed to update the model G by $\omega_G \leftarrow \omega_G - \gamma_G \nabla_G J$ where

$$\nabla_G J = \frac{\partial}{\partial \omega_G} E_{z \sim p_{noise}(z)} \log(1 - D(G(z, \omega_G), \omega_D)) \qquad (2)$$

- We let the G fixed to update the model D by $\omega_D \leftarrow \omega_D + \gamma_D \nabla_D J$ where

$$\nabla_D J = \frac{\partial}{\partial \omega_D} \{ E_{x \sim p_{data}(x)} \log(D(x, \omega_D)) + E_{z \sim p_{noise}(z)} \log(1 - D(G(z, \omega_G), \omega_D)) \} \qquad (3)$$

In this paper, we use WGANs to verify the advantages of generating and discriminating the image using adversarial training process.

2.2   Model Design

We introduce a model that we called SSGAN, which contains a generative network, and two discriminative networks. The model can be described as Fig. 1:

Since we want the G to generate realistic images that could be used as secure covers for steganography, we force G to compete against the D and S at the same time. We use $S(x)$ to represent the output of the steganalysis network, then the game can be shown as follows:

$$\begin{aligned} \min_G \max_D \max_S J = {}& \alpha \left(E_{x \sim p_{data}(x)} \log(D(x)) + E_{z \sim p_{noise}(z)} \log(1 - D(G(z))) \right) \\ & + (1 - \alpha) E_{z \sim p_{noise}(z)} [\log S(Stego(G(z))) + \log(1 - S(G(z)))] \end{aligned} \qquad (4)$$

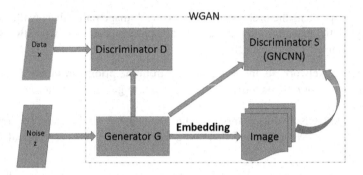

Fig. 1. The SSGAN model

To control the trade-off between the realistic of the generated images and the evaluation of the steganalysis, we use a convex combination which includes the D and S network with parameters $\alpha \in [0, 1]$. And we show that when we give $\alpha \le 0.7$, the results are closer to the noise.

2.2.1 Generator G

For the generator G, it is used to generate the secure covers. And we use a fully connected layer, and four fractionally-strided convolution layers, and then a Hyperbolic tangent function layer. This network structure can be described as Fig. 2:

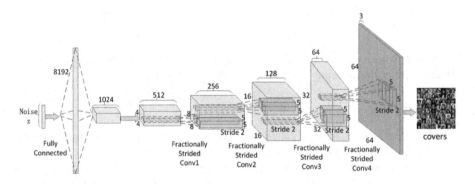

Fig. 2. The generative network structure

2.2.2 Discriminator D

For the discriminator D, it is used to evaluate the visual quality of the generated images. And we use four convolutional layers, and then a fully connected layer. This network structure can be described as Fig. 3:

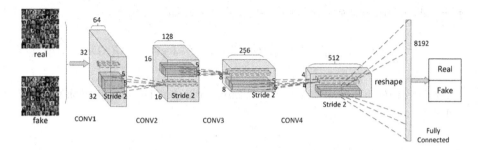

Fig. 3. The discriminative network structure

2.2.3 Discriminator S

For the S network, it is used to assess the suitableness of the generated images. And we first use a predefined high-pass filter to make a filtering operation, which is mainly for steganalysis. And then four convolutional layers. Finally we use a classification layer, which includes several fully connected layers. This network structure can be described as Fig. 4.

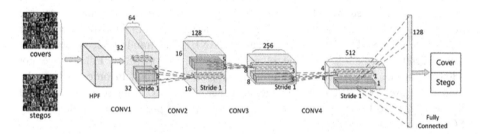

Fig. 4. The steganalysis network structure

2.2.4 Update Rules

And we can show that the SGD update rules:

- For the generator G: $\omega_G \leftarrow \omega_G - \gamma_G \nabla_G J$ it is calculated by

$$
\begin{aligned}
\nabla_G J = &\frac{\partial}{\partial \omega_G} E_{z \sim p_{noise}(z)}[\log(1 - D(G(z, \omega_G), \omega_D))] \\
&+ \frac{\partial}{\partial \omega_G}(1 - \alpha)E_{z \sim p_{noise}(z)}[\log(S(Stego(G(z, \omega_G), \omega_S)))] \\
&+ \frac{\partial}{\partial \omega_G}(1 - \alpha)E_{z \sim p_{noise}(z)}[\log(1 - S(G(z, \omega_G), \omega_S))]
\end{aligned}
\tag{5}
$$

- For the discriminator D: $\omega_D \leftarrow \omega_D + \gamma_D \nabla_G J$ it is calculated by

$$
\nabla_G J = \frac{\partial}{\partial \omega_D}\{E_{z \sim p_{data}(x)}[\log D(x, \omega_D)] + E_{z \sim p_{noise}(z)}[\log(1 - D(G(z, \omega_G), \omega_D))]\}
\tag{6}
$$

- For the discriminator S: $\omega_S \leftarrow \omega_S + \gamma_S \nabla_S J$ it is calculated by

$$\nabla_S J = \frac{\partial}{\partial \omega_S} E_{z \sim p_{noise}(z)} [\log S(Stego(G(z, \omega_G)), \omega_S) + \log(1 - S(G(z, \omega_G), \omega_S))] \quad (7)$$

We update G to not only maximize the errors of D, but the normalization errors of D and S.

3 Experiments

3.1 Data Preparation

All experiments are performed in TensorFlow [1], on a workstation with a Titan X GPU. In our experiments, we use the CelebA dataset which contains more than 200,000 images.

We pre-process the image, and all images are cropped to 64×64 pixels.

For the purpose of the steganalysis, we use 90% of the data to construct a training set, and regard the rest as testing set. The training set is denoted by TRAIN, and the testing set is denoted by TEST. We use Stego(x) to represent the steganographic algorithm used to hide information. Two datasets are involved in the experiments. One is TRAIN + Stego(TRAIN), where Stego(TRAIN) is the training set embedded in some secret information, and the other is TEST + Stego(TEST). Finally, we got 380,000 images for steganography training, 20,000 for testing. In order to train the model, we use 200,000 cropped images to generate images. After seven epochs, the images generated by our generative model and the model proposed in [5], denoted by SGAN, are shown in the Fig. 5.

Fig. 5. Examples of images, generated by SSGAN and SGAN after training for 7 epochs on the CelebA dataset, the left is generated by SSGAN, the right is generated by SGAN.

Meanwhile, we use the LSB Matching algorithm which is ± 1-embedding algorithm with a payload size to 0.4 bits per pixel to embed information, which we use a text from casual articles.

The experimental results are as follows, the visual quality of images generated by our SSGAN model are higher than its counterpart.

Experimental results show that through the use of WGAN, the convergence speed is faster than DCGAN, and the effect is more obvious, as is shown in Table 1.

Table 1. The contrast of two methods' time for running for seven epochs

Method	Time (mins)
SSGAN	227.5
SGAN	240.3

3.2 Experimental Setup

The generative network G is designed with one fully connected layer, four Fractionally − Strided $Conv2D \rightarrow Batch\,Normalization \rightarrow Leaky\,ReLU$ layers, and one Hyperbolic tangent function layer. The discriminative network D comprises four $Conv2D \rightarrow Batch\,Normalization \rightarrow Leaky\,ReLU$ layers, one fully connected layer. As for the steganalyser network S, we use a predefined high-pass filter to make a filtering operation, which is kept fixed while training, and four convolutional layers corresponding to three kinds of operations, i.e. convolution, non-linearity, and pooling, followed by a fully connected layer and a softmax layer for classification.

We train the model using RMSProp optimization algorithm with the learning rate 2×10^{-4} and update parameters $\beta_1 = 0.5$ and $\beta_2 = 0.99$. We update the weights of D and S once, while update weights of G twice in each mini-batch. In steganalysis, we call S the Steganalyser. In addition to the S network, we also use an independent network which is called S* [17]. To make the network S effective, we also use the filter in [17], which defines as follows:

$$F^{(0)} = \begin{pmatrix} -1 & 2 & -2 & 2 & -1 \\ 2 & -6 & 8 & -6 & 2 \\ -2 & 8 & -12 & 8 & -2 \\ 2 & -6 & 8 & -6 & 2 \\ -1 & 2 & -2 & 2 & -1 \end{pmatrix}$$

We also train the S* network using RMSProp optimization algorithm with the learning rate 5×10^{-6} and update parameters $\beta_1 = 0.9$ and $\beta_2 = 0.99$. And we use the format of binary cross-entropy to calculate the loss.

We conduct experiments on real images and generative images respectively, and the results are as follows:

In our first experiment, we compare the security of the generated images with that of real images. We embed secret message into real images and use the steganalysis network on real images first, then we embed secret message into generative images and use the steganalysis network on generative images.

We train the S network on real images and from the results we conclude that even if the usual WGAN can generate a synthetic image, it can be easily detected by a steganalyser. And our method increase the results of the classification error rates, which means the images generated by our model is more secure to be the carrier of the steganography images (Table 2).

Table 2. Accuracy of the steganalyser trained on real images

Type of images	SSGANs	SGANs
Real images	0.87	0.92
Generated images	0.72	0.90

We also use HUGO steganography scheme on real images and generative images.

In our second experiment, we investigate the security of generated images under different seed values. We conduct the experiment on generative images generated by different setups.

In this group of experiments, we use Qian's network [17] which is called steganalyser S* on generated images generated by SSGAN. The input is the prior noise distribution $p_{noise}(z)$ for some fixed seed value. We test the S* on images. The experimental setups are as follows:

S1. We use same seed value;
S2. We use some randomly selected seed value.
S3. We use the same seed value, as in S2, and we additionally tune the WGAN model for several epochs.

As is shown in Table 3, we can see that through using different seed values when generating images, can make it easier to deceive the steganalysis network.

Table 3. Trained on generated images according to experimental conditions S1-S3

Experimental conditions	Accuracy
S1	0.87
S2	0.72
S3	0.71

3.3 Discussion

As demonstrated in the experiments, the method proposed in [5] has some limitations, the experiments show that the steganography is not secure enough. The experiments show that the steganalysis network in Denis's article is suitable for embedding with the same key, but when using the random key, their network is not so useful. So we use GNCNN [17]. And we have confirmed that the steganalysis network they used was not so useful. Our results show that on the one hand, the generated images are more difficult to detect, indicating that the security performance is higher. On the other hand, the generated images' visual quality is better and more realistic.

4 Conclusion and Future Work

In this paper, we introduce generative adversarial networks for steganography to generate more suitable and secure covers for steganography. Based on the WGANs, we have proposed a model called SSGAN for steganography. The proposed model is efficient to generate images, which have higher visual quality. And our model is suitable for embedding with the random key. Mostly, it can generate more secure covers for steganography. We have evaluated the performance of our model using CelebA datasets. Results show the effectiveness of the SSGAN model through the classification accuracy, and we think it could be used for adaptive steganographic algorithm for social network in the future. We believe that, by exploring more steganography properties, better performance can be achieved.

Acknowledgement. This work is supported by the National Natural Science Foundation of China (No. 61501457, U1536120, U1636201, 61502496) and the National Key Research and Development Program of China (No. 2016YFB1001003).

References

1. Abadi, M., Agarwal, A., Barham, P., Brevdo, E., Chen, Z., Citro, C., Corrado, G.S., Davis, A., Dean, J., Devin, M., et al.: TensorFlow: large-scale machine learning on heterogeneous distributed systems. arXiv preprint arXiv:1603.04467 (2016a)
2. Ker, A.D.: Resampling and the detection of LSB matching in color bitmaps. In: Eletronic Imaging 2005, pp. 1–15. International Society for Optics and Photonics (2005)
3. Arjovsky, M., Chintala, S., Bottou, L.: Wasserstein GAN. ArXiv e-prints, January 2017
4. Browne, M., Ghidary, S.S.: Convolutional neural networks for image processing: an application in robot vision. In: Gedeon, T.D., Fung, L.C.C. (eds.) AI 2003. LNCS (LNAI), vol. 2903, pp. 641–652. Springer, Heidelberg (2003). https://doi.org/10.1007/978-3-540-24581-0_55
5. Volkhonskiy, D., Borisenko, B., Burnaev, E.: Generative adversarial networks for image steganography. In: ICLR 2016 Open Review (2016)
6. Fridrich, J., Goljan, M., Du, R.: Detecting LSB steganography in color, and gray-scale images. IEEE Multimedia **8**(4), 22–28 (2001)
7. Fridrich, J., Kodovsky, J.: Rich models for steganalysis of digital images. IEEE Trans. Inf. Forensics Secur. **7**(3), 868–882 (2012)
8. Holub, V., Fridrich, J.: Designing steganographic distortion using directional filters. In: 2012 IEEE International Workshop on Information Forensics and Security (WIFS), pp. 234–239. IEEE (2012)
9. Holub, V., Fridrich, J., Denemark, T.: Universal distortion function for steganography in an arbitrary domain. EURASIP J. Inf. Secur. **2014**(1), 1 (2014)
10. Goodfellow, I., Pouget-Abadie, J., Mirza, M., Xu, B., Warde-Farley, D., Ozair, S., Courville, A., Bengio, Y.: Generative adversarial nets, pp. 2672–2680 (2014)

11. Mielikainen, J.: LSB matching revisited. IEEE Signal Process. Lett. **13**(5), 285–287 (2006)
12. Pevný, T., Filler, T., Bas, P.: Using high-dimensional image models to perform highly undetectable steganography. In: Böhme, R., Fong, P.W.L., Safavi-Naini, R. (eds.) IH 2010. LNCS, vol. 6387, pp. 161–177. Springer, Heidelberg (2010). https://doi.org/10.1007/978-3-642-16435-4_13
13. Ranzato, M., Huang, F.J., Boureau, Y.-L., LeCun, Y.: Unsupervised learning of invariant feature hierarchies with applications to object recognition. In: IEEE Conference on Computer Vision and Pattern Recognition, pp. 1–8. IEEE (2007)
14. Radford, A., Metz, L., Chintala, S.: Unsupervised representation learning with deep convolutional generative adversarial networks. CoRR, abs/1511.06434 (2015). http://arxiv.org/abs/1511.06434
15. Shi, Y.Q., Sutthiwan, P., Chen, L.: Textural features for steganalysis. In: Kirchner, M., Ghosal, D. (eds.) IH 2012. LNCS, vol. 7692, pp. 63–77. Springer, Heidelberg (2013). https://doi.org/10.1007/978-3-642-36373-3_5
16. Reed, S., Akata, Z., Yan, X., Logeswaran, L., Schiele, B., Lee, H.: Generative adversarial text to image synthesis. arXiv preprint arXiv:1605.05396 (2016)
17. Qian, Y., Dong, J., Wang, W., Tan, T.: Deep learning for steganalysis via convolutional neural networks. In: IS&T/SPIE Electronic Imaging, p. 94090J. International Society for Optics and Photonics (2015a)

Generating Chinese Poems from Images Based on Neural Network

Shuo Xing, Xueliang Liu[✉], Richang Hong, and Ye Zhao

Hefei University of Technology, Hefei, China
liuxueliang@hfut.edu.cn

Abstract. Chinese classical poetry generation from images is an overwhelmingly challenging work in the field of artificial intelligence. Inspired by recent advances in automatically generating description of an image and Chinese poem generation, in this paper, we present a generative model based on deep recurrent framework that describes images in the form of poems. Our model consists of two parts, one is to extract information according to the semantics presented in images, and the other is to generate each line of the poem incrementally according to the extracted semantic information from the images by a recurrent neural network. Experimental results thoroughly demonstrate the effectiveness of our approach by manual evaluation.

Keywords: Chinese poems · Image semantics · Automatic generation

1 Introduction

Describing the content of an image is casual for human, however, it's significantly hard for a computer, since it requires the computers to have such a capacity that capture the content of an image on the semantic level and then output the semantic information sequentially just liking a human being. Automatically describing an image is an important issue in the computer vision domain [1, 2, 27, 29], which has attracted increasing attentions. Many approaches have been raised to address this issue. Some of the previous work produces descriptions for images using template-based approaches that are constructed with linguistically motivated constraints based on salient syntactic patterns [3–6]. Some other attempts consider the descriptions generation as a retrieval problem and merge the annotation of similar images semantically [4, 7, 8, 28]. The above approaches have been able to generate descriptions, yet they restrict the diversity of the descriptions and lack of flexibility due to excessive artificial designs. With the development of deep learning, advanced approaches based on deep neural network begin to emerge [9–11, 26]. Karpathy et al. [10] and Vinyals et al. [9] pose models that map images and corresponding sentences to the same embedding space leveraging a convolution neural network (CNN) and a recurrent neural network (RNN) to maximize the probability distribution of the next word in the sentence. These methods overcome shortcomings of previous methods to a certain extent and can generate effective and rich descriptions.

Chinese ancient poetry is one of the most precious jewels in Chinese civilization, which has a history of thousands of years. Automated poetry generation is a hot issue

© Springer International Publishing AG, part of Springer Nature 2018
B. Zeng et al. (Eds.): PCM 2017, LNCS 10735, pp. 545–554, 2018.
https://doi.org/10.1007/978-3-319-77380-3_52

that has been explored for a long time [15]. Benefiting from the development of deep learning, Chinese poems generation based on neural networks recently has made some new breakthroughs [12–14], which captures the semantic, structure and coherence naturally instead of constructing poems according to a series of rules. Compared with the methods based on neural networks, the approaches based on grammar templates [15–17], genetic algorithms [20] and statistical machine translation [18, 19] are constrained by the given rules and patterns, lacking of semantic coherence between sentences and flexibility.

Inspired by recent advances in automatically generating description of an image and Chinese poems generation, we propose a generative model based on deep recurrent framework that describes the image in the form of Chinese poems. There are many different types and forms in Chinese poems, and the quatrain is the most classical one. Figure 1 is an example of a quatrain. Quatrains contain four lines and each line consists of five or seven characters. Moreover, quatrains are required to follow specific structural forms and rhyme schemes, where the last characters of the second line and the last line obey the same rhyme and every characters has a tone, Ping (the level tone) or Ze (the downward tone) [21]. Chinese classical poetry must meet these strict restrictions, which in turn also make the poetry full of artistic beauty, hence it is a more tough work to generate poetry according to images content than automatically describing images or poetry generation.

Fig. 1. An example of classic quatrain. The tone is shown at the end of each line, where P represents the level tone, Z represents the downward tone and * indicates that both are OK. Rhyming characters are in boldface.

In this paper, we address the problem of utilizing Chinese poems to describe images automatically. To this end, we propose a model based on deep recurrent framework. Our model consists of two parts, one is to extract information according to the semantics presented in images by combining deep convolution networks over images with recurrent networks over sentences, and the other is to generate each line of the poem incrementally base on recurrent neural network by taking into account the semantic information of the image and what has been generated so far. As we know, CNNs are powerful and effective for extracting features of images and embedding them into a fixed-length vector space, and RNNs have also achieved promising results in sequence information processing. Therefore, our system uses CNNs [22] as image 'encoder' to read the content information and output a feature vector to represent the image in a semantic space, and then utilizes a RNN model to embed the corresponding sentence to the same space. We maximize the probability of correct description given the image through a multi-model embedding to conduct the description of the image. This implementation is similar to captioning models described in Karpathy et al. [10] and Vinyals et al. [9]. To establish the corresponding relations between images and poems, we extract semantic information from the generated description as the keywords of given image by mapping them to relevant Chinese words that may appear in ancient poetry. Finally, we conduct the poem incrementally according to the semantic information of the image using a Long-Short Term Memory (LSTM) network.

Our approach is evaluated by manual judgment. Experimental results thoroughly demonstrate the effectiveness of our approach.

2 Our Model

2.1 Overview

On the purpose of automatically describing images by Chinese poems, a model based on deep neural network is designed in this paper. First we extract the semantics of images in the form of textual keywords by a multimodal recurrent neural network. And then we import these keywords to a recurrent neural network to generate poems. In this section, we first introduce the multimodal recurrent neural network to get the semantic meaning and then describe a multi-layer LSTM to conduct poems (see Fig. 2).

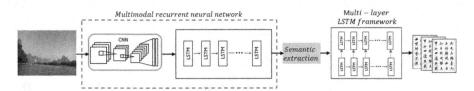

Fig. 2. Diagram of generating Chinese poems from images based on a multimodal recurrent neural network and a multi-layer LSTM framework. Our model consists of two parts, first extracting information of the image and then generating each line of the poem incrementally.

2.2 Image Semantic Generation

2.2.1 Description Generation

Given an image, we follow the method of Krizhevsky et al. [22] to detect objects and generate representation of the image with a CNN. The CNN is pre-trained on ImageNet [23]. The deep features of images extracted by the pre-trained network have a better generalization capability than traditional hand-craft features such as scale invariant feature transform (SIFT) and bag of words, which is widely used in many computer vision tasks. In our proposal, we use the last hidden layer of the pre-trained CNN framework to compute the representation of image as follows:

$$x' = W_c[CNN(I)] \tag{1}$$

Where $CNN(I)$ denotes the conversion of an image into a 4096-dimensional vector. The weights W_c signify an image embedding matrix that has dimensions of h × 4096, where h is the size of the embedding space. Thus, each image is represented as a feature vector.

Given the sentence of an image, we first represent each word as a one-hot vector, and then embed them to the same vector space as follows:

$$x_t = W_e O_t \qquad t \in (1, \ldots, N) \tag{2}$$

Here, O_t denotes a one-hot vector of the t-th word in the sentence and has a dimension equal to the size of dictionary D. The length of the sentence is N and W_e represents the embedding matrix with dimension of h × D. The image and the corresponding words thus are encoded in feature spaces with the same dimension.

A recurrent neural network is effective to model temporal dynamics in sequences. However, traditional RNNs have a problem of vanishing and exploding gradients [24], that is, RNN can only remember the contents of a limited time unit. To address this problem, a special RNN architecture called LSTM is described in [24] and has shown state-of-art performance on sequence work. Therefore, we feed images and words that are encoded into the same vector space to the LSTM for description generation. Given an image and the corresponding sentence, the LSTM takes a vector of the image x' and a set of word vectors x $= \{x_0, x_1, \ldots, x_N\}$ sequentially in time and is trained to produce the description. The definition of the LSTM is shown as follows:

$$i_t = \sigma(W_{ix}x_t + W_{ih}h_{t-1}) \tag{3}$$

$$f_t = \sigma\left(W_{fx}x_t + W_{fh}h_{t-1}\right) \tag{4}$$

$$o_t = \sigma(W_{ox}x_t + W_{oh}h_{t-1}) \tag{5}$$

$$g_t = \tanh\left(W_{gx}x_t + W_{gh}h_{t-1}\right) \tag{6}$$

$$c_t = c_{t-1} \odot f_t + g_t \odot i_t \tag{7}$$

$$h_t = o_t \odot c_t \tag{8}$$

$$y_{t+1} = Softmax(h_t) \tag{9}$$

Here, $\odot$ represents the element-wise multiplication, $\sigma(\cdot)$ and $\tanh(\cdot)$ indicate respectively the sigmoid function and the hyperbolic tangent function. h_t is the hidden state and W matrices are trained parameters. Using the softmax function, probability distribution y_t over all words are generated according to Eq. (9). The LSTM consists of a cell state c_t and three gates, namely the input gate i_t, the output gate f_t and the forgotten gate o_t, and the three gates are used to allow the network to learn whether to read the new input, when to forget previous hidden states and whether to output the new hidden states (see Fig. 3). This mechanism thus makes LSTM solve the issue of vanishing and exploding gradients. In the training process, the goal is to maximize the log-likelihood of the correct description given an image over the whole training dataset, defined as:

$$\mathrm{argmax}_{\Theta_\alpha} \sum\nolimits_{(I,S)} \log p(S|I; \Theta_\alpha) \tag{10}$$

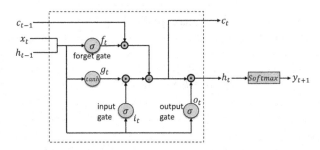

Fig. 3. Diagram of the LSTM memory cell. The core of the LSTM is a cell state c_t which is controlled by three gates; the hidden state h_t is used for word prediction by the softmax function.

Applying chain rule to $\log p(S|I)$ in Eq. (10), we can get the following equation:

$$\log p(S/I) = \sum\nolimits_{t=0}^{N} \log p(S_t|I, S_0, \ldots, S_{t-1}) \tag{11}$$

Where I and S denote images and sentences, respectively. Θ_α is the model parameter to be learned. We use the stochastic gradient descent (SGD) to optimize the goal function and the feature vector of a given image is only feed at the beginning of the LSTM according to Vinyals et al. [9] at training time.

2.2.2 Semantic Extraction
Since image caption generation can describe the relationship between objects and the high-level semantic meaning in addition to the objects in the image, we can easily get an image semantic meaning by its description. The LSTM framework described in Sect. 2.2.1 computes a probability distribution y_t of each word in target sentence. Therefore, we extract the high probability words according to y_t and remove the stop-words such as 'a', 'the' and so on, and then map them to relevant Chinese words that may appear in ancient poetry. We thus obtain the semantic meaning as keywords for poem generation described in next part.

2.3 Poem Generation

The traditional approaches of poetry generation [15–20] depend on professional knowledge in the field of poetry and need experts to design a large quantity of artificial rules to obtain high quality poems. To generate high quality poems automatically, we utilize multi-layer LSTM for poetry generation. In the stage of generating poetry, our model uses the keywords extracted in Sect. 2.2 and the previously generated verses to generate the poem from an image sequentially, and the generation process is achieved by calculating the probability distribution of the next character over the entire vocabulary. This procedure can be described in Fig. 4. We use the first keyword to feed the multi-layer LSTM model at the beginning of generating, and then the model iteratively generates the next character Y_t by maximize its probability at the each generation step t following the equation defined below:

$$Y_t = \text{argmax}_Y \, p(Y|s_t, Y_{t-1}, k_t) \tag{12}$$

Where

$$s_t = f(s_{t-1}, Y_{t-1}, k_t) \tag{13}$$

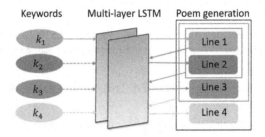

Fig. 4. Illustration of poem generation based a multi-layer LSTM with the keywords and poem lines that have been generated.

Here, s_t denotes the internal hidden state, and k_t represents the keyword vector encoded by a LSTM. Y_{t-1} is the previous generated output. $f(\cdot)$ is the activate function of the multi-layer LSTM. The multi-layer LSTM produces the poem one character at a time, conditioned on the previous outputs, the previous recurrent state and initial keywords. The multi-layer LSTM is trained by maximize the log-likelihood as follows:

$$\text{argmax}_{\Theta_\beta} \sum_{m=1}^{M} \log P(Y_m|x_m; \Theta_\beta) \tag{14}$$

In the training process, we utilize a two-layer LSTM for poem generation and the M represents the length of poem line and Θ_β is the parameter to be trained of the two-layer LSTM.

3 Experiments

3.1 Data and Training

In the semantics of images extraction stage, we used the Flickr30k dataset for learning the contents of images. Flickr30k contains 31K images and each image is described with 5 sentences in English. We used 1000 images for validation and the rest for training. The dimension of the embedding space was 256. The hidden layers of the LSTM contained 256 hidden units. We trained all the parameters using the SGD, and the size of the mini-batch was set 128. All the parameters were randomly initialized over a uniform distribution [–0.1, 0.1] except for the CNN parameters that were initialized with a pre-trained model.

In the poem generation stage, we collected 50000 poems and we used 2500 poems as the validation set and the rest as the training set, each line of which consists of five or seven characters. We took the 3000 highest frequency characters occurring in training set as the vocabulary. The size of the two-layer LSTM internal state was 500, the parameters of the model were trained using the RMSProp algorithm with the mini-batch of 100 poems and initialized randomly over a uniform distribution [–0.08, 0.08].

3.2 Evaluation

3.2.1 Evaluation Metrics

Evaluating machine-generated poetry from images precisely is a difficult work. Thousands of relevant poems can be used to describe the given image, hence limited rating metrics cannot cover all the correct expression. Liu et al. [25] has shown that some automatic evaluation metrics such as BLEU and METERO used for dialog responses have little correlation with human evaluation. Therefore, we carried out human judgments to rate the generated poems from images. Specifically, we chosen twenty images and then generated twenty poems with our system to evaluate our system. With respect to image-poem pairs, we adopted three grades to evaluate the degree of consistency between images and poems, i.e. 'poor', 'acceptable' and 'good', which denote 0, 50, and 100 points respectively. With respect to the generated poems separately, we evaluated them on four dimensions shown in Table 1 and the participants scored for each dimension ranging from 1 to 5 (the higher the better). We calculated the average score as the final score.

Table 1. Four dimensions for poem evaluation

Dimensions	Explanation
Fluency	Whether the generated poem is smooth and syntactically well-formed?
Coherence	Whether each character in the generated sequence is consistent with each other?
Meaning	Whether the generated poem expresses a clear purpose?
Structure	Whether the generated poem meets the patterns of the classic poetry?

3.2.2 Evaluation Results

The evaluation results of image-poem pairs are shown in Table 2, where the second column and third column report average scores of five-character poems and seven-character poems respectively. To verify the effectiveness of the two-layer LSTM framework, we compared it with different layers of LSTM, i.e. one-layer LSTM and three-layer LSTM. The values of average score in Table 2 show that our two-layer LSTM performs better than other LSTM structures. Table 2 shows that the most participants accept the generated poems from images by our system, which demonstrates the effectiveness of our model. From Table 2, we can also see that the average score of the five-character poems is higher than that of the seven-character poems. This is because the seven-character poems express more complex, complete meaning, which makes the model more difficult to capture the underlying rules of seven-character poems.

Table 2. Human evaluation for image-poem pairs

Quatrain	Five-character	Seven-character
LSTM-1	60.00	52.50
LSTM-2	68.75	53.75
LSTM-3	58.75	46.25

The evaluation results of generated poems are shown in Table 3, where each column reports average rating for different dimensions. As shown in Table 3, the poems generated by the two-layer LSTM are better evaluated on four dimensions than the one-layer LSTM and three-layer LSTM. We can see from Table 3 that the scores on four dimensions suggest the generated poems by our model basically meet the standard of Chinese classical poetry.

Table 3. Human evaluation for generated poems

Dimensions	Fluency	Coherence	Meaning	Structure
LSTM-1	3.48	3.32	3.45	3.39
LSTM-2	4.05	3.82	4.05	3.81
LSTM-3	3.42	3.35	3.21	3.29

Some samples of the generated results using our method are shown in Fig. 5. The number of the keywords extracted from an image ranges from 1 to 4. And the keywords are used in different poem lines for generation, i.e. the first keyword for the first poem line, the second keyword for the second line and so on, which promote the poem generating following the semantics of the image.

犬吠春水上，
The dog is barking on the water.
山色满江村。
The village is full of scenery.
野客无人问，
Visitors can not find people to ask for directions.
渔舟不可寻。
They can not find the fishing boat.

江水东流水，
The river flows to the east.
悠悠天山间。
Quietly stands among the mountains.
不知何处去，
Do not know where it goes.
空有钓鱼船。
There are only fishing boats on the river.

Fig. 5. Example poems from images generated by our model.

4   Conclusions

In this paper, we proposed a novel system that transform images into poems. Our system first extracts the semantic information of a given image as keywords according to a probability distribution of each word in target description based on a multimodal recurrent neural network, and then generates description in the form of poetry sequentially according to the keywords based on a multi-layer LSTM framework. Our model is trained by maximize the log-likelihood. Human evaluation is adopted to rate our model. We used two metrics to evaluate the results and the experimental results strongly suggest our model can produce appropriate and relevant poems to describe images.

Acknowledgments. This work was supported by the National Natural Science Foundation of China (NSFC) under grants 61472116 and 61502139.

References

1. Russakovsky, O., Deng, J., Su, H., Krause, J., Satheesh, S., Ma, S., Huang, Z., Karpathy, A., Bernstein, M., Khosla, A., Berg, A.C., Fei-Fei, L.: ImageNet large scale visual recognition challenge. IJCV **115**, 211–252 (2015)
2. Farhadi, A., Endres, I., Hoiem, D., Forsyth, D.: Describing objects by their attributes. In: CVPR, pp. 1602–1605 (2009)
3. Kulkarni, G., Premraj, V., Dhar, S., Li, S., Berg, A., Choi, Y., Berg, T.: Baby talk: understanding and generating simple image descriptions. In: CVPR (2011)
4. Farhadi, A., Hejrati, M., Sadeghi, M.A., Young, P., Rashtchian, C., Hockenmaier, J., Forsyth, D.: Every picture tells a story: generating sentences for images. In: ECCV (2010)
5. Yao, B.Z., Yang, X., Lin, L., Lee, M.W., Zhu, S.C.: I2T: image parsing to text description. Proc. IEEE **98**(8), 1485–1508 (2010)
6. Elliott, D., Keller, F.: Image description using visual dependency representations. In: EMNLP, pp. 1292–1302 (2013)

7. Li, S., Kulkarni, G., Berg, T.L., Berg, A.C., Choi, Y.: Composing simple image descriptions using web-scale n-grams. In: CoNLL (2011)
8. Hodosh, M., Young, P., Hockenmaier, J.: Framing image description as a ranking task: data, models and evaluation metrics. J. Artif. Intell. Res. **47**(1), 853–899 (2013)
9. Vinyals, O., Toshev, A., Bengio, S., Erhan, D.: Show and tell: a neural image caption generator. arXiv preprint arXiv:1411.4555 (2014)
10. Karpathy, A., Fei-Fei, L.: Deep visual-semantic alignments for generating image descriptions. In: CVPR (2015)
11. Xu, K., Ba, J., Kiros, R., Cho, K., Courville, A.C., Salakhutdinov, R., Zemel, R.S., Bengio, Y.: Show, attend and tell: neural image caption generation with visual attention. arXiv preprint arXiv:1502.03044 (2015)
12. Zhang, X., Lapata, M.: Chinese poetry generation with recurrent neural networks. In: EMNLP, pp. 670–680 (2014)
13. Wang, Q., Luo, T., Wang, D., Xing, C.: Chinese song iambics generation with neural attention-based model. CoRR, abs/1604.06274 (2016)
14. Yi, X., Li, R., Sun, M.: Generating Chinese classical poems with RNN encoder-decoder. CoRR, abs/1604.01537 (2016)
15. Colton, S., Goodwin, J., Veale, T.: Full FACE poetry generation. In: ICCC, pp. 95–102 (2012)
16. Oliveira, H.: Automatic generation of poetry: an overview. Universidade de Coimbra (2009)
17. Oliveira, H.: Poetryme: a versatile platform for poetry generation. Comput. Creat. Concept Inven. Gen. Intell. **1**, 21 (2012)
18. Jiang, L., Zhou, M.: Generating Chinese couplets using a statistical MT approach. In: Proceedings of the 22nd International Conference on Computational Linguistics, pp. 377–384 (2008)
19. He, J., Zhou, M., Jiang, L.: Generating Chinese classical poems with statistical machine translation models. In: AAAI, pp. 1650–1656 (2012)
20. Zhou, C.L., You, W., Ding, X.: Genetic algorithm and its implementation of automatic generation of Chinese songci. J. Softw. **21**(3), 427–437 (2010)
21. Wang, L.: A Summary of Rhyming Constraints of Chinese Poems (in Chinese). Beijing Press, Beijing (2002)
22. Krizhevsky, A., Sutskever, I., Hinton, G.: Imagenet classification with deep convolutional neural networks. In: NIPS (2012)
23. Deng, J., Dong, W., Socher, R., Li, L.-J., Li, K., Fei-Fei, L.: Imagenet: a large-scale hierarchical image database. In: CVPR (2009)
24. Hochreiter, S., Schmidhuber, J.: Long short-term memory. Neural Comput. **9**, 1735–1780 (1997)
25. Liu, C.W., Lowe, R., Serban, I.V., Noseworthy, M., Charlin, L., Pineau, J.: How not to evaluate your dialogue system: an empirical study of unsupervised evaluation metrics for dialogue response generation. arXiv preprint arXiv:1603.08023 (2016)
26. Wu, Q., Shen, C., Liu, L., Dick, A., van den Hengel, A.: What value do explicit high level concepts have in vision to language problems? In: CVPR (2016)
27. Hong, R., Yang, Y., Wang, M., Hua, X.-S.: Learning visual semantic relationships for efficient visual retrieval. IEEE Trans. Big Data **1**(4), 152–161 (2015)
28. Zhang, H., Shang, X., Luan, H.-B., Wang, M., Chua, T.-S.: Learning from collective intelligence: feature learning using social images and tags. TOMCCAP **13**(1), 1:1–1:23 (2016)
29. Zhang, H., Kyaw, Z., Chang, S.-F., Chua, T.-S.: Visual translation embedding network for visual relation detection. In: CVPR (2017)

Detail-Enhancement for Dehazing Method Using Guided Image Filter and Laplacian Pyramid

Dong Zhao and Long Xu$^{(\boxtimes)}$ (ID)

Key Laboratory of Solar Activity, National Astronomical Observatories,
Chinese Academy of Sciences, Beijing 100101, China
{dzhao,lxu}@nao.cas.cn

Abstract. Using dark channel prior (DCP) with guided image filter (GIF) is one of the most attention haze removal methods in recent years. However, this method may lead to blurring phenomenon in the dehazed image. This work focus on address this issue by constructing a differential model to look for the causes of the blurry vision. Inspired by this model, we proposed a detail-enhancement method using Laplacian pyramid technology. One of the advantages of this method is that, it can simultaneously achieve dehazing and detail-enhancing while without additional computational complexity. The experimental results show that the proposed method can effectively enhance the edge of the dehazed image.

Keywords: Single image dehazing · Guided image filtering
Laplacian pyramid · Image restoration

1 Introduction

The additional suspended particles, such as aerosols and liquid droplets in bad weather condition, affect atmospheric absorption and scattering of lights, leading to less visible objects in the distance. The images captured in such weather condition are called hazed images, which are characterized by faded colors and low contrast. Accordingly, removal of hazy effects is named dehazing. Dehazing has many applications in scene understanding and has caught increasing attention.

The state-of-the-art methods, such as Tan [1], Fattal [2], He et al. [3], Tarel [4] and Nishino et al. [5] etc., often depend on a physical haze model for more accurate haze removal. In recent years, novel dehazing methods [6–12] were proposed. Zhu et al. [6] recovered the depth information by proposing a color attenuation prior with a supervised learning method. Berman et al.'s [7] approach relies on the assumption that colors of a haze-free image are well approximated by a few hundred distinct colors. Bahat et al. [8] proposed a blind dehazing method by exploiting the deviations from the ideal patch, recovering the unknown haze parameters. Chen et al. [9] proposed a new method for reliable suppression of

© Springer International Publishing AG, part of Springer Nature 2018
B. Zeng et al. (Eds.): PCM 2017, LNCS 10735, pp. 555–563, 2018.
https://doi.org/10.1007/978-3-319-77380-3_53

different types of visual artifacts in image and video dehazing. Although these novel dehazing methods can achieve well and encouraging result, unavoidable imperfections still exist in each of them.

Among of these single image dehazing methods, the DCP [3] approach have been achieved more effective and better visually result in most cases. However, it is inaccurate in handling the halo artifacts in images, computationally intensive and the blurring phenomenon. Some algorithms are proposed to improve the DCP model. For efficiency, Gibson et al. [13], He et al. [14], Li et al. [15] replace the time-consuming soft matting [16] with standard median filtering [13], guided image filtering (GIF) [14] and weighted GIF [15], respectively. In terms of halo suppressing, Meng et al. [17] proposed an effective regularization dehazing method to restore the haze-free image by exploring the inherent boundary constraint. However, there are less outstanding works focus on the blurring phenomenon in DCP dehazing method using guided image filter.

The phenomenon of blurring is the issue that: when the guided image filter is used to refine the raw transmission map, the restored image may display edge-blurring. In this work, in odder to find the reason of the blurring phenomenon, we first set up a differential model about the transmission, hazy and dehazed image. Then, based on this model, we proposed our detail-enhancement method using the Laplacian pyramid technology. The striking advantage of the proposed method is that: it can not only simultaneously achieve haze removal and detail-enhancement, but also without additional computational complexity.

2   Related Works

2.1   Dehazing Model

The haze model can be mathematically described as [2,3]:

$$I(x) = J(x) \cdot t(x) + A(1 - t(x)) \tag{1}$$

where I is the observed intensity (i.e. hazy image), J is the scene radiance (i.e. dehazed image), A is the global atmospheric light, and t is the medium transmission, which describes the portion of the light that is not scattered and reaches the camera. The goal of dehazing is to restore J from I, by estimating A and t.

To estimate A [3], the top 0.1 percent brightest pixels in the dark channel I_{dark} are first selected. Among these pixels, the value of A is set as the highest intensity in the color image I along each color channel.

To estimate transmission map t, [3] proposed dark channel prior, which is based on the observation that, in most non-sky patches of the haze free images, at least one color channel has some pixels with very low intensity. For an arbitrary image F, its dark channel F_{dark} is obtained by [3]:

$$F_{dark}(x) = \min_{y \in \Omega(x)} [\min_{c \in \{r,g,b\}} F_c(y)], \tag{2}$$

where F_c is a color channel of $\boldsymbol{F}$ and $\Omega(\boldsymbol{x})$ is a local patch centered at $\boldsymbol{x}$.

Operating the dark channel prior on both sides of (1), the value of t can be initially estimated as [3]:

$$\tilde{t}(\boldsymbol{x}) = 1 - \min_{\boldsymbol{y} \in \Omega(\boldsymbol{x})} [\min_{c \in \{r,g,b\}} I_c(\boldsymbol{y})/A_c]. \tag{3}$$

Then, the GIF is employed to remove the block artifacts from $\tilde{t}$ [14]: $t_g = max\{G[\tilde{t}, \boldsymbol{I}], 0\}$, where $G[\cdot, \boldsymbol{I}]$ is the guided filter with the guidance as $\boldsymbol{I}$.

With the estimated t and $\boldsymbol{A}$, the scene radiance is restored according to (1)

$$\boldsymbol{J}_g(\boldsymbol{x}) = (\boldsymbol{I}(\boldsymbol{x}) - \boldsymbol{A})/t_g(\boldsymbol{x}) + \boldsymbol{A}. \tag{4}$$

2.2 Guided Image Filtering

The guided image filter (GIF) [14] can be used to refine the raw transmission map $\tilde{t}$, in which the refined transmission map t_g is a linear transform of the guidance image $\boldsymbol{I}$ in the window $\Omega_r(k)$ centered at the pixel k of a radius r: $t_g(\boldsymbol{x}) = \boldsymbol{a}_k \boldsymbol{I}(\boldsymbol{x}) + \boldsymbol{b}_k$, where $(\boldsymbol{a}_k, \boldsymbol{b}_k)$ are some constant linear coefficients in $\Omega_r(k)$. $(\boldsymbol{a}_k, \boldsymbol{b}_k)$ is obtained by minimizing a cost function [14]

$$E(\boldsymbol{a}_k, \boldsymbol{b}_k) = \sum_{\boldsymbol{x} \in \Omega_r(k)} (\boldsymbol{a}_k \boldsymbol{I}(\boldsymbol{x}) + \boldsymbol{b}_k - \tilde{t}(\boldsymbol{x}))^2 + \epsilon \boldsymbol{a}_k^2, \tag{5}$$

where ϵ is a regularization parameter penalizing large $\boldsymbol{a}_k$. The optimal values of $\boldsymbol{a}_k$ and $\boldsymbol{b}_k$ are computed as [14]:

$$\boldsymbol{a}_k = \frac{\mu_{\boldsymbol{I} \odot \tilde{t}, r}(k) - \mu_{\boldsymbol{I}, r}(k) \cdot \mu_{\tilde{t}, r}(k)}{\sigma_{\boldsymbol{I}, r}^2(k) + \epsilon}, \quad \boldsymbol{b}_k = \mu_{\tilde{t}, r}(k) - \boldsymbol{a}_k \cdot \mu_{\boldsymbol{I}, r}(k), \tag{6}$$

where $\odot$ is the element-wise product of two matrices. $\mu_{\boldsymbol{I} \odot \tilde{t}, r}(k)$, $\mu_{\boldsymbol{I}, r}(k)$ and $\mu_{\tilde{t}, r}(k)$ are the mean value of $\boldsymbol{I} \odot t$, $\boldsymbol{I}$ and $\tilde{t}$ in the window $\Omega_r(k)$, respectively.

Then, the final output is derived as [14]

$$t_g(\boldsymbol{x}) = \overline{\boldsymbol{a}}(\boldsymbol{x}) \cdot \boldsymbol{I} + \overline{\boldsymbol{b}}(\boldsymbol{x}), \tag{7}$$

where $\overline{\boldsymbol{a}}(\boldsymbol{x})$ and $\overline{\boldsymbol{b}}(\boldsymbol{x})$ are the mean value of $\boldsymbol{a}(\boldsymbol{x})$ and $\boldsymbol{b}(\boldsymbol{x})$ in the window $\Omega_r(\boldsymbol{x})$.

3 Detail-Enhanced Dehazing Method

In Subsect. 3.1, we give a mathematical explanation on the reason of blurring phenomenon generated in the GIF dehazing method. The detail-enhanced dehazing method presented in Subsect. 3.2 is based on this analysis.

3.1 Analysis on the Blurring-Phenomenon

Since $t_g = max\{G[\tilde{t}, \boldsymbol{I}], 0\}$, with the modification in (7), in the local domain Ω_r we have

$$\frac{\partial t_g}{\partial x_c} \approx \bar{a}_{g,c} \cdot \frac{\partial I_c}{\partial x_c}, \quad c \in \{r, g, b\}. \tag{8}$$

To analysis the reason of the blurring phenomenon, we take the derivative of equation (4); and according to (8), in the local domain Ω_r we can gain:

$$|\frac{\partial J_{g,c}}{\partial x_c}| = |\frac{1}{t_g} \cdot \frac{\partial I_c}{\partial x_c} + \frac{(A_c - I_c)}{t_g^2} \cdot \frac{\partial t_g}{\partial x_c}| \approx |\underbrace{\frac{1}{t_g} \cdot \frac{\partial I_c}{\partial x_c}}_{\Phi_{g1}} + \underbrace{\frac{(A_c - I_c)}{t_g^2} \cdot \bar{a}_{g,c} \cdot \frac{\partial I_c}{\partial x_c}}_{\Phi_{g2}}|, \tag{9}$$

where $c \in \{r, g, b\}$ presents the RGB color channels.

Since $0 < t_g < 1$, we have $\Phi_{g1} > 1$. Additionally, we observed that $\boldsymbol{a}_g(\boldsymbol{x})$ is often less than zero for most of $\boldsymbol{x}$, as the $\boldsymbol{a}_g$ map demonstrated in Fig. 1(b), in which the black region are the pixels with negative value, specially at the mountains and forest regions. These regions contain majority detail information, known as 'visual edges' regions. The histograms of $\boldsymbol{a}_g(\boldsymbol{x})$ illustrated in Fig. 1(d) also verify this observation. Since $\boldsymbol{I}$ is always less then $\boldsymbol{A}$, we have $\Phi_{g2} < 0$, thus the two terms at right side of (9) get opposite signal. Consequently, the $|\partial J_{g,c}/\partial x_c|$ gets less value, meaning that the radiance $\boldsymbol{J}_g$ has less gradient. That is the blurring reason for $\boldsymbol{J}_g$.

3.2 Detail-Enhanced Dehazing Using GIF and Laplacian Pyramid

Inspired by the model (9), our strategy is to modulate Φ_{g1} and Φ_{g2} to have same sign in most of regions, specially where the contents play a vital role in visual effect of the image, such as the mountains and forest in Fig. 1(a). To achieve this, a simply way is let t_g plus the lightness of the bottom-most level Laplacian pyramid of the input image $\boldsymbol{I}$ (i.e. the $0th$ level of Laplacian pyramid and it is noted as $L_{I,0}$ in this work), since $L_{I,0}$ can represent the most visible details at original spatial scales. That is:

$$t_l'(\boldsymbol{x}) = t_g(\boldsymbol{x}) + L_{I,0}(\boldsymbol{x}). \tag{10}$$

In such way, $\partial(t_g + L_{I,0})/\partial x_c$ contains more detail structure of $\boldsymbol{I}$, and it can help enlarge the regions where Φ_{g1} and Φ_{g2} with same sign. However, the obtained $\boldsymbol{J}_l'$ is unnatural with rough edges, as presented in Fig. 2(a). That is because of the $L_{I,0}$ can only represent one spatial scale detail. Directly adding Laplacian pyramid on the t_g may yield discontinuous edges, as the zoom-in yellow block in Fig. 2(a).

In this work, we replace the $L_{I,0}$ as the $G[L_{I,0}, \boldsymbol{I}]$ in (10), i.e.

$$t_l = max\{G[\tilde{t}, \boldsymbol{I}] + G[\eta \cdot L_{I,0}, \boldsymbol{I}], 0\}, \tag{11}$$

Fig. 1. Traditional dehazing results using GIF. (a) is the input image. (b) and (c) are $\boldsymbol{a}_g$ and $\boldsymbol{b}_g$, respectively. (d) is the histogram of $\boldsymbol{a}_g$. (e) is the transmission map t_g. (f) is the result $\boldsymbol{J}_g$.

where η is a constant parameter. Since the GIF is a local linear filer, it is easily to proof that:

$$t_l = max\{G[\tilde{t} + \eta \cdot L_{I,0}, \boldsymbol{I}], 0\}. \tag{12}$$

This mean that, the proposed method only operate GIF one time without additional computational complexity.

Then, the final scene radiance is $\boldsymbol{J}_l(\boldsymbol{x}) = (\boldsymbol{I}(\boldsymbol{x}) - \boldsymbol{A})/t_l(\boldsymbol{x}) + \boldsymbol{A}$. In this strategy, GIF is employed to smooth the $L_{I,0}$, and the radiance $\boldsymbol{J}_l(\boldsymbol{x})$ looks more naturally and significantly enhanced.

Similarly as (9), we have

$$|\frac{\partial J_{l,c}}{\partial x_c}| = |\frac{1}{t_l} \cdot \frac{\partial I_c}{\partial x_c} + \frac{(A_c - I_c)}{t_l^2} \cdot \frac{\partial t_l}{\partial x_c}| \approx |\underbrace{\frac{1}{t_l} \cdot \frac{\partial I_c}{\partial x_c}}_{\Phi_{l1}} + \underbrace{\frac{(A_c - I_c)}{t_l^2} \cdot \overline{a}_{l,c} \cdot \frac{\partial I_c}{\partial x_c}}_{\Phi_{l2}}|, \tag{13}$$

where $c \in \{r, g, b\}$.

Figure 2(b) shows the $\boldsymbol{a}_l$ map calculated by (12). From Fig. 2(b) and (d) we can find that, at the 'visual edge' regions $\boldsymbol{a}_l$ normally get positive value, implying that $\Phi_{l2} > 0$, i.e. Φ_{l1} and Φ_{l2} have same sign. Ulteriorly, comparing with (9), $|\partial J_{l,c}/\partial x_c|$ gets higher value than $|\partial J_{g,c}/\partial x_c|$ in these regions, i.e. $\boldsymbol{J}_l$ is more contrast than $\boldsymbol{J}_g$.

Fig. 2. Detail-enhancement results. (a) is the results by using (10). (b) and (c) are a_l and b_l , respectively. (d) is the histogram of a_l . (e) is the transmission map t_l . (f) is the result J_l . (Color figure online)

4 Experiments

To evaluate the proposed method, both qualitative and quantitative performances are presented, comparing with several state-of-the-art methods, including He et al. [14], and some newly developed methods, including Meng et al. [17],
Zhu et al. [6], Berman et al. [7,20], Chen et al. [9], Bahat et al. [8]. The configurations of the benchmark methods strictly follow the authors' recommendations
in their papers. The parameters in this work are set as: the windows of GIF and
Laplacian pyramid are 35 and 5, respectively; parameter in (12) is $\eta = 1$.

4.1 Qualitative Evaluation

Figure 3 shows the qualitative comparisons on state-of-the-art methods and
newly improved dehazing methods. He et al. [14] results are not satisfactory
in processing details, compared with other methods. Meng et al. [17] method
can generate visually pleasing results with faithful color as well as finer image
structures and details. However, this method is poor robustness at white objects
or bright sky region, as illustrated in Fig. 3(c). Zhu et al.'s [6] approach achieves
high efficiency. While this method is prone to misestimating the transmission in
some cases, leading to over-saturation as shown in Fig. 3(d)(top). Compared with

(a)   (b)   (c)   (d)   (e)

Fig. 3. Qualitative Evaluation I. (a) is the input image. (b) and (e) are the dehazing results of [14], Meng et al. [17], Zhu et al. [6] and the proposed method, respectively.

these methods, the outstanding feature of the proposed method is that the results have more clear edge and finer contrast.

Figure 4 shows the comparisons with other newly dehazing methods. Berman et al. [7] method can obtain more accurate estimation of the transmission for most cases and achieve the least transmission estimation error at medium haze level. However, in near clean (low haze level) or heavily hazy scenarios, the haze lines found may not be reliable, as the distance mountains in the Fig. 4(b)(bot.) The Chen et.al [9] results maintain subtle image features while at the same time successfully avoids boosting these artifacts. Nevertheless, in order to remove the noise and artifacts, it mistakenly removes the distant objects to produce over-smoothed results, as the distance smoothed scene in Fig. 4(c)(top). The blind dehazing method [8] can effectively remove haze from single image, while the color preset quite unnatural for some dehazed image, as shown in Fig. 4(d)(top). The proposed method has good robustness for these different scenarios, and achieves outstanding dehazing effects.

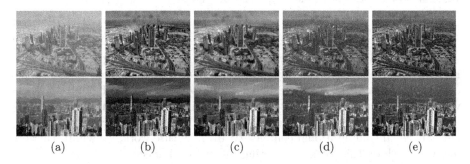

(a)   (b)   (c)   (d)   (e)

Fig. 4. Qualitative Evaluation II. (a) is the input image. (b) and (e) are the dehazing results of Berman et al. [7], Chen et al. [9], Bahat et al. [8] and the proposed method, respectively.

4.2   Quantitative Evaluation

In our quantitative comparisons, three objective indicators, e, r, and p defined in [19], are employed to assess the corresponding results quantitatively. Indicator e represents the rate of edges newly visible after restoration. Indicator r expresses the contrast restoration, which is the mean of normalized gradients of visible edges. Indicator p is the occurrence probability of oversaturated pixels (completely black or white, but not existed in input) produced by the restoration method. Generally supposed that, higher values of e and r, and lower value of p are expected for a better dehazed image. The quantitative evaluations of the aforementioned methods applied to Figs. 3 and 4 are given in Table 1, with the optimal values are highlighted in bold.

Table 1. BCEA [19] Qualitative Evaluations.

		Fig. 3				Fig. 4			
		He et al.	Meng et al.	Zhu et al.	Our	Berman et al.	Chen et al.	Bahat et al.	Our
top	e	2.002	1.176	0.198	*2.193*	0.392	0.632	0.336	*0.932*
	p	*0.000*	*0.000*	*0.000*	*0.000*	*0.000*	0.031	0.002	*0.000*
	r	1.550	1.527	0.612	*1.693*	1.175	*2.753*	1.082	2.337
bot.	e	2.803	2.660	1.291	*3.109*	0.031	0.225	0.271	*0.311*
	p	*0.000*	*0.000*	*0.000*	*0.000*	0.001	0.034	*0.000*	0.002
	r	3.535	2.155	1.536	*5.580*	1.040	*1.943*	1.190	1.394

It is observed from this table that our method performs well in e and r, especially the e are better than the others algorithms. Comparing with He et al.'s [3] results, the indexes e and r are significantly enlarged, which means our method can restored dehazed images with more local details and present higher contrast. He et al.'s [3], Zhu et al.'s [6] and Chen et al.'s [9] results are always with little p, which means that they are free from oversaturation effectively; however their results are less contrast with lower e and r values than ours. For our method, although the performance in r is not the best for Figs. 4(top) and 4(bot.), the value is closer to the best one than other methods.

5   Conclusion

An effective and considerable practical refining method for single image dehazing is proposed to solve the blurring problem in DCP dehazing method. The detail-enhancement dehazing method is proposed based on a differential model, which can reflect the main reason of the blurring phenomenon. The proposed method not only effectively enhance the blurred deahzed image, but also without additional computational complexity. In the future work, we will further do more research on this work considering the artificial affect.

Acknowledgments. This work was partially supported by the National Natural Science Foundation of China (NSFC) under Grants 61232016, 61572461, 11790305, CAS '100-Talents' (Dr. Xu Long).

References

1. Tan, R.T.: Visibility in bad weather from a single image. In: IEEE Conference on Computer Vision and Pattern Recognition, 2008, CVPR 2008, pp. 1–8. IEEE (2008)
2. Fattal, R.J.: Single image dehazing. ACM Trans, Graph. (TOG) **27**(3), 72 (2008)
3. He, K., Sun, J., Tang, X.: Single image haze removal using dark channel prior. IEEE Trans. Pattern Anal. Mach. Intell. **33**(12), 2341–2353 (2011)
4. Tarel, J.P., Hautiere, N.: Fast visibility restoration from a single color or gray level image. In: 2009 IEEE 12th International Conference on Computer Vision (ICCV), pp. 2201–2208. IEEE Press (2009)
5. Nishino, K., Kratz, L., Lombardi, S.: Bayesian defogging. Int. J. Comput. Vis. **98**(3), 263–278 (2012)
6. Zhu, Q., Mai, J., Shao, L.: A fast single image haze removal algorithm using color attenuation prior. IEEE Trans. Image Process. **24**(11), 3522–3533 (2015)
7. Berman, D., Avidan, S.: Non-local image dehazing. In: Proceedings of the IEEE Conference on Computer Vision and Pattern Recognition, pp. 1674–1682 (2016)
8. Bahat, Y., Irani, M.: Blind dehazing using internal patch recurrence. In: 2016 IEEE International Conference on Computational Photography (ICCP), pp. 1–9. IEEE (2016)
9. Chen, C., Do, M.N., Wang, J.: Robust image and video dehazing with visual artifact suppression via gradient residual minimization. In: Leibe, B., Matas, J., Sebe, N., Welling, M. (eds.) ECCV 2016. LNCS, vol. 9906, pp. 576–591. Springer, Cham (2016). https://doi.org/10.1007/978-3-319-46475-6_36
10. Cai, B., Xu, X., Jia, K., Qing, C., Tao, D.: DehazeNet: an end-to-end system for single image haze removal. IEEE Trans. Image Process. **25**(11), 5187–5198 (2016)
11. Ren, W., Liu, S., Zhang, H., Pan, J., Cao, X., Yang, M.-H.: Single image dehazing via multi-scale convolutional neural networks. In: Leibe, B., Matas, J., Sebe, N., Welling, M. (eds.) ECCV 2016. LNCS, vol. 9906, pp. 154–169. Springer, Cham (2016). https://doi.org/10.1007/978-3-319-46475-6_10
12. He, L., Zhao, J., Zheng, N., Bi, D.: Haze removal using the difference-structure-preservation prior. IEEE Trans. Image Process. **99**, 1–1 (2017)
13. Gibson, K.B., Vo, D.T., Nguyen, T.Q.: An investigation of dehazing effects on image and video coding. IEEE Trans. Image Process. **21**(2), 662–673 (2012)
14. He, K., Sun, J., Tang, X.: Guided image filtering. IEEE Trans. Pattern Anal. Mach. Intell. **35**(6), 1397–1409 (2013)
15. Li, Z., Zheng, J., Zhu, Z., et al.: Weighted guided image filtering. IEEE Trans. Image process. **24**(1), 120–129 (2015)
16. Levin, A., Lischinski, D., Weiss, Y.: A closed form solution to natural image matting. In: Proceedings of IEEE Conference on Computer Vision and Pattern Recognition. vol. 1, pp. 61–68 (2006)
17. Meng, G., Wang, Y., Duan, J., et al.: Efficient image dehazing with boundary constraint and contextual regularization. In: Proceedings of the IEEE International Conference on Computer Vision, pp. 617–624 (2013)
18. Burt, P., Adelson, E.: The Laplacian pyramid as a compact image code. IEEE Trans. Commun. **31**(4), 532–540 (1983)
19. Hautiere, N., Tarel, J.P., Aubert, D., et al.: Blind contrast enhancement assessment by gradient ratioing at visible edges. Image Anal. Stereol. **27**(2), 87–95 (2011)
20. Non-Local Dehazing. http://www.eng.tau.ac.il/~berman/NonLocalDehazing/

Personalized Micro-Video Recommendation via Hierarchical User Interest Modeling

Lei Huang[(⊠)] and Bin Luo

State Key Laboratory for Novel Software Technology,
Nanjing University, Nanjing, China
{leihuang,luobin}@nju.edu.cn

Abstract. The increasing prevalence of micro-videos on the Internet requires efficient recommendation mechanisms to help users to find interesting micro-videos. In this paper, we propose a novel personalized micro-video recommendation method using hierarchical user interest modeling based on multi-modal features. Specifically, multi-modal features, including visual, acoustic, textual, emotional and social features, are extracted from micro-videos to model user interests on three levels. The user interest scores on different levels are fused to recommend the micro-videos satisfying users' personalized interests. The experimental results on a micro-video dataset crawled from Vine show that our method outperforms the state-of-the-art methods.

Keywords: Micro-video · Personalized recommendation
User interest · Hierarchical modeling · Multi-modal features

1 Introduction

Video, benefiting from its natural advantages in multi-modality representation, becomes increasingly popular on social network websites and online video sharing platforms [1–3]. Since 2012, the emergence of micro-video, a new type of videos with bite-sized lengths, promotes the popularity of videos in communication, because of the convenience of micro-videos in capturing, sharing and viewing [4]. Many micro-video sharing platforms appear on the Internet. For example, Twitter reached 12 million daily micro-video posting [5], and Snapchat had 7 billion video views every day in 2016 [4].

Compared to the traditional videos with the lengths of dozens minutes even a few hours, micro-videos only last several seconds. For example, the maximum lengths of micro-videos on Vine, Snapchat and Instagram are 6 s, 10 s and 15 s, respectively. It will be terrible experience for a user if she/he needs to select an interesting micro-video manually from a lot of videos and view it for only several seconds. Hence, it is important to reduce manual micro-video selection and recommend the most interesting ones for each user automatically according

© Springer International Publishing AG, part of Springer Nature 2018
B. Zeng et al. (Eds.): PCM 2017, LNCS 10735, pp. 564–574, 2018.
https://doi.org/10.1007/978-3-319-77380-3_54

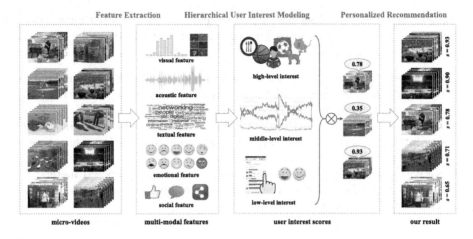

Fig. 1. An overview of our personalized micro-video recommendation method.

to her/his personalized interests. Similar to other recommendation tasks [6], the key issue in micro-video recommendation is to model user interests and the correspondences between user interests and video content [7]. They are usually derived from user viewing history and feedbacks on social network websites, such likes and comments [8].

As an attractive topic, video recommendation has been widely studied and applied in real video sharing platforms, such as YouTube [9]. However, since micro-video is a new medium type, there are few works on micro-video recommendation. The current micro-video recommendation methods only focus on the popularity of micro-videos [8], which ignores the diversities of user interests, or consider that the interests of a user is unchangeable [7]. They cannot satisfy the requirements of user interests in micro-video viewing.

In this paper, we propose a novel micro-video recommendation method based on hierarchical user interest modeling. The interests of each user to micro-videos are modeled on three layers in our method: high-level, middle-level and low-level. Specifically, high-level interests describe the topics that a user is interested in, such as football and cooking. These topics are usually related to a user's occupation or hobby, which may be constant in a long duration. Low-level interests indicate the temporary interests of a user, such as a specific hot spot. They are continuously changeable even during the viewing of micro-videos. Middle-level interests are the intermediates between high-level interests and low-level interests. They are the popular things, such as products or events, belonging to the high-level topics that a user is interested in, but they are not confirmed by the user whether she/he wishes to watch in the current viewing. Figure 1 shows an overview of our method. We first extract multi-modal features from the candidate micro-videos, including visual, acoustic, textual, emotional and social features. Next, we model the high-level, middle-level and low-level user interests of a user on micro-videos based on these features. Finally, we fuse the scores on three levels to calculate the user interest score on each micro-video, and recommend the micro-videos with the highest scores to the user.

Our contributions mainly include:

- We propose a hierarchical model to describe user interests in viewing micro-videos, which can describe both the long-term interests related to users' hobby and temporal interests in a certain viewing.
- We present a micro-video recommendation method based on hierarchical user interest modeling, which can recommend micro-videos for different users according to their personalized interests.
- We construct a micro-video dataset and validate our proposed method on the dataset. The experimental results show that our method outperforms the state-of-the-art methods.

2   Related Work

2.1   Video Recommendation

Video recommendation has been widely studied and served in many online video sharing platforms, such as YouTube [9] and Tecent [10]. Recent efforts on video recommendation focus on solving the real problems in applications. For example, Krishnappa et al. [11] improved the performance of server caches by taking advantage of the user habit in viewing the top recommended video. Huang et al. [10] presented several techniques, such as scalable online collaborative filtering algorithm, to provide real-time and accurate recommendations. Zhou et al. [12] presented a cloud-assisted differentially private video recommendation system to handle the problems in user privacy and service repository. Sun et al. [13] proposed a social-aware group recommendation method to model both group preference and model group members' tolerance characteristics by jointly using social relationships and social behaviors.

2.2   Micro-video Recommendation

As compared to traditional video recommendation, there are few works on micro-video recommendation. Chen et al. [8] proposed a micro-video popularity prediction method based on a transductive model, which can only recommend micro-videos according to their popularity rather than provide personalized recommendation. Ma et al. [7] proposed a micro-video recommendation method using a latent genre aware model, but they did not consider the changeability of user interests. There are also several works about micro-video characteristics analysis, such as loop assessment [14] and creativity classification [15]. These works cannot be used to provide recommendation services directly.

3 Our Method

3.1 Feature Extraction

Inspired by the previous works in micro-video recommendation [7,8], we extract the features for videos in multiple modalities, including visual feature, acoustic feature, textual feature, emotional feature and social feature. In our method, we simplify user profiling, *i.e.*, we treat each user as an individual without considering their relationships.

Visual Feature Extraction. Visual feature is used in micro-video popularity prediction and tag refinement in our method. We select a keyframe per second uniformly from micro-videos, and extract low level features on the keyframes, including color histogram, edge direction histogram, wavelet texture, and block-wise color moments extracted over 5×5 grid partitions [16]. For popularity prediction, we extract aesthetic features and visual quality features besides color histogram [8] with the released tools[1,2], and the visual sentiment features based on a deep CNN model trained on SentiBank dataset [17]. For tag complement, we extract object appearance features using VGG-16 model [18] and motion features using improved dense track (iDT) with HoF, HoG and MBH [19] besides the low level features on keyframes by referring to [16].

Acoustic Feature Extraction. Acoustic feature is used in micro-video popularity prediction in our method. We extract Mel-Frequency Cepstral Coefficients (MFCC) [20] and Audio-Six [21] by referring to [8].

Textual Feature Extraction. Textual feature is the dominant feature for user interest modeling in our method, which can be extracted from user comments to micro-videos. We use the hashtags contained in user comments, because they usually highlight micro-videos' content. However, a statistic on a large micro-video dataset shows that over half micro-videos do not have the associated hashtags [5]. Hence, we refine the tags of micro-videos with tag transfer, tag complement and tag denoising in [16], which use external datasets to refine micro-video tags based on visual features.

Emotional Feature Extraction. Emotional feature is used in both micro-video popularity prediction and micro-video similarity measurement in our method. We extract the emotional feature using the visual sentiment features from visual feature extraction based on SentiBank dataset [17], which represents 2,089 types of sentiments.

---

[1] http://www.ee.columbia.edu/~subh/Software.php.
[2] http://live.ece.utexas.edu/.

Social Feature Extraction. Social feature represents the interaction between micro-videos with a specific user or all users. To each micro-video, we extract its four indicators, namely the numbers of reposts, comments, likes and loops. Besides, we extract the posting history including reposting for each user, which represents the viewing history of each micro-video.

3.2 Hierarchical User Interest Modeling

High-Level Interests. Since high-level interests aim to describe the topics that a user is interested in, a topic list covering the high-level interests of all users is required. A straightforward solution to obtain the topic list is to define it manually, just as the predefined video categories provided in many video sharing platforms in video navigation, including sport, comic, finance, and music. However, such a hand-crafted solution is time-cost and ineffective sometimes. For instance, a user may be only interested in football but not any other sports. Hence, we use the representative tags instead of manually defined categories in describing the micro-video topics that users are interested in. Specifically, we use the 40 tags in MV-40 dataset construction in [5], which can be adjusted or extended dynamically in real applications. Considering the incompleteness of tags, we construct a weight matrix between all the tags and the 40 topics. Each tag is embedded with Word2Vec [22] and the similarity between each tag and each one in the 40 topics is calculated based on the cosine distance of their vectors. In this way, the degree that a micro-video belonging to a topic is calculated as the sum of the similarities between its tags and topics.

To each user, we make a statistic of the number of her/his interested micro-videos on each topic in a long duration, such as in the past six months. We calculate the high-level interest score of the ith user on the jth topic of micro-videos with Sigmoid function as follows:

$$s_{i,j}^h = \frac{1}{1 + e^{-(n_{i,j} - \bar{n}_i)}}, \tag{1}$$

where $n_{i,j}$ is the degree sum of micro-videos which the ith user is interested on the jth topic in the duration; $\bar{n}_i$ is the average number of micro-videos the ith user is interested on all the topics in the duration.

Middle-Level Interests. Middle-level interests are the connects between high-level user interests and low-level user interests, *i.e.*, they aim to provide the candidate micro-videos to explore a user's current interests while they should be under the constraints of the topics that the user is interested in a long duration. We assume that the users interested in the same topic may have similar interests in this topic. Hence, we use the popularity of micro-videos in each topic to model the middle-level user interests on each micro-video.

Inspired by [8], we represent the popularity of each micro-video by linearly fusing its four indicators, namely the numbers of reposts, comments, likes and loops. To eliminate the unbalance of popularity caused by posting time, we also predict the potential popularity with a method similar to [8]. In our popularity prediction, we use the visual, acoustic, textual, emotional and social features presented in Sect. 3.1 to replace the original ones in [8], which obtains the results with similar performance in our experiments. Based on the actual popularity and the potential popularity of each micro-video, we calculate the middle-level interest score of the ith user on the kth micro-video as follows:

$$s_{i,k}^m = \frac{1}{|\Omega_k|} \sum_{t_j \in \Omega_k} s_{i,j}^h \left(\alpha\, p_k^a + (1 - \alpha)\, p_k^p \right), \qquad (2)$$

where Ω_k is the set of topics that the kth micro-video belongs to; t_j is the jth topic; $s_{i,j}^h$ is the high-level interest of the ith user on the jth topic of micro-videos, which is defined in Eq. (1); p_k^a and p_k^p are the actual popularity and the potential popularity of the kth micro-video, respectively; α is a parameter to adjust the weights of p_k^a and p_k^p, which equals $\min(T_k, T_h)/T_h$, here T_k is the time that the kth micro-video has been posted and T_h is the duration length in high-level interest calculation, which equals 3 months in our experiments.

Low-Level Interests. Low-level interests aim to indicate the temporary interests of a user, which is changeable when a user views micro-videos. Hence, we model the low-level interests of a user based on the similarities to the micro-videos she/he is interested in recently.

In micro-video similarity measurement, we only use the textual and emotional features of micro-videos, because the usage of visual and acoustic features does not bring obvious performance improvement in our experiments. It may be caused by that we have used visual and acoustic features in textual feature completion. To emphasize the temporary characteristic of low-level interests, we filter the tags for topic description in textual feature and weight the rest tags with a strategy similar to TF-IDF (term frequency - inverse document frequency) [23], i.e., highlighting the specific tags. Based on the textual and emotional features, we calculate the low-level interest score of the ith user on the kth micro-video v_k as follows:

$$s_{i,k}^l = \frac{1}{|\Phi_i|} \sum_{v_m \in \Phi_i} \left(\beta\, sim^t(v_k, v_m) + (1 - \beta)\, sim^e(v_k, v_m) \right), \qquad (3)$$

where Φ_i is the set of micro-videos that the ith user is interested in recently, which contains the recent 3 micro-videos in our experiments; v_m is a micro-video belonging to the set Φ_i; $sim^t(,)$ and $sim^e(,)$ denote the cosine distances between two micro-videos on textual and emotional features weighted by the matrixes generated based on Word2Vec [22] for word embedding, respectively; β is a parameter to adjust the weights of textual and emotional similarities, which equals 0.5 in our experiments.

3.3 Personalized Video Recommendation

Based on the high-level, middle-level and low-level user interests modeled in Eqs. (1–3), we calculate the interest score of the ith user on the kth micro-video as follows:

$$s_{i,k} = \gamma\, s_{i,k}^m + (1 - \gamma) \frac{(s_{i,k}^h + \varepsilon)s_{i,k}^l}{1 + \varepsilon}, \tag{4}$$

where γ is a parameter to adjust the weights of middle-level and low-level user interests, which equals 0.3 to emphasize low-level user interests; $s_{i,k}^h$ is used to filter the micro-videos belonging to the uninterested topics; ε is used to allow some exceptions in filtering, which equals 1 in our experiments.

Once obtaining the interest score between each user and each micro-video, we rank the micro-videos for each user based on their interest scores in a descending order. Because the scores on high-level and middle-level user interests need not to be updated online and the similarities between micro-videos for low-level interest modeling can be previously calculated, our method is practicable in real applications.

4   Experiments

4.1   Dataset and Experiment Settings

Inspired by [8], we constructed a micro-video dataset crawled from Vine. We first randomly select 500 active Vine users from Rankzoo[3] as the seed users, and retained the top 1,000 followers for each seed users. We removed the repeated users and crawled the timeline for each user, *i.e.*, her/his micro-video posting history including reposting, in the duration from July 2015 to December 2015. Because our method needs to model user interests in temporal, we analyzed the timelines of all the users and only retained the users who post no less than 5 micro-videos in every month. In this way, we obtained a dataset consisted of 2,738 users, 10,453 micro-videos and 101,896 posting records. To each micro-video, we crawled its numbers of reposts, comments, likes and loops for popularity prediction. We randomly selected 80% posting records of each user in every month for training, and used the rest ones for testing. Finally, we obtained the training data with 80,362 posting records associated to 9,877 micro-videos and the test data with 21,534 posting records associated to 7,108 micro-videos. Note here, to void the leaking of user interests, we divided the training data and the test data according the time of posting records on month level. In Tables 1 and 2, $T = k$ denotes that the training data and the test data in the first k month(s) were used in our experiments.

In our evaluation, we adopted hit ratio and precision as the metrics, and accessed the performance of the top 10 results for each method. Specifically, hit ratio measures whether one or more interesting micro-videos are provided, while precision measures how many interesting micro-videos are proposed.

All the experiments were conducted on a computer with 3.5 GHz CPU and 32 GB memory. In deep feature extraction, we used a server with a Titan X GPU.

---

[3] https://rankzoo.com/.

4.2 Component Analysis

We first validate the effects of different components in our method. In component analysis, we generate four baselines, including: (1) **Our-H**: ranking the micro-videos based on high-level interests in recommendation; (2) **Our-M\H**: ranking the micro-videos based on middle-level interests without the weighting from high-level interests, *i.e.*, only depending on micro-video popularity; (3) **Our-L**: ranking the micro-videos based on low-level interests, *i.e.*, only depending on users' temporal viewing histories; (4) **Our-M**: ranking the micro-videos based on middle-level interests, in which high-level interests have been contained.

Table 1 shows the performance of different baselines and our method. We can see that: (1) our method outperforms other combinations of different components on both hit ratio and precision, which shows that all the components in our method are effective; (2) Our-M\H obtains the worst performance among all the methods, which shows that only micro-video popularity is insufficient for micro-video recommendation; (3) both Our-H and Our-L obtain acceptable performance, which shows that personal interests, no matter long-term or short-term, are important to micro-video recommendation; (4) Our-M obtains better performance than Our-H by recommending the popular micro-videos belonging to the topics that a user is interested in, which shows that micro-video popularity is effective under the constraint of high-level user interests.

Table 1. Evaluation of our method with different components on Hit Ratio (HR) and Precision (Pre). $T = k$ denotes that the training data and the test data in the first k month(s) were used in our experiments.

	Our-H		Our-M\H		Our-L		Our-M		Our	
	HR	Pre	HR	Pre	HR	Pre	HR	Pre	HR	Pre
$T = 1$	0.043	0.005	0.032	0.004	0.094	0.010	0.056	0.006	**0.102**	**0.011**
$T = 2$	0.077	0.009	0.034	0.005	0.104	0.011	0.091	0.015	**0.140**	**0.024**
$T = 3$	0.116	0.020	0.037	0.005	0.115	0.012	0.131	0.038	**0.197**	**0.059**
$T = 4$	0.145	0.024	0.037	0.005	0.137	0.015	0.198	0.062	**0.286**	**0.083**
$T = 5$	0.144	0.025	0.033	0.005	0.134	0.015	0.266	0.074	**0.348**	**0.113**
$T = 6$	0.147	0.026	0.043	0.006	0.142	0.015	0.310	0.094	**0.356**	**0.137**

Note here, the performance of Our-M\H may be conflict to our institutive feeling, since the popular micro-videos easily attract our interests to view them in daily life. The reason is that a more strict definition of "a user is interested in a micro-video" is used, *i.e.*, we only consider that a user is interested in a micro-video if she/he does some operation, such as click "like" after viewing. Moreover, the micro-video popularity are collected or predicted from all the users, which may confuse the interests of different types of users. It will be better to cluster users into groups and use the popularity within each group.

4.3   Comparison Results

To illustrate the effectiveness of our method, we compare it with several state-of-the-art methods, including: (1) **LGA**: recommending micro-videos with a latent genre aware model [7]; (2) **MP**: recommending videos using graph-based iterative message propagation, in which we used the viewing history as user behaviors information [24]; (3) **PP**: predicting the popularity of micro-videos based on multi-modal features [8]. We also use actual popularity (**AP**) as a baseline, which ranks micro-videos in a descending order according to their actual popularity. For fair comparison, we used the same extraction approach for each type feature and the default settings of all the other methods suggested by their authors.

Table 2 shows the performance of different baselines and our method. We can see that: (1) our method outperforms other methods on both hit ratio and precision, which illustrate the effectiveness of our method; (2) the methods based on micro-video popularity, both AP and PP, obtain worse performance than other methods; (3) LGA and MP obtain worse performance than our method because they cannot model the changeable user interests, and their performance is poor when the size of training dataset is small.

Table 2. Comparison of micro-video recommendation with different methods on Hit Ratio (HR) and Precision (Pre).

	AP		LGA [7]		MP [24]		PP [8]		Our	
	HR	Pre	HR	Pre	HR	Pre	HR	Pre	HR	Pre
T = 1	0.032	0.004	0.023	0.003	0.047	0.006	0.024	0.003	**0.102**	**0.011**
T = 2	0.033	0.005	0.059	0.010	0.065	0.016	0.038	0.006	**0.140**	**0.024**
T = 3	0.037	0.006	0.115	0.027	0.116	0.026	0.035	0.004	**0.197**	**0.059**
T = 4	0.029	0.004	0.189	0.046	0.169	0.043	0.039	0.006	**0.286**	**0.083**
T = 5	0.034	0.006	0.250	0.069	0.228	0.063	0.033	0.005	**0.348**	**0.113**
T = 6	0.030	0.005	0.312	0.093	0.289	0.077	0.041	0.007	**0.356**	**0.137**

5   Conclusion

We presented a personalized micro-video recommendation method, which models user interests hierarchically based on multi-modal features. Specifically, the visual, acoustic, textual, emotional and social features are extracted from micro-videos, and the scores of user interests on three levels are automatically calculated. These scores are fused to calculate the final interest scores of a user to different micro-videos, and the micro-videos with the highest scores are recommended to the user. We validated the performance of our method on a micro-video dataset crawled from Vine. It shows that our method is superior to the state-of-the-art methods.

Acknowledgements. This work is supported by National Science Foundation of China (61321491, 61202320), and Collaborative Innovation Center of Novel Software Technology and Industrialization.

References

1. Xu, Q., Huang, Q., Jiang, T., Yan, B., Lin, W., Yao, Y.: Hodgerank on random graphs for subjective video quality assessment. IEEE Trans. Multimedia **14**(3), 844–857 (2012)
2. Bao, B.K., Liu, G., Xu, C., Yan, S.: Inductive robust principal component analysis. IEEE Trans. Image Process. **21**(8), 3794–3800 (2012)
3. Liu, S., Liang, X., Liu, L., Lu, K., Lin, L., Cao, X., Yan, S.: Fashion parsing with video context. IEEE Trans. Multimedia **17**(8), 1347–1358 (2015)
4. Chen, J.: Multi-modal learning: study on a large-scale micro-video data collection. In: ACM International Conference on Multimedia. ACM, pp. 1454–1458 (2016)
5. Nguyen, P.X., Rogez, G., Fowlkes, C., Ramanan, D.: The open world of micro-videos. arXiv preprint arXiv:1603.09439 (2016)
6. Min, W., Bao, B.K., Xu, C., Hossain, M.S.: Cross-platform multi-modal topic modeling for personalized inter-platform recommendation. IEEE Trans. Multimedia **17**(10), 1787–1801 (2015)
7. Ma, J., Li, G., Zhong, M., Zhao, X., Zhu, L., Li, X.: LGA: latent genre aware micro-video recommendation on social media. Multimedia Tools Appl. **77**, 2991–3008 (2017)
8. Chen, J., Song, X., Nie, L., Wang, X., Zhang, H., Chua, T.S.: Micro tells macro: predicting the popularity of micro-videos via a transductive model. In: ACM International Conference on Multimedia, pp. 898–907 (2016)
9. Yan, M., Sang, J., Xu, C., Hossain, M.S.: A unified video recommendation by cross-network user modeling. ACM Trans. Multimedia Comput. Commun. Appl. **12**(4), 1–24 (2016). Article No. 53
10. Huang, Y., Cui, B., Jiang, J., Hong, K., Zhang, W., Xie, Y.: Real-time video recommendation exploration. In: ACM International Conference on Management of Data, pp. 35–46 (2016)
11. Krishnappa, D.K., Zink, M., Griwodz, C., Halvorsen, P.: Cache-centric video recommendation: an approach to improve the efficiency of Youtube caches. ACM Trans. Multimed. Comput. Commun. Appl. (TOMM), **11**(4) (2015). Article No. 48
12. Zhou, P., Zhou, Y., Wu, D., Jin, H.: Differentially private online learning for cloud-based video recommendation with multimedia big data in social networks. IEEE Trans. Multimedia **18**(6), 1217–1229 (2016)
13. Sun, L., Wang, X., Wang, Z., Zhao, H., Zhu, W.: Social-aware video recommendation for online social groups. IEEE Trans. Multimedia **19**(3), 609–618 (2017)
14. Sano, S., Yamasaki, T., Aizawa, K.: Degree of loop assessment in microvideo. In: IEEE International Conference on Image Processing, pp. 5182–5186 (2014)
15. Redi, M., O'Hare, N., Schifanella, R., Trevisiol, M., Jaimes, A.: 6 seconds of sound and vision: Creativity in micro-videos. In: IEEE Conference on Computer Vision and Pattern Recognition, pp. 4272–4279 (2014)
16. Huang, L., Luo, B.: Tag refinement of micro-videos by learning from multiple data sources. Multimedia Tools Appl. **76**(19), 20341–20358 (2017)
17. Borth, D., Ji, R., Chen, T., Breuel, T., Chang, S.F.: Large-scale visual sentiment ontology and detectors using adjective noun pairs. In: ACM International Conference on Multimedia, pp. 223–232 (2013)

18. Simonyan, K., Zisserman, A.: Very deep convolutional networks for large-scale image recognition. arXiv preprint arXiv:1409.1556 (2014)
19. Wang, H., Schmid, C.: Action recognition with improved trajectories. In: IEEE International Conference on Computer Vision, pp. 3551–3558 (2013)
20. Logan, B.: Mel frequency Cepstral coefficients for music modeling. In: International Symposium on Music Information Retrieval (2000)
21. Wu, B., Zhong, E., Horner, A., Yang, Q.: Music emotion recognition by multi-label multi-layer multi-instance multi-view learning. In: ACM International Conference on Multimedia, pp. 117–126 (2014)
22. Mikolov, T., Sutskever, I., Chen, K., Corrado, G.S., Dean, J.: Distributed representations of words and phrases and their compositionality. In: Advances in Neural Information Processing Systems, pp. 3111–3119 (2013)
23. Salton, G., Buckley, C.: Term-weighting approaches in automatic text retrieval. Inf. Proces. Manage. **24**(5), 513–523 (1988)
24. Huang, Q., Chen, B., Wang, J., Mei, T.: Personalized video recommendation through graph propagation. ACM Trans. Multimed. Comput. Commun. Appl. (TOMM), **10**(4) (2014). Article No. 32

3D and Panoramic Vision

MCTD: Motion-Coordinate-Time Descriptor for 3D Skeleton-Based Action Recognition

Qi Liang and Feng Wang[✉]

Shanghai Key Laboratory of Multidimensional Information Processing,
Department of Computer Science and Technology, East China Normal University,
Shanghai, China
fwang@cs.ecnu.edu.cn

Abstract. During the past few years, 3D-skeleton based action recognition has received increasing research attentions. Numerous approaches have been proposed. Most existing approaches extract the pose features in each frame along the video sequence for recognizing different actions. However, the motion information between adjacent poses is missing. In this paper, we propose a new descriptor by employing motion for action recognition. In our approach, the Lie algebra is employed to extract the motion between neighboring poses. The spatial coordinate and the timestamp information are also used to describe the space-temporal distribution of motion in the video sequence. For classification, we modify the SVM kernel to measure the distance between different action instances. Our experiments on three common datasets show that the proposed descriptor outperforms the state-of-the-art approaches.

Keywords: 3D skeleton · Action recognition · MCTD descriptor

1 Introduction

Human action recognition plays an extremely important role in many applications such as video surveillance, human-computer interaction, and sports training assistance. A lot of efforts have been devoted to this topic. During the past few decades, numerous approaches are proposed based on RGB videos. With the wide use of depth sensors such as Microsoft Kinect, some works investigate action recognition using 3D data. Johansson [5] demonstrates that human action can be recognized by using the evolution of key joints of human body, and a lot of efforts have been devoted to 3D skeleton based action recognition. Compared with 2D action recognition, 3D skeleton based action recognition has some advantages. First, 3D data has extra depth dimension which can be used to remove the effect of background. Second, the data captured by depth equipment is more reliable and less sensitive to the illumination changes. Especially with the advances of estimating technologies, 3D skeleton action recognition becomes less sensitive to the self-occlusion and the corrupted data.

© Springer International Publishing AG, part of Springer Nature 2018
B. Zeng et al. (Eds.): PCM 2017, LNCS 10735, pp. 577–587, 2018.
https://doi.org/10.1007/978-3-319-77380-3_55

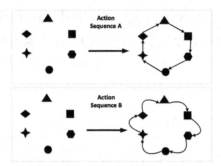

Fig. 1. Two action sequences with similar pose features but different motion. The nodes represent different pose features, while the curves represent the motion between poses.

In the past few years, numerous approaches have been proposed for 3D skeleton action recognition. Given a video, discriminate features are extracted to describe the skeleton pose in each frame. An action is then expressed by using the temporal evolution of these features over the video sequence. In [14], the concatenated 3D geometric features between different body parts are proposed to describe the pose in each frame. In [17], the skeleton is featured by using relative positions between pairwise joints. This kind of approaches extract discriminative features to describe poses, while the motion information between the adjacent poses is ignored. In fact, an action is a dynamic process and the motion of human body is important for action recognition. The pose describes the static state of an action at each moment, while motion describes the dynamic process between the adjacent poses. Both of them are important to describe an action completely. An example is illustrated in Fig. 1 where two actions show the same pose sequences and thus cannot be discriminated with only pose features. However, the motion between poses is different in these two sequences. This motivates us to incorporate motion features into skeleton based action recognition. Furthermore, motion information can be used to alleviate the problem of intra-class variance. The same action performed by different people may show slightly different poses, while the motion trajectories could be similar.

In this paper, we propose a new feature descriptor by employing motion information for action recognition. In our approach, the Lie algebra is used to extract the motion between the adjacent poses. The normalized coordinate and timestamp information are then employed to describe the space-time locations of the motion in the video sequence. Finally, we modify the kernel in [6] for SVM classification.

The remaining of this paper is organized as follows. We briefly review the related works in Sect. 2, and then present the proposed descriptor in Sect. 3. Section 4 modifies the SVM kernel for classification. The experimental results are presented in Sect. 5. Finally, Sect. 6 concludes this paper.

2   Related Works

Actions are usually expressed as the dynamic process in the space-time domain. For action recognition, space-time features are extracted to represent and discover the dynamic patterns. Existing approaches can be grouped into two categories.

Pose Sequence Based Approaches: This kind of approaches extracts features to describe the skeleton pose in each frame and an actions is then represented by the evolution of these features. The skeleton pose can be described by the connected rigid segments (bones) or the joints between the bones. In [14], the skeleton pose is represented by the geometric relationships between different body parts. The similar idea is used in [2] to extract geometrical features. In [4], human skeleton is represented by 3D joint location covariances. In [3], human skeleton is represented by 3D joint angles. In [13], one joint is selected as a root and a coordinate system attached to the root joint is built. The other joints are represented using the orientations with respect to this coordinate system. In [20], the human skeleton is represented by a histogram of the joint orientations. The above approaches focus on feature extraction for describing the skeleton poses, which are effective to discriminate actions with different poses. However, the motion between poses is missing.

Model Based Approaches: This kind of approaches attempts to model the dynamic process of actions. In [11], Hidden Markov Model (HMM) is used on the 3D relative positions. Linear dynamical system is proposed to model the dynamics of joints in [1]. However, since the common datasets are usually small and the number of training data is not enough for model training, the complex models can easily get over-fitting.

In this paper, we propose a new feature descriptor, named Motion-Coordinate-Time Descriptor (MCTD). This descriptor directly employs the motion between the neighboring poses for action recognition, which can capture the dynamic process of an action. Meanwhile, our approach does not suffer from the small scales of the datasets.

3   Proposed MCTD Descriptor

Our proposed descriptor employs motion along the pose sequence to represent actions. The spatial coordinate and timestamp features are also used to describe the distributions of motion on the space-time dimensions. In this section, we present the extraction of each feature and then integrate them into the final descriptor.

3.1   Pre-processing

Given a video with N frames, the raw 3D skeleton with n joints $o_1, o_2, \cdots, o_n$ is denoted as $V = (F_1, F_2, \cdots, F_N)$, and the $t - th$ frame

$$F_t = \{o_{kt} = (u_{kt}, v_{kt}, d_{kt}) | k = 1, 2, \cdots, N\} \tag{1}$$

where o_k is a joint of the skeleton, and (u_{kt}, v_{kt}, d_{kt}) records the 3D coordinate of o_k at the $t - th$ frame. We follow the approach in [14] to normalize the raw data and thus the normalized coordinates are invariant to scales and viewpoints.

3.2   Motion Features

As discussed in Sect. 1, the motion between poses provides discriminative information. Some approaches extract the differences between poses of adjacent frames to form descriptors. In [21], the distances between neighboring joints are used for action recognition. However, these descriptors are weak to represent motion information of skeletons. According to the structure of the human skeleton, we consider the skeleton as a combination of rigid segments, i.e. bones. Motion is produced by the rotation and the displacement of bones, which are used to describe the motion between adjacent poses in our descriptor. For convenience of presentation, we use B={b^1,b^2,...,b^j} to denote a set of j bones.

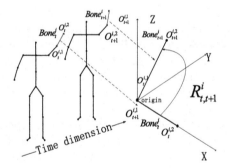

Fig. 2. An illustration to calculate the translation from b_t^i to b_{t+1}^i. We use one joint of b_t^i as the origin of the new system and b_t^i coincides with the x-axis. b_{t+1}^i is then represented in this system. The translation is calculated by taking b_t^i to the position and orientation of b_{t+1}^i.

In our approach, we use special Euclidean group SE(3) to extract the motion of bones. SE(3) is a set of 4-by-4 matrices of the following form

$$P(r, \overrightarrow{d}) = \begin{bmatrix} r & \overrightarrow{d} \\ 0 & 1 \end{bmatrix}, \tag{2}$$

where r $\in R^{3*3}$ is a rotation matrix and denotes the rotation of a rigid segment, and $\overrightarrow{d} \in R^{3*1}$ denotes the displacement change. Let $M_{t1,t2}^i$ denote the motion information of the i-*th* bone between neighboring frames t_1 and t_2. Given a bone b^i at frame t, suppose two joints at two ends of the bone are o^i_{1t}, o^i_{2t}. For normalization, we calculate the relative translation from b^i_t to b^i_{t+1}. We build a local coordinate system attached to b^i_t. Let o^i_{1t} be the origin of the coordinate system and b^i_t coincides with the x-axis. Let $o^i_{1,t+1}$, $o^i_{2,t+1} \in R^{3*1}$ denote the two joints of the bone b^i_{t+1} represented in the local coordinate system. Thus

$$
\begin{bmatrix} o^i_{1,t+1} & o^i_{2,t+1} \\ 1 & 1 \end{bmatrix} = \begin{bmatrix} r^i_{t,t+1} & \overrightarrow{d}^i_{t,t+1} \\ 1 & 1 \end{bmatrix} \begin{bmatrix} 0 & l^i \\ 0 & 0 \\ 0 & 0 \\ 1 & 1 \end{bmatrix} .
\tag{3}
$$

where l^i denotes the length of b^i and $r^i_{t,t+1}$, and $\overrightarrow{d}^i_{t,t+1}$ are the rotation and the displacement required to transform b^i_t to the position and orientation of b^i_{t+1}, which is illustrated in Fig. 2. The motion feature of b^i between two neighboring frames t_1 and t_2 can then be described as

$$
P^i_{t,t+1} = \begin{bmatrix} r^i_{t,t+1} & \overrightarrow{d}^i_{t,t+1} \\ 0 & 1 \end{bmatrix} \in SE(3) .
\tag{4}
$$

Since it is difficult to directly use SVM on SE(3), we map the motion information from SE(3) to its Lie algebra, which is the tangent space at the identity element as presented in [14]. The motion of bone i from frame t to frame $t+1$ is then formulated as

$$
M^i_{t,t+1} = vec(log(P^i_{t,t+1})) .
\tag{5}
$$

3.3   Coordinate Features

Motion can capture the dynamic process of an action. However, only using motion information would cause confusions. The same motion pattern of different body parts may represent different actions. An example is illustrated in Fig. 3(a) where the curve denotes the motion trajectory. When the motion is performed by the upper body, it may represent the action *raising the arm*. When the curve lies in the lower body, it may represent another action *raising the leg*. Therefore, we use the spatial coordinate to describe the distribution of motion on the space dimension. In our implementation, the normalized skeleton coordinate is used.

A bone links two joint points and a joint may appear on two different bones. In our approach, we use a unique joint to locate the corresponding bone. If we consider the hip-center joint as a root, the skeleton can be represented by using a tree structure as illustrated in Fig. 3(b). In this way, each node (i.e. joint) can be uniquely assigned to one bone. We use the coordinate of the child node joint to locate motion. In this way, we can avoid the confusion caused by using the same joint for different bones. The coordinate feature for motion $M^i_{t,t+1}$ is formulated as

$$
C^i_{t+1} = (x^{node}_{t+1}, y^{node}_{t+1}, z^{node}_{t+1})
\tag{6}
$$

where the node indicates the node joint of the bone i.

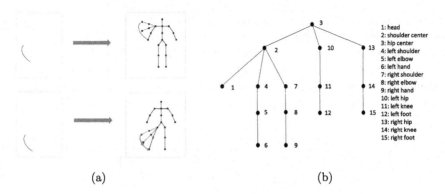

Fig. 3. (a) Two actions with the same motion pattern but different spatial coordinates. (b) An illustration of a joint tree. Each bone is represented as a path and each joint is represented by a node.

3.4   Timestamp Features

An action usually consists of several motion pieces. Different actions may have the same motion piece, but the locations on the time dimension of the motion piece are different. For instance, a motion piece appears at the beginning of action A, while appears at the end of another action B. Thus, the temporal locations of motion pieces could be used to discriminate different actions. To employ the time information for action recognition, in [9,16], space-time pyramids is proposed as a pooling step. However, the dimensions of features after pooling are much higher. In fact, the time that motion appears itself is discriminative. The success of Space-Time Extended Descriptor in 2D video action recognition [8] demonstrates the effectiveness by using the spatio-temporal locations to describe the distribution of features. In our approach, we directly use the temporal locations in our descriptor. The timestamp feature for motion $M_{t,t+1}^i$ in an action sequence is formulated as

$$T_{t+1}^i = (t+1)/N \ . \tag{7}$$

where N is the total number of frames of the corresponding action sequence.

3.5   Final MCTD Descriptor

Finally, by combining the motion, coordinate, and timestamp features, our descriptor for bone i at frame t in an action is formulated as

$$D_{t-1,t}^i = \{M_{t-1,t}^i, C_t^i, T_t^i\} \tag{8}$$

where N is total number of frames in the sequence. An action is then represented as

$$MCTS = \{D_{1,2}, D_{2,3}, ..., D_{N-1,N}\} \tag{9}$$

where

$$D_{t-1,t} = (D_{t-1,t}^1, D_{t-1,t}^2, \cdots, D_{t-1,t}^k)^{\mathrm{T}}. \tag{10}$$

4 Kernel Measures

In order to deal with the unreliable data and to measure the distances between the spatio-temporal coordinates exhaustively, we modify the kernel in [6] for classification. Given the MCTD descriptors of two action sequences M_1 and M_2 with k bones, let N_1 and N_2 be the numbers of frames respectively. The kernel can be formulated as

$$K(M_1, M_2) = \sum_{i=1}^{k} \sum_{t1=1}^{N_1} \sum_{t2=1}^{N_2} (G_{\sigma 1}(T_{t1}^i - T_{t2}^i)$$
$$+G_{\sigma 2}(C_{t1}^i - C_{t2}^i) + G_{\sigma 3}(t1/N_1 - t2/N_2))^3 \tag{11}$$

where G_{σ_1} captures the compatibility of motion, G_{σ_2} captures the compatibility of locations, and G_{σ_3} captures the time compatibility. The kernel could be approximated with the sum over Z pivots $\zeta_1, ..., \zeta_z$ according to the approach proposed in [7].

$$G_\sigma(u - v) \approx < \sqrt{c}\phi(u), \sqrt{c}\phi(v) > \tag{12}$$

$$\phi(u) = [G_{\sigma/\sqrt{2}}(u - \zeta_1), ..., G_{\sigma/\sqrt{2}}(u - \zeta_z)] \tag{13}$$

In order to utilize the relation of the translation and the coordinate, we put the three-order occurrence pooling on the kernel linearization. The Eigenvalue Power Normalization symbolized by g is then used to deal with burstiness, i.e. dealing with different lengths of the same action [7]. In this way, our kernel can be rewritten as:

$$K(M_1, M_2) = \sum_{i=1}^{k} \sum_{t1=1}^{N_1} \sum_{t2=1}^{N_2} (\begin{bmatrix} \phi(T_{t1}^i) \\ \phi(C_{t1}^i) \\ \phi(t_1/N_1) \end{bmatrix}^{\mathrm{T}} \cdot \begin{bmatrix} \phi(T_{t2}^i) \\ \phi(C_{t2}^i) \\ \phi(t_2/N_2) \end{bmatrix})^3$$

$$\approx \sum_{i=1}^{k} < g(\sum_{t1=1}^{N_1} \uparrow \otimes 3 \begin{bmatrix} \phi(T_{t1}^i) \\ \phi(C_{t1}^i) \\ \phi(t_1/N_1) \end{bmatrix}), g(\sum_{t2=2}^{N_2} \uparrow \otimes 3 \begin{bmatrix} \phi(T_{t2}^i) \\ \phi(C_{t2}^i) \\ \phi(t_2/N_2) \end{bmatrix}) > . \tag{14}$$

Finally, Support Vector Machine (SVM) with the above kernel is used for classification.

5 Experiments

5.1 Datasets

For experiments, we use three common databases: MSR-Action3D [10], MSR-Action Pairs [20], and G3D-Gaming [1].

MSR-Action3D Dataset: This dataset includes 557 action instances with 20 categories. 3D locations of 20 joints are provided. Each instance is performed two or three times by 10 different subjects. For experiments, we follow the cross-subject settings in [18]. Half of the subjects are used for training and another half for testing.

MSR-Action Pairs Dataset: This is a paired action dataset which consists of six action pairs such as *Lift a box/Place a box*, *Push a chair/Pull a chair*, etc. Each action is performed two or three times by 10 different subjects.

G3D-Gaming Dataset: This dataset includes 663 action instances. There are 20 different gaming actions performed three or more times by 10 subjects. The 3D locations of 20 joints are provided.

5.2 Experimental Settings and Results

Figure 4 shows the recognition accuracy with different parameter settings on MSR-Action 3D dataset. From Fig. 4(a), we can see that smaller σ_2, σ_3 would lead to slightly better results, while a larger σ_1 is better. Overall, the selection of these three parameters does not greatly affect the performances. In Fig. 4(b), Z_1, Z_2, Z_3 represent the numbers of pivots for approximating $G_{\sigma 1}(T_{t1}^i - T_{t2}^i)$,

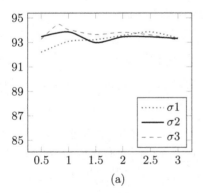 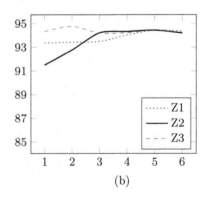

Fig. 4. (a) Recognition accuracy with different settings for σ_1, σ_2 and σ_3 on MSR-Action 3D dataset. (b) Recognition accuracy with different settings for Z_1, Z_2 and Z_3 on MSR-Action 3D dataset.

$G_{\sigma 2}(C_{t1}^i - C_{t2}^i)$, and $G_{\sigma 3}(t_1/N_1 - t_2/N_2)$. In our experiments, the pivots are distributed uniformly within the intervals of [-3:3], [-1:1], and [0:1]. From Fig. 4(b), we can see that different settings of Z_1 and Z_3 do not affect the performance much, while a larger Z_3 can lead to better performance. Table 1 shows all parameters for the best performances on three datasets.

Table 1. The parameters for the best performances on three datasets.

Dataset	γ_1	γ_2	σ_1	σ_2	σ_3	Z_1	Z_2	Z_3	Accuracy (%)
MSR-Action 3D	0.36	0.83	2.5	1	0.8	5	5	2	94.77
MSRAction Pair	0.36	0.86	0.5	1.5	1.5	2	4	6	97.73
G3D	0.36	0.90	3.5	1	2.3	5	5	6	91.21

Table 2. Comparison between our proposed MCTD descriptor with the state-of-the-art approaches. The performances are evaluated by the recognition accuracy (%).

	MSR-Action3D	MSR Pairs	G3D
Lie group [14]	89.48	93.65	–
Tensor representation [6]	91.45	–	-
RBM+HMM [12]	80.20	–	86.40
Rolling rotations [15]	–	94.67	90.94
Ours	**94.77**	**97.73**	**91.21**

Table 3. Actions for which the recognition accuracies are significantly improved with our approach. The numbers are the accuracies (%) of our approach versus the other approaches.

MSR-Action3D	MSR Pairs	G3D
draw circle (92.67 vs 64.00 [14])	pick up a box (97.33 vs 33.00 [18])	punch right (96.00 vs 93.00 [19])
High arm wave (83.00 vs 79.83 [14])	Put down a box (98.67 vs 47.00 [18])	Tennis swing forehand (68.67 vs 67.00 [19])
Hammer (82.00 vs 75.00 [14])	Take off hat (99.33 vs 40.00 [18])	Tennis serve (82.67 vs 80.00 [19])

Table 2 compares our approach to the state-of-the-art approaches. We can see that our approach outperforms the other approaches on all three datasets. Table 3 lists some actions for which the recognition accuracies are significantly improved with our approach on three datasets. As discussed in Sect. 1, by employing motion between different poses to represent action sequences, our proposed MCTD descriptor is more discriminative for recognizing different actions.

6   Conclusion

In this paper, we propose a new descriptor by employing the motion information along the pose sequences for 3D skeleton based action recognition. The spatial coordinates and temporal locations of the motion are used to describe the spatial-temporal distributions of motion. Our experiments on three common datasets demonstrate the effectiveness of our approach. For future work, we will model the relation of translation and space coordinate to better represent actions.

Acknowledgments. The work described in this paper was supported by the National Natural Science Foundation of China (No. 61103127 and No. 61375016).

References

1. Chaudhry, R., Ofli, F., Kurillo, G., Bajcsy, R., Vidal, R.: Bio-inspired dynamic 3D discriminative skeletal features for human action recognition. In: Conference on Computer Vision and Pattern Recognition Workshops, pp. 471–478 (2013)
2. Eweiwi, A., Cheema, M.S., Bauckhage, C., Gall, J.: Efficient pose-based action recognition. In: Cremers, D., Reid, I., Saito, H., Yang, M.-H. (eds.) ACCV 2014. LNCS, vol. 9007, pp. 428–443. Springer, Cham (2015). https://doi.org/10.1007/978-3-319-16814-2_28
3. Gavrila, D., Davis, L., et al.: Towards 3-D model-based tracking and recognition of human movement: a multi-view approach. In: International workshop on automatic face and gesture recognition, pp. 272–277. Citeseer (1995)
4. Hussein, M.E., Torki, M., Gowayyed, M.A., El-Saban, M.: Human action recognition using a temporal hierarchy of covariance descriptors on 3D joint locations. In: International Joint Conference on Artificial Intelligence IJCAI, vol. 13, pp. 2466–2472 (2013)
5. Johansson, G.: Visual perception of biological motion and a model for its analysis. Percept. psychophys. **14**(2), 201–211 (1973)
6. Koniusz, P., Cherian, A., Porikli, F.: Tensor representations via kernel linearization for action recognition from 3D skeletons. In: Leibe, B., Matas, J., Sebe, N., Welling, M. (eds.) ECCV 2016. LNCS, vol. 9908, pp. 37–53. Springer, Cham (2016). https://doi.org/10.1007/978-3-319-46493-0_3
7. Koniusz, P., Yan, F., Gosselin, P.H., Mikolajczyk, K.: Higher-order occurrence pooling for bags-of-words: visual concept detection. IEEE Trans. Pattern Anal. Mach. Intell. **39**(2), 313–326 (2017)
8. Lan, Z., Hauptmann, A.G.: Beyond spatial pyramid matching: space-time extended descriptor for action recognition. arXiv preprint arXiv:1510.04565 (2015)
9. Laptev, I., Marszalek, M., Schmid, C., Rozenfeld, B.: Learning realistic human actions from movies. In: IEEE Conference on Computer Vision and Pattern Recognition CVPR, pp. 1–8. IEEE (2008)
10. Li, W., Zhang, Z., Liu, Z.: Action recognition based on a bag of 3D points. In: IEEE Computer Society Conference on Computer Vision and Pattern Recognition Workshops, pp. 9–14. IEEE (2010)
11. Lv, F., Nevatia, R.: Recognition and segmentation of 3-D human action using HMM and multi-class AdaBoost. In: Leonardis, A., Bischof, H., Pinz, A. (eds.) ECCV 2006. LNCS, vol. 3954, pp. 359–372. Springer, Heidelberg (2006). https://doi.org/10.1007/11744085_28

12. Nie, S., Ji, Q.: Capturing global and local dynamics for human action recognition. In: International Conference on Pattern Recognition, pp. 1946–1951. IEEE (2014)
13. Shao, Z., Li, Y.: A new descriptor for multiple 3D motion trajectories recognition. In: IEEE International Conference on Robotics and Automation ICRA, pp. 4749–4754. IEEE (2013)
14. Vemulapalli, R., Arrate, F., Chellappa, R.: Human action recognition by representing 3D skeletons as points in a lie group. In: IEEE Conference on Computer Vision and Pattern Recognition (2014)
15. Vemulapalli, R., Chellapa, R.: Rolling rotations for recognizing human actions from 3D skeletal data. In: IEEE Conference on Computer Vision and Pattern Recognition, pp. 4471–4479 (2016)
16. Wang, J., Liu, Z., Wu, Y.: Learning Actionlet ensemble for 3D human action recognition. Human Action Recognition with Depth Cameras. SCS, pp. 11–40. Springer, Cham (2014). https://doi.org/10.1007/978-3-319-04561-0_2
17. Wang, J., Liu, Z., Wu, Y., Yuan, J.: Mining Actionlet ensemble for action recognition with depth cameras. In: IEEE Conference on Computer Vision and Pattern Recognition (CVPR), pp. 1290–1297. IEEE (2012)
18. Wang, P., Li, W., Ogunbona, P., Gao, Z., Zhang, H.: Mining mid-level features for action recognition based on effective skeleton representation. In: DICTA, pp. 1–8. IEEE (2014)
19. Wang, P., Li, Z., Hou, Y., Li, W.: Action recognition based on joint trajectory maps using convolutional neural networks. In: ACM on Multimedia Conference, pp. 102–106. ACM (2016)
20. Xia, L., Chen, C.C., Aggarwal, J.: View invariant human action recognition using histograms of 3D joints. In: IEEE Computer Society Conference on Computer Vision and Pattern Recognition Workshops (CVPRW), pp. 20–27. IEEE (2012)
21. Yang, X., Tian, Y.L.: Eigenjoints-based action recognition using naive-bayes-nearest-neighbor. In: Computer vision and pattern recognition workshops (CVPRW), pp. 14–19. IEEE (2012)

Dense Frame-to-Model SLAM
with an RGB-D Camera

Xiaodan Ye[1,2(✉)], Jianing Li[1,2], Lianghao Wang[1,2,3(✉)], Dongxiao Li[1,2],
and Ming Zhang[1,2]

[1] College of Information Science and Electronic Engineering,
Zhejiang University, Hangzhou, China
{yexiaodan,lijianing,wanglianghao,lidx,zhangm}@zju.edu.cn
[2] Zhejiang Provincial Key Laboratory of Information Processing,
Communication and Networking, Zhejiang, China
[3] State Key Lab for Novel Software Technology, Nanjing University, Nanjing, China

Abstract. In this paper, a dense frame-to-model Simultaneous Localization And Mapping (SLAM) with an RGB-D camera is proposed, which
achieves a more accurate trajectory in contrast to traditional frame-to-
model methods. In the frontend, dense photometric information and geometric information are combined to perform a more robust tracking. In
the backend, we add volume to loop closure detection to reject false loop.
A novel volume-camera pose graph is proposed to effectively reduce drift.
Experimental results on some RGB-D SLAM datasets show a reduction
of global trajectory error by 18.60% in comparison to Kinituous, 84.43%
in comparison to Kinfu.

Keywords: Frame-to-model · Dense · RGB-D · Graph optimization

1 Introduction

Simultaneous Localization And Mapping (SLAM) is one of the hottest topics
in multimedia research, which consists of two parts: frontend for tracking and
backend for loop optimization. Recently, RGB-D SLAM, as a branch of SLAM,
becomes a mainstream. In RGB-D SLAM, there were lots of methods proposed
for tracking, but most of them either utilized sparse feature or did not use
photometric information. To be specific, in some RGB-D SLAM systems [3],
camera tracking mainly relied on sparse features, while depth value of them was
only used for 3D-coordinate acquiring. On the other side, the performance of
dense tracking such as Kinect Fusion [10] and Point Cloud Library (PCL) [12]
is comparable to sparse tracking. Kinect Fusion is a well-known frame-to-model
method. However, it is only applicable for small scale scenes due to memory
limitation and only geometric information was used. To work in large scale scene,
operating region was extended by volume-shift in previous work [9] and main
idea was to minimize geometric error of 3D points using Iterative Closest Point

© Springer International Publishing AG, part of Springer Nature 2018
B. Zeng et al. (Eds.): PCM 2017, LNCS 10735, pp. 588–597, 2018.
https://doi.org/10.1007/978-3-319-77380-3_56

(ICP) [1]. Compared to sparse depth of features introduced in [3], frame-to-model method used dense depth, but photometric information was not applied.

It was proven that making full use of geometric and photometric information improved accuracy of trajectory [13]. Kerl [6] proposed a dense SLAM, which optimized both intensity and depth errors over every pixel frame-to-frame. But it was a frame-to-frame method that did not utilize previous frames. Whelan [15] fused previous frames to model, but its backend was complex.

In the backend, drift correction is a main challenge for a dense RGB-D SLAM. Drift is the accumulated error in trajectory. To correct drift, optimization is performed after loop closure detection. The error correction is distributed over the edge in the loop. Plenty of methods were proposed to reduce drift, but few of them took into account the map consistency and complexity. Some methods [2,6] built up a camera pose graph and optimized it using the general framework for graph optimization (g2o) [8], but map consistency is not considered. Whelan [15] added dense map points into the camera pose graph, but it was complex.

In this paper, a novel dense frame-to-model SLAM system using an RGB-D camera is proposed. In the frontend, this system tracks with dense photometric and dense geometric information. In the backend, multistage consistent loop closure detection and a novel volume-camera pose graph are proposed to effectively reduce drift. The pose graph consists of camera poses and volume poses, where the number of volume poses is not worthy mentioning compared to the number of map points. In this case, this method takes into account the map consistency and computational complexity. We add volume poses instead of dense depth point poses into the pose graph, effectively reducing the number of parameters and maintaining a better result. This method is tested on the widely used RGB-D benchmark with comparison to several state-of-the-art frame-to-model approaches. Experimental results demonstrate that this method achieves significant improvement on trajectory estimation.

In summary, the main contributions are two folds: (1) We use dense information in tracking part of this frame-to-model SLAM. Dense photometric and dense geometric information are utilized to improve the accuracy of trajectory. (2) We apply the volume to loop closure detection and pose graph optimization. False loop will be rejected after adding volume poses. The new volume-camera pose graph optimization improves accuracy of trajectory with limited complexity.

2   Proposed Method

Figure 1 shows the framework of the proposed dense frame-to-model SLAM.

In Sect. 2.1, where the frontend is introduced, photometric information and geometric information make the tracking more robust. In Sect. 2.2, where the backend is discussed, a volume-camera pose graph is presented. Loop closure is detected among key frames. Loop frame is linked to current frame with a red line in Fig. 1. Map is increased piece by piece as operating volume moves. The concept of operating volume comes from the previous work [9], referring to the local model where the current scene is. A operating volume is represented as a

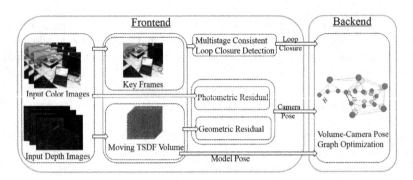

Fig. 1. Dense frame-to-model RGB-D SLAM framework.

graph vertex. Each operating volume is linked with the camera poses that belong to the volume. Adjacent operating volumes are linked as well.

2.1   Frame-to-Model Visual Odometry

Truncated Signed Distance Function (TSDF) volume consists of voxels. Each voxel stores a signed distance from the voxel to the surface and a weight value that shows the stability of the voxel. In our previous work [9], a moving TSDF volume is built for tracking part, which is the basis of this work.

In this work, when a image frame comes, $\mathcal{F}_k = \{V_k, N_k, W_k, I_k, H_k\}$ is obtained. k is the index of frame. $\mathcal{F}_k$ is represented as a reference model frame where I_k represents the k_{th} color image (640×480). Previous k frames are integrated in TSDF volume. Assume there are M pixels x_m ($m = 1, \ldots, M$) in the reference model frame, where x_m is a 2D point in image coordinate. Then corresponding 3D point P_m in the world coordinate is stored in Vertex map V_k, i.e. $P_m = V_k(x_m)$. Every 3D point P_m has a weight that is stored in W_k, i.e. $\omega_m = W_k(P_m)$. The corresponding normal vector is stored in normal map N_k, i.e. $n_m = N_k(P_m)$. H_k transforms the point from the camera coordinate to the world coordinate. H_k comprises a rotation matrix and a translation vector:

$$H_k = \begin{bmatrix} R_k & t_k \\ 0 & 1 \end{bmatrix}, \tag{1}$$

where R_k is a 3×3 rotational matrix and t_k is a 3×1 translational vector.

We aim to estimate H_k solely from color and depth image streams. Trajectory consists of camera poses and camera poses comes from H_k. A frame-to-model visual odometry based on geometric and photometric information is proposed to obtain a more robust trajectory.

Geometric Residual. With a reference model frame $\mathcal{F}_{k-1}$ got from the model, we match it with current color image I_k and depth image D_k to estimate H_k. For each pixel x_m ($m = 1, \ldots, M$) in I_{k-1}, its corresponding 3D point P_m defined in homogeneous coordinate is found in V_{k-1} and normal vector n_m in N_{k-1}.

Ideally the same point in image coordinate of D_k and D_{k-1} are equal. More robustly, error of point in camera coordinate of D_k and D_{k-1} can be defined as point-plane residual, i.e., the distance from P'_m to the plane where P_m is. P'_m is the corresponding 3D point of P_m in current camera coordinate. P'_m is a camera coordinate. Therefore, geometric residual can be computed as follows:

$$e_{m,icp}(H_k) \triangleq \left(H_k^{-1} P_m - \pi^{-1}\left(x'_m, Z\left(x'_m \right) \right) \right) R_k^{-1} n_m = \left(H_k^{-1} P_m - P'_m \right) R_k^{-1} n_m, \quad (2)$$

where $Z\left(x'_m \right)$ represents the depth value of x'_m. π is projection function from camera coordinate to image coordinate. P'_m is calculated using π^{-1}.

Photometric Residual. Method with only geometric information is likely to fail in little-structured scene. A 3D point has the same color in all frames as long as the sensor is noiseless, the scene is static and the illumination is constant. This is known as *photo-consistency*. Based on this principle, H_k is estimated by maximizing the photo-consistency between images, i.e. minimizing photometric residual. Given color images I_{k-1} and I_k, photometric residual can be obtained:

$$e_{m,rgb}(H_k) \triangleq I_k\left(x'_m \right) - I_{k-1}(x_m) = I_k\left(\pi\left(H_k^{-1} P_m \right) \right) - I_{k-1}(x_m). \quad (3)$$

Information Combination and Optimization. Subsequently, residuals in Eqs. (2) and (3) are combined as: $e_m(H_k) = [e_{m,icp}(H_k), e_{m,rgb}(H_k)]^T$. For simplicity, $e_m = [e_{m,icp}, e_{m,rgb}]^T$. $p(e_m|H_k)$ is the distribution of e_m and it depends on the noise probability conditioned on H_k. $p(e_m|H_k)$ follows a Gaussian distribution: $p(e_m|H_k) \sim N(0, \Sigma)$. When noise of each pixel is independent identically distributed (i.i.d), the problem turns to:

$$H_k^* = arg \min_{H_k} - \sum_m \log p(e_m|H_k) = arg \min_{H_k} \sum_m e_m^T \Sigma^{-1} e_m, \quad (4)$$

where Σ^{-1} is a information matrix. In contrast to traditional ICP method, varying noise is taken into account on the point extracted from model. Since P_m is updated from fusion volume, the points with less noise are more convincing. Therefore, weight coefficient is set from weight map W_k:

$$e_m = [\omega_m e_{m,icp}, e_{m,rgb}]^T, \quad (5)$$

where ω_m is $W_k(x_m)$ normalized by the average of W_k. $W_k(x_m)$ is the value of x_m in W_k. ω_m will be larger if the location is updated more and less noisy [9].

Note that our formulation is substantially different from previous ones [6]. Weight is obtained from volume, which varies as tracking goes. Weight is not constant and needs no extra complexity. If the volume is more stable, ω_m is larger and $e_{m,icp}$ is more convincing. The problem can be linearized and optimized. H_k^{-1} is a 4×4 matrix and there is a representation ξ given by the Lie algebra se(3) [7] associated with the Lie Group SE(3). ξ is a six-vector. H_k^{-1} is represented as: $H_k^{-1} \triangleq exp(\xi)$. We seek for motion parameter ξ that minimizes $f(\xi)$:

$$f(\xi) = \sum_m e_m(\xi)^T \Sigma^{-1} e_m(\xi).\tag{6}$$

Equation (6) is a nonlinear least-squares objective and Quasi-newton is chosen considering the compromise between accuracy and efficiency. After adding a slight disturbance $\Delta\xi$ to ξ, normal equations of minimizing $f(\xi)$ are:

$$\sum_m \left(J_m^T \Sigma^{-1} J_m\right) \Delta\xi = -\sum_m J_m^T \Sigma^{-1} e_m(\xi),\tag{7}$$

where J_m is the combination of $J_{m,rgb}$ and $J_{m,icp}$. $J_{m,rgb}$ and $J_{m,icp}$ are 2×6 Jacobian matrices of $e_{m,rgb}(\xi)$ and $e_{m,icp}(\xi)$, respectively. In order to adapt to rapid movements of camera, a three-layer image pyramid for coarse-to-fine hierarchical matching is built. Pyramid is applied to both color and depth images. Several iterations are performed for each image. H_k is updated in each iteration and used as initial value for next iteration. Figure 2 shows three level coarse-to-fine residual images on fr1/room dataset. The finer and clearer the edge is, the smaller the error is. This figure shows that this method reduces the error.

2.2   Loop Closure Optimization

Visual odometry inherently accumulates drift because there is always a small error in estimation of H_k. The error is caused by the noise of camera and the inaccuracy of model. To deal with drift, a novel loop closure optimization is proposed. When the camera revisits the same place and the revisiting is identified, an additional constraint can be established to reduce the drift. The constraint is *loop closure*. The loop closure optimization includes three steps: choosing key frames, detecting loop closure, optimizing camera poses and map pieces.

Choose Key Frames. There are three strategies adopted for key frames choosing: (1) Current frame is added as a new key frame if the norm of rotational or translational distance between current frame and the previous one exceeds a certain threshold. (2) If the nearest N frames are not chosen as key frames, current frame is added as key frame. (3) If the similarity of current frame against every key frame is smaller than a certain threshold, current frame is regarded as a key frame. The computation of the similarity is introduced in the next section.

Detect Loop Closure. To detect loop closure, a multistage consistent detection is employed, where the model plays an important role.

Firstly, one of the appearance based methods: the bag of words is adopted [4,5]. A codebook is computed based on a given image set. Each column of the codebook can be interpreted as a visual vocabulary. Then every image can

(a) RGB-D image(640×480)   (b) Initial residual   (c) Residual after iterations

Fig. 2. (a) is a color image and corresponding reconstructed model surface. (b)–(c) shows the initial and final residual images of three levels coarse-to-fine method on fr1/room. Top row of (b)–(c) is photometric residual and bottom row is geometric residual.

be represented by the vocabularies of the codebook. Bag of words vector B_i of current color image is got and the similarity $s\left(B_i, B_{k_t}\right)$ for every key frame $B_{k_t} \in \left\{B_{k_1}, \ldots, B_{k_k}\right\}$ is computed. Then the most similar frame B_{k_j} and the highest score $s\left(B_i, B_{k_j}\right)$ can be obtained. It is more robust to normalize the highest score to the similarity score of the most recently key frame $s\left(B_i, B_{k_k}\right)$:

$$\eta\left(B_i, B_{k_j}\right) = s\left(B_i, B_{k_j}\right)/s\left(B_i, B_{k_k}\right). \tag{8}$$

Large loop closure is more conducive to drift reduction. Normalized similarity can effectively eliminate loop frames that are too close. When η is greater than the threshold, the frame is a loop frame candidate and sent to the next step.

Afterwards, transformation matrix H_{loop} from current frame to the loop frame candidate is coarsely estimated with Random Sample Consensus (RANSAC) after feature extraction and matching. If there are enough inliers and features, the transformation matrix is reserved. On feature extraction, binary features that are competitively robust and less time-consumed have been widely adopted for loop closure detection. Hence Oriented Brief (ORB) [11] is adopted.

The transformation matrix H_{loop} obtained in the previous step is rather crude, which can be regarded as an initial value. The coarse initial matrix H_{loop} will be further optimized. The frame-to-model method mentioned in Sect. 2 will generate a reference model frame $\mathcal{F}_{loop}$ for loop frame candidate. $\mathcal{F}_{loop}$ is more stable than a single captured frame and it reflects the benefit of frame-to-model system. We utilize $\mathcal{F}_{loop}$ to estimate precise H_{loop} with the same method as Sect. 2.1. If $J_m^T \Sigma^{-1} J_m$ from the Eq. (7) is reversible, precise H_{loop} can be got iteratively, otherwise the loop closure is rejected.

Optimize Camera Poses and Map Pieces. Final step is to optimize camera poses and map pieces with the loop constraint. The volume-camera pose graph optimization framework is shown in the backend part of Fig. 1, which has been introduced in the beginning of Sect. 2.

To correct the accumulated error of trajectory, the optimization is performed after loop closure detection. The correction is distributed over the edge in the loop. A wrong loop closure will increase the error. Adding operating volumes to the graph can curb the error from the false loop.

As described above, volume-based pose graph composes two kinds of vertices: camera pose vertex and operating volume pose vertex. An operating volume corresponds to several camera poses, so the operating volume and its corresponding camera poses are linked with edges. When operating volume shifts, a new operating volume is got and these two adjacent volumes are linked with an edge.

Traditional key-frame-based SLAM takes each key frame as a vertex and takes the transformation between adjacent key frames as an edge. Different from that, three constraints are obtained in the volume-camera pose graph: constraint between adjacent key frames, constraint between adjacent operating volumes, constraint between operating volume and its corresponding key frames. Constraint between adjacent key frames and constraint between operating volume and its corresponding key frames unify all camera poses error of key frames under the same operating volume on the local model. As a result, accumulated errors are suppressed. Note that the reconstructed map is a combination of map pieces from different operating volumes. Camera poses before optimization are estimated by the model frame. Each map piece is generated by fused TSDF volume and map pieces are continuous. But there are cracks among map pieces after optimization. Constraint between adjacent operating volumes allows optimized operating volumes continuous, preventing cracks between map pieces. To get a globally consistent trajectory, the pose graph is optimized with g2o [8].

3   Experiment

In the experiment, RGB-D benchmark provided by the Technical University of Munich [14] is used to evaluate the performance of proposed method and two state-of-the-art methods. The benchmark provides synchronized ground truth poses of the sensor captured by a highly precise motion capture system.

3.1   Evaluation on Global Trajectory

Our dense frame-to-model RGB-D SLAM is compared to some state-of-the-art frame-to-model methods on nine datasets. In trajectory estimation performance, the method is compared to Kintinuous [15] and Kinfu [12]. Table 1 summarizes the Absolute Trajectory Errors (ATE) obtained by these three methods including ours. The first column contains names of the datasets, the second, third and fifth columns show the Root Mean Square Error (RMSE) of ATE for different methods. On these nine sequences, our method improves the performance by 18.60% in comparison to Kintinuous, 84.43% in comparison to kinfu. Overall, our method outperforms other leading frame-to-model approaches. Note that Kinfu is developed by PCL organization based on Kinect Fusion. Kintinuous is one of the state-of-the-art frame-to-model SLAMs.

Table 1. RMSE of ATE for some state-of-the-art frame-to-model systems on nine datasets. All units are given in meters.

Dataset	Kinfu [12]	Kintinuous [15]	Ours-no-loop-closure-optimization	Ours
fr1/rpy	0.133	0.031	0.046	0.026
fr1/desk2	0.420	0.075	0.107	0.050
fr1/xyz	0.026	0.018	0.020	0.015
fr1/room	0.313	0.081	0.186	0.063
fr1/desk	0.057	0.041	0.070	0.040
fr1/plant	0.598	0.050	0.092	0.048
fr2/desk	0.170	0.038	0.132	0.034
fr2/xyz	0.034	0.034	0.034	0.020
fr3/long	-	0.033	0.084	0.030
Average	0.2189	0.0446	0.086	0.0363

3.2 Performance Analysis of Two Contributions

The first contribution is that the tracking part is frame-to-model with dense information, where both dense photometric and dense geometric information are utilized to improve the accuracy of trajectory. Table 2 shows the results of the method on different scenes. Results of tracking with photometric only, geometric only and photometric and geometric combined methods are listed in the table. It can be seen that photometric and geometric combined method works the best.

Table 2. Comparison of photometric, geometric and combined methods based on the RMSE of ATE. All units are given in meters.

Dataset	Photometric	Geometric	Photometric+Geometric
fr3/st-near	0.1365	0.0943	0.0454
fr3/st-far	0.0943	0.0754	0.0419

The second contribution is that volume is applied to loop closure detection and pose graph optimization. The new loop closure detection method and volume-camera pose graph optimization improve accuracy of trajectory with limited increase of complexity. Table 3 and part of Table 1 show the improvement. Table 1 shows that the method with loop optimization improves the performance by 58.14% in comparison to no-loop-closure-optimization method. It shows that loop closure detection and volume-camera graph optimization are very effective. Since Kintinuous [15] did not give the evaluation of no-loop-closure-optimization, the effectiveness of our tracking part and loop optimization part cannot be compared to theirs, respectively. But one thing is for sure, combination of our contributions outperforms Kintinuous [15]. In order to evaluate the benefit of the volume-camera pose optimization in detail, we compare the performance of no-loop-closure–optimization, only-camera-pose-graph-optimization and volume-camera-graph-optimization. Results of evaluation on fr1/room dataset are listed in Table 3. The volume-camera achieves significant improvement in RMSE, min error and max error of ATE. For RMSE, volume-camera-graph-optimization improves the performance by 65.05% in comparison to no-loop-optimization, 28.57% in comparison to only-camera-pose-graph-optimization. Figure 3 shows the measured trajectory errors using hessian uncertainty method [14]. Figure 3 supports the conclusion of Table 3, where volume-camera graph optimization achieves the most accurate trajectory. The two stages of our method are both effective and improve accuracy of trajectory significantly.

Table 3. RMSE, min error, max error of ATE with different backend methods. All units are given in meters.

	RMSE	Min	Max
No-loop-closure-optimization	0.186	0.059	0.364
Only-camera-pose-graph-optimization	0.091	0.008	0.184
Volume-camera graph optimization	0.065	0.008	0.125

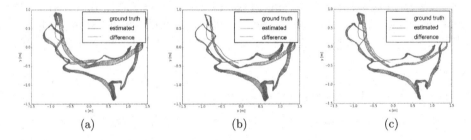

| (a) | (b) | (c) |

Fig. 3. ATE Trajectory error on dataset fr1/room. From (a) to (c) are the results of no-loop-closure-optimization, only-camera-pose-graph-optimization and our volume-camera graph optimization, respectively.

4   Conclusion

In this paper, a dense frame-to-model RGB-D SLAM that combines geometric and photometric information is proposed. A novel loop closure detection and volume-camera pose graph optimization effectively reduce drift. In experiments on publicly available datasets, this method outperforms other state-of-the-art frame-to-model methods, and both of our contributions are effective. Our method yields a reduction of global trajectory error by 18.60% in comparison to Kinituous, 84.43% in comparison to Kinfu.

Acknowledgments. This work is supported in part by the National Natural Science Foundation of China (Grant No. 61401390).

References

1. Besl, P.J., McKay, N.D.: A method for registration of 3-D shapes. IEEE Trans. Pattern Anal. Mach. Intell. **14**(2), 239–256 (1992)
2. Endres, F., Hess, J., Engelhard, N., Sturm, J., Cremers, D., Burgard, W.: An evaluation of the RGB-D SLAM system. In: 2012 IEEE International Conference on Robotics and Automation, pp. 1691–1696 (2012)
3. Endres, F., Hess, J., Sturm, J., Cremers, D., Burgard, W.: 3-D mapping with an RGB-D camera. IEEE Trans. Rob. **30**(1), 177–187 (2014)
4. Galvez-López, D., Tardos, J.D.: Bags of binary words for fast place recognition in image sequences. IEEE Trans. Rob. **28**(5), 1188–1197 (2012)
5. Glvez-López, D., Tards, J.D.: Real-time loop detection with bags of binary words. In: 2011 IEEE/RSJ International Conference on Intelligent Robots and Systems, pp. 51–58 (2011)
6. Kerl, C., Sturm, J., Cremers, D.: Dense visual SLAM for RGB-D cameras. In: 2013 IEEE/RSJ International Conference on Intelligent Robots and Systems, pp. 2100–2106 (2013)
7. Kerl, C., Sturm, J., Cremers, D.: Robust odometry estimation for RGB-D cameras. In: 2013 IEEE International Conference on Robotics and Automation, pp. 3748–3754 (2013)
8. Kümmerle, R., Grisetti, G., Strasdat, H., Konolige, K., Burgard, W.: G2o: a general framework for graph optimization. In: 2011 IEEE International Conference on Robotics and Automation, pp. 3607–3613 (2011)
9. Li, J.N., Wang, L.H., Li, Y., Zhang, J.F., Li, D.X., Zhang, M.: Local optimized and scalable frame-to-model SLAM. Multimedia Tools Appl. **75**(14), 8675–8694 (2016)
10. Newcombe, R.A., Izadi, S., Hilliges, O., Molyneaux, D., Kim, D., Davison, A.J., Kohi, P., Shotton, J., Hodges, S., Fitzgibbon, A.: KinectFusion: real-time dense surface mapping and tracking. In: 2011 10th IEEE International Symposium on Mixed and Augmented Reality, pp. 127–136 (2011)
11. Rublee, E., Rabaud, V., Konolige, K., Bradski, G.: ORB: An efficient alternative to sift or surf. In: 2011 International Conference on Computer Vision, pp. 2564–2571 (2011)
12. Rusu, R.B., Cousins, S.: 3D is here: Point cloud library (PCL), pp. 1–4 (2011)
13. Stückler, J., Behnke, S.: Integrating depth and color cues for dense multi-resolution scene mapping using RGB-D cameras. In: 2012 IEEE International Conference on Multisensor Fusion and Integration for Intelligent Systems (MFI), pp. 162–167 (2012)
14. Sturm, J., Engelhard, N., Endres, F., Burgard, W., Cremers, D.: A benchmark for the evaluation of RGB-D SLAM systems. In: 2012 IEEE/RSJ International Conference on Intelligent Robots and Systems, pp. 573–580 (2012)
15. Whelan, T., Kaess, M., Johannsson, H., Fallon, M., Leonard, J.J., McDonald, J.: Real-time large-scale dense RGB-D SLAM with volumetric fusion. Int. J. Robot. Res. **34**(4–5), 598–626 (2015)

Parallax-Robust Hexahedral Panoramic Video Stitching

Sha Guo, Ronggang Wang$^{(\boxtimes)}$, Xiubao Jiang, Zhenyu Wang, and Wen Gao

Shenzhen Graduate School, Peking University, Shenzhen 518055, China
rgwang@pkusz.edu.cn

Abstract. In this paper, we present a parallax-robust hexahedral panoramic video stitching method. An efficient three-stage stitching procedure is proposed. In the preprocessing stage, layered feature points matching strategy extracts feature matches lying in different depth layers. In the rough alignment stage, based on the first layer of feature matches, global projective warping estimates and refines camera parameters by considering the constraints among all cameras to avoid accumulated errors. With camera parameters, image pixels are roughly mapped onto a spherical surface. In the refined alignment stage, based on multiple layers of feature matches, layered content-preserving warping further aligns abundant feature pairs exploited from multiple depth layers, so as to alleviate ghosting caused by large parallax. Experimental results show that our method can effectively stitch panoramic video without noticeable parallax errors.

Keywords: Hexahedral panoramic stitching · Video stitching
Layered content-preserving warping

1 Introduction

A panoramic video records omni-directional lights from the surrounding environment, which allows viewers to interactively look around the scene, providing a strong sense of presence. This potential change of the viewing paradigm inspires content creators to produce panoramic video. Several freewares and commercial softwares are available for panoramic video stitching, such as AutoStitch[1] and Kolor Autopano[2].

One of the most popular methods utilizes a structured hexahedral panoramic rig and multiple wide-angle cameras (*e.g.* GoPro, see Fig. 1(a)) to capture images of different views. Then panoramic stitching algorithms follow to stitch captured

---

S. Guo—Thanks to National Natural Science Foundation of China 61672063, 61370115, China 863 project of 2015AA015905, Shenzhen Peacock Plan, Shenzhen Research Projects of JCYJ20160506172227337 and GGFW2017041215130858, and Guangdong Province Projects of 2014B010117007 and 2014B090910001 for funding.

[1] http://matthewalunbrown.com/autostitch/autostitch.html.
[2] http://www.kolor.com.

© Springer International Publishing AG, part of Springer Nature 2018
B. Zeng et al. (Eds.): PCM 2017, LNCS 10735, pp. 598–608, 2018.
https://doi.org/10.1007/978-3-319-77380-3_57

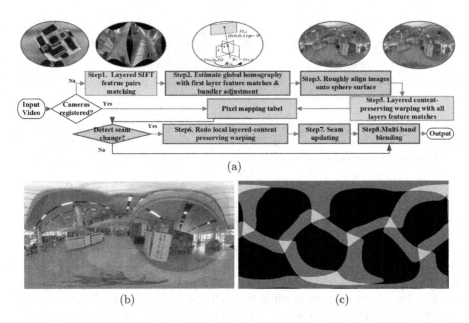

(a)

(b)   (c)

Fig. 1. (a) The pipeline of our proposed method. (b) Roughly aligned panoramic result, which is rendered on a spherical surface and expanded as a latitude-longitude image. (c) The non-overlapping region and the overlapping region in (b) are filled with black and gray, respectively.

images. Since more than half of the areas are non-overlapping in images captured by hexahedral panoramic rig (see Fig. 1(c)), algorithms based on optical flow estimation, such as Facebook Surround360[3] and Jump [1], are not applicable in this scenario. Other panoramic stitching pipelines, such as AutoStitch (See footnote 2) and Automatic Panoramic Stitching [2], solve stitching problem by estimating a 2D perspective warp (typically 3×3 homography matrix) to align the input images. However, Homography alignment is correct only if the scene is planar or the views differ only by rotation [8]. In practice, such conditions are usually hard to satisfy. Therefore, global homography based image stitching algorithms can not account for parallax errors. Recent studies use spatially-varying warping to handle parallax [3,10,11]. These methods generally divide image into mesh grids and perform flexible warping in each mesh cell. Zhang [11] adopted content-preserving warping to provide flexibility for handling parallax, but this method stitches images one by one using local aligned homography. This disregards multiple constraints between images, and therefore causes accumulated errors. Besides, spatially-varying warping relies on a set of feature correspondences computed by SIFT. However, different from common stitching data sets[4], the hexahedral panoramic rig offers quite narrow overlap regions

---

[3] https://github.com/facebook/Surround360.
[4] http://cs.adelaide.edu.au/~tjchin/apap/#Datasets.

(a)   (b)

Fig. 2. An example of ghosting artifacts caused by parallax. (a) For images with large parallax and repeated textures, spatially varying methods like APAP [10] fail to align the image. (b) Our method generates a well-aligned result.

(See Fig. 1(c)) and thus provides very few feature point pairs, especially in scenes with smooth or repeated textures (*e.g.* sky and ceiling). This adversely affects the result (See Fig. 2(a)).

In this paper, we propose an efficient parallax-robust hexahedral panoramic video stitching method, which consists of three stage. Firstly, because the overlapping region is narrow, we utilize layered feature point matching to extract as many feature point pairs as possible. Secondly, based on the first layer of feature matches, we adopt global projective warping to calculate the position and orientation of cameras. This takes constraints among all cameras into account to avoid accumulated errors. Finally, based on multiple layers of feature matches, we utilize a layered content-preserving warping method to alleviate parallax errors. Experimental results testify the effectiveness of our proposed method over state-of-the-art methods.

2 Proposed Approach

Given initial frames, we first extract feature matches lying in different depth layers. Based on the first layer of feature matches, we work out extrinsic and intrinsic parameters of all the six cameras. Then image pixels are mapped to 3D coordinates and roughly aligned onto a spherical surface. Finally, based on multiple layers of feature matches, we refine alignment utilizing layered content-preserving. The pipeline of our proposed method is shown in Fig. 1(a).

2.1 Layered Feature Points Matching

Inspired by Gao [3] and He [4], we assume that different objects in a scene usually lie in different depth layers, and the objects in the same layer (plane) shall be consistent with each other in a homography transformation. Based on this, we replace single layer homography in typical stitching pipeline with layered homography (See Fig. 3(b)).

Taking two adjacent images I_1 and I_2 for example, We extract the matched feature point pairs $P = \{(p_i^1, p_i^2)\}_{i=1}^{N}$ using a kd-tree, where p_i^1 and p_i^2 mean the coordinate of the i-th matched feature point from I_1 and I_2 respectively.

(a)   (b)   (c)

Fig. 3. Example of improving alignment using our method. (a) Alignment result of global homography. (b) Layered matched feature pairs, different colors indicate different layers. (c) Refined result with layered content preserving warping. (Color figure online)

Given the matched feature pairs, we iteratively utilize Random Sample Consensus (RANSAC) algorithm to robustly group the feature pairs into different layers. Denote the matched feature pairs of layer m as L_m and its corresponding homography as H_m. For each layer, there are a set of feature point pairs that are geometrically consistent with H_m (RANSAC inliers) while others not (RANSAC outliers). To guarantee the H_m correct, Eq. 1 gives a probabilistic model using the same method as [2].

$$p(H_m iscorrect) = \frac{n_i^m}{\alpha + \beta n_f^m}, \tag{1}$$

where $p(H_m iscorrect)$ is the probability of finding the correct homography, n_f^m is the total number of feature point pairs in L_m, n_i^m is the number of inlier, $\alpha = 8.0$, $\beta = 0.3$. Layers whose probability is smaller than threshold $t_{min} = 0.8$ are simply dropped. The detailed layered feature point pairs match process is presented in Algorithm 1.

Algorithm 1. Layered feature points matching

Require: Initial pair set $P_1 = P$, iteration index $m = 0$;
Ensure: Each layers matching feature pair set L_m;
1: **repeat**$m \leftarrow m + 1$
2:     RANSAC in pair set P_m for model $\{p_i^1 = Hp_i^2\}_{i=1}^N$, where $(p_i^1, p_i^2) \in P_m$;
3:     Divide outliers V_{out} and inliers V_{in} according to H_m;
4:     **if** $p(H_m iscorrect) \geqslant t_{min}$ **then**
5:         Set matching pair set of m-th layer as $L_m = V_{in}$;
6:         Set homography of the m-th layer as $H_m = H$;
7:     **end if**
8:     Set the pair set of next iteration as $P_{m+1} = V_{out}$;
9: **until** $p(H_m iscorrect) \leqslant t_{min}$

2.2   Global Projective Warping

It is well studied [8] that a 3D point $p = (X, Y, Z, 1)$ gets mapped to an image coordinate $\hat{x}_0 = (x, y, 1, d_0)$ in camera 0 through the combination of a 3D rigid-body motion E_0,

$$x_0 = \begin{bmatrix} R_0 & t_0 \\ 0^T & 1 \end{bmatrix} p = E_0 p, \tag{2}$$

and a perspective projection P_0,

$$\hat{x}_0 \sim \begin{bmatrix} f_0 & & \\ & f_0 & \\ & & 1 \\ & & & 1 \end{bmatrix} E_0 p \sim \begin{bmatrix} K_0 & 0 \\ 0^T & 1 \end{bmatrix} E_0 p \sim P_0 E_0 p, \tag{3}$$

where R_0 and t_0 are the rotation matrix and translation matrix of camera0 extrinsic parameters, respectively; K_0 is the matrix of camera0 intrinsic parameters; f_0 is the focal of camera0; d_0 is the depth of pixel $\hat{x}_0$.

Theoretically, we can calculate the 3D coordinates of a scene by triangulation of corresponding feature matches, using the geometry of the two cameras. However, most visual field is not overlapping in images captured by the hexahedral panoramic rig. As shown in Fig. 1(c), the black filled area denotes the non-overlapping area, whose 3D coordinates can not be calculated by triangulation. Thus, we assume 3D scene is planar and replace the last row of E_0 in Eq. 2 with a genera plane equation, $\hat{n}_0 \cdot p + c_0 = 0$ that maps points on the plane to image pixels $d_0 = 0$. The mapping equation Eq. 3 thus reduces to

$$\hat{x}_0 \sim K_0 R_0 p. \tag{4}$$

Since we know the z-buffer value d_0 is 0, we can map an image pixel $\hat{x}_0 = (x, y, 1, d_0)$ back to a 3D coordinate p using

$$p \sim R_0^{-1} K_0^{-1} \hat{x}_0, \tag{5}$$

and then project it into adjacent image captured by camera1

$$\hat{x}_1 \sim K_1 R_1 R_0^{-1} K_0^{-1} \hat{x}_0 \sim K_1 R_{10} K_0^{-1} \hat{x}_0 \sim H_{10} \hat{x}_0, \tag{6}$$

where H_{10} is a general 3×3 homography matrix, which can be calculated by the first layer of feature matches L_1 according to Algorithm 1.

From Eq. 6 we obtain

$$R_{10} \sim K_1^{-1} H_{10} K_0 \sim \begin{bmatrix} h_{00} & h_{01} & f_0^- 1 h_{02} \\ h_{10} & h_{11} & f_0^- 1 h_{12} \\ f_1 h_{20} & f_1 h_{21} & f_0^{-1} f_1 h_{22} \end{bmatrix}. \tag{7}$$

Using the orthonormality properties of the rotation matrix R_{10}, we can calculate f_0, f_1 and R_{10}. Take camera0 as a reference, we then define $R_0 = \begin{bmatrix} 1 & & \\ & 1 & \\ & & 1 \end{bmatrix}$, and thus calculate R_1 according to $R_{10} = R_1 R_0^{-1}$. In the same method, we work out extrinsic and intrinsic parameters of all the six cameras. Then bundler adjustment [9] is employed to refine the intrinsic and extrinsic parameters.

With the solved intrinsic and extrinsic parameters, image pixels can be mapped back to 3D coordinates according to Eq. 5.

Then we render the roughly aligned panorama. In our hexahedral panoramic rig, the final panorama includes a full sphere of views, so we project 3D coordinates onto a spherical surface. In this case, the sphere is parameterized by two angles (θ, ϕ), with 3D spherical coordinates given by

$$(sin\theta cos\phi, sin\phi, cos\theta cos\phi) \propto (X, Y, Z), \tag{8}$$

as shown in Fig. 4. For the sake of watching, the spherical surface is expanded as a latitude-longitude image. The correspondence between coordinates is given by

$$x' = s\theta = s \cdot tan^{-1}\frac{X}{Z}, \tag{9}$$

$$y' = s\phi = s \cdot tan^{-1}\frac{Y}{\sqrt{X^2 + Z^2}}, \tag{10}$$

where (x', y') is the latitude-longitude image coordinate and (X,Y,Z) is the 3D coordinate. Figures 1(b) and 3(a) show the roughly aligned result, which can be refined by content-preserving warping.

Before content-preserving warping, we should discard erroneous matches in feature point pairs acquired by Algorithm 1. One or two erroneous matches can adversely influence the performance of spatially-varying warping [10,11]. Thanks to the global projective warping, we can distinguish erroneous matches whose Euclidean distance is larger than a threshold in the roughly aligned images.

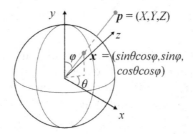

Fig. 4. Projection from 3D coordinates to spherical coordinates

2.3 Layered Content-Preserving Warping

After global projective warping, some feature pairs from multiple layers are still not aligned perfectly, as shown in Fig. 3(b). Therefore, we employ content-preserving warping to refine the alignment.

We use I and $\hat{I}$ to denote the roughly aligned image and the refined image with content-preserving warping, respectively. We divide I into $M \times N$ uniform grids. The vertices in I and $\hat{I}$ are denoted by v and $\hat{v}$, respectively. Then the content-preserving is formulated as an optimization problem that aims to align multiple layer feature pairs in I into their corresponding positions in adjacent images, so that they can be well aligned. $\hat{v}$ are the unknowns in this problem.

For each feature point p_i^k in the i-th image I_i, we find the mesh cell contains it and present it using a liner combination of the four cell vertices of corresponding mesh cell in the image I_i. The linear combination coefficients are computed using the inverse bi-linear interpolation method. These coefficients $\alpha_{m,i}^k$ can be used to combine the vertices in the output image $\hat{I}_i$ to compute $\hat{p}_i^k$.

Our content-preserving warping aims to align p_i^k in I_i to the corresponding point p_j^k in I_j, where I_i and I_j are adjacent to each other. The alignment term is formulated as follows.

$$
\begin{aligned}
E_p &= \sum_{i=1}^{n-1} \sum_{j=i+1}^{n} N_{ij} \sum_{k} \left\| \hat{p}_i^k - \hat{p}_j^k \right\|^2, \\
&= \sum_{i=1}^{n-1} \sum_{j=i+1}^{n} N_{ij} \sum_{k} \sum_{m=1}^{4} \left\| \alpha_{m,i}^k \hat{v}_{m,i} - \alpha_{m,j}^k \hat{v}_{m,j} \right\|^2,
\end{aligned}
\tag{11}
$$

where n is the number of images, k is the total number of feature pairs gathered from multiple layers, $\alpha_{m,i}^k$ and $\alpha_{m,j}^k$ are the bi-linear combination coefficient, $\hat{v}_{m,i}$ and $\hat{v}_{m,j}$ are the vertices of the mesh grid that contain $\hat{p}_i^k$ and $\hat{p}_j^k$. If image $\hat{I}_i$ is adjacent to $\hat{I}_j$, $N_{ij} = 1$; otherwise, $N_{ij} = 0$.

For regions without matched feature pairs, our method maintains vertices of mesh cell in $\hat{I}$ to be as close to I as possible, which is described as follows.

$$
E_g = \gamma \sum_{i} \left\| v_i - \hat{v}_i \right\|^2,
\tag{12}
$$

where v_i and $\hat{v}_i$ are the corresponding vertices in I and $\hat{I}$. If there is no feature point in the neighborhood of v_i, $\gamma = 1$; otherwise, $\gamma = 0$.

To smoothen the local distortion during warping, we add a similarity transformation term [5] that has been widely employed as a metric for local shape distortions,

$$
E_s = \eta \sum_{i} \left\| \hat{v}_{i,1} - (\hat{v}_{i,2} + u(\hat{v}_{i,3} - \hat{v}_{i,2}) + w R_{90}(\hat{v}_{i,3} - \hat{v}_{i,2})) \right\|^2,
\tag{13}
$$

where $(\hat{v}_{i,1}, \hat{v}_{i,2}, \hat{v}_{i,3})$ denote the vertices comprising a triangle and R_{90} is a $90°$ rotation matrix. u and w are computed from the initial uniform mesh in I. η is the weight for similarity transformation term of each triangle using the same method as [5].

In order to prevent visible jitter in temporal domain, the following energy function is added, which takes temporal smoothness into account.

$$E_t = \sum_i \left\| \hat{v}_i^t - \frac{1}{t_w} \sum_{j \in T(i,t)} \hat{v}_j \right\|^2, \tag{14}$$

where t_w is the temporal window size and $T(i,t)$ denotes a set of indices to the temporal neighbor vertices of v_i^t from $t - t_w$ to t. t_w is set to 5 in our experiments.

Finally, we combine the sum of the above energies into the following energy minimization problem

$$E = \arg \min E_p + \alpha E_g + \beta E_s + \theta E_t, \tag{15}$$

where the weight of α, β and θ are set to 0.01, 0.005, 0.01 respectively. Equation 15 is solved to get the mesh grid coordinates. We use these coordinates for rendering the final panoramic result and store them in an index table to be re-used in rendering the following frames.

2.4   Postprocessing

After content-preserving warping, the panoramic video is overall pre-aligned. We adopt the graph-cut seam finding method [6] to relieve artifacts. After seam-cutting, we perform multi-band blending and exposure adjustment [8] to create a seamless panoramic image.

3   Experiments

To evaluate the performance of our proposed video stitching method, we conduct both qualitative and quantitative experiments. The inputs are 2704×2028 fisheye videos captured by hexahedral panoramic rig. Before experiments, we utilize algorithm [7] to correct the geometrical distortion.

3.1   Qualitative Comparison

To evaluate the proposed layered content-preserving algorithm, we compared our method to two state-of-the-art methods of APAP [10] and Kolor Autopano Giga (See footnote 2) in Fig. 5(a)–(f).

APAP [10] applies spatially-varying warping but highly depends on the performance of the feature point pairs. In Fig. 2(a), the repeated patterns on the floor disturb the result of APAP [10]. In green and blue box of Fig. 5(d), APAP [10] suffers from structural distortion caused by erroneous matches. APAP [10] can neither handle large parallax when it lacks of sufficient point matches, as shown in blue box of Fig. 5(a) and purple box of Fig. 5(d).

Fig. 5. Comparisons among APAP, Kolor Autopano Giga (See footnote 2), and Our method (Correspondences are color-coded). (Color figure online)

Kolor Autopano Giga (See footnote 2) is a state-of-the-art commercial software in image stitching. However, it is not robust enough to account for indoor large parallax and causes apparent ghosting, as indicated by the red circle in Fig. 5(b) and (e).

Our method combines the advantages of both global projective warping and content preserving warping. We preserve image structures, explore abundant feature pairs from multiple layers and align them through content-preserving warping. From Fig. 5(c) and (f) we can see that the stitching results of our algorithm are more visually pleasing than others.

3.2   Quantitative Comparison

We compute the root mean square error (RMSE) on matched points in the final warped result of APAP [10], Kolor Autopano (See footnote 2) and our method, respectively. For a fair comparison, we use the same matched points extracted from Kolor Autopano (See footnote 2). Table 1 shows that APAP [10] performs generally better than Kolor in Figs. 1(a, b) and 5(a, b, c), but it makes an apparent error in Fig. 5(d), which results from the wrong feature point matches. The result indicates that our method outperforms other two methods.

Table 1. Quantitative evaluation (pixel unit).

Datasets	APAP	Kolor Autopano Giga	Ours
Figure 1(a, b)	3.56	3.72	**2.09**
Figure 5(a, b, c)	3.28	3.48	**1.95**
Figure 5(d, e, f)	5.89	4.67	**2.52**

4   Conclusion

This paper presents a parallax-robust hexahedral panoramic video stitching method. We propose a hybrid strategy which combines global projective warping and spatial-vary warping to improve panoramic video quality. We first extract feature matches lying in different depth layers. After that, we give full play to global projective warping, which estimates the position and orientation of cameras jointly based on the first layer of the feature matches. Then we render images onto a spherical surface. Erroneous matches are discarded and layered content-preserving warping is performed to align feature points subtly. Both subjective and objective experiments are conducted to testify the effectiveness of our method over some state-of-the-art methods.

References

1. Anderson, R., Gallup, D., Barron, J.T., Kontkanen, J., Snavely, N., Hernández, C., Agarwal, S., Seitz, S.M.: Jump: virtual reality video. ACM Trans. Graph. **35**(6), 198 (2016)
2. Brown, M., Lowe, D.G.: Automatic panoramic image stitching using invariant features. Int. J. Comput. Vis. **74**(1), 59–73 (2007)
3. Gao, J., Kim, S.J., Brown, M.S.: Constructing image panoramas using dual-homography warping. In: 2011 IEEE Conference on Computer Vision and Pattern Recognition (CVPR), pp. 49–56. IEEE (2011)
4. He, B., Yu, S.: Parallax-robust surveillance video stitching. Sensors **16**(1), 7 (2015)
5. Igarashi, T., Moscovich, T., Hughes, J.F.: As-rigid-as-possible shape manipulation. ACM Trans. Graph. (TOG) **24**, 1134–1141 (2005)
6. Kwatra, V., Schödl, A., Essa, I., Turk, G., Bobick, A.: Graphcut textures: image and video synthesis using graph cuts. ACM Trans. Graph. (ToG) **22**, 277–286 (2003)
7. Rufli, M., Scaramuzza, D., Siegwart, R.: Automatic detection of checkerboards on blurred and distorted images. In: IEEE/RSJ International Conference on Intelligent Robots and Systems, IROS 2008, pp. 3121–3126. IEEE (2008)
8. Szeliski, R.: Image alignment and stitching: a tutorial. Found. Trends® Comput. Graph. Vis. **2**(1), 1–104 (2006)
9. Triggs, B., McLauchlan, P.F., Hartley, R.I., Fitzgibbon, A.W.: Bundle adjustment —a modern synthesis. In: Triggs, B., Zisserman, A., Szeliski, R. (eds.) IWVA 1999. LNCS, vol. 1883, pp. 298–372. Springer, Heidelberg (2000). https://doi.org/10.1007/3-540-44480-7_21
10. Zaragoza, J., Chin, T.J., Brown, M.S., Suter, D.: As-projective-as-possible image stitching with moving DLT. In: Proceedings of the IEEE Conference on Computer Vision and Pattern Recognition, pp. 2339–2346 (2013)
11. Zhang, F., Liu, F.: Parallax-tolerant image stitching. In: Proceedings of the IEEE Conference on Computer Vision and Pattern Recognition, pp. 3262–3269 (2014)

Image Formation Analysis and Light Field Information Reconstruction for Plenoptic Camera 2.0

Li Liu, Xin Jin$^{(\boxtimes)}$, and Qionghai Dai

Graduate School at Shenzhen, Tsinghua University, Beijing, China
jin.xin@sz.tsinghua.edu.cn

Abstract. This paper builds an image formation model of plenoptic camera 2.0 and reconstructs the light field via solving a regularized optimization problem. The image formation model is built based on the cognition that the plenoptic camera 2.0 is a linear forward imaging system, which is also verified via the derivation of the impulse response of plenoptic camera 2.0. Based on the proposed image formation model, the method to reconstruct the light field is analyzed by solving an inverse optimization problem. Simulation results for plenoptic camera 2.0 with a single microlens and a microlens array all indicate that the reconstructed the light field has more details and conveys more objects' information.

Keywords: Plenoptic camera 2.0 · Image formation model
Linear inverse problem

1 Introduction

Light field camera, also known as plenoptic camera, develops quickly and attracts much attention in recent years. As a device for recording the distribution of four-dimension light field rays, light field camera inserts a microlens array in front of the sensor to discriminate the light from different directions [1, 2]. Combined with proper rendering algorithms, light field cameras can reconstruct images with small viewpoint changes, estimate the depth map and refocus the images at different depths with a single shot [3]. Based on the optical structure and image formation properties, light field cameras can be mainly divided into two categories: plenoptic camera 1.0 [4] and plenoptic camera 2.0 [5]. Plenoptic 1.0 inserts a microlens array directly at the focused plane of the main lens to sample a set of rays' directions at a single spatial point, which limits the spatial resolution to the number of microlenses. Plenoptic camera 2.0, which inserts a microlens array as micro-cameras to reimage the object, samples dense positional information and benefits the spatial resolution increment compared with plenoptic camera 1.0 [6–8].

Although plenoptic camera 2.0 increases the spatial resolution, it still suffers from the loss of light field information, which results in the decrement of depth of field. Some existing works tried to reconstruct the light field for plenoptic cameras. Bishop *et al.* derived the space-varying PSF of plenoptic cameras, which is investigated in a Bayesian

© Springer International Publishing AG, part of Springer Nature 2018
B. Zeng et al. (Eds.): PCM 2017, LNCS 10735, pp. 609–618, 2018.
https://doi.org/10.1007/978-3-319-77380-3_58

deconvolution approach to estimate a larger depth of field image [9, 10]. However, in their work, the space-varying PSF was calculated with the assumption that both PSFs of the main lens and the microlens are defocused PSFs, which cannot describe the accurate image formation properties of plenoptic cameras. S. Shroff and K. Berkner built an image formation model for plenoptic camera 1.0 to recover the spatial resolution, while their work was only applicable to plenoptic camera 1.0 [11–13]. Ng used the focal stack to extend the depth of field of plenoptic cameras by fusing refocused images at different depths, which requires high computational complexity [4]. Broxton *et al.* derived the optical model of the light field microscope, which has similar optical structure with the plenoptic cameras, and reconstructed the light field via the linear inverse problem. However, their models are not capable for plenoptic camera 2.0 [14].

Consequently, this paper tries to reconstruct the light field for plenoptic camera 2.0 by solving a regularized optimization problem. Modeling the image formation process of plenoptic camera 2.0 as a linear process, PSF derived in our previous work [15] based on wavefront propagation is used to calculate the linear forward mapping. Then, a regularized inverse optimization model is built to minimize the residual between the imaging results and the reconstructed imaging results, and maximize the smoothness of the reconstructed the light field simultaneously. Experimental results demonstrate that the reconstructed the light field are clearer with richer details compared with the plenoptic imaging results.

The rest of this paper is organized as follows. Section 2 describes the linear forward imaging model of plenoptic camera 2.0. Section 3 provides the regularized inverse optimization model to reconstruct the light field together with the analysis. Experimental results of the reconstructed light field are provided in Sect. 4 followed by the conclusions in Sect. 5.

2   Image Formation Model of Plenoptic Camera 2.0

2.1   Image Formation Analysis of Plenoptic Camera 2.0

The image formation models for the imaging systems with a microlens array have been discussed in some previous works. In [9–14], the fundamental formations of the models are considered as a linear forward imaging model, which shows a possibility to retrieve the original object information by solving a linear inverse problem. In this paper, the linear forward imaging model is also investigated to represent the image formation properties of plenoptic camera 2.0. The matrix formation of the linear imaging system is:

$$I_m = H_{PSF}I_{m0}, \tag{1}$$

where I_m and I_{m0} are column vectors by rearranging $P \times Q$ initial sensor data and $M \times N$ object data, respectively; H_{PSF} is the impulse response of the imaging system, i.e. the point spread function (PSF). The detailed rearrangement of Eq. (1) is shown as:

$$
\begin{bmatrix} I_m(1,1) \\ I_m(1,2) \\ \vdots \\ I_m(2,1) \\ I_m(2,2) \\ \vdots \\ I_m(P,Q) \end{bmatrix} = \begin{bmatrix} H_{PSF}(1,1,1,1) & H_{PSF}(1,1,1,2) & \cdot & H_{PSF}(1,1,M,N) \\ H_{PSF}(1,2,1,1) & H_{PSF}(1,2,1,2) & \cdot & H_{PSF}(1,2,M,N) \\ \vdots & \vdots & & \vdots \\ H_{PSF}(2,1,1,1) & H_{PSF}(2,1,1,2) & \cdot & H_{PSF}(2,1,M,N) \\ H_{PSF}(2,2,1,1) & H_{PSF}(2,2,1,2) & \cdot & H_{PSF}(2,2,M,N) \\ \vdots & \vdots & & \vdots \\ H_{PSF}(P,Q,1,1) & H_{PSF}(P,Q,1,2) & \cdot & H_{PSF}(P,Q,M,N) \end{bmatrix} \begin{bmatrix} I_{m0}(1,1) \\ I_{m0}(1,2) \\ \vdots \\ I_{m0}(2,1) \\ I_{m0}(2,2) \\ \vdots \\ I_{m0}(M,N) \end{bmatrix}. \tag{2}
$$

Based on the Eq. (2), the imaging results can be calculated by accumulating all points' PSF together, which also implies that imaging results of a single point is spread out over several pixels.

Based on the above analysis, the key points to reconstruct light fields of the objects are to derive the accurate H_{PSF} for plenoptic camera 2.0 and to calculate the linear inverse optimization process.

2.2 Point Spread Function for Plenoptic Camera 2.0

H_{PSF} of plenoptic camera 2.0 has been derived and verified in our previous work [15] based on the analysis of the wavefront propagation process. We first divide plenoptic camera 2.0 into two subsystems: Subsystem 1 represents ray propagation from the object plane (x_0, y_0) to the image plane (x_1, y_1) of the main lens; Subsystem 2 represents ray propagation from image plane (x_1, y_1) to the sensor (x, y). The optical structure and corresponding coordinate system settings are shown in Fig. 1.

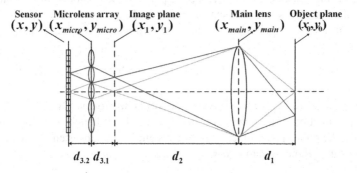

Fig. 1. Optical structure of plenoptic camera 2.0 and coordinate system settings.

For subsystem 1, the PSF $h_1(x_1, y_1, x_0, y_0)$ can be formulated by [15]:

$$
\begin{aligned}
h_1(x_1, y_1, x_0, y_0) = \frac{\exp[ik(d_1 + d_2)]}{-\lambda^2 d_1 d_2} \int\limits_{-\infty}^{+\infty} \int \int t_{main}(x_{main}, y_{main}) \\
\times \exp\{\frac{ik}{2d_1}[(x_0 - x_{main})^2 + (y_0 - y_{main})^2]\} \\
\times \exp\{\frac{ik}{2d_2}[(x_1 - x_{main})^2 + (y_1 - y_{main})^2]\} \mathrm{d}x_{main} \mathrm{d}y_{main},
\end{aligned} \tag{3}
$$

where λ is the wavelength of the light; k is the wavelength number and equals to $2\pi/\lambda$; d_1 is the distance between the object and the main lens; d_2 is the distance between the main lens and the image plane; and t_{main} (x_{main}, y_{main}) is the phase correction factor of the main lens, which represents the optical characteristic of the main lens. The formulation of t_{main} (x_{main}, y_{main}) is:

$$t_{main}(x_{main}, y_{main}) = P_1(x_{main}, y_{main}) \exp[\frac{-ik}{2f_1}(x_{main}^2 + y_{main}^2)], \qquad (4)$$

where (x_{main}, y_{main}) is the coordinate system of the main lens plane; P_1 (x_{main}, y_{main}) is the pupil function of the main lens; and f_1 is the focal length of the main lens.

For Subsystem 2, the point spread function $h_2(x, y, x_1, y_1)$ is given by [15]:

$$h_2(x, y, x_1, y_1) = \frac{\exp[ik(d_{3.1} + d_{3.2})]}{-\lambda^2 d_{3.1} d_{3.2}} \sum_m \sum_n \int_{-\infty}^{+\infty} \int t_{micro}(x_{micro} - mD, y_{micro} - nD)$$

$$\times \exp\{\frac{ik}{2d_{3.1}}[(x_1 - x_{micro})^2 + (y_1 - y_{micro})^2]\}$$

$$\times \exp\{\frac{ik}{2d_{3.2}}[(x - x_{micro})^2 + (y - y_{micro})^2]\} dx_{micro} dy_{micro}.$$

$$(5)$$

where $d_{3.1}$ is the distance between the image plane to the microlens; $d_{3.2}$ is the distance between the microlens and the sensor plane; and t_{micro} (x_{micro}, y_{micro}) is the phase correction factor of the single microlens. The formulation of t_{micro} (x_{micro}, y_{micro}) is:

$$t_{micro}(x_{micro}, y_{micro}) = P_2(x_{micro}, y_{micro}) \exp[\frac{-ik}{2f_2}(x_{micro}^2 + y_{micro}^2)], \qquad (6)$$

where (x_{micro}, y_{micro}) is the coordinate system of the microlens plane; P_2 (x_{micro}, y_{micro}) is the pupil function of the microlens; and f_2 is the focal length of a single microlens.

Having the point spread function of Subsystem 1 and Subsystem 2, the point spread function of the whole system $h(x, y, x_0, y_0)$ can be written as:

$$h(x, y, x_0, y_0) = \frac{\exp[ik(d_1 + d_2 + d_{3.1} + d_{3.2})]}{\lambda^4 d_1 d_2 d_{3.1} d_{3.2}} \sum_m \sum_n \int_{-\infty}^{+\infty} \int \int \int t_{micro}(x_{micro} - mD, y_{micro} - nD)$$

$$\times \exp\{\frac{ik}{2d_{3.1}}[(x_1 - x_{micro})^2 + (y_1 - y_{micro})^2]\}$$

$$\times \exp\{\frac{ik}{2d_{3.2}}[(x - x_{micro})^2 + (y - y_{micro})^2]\} dx_{micro} dy_{micro}$$

$$\times \int\int t_{main}(x_{main}, y_{main}) \exp\{\frac{ik}{2d_1}[(x_0 - x_{main})^2 + (y_0 - y_{main})^2]\}$$

$$\times \exp\{\frac{ik}{2d_2}[(x_1 - x_{main})^2 + (x_1 - y_{main})^2]\} dx_{main} dy_{main} dx_1 dy_1.$$

$$(7)$$

For a real imaging system, the image on the sensor for a point light source is the intensity of the PSF, or absolute square of the PSF $|h(x, y, x_0, y_0)|^2$. The intensity of the sensor data $I(x, y)$ is formulated as:

$$I(x, y) = \iint I(x_0, y_0) |h(x, y, x_0, y_0)|^2 \mathrm{d}x_0 \mathrm{d}y_0. \tag{8}$$

where $I(x_0, y_0)$ is the intensity of the objects. Thus, H_{PSF} can be obtained by rearranging $|h(x, y, x_0, y_0)|^2$ of all the points into the column vectors and combining the vectors together. Besides, Eq. (8) also indicates the correctness of the assumption that plenoptic camera 2.0 can be considered as a linear imaging system.

3 Light Field Information Reconstruction

Based on the image formation model of plenoptic camera 2.0, the light field reconstruction algorithm is to solve the linear inverse problem of Eq. (1), which also corresponds to estimating I_{m0} in Eq. (1) by calculating the following optimization problem:

$$\arg \min_{I_{m0}} \|H_{PSF} I_{m0} - I_m\|. \tag{9}$$

Solutions of this optimization problem is not complicated by using the existing optimization algorithms based on the choice of the norm $\|\cdot\|$ and the limitation on I_{m0}. For the noise-free cases, the results of the above optimization problem can be solved directly by using generalized inverse of H_{PSF}, which is denoted by H_{PSF}^{-1}. However, as the size of H_{PSF} increases, which is $(P \times Q) \times (M \times N)$ in this paper, the computation complexity of H_{PSF}^{-1} makes an exponential increase. Besides, if the noise is added in the system, the generalized inverse H_{PSF}^{-1} does not work well on the image formation model, which can be rewritten as:

$$I_m = H_{PSF} I_{m0} + N, \tag{10}$$

where N is the noise in the imaging system.

Based on the above discussions, Eq. (9) is solved as a ℓ_2 regularized problem [17–19] in our paper instead of the direct using generalized inverse. The optimization problems in Eq. (9) is rewritten as:

$$\arg \min_{I_{m0}} \|H_{PSF} I_{m0} - I_m\|_2^2 + \tau^2 \|I_{m0}\|_2^2 \tag{11}$$

where τ is a scalar regularization parameter. If $\tau > 0$, a unique solution always exists, and $\|I_{m0}\|$ is bounded. Meanwhile, as the τ increases, the final solutions become smoother while computation complexity decreases. The influence of the scalar regularization parameter τ is discussed in the Sect. 4.

4 Experiments

The correctness of the proposed light field reconstruction algorithm is verified via simulated results calculated by Eq. (11). Three planar objects with different complexities, as shown in column (a) in Fig. 2, are tested in the simulations. To analyze the efficiency of the light field reconstruction, two optical configurations of plenoptic camera 2.0 are evaluated: plenoptic camera 2.0 with a single microlens and an array with 3×3 microlenses.

(a) Objects   (b) d_1=95mm   (c) Retrieved object   (d) d_1=105mm   (e) Retrieved object

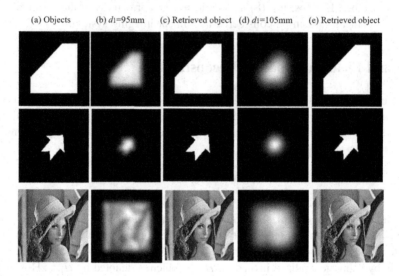

Fig. 2. Light field reconstruction for plenoptic camera 2.0 with a single microlens in noise free case. Columns (a) shows the three objects used in the simulation. Column (b) and (d) are the imaging results calculated at $d_1 = 95$ mm and $d_1 = 105$ mm, respectively. Column (c) and (e) are the reconstructed light field information corresponding to Column (b) and (d), respectively.

For plenoptic camera 2.0 with a single microlens, the simulation system consists of a main lens with the 30 mm focal length and the 12.7 mm radius, and a microlens with the 10 mm focal length and the 5 mm radius. Here, a much bigger microlens is used compared with the microlens in [5, 6]. The reason is mainly based on the considerations that the increase of the microlens size enables much more rays passing through which increases the imaging areas on the sensor and provides a brighter imaging results to facilitate the verification, while the image formation properties are not changed. The distance d_2, $d_{3.1}$, and $d_{3.2}$ is 45 mm, 30 mm and 15 mm, respectively, which indicates the focal plane of the whole systems is 90 mm in front of the main lens. In the noise-free cases, simulation results of the three objects with single microlens are shown in Fig. 2. Since the focal plane corresponds to $d_1 = 90$ mm, sensor data obtained by placing the object at depths 95 mm and 105 mm are obviously blurry as shown in column (b) and column (d) in Fig. 2. Meanwhile, the sizes of the objects in the images are changed. The blurry edges and changed size all indicate the object's light field information loss. After solving the linear inverse problem, the reconstructed light fields of objects are shown in the column (c) and column (e) in Fig. 2, which have more detailed information and more accurate size compared with the imaging results in column (b) and column (d). The noise free cases are the ideal conditions, in which all the details of objects are reconstructed while no aliasing exists. After adding some noises to the system, the simulation results for a single microlens are shown in Fig. 3. Gaussian noise of power 10dBW is added to the sensor data. By solving the optimization problem in Eq. (10), the reconstructed light fields of objects are shown in the column (c) (d) and column (f) (g) in Fig. 3, which correspond to the imaging results in the column (b) and column (e) for different scalar regularization parameter τ, respectively. Although the reconstructed light fields of objects are not as good as that in the Fig. 2, more details and more accurate information can still be observed. Besides, as the scalar regularization parameter τ increases, the retrieved results becomes smoother while the detail information losses.

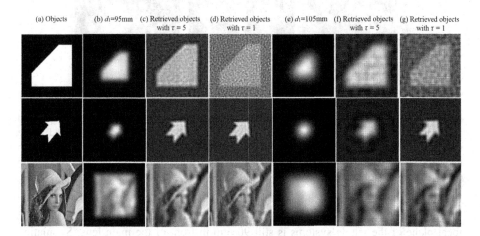

| (a) Objects | (b) d_1=95mm | (c) Retrieved objects with τ = 5 | (d) Retrieved objects with τ = 1 | (e) d_1=105mm | (f) Retrieved objects with τ = 5 | (g) Retrieved objects with τ = 1 |

Fig. 3. Light field reconstruction for plenoptic camera 2.0 with a single microlens added with the Gaussian noise of power 10 dBW. Columns (a) shows the three objects used in the simulation. Column (b) and (e) is the imaging results calculated at $d_1 = 95$ mm and $d_1 = 105$ mm, respectively, which are added with the Gaussian noise of power 10 dBW. Column (c) and (f) are the reconstructed light field information corresponding to Column (b) and (e) respectively when scalar regularization parameter τ equals to 5. Column (d) and (g) are the reconstructed light field information when scalar regularization parameter τ equals to 1.

For plenoptic camera 2.0 with a microlens array, a 3×3 microlens array is used, which can be extended to a microlens array with more lenses easily without influence on the reconstruction efficiency. Parameter settings of the main lens are the same with that used for plenoptic camera 2.0 with a single microlens. For each microlens, the focal length and the radius of the microlens are 2.057 mm and 150 μm, respectively.

(a) object   (b) d_1=90mm   (c) Retrieved object

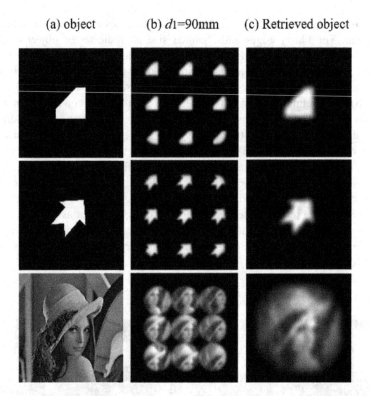

Fig. 4. Light field reconstruction for plenoptic camera 2.0 with a 3 × 3 microlens array added with the Gaussian noise of power 10 dBW. Columns (a) shows the three objects used in the simulation. Column (b) are the imaging results calculated at d_1 = 90 mm, which are added with the Gaussian noise of power 10 dBW. Column (c) are the reconstructed light field information corresponding to Column (b).

The distance d_2, $d_{3.1}$, and $d_{3.2}$ is 45 mm, 4.117 mm and 4.117 mm, respectively. The focal plane of the whole systems is still 90 mm in front of the main lens. Simulation results for the microlens array are shown in the Fig. 4. Column (a) are the objects, which are same as the objects used for plenoptic camera 2.0 with the single microlens. Column (b) are the initial images by placing the objects at d_1 = 90 mm and adding the Gaussian noise of power 10 dBW. Here, as the size of our objects are small, we can also observe some blurry situations. The reason is that the point spread function of the imaging system cannot cover only one pixel even as imaging a point light source on the focal plane. Column (c) are the reconstructed light fields corresponding to the imaging results in column (b). Results show that reconstructed light fields become clearer and convey much more details compared with the imaging results. Although there are some aliasing and unrecovered information between the microlenses, the reconstructed light fields of objects have already been closer to the original objects.

5 Conclusions

In this paper, an algorithm to reconstruct the light field for plenoptic camera 2.0 by solving a regularized optimization problem is proposed. The image formation process of plenoptic camera 2.0 is investigated as a linear forward imaging process, in which the linear forward mapping is calculated based on the PSF of plenoptic camera 2.0, which is derived in our previous work [15]. Based on the proposed linear forward imaging model, a regularized inverse optimization model is built to reconstruct the light field. Experimental results verify that the reconstructed light field images are clearer and have richer details compared with the plenoptic imaging results, which is beneficial to the imaging quality improvement and the depth of field extension.

Acknowledgement. This work was supported by the Natural National Science Foundation of China under Grant 61371138, National Science Foundation of Guangdong under Grant 2014A030313733, and Youth Top-notch Talent of Guangdong Special Support Program under Grant 2016TQ03X998, China.

References

1. Adelson, E.H., Wang, J.Y.A.: Single lens stereo with a plenoptic camera. IEEE Trans. Pattern Anal. Mach. Intell. **14**(2), 99–106 (1992)
2. Ng, R., Levoy, M., Bredif, M., et al.: Light Field Photography with a Hand-Held Plenopic Camera, Technical Report. Stanford University (2005)
3. Lam, E.: Computational photography with plenoptic camera and light field capture: tutorial. J. Opt. Soc. Am. A **32**, 2021–2032 (2015)
4. Ng, R.: Digital light field photography, Ph.D. thesis. Stanford University (2006)
5. Lumsdaine, A., Georgiev, T.: The focused plenoptic camera. In: 2009 IEEE International Conference on Computational Photography (ICCP), San Francisco, CA, pp. 1–8 (2009)
6. Georgiev, T., Lumsdaine, A.: Focused plenoptic camera and rendering. J. Electron. Imaging **19**(2), 021106 (2010)
7. Lumsdaine, A., Georgiev, T.: Full resolution light field rendering, Technical report. Adobe Systems (2008)
8. Georgiev, T., Lumsdaine, A.: Superresolution with Plenoptic 2.0 cameras. In: Frontiers in Optics 2009/Laser Science XXV/Fall 2009 OSA Optics & Photonics Technical Digest, OSA Technical Digest (CD) (Optical Society of America), paper STuA6 (2009)
9. Bishop, T.E., Favaro, P.: The light field camera: extended depth of field, aliasing, and superresolution. IEEE Trans. Pattern Anal. Mach. Intell. **34**(5), 972–986 (2012)
10. Bishop, T.E., Zanetti, S., Favaro, P.: Light field superresolution. In: 2009 IEEE International Conference on Computational Photography (ICCP), San Francisco, CA, pp. 1–9 (2009)
11. Shroff, S., Berkner, K.: Plenoptic system response and image formation. In: Imaging and Applied Optics, OSA Technical Digest (online), paper JW3B.1. Optical Society of America (2013)
12. Shroff, S., Berkner, K.: High resolution image reconstruction for plenoptic imaging systems using system response. In: Imaging and Applied Optics Technical Papers, OSA Technical Digest (online), paper CM2B.2. Optical Society of America (2012)
13. Shroff, S., Berkner, K.: Wave analysis of a plenoptic system and its applications. In: Proceedings of SPIE 8667, Multimedia Content and Mobile Devices 86671L (2013)

14. Broxton, M., Grosenick, L., Yang, S., Cohen, N., Andalman, A., Deisseroth, K., Levoy, M.: Wave optics theory and 3-D deconvolution for the light field microscope. Opt. Express **21**, 25418–25439 (2013)
15. Jin, X., Liu, L., Chen, Y., Dai, Q.: Point spread function and depth-invariant focal sweep point spread function for plenoptic camera 2.0. Opt. Express **25**, 9947–9962 (2017)
16. Turola, M.: Investigation of plenoptic imaging systems: a wave optics approach, PhD dissertation. City University London (2016)
17. Voelz, D.: Computational Fourier Optics: A MATLAB Tutorial (2011)
18. Arioli, M., Gratton, S.: Least-squares problems, normal equations, and stopping criteria for the conjugate gradient method, Technical Report RAL-TR-2008-008. Rutherford Appleton Laboratory, Oxfordshire (2008)
19. Figueiredo, M.A.T., Nowak, R.D., Wright, S.J.: Gradient projection for sparse reconstruction: application to compressed sensing and other inverse problems. IEEE J. Sel. Top. Signal Process. **1**(4), 586–597 (2007)
20. Paige, C.C., Saunders, M.A.: LSQR: an algorithm for sparse linear equations and sparse least squares. ACM Trans. Math. Softw. **8**(1), 43–71 (1982)
21. Fong, D., Saunders, M.: LSMR: an iterative algorithm for sparse least-squares problems. SIAM J. Sci. Comput. **33**(5), 2950–2971 (2010)

Part Detection for 3D Shapes
via Multi-view Rendering

Youcheng Song, Zhengxing Sun$^{(\boxtimes)}$, Mofei Song, and Yunjie Wu

State Key Laboratory for Novel Software Technology, Nanjing University,
Nanjing, People's Republic of China
szx@nju.edu.cn

Abstract. This paper presents a novel way of shape structure analysis
namely part detection, which provides the positions and categories of all
potential parts for any input shape. Different from segmentation, part
detection does not provide precise shape part boundaries, but rather
gives the bounding boxes and semantic labels of shape parts. This is
useful for applications like style discovery, retrieval, visualization, etc.
Part detection is achieved by multi-view rendering in this paper. Firstly,
our method renders 3D shape into images under different perspectives,
and detects the potential parts (as boxes) in the images using Faster R-
CNN. Then, each detection result votes for the visible vertices in its own
box under the corresponding perspective. Finally, we select the vertices
for each part category according to the voting result, and generate the
bounding boxes. The performance of this approach on a database of 16
shape categories is demonstrated in the end of paper.

Keywords: Part detection · Shape Analysis · Multi-view rendering

1 Introduction

Shape structure analysis is a basic task in computer graphics [7], and is the
foundation of many high-level shape processing applications, such as style discovery [5], shape synthesis [12], etc. Shape structure analysis is often utilized
using segmentation and labeling methods. These methods follow a bottom-up
procedure, which extracts low-level features first and then abstract high-level
information from them. This makes them feature sensitive and less generic. These
methods have another thing in common, that is, they all focus on extracting
precise shape part boundaries. However, some applications requires universality
instead of precise shape part boundaries. In the semantic retrieval, it is necessary to extract structural knowledge for 3D shapes [1], which focuses on the
relationship between shape parts, instead of the parts themselves. In shape set
organization, meta-representation [3] even directly uses bounding boxes to represent shape parts.

Therefore, we propose a 3D shape part detection method, and achieve better universality by relaxing the constraint of precise shape part boundaries.

© Springer International Publishing AG, part of Springer Nature 2018
B. Zeng et al. (Eds.): PCM 2017, LNCS 10735, pp. 619–628, 2018.
https://doi.org/10.1007/978-3-319-77380-3_59

Our objective is to quickly and accurately detect the location (bounding box) and category (label) of each part for 3D shapes from different categories. However, the representation, learning and detecting in 3D space is very complicated. Treating a 3D shape as a collection of 2D projections rendered from multiple directions is an effective method [10], and there are some mature object detection technologies [9] in the image processing filed. Rendering a shape to images have a number of desirable properties: they are relatively low-dimensional, efficient to evaluate, and robust to 3D shape representation artifacts, such as holes, imperfect polygon mesh tessellations, noisy surfaces. Therefore, we construct a map from 3D shape to 2D images by multi-view projection, and transform the part detection of 3D shape into object detection problem for each view.

According to the above, we propose a 3D part detection method based on multi-view projection. Firstly, we render a 3D shape into images under different perspectives, and detect the potential parts (as boxes) in the images using Faster R-CNN [9]. Then, each detection result votes for the vertices in its own box under the corresponding perspective. Finally, we select the vertices for each part category by the vote result, and generate the bounding boxes. In the last step, we introduce a category-specific threshold for selecting vertices, which achieves a significant improvement on the performance of our method.

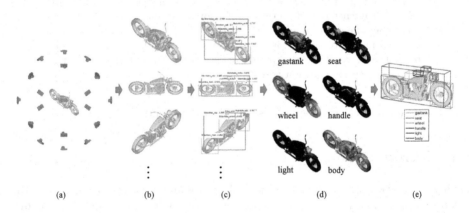

Fig. 1. Pipeline. (a) 24 view-directions. (b) Rendered images. (c) Detection results on the images. (d) Voting results on the shape. (e) The final part detection result

2   Part Detection

The detection procedure is shown as Fig. 1. Firstly, we generate images by rendering input shape in different view-directions. Next, we perform object detection on the images through a pre-trained Faster-RCNN model, so that we get several bounding boxes with labels and confidences for each view-direction. Then, each bounding box votes for the visible vertices within its boundary to its corresponding category. Finally, we select vertices belonging to each shape part category based on the voting result, and construct bounding boxes with labels for them.

We have to train a special Faster R-CNN model to detect shape parts in the rendering image. The training set includes a collection of images rendered from various 3D shapes at different directions, with shape part labels for each image. We collect images by rendering 3D shapes from ShapeNetCore [2] dataset, and generate labels by the labeling ground truth on the same dataset provided by Yi et al. [11]. Our training set contains nearly 20000 images rendered from 800 shapes in 16 categories, including Airplane, Bag, Cap, Car, Chair, Earphone, Guitar, Knife, Lamp, Laptop, Motorbike, Mug, Pistol, Rocket, Skateboard, and Table. Each category has 2 to 6 kinds of shape parts. We have 50 categories of shape parts in total. We denote L_s as the collection of shape category labels, and L_p as the collection of part category labels. After collecting training set, we follow the standard training procedure of Faster R-CNN [9] to train our model.

2.1   Input

We assume that the input shapes are upright oriented along a consistent axis (e.g., y-axis). Even if some of the shapes are not oriented correctly, there is existing method to amend them [4]. In addition, all shapes are normalized into the unit sphere. In our procedure, voting and generating bounding boxes are based on vertices. In order to handle shapes with uneven distribution of vertices, we uniformly sample N_P points on each shape (in this paper $N_P = 3000$). So we can represent each shape S as a triple (V, F, P). The three elements are all matrixes with 3 rows, each column of V is the coordinate of a vertex, each column of F is 3 vertex indexes of a face, and each column of P is the coordinate of a sampled point. We use N_V and N_F to represent the number of columns of V and F.

In our approach, the polygonal structure (V, F) of shapes are used only for rendering, and the sampled points P are used for detection. Therefore, our method does not require input shape to be manifold or watertight.

2.2   Multi-view Rendering

To generate rendered views of shapes, we use the Phong reflection model [8]. The shapes are rendered under a perspective projection and the pixel color is determined by interpolating the reflected intensity of the vertices. To perform our multi-view rendering, we need to setup multiple view-directions. Since our final results are axis-aligned bounding boxes, view-directions paralleled to any axis are more helpful to our detection. For simplicity, we select four directions that are parallel to x-axis and z-axis, along with some other interpolated directions between them.

We define our multi-view as a set of rotation matrix $R = \left\{ r_\psi^\theta | \psi \in \Psi, \theta \in \Theta \right\}$. r_ψ^θ represents the view-direction by rotating the yaw angle ψ around the y-axis, followed by rotating the pitch angle θ around the x-axis. Here r_0^0 is the initial view-direction, which represents viewing the origin from the positive direction of the z-axis. According to the definition, we can calculate r_ψ^θ as follow:

$$r_\psi^\theta = \begin{pmatrix} 1 & 0 & 0 \\ 0 & \cos\psi & \sin\psi \\ 0 & -\sin\psi & \cos\psi \end{pmatrix} \cdot \begin{pmatrix} \cos\theta & 0 & -\sin\theta \\ 0 & 1 & 0 \\ \sin\theta & 0 & \cos\theta \end{pmatrix} \qquad (1)$$

In our paper, we let $\Psi = \left\{ \frac{i}{4}\pi | 0 \leqslant i < 8, i \in \mathbb{N} \right\}$, and $\Theta = \left\{ -\frac{\pi}{4}, 0, \frac{\pi}{4} \right\}$. That is, we uniformly select 8 groups of directions around the y-axis, each group contains 3 directions that are $45°$ above the x-z plane, on the x-z plane and $45°$ below the x-z plane. Then we have 24 view-directions, which construct our multi-view (see Fig. 1(a)).

The input shape is rendered under each rotation matrix in R, with the shape color set to white. These rendered images form a set $I = \{img_r | r \in R\}$, here img_r is the image rendered with the rotation matrix r.

2.3   Detection on Rendered Images

In this step, we perform Faster R-CNN object detection on each image in set I. We formulate the detection as a function $B_r = \text{Detect}(img_r)$. img_r is the image to be detected, and B_r is a collection of quaternions (b, l, p, r). The elements of the quaternion represent bounding box, label, confidence and rotation matrix respectively. The bounding box b is a quaternion consisting of 4 integers, denoting the upper, lower, left and right position of the bounding box. The label l is a tuple (l_s, l_p), $l_s \in L_s$ is the label of shape category, and $l_p \in L_p$ is the label of part category. For example, the table legs have the label (table,table_leg), and the chair legs have the label (chair,chair_leg). We introduce the shape label in the part label to facilitate the classification of part labels. The confidence p is a decimal between 0 and 1, representing the confidence of the detection result. Here b, l, and p are provided by the Faster R-CNN, while the rotation matrix r is inherited from the rendered image img_r.

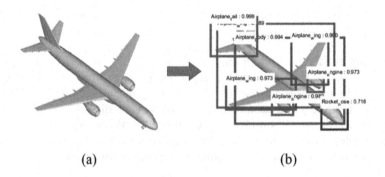

(a)   (b)

Fig. 2. Detection on rendered image. (a) Rendered image. (b) Detection result.

After performing detection on all the rendered images, we have a set of detection results $B = \bigcup_{img_r \in I} \text{Detect}(img_r)$. As mentioned above, each element of B

is a quaternion (b, l, p, r). As our method handles multi-category shapes, there may be parts from other shape category detected in the image. For example, in Fig. 2, we detect a rocket nose in the airplane image. We choose the correct shape category based on the sum of confidence, and filter out the bounding boxes belonging to other shape categories:

$$l_{shape} = \arg\max_{l \in L_s} \sum_{(b,(l_s,l_p),p,r) \in B, l_s = l} p \tag{2}$$

$$B' = \{(b, (l_s, l_p), p, r) \mid (b, (l_s, l_p), p, r) \in B, l_s = l_{shape}\} \tag{3}$$

Here l_{shape} is the label of predicted shape category, and $B_{2D}{}'$ is the collection of filtered bounding boxes.

2.4 Voting

After detecting the parts for each rendered image, now we enter the voting process. The sampled points are to be voted, each point has a vector to record the number of votes for each part category. All the vectors form a matrix $Vote$ with $|L_p|$ rows and N_P columns, and the matrix element $Vote_{c,i}$ denotes the voting result for point i of belonging to part category c. Since the detection results are in the image space, while the sampled points are in the 3D space, we have to map the sampled points to the image pixels. The mapping is acquired by coding point indexes into colors and rendering without lighting model. This method is widely used for picking 3D objects from a 2D view. Note that a 24-bit color value can encode an integer smaller than 2^{24}, which is far enough for our 3000 sampled points.

With the mapping, wa can select a collection of sampled points S_b which are inside the bounding box b for each $b \in B'$. Now we can proceed the voting:

$$Vote_{c,i} = \sum_{(b,(l_s,l_p),p,r) \in B', c = l_p, i \in S_b} p \tag{4}$$

That is to say, a bounding box b votes for a sampled point i with a specified label c only if the box has the same label and the box contains the point in the rendered image, and the value of this vote equals the detection confidence p.

2.5 Bounding Box Generation

After the voting process, we can get the category information for each vertex by setting a threshold. However, a global threshold cannot be suitable for all categories. For example, when we handling a car shape, the body appears in almost every view-directions while the wheel only appears in a small amount of view-directions, so the threshold for selecting body points should be larger than that for selecting wheel points. In our approach, we introduce a category-specific threshold. We determine the thresholds for each category once the training of Faster R-CNN model is finished, so when we performing part detection on shapes, we can directly use the thresholds. How to determine the category-specific thresholds will be explained after we introduce the procedure for generating the bounding boxes, and now we assume that all the thresholds are known. Here we use t_c to represent the threshold for the part category c. We select the points that belonging to each category:

$$P_c = \left\{ i | i \in [1, N_P], Vote_{c,i} \geq t_c \times \max_{j \in [1, N_P]} Vote_{c,j} \right\} \tag{5}$$

These points belong to the same part category, but may not belong to the same shape part. We add an edge between two points if the distance between them is smaller than the threshold d to construct a graph, and consider each connected component to be a separate part. The threshold d id related to the density of the sampled points. In our settings with shapes normalized to unit sphere and 3000 points sampled from each shape, we let $d = 0.05$ as an experimental value. Then we can generate a bounding box with label c for each connected component. After generating bounding boxes for each category, we have a collection of boxes B_{3D} as our final result, each element of B_{3D} is a tuple (b_{3D}, c) denoting the bounding box and its label.

Determining the Category-Specific Thresholds. As mentioned above, we need to determine the thresholds for each category after training the Faster R-CNN. We define an objective function and perform a simple optimization to achieve this goal. We select 10 shapes from each shape category to form our training set S, and generate the ground truth. Then we calculate the thresholds for each part category separately. For category c, we define the objective function:

$$E_c(t) = \frac{\sum_{s \in S} \text{Area} \left(\left(\bigcup B_t(c,s) \right) \cap \left(\bigcup B_{GT}(c,s) \right) \right)}{\sum_{s \in S} \text{Area} \left(\left(\bigcup B_t(c,s) \right) \cup \left(\bigcup B_{GT}(c,s) \right) \right)} \tag{6}$$

Where $B_{GT}(c,s)$ denotes the collection of ground truth bounding boxes in category c on shape s. $B_t(c,s)$ denotes the collection of detected bounding boxes in category c on shape s using the method described in previous sections with the threshold t. Area (B) denotes the total area of all the faces inside the bounding boxes. $E_c(t)$ can be understood as a measure of the detection accuracy of shape part c for all the shapes with threshold t. We can determine the threshold for category c by solving $t_c = \arg\max_{t \in (0,1)} E_c(t)$.

3 Experiments

In this section, we describe experimental validation and analysis of our approach. As far as we know, there is only one proposed method [6] which aims at part detection for 3D shapes. However, their method detects only one vertex for each shape part, while ours detects a bounding box. We can not find a suitable evaluation to compare with their methods fairly. Therefore only our results are shown in the experiment.

3.1   Dataset and Evaluation

As mentioned in Sect. 2, we select 50 shapes from each of 16 categories in ShapeNetCore [2] to construct our dataset for training the Faster R-CNN [9] model, and use the annotation ground truth provided by Yi et al. [11] to generate our detection ground truth. Here, we randomly select 10 shapes from each category to form our testing set (5 shapes for the Cap category, because it contains only 55 shapes with annotations and 50 of them are already used for training), and we make sure that the training set and the testing set do not intersect. Eventually, we have a testing set of 155 shapes from 16 categories.

To analyze the results quantitatively, we use accuracy, precision and recall together to measure the resulting performance. Referring to the region differencing metrics in segmentation and labeling, we define our metrics:

$$Accuracy = \frac{\sum_{l \in L_p} \text{Area}\left(\left(\bigcup B_d\left(l\right)\right) \cap \left(\bigcup B_{GT}\left(l\right)\right)\right)}{\sum_{l \in L_p} \text{Area}\left(\left(\bigcup B_d\left(l\right)\right) \cup \left(\bigcup B_{GT}\left(l\right)\right)\right)} \tag{7}$$

$$Precision = \frac{\sum_{l \in L_p} \text{Area}\left(\left(\bigcup B_d\left(l\right)\right) \cap \left(\bigcup B_{GT}\left(l\right)\right)\right)}{\sum_{l \in L_p} \text{Area}\left(\bigcup B_d\left(l\right)\right)} \tag{8}$$

$$Recall = \frac{\sum_{l \in L_p} \text{Area}\left(\left(\bigcup B_d\left(l\right)\right) \cap \left(\bigcup B_{GT}\left(l\right)\right)\right)}{\sum_{l \in L_p} \text{Area}\left(\bigcup B_{GT}\left(l\right)\right)} \tag{9}$$

Where Area() denotes the total area of shape faces (triangles) inside the bounding boxes, $B_{GT}\left(l\right)$ denotes the ground truth bounding boxes with label l, and $B_d\left(l\right)$ denotes the detection results with label l.

3.2   Performance of Our Proposed Method

We perform part detection on all the 155 shapes from our testing set, and calculate the precision, recall and accuracy of our method for each category (see Table 1). Part of our detection results are shown in Figs. 3 and 4. Figure 3 shows that our method can perform part detection on shapes from different categories, and can detect some small parts like airplane engines, motorbike handles, skateboard axles, etc. Figure 4 shows that our method can achieve consistent detection results for shapes in the same category, even though their shape or structure may be very different form each other. Note that the labels shown in the figures are abbreviated. The complete form of the labels are shape category name followed by shape part name. Since we have a constraint explained in Sect. 2.3 that the parts detected in one shape should come from the same category, we can cut off the shape category name. Therefore, the 'same' label appeared in different categories does represent different shape parts. For example, most categories have a part named 'body', but they mean different 'body'.

Table 1 shows the performance of our method on different shape categories ordered by accuracy. Our method have a poor performance on the Lamp and Table because the lamp support and the table legs are too diverse. It is difficult to identify them using visual methods like our multi-view rendering.

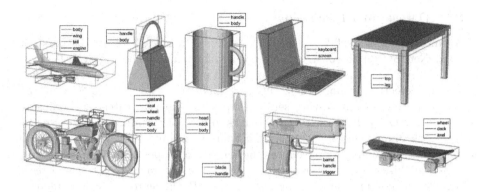

Fig. 3. Detection results on shapes from different categories

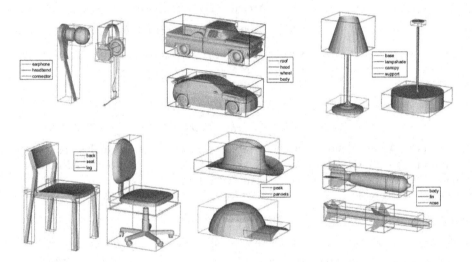

Fig. 4. Detection results on dissimilar shapes from the same category

Table 1. Precision, recall and accuracy on different shape categories

Category	Precision	Recall	Accuracy	Category	Precision	Recall	Accuracy
Mug	0.9919	0.9558	0.9484	Motorbike	0.9207	0.9380	0.8679
Guitar	0.9761	0.9699	0.9474	Car	0.8962	0.9495	0.8555
Bag	0.9535	0.9888	0.9433	Earphone	0.8985	0.8815	0.8016
Cap	0.9707	0.9643	0.9370	Rocket	0.8134	0.9631	0.7888
Pistol	0.9525	0.9688	0.9241	Chair	0.9085	0.8139	0.7523
Laptop	0.9367	0.9644	0.9054	Airplane	0.8856	0.8158	0.7380
Skateboard	0.9302	0.9380	0.8763	Lamp	0.8536	0.7248	0.6447
Knife	0.8996	0.9678	0.8735	Table	0.7986	0.6923	0.5894
				Average	0.9188	0.9092	0.8416

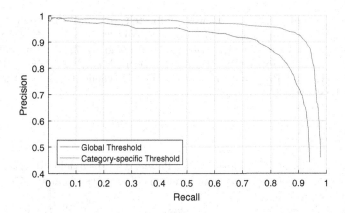

Fig. 5. Precision-Recall curve of the global threshold and category-specific threshold

3.3 Global Threshold vs. Category-Specific Threshold

As mentioned in Sect. 2.5, we can set a threshold for our voting result to generate bounding boxes. Here we compare the performance between the category-specific threshold and the global threshold using Precision-Recall curve. We plot the PR curve for the global threshold by setting the threshold to be 0 to 1 stepping 0.01. The category-specific threshold is essentially a group of thresholds, so we can plot the PR curve by varying the group from 0 to 1. For each threshold t in the group, we can define a monotonic function $f_t(x) \in [0,1]$ for $x \in [0,1]$, which meats $f_t(0.5) = t$. Here we use $f_t(x) = x^{\lg \frac{1}{t}}$, and we can plot the curve by varying x from 0 to 1 and using $f_t(x)$ to replace t as the threshold.

The PR curves for the two kinds of thresholds are shown in Fig. 5. It is obvious that the category-specific threshold has a great performance enhancement over the global threshold.

4 Conclusions

We present a novel approach for part detection on 3D shapes. We construct a mapping between 3D shape and images for transforming information and solve the detection problem with the help of image object detection technology. We also introduce a category-specific threshold strategy for generating bounding boxes. Experimental results show that our approach can detect parts correctly on most 3D shapes, and the category-specific threshold does improve the performance of our approach.

The main limitation of our work is that some shape parts with large internal differences are hard to detect. In order to overcome the weakness, we plan to introduce shape features into visual methods. Another direction to explore in future work is to set different weights for each view-direction, because some good views should provide more information for the detection.

Acknowledgements. This work was supported by National High Technology Research and Development Program of China (No. 2007AA01Z334), National Natural Science Foundation of China (Nos. 61321491 and 61272219), Innovation Fund of State Key Laboratory for Novel Software Technology (Nos. ZZKT2013A12 and ZZKT2016A11), and Program for New Century Excellent Talents in University of China (NCET-04-04605).

References

1. Attene, M., Biasotti, S., Mortara, M., Patanè, G., Spagnuolo, M., Falcidieno, B.: Computational methods for understanding 3D shapes. Comput. Graph. **30**(3), 323–333 (2006)
2. Chang, A.X., Funkhouser, T., Guibas, L., Hanrahan, P., Huang, Q., Li, Z., Savarese, S., Savva, M., Song, S., Su, H., et al.: Shapenet: an information-rich 3D model repository. arXiv preprint arXiv:1512.03012 (2015)
3. Fish, N., Averkiou, M., van Kaick, O., Sorkine-Hornung, O., Cohen-Or, D., Mitra, N.J.: Meta-representation of shape families. ACM Trans. Graph. **33**(4), 1–11 (2014)
4. Fu, H., Cohen-Or, D., Dror, G., Sheffer, A.: Upright orientation of man-made objects. ACM Trans. Graph. **27**(3), 1 (2008)
5. Han, Z., Liu, Z., Han, J., Bu, S.: 3D shape creation by style transfer. Vis. Comput. **31**, 1147–1161 (2014)
6. Makadia, A., Yumer, M.E.: Learning 3D part detection from sparsely labeled data. In: 2014 2nd International Conference on 3D Vision, pp. 311–318. IEEE, December 2014
7. Mitra, N., Wand, M., Zhang, H.R., Cohen-Or, D., Kim, V., Huang, Q.X.: Structure-aware shape processing. In: SIGGRAPH Asia 2013 Courses on - SA 2013, pp. 1–20. ACM Press, New York (2013)
8. Phong, B.T.: Illumination for computer generated pictures. Commun. ACM **18**(6), 311–317 (1975)
9. Ren, S., He, K., Girshick, R., Sun, J.: Faster R-CNN: towards real-time object detection with region proposal networks. In: Cortes, C., Lawrence, N.D., Lee, D.D., Sugiyama, M., Garnett, R. (eds.) Advances in Neural Information Processing Systems 28, pp. 91–99. Curran Associates, Inc. (2015)
10. Su, H., Maji, S., Kalogerakis, E., Learned-Miller, E.: Multi-view convolutional neural networks for 3D shape recognition. In: 2015 IEEE International Conference on Computer Vision (ICCV), pp. 945–953. IEEE, December 2015
11. Yi, L., Kim, V.G., Ceylan, D., Shen, I.C., Yan, M., Su, H., Lu, C., Huang, Q., Sheffer, A., Guibas, L.: A scalable active framework for region annotation in 3D shape collections. In: SIGGRAPH Asia (2016)
12. Zheng, Y., Cohen-Or, D., Mitra, N.J.: Smart variations: functional substructures for part compatibility. Comput. Graph. Forum **32**(2pt2), 195–204 (2013)

Benchmarking Screen Content Image Quality Evaluation in Spatial Psychovisual Modulation Display System

Yuanchun Chen[1]([✉]), Guangtao Zhai[1], Ke Gu[2], Xinfeng Zhang[3], Weisi Lin[3], and Jiantao Zhou[4]

[1] Institute of Image Communication and Information Processing,
Shanghai Jiao Tong University, Shanghai, China
{chenyuanchun,zhaiguangtao}@sjtu.edu.cn
[2] BJUT Faculty of Information Technology,
Beijing University of Technology, Beijing, China
[3] Nanyang Technological University, Singapore, Singapore
[4] University of Macau, Macau, China

Abstract. Spatial Psychovisual Modulation (SPVM) is a novel information display technology which aims to simultaneously generate multiple visual percepts for different viewers on a single display. The SPVM system plays an important role in information security. In a SPVM system, the viewers wearing polarized glasses can see a specific image (called *personal view*), and meanwhile the viewers not wearing glasses can also see a semantically meaningful image (called *shared view*). Researches on screen content image (SCI) are very hot recently, which have received a great amount of attention from multiple fields in multimedia signal processing. In this paper, we focus our gaze on how the users' quality-of-experience on SCIs is influenced under the SPVM display system. To this aim, we implement a comprehensive subjective quality assessment of SCIs by building a database which contains the distorted SCIs generated by a SPVM system. We run prevailing image quality methods on the newly established database, and results of experiments indicate that existing image quality metrics cannot reach a good performance, possibly due to some unique distortions, e.g. false contour and ghosting artifacts of SPVM-generated SCIs. Furthermore, we also point out some potential features which may lead to a high-performance metric by some appropriate modification and combination.

Keywords: Spatial Psychovisual Modulation (SPVM)
Display technology · Screen Content Image (SCI)
Quality-of-experience · Image quality metrics

1 Introduction

With the newly arising paradigm of information display, called Spatiotemporal Psychovisual Modulation (STPVM) [1,2], which is conceived as an ingenious

© Springer International Publishing AG, part of Springer Nature 2018
B. Zeng et al. (Eds.): PCM 2017, LNCS 10735, pp. 629–640, 2018.
https://doi.org/10.1007/978-3-319-77380-3_60

interplay of signal processing, optoelectronics, and psychophysics. The rationale behind STPVM system is that, the refresh rate and resolution of modern display become more and more higher, but the discrimination capacities of human visual system (HVS) in spatial and temporal domain are limited. So the spatial and temporal redundancies of modern display can be explored to achieve duel-view or even multi-view display. STPVM system aims to generate multiple percepts for different viewers simultaneously on the same medium. It means the dual-view or multi-view display can be implemented in two domains: temporal domain and spatial domain. In the current work, we focus our gaze on the Spatial Psychovisual Modulation (SPVM). Moreover, in SPVM system, as shown in Fig. 1, the viewers wearing a pair of polarized glasses can see the specific image (called *personal view*). The viewers without any glasses can also see a semantically meaningful image (called *shared view*). By this idea, as shown in Fig. 1(b), SPVM system can serve for information security protection. Users with specific glasses can see the secret information and those bystanders without the glasses only see mask/disguise images, which can be semantically meaningful but irrelevant to the secret information. It should be pointed out that the *personal view* is inclined to process a good quality, while the quality of *shared view* is affected greatly by some distinctive factors, e.g. the ghosting artifacts and contrast change. So we focus the most attention on assessing the performance of *shared view*.

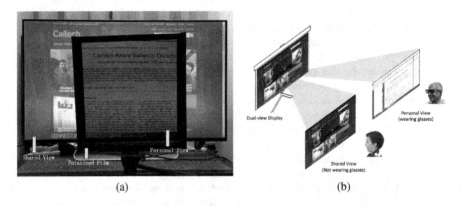

(a)   (b)

Fig. 1. (a) The prototype of the SPVM system. We denote the view through this polarized glasses or polarizing film as the personal view and the naked-eye view watched directly from the screen as the shared view. (b) Dual-view display system.

Since the emergence of SPVM system, many researches have been conducted and some applications have been implemented. In [3], a backward compatible stereoscopic display technology is proposed for the concurrent 3D and 2D exhibitions with the same physical display. Meanwhile, a dual-view medical image visualization prototype based on SPVM is developed in [4]. In order to prevent

Fig. 2. Samples of the 22 source SCIs in the QADSS database

camcorder privacy, The literature [5] presents a new video projection technology. What is more, the SPVM system can be widely used in many applications, such as browsing the web and viewing documents concurrently. Here we take one concrete case as an example, as shown in Fig. 1(b), we may be very cautious when viewing some confidential documents in the public in case of peeping by people around. However, when wearing the specific glasses we can see the confidential content and others can only see the disguised content not wearing glasses in SPVM system. We have found the quality of screen content image (SCI) in SPVM system determines the interactivity performance and plays a great impact on users' quality-of-experience because the SPVM-generated SCIs contain false contour and ghosting artifacts between two kinds of views. At the same time, there is no standard and clear Screen Content Image Quality Assessment (SCIQA) method used to assess the performance of SPVM system. Therefore, developing accurate SCI quality measures is an urgent need, as it can further serve as a benchmark for adjusting and optimizing the quality of SPVM system.

What is more, recently quality assessment of SCIs has also emerged as a hot topic on account of the exponential increase in the great demand for these graphically rich services. However, the properties of SCIs are usually discrepant compared with the natural image [6,7]. Simultaneously traditional IQA algorithms were usually devised relying on the statistics of natural images, which are making the image quality assessment (IQA) task of SCIs a non-trivial problem. In [8], a database of distorted screen images and associated subjective quality ranking results have been provided, showing that classical IQA methods do not work effectively in predicting the subjective quality of screen images. In view of

632 Y. Chen et al.

the distinctive features of SCIs, especially the SPVM-generated SCIs also distinguished from the general SCIs, it is highly desirable to study the subjective and objective quality of the SCIs containing false contour and ghosting artifacts, which can further provide essential guidance in devising, monitoring and optimizing the advanced SPVM system [9,10].

In particular, in view of the special properties of the SPVM system, we firstly build a screen content quality assessment database of SPVM-generated SCIs, including 2 types of images and 360 SPVM-generated SCIs. One type is of webpage, and the other one belongs to graphic type, which are 240 and 120 SCIs respectively. To obtain the perceived quality scores of these SCIs, a comprehensive subjective experiment is conducted. Then we will investigate and develop the screen content image quality metrics for SPVM display system with most mainstream SCIQA algorithms. Such database allows us to directly investigate the perceptual quality of the SCIs generated by SPVM system, which services the complementary SCI database and the design of more advanced quality measures in the future.

The remainder of this paper is organized as follows: Sect. 2 details the process of constructing the screen content image database and subjective experiment. In Sect. 3, we run prevailing image quality metrics on the newly established database, and present the associated results and analyses on experiments. At last, the conclusion and future works are given in Sect. 4.

2 Subjective Quality Assessment of SCIs

2.1 Database Construction

To the best of our knowledge, so far there have been just two SCI databases dedicated to the screen content IQA, which are called Screen Image Quality Assessment Database (SIQAD) [11] and quality assessment of Screen Content Database (QASC) [12]. The former includes 980 distorted SCIs generated by corrupting 20 source SCIs with seven distortion types at seven distortion levels. The latter includes up to 528 distorted SCIs which are generated by 24 pristine SCIs that compressed with 11 QP values ranging from 30 to 50 by Intra coding of HEVC SCC extension [13], which have three typical image resolutions of 2560 × 1440, 1920 × 1080 and 1280 × 720.

In order to make the research convenient, we have constructed a prototype SPVM system, which consists of polarized glasses and a interlaced polarization 3D LCD display. The viewers can percept the shared views without glasses and the personal view with glasses when the SPVM system is running. So we can directly obtain the SPVM-generated SCIs as the 1920 × 1080 format in SPVM system by screen snapshots. By this way, we have built a new screen content Quality Assessment Database of SPVM-generated SCIs (QADSS).

Image materials of our QADSS database are composed of a total of 360 SPVM-generated SCI images which includes two kinds of pristine SCIs. As illustrated in Fig. 2, it gives some pristine SCIs materials for building the QADSS database. These pristine SCIs were gathered from webpages, graphic and digital magazines by screen snapshots, and were cropped to the proper sizes so they can be natively displayed on computer screens during the subjective experiment. Then we obtain our specific SPVM-generated SCIs when these pristine SCIs are run in SPVM system by screen snapshots. The SCIs in our database can be divided into 2 groups, the first group selects webpages as the source images and the second one chooses graphic images as the pristine images, which are 240 and 120 SCIs respectively. The SPVM-generated SCIs have a unique characteristic that the *shared view* contain some artifacts of edge contours from the *personal view*, which reduces the visual quality greatly. However, the *personal view* always keeps the good quality because it dose not contain any artifacts. Therefore, we will focus the attention on the quality of *shared view*. Here, the quality of each SCI of this database varies with three typical factors, i.e., image dynamic range, ghosting artifacts and image complexity. When the *personal view* and image dynamic range keep the same of different SCIs, the quality of each SCI depends on the image complexity of the *shared view*. While the *shared view* and the *personal view* are the same, the quality of SCIs varies with different image dynamic ranges. The above three factors substantially affect human perceptions of image/video quality. Here we introduce the three main impact factors briefly as follows.

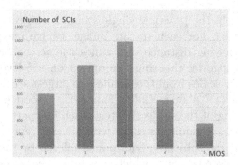

Fig. 3. Histogram of the MOS values in the QADSS database

(1) Image dynamic range: it will make a significant impact on perceived SCIs quality in SPVM system. Meanwhile, it is a trade-off coefficient to balance the visual qualities between the *personal view* and the *shared view*. The SCIs in QADSS database are divided into six groups by different image dynamic ranges. For an 8-bit SCIs, if we set the coefficient of the image dynamic range equal to 0.5, the dynamic range is from 0 to 127 for *shared view*, and 128 to 255 for *personal view*.

(2) Ghosting artifacts: the artifacts play a great important role in the perceived visual quality of SCIs. Due to the mechanism of the SPVM system, the *shared view* contains some artifacts of edge contours from the *personal view*. Whether the artifacts are obvious or not depend on the complexity of the *personal view*.

(3) Image complexity: the complexity of an image tells many aspects of the image content and it is an important factor in the selection of source SCI materials for the QADSS database. The higher of the image complexity, the more spatial information in this image. The image complexity will make a remarkable effect on the performance of the SPVM system.

2.2   Subjective Study of the SPVM-Generated SCIs

In SIQAD and QASC, guided by the suggestions from ITU-R BT.500-13 [14], they take a single stimulus (SS) method as the testing strategy with 11 point discrete scales ranging from the worst 0 to the best 10. Twenty inexperienced subjects were invited for the assessment task. The subjects are asked grade each distorted SCI. The specific viewing distance is 2–2.5 times of the screen height. Before the subjective testing process, the subjects are firstly trained with various distortion types at different levels.

Here we performed the subjective test on our QADSS database to gather subjective quality evaluations. During the subjective testing process, similar to the previous approach, the practical single-stimulus subjective testing methodology [14] is also used. For each testing image, twelve inexperienced subjects were invited at a viewing distance of 2 times the screen height to offer their personal quality ratings by choosing one option on a 5-level discrete scale, in which the five quality scales from the smallest to largest scores were successively labeled to be "Bad (1)", "Poor (2)", "Fair (3)", "Good (4)" and "Excellent (5)". At the beginning of the subjective test, each inexpert subject was to have undergone a particular training session with several representative examples. Then we will record the subjective viewpoints offered by the subjects with the help of 5-category discrete scale, which can make the subjective values more distinguishable. However, it is widely acknowledged that different subjects have different understandings on the quality of the perceived SCIs. Considering most of the twelve subjects should have similar but not exactly the same agreements on the perceived quality, it is acceptable that we allow the dissimilarities of the subjective score to a certain degree. However if the dissimilarities are too high to exceed the tolerance, the SCI should be rejected to ensure that only reliable MOS values are adopted in the database.

Specifically, referred to the methodology in [15], the 25% and 75% of subjective ratings of the sorted subjective scores can be obtained for each SCI. It means that the half of subject ratings lie within the range from 25% to 75%. If the interval of these ratings are constrained into 1, we can come to the conclusion that the subjects have reached consensus of the perceived SCI quality. In this way, in total 24 out of 360 outlier SCIs are rejected, which making the rest of 336 SCIs used in the database. Finally the raw scores we collected will

(a) MOS: 4.428   (b) MOS: 3.571   (c) MOS: 3.286

(d) MOS: 4.587   (e) MOS: 2.714   (f) MOS: 1.978

(g) MOS: 4.143   (h) MOS: 2.857   (i) MOS: 1.741

(j) MOS: 4.728   (k) MOS: 3.228   (l) MOS: 2.152

Fig. 4. Twelve SPVM-generated SCIs with resolutions of 1920 × 1080 in the QADSS database. First row, the SCIs with the same *shared view* and dynamic range degree but different *personal views* in QADSS database. Second row, the SCIs with the same *personal view* and dynamic range degree but different *shared views*. Third row, the SCIs with the same *shared view* and *personal view* but different dynamic range degrees. Fourth row, the graphic SCIs with different dynamic range degrees.

be further processed to generated the final mean opinion score (MOS) for each SCI. The final MOS will be computed by averaging the subjective ratings for each SPVM-generated SCI, which is given by

$$\mathbf{S}_j = \frac{1}{N} \sum_{i=1}^{N} \mathbf{S}_{i,j} \tag{1}$$

where N denotes the number of subjects and $S_{i,j}$ denotes the rating by the subject i when viewing the jth SPVM-generated SCI. As shown in Fig. 3, the histogram of the MOS values is illustrated, where we can observe that the perceptual quality of the SCIs has a distribution in a wide MOS value range.

The separation of the visual quality can also facilitate the future investigation on the perceptual feature of SCIs and the design of trusted SCI IQA algorithms.

3   Experimental Results and Discussions

In this section, we will investigate the performance of the SPVM-generated SCIs to evaluate the corresponding visual quality when we apply existing mainstream objective traditional IQA and SCI-IQA metrics respectively to the QADSS database. After that we will give the experimental results and analysis.

In order to evaluate the performance when applying the traditional IQAs for natural images to the QADSS database, we have applied the following ten represented objective IQA methods: ARISM [16], CPBD [17], S_3 [18], $FISH_{bb}$ [19], NIQMC [20], SISBLIM [21], NIQE [22], BQMS [23], RQMSH [12] and RWQMS [24].

When calculating performance, we firstly mapped the results of the objective quality metric to subjective ratings through nonlinear regression of a five-parameter logistic function as suggested by VQEG:

$$f(x) = \beta_1 \left(\frac{1}{2} - \frac{1}{1 + e^{\beta_2(x - \beta_3)}} \right) + \beta_4 x + \beta_5 \qquad (2)$$

where x denotes the predicted score; $f(x)$ denotes the corresponding subjective score; β_i $\{i = 1, 2, 3, 4, 5\}$ are the parameters to be fitted.

Meanwhile, we have employed five statistical indexes, which are Kendall's rank correlation coefficient (KRCC), Spearman Rank order Correlation coefficient (SRCC), Pearsons linear correlation coefficient (PLCC), Root mean square error (RMSE) and Mean absolute error (MAE) respectively. The SRCC and KRCC values can indicate the prediction monotonicity of the quality metric, PLCC reflects the prediction accuracy, RMSE points out the prediction consistency and MAE is a quantity used to measure how close forecasts or predictions are to the eventual outcomes. Therefore, these five indexes demonstrate the prediction performance from different aspects. A superior IQA metric is expected to achieve values close to 1 in SRCC, KRCC and PLCC, while values close to 0 in RMSE and MAE.

As the QADSS database is composed of the webpages and graphic SCIs, we have listed the performance results of objective assessment quality methods on the webpages, graphic SCIs and overall SCIs respectively in Tables 1, 2 and 3. The validation results of the QADSS database are shown in Tables 1, 2 and 3, where it can be observed that a direct comparison among these traditional mainstream IQA methods. From the three tables, on one hand, we have found that they have a poor performance as the most values in SRCC, KRCC and PLCC are lower than 0.5 and some of them even close to 0. On the other hand, the values in RMSE and MAE are relative higher and even close to 1. We can get that the most mainstream IQA objective assessment methods do not work for the QADSS database.

Table 1. Performance of ten IQA models in terms of PLCC, SRCC, KRCC, RMSE, MAE metrics for the webpages in the QADSS database.

Method	PLCC	SRCC	KRCC	RMSE	MAE
ARISM	0.2134	0.2162	0.1531	0.7030	0.8830
CPBD	0.1386	0.1443	0.0957	0.7105	0.8951
S_3	0.1409	0.1541	0.1063	0.7198	0.8948
$FISH_{bb}$	0.1570	0.1599	0.1136	0.7171	0.8926
NIQMC	0.0905	0.0806	0.0545	0.7237	0.9001
SISBLIM	0.1400	0.1166	0.0819	0.7173	0.8949
NIQE	0.2739	0.2306	0.1624	0.7118	0.8692
BQMS	0.4253	0.4008	0.2732	0.6515	0.8180
RQMSH	0.2020	0.1922	0.1396	0.7129	0.8852
RWQMS	0.3465	0.1346	0.0882	0.6751	0.8478

Table 2. Performance of ten IQA models in terms of PLCC, SRCC, KRCC, RMSE, MAE metrics for the graphic SCIs in the QADSS database.

Method	PLCC	SRCC	KRCC	RMSE	MAE
ARISM	0.4712	0.4753	0.3425	0.5157	0.6536
CPBD	0.6524	0.6530	0.4833	0.4367	0.5616
S_3	0.2805	0.1999	0.1428	0.5814	0.7113
$FISH_{bb}$	0.4025	0.3869	0.2685	0.5325	0.6784
NIQMC	0.3913	0.3804	0.2641	0.5500	0.6820
SISBLIM	0.4684	0.2372	0.1815	0.5269	0.6547
NIQE	0.5427	0.5293	0.3883	0.4809	0.6225
BQMS	0.3464	0.2188	0.1521	0.5452	0.6952
RQMSH	0.2065	0.1920	0.1319	0.5827	0.7251
RWQMS	0.1893	0.1273	0.0897	0.5826	0.7277

However, it is surprising to find that the SISBLIM cannot discriminate the images' differences while the ARISM and BQMS based on free-energy principle have a relative better performance among all the computing IQA models, which can be considered to be used in subsequent research of objective algorithm. What is more, the results of the experiment have indicated that the three impact factors, namely image dynamic range, ghosting artifacts and image complexity, play a remarkable impact on the performance on the QADSS database. The SCIs in QADSS contain varying degrees of ghosting artifacts and the contrast distortion because of these impact factors. As shown in Fig. 4, it shows some SCIs with corresponding MOS in QASSD database. The three SCIs in the first two rows are of the same dynamic rang degree, the quality of these SCIs varies

Table 3. Performance of ten IQA models in terms of PLCC, SRCC, KRCC, RMSE, MAE metrics for the overall SCIs in the QADSS database.

Method	PLCC	SRCC	KRCC	RMSE	MAE
ARISM	0.3017	0.3127	0.2171	0.6497	0.8256
CPBD	0.1704	0.1126	0.0774	0.6841	0.8533
S_3	0.0763	0.0572	0.0392	0.6884	0.8635
$FISH_{bb}$	0.0958	0.0825	0.0565	0.6897	0.8620
NIQMC	0.1151	0.1373	0.0922	0.6850	0.8602
SISBLIM	0.2739	0.1819	0.1204	0.6665	0.8329
NIQE	0.2414	0.2025	0.1376	0.6743	0.8404
BQMS	0.3683	0.3698	0.2531	0.6320	0.8051
RQMSH	0.1441	0.0612	0.0393	0.6905	0.8569
RWQMS	0.3219	0.2026	0.1403	0.6562	0.8199

with the image complexity. The higher of the image complexity of *personal view*, the worse of the quality of *shared view*, and vice versa. In the latter two rows, the performance of the SCIs varies with the image dynamic range when the image complexity of *personal view* and *shared view* is the same. In the future work, we aim to propose a specific objective quality method for the QADSS database based on the free-energy model and the above three impact factors.

4   Conclusion

In this paper, we have investigated into the problem of quality assessment of SCIs generated by SPVM system. Firstly, the new SCI image database QADSS, which includes two kinds of type pristine SCIs and a total of 360 SPVM-generated SCI images, has been constructed to investigate the subjective quality of SCIs. In order to ensure the reliability of the results for the subjective viewing, the SS method has been employed. Afterwards, we have applied the ten traditional mainstream IQA objective assessment methods to evaluate the quality of the SCIs in QADSS database. By observing the experimental results, we have found the performance of these mainstream methods conducted on the QADSS database have relative substantial discrepancy compared with the subjective evaluations. According to the correlation analysis and comparison of the ten IQA scores and the MOS values, we can conclude that some distinctive factors, such as image dynamic range, ghosting artifacts and image complexity, cause the false contours and ghosting artifacts in SCIs.

Acknowledgement. This work was supported by the NSFC (61422112, 61371146, 61521062, 61527804), National High-tech R&D Program of China (2015AA015905) and STCFM (15DZ0500200). This work was supported in part by the Research Committee at University of Macau under grant MYRG2016-00137-FST and MYRG2015-00056-FST.

References

1. Wu, X., Zhai, G.: Temporal psychovisual modulation: a new paradigm of information display [Exploratory DSP]. IEEE Sign. Process. Mag. **30**(1), 136–141 (2013)
2. Zhai, G., Wu, X.: Multiuser collaborative viewport via temporal psychovisual modulation [Applications Corner]. IEEE Sign. Process. Mag. **31**(5), 144–149 (2014)
3. Wu, X., Zhai, G., Backward compatible stereoscopic displays via temporal psychovisual modulation. In: SIGGRAPH Asia 2012 Emerging Technologies, vol. 4. ACM (2012)
4. Gao, Z., Zhai, G., Hu, C., et al.: Dual-view medical image visualization based on spatial-temporal psychovisual modulation. In: ICIP, pp. 2168–2170 (2014)
5. Zhai, G., Wu, X.: Defeating camcorder piracy by temporal psychovisual modulation. J. Disp. Technol. **10**(9), 754–757 (2014)
6. Lan, C., Shi, G., Wu, F.: Compress compound images in H.264/MPGE-4 AVC by exploiting spatial correlation. IEEE Trans. Image Process. **19**(4), 946–957 (2010)
7. Lin, T., Zhang, P., Wang, S., et al.: Mixed chroma sampling-rate high efficiency video coding for full-chroma screen content. IEEE Trans. Circuits Syst. Video Technol. **23**(1), 173–185 (2013)
8. Yang, H., Fang, Y., Lin, W., Wang, Z.: Subjective quality assessment of screen content images. In: QoMEX, September 2014
9. Wang, S., Gu, K., Zeng, K., et al.: Objective quality assessment and perceptual compression of screen content images. IEEE Comput. Graph. Appl. **38**, 47–58 (2016)
10. Wang, S., Gu, K., Zeng, K., Wang, Z., Lin, W.: Objective quality assessment and perceptual compression of screen content images. IEEE Comput. Graph. Appl. (to be published)
11. Yang, H., Fang, Y., Lin, W.: Perceptual quality assessment of screen content images. IEEE Trans. Image Process. **24**(11), 4408–4421 (2015)
12. Wang, S., Gu, K., Zhang, X., et al.: Subjective and objective quality assessment of compressed screen content images. IEEE J. Emerg. Sel. Top. Circuits Syst. **6**, 532–543 (2016)
13. Xu, J., Joshi, R., Cohen, R.A.: Overview of the emerging HEVC screen content coding extension. IEEE Trans. Circuits Syst. Video Technol. **26**(1), 50–62 (2016)
14. ITU-R: Bt. 500–12, methodology for the subjective assessment of the quality of television pictures, International Telecommunication Union (2009)
15. Ma, L., Lin, W., Deng, C., Ngan, K.N.: Image retargeting quality assessment: a study of subjective scores and objective metrics. IEEE J. Sel. Top. Sign. Process. **6**(6), 626–639 (2012)
16. Gu, K., Zhai, G., Lin, W., Yang, X., Zhang, W.: No-reference image sharpness assessment in autoregressive parameter space. IEEE Trans. Image Process. **24**(10), 3218–3231 (2015)
17. Narvekar, N.D., Karam, L.J.: A no-reference image blur metric based on the cumulative probability of blur detection (CPBD). IEEE Trans. Image Process. **20**(9), 2678–2683 (2011)
18. Vu, C.T., Phan, T.D., Chandler, D.M.: A spectral and spatial measure of local perceived sharpness in natural images. IEEE Trans. Image Process. **21**(3), 934–945 (2012)
19. Vu, P., Chandler, P.: A fast wavelet-based algorithm for global and local image sharpness estimation. IEEE Sign. Process. Lett. **19**(7), 423–426 (2012)

20. Gu, K., Lin, W., Zhai, G., et al.: No-reference quality metric of contrast-distorted images based on information maximization. IEEE Trans. Cybern. **47**, 4559–4565 (2016)
21. Gu, K., Zhai, G., Yang, X., Zhang, W.: Hybrid no-reference quality metric for singly and multiply distorted images. IEEE Trans. Broadcast. **60**(3), 555–567 (2014)
22. Mittal, A., Soundararajan, R., Bovik, A.C.: Making a completely blind image quality analyzer. IEEE Sign. Process. Lett. **20**(3), 209–212 (2013)
23. Gu, K., Zhai, G., Lin, W., et al.: Learning a blind quality evaluation engine of screen content images. Neurocomputing **196**, 140–149 (2016)
24. Wang, S., Gu, K., Zhang, X., et al.: Reduced-reference quality assessment of screen content images. IEEE Trans. Circuits Syst. Video Technol. **28**, 1–14 (2016)

A Fast Sample Adaptive Offset Algorithm for H.265/HEVC

Yan Zhou and Zhenzhong Chen[(⊠)]

State Key Laboratory of Software Engineering, School of Computer,
Wuhan University, Wuhan 430072, China
{zapply,zzchen}@whu.edu.cn

Abstract. In this paper, a fast Sample Adaptive Offset (SAO) method is proposed to reduce the high computational complexity in SAO estimation process. On the frame level, the relationship between SAO and the quantization parameter or the layer information due to the hierarchical coding structure is explored. A fuzzy control method is proposed to decide how to perform the SAO operation. On the CTU level, an asymmetric EO/BO skipping method is proposed. The complexity measurement of a coding tree unit (CTU) is inferred by the number of coding units (CU). Edge offset (EO) or band offset (BO) is asymmetrically skipped while the CTU is of low complexity, thus the SAO process time can be reduced. Experimental results show that the proposed method can reduce about 63.89% SAO encoding time on average under the common test conditions with negligible loss compared with the original SAO method in HEVC reference software HM16.2.

Keywords: H.265/HEVC · Sample adaptive offset
Fuzzy control · Texture complexity

1 Introduction

The High Efficiency Video Coding (HEVC) or H.265 is the latest video coding standard, which is developed by the Joint Collaborative Team on Video Coding (JCT-VC). It achieves about 50% bit rate reduction compared with the advanced video coding (AVC) or H.264, under the same visual quality. JCT-VC announced the final draft international standard of H.265/HEVC in 2013 [1].

Block-based discrete cosine transform (DCT) is still used in H.265/HEVC, and the transform coefficients are quantized in the frequency domain [2]. For the strong edges in the picture, due to the quantization distortion of the high frequency AC coefficients, ringing artifacts are produced [3]. In order to reduce these artifacts, sample adaptive offset (SAO) is adopted in H.265/HEVC. As a new in-loop filter tool, SAO brings significant improvement in coding efficiency, especially in low delay B and low delay P encoder's configurations. But there still exists the problem of high computational complexity. In order to derive the best SAO parameters for each CTU, many exhaustive operations like comparisons

© Springer International Publishing AG, part of Springer Nature 2018
B. Zeng et al. (Eds.): PCM 2017, LNCS 10735, pp. 641–651, 2018.
https://doi.org/10.1007/978-3-319-77380-3_61

and computations are needed in the SAO parameter estimation process, which take a lot of time in the encoding process. Due to the increasing demand for high-definition (HD, 1920 × 1080) and ultra-high-definition (UHD, 3840 × 2160) resolution videos, the SAO process is time consuming as there are more CTUs in a picture. Therefore, it is very important to develop more efficient SAO algorithms with less computation.

In this paper, a fast SAO algorithm is proposed to reduce the complexity of the SAO process. On the frame level, we found that whether the SAO filter is efficient or not has a great relationship with the quantization parameter and the layer information. Thus, a fuzzy control method is proposed to decide how to perform the SAO operation. We use the fuzzy control method because the fuzzy control method makes it easy to understand the control strategy and it is more robust. On the CTU level, for each CTU, the complexity measurement of a CTU can be evaluated from the number of CUs in the CTU. After deriving the complexity measurement, EO or BO operation is asymmetrically skipped to reduce the SAO encoding time. Our proposed method can achieve a significant reduction of SAO encoding time with negligible loss of coding quality.

The rest of the paper is organized as following. An overview of SAO in H.265/HEVC and some related work is given in the next section. In Sect. 3 the fast SAO algorithm is proposed. Section 4 shows the experiment results, and finally Sect. 5 concludes the paper.

2   Overview of SAO and Related Work

Sample adaptive offset (SAO) is a new in-loop filter technique. The key idea of SAO is to reduce the mean sample distortion by adding an offset value to each sample. There are two kinds of offset techniques adopted in SAO: edge offset (EO) and band offset (BO) [4]. For edge offset operation, firstly the pixel samples are classified by comparing the current pixel value and the neighbouring pixel value. After that, the offset values are calculated based on the classification. Then different offset values are added to different samples. According to the location of the sample, four 1-D directional offset types are used: horizontal (EO_0), vertical (EO_1), 135° diagonal (EO_2), and 45° diagonal (EO_3), as shown in Fig. 1(a).

One of the four EO classes is selected as the best EO mode by rate-distortion optimization [5]. For each EO class, the samples in each CTU are classified into

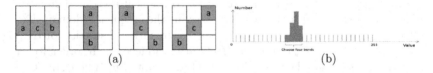

(a)   (b)

Fig. 1. (a) Four 1-D directional offset types for EO sample classification: horizontal (EO_0), vertical (EO_1), 135° diagonal (EO_2), and 45° diagonal (EO_3). (b) Band offset in H.265/HEVC.

Table 1. Sample category classification for each EO class.

Category	Conditions
1	c < a && c < b
2	c < a && c == b or c == a && c < b
3	c > a && c == b or c == a && c > b
4	c > a && c > b
0	None of the above

Table 2. Summarization of the fuzzy rules.

SAO mode	QP			
	NL	NS	PS	PL
Layer NL	S	S	S	S
NS	S	S	S	N
PS	S	S	N	L
PL	S	N	L	L

five categories according to the comparison between the current sample value and its two neighbours. The classification rules are shown in Table 1. In order to get a smoothing effect in the EO mode, for categories 1 and 2, the offset values are always positive. And for categories 3 and 4 are negative [4]. Thus the distortion can be effectively reduced. The selected best EO mode and four offset values are signalled to the decoder.

For band offset, all the samples are classified into 32 segments based on the pixel value of the samples. For an 8-bit sample, pixel value ranges from 0 to 255. The width of each band is 8. Thus for pixel value ranging from $8n$ to $8n + 7$, they belong to band n and n ranges from 0 to 31. As shown in Fig. 2. Four adjacent bands are selected to do the band offset. Four offset values are added to the samples belonging to the selected four bands and the rate-distortion optimization is used to decide which four bands are to do the band offset. The start band position and the four offset values are signalled to the decoder [6].

There are some related work about SAO in the past few years. Joo *et al.* proposed a fast SAO algorithm which reduces SAO encoding time about 77.3% in HM10.0, they proposed a good idea of making the decision of the best SAO edge offset class by exploiting intra prediction mode information instead of exhaustive RD cost calculation for all classes [8]. But the 0.8% BD-rate degradation is a little big. A fast SAO parameter estimation algorithm was proposed by Joo *et al.* [9], which uses the Sobel edge operator to predict the best EO mode. Chen *et al.* proposed a low complexity SAO algorithm based on EO class combination, BO pre-decision and merge separation [10], which can calculate the four EO mode at the same time and decrease the number of BO offset category from 29 to 4. In [11], Choi *et al.* explored various SAO encoding policies including complexity reduction in the SAO parameter estimation and efforts to remove inefficiency caused by its implementation in a pipelined manner through numerous experimental tests. Gendy *et al.* proposed an algorithm that reduces the SAO parameter estimation complexity by adaptively reusing the dominate mode of corresponding set of CTUs [12]. There are two GPU-based SAO optimization algorithm proposed in [13,14], which bring both coding efficiency gain and encoding time reduction. In [15], a dual-clock VLSI design for SAO estimation is proposed to reduce the complexity.

3 Proposed Fast SAO Method

In this paper, we propose a fast SAO algorithm to reduce the complexity of SAO in H.265/HEVC. We aim to design a fast SAO algorithm mainly for random access configuration, it also can be used in other configurations. On the frame level, a fuzzy control method is proposed to decide how to perform the SAO operation for each CTU in a frame. While on the CTU level, an asymmetric EO/BO skipping method is proposed to decide whether the EO operation or BO operation is skipped when performing the SAO operation.

3.1 Low Complexity SAO Based on Fuzzy Controller

As in the prior video coding standard, the artifacts are commonly seen at medium and low bit rates, and the quality is more important for the pictures at lower layers. How to perform the SAO operation can be decided by the quantization parameters and the layer information due to the hierarchical coding structure. Thus we propose a low complexity SAO method based on fuzzy controller on the frame level.

Fuzzy systems are knowledge or principle based systems. The main idea of a fuzzy system is a knowledge station that consists of fuzzy if-then rules [16]. The general structure of a fuzzy system is summarized in three basic forms: fuzzification (inputs related parts), inference engine based on fuzzy rules and defuzzification (output related parts) [17]. As shown in Fig. 2(a). We use the fuzzy control method to decide how to perform the SAO operation because it is easier to design, cheaper to produce, and more robust.

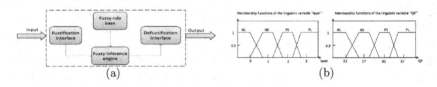

Fig. 2. (a) The general structure of a fuzzy system. (b) Membership function of the linguistic variables.

As artifacts are more probably produced in video coding at medium and low bit rates, the SAO filter is more efficient for the medium and low bit rate videos. So whether the SAO operation should be performed has a great relationship with the quantization parameter. Besides, as the pictures at the lower layers are used for the prediction of the pictures at the higher layers, the improvement of coding quality is more important for the pictures at lower layers. Therefore we choose the quantization parameter (QP) and the layer information as the two input signals of the fuzzy control system.

The output of the fuzzy system is how to perform the SAO operation. As mentioned in Sect. 2, for a CTU, to decide whether to use the SAO filter, many exhaustive calculations are done to derive the RD cost. In this paper, we use the fuzzy control system to decide how to do the SAO filter on a CTU. In some cases, the whole SAO operation is skipped or some EO operation is skipped. Thus many exhaustive operations in the SAO process can be skipped and the SAO encoding time can be reduced.

We use a well-known and simple fuzzy system with two input signals using "Product Inference Engine", singleton fuzzifier, and central average defuzzifier [18]. For the input membership function, the two input signals are layer and QP, which are specified by their fuzzy membership functions (MSF). MSF of a fuzzy system is generalized form of determined function in classic systems. As shown in Fig. 2(b), the layer ranges from 0–3, the letters NS, NL, PS, PL represent negative small, negative large, positive small and positive large. The QP value ranges from 0–51 for 8-bit video sequences in H.265/HEVC, in this paper, we set four typical QP values according to the common test condition.

The output is how to perform the SAO operation. According to our analysis and statistical work, most of the SAO modes in the large QP value and high layer are off, which means the SAO filter is not necessary in these pictures. What's more, the statistical results in Table 3 show that the EO mode is more probable to be EO_0 or EO_1 in the medium QP value and lower layer conditions. Based on these results, we define three kinds of SAO mode. The first one is NORMAL_SAO mode, which means we perform the regular SAO operation. The second one is HALF_SAO mode, in this SAO mode, only EO_0 and EO_1 are selected while performing EO operation, EO_2 and EO_3 are skipped. The last one is SKIP_SAO mode, which means the whole SAO operation is skipped.

After input and output membership functions are determined, a set of principles must be determined that are able to relate the input to the output. We define a fuzzy rule as *if x and y then z* [19], all fuzzy rules are summarized in Table 2. As an example from the table it can be expressed as: *if (QP is PL and layer is PL) then (output is L)*. The letter S, N, L represent small, normal and large, which means we should do NORMAL_SAO mode, HALF_SAO mode and SKIP_SAO mode.

All these fuzzy rules in Table 2 are summarized based on our theoretical analysis and experiment results. Statistical results have been provided in Tables 3 and 4 to support the fuzzy rules in Table 2. The sequences are encoded under random access configuration. In Table 3, we only show the statistical results of the frames whose slice_sao_luma_flag is true. The EO_0/EO_1 mode CTU number and the EO mode CTU number under different QP and layer conditions are presented, the Rate is the ratio between the EO_0/EO_1 mode CTU number and the EO mode CTU number. It is easy to get the conclusion that, the EO mode of most CTUs under these QP and layer conditions in Table 3 are selected as EO_0/EO_1 mode. So EO_2 and EO_3 process can be skipped under these QP and layer conditions. The number of CTUs which have performed SAO operation and the total CTU number in each sequence under different QP and layer conditions are provided in Table 4. It is obvious that the SAO filter is rarely used under these QP and layer conditions. Thus the whole SAO operation is

Table 3. The statistical results of CTU SAO EO mode selection under certain QP and layer conditions.

Sequence	Total frames	QP = 27 && layer = 3			QP = 32 && layer = 2			QP = 37 && layer = 1		
		EO_0/ EO_1	EO mode	Rate	EO_0/ EO_1	EO mode	Rate	EO_0/ EO_1	EO mode	Rate
PeopleOnStreet	150	11826	15831	74.70%	5881	12420	47.35%	4011	4979	80.56%
Traffic	150	0	0	-	0	0	-	3992	3992	100.00%
BasketballDrive	500	12701	13295	95.53%	861	1160	74.22%	13922	14100	98.74%
BQTerrace	600	23533	23865	98.61%	953	955	99.79%	18816	18821	99.97%
Cactus	500	24	26	92.31%	0	0	-	9714	9729	99.85%
BasketballDrill	500	6035	6119	98.63%	214	311	68.81%	4167	4227	98.58%
BQMall	600	661	665	99.40%	403	408	98.77%	6003	6023	99.67%
PartyScene	500	6602	7587	87.02%	962	1126	85.44%	5799	5951	97.45%
BasketballPass	500	971	1156	84.00%	657	868	75.69%	1215	1291	94.11%
BQSquare	600	2084	2095	99.47%	532	532	100.00%	819	819	100.00%
RaceHorses	300	974	1133	85.97%	916	1307	70.08%	745	850	87.65%
FourPeople	600	0	0	-	0	0	-	4759	4760	99.98%
Johnny	600	0	0	-	0	0	-	4284	4284	100.00%
ChinaSpeed	300	15575	18489	84.24%	5843	7292	80.13%	4198	4655	90.18%
SlidEditing	300	475	475	100.00%	63	80	78.75%	3080	3090	99.68%
SlideShow	200	1199	1383	86.70%	815	1028	79.28%	1821	1921	94.79%

Table 4. The statistical results of CTU SAO performed information under certain QP and layer conditions.

Sequence	Total frames	QP = 32 && layer = 3		QP = 37 && layer = 2		QP = 37 && layer = 3	
		SAO on	Total	SAO on	Total	SAO on	Total
PeopleOn Street	150	1	75000	0	37000	0	75000
Traffic	150	0	75000	0	37000	0	750002
BQTerrace	600	0	15300	0	76500	0	15300
BQMall	600	0	31200	0	15600	0	31200
BQSquare	600	0	8400	0	4200	0	8400
Johnny	600	0	72000	0	36000	0	72000
SlideShow	200	240	24000	268	12000	476	24000

Table 5. The statistical results about the SAO information of the CTUs whose CU number is 1.

Sequences	CTUs whose CU number is 1		
	SAO off CTU number	Total CTU number	Rate
PeopleOn Street	16725	21173	78.99%
Traffic	11543	15341	75.24%
BQTerrace	23953	37056	64.64%
BQMall	3535	4331	81.62%
BQSquare	1383	1543	89.63%
Johnny	16215	19089	84.94%
SlideShow	8434	11166	75.53%

skipped at high QP and high layer to save the SAO encoding time. While at low layer and low QP conditions, the original SAO process is selected, which can guarantee the quality improvements from the SAO filter for H.265/HEVC coding.

3.2 Asymmetric EO/BO Skipping Based on CTU Complexity

The SAO filter is used to improve visual quality by preventing ringing artifacts which appear when using large transform size or large numbers of taps in the interpolation filter. While large number taps interpolation filter is more efficient in the picture of low texture complexity, thus the SAO filter is more efficient in the CTUs of high texture complexity. Our statistical work also demonstrates that the SAO operation is done more on those CTUs of high complexity. In order to reduce the complexity of SAO operation, the asymmetric EO/BO skipping is a good method.

Our statistical results show that if a CTU has only one CU, the SAO operation mode for this CTU is more probably to be off, namely no SAO operation. As show in Table 5, these sequences are all encoded under the random access configuration and the quantization parameter value is 32. In the most CTUs whose CU number is 1, the SAO operation is off, which means the SAO filter is not efficient on these CTUs. The Rate in the table is a ratio between the SAO off CTU number and the Total CTU number. According to the statistical results, both the BO and EO operations can be skipped while the CU number in a CTU is 1 to reduce the computational complexity.

In the whole SAO process, EO category calculation takes the most SAO processing time [11]. It takes a great deal of time to calculate the EO_0 mode to EO_3 mode one by one to get the best EO mode. If we want to reduce the complexity of SAO, the EO operation is vital. For the video with more low complexity CTUs, if EO operation can be skipped when doing SAO filter, the computational complexity would be reduced greatly with negligible coding quality loss. In order to control quality loss in a certain range, EO operation is skipped while the CU number in a CTU is between 1 and 8, only BO operation is considered in the SAO process.

Thus on the CTU level, the asymmetric EO/BO skipping method is proposed. Firstly the complexity measurement is refered by calculating the CU number of the CTU. If the CU number of the current CTU is 1, the whole SAO operation is skipped. If the CU number is between 1 and 8, EO operation is skipped. If the CU number is more than 8, the whole SAO operation is performed.

4 Experimental Results

In this section, the experimental results are presented. The proposed algorithm is implemented in the H.265/HEVC reference software HM16.2 [20]. The test sequences are HEVC full test sequences. In order to show the performance of our proposed method comprehensively, all intra (AI), random access (RA), low delay P (LP) and low delay B (LB) group of pictures (GOP) structure are used.

Table 6 shows the comparison results between the original SAO algorithm in H.265/HEVC and our proposed fast SAO algorithm. We also give the experimental results without SAO filter in H.265/HEVC for comparison. The Bjontegaard-Delta bitrate (BD-rate) [21] measure is used to evaluate objective coding efficiency, which represents the average differences in rate distortion performance.

Table 6. Sequence by sequence Y BD-rates degradation under different GOP structure and time saving.

Class	Sequence	SAO off				Proposed fast SAO				SAO time saving			
		AI	RA	LP	LB	AI	RA	LP	LB	AI	RA	LP	LB
Class A	Nebuta	0.23%	2.92%	-	-	0.08%	0.29%	-	-	61.28%	76.27%	-	-
	PeopleOnStreet	1.27%	2.13%	-	-	0.19%	0.06%	-	-	37.18%	47.82%	-	-
	SteamLocomotive	0.25%	2.94%	-	-	0.10%	0.56%	-	-	71.66%	87.08%	-	-
	Traffic	0.94%	1.21%	-	-	0.12%	0.17%	-	-	39.84%	73.28%	-	-
Class B	BasketballDrive	0.18%	1.54%	9.79%	1.40%	0.03%	0.41%	1.61%	0.54%	49.34%	71.44%	66.36%	69.90%
	BQTerrace	0.49%	4.89%	23.31%	3.92%	0.07%	0.51%	1.03%	0.56%	42.52%	70.64%	62.51%	68.86%
	Cactus	0.44%	2.40%	11.54%	2.95%	0.09%	0.41%	0.86%	0.85%	41.63%	69.30%	65.07%	68.26%
	Kimono	0.46%	0.63%	8.51%	0.84%	0.20%	0.19%	0.94%	0.21%	62.97%	77.28%	70.26%	75.63%
	ParkScene	0.66%	0.85%	9.85%	1.38%	0.08%	0.16%	0.30%	0.13%	44.08%	67.52%	57.98%	61.93%
Class C	BasketballDrill	1.04%	1.61%	6.75%	2.75%	0.06%	0.17%	0.52%	0.39%	23.67%	60.47%	61.06%	65.87%
	BQMall	0.33%	0.61%	8.88%	1.71%	-0.01%	0.08%	0.31%	0.27%	38.68%	66.15%	58.22%	62.38%
	PartyScene	0.15%	-0.21%	4.22%	0.68%	-0.01%	0.02%	0.11%	0.01%	41.27%	59.26%	45.53%	46.82%
	RaceHorses	0.54%	2.06%	10.82%	1.82%	0.09%	0.11%	0.54%	0.17%	40.48%	50.39%	45.21%	47.37%
Class D	BasketballPass	0.25%	0.45%	4.90%	1.24%	-0.03%	0.05%	0.27%	0.21%	42.32%	49.38%	42.28%	44.70%
	BlowingBubbles	0.23%	-0.48 %	2.90%	0.02%	0.00%	0.00%	0.09%	0.08%	36.27%	50.66%	40.01%	37.00%
	BQSquare	0.52%	-0.03%	3.91%	0.83%	0.11%	0.03%	-0.02%	0.09%	38.72%	57.47%	39.60%	44.46%
	RaceHorses	0.55%	1.14%	6.75%	1.34%	0.08%	0.08%	0.16%	0.06%	36.24%	39.93%	37.00%	37.83%
Class E	FourPeople	0.71%	1.92%	9.84%	3.12%	0.03%	0.35%	1.09%	0.65%	39.02%	83.15%	81.05%	82.95%
	Johnny	0.38%	0.88%	15.81%	2.53%	0.03%	0.20%	1.63%	0.42%	58.24%	88.73%	86.60%	88.68%
	KristenAndSara	0.59%	1.57%	12.51%	2.53%	0.04%	0.27%	1.67%	0.53%	51.23%	86.24%	84.06%	86.33%
Class F	BasketballDrillText	1.10%	1.83%	7.20%	3.98%	0.04%	0.21%	0.44%	0.30%	34.38%	57.70%	59.29%	61.65%
	ChinaSpped	1.37%	3.57%	9.62%	6.82%	0.25%	0.23%	0.58%	0.42%	60.06%	62.13%	58.53%	62.78%
	SlideEditing	1.53%	2.96%	5.58%	4.83%	0.21%	1.11%	2.24%	2.40%	56.45%	88.35%	92.37%	92.08%
	SlideShow	1.64%	2.64%	6.51%	5.70%	0.38%	0.52%	1.74%	1.78%	80.15%	82.45%	81.93%	82.45%
Summary	Class A	0.67%	2.30%	-	-	0.12%	0.27%	-	-	52.49%	71.11%	-	-
	Class B	0.45%	2.06%	12.60%	2.10%	0.09%	0.34%	0.95%	0.46%	48.11%	71.24%	64.44%	68.92%
	Class C	0.51%	1.02%	7.67%	1.74%	0.03%	0.09%	0.37%	0.21%	36.03%	59.07%	52.51%	55.61%
	Class D	0.39%	0.27%	4.61%	0.86%	0.04%	0.04%	0.12%	0.11%	38.39%	49.36%	39.72%	41.00%
	Class E	0.56%	1.46%	12.72%	2.72%	0.03%	0.27%	1.46%	0.54%	49.50%	86.04%	83.90%	85.99%
	Class F	1.41%	2.75%	7.23%	5.33%	0.22%	0.52%	1.25%	1.22%	57.76%	72.66%	73.03%	74.74%
Avg		0.66%	1.64%	8.96%	2.52%	0.09%	0.26%	0.81%	0.50%	48.99%	71.05%	66.42%	69.11%

Please note that a positive BD-rate number means the proposed SAO method has coding loss. Time saving represents the SAO processing time compared with the original SAO method in H.265/HEVC. And the SAO time saving here is defined as

$$timesaving = \frac{(SAOTime_{org} - SAOTime_{prop})}{SAOTime_{org}} \times 100\%$$

The experimental results show that about 48.99%, 71.05%, 66.42% and 69.11% time can be saved in the AI, RA, LP and LB configurations with the proposed algorithm. Accordingly it brings about 0.09%, 0.26%, 0.81% and 0.50% BD-rate loss for luma component at those conditions. From Table 6 we can see, for each class, the proposed fast SAO algorithm achieves saving different SAO encoding time.

In Table 7, we make a comparison with other fast SAO algorithms proposed in recent years. As shown in the table, the average Y BD-rate degradation for each class (except Class A) under LP configuration is presented. We also show the average Y BD-rate degradation results for AI, RA, LP, LB configurations. The SAO encoding time saving in Table 7 is an average result of the

Table 7. Comparison with previous work in terms of luma BD-rate degradation and SAO encoding time saving.

Y BD-rate degradation		Method A [11]	Method B [8]	Method C [12]	Proposed
LP	Class B	2.2%	1.6%	1.8%	1.0%
	Class C	1.3%	1.1%	1.6%	0.4%
	Class D	1.2%	1.0%	1.1%	0.1%
	Class E	2.9%	2.9%	0.7%	1.5%
	Class F	4.2%	4.0%	1.0%	1.3%
	Avg.	2.36%	2.12%	1.2%	0.8%
LB	Avg.	1.5%	1.3%	0.9%	0.5%
RA	Avg.	0.7%	0.5%	0.7%	0.3%
AI	Avg.	0.3%	0.2%	0.5%	0.1%
SAO encoding time saving relative to anchor					
	Avg.	75.5%	69.6%	75.0%	63.9%

SAO encoding time saving for each sequence under the four common test configurations. The three other fast SAO methods achieve about 75.5%, 69.6%, and 75.0% SAO encoding time reduction compared with the original SAO method in H.265/HEVC, but the problem in these methods is that the encoding quality loss is also high. For example, under the LB configuration, the encoding quality loss for method A, B and C are 1.5%, 1.3% and 0.9%, while our proposed method achieves only 0.5% loss. Whilst achieving much smaller quality loss compared with other methods under the common test conditions, we also achieve about 63.9% SAO encoding time saving. Therefore, we keep a better balance between the encoding quality and the encoding time.

5   Conclusion

In this paper, we propose a fast SAO algorithm to reduce the high complexity of the SAO encoding process for H.265/HEVC. On the frame level, the relationship between the SAO filter and the quantization parameter or the layer information is explored. A fuzzy control method is proposed to decide how to perform the SAO operation for each frame, which can reduce much SAO encoding time. On the CTU level, the complexity measurement of each CTU is decided by the CU number in each CTU. According to the different CU split information, EO operation or BO operation is skipped when doing SAO filtering. In order to keep a better balance between encoding time and video quality, the EO/BO skipping is asymmetric instead of skipping symmetrically as designed in the most of traditional methods. Experiment results show that our proposed algorithm can reduce about 63.89% SAO coding time with only 0.42% BD-rate loss on average under the common test condition on the H.265/HEVC full test sequences.

Acknowledgments. This work was supported by National Hightech R&D Program of China (863 Program, 2015AA015903).

References

1. Bross, B., Han, W.J., Ohm, J.R., Sullivan, G.J., Wang, Y.K., Wiegand, T.: High efficiency video coding (HEVC) text specification draft 10. In: ITU-T/IEC/ISO JCTVC-L1003, pp. 1–88 (2013)
2. Sullivan, G.J., Ohm, J.R., Han, W.J., Wiegand, T.: Overview of the high efficiency video coding (HEVC) standard. IEEE Trans. Circ. Syst. Video Technol. **22**(12), 1649–1668 (2012)
3. Yuan, M., Wu, H.: A survey of hybrid MC/DPCM/DCT video coding distortions. Sig. Process. **70**(3), 247–278 (1998)
4. Fu, C.M., Alshina, E., Alshin, A., Huang, Y.W., Chen, C.Y., Tsai, C.Y., Hsu, C.W., Lei, S.M., Park, J.H., Han, W.-J.: Sample adaptive offset in the HEVC standard. IEEE Trans. Circ. Syst. Video Technol. **22**(12), 1755–1764 (2012)
5. Sullivan, G.J., Wiegand, T.: Rate-distortion optimization for video compression. IEEE Sig. Process. Mag. **15**(6), 74–90 (1998)
6. Maani, E., Nakagami, O.: Flexible band offset mode in SAO. Joint Collaborative Team on Video Coding (JCT-VC), Document JCTVC-H0406 (2012)
7. Yin, S., Zhang, X., Gao, Z.: Efficient SAO coding algorithm for x265 encoder. In: 2015 IEEE Visual Communications and Image Processing (VCIP), pp. 1–4 (2015)
8. Joo, J., Choi, Y., Lee, K.: Fast sample adaptive offset encoding algorithm for HEVC based on intra prediction mode. In: 2013 IEEE The Third International Conference on Consumer Electronics (ICCE), pp. 1–4 (2013)
9. Joo, J., Choi, Y.: Dominant edge direction based fast parameter estimation algorithm for sample adaptive offset in HEVC. In: 2014 IEEE International Conference on Image Processing (ICIP), pp. 3749–3752 (2014)
10. Chen, G., Pei, Z., Liu, Z., Ikenaga, T.: Low complexity SAO in HEVC base on class combination, pre-decision and merge separation. In: 2014 19th International Conference on Digital Signal Processing (DSP), pp. 259–262 (2014)
11. Choi, Y., Joo, J.: Exploration of practical HEVC/H. 265 sample adaptive offset encoding policies. IEEE Sig. Process. Lett. **22**(4), 465–468 (2015)
12. Gendy, S.E., Shalaby, A., Sayed, M.S.: Fast parameter estimation algorithm for sample adaptive offset in HEVC encoder. In: 2015 IEEE Visual Communications and Image Processing (VCIP), pp. 1–4 (2015)
13. Wang, Y., Guo, X., Lu, Y., Fan, X., Zhao, D.: GPU-based optimization for sample adaptive offset in HEVC. In: 2016 IEEE International Conference on Image Processing (ICIP), pp. 829–833 (2016)
14. Luo, F., Wang, S., Zhang, N., Ma, S., Gao, W.: GPU based sample adaptive offset parameter decision and perceptual optimization for HEVC. In: 2016 IEEE International Symposium on Circuits and Systems (ISCAS), pp. 2687–2690 (2016)
15. Zhou, J., Zhou, D., Wang, S., Zhang, S., Yoshimura, T., Goto, S.: A dual-clock VLSI design of H.265 sample adaptive offset estimation for 8k ultra-HD TV encoding. IEEE Trans. Very Scale Integr. (VLSI) Syst. **25**(2), 714–724 (2017)
16. Kamran, R., Rezaei, M., Fani, D.: A new fuzzy rate control scheme for variable bit rate video applications of HEVC. In: IEEE 2015 4th Iranian Joint Congress on Fuzzy and Intelligent Systems, pp. 1–5 (2015)
17. Rezaei, M., Hannuksela, M.M., Gabbouj, M.: Semi-fuzzy rate controller for variable bit rate video. IEEE Trans. Circ. Syst. Video Technol. **18**(5), 633–645 (2008)

18. Bezdek, J.C.: Fuzzy models what are they, and why? [Editorial]. IEEE Trans. Fuzzy Syst. **1**(1), 1–6 (1993)
19. Simon, D., El-Sherief, H.: Fuzzy logic for digital phase-locked loop filter design. IEEE Trans. Fuzzy Syst. **3**(2), 211–218 (1995)
20. HEVC test model reference software (HM). https://hevc.hhi.fraunhofer.de/svn/ svn_HEVCSoftware/tags/HM-16.2/
21. Bjontegaard, G.: Calculation of average PSNR differences between RD-curves. In: ITU-T VCEG-M33, p. 14 (2001)

Blind Quality Assessment for Screen Content Images by Texture Information

Ning Lu$^{(\boxtimes)}$ and Guohui Li

School of Computer Science and Technology, Huazhong University of Science and Technology, Wuhan, China
jiangxiluning@gmail.com

Abstract. Most image quality assessment (IQA) methods designed for screen content images (SCIs) require the reference information, and existing blind IQA metrics can not obtain consistent results with subjective ratings. In this study, we propose a novel blind image quality assessment method for SCIs based on orientation selectivity mechanism by which the primary visual cortex performs visual texture information extraction for scene understanding. First, we extract the orientation features to perceive the visual distortion of degraded SCIs. Second, the structure features are extracted from the derivatives as the complementary information of orientation features. Finally, we employ support vector regression (SVR) as the mapping function from the features to quality scores. Experimental results show that the proposed method can obtain better performance than other existing related methods.

Keywords: Visual quality assessment · Screen content image
No reference quality assessment

1 Introduction

With the development of multimedia technology, the amount of multimedia interactive devices has increased dramatically in recent years. And the screen content images (SCIs) are often treated as the medium of signal transmission. Subject to bandwidth and other factors, various processing technologies might be involved, such as segmentation [1], compression [2], *etc.* During the SCI processing, many visual distortions might be introduced. The visual quality degradation of SCIs has great influence on quality of experiences from viewers. It is import to adjust the parameters or settings of various applications dynamically according to the quality of SCIs, and thus, perceptual quality assessment of SCIs is highly desired for different SCI processing applications.

In the past decades, there have been many image quality assessment (IQA) methods proposed in the literature. Among these methods, peak signal to noise (PSNR) and mean square error (MSE) are well-known for its low-complexity. However, they can not obtain promising quality prediction performance, since they do not consider the visual characteristics of the human visual systems

© Springer International Publishing AG, part of Springer Nature 2018
B. Zeng et al. (Eds.): PCM 2017, LNCS 10735, pp. 652–661, 2018.
https://doi.org/10.1007/978-3-319-77380-3_62

(HVS). Apart from PSNR and MSE, many other IQA metrics have been designed by considering the properties of the HVS, such as structure similarity (SSIM) [3], GSMD [4], IR-SSIM [5], information fidelity criterion (IFC) [6]. These methods require the full reference (FR) information. Some studies also introduce reduced-reference (RR) IQA methods [7] which require part of reference information for quality prediction. Besides, there have been some no reference (NR) methods designed without any reference information [8,9].

These aforementioned methods are designed for IQA of natural images. As shown in the initial study on IQA of SCIs [10], the properties of SCIs are different from those of natural images in naturalness. Applying IQA methods designed for natural images to predict the visual quality of SCIs directly can not obtain consistent prediction results as human beings perceive. According to different perceptual properties of textual and pictorial regions, Yang et al. adopted two different manners to calculate the visual quality of textual and pictorial regions, and a weighted activity map is employed to combine the quality scores of textual and pictorial regions to get the final quality of SCI [10]. Gu et al. proposed a structure-induced quality metric (SIQM) by weighting SSIM with the structural degradation model [11]. In [2], Wang et al. designed an IQA method for SCIs by incorporating viewing field adaption. Fang et al. developed a FR IQA metric for SCIs by uncertainty weighting with the consideration that the HVS is more sensitive to high-frequency information (such as edge information) than other smooth regions in SCIs [12]. Ni et al. designed IQA models to evaluate the perceptual quality of SCIs based on gradient direction [13] and edge information [14]. Wang et al. proposed a RR IQA method from the perspective of SCI visual perception [15]. All these methods require the reference information which is always unavailable in practical applications.

In [16], Gu et al. established a blind quality evaluation engine of SCIs with the free energy based brain theory and structural degradation model. Meanwhile, a large scale database without human ratings was applied to train the IQA model in order to avoid the over-fitting problem [16]. However, these distorted SCIs in the training database are labeled by an objective FR IQA method [11], thus the IQA model may exist deviations with the actual model obtained by training with the labels obtained by subjective experiments. Shao et al. designed a NR IQA model for SCIs from the perspective of sparse representation in which both local and global properties are taken into account. However, these two methods can not get high accuracy in predicting the visual quality of distorted SCIs. Thus, how to design an effective NR IQA method for SCIs is still challenging.

In this paper, we propose a novel blind IQA model based on visual texture information inspired by orientation selectivity mechanism [18] with which the primary visual cortex performs visual information extraction for scene under-standing. In the local receptive field, pixels with similar gradient directions are regarded as excitatory and vice versa, and the pattern calculated by local ori-entation will be degraded by the distortion [18]. The orientation information is also used for IQA in other existing study [13]. As shown in the study [3], the HVS is sensitive to the structure information. There also many existing studies of IQA focused on structure degradation. In [19], Gu *et al.* designed a structural similarity weighted SSIM metric by locally weighting SSIM map with local structure similarities computed by SSIM itself. In this work, we employ the structure features to capture the distortion of SCIs which can be regared as the complementary information of orientation features. We calculate the gradient magnitudes based on the deviations of four adjacent pixel pairs and pixel pairs in the corresponding positions around the centre pixel along four directions and another gradient map by convolution operators. As shown in existing studies [20], the histograms of second order gradients are powerful in capturing the curvature related geometric properties of the neural landscape. There are also some studies applying high order gradients in IQA task [21,22]. Different from these existing studies, we applied the local binary pattern (LBP) [23] to calculate the second order. derivatives based on nine gradient maps, and the structure features are represented in the form of histogram. Finally, support vector regression (SVR) is adopted as the mapping function from the features to subjective scores. Experiments are conducted on the large-scale database to demonstrate the high performance of the proposed method.

The remaining of this paper is organized as follows. In Sect. 2, we introduce the proposed method step by step. In Sect. 3, we provide the experimental results to demonstrate the advantages of the proposed method. The final section summarizes the paper.

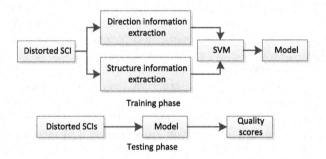

Fig. 1. The proposed framework.

2   Proposed Method

Inspired by the orientation selectivity mechanism [18], we extract orientation features as an indictor of quality degradation of SCIs. Meanwhile, structure features are used as the complementary information to predict the visual quality of SCIs. As shown in Fig. 1, we first train the quality prediction model of SCIs and then use this model to predict visual quality of SCIs. In the training phase, we select the training samples from the database randomly and the corresponding labels are the subjective quality scores, SVR is adopted to train the model. In the testing phase, objective quality scores of testing SCIs are calculated based on the model calculated in the training phase. When extracting the orientation information, we calculate the orientation of each pixel, then we compare the orientation features of the surrounding pixels with centre pixel, if the deviation between the orientation values of centre pixel and one surrounding pixel is less than the threshold, the pattern of the surrounding pixel is set to excitatory and denoted by '+', otherwise inhibitory which is denoted by '−'. The detailed description can refer to [18]. According to the number of '+' of the binary pattern for each pixel, we can get the histogram features of the orientation information of each SCI which represent the first part of quality aware features. For the structure features, first, we calculate the gradient magnitudes from both the adjacent pixels and pixel pairs in the corresponding positions around the central pixel along four directions and another gradient map by the convolution operators, these gradient maps represent the first order derivatives, while LBP is used to calculate the second order derivatives.

2.1 Orientation Feature Extraction

As mentioned in the previous section, we extract orientation and structure features to capture the visual degradation of SCIs. First, the orientation of each pixel is calculated as below.

$$d = \arctan \frac{P_v}{P_h} \tag{1}$$

$$P_v = P \otimes c_v \tag{2}$$

$$P_h = P \otimes c_h \tag{3}$$

$$c_v = \frac{1}{3} \begin{bmatrix} 1 & 1 & 1 \\ 0 & 0 & 0 \\ -1 & -1 & -1 \end{bmatrix} \tag{4}$$

$$c_h = \frac{1}{3} \begin{bmatrix} 1 & 0 & -1 \\ 1 & 0 & -1 \\ 1 & 0 & -1 \end{bmatrix} \tag{5}$$

where d represent orientation information map of image P; P_v and P_h are the orientation information maps along vertical and horizontal directions which are calculated based on filtering operations c_v and c_h, respectively. $\otimes$ represents the convolution operator.

After calculating the orientation information map d, we compare the value of each central pixel in d with the values of the surrounding pixels in local region. If the deviation between the central pixel and one surrounding pixel is smaller than the threshold (set to 6°), the pattern of this surrounding pixel will be set as '+', otherwise it is set as '−'. After calculating the transformed image d, each pixel of image d will be represented by a binary pattern according to the symbols of the surrounding pixels [18]. We set the size of local region as $3 * 3$, and each central pixel can be represented by a 8-bit binary pattern. These binary patterns with the same number of excitations are combined together for feature representation [18]. Thus, we can obtain 9 features to represent the orientation information as below.

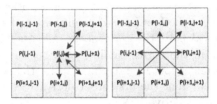

Fig. 2. The operators for calculating structure features.

$$f_m = \sum_{n=1}^{N} \sigma(d_n)\theta(d_n', m) \tag{6}$$

$$\theta(d_n', m) = \begin{cases} 1, & \text{if } d_n' = m \\ 0, & \text{otherwise.} \end{cases} \tag{7}$$

where d_n represents the n-th pixel in image d and $\sigma(d_n)$ is the local variance of d_n; N is the pixel number of image d; d_n' represents the number of '+' of the binary pattern; m is in the range of 0 and 8. Finally, we normalize the features as follows.

$$f_m' = \frac{f_m}{\sum_{f=0}^{8} f_m} \tag{8}$$

The orientation features of each SCI are combined together to obtain a feature vector: $\{f_0', f_1' ..., f_8'\}$.

2.2   Structure Feature Extraction

Considering that the HVS is sensitive to the structure features which is complicated in textual region and the high-frequency region of pictorial region. It also can be treated as the complementary features of orientation information in capturing the distortion of SCIs. The structure features are extracted by two steps in this study. First, we calculate the magnitudes of deviations of two adjacent pixels and pixel pairs in the corresponding positions around the central pixel along four orientations as shown Fig. 2, the gradient operators defined in Fig. 2 can only capture the variations of two pixels in a local region, so we employ the laplacian filter to calculate the deviations of all pixels in the local region. The operations are conducted as follows:

$$H(i,j) = \frac{1}{2}|P(i,j) - P(i,j+1)| \tag{9}$$

$$V(i,j) = \frac{1}{2}|P(i,j) - P(i+1,j)| \tag{10}$$

$$ld(i,j) = \frac{1}{2}|P(i,j) - P(i+1,j+1)| \tag{11}$$

$$lu(i,j) = \frac{1}{2}|P(i,j) - P(i-1,j+1)| \tag{12}$$

$$H1(i,j) = \frac{1}{2}|P(i,j+1) - P(i,j-1)| \tag{13}$$

$$V1(i,j) = \frac{1}{2}|P(i+1,j) - P(i-1,j)| \tag{14}$$

$$ld1(i,j) = \frac{1}{2}|P(i+1,j+1) - P(i-1,j-1)| \tag{15}$$

$$lu1(i,j) = \frac{1}{2}|P(i,j) - P(i+1,j-1)| \tag{16}$$

$$L = P \otimes \frac{1}{3} \begin{bmatrix} \frac{1}{2} & 2 & \frac{1}{2} \\ 2 & -10 & 2 \\ \frac{1}{2} & 2 & \frac{1}{2} \end{bmatrix} \tag{17}$$

where $i \in \{1, 2..., I-1\}$ and $j \in \{1, 2..., J-1\}$; I and J represent image height and width, respectively. In total, we obtain 9 gradient maps which are denoted as the first order derivatives, These gradient maps are used to calculate the second order derivatives based on LBP [23] from which the structure features are calculated. The local rotation invariant uniform LBP operator can be formulated as:

$$RIULBP_{E,R} = \begin{cases} \sum_{i=0}^{E-1} t(I_i - I_c), T(LBP_{E,R}) \leq 2 \\ \\ E+1, Otherwise \end{cases} \tag{18}$$

$$T(LBP_{E,R}) = \|t(I_{(E-1)} - I_c) - t(I_0 - I_c)\| + \\ \sum_{i=0}^{K-1} \|t(I_i - I_c) - t(I_{(i-1)} - I_c)\| \tag{19}$$

$$t(I_i - I_c) = \begin{cases} 1, (I_i - I_c) \geq 0 \\ \\ 0, (I_i - I_c) < 0 \end{cases} \tag{20}$$

where $RIULBP$ represents the local rotation invariant uniform LBP operator; E denotes the number of neighbors and R denotes the radius of the neighborhood;

I_c and I_i represent the intensity value of the center pixel and circularly symmetric neighborhood in the local region of gradient map; T is used to calculate the number of bitwise transitions. $RIULBP$ would have $E + 2$ distinct patterns, and we set E and R to 8 and 1, respectively. Thus, the gradient maps denoted by H, V, ld, lu, $H1$, $V1$, $ld1$, $lu1$, and L can be mapped to the feature maps denoted by g_1, g_2, g_3, g_4, g_5, g_6, g_7, g_8, g_9 in which the intensity of pixels is in the interval $\{0, 1..., 9\}$. We extract the structure features from the mapped gradient maps as follows.

$$s_m = \frac{\sum_{i=1}^{NUM_m} f(g_m(i), n)}{NUM_m} \tag{21}$$

$$f(g_m(i), n) = \begin{cases} 1, & \text{if } g_m(i) = n \\ 0, & \text{otherwise.} \end{cases} \tag{22}$$

where g_m represents the mapped feature maps; m is in the range of 1 and 9; n represents the intensity of pixel in g_m which is in the range of 0 and 9; NUM_m is the number of pixel of g_m. Thus, we can get 9-element feature vector s_m which represents the structure features for each gradient map g_m. In total, we can get 90 features to represent structure information of each SCI.

2.3   Regression Model for Quality Prediction

In the final step, SVR with radial basis function (RBF) kernel is adopted by using LIBSVM package [24] as the mapping function from quality aware features to subjective quality scores. For each distorted SCI, we obtain 97 features including 9 features for orientation information and 90 features for structure information. In our implementation, orientation and structure features are calculated in three scales. Thus, each SCI has 297 features totally. The database are divided into training and testing subsets randomly for 1000 times, with 80% as the training dataset and the rest as testing dataset, and the median performance is reported.

3   Experimental Results

3.1   Database Description and Evaluation Methodology

The comparison experiments are conducted on a large scale SCI database SIQAD [10]. Twenty SCIs are collected from webpages, slides, PDF files and digital magazines, with seven degradation types are introduced to generate distorted distorted images including Gaussian Noise (GN), Gaussian Blur, Motion Blur, Contrast Change, JPEG, JPEG 2000, and Layer Segmentation Based Coding, each of which includes seven levels. Thus, there are 980 distorted SCIs in total in the database. Three different criteria are used to evaluate the performance of the IQA metrics including: Pearson linear correlation coefficient (PLCC), Spearman rank order correlation coefficient (SRCC) and root mean squared error (RMSE). PLCC and SRCC are used to calculate the prediction accuracy, RMSE measures the deviation between the objective prediction and subjective ratings.

Table 1. Experimental results of the proposed method and other existing FR methods.

Components	PSNR	SSIM	IFC	GMSD	SPQA	SQI	GSS	EMSQA	Proposed
PLCC	0.5869	0.5912	0.6395	0.7259	0.8584	0.8644	0.8461	0.8648	**0.8306**
SRCC	0.5608	0.5836	0.6011	0.7305	0.8416	0.8548	0.8359	0.8504	**0.8007**
RMSE	11.5859	11.5450	10.9920	9.4684	7.3421	7.1782	7.6310	7.1860	**7.9331**

Table 2. Experimental results of the proposed method and other existing NR methods.

Components	BRISQUE	RR-IQA	BLIQUP-SCI	BQMS	Proposed
PLCC	0.8113	0.8014	0.7705	0.8115	**0.8306**
SRCC	0.7749	0.7655	0.7990	0.8005	**0.8007**
RMSE	8.2565	8.5620	10.0200	9.3042	**7.9331**

3.2 Comparison Experiments

In this section, we compare the proposed method with the following existing visual quality metrics: PSNR, SQI [2], SSIM [3], GMSD [4], IFC [6], BRISQUE [8], SPQA [10], GSS [13], EMSQA [14], RR-IQA [15], BQMS [16] and BLIQUP-SCI [17]. Among these metrics, PSNR, IFC, GMSD, SPQA, SQI, GSS and EMSQA are FR VQA metrics. Specifically, SPQA, SQI, GSS and EMSQA are designed for quality assessment of SCIs. RR-IQA is RR IQA methods designed for quality prediction of SCIs. BRISQUE, BLIQUP-SCI and BQMS are NR IQA metrics. Specifically, BLIQUP-SCI and BQMS are proposed for blind quality prediction of SCIs. It should be noted that the performance of BRISQUE is calculated in the same way as the proposed method, the results of the metrics including SPQA, GSS, EMSQA, RR-IQA, BQMS and BLIQUP-SCI are taken from the original paper.

The experimental results are shown in Tables 1 and 2. From Table 1. We can observe that GMSD can obtain better performance than PSNR, SSIM and IFC in visual quality prediction of SCIs, the deviation of gradient magnitude is mainly considered in GMSD which demonstrates that the structure information is useful in capturing visual distortion of SCIs. It is also consistent with the fact that the textual region which contains much gradient information and the pictorial region containing high-frequency information would attract more attention than other regions. The performance of quality prediction of SCIs from PSNR is poor for the reason that it only calculates the deviation of pixel-pair in corresponding locations of reference and distorted images, while it does not consider the characteristics of the HVS. Among all the compared metrics, the proposed method can obtain competitive performance on visual quality prediction of SCIs compared with other existing ones, even including some FR IQA methods designed for SCIs such as SPQA, SQI, GSS and EMSQA.

4   Conclusion

In this paper, we propose a novel blind quality assessment method for SCIs based on orientation selectivity mechanism with which the primary visual cortex performs visual texture information extraction for scene understanding. The proposed method first extracts orientation information based on orientation selectivity mechanism and the structure features are also extracted as another quality indictor of SCIs. After the features are extracted, SVR is adopted as the mapping function from the features space to subjective scores. Experimental results demonstrate that the proposed method can obtain superior performance against state-of-the-art approaches, even including some FR IQA metrics.

References

1. Yang, H., Wu, S., Deng, C., Lin, W.: Scale and orientation invariant text segmentation for born-digital compound images. IEEE Trans. Cybern. **45**(3), 533–547 (2015)
2. Wang, S., Gu, K., Zeng, K., Wang, Z., Lin, W.: Objective quality assessment and perceptual compression of screen content images. IEEE Comput. Graph. Appl. **38**(1), 47–58 (2016)
3. Wang, Z., Bovik, A.C., Sheikh, H.R., Simoncelli, E.P.: Image quality assessment: from error visibility to structural similarity. IEEE Trans. Image Process. **13**(4), 600–612 (2004)
4. Xue, W., Zhang, L., Mou, X., Bovik, A.C.: Gradient magnitude similarity deviation: a highly efficient perceptual image quality index. IEEE Trans. Image Process. **23**(2), 684–695 (2014)
5. Fang, Y., Zeng, K., Wang, Z., Lin, W., Fang, Z., Lin, C.-W.: Objective quality assessment for image retargeting based on structure similarity. IEEE J. Emerg. Sel. Top. Circuits Syst. **4**(1), 95–105 (2014)
6. Sheikh, H.R., Bovik, A.C., de Veciana, G.: An information fidelity criterion for image quality assessment using natural scene statistics. IEEE Trans. Image Process. **14**(12), 2117–2128 (2005)
7. Rehman, A., Wang, Z.: Reduced-reference image quality assessment by structural similarity estimation. IEEE Trans. Image Process. **21**(8), 3378–3389 (2013)
8. Mittal, A., Moorthy, A.K., Bovik, A.C.: No-reference image quality assessment in the spatial domain. IEEE Trans. Image Process. **21**(12), 4695–4708 (2012)
9. Fang, Y., Ma, K., Wang, Z., Lin, W., Fang, Z., Zhai, G.: No-reference quality assessment for contrast-distorted images based on Natural scene statistics. IEEE Signal Process. Lett. **22**(7), 838–842 (2015)
10. Yang, H., Fang, Y., Lin, W., Wang, Z.: Perceptual quality assessment of screen content images. IEEE Trans. Image Process. **24**(11), 4408–4421 (2015)
11. Gu, K., Wang, S., Zhai, G., Ma, S., Lin, W.: Screen image quality assessment incorporating structural degradation measurement. In: IEEE International Symposium on Circuits and Systems, pp. 125–128 (2015)
12. Fang, Y., Yan, J., Liu, J., Wang, S., Li, Q., Guo, Z.: Objective quality assessment of screen content images by uncertainty weighting. IEEE Trans. Image Process. **26**(4), 2016–2027 (2017)
13. Ni, Z., Ma, L., Zeng, H., Cai, C., Ma, K.-K.: Gradient direction for screen content image quality assessment. IEEE Signal Process. Lett. **23**(10), 1394–1398 (2016)

14. Ni, Z., Ma, L., Zeng, H., Cai, C., Ma, K.-K.: Screen content image quality assessment using edge model. In: IEEE International Conference on Image Processing (2016)
15. Wang, S., Gu, K., Zhang, X., Lin, W., Ma, S., Gao, W.: Reduced reference quality assessment of screen content images. IEEE Trans. Circuits Syst. Video Technol. **28**(1), 1–14 (2016)
16. Gu, K., Zhai, G., Lin, W., Yang, X., Zhang, W.: Learning a blind quality evaluation engine of screen content images. Neurocomputing **196**, 140–149 (2016)
17. Shao, F., Gao, Y., Li, F., Jiang, G.: Toward a blind quality predictor for screen content images. IEEE Trans. Syst. Man Cybern. Syst. (99), 1–10 (2017)
18. Wu, J., Lin, W., Shi, G., Zhang, Y., Dong, W., Chen, Z.: Visual orientation selectivity based structure description. IEEE Trans. Image Process. **24**(11), 4602–4613 (2015)
19. Gu, K., Zhai, G., Yang, X., Zhang, W., Liu, M.: Structural similarity weighting for image quality assessment. In: IEEE International Conference on Multimedia and Expo Workshops (2013)
20. Huang, D., Zhu, C., Wang, Y., Chen, L.: HSOG: a novel local image descriptor based on histograms of the second-order gradient. IEEE Trans. Image Process. **23**(11), 4680–4695 (2014)
21. Li, Q., Lin, W., Fang, Y.: No-reference image quality assessment based on high order derivatives. In: IEEE International Conference on Multimedia and Expo, pp. 1–6 (2016)
22. Du, S., Yan, Y., Ma, Y.: Blind image quality assessment with the histogram sequences of high-order local derivative patterns. Digit. Signal Process. **55**, 1–12 (2016)
23. Ojala, T., Pietikainen, M., Maenpaa, T.: Multiresolution gray-scale and rotation invariant texture classification with local binary pattern. IEEE Trans. Patt. Anal. Mach. Intell. **24**(7), 971–987 (2002)
24. Chang, C.-C., Lin, C.-J.: LIBSVM: a library for support vector machines. ACM Trans. Intell. Syst. Technol. **2**(3), 27 (2011)

Assessment of Visually Induced Motion Sickness in Immersive Videos

Huiyu Duan[(✉)], Guangtao Zhai, Xiongkuo Min, Yucheng Zhu, Wei Sun, and Xiaokang Yang

Institute of Image Communication and Network Engineering,
Shanghai Jiao Tong University, Shanghai, China
hyuduan@gmail.com, zhaiguangtao@gmail.com, minxiongkuo@gmail.com,
{zyc420,sunguwei,xkyang}@sjtu.edu.cn

Abstract. Immersive videos are important components of virtual reality. However, when watching immersive videos, simulator sickness (SS) sometimes occurs. In addition, when there are visual oscillations (VOs) in immersive videos, visually induced motion sickness (VIMS) will make the videos' quality of experience (QoE) worse. Most of existing VIMS studies under controlled experimental conditions use virtual patterns, e.g., black and white stripes. However, QoE of immersive real scenes are far more complicate than visual patterns. Therefore, in this paper, we mainly concern QoE degradations caused by VIMS in immersive videos with real scenes. To get controlled VOs, we add shake to panoramic videos captured by still camera and conduct subjective experiments among 15 individuals. We find that the velocity (frequency) of VOs, the time we immersed and the scenes' contents will all influence the level of VIMS. And the QoE of immersive videos with real life content will be influenced correspondingly.

Keywords: Immersive videos · Simulator sickness
Visual oscillations · Visually induced motion sickness · QoE

1 Introduction

Virtual reality (VR) technology is a new display technology, which will bring real experience to individuals. VR can provide users a new interactive experience. The contents of virtual reality can approximately be divided into three kinds: composed completely by graphics, entirely come from reproduction of real world image and blend graphics from virtual world and images from real world. Immersive videos are video recordings where the scene in every direction is recorded at the same time and they are important components of virtual

This work was supported by the National Science Foundation of China (61422112, 61371146, 61521062, 61527804), National High-tech R&D Program of China (2015AA015905), and Science and Technology Commission of Shanghai Municipality (15DZ0500200).

© Springer International Publishing AG, part of Springer Nature 2018
B. Zeng et al. (Eds.): PCM 2017, LNCS 10735, pp. 662–672, 2018.
https://doi.org/10.1007/978-3-319-77380-3_63

reality. In some cases, when using head-mounted displays (HMDs) to experience immersive videos, users may undergo simulator sickness (SS). Usually SS will be slight when immersive videos are shot by still camera. However, when immersive videos are captured by moving camera, visual oscillations (VOs) could lead to visually induced motion sickness (VIMS). Quality of experience (QoE) of immersive videos captured by still camera mainly depends on the quality of videos. Meanwhile QoE of immersive videos captured by moving camera mainly depends on the quality of videos and the level of VIMS. We will mainly discuss VIMS in this paper.

Image and video quality assessment has always been a hot topic in recent years [6,7,12,13,22]. With the fast development of video technologies, studies of video quality assessment also make much progress [4,19–21]. Furthermore, when evaluating a video, Besides video quality, QoE of individuals should be considered as well. Nowadays, video technologies have developed into virtual reality era and virtual reality environment is regarded as a new generation of media of video display. Therefore, it is important to study the QoE of immersive videos.

SS is a byproduct of modern simulator technology and sometimes occurs in high-fidelity simulators. SS tends to happen when users immerse into virtual reality environment which is a new type of stereoscopic high-fidelity simulator. The level of SS is measured by simulator sickness questionnaire (SSQ) [9] in our experiments. QoE of immersive videos with VOs is mainly relevant to the quality of immersive videos and the level of VIMS of immersive videos. Therefore, It is important to introduce the concept of VIMS. Motion sickness is general in passengers and it is definitely an unpleasant experience. Unfortunately, this unpleasant experience does not exclusively affect passengers. A person exposed to visual environments with visual oscillations may also sense motion sickness [8,15]. This kind of case is often called VIMS. Symptoms of VIMS mainly include dizziness, nausea, fatigue, eye strain etc. Some studies have shown that these symptoms would impair user's visual experience and performance, such as [1,14].

There are many studies research frequency responses of VIMS. In VIMS studies, frequency of VOs could be controlled in two methods:

– Changing the amplitude of VOs while keeping the rms velocity constant.
– Changing the rms velocity of VOs while keeping the amplitude constant.

There were many past studies such as [2,3] researching the frequency responses of VIMS. Chen et al. [2] summarised the parameters and findings of VOs in these studies. As shown in [2], the frequency responses of VIMS are influenced by motion axis [11], scene content [17] and other latency [10]. Schrater et al. [16] have shown that human visual systems are more sensitive to velocity than acceleration. [2] concluded that the level of VIMS mainly relevant to rms velocity rather than amplitude. Based on the conclusion above, we design an experiment in which we change the rms velocity while keeping the amplitude constant.

Assessment of QoE is a necessary component of VR technology. Immersion and interactive are two important influence factors of QoE. There are two main

factors which will influence the sense of immersion: the quality of VR environment such as resolutions, frame rate. and SS. SS sometimes could also cause
VIMS. In this paper, we talk about the effect of SS and VIMS to immersion,
which will finally influence the QoE of immersive videos. We conducted a rigorous experiment to obtain subjective scores of VIMS and SS. In this paper, to
simulate the VO in virtual environment, we add translation shake in two directions: left-and-right axis and up-and-down axis. We change the velocity of VOs
while keeping the amplitude constant. Similarly, time and scenes are also the
factors we considered, which will be described detailedly in Sect. 2. By using our
results, researchers could study the objective assessment of QoE of immersive
videos with VOs easily.

This topic is of great significance and our experimental design could guide
subsequent researchers. Firstly, the subjective assessment results of immersive
videos with VOs could facilitate the research of objective assessment. In the
second place, through the rating of VIMS, we propose to limit the VOs of VR
contents under a certain range. We can grade the immersive videos and give a
warning when an immersive video may cause uncomfortable VIMS. Meanwhile,
the time we immersed in virtual environment should be limited too. The length
of this time is relevant to the contents. Last but not least, Our results could
direct game development to some extent. Though we use real scenes to research,
VIMS of virtual scenes may be similar to that of real scenes.

The rest of this papers is organised as follows. Section 2 describes detailed
experimental procedures. Section 3 shows and analyses the experimental results,
and make a discussion. Section 4 concludes the paper.

2   Experimental Procedures

In our experiment, there are 10 raw videos. Then we add shake with different
levels to them. We conducted an experiment covered 15 subjects, which were
healthy college students. There are many items should be noticed when conducting this experiment. Detailed items will be discussed later.

2.1   Shooting and Processing

10 raw video streams are captured by Insta 360 4K Spherical VR Video Camera
with resolution of 4096 × 2048 and file format MPEG-4, which are fit for playing
in virtual reality environment. All 10 scenes are shot in one university campus
with still camera. To avoid the influence of sound, we eliminate the audio track
of the videos. And then 15 seconds' video streams are cut from 10 raw videos.
The length of time of each video stream comes from the preliminary experiment,
which will be explained detailedly in Sect. 2.

A total of 15 subjects are exposed to sinusoidal motion VOs along left-and-
right axis and up-and-down axis. The methods we used to add shake along
left-and-right axis or up-and-down axis are similar. We use up-and-down axis
for illustration. Figure 1 shows the model we used. Usually, we paste a frame of

immersive video on a sphere to play. When we watch immersive videos, the image on the sphere could reflect the scenes all around. From Fig. 1, we notice that when the amplitude of VOs is small, we could stimulate VOs through shifting the virtual camera in the sphere. The new frames are stitched on the sphere around the new position of virtual camera. The new latitude of each pixel is computed as follows:

$$\theta = \arctan \frac{r_{xoz}}{y - \Delta y} \quad (y > \Delta y), \tag{1}$$

$$\theta = \pi - \arctan \frac{r_{xoz}}{\Delta y - y} \quad (y < \Delta y), \tag{2}$$

$$\theta = \pi/2 \quad (y = \Delta y). \tag{3}$$

In the expressions above, r_{xoz} is computed as:

$$r_{xoz} = x^2 + z^2, \tag{4}$$

where x, y, z is the coordinate of the pixels on the sphere; Δy is the shift distance of virtual camera. When we get the latitude (θ) of the position of new pixels, the new coordinate of x, y, z could be computed correspondingly.

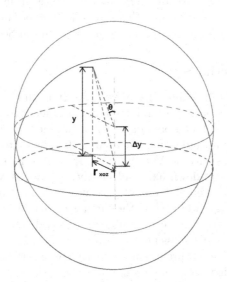

Fig. 1. The model of adding shake we used (y is the distance between the original pixel and the plane xoz, Δy is the shift distance of virtual camera, r_{xoz} is the distance between the pixel and the y axis, θ is the angle of y axis, center of new sphere and the pixel).

2.2   Preliminary Experiments

Fifteen healthy individuals aged between 20 and 27 years old participated in our experiment and all participants consented to take part in our formal experiments and preliminary experiments. Before the first preliminary experiment, we had investigated the physical conditions of all subjects. All subjects responded that they have normal or corrected-to-normal vision, intact vestibular function. And two people reflected that they have slight travel sickness. All participants were told that once they want to stop they could take off the HMD immediately. In the first preliminary experiment, we discuss the length settings of the time of each video stream. From the feedback, we noticed that the emergency of VIMS usually happen in 15 s. Although as time goes, symptoms of VIMS and SS would increase, the variation would be small after 30 s. Additional research on this point is needed. In the second preliminary experiment, we concern the velocity settings of shake. Velocity settings of shake are important in our experiments. We use percentage average velocity to describe the velocity settings. It could be computed by:

$$v_{pav} = \frac{\Delta y}{r \cdot t_{\Delta y}}. \tag{5}$$

Several levels of shake are manipulated with one scene. Based on this preliminary experiment, we selected five different velocity levels from them according to rough boundary. The procedure of this preliminary experiment is similar to the formal experiment, and detailed items could be found in Sect. 3.

2.3   Formal Experiments

In order to investigate the influence of velocity, time and scenes on VIMS when watching immersive videos, we conducted an experiment to obtain faithful data. There are many items should be noticed when conducting the experiments, such as rest time, drink time and so on. There are 110 videos altogether in our experiments. 10 raw videos with no VOs captured from 10 different scenes. 50 videos with VOs along up-and-down axis and another 50 videos with VOs along left-and-right axis. Five different levels of percentage average velocity are listed in the Table 1. The device we used as the virtual reality head-mounted display is HTC Vive. The order of 10 scenes subjects exposed to was randomised. The model we used to rate dizziness and nausea is similar to the 7-point Likert scale used in [5]. However, in our preliminary experiment, Some subjects reported that they only have vertigo symptoms, some other subjects reflected that they only have nausea symptoms, while others said that they have both vertigo symptoms and nausea symptoms. Since our final goal is to evaluate the QoE of immersive videos with VOs, we redefined the 7-point scale: 0 - no symptom, 1 - any slight symptom (dizziness), 2 - mild symptoms but no vertigo and nausea, 3 - mild vertigo or mild nausea, 4 - mild to moderate vertigo or mild to moderate nausea, 5 - moderate vertigo or moderate nausea but can continue and 6 - moderate vertigo or moderate nausea and want to stop. The experiment was terminated when the level of 6 was reached whenever during the trial.

Before each experiment, subjects were requested to eat normal food and keep good spirits. And they were notified the process of experiment and the rating announcements before the first experiment. Detailed rating scale were explained in this procedure, such as the contents of dizziness and the difference between dizziness and vertigo. All subjects were informed that they could quit the experiment at any moment and stop whenever they want. The contents of SSQ were also explained. First of all, subjects were immersed into 10 raw immersive videos with no VOs. At the end of each video, they should give the rating of VIMS. When this group of immersive videos were all played, they were asked to fill in the SSQ. After a rest time, the next group of 10 videos with VOs along up-and-down axis or left-and-right axis were played. Similarly, at the end of each video stream, we recorded the rating score given by each subject. After rating of each group of immersive videos, subjects were asked to fill in the SSQ. And then we provided a break time. The length of break time should be appropriate. In our experiment, at least 30 minutes' break time were needed while according to the feedback of subjects, it could be extended. During the rest time, subjects could drink some water, but other drinks are not permitted. The order of video groups with different velocity levels was random and the videos' order in each group is random too. To ensure the length of time, subjects were demanded to experience the whole video. The trial was conducted with subjects standing. Because when we experience VR environment, we often stand rather than other position so as to look around convenient.

Table 1. Velocity settings of the experiment.

Level	1	2	3	4	5
Percentage average velocity (%/s)	77.333	40.000	25.777	20.000	13.333
Frequency (Hz)	1.933	1.000	0.644	0.500	0.333

3   Data Analysis

Before analyzing the data, there is an important circumstance to say. There are 15 individuals involved in our experiment, However, 3 subjects did not complete the trial because the physical cause. Detailed illustration will be discussed in Subsect. 3.2.

3.1   VIMS Ratings and Elements Analysis

When discussing the ratings of VIMS, we should find out the main factors which will influence the level of VIMS first. We discovered that when we experience immersive videos with VOs, the velocity (frequency) of VOs, the time we immersed and the scenes' contents will all influence the level of VIMS. The

Table 2. Overall MOS of VIMS of 10 scenes with different VOs along up-and-down axis or along left-and-right axis.

Orientation		Up-and-down axis					Left-and-right axis				
Frequency (Hz)		0.333	0.500	0.644	1.000	2	0.333	0.500	0.644	1.000	2
MOS of ratings	Scene 1	0.63	1.72	2.27	3.363	4.45	0.63	1.72	2.27	3.363	4.45
	Scene 2	0.81	1.63	2.63	3.45	4.36	1	1.27	2.09	3.09	4.27
	Scene 3	1.09	2	2.72	3.27	4.54	1.36	1.45	2.45	3	4.72
	Scene 4	1.36	2.09	2.63	3.54	4.90	1	1.72	2.63	3.72	4.72
	Scene 5	1.18	1.72	2.36	3.18	4.72	0.81	1.36	2.27	3.27	4.54
	Scene 6	0.81	1.81	2.54	3.27	4.81	0.63	1.54	2.18	3.36	4.72
	Scene 7	1.18	1.90	2.54	3.36	5.09	0.72	1.27	2.45	3.18	5
	Scene 8	1.63	2.18	2.72	4.09	5.27	1.09	1.81	2.63	3.81	5.09
	Scene 9	1.54	1.90	2.45	3.90	5.45	0.81	1.54	2.27	3.27	5.09
	Scene 10	1.27	2	2.45	4	5.09	1	1.36	2.27	3.63	5

rating of VIMS could be impacted relevant. Therefore, in this subsection, we will evaluate the level of VIMS and analyse the effect of three aspects.

First of all, the Mean opinion Scores (MOS) of each videos was computed as follows:

$$MOS_j = \frac{\sum_{i=1}^{N} m'_{ij}}{N}. \tag{6}$$

In the expression above, N is the number of subjects and m'_{ij} is the score assigned by subject i to video j with various conditions.

Before computing the MOS, there is an important step: Removing outliers. Sometimes, a few subjects will give a score which is far away the mean value. And these outliers should be removed. However, because of the specificity of this experiment, some subjects could give special scores indeed. So we mainly remove outliers produced by unconscious fault. To avoid removing useful data, we would observe overall data of this subject and make sure whether it is natural before removing it. We used 3σ principle to remove outliers.

In this experiment, amplitude was kept a constant of 0.1. Therefore, the variation of frequency is corresponding to the change of velocity. Table 2 shows all MOS of the VIMS. From the table, we noticed that as the increase of frequency (velocity), the level of VIMS would also increase. And it is obvious that the scene could influence the rating of VIMS to some extend. The axis of VOs will also influence the experimental results reflected from the Table 2. Detailed explanation will be given later.

Figure 2 shows the MOS of one scene ratings. The trend could be observed obviously. Through analyzing the overall situations in the experiment, we found that exposed to immersive videos with VOs along up-and-down axis could cause the larger VIMS than VOs along left-and-right axis, especially in the situation

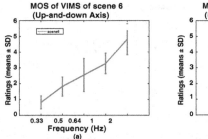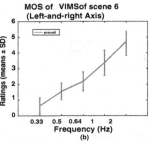

Fig. 2. Rating of scene 6 with different velocity (frequency).

that the velocity of VOs is small. The reason we believe is that when subjects experience the immersive videos with VOs along left-and-right axis, they could waggle with the shake which could alleviate the VIMS.

Except the velocity (frequency) and the orientation of VOs, the contents of scenes could also influence the rating of VIMS. There are 10 scenes in our experiment. And through the comparison of the MOSs of 10 scenes, we believe that the brightness of the environment, the movement speed of the surroundings and the distance between the scene and the camera could all influence the level of VIMS. Figure 3 shows the MOSs of scene 2 and scene 4. From the figure, we noticed that nearly all of the average ratings of scene 2 is less than that of scene 4 whatever the velocity (frequency) or orientation of VO are. The main difference between scene 2 and scene 4 is that the shooting place in scene 4 is football playing while that of scene 2 is pedestrian. The people in two videos have different movement speed. So we could conclude that the scene with faster moving objects will cause more serious VIMS. By similar methods, we derived that as the increase of brightness of immersive videos with VOs, the VIMS will be more serious. Though if there were no VOs, the QoE would increase. The distance between the scene and the camera could also influence the level of VIMS. The level of VIMS will increase when shortening the distance. Additional research is needed in this direction.

Because the order of the videos in each group is random, in this experiment, we could obtain the data of the relation between VIMS rating and immersion time. As time pass by, the level of VIMS would increase in a short time and then fluctuate around a certain value. The main cause of fluctuation is the contents of the scene. That is an interesting findings, we believe that an abrupt shake which could up to a certain level will cause an abrupt VIMS.

3.2 Exceptional Case

Although we considered many Precautions, some exceptional cases still happen. First of all, there are 12 people completing the trial including one individual with slight travel sickness. 3 subjects did not complete the experiment altogether because of the discomfort. Another subject with slight travel sickness

MOS of VIMS of scene 2 and scene 4

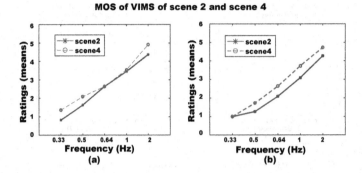

Fig. 3. The comparison between scene 2 and scene 4 with different velocity (frequency) ((a) up-and-down axis, (b) left-and-right axis).

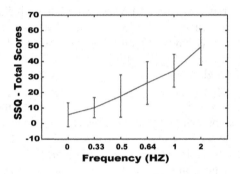

Fig. 4. Frequency responses of SSQ results.

only experienced one group of immersive videos with the minimum VOs and then he said it is unbearable. The situation of other two subjects may be better but they also can not stand finally. Indeed, Motion sickness is common in passengers and has occupied a great proportion [18]. Therefore, we suggest that we should grade the contents in VR environment. The scores given by 3 subjects who did not complete the trial also make sense. Further research is needed.

From the feedback of subjects, some individuals report that they think the VOs along left-and-right axis will cause more VIMS than VOs along up-and-down axis. Some subjects feel that when the velocity (frequency) is too large, they feel less dizziness than lower velocity because they think the VO is untruthful.

3.3   SSQ Scores

Before and after each trial participants were required to fill in an SSQ. As shown in Fig. 4, we noticed that the increases in velocity (frequency) resulted in a significance increase in the SSQ total scores.

4 Conclusion

In this paper, we conducted an experiment to evaluate the QoE of immersive videos with VOs. In order to get videos with controlled VOs, we add shake to panoramic videos captured by still camera through spherical transform. VOs along up-and-down axis or left-and-right axis in our experiment were added. Changing velocity while keeping the amplitude constant will cause different levels of dizziness. We find that the velocity (frequency) of VOs, the time we immersed and the scenes' contents will all influence the level of VIMS when we experience immersive videos. In detail, increases in velocity (frequency) could result in a significance increase in the level of VIMS and SSQ total scores. Similarly, increasing brightness and movement speed or shortening the distance between scene and camera will also increase VIMS. With time pass by, VIMS would increase in a short time and then fluctuate around a certain value.

References

1. Caroux, L., Le Bigot, L., Vibert, N.: Impact of the motion and visual complexity of the background on players' performance in video game-like displays. Ergonomics **56**(12), 1863–1876 (2013)
2. Chen, D.J., Bao, B., Zhao, Y., So, R.H.: Visually induced motion sickness when viewing visual oscillations of different frequencies along the fore-and-aft axis: keeping velocity versus amplitude constant. Ergonomics **59**(4), 582–590 (2016)
3. Diels, C., Howarth, P.A.: Frequency characteristics of visually induced motion sickness. Hum. Factors J. Hum. Factors Ergon. Soc. **55**(3), 595–604 (2013)
4. Duan, H., Zhai, G., Yang, X., Li, D., Zhu, W.: IVQAD 2017: an immersive video quality assessment database. In: 2017 International Conference on Systems, Signals and Image Processing (IWSSIP), pp. 1–5. IEEE (2017)
5. Golding, J.F., Kerguelen, M.: A comparison of the nauseogenic potential of low-frequency vertical versus horizontal linear oscillation. Aviat. Space Environ. Med. **63**, 491–497 (1992)
6. Gu, K., Li, L., Lu, H., Min, X., Lin, W.: A fast reliable image quality predictor by fusing micro-and macro-structures. IEEE Trans. Ind. Electron. **64**(5), 3903–3912 (2017)
7. Gu, K., Zhai, G., Yang, X., Zhang, W.: Using free energy principle for blind image quality assessment. IEEE Trans. Multimed. **17**(1), 50–63 (2015)
8. Hettinger, L.J., Berbaum, K.S., Kennedy, R.S., Dunlap, W.P., Nolan, M.D.: Vection and simulator sickness. Mil. Psychol. **2**(3), 171 (1990)
9. Kennedy, R.S., Lane, N.E., Berbaum, K.S., Lilienthal, M.G.: Simulator sickness questionnaire: an enhanced method for quantifying simulator sickness. Int. J. Aviat. Psychol. **3**(3), 203–220 (1993)
10. Kinsella, A.: The effect of 0.2 Hz and 1.0 Hz frequency and 100 ms and 20–100 ms amplitude of latency on simulatory sickness in a head mounted display (2014)
11. Lo, W., So, R.H.: Cybersickness in the presence of scene rotational movements along different axes. Appl. Ergon. **32**(1), 1–14 (2001)
12. Min, X., Ma, K., Gu, K., Zhai, G., Wang, Z., Lin, W.: Unified blind quality assessment of compressed natural, graphic and screen content images. IEEE Trans. Image Process. **26**, 5462–5474 (2017)

13. Min, X., Zhai, G., Gu, K., Fang, Y., Yang, X., Wu, X., Zhou, J., Liu, X.: Blind quality assessment of compressed images via pseudo structural similarity. In: Proceedings of IEEE International Conference Multimedia and Expo, pp. 1–6, July 2016

14. Read, J.C., Bohr, I.: User experience while viewing stereoscopic 3d television. Ergonomics **57**(8), 1140–1153 (2014)

15. Reason, J.T.: Motion sickness adaptation: a neural mismatch model. J. R. Soc. Med. **71**(11), 819 (1978)

16. Schrater, P.R., Knill, D.C., Simoncelli, E.P.: Mechanisms of visual motion detection. Nat. Neurosci. **3**(1), 64–68 (2000)

17. So, R.H., Ho, A., Lo, W.: A metric to quantify virtual scene movement for the study of cybersickness: definition, implementation, and verification. Presence Teleoperators Virtual Environ. **10**(2), 193–215 (2001)

18. Turner, M., Griffin, M.J.: Motion sickness in public road transport: passenger behavior and susceptibility. Ergonomics **42**, 444–461 (1999)

19. Zhai, G.: Recent advances in image quality assessment. In: Deng, C., Ma, L., Lin, W., Ngan, K.N. (eds.) Visual Signal Quality Assessment, pp. 73–97. Springer, Cham (2015). https://doi.org/10.1007/978-3-319-10368-6_3

20. Zhai, G., Cai, J., Lin, W., Yang, X., Zhang, W.: Three dimensional scalable video adaptation via user-end perceptual quality assessment. IEEE Trans. Broadcast. **54**(3), 719–727 (2008)

21. Zhai, G., Cai, J., Lin, W., Yang, X., Zhang, W., Etoh, M.: Cross-dimensional perceptual quality assessment for low bit-rate videos. IEEE Trans. Multimed. **10**(7), 1316–1324 (2008)

22. Zhai, G., Wu, X., Yang, X., Lin, W., Zhang, W.: A psychovisual quality metric in free-energy principle. IEEE Trans. Image Process. **21**(1), 41–52 (2012)

Hybrid Kernel-Based Template Prediction and Intra Block Copy for Light Field Image Coding

Deyang Liu, Ping An[✉], Ran Ma, Xinpeng Huang, and Liquan Shen

School of Communication and Information Engineering,
Shanghai University, Shanghai 200072, China
anping@shu.edu.cn

Abstract. Light field (LF) technology can capture both spatial and angular information of a 3D scene, and enable new possibilities for digital imaging. However, one problem that occupies an important position to deal with the LF data is the sheer size of data volume. Therefore, in this paper, we propose an effective LF image coding scheme by combining the kernel-based template prediction method and intra block copy method. In the proposed method, intra block copy method is used to predict the unknown blocks where kernel-based template prediction method fails under the Rate-Distortion (RD) based decision mechanism. Experimental results show that the LF data can be efficiently compressed by the proposed method and the execution time in decoder side can also be reduced by about 35% compared to kernel-based template prediction method.

Keywords: Light field image · Image coding · Template prediction
Intra block copy · HEVC

1 Introduction

Light fields (LFs) represent the intensity and direction of the light rays emanated from a 3D scene. With the advances in computational photography, the LFs can be explored from the digital perspective [1]. Light field imaging, also referred to as plenoptic imaging, holoscopic imaging and integral imaging, can capture both spatial and angular information of a 3D scene, and enable new possibilities for digital imaging [2].

Several techniques, such as by using coded apertures, multi-camera arrays and micro-lens arrays, can be utilized to capture a light field image. The capture technique by using micro-lens arrays can be further categorized into two approaches: standard plenoptic capturing and plenoptic 2.0 techniques. The commercially available plenoptic cameras by using these two techniques are first produced by Lytro. So far, many research groups have considered the standardization of light field application. The JPEG working group starts a new

© Springer International Publishing AG, part of Springer Nature 2018
B. Zeng et al. (Eds.): PCM 2017, LNCS 10735, pp. 673–682, 2018.
https://doi.org/10.1007/978-3-319-77380-3_64

study, known as JPEG Pleno [3], aiming at richer image capturing, visualization, and manipulation. The MPEG group has also started the third phase of Free-viewpoint Television (FTV) since 2013, targeting super multiview, free navigation and full parallax imaging applications [4].

LF data captured by using the micro-lens arrays has two main features. One is that arbitrary views and views at different focused planes can be generated by combining the pixels from the captured micro-lens images, also called elementary images (EI). The other is that end users can enjoy a more immersive glassless 3D experience by placing the same micro-lens array on top of the visualization display. An example of light field image captured by the plenoptic 2.0 technique is shown in Fig. 1.

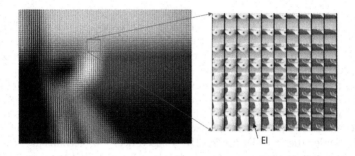

EI

Fig. 1. Light field image "seagull": (a) full image (b) partial enlargement

One problem that occupies an important position to deal with the LF data is the sheer size of data volume, which brings new challenges on how to efficiently store and transmit such particular type of complex data [5]. Since the LF data exhibits a more complex and unique structure compared to the natural 2D image, the existing image coding method, e.g., JPEG, H.264 and HEVC can not achieve a high coding efficiency. Due to the fact that the EIs exhibit repetitive patterns and a large amount of redundancy exists between the neighboring EIs, several light field image coding schemes have been proposed, which can be categorized into two different groups: template matching prediction (TMP) based coding methods and intra displacement compensation (IDC) based coding methods. In the TMP based coding methods, our previous work [6] puts forward a disparity compensation based light field image coding algorithm to derive a better prediction. In [7], a coding method combining the locally linear embedding (LLE) is proposed to predict the coding block. We further improved this work by using kernel-based minimum mean-square-error estimation prediction [8] and Gaussian process regression based prediction method [9]. In the IDC based coding methods, Conti et al. introduced the Self-Similarity (SS) mode [10] into HEVC to improve the coding efficiency of light field image [11]. The SS mode is similar to the Block Copying (BC) mode [12] which is incorporated into the HEVC range extension to code the screen contents. A displacement intra prediction scheme for light field contents is proposed in [13,14], where more than one hypothesis is used to reduce prediction errors.

Although good predictions can be achieved by using the coding schemes mentioned above, a few underlying shortcomings still exist. Firstly, the computational load of the TMP based coding methods is very high. Since the decoder side usually has to perform the same template prediction process as the encoder side in the TMP based coding methods, the time ratio on the decoder side is much higher than that on the encoder compared to the existing image-encoder, such as HEVC. Secondly, the IDC based coding methods have to send the obtained displacement vectors to the decoder side. Although the computational load in the decoder side is low, the additional overhead will reduce the coding efficiency.

In order to alleviate the shortcomings, in this paper, we proposed a hybrid kernel-based template prediction and intra block copy algorithm to compress the light field image. The proposed coding method explores the idea of using the intra block copy (IntraBC) scheme which performs block matching on the current frame to find repeated patterns [15] in the image areas when kernel-based template prediction method fails. The main goal of the proposed coding method is to further improve the coding efficiency with desirable computational loads both in encoder and decoder sides.

The remainder of the paper is organized as follows. Section 2 presents the proposed 3D holoscopic image coding scheme. The experimental results are presented and analyzed in Sect. 3, while the concluding remarks are given in Sect. 4.

2   Proposed Coding Scheme

In our previous work [8], a light field image coding method with kernel-based minimum mean square error (MMSE) estimation is proposed. In the proposed scheme, the coding block is predicted by an MMSE estimator under statistical modeling. Although the kernel-based MMSE estimation method can achieve a high coding efficiency, it does not always necessarily lead to a good prediction for the unknown block to be predicted, especially in non homogenous texture areas. Fortunately, unknown blocks located in such areas can be better predicted by using a direct match with the block to be predicted. Therefore, in this paper, we combine the kernel-based MMSE estimation method with the IntraBC mode to further improve the whole coding efficiency. In order to avoid the strong impact of the displacement vectors cost on the rate-distortion performance of the complete compression algorithm, IntraBC mode is used only for blocks where kernel-based MMSE estimation method fails. The advantage of the proposed coding method mainly lies in two aspects. One is that a better prediction of the unknown blocks can be achieved by combining the kernel-based MMSE estimation method with the IntraBC mode. The other is that the execution time in decoder side can be reduced. The proposed coding scheme is realized in the screen content coding (SCC) extension to HEVC (HEVC-SCC). In the following subsections, we first introduce the kernel-based MMSE estimation method, and then present a method to integrate the kernel-based MMSE estimation method into the HEVC-SCC standard.

2.1 Kernel-Based MMSE Estimation Method

Let the pixel values in the current coding block be stacked in a column vector $\mathbf{x}_0$, and the pixel values in its neighbor templates with template thickness being T are compacted in a column vector $\mathbf{y}_0$, shown in Fig. 2(a). The current coding block and its neighbor templates with template thickness being T are called the prototype region in this paper. Therefore, the main goal of the prediction method can be expressed as to derive the MMSE estimate $E[\mathbf{x}|\mathbf{y}_0]$ of vector $\mathbf{x}_0$ given its context $\mathbf{y}_0$. In order to do so, we arrange the vector $\mathbf{x}_0$ and $\mathbf{y}_0$ into a multidimensional vector $\mathbf{z}_0 = (\mathbf{x}_0, \mathbf{y}_0)$, and a random vector variable $\mathbf{z} = (\mathbf{x}, \mathbf{y})$ which has the same configuration as $\mathbf{z}_0$ is considered to obtain the signal statistical behavior. If the PDF of $\mathbf{z}$ is acquired, the MMSE estimator $E[\mathbf{x}|\mathbf{y}_0]$ can be derived from it. In our scheme, we propose to utilize kernel density estimation (KDE) to estimate the PDF of $\mathbf{z}$ given a set of observed vectors $\{\mathbf{z}_k | k = 1, ..., K\}$. Here, the observed vectors are composed of K-NN patches, the top K closest templates that have the same configuration as the prototype region in terms of Euclidean distance. Note that, the K-NN patches are derived within the specified horizontal and vertical search windows, shown in Fig. 2(b). Since the coding block in prototype region is unknown in the K-NN patches searching procedure, its neighbor blocks are used for searching. In searching procedure, we set the template thickness to T_1 which equals to the size of the current coding block to increase the searching accuracy, shown in Fig. 2(b).

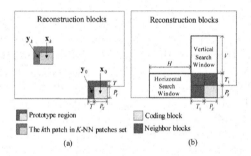

Fig. 2. Multidimensional vector construction: (a) the prototype region and kth observed vector in its K-NN set; (b) searching windows used to derive the K-NN set of prototype region.

Given the observed vectors, the estimator of the PDF of $\mathbf{z}$ using KDE with a Gaussian kernel $\mathcal{K}(\mathbf{u}) = exp(-\mathbf{u}^T\mathbf{u}/2)/\sqrt{2}$ can be defined by [16]

$$\mathcal{P}(\mathbf{z}) = \frac{1}{K\mathbf{H}} \sum_{k=1}^{K} \mathcal{K}(\frac{\mathbf{z} - \mathbf{z}_k}{\mathbf{H}}) = \frac{1}{K} \sum_{k=1}^{K} \mathcal{K}_Z^{(k)}(\mathbf{z}) \qquad (1)$$

where matrix $\mathbf{H}$ is called bandwidth, controlling the smoothness of the resulting PDF. $\mathcal{K}_Z^{(k)}(\mathbf{z})$ can be seen as a multivariate Gaussian with mean $\mathbf{z}_k$ and covariance matrix $\mathcal{H} = \mathbf{H}\mathbf{H}^T$. The covariance matrix $\mathcal{H}$ is also called as bandwidth for simplicity, which can be decomposed as

$$\mathcal{H} = \begin{bmatrix} \mathcal{H}_{XX} & \mathcal{H}_{XY} \\ \mathcal{H}_{YX} & \mathcal{H}_{YY} \end{bmatrix} \tag{2}$$

With the knowledge of $\mathcal{P}(\mathbf{z})$, we can calculate the MMSE estimator $E[\mathbf{x}|\mathbf{y}_0]$ of vector $\mathbf{x}_0$. From Eq. (1), we find that $\mathcal{P}(\mathbf{z})$ has the form of Gaussian mixture model (GMM) with a priori probabilities $1/K$ and covariance matrices $\mathcal{H}$. Therefore, it is reasonable to utilize the expressions of MMSE estimation under GMM modeling [16,17]. For our case, the MMSE estimator can be expressed as

$$\hat{\mathbf{x}}_0 = E[\mathbf{x}|\mathbf{y}_0] = \sum_{k=1}^{K} \mathbf{w}_k(\mathbf{y}_0)\mu_{X|Y}^{(k)}(\mathbf{y}_0) \tag{3}$$

$$\mathbf{w}_k(\mathbf{y}_0) = \frac{\mathcal{K}_Y^{(k)}(\mathbf{y}_0)}{\sum_{k=1}^{K} \mathcal{K}_Y^{(k)}(\mathbf{y}_0)} \tag{4}$$

$$\mu_{X|Y}^{(k)}(\mathbf{y}_0) = E[\mathbf{x}|\mathbf{y}_0, \mathbf{y}_k] = \mathbf{x}_k + \mathcal{H}_{XY}\mathcal{H}_{YY}^{-1}(\mathbf{y}_0 - \mathbf{y}_k) \tag{5}$$

where $\mathcal{K}_Y^{(k)}(\mathbf{y})$ is the marginal kernel for $\mathbf{y}$, with mean $\mathbf{y}_k$ and covariance $\mathcal{H}_{YY}$. According to the Eqs. (3)–(5), we can obtain the prediction of the coding block and the estimation method is referred as the kernel-based MMSE (K-MMSE) estimation. For simplicity, the K-MMSE estimation can be rewritten as

$$\hat{\mathbf{x}}_0 = \tilde{\mathbf{x}}_0 + \mathcal{H}_{XY}\mathcal{H}_{YY}^{-1}(\mathbf{y}_0 - \tilde{\mathbf{y}}_0) \tag{6}$$

where $\tilde{\mathbf{x}}_0$ and $\tilde{\mathbf{y}}_0$ express the linear predictions of $\mathbf{x}_0$ and $\mathbf{y}_0$ from the sets of vectors $\mathbf{z}_k(k = 1, ..., K)$ by

$$\tilde{\mathbf{x}}_0 = \sum_{k=1}^{K} \mathbf{w}_k(\mathbf{y}_0)\mathbf{x}_k, \quad \tilde{\mathbf{y}}_0 = \sum_{k=1}^{K} \mathbf{w}_k(\mathbf{y}_0)\mathbf{y}_k \tag{7}$$

There are two problems should be tackled in kernel-based MMSE estimation method. One is to derive weight vector $\mathbf{w}_k(\mathbf{y}_0)$. The other is to estimate kernel bandwidth matrix $\mathcal{H}$.

For the first problem, we adopt a more direct way to obtain the weight vector. That is to minimize the residual energy $\epsilon(\mathbf{w})$ by solving a squared error function, where $\epsilon(\mathbf{w})$ is given by

$$\epsilon(\mathbf{w}) = \left\| \mathbf{y}_0 - \sum_{k=1}^{K} \mathbf{w}_k(\mathbf{y}_0)\mathbf{y}_k \right\| \tag{8}$$

In order to estimate the kernel bandwidth matrix, we propose a new BE method which is based on the analysis of physical interpretation of the K-MMSE estimation method. From Eq. (6), we find that the K-MMSE estimator consists of two parts. The first part is a linear prediction of vector $\mathbf{x}_0$, and the second part is a correction vector representing the unpredictable part of $\mathbf{y}_0$ is transformed into subspace $\mathbf{x}$ [16]. The physical interpretation of the second part can be understood as the vector $\mathbf{x}_0$ close to vector $\mathbf{y}_0$ is likely to have a similar unpredictable part as vector $\mathbf{y}_0$. The matrix $\mathcal{H}_{XY}\mathcal{H}_{YY}^{-1}$ can be regarded as a transfer matrix used to transfer the unpredictable part of $\mathbf{y}_0$ to subspace $\mathbf{x}$. It is reasonable to infer that the bandwidth matrix $\mathcal{H}$ in K-MMSE estimation is used to measure the similarity of the subspace $\mathbf{x}$ and subspace $\mathbf{y}$. Therefore, we propose to utilize Eq. (9) to estimate the bandwidth matrix $\mathcal{H}$ approximately.

$$\mathcal{H} = l^2(1 + \mathbf{x}^T\mathbf{y}) \tag{9}$$

where l is a hyper parameter and is specified to 1.0 in our system.

A special case is that subspace $\mathbf{x}$ and subspace $\mathbf{y}$ have a low correlation, which means that the vector $\mathbf{x}_0$ and vector $\mathbf{y}_0$ may have a different unpredictable part. In this case, we propose to discard the correction vector and only use the prediction vector $\tilde{\mathbf{x}}_0$ to estimate $\mathbf{x}_0$. The gradient information of the top nearest patch of the prototype region in K-NN patches is utilized to judge such correlation. Let $\mathbf{z}_1 = (\mathbf{x}_1, \mathbf{y}_1)$ be the vector form of the top nearest patch of the prototype region in K-NN patches. Suppose $G_{\mathbf{z}1}$, $G_{\mathbf{x}1}$ and $G_{\mathbf{y}1}$ represent the gradient of vector $\mathbf{z}_1$, $\mathbf{x}_1$, and $\mathbf{y}_1$, respectively. If $\|G_{\mathbf{x}1} - G_{\mathbf{y}1}\| > G_{\mathbf{z}1}$, the correlation between the coding block and its neighbor templates is considered to be low. Bandwidth matrix $\mathcal{H}$ is set to 0. Otherwise bandwidth matrix is computed by Eq. (9).

2.2   Integration of Proposed Method into HEVC-SCC

Since HEVC-SCC incorporates the intraBC coding tool, HEVC-SCC standard promises to be a better choice incorporating the proposed prediction scheme. In order to avoid modifying the bit stream structure, the proposed prediction framework is implemented in HEVC-SCC by replacing one of the 35 intra prediction modes. In other words, the prediction samples that generated by the substituted directional mode are replaced by the outputs produced by the proposed method. Note that, the least statistically used mode of the 35 intra prediction modes is replaced by the K-MMSE estimation method and a precoding procedure of the light field image test set in HEVC-SCC is needed to find the least statistically used mode. Since PU size 64×64 is seldom chosen as the intra prediction block size for LF image, we only choose four prediction block sizes ranging form 32×32 to 4×4 for PU.

Rate-distortion optimization (RDO) procedure is adopted to choose the optimal block partition and the prediction modes. In addition, the proposed framework can also be used to predict chrominance blocks.

3   Experiment Results

Light field image [18] Bike, Fountain, Jeff and Seagull, captured by the plenoptic 2.0 technique, are used in the test. For simplicity, we cut all the test images into size of 3840×2160, and all images are transformed into YUV 4:2:0 formats. The HEVC-SCC reference software SCM-8.0 [19] is used. The configuration parameter is set as the "All Intra", which is defined in [20]. Four tested Quantization Parameters 22, 27, 32 and 37 are used. The proposed prediction method is compared with three prediction schemes: the original HEVC standard (referred to as HEVC), the screen content coding (SCC) extension to HEVC (referred to as HEVC-SCC) and the K-MMSE estimation method (referred to as K-MMSE).

The template thickness T is set to 4. The dimensions of the searching windows used in the proposed method are given by $V = 128$ and $H = 128$, shown in Fig. 2(b).

Table 1. Rate distortion gains over HEVC intra standard

Images	Coding methods	BD-PSNR (dB)	BD-Rate (%)
Bike	HEVC-SCC	1.85	−20.09
	K-MMSE	2.38	−26.87
	Proposed	**2.63**	**−29.32**
Fountain	HEVC-SCC	2.07	−29.22
	K-MMSE	2.79	−36.59
	Proposed	**2.96**	**−39.59**
Jeff	HEVC-SCC	1.67	−26.10
	K-MMSE	2.27	−32.08
	Proposed	**2.45**	**−35.56**
Seagull	HEVC-SCC	2.32	−38.14
	K-MMSE	2.99	−43.66
	Proposed	**3.27**	**−48.40**

Table 1 shows the rate distortion gains of the three prediction methods over HEVC intra standard. From Table 1, we can see that the proposed method is clearly superior to the other methods. An average gain of up to 0.63 dB has been achieved by the K-MMSE method to HEVC-SCC, which means that the K-MMSE method can achieve a higher coding efficiency compared to the HEVC-SCC. We have mentioned above that the K-MMSE method can not predict the unknown blocks better in some non homogenous texture areas. And in this paper, we try to combine the kernel-based MMSE estimation method with the IntraBC mode to further improve the whole coding efficiency. The results in Table 1 demonstrate the validity of the proposed method. About 0.22 dB average gain has been achieved by the proposed method compared to the K-MMSE method. This further confirm that a better prediction of unknown blocks in non homogenous texture areas can be obtained by combining the K-MMSE method with the IntraBC mode.

Table 2 gives the coding time ratios of HEVC-SCC, K-MMSE and the proposed method to HEVC. From Table 2 we see that around 2.7 times and 1.2

Table 2. Coding time ratios to HEVC at the encoder side and decoder side

Images	Coding methods	Encoder side	Decoder side
Bike	HEVC-SCC	7.5	1.13
	K-MMSE	10.6	53.2
	Proposed	16.2	34.2
Fountain	HEVC-SCC	4.4	1.1
	K-MMSE	15.9	84.2
	Proposed	16.0	55.1
Jeff	HEVC-SCC	4.8	1.3
	K-MMSE	14.6	74.5
	Proposed	14.9	48.4
Seagull	HEVC-SCC	7.9	1.2
	K-MMSE	15.1	97.2
	Proposed	19.3	60.9

times coding complexity are needed in the encoder side for the proposed method compared to HEVC-SCC and K-MMSE, respectively. In the decoder side, the coding time ratios of the K-MMSE and the proposed method are tens of times than HEVC-SCC. Moreover, the results in Table 2 also demonstrate that the execution time of the proposed method in decoder side can be reduced by about 35% compared to the K-MMSE. The reason mainly lies in that decoding an unknown block which selects the IntraBC mode needs less time than decoding an unknown block who selects the K-MMSE mode.

Table 3. The average frequency of prediction mode selected for light field image Fountain over the tested QP range

K-MMSE	IntraBC	Planar	DC	Others
40.23	25.84	4.99	15.2	13.74

Table 3 gives the average frequency of prediction mode selected for light field image Fountain over the tested QP range. From Table 3, we find that the K-MMSE mode is selected in more than 40% of the time by the RD-optimization routine. And average frequency of IntraBC mode selected by the RD-optimization routine is also more than 25%. This further confirms the feasibility and rationality of the proposed coding method.

4   Conclusion

This paper puts forward a hybrid kernel-based template prediction and intra block copy algorithm to compress the light field image. The IntraBC mode is used for unknown blocks where K-MMSE method fails. The experimental results show that the proposed coding scheme can achieve a higher coding efficiency, and the execution time in decoder side can be reduced by about 35% compared to the K-MMSE method.

Acknowledgement. This work was supported in part by the National Natural Science Foundation of China, under Grants 61571285, U1301257, and 61301112.

References

1. Levoy, M.: Light fields and computational imaging. Computer **39**, 46–55 (2006)
2. Yang, R., Huang, X., Li, S., Jaynes, C.: Toward the light field display: autostereoscopic rendering via a cluster of projectors. IEEE Trans. Vis. Comput. Graph. **14**(1), 84–96 (2008)
3. Ebrahimi, T.: JPEG PLENO Abstract and Executive Summary, ISO/IEC JTC 1/SC 29/WG1 N6922, Sydney (2015)
4. Tehrani, M.P., Shimizu, S., Lafruit, G., Senoh, T., Fujii, T., Vetro, A., et al.: Use Cases and Requirements on Free-viewpoint Television (FTV), ISO/IEC JTC1/SC29/WG11 MPEG N14104, Geneva (2013)
5. Levoy, M., Hanrahan, P.: Light field rendering. In: Proceedings of SIGGRAPH, New York, pp. 31–42, August 1996
6. Liu, D., An, P., Ma, R., Shen, L.: Disparity compensation based 3D holoscopic image coding using HEVC. In: IEEE China Summit and International Conference Signal and Information Processing (ChinaSIP), pp. 201–205, July 2015
7. Lucas, L.F.R., Conti, C., Nunes, P., Soares, L.D., Rodrigues, N.M.M., Pagliari, C.L., da Silva, E.A.B., de Faria, S.M.M.: Locally linear embedding-based prediction for 3D holoscopic image coding using HEVC. In: Proceedings of the 22nd European Signal Processing Conference (EUSIPCO), pp. 11–15, 1–5 September 2014
8. Liu, D., An, P., Ma, R., Yang, C., Shen, L., Li, K.: Three-dimensional holoscopic image coding scheme using high-efficiency video coding with kernel-based minimum mean-square-error estimation. J. Electron. Imaging **25**(4), 043015-1–043015-9 (2016)
9. Liu, D., An, P., Ma, R., Yang, C., Shen, L.: 3D holoscopic image coding scheme using HEVC with Gaussian process regression. Signal Process. Image Commun. **47**, 438–451 (2016)
10. Conti, C., Soare, L.D., Nunes, P.: Influence of self-similarity on 3D holoscopic video coding performance. In: Proceedings of the 18th Brazilian Symposium on Multimedia and the Web, pp. 131–134, October 2012
11. Conti, C., Nunes, P., Soares, L.D.: New HEVC prediction modes for 3D holoscopic video coding. In: 19th IEEE International Conference on Image Processing, pp. 1325–1328, September 2012
12. Flynn, D., Sole, J., Suzuki, T.: High Efficiency Video Coding (HEVC) Range Extensions Text Specification: Draft 4, Joint Collaborative Team Video Coding (JCT-VC), Document JCTVC-N1005, April 2013
13. Li, Y., et al.: Efficient intra prediction scheme for light field image compression. In: IEEE International Conference on Acoustics, Speech and Signal Processing, pp. 539–543 (2014)
14. Li, Y., et al.: Coding of focused plenoptic contents by displacement intra prediction. IEEE Trans. Circuits Syst. Video Technol. **26**(7), 1308–1319 (2015)

15. AHG8: Video Coding Using Intra Motion Compensation, JCTVC-M0350, ITU-T/ISO/IEC Joint Collaborative Team on Video Coding, Incheon, April 2013
16. Koloda, J., Peinado, A.M., Sanchez, V.: Kernel-based MMSE multimedia signal reconstruction and its application to spatial error concealment. IEEE Trans. Multimed. **16**(6), 1729–1738 (2014)
17. Persson, D., Eriksson, T., Hedelin, P.: Packet video error concealment with Gaussian mixture models. IEEE Trans. Image Process. **17**(2), 145–154 (2008)
18. Georgiev, T.: January 2013. http://www.tgeorgiev.net
19. HEVC SCC Reference Software Ver. 8.0 (SCM-8.0). https://hevc.hhi.fraunhofer.de/
20. Yu, H., Cohen, R., Rapaka, K., Xu, J.: Common Test Conditions for Screen Content Coding, Document JCTVC-X1015, June 2016

Asymmetric Representation for 3D Panoramic Video

Guisen Xu, Yueming Wang, Zhenyu Wang, and Ronggang Wang[✉]

Shenzhen Graduate School, Peking University, Beijing, China
rgwang@pkusz.edu.cn

Abstract. The 3D panoramic video provides an immersive stereo visual experience by presenting 3D omnidirectional videos of real-world scenes. The key challenge is to develop an efficient representation of 3D panoramic video in order to maximize coding efficiency. In this paper, we propose an asymmetric representation based on the binocular suppression theory that in a stereo sequence, where the sharpness of left-eye and right-eye view differ, the perceived binocular quality of a stereoscopic sequence is rated close to the sharper view. According to the theory, in our method, one view is down-sampled to half size of original sequence in horizontal and vertical direction, and the other keeps the original resolution. To improve the quality of the reconstructed 3D panoramic video, we propose an anti-aliasing method based on detail blurring. Experimental results show that our representation can get significant coding gains (26.13%) over side-by-side and top-and-bottom method with full resolution.

Keywords: Virtual reality · 3D panoramic image · Asymmetric representation

1 Introduction

Virtual reality (VR) refers to creating an artificial environment with immersive 3D visual experience. Generally, VR with head-mounted displays (HMDs) is associated with gaming applications and computer-generated content. However, based on the ability to display wide-field-of-view content at high resolution, and track user head motion and update the displayed content with low latency, HMDs can be used to provide immersive visual experiences involving real-world scenes. Such applications are called Cinematic VR. In order to provide a fully immersive experience, a real-world environment has to be captured in all directions (e.g., with a camera rig) resulting in an omnidirectional video corresponding to a viewing sphere. To achieve 3D effects, a separate view is generated and presented to each eye, which leads to stereoscopic omnidirectional video with the corresponding parallax between the two views. Generally, the 3D panoramic video consists of two storage formats: side-by-side and top-and-bottom. And it's common to store 3D video in equirectangular format.

Due to the parallax between two views, 3D panoramic video means doubling the amount of raw data compared to 2D video. Therefore, transmitting 3D panoramic video consumes a lot of bandwidth.

© Springer International Publishing AG, part of Springer Nature 2018
B. Zeng et al. (Eds.): PCM 2017, LNCS 10735, pp. 683–690, 2018.
https://doi.org/10.1007/978-3-319-77380-3_65

In order to save the bandwidth for transmitting 3D video, we represent 3D panoramic video in mixed resolution method (MR) instead of full resolution method (FR) by down-sampling right-eye frames vertically and horizontally to half. Furthermore, we applied anti-aliasing method based on detail blurring as pre-process to the down-sampled right-eye frames, which can further decrease the bit rate without increasing the computational complexity of rendering. Finally, we evaluate the coding efficiency and the perceived binocular quality of our representation.

The contributions of this paper are as follows.

- We propose an asymmetric representation to improve the coding performance of 3D panoramic video.
- In order to improve the quality of reconstructed 3D panoramic video and further decrease bit rate, we propose an anti-aliasing method based on detail blurring.

2 Related Work

In this section, we briefly review the relevant researches on 3D panoramic video representation. Since 3D panoramic videos need to be played in real-time, those complex methods, such as Depth-Image-Based Rendering (DIBR) [1], aren't suitable for 3D panoramic video. In order to find a more efficient representation, some researchers try to exploit the spatio-temporal correlation of the left-eye and right-eye frames of a given 3D panoramic video, as is done in the Multiview Profile of MPEG-2 [2, 3]. The concept of mixed-resolution coding (MR), which was first introduced by Perkins in 1992 [4], indicates that mixed-resolution stereo image sequences can provide acceptable image quality, although the latter comments were based on informal observations. In 2000, Stelmach *et al.* explored the response of the human visual system to mixed-resolution stereo video sequences, and concluded that spatial filtering of one channel of a stereo video sequence may be an effective means of reducing storage and transmission bandwidth [5]. Therefore, in a stereo sequence, where the sharpness of left-eye and right-eye view differ, the perceived binocular quality of a stereoscopic sequence was rated close to the sharper view.

According to the mixed-resolution theory, we down-sampled right-eye view vertically and horizontally at half. In order to perform anti-aliasing in down-sampled right-eye view, we proposed an anti-aliasing method based on detail blurring, which used the structure extraction method proposed by Xu *et al.* [6]. First, we divided the down-sampled frame into structure image and detail image. And then we used the Gaussian filter to blur the detail images for anti-aliasing. Finally, left-eye and right-eye view are spliced to a complete 3D panoramic image.

3 Approach

According to the principle of mixed-resolution coding, a 3D panoramic video, in which one view has a reduced resolution (mixed-resolution representation, MR), yields the same subjective quality in comparison to the full-resolution representation (FR). Thus, a lower bit rate at equal quality is achieved for MR. Therefore, we propose an asymmetric representation (mixed resolution with anti-aliasing, MRAA) to improve the coding performance of 3D panoramic video. The framework of our method is shown in Fig. 1. First, we keep the left-eye view in full resolution and down-sample the right-eye view by the factor of two in horizontal and in vertical direction. When rendering the right-eye view, the frames are up-sampled to the original resolution again. Unfortunately, up-sampling leads to alias in right-eye view, which influences the perceived binocular quality of a 3D panoramic sequence. In order to solve this problem, we apply structure extraction technology and Gaussian filter to the right-eye view to perform anti-aliasing. Finally, we splice left-eye view and right-eye view together.

In this paper, we down-sampled the right-eye view. In fact, both left-eye and right-eye view can be used as down-sampled view.

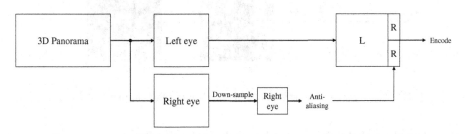

Fig. 1. Framework of asymmetric splicing method for 3D panoramic image

3.1 Anti-alias Method Based on Detail Blurring

When rendering the right-eye view, recovering down-sampled view to original resolution results in aliasing. After analysis, the alias is obvious in Y component of right-eye and almost impossible to be observed in U and V component. Therefore, we mainly solve the problems of aliasing in Y component. Super-resolution image reconstruction is an effective anti-aliasing technology. However, most super-resolution methods are too time-consuming to be employed in 3D panoramic video rendering. In order to render video in real-time, we propose the anti-aliasing method based on detail blurring and applied our method as a pre-process step, which doesn't increase the computation complexity of rendering and saves more bit rate.

Anti-aliasing method Based on Gaussian Filter. Blurring images with Gaussian filter is a simple anti-aliasing method. However, Gaussian filter only considers the spatial correlation between pixels, and does not consider the similarity between pixels. Therefore, the image blurred by Gaussian filter will lose the boundary information. To solve this problem, we propose the anti-aliasing method based on detail blurring.

Anti-aliasing method Based on Detail Blurring. Inspired by the method of structure extraction from texture, proposed by Xu *et al.* [6], we utilize structure extraction method to divide down-sampled image into base image and detail image. After blurring detail image by Gaussian filter, we add base image and detail image to a complete right-eye image. Because detail image contains details of down-sampled image, blurring detail image will also blur alias. The framework of anti-aliasing based on detail blurring is shown as Fig. 2.

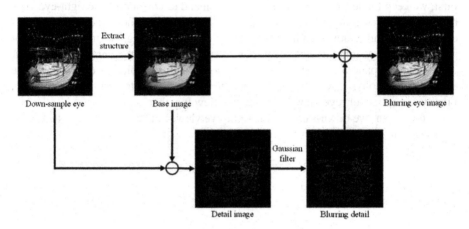

Fig. 2. Framework of anti-alias based detail blurring

3.2 The Method of Splicing Left-Eye and Right-Eye View

After down-sampling and anti-aliasing, we splice left-eye and right eye view together. Our method can be applied to side-by-side and top-and-bottom 3D panoramic videos. The method of splicing is shown in Fig. 3. Supposed A and B are the view of two eyes. The splicing method for the side-by-side 3D panoramic image is shown in Fig. 3(a) and (b). First, we divide B into B1 and B2. After down-sampling, B1′ and B2′ are spliced in the vertical direction. And then A and B are spliced in the horizontal direction. The splicing method for the top-and-bottom 3D panoramic image is shown in Fig. 3(c) and (d). First, we divide B into B1 and B2. After down-sampling, B1′ and B2′ are spliced in the horizontal direction. And then A and B are spliced in the vertical direction.

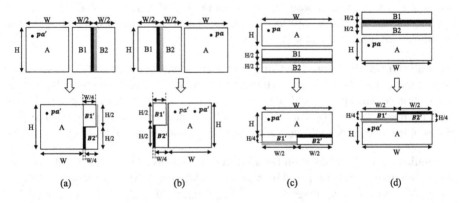

Fig. 3. (a), (b) Splicing method for side-by-side. (c), (d) Splicing method for top-and-bottom

3.3 Padding

According to splicing method mentioned in Sect. 3.2, the down-sampled view B isn't a continuous image after splicing. Due to filtering in encoding and decoding, the pixels at the right edge of B1′ and the left edge of B2′ are affected. Taking Fig. 3(a) as an example, the right-edge of B1 and the left-edge of B2 should be continuous. However, the splicing method leads to that the right edge of B1′ and the left edge of B2′ isn't continuous, which causes seam in right-eye view after encoding and decoding. In order to solve the problem, we pad 8-line pixels in the right edge of B1′ to the left edge of B2′; pad 8-line pixels in the left edge of B2′ to the right edge of B1′. Padding can avoid the impact of filtering in encoding and decoding, as shown in Fig. 4.

Fig. 4. (a) Before padding, the seam in the middle of right-eye view; (b) After padding, the seam in the middle of right-eye view is eliminated

4 Experiments and Analysis

We evaluated the coding efficiency of the proposed representation on test sequence set. The test set contains two 180° side-by-side 3D panoramic sequences in the equirectangular format at 4096 × 2048 resolution, the duration of each sequence is 10 s and the frame rate of each sequence is 30 fps. Figure 5 shows some sample frames of the test set. Finally, a subjective test is carried out to evaluate the perceived binocular quality of 3D panoramic sequences.

Fig. 5. Sample frames of the test sequence set. (a) Frame of Kunlunjue_1. (b) Frame of Wuxiubo_1

4.1 Experiment for Evaluating the Coding Efficiency

In our experiments, we compared the bit rate of our method (MRAA) with that of MR using FR as the anchor.

The standard deviation of Gaussian filter was set to 0.8. Parameters of structure extraction method [6] were set to follows: $\lambda = 0.01$, $\delta = 3$, sharpness $= 0.03$, maxIter $= 4$. λ controls the degree of smooth, increasing λ causes more blurriness. To make the image sharper, λ was set as a very small value (0.01). The factors of down-sampling in horizontal and in vertical direction were both 2. To improve the fairness of comparison, we utilized HM16.0 to encode anchor sequences and testing sequences. The result is shown in Table 1.

Table 1. The saving bit rate of two methods compared with full-resolution sequences

FR (anchor)	QP	Save bit rate (%)	
		MR	MRAA
Kunlunjue_1	22	21.70	24.13
	27	21.75	24.36
	32	22.75	25.30
	37	24.27	26.57
Wuxiubo_1	22	26.81	30.30
	27	25.95	30.21
	32	25.46	30.81
	37	26.45	31.29
Average	–	24.39	27.87

According to Table 1, both MR and MRAA save bit rate. For MR method, the average proportion of saving bit rate is 24.39%. For MRAA method, the average proportion is 27.87%, which saves more bit rate (3.48%) than MR. Because the anti-aliasing pre-process utilizes the structure extraction and Gaussian filter, which will blur the image. Therefore, it can save bit rate when encoding.

4.2 Subjective Test

Under the same bit rate, the sampled frames of FR, MR and MRAA are shown in Fig. 6. The results are captured from VR player in the mobile phone. Due to all left-eye views are full-resolution in the same sequence, we only show the right-eye views. To show more detail of right-eye, we captured the main region of right-eye image to show the results. According to Fig. 6(c) and (d), our anti-aliasing method based on detail blurring can slightly improve the quality of down-sampled view.

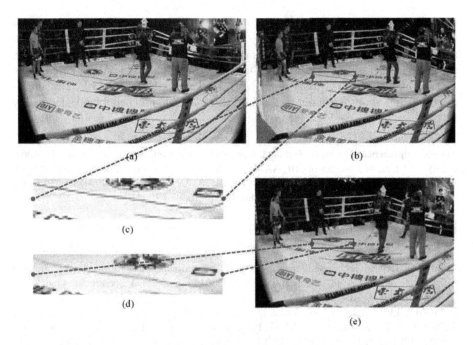

Fig. 6. (a) Right-eye full resolution image. (b) Right-eye mixed resolution image. (c) Alias in (b). (d) Alias in (e). (e) Right-eye mixed resolution image with anti-aliasing.

To assess the binocular quality, we carried out the subjective tests. Because MRAA can save more bit rate than MR, we compare the perceived binocular quality between MRAA and FR. The decoded 3D panoramic sequences with the following total bit rates were used: Kunlunjue: 1.5 M/s, 2 M/s, 3.5 M/s. In our experiment, Samsung Gear VR headset was used to display test sequences. The results of these tests are shown in Table 2. It can be seen that MRAA has a slightly better binocular quality than FR. Comparing the results of different bit rate, we found that the smaller the bit rate is, the more obvious the difference between MRAA and FR.

Table 2. Results of subjective tests with coded sequences (sum of votes)

Bit rate	MRAA better	No difference	FR better
1.5 M/s	5	3	2
2 M/s	2	5	3
3.5 M/s	1	6	3

5 Conclusion

In this paper, we proposed an asymmetric representation of 3D panoramic video based on the mixed resolution theory. In order to solve the problems of aliasing, we proposed an anti-aliasing method based on detail blurring, which is a pre-processing step.

Objective and subjective evaluations for 3D panoramic videos with mixed and full resolution have been carried out. The objective evaluation showed that mixed resolution method is an effective representation, and the average proportion of saving bit rate, compared to full resolution, is 26.13%. Due to the anti-aliasing pre-process based on the structure extraction and Gaussian filter, MRAA save more bit rate (3.48%). The subjective evaluation showed that our method (MRAA) has a slightly better binocular quality than FR.

Acknowledgement. Thanks to National Natural Science Foundation of China 61672063, 61370115, China 863 project of 2015AA015905, Shenzhen Peacock Plan, Shenzhen Research Projects of JCYJ20160506172227337 and GGFW2017041215130858, and Guangdong Province Projects of 2014B010117007 and 2014B090910001 for funding.

References

1. Fehn, C.: Depth-image-based rendering (DIBR), compression, and transmission for a flexible approach on 3DTV. In: Electronic Imaging 2004, International Society for Optics and Photonics, pp. 93–104 (2004)
2. ISO/IEC 13818-2: Draft Amendment 3, September 1996
3. Puri, A., Kollarits, B.G., Haskell, B.G.: Basics of stereoscopic video, new compression results with MPEG-2 and a proposal for MPEG-4. Signal Process. Image Commun. **10**(1–3), 201–234 (1997)
4. Perkins, M.G.: Data compression of stereopairs. IEEE Trans. Commun. **40**(4), 684–696 (1992)
5. Stelmach, L., Tam, W.J., Meegan, D., Vincent, A.: Stereo image quality: effects of mixed spatio-temporal resolution. IEEE Trans. Circuits Syst. Video Technol. **10**(2), 188–193 (2000)
6. Xu, L., Yan, Q., Jia, J.: Structure extraction from texture via relative total variation. ACM Trans. Graph. (TOG) **31**(6), 139 (2012)

Deep Learning for Signal Processing and Understanding

Shallow and Deep Model Investigation for Distinguishing Corn and Weeds

Yu Xia, Hongxun Yao$^{(\boxtimes)}$, Xiaoshuai Sun, and Yanhao Zhang

School of Computer Science and Technology,
Harbin Institute of Technology, Harbin, China
{xiayu1,h.yao,xiaoshuaisun,yhzhang}@hit.edu.cn

Abstract. Nowadays, the development of agriculture is growing very fast. The yields of corn is also an important indicator and a great part in the agriculture, which makes automatic weeds removal a necessary and urgent task. There are many challenges to distinguish the corn and weed, the biggest one is the similarity in both color and shape between corn and weeds. The processing speed is also very important in practical application. In this paper, we investigate two methods to fulfill this task. The first one is training and computing the SIFT and HARRIS feature descriptors, then using the SVM classifier to distinguish the corn and weeds. The second one is an End-to-End solution based on the faster R-CNN model. In addition, we design a specific module in order to improve the processing speed and ensure the accuracy at the same time. The experiment results conducted on our dataset demonstrate that detection based on improved Faster R-CNN model can better handle the problem.

Keywords: SIFT/HARRIS · Faster R-CNN · Weed detection
Image classification

1 Introduction

The healthy growth of the corn seeding is very important to the agricultural development. Although the detection problem has been solved very well in some fields such as pedestrian detection and face detection, the detection work for identifying weeds is still relatively small. Unfortunately, if there are many weeds around the corn, it will cause a bad effect on the growth of the corn, so a very important thing is how to distinguishing the corn and the weed. In traditional way, people use the herbicide to remove weeds, which causes serious environmental pollution and huge human resources. We resort the automatic way for distinguishing corn and weeds. Although there are some methods have been proposed in some works of the leaf detection, such as ANN and PNN [1] and so on, yet there is no good method for detecting the weed until now. So we want to use the detection methods in the field of computer vision to detect the corn and the weed efficiently and environmentally.

© Springer International Publishing AG, part of Springer Nature 2018
B. Zeng et al. (Eds.): PCM 2017, LNCS 10735, pp. 693–702, 2018.
https://doi.org/10.1007/978-3-319-77380-3_66

The main work of the detection is composed of two parts, region proposal and classification. In addition, most existing work on detection fall into two categories. The first one is using manually designed shallow features (like SIFT), these methods ignore the color and texture information, which is very likely to cause false detections of non-human objects. This kind of methods can achieve relatively good results with less training time and data compared with conventional network. In addition, the method of feature fusion appears later and this method is widely used in the detection field, such as human detection [2], face detection [3] and so on, there are many methods have been proposed to fuse the features [4]. The other categories is to train the deep neural network for the region proposal and classification. So far, there are many methods have been applied to detection. For example, one of the popular methods is the method of Regions with CNN features (R-CNN) [5]. There is another work called Fast Region-based Convolutional Network method (Fast R-CNN) [6], which employs several innovations to improve training and testing speed while also increasing detection accuracy. Furthermore, there is another method which is called Towards Real-Time Object Detection with Region Proposal Networks (Faster R-CNN) [7]. For the very deep VGG-16 model [8], the detection system has a frame rate of 5fps (including all steps) on a GPU, which achieving state-of-the-art object detection accuracy on PASCAL VOC2007, 2012, and MS COCO datasets [9] with only 300 proposals per image. Faster R-CNN is undoubtedly a big improvement in the detection field. Recently, there is another good method which is called You Look only once (YOLO) [10], it is a very efficient method.

Now we talk about the problem we want to solve in this paper. There are some important indicators in this problem. The first one is the classification accuracy, there is another important indicators which is the processing speed because in practical applications we want to remove the weeds efficiently. So based on the above two points, we make three contributions. Firstly we use the SIFT feature descriptors and HARRIS corner detector combined with SVM classifier to accomplish this work. At the same time, we use the Faster R-CNN architecture to finish it. In addition, we improve the Faster R-CNN method in view of our problem to improve the processing speed and maintain the high accuracy. The main idea of our paper is shown in Fig. 1.

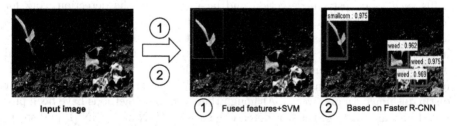

Fig. 1. Illustrating for our work. We use two ways to distinguish the corn and weeds, the first is using the hand-crafted feature, the second is using the method based on the Faster R-CNN model.

2 Creation of the Weed Detection Dataset

As we know, a good dataset is very important to study the detection problem. So far, there are many impeccable datasets such as VOC2007, 2010, and 2012 and many other good datasets. Unfortunately there is not a popular dataset for the detection of corn and weed. So it is very necessary to set up a dataset for corn & weed detection. We take about 400 high definition photos of corns and weeds in the greenhouse covering many situations. The photos consist of different sizes of the samples and the situations of lighting and occlusions. We use these photos to build the datasets for our work.

3 Detection Based on Hand-Crafted Feature

Firstly, we used the Scale-invariant feature transform (SIFT) [11] feature descriptors combined with HARRIS corner detector as our main feature extraction method, because we find that there are some differences in the corner between the corn and the weed. We adopt the SIFT+HARRIS feature descriptors combined with the SVM classifier to fulfill the work. The main idea of our approach is shown in Fig. 2.

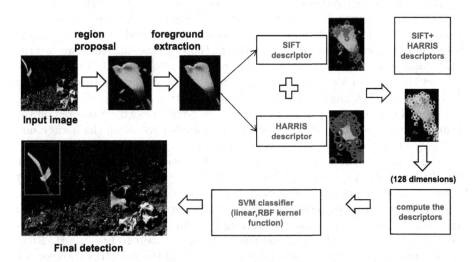

Fig. 2. Feature extraction method based on hand-crafted features. We extract SIFT descriptors for each sample, and fuse the two descriptors. Then we compute the descriptors and use the SVM classifier to train the model we need.

3.1 Region Proposal

The first step is the preprocessing of the pictures we take. We observe that the difference between the background and the samples is very obvious. So the work of the region proposal in this problem is not very difficult. We find the location of the samples whether it is corn or weed based on RGB channels because both corn and weed can be located by thresholding the green channel. The threshold we set is that we maintain the pixel value from 140 to 250 of the green channel, 30 to 100 of the blue channel, 90 to 145 of the red channel. The next step, we do the operation of the expansion and corrosion. After getting the images of single samples, we label the class of the samples manually so that we can extract features of each samples and train our classifier afterwards.

3.2 Feature Extraction and Training

After confirming the category of each samples, the next task is to choose a kind of feature or some features combined with each other. Meanwhile, the SIFT descriptors [11] is a widely used descriptors in image processing. In addition, it has strong matching ability and rotation invariant and also the sift features can be generated for even small objects. There is another important reason is that SIFT [11] uses a 128-dimensional vector to describe each keypoint, so that the length of each keypoint vector is fixed. So we can save the work of feature coding later. Based on the above reasons, we choose the SIFT features first and compute the descriptors.

Before feature extraction, we use the method of grabcut and the HSV color space to do the foreground extraction. Because the work of the foreground extraction can reduce the interference elements of the background. In the work of the foreground extraction, we firstly use the method of Grabcut, then we use the HSV color space. Firstly we convert the color space from the RGB to HSV. We extract the information of H, S, V separately, and maintain the threshold from 60 to 80 of the H channel and set the rest of the pictures to black color. After the foreground extraction, we make all the feature points we extract covered on the samples, otherwise there will be some feature points covered on the background and cause the interference of the processing accuracy.

Unfortunately, after training the SVM classifier, as we had expected, the classification accuracy is not very well, because only one kind of feature can not cover many differentiated information. It can also be inferred via visualizing the feature points. We discovered that there are no feature points in many place in the corn and the weed samples. Meanwhile, we find that there are some differences in the corner of the corn and the weed. So we want to fuse the HARRIS corner detector. We redefine the feature structure of the HARRIS detector, we add the structure information of size, angle and so on to make the feature structure of the two features unitive. Then we can compute the descriptors of the fused descriptor using the method of computing the SIFT descriptor [11] and combined with SVM classifier to distinguish the corn and the weed. The dimension of the two descriptors unified to 128 dimensions. The processing accuracy is better but it is also an unsatisfactory accuracy, so we should regard it as the baseline accuracy of our problem and explore other methods.

4   Detection Based on Improved Faster R-CNN Model

The method we have proposed in Sect. 3 did not give us a satisfactory result. We want to improve the accuracy further. As we know, the convolutional neural network is widely used in the detection problem. In addition, a number of following works have made many improvements on the basis of the convolutional neural network, the method of faster R-CNN [7] and YOLO [10] both have a good result in the accuracy and processing speed. As we know, the Faster R-CNN detection system is composed of two modules, the region proposal network and Fast R-CNN detector that uses the proposed regions. Firstly, we want to train a model to distinguish the corn and weeds using the method of Faster R-CNN [7] and improve the method in processing speed later. The main idea of the work is shown in Fig. 3.

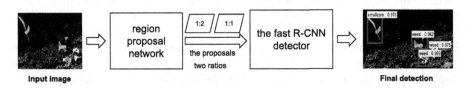

Fig. 3. The main idea of the Improved faster R-CNN model. It consists of the RPN network and the Fast R-CNN detector, we use 2 aspect ratios of 1:1 and 1:2 to generate the region proposals.

4.1   Preparing the Training Data

The Faster R-CNN [7] evaluate the method on the PASCAL VOC2007 detection benchmark. The VOC2007 dataset consists of over 20 categories. Unfortunately, there is no categories of corn and weed. So we should label our dataset by ourselves to give them the annotations we appoint. Firstly we want to make our dataset the same format as the dataset of PASCAL VOC2007. The first step is to make annotations to our dataset. We divide our dataset into four classes which is big corn, small corn, weed and one class of the background according to the actual situation. We label the dataset manually by using the tools for labeling the image. In addition to this, we should also appoint the percentage of the training data and testing data. The next step, we make the format of our dataset the same as the dataset of the PASCAL VOC2007. So far, we have prepared the training dataset of our task.

4.2   The Improved Faster R-CNN Model

The proposed Faster R-CNN model mainly composed of the fully convolutional network for region proposal and the Fast R-CNN detector. We follow the method of the region proposal network. The work of the Faster R-CNN investigate two models, ZF model and VGG model. In our work, we use the Zeiler and Fergus

(ZF) model of the Faster R-CNN [7]. Another important work of the Faster R-CNN is to generate the reference boxes, which called anchors. By observing we found that the implement details for anchors, the original work used the method of 3 scales with boxes. In addition, it used 3 aspect ratios of 1:1, 1:2 and 2:1. For our practical problem, the shape of the samples, both the positives and the negatives, has the length-to-width ratios of 1:1 and 1:2, none of the samples has the length-to-width ratios of 2:1. So we use 2 aspect ratios, 1:1 and 1:2, and abandon the ratio of 2:1 in order to improve the processing speed and remain the processing accuracy at the same time.

5   Experimental Results and Analyses

In this section, we will illustrate the experiments we set and the results of the method we use. We implemented our method using the visual studio 2013 and MATLAB R2012a on a Windows 7 operating system. For the method of feature extraction combined with SVM classifier, we combined different maximum iterations with the same kernel of the SVM classifier. In addition, we combine the experiment results trained by different SVM kernel with the same maximum iterations. For the method of Faster R-CNN [7], we combined the experiment result with the original and the method of improved Faster R-CNN model.

5.1   Hand-Crafted Feature Combined with SVM Classifier

We combined the experiment result of different features and different kernel function of the SVM classifier. We use the SIFT descriptors [11] combined with the linear kernel function of the SVM classifier. In addition, we visualize the feature points on the samples, then we keep the state of the linear kernel function of the SVM. We compare the influence by the maximum iterations and also the feature we choose. The first step we explore the influence to the experiment result caused by the maximum iterations of the SVM classifier. We maintain the same kernel (linear kernel) function of the SVM classifier and use the SIFT descriptors [11] firstly. We set the parameter of the maximum to 5000 and 10000 respectively and observe the classification rate, we found that the classification rate with the maximum iterations of 10000 gets a higher accuracy than the one with maximum iterations of 5000. The experiment result is shown in Table 1.

In addition to this experiment, we change different types of the kernel of the SVM classifier. As we know, the amount of the parameter of the linear kernel function is very small, and the linear kernel function has a advantage of the fast processing speed. But the linear kernel function can obtain a good result with the samples which are detachable linearity. For the large amount of samples, people usually use the RBF kernel function. We want to explore whether the RBF kernel function is a better choice for our work. As we know, the expression of the RBF kernel function is $K(x,y) = e^{-\gamma\|xi-xj\|^2}$, $\gamma > 0$, firstly, we should confirm the parameter γ. We use the sift descriptors and set the maximum iterations of the

Table 1. Experiment results caused by the maximum iterations of the SVM classifier

Features	Positive samples for training	Negative samples for training	Maximum iterations	Kernel function	Classification rate (%)
SIFT	200	200	5000	LINEAR	63.3
SIFT	300	300	5000	LINEAR	76.1
SIFT	200	200	10000	LINEAR	76.2
SIFT	300	300	10000	LINEAR	79.2

Table 2. The classification rate influence by the parameter γ

The parameter γ	0.00005	0.00001	0.000005	0.000001
Classification rate (%)	20.1	74.3	76.2	66.0

SVM classifier to 10000, the classification rate influence by the parameter γ is shown in Table 2.

So we know that the parameter should be set to 0.000005. The next step we compare the classification rate with the feature descriptors of only using the SIFT descriptors [11] and the feature descriptors of SIFT descriptors [11] combined with the HARRIS descriptors. We references set the parameter γ to 0.00005 and the maximum iterations to 10000 and the classification rate is shown in Table 3.

Table 3. Classification rate influenced by the features

Features	Positive samples for training	Negative samples for training	Maximum iterations	Kernel function	The parameter γ	Classification rate (%)
SIFT	200	200	10000	RBF	0.000005	77.6
SIFT	300	300	10000	RBF	0.000005	81.2
SIFT+HARRIS	200	200	10000	RBF	0.000005	83.6
SIFT+HARRIS	300	300	10000	RBF	0.000005	87.1

Some of the experiment result is shown in Fig. 4. The green bounding box represents the class of the corn, the blue bounding box represents the class of the weed. We found that there are some mistakes in the samples which is very small. It may be caused by the non obvious texture feature.

5.2 Experiments of the Improved Faster R-CNN Model

In this section, we do the experiments to observe the classification rate and the processing speed using the method of the Faster R-CNN model. In addition

Fig. 4. Some experimental results of the method based on hand-crafted features combined with SVM classifier. The yellow boxes represent the corn and the red boxes represent weeds. (Color figure online)

Fig. 5. Some experiment results of the method based on Faster R-CNN model. The blue boxes represent the class of small corns, the green boxes represent the class of big corns and the red boxes represent weeds. (Color figure online)

to this, we compare the classification rate and the processing speed with the method of the feature extraction combined with the SVM classifier. Firstly, we do the experiment with the combination of the region proposal network and the Zeiler and Fergus model. We make annotations to our datasets manually using the tools for labeling images. For the whole 400 pictures in the datasets. We appoint 300 pictures for training and the rest 100 of them for testing. For the region proposal network, we produce about 300 proposals. The next step, we run the faster R-CNN model and observe the processing accuracy and the processing speed. The experiment result is shown in Table 4.

Table 4. The classification rate by the Faster R-CNN model compared with the SVM classifier.

Method	Max bounding box	max_iter	Classification rate (%)
RPN+ZF	300	40000	95.2
Feature+SVM	-	10000	87.1

In addition, we abandon the ratios of 2:1 scale in the region proposal network and remain the ratios of 1:1 and 1:2. We keep the other parameters and the training environment the same as the front experiment in order to see whether we make an improvement in the processing speed. According to the experiments, we found that the processing speed has been improved. We also compare the processing speed with the method of SIFT+SVM classifier. The experimental result is shown in Table 5. Some of the localization results are shown in Fig. 5.

Table 5. The classification rate and processing speed of 3 methods.

Method	Two features combined with SVM	Faster R-CNN model (3 ratios anchors)	Faster R-CNN model (2 ratios anchors)
Classification rate (%)	87.1	95.2	95.1
Processing speed (sec. per image)	2	3	1.6

We found that for our problem, the method based on the deep learning method can achieve a higher accuracy than the method of choosing the features manually, the method based on the Faster R-CNN achieve an accuracy better than the best result of the method based on the SVM classifier. But the method of hand-crafted feature combined with SVM classifier can save the time of training. In addition to this, the demanding for the hardware condition is lower. When we have finished training a model, for the test data, there is no obvious difference in processing time of the three method. In the future, we can choose different method according to the different situations.

6   Conclusion

In this paper, we attempt to distinguish the corn seeding and the weed efficiently. Firstly, we adopt the method of the traditional hand-crafted feature combined with the SVM classifier. We choose the SIFT descriptors combined with the HARRIS corner detector as the feature extractor. Secondly, we adopt the method of the Faster R-CNN [7] and make an improvement of the model. We found that the method based on the improved Faster R-CNN model get a higher accuracy than the first one, but it also has a disadvantage of slower processing speed. In the future, we will collect more datasets covering more complicated situations to make our experiment results more reliable.

Acknowledgement. This work was supported by the National Natural Science Foundation of China under Project No. 61472103.

References

1. Wu, S.G., Bao, F.S., Xu, E.Y., Wang, Y., Chang, Y., Xiang, Q.: A leaf recognition algorithm for plant classification using probabilistic neural network, CoRR abs/0707.4289 (2007)
2. Jiang, Y., Ma, J.: Combination features and models for human detection. In: CVPR, pp. 240–248. IEEE Computer Society (2015)
3. Fusek, R., Sojka, E., Mozdren, K., Surkala, M.: Energy-transfer features and their application in the task of face detection. In: AVSS, pp. 147–152. IEEE Computer Society (2013)
4. Wang, J., Zhu, H., Yu, S., Fan, C.: Object tracking using color-feature guided network generalization and tailored feature fusion. Neurocomputing **238**, 387–398 (2017)
5. Girshick, R.B., Donahue, J., Darrell, T., Malik, J.: Rich feature hierarchies for accurate object detection and semantic segmentation. In: CVPR, pp. 580–587. IEEE Computer Society (2014)
6. Girshick, R.B.: Fast R-CNN. In: ICCV, pp. 1440–1448. IEEE Computer Society (2015)
7. Ren, S., He, K., Girshick, R.B., Sun, J.: Faster R-CNN: towards real-time object detection with region proposal networks. In: NIPS, pp. 91–99 (2015)
8. Simonyan, K., Zisserman, A.: Very deep convolutional networks for large-scale image recognition, CoRR abs/1409.1556 (2014)
9. Lin, T.-Y., Maire, M., Belongie, S., Hays, J., Perona, P., Ramanan, D., Dollár, P., Zitnick, C.L.: Microsoft COCO: common objects in context. In: Fleet, D., Pajdla, T., Schiele, B., Tuytelaars, T. (eds.) ECCV 2014. LNCS, vol. 8693, pp. 740–755. Springer, Cham (2014). https://doi.org/10.1007/978-3-319-10602-1_48
10. Redmon, J., Divvala, S.K., Girshick, R.B., Farhadi, A.: You only look once: unified, real-time object detection. In: CVPR, pp. 779–788. IEEE Computer Society (2016)
11. Lowe, D.G.: Distinctive image features from scale-invariant keypoints. Int. J. Comput. Vis. **60**(2), 91–110 (2004)

Representing Discrimination of Video by a Motion Map

Wennan Yu, Yuchao Sun, Feiwu Yu, and Xinxiao Wu[✉]

Beijing Laboratory of Intelligent Information Technology,
School of Computer Science, Beijing Institute of Technology, Beijing, China
{yuwennan,sunyuchao,yufeiwu,wuxinxiao}@bit.edu.cn

Abstract. Representing the content of the video by a motion map is a challenging problem in video analysis. This paper proposes to integrate the discriminative information of a video into a map by optimizing the recognition accuracy of the original video in the action recognition task. The motion map represents a prefix of video frames sequence. A motion map and the next video frame can be integrated to a new motion map by the proposed 3-dimensional convolution based model. This model can be trained by incremental length clips from training videos iteratively, and the final acquired network can be used for generating the motion map of the whole video. Experimental results on the UCF101 and the HMDB51 datasets show that our method achieves better results compared with other related methods.

Keywords: Video-to-Image · Video analysis · Action recognition
CNN · Discriminative information

1 Introduction

Representing a video by a motion map is an important topic in video analysis. A motion map is a powerful and compact representation of a video which can be used in video retrieval and video surveillance. The motion map has many distinct applications such as visualization of video, redundancy removal of information, and discovery of the discriminative information. The calculation of the motion map is fast and requires less memory resources. Hence using a map to represent the video has realistic requirements.

There are three main challenges to be solved when we generate a motion map to represent a video: 1. How to acquire the temporal information in the video, which can reflect the dynamic content; 2. How to solve the problem of variable video lengths when generating a map representation from a video; 3. How to integrate the temporal information of the video into a map without losing the discriminative information, so as to effectively represent the video content.

Recently, many methods have been proposed to solve these problems respectively. As for the problem of acquiring temporal information in the video, many researches have been done in the field of action recognition. For example, the

© Springer International Publishing AG, part of Springer Nature 2018
B. Zeng et al. (Eds.): PCM 2017, LNCS 10735, pp. 703–711, 2018.
https://doi.org/10.1007/978-3-319-77380-3_67

LSTM [4] and RNN [2] models are used to identify the temporal pattern of the features acquired by convolutional neural networks (CNNs) [8]. The slow fusion method [7] is used to extend the connectivity of the network in temporal dimension to learn spatio-temporal features. The two stream network [11] learns the spatio-temporal features by using the optical flow and the original image at the same time. The C3D method [6,7,15] exploits a 3-dimensional convolution kernel to directly extend the convolution operation of the image to the operation of the frame sequence. These methods can process temporal information effectively, but can not generate motion maps. To address the problem of variable video lengths, some useful schemes have been developed. Typically, features can be encoded by a coding method such as Fisher Vector [10], or a video can be iteratively integrated by various pooling methods, such as rank pooling [3]. To solve the problem of integrating the temporal information, there are few methods using videos for map generation and preserving the discriminative information simultaneously. Taylor *et al.* [14] use the convolutional gated restricted Boltzmann machine to generate a flow field of the adjacent two frames in the video for action recognition, yet can not generate a single map to represent a video. Bilen *et al.* [1] use the dynamic image network to generate dynamic images for action videos, which use the order of video frames as the supervisory information without considering the category information, thus this method loses some discriminative information of videos. Different from the above methods, we propose the Motion Map Network (MMN) to cope with these three challenges simultaneously in this paper.

The MMN based on 3-dimensional convolution (3Dconv) neural network [5] is proposed to acquire and integrate the temporal information of variable-length videos. The 3Dconv can model appearance and motion information effectively, therefore it has achieved good performances on various video analysis tasks, such as action recognition, action localization, and event analysis. Our model integrates the motion map of the previous frames with the next frame to generate a new motion map. The motion map of the whole video can be obtained after the repetitive integration of the next frame frame-by-frame for variable-length videos. Besides, the video category labels are used as the supervisory information to train the model, so that the generated motion maps can optimize the classification results. Optimizing with category labels makes the final motion maps most likely to retain the discriminative information of the videos. In general, the proposed method can acquire the temporal information effectively, deal with variable-length videos, and integrate the temporal information into a map without losing the discriminative information of videos.

The main contributions of this paper are twofold: 1. We propose the Motion Map Network which can discover and integrate the temporal information of the video; 2. We propose an iterative training method for our network to generate a motion map from a video with an arbitrary video length.

2   Method

In this section, we first introduce the concept of motion maps which integrate the spatio-temporal information of the prefixes of video frame sequences. Then, we describe the architecture of the MMN in detail. Finally, we elaborate the training procedure for the MMN.

2.1   Motion Map

A motion map is a representation for a prefix of video frame sequences. For a video V with N frames, we define the video frames of V as f_i, $i \in \{1...N\}$. F_i denotes the motion map of f_1 to f_i. In this paper, in order to retain the action and appearance information, we propose an iterative method to generate the motion map by combining the motion map F_i with the video frame f_{i+1} through the MMN:

$$F_{i+1} = F_i \oplus f_{i+1}. \tag{1}$$

After the iteration, the final motion map F_N of video V can be obtained. The discriminative information embodied in the single motion map F_N can be applied to the action recognition tasks.

Fig. 1. The motion maps generated by the MMN represent the motions and static objects of video in various categories. The discriminative information integrated in the motion map can be used to classify the categories of videos.

Some motion maps of various categories are listed in Fig. 1. Figure 1(a) shows that the static objects such as windows and floors are presented as what they are and the superposed silhouette incarnates the different location and posture of the man when he raises and lowers the body using the arms; Fig. 1(d) shows that the woman's body and cello are barely moving, while the location of her head, arms, and fiddlestick are changing, hence the superposed shadows reflect the action of playing cello; Fig. 1(l) shows that the arms and yo yo ball are the main features of this motion map while the rest of the motion map is diluted, which shows the relationship between the arms movements and playing yo yo ball. It proves that dynamic information is reflected by the superposition of different frames, when the static information in the video frame sequences can be retained. Thus, the motion map can incarnate the discriminative information effectively.

2.2 Motion Map Network

The architecture of the MMN is illustrated in Fig. 2. A motion map and the next video frame are combined into a video frame sequence as an input, then a single 2D-feature map is extracted following two 3DConv layers and pooling in temporal dimension. After that, we perform a simple convolutional neural network that has two 2Dconv layers and two fully connected layers for image classification, following the output of layer 3DConv2. Concatenating these two parts, the MMN is structured as an end-to-end network.

The special structure of layer 3DConv2 can generate a motion map that integrates the information of input. Firstly, we consider the MMN as an action recognition network that exploits the information of both previous motion map and the next video frame. After training with the label of videos, the output is based on the information provided by the input pair of motion map and the next frame. Then ignoring the generation part (layer Input to layer 3DConv2), we regard the MMN as an image classification network, and the output given by the well trained network shows that the single motion map provides enough discriminative information for distinguishing actions. Finally, we focus on the

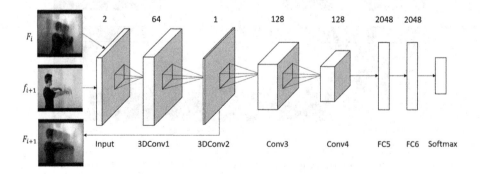

Fig. 2. The architecture of the motion map network.

generation part. When the network is well trained, the effect of using a pair of images and using a single motion map as input is consistent. It indicates that the function of the generation part is to represent and integrate the information of input. The output of the generation part is called motion map. As we described earlier, the special structure can be used to generate a motion map.

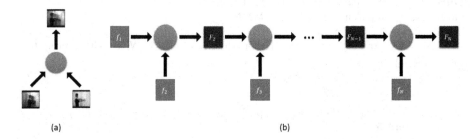

(a)   (b)

Fig. 3. (a) The MMN takes two images as input, and generates a motion map by integrating the temporal information of input; (b) A motion map of a video is generated by using the MMN iteratively.

Using the MMN to integrate two images into one, the motion map of a whole video can be iteratively generated. As shown in Fig. 3(a), the MMN accepts two images including a motion map and a next video frame, and produces a new motion map. According to Eq. 1, we use the MMN iteratively to get the final motion map, and the whole process is shown in Fig. 3(b).

2.3   Training

We propose an iterative method to train the MMN. Video database V with N frames and video labels L are used to train the MMN. S is defined as the maximum training iteration length, and we train the MMN using training length s from 2 to S. The meaning of training length s is that in a round of iteration we cut the training video V_i into s-length clips $C_j^i (j \in 1...N_i/s)$ with overlap 0.5 and assign the labels L_i to clip C_j^i. We define the MMN as a function $G_{\theta_s}(I_a, I_b)$, where θ_s denotes the parameters of the MMN after the iteration of training length s. The initial parameters of the MMN is defined as θ_1. For each s, we generate the motion map $F_{1 \sim s-1}^{C_j^i}$ using the $G_{\theta_{s-1}}$, and train the MMN using the motion map $F_{s-1}^{C_j^i}$, video frame $f_s^{C_j^i}$ and video clip label L_i. Finally, we can get θ_S which is the parameters of the well trained MMN mentioned above.

The detailed training procedure is summarized in Algorithm 1.

3   Experiment

We explore the proposed models on the UCF101 [13] and HMDB51 [9] datasets for evaluating the discrimination of the motion map generated by the MMN on action recognition tasks.

Algorithm 1. The training algorithm for Motion Map Network

Input: The video dataset, V;

The frames number of video dataset, N;

The video labels, L;

The maximum training iteration length, S;

The parameters of the MMN, θ_1;

Output: The final parameters of the MMN, θ_S;

1: Initialize the parameter θ_1 for the MMN;

2: **for** each $s \in 2, 3, ..., S$ **do**

3:     Cut the training video V_i into s-length clips $C_j^i (j \in 1...N_i/s)$ with overlap 0.5;

4:     Extract the video frames from C_j^i as $f^{C_j^i}$;

5:     **for** each $j \in 1, 2, ..., N/s$ **do**

6:         **for** each $k \in 1, 2, ..., s - 1$ **do**

7:             Generate the motion map $F_k^{C_j^i}$ using the $G_{\theta_{s-1}}(F_k^{C_j^i} - 1, f_k^{C_j^i})$;

8:         **end for**

9:         Train the MMN using $F_{s-1}^{C_j^i}$, $f_s^{C_j^i}$ and L_i;

10:     **end for**

11:     Get the MMN parameters θ_s;

12: **end for**

3.1 Datasets

UCF101. The UCF101 dataset [13] comprises of 101 action categories, over 13 k clips and 27 h of video data, and the mean clip length is 7.21 s. The database consists of realistic user-uploaded videos containing camera motion and cluttered background, such as surfing, ice dancing. The dataset is trimmed, thus each frame of a video is related to its category.

HMDB51. The HMDB51 dataset [9] comprises of 51 action categories, which in total contains around 7,000 manually annotated clips extracted from a variety of sources ranging from digitized movies to YouTube. Comparing with UCF101 dataset, the HMDB51 dataset includes more complex background and more intra class differences.

3.2 Implement Details

Video Frames. Since the network can only deal with video frames, the videos need to be processed to video frames. Some methods directly split the videos ignoring the different frame rate, which may result in the time inconsistent dynamic information. Therefore, we extract a fixed number video frames on each second according to the frame rate of videos, which improves the generalization performance of the network. To make the network better capture the changes in the action, we extract two frames per second. As for some short videos, we loop the extracted frames, and fill up to 16 frames per video.

Motion Map. As described in Sect. 2.2, the output of layer 3DConv2 is regarded as the motion map generated by input. Nevertheless, the motion map is not directly obtained by the network. We propose to scale the value in feature map and perform histogram equalization to generate the motion map.

3.3 Results

We trained the MMN on the UCF101 and HMDB51 datasets. Firstly, we utilize the Algorithm 1 to train a MMN which is used to generate a single motion map for each video in each dataset. Then we use the motion maps to finetune the VGG network [12] for action recognition task. The result is shown in Tables 1 and 2.

Table 1. Results on UCF101 dataset

Approach	Split1	Split2	Split3	Average
Average image	52.6	53.4	51.7	52.6
SDI [1]	57.2	58.7	57.7	57.9
Ours	**61.2**	**61.4**	**60.5**	**61.0**

Table 2. Results on HMDB51 dataset

Approach	Split1	Split2	Split3	Average
Average image	34.1	33.8	33.9	33.9
SDI [1]	37.2	36.4	36.9	36.8
Ours	**39.3**	**37.1**	**37.0**	**37.8**

We use the motion maps generated by the MMN to compare with the Average image and the SDI proposed by Hakan *et al.* [1]. Average image is the average of each video frame on pixel-level. The comparison results show that the motion map outperforms the Average image and the SDI.

Table 3. The accuracy of some categories from the HMDB51 dataset

Categories	Accuracy	Categories	Accuracy
ShootBall	83.3	Pick	6.7
PullUp	83.3	FallFloor	6.7
Golf	76.7	KickBall	10.0
Walk	63.3	Wave	13.3
Jump	63.3	Smoke	13.3

Table 3 lists the top 5 categories with the highest accuracy and lowest accuracy. We can find that the categories with similar background (e.g. the action of "Gol") or regular movement (e.g. the actions of "Jump" and "PullUp") are easy to be recognized. We have some failure cases as well when the background is complex, the action objects are not prominent, or the same action concept has different forms of entity expression. Taking the action of "FallFloor" for example, some people are squatting on the floor, while some people are thrown to the floor. As for the significant difference between the action of "ShootBall" and the action of "KickBall", most of the videos in the action of "ShootBall" have few camera moving and simple scenes, while most of the videos in the action of "KickBall" have complex backgrounds and more than one person on camera. Therefore, the experimental results of these two categories are not as similar as the description of them. We can conclude that the MMN is more suitable for the categories featured by motion patterns and obvious static features.

4   Conclusion

In this paper, we have proposed a 3DConv based model MMN and its iterative training method to integrate the discriminative information of a video into a single motion map. Experiments on action recognition datasets prove that the motion maps generated by our model retain more discriminative information. A visual inspection reflects that the motion map intuitively integrates the dynamic information, thus the motion maps retain sufficient identifiability.

Acknowledgments. This work was supported in part by the Natural Science Foundation of China (NSFC) under Grants No. 61673062, No. 61472038 and No. 61375044.

References

1. Bilen, H., Fernando, B., Gavves, E., Vedaldi, A., Gould, S.: Dynamic image networks for action recognition. In: Proceedings of the IEEE Conference on Computer Vision and Pattern Recognition, pp. 3034–3042 (2016)
2. Donahue, J., Anne Hendricks, L., Guadarrama, S., Rohrbach, M., Venugopalan, S., Saenko, K., Darrell, T.: Long-term recurrent convolutional networks for visual recognition and description. In: Proceedings of the IEEE Conference on Computer Vision and Pattern Recognition, pp. 2625–2634 (2015)
3. Fernando, B., Gavves, E., Oramas, J.M., Ghodrati, A., Tuytelaars, T.: Modeling video evolution for action recognition. In: Proceedings of the IEEE Conference on Computer Vision and Pattern Recognition, pp. 5378–5387 (2015)
4. Hochreiter, S., Schmidhuber, J.: Long short-term memory. Neural Comput. **9**(8), 1735–1780 (1997)
5. Ji, S., Xu, W., Yang, M., Yu, K.: 3D convolutional neural networks for human action recognition. IEEE Trans. Pattern Anal. Mach. Intell. **35**(1), 221–231 (2013)
6. Jia, Y., Shelhamer, E., Donahue, J., Karayev, S., Long, J., Girshick, R., Guadarrama, S., Darrell, T.: Caffe: convolutional architecture for fast feature embedding. In: Proceedings of the 22nd ACM International Conference on Multimedia, pp. 675–678. ACM (2014)

7. Karpathy, A., Toderici, G., Shetty, S., Leung, T., Sukthankar, R., Fei-Fei, L.: Large-scale video classification with convolutional neural networks. In: Proceedings of the IEEE Conference on Computer Vision and Pattern Recognition, pp. 1725–1732 (2014)

8. Krizhevsky, A., Sutskever, I., Hinton, G.E.: Imagenet classification with deep convolutional neural networks. In: Advances in Neural Information Processing Systems, pp. 1097–1105 (2012)

9. Kuehne, H., Jhuang, H., Garrote, E., Poggio, T., Serre, T.: HMDB: a large video database for human motion recognition. In: 2011 IEEE International Conference on Computer Vision (ICCV), pp. 2556–2563. IEEE (2011)

10. Perronnin, F., Sánchez, J., Mensink, T.: Improving the fisher kernel for large-scale image classification. In: Daniilidis, K., Maragos, P., Paragios, N. (eds.) ECCV 2010. LNCS, vol. 6314, pp. 143–156. Springer, Heidelberg (2010). https://doi.org/10.1007/978-3-642-15561-1_11

11. Simonyan, K., Zisserman, A.: Two-stream convolutional networks for action recognition in videos. In: Advances in Neural Information Processing Systems, pp. 568–576 (2014)

12. Simonyan, K., Zisserman, A.: Very deep convolutional networks for large-scale image recognition. arXiv preprint arXiv:1409.1556 (2014)

13. Soomro, K., Zamir, A.R., Shah, M.: UCF101: a dataset of 101 human actions classes from videos in the wild. arXiv preprint arXiv:1212.0402 (2012)

14. Taylor, G.W., Fergus, R., LeCun, Y., Bregler, C.: Convolutional learning of spatio-temporal features. In: Daniilidis, K., Maragos, P., Paragios, N. (eds.) ECCV 2010. LNCS, vol. 6316, pp. 140–153. Springer, Heidelberg (2010). https://doi.org/10.1007/978-3-642-15567-3_11

15. Tran, D., Bourdev, L., Fergus, R., Torresani, L., Paluri, M.: Learning spatiotemporal features with 3D convolutional networks. In: The IEEE International Conference on Computer Vision (ICCV) (2015)

Multi-scale Discriminative Patches for Fined-Grained Visual Categorization

Wenbo Tang, Hongxun Yao$^{(\boxtimes)}$, Xiaoshuai Sun, and Wei Yu

School of Computer Science and Technology,
Harbin Institute of Technology, Harbin, China
wenbotang@stu.hit.edu.cn, {h.yao,xiaoshuaisun,w.yu}@hit.edu.cn

Abstract. Fine-grained visual categorization (FGVC) is a challenging vision problem since the similar appearance between object classes. It is important to note that human visual recognition system generally focuses on the specific part to distinguish those confused classes, which is also the breakthrough point for FGVC. In this paper, we will introduce the feedback mechanism of CNN to extract multi-scale discriminative patches. The extracted patches show more significance than the whole object region. Compared with tradition methods, we only require the object-level label rather than part-level annotations. Experiments on Caltech-UCSD Birds-200-2011 demonstrate the effectiveness of our method in solving FGVC.

Keywords: Discriminative patches
Fine-grained visual categorization · Multi-scale

1 Introduction

In recent years, FGVC has received increased interest in computer vision community. FGVC is a sub-field of object classification. The goal of FGVC is to distinguish subordinate categories within an entry-level category, therefore, there are two major problems for FGVC. One is the high inter-class similarity and the other is high intra-class variance. In order to handle these two challenges, most works rely on extra annotations of bounding boxes and part landmarks more or less.

Early works require the annotation of fine-grained datasets at both training and test stage. Some works use not only the bounding box information but also part-level annotations [2,4,7,10,15]. There is no doubt that these works' setting is demanding. Meanwhile, it's almost impossible to apply these methods to practical application. But it is acceptable to use only the object bounding box information. Berg and Belhumeur [2] introduced a part-based one-vs-one feature for fine-grained categorization, which pairwise parts are used for discovering discriminative areas. Huang et al. [7] propose a Part-Stacked CNN framework which requires both bounding box and part annotations at training time, and even need the bounding boxes during test time. Chai et al. [4] propose a method

© Springer International Publishing AG, part of Springer Nature 2018
B. Zeng et al. (Eds.): PCM 2017, LNCS 10735, pp. 712–721, 2018.
https://doi.org/10.1007/978-3-319-77380-3_68

by combine segmentation and detection to improve both part localization and segmentation accuracy.

Later works only use object-level and part-level annotations during the training stage and do not use annotations in the testing phase. Branson et al. [3] propose a graph-based clustering algorithm for pose normalization space, which can train a strongly supervised model. Zhang et al. [16] use the R-CNN [6] framework to detect part information and the object-level regions. Krause et al. [8] propose a method which only needs bounding box annotations at training time, and is unsupervised at part-level information.

Recent years, there are lots of universal methods appeared which don't use any object-level or part-level annotations during both training time and test time. These methods don't need too many labeled information about the fine-grained object, therefore it is a major step for apply fine-grained classification to practical application. Simon and Rodner [11] propose a method which incorporates CNN into deformable part model [5] and localize parts with constellation model. Xiao et al. [14] combine two deep convolutional network models, one of them is used to select interrelated patches about an object, and the other model is used to select discriminative patches within a picture. Zhang et al. [17] proposes a method which is free of any object-level or part-level annotations at both training and test time.

Our method (Fig. 1) belongs to the last kind and does not use any object-level or part-level annotations at both training time and test time. We propose a novel method which can automatically extract multi-scale discriminative patches of a fine-grained image. Compared with [17] our method does not need to produce lots of candidate parts, besides, we do not need to screen them for finding discriminative patches.

Most existing FGVC methods [1,2,4,14] can be divided into two steps: feature extraction and classification. Because these two steps are independent, it's hard for people to find the best way to combine the feature and the classifier. Generally, the performance of two steps methods are worse than those End-to-End Convolutional Neural Networks (CNN) which can be globally optimized through back-propagation. Therefore, in this work, we adopt an End-to-End CNN-based method for FGVC. In summary, our method has three merits: (1) At both training time and test time, we do not need any part-level or object-level annotations. (2) We propose a novel method which can extract multi-scale discriminative patches of a fine-grained object. (3) We combine several different scales patches based End-to-End CNN models to improve performance.

We detail our extracting discriminative patches method in Sect. 2. In Sect. 3 we present the experimental detail and results. Finally, we conclude our work in Sect. 4.

2   Extracting Discriminative Patches

Previous works demonstrate that object-level and part-level annotations of fine-grained objects could significantly boost the accuracy of fine-grained recognition

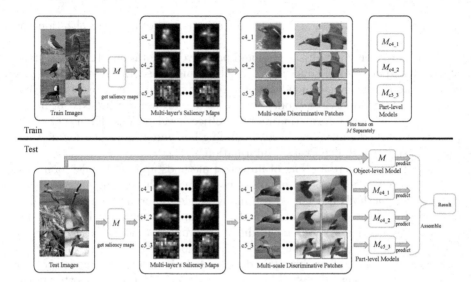

Fig. 1. The pipeline of our proposed method. Notice that all of the images in our pipeline are resize to 224×224. Our method includes the training and testing stages. At the training stage, we first fine tuning a pre-trained model on ImageNet dataset with Caltech-UCSD Birds-200-2011 denoted as M, then feed all training images and corresponding labels to M to get the multi-layer's saliency maps. Then for every saliency map, we choose top-k activations to extract corresponding receptive fields as discriminative patches. Finally, we fine tuning M separately with different layers' training images' patches and get different part-level models. At testing time, we get testing images' patches as same as what we do at training time, then feed these patches to corresponding part-level models, we also feed source testing images to object-level model M, then assemble these models' results as the final result.

[14,17], and those part-level annotations include discriminative patches in general. In this section, we target to extract discriminative patches automatically. Our strategy consists two modules: generate the saliency map and get discriminative patches. In the first module, we extract all saliency maps of both training data and testing data. In the second module, we compute the discriminative patches of all data according to the saliency maps which we get in the first module.

2.1 Generate Saliency Map

In our method, saliency map shows the response of CNN model for an input image. We can train a CNN model by feeding it with lots of fine-grained images and class label (no any object-level or part-level annotations), denoted as M, and then M has the ability which classifies specify images. In other words, M can capture specific features which belong to training data. Since there are multiple components in CNN such as the convolutional layer, pooling layer, fully connected layer, and activation function, a CNN model can imitate any complex non-linear function. When it comes to forward propagation, the computing process from input picture I to evidence output $E_c(I)$ can be regarded as a linear function:

$$E_c(I) = w_c I + b_c \tag{1}$$

where c is class number, $E_c(I)$ is the evidence which M model predict for class c, and w_c and b_c are respectively the weight vector and the bias of the total model. We will prove Eq. 1 is a liner function later. Take VGG-VD [12] model as an example, there are five kind of operations: convolution, Max-Pooling, Relu, fully connected and Softmax. Then we discuss these operations separately.

Convolution operation can be expressed as:

$$m_{i+1} = w_i m_i \tag{2}$$

where w_i is a filter weight matrix of layer i, m_i is input image or input feature map and m_{i+1} is output feature map. Both m_i and m_{i+1} are matrices, so convolution operation is a liner operation.

Max-Pooling can retain the max number and it's a special convolution operation, it can be wrote as:

$$m_{i+1} = w_{i(n,n)} m_i \tag{3}$$

$$w_{i(p,q)} = \begin{cases} 0 & \text{other conditions} \\ 1 & \text{if } m_{i(p,q)} \text{ is the maximum number} \end{cases} \tag{4}$$

where $w_{i(n,n)}$ is a $n \times n$ size matrix and it's value depends on Eq. 4 and $w_{i(p,q)}$ is p row q column value of $w_{i(n,n)}$ $(1 \le p, q \le n)$.

Relu also can be regarded as a special convolution operation, it retention nonnegative number and assignment 0 for negative number. It can be wrote as Eq. 3 and $w_{i(n,n)}$ values depend on:

$$w_{i(p,q)} = \begin{cases} 0 & m_{i(p,q)} < 0 \\ 1 & m_{i(p,q)} \ge 0 \end{cases} \tag{5}$$

Where $1 \le p, q \le n$, since we have proved that both Max-Pooling and Relu are convolution operations at forward time, so both of them are liner operations.

As for fully connected, it's also a liner operation, it can be wrote as:

$$y_j = \sum_{i=1}^{n} w_{i,j} x_i + b_j \tag{6}$$

where y_j is the number j node's input in vector y, x_i is the number i node's output in vector x, $w_{i,j}$ is a weight between y_j and x_i and b_j is the corresponding bias. So fully connected also is a liner operation.

Softmax is the last operation in VGG-VD [12] model, and it just normalizes the evidence output use:

$$\text{softmax(x)}_i = \frac{e^{x_i}}{\sum_{j=1}^{n} e^{x_j}} \tag{7}$$

where n is the output class number of the model, it's obvious that softmax do not change the result of predict. So we can ignore this operation and consider the forward propagation only consist of convolution, Max-Pooling, Relu, and fully connected. Now that all of these four operations are liner operations, Eq. 1 is a liner function.

For an input image I, we know it belong to class c, we can compute the w_i which is the derivative of E_c with respect to i-th layer feature map m_i:

$$w_i = \frac{\partial E_c}{\partial m_i} \tag{8}$$

Let us assume that the i-th layer feature map m_i (with k filter channels, n rows and n columns) size is $k \times n \times n$. Because w_i have the same size as feature map m_i, m_i is a $k \times n \times n$ size tensor. Let us assume that the filter channel c of the pixel (p, q) of the feature map m_i corresponds to w_i with the index $h(c, p, q)$. To derive a single class saliency value for each pixel (p, q), we compute the average of w_i across all filter channels: $W_{i,p,q} = (\sum_c w_{i,h(c,p,q)})/k$. W_i (with n rows and n columns) is the i-th layer saliency map we compute in this section.

2.2 Get Discriminative Patches

In the above section, we have generated all images' saliency maps, and for a saliency map W_i, there are different values in the matrix. Different values represent different response for the input image I. From Eq. 8 we can know that w_i represent the importance of E_c, they have positive correlation. We take top-k points from the W_i as candidate points. Since every point on the feature map has a receptive field on input image I, top-k points corresponding to those points which have same position as top-k points on feature map. We can compute top-k points' receptive fields according to model structure. Since these candidate points represent the highest response for input image I, in other words, those receptive fields corresponding to candidate points attach great importance to model M, model M think these receptive fields are discriminative patches for input image I.

By computing top-k points' receptive fields we can get discriminative patches. Moreover, we can get every layer's saliency map for input image I, and the point on different layer feature map corresponding to different scales receptive fields. So we can get different scales discriminative patches for an image I by derivative with respect to different layer's feature maps.

It is important to notice that our method extracting discriminative patches only use a CNN model trained on the image label, so no any additional annotations are required (such as bounding box of objects or part-level annotations). And the computing process is quick because it just needs once forward-propagation.

3   Experiments

We test our method with VGG-VD [12] on the benchmark dataset: Caltech-UCSD Birds-200-2011 (Bird-200-2011) [13], which is the most competitive and extensive dataset in the fine-grained domain. Bird-200-2011 consists of 11788 images for 200 species of birds. It's difficult to classify this dataset due to the high variations of light, views and object poses. In our experiments, we only use training images' class label at training time and generate discriminative patches of both training images and testing images. We show the saliency map, discriminative patches and recognition result separately.

3.1 Saliency Map Results

First, we fine tune VGG-VD [12] which pre-trained on the ImageNet dataset to get a new model denote as M, then we feed training images and corresponding class label to M, and use the method we proposed in Sect. 2.1 to compute saliency maps for different layers. As for testing images, we feed them to M first and do a forward propagation to get the predict class label, then use the predict class label to get the saliency map as same as training images. The results of training images and testing images' saliency maps are shown in Fig. 2. All of the images are resized to 224×224 for better visualization.

One hand, we chose 4 kinds of images which have different complexities of background to show the effectiveness of our generate saliency map method. On the other hand, we take 3 layers (c4_1, c4_3, c5_1) to show the difference between different saliency maps. The results are shown in Fig. 2.

From Fig. 2 we can clearly see that all of different layers' saliency maps expression the fine-grained object outline no matter how complex the background is. Since M captures the fine-grained object and our method is effective for getting the saliency maps. Besides, different values of the pixel in saliency map show different significance for recognition. In other words, our method can compute and express which parts are the model most focus on. Low layers' (c4_1, c4_3) saliency map can express more accurate different importance for different parts of a fine-grained object, and high layer's (c5_1) saliency map mainly express the location of fine-grained object in an image.

3.2 Discriminative Patches Results

We compute discriminative patches according to saliency maps. In this experiment, we chose top 16 response points from c4 layers' saliency map and top 4 response points from c5. Then use these points to compute corresponding receptive fields, at last, we get the discriminative patches by crop original image according to these receptive fields.

Figure 2 illustrates the discriminative patches computed by corresponding saliency map. We can see that from low layer (c4_1) to high layer (c5_1) the patch size is becoming bigger, and low layer discriminative patches mainly locate in some semantic parts, like head, nape, and leg. While high layer discriminative patches locate in the whole fine-grained object. Take the last column of Fig. 2 as an example, although the bird's feather is similar with the background, it's hard to find the bird and distinguish the border of bird and background, our

images

c4_1

c4_3

c5_1

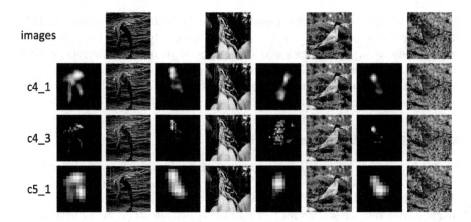

Fig. 2. Saliency map and discriminative patches. The odd column of images are saliency maps and the even column of images are corresponding patches results. Different rows show different layers' results for one image. Every image's discriminative patches are marked by different color rectangles. (Color figure online)

method can locate this bird's head, nape, leg, and the body. Thus our method is effective on extracting discriminative patches.

3.3 Recognition Results

Notice that we don't use any part annotations or bounding-boxes at training and test time. We first get discriminative patches for every image using our extracting discriminative patches method. Since we can get different scales patches according to different layers' saliency map. We fine tune M to get several models using different scales patches separately. These new models denoted as M_{c4_1}, M_{c4_2}, M_{c4_3}, M_{c5_1}, M_{c5_2}, and M_{c5_3} according to layer name.

At test time, we can also get corresponding different scales patches for every test image, then test different models using corresponding layers' patches, we feed one image's different layers' patches to the corresponding model, then average the confidence score to get the final result.

Table 1 shows different models' performance of recognition on Bird-200-2011 dataset. All of these models use default training test partition and all models use corresponding patches to test except for M which use source images. We can see different models have different performance and M_{c4_3} achieves an improvement of 7.5% in terms of recognition accuracy as compared to M.

In order to fully use different scales patches and improve the performance. We assemble several models' results together. At last we choose M, M_{c4_1}, M_{c4_3} and M_{c5_1}. Since these models can capture different scales information and form a complementary relationship in recognition, the performance on recognition improve to 83.3% by setting these four models confidence score weights by 0.1, 0.4, 0.3 and 0.2.

For M, M_{c4_1}, M_{c4_3} and M_{c5_1}, in order to further study every model's contribution to accuracy, we increase one model's weight x from 0 to 1 and set other three models' weights by $(1-x)/3$. Figure 3 shows the result of this experiment. We can see that M model 's weight have a huge impact on the accuracy. The performance is becoming worse with the M model's weight increase. While the other three part-level models performance have a weak relation between performance and weights. In other words, those part-level models are helpful to improve the recognition performance.

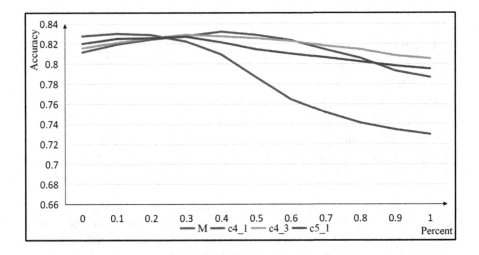

Fig. 3. Relationship between weights and accuracy

Table 2 shows the recognition results of different methods on Birds-200-2011 dataset. It is easy to see that our method is comparable to those state-of-the-art approaches. Notice that PD+FC+SWFV-CNN and B-CNN outperform our

Table 1. Recognition results of different models on Birds-200-2011 dataset

Models	Accuracy(%)
M	73.0
M_{c4_1}	78.7
M_{c4_2}	80.0
M_{c4_3}	80.5
M_{c5_1}	79.5
M_{c5_2}	78.3
M_{c5_3}	75.9
$M + M_{c4\_1} + M_{c4\_3} + M_{c5\_1}$	**83.3**

Table 2. Comparisons of different methods on Birds-200-2011 dataset. "EDP-CNN" is M_{c4_3} model result and "EDP-CNN+assemble" is $M + M_{c4\_1} + M_{c4\_3} + M_{c5\_1}$ result.

Methods	Train		Test		Accuracy(%)
	BBox	Parts	BBox	Parts	
FC-CNN	✓		✓		76.4
FC-CNN					70.4
FV-CNN	✓		✓		77.5
FV-CNN					74.7
PG-Alignment [8]	✓		✓		82.8
Part R-CNN [16]	✓	✓			73.9
Part R-CNN [16]	✓	✓	✓		76.4
PoseNorm CNN [3]	✓	✓			75.7
B-CNN [9]					84.1
PD+FC+SWFV-CNN [17]					84.5
PD+FC-CNN [17]					82.6
EDP-CNN (Ours)					**80.5**
EDP-CNN+assemble (Ours)					**83.3**

method, since we only use discriminative patches. PD+FC+SWFV-CNN use not only patches but also an additional spatially weighted FV-CNN method. Compared with B-CNN, our method only combines several models' confidence score simply. B-CNN assembles two models' CNN features by the complicated kroneker product. We have reason to believe that we can get a better performance by their additional methods.

4   Conclusion

In this paper, we propose a novel extracting multi-scale discriminative patches method for fine-grained recognition. We introduce a extracting multi-scale saliency map method which doesn't use any part-level or object-level information except for image class label. Since the multi-scale saliency map, we can compute corresponding multi-scale discriminative patches directly, the computing process is fast and the result is reliable. At last, we fine tune several patches based model by these multi-scale patches we compute, and combine several models together by different weights as the final result. The experiment demonstrated that our method is comparable to the competitors on recognition benchmarks.

References

1. Angelova, A., Zhu, S.: Efficient object detection and segmentation for fine-grained recognition. In: Proceedings of the IEEE Conference on Computer Vision and Pattern Recognition, pp. 811–818 (2013)

2. Berg, T., Belhumeur, P.N.: POOF: part-based one-vs.-one features for fine-grained categorization, face verification, and attribute estimation. In: Proceedings of the IEEE Conference on Computer Vision and Pattern Recognition, pp. 955–962 (2013)
3. Branson, S., Van Horn, G., Belongie, S., Perona, P.: Bird species categorization using pose normalized deep convolutional nets. arXiv preprint arXiv:1406.2952 (2014)
4. Chai, Y., Lempitsky, V., Zisserman, A.: Symbiotic segmentation and part localization for fine-grained categorization. In: Proceedings of the IEEE International Conference on Computer Vision, pp. 321–328 (2013)
5. Felzenszwalb, P., McAllester, D., Ramanan, D.: A discriminatively trained, multiscale, deformable part model. In: IEEE Conference on Computer Vision and Pattern Recognition, CVPR 2008, pp. 1–8. IEEE (2008)
6. Girshick, R., Donahue, J., Darrell, T., Malik, J.: Rich feature hierarchies for accurate object detection and semantic segmentation. In: Proceedings of the IEEE Conference on Computer Vision and Pattern Recognition, pp. 580–587 (2014)
7. Huang, S., Xu, Z., Tao, D., Zhang, Y.: Part-stacked CNN for fine-grained visual categorization. In: Proceedings of the IEEE Conference on Computer Vision and Pattern Recognition, pp. 1173–1182 (2016)
8. Krause, J., Jin, H., Yang, J., Fei-Fei, L.: Fine-grained recognition without part annotations. In: Proceedings of the IEEE Conference on Computer Vision and Pattern Recognition, pp. 5546–5555 (2015)
9. Lin, T.Y., RoyChowdhury, A., Maji, S.: Bilinear CNN models for fine-grained visual recognition. In: Proceedings of the IEEE International Conference on Computer Vision, pp. 1449–1457 (2015)
10. Liu, J., Kanazawa, A., Jacobs, D., Belhumeur, P.: Dog breed classification using part localization. In: Fitzgibbon, A., Lazebnik, S., Perona, P., Sato, Y., Schmid, C. (eds.) ECCV 2012. LNCS, vol. 7572, pp. 172–185. Springer, Heidelberg (2012). https://doi.org/10.1007/978-3-642-33718-5_13
11. Simon, M., Rodner, E.: Neural activation constellations: unsupervised part model discovery with convolutional networks. In: Proceedings of the IEEE International Conference on Computer Vision, pp. 1143–1151 (2015)
12. Simonyan, K., Zisserman, A.: Very deep convolutional networks for large-scale image recognition. arXiv preprint arXiv:1409.1556 (2014)
13. Wah, C., Branson, S., Welinder, P., Perona, P., Belongie, S.: The Caltech-UCSD Birds-200-2011 Dataset (2011)
14. Xiao, T., Xu, Y., Yang, K., Zhang, J., Peng, Y., Zhang, Z.: The application of two-level attention models in deep convolutional neural network for fine-grained image classification. In: Proceedings of the IEEE Conference on Computer Vision and Pattern Recognition, pp. 842–850 (2015)
15. Xie, L., Tian, Q., Hong, R., Yan, S., Zhang, B.: Hierarchical part matching for fine-grained visual categorization. In: Proceedings of the IEEE International Conference on Computer Vision, pp. 1641–1648 (2013)
16. Zhang, N., Donahue, J., Girshick, R., Darrell, T.: Part-based R-CNNs for fine-grained category detection. In: Fleet, D., Pajdla, T., Schiele, B., Tuytelaars, T. (eds.) ECCV 2014. LNCS, vol. 8689, pp. 834–849. Springer, Cham (2014). https://doi.org/10.1007/978-3-319-10590-1_54
17. Zhang, X., Xiong, H., Zhou, W., Lin, W., Tian, Q.: Picking deep filter responses for fine-grained image recognition. In: Proceedings of the IEEE Conference on Computer Vision and Pattern Recognition, pp. 1134–1142 (2016)

Chinese Characters Recognition from Screen-Rendered Images Using Inception Deep Learning Architecture

Xin Xu[1,2(✉)] [iD], Jun Zhou[1], Hong Zhang[1,2], and Xiaowei Fu[1,2]

[1] School of Computer Science and Technology, Wuhan University
of Science and Technology, Wuhan 430065, China
xuxin0336@163.com
[2] Hubei Province Key Laboratory of Intelligent Information Processing
and Real-Time Industrial System, Wuhan University of Science
and Technology, Wuhan 430065, China

Abstract. Text recognition from images can substantially facilitate a wide range of applications. However, screen-rendered images pose great challenges to current methods due to its low resolution and low signal to noise ratio properties. This paper proposed a Chinese characters recognition model using inception module based convolutional neural networks. Chinese characters were firstly extracted using vertical projection and error correction; then it can be recognized via inception module based convolutional neural networks. The proposed model can effectively segment Chinese characters from screen-rendered images, and significantly reduce the training time. Extensive experiments have been conducted on a number of screen-rendered images to evaluate the performance of the proposed model against state-of-the-art models.

Keywords: Optical Character Recognition · Screen-rendered image
Chinese character recognition · Inception module
Convolutional neural networks

1 Introduction

Optical Character Recognition (OCR) is a key technique in computer vision, it is widely applied in various scenarios, such as vehicle license plate recognition [1] and receipt recognition [2]. Previous Chinese OCR models were generally designed for Handwritten Chinese Character Recognition (HCCR) [3–7]. As illustrated in Fig. 1, few efforts have been made towards screen-rendered text recognition. Although there are some OCR methods for scene-rendered English text recognition [8–12], these methods face great challenges in Chinese characters Recognition from Screen-Rendered images due to large Chinese characters library and complicated feature of Chinese character except for the low resolution and low signal to noise ratio [13, 14].

Since LeCun [15] put forward the Convolutional Neural Network (CNN) structure for deep learning, recent years have witness the emerging of numerous CNN models such as AlexNet [16], VGGNet [17], GoogLeNet [18], ResNet [19], and etc. These CNN models have achieved significant performance over traditional models in a

© Springer International Publishing AG, part of Springer Nature 2018
B. Zeng et al. (Eds.): PCM 2017, LNCS 10735, pp. 722–732, 2018.
https://doi.org/10.1007/978-3-319-77380-3_69

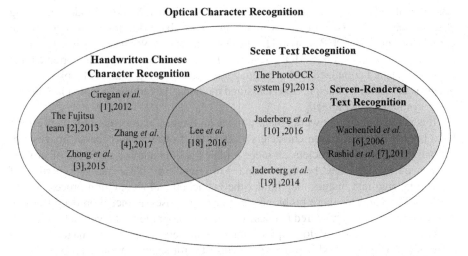

Fig. 1. Overview of the state-of-the-art OCR schemes.

wide range of applications, including image classification, object detection, object recognition, and etc. For example, Ciregan et al. [3] proposed a Multi-Column Deep Neural Network (MCDNN) for HCCR. MCDNN utilized different preprocessing results of the input image as the input of different deep neural networks, and then it averaged the outputs to obtain the final recognition result. The network proposed by Fujitsu team [3] won the ICDAR offline HCCR competition. This model required a dictionary storage size of 2.46 GB. Afterward, traditional feature extraction methods are gradually applied in CNN to improve the accuracy of HCCR. Zhong et al. [5] designed a GoogLeNet based streamlined network (HCCR-GoogLeNet) with four inception-v1 modules. They combined the Gabor and gradient feature maps with original images as the input of HCCR-GoogLeNet. Finally, they obtained the recognition accuracy of 96.35% on offline HCCR dataset of ICDAR2013. Zhang et al. [6] utilized the character shape normalization and direction-decomposed feature maps to enhance the performance of CNN. So far, most OCR methods paid more attention to improve the accuracy of CNN, but in practical applications, the speed and storage size of CNN model are also crucial. Aiming at this, Xiao et al. [7] presented a Global Supervised Low-rank Expansion to accelerate the calculation in convolutional layers, and introduced an Adaptive Drop-weight method to remove redundant connections between each layer.

However, HCCR methods mainly focused on designing classifier to recognize single character. They may face great challenges in recognizing text lines or characters segmented from screen-rendered text images. Generally, screen-rendered text recognition contains two stages: text detection and text recognition. The earliest screen-rendered text recognition method was proposed by Wachenfeld et al. [8]. They used the segmentation correction strategy based on the recognition result to segment the screen-rendered character correctly, and their method classified the character using the European distance between the character image and subclass in sample space.

Rashid et al. [9] constructed a classifier by means of Hidden Markov Models modeling character, and achieved a higher accuracy in the database developed by Wachenfeld et al. [10]. The PhotoOCR system [11] proposed a seven-layer neural network to train the classifier based on the HOG feature of the character image. It corrected the recognition result combined with a language model. Jaderberg et al. [12] took the word image as the input. Unlike previous classified methods, they trained a word classifier by using synthesize data directly.

It is noted that current works mainly focus on English text recognition. Few efforts have been made on Chinese characters recognition from screen-rendered images. On the one side, Chinese characters are more complex both in number and types of strokes; on the other side, low resolution and low signal to noise ratio properties of screen-rendered text images may hinder the extraction and recognition processes.

In order to address these problems, this paper proposes an inception deep learning architecture for screen-rendered Chinese characters recognition. The vertical projection method is firstly adopted to acquire single characters from input image. Then, a word-width fusion method is proposed to correct error segmentation characters. Next, the training dataset is synthesized by a data generation engine. Finally, the CNN model with inception-v2 [20] module is designed based on HCCR-GoogLeNet. Extensive experiments have been conducted on a number of screen-rendered images to evaluate the performance of the proposed network against the state-of-the-art models.

2 The Proposed Method

As shown in Fig. 2, the proposed method contains two stages: character extraction and character recognition.

In the step of character extraction, initial segmented characters are obtained by a series of image processing methods, such as binarization, inverse color, dilation, and connected domain detection. However, there are some error characters in initial segmentation results, for example, '神' is divided into '礻' and '申', '脂' is divided into '月' and '旨'. Therefore, the word-width fusion method is presented to correct the error segmentation characters in this paper.

In the step of character recognition, a data generation engine is designed to generate dataset, and then, a novel CNN based on HCCR-GoogLeNet is proposed for screen-rendered Chinese character recognition. After character segmentation and network training, the character image is identified by the proposed network.

2.1 Character Extraction

As shown in Fig. 2, the character extraction step is divided into two sub-steps: initial segmentation and error segmentation corrected.

In the first step, binarization and inverse color operation are performed to pre-process input screen-rendered images. Subsequently, the initial multiple text candidates in each line are acquired by dilation and connected domain detection operation. Thereafter, a connected domain confusion is utilized to guarantee that there is only one text area per line. We divide a large character extraction task into a set of similar small

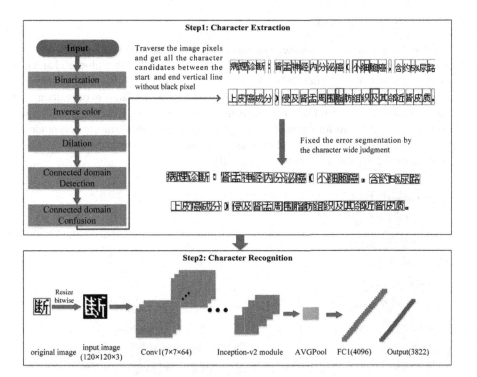

Fig. 2. Overview of the proposed method.

tasks by getting the text line candidates. Finally, single characters are segmented by vertical projection method.

In the next step, the proposed word-width fusion method is adopted to deal with the error character: traverse all character candidates, and then judge whether two consecutive characters are separated from one whole character by comparing their total width with the character width threshold T_w.

For different input images, the value of T_w is different due to different font size or different shooting methods. In this paper, T_w is calculated adaptively as follows:

$$T_w = \frac{1}{len(\Omega_l)} \sum_{w \in \Omega_l} w, l = \max_i \{len(\Omega_i)\}, \tag{1}$$

where, $len(\bullet)$ is the number of elements in a finite set. $\Omega_i, i = 1, 2, \cdots, M$ represents the set of character width w, satisfying $\Omega_i = \{w|w \in [(i-1)*10, i*10]\}$. M represents the total number of subintervals obtained by dividing the interval $[0, J]$ in steps of 10. J is given by the following formula:

$$J = \left\lfloor \frac{\max\_w}{10} \right\rfloor \times 10, \tag{2}$$

where, max_w is the max width of all character candidates.

2.2   Character Recognition

CNN has been widely investigated for image classification due to its weight sharing and local connection. In [8], GoogLeNet is applied for handwrite Chinese characters recognition and achieved a desired performance. Literature [8, 9] solved the problem of screen-rendered English text recognition. However, few research works focus on Chinese characters recognition from screen-rendered images. Therefore, a modified GoogLeNet is presented for Chinese and English text recognition from screen-rendered images in this paper. Figure 3(a) shows the structure of the proposed network, where the inception-v2 structure is shown in Fig. 3(b).

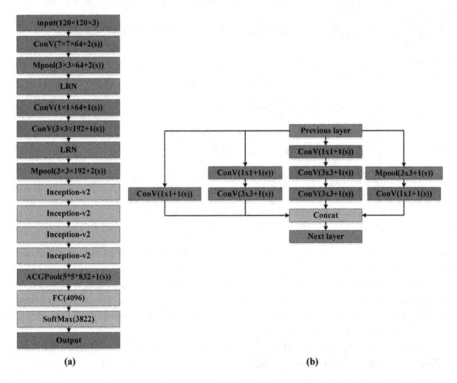

(a)   (b)

Fig. 3.   The proposed network. (a) structure of the proposed network. (b) inception-v2 module.

Convolutions with larger spatial filters (e.g. 5×5 or 7×7) tend to be more time-consuming [20]. For example, the time cost by a 5×5 convolution is $25 \div 9 = 2.78$ times than that of 3×3 convolution. Nevertheless, as shown in Fig. 3, two consecutive 3×3 convolutional layers have a same receptive field as a 5×5 convolutional layer, which guarantee that a 5×5 convolution can be replaced by two 3×3 convolution with the same input size and output depth. Motivated by this, the 5×5 convolution in the inception-v1 module of HCCR-GoogLeNet is decomposed into two 3×3 convolutional layers to improve the performance of HCCR-GoogLeNet in [5].

The output of convolutional layer can resort to an activation layer to increase non-linear factors of CNN. By stacking the 3×3 convolutional layer, CNN become deeper and introduce more non-linear factors, which can improve the feature expression ability of CNN.

The change of the feature maps should be a smooth process [20], when increasing number of the feature maps, the size of the feature maps should be reduced. Based on this, the change of the feature maps should not be too abrupt to keep useful information. Nevertheless, the HCCR-GoogLeNet violates this point. Between the last average pool layer and the subsequent convolutional layer, there is a reduced process for the number of feature maps without any size change. Therefore, we removed the last convolutional layer (kernel size is 1×1, kernel number is 128) between last AVE Pool layer (kernel size is 5×5, stride is 3) and first fully connected layer (output number is 1024). In the HCCR-GoogLeNet, the size of feature maps from the last AVE pool layer is $2 \times 2 \times 832$, but it changes into $2 \times 2 \times 128$ after the convolutional layer, the output of first fully connected layer is 1024. In other words, the number of feature maps directly reduce by $832/128 = 6.5$ times firstly, and then it increases $1024/(2 \times 2 \times 128) = 2$ times. During this process, many useful information will be lost. In the proposed network, the size of feature maps changes more smoothly ($3 \times 3 \times 832$ to 4096).

3 Experimental Results

In this section, the proposed network is compared with HCCR-AlexNet [5], HCCR-GoogLeNet [5] and the network in Ref. [12]. Experiments are conducted on real screen-rendered text images to demonstrate the practicability of the proposed method. Since there is no public training dataset of printed character, we firstly generate three groups of character images as training sample, described in Sect. 3.1. And then, the proposed character extraction method is applied to segment a screen-rendered text image into multiple character images. Lastly, all character images are identified by the proposed network. All networks are trained on an open deep learning framework named CAFFE with a GTX1080ti graphics card, and all testing experiments are conducted under Pycharm2017.1 platform (the intel Pentium dual-core CPU G3420 3.20 GHz).

3.1 Generated Dataset

Due to large Chinese characters library (there are 3755 Chinese characters and each character has different fonts) and complicated feature of Chinese character, it is very difficult to train a large Chinese character classifier in the absence of training samples. Therefore, following some success synthetic character datasets [21, 22], a synthetic character engine is designed to generating training and validation dataset for the proposed network. The goal number of the classifier is 3822, including 3755 Chinese characters, 52 English characters, 10 digits and 5 punctuations.

Whole dataset is comprised of three types of character images. Firstly, in order to guarantee that the proposed network can identify each character of different fonts and size, we synthetic six clean images with different sizes (40×40, 50×50, 60×60, 70×70, 80×80) for each character of different font (24 light and 4 bold). There are $3822 \times 28 \times 6 = 642,096$ images totally generated as part of the dataset.

Besides, in order to reduce the sensitiveness to noise of the proposed network, we generate a group of simulated images corrupted by random noise ($3822 \times 28 \times 5$ $2 = 1,070,160$ images). The generation process is: firstly, five original images are generated with different sizes (70×70, 73×73, 76×76, 79×79, 82×82); And then, we added noise of two levels (randomly chosen from 0.1% to 0.5%) to these images.

Lastly, in daily experiments, screen-rendered images are conducted the binary operation to avoid the effect of uneven illumination, which will lead to character strokes break. In this case, images are generated by erode and blur operations on clean images with size 70×70 ($3822 \times 28 \times 2 = 214,032$ images).

After data cleaning, we divided the dataset into a training dataset including 1,711,277 images and a validation dataset of 123,400 images. All the training is resized to 120×120 with a 5-pixel border around.

3.2 Character Extraction Result

The character extraction result is vital to subsequent character recognition, therefore, we test the proposed character extraction method on real screen-rendered images obtained by 13.0 megapixels' mobile phone (MEIZU M5 note).

Figure 4 shows character extraction results of the proposed method. The input image and its local region in red box are shown in Fig. 4(a) and (b). Figure 4(c)–(d) show the result of connected domain detection and the connected domain confusion on Fig. 4(b). Figure 4(e)–(f) give the initial character segmentation result by vertical projection method and error segmentation corrected result, respectively. Seen from Fig. 4(e), it can be observed that there are some error segmentation characters (marked with a red box), such as the characters '神', '小', '细', '肥' and '及'. By means of the proposed word-width fusion method, we can extract all correct characters, as shown in Fig. 4(f). Eventually, the proposed character extraction method can successfully segment screen-rendered text images into multiple characters, which facilitate following character recognition.

3.3 Character Recognition Result

In this subsection, four networks are trained on the training dataset and evaluated on the validation dataset. These datasets are generated as describe in Sect. 3.1.

The validation dataset is utilized to demonstrate the performance of the proposed network by comparison with other networks. With the increasing of iterations, we record the training time when each epoch finishing, where a training epoch includes 13500 iterations.

Figure 5(a) shows the accuracy curve on the validation dataset by the above networks of different training epoch. Objectively, the proposed network obtains the higher accuracy on the validation dataset and converges quicker. It is more stable that the other networks. In the first epoch, the proposed network achieves 98.5% accuracy on the validation dataset, while the best accuracy of the other networks is 95.5%. After converging, the accuracy on the validation dataset obtained by HCCR-AlexNet,

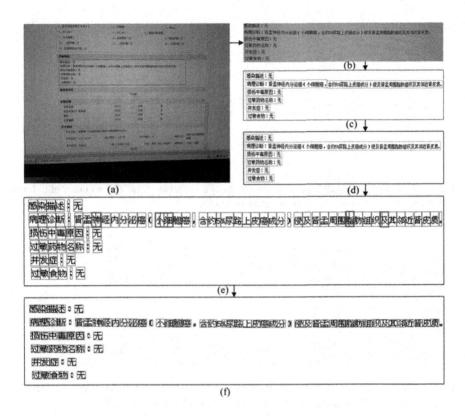

Fig. 4. Character extraction results. (a) input image; (b) the detail of red box in (a); (c)–(f) represent the result of connected domain detection, connected domain confusion, vertical projection method and the proposed word-width fusion, respectively. (Color figure online)

HCCR-GoogLeNet and Ref. [12] are 98.69%, 98.81% and 98.70, respectively. While the proposed network can achieve a better performance of 99.37%.

Figure 5(b) gives the training time curve of these networks. Seen from Fig. 6(b), it can be seen that the HCCR-GoogLeNet takes the longest training time. However, the proposed network reduces the training time significantly, it has similar computation complexity to HCCR-AlexNet. In other words, compared to the HCCR-GoogLeNet, the proposed network improves the feature expression ability and reduces the computational complexity significantly.

After character extraction, character images are took as input of the proposed network to identify the text information. Since test images may contain some punctuations that are not a part of the training sample, these punctuations are considered to be identified correctly in this paper.

Figure 6 shows the recognition results obtained by HCCR-GoogLeNet, Ref. [12], HCCR-AlexNet and proposed network. The characters in red box represent error recognition result. The numbers of red boxes of HCCR-AlexNet, HCCR-GoogLeNet, Ref. [12] and the proposed network are 62, 35, 48 and 21, respectively.

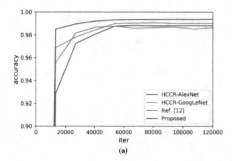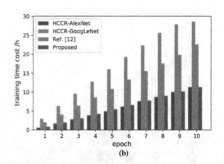

(a)   (b)

Fig. 5. The training time and the accuracy curves of each network. (a) The accuracy of different networks; (b) The training times of different networks.

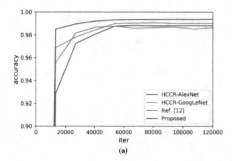

| (a) HCCR-AlexNet | (b) HCCR-GoogLeNet | (c) Ref. [12] | (d) Propsoed |

Fig. 6. The recognition results of different network. (a) HCCR-AlexNet; (b) HCCR-GoogLeNet; (c) Ref. [12]; (d) the proposed network. (Color figure online)

Table 1 gives the recognition accuracy on our testing images. As seen from Fig. 6 and Table 1, the proposed network can achieve the best performance on screen-rendered text images than HCCR-AlexNet, HCCR-GoogLeNet and Ref. [12].

Table 1. Average accuracy of different networks.

Methods	HCCR-AlexNet	Ref. [12]	HCCR-GoogLeNet	Proposed
Average (%)	85.74	91.12	91.88	**94.83**

4 Conclusions

In this paper, we present a novel Chinese character recognition method for screen-rendered text recognition. The vertical projection method is adopted to acquire single characters from input image. Then, a word-width fusion method is proposed to correct error segmentation characters. Finally, the network with inception-v2 module is designed based on HCCR-GoogLeNet for single characters recognition, which trained on a dataset synthesized by a proper data generation engine. The experimental results demonstrate that the proposed network can reduce the computational complexity significantly and achieve a better generalization ability by comparison with the state-of-the-art models.

Acknowledgments. This work was supported by the National Natural Science Foundation of China (61602349, 61440016, 61373109) and the Hubei Chengguang Talented Youth Development Foundation (2015B22).

References

1. Masood, S.Z., Shu, G., Dehghan, A., Ortiz, E.G.: License plate detection and recognition using deeply learned convolutional neural networks. arXiv preprint arXiv:1703.07330 (2017)
2. Yang, F., Jin, L., Yang, W., Feng, Z., Zhang, S.: Handwritten/printed receipt classification using attention-based convolutional neural network. In: 15th International Conference on Frontiers in Handwriting Recognition, pp. 384–389 (2016)
3. Ciregan, D., Meier, U., Schmidhuber, J.: Multi-column deep neural networks for image classification. In: Proceedings of the IEEE Conference on Computer Vision and Pattern Recognition, pp. 3642–3649 (2012)
4. Yin, F., Wang, Q.F., Zhang, X.Y., Liu, C.L.: ICDAR 2013 Chinese handwriting recognition competition. In: 12th International Conference on Document Analysis and Recognition, pp. 1464–1470 (2013)
5. Zhong, Z., Jin, L., Xie, Z.: High performance offline handwritten Chinese character recognition using GoogLeNet and directional feature maps. In: 13th International Conference on Document Analysis and Recognition, pp. 846–850 (2015)
6. Zhang, X.-Y., Bengio, Y., Liu, C.-L.: Online and offline handwritten chinese character recognition: a comprehensive study and new benchmark. Pattern Recognit. **61**, 348–360 (2016)
7. Xiao, X., Jin, L., Yang, Y., Yang, W., Sun, J., Chang, T.: Building fast and compact convolutional neural networks for offline handwritten chinese character recognition. arXiv preprint arXiv:1702.07975 (2017)
8. Wachenfeld, S., Klein, H.U., Jiang, X.: Recognition of screen-rendered text. In: 18th International Conference on Pattern Recognition, pp. 1086–1089 (2006)
9. Rashid, S.F., Shafait, F., Breuel, T.M.: An evaluation of HMM-based techniques for the recognition of screen rendered text. In: 11th International Conference on Document Analysis and Recognition, pp. 1260–1264 (2011)
10. Wachenfeld, S., Klein, H.U., Jiang, X.: Annotated databases for the recognition of screen-rendered text. In: 9th International Conference on Document Analysis and Recognition, pp. 272–276 (2007)
11. Bissacco, A., Cummins, M., Netzer, Y., Neven, H.: Photoocr: reading text in uncontrolled conditions. In: Proceedings of the IEEE International Conference on Computer Vision, pp. 785–792 (2013)
12. Jaderberg, M., Simonyan, K., Vedaldi, A., Zisserman, A.: Reading text in the wild with convolutional neural networks. Int. J. Comput. Vision **116**(1), 1–20 (2016)
13. Xu, X., Mu, N., Zhang, X., Li, B.: Covariance descriptor based convolution neural network for saliency computation in low contrast images. In: International Joint Conference on Neural Networks, pp. 616–623 (2016)

14. Xu, X., Mu, N., Zhang, H., Fu, X.: Salient object detection from distinctive features in low contrast images. In: IEEE International Conference on Image Processing, pp. 3126–3130 (2015)
15. LeCun, Y., Bottou, L., Bengio, Y., Haffner, P.: Gradient-based learning applied to document recognition. Proc. IEEE **86**(11), 2278–2324 (1998)
16. Krizhevsky, A., Sutskever, I., Hinton, G.: Imagenet classification with deep convolutional neural networks. In: Advances in Neural Information Processing Systems 25, pp. 1106–1114 (2012)
17. Simonyan, K., Zisserman, A.: Very deep convolutional networks for large-scale image recognition. arXiv preprint arXiv:1409.1556 (2015)
18. Szegedy, C., Liu, W., Jia, Y., Sermanet, P., Reed, S., Anguelov, D., Erhan, D., Vanhoucke, V., Rabinovich, A.: Going deeper with convolutions. In: Proceedings of the IEEE Conference on Computer Vision and Pattern Recognition, pp. 1–9 (2015)
19. He, K., Zhang, X., Ren, S., Sun, J.: Deep residual learning for image recognition. arXiv preprint arXiv:1512.03385 (2015)
20. Szegedy, C., Vanhoucke, V., Ioffe, S., Shlens, J., Wojna, Z.: Rethinking the inception architecture for computer vision. arXiv preprint arXiv:1512.00567 (2015)
21. Jaderberg, M., Simonyan, K., Vedaldi, A., Zisserman, A.: Synthetic data and artificial neural networks for natural scene text recognition. arXiv preprint arXiv:1406.2227 (2014)
22. Ren, X., Chen, K., Sun, J.: A CNN based scene Chinese text recognition algorithm with synthetic data engine. arXiv preprint arXiv:1604.01891 (2016)

Visual Tracking by Deep Discriminative Map

Wenyi Tang, Bin Liu$^{(\boxtimes)}$, and Nenghai Yu

CAS Key Laboratory of Electromagnetic Space Information,
University of Science and Technology of China, Hefei, China
flowice@ustc.edu.cn

Abstract. Deep neural networks which widely used in image classification and speech recognition have been successfully applied to model-free object tracking. However, during tracking, it easily falls into over-fitting problem, when the object size is either over-estimated or under-estimated during tracking. Besides, the increasingly complicated discriminative model which strengthens the ability to identify object under highly occlusion also raises the opportunity of getting poor samples for training. In this paper, we propose a visual tracking algorithm based on deep discriminative map. The method guides the tracking algorithm by estimating the object's size and shape, and whether it is proper to gather training samples. Our method utilises two neural networks, one focusing on the center of object and one focusing on the object appearance. Experimental result on 13 public challenging tracking sequences shows that our proposed framework is effective and produces state-of-art tracking performance.

Keywords: Visual tracking · Convolutional Neural Network
Global average pooling

1 Introduction

Visual tracking is one of the most fundamental problems in the field of computer vision and plays an increasingly important role in many fields, such as public surveillance, intelligent transport system and self-driving cars. Although visual tracking has been researched for years, it is still a challenging problem, since it is model-free, which means given a initial bounding box of target in the first frame, we need to estimate its size and position in the following sequence of video. Furthermore, these videos are full of challenges, including illumination and scale variation, occlusion, deformation, motion blur and so on. For several years, track-by-detection framework has been successfully applied in tracking, which decomposes such problem into two small ones, appearance and motion.

Recently, an increasingly number of Discriminative Correlation Filter (DCF)-based methods are proposed. These approaches train a correlation filter to estimate the target confidence at different places. Due to considering all the training and test samples as convolution and the utility of fast Fourier transform

© Springer International Publishing AG, part of Springer Nature 2018
B. Zeng et al. (Eds.): PCM 2017, LNCS 10735, pp. 733–742, 2018.
https://doi.org/10.1007/978-3-319-77380-3_70

(FFT), the DCF-based method shows great performance at visual tracking. These trackers have great flexibility in feature choice, such as hand-craft features [4,6] or deep Convolutional Neural Network [5] as feature extractor. On the other hand, Convolutional Neural Networks (CNN) has also been applied in tracking. Inspired by transfer learning [17], they fine tune the deep CNN pre-trained at ILSVRC2012 ImageNet [14] classification dataset. These pre-trained convolutional features are of excellent generalization ability and are suitable for distinguishing object and background.

Those aforementioned trackers, have great ability to discriminate target from other disturbance in the same video. However, such ability means it is difficult for them to find the scale variance of object or the ratio variance due to out-of-plain rotation. They usually use a simple Gaussian model to estimate scale change based on Histogram of oriented gradients (HoG) feature or spacial pyramid.

In recent years, many sophisticated neural networks perform well at object detection [7,19] and semantic segmentation [15], it is quite straightforward to ask whether we can build a CNN to estimate the current target size. Since sophisticated network needs large number of training data, we should find a way to get more positive and negative samples, besides the initial bounding box. In other word, we need weakly supervised data. As the development of deep learning, global average pooling (GAP) has shown the power of handle weakly supervised data. [27] add a convolutional layer followed by a GAP layer and a softmax layer after VGG [20] conv5-3 layer and put forward a weakly object localization algorithm.

We argue that global average pooling forces the network to learn information about object position in the image, and class activation mapping (CAM) structure should be utilized in a proper manner for visual tracking. It is observed that, networks trained with some weakly supervised bounding boxes sampled around the initial ground truth, could output proper heat map indicates the position and the size of target (see Fig. 1).

In this paper, we propose a tracking framework based on deep discriminative map (Discriminative map tracker, DMT), which consists of two neural networks. One discriminatingly determines the center of current target at the time. The other learns the target appearance and generates a heat map reflecting the object size. When it comes to tracking-by-detection routine, the former network represents both appearance model (find the object from objects in the video) and motion model (tell the probability of whether the object is here). The latter network represents the appearance model (display the size of target). Recent trackers which use neural network, only have one network, but such scheme has immanent contradiction. Because, the scale estimation task requires the net is sensitive to appearance changes, while positioning task demand invariance feature. Different from these algorithms, the position network of our method is relived from the task of estimating the scale variance. On the other hand, the size network becomes quite easily being misled by inaccurate training sample. As a result, the size network parameters should keep fixed when object is under occlusion or fast moving.

The contribution of our method can be summarised as:

(1) We propose an activation map network, which can effectively sense the scale and ratio change of the target.
(2) We propose a novel framework consists of two networks, one for positioning and one for size change estimation, which overcomes the immanent contradiction of one network routine.
(3) Both networks cooperate with each other to handle occlusion or drift during tracking and to reduce the possibility of noisy updates.

The rest of the paper is organised as follows. In Sect. 2, we first review related work. The details of the proposed method are provided in Sect. 3. In Sect. 4, we would present and discuss the experimental results on 13 challenging sequences. Section 5 provides conclusions.

2   Related Work

Tracking-by-detection [13] procedure mainly contains two important parts: an appearance model to differentiate the target from the background and a motion model to tell where is the target right now. There are two kinds of appearance model, generation model and discriminative model. Generation model estimates the likelihood of target candidates by reconstruction error. These methods utilizes raw pixel information [1] or sparse feature space [12] to describe the appearance model. Discriminative model finds the most discriminative feature to distinguish object and background. Recently, discriminative tracking methods typically train a model to simultaneously filter out candidates and estimate the position of target. Online learning framework based on structured SVM [9], multiple instance learning [2] and correlation filters [4,6] are applied and they performs better than generation models. DCF-based tracker initially uses low level feature, such as HOG feature [4]. Resent DCF-based trackers [5] utilize CNN as robust feature extractor. [4] proposes an algorithm to estimate the scale changes based on the Gaussian model and [22] reimplements it by deep features. These two scale estimator omit the possibility of ratio changes and could not detect occlusion. We build a network by appending CAM-like structure after conv4-3 of VGG to estimate the target shape and size.

As the development of GPU, convolutional neural network performs well in computer vision, for example, image classification [14], object detection [7,19] and semantic segmentation [15]. Existing methods also explore the usage of CNN in model-free tracking. In [8], two-stream CNN is used to build a classifier tracking. By using auxiliary images, [24] presents an auto-encoder tracker. [16] utilizes auxiliary tracking sequences to build a multi-domain network. To reduce overfitting, [22] uses a sequential ensemble learning strategy. [18] tries to use multi level feature from stacks of convolutional networks. We follow these outcomes of CNN trackers, design a network which most weight is transferred from image classification domain and append it with a few layers for fine-tuning.

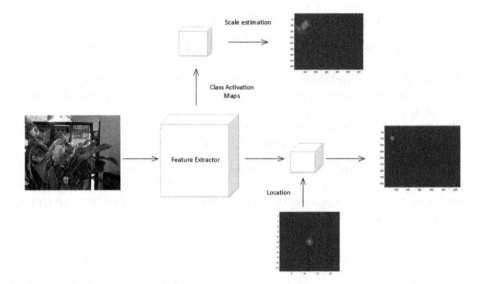

Fig. 1. The structure of proposed algorithm. Our algorithm consists of three main steps: (1) extract robust features from CNN layers; (2) use location network to detect the object center; (3) use class activation mapping to estimate the scale change

3   Discriminative Map Tracker

Before describing the details of proposed discriminative map tracker, we first introduce some background of class activation map.

3.1   Class Activation Map

When a convolutional network, like VGG, tries to classify an object, it first uses its convolution kernels to slide across the object and produces heat maps indicating what kernels response to this structure. After the last convolutional layer, VGG would connect all its heat map unit to all the unit of fully connection (fc) layer to learn every unit's contribution to the final decision. However, as described in [27], if we remove all the fully-connected (fc) layers, and append a global average layer after the convolutional layers, things would change.

For a given image consisting object of class c, assuming $f_k(x, y)$ represent the activation of convolution filter (k) at relative location (x, y). If the loss function is softmax, the output of the probability of class c is $\frac{exp(F_c)}{\Sigma_c exp(F_c)}$, where F_c is the output of global average layer $\Sigma_k \Sigma_{x,y} f_k(x, y) \omega_k^c$.

Unlike the fc layers symmetrically view all the feature map unit, global average layer keep the sequence of feature map unit in the same channel, which means every channel share the same weight. Conversely, weight of each channel represents channel's contribution to the final decision. Since convolutional layers guarantee activation unit in the same feature map is generated by the same set of convolution filters, the weight of each channel also represents the contribution of a particular set of convolution filters or, in another speaking, a particular feature. If a feature is sensitive to a class of object or a structure of texture, it would produce higher response on the feature map and the response's position on the feature map is accordance to the position of the object or the pattern of pixels at the image. Furthermore, the weight of channel could also regulate the final decision. As a result, if we multiply the feature map which is produced by the last convolutional layer by the class-specific weight of such channel, then summarize all the feature map channels, we would get a class activation map which presents where the object of that class is.

3.2 Build the Size-CNN

Since we need a size-sensitive CNN, we should consider the resolution of CAM. For VGG-16 network, conv5-3 outputs a $14 \times 14 \times 512$ feature map if we input a 224×224 image, it is not enough for tracking, since almost every tracking target is no larger than 100×100, which means we need do some image resize and loss a lot of detail. According to initial experiment, we choose conv4-3 as feature extractor and append a conv layer with kernel size 3 and stride 1 as in [27].

Then we should do data augmentation and gather weakly labelled samples. According to [16], we sample 100 positive data around the initial ground truth using Gaussian model. All the positive data should have over 0.8 IoU with initial ground truth. Then we sample 1000 negative data all over the image and guarantee their IoU with initial ground truth is less than 0.2. Next, all the data should be learnt over twice in a batch of 32 to fine-tune the network. After every mini batch, we also gather hard negative samples to reduce the impact of other similar objects.

When tracking, size-CNN produces class activation maps and we binarize it with a threshold of 20% of the peak of CAM. When target scale changes, the area of class activation map would change. When target is occluded by other object, the class activation map would break into pieces. Therefore, we could use class activation maps to estimate scale change and whether occlusion happens.

3.3 Build the Position-CNN

In order to make our position-CNN as discriminative as possible, we choose one of the best CNN classifiers [10] as feature extractor, we transfer the 51-layer version ResNet pre-trained on ILSVRC2012 dataset, and fix parameters of layers before res4a (including res4a) as feature extractor. Then we append two conv layers with kernel size 3×3 and stride 1 to it and the former is followed by a ReLU layer. In order to estimate the position of target, we follow the method of Discriminative Correlation Filter [4]: forcing the network to produce a compact 2-D Gaussian shaped peak centered at the target in training image. Since target position plays the most important role in tracking, we should not use weakly labelled data.

The last appended layers of the network is updated 100 times using the initial ground truth. This is achieved by minimizing following loss function:

$$L = \|F(I) - g\|^2 + \lambda \Sigma \|w\|^2 \tag{1}$$

F function is the position-CNN. If fed with image patch I, it would produce a 2-D heat map. The parameter λ balances importance of L2 loss and regularization term.

3.4   Tracking Algorithm

Overview. The overall tracking procedure is presented in Algorithm 1.

Algorithm 1. Online tracking algorithm

Input: The initial bounding box $bbox_1$ fine-tuned *size-CNN* fine-tuned *position-CNN*
Output: current bounding box $bbox_t$
1: **repeat**
2:     Crop region I_t centered at last location and two time larger in size
3:     Use *position- CNN* to estimate current center $center_t$ of target. Crop region I_t' centered at $center_t$ with the same size as I_t
4:     Pass I_t' through *size- CNN*, produce class activation map CAM_t of target
5:     Binarize CAM_t, and compute the area of largest contour's rigid bounding-box
6:     **if** Occlusion happens **then**
7:         Keep the scale variance to 1. set *update*=0
8:     **else if** Area of bounding box is larger than area of previous bounding box $bbox_{t-1}$ **then**
9:         Scale up the bounding box, set *update*=1
10:    **else**
11:         Scale down the bounding box, set *update*=1
12:    **end if**
13:    **if** Ratio of bounding box varies a lot **then**
14:         Change the ratio of $bbox_t$
15:    **end if**
16:    **if** *update*==1 and *position-CNN* has not been updated for 10 iteration **then**
17:         Update *position-CNN*
18:    **end if**
19: **until** B

Tracking and Update. We use position-CNN to get the center of object, while use size-CNN to estimate the ratio and scale. To get the center of object, we find the maximum heat map value and convert relative position to pixel position.

To avoid updated by inaccurate samples, we propose two update requirement: (1) no occlusion occurs; (2) high confidence position result. The former one requires size-CNN produces non-broken class activation map, since once object is occluded, parts blocked by background would not produce bright signal on the heat map. We use the size of binarized map divided by the rigid bounding box. If the ratio is less than 0.5, occlusion happens and parameter update stops. The latter criteria is measured by ways as in [23], we treat the maximum heat map value as current confidence. If it is less than a threshold 0.1, we would stop parameter update. Once scale or size needs update, they vary by one step (1.02 for scale and ratio).

4 Experiment

4.1 Experiment Setup

The proposed framework is implmented in Caffe with MATLAB interface and runs at 2 frames per second. Our tracker runs on a PC with 3.0 GHz CPU and a TITAN X GPU. All of networks are trained with SGD solver at learning rate 1e-7 with momentum of 0.9.

Our tracker is evaluated on 13 public challenging video sequences from OTB benchmark [25]. We compare our tracker result with 10 state-of-art trackers, consisting of 3 deep learning based trackers, including FCNT [23], SiamFC [3], SINT [21], 4 DCF-based trackers, including SRDCF [6], DSST [4], HDT [18], DeepSRDCF [5] and 3 classic trackers, including MEEM [26], MUSTer [11] and Struck [9]. For the fairness, we adopt the source codes or result files provided by the authors.

4.2 Experiment Result

Evaluation Results. Figure 2 demonstrate the average precision plots and success plots on 13 sequences containing various challenging factors including fast motion, scale and illumination variation, background clutter, and occlusion. And Tables 1 and 2 illustrate the detail result of each sequence. We use the precision plot and the success plot to evaluate all the trackers. The precision plot demonstrates the percentage of frames where the distance between the predicted target location and the ground truth location is within a given threshold from 0 pixel to 50 pixels. Whereas the success plot illustrates the percentage of frames where the overlap ratio between the predicted bounding box and the ground truth bounding box is higher than each threshold from 0% to 100%. The area under curve (AUC) is used to rank the tracking algorithms in each plot. Our method achieves the competitive performance in terms of both evaluation metrics compared to state-of-art trackers.

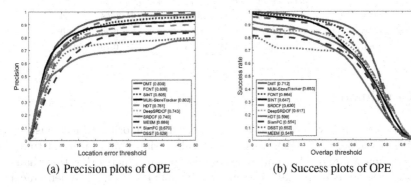

(a) Precision plots of OPE   (b) Success plots of OPE

Fig. 2. Result curve of proposed tracker and 10 state-of-art trackers on 13 challenging videos

740   W. Tang et al.

Table 1. Comparison of 11 trackers on 13 video sequences in terms of central location error (in pixels). Red fonts indicate the best performance while the blue fonts indicate the second best.

	FCNT	SRDCF	DSST	SiamFC	MEEM	SINT	Struck	HDT	MUSTer	DeepSRDCF	DMT
singer2	13.2	8.6	7.8	172.4	173.5	17.1	174.3	173.9	9.1	183.0	15.7
carDark	4.3	1.6	1.5	20.4	1.3	3.1	1.0	5.3	2.3	1.2	1.9
car4	4.7	1.7	1.8	5.6	18.0	3.3	8.7	7.4	1.9	1.9	1.9
jogging-2	15.3	3.7	150.8	6.1	8.2	4.1	107.7	2.9	4.8	5.7	2.8
jumping	5.0	4.5	36.9	4.2	4.5	4.7	6.5	3.9	6.9	3.0	7.1
woman	9.5	4.8	10.0	14.9	4.1	11.1	4.2	10.9	9.4	3.7	2.9
mountainBike	6.4	9.0	7.8	6.1	13.2	10.3	8.6	8.4	8.1	9.7	7.0
couple	3.5	4.0	125.6	5.0	6.5	9.6	11.3	8.5	9.2	5.4	6.3
Bolt	8.4	402.5	4.5	404.8	10.0	6.8	398.8	5.0	3.7	6.3	3.9
FaceOcc1	22.3	14.8	13.8	11.7	16.4	13.8	18.8	17.4	14.3	12.9	11.2
Deer	7.7	4.0	16.7	5.5	4.5	5.3	5.3	5.1	7.2	4.6	4.3
CarScale	10.6	19.7	19.1	15.4	30.1	31.5	36.4	29.9	18.7	25.2	10.0
MotorRolling	12.5	247.1	296.9	87.9	170.9	24.0	145.7	14.1	110.4	200.8	16.7
avg	9.5	55.8	53.3	58.4	35.5	11.1	71.3	22.5	15.8	35.7	8.1

Table 2. Average overlap rate. Red fonts indicate the best performance while the blue fonts indicate the second best.

	FCNT	SRDCF	DSST	SiamFC	MEEM	SINT	Struck	HDT	MUSTer	DeepSRDCF	DMT
singer2	0.69	0.74	0.78	0.04	0.04	0.62	0.04	0.04	0.76	0.03	0.72
carDark	0.66	0.85	0.85	0.58	0.86	0.76	0.89	0.66	0.80	0.86	0.81
car4	0.82	0.87	0.91	0.78	0.46	0.78	0.49	0.49	0.90	0.88	0.80
jogging-2	0.67	0.71	0.14	0.70	0.63	0.75	0.20	0.79	0.75	0.60	0.80
jumping	0.69	0.67	0.14	0.62	0.71	0.63	0.62	0.73	0.63	0.74	0.62
woman	0.69	0.67	0.69	0.54	0.71	0.62	0.73	0.74	0.69	0.72	0.76
mountainBike	0.77	0.69	0.73	0.76	0.60	0.63	0.71	0.70	0.73	0.69	0.78
couple	0.66	0.71	0.09	0.67	0.61	0.63	0.54	0.58	0.63	0.69	0.62
Bolt	0.65	0.01	0.72	0.03	0.59	0.57	0.01	0.74	0.78	0.58	0.75
FaceOcc1	0.64	0.77	0.77	0.76	0.75	0.75	0.73	0.74	0.76	0.79	0.78
Deer	0.71	0.81	0.64	0.73	0.75	0.71	0.74	0.75	0.75	0.77	0.78
CarScale	0.52	0.72	0.74	0.69	0.41	0.54	0.41	0.41	0.68	0.69	0.75
MotorRolling	0.58	0.09	0.09	0.37	0.10	0.52	0.15	0.52	0.29	0.10	0.54
avg	0.67	0.64	0.56	0.56	0.55	0.65	0.48	0.61	0.70	0.63	0.72

5   Conclusion

In this paper, we have proposed a two-CNN based algorithm for robust visual tracking. To make the tracker sensitive to scale variance and invariant to occlusion, deformation and other noises, we build two neural network rather than one and use class activation map to estimate the shape of target. When tracking, one CNN produces location estimation and the other produces scale estimation. When occlusion or fast moving happens, the size-CNN would detect it and stop online-training to avoid poor tracking samples. We have tested our method extensively on 13 challenging video sequences, and experimental results demonstrate the superiority of our method when compared with 10 state-of-the-art trackers.

Acknowledgement. This work is supported by the National Natural Science Foundation of China (Grant No. 61371192), the Key Laboratory Foundation of the Chinese Academy of Sciences (CXJJ-17S044) and the Fundamental Research Funds for the Central Universities (WK2100330002).

References

1. Adam, A., Rivlin, E., Shimshoni, I.: Robust fragments-based tracking using the integral histogram. In: 2006 IEEE Computer Society Conference on Computer Vision and Pattern Recognition, vol. 1, pp. 798–805. IEEE (2006)
2. Babenko, B., Yang, M.H., Belongie, S.: Visual tracking with online multiple instance learning. In: IEEE Conference on Computer Vision and Pattern Recognition, CVPR 2009, pp. 983–990. IEEE (2009)
3. Bertinetto, L., Valmadre, J., Henriques, J.F., Vedaldi, A., Torr, P.H.S.: Fully-convolutional siamese networks for object tracking. In: Hua, G., Jégou, H. (eds.) ECCV 2016. LNCS, vol. 9914, pp. 850–865. Springer, Cham (2016). https://doi.org/10.1007/978-3-319-48881-3_56
4. Danelljan, M., Häger, G., Khan, F., Felsberg, M.: Accurate scale estimation for robust visual tracking. In: British Machine Vision Conference, Nottingham, 1–5 September 2014. BMVA Press (2014)
5. Danelljan, M., Hager, G., Shahbaz Khan, F., Felsberg, M.: Convolutional features for correlation filter based visual tracking. In: Proceedings of the IEEE International Conference on Computer Vision Workshops, pp. 58–66 (2015)
6. Danelljan, M., Hager, G., Shahbaz Khan, F., Felsberg, M.: Learning spatially regularized correlation filters for visual tracking. In: Proceedings of the IEEE International Conference on Computer Vision, pp. 4310–4318 (2015)
7. Girshick, R.: Fast R-CNN. In: The IEEE International Conference on Computer Vision (ICCV), December 2015
8. Gladh, S., Danelljan, M., Khan, F.S., Felsberg, M.: Deep motion features for visual tracking. arXiv preprint arXiv:1612.06615 (2016)
9. Hare, S., Golodetz, S., Saffari, A., Vineet, V., Cheng, M.M., Hicks, S.L., Torr, P.H.: Struck: structured output tracking with kernels. IEEE Trans. Pattern Anal. Mach. Intell. **38**(10), 2096–2109 (2016)
10. He, K., Zhang, X., Ren, S., Sun, J.: Deep residual learning for image recognition. In: Proceedings of the IEEE Conference on Computer Vision and Pattern Recognition, pp. 770–778 (2016)
11. Hong, Z., Chen, Z., Wang, C., Mei, X., Prokhorov, D., Tao, D.: Multi-store tracker (muster): A cognitive psychology inspired approach to object tracking. In: Proceedings of the IEEE Conference on Computer Vision and Pattern Recognition, pp. 749–758 (2015)
12. Jia, X., Lu, H., Yang, M.H.: Visual tracking via adaptive structural local sparse appearance model. In: 2012 IEEE Conference on Computer Vision and Pattern Recognition (CVPR), pp. 1822–1829. IEEE (2012)

13. Kalal, Z., Mikolajczyk, K., Matas, J.: Tracking-learning-detection. IEEE Trans. Pattern Anal. Mach. Intell. **34**(7), 1409–1422 (2012)
14. Krizhevsky, A., Sutskever, I., Hinton, G.E.: Imagenet classification with deep convolutional neural networks. In: Advances in Neural Information Processing Systems, pp. 1097–1105 (2012)
15. Long, J., Shelhamer, E., Darrell, T.: Fully convolutional networks for semantic segmentation. In: Proceedings of the IEEE Conference on Computer Vision and Pattern Recognition, pp. 3431–3440 (2015)
16. Nam, H., Han, B.: Learning multi-domain convolutional neural networks for visual tracking. In: Proceedings of the IEEE Conference on Computer Vision and Pattern Recognition, pp. 4293–4302 (2016)
17. Oquab, M., Bottou, L., Laptev, I., Sivic, J.: Learning and transferring mid-level image representations using convolutional neural networks. In: The IEEE Conference on Computer Vision and Pattern Recognition (CVPR), June 2014
18. Qi, Y., Zhang, S., Qin, L., Yao, H., Huang, Q., Lim, J., Yang, M.H.: Hedged deep tracking. In: Proceedings of the IEEE Conference on Computer Vision and Pattern Recognition, pp. 4303–4311 (2016)
19. Ren, S., He, K., Girshick, R., Sun, J.: Faster R-CNN: towards real-time object detection with region proposal networks. In: Advances in Neural Information Processing Systems, pp. 91–99 (2015)
20. Simonyan, K., Zisserman, A.: Very deep convolutional networks for large-scale image recognition. arXiv preprint arXiv:1409.1556 (2014)
21. Tao, R., Gavves, E., Smeulders, A.W.: Siamese instance search for tracking. In: Proceedings of the IEEE Conference on Computer Vision and Pattern Recognition, pp. 1420–1429 (2016)
22. Wang, L., Ouyang, W., Wang, X., Lu, H.: STCT: sequentially training convolutional networks for visual tracking. In: 2016 IEEE Conference on Computer Vision and Pattern Recognition (CVPR), pp. 1373–1381, June 2016
23. Wang, L., Ouyang, W., Wang, X., Lu, H.: Visual tracking with fully convolutional networks. In: Proceedings of the IEEE International Conference on Computer Vision, pp. 3119–3127 (2015)
24. Wang, N., Li, S., Gupta, A., Yeung, D.Y.: Transferring rich feature hierarchies for robust visual tracking. arXiv preprint arXiv:1501.04587 (2015)
25. Wu, Y., Lim, J., Yang, M.H.: Online object tracking: a benchmark. In: IEEE Conference on Computer Vision and Pattern Recognition (CVPR) (2013)
26. Zhang, J., Ma, S., Sclaroff, S.: MEEM: robust tracking via multiple experts using entropy minimization. In: Fleet, D., Pajdla, T., Schiele, B., Tuytelaars, T. (eds.) ECCV 2014. LNCS, vol. 8694, pp. 188–203. Springer, Cham (2014). https://doi.org/10.1007/978-3-319-10599-4_13
27. Zhou, B., Khosla, A., Lapedriza, A., Oliva, A., Torralba, A.: Learning deep features for discriminative localization. In: Proceedings of the IEEE Conference on Computer Vision and Pattern Recognition, pp. 2921–2929 (2016)

Hand Gesture Recognition by Using 3DCNN and LSTM with Adam Optimizer

Siyu Jiang and Yimin Chen[✉]

School of Computer Engineering and Science,
Shanghai Institute for Advanced Communication and Data Science,
Shanghai University, Shanghai, China
1326260332501163.com, ymchen@shu.edu.cn

Abstract. A two-step hand gesture recognition system is proposed to classify gestures from different subjects performed under widely varying lighting conditions. First, 3D Convolutional neural network are fine-tuned to classify each hand gesture. Then, the fine-tuned 3D Convolutional neural network are used to learn spatio-temporal features for Long short-term memory automatically. We also perform spatiotemporal data augmentation for more effective training to reduce potential overfitting. In addition, Adam optimizer is employed to improve training speed in both steps. On the VIVA challenge dataset, our method achieves a correct classification rate of 94.5%, and experimental result shows that Adam optimizer outperforms the most commonly used optimizer SGD. Moreover, our system has strong robustness in different lighting conditions.

Keywords: 3DConvolutional neural network
Long short-term memory · Adam · VIVA challenge dataset

1 Introduction

As a human-computer interaction, dynamic hand gesture recognition has attracted more and more scholars' attention in the last years, due to its potential application in a variety of domains. In the AR/VR system, dynamic gesture recognition based on computer vision not only provides users with convenient and natural way to interact with computer, but also improves the user's sense of immersion. In the last decade, many vision-based dynamic hand gesture recognition algorithms have been introduced [20,21]. Hidden Markov model (HMM) [1], Conditional Random Fields [2] and Support Vector Machines (SVM) [3] are the most common used classifiers which are combined with handcraft features to recognize hand gestures. In some papers, single hand-crafted features were used for developing the gesture recognition system, Elme-zain et al. proposed a system to recognize both isolated and continuous gestures [5]. They used orientation feature in the feature extraction stage which provided the direction of motion between consecutive trajectory points. The angle of orientations was quantized using codeword ranging from 1 to 18, finally, the gestures were classified by using

© Springer International Publishing AG, part of Springer Nature 2018
B. Zeng et al. (Eds.): PCM 2017, LNCS 10735, pp. 743–753, 2018.
https://doi.org/10.1007/978-3-319-77380-3_71

HMM. Ohn-Bar and Trivedi [4] evaluated various hand-crafted spatio-temporal features and classifiers for in-car hand gesture recognition with RGBD data. They reported the best performance with a combination of histogram of gradient (HOG) features and an SVM classifier is the most outperform combination. However, robust classification of hand gestures under widely varying lighting conditions, and from different subjects is still challenging [22–24]

Recent work using deep Convolution Neural Networks (CNNs) has significantly advanced the accuracy of dynamic hand gesture [6,25], and had been proved useful for gesture recognition in challenging lighting conditions [26]. However, their extension to the video case is still an open issue. To recognize human actions with depth video dataset, Moez Baccouch [7] extended Convolution Neural Network to 3D case (3DCNN), which can automatically learn spatio-temproal features for Long Short-Term Memory (LSTM) [8]. Similarly, In order to recognize dynamic Molchanov used 3D Convolutional Neural Networks to learn spatio-temproal features for Recurrent Neural Networks (RNN) [11], and Tran D chose Support Vector Machine as the classifier [9]. But 3D Convolutional Neural Networks can be regarded as classifier too. Ji [10] utilizes 3D Convolutional Neural to recognize human actions. Molchanov [12] use 3D Convolutional Neural Networks challenging on VIVA hand gesture dataset [4], and get better recognition rate than Ohn-Bar using combination of histogram of gradient (HOG) features and an SVM classifier [4]. But neither of these methods achieve a satisfactory recognition rate. Inspired by Moez Baccouch [7], our system achieves an accuracy of 94.5%, outperforms competing state-of-the-art methods.

However, deep convolution neural network(CNN) need large datasets to fine tune the model, which will cost a lot of time. Thus, it is necessary to choose algorithms to speed up training. Stochastic gradient descent (SGD) is one of the most popular gradient descent algorithms to perform optimization [16–19]. However, objectives may also have other sources of noise than data subsampling, such as Dropout [13] and regularization. For all such noisy objectives, efficient stochastic optimization techniques are required. Diederik P. Kingma proposed a new method named Adaptive Moment Estimation(Adam) for efficient stochastic optimization that only requires first-order gradients with little memory requirement [14].

In this paper, we propose a new two-step neural-based deep model for hand gesture recognition. The first part, we propose a new 3DCNN model, which will be trained with augmented dataset. The second part, similar to Moez Baccouch [8], using fine-tuned 3DCNN learns spatio-temporal features for LSTM automatically. The optimizer Adam [14] is employed for both parts. We demonstrate that the first part of our system outperforms both Molchanov and Ohn-Bar on the VIVA challenge dataset. And the second part of our model, we get an accuracy of 94.7%, which is much better than using 3DCNN only.

2   Method

In this section, the proposed 3DCNN will be introduced in detail, and we will describe Adaptive Moment Estimation (Adam) [14] briefly. Then, we focus on

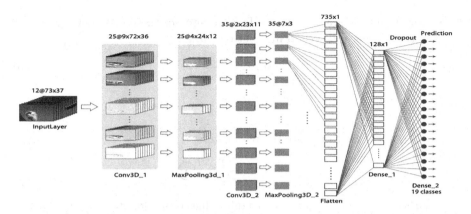

Fig. 1. The first layer is input layer with 12 successive images, and the size of images is 73 × 37 pixels. The Conv3D1 and Conv3D2 are convolutional layers, the filter size of both layer is 4 × 2 × 2 and 2 × 3 × 3 respectively. Maxpooling3d1 and MaxPooling3D2 are 3D maxpooling layers, both pooling sizes are 2 × 3 × 3. We apply dropout between the two dense layers Dense1 and Dense2 and set the fraction of the input units to drop as 0.5. Note that we only apply regularization method on dense2 layer. We performed visualization method to visualize the weights of Conv3D1 and Maxpooling3d1 layers, which are presented in this figure.

how to use 3DCNN to produce spatio-temporal features for Long Short-Time Memory model.

2.1 3DConvolutional Neural Network

The 3DCNN we propose have 8 layers including input layer, illustrated in Fig. 1. We only apply Regularization method on Dense2 layer, and employ Softmax to predict gestures. Motivated by Kingma [14], we choose Adam optimizer for our 3DCNN model, which is aimed towards machine learning problems with large datasets or high-dimensional parameter spaces. The method not only have the ability of AdaGrad [16] to deal with sparse gradients, but also have the ability of RMSProp [15] to deal with non-stationary objectives. And being similar to AdaGrad and RMSProp, Adam stores an exponentially decaying average of past squared gradients v_t. In addition, Adam also keeps an exponentially decaying average of past gradients m_t, which is similar to momentum:

$$m_t = \beta_1 m_t - 1 + (1 - beta_1)g_t \tag{1}$$

$$v_t = \beta_2 v_t - 1 + (1 - \beta_2)g_t^2 \tag{2}$$

m_t and v_t are estimates of the first moment (the mean) and the second moment (the uncentered variance) of the gradients respectively. As m_t and v_t are initialized as vectors of 0 s, the authors of Adam observe that they are biased towards zero, especially during the initial time steps, especially when the decay rates are small(i.e. β_1 and β_2 are close to 1). They counteract these biases by computing bias-corrected first and second moment estimates:

$$\hat{m}_t = \frac{m_t}{1 - \beta_1^t} \tag{3}$$

$$\hat{v} = \frac{v_t}{1 - \beta_2^t} \tag{4}$$

They then use these to update the parameters:

$$\theta_{t+1} = \theta_t - \frac{\eta}{\sqrt{\hat{v}_t} + \varepsilon} \bigodot \hat{m}_t \tag{5}$$

The author of Adam suggests the default values of 0.9 for β_1, 0.999 for β_2, and 10^{-8} for ε. Where η is the learning rate, θ is the parameter we aim to tune, g_t is the gradient of the objective function w.r.t to the parameter θ_t at time t. The author shows that Adam works well in practice and compares favorably to other adaptive learning-method algorithms. Thus, we compared performance of Adam and SGD in Sect. 4.1, and analysed the result of classification by using 3DCNN to challenge on VIVA hand gesture dataset.

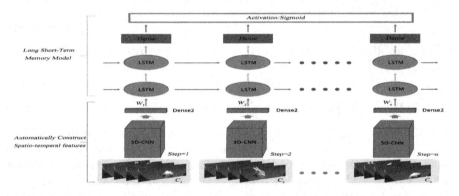

Fig. 2. The bottom part is fine-tuned 3DConvolutional Neural Network, which is used to learn spatio-temporal features. C_i is a clip of hand gesture video, and is the ith step input data of 3DConvolutional Neural Network. The output W_i of Dense2 is the spatio-temporal features, and it is the ith step input data of LSTM.

2.2 Automated Space-Time Feature Construction with 3DConvolutional Neural Network

In this section, we describe how to use 3DCNN, which was proposed in Sect. 2.1, automatically constructing spatio-temporal features for LSTM [8], illustrated in Fig. 2. The outputs of layer Dense2 are probability of each gesture. Supposing that there are n kinds of gestures and define each probability as $p_{it}(i \in \{1, 2, \ldots, n\})$, the one time step input data of LSTM is defined as

$W_t = \{p_{1t}, p_{2t}, ..., p_{nt}\}$. If there are α time steps, the all spatio-temporal features of a video is described as $Seq = \{W_1, W_2, .., W_\alpha\}$ $(t \in \{1, 2, ..., \alpha\})$. However, the image sequences of hand gesture videos should not be input directly, because if a image sequence of a hand gesture video is input into 3DCNN, there will only one time step input data of LSTM be manufactured. Thus, we propose a method to reorganize the sequences in Sect. 3.3.

Fig. 3. Samples of augmented dataset

3 Dataset

The VIVA challenge dataset is composed of 885 intensity and depth videos, and there are 19 different dynamic hand gestures performed by 8 subjects inside a vehicle [4]. Both channels are recorded with the Microsoft Kinect device and have a resolution of 115×250 pixels. The dataset is organized to evaluate and advance the state-of-the-art in multi-modal dynamic hand gesture recognition under challenging variable lighting and multiple subjects. The gesture which involve hand and/or finger movements is performed by the left hand of the driver and right hand of the front passenger.

3.1 Preproccesing

Each hand gesture sequence in the VIVA dataset has a different duration. To normalize the temporal lengths of the gestures, we first resampled each gesture sequence to 12 frames dropping or repeating frames. We also spatially down sampled the original intensity images by a factor of 2 to 73×37 pixels. We normalized each channel of a particular gesture's video sequence to be of zero mean and unit variance. This helped our gesture classifier converge faster. The final inputs to the gesture classifier were $12 \times 73 \times 37$ sized columns. However, we only challenged on intensity videos, because the depth videos have no information of lighting conditions.

3.2   Data Augmentation

The VIVA challenge dataset contains less than 750 gestures for training, which are not enough to prevent overfitting. Therefore, we performed offline spatio-temporal data augmentation to increase training samples. Note that we did not augment the validation dataset, and the augmented training dataset is used to train 3DCNN only. Motivated by existing methods [12], augmentation datasets are comprised of four operations: adjust brightness, adjust saturation, horizontal flipping, and rotating 90°, and we also apply both operations together. For example (Fig. 3), applying horizontal flipping on original *Swipe to right*, we get the new sample of gesture *Swipe to left*. We adjust the brightness on original data to increase the training dataset under different lighting conditions.

3.3   Reorganize Dataset

We propose a method to organize dataset as input data of 3DCNN to generate spatio-temporal features. First step: Assuming that m images are sampled from a hand gesture video, and marked as $S = \{M_1, M_2, ..., M_m\}$. According to the depth (we define it as d) of filter in 3Dconv1, then we get the first subsequence of S as $K_1 = \{M_1, M_2, ..., M_d\}$, similarly we get the second subsequence of S as $K_2 = \{M_2, M_3, ..., M_{d+1}\}$, repeat such steps to produce subsequence K_j till $j = m$. At last, there is such result: $\{K_1, K_2, ..., K_j\}$. Second step: define $h = m/d$, and there are $/alpha$ steps input data of LSTM. Then each step of input data is defined as $c_i = \{K_i, K_{i+1}, ..., K_{i+h-1}\}$ $(1 \leq i \leq \alpha)$, so the all spatio-temporal features are organized as $Input = \{c_i, c_{i+1}, ..., c_\alpha\}$. Once the input data is taken to 3DCNN under validation model, we would automatically get the input sequence $Seq = \{W_1, W_2, .., W_\alpha\}$, which is defined in Sect. 2.2.

Table 1. The classification results of LSTM, results show that LSTM outperforms 3DConvolutional Neural Network by 12.47%. Our final classifies resulted in the best performance.

Method	HOG [4]	LRN [12]	HRN [12]	LRN+HRN [12]	3DCNN
Accuracy	64.5%	74.0%	70.0%	77.5%	**82.03%**

4   Training and Results

In this section we describe the details of our experiments. Firstly, We train 3DCNN and analyze the performances of Adam and SGD applied on our 3DCNN model. Secondly, the accuracy of our model are compared with Molchanov [12] and Ohn-Bar [4], the results are listed in Table 1. Finally, we report the training result of LSTM, and present the parameter we used in both model.

Table 2. The confusion matrix for our 3DConvolutional Neural Network. Abbreviations:L-left, R-right, D-down, U-up, CW/CCW-clock/counter-clock wise.

Class	1.Swipe R	2.Swipe L	3.Swipe D	4.Swipe U	5.Swipe V	6.Swipe X	7.Swipe +	8.Scroll R	9.Scroll L	10.Scroll D	11.Scroll U	12.Tap-1	13.Tap-3	14.Pinch	15.Expand	16.Rotate CCW	17.Rotate CW	18.Open	19.Close
1	**85**	0	0	1	0	0	1	2	0	0	0	0	0	0	0	0	1	0	0
2	1	**88**	1	0	3	0	0	0	3	1	0	0	1	0	2	2	3	0	0
3	0	0	**73**	2	2	0	0	0	0	4	0	0	0	1	0	0	1	0	1
4	0	0	1	**80**	0	0	0	0	0	0	0	0	0	0	0	0	0	1	0
5	0	0	1	0	**78**	4	0	0	1	1	0	0	0	0	0	3	0	0	0
6	0	0	2	0	4	**87**	0	0	0	0	0	0	1	0	0	0	1	0	0
7	0	2	0	0	0	1	**91**	0	0	0	0	0	0	0	0	0	1	0	0
8	5	0	0	1	0	0	0	**91**	0	0	0	0	0	0	0	0	1	0	0
9	0	4	0	0	0	1	2	0	**89**	1	1	0	0	0	0	2	0	0	0
10	0	0	2	0	1	0	0	1	0	**74**	0	0	0	0	0	0	1	0	0
11	0	0	0	2	1	0	0	0	0	0	**94**	0	0	0	0	0	1	0	0
12	0	0	1	1	0	0	0	0	0	1	0	**70**	3	0	0	1	0	0	0
13	0	0	0	2	1	0	0	0	0	1	0	11	**73**	5	2	1	1	0	0
14	1	0	0	0	0	0	0	0	0	0	1	1	6	**84**	1	1	3	0	0
15	0	0	0	0	0	0	0	0	0	0	0	0	1	0	**84**	1	0	0	0
16	0	0	1	0	0	0	0	0	0	0	0	0	0	0	0	**68**	0	0	0
17	0	0	0	0	0	0	0	0	0	0	1	1	1	1	0	1	**68**	0	0
18	0	0	0	1	0	0	0	0	0	0	1	0	0	1	0	0	3	**98**	2
19	0	0	0	0	0	0	0	0	0	0	0	0	0	0	0	0	2	1	**92**

4.1 Results of 3DConvolutional Neural Network

The aim of training a 3DCNN is to optimize the values of θ, and minimize a cost function for the dataset. We perform categorical cross entropy [27] as cost function, select normal initialization function to initialize all parameters, set the values of learning rate as 1×10^{-3} and set the batch size as 3.

In order to compare the performance of Adam with SGD, we use same training dataset, which was augmented in Sect. 3.1, to train a 3DCNN with Adam optimizer and SGD optimizer respectively. There are four aspects to be compared: training accuracy, training loss, validation accuracy and validation. After 100 training epochs, we get such results (Fig. 4). Results show that no matter which aspect is compared, the model using Adam as optimizer has a higher convergence rate than the model using SGD, We can notice that the both validation accuracy and training accuracy of Adam are higher than SGD does. In addition,

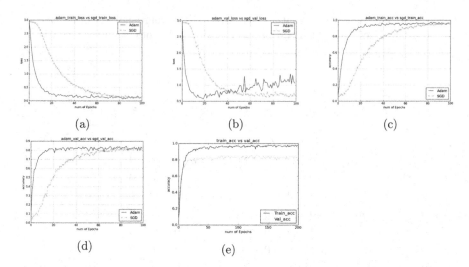

Fig. 4. The figure (a) shows the change in **Training Loss**, the figure (b) shows the change in **Validation Loss**, the figure (c) shows the change in **Training Accuracy**, the figure (d) shows the change in **Validation Accuracy**. All figures show that Adam has a faster convergence rate than SGD does. (e)shows that after 200 training epochs, the training accuracy is 97%. And the curves show that our deep model is very stable.

Adam only used 20 training epochs to get 80% validation accuracy, but SGD took nearly 40 training epochs. But, as for validation loss, SGD presented a stabler performance than Adam did. In summary we demonstrated that it is better to use Adam as optimizer for a 3DCNN than SGD. To get the accuracy of our 3DCNN with Adam optimizer, we trained the model again by using 200 training epochs. The result is presented in Fig. 4e. The average validation accuracy of our 3DCNN is 82%, and the average of training accuracy is 97%. We compared our result with Molchanov [12] and the baseline method proposed by Ohn-Bar and Trivedi [4], the classification rates are listed in Table 1. Ohn-Bar and Trivedi, which employs HOG + HOG^2 features, get 64.5% accuracy. Molchanov proposed his 3DConvolutional Neural Network, he use HRN to classify intensive hand gesture videos and get 70.0% classification accuracy, and use LRN training on depth videos get 74.4% classification accuracy. He combines LRN and HRN, and gets a better accuracy of 77.5%. However, the 3DCNN model we proposed get the highest accuracy of 82.03%. Additionally, Molchanov augmented more training datasets than us, and it took 300 training epochs to tune the model he proposed. In short, our approach not only has a higher recognition rate than his model, but also has a faster training speed.

In order to analyze the accuracy of each hand gesture, we augmented validation videos, because the results cannot be accurately described as there are less than 300 validation videos. Then, we use fine-tuned 3DCNN to validate the augmented validation datasets, and draw a confusion matrix (Table 2), which is the same as Molchanov. We can notice that the highest classification rate 98%

Table 3. The classification results of our LSTM, and outperformed 3DConvolutional Neural Network by 12.47%. Our final classifier resulted in the best performance.

Method	HOG [4]	LRN+HRN [12]	3DCNN	LSTM
Accuracy	64.5%	77.5%	82.03%	**94.5%**

is the gesture *Open*, and there are five gestures can be correctly classified more than 90% accuracy. The *Rotate CW/CCW* gestures are difficult for classifier, and this result is similar to Molchanov.

4.2 Results of LSTM

Regarding 3DConvolutional Neural Network as a spatio-temporal features extractor is the most common way to use 3DCNN [8,9,11]. The reorganize dataset method is performed on the original dataset, which we proposed in Sect. 3.3. The fine-tuned 3DCNN is used to generate spatio-temporal features. The Binary Cross Entropy [27] is employed as cost function, and the Sigmoid as activation function. Set the value of learning rate as 1×10^{-6} and the value of batch size as 20. After 50 training epochs, we use this LSTM model get a satisfied 94.5% classification rate presented in Table 3. Our LSTM outperforms the method of Ohn-Bar and Trived by 30%, and outperforms the method of Molchanov by 17%.

5 Conclusions

We developed an effective method for dynamic hand gesture recognition with 3DCNN and LSTM, challenging VIVA dataset. We fine-tuned the 3DCNN as classifier and got a average accuracy of 82.04%. With the fine-tuned 3D convolutional neural networks, excellent spatio-temporal features are learned automatically to describe the hand gestures video, and the result of LSTM got pretty satisfied average accuracy of 94.7%. In the future work, we will challenge the higher level dynamic gestures including activities and motion contexts. And we will investigate the possibility of using a single-step model, in which the 3D convolutional neural networks model described in this paper is directly connected to the LSTM sequence classifier.

Acknowledgments. This work is partially supported by Shanghai Innovation Action Plan Project under the grant No. 16511101200 and the Natural Science Foundation of Shanghai, China (Grant No. 14ZR1419700).

References

1. Starner, T., Weaver, J., Pentland, A.: Real-time american sign language recognition using desk and wearable computer based video. IEEE Trans. Pattern Anal. Mach. Intell. **20**(12), 1371–1375 (1998)
2. Wang, S.B., Quattoni, A., Morency, L.P., et al.: Hidden conditional random fields for gesture recognition. In: 2006 IEEE Computer Society Conference on Computer Vision and Pattern Recognition, vol. 2, pp. 1521–1527. IEEE (2006)
3. Dardas, N.H., Georganas, N.D.: Real-time hand gesture detection and recognition using bag-of-features and support vector machine techniques. IEEE Trans. Instrum. Meas. **60**(11), 3592–3607 (2011)
4. Ohn-Bar, E., Trivedi, M.M.: Hand gesture recognition in real time for automotive interfaces: a multimodal vision-based approach and evaluations. IEEE Trans. Intell. Transp. Syst. **15**(6), 2368–2377 (2014)
5. Elmezain, M., Al-Hamadi, A., Appenrodt, J., et al.: A hidden markov model-based continuous gesture recognition system for hand motion trajectory. In: 19th International Conference on Pattern Recognition, ICPR 2008, pp. 1–4. IEEE (2008)
6. Neverova, N., Wolf, C., Taylor, G.W., Nebout, F.: Multi-scale deep learning for gesture detection and localization. In: Agapito, L., Bronstein, M.M., Rother, C. (eds.) ECCV 2014. LNCS, vol. 8925, pp. 474–490. Springer, Cham (2015). https://doi.org/10.1007/978-3-319-16178-5_33
7. Baccouche, M., Mamalet, F., Wolf, C., Garcia, C., Baskurt, A.: Sequential deep learning for human action recognition. In: Salah, A.A., Lepri, B. (eds.) HBU 2011. LNCS, vol. 7065, pp. 29–39. Springer, Heidelberg (2011). https://doi.org/10.1007/978-3-642-25446-8_4
8. Gers, F.A., Schraudolph, N.N., Schmidhuber, J.: Learning precise timing with LSTM recurrent networks. J. Mach. Learn. Res. **3**, 115–143 (2002)
9. Tran, D., Bourdev, L., Fergus, R., et al.: Learning spatiotemporal features with 3d convolutional networks. In: Proceedings of the IEEE International Conference on Computer Vision, pp. 4489–4497 (2015)
10. Ji, S., Xu, W., Yang, M., et al.: 3D convolutional neural networks for human action recognition. IEEE Trans. Pattern Anal. Mach. Intell. **35**(1), 221–231 (2013)
11. Molchanov, P., Yang, X., Gupta, S., Kim, K., Tyree, S., Kautz, J.: Online detection and classification of dynamic hand gestures with recurrent 3D convolutional neural networks
12. Molchanov, P., Gupta, S., Kim, K., et al.: Hand gesture recognition with 3D convolutional neural networks. In: Proceedings of the IEEE Conference on Computer Vision and Pattern Recognition Workshops, pp. 1–7 (2015)
13. Hinton, G.E., Srivastava, N., Krizhevsky, A., et al.: Improving neural networks by preventing co-adaptation of feature detectors. arXiv preprint arXiv:1207.0580 (2012)
14. Kingma, D., Ba, J.: Adam: a method for stochastic optimization. arXiv preprint arXiv:1412.6980 (2014)
15. Duchi, J., Hazan, E., Singer, Y.: Adaptive subgradient methods for online learning and stochastic optimization. J. Mach. Learn. Res. **12**, 2121–2159 (2011)
16. Tieleman, T., Hinton, G.: Lecture 6.5-rmsprop: divide the gradient by a running average of its recent magnitude. COURSERA Neural Netw. Mach. Learn. **4**(2), 26–31 (2012)
17. Hinton, G.E., Salakhutdinov, R.R.: Reducing the dimensionality of data with neural networks. Science **313**(5786), 504–507 (2006)

18. Krizhevsky, A., Sutskever, I., Hinton, G.E.: Imagenet classification with deep convolutional neural networks. In: Advances in Neural Information Processing Systems, pp. 1097–1105 (2012)
19. Kim, Y.: Convolutional neural networks for sentence classification. arXiv preprint arXiv:1408.5882 (2014)
20. Pavlovic, V.I., Sharma, R., Huang, T.S.: Visual interpretation of hand gestures for human-computer interaction: a review. IEEE Trans. Pattern Anal. Mach. Intell. **19**(7), 677–695 (1997)
21. Trindade, P., Lobo, J., Barreto, J.P.: Hand gesture recognition using color and depth images enhanced with hand angular pose data. In: 2012 IEEE Conference on Multisensor Fusion and Integration for Intelligent Systems (MFI), pp. 71–76. IEEE (2012)
22. Zobl, M., Nieschulz, R., Geiger, M., Lang, M., Rigoll, G.: Gesture components for natural interaction with in-car devices. In: Camurri, A., Volpe, G. (eds.) GW 2003. LNCS (LNAI), vol. 2915, pp. 448–459. Springer, Heidelberg (2004). https://doi.org/10.1007/978-3-540-24598-8_41
23. Althoff, F., Lindl, R., Walchshausl, L., et al.: Robust multimodal hand-and-head gesture recognition for controlling automotive infotainment systems. VDI BERICHTE **1919**, 187 (2005)
24. Parada-Loira, F., Gonzlez-Agulla, E., Alba-Castro, J.L.: Hand gestures to control infotainment equipment in cars. In: 2014 IEEE Intelligent Vehicles Symposium Proceedings, pp. 1–6. IEEE (2014)
25. Karpathy, A., Toderici, G., Shetty, S., et al.: Large-scale video classification with convolutional neural networks. In: Proceedings of the IEEE Conference on Computer Vision and Pattern Recognition, pp. 1725–1732 (2014)
26. Molchanov, P., Gupta, S., Kim, K., et al.: Multi-sensor system for driver's hand-gesture recognition. In: Automatic Face and Gesture
27. Hoskisson, R.E., Hitt, M.A., Johnson, R.A., et al.: Construct validity of an objective (entropy) categorical measure of diversification strategy. Strateg. Manag. J. **14**(3), 215–235 (1993)

Learning Temporal Context
for Correlation Tracking
with Scale Estimation

Yuhao Cui[1]([✉]), Haoqian Wang[1,3], Xingzheng Wang[1], and Yi Yang[2]

[1] Key Laboratory of Broadband Network and Multimedia,
Graduate School at Shenzhen, Tsinghua University, Shenzhen 518055, China
cuiyuhao001@foxmail.com
[2] LUSTER LightTech Co., Ltd., Beijing 100094, China
[3] Shenzhen Institute of Future Media Technology, Shenzhen 518071, China

Abstract. Visual object tracking is a fundamental task in computer
vision with its wide range of applications. In this paper, we propose a
robust algorithm based on the kernelized correlation filter framework to
handle occlusions or scale variations. Our algorithm takes into account
the relationships between the target object and its surrounding context,
and learns a discriminative correlation filter for the estimation of the
new position. Another discriminative regression model via constructing
the target pyramid is introduced to estimate the optimal scale. The proposed algorithm integrated with two discriminative regression models
can track complex targets with occlusion and deformation at real-time.
The competitive experimental results on the dataset sequences show that
the proposed tracker outperforms other state-of-the-art methods, in both
the precision and the success rate.

Keywords: Object tracking · Correlation filter · Temporal context
Scale pyramid · Fast Fourier Transform (FFT)

1 Introduction

Visual object tracking is one of the significant research in computer vision with its
wide range of applications in video surveillance, motion analysis, activity recognition, and human-computer interaction. Object tracking focuses on assigning
consistent labels to the tracked objects in different video frames [18]. In other
words, the tracker is expected to estimate the exact location of an unknown
object which has been initialized first, in each frame of an image sequence. The
benchmark datasets [17], which contain large numbers of image sequences and
standardized quantitative evaluation metrics, accelerate the pace of development
in tracking algorithm. However, it is still hard to design an efficient tracker due
to several challenging problems, such as partial occlusion, background clutter,
scale variations, deformation, motion blur, fast motion, illumination variation,
and so on.

© Springer International Publishing AG, part of Springer Nature 2018
B. Zeng et al. (Eds.): PCM 2017, LNCS 10735, pp. 754–763, 2018.
https://doi.org/10.1007/978-3-319-77380-3_72

Fig. 1. Qualitative comparison of our approach with KCF [11], DSST [6] and Struck [9] on 8 challenging sequences: matrix, carscale, basketball, david3, dog1, football, singer1 and skating1. Our approach provides consistent results in challenging scenarios, such as occlusions, scale variation, background clutter and illumination variation.

Over the past decade, various approaches have been proposed to cope with the challenges. They can be categorized into generative [2,5,12,15,22] and discriminative [1,9,13,19,20] approaches. Generative methods aim to construct an effective appearance model so as to represent the target and search for the regions that are most similar to the target, while discriminative methods focus on learning a classifier to distinguish the target from backgrounds with local search. The background information has been proved to be beneficial for effective tracking in [17], which indicates that the discriminative trackers are more competitive than the generative ones. The powerful discriminative approaches proceed by specifying the task of target localization as a binary classification problem, and the discriminative classifier is learned by using image patches from both the target and the background, to get the decision boundary.

Recently, the correlation filter-based discriminative tracking algorithms have made breakthrough [4]. In correlation filter-based trackers, adoption of the fast Fourier transform (FFT) makes it possible to track the targets with unparalleled speed. In particular, the KCF tracker [11], which achieves top-performing results on Visual Tracker Benchmark, has already attracted researchers' attention with the high efficiency. The tracker learns a kernelized least squares classifier of a target from a single image patch. The key for its outstanding performance is that the structure of circulant matrix makes it possible to train a discriminative classifier with dense sampling scheme. More specifically, the augmentation of training samples is employed to enhance the discriminative ability, and the exploration of the circulant structure that appears from the periodic assumption of the local image patch brings about the high efficiency [14]. However, the KCF tracker can't work well when it encounters with heavy occlusions in complex image sequences. Besides, only estimating the target translation is a vital limitation on the ability of tracking. These imply inferior performance when processing the sequences with occlusions or scale variations.

In this paper, we propose a robust algorithm based on the kernelized correlation filter framework. In order to learn a discriminative correlation filter, we take advantage of the information that contains the target object and its surrounding context which is favorable for predicting the position of the target. Moreover, exploration of the temporal context by greatly reducing the impact of occlusion on the process, is not prone to drifting in visual tracking. In addition, our method introduces another discriminative regression model via constructing the target pyramid to estimate the optimal scale of target object. It provides an efficient approach for the tracker by the multiple scales searching strategy. As shown in Fig. 1, the proposed tracker outperforms other state-of-the-art methods in several scenarios. Meanwhile, adoption of the fast Fourier transform (FFT) makes the proposed algorithm operating complex targets with occlusion and deformation at real-time. Finally, we compare our method with state-of-the-art trackers and show the highly competitive experimental results on the benchmark sequences.

2   Related Work

In this section, we discuss the tracking-by-detection approaches and the correlation filter-based trackers. Discriminative tracking-by-detection methods have demonstrated superior performances on OTB benchmarks [17] recently. The model of the target appearance within a tracking-by-detection framework, typically depends on a discriminatively trained classifier or regressor which is inspired by machine learning algorithms. MIL tracker [1] explores the idea about a bag of positive samples with a boosting variant algorithm to construct the tracker. TLD algorithm [13] exploits two independent experts to identify the false classification of the boosting detector, which can give assistance to the tracker. In compressive tracker [20], Zhang et al. train a Naive Bayes classifier using the compressive features projected from the original space, inspired by compressive sensing techniques. MEEM method [19] proposes a multi-expert restoration scheme to address the model drift problem. As one of the most typical discriminative trackers, Struck [9] employs the structured SVM which connects the target location space to the training samples.

Our proposed tracker is closely related to the correlation filter-based approaches. Adoption of the correlation filter in traditional signal processing technique into the tracking applications makes them more appealing than the methods mentioned in the last paragraph, since their computational cost is low. Specifically, converting the operation to the Fourier domain bring about a speed reaching several hundreds frames per second. Bolme et al. [3] first proposed the first tracking method using correlation filter in the paper. It formulated the problem in the view of learning a correlation filter by minimizing the output sum of squared error (MOSSE) with gray-scale images. Then, STC algorithm [21] models the statistical correlation between the simple low-level features from the target and its surrounding regions in a Bayesian framework. CSK [10] is proposed to employ the circulant structure to enhance the discriminative ability of the classifier by the augmentation of negative samples, and the exploration of kernel trick brings about the high precision. Based on CSK, KCF tracking algorithm [11] extends to multiple feature channels and adopts the HOG feature instead of raw pixel to reach the peak of both the accuracy and robustness. Meanwhile, Danelljan et al. [8] applied the color attributes of object [16] to the tracking task in order to further boost the performance of CSK tracker, which is a powerful color feature. In addition, to solve the scale change issue in object tracking, the DSST tracker [6] integrates a multi-scale template for the estimation of the scale employing a 1D correlation filter, while the SAMF tracker [14] samples the target at different scales, and resizes the samples into a fixed size to compare with the responses at each frame to obtain the optimal scale. Recently, the Spatially Regularized (SRDCF) [7] formulation learns to assign penalty coefficients to the correlation filter depending on their spatial location. It has demonstrated excellent tracking results, but this is achieved at the expense of efficiency.

3   Proposed Method

In this section, we detail the proposed method to track the target object with severe occlusions or significant scale variations. In order to prevent drifting, the process of tracking can be viewed as estimation of the translation and the scale, and two regression models are trained to carry out the task. According to the relationships between the target object and its surrounding context, a correlation filter is learned to predict the new position of the target. After that, another discriminative regression model learned from the most reliable tracked targets estimates the optimal scale of the object.

3.1   The KCF Tracker

Our approach is built on kernelized correlation filter framework. Here, we briefly review the main idea of the KCF method [11]. The tracker extracts dense samples over the base sample of target appearances. The ridge regression model is learned by finding a function $f(x) = w^T x$ to minimize the squared error, and the minimization problem can be expressed as:

$$\min_{w} \sum_{i} (f(x_i) - y_i)^2 + \lambda \|w\|^2 \tag{1}$$

where x_i, y_i are samples and their regression targets respectively. λ is a regularization parameter and $\lambda \geqslant 0$. The close-form solution of this optimization problem is easy to get: $w = (X^T X + \lambda I)^{-1} X^T y$, X^T denotes the transpose of X.

Considering a vector $x = [x_1, x_2, \ldots, x_n]$, a cyclic shift of x can be donated as $Px = [x_n, x_1, x_2, \ldots, x_{n-1}]$. All the possible cyclic shifts $\{P_u x | u = 0, \ldots, n-1\}$ are concatenated to constitute the circulant matrix $X = C(x)$.

Every circulant matrix X can be made diagonal by the Discrete Fourier Transform (DFT):

$$X = F^H diag(\hat{x}) F \tag{2}$$

where, F denotes the DFT matrix, which is known as the constant matrix, F^H is the Hermitian transpose of F, and $\hat{x}$ denotes the DFT of vector x.

So, the solution can be expressed as below:

$$\hat{w}^* = \frac{\hat{x}^* \odot \hat{y}}{\hat{x}^* \odot \hat{x} + \lambda} \tag{3}$$

where, $\hat{x}$ denotes the DFT of x, $\hat{x}^*$ denotes the complex-conjugate of $\hat{x}$, and $\odot$ denotes the element-wise product. Only dot-product and DFT/IDFT are required, and so the time complexity of the algorithm is only a nearly-linear $O(nlogn)$.

Map the inputs of a linear problem to a non-linear feature-space with the kernel trick, and get the classifier with better performance:

$$f(z) = w^T z = \sum_{i=1}^{n} \alpha_i \mathcal{K}(z, x_i) \tag{4}$$

The dual space coefficients α are learned in Fourier domain:

$$\hat{\alpha}^* = \frac{\hat{y}}{\hat{k}^{xx} + \lambda} \tag{5}$$

where the k^{xx} is the first row of the kernel matrix K, and usually we choose the Gaussian kernel:

$$k^{xx'} = exp(-\frac{1}{\sigma^2}(\|x\|^2 + \|x'\|^2) - 2F^{-1}(\hat{x} \odot \hat{x}'^*)) \tag{6}$$

As a Gaussian function, the training label y takes the smoothly decreasing value from 1 for the center of the target to 0 for other shifts. In order to include more negative samples, we set the size of window 2.8 times the original target box when training, in our method.

The circulant matrix also contributes to accelerating the process of detection. The response map can be computed for all candidate patches z:

$$f(z) = F^{-1}[(\hat{k}^{\tilde{x}z})^* \odot \hat{\alpha}] \tag{7}$$

where, $\tilde{x}$ denotes the learned target appearance model. The translation with respect to the maximum response is considered as the movement of the tracked target.

3.2   Estimation of Translation

We employ the kernelized correlation filter to train the first classifier f_t for the estimation of translation, but there is vital difference between our approach and KCF.

In visual tracking, the local context is composed of the target rectangle and its surrounding background in the determined area, and there exists a reliable

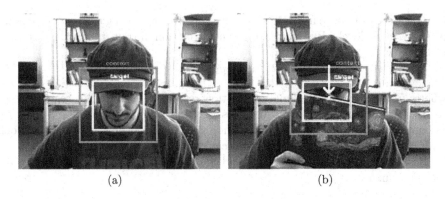

(a)   (b)

Fig. 2. The proposed method can deal with severely occlusion well by exploiting the spatio-temporal context information. The region inside the yellow rectangle is the context region containing the target and its surrounding background. (Color figure online)

spatio-temporal relationship between the local scenes containing the object. As the time interval between two consecutive frames is small, we can assume that there is no significant change. What's more, the local context around the object which stays the same can be used for localization even if the target is occluded heavily. Even if the appearance of the scene changes rapidly, the spatial relationship between the target and its local context can provide specific information about the scene configuration, which gives more information to contribute to locating the center of target in the next frame. Zhang et al. [21] has shown that it is impactful to model the temporal relationship of appearance using a target object and its context for visual tracking. Therefore, our algorithm takes into account the relationship between the target object and its surroundings to learn the discriminant correlation filter used for the estimation of the new position. For instance, the target person in Fig. 2 undergoes severe occlusion, but the spatial relationship between the person and the surrounding locations in the context region is almost unchanged. We model the appearance of the target and the context to look for the center of the object.

3.3   Estimation of Scale

Another improvement is that we train an extra discriminative regression model f_s from the most reliable tracked targets $\tilde{y}$. A target pyramid is structured to provide an efficient approach for the tracker by the multiple scales searching strategy, in order that we estimate the target scale independently after the optimal translation is found. Specifically, consider $P \times R$ as the target size in a test frame and N indicates the number of scales. $S = \{a^n | n = \lfloor -\frac{N-1}{2} \rfloor, \lfloor -\frac{N-3}{2} \rfloor, \ldots, \lfloor \frac{N-1}{2} \rfloor\}$, here, a denotes the scale factor between feature layers. For each $s \in S$, we extract an image patch Js of size $sP \times sR$ centered around the estimated location and resize all patches with size $P \times R$ again.

Here, it's the difference from DSST tracker [6] when operating the training examples at n scale levels. By maximizing the correlation output, the optimal scale $\tilde{s}$ is as below:

$$\tilde{s} = \arg\max_{s}(\tilde{y}_1, \tilde{y}_2, \ldots, \tilde{y}_S) \tag{8}$$

where, $\tilde{y}_S$ denotes the maximal correlation response of the target regression f_t to Js. Note that the cosine window is used for elimination of the boundary discontinuity of the target and surrounding context in translation filter model f_t, but there is no need to weight the scale filter f_s.

Besides, the translation model f_t and the scale model f_s are updated by same formulation:

$$\tilde{x}^t = (1 - l)\tilde{x}^{t-1} + lx^t \tag{9a}$$
$$\tilde{A}^t = (1 - l)\tilde{A}^{t-1} + lA^t \tag{9b}$$

where l is the learning rate, t is the index of the current frame, and $A = F(a)$.

As for the features, we exploit the powerful HOG feature in this algorithm, for the temporal context regressor f_t and the scale model f_t.

4   Experimental Results

Here, evaluation of our proposed tracker on the OTB-2013 benchmark datasets with 51 video sequences is shown.

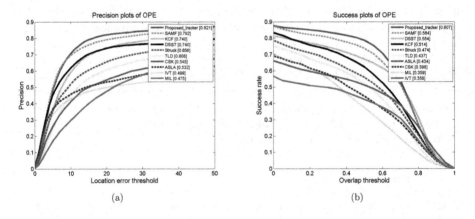

(a)   (b)

Fig. 3. Precision and success plots on OTB-2013.

Considering the real-time requirements of tracking application, some algorithms with low efficiency are discarded. We provide a comparison of our tracker with 9 state-of-art trackers from the literature: IVT [15], ASLA [12], TLD [13], MIL [1], Struck [9], CSK [10], KCF [11], SAMF [14] and DSST [6]. Note that IVT [15] and ASLA [12] are almost the best in generative methods while others

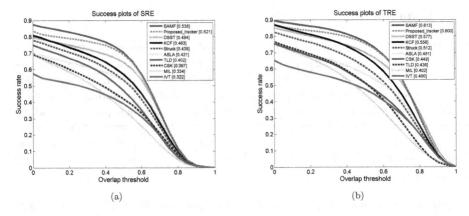

Fig. 4. Comparison with respect to robustness to initialization on OTB-2013. We show success plots for both the spatial (SRE) and temporal (TRE) robustness.

are impressive discriminative methods. Among the discriminative algorithms, CSK [10], KCF [11], SAMF [14] and DSST [6] algorithms are outstanding correlation filter-based approaches. Different evaluation methodologies are adopted respectively in order to show both the accuracy and robustness of the trackers.

Our regularization parameter is set to $\lambda = 0.0001$ in Eq. 1. The filter size is set to 2.8 times the initial target size and the Gaussian kernel width is set to 0.1. We use S = 33 number of scales with a scale factor of a = 1.02. The base learning rate is set to 0.01 for the translation model and scale model. And the same parameter values are used for all the sequences.

Figure 3(a) contains the precision plots based on center location error. The Struck algorithm, based on structured SVM, obtains a mean distance precision of 0.656. The DSST method obtains a mean distance precision of 0.740, the same as KCF tracker. SAMF tracker get a high precision of 0.792. Our tracker performs better than all these methods, reaching a mean distance precision of 0.821. The success plot showing the overlap precision over the range of thresholds is in Fig. 3(b). Among the compared tracking methods, DSST and SAMF provide the best results with AUC scores of 0.554 and 0.584 respectively. Our tracker achieves score of 0.607, slightly outperforming SAMF with 2.3%. Other compared trackers can not come up to these three methods with the score of overlap precision. It clearly illustrates that our algorithm outperforms the state-of-the-art trackers significantly in accuracy.

Furthermore, visual tracking algorithms are sensitive to initialization. We evaluate the robustness of our tracker by two different types of initialization criteria, namely: temporal robustness (TRE) and spatial robustness (SRE). Figure 4 shows the success plots for TRE and SRE on the OTB-2013 dataset. Among the provided methods, SAMF and our approach provide the top-performing results. Our proposed algorithm still achieves a desirable performance over these state-of-the-art trackers on robustness evaluations.

5 Conclusions

In this paper, we propose an efficient and robust algorithm based on the kernelized correlation filter framework to deal with occlusions and scale variations. Our method decomposes the task of tracking into translation and estimation of the scale. Relationships between the target and its surrounding context are employed to learn a correlation filter for prediction of the new position. Also, we construct another discriminative regression model from the most reliable tracked targets to estimate the optimal scale of the object. Finally, extensive experimental results on the OTB tracking benchmark prove that our proposed approach achieves superior performances.

Acknowledgements. This work is partially supported by the NSFC fund (61571259, 61531014, 61471213), Shenzhen Fundamental Research fund (JCYJ201703071530 51701), Shenzhen Public Technology Platform fund (GGFW2017040714161462).

References

1. Babenko, B., Yang, M.H., Belongie, S.: Visual tracking with online multiple instance learning. In: IEEE Conference on Computer Vision and Pattern Recognition (CVPR 2009), pp. 983–990. IEEE (2009)
2. Bao, C., Wu, Y., Ling, H., Ji, H.: Real time robust L1 tracker using accelerated proximal gradient approach. In: IEEE Conference on Computer Vision and Pattern Recognition (CVPR), pp. 1830–1837. IEEE (2012)
3. Bolme, D.S., Beveridge, J.R., Draper, B.A., Lui, Y.M.: Visual object tracking using adaptive correlation filters. In: IEEE Conference on Computer Vision and Pattern Recognition (CVPR), pp. 2544–2550. IEEE (2010)
4. Chen, Z., Hong, Z., Tao, D.: An experimental survey on correlation filter-based tracking. arXiv preprint arXiv:1509.05520 (2015)
5. Comaniciu, D., Ramesh, V., Meer, P.: Kernel-based object tracking. IEEE Trans. Pattern Anal. Mach. Intell. **25**(5), 564–577 (2003)
6. Danelljan, M., Hager, G., Khan, F.S., Felsberg, M.: Discriminative scale space tracking. IEEE Trans. Pattern Anal. Mach. Intell. **39**(8), 1561–1575 (2017)
7. Danelljan, M., Hager, G., Khan, F.S., Felsberg, M.: Learning spatially regularized correlation filters for visual tracking. In: Proceedings of the IEEE International Conference on Computer Vision, pp. 4310–4318 (2015)
8. Danelljan, M., Khan, F.S., Felsberg, M., Van de Weijer, J.: Adaptive color attributes for real-time visual tracking. In: Proceedings of the IEEE Conference on Computer Vision and Pattern Recognition, pp. 1090–1097 (2014)
9. Hare, S., Golodetz, S., Saffari, A., Vineet, V., Cheng, M.M., Hicks, S.L., Torr, P.H.: Struck: structured output tracking with kernels. IEEE Trans. Pattern Anal. Mach. Intell. **38**(10), 2096–2109 (2016)
10. Henriques, J.F., Caseiro, R., Martins, P., Batista, J.: Exploiting the circulant structure of tracking-by-detection with kernels. In: Fitzgibbon, A., Lazebnik, S., Perona, P., Sato, Y., Schmid, C. (eds.) ECCV 2012. LNCS, vol. 7575, pp. 702–715. Springer, Heidelberg (2012). https://doi.org/10.1007/978-3-642-33765-9_50
11. Henriques, J.F., Caseiro, R., Martins, P., Batista, J.: High-speed tracking with kernelized correlation filters. IEEE Trans. Pattern Anal. Mach. Intell. **37**(3), 583–596 (2015)

12. Jia, X., Lu, H., Yang, M.H.: Visual tracking via adaptive structural local sparse appearance model. In: IEEE Conference on Computer Vision and Pattern Recognition (CVPR), pp. 1822–1829. IEEE (2012)
13. Kalal, Z., Mikolajczyk, K., Matas, J.: Tracking-learning-detection. IEEE Trans. Pattern Anal. Mach. Intell. **34**(7), 1409–1422 (2012)
14. Li, Y., Zhu, J.: A scale adaptive kernel correlation filter tracker with feature integration. In: Agapito, L., Bronstein, M.M., Rother, C. (eds.) ECCV 2014. LNCS, vol. 8926, pp. 254–265. Springer, Cham (2015). https://doi.org/10.1007/978-3-319-16181-5_18
15. Ross, D.A., Lim, J., Lin, R.S., Yang, M.H.: Incremental learning for robust visual tracking. Int. J. Comput. Vis. **77**(1), 125–141 (2008)
16. Van De Weijer, J., Schmid, C., Verbeek, J., Larlus, D.: Learning color names for real-world applications. IEEE Trans. Image Process. **18**(7), 1512–1523 (2009)
17. Wu, Y., Lim, J., Yang, M.H.: Online object tracking: a benchmark. In: Proceedings of the IEEE Conference on Computer Vision and Pattern Recognition, pp. 2411–2418 (2013)
18. Yilmaz, A., Javed, O., Shah, M.: Object tracking: a survey. ACM Comput. Surv. (CSUR) **38**(4), 13 (2006)
19. Zhang, J., Ma, S., Sclaroff, S.: MEEM: robust tracking via multiple experts using entropy minimization. In: Fleet, D., Pajdla, T., Schiele, B., Tuytelaars, T. (eds.) ECCV 2014. LNCS, vol. 8694, pp. 188–203. Springer, Cham (2014). https://doi.org/10.1007/978-3-319-10599-4_13
20. Zhang, K., Zhang, L., Yang, M.-H.: Real-time compressive tracking. In: Fitzgibbon, A., Lazebnik, S., Perona, P., Sato, Y., Schmid, C. (eds.) ECCV 2012. LNCS, vol. 7574, pp. 864–877. Springer, Heidelberg (2012). https://doi.org/10.1007/978-3-642-33712-3_62
21. Zhang, K., Zhang, L., Yang, M.H., Zhang, D.: Fast tracking via spatio-temporal context learning. arXiv preprint arXiv:1311.1939 (2013)
22. Zhang, T., Ghanem, B., Liu, S., Ahuja, N.: Robust visual tracking via multi-task sparse learning. In: IEEE Conference on Computer Vision and Pattern Recognition (CVPR), pp. 2042–2049. IEEE (2012)

Deep Combined Image Denoising
with Cloud Images

Sifeng Xia[1], Jiaying Liu[1(✉)], Wenhan Yang[1], Mading Li[1],
and Zongming Guo[1,2]

[1] Institute of Computer Science and Technology, Peking University, Beijing, China
liujiaying@pku.edu.cn
[2] Cooperative Medianet Innovation Center, Shanghai, China

Abstract. Image denoising methods essentially lose some high-frequency (HF) information in denoising. To address this issue, we propose an end-to-end trainable deep network to additionally utilize online retrieved cloud images to compensate for the HF information loss based on the internal inferred results. In particular, the noise inference network first infers a noise map from the noisy image and derives an intermediate image by removing the noise map from the noisy image. Then the external online compensation is performed based on the intermediate image. The final results are obtained by fusing the intermediate image with external HF maps extracted by the external HF compensation network. Extensive experimental results demonstrate that our method achieves notably better performance than state-of-the-art denoising methods.

Keywords: Image denoising · High-frequency information loss
Online compensation · External high-frequency map

1 Introduction

Image denoising aims to obtain a clean image from a noisy one and it is widely applied in practical issues. Due to the information loss caused by the noise contamination, image denoising is an ill-posed problem. Early image denoising methods estimate and remove the noise based on local statistics of the noisy image. For example, Li *et al.* [9] proposed a method that removes the noise by studying both signal and noise characteristics under overcomplete expansion. An adaptive denoising method for images decomposed in overcomplete oriented pyramids is proposed in [7]. The sparse representation based method [4] groups similar 2D image fragments in the noisy image into 3D data arrays to enhance the sparse representation. In these methods, only limited local signal of the noisy image is utilized for removing the noise.

For the purpose of better denoising performance, many methods are successively proposed utilizing additional external data to bring more information

---

This work was supported by National Natural Science Foundation of China under contract No. U1636206.

© Springer International Publishing AG, part of Springer Nature 2018
B. Zeng et al. (Eds.): PCM 2017, LNCS 10735, pp. 764–772, 2018.
https://doi.org/10.1007/978-3-319-77380-3_73

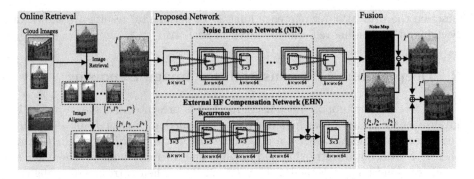

Fig. 1. The framework of the proposed deep denoising method with online compensation.

for image denoising. The K-SVD algorithm is used in [6] to obtain a dictionary that describes the image content effectively based on the noisy image and a high-quality image dataset. Mairal *et al.* [12] proposed to combine a learned dictionary from external data with self-similarities of natural images for image denoising. Context-aware sparsity prior was proposed in [13] to facilitate the sparsity-based regularization for image denoising. Dong *et al.* [5] proposed a method that introduces the concept of sparse coding noise and try suppressing the noise over a learned dictionary. Besides, Yue *et al.* [18] combined spatial and frequency filtering with the assistance of retrieved web images to preserve details.

Recently, many learning based methods have been proposed and they posses impressive performance. A random field-based architecture is constructed in [14] combining the image model and the optimization algorithm in a single unit for image denoising. Chen and Pock [3] described a flexible learning framework that simultaneously learns all the parameters including the filters and the influence functions from the training data through a loss based approach. Besides, a feedforward convolutional network (CNN) is constructed by Zhang *et al.* to infer a map from the noisy image for denoising [19], which obtains state-of-the-art performance. However, despite the impressive result Zhang has achieved, some high-frequency (HF) information is still lost due to the ambiguity nature of image denoising and the problem that mean squared error leads to "regression to mean" [15].

To address the above issues, we propose a unified deep network that utilizes additional online retrieved cloud images to facilitate image denoising. Specifically, our work first initially removes an inferred noise map from the noisy image to obtain an intermediate image. Then the intermediate image is utilized to retrieve and align multiple reference images. The final result with well recovered HF detail is derived by extracting external HF (EHF) maps with the external HF compensation network and fusing the maps with the intermediate image.

The rest of the paper is organized as follows. Section 2 introduces the proposed denoising method. The unified network is first illustrated and then we describe the utilization of reference images. Experimental results are shown in Sect. 3 and concluding remarks are given in Sect. 4.

2   Deep Online Compensation for Image Denoising

In this section, the proposed denoising method is presented. As shown in Fig. 1, given a noisy image $\tilde{I}$, we first derive an intermediate image I^t by removing the noise map inferred with the noise inference network (NiNet) from $\tilde{I}$. And then I^t is utilized for retrieving and aligning the reference images. There are K reference cloud images defined as $\{I^{r_1}, I^{r_2}, ..., I^{r_K}\}$. Their corresponding aligned images are represented by $\{\hat{I}^{r_1}, \hat{I}^{r_2}, ..., \hat{I}^{r_K}\}$. For each $\hat{I}^r$ of $\{\hat{I}^{r_1}, \hat{I}^{r_2}, ..., \hat{I}^{r_K}\}$, it is taken as an input of the external HF compensation network (EhNet), which extracts the EHF map $\hat{I}_m^r$. Finally, the extracted EHF maps $\{\hat{I}_m^{r_1}, \hat{I}_m^{r_2}, ..., \hat{I}_m^{r_K}\}$ are fused with the intermediate image I^t based on the patch matching results between each $\hat{I}^r$ and I^t.

2.1   The Proposed Network

As can be observed in Fig. 1, the proposed network consists of two components: the noise inference network (NiNet) and the external high-frequency compensation network (EhNet). The first component NiNet proposed by [19] is utilized to infer a noise map from the noisy image $\tilde{I}$. As shown in Fig. 1, $\tilde{I}$ is directly used as the input of NiNet. The size of convolutional layers is $h \times w \times *$, where h and w are the height and the width of the input image, respectively. Except for the last layer, there are 64 filters with the size $3 \times 3 \times c$ to generate feature maps in each layer. c is 1 in the first layer and 64 for the rest. The rectified linear units (ReLU) are utilized for nonlinearity and batch normalization is utilized between convolution and Relu in the intermediate layers. One $3 \times 3 \times 64$ filter is used in the last layer to estimate the noise map.

With the inferred noise map, the intermediate image I^t is then generated as follows:

$$I^t = \tilde{I} \ominus \varphi(\tilde{I}), \tag{1}$$

where $\ominus$ is the direct minus operation between $\tilde{I}$ and $\varphi(\tilde{I})$. $\varphi(\tilde{I})$ represents the process that infers the noise map from $\tilde{I}$ using NiNet. The training loss function of NiNet is defined by the MSE between I^t and the ground truth signal.

NiNet works well in predicting the noise map and removing the noise from the input image. However, during the removal process, it also essentially leads to losing some HF information, as shown in Fig. 2(b). This inspires us to construct EhNet to extract a significant EHF map $\hat{I}_m^r$ from each aligned reference image $\hat{I}^r$ for further compensation.

During the training process of EhNet, $\hat{I}^r$ is utilized as the input. In particular, $\hat{I}^r$ is generated from the ground truth image in the training process of NiNet. The settings of convolutional layers and filters are the same as NiNet, and ReLU is also used for nonlinearity. Besides, the recurrent network is utilized here to accelerate training. With the EHF maps extracted by EhNet, the intermediate image can be enhanced as follows:

$$I^d = I^t \bar{\oplus} \psi(\hat{I}^r), \qquad (2)$$

where ψ is the formulation of the process that extracts the HF map $\hat{I}^r_m$. I^d represents the final result. The operation $\bar{\oplus}$ represents the combination of I^t and $\hat{I}^r_m$. In the training process, operation $\bar{\oplus}$ directly adds $\hat{I}^r_m$ to I_t. In the practical testing process, the EHF maps will be utilized based on patch matching results, which will be elaborated in Sect. 2.3. The training loss function of EhNet is defined as MSE between I^d and the ground truth image.

2.2 References Retrieval and Registration

In the practical testing process, we search for K reference images to extract EHF maps for compensation. The method mentioned in [10] is utilized for retrieving and the immediate image I^t is used as the query image. During the searching process, the SURF detector [2] is first used to detect key points. Then a 144-dimension vector that contains discriminative information is extracted for each patch centered at the key point. Finally, the BOW model [8] is used for indexing and retrieving the reference images with extracted feature vectors.

However, considering different scales and viewpoints factors between I^t and reference images, we cannot directly extract EHF maps from the references and add them to I^t for compensation. As a result, each reference image I^r is aligned to I^t before we extract EHF maps. In order to align these reference images, we first detect SIFT features [11] of I^t and I^r and match their feature points. Then the RANSAC algorithm is performed over the matched points to find the best homography transformation matrix. Finally, the aligned reference images $\{\hat{I}^{r_1}, \hat{I}^{r_2}, ..., \hat{I}^{r_K}\}$ are derived from $\{I^{r_1}, I^{r_2}, ..., I^{r_K}\}$ based on the transformation matrix.

2.3 External High-Frequency Maps Fusion

After obtaining the aligned reference images, the EHF maps are then extracted from each $\hat{I}^r$ by EhNet for compensation. As pixels in the aligned references are still not exactly corresponding to those pixels at the same position in I^t, patch matching is further performed to find corresponding pixels between I^t and each aligned reference image $\hat{I}^r$ to guide the combination between I^t and the extracted EHF maps.

Specifically, I^t is first split into $\sqrt{n} \times \sqrt{n}$ query patches with 4-pixel overlapping. And then for each aligned reference image $\hat{I}^r$, we search for its best matching patch of each query patch within a search window. Since small patches contain little structural information of raw images, patch matching results with small patch sizes are not accurate. Thus we perform the patch matching with large patch sizes. Considering that it is impossible for each large patch in I^t to have an exact corresponding large patch in $\hat{I}^r$, a method that adaptively adjusts

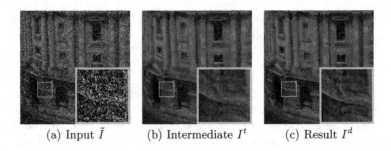

(a) Input $\tilde{I}$ (b) Intermediate I^t (c) Result I^d

Fig. 2. An example of our denoising method at noise level 50.

patch sizes according to patch difference [17] is adopted for more accurate patch matching.

Let $\mathbf{P}_i$ denote the query patch of size $\sqrt{n} \times \sqrt{n}$ in I^t centered at position i and $\mathbf{Q}_j^i$ denote the matching candidate in $\hat{I}^r$ centered at j. For a query patch $\mathbf{P}_i$, we search for its best matching candidate patch with the minimum patch difference within the search window of size $3\sqrt{n} \times 3\sqrt{n}$ centered at i in $\hat{I}^r$. The patch difference between $\mathbf{P}_i$ and $\mathbf{Q}_j^i$ is defined as:

$$d(\mathbf{P}_i, \mathbf{Q}_j^i) = ||\mathbf{P}_i - \mathbf{Q}_j^i||_2^2 + \rho||\nabla(\mathbf{P}_i) - \nabla(\mathbf{Q}_j^i)||_2^2, \tag{3}$$

where ∇ is the operation that calculates the gradient of the patches and ρ is the weighting parameter that controls the relative importance of pixel value differences and their gradient differences, which is empirically set to be 10. Then the value of $d(\mathbf{P}_i, \mathbf{Q}_j^i)/(\sqrt{n} \times \sqrt{n})$ is defined as the gradient mean square error (GMSE) and G_i^{min} is set as the minimum GMSE value between the query patch $\mathbf{P}_i$ and the best candidate patch $\mathbf{Q}_j^i$. In particular, the value of G_i^{min} is consistent with the quality of patch matching. In order to improve the quality of patch matching, patch sizes are then adaptively adjusted according to G_i^{min} as follows:

$$\sqrt{n} = \begin{cases} 21, & G_i^{min} <= 400, \\ 17, & 400 < G_i^{min} <= 600, \\ 13, & 600 < G_i^{min} <= 800, \\ 9, & G_i^{min} > 800. \end{cases} \tag{4}$$

Patch matching is performed at initial size 21×21 and will be adjusted if the value of G_i^{min} is too large according to Eq. 4. Finally the best candidate patch $\mathbf{Q}_{j_0}^i$ will be found.

After patch matching, pixels at the same position in the matched patches between I^t and each $\hat{I}^r$ are matched. Note that since the EHF maps are directly derived from the aligned reference images, the pixel-wise matching correlation between I^t and each $\hat{I}_m^r$ is the same as that of I^t and each $\hat{I}^r$. For pixel $\mathbf{p}$ in I^t, we define the set of its matching pixels in K EHF maps as $\Omega_{\mathbf{p}}$. The final result image I^d is then obtained by combining I^t with the EHF maps as follows:

$$I_{\mathbf{p}}^d = I_{\mathbf{p}}^t + \begin{cases} \dfrac{\displaystyle\sum_{\mathbf{q}\in\Omega_{\mathbf{p}}} \hat{I}_{m,\mathbf{q}}^r \cdot e^{\frac{-d(\mathbf{p},\mathbf{q})}{100}}}{\displaystyle\sum_{\mathbf{q}\in\Omega_{\mathbf{p}}} e^{\frac{-d(\mathbf{p},\mathbf{q})}{100}}}, & |\Omega_{\mathbf{p}}| \neq 0, \\[6pt] 0, & |\Omega_{\mathbf{p}}| = 0, \end{cases} \tag{5}$$

where $I_{\mathbf{p}}^d$ and $I_{\mathbf{p}}^t$ are the values of the pixel $\mathbf{p}$ in image I^d and I^t, respectively. Similarly, $\hat{I}_{m,\mathbf{q}}^r$ is the value of pixel $\mathbf{q}$ in map $\hat{I}_m^r$. $|\Omega_{\mathbf{p}}|$ represents the number of elements in set $\Omega_{\mathbf{p}}$. $d(\mathbf{p},\mathbf{q})$ is the GMSE value between the patches that p and q belong to.

Fig. 3. Testing images from 'a' to 'f'.

3 Experimental Results

We train our EhNet based on 91 images in [16] and 200 training images in *BSD500* [1]. The noisy images are generated by adding Gaussian noise with a random standard deviation of $\sigma \in [0, 55]$. With the mentioned 291 images, we first transfer the images to gray images. Then we generate sub-images at the size of 50×50 from the 291 images with the stride step of 25 pixel. As a result, 45824 sub-images are obtained for training. The learning rate is initially set as 10^{-3}. As for NiNet, weights provided by [19] are directly used.

Table 1. PSNR values of the denoising results of 6 images at noise level 40 by different methods.

Images	BM3D	NCSR	DnCNN	Proposed
a	29.11	29.68	30.45	**30.61**
b	28.26	28.48	29.05	**29.26**
c	27.20	27.57	**28.15**	**28.15**
d	25.90	26.67	27.09	**27.27**
e	26.39	26.75	27.31	**27.43**
f	28.69	28.99	29.52	**29.70**
Avg.	27.67	28.11	28.68	**28.85**

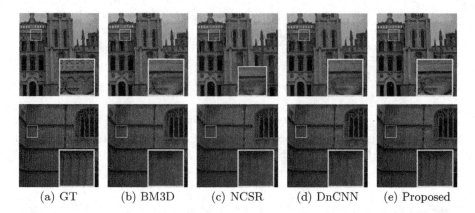

(a) GT   (b) BM3D   (c) NCSR   (d) DnCNN   (e) Proposed

Fig. 4. Subjective results of different methods at noise level 40 for images 'a' and 'f'. The regions with HF signals have been highlighted in the red rectangle and enlarged for comparison. (Color figure online)

Table 2. Average PSNR and SSIM values of the results at noise level 30, 40 and 50 by different methods.

Noise level	BM3D	NCSR	DnCNN	Proposed
30	28.07	29.37	29.93	**30.12**
	0.7599	0.8068	0.8232	**0.8392**
40	27.67	28.11	28.68	**28.85**
	0.7490	0.7661	0.7844	**0.7998**
50	27.27	27.21	27.77	**27.89**
	0.7356	0.7353	0.7529	**0.7662**

We compare our algorithm with different denoising methods including a single image based denoising method BM3D [4] and a dictionary based method NCSR [5]. Besides, the intermediate images derived by NiNet [19] are also shown and named as DnCNN. DnCNN is one of the newest deep based denoising methods without using external references. The Oxford Building dataset[1] is utilized to simulate the web images. There are totally 6 testing images named from 'a' to 'f' for comparison, as shown in Fig. 3. The reference images number K is set to be 4.

Table 1 shows the objective results of the 6 testing images at noise level 40. Our proposed method has obtained the best PSNR values for all of the 6 images. We also show average PSNR and SSIM values for the 6 images at different noise levels in Table 2. Our method outperforms all the other methods at each noise level in PSNR and SSIM values.

---

[1] http://www.robots.ox.ac.uk/~vgg/data/oxbuildings/.

Subjective results are shown in Fig. 4. The other three methods all fail to preserve some HF signal while removing the noise. On the contrary, our method successfully extracts some HF information from the reference images and compensates for the HF loss in noise removal, which is well identified by the subjective results. Our method indeed achieves a much better success in visual quality recovering the lost HF signal.

4 Conclusion

In this paper, we propose a deep online compensation network for image denoising. With the noise map estimated by NiNet, we initially obtain an intermediate image by removing the noise map. Then the EHF maps of the aligned reference images are further extracted for compensation. The final compensated denoising result is obtained by fusing the EHF maps with the intermediate image. Extensive experimental results demonstrate that the proposed method can well extract external HF maps from the reference images and significantly improve the denoising results via compensating for HF information loss with EHF maps.

References

1. Arbelaez, P., Maire, M., Fowlkes, C., Malik, J.: Contour detection and hierarchical image segmentation. IEEE Trans. Pattern Anal. Mach. Intell. **33**(5), 898–916 (2011)
2. Bay, H., Ess, A., Tuytelaars, T., Gool, L.V.: Speeded-up robust features (SURF). Comput. Vis. Image Understanding **110**(3), 346–359 (2008)
3. Chen, Y., Pock, T.: Trainable nonlinear reaction diffusion: a flexible framework for fast and effective image restoration. IEEE Trans. Pattern Anal. Mach. Intell. **PP**(99), 1 (2016)
4. Dabov, K., Foi, A., Katkovnik, V., Egiazarian, K.: Image denoising by sparse 3-D transform-domain collaborative filtering. IEEE Trans. Image Process. **16**(8), 2080–2095 (2007)
5. Dong, W., Zhang, L., Shi, G., Li, X.: Nonlocally centralized sparse representation for image restoration. IEEE Trans. Image Process. **22**(4), 1620–1630 (2013)
6. Elad, M., Aharon, M.: Image denoising via sparse and redundant representations over learned dictionaries. IEEE Trans. Image Process. **15**(12), 3736–3745 (2006)
7. Guerrero-Colon, J.A., Portilla, J.: Two-level adaptive denoising using Gaussian scale mixtures in overcomplete oriented pyramids. In: Proceedings of IEEE International Conference Image Processing, vol. 1, pp. 105–108, September 2005
8. Li, F., Perona, P.: A Bayesian hierarchical model for learning natural scene categories. In: Proceedings of IEEE International Conference Computer Vision and Pattern Recognition, pp. 524–531 (2005)
9. Li, X., Orchard, M.T.: Spatially adaptive image denoising under overcomplete expansion. In: Proceedings of IEEE International Conference Image Processing, vol. 3, pp. 300–303 (2000)
10. Liu, J., Yang, W., Zhang, X., Guo, Z.: Retrieval compensated group structured sparsity for image super-resolution. IEEE Trans. Multimedia **19**(2), 302–316 (2017)

11. Lowe, D.: Distinctive image features from scale-invariant keypoints. Int. J. Comput. Vis. **60**(2), 91–110 (2004)
12. Mairal, J., Bach, F., Ponce, J., Sapiro, G., Zisserman, A.: Non-local sparse models for image restoration. In: 2009 IEEE 12th International Conference on Computer Vision, pp. 2272–2279, September 2009
13. Ren, J., Liu, J., Guo, Z.: Context-aware sparse decomposition for image denoising and super-resolution. IEEE Trans. Image Process. **22**(4), 1456–1469 (2013)
14. Schmidt, U., Roth, S.: Shrinkage fields for effective image restoration. In: Proceedings of IEEE International Conference Computer Vision and Pattern Recognition, pp. 2774–2781, June 2014
15. Timofte, R., Smet, V., Gool, L.: Semantic super-resolution: when and where is it useful? Comput. Vis. Image Underst. **142**, 1–12 (2016)
16. Yang, J., Wright, J., Huang, T., Ma, Y.: Image super-resolution via sparse representation. IEEE Trans. Image Process. **19**(11), 2861–2873 (2010)
17. Yue, H., Sun, X., Yang, J., Wu, F.: Landmark image super-resolution by retrieving web images. IEEE Trans. Image Process. **22**(12), 4865–4875 (2013)
18. Yue, H., Sun, X., Yang, J., Wu, F.: CID: combined image denoising in spatial and frequency domains using web images. In: Proceedings of IEEE International Conference Computer Vision and Pattern Recognition, pp. 2933–2940, June 2014
19. Zhang, K., Zuo, W., Chen, Y., Meng, D., Zhang, L.: Beyond a gaussian denoiser: residual learning of deep CNN for image denoising. IEEE Trans. Image Process. **26**(7), 3142–3155 (2017)

Vehicle Verification Based on Deep Siamese Network with Similarity Metric

Qian Zhang[1], Mingtao Pei[1(✉)], Mei Chen[2], and Yunde Jia[1]

[1] Beijing Lab of Intelligent Information, School of Computer Science,
Beijing Institute of Technology, Beijing 100081, China
{zhang_qian,peimt,jiayunde}@bit.edu.cn
[2] Department: Electrical and Computer Engineering,
State University of New York at Albany, Albany, NY 12222, USA
meichen@albany.edu

Abstract. Vehicle verification is a challenging research problem with important practical applications. Most prior work focused on either feature learning or distance metric learning, which could not guarantee the compatibility of the learned feature and the distance metric. In this paper, we propose an end-to-end model based on the Siamese Convolutional Neural Network (CNN), which integrates distance metric learning and feature learning into a unified framework. The network is trained by contrastive loss and a similarity metric loss defined by joint Bayesian to learn more discriminative features for vehicle verification. The experimental results demonstrate the effectiveness of the proposed method.

Keywords: Vehicle verification · Siamese network
Joint Bayesian · Similarity metric

1 Introduction

Vehicle verification is the problem of determining whether two images are of the same vehicle. It has wide applications in public security systems. Many factors make it challenging to identify a vehicle when the license plate is unavailable, such as illumination variations and different viewing angles. In addition, the lack of available vehicle datasets also brings difficulty on the further exploration of vehicle verification task, as mentioned in [13]. Compared with face verification or person re-identification, vehicle verification is considerably more challenging due to often higher intra-vehicle variations and lower inter-vehicle variations.

Recent works in verification mainly consider two components: feature extraction and distance metric learning, and methods employing the deep learning framework typically outperform those based on handcrafted features. However, most researchers focus on either distance metric learning or deep feature extraction, which cannot guarantee the compatibility between the feature and the metric.

© Springer International Publishing AG, part of Springer Nature 2018
B. Zeng et al. (Eds.): PCM 2017, LNCS 10735, pp. 773–782, 2018.
https://doi.org/10.1007/978-3-319-77380-3_74

In this paper, we propose an end-to-end model based on the deep Siamese network [5], which integrates metric learning and feature learning into a unified framework, as shown in Fig. 1. The input of our network is a pair of images, and the output is whether the two images are of the same vehicle. We use two loss functions to train the deep Siamese network. One is the original contrastive loss, and the other is a similarity metric loss defined by joint Bayesian [2]. In this way, we can train the network in an end-to-end manner to guarantee the compatibility of the learned feature and the learned distance metric.

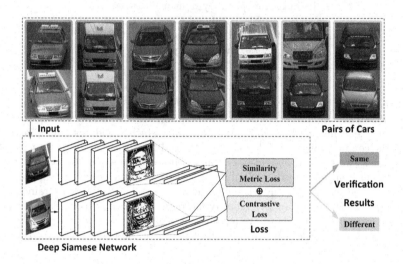

Fig. 1. Our proposed model for vehicle verification.

2   Related Work

Vehicle verification is quite a challenging task to achieve satisfactory results due to many complex factors such as scene illumination variation and alterable viewing angle. The lack of available vehicle datasets results in less effective research work. Fortunately, these problems also occur in face verification [4,8,20] and person re-identification [15,24], and a common solution has been given which can be divided into feature extraction and distance metric learning.

2.1   Feature Extraction

Previous research on verification or re-identification primarily makes use of hand-crafted features to model the transformation of person's appearance, such as color and texture histograms, local binary patterns and local patches. Lu et al. [14] proposed a principled multi-task learning approach based on Gaussian-Face. Li [17] and Chen [2,3] depicted the face image as a summation of extra-person and inner-person variations. However, complex illumination variation and changeable viewing angle could impact on the feature descriptors so heavily that the performance of these methods seems not very satisfactory. Especially, it even requires deep domain knowledge to select suitable features to cope with individual variations in person re-identification.

Thanks to the success of deep learning, we can use deep features rather than handcrafted ones to make the verification model more adaptive. Sun et al. [19] learned features of face images by multiple convolutional network groups for face verification. Ahmed et al. [1] proposed a specifically designed deep neural network, by which the person re-identification task is formulated as a binary classification problem and the final estimate can be obtained from a softmax function in the last layer. As for vehicle image processing, there are more researches dealing with vehicle model recognition. Liang et al. [12] counted and classified highway vehicles based on regression analysis. In [21], Wang et al. achieved vehicle categorization by using an audio-visual sensing system. To handle automatic vehicle recognition in multiple cameras, Rao [18] proposed a level-based region comparison algorithm.

2.2   Distance Metric Learning

The distance metric also plays a role in verification or re-identification tasks. In face verification, Taigman et al. [20] concentrated on the classification of differences between two face images. Ding et al. [6] proposed a triplet based model which takes a large number of triplet units as input to generate layered representations, and maximized the relative $L2$ distance between any pair of faces for each unit by optimizing a triplet loss function [10]. By using an effective triplet generation scheme and an optimized gradient descent algorithm, it makes the number of images instead of triplets matter the computational load. In [2], joint Bayesian method modeled the joint distribution of the face pairs rather than the difference only, and considered the ratio of intra-personal and extra-personal variation as distance metric. In person re-identification, Zheng et al. proposed a Probabilistic Relative Distance Comparison (PRDC) model [25] to maximize the likelihood such that the similarity of pairs can be measured directly by distance. Mignon et al. exploited Pairwise Constrained Component Analysis (PCCA) [16] and projected the original data into a lower dimension space to represent the actual relationship between two images. Li et al. [11] introduced a decision function as a joint model of a distance metric and a locally adaptive thresholding rule, which performed well on both human body verification and face verification tasks.

Based on the distance metric algorithms [22,23] applied in face verification and person re-identification problems, more reliable distance metric can be adopted in vehicle verification combined with feature extraction. The most closely related approach [13] of vehicle re-identification provided a Deep Relative Distance Learning (DRDL) model which projected the raw vehicle images into an Euclidean space and measured the difference by $L2$ distance. Liu et al. [13] introduced the coupled clusters loss function and the mixed difference network structure to the framework to maximize the relative distance between two sample features. Nevertheless, the model requires plenty of positive samples to construct the center point used in coupled clusters loss function despite it has validity in testing stage.

3   Proposed Method

We train our model in an iterative way. First, we use the network pre-trained by the contrastive loss to extract features from the training data, and compute the parameters of the similarity metric loss. Then, we fix the parameters in the similarity metric loss function and train the network by both of them. After that, we use the retrained network to extract features before updating the parameters in the similarity metric loss function and retrain the network again.

3.1   The Contrastive Loss

The network takes pairs of vehicle images as input during the forward propagation, and the contrastive loss function [7] is defined as

$$L_c(w, y, \overrightarrow{x_1}, \overrightarrow{x_2}) = \frac{1}{2N} \sum_{n=1}^{N} y d_w(\overrightarrow{x_1}, \overrightarrow{x_2})^2 + (1 - y)\{\max(margin_1 - d_w(\overrightarrow{x_1}, \overrightarrow{x_2}), 0)\}^2,$$

(1)

where $d_w(\overrightarrow{x_1}, \overrightarrow{x_2})$ is the Euclidean distance between two sample features x_1 and x_2, and y is a binary label. The $margin_1$ as the pre-set threshold is a positive number, which defines a radius around the value of sample features. The symmetric architecture with contrastive loss function remains the relationship between the input vehicle image pairs in feature space.

3.2   Similarity Metric Loss

As the contrastive loss only estimates the Euclidean distance between samples, it does not consider the intra-vehicle and inter-vehicle variations. We propose a similarity metric loss defined by joint Bayesian [2] to enhance the discriminative power of the learned feature.

The feature representation of a vehicle is made up of two parts, including identity μ to denote different vehicles, and intra-vehicle variations ε to capture the same vehicle under various conditions. We assume both μ and ε can be represented by a Gaussian distribution. For the input vehicle features x_1 and x_2, we have two hypotheses: H_i means they are intra-vehicle, i.e., they represent the same vehicle; and H_e means they are extra-vehicle, i.e., they represent different vehicles.

Based on the above assumptions, log-likelihood ratio obtained after an algebraic transformation is given by

$$r(x_1, x_2) = log\frac{P(x_1, x_2|H_I)}{P(x_1, x_2|H_E)} = x_1^T A x_1 + x_2^T A x_2 - 2x_1^T G x_2,$$

(2)

where A is a positive semi-definite matrix defined as

$$A = (S_\mu + S_\varepsilon)^{-1} - (F + G). \tag{3}$$

Now the unknown covariance matrices S_μ and S_ε need to be solved by model training, in which an EM-like algorithm is adopted. In E-step, F and G are calculated as

$$F = S_\varepsilon^{-1}, \tag{4}$$

$$G = -(mS_\mu + S_\varepsilon)^{-1} S_\mu S_\varepsilon^{-1}, \tag{5}$$

then F and G are used to solve the latent variables μ and ε. In M-step, the parameter $\{S_\mu, S_\varepsilon\}$ is updated as

$$S_\mu = cov(\mu) = n^{-1} \sum_i \mu_i \mu_i^T, \tag{6}$$

$$S_\varepsilon = cov(\varepsilon) = n^{-1} \sum_i \sum_j \varepsilon_{ij} \varepsilon_{ij}^T, \tag{7}$$

where the two steps are repeatedly executed until S_μ and S_ε converge.

The joint Bayesian ratio $r(x_1, x_2)$ between two sample features x_1 and x_2 can be described as a log-likelihood ratio with any value in the range from negative infinity to positive infinity. Based on the joint Bayesian ratio, most methods learn distance metric from extracted features independently, thus cannot guarantee the compatibility of the learned feature and the distance metric.

In our framework, we employ the ratio as a distance measurement of the input image pairs, and add a new loss defined by joint Bayesian to our two-branch Siamese network. Specifically, we map the ratio into zero to positive infinity using an exponential function, and define our *similarity metric loss* as

$$L_{sm}(\vec{x_1}, \vec{x_2}, y) = \frac{1}{2N} \sum_{n=1}^{N} y e^{-r(x_1, x_2)} + (1 - y)\left\{\max\left(margin_2 - e^{-r(x_1, x_2)}, 0\right)\right\}, \tag{8}$$

where $r(x_1, x_2)$ is the joint Bayesian ratio as in Eq. 2, and y is a binary label. The $margin_2$ is a pre-set threshold which is a positive number, and also defines a radius around the ratio value of learned feature. The similarity metric loss function produces a loss whose value influences weight updates in the network.

By applying the original contrastive loss as well as the similarity metric loss, we describe the final loss function to be

$$L_{final} = L_c(w, y, \vec{x_1}, \vec{x_2}) + \alpha L_{sm}(\vec{x_1}, \vec{x_2}, y), \tag{9}$$

where α is chosen to multiply L_{sm} to a more suitable scale.

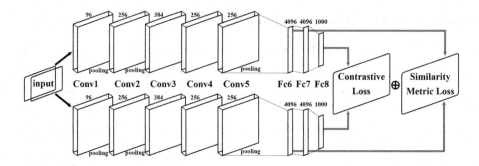

Fig. 2. The proposed network structure.

3.3 Integrated Model Structure

Figure 2 shows the proposed network structure. Our network contains 5 convolutional layers and 3 fully connected layers. The parameters in each convolutional layer are shared between the two branches. The dimension of "Fc6", "Fc7" and "Fc8" is 4096, 4096 and 1000, respectively.

The contrastive loss is added to the "Fc8" layer, and the proposed similarity metric loss is added to the "Fc6" layer to better supervise early feature extraction processes. We find that adding the proposed similarity metric loss to the "Fc6" layer rather than "Fc7" and "Fc8" can obtain 10%–15% improvement in accuracy.

4   Experiments

4.1 Experimental Settings

DataSets. We build a vehicle verification dataset called CarCP which includes 1000 image pairs of different vehicles. The images are captured from two different cameras located at the entrance and the exit of a public parking lot. The resolution of the images is 1600×1200 pixels. The dataset contains changes in illumination, scale, and viewpoint. We split the 1000 image pairs (a total of 2000 images) into a probe set and a gallery set. In our case, the probe set contains 1000 vehicle images to be recognized, and the gallery set consists of 1000 images against which a probe image is matched.

We also test our method on the VehicleID dataset [13] which contains over 200,000 images of about 26,000 vehicles. We use the same data split as [13]. The training data contains 110,178 images of 13,134 vehicles, and the testing data contains three subsets (small, medium and large) ordered by their size. Table 1 shows the details of these two datasets. All samples are scaled to 227×227 pixel gray-scale images to train and test the network, and the license plate area in each image is blocked.

Table 1. Detailed information of two datasets

Detail of datasets	VehicleID			CarCP
	Small	Medium	Large	
Number of vehicles	800	1600	2400	1000
Number of images	6492	13377	19777	2000
Gallery size	800	1600	2400	1000
Probe size	5692	11777	17377	1000

Deep Siamese Network Training. Our network is trained on VehicleID using the deep learning framework Caffe. Specifically, there are 450,000 pairs of samples in the training data, including 300,000 negative pairs and 150,000 positive pairs. The network is trained by the stochastic gradient descent with momentum of 0.9 and weight decay of 2×10^{-4}. The optimal batch-size is 32 and the learning rate decreased according to the polynomial policy is set as 0.01.

4.2   Comparison with Baseline Methods

We construct four baselines to evaluate the proposed method. The first baseline uses a single-branch network BvlcNet [9] with softmax loss to extract features, and uses the Euclidean distance as the distance metric for vehicle verification. The second one uses the same BvlcNet with softmax loss to extract features and joint Bayesian as the distance metric. The third one uses the Siamese network with the original contrastive loss to learn features and the Euclidean distance as the distance metric. The fourth one uses the same Siamese network with contrastive loss to learn features and joint Bayesian as the distance metric. These baseline methods are trained on the same training data of the VehicleID dataset.

We evaluate the four baselines and our method on the CarCP dataset. The comparison results are listed in Table 2. We can see that the two-branch Siamese network performs better than single branch BvlcNet as a whole, both on the Euclidean distance and joint Bayesian distance metric.

Table 2. Comparisons of matching rate with other solutions on CarCP dataset

Match rate	Accuracy rank				
	Top 1	Top 3	Top 5	Top 8	Top 10
Siamese+Similarity metric loss (ours)	**0.764**	**0.825**	**0.869**	**0.894**	**0.912**
Siamese+JointBayes	0.694	0.749	0.766	0.781	0.792
Siamese+Euclidean	0.494	0.659	0.759	0.824	0.841
BvlcNet+JointBayes	0.541	0.70	0.776	0.829	0.859
BvlcNet+Euclidean	0.294	0.406	0.459	0.535	0.565

It is noticed that two-branch Siamese network achieves higher accuracy as pairwise images are employed as input which contributes to feature learning. In addition, joint Bayesian distance metric performs better than the Euclidean distance on both the Siamese network and the Bvlcnet as it takes both intra-vehicle and inter-vehicle variations into consideration. Our proposed method works better than all the baselines because it makes the learned feature more compatible with joint Bayesian distance metric.

4.3   Comparison with State-of-the-Art Methods

We compare our method with several state-of-the-art methods, including VGG+Triplet Loss [6], VGG+CCL [13] and Mixed Diff+CCL [13]. The comparison results show that our method outperforms VGG+Triplet Loss and VGG+CCL, and obtains comparable results as Mixed Diff+CCL, as shown in Table 3.

Table 3. Comparisons of matching rate with state-of-the-art results on VehicleID dataset

Match rate		Small	Medium	Large
VGG+Triplet loss [6]	Top 1	0.404	0.354	0.319
VGG+CCL [13]		0.436	0.370	0.329
Mixed Diff+CCL [13]		0.490	0.428	0.382
Siamese+Similarity metric loss (ours)		**0.488**	**0.427**	**0.380**
VGG+Triplet loss [6]	Top 5	0.617	0.546	0.503
VGG+CCL [13]		0.642	0.571	0.533
Mixed Diff+CCL [13]		0.735	0.668	0.616
Siamese+Similarity metric loss (ours)		**0.734**	**0.671**	**0.614**

The triplet loss used in [6] can generate more constrains for distance metric learning, but the loss function is sensitive to the selection of anchor points. This means that poorly selected anchors might result in interference in the training stage and lead to slow convergence. The Coupled Clusters Loss used in [13] is defined over multiple samples and needs to estimate the center point. When there is not enough samples per vehicle, it reduces to the triplet loss. In contrast, our similarity metric loss is trained on image pairs, which does not need the generation of triplet units and the selection of anchor point. Our method achieves results comparable to the state-of-the-art with easily collected image pairs.

5   Conclusion

In this paper, we propose a two-branch deep convolutional network for vehicle verification, with contrastive loss and a similarity metric loss derived from joint

Bayesian. Joint Bayesian considers both inter-vehicle and intra-vehicle variations to preserve the discriminative information. Feature extraction and distance metric learning are integrated in our network, which are jointly optimized to guarantee the compatibility of the learned feature and the distance metric. The experiments demonstrate that by incorporating the proposed similarity metric loss, our model achieves performance on par with the state-of-the-art methods.

Acknowledgments. This work was supported in part by the Natural Science Foundation of China (NSFC) under Grant No. 61472038 and No. 61375044.

References

1. Ahmed, E., Jones, M., Marks, T.K.: An improved deep learning architecture for person re-identification. In: IEEE Conference on Computer Vision and Pattern Recognition (CVPR), pp. 3908–3916 (2015)
2. Chen, D., Cao, X., Wang, L., Wen, F., Sun, J.: Bayesian face revisited: a joint formulation. In: Fitzgibbon, A., Lazebnik, S., Perona, P., Sato, Y., Schmid, C. (eds.) ECCV 2012. LNCS, vol. 7574, pp. 566–579. Springer, Heidelberg (2012). https://doi.org/10.1007/978-3-642-33712-3_41
3. Chen, D., Cao, X., Wen, F., Sun, J.: Blessing of dimensionality: high-dimensional feature and its efficient compression for face verification. In: IEEE Conference on Computer Vision and Pattern Recognition (CVPR), pp. 3025–3032 (2013)
4. Chen, J.C., Patel, V.M., Chellappa, R.: Unconstrained face verification using deep CNN features. In: IEEE Winter Conference on Applications of Computer Vision (WACV), pp. 1–9. IEEE (2016)
5. Chopra, S., Hadsell, R., LeCun, Y.: Learning a similarity metric discriminatively, with application to face verification. In: IEEE Conference on Computer Vision and Pattern Recognition (CVPR), vol. 1, pp. 539–546. IEEE (2005)
6. Ding, S., Lin, L., Wang, G., Chao, H.: Deep feature learning with relative distance comparison for person re-identification. Pattern Recogn. 48(10), 2993–3003 (2015)
7. Hadsell, R., Chopra, S., LeCun, Y.: Dimensionality reduction by learning an invariant mapping. In: IEEE Conference on Computer Vision and Pattern Recognition (CVPR), vol. 2, pp. 1735–1742. IEEE (2006)
8. Hu, J., Lu, J., Tan, Y.P.: Discriminative deep metric learning for face verification in the wild. In: IEEE Conference on Computer Vision and Pattern Recognition (CVPR), pp. 1875–1882 (2014)
9. Jia, Y., Shelhamer, E., Donahue, J., Karayev, S., Long, J., Girshick, R., Guadarrama, S., Darrell, T.: Caffe: convolutional architecture for fast feature embedding. In: the 22nd ACM International Conference on Multimedia (ACM MM), pp. 675–678. ACM (2014)
10. Kwong, K., Kavaler, R., Rajagopal, R., Varaiya, P.: Arterial travel time estimation based on vehicle re-identification using wireless magnetic sensors. Transp. Res. Part C: Emerg. Technol. 17(6), 586–606 (2009)
11. Li, Z., Chang, S., Liang, F., Huang, T.S., Cao, L., Smith, J.R.: Learning locally-adaptive decision functions for person verification. In: IEEE Conference on Computer Vision and Pattern Recognition (CVPR), pp. 3610–3617 (2013)
12. Liang, M., Huang, X., Chen, C.H., Chen, X., Tokuta, A.: Counting and classification of highway vehicles by regression analysis. IEEE Trans. Intell. Transp. Syst. (TITS) 16(5), 2878–2888 (2015)

13. Liu, H., Tian, Y., Yang, Y., Pang, L., Huang, T.: Deep relative distance learning: tell the difference between similar vehicles. In: IEEE Conference on Computer Vision and Pattern Recognition (CVPR), pp. 2167–2175 (2016)
14. Lu, C., Tang, X.: Surpassing human-level face verification performance on LFW with GaussianFace. In: Twenty-Ninth AAAI Conference on Artificial Intelligence (AAAI) (2015)
15. Martinel, N., Micheloni, C., Foresti, G.L.: Saliency weighted features for person re-identification. In: Agapito, L., Bronstein, M.M., Rother, C. (eds.) ECCV 2014. LNCS, vol. 8927, pp. 191–208. Springer, Cham (2015). https://doi.org/10.1007/978-3-319-16199-0_14
16. Mignon, A., Jurie, F.: PCCA: a new approach for distance learning from sparse pairwise constraints. In: IEEE Conference on Computer Vision and Pattern Recognition (CVPR), pp. 2666–2672. IEEE (2012)
17. Prince, S., Li, P., Fu, Y., Mohammed, U., Elder, J.: Probabilistic models for inference about identity. IEEE Trans. Pattern Anal. Mach. Intell. (PAMI) **34**(1), 144–157 (2012)
18. Rao, Y.: Automatic vehicle recognition in multiple cameras for video surveillance. Vis. Comput. **31**(3), 271–280 (2015)
19. Sun, Y., Wang, X., Tang, X.: Hybrid deep learning for face verification. In: IEEE International Conference on Computer Vision (ICCV), pp. 1489–1496 (2013)
20. Taigman, Y., Yang, M., Ranzato, M., Wolf, L.: Deepface: closing the gap to human-level performance in face verification. In: IEEE Conference on Computer Vision and Pattern Recognition (CVPR), pp. 1701–1708 (2014)
21. Wang, T., Zhu, Z., Hammoud, R.: Audio-visual feature fusion for vehicles classification in a surveillance system. In: IEEE Conference on Computer Vision and Pattern Recognition Workshops (CVPRW), pp. 381–386 (2013)
22. Weinberger, K.Q., Saul, L.K.: Distance metric learning for large margin nearest neighbor classification. J. Mach. Learn. Res. **10**(Feb), 207–244 (2009)
23. Xiang, S., Nie, F., Zhang, C.: Learning a Mahalanobis distance metric for data clustering and classification. Pattern Recogn. **41**(12), 3600–3612 (2008)
24. Zhang, Z., Chen, Y., Saligrama, V.: A novel visual word co-occurrence model for person re-identification. arXiv preprint arXiv:1410.6532 (2014)
25. Zheng, W.S., Gong, S., Xiang, T.: Person re-identification by probabilistic relative distance comparison. In: IEEE Conference on Computer Vision and Pattern Recognition (CVPR), pp. 649–656. IEEE (2011)

Style Transfer with Content Preservation from Multiple Images

Dilin Liu$^{(\boxtimes)}$, Wei Yu, and Hongxun Yao

Harbin Institute of Technology, Harbin, China
{liudilin,h.yao}@hit.edu.cn, yuwei.hit@outlook.com

Abstract. Artistic style transfer is an image synthesis problem where the style of input image is reproduced with the style of given examples. Recent works show that artistic style transfer can be achieved by using hidden activations of a pretrained model. However, most existing methods only allow one example image representing style. In this work, we propose a framework based on neural patches matching that combines the content structure and style textures in a fusion layer of the network. Our method is capable to extract the style from a group of images, such as the paintings of specific painter. In particular, our method can preserve the original content information. Furthermore, by using multiple style images our approach can obtain desirable synthesis results in foreground objects.

Keywords: Texture synthesis · Style transfer
Convolutional neural network

1 Introduction

Famous artists are typically renowned for a particular artistic style and create literatures with their certain style. This motivates us to explore efficient computational strategies to create artistic images by examples. Many approaches focus on the problem of transferring the desired style from single painting to other images with similar content, mostly photographs. These are known as artistic style transfer in computer graphics and vision.

The key challenges of artistic style transfer problem are to capture the structure and color information of complex paintings. There have been many efforts to develop efficient methods for automatic style transfer. Many classic data-driven approaches [1–3] to the task are based on Markov Random Field that models characterize from images by statistics of local patches of pixels. Recently, deep neural networks models have shown exciting new perspective for image synthesis [4,5]. Subsequent work has improved both speed [6] and quality [7]. However, we found that most existing deep learning based approaches are designed to synthesis texture from only one single image. Their approaches only extract feature from one style image and the models are lack of ability to learn the common style of multiple paintings.

© Springer International Publishing AG, part of Springer Nature 2018
B. Zeng et al. (Eds.): PCM 2017, LNCS 10735, pp. 783–791, 2018.
https://doi.org/10.1007/978-3-319-77380-3_75

(a) Content image   (b) Style images   (c) Our transfer result

(d) Different results using single style image in transfer

Fig. 1. Overview of our synthesis result using multiple example images. (a) Is the input content image. (b) Is three style images from *Vincent Willem van Gogh*. (c) Our result are generated with multiple style inputs where edges of the squirrel is well preserved. (d) Are the synthesis results using corresponding style image from content image.

In this paper, we propose an architecture of discriminative network which can extract the unified style from multiple images. Figure 1 shows the comparison of different synthesis results. Our idea is to evaluate the similarity between fused neural patch features sampled from the synthesis image and from different example images. The features are extracted from different networks with combination of both style and content information.

2   Related Work

Style transfer is an active topic in both academia and industry. Traditional methods mainly focus on generating new images by resampling either pixels [2,8] or whole patches [9,10] of the source texture images. Different methods were proposed to improve the quality of the synthesis image.

More recently, neural style transfer [4] has demonstrated impressive results in example-based image stylisation. The method is based on deconvolution on a parametric texture model [11,12] by summarising global covariance statistics of feature vectors on higher network layers. Most prominently, during the stylisation it displays a greater flexibility than traditional models to reconstructs the content that are not present in the source images. However, the representation of image style within the parametric neural texture model allows far less intuitive control and extension than patch-based methods. Our model works on calculating the similarities between neural patches to control the transformation in the guidance of content information. On the theory side, Xie [13] have proved that a generative random field model can be derived from the discriminative networks, and show some applications to unguided texture synthesis.

In very recent, there are a serious of approaches that employ specially trained auto-encoders as generative networks. Generative Adversarial Networks(GANs) use two different networks, one as the discriminator and the other as the generator, to iteratively improve the model by playing a minimax game [14]. The adversarial network models can offer perceptual metrics [15,16] that allows auto-encoders to be training more efficiently. Previous works have trained GANs on kinds of datasets, including discrete labels, text and images. Additionally, Li use GANs to obtain real-time texture synthesis in one-image style transfer [17]. As far as we know, we are the first to generate synthesis image from multiple style examples and learn discriminative features for a specific style.

3   Our Approach

We first introduce our model to perform style transfer on multiple example images. Our goal is to control the stylization to preserve the sematic information in the content image. The main component of our proposed method is a content guidance channel calculated from the content network and serving to texture neural patches matching.

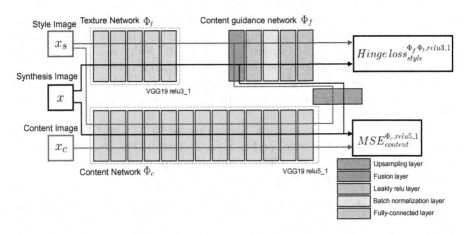

Fig. 2. Overview of our style transfer model. Our model contains a texture network, a content network, and the content guidance network. The content guidance network consists of fusion layer, batch normalization layer, leaky relu layers, and fully-connected layer.

The pipeline of our model is visualized in Fig. 2. The discriminative image synthesizer contains three parts: the texture network and the content network

work on different feature patches extraction and the content guidance network extracts the content guidance feature to the style patches.

The texture network is trained to distinguish between neural patches sampled from the synthesis image and sampled from the example images. It outputs a classification score for each neural patch, indicating the similarity of the patch matched with training data. For each patch sampled from the synthesized image, its similarity to patches from example images is maximized. The fusion layer consists of the output on layer relu3_1 of VGG_19 and the output of our proposed content guidance channel.

The content guidance network is connected to layer relu5_1 of VGG_19 and upsampling by using the nearest neighbour technique so that the output is the same size of the neural patches in texture network. The convolutional and upsampling layers ensure that features corresponding to neural patches contain the content information from a larger region than the representation of texture neural patches. Thus the output of the fusion layer for texture loss calculation is written as:

$$\Phi(x_f) = \sigma \left(\mathbf{b} + W \begin{bmatrix} \Phi(x) \\ \Phi(x_t) \end{bmatrix} \right) \tag{1}$$

where $\Phi(x_f)$ is the fused feature, $\Phi(x)$ represent the neural patches of the iterative image and $\Phi(x_t)$ is the corresponding content guided feature from layer relu5_1 of VGG_19. $\sigma(\cdot)$ is the Sigmoid non-linear transfer function and W is the weight matrix of the fusion layer, b is a bias. Here both W and b are learnable part of the network. Our style transfer approach concatenates the content and style information into the fused feature vector. The deconvolution progress back-propagates the loss to pixels in the synthesis image until the discriminative network recognize the patches as samples from the example images with similar content. We use batch normalization layer (BN) and leaky ReLU (LReLU) to decline the overfitting in the iteration progress as Radford [18] did.

The content network calculate the Mean Squared Error (MSE) between the synthesis image and the content image from the output on the abstract layer Relu5_1 as the content loss function.

Formally, we denote the example texture image by x_t, and the synthesized image by x. We initialize x with random noise and iterate the image in the guidance from the content image x_c. The deconvolution progress iteratively updates x until the following energy is minimized:

$$x^* = \arg\min_x E_t(x, x_t) + \alpha_1 E_c(x, x_c) + \alpha_2 \gamma(x) \tag{2}$$

E_t denotes the texture loss, in which x_f is the output of fusion feature layer. We sample nerual patches from the synthesized image x, and compute E_t using the Hinge loss with their guidance features fixed to the most similar patch in content:

$$E_t(x, x_t) = \frac{1}{N} \sum_{i=1}^{N} \max(0, 1 - s(\Phi_i(x_f))) \tag{3}$$

where $s(\Phi_i(x_f))$ is the classification score of i-th fusion feature that consists of the texture neural patch and the content guidance feature. N is the total number of sampled patches.

The content loss is the Mean Squared Error between the two feature maps x and x_c. By minimizing an additional content loss E_c, the network can generate an image that is contextually related to a guidance image x_c.

To perform the training of proposed discriminative network, the parameters are randomly initialized and then updated after each iteration. The synthesis image will go through both three parts in each iteration then the networks will back-propagate the loss to pixels. We set the weights with $\alpha_1 = 1$ and $\alpha_2 = 0.0001$, and minimize Eq. 2 using back-propagation. The additional regularizer $\gamma(x)$ is a smoothness prior for the synthesis image [19].

4 Experimental Results and Analyses

In this section, we analyze the improvement of proposed content preserving style transfer model. We use the Torch7 framework [20] to implement our model and use existing open source implementations of prior works [1,4,17] for comparison. We choose two groups of *Vincent Willem van Gogh's* painting in different theme ("night star" and "yellow field") as example images. For the transferred images producing we iterated the synthesis image from the content image as initialization.

First experiment is the comparison of transferring the style of Vincent's painting onto a photo with building content. We use each image in the group of example images as input to get the baseline synthesis image. For comparison we choose Vincent's another painting with building to simulate the condition of transferring from the style image with same content information. Figure 3 shows different results between using one example image and using multiple example images in our method. In the synthesis image of column (a), ceiling lights are almost unrecognized. In the results of column (b)(c), the shape of the building is messed up with the background. By using multiple example images, our style transfer result in column (d) obtain advantages in generating the edges of building where the ceiling lights is clear and the edges of the building is preserved as the original image. With the comparison to the synthesis image of column (e), our method can preserve the building content in style transfer. In Fig. 4 we show more qualitative examples using different groups of style images.

Secondly, in Fig. 5 we compare our synthesis result with existing neural style transfer methods. Since most approaches focus on using only one example images, we choose a group of Vincent's painting in the same theme as example images. The synthesis result from Li [17] is failed to preserve detail of the house content. Gatys's method [4] transfers some houses to black cypress in the style image and colorize the houses with cold color tone. More obviously, the synthesis image from Elad [1] is divided into two kinds of style where houses almost stay in the style of original image with only colorization. In our result, the houses stay the warm color tone as content image and obtain the style of given oil paintings. Our method choose to synthesis sky regions with uniform texture instead

Style images:

(a) Content image   (b)(c)(d) Synthesis result using style image without building

(e) Our synthesis result   (f) Using style image with building

Fig. 3. The comparison of different synthesis strategies using corresponding style images. (b)(c)(d) Are the synthesis results using style images without building from (a) content image. (e) Our synthesis image is comparable to the synthesis image (f) using the style image with building content.

Fig. 4. More qualitative synthesis results using different groups of style inputs.

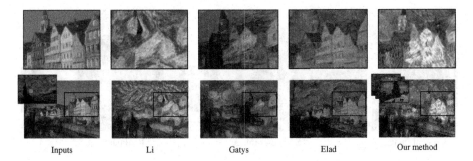

Fig. 5. The comparison of different synthesis strategies using our style transfer method and existing neural network based methods. The results in each column of images are given by (left-to-right): Li [17], Gatys [4], Elad [1] and our method. (Color figure online)

of stars because sky regions in original image match uniform style patches rather than patches sampled from stars. More comparisons of style transfer results are shown in Fig. 6.

Fig. 6. More comparisons with style transfer methods: Chen [21], John [6] and Gatys [4] (Color figure online).

To explore deficiency in our synthesis method, we choose a photo of street cafe for content image because it is similar with Vincent's painting (*Night coffee shop*). We use three painting from Vincent in the same theme of "night star" as style input. The synthesis results are shown in Fig. 7. Our method can transfer the eave and tables to the one in real painting. The colorization of the coffee shop is not real enough. We considerate that cold color patches from style images occupy the majority and the network is in high probability to iterate the synthesis image with cold color tone building.

Content image   Synthesis image   Real painting

Fig. 7. The result of matching the content representation through the network. Texture of the painting and content of the photograph are merged together such as the real painting. (Color figure online)

5 Conclusion

We present a new CNN-based method of artistic style transfer that focus on preserving the content information and adaptability to arbitrary content. Our model concatenates both content and style information into a fusion layer by upsampling features from the content network. It is capable to transfer the style from a group of example images with preserving complex content. Our method is only one step in the direction of learning the relationship between style and content from images. An important avenue for future work would be to study the semantic representation of the style in some certain theme.

Acknowledgement. This work was supported by the National Natural Science Foundation of China under Project No. 61472103.

References

1. Elad, M., Milanfar, P.: Style-transfer via texture-synthesis, arXiv preprint arXiv:1609.03057
2. Efros, A.A., Leung, T.K.: Texture synthesis by non-parametric sampling. In: The Proceedings of the Seventh IEEE International Conference on Computer Vision, vol. 2, pp. 1033–1038. IEEE (1999)
3. Paget, R., Longstaff, I.D.: Texture synthesis via a noncausal nonparametric multiscale markov random field. IEEE Trans. Image Process. 7(6), 925–931 (1998)
4. Gatys, L.A., Ecker, A.S., Bethge, M.: Image style transfer using convolutional neural networks. In: Proceedings of the IEEE Conference on Computer Vision and Pattern Recognition, pp. 2414–2423 (2016)
5. Li, C., Wand, M.: Combining Markov random fields and convolutional neural networks for image synthesis. In: Proceedings of the IEEE Conference on Computer Vision and Pattern Recognition, pp. 2479–2486 (2016)
6. Johnson, J., Alahi, A., Fei-Fei, L.: Perceptual losses for real-time style transfer and super-resolution. In: Leibe, B., Matas, J., Sebe, N., Welling, M. (eds.) ECCV 2016 Part II. LNCS, vol. 9906, pp. 694–711. Springer, Cham (2016). https://doi.org/10.1007/978-3-319-46475-6_43

7. Ulyanov, D., Vedaldi, A., Lempitsky, V.: Improved texture networks: maximizing quality and diversity in feed-forward stylization and texture synthesis, arXiv preprint arXiv:1701.02096
8. Wei, L.-Y., Levoy, M.: Fast texture synthesis using tree-structured vector quantization. In: Proceedings of the 27th Annual Conference on Computer Graphics and Interactive Techniques, pp. 479–488. ACM Press/Addison-Wesley Publishing Co. (2000)
9. Efros, A.A., Freeman, W.T.: Image quilting for texture synthesis and transfer. In: Proceedings of the 28th Annual Conference on Computer Graphics and Interactive Techniques, pp. 341–346. ACM (2001)
10. Kwatra, V., Schödl, A., Essa, I., Turk, G., Bobick, A.: Graphcut textures: image and video synthesis using graph cuts. In: ACM Transactions on Graphics (ToG), vol. 22, pp. 277–286. ACM (2003)
11. Heeger, D.J., Bergen, J.R.: Pyramid-based texture analysis/synthesis. In: Proceedings of the 22nd Annual Conference on Computer Graphics and Interactive Techniques, pp. 229–238. ACM (1995)
12. Portilla, J., Simoncelli, E.P.: A parametric texture model based on joint statistics of complex wavelet coefficients. Int. J. Comput. Vis. **40**(1), 49–70 (2000)
13. Xie, J., Lu, Y., Zhu, S.-C., Wu, Y.N.: A theory of generative convnet, arXiv preprint arXiv:1602.03264
14. Goodfellow, I., Pouget-Abadie, J., Mirza, M., Xu, B., Warde-Farley, D., Ozair, S., Courville, A., Bengio, Y.: Generative adversarial nets. In: Advances in neural information processing systems, pp. 2672–26800 (2014)
15. Dosovitskiy, A., Brox, T.: Generating images with perceptual similarity metrics based on deep networks. In: Advances in Neural Information Processing Systems, pp. 658–666 (2016)
16. Larsen, A.B.L., Sønderby, S.K., Larochelle, H., Winther, O.: Autoencoding beyond pixels using a learned similarity metric, arXiv preprint arXiv:1512.09300
17. Li, C., Wand, M.: Precomputed real-time texture synthesis with markovian generative adversarial networks. In: Leibe, B., Matas, J., Sebe, N., Welling, M. (eds.) ECCV 2016 Part III. LNCS, vol. 9907, pp. 702–716. Springer, Cham (2016). https://doi.org/10.1007/978-3-319-46487-9_43
18. Radford, A., Metz, L., Chintala, S.: Unsupervised representation learning with deep convolutional generative adversarial networks, arXiv preprint arXiv:1511.06434
19. Mahendran, A. Vedaldi, A.: Understanding deep image representations by inverting them. In: Proceedings of the IEEE Conference on Computer Vision and Pattern Recognition, pp. 5188–5196 (2015)
20. Collobert, R., Kavukcuoglu, K., Farabet, C.: Torch7: a Matlab-like environment for machine learning. In: BigLearn, NIPS Workshop, no. EPFL-CONF-192376 (2011)
21. Chen, D., Yuan, L., Liao, J., Yu, N., Hua, G.: StyleBank: an explicit representation for neural image style transfer, arXiv preprint arXiv:1703.09210

Task-Specific Neural Networks for Pose Estimation in Person Re-identification Task

Kai Lv[1], Hao Sheng[1(✉)], Yanwei Zheng[1], Zhang Xiong[1],
Wei Li[1], and Wei Ke[2]

[1] State Key Laboratory of Software Development Environment,
School of Computer Science and Engineering, Beihang University, Beijing, China
{lvkai,shenghao,zhengyw,xiongz}@buaa.edu.cn, liwei@nlsde.buaa.edu.cn
[2] Macao Polytechnic Institute, Macao, China
wke@ipm.edu.mo

Abstract. Person re-identification is a challenging task because of severe appearance changes of a person due to diverse camera viewpoints and person poses. To alleviate the impact of different poses, more and more studies have been done in pose estimation. In this work, we present three task-specific neural networks (TNN) algorithm designed to address the problem of pose estimation for re-identification in both single-shot and multi-shot matching. In order to recognize the human pose as one of the four classes (front, back, left, right), a PoseNet-A is first required to estimate the pose as class front-back or class left-right. Based on the results, we select the appropriate network (PoseNet-B1, PoseNet-B2) to obtain the final pose. According to the results, our method achieves very good results on a large data set (CUHK03-Pose). One thing that needs to be pointed out is that we build the dataset CUHK03-Pose which is based on the person re-identification dataset CUHK03.

Keywords: Re-identification · Pose estimation · Single-shot
Deep learning

1 Introduction

Person re-identification (re-id) is of great importance in security, human computer interaction and many other systems. A typical scenario of person re-id is to identify people across images that have been taken using different cameras, or across time using a single camera. However, re-id still remains a challenging problem due to illumination, pose and viewpoint changes for the people across images that have been taken using different cameras. Thereinto, the pose diversity is one of the most prominent problems.

We classify previous person re-id methods into single-shot and multi-shot matching-based methods. For single-shot matching, most of the works have focused on appearance-based techniques such as feature and metric learning

© Springer International Publishing AG, part of Springer Nature 2018
B. Zeng et al. (Eds.): PCM 2017, LNCS 10735, pp. 792–801, 2018.
https://doi.org/10.1007/978-3-319-77380-3_76

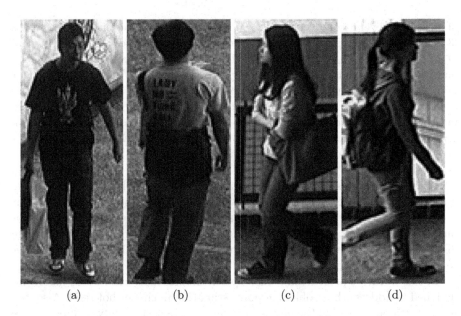

(a)   (b)   (c)   (d)

Fig. 1. Sample images from the CUHK03 dataset [13]. We have roughly divided the pose into four categories: (a) front, (b) back, (c) left and (d) right.

for the efficient person re-id. Farenzena *et al.* [6] presented an appearance-based method for person re-id. It consists in the extraction of features that model three complementary aspects of the human appearance. Feature learning methods that select or weight discriminative features have been proposed in [15,19]. Xiao *et al.* [18] presented a pipeline for learning deep feature representations from multiple domains with Convolutional Neural Networks (CNNs). Several methods have been applied to the re-id problem, such as KISSME [11], LMNNR [5]. Köstinger *et al.* [11] raised important issues on scalability and the required degree of supervision of existing Mahalanobis metric learning methods. Dikmen *et al.* [5] used a metric learning framework to obtain a robust metric for large margin nearest neighbor classification with rejection.

Regarding the multi-shot matching, several person re-id methods have been proposed in recent years. Farenzena *et al.* [6] provided multi-shot matching results by comparing each possible pair of histograms between different signatures (a set of appearances) and selecting the obtained lowest distance for the final score of matching. Wang et al. [16] presented a novel model to automatically select the most discriminative video fragments from noisy image sequences of people where more reliable space-time features can be extracted, whilst simultaneously to learn a video ranking function for person re-id. Li *et al.* [14] also proposed an algorithm based on the Fisher criterion to learn a representative and discriminative feature sub-space from image sequences in person re-id task.

As shown in Fig. 1, it is quite challenging for person re-id due to target pose variations. However, it is reasonable to explore and utilize the pose priors of targets in every non-overlapping camera in advance. Recently, a few works [3,4,17] used target pose priors (pose cues) for person re-id very recently. Bąk *et al.* [3] proposed to learn a generic metric pool which consists of metrics, each one learned to match specific pairs of poses. Wu *et al.* [17] built a model for human appearance as a function of pose, using training data gathered from a calibrated camera and then applied this pose prior in online re-id to make matching and identification more robust. Cho *et al.* [4] propose a novel framework for by analyzing camera viewpoints and person poses, which robustly estimates target poses and efficiently conducts multi-shot matching based on the target pose information.

However, previous works [3,4,17] estimated the pose only by using 3D scene information and motion of the target. Pose orientation is computed as a dot product between the viewpoint vector and the motion vector. It is viable for multi-shot matching, which enables us to extract additional cues such as the 3D position of the targets. Because of the lack of additional cues for single-shot re-id, pedestrian pose estimation is a quite difficult task.

In this work, we present three task-specific neural networks (TNN) algorithm designed to address the problem of pose estimation in single-shot re-id. Also, the method can be applied in the multi-shot matching task since only an input image is required to estimate pose. Another contribution is that we build the dataset CUHK03-Pose which is based on the re-id dataset CUHK03. The CUHK03-Pose dataset contains 13,164 images of 1,360 pedestrians and each image has a pose label.

2   Task-Specific Neural Networks

In order to recognize the human pose as one of the four classes (front, back, left, right), three PoseNets (PoseNet-A, PoseNet-B1, PoseNet-B2) are required. In this section, we describe the proposed framework for the pose estimation. First, we show the overall framework of PSE for person re-identification. (Sect. 2.1). Second, we introduce the two pose classes (front-back and left-right) we classified for pedestrians Sect. 2.2). Third, we present the deep neural network architecture of PoseNet-A and PoseNet-B (Sect. 2.3). Finally, we introduce the dataset CUHK03-Pose which is built for the pedestrain pose estimation problem (Sect. 2.4).

2.1   Overall Framework

As shown in Fig. 2, we have several images in appearance pool A and we eventually classify them into four categories: front, back, left and right. The PoseNet-A of TNN is first needed to estimate the pose as front-back or left-right. The class front-back images are put into the appearance pool B1 and the class left-right images are put into the appearance pool B2. Based on the first classification, we then select the corresponding network. PoseNet-B1 is designed and trained to divide the class front-back into the class front and class back while PoseNet-B2

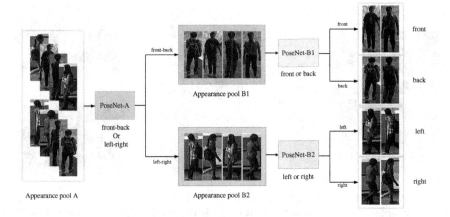

Fig. 2. Overall framework. PoseNet-A, PoseNet-B1 and PoseNet-B2 have the same architecture but different tasks. A group of images are classified into four categories using the proposed algorithm.

is to divide the class left-right into the class left and right. Finally, we yield the final estimation of which class the input images are. It should be pointed out that the three PoseNets have the same architecture but are different in classification use. 1

2.2 Front-Back and Left-Right

As shown in Fig. 1, pedestrian pose estimation is a problem of dividing the pose into four categories (front, back, left and right). It is quite reasonable and valid to turn the question into two binary problems. First, we estimate the pose as class front-back or class left-right using PoseNet-A. The poses are classified like this for the reason that more parts of the body are exposed to the class front and class back images. Moreover, the body silhouette of the class front and class back ones are relatively fixed. After the first binary classification, TNN can get the class front-back or class left-right and choose the corresponding PoseNet-B1 or PoseNet-B2. We regard the TNN as three experts, who have an advantage in their own field. By dividing the pose into two classes (front-back, left-right), TNN split the big task into small tasks. Thus, the experts (PoseNets) can work better in their respective fields by which the network architecture can also be designed lighter and work faster.

2.3 Network Architecture of TNN

As the three PoseNets of TNN are of the same architecture, we describe the PoseNet-A as an example in this subsection. As shown in Fig. 3, to determine whether the pose is the class front-back or class left-back, we need to design an appropriate architecture to solve the binary classification problem.

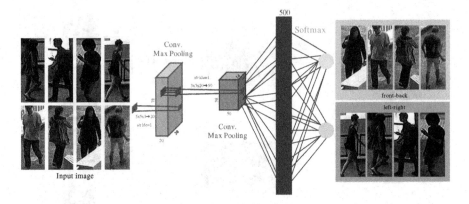

Fig. 3. Proposed architecture. An input image is passed through the network. PoseNet-A's outputs means class front-back or class left-right, while the PoseNet-B1 (PoseNet-B2) network means front (left) or back (right). The number and size of convolutional filters that must be learned are shown. For example, in the first convolution layer, $5 \times 5 \times 3 \rightarrow 20$ indicates that there are 20 convolutional features in the layer, each with a kernel size of $5 \times 5 \times 3$.

In the deep learning literature, convolutional features have proven to provide representations that are useful for a variety of classification tasks. The first layer is convolution layers, which we use to compute higher-order features. In the first convolution layer, we pass an input RGB image of size $64 \times 160 \times 3$ through 20 learned filters of size $5 \times 5 \times 3$. The resulting feature maps are passed through a max-pooling kernel that halves the width and height of features. Then the features are passed through another convolutional layer that uses 50 learned filters of size $3 \times 3 \times 50$, followed by a max-pooling layer that again decreases the width and height of the feature map by a factor of 2. At the end of the two layers, each input is represented by 50 features maps of size 14×38. We then apply a fully connected layer. The resultant feature vector of size 500 is passed through a ReLu nonlinearity. These 500 outputs are then passed to another fully connected layer containing 2 softmax units, which represent the probability that the image is class front-back or class left-back.

2.4   CUHK03-Pose Dataset

In this paper, a pose estimation dataset, the "CUHK03-Pose" dataset, is proposed. The CUHK03-Pose dataset is based on the large dataset CUHK03 [13] which includes 13,164 images of 1360 pedestrians. The whole dataset captured with ten surveillance cameras. Each identity is observed by two disjoint camera views and has an average of 4.8 images with pose labels in each view. Overall, there are two reasons to utilize CUHK03 dataset.

First, a large amount of images are required for deep learning task. There are many specialized datasets for person identification such as Market-1501 [20], CUHK03 [13], CUHK01 [12], VIPeR [7], PRID2011 [8], 3DPeS [2], i-LIDS [21]

Table 1. Details of existing datasets [2,7,8,12,13,21].

Datasets	CUHK03 [13]	CUHK01 [12]	VIPeR [7]	PRID [8]	3DPeS [2]	i-LIDS [21]
Cameras	10	2	2	2	8	2
Identities	1360	971	632	934	193	119
Images	13,164	1,552	1264	1,134	1,012	476

and Shinpuhkan [10]. As we can see in Table 1, the identities and images of CUHK03 dataset are larger than the other four datasets.

Second, when observing the CUHK03 dataset, we found the dataset has two characteristics: there exist no more than 10 images per person and the poses of image 1–5 are always left-right while the rest are front-back. Then, it is reasonable to label the images as front-back and left-right respectively. Finally, each image of the CUHK03 dataset is labeled as front, back, left or right. At the same time, because there are also very few obvious false labels, we have made a manual correction. To the best of our knowledge, this is the first attempt to build a large dataset for pedestrian pose estimation. Sample images are shown in Fig. 4.

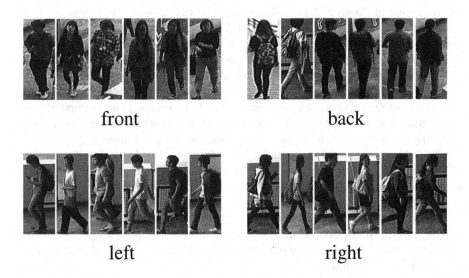

Fig. 4. Sample images of the "CUHK03-Pose" dataset.

3 Experiments

3.1 Data Preparation

We regard the pedestrian pose estimation problem as binary classification. All the images of CUHK03-Pose are labeled as front, back, left, right. However, the

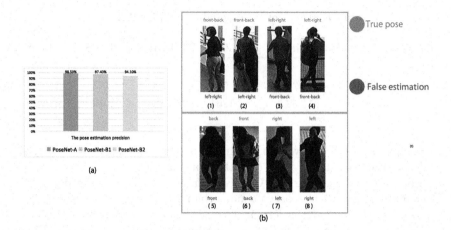

Fig. 5. Experimental results. (a) Shows the precision of the three PoseNet. (b) Have listed several wrong estimates. The true pose is listed upon every picture with green color and the words under each picture with red color mean a false estimation. (Color figure online)

training data of PoseNet-A consist of images labeled as positive (front-back) and negative (left-right). Indeed, the front-back images are the union of class front images and class back images while the left-right images are the union of class left images and class right images. When training the PoseNet-B1 or PoseNet-B2, we only use the front-back or left-right images to achieve the specific network.

In order to train the network in caffe [9], training data are randomly divided into mini-batches. The model performs forward propagation on the current mini-batch and computes the output and loss. Backpropagation is then used to compute the gradients on this batch, and network weights are updated.

To reduce overfitting, we artificially augment the data by performing random 2D translation, as also done in [1]. For an original image of size $W \times H$, we sample 5 images around the image center, with translation drawn from a uniform distribution in the range $[-0.05H, 0.05H] \times [-0.05W, 0.05W]$.

We start with a base learning rate of $\gamma^{(0)} = 0.01$ and gradually decrease it as the training progresses using the "inv" policy: $\gamma^{(i)} = \gamma^{(0)}(1 + \gamma \cdot i)^{-p}$ where $\gamma = 10^{-4}, p = 0.75$. The momentum and weight decay in our experiment are $u = 0.9$ and $\lambda = 0.0001$.

3.2   Evaluation

Results of Three PoseNets. We evaluate TNN in CUHK03-Pose by calculating the precision of each PoseNet. As shown in Fig. 5(a), the three PoseNets get a good performance, although there exist some false pose estimations. The precisions of the three networks ranges from 94.1% to 98.5%. However, our network have some shortcomings as we can see in Fig. 5(b). The true pose is listed upon every picture with green color and the words under each picture with red color mean a false estimation. Through image (5) (6), we can draw conclusions that we may get false estimation when the light is too dark. Also, image (2) (7) shows that the pose estimation results are easy to be affected by occlusion.

Overall Results. In this paper, TNN divides the pose of pedestrians into front-back and left-right at first. To evaluate the effectiveness of our two-stage approach, a classifier that directly decomposed into the four classes is trained. This classifier has the same network architecture and parameters but with four outputs. In our experiment, the overall precision of this four-class classifier is 90.1%. However, the final precision of TNN can be achieved by calculating the three PoseNets' precision. The overall precision of TNN is 94.6% which has a 4% improvement than the four-class classifier.

4 Conclusion

Previous works estimate pedestrian pose by using 3D scene information and motion of the target in multi-shot matching which is not viable in single-shot scenario. To estimate pose in both single-shot and multi-shot matching, we solve the pedestrian pose estimation problem by using three PoseNets of TNN. In order to recognize the human pose as one of the four classes (front, back, left, right), a PoseNet-A is first required to estimate the pose as class front-back or class left-right. Based on the results obtained, we then select the appropriate network (PoseNet-B1, PoseNet-B2) to obtain the final pose. Experiments show that our method is very effective and also have a high precision. In this paper, although the algorithm performs well at CUHK03-Pose dataset, there are a lot of works to do to apply this algorithm to other datasets. Moreover, we need to use the pose cues for person re-identification works. In future, we plan to explore the potential of using pose cues to solve the re-identification problem.

Acknowledgement. This study is partially supported by the National Natural Science Foundation of China (No. 61472019), the National Key Research and Development Program of China (No. 2017YFC0806502), the Macao Science and Technology Development Fund (No. 138/2016/A3), the Programme of Introducing Talents of Discipline to Universities, the Open Fund of the State Key Laboratory of Software Development Environment under grant SKLSDE-2017ZX-09 and HAWKEYE Group.

References

1. Ahmed, E., Jones, M., Marks, T.K.: An improved deep learning architecture for person re-identification. In: Computer Vision and Pattern Recognition, pp. 3908–3916 (2015)
2. Baltieri, D., Vezzani, R., Cucchiara, R.: 3DPeS: 3D people dataset for surveillance and forensics. In: International ACM Workshop on Multimedia Access To 3D Human Objects, pp. 59–64 (2011)

3. Bąk, S., Martins, F., Bremond, F.: Person re-identification by pose priors. In: Proceedings of SPIE - The International Society for Optical Engineering, vol. 9399, pp. 93990H–93990H-6 (2015)
4. Cho, Y.J., Yoon, K.J.: Improving person re-identification via pose-aware multi-shot matching. In: IEEE Conference on Computer Vision and Pattern Recognition, pp. 1354–1362 (2016)
5. Dikmen, M., Akbas, E., Huang, T.S., Ahuja, N.: Pedestrian recognition with a learned metric. In: Kimmel, R., Klette, R., Sugimoto, A. (eds.) ACCV 2010 Part IV. LNCS, vol. 6495, pp. 501–512. Springer, Heidelberg (2011). https://doi.org/10.1007/978-3-642-19282-1_40
6. Farenzena, M., Bazzani, L., Perina, A., Murino, V., Cristani, M.: Person re-identification by symmetry-driven accumulation of local features. In: Computer Vision and Pattern Recognition, pp. 2360–2367 (2010)
7. Gray, D., Brennan, S., Tao, H.: Evaluating appearance models for recognition, reacquisition, and tracking (2007)
8. Hirzer, M., Beleznai, C., Roth, P.M., Bischof, H.: Person re-identification by descriptive and discriminative classification. In: Heyden, A., Kahl, F. (eds.) SCIA 2011. LNCS, vol. 6688, pp. 91–102. Springer, Heidelberg (2011). https://doi.org/10.1007/978-3-642-21227-7_9
9. Jia, Y., Shelhamer, E., Donahue, J., Karayev, S., Long, J., Girshick, R., Guadarrama, S., Darrell, T.: Caffe: convolutional architecture for fast feature embedding. arXiv preprint arXiv:1408.5093 (2014)
10. Kawanishi, Y., Yang, W., Mukunoki, M., Minoh, M.: Shinpuhkan2014: a multi-camera pedestrian dataset for tracking people across multiple cameras. In: The Korea-Japan Joint Workshop on Frontiers of Computer Vision, FCV (2014)
11. Köstinger, M., Hirzer, M., Wohlhart, P., Roth, P.M.: Large scale metric learning from equivalence constraints, pp. 2288–2295 (2012)
12. Li, W., Wang, X.: Locally aligned feature transforms across views. In: Computer Vision and Pattern Recognition, pp. 3594–3601 (2013)
13. Li, W., Zhao, R., Xiao, T., Wang, X.: DeepReID: deep filter pairing neural network for person re-identification. In: IEEE Conference on Computer Vision and Pattern Recognition, pp. 152–159 (2014)
14. Li, Y., Wu, Z., Karanam, S., Radke, R.J.: Multi-shot human re-identification using adaptive fisher discriminant analysis. In: British Machine Vision Conference, pp. 73.1–73.12 (2015)
15. Liu, C., Gong, S., Loy, C.C., Lin, X.: Person re-identification: what features are important? In: Fusiello, A., Murino, V., Cucchiara, R. (eds.) ECCV 2012 Part I. LNCS, vol. 7583, pp. 391–401. Springer, Heidelberg (2012). https://doi.org/10.1007/978-3-642-33863-2_39
16. Wang, T., Gong, S., Zhu, X., Wang, S.: Person re-identification by video ranking. In: Fleet, D., Pajdla, T., Schiele, B., Tuytelaars, T. (eds.) ECCV 2014 Part IV. LNCS, vol. 8692, pp. 688–703. Springer, Cham (2014). https://doi.org/10.1007/978-3-319-10593-2_45
17. Wu, Z., Li, Y., Radke, R.J.: Viewpoint invariant human re-identification in camera networks using pose priors and subject-discriminative features. IEEE Trans. Pattern Anal. Mach. Intell. 37(5), 1095–1108 (2015)
18. Xiao, T., Li, H., Ouyang, W., Wang, X.: Learning deep feature representations with domain guided dropout for person re-identification (2016)
19. Zhao, R., Ouyang, W., Wang, X.: Learning mid-level filters for person re-identification. In: Computer Vision and Pattern Recognition, pp. 144–151 (2014)

20. Zheng, L., Shen, L., Tian, L., Wang, S., Wang, J., Tian, Q.: Scalable person re-identification: a benchmark. In: IEEE International Conference on Computer Vision, pp. 1116–1124 (2015)
21. Zheng, W.S., Gong, S., Xiang, T.: Associating groups of people. In: Proceedings of British Machine Vision Conference, BMVC 2009, London, UK, 7–10 September 2009 (2009)

Mini Neural Networks for Effective and Efficient Mobile Album Organization

Lingling Fa[✉], Lifei Zhang, Xiangbo Shu, Yan Song, and Jinhui Tang

School of Computer Science and Engineering, Nanjing University of Science and Technology, Nanjing, China
linglingfa12@gmail.com, zlfyouxiang@gmail.com,
{shuxb,songyan,jinhuitang}@njust.edu.cn

Abstract. In this paper, we present an auto mobile album organization system, which can automatically classify daily photos in mobile devices into six daily categories, e.g., *Baby, Food, Party, Scenery, Selfie,* and *Sport*. Recently, deep convolutional neural networks have been used to build powerful classifiers by learning high-level representations of images. However, such models are limited to be implemented in the mobile album organization system due to the computational complexity of these networks with millions of parameters. To address these problems, we propose Mini Neural Networks (MiniNN) customized for mobile devices to improve computational efficiency of the album organization system, which is not sacrificed for performance a lot. We train the MiniNN model on the collected datasets as the classifier. Users can choose photos of any size as the input to the system, which will return the predicted tags. Experimental results show that the proposed MiniNN have an advantage over the CaffeNet with comparable classification accuracy but high computational efficiency. It can help us to organize daily photos in the mobile devices effectively and efficiently.

Keywords: Mobile album organization
Convolutional neural network · Mini Neural Networks

1 Introduction

While the possibility of sharing one's lives with the community is compelling enough, the usage of phones or cameras for life logging is also on the rise. However, these albums in our mobiles are scattered across our hard drives, mismatched, poorly named and utterly disorganized. Currently, the main way to search digital photo libraries is using keywords given by the user. An ideal system for image browsing should allow an automatic organization of pictures based on the semantic of images by the keyword. Most album organization softwares use the traditional methods by sorting in time-line or presenting the folders of storage path in the mobile devices. There are several tools which manage photos in albums based on the content by traditional machine learning methods.

© Springer International Publishing AG, part of Springer Nature 2018
B. Zeng et al. (Eds.): PCM 2017, LNCS 10735, pp. 802–810, 2018.
https://doi.org/10.1007/978-3-319-77380-3_77

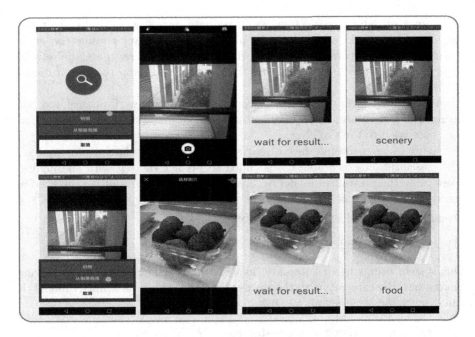

Fig. 1. The interface of our mobile album organization system. The top row shows the classification result when the user takes a photo. The second row shows the classification result with photos in the album.

Recently, Convolutional Neural Networks (CNNs) have been demonstrated as an effective class of models for understanding image content, giving state-of-the-art results on image recognition, segmentation, detection and retrieval tasks [1–6]. The key factors behind these results are the techniques of scaling up the networks to millions of parameters, which can be learned on a large-scale labeled datasets.

It is the right time to equip smart portable devices (i.e., tablet or mobile phone) with the power of state-of-the-art recognition systems. As CNN based recognition systems perform well on expensive GPU based machines, they need large amounts of memory and computational power. For example, AlexNet [7] has 61 M parameters (249 MB of memory) and performs 1.5 B high accuracy operations to classify one image. These numbers are even higher for deeper CNNs, e.g., VGG [7], GoogleNet [8], ResNet [9,10]. Hense, these networks are often unsuitable to embed in smaller devices like mobile phones and tablet.

From a practical standpoint, there is currently no existing photo classification benchmark that matches the daily content for the album organization. These data mainly scatter on social media platforms and it is labor intensive to collect a large amount of accurate annotation. Thereby, we firstly collect a new dataset from the web and several available databases, and then obtain 60000 images covering six categories, e.g. *Baby, Food, Party, Scenery, Selfie* and *Sport*.

From a modeling perspective, we investigate several ways to speed up the deep neural networks and reduce the model size with fewer parameters, while maintaining a comparable accuracy with a model such as the CaffeNet. To achieve this goal, we propose an effective approach to improve computational efficiency of CNNs.

As a consequence, we observe 7x increase in runtime performance and 33x decrease in cost of memory requirement while maintaining the classification accuracy compared to the CaffeNet.

Figure 1 shows the interface of our auto photo album classification system. The classification executable file is called to predict the tag with the highest score using the pretrained model by the MiniNN, and the result is visualized in the system.

Overall, our system has these advantages:

(1) Automatic & High accuracy

Our system brings in an automatic image management method by classifying images into the category with the max score returned by the MiniNN model. It can acquire the accuracy above 90%.

(2) Real-time processing & Small storage

The classification process is particularly effective and efficient. The MiniNN model takes nearly 2 s to classify per 100 images without using the GPU devices. The speed is 7x faster than the CaffeNet under the same hardware configuration. It is small enough to fit into the memory of portable devices.

2 Related Work

Convolutional Network: These years, approaches taking advantage of deep learning for image recognition have been gaining an increasing amount of attention, especially the convolutional networks [11]. The use of convolutional neural networks (CNNs) have been particularly successful, since they are able to jointly learn image features optimized for the task based on their training data. It is not only a consequence of new ideas, algorithms and improved network architectures, but also the result of more powerful hardware, larger annotated datasets and bigger models [8]. Under these conditions, CNNs are able to learn powerful and interpretable image features [12–16].

The most straightforward way of improving the performance of deep neural networks is to increase their sizes. This includes increasing the depth and its width, such as the number of network levels and the number of units at each level [8]. However, this solution dramatically cost a large number of computational resources.

Compact CNN: Estimating a deep neural network with a shallower model reduces the size of a network. Early theoretical work by Cybenko shows that decision boundary can be approximated by a shallow network with a large enough single hidden layer of sigmoid units [17]. However, shallow networks cannot compete with deep models [18] in several areas (e.g., vision and speech). Rastegari et al. [10] introduce XNOR-Networks where both the weights and the inputs to the convolutional and fully connected layers are approximated with binary values. Iandola et al. [19] describe and evaluate the SqueezeNet architecture which can help to understand how CNN architectural design choices impact model size and accuracy.

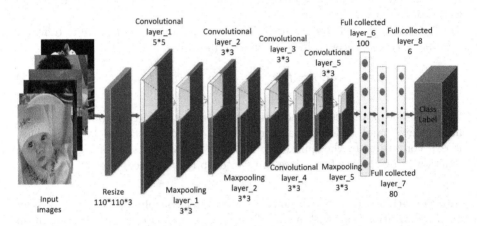

Fig. 2. The architectures of the MiniNN. The MiniNN are modified from the CaffeNet in the several convolution layers and the full connected layers.

3 Mini Neural Networks Architectures

In this section, we propose our design strategies for MiniNN architectures to reduce the number of parameters and improve speed while preserve accuracy. The MiniNN use the full network as the CaffeNet [20]. It comprises of five convolutional layers, each of which is followed by a pooling layer, and three full connected layers.

We take advantage of the architectures of CaffeNet and extend them to the MiniNN. Our proposed speed-up mobile album organization framework contains two improvements. The first one is that we resize the input images to $110 \times 110 \times 3$, which cuts back nearly half of the computation complexity in the network. The second one is that we modify the CaffeNet from several aspects to greatly reduce the size of the classification model stored in the hardware and dramatically accelerate the organization of photos. Overall, there are four main characteristics of the proposed MiniNN, which are summarized as follows:

Resizing Images: Since we take a picture at different shooting angle by the camera embedded in the mobile, the image size in the album can be arbitrary. We add a preprocess step to resize the input picture to fix size as $110 \times 110 \times 3$ to be the input into the MiniNN. The resize step is built in the mobile album organization system so that it can be a single coherent classification framework. Training with images of lower resolution can speed up the model when the image size changes from $256 \times 256 \times 3$ in the CaffeNet to $110 \times 110 \times 3$ in the MiniNN.

Smaller Kernel Size: To match the smaller size of input, we reduce the kernel size from 11 in the CaffeNet to 5 in the MiniNN in the first convolution layer. In the same way, we use 3×3 filter to replace the 5×5 filter in the CaffeNet in the second convolution layer.

The smaller kernel size is able to learn the discriminative feature to differentiate between categories, which is computed as follows:

$$h_{W,b} = f(W^T x) = f(\sum_i W_i x_i + b) \tag{1}$$

where W and b are the learned weights and biases from the input layer to the hidden layer, and x_i is the patch defined in the convolutional layer. Besides, it can contribute to the quicker convolution process as computing activation function using smaller filter sizes can speed up forward feedback.

Smaller Stride: In a convolutional network, each convolution layer produces an output activation map with a spatial resolution. Because the spatial resolution of the input is dropped, we set smaller strides in the early convolution layer. If early layers in the network have smaller strides, then many layers in the end of network will have large activation maps. It can compensate for the performance of classification accuracy [19].

Minimizing the Number of Output: From conv2 to conv5, we minimize the number of output of the layer, the number output changes to 192, 320, 320, 192 correspondingly. Besides, the full connected layers can identify different categories but have over 80% of the number of parameters. Hence, we reduce the number of output in fc6 from 4096 to 100 and similarly reduce the output in fc7 from 4096 to 80, which decreases parameter size.

The architectures of the MiniNN are shown in Fig. 2.

4   Experiment

4.1   Data Collection

We check the images people shared with others in the social networks and obtain six categories concerning to multiple aspects such as *Baby, Food, Party, Scenery, Selfie,* and *Sport*. Specially, we download a large number of images covering

| Baby | Food | Party | Scenery | Selfie | Sport |

Fig. 3. The diversity of the dataset.

six classes from Bing and Google, and also other two available datasets: the ImageNet Large Scale Visual Rection Challenge (ILSVRC) database [21] and the NUS-WIDE-128 database [22]. We choose images with high diversities and relatively natural illumination. For example, the category *Baby* includes babies at various periods under age five and from all over the world. The category *Sport* contains different types of sport like horsing, boxing, tennis, swimming and so on to extend the parent-level semantics. Figure 3 visualizes the diversity of the dataset.

Then we manually check and clean all image data to provide higher label quality. The dataset for album organization consists of 60000 photos by six classes, 70% of which used for the training and the rest ones are used for testing.

4.2 Implementation Details

In the training phase, we use the Caffe framework on a NVIDIA Tesla GPU K20 with 4GB memory on the server. We train the MiniNN and the original CaffeNet as the basic network on the training set.

We first apply a normalization preprocessing step to resize the images to $110 \times 110 \times 3$ as the input to the MiniNN using opencv with the interpolation of INTER_AREA, because it is better to use it for shrinking images and the accuracy is higher compared to the interpolation of INTER_LINEAR. We use a mini-batch of 256 images where patches of 100×100 pixels are randomly cropped from images for training the MiniNN. We adopt the 'step' as the learning policy. A momentum of 0.9 is used.

Here, to compare the performance, we also train the CaffeNet. The images input to the CaffeNet are resized to $256 \times 256 \times 3$. For the CaffeNet, a 227×227 sub-image is randomly cropped from the selected image with a batch size of 60. In practice, we choose the ImageNet models as the initialization for the network. The initial learning rate is 0.00001. It converges at 100000 iterations.

In the testing phase, for fair comparison, all models including the baseline are tested on the same device using the same framework with CPU. The whole classification algorithm for batch processing of large number of image files is implemented in C++ with Caffe framework, which can take photos with any size as input. We measure the classification performance via the Top-1 accuracy. Besides, we record the memory consumption and runtime of the proposed MiniNN by comparing with other deep learning based on classification method.

5   Evaluations

In this section, we evaluate the performance of the proposed MiniNN and the CaffeNet for mobile album organization on the collected dataset. Three evaluations including the classification accuracy, the computational speed and the memory consumption are considered into the measure evaluation in this work.

Table 1. Comparison of classification accuracies per class between the CaffeNet and MiniNN.

Class	CaffeNet (%)	MiniNN (%)
Baby	82.67	92.97
Food	98.83	95.63
Party	92.87	85.93
Scenery	98.77	97.70
Selfie	97.97	91.53
Sport	89.57	83.53
Average	93.44	91.22

Table 2. Comparison of accuracy, speed and storage space for the CaffeNet and the MiniNN.

	Precision (%)	Speed (s/100 image)	Storage space (M)
CaffeNet	93.44	15	217
MiniNN	91.22	2	6.52

Accuracy: To evaluate the effectiveness of the MiniNN model, we report the results of classification per class in Table 1. CaffeNet achieves an average accuracy of 93.44%. Classes such as *Food, Scenery* and *Selfie* achieve near perfect accuracy. On the other hand, our MiniNN model achieve an average accuracy of 91.22%, which is still better than the product on the market.

Speed and Space: In addition to comparing classification accuracy between the CaffeNet and the MiniNN, we also report the computational speed and memory requirement. The comparison of accuracy, runtime and memory requirement is summarized in Table 2. We can see that, the proposed MiniNN method not only leads to speed up, but also benefits in terms of memory requirement compared to the CaffeNet.

For the running time, the proposed MiniNN model only takes 2 s to classify per 100 images, which is 7x faster than the CaffeNet. Moreover, the memory size of the proposed model is nearly 6M, which is 33x reduced than the traditional CaffeNet model. These advantages enable the proposed MiniNN model to be embedded in the portable devices like mobile phones or digital cameras.

6 Conclusion

In this paper, we propose an auto mobile album organization system. This system can automatically organize digital photos in the album based on the image content by the MiniNN effectively and efficiently. It can help us organize photos based on the content into six categories, e.g., *Baby, Food, Party, Scenery, Selfie,* and *Sport*. We have shown in the experiments that the MiniNN enable the possibility of running the inference of deep neural networks on CPU without large cost in terms of memory requirement and speed while maintaining the same level of accuracy. It can be embedded in the mobiles.

Acknowledgement. This work was supported in part by the 973 Program (Project No. 2014CB347600), the National Nature Science Foundation of China (Grant No. 61672285 and 61702265) and the Natural Science Foundation of Jiangsu Province (Grant No. BK 20170856).

References

1. Krizhevsky, A., Sutskever, I., Hinton, G.E.: ImageNet classification with deep convolutional neural networks. In: International Conference on Neural Information Processing Systems, pp. 1097–1105 (2012)
2. Farabet, C., Couprie, C., Najman, L., Lecun, Y.: Learning hierarchical features for scene labeling. IEEE Trans. Pattern Anal. Mach. Intell. **35**(8), 1915–1929 (2013)
3. Cireşan, D.C., Giusti, A., Gambardella, L.M., Schmidhuber, J.: Deep neural networks segment neuronal membranes in electron microscopy images. In: Advances in Neural Information Processing Systems, vol. 25, pp. 2852–2860 (2012)
4. Sermanet, P., Eigen, D., Zhang, X., Mathieu, M., Fergus, R., LeCun, Y.: OverFeat: integrated recognition, localization and detection using convolutional networks. Eprint Arxiv (2013)
5. Girshick, R., Donahue, J., Darrell, T., Malik, J.: Rich feature hierarchies for accurate object detection and semantic segmentation, pp. 580–587 (2014)
6. Razavian, A.S., Azizpour, H., Sullivan, J., Carlsson, S.: CNN features off-the-shelf: an astounding baseline for recognition, pp. 512–519 (2014)
7. Simonyan, K., Zisserman, A.: Very deep convolutional networks for large-scale image recognition. In: Computer Science (2014)

8. Szegedy, C., Liu, W., Jia, Y., Sermanet, P., Reed, S., Anguelov, D., Erhan, D., Vanhoucke, V., Rabinovich, A.: Going deeper with convolutions, pp. 1–9 (2015)

9. He, K., Zhang, X., Ren, S., Sun, J.: Deep residual learning for image recognition, pp. 770–778 (2015)

10. Rastegari, M., Ordonez, V., Redmon, J., Farhadi, A.: XNOR-Net: ImageNet classification using binary convolutional neural networks. In: Leibe, B., Matas, J., Sebe, N., Welling, M. (eds.) ECCV 2016. LNCS, vol. 9908, pp. 525–542. Springer, Cham (2016). https://doi.org/10.1007/978-3-319-46493-0_32

11. LeCun, Y., Boser, B., Denker, J.S., Henderson, D., Howard, R.E., Hubbard, W., Jackel, L.D.: Backpropagation applied to handwritten zip code recognition. Neural Comput. 1(4), 541–551 (1989)

12. Zeiler, M.D., Fergus, R.: Visualizing and understanding convolutional networks. In: Fleet, D., Pajdla, T., Schiele, B., Tuytelaars, T. (eds.) ECCV 2014. LNCS, vol. 8689, pp. 818–833. Springer, Cham (2014). https://doi.org/10.1007/978-3-319-10590-1_53

13. Karpathy, A., Toderici, G., Shetty, S., Leung, T., Sukthankar, R., Fei-Fei, L.: Large-scale video classification with convolutional neural networks. In: IEEE Conference on Computer Vision and Pattern Recognition, pp. 1725–1732 (2014)

14. Shu, X., Tang, J., Qi, G.-J., Li, Z., Jiang, Y.-G., Yan, S.: Image classification with tailored fine-grained dictionaries. IEEE Trans. Circuits Syst. Video Technol. 28, 454–467 (2016)

15. Shu, X., Tang, J., Lai, H., Liu, L., Yan, S.: Personalized age progression with aging dictionary, pp. 3970–3978 (2015)

16. Dai, J., Li, Y., He, K., Sun, J.: R-FCN: Object detection via region-based fully convolutional networks (2016)

17. Cybenko, G.: Approximation by superpositions of a sigmoidal function. Math. Control Signals Syst. 5(4), 455 (1992)

18. Seide, F., Li, G., Yu, D.: Conversational speech transcription using context-dependent deep neural networks. In: Interspeech, pp. 437–440 (2011)

19. Iandola, F.N., Han, S., Moskewicz, M.W., Ashraf, K., Dally, W.J., Keutzer, K.: SqueezeNet: AlexNet-level accuracy with 50x fewer parameters and <0.5MB model size (2016)

20. Jia, Y., Shelhamer, E., Donahue, J., Karayev, S., Long, J.: Caffe: convolutional architecture for fast feature embedding. Eprint Arxiv, pp. 675–678 (2014)

21. Deng, J., Dong, W., Socher, R., Li, L.J., Li, K., Fei-Fei, L.: ImageNet: a large-scale hierarchical image database. In: 2009 IEEE Conference on Computer Vision and Pattern Recognition, CVPR 2009, pp. 248–255 (2009)

22. Tang, J., Shu, X., Li, Z., Qi, G.J., Wang, J.: Generalized deep transfer networks for knowledge propagation in heterogeneous domains. ACM Trans. Multimed. Comput. Commun. Appl. 12(4s), 68 (2016)

Sweeper: Design of the Augmented Path in Residual Networks

Kang Shi[✉] and Weiqiang Wang

School of Computer and Control Engineering,
University of Chinese Academy of Sciences, Beijing, China
shikang15@mails.ucas.ac.cn, wqwang@ucas.ac.cn

Abstract. In recent years, the residual networks (ResNets) have become popular in training very deep neural networks due to its impressive applications in multiple tasks of ILSVRC 2015. In this work, we propose a new network architecture called Sweeper which augments another path in residual block to control the information in residual networks. The proposed architecture is suitable for improving various ResNets. Our experimental results on CIFAR-10 and CIFAR-100 datasets show that the proposed module can bring stable classification accuracy improvement for ResNets and present a new possibility to enhance performance of ResNets differing from deepening and widening it.

Keywords: Classification · Convolutional neural networks
Deep learning

1 Introduction

Convolutional neural networks (CNNs) have evolved dramatically in recent years. From "AlexNet" [1] to "VGGNet" [2], CNNs grow increasingly in depth. Going deeper is a trend that could be explained by a view that adding same number parameters in depth is more effective than that in width in offering deep neural networks (DNNs) more capability [3,4]. And until recently, ResNets have already shown the expressivity of an 1001-layer architecture [6], which booms the study of ultra deep neural networks.

Deep neural networks are more data-driven compared with traditional machine learning models. However, with explosive growth in depth, it is increasingly difficult to design structure of each layer respectively in DNNs. Thus a plenty of works have made general contribution in constructing a robust deep neural network more easily. Some of them study how to simply stack blocks with the same topology, for example, 3×3 convolution layers [2], inception modules [7] and residual blocks [5]. The modularized way in building DNNs enables us to solve complicated machine learning problems. The others bring some regular and practical tricks ranging from 1×1 convolution [3] to batch normalisation [8].

These significant studies can be summarized as doing the same thing, i.e. constructing trainable but deeper neural networks. And it is always hindered by

© Springer International Publishing AG, part of Springer Nature 2018
B. Zeng et al. (Eds.): PCM 2017, LNCS 10735, pp. 811–821, 2018.
https://doi.org/10.1007/978-3-319-77380-3_78

the problem of gradients vanishing. The problem has existed since the birth of deep learning, until today this is still a difficult hot spot. Currently, the residual networks use identity shortcuts to learn layers in CNNs to ease the problem of gradients vanishing and have achieved striking results.

However, identity mappings in ResNets don't learn anything. All the features are learnt by specific residual pathes. Considering this may limit the expressivity due to lacking the capability of regulating an input of each layer, we design a generalized new module called Sweeper. Sweeper module is actually a residual block with an augmented path, and it targets on two things directly: (1) regulate the input of each layer, (2) communicate information of the input from different channels. Inspired by the forgetting gate of long short-term memory (LSTM) unit, we have a natural idea of combining forgetting gate with residual block. However, using forgetting gate on shortcuts directly can cause the problem of gradients vanishing in ResNets when depth increased. To tackle this problem, we carefully design an augmented path, which leverage the idea of residual learning to learn the function of forgetting gate. The augmented path applies element-wise addition instead of multiplication to modulate the input of each layer. Addition module avoids successive multiplication on highway[1] to ease the problem of gradients vanishing in back propagation. We think proposed architecture allows supplementary information-control function to ResNets.

We use ResNets with pre-activation techniques as benchmark. In the following parts, we refer this with ResNetV2. Through experiments, we find that shortcuts with proposed module bring improvements to benchmark networks with various depth, width and architectures. These results reveal the effectiveness of the proposed architecture.

In summary, the main contributions of this paper are summarized as follows:

- We design an augmented path to enhance the capability of information control on shortcuts.
- We carry out experiments to demonstrate that the ResNets with Sweeper module perform better than the benchmark networks with various designs.
- We analyse the difference of the proposed method from deepening or widening the network. This is a new possibility in designing high-performance neural networks.

2 Related Works

Long Short-term Memory. LSTM network [9] is an advanced version of RNN (Recurrent Neural Network). It keeps a 'cell state' throughout time, this is a shortcut indeed. In vanilla version, LSTM module doesn't have gates. Thus in such condition, the cell state can only be changed by element-wise addition from learnable weights. The cell state can't learn anything, this differs most from

---

[1] We refer all shortcuts from the initial layer to global average pooling in ResNets with *highway*.

that in RNNs. Such kind of settings make gradients comparatively stable when Back Propagation Through Time (BPTT). The cell state can be considered as a recursive link with a constant factor of 1 through time called CEC (constant error carousel). Advanced LSTM module has forgetting gates. Forgetting gates regulate information on cell state by element-wise multiplication, thus trap the error continuously to each gate from error carousel. The LSTM with forgetting gates usually performs better than vanilla version.

Highway Network. The highway network is the first successful try in training an ultra deep convolutional neural network. It actually draws experience from LSTM. The researchers use the idea of shortcuts (skip connections), forgetting gates, sigmoid activations and coupled connections just like that in LSTM. However the highway network applies these in CNNs [10]. Using shortcuts makes it possible to train a CNN with deeper structure compared with traditional connection design, although highway networks need teacher networks and achieve mediocre performance.

Residual Networks. The first version of ResNets makes an outstanding performance in ILSVRC 2015 [5], where researchers claim that identity mappings are quite important in training such a network. This is similar to the CEC in vanilla LSTM and opposite to the highway network. The work thinks forgetting gates on shortcuts block the back propagation on highway. The second version of ResNets uses pre-activation and puts forward bottleneck structure to make the network deeper with the same parameters. In that work, an ultra deep neural network–1001-layer ResNet achieves state-of-the-art performance at that time [6]. ResNets control information on highway by residual learning, and shortcuts with identity mappings learn nothing, which is similar to of CEC in vanilla LSTM. In our paper, proposed Sweeper module actually brings a residual version of forgetting gate to the highway networks. Or to say, compared with Residual Networks, it has another path for learning information control capability.

3   Sweeper Module

3.1   Module Description

ResNet is constructed by simply stacking residual blocks, each block can be formulated as

$$\mathbf{y}_l = \mathbf{x}_l + \mathcal{F}(\mathbf{x}_l, \mathcal{W}_{l,F}), \tag{1}$$

where $\mathbf{x}_l$ is the input feature, $\mathcal{W}_{l,F}$ is a specific set of learnable weights of the l-th layer. $\mathcal{F}$ denotes the residual learning function, usually $B(3,3)$ or $B(1,3,1)^2$. $\mathbf{y}_l$ (also noted as $\mathbf{x}_{l+1}$) is the output of layer l. It has the same dimension as input and is obtained by element-wise adding $\mathbf{x}_l$ with $\mathcal{F}$.

---

[2] We refer the design of 3×3 convolution after 3×3 convolution in residual path with $B(3,3)$. Similarly, bottleneck design $\begin{bmatrix} 1 \times 1conv \\ 3 \times 3conv \\ 1 \times 1conv \end{bmatrix}$ is noted as $B(1,3,1)$.

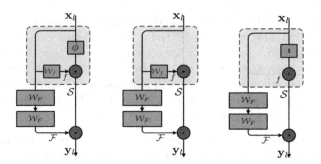

Fig. 1. From the left to right is Sweeper, Highway and Residual block respectively.

We propose a new form $\mathcal{S}$ to substitute the identity mapping $\mathbf{x}_l$ in ResNets, i.e.

$$\mathcal{S}(\mathbf{x}_l, \mathcal{W}_{l,f}) = \phi \mathbf{x}_l + f(\mathbf{x}_l, \mathcal{W}_{l,f}), \tag{2}$$

where $\mathcal{S}$ denotes the output of Sweeper module as shown in Fig. 1. It is the middle output of a layer. $\mathcal{W}_{l,f}$ is a set of learnable weights. f denotes Sweeper learning function. ϕ is a two-valued parameter defined manually. When $\phi = 0$, ϕ masks the input and f regulates the input gate-like as the highway network does. When $\phi = 1$, module $\mathcal{S}$ reserves the input and regulates by adding input with Sweeper path f element-wise.

The proposed module $\mathcal{S}$ diversifies the expressivity of the counterpart $\mathbf{x}_l$ in ResNets. For example, when $\phi = 1$, and f is zero mapping, $\mathcal{S} = \mathbf{x}_l$, the proposed block is equivalent to basic residual block with identity mapping shortcuts. Thus we could say that residual block in ResNet is a special case of Sweeper block.

With the careful design of Sweeper learning function, we think Sweeper module will gain improvements to ResNets.

3.2   Details of the Module

As described above, we design our Sweeper learning function with inferences and experiments.

Learnable Weights. For simplicity, we use M to denote feature map size, F to denote filter size and C to denote the number of channels.

Since our idea originates from the forgetting gate in LSTM, we naturally follow its setting to design parameters. It has the number of parameters $M \times C$ to element-wise multiply the input feature maps. It should be denoted the output of Sweeper element-wise add with the input feature maps instead of multiplying them. We refer such layer with pixel-level weight layer, because no weight sharing is used. In contrast to this kind of setting, we have weight sharing layer—channel-level weight layer. If we use R to denote weights in this layer, R has same dimension as C. $R^{(i)}$ represents the i-th dimension of R and it is scalar-multiplied with the i-th feature map.

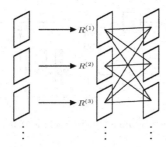

Fig. 2. Channel-level weight layer is used to modulate the feature map channel-wisely, we call this Redundant layer. Each dimension of $R^T = (R^{(1)}, R^{(2)}, ..., R^{(C)})$ is a modulating scalar.

In our experiments, the pixel-level weights not only make no contribution to the result, but also make it worse. We can expect this result, since concept such as local connection and weight sharing has shown their great power in deep learning. Channel-level layer only makes a little improvement to benchmark ResNetV2, probably because it has too little parameters to influence the whole network.

We notice that 1×1 convolution actually satisfies our two main purposes. It has the ability that channel-level layer has, and also communicates information from different channels. However, we find that if we set a channel-level layer before 1×1 convolution as shown in Fig. 2, the result will obtain a further improvement. This is somehow uncommon, since such layer before 1×1 convolution (without non-linear between them) seems to be redundant in traditional MLP. So we call it Redundant layer. We will explain this more in Sect. 3.3.

We carry out experiments under different settings mentioned above on CIFAR-100 datasets and the corresponding results are summarized in Table 1. The augmented path with "Redundant layer + 1×1 convolution" works best. For fair comparison and simplicity, we don't change the downsampling layers. We only use the Sweeper module to replace the identity mappings in residual block. It should be noted that the augmented path doesn't include any convolution with filter size larger than 1, thus no concept such as Local receptive field really exists. This differs a lot from the augmented channels in Wide Residual Network [11], where they copy regular residual path with 3×3 convolution kernels. It can be considered as an augmentation for feature extraction.

Table 1. Experiments of Sweeper path with different designs.

	Design	Error rate (%)
ResNet	-	24.33
ResNet + Sweeper	Redundant	24.16
	conv 1	24.05
	Redundant + conv 1	**23.29**

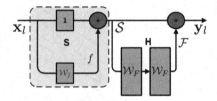

Fig. 3. Sweeper module as an independent layer in ResNets.

Plug in. The proposed module can be easily embedded in ResNets. We evaluate the proposed architecture in various residual networks to check the add-in flexibility of Sweeper module. The experiments are carried out on ResNets with different depths, residual paths, and channels[3]. We design our experiments with maximum width factor $k = 2$ for simplicity. Some of the results are shown in Table 2. They show that the proposed Sweeper module can improve the performance of ResNets with various designs. Moreover, width or depth growing is not the only method to enhance the performance, at least for $B(1, 3, 1)$-designed residual network, the proposed module with less parameters achieves better performance than wider one.

It is noted that if we add Sweeper module in ResNet with the connection shown in Fig. 3, we get a worse result compared with the benchmark ResNetV2. This plug-in mode actually makes the Sweeper module an independent layer and cannot fulfill the purpose of regulating the input layer-wise. According to the conclusion that residual networks behave like ensemble models [12], widening the ResNet would bring similar improvement as deepening it. If the augmented path is the copy of the residual path itself (widening), it should not bring damage to the performance to let this augmented path an independent layer (deepening). Thus the observation indicates that the proposed module differs from widening or deepening the networks.

Table 2. Experimental results on datasets CIFAR-10 of proposed architecture and benchmarks.

	Architecture	Params	Error rate (%)
ResNet	B(3, 3)-1	0.48M	7.45
	B(3, 3)-2	1.92M	5.99
	B(1, 3, 1)-1	0.48M	7.55
	B(1, 3, 1)-2	1.92M	6.70
ResNet + Sweeper	B(3, 3)-1	0.51M	7.21
	B(3, 3)-2	1.98M	5.78
	B(1, 3, 1)-1	0.93M	6.51
	B(1, 3, 1)-2	3.72M	5.91

---

[3] For a widened ResNet, we denote the network with k-times width in the form of, for example, B(3, 3)-2 [11].

Number of Parameters. The detailed setting of our Sweeper module is shown in Fig. 4. It is easy to calculate the number of parameters the proposed module import compared with benchmark. For each residual path with B(3, 3), the number of parameters needed to learn is: $C \times C \times F \times 2$, and the increased parameters brought by Sweeper module is: $C \times C + C$. Compared with a residual block with B(3, 3), the proposed architecture only uses about 5% more parameters (assuming filter size is 3×3). Considering the number of parameters corresponding to the layers outside highway and downsampling layers, this proportion can further decrease. However, for the design B(1, 3, 1), since it uses 1×1 convolution to reduce the parameters in residual path, the corresponding imported parameters increase to 94%.

3.3   Discussion

Effectiveness of Our Module. Actually the Sweeper module learns the capability of forgetting gate in the highway network by residual learning. That is, we use Eq. (2) to substitute $f(\mathcal{W}_l) \cdot \mathbf{x}_l$, where the forgetting gate element-wise multiplies the layer-wise input $\mathbf{x}_l$ in the highway networks. Thus proposed module supplies ResNets more capability to control the information highway without blocking the back propagation.

If we imagine the information flow in networks as the traffic flow on highways, the multiplicative weights (gate) on highways perform like checkpoints. They have the strong ability to control information but easily block the traffic. However, Addition module could regulate information in a more soft way without blocking the highway. As explained above, the addition operation eases gradients vanishing but has the function that the forgetting gate has.

The effectiveness of Redundant layers is beyond our expectation. It seems that a single 1×1 convolution layer can learn equivalent knowledge to the combination of 'Redundant layer $+ 1 \times 1$ convolution'. In fact, weight decay makes these two methods not strictly equal, additional weights imported by Redundant layer may cause the $l2$ penalty different.

Tanh. Due to the addition operation in Sweeper module, we expect it has the ability to remove or add information on highway. Thus in Sweeper path, Tanh is

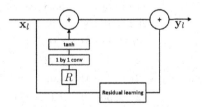

Fig. 4. A closer look at the augmented path. R represents the Redundant layer, which is a channel-level weights layer.

a good choice in activation function, since it has the property of axial symmetric. On the other hand, the output values of each layers in ResNets are distributed around zero mean, as reported in ResNetsV2. This makes it less likely to fall into the saturation area of function Tanh. These two reasons make Tanh a best candidate in proposed module.

4   Experiments

We evaluate our module on public datasets CIFAR [13]. By simply replacing the basic blocks in ResNetV2 with the proposed architecture as introduced in Sect. 3.2, we obtain significant improvements. Regularizer techniques such as dropout are not applied in our experiments. Unless stated specifically, all layers follow the settings of ResNetV2. We take 3×3 convolution with stride 2 at the first layer, then simply stack the blocks with the proposed architecture. And after every N blocks we conduct downsampling operation. Details of experiments are introduced in Sect. 4.2.

We compare several state-of-the-art results with our approach in the same environment. We notice that some of the results we re-implemented differ from the ones that in original papers. This may results from the difference of implementing hardware as well as software. Also learning schedule and weight decay

Table 3. Experimental results in comparison with the state-of-the-art methods; Re-implementations by our own environment with the same hyper-parameters and learning schedule are marked with '*' in parentheses, trained with batch size 128 except results with tag '†' with batch size 64; Our results in bold are the medians over 5 runs. Our highest quality version is Sweeper module with B(1, 3, 1)-designed residual blocks.

	Depth	Params	CIFAR10	CIFAR100
Highway [10]	-	-	7.72	32.39
ResNetV1 [5]	110	1.7M	6.61	-
	164	1.7M	5.93	25.16
ResNetV2 [6]	110	1.7M	6.37(6.35*)	−(28.64*)
	164	1.7M	5.46(**5.40***)	24.33(**24.34***)
	1001	10.2M	4.92	22.71
ResNetSD [14]	110	1.7M	5.23	24.58
	1202	10.2M	4.91	-
RiR [15]	18	10.3M	5.01	22.90
FractalNet [16]	21	38.6M	5.22	23.30
FractalNet (Droupout)	21	38.6M	4.60	23.73
Wide ResNet [11]	28	36.5M	4.17(4.87†*)	20.50(21.67†*)
Our approach	164	3.2M	**5.11**	**23.29**
	488	9.5M	**4.65**	**22.31**

rate also matter the results. For fair comparison, we use consistent hyper-parameters, and re-implement some of the sate-of-the-art results under the same environment.

The experimental results in comparison with state-of-the-art methods are reported in Table 3. Combining the results from Table 2, we can demonstrate that with our Sweeper module as plugin, ResNets can achieve significant and consistent performance improvements. Our results with less parameters out-perform most of state-of-the-art methods, which validates the purpose of the proposed architecture.

4.1 Datasets

CIFAR datasets are labeled subsets of the 80 million tiny images datasets [13]. CIFAR datasets are often used as benchmark datasets for comparing the performance of a neural network especially in image classification tasks.

CIFAR-10: The CIFAR-10 dataset consists of 60000 colour images of size 32×32. It contains in 10 classes with 6000 images per class. There are 50000 training images and 10000 test images.

CIFAR-100: Similar to CIFAR-10, CIFAR-100 contains 100 classes, with 500 images per class for training and 100 images per class for testing.

4.2 Details of Experiments

We take ResNetV2 as a baseline and follow the implementation details of it [6].

Preprocessing. We adopt the basic data augmentation strategy. Firstly we zero pad the input images from size 32×32 to 36×36 and then randomly crop it to the original size. After that we randomly mirror the images. No other data augmentation is applied and our data augmentation is done before training without enlarging the number of samples per epoch. Finally we do per image whitening.

Training. We randomly shuffle the training sets every epoch. We use cross-entropy loss to evaluate our model, and use SGD with momentum 0.9 as opti-mizer. We train both CIFAR-10 and CIFAR-100 with total 200 epochs on two GPUs (NVIDIA Tesla K80) and with batch size 128. Starting from learning rate 0.1, we reduce it with a factor of 0.1 after 120 and 160 epochs respectively. Weight decay is 0.0001. The weights initialization of our Sweeper module is Xavier ini-tializer [17]. It should be noted that we train our model from scratch without teacher network or any fine-tuning, and no other manually-set parameters are used except we mentioned.

Testing. We evaluate our model with test datasets provided by CIFAR. Both of the CIFAR-10 and CIFAR-100 test sets have 10000 images, we use a test batch size 50 with 200 batches to cover the whole sets. We test our model after every training epoch. And for each run we reserve the best precision and round the results to two decimal places. For rationality, our final result is the median over 5 runs. It should be noted that no tricky methods are used in implementation or evaluation process by comparison to ResNetV2.

5   Conclusions

In this paper, we introduce an architecture called Sweeper, which utilizes an augmented path to transfer the capability of forgetting gate from LSTM networks to ResNets while eases the gradients vanishing problem by using the idea of residual learning. The Experimental results on CIFAR-10 and CIFAR-100 datasets demonstrate that the proposed design can bring more expressivity in image recognition task. Also, except increase in width or depth, it provides a new possible method for enhancing the performance of a neural network.

References

1. Krizhevsky, A., Sutskever, I., Hinton, G.E.: ImageNet classification with deep convolutional neural networks. In: Advances in Neural Information Processing Systems, pp. 1097–1105 (2012)
2. Simonyan, K., Zisserman, A.: Very deep convolutional networks for large-scale image recognition. arXiv preprint arXiv:1409.1556 (2014)
3. Lin, M., Chen, Q., Yan, S.: Network in network. arXiv preprint arXiv:1312.4400 (2013)
4. Raghu, M., Poole, B., Kleinberg, J., Ganguli, S., Sohl-Dickstein, J.: On the expressive power of deep neural networks. arXiv preprint arXiv:1606.05336 (2016)
5. He, K., Zhang, X., Ren, S., Sun, J.: Deep residual learning for image recognition. In: Proceedings of the IEEE Conference on Computer Vision and Pattern Recognition, pp. 770–778 (2016)
6. He, K., Zhang, X., Ren, S., Sun, J.: Identity mappings in deep residual networks. In: Leibe, B., Matas, J., Sebe, N., Welling, M. (eds.) ECCV 2016. LNCS, vol. 9908, pp. 630–645. Springer, Cham (2016). https://doi.org/10.1007/978-3-319-46493-0_38
7. Szegedy, C., Liu, W., Jia, Y., Sermanet, P., Reed, S., Anguelov, D., Erhan, D., Vanhoucke, V., Rabinovich, A.: Going deeper with convolutions. In: Proceedings of the IEEE Conference on Computer Vision and Pattern Recognition, pp. 1–9 (2015)
8. Ioffe, S., Szegedy, C.: Batch normalization: accelerating deep network training by reducing internal covariate shift. In: Computer Science (2015)
9. Hochreiter, S., Schmidhuber, J.: Long short-term memory. Neural Comput. **9**(8), 1735–1780 (1997)
10. Srivastava, R.K., Greff, K., Schmidhuber, J.: Highway networks. In: Computer Science (2015)
11. Zagoruyko, S., Komodakis, N.: Wide residual networks. arXiv preprint arXiv:1605.07146 (2016)

12. Veit, A., Wilber, M.J., Belongie, S.: Residual networks behave like ensembles of relatively shallow networks. In: Advances in Neural Information Processing Systems, pp. 550–558 (2016)
13. Krizhevsky, A., Hinton, G.: Learning multiple layers of features from tiny images (2009)
14. Huang, G., Sun, Y., Liu, Z., Sedra, D., Weinberger, K.Q.: Deep networks with stochastic depth. In: Leibe, B., Matas, J., Sebe, N., Welling, M. (eds.) ECCV 2016. LNCS, vol. 9908, pp. 646–661. Springer, Cham (2016). https://doi.org/10.1007/978-3-319-46493-0_39
15. Targ, S., Almeida, D., Lyman, K.: Resnet in Resnet: generalizing residual architectures. arXiv preprint arXiv:1603.08029 (2016)
16. Larsson, G., Maire, M., Shakhnarovich, G.: FractalNet: ultra-deep neural networks without residuals. arXiv preprint arXiv:1605.07648 (2016)
17. Glorot, X., Bengio, Y.: Understanding the difficulty of training deep feedforward neural networks. In: AISTATS, vol. 9, pp. 249–256 (2010)

Large-Scale Multimedia Affective Computing

Sketch Based Model-Like Standing Style Recommendation

Ying Zheng[1,2], Hongxun Yao[1(✉)], and Dong Wang[1,3]

[1] School of Computer Science and Technology,
Harbin Institute of Technology, Harbin, China
{zhengying,h.yao,dwang89}@hit.edu.cn
[2] Research School of Engineering,
Australian National University, Canberra, Australia
[3] State Key Laboratory of Robotics and System,
Harbin Institute of Technology, Harbin, China

Abstract. Various mobile devices with high-quality cameras are very popular in human daily life. Appropriate directions about the standing postures can greatly improve the user experience while taking photos. In this paper, we propose a method to recommend custom model-like standing style based on model sketches. We first translate the real images of splendid models into sketches by fast person detection and model sketching. The generated sketches are represented by the deep feature vectors. We design an iterative detection approach to finding the most representative model sketches. For a user-input image, the model-like standing styles are recommended in form of the sketch. Besides, we introduce a novel method to score the standing posture of the input image through multi-Gaussian functions. Finally, the experimental results on the Model Standing Style (MSS) dataset demonstrate the effectiveness of the proposed approach.

Keywords: Model sketch · Iterative detection
Model Standing Style · Multi-Gaussian function

1 Introduction

With the rapid development of science and technology, various mobile devices with high-quality cameras have already become very widespread, such as iPhone, iPad. More and more people use the portable devices to take photos in different places [13], especially in tourist attractions. However, many people are no longer satisfied with simply relying on pictures, but choose short video applications like Vine to share their life. Compared to pictures, short videos can obviously better record and convey the colorful moments which make everyone be director and star of their life. Both in pictures and short videos, an elegant standing posture is very important for the users. Therefore, the appropriate directions about their standing postures can give the users an emotional pleasure

© Springer International Publishing AG, part of Springer Nature 2018
B. Zeng et al. (Eds.): PCM 2017, LNCS 10735, pp. 825–833, 2018.
https://doi.org/10.1007/978-3-319-77380-3_79

Fig. 1. Illustration of model standing sketch.

[16,17]. Yet unfortunately, there are still limited studies revolving the problem of standing style recommendation.

While standing can be seen as one kind of action, researchers mainly focus on the task of action segmentation and recognition. Some interesting studies related to our work are photo quality assessment [11], image memorability [5,6] and interestingness prediction [2]. There also exist other relevant works, such as action quality assessment [7,12]. They introduce a learning-based framework for assessing the quality of actions in videos and provide feedback for how the performer can improve. Another work similar to ours is human position recommendation in mobile photographing [14]. They propose a learning-based method to recommend good human position from massive web images. Differently, we aim to address the problem of how to stand like a model. To the best of our knowledge, this is the first work that designs explicitly for custom model-like standing style recommendation.

In this paper, we propose an approach to recommend the model-like standing style based on model sketch for users. As shown in Fig. 1, sketch or cucoloris can be an effective way to express human standing style or posture. We first apply the fast person detection and real-time model sketching to generate the model sketch. Then we extract deep features from the fully-connected layer of VGG-19 Net [9] to represent the model sketch. To discover the representative model sketches, a fully unsupervised iterative detection method is implemented. After that, we propose a method of recommending the custom model-like standing style for user-input image and evaluating the score of the standing posture through multi-Gaussian functions. Finally, we demonstrate the effectiveness of our approach on a new dataset named Model Standing Style (MSS).

2   Model Sketch Generation

It is generally known that sketch can effectively extract the character's posture and eliminate the disturbing information such as color and illumination. Therefore, we regard sketch as the foundation of expressing human standing postures. We follow our previous work of distinctive action sketch [18] to convert real standing images into model sketches. We divide the method of model sketch generation into two parallel stages: person detection and model sketching.

The action sketch [18] use the method of structured output tracking with kernels (Struck) [4] to obtain the person location in each frame. However, the tracking based person detection requires the bounding box of human in the first frame and usually has the problem of target lost. Instead of Struck [4], we use the method called Faster R-CNN [8] as an accurate and efficient tool for person detection. It depends on the region proposal network (RPN) that shares full-image convolutional features with the detection network, which makes it become the state-of-the-art object detection network. In practice, we filter out the detection results with too small size and unsatisfied aspect ratio for better person detection. The first line in Fig. 4 gives 10 examples of person detection.

For model sketching, we also adopt the fast edge detection method [3] which depends on a kernelized structured output support vector machine (SVM). In this stage, we can transform each model image to sketch in real time. After that, we will get the corresponding sketch (see Fig. 4) only associated with the person for each model image when combining person detection and model sketching together.

3   Custom Model-Like Standing Style Recommendation

There are diverse types of standing style in model sketches. Firstly we describe the deep feature representation of model sketches. Then we introduce an iterative detection approach to discover the most representative sketches on behalf of standing style. For a user-input image, model-like standing style will be recommended in the form of sketch. We also give a score of the model-like degree to user's standing posture by multi-Gaussian functions.

3.1   Deep Feature Representation

The recent work of Sketch-a-Net proposed by Yu et al. [15] presents powerful evidence that deep model is a super choice for representation of sketch. To get better representative features, we employ the VGG-19 Net [9] and extract features of each sketch from the fully-connected (FC) layer. We divide each sketch into $m = 25$ overlapped parts and compute deep feature in the full sketch image and its parts. So we total obtain 26 feature vectors f with 4096 dimensions for each model sketch.

3.2   Representative Model Sketch Mining

Inspired by the method proposed by Zheng et al. [19], we implement an iterative detection process to discover the most representative model sketches. We first divide the dataset D into two equal sized disjoint sets $D1, D2$. The set $D1$ is regarded as the training set, and $D2$ is the testing set for searching representative sketches.

Among the training dataset $D1$, K-means clustering is applied to obtain the initial K clusters by clustering all model sketches. To get better input for our approach, we refine the initial clusters by removing the clusters with a small number of sketches. After obtaining the refined K' initial clusters, we propose an iterative detection method to find the most representative model sketches. In experiment, we set $K = 100$ and $K' = 27$ clusters survived. All sketches in cluster $K'(i)$ are thrown into testing dataset $D2$ to discover the most similar sketches. The distance d between $K'(i)$ and the sketch in $D2$ is defined as,

$$d = \sum_{i=1}^{n}(\varphi_0 + \frac{\sum_{j=1}^{t}\varphi_j}{m})/n, \tag{1}$$

where φ_0 is the Euclidean distance between vector f of model sketches, φ_j is the distance between the corresponding parts of two sketches, and n means the number of sketches in cluster $K'(i)$. In experiment, we select top $t = 10$ similar parts of sketch for computation. The similarity is considered as the opposite of distance d.

At each iteration, the top k similar sketches are selected to form new clusters $C(i)$. When all clusters have been used to detect representative sketches, we can obtain new clusters based on the similarity. After that, we swap the training dataset $D1$ and the testing dataset $D2$ for the next iteration. The iterative process will be terminated when the convergence criteria is satisfied. To obtain new clusters K'' with better expression ability on the whole dataset D, we merge the clusters $K'(D1)$ and $K'(D2)$ created in last two iterations according to the similarity of cluster members. Finally, the top k representative sketches are returned. Figure 4 shows the most representative model sketches and real images of 10 clusters discovered on the MSS dataset.

3.3   Custom Standing Style Recommendation

To recommend custom model-like standing style for user-input images, we compute the distances between all model sketches and the clusters obtained in Sect. 3.2. We count the numbers of distance dropped in each interval with a step 0.5 and normalize it into the range $[0, 1]$. Data points are fitted with 4 kinds of multi-Gaussian functions as shown in Fig. 2. The multi-Gaussian function is defined as,

$$\varphi(x) = \sum_{i=1}^{p}(a_i \times e^{-(\frac{x-b_i}{c_i})^2}), \tag{2}$$

where p is the number of terms in Gaussian function, while a_i, b_i, c_i are parameters. From the figure, we can see that multi-Gaussian function are the best of fitting statistic data points when combining 4 Gaussian functions.

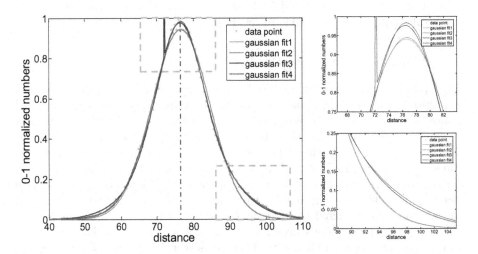

Fig. 2. Data points and four multi-Gaussian fit curves. Gaussian Fit1-4 means the number of Gaussian functions. We enlarge the parts in the dotted line box of curves on right to make a clear illustration. Best viewed in color and please zoom in for clear detail.

Clearly, there are more model sketches around the center of Gaussian distribution. This suggests that those sketches with small distance distributed over the left bottom of Gaussian curve. That is to say, we can score the sketch through its position in the Gaussian distribution. From Eq. 2, we can get the formation of Gaussian distribution,

$$\Phi(d) = \sum_{i=1}^{p} a_i \int_0^d e^{-(\frac{t-b_i}{c_i})^2} dt. \tag{3}$$

Considering that the relation between Gaussian distribution and model-like similarity, we get the way as Eq. 4 defined to score the standing posture in user-input image.

$$\omega = 1 - \Phi(d). \tag{4}$$

Given a user-input image, we first detect the person and transform it into sketch, and then we search those representative model sketches to find the most similar sketch as the model standing style recommendation. After that, we compute the distance $\hbar$ between the sketch and the cluster it belongs. According to Eq. 4, we provide a model-like score for the standing posture.

4 Experiments

In this section, we describe the Model Standing Style (MSS) dataset and demonstrate the effectiveness of our approach. The experimental results on the MSS dataset are shown in Figs. 4 and 5. Besides, we make a further discussion about the results and describe possible future work.

4.1 Model Standing Style Dataset

Most popular large-scale image benchmarks such as the ImageNet [1] are not appropriate for evaluating our method. In addition, others like UCF 101 [10] dataset adopted by action recognition methods are also clearly limited for our research. To our knowledge, there is no benchmark dataset consisting of model-like standing style. To address this problem, we construct a new dataset named Model Standing Style (MSS). We first collect a number of videos from the world top-level modern fancywork like Milan fashion show. The videos provide a huge number of model standing images. More importantly, the standing postures of models can be considered to be designed by professionals which show fashion breath. We segment these videos into small clips and removed those only contained background or auditorium. Then we select images which show model standing style from the surviving clips. The MSS dataset consists of 5859 images with a uniform resolution of 640 × 360 pixels. Figure 3 illustrates 8 sample images of the MSS dataset.

Fig. 3. Model Standing Style dataset.

4.2 Results on Model Standing Style Dataset

To discover the representative model sketches, we implement a fully unsupervised iterative detection process on the MSS dataset and obtain 27 clusters containing 10 most representative model sketches each. Figure 4 gives 10 most representative model sketches and the corresponding real images. The experimental results show that our approach has a promising potential.

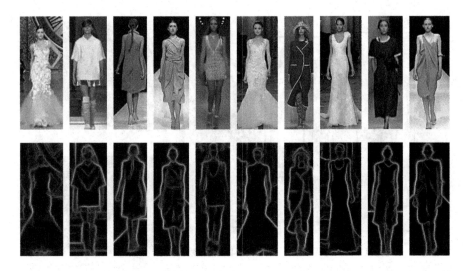

Fig. 4. 10 most representative model sketches. Top line: corresponding real model standing images. Bottom line: representative sketches of model standing discovered by our method.

Figure 5 illustrates the result of custom standing style recommendation and model-like scores for user-input image. The left is user-input image with four standing people detected in red boxes. Under the real images, we give the model-like scores of each person. On the right, we show the sketches generated by our method and the recommended sketches as the model-like standing style. Looking at the number 4 person who get the lowest score, she can change her pose based on the recommended sketch to stand like a model. One additional point we can capture from Fig. 5 is that both the profile of standing person and the cloth appearance affect the degree of model-like. Finally, we can conclude that our method make a contribution on the task of how to stand like a model by custom model-like standing style recommendation.

4.3   Discussions

We mainly focus on the problem of model standing style recommendation in this paper. The condition also can be customized for other special applications, such as the sacred walking style in wedding, the joyous action types in graduation photos. All these novel applications can help users to enjoy more wonderful experience while taking various kinds of pictures or videos. As the MSS dataset only contains female models now, we will add male models into it and take more kinds of styles into the recommendation system in the future. Furthermore, we also will add other attributes like color and cloth to enrich semantic information of images.

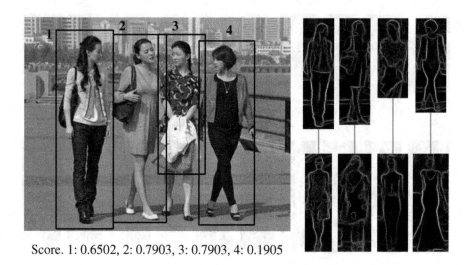

Score. 1: 0.6502, 2: 0.7903, 3: 0.7903, 4: 0.1905

Fig. 5. Illustration of custom standing style recommendation and model-like scores.

5   Conclusions

We propose a method for the novel task of custom model-like standing style recommendation. To better explore the problem, we construct the MSS dataset which consists of a large number of standing postures of professional models. We translate model images into sketches and use deep features to represent them. To discover the representative model sketches, a fully unsupervised iterative detection process is implemented. We introduce an approach to recommend model-like standing style. Through multi-Gaussian function, we provide a model-like score for the standing posture of user-input image. Finally, we demonstrate the encouraging performance over the MSS dataset.

Acknowledgements. The work was supported in part by the National Science Foundation of China (No. 61472103). We especially would like to thank the China Scholarship Council (CSC) for funding the first author to conduct the partially of this project at Australian National University.

References

1. Deng, J., Dong, W., Socher, R., Li, L.J., Li, K., Fei-Fei, L.: Imagenet: a large-scale hierarchical image database. In: IEEE Conference on Computer Vision and Pattern Recognition, pp. 248–255 (2009)
2. Dhar, S., Ordonez, V., Berg, T.L.: High level describable attributes for predicting aesthetics and interestingness. In: IEEE Conference on Computer Vision and Pattern Recognition, pp. 1657–1664 (2011)
3. Dollár, P., Zitnick, C.: Structured forests for fast edge detection. In: IEEE International Conference on Computer Vision, pp. 1841–1848 (2013)

4. Hare, S., Saffari, A., Torr, P.H.: Struck: structured output tracking with kernels. In: IEEE International Conference on Computer Vision, pp. 263–270 (2011)
5. Isola, P., Xiao, J., Parikh, D., Torralba, A., Oliva, A.: What makes a photograph memorable? IEEE Trans. Pattern Anal. Mach. Intell. **36**(7), 1469–1482 (2014)
6. Isola, P., Xiao, J., Torralba, A., Oliva, A.: What makes an image memorable? In: IEEE Conference on Computer Vision and Pattern Recognition, pp. 145–152 (2011)
7. Pirsiavash, H., Vondrick, C., Torralba, A.: Assessing the quality of actions. In: Fleet, D., Pajdla, T., Schiele, B., Tuytelaars, T. (eds.) ECCV 2014. LNCS, vol. 8694, pp. 556–571. Springer, Cham (2014). https://doi.org/10.1007/978-3-319-10599-4_36
8. Ren, S., He, K., Girshick, R., Sun, J.: Faster R-CNN: towards real-time object detection with region proposal networks. In: Advances in Neural Information Processing Systems, pp. 91–99 (2015)
9. Simonyan, K., Zisserman, A.: Very deep convolutional networks for large-scale image recognition. arXiv preprint arXiv:1409.1556 (2014)
10. Soomro, K., Zamir, A.R., Shah, M.: UCF101: a dataset of 101 human actions classes from videos in the wild. arXiv preprint arXiv:1212.0402 (2012)
11. Tang, X., Luo, W., Wang, X.: Content-based photo quality assessment. IEEE Trans. Multimed. **15**(8), 1930–1943 (2013)
12. Tao, L., Paiement, A., Damen, D., Mirmehdi, M., Hannuna, S., Camplani, M., Burghardt, T., Craddock, I.: A comparative study of pose representation and dynamics modelling for online motion quality assessment. Comput. Vis. Image Underst. **148**, 136–152 (2016)
13. Wang, F., Qi, S., Gao, G., Zhao, S., Wang, X.: Logo information recognition in large-scale social media data. Multimed. Syst. **22**(1), 63–73 (2016)
14. Xu, P., Yao, H., Ji, R., Liu, X.M., Sun, X.: Where should i stand? learning based human position recommendation for mobile photographing. Multimed. Tools Appl. **69**(1), 3–29 (2014)
15. Yu, Q., Yang, Y., Song, Y.Z., Xiang, T., Hospedales, T.M.: Sketch-a-net that beats humans. In: British Machine Vision Conference, pp. 1–12 (2015)
16. Zhao, S., Yao, H., Gao, Y., Ding, G., Chua, T.S.: Predicting personalized image emotion perceptions in social networks. IEEE Trans. Affect. Comput. (2016)
17. Zhao, S., Yao, H., Gao, Y., Ji, R., Ding, G.: Continuous probability distribution prediction of image emotions via multitask shared sparse regression. IEEE Trans. Multimed. **19**(3), 632–645 (2017)
18. Zheng, Y., Yao, H., Sun, X., Zhao, S.: Distinctive action sketch. In: IEEE International Conference on Image Processing, pp. 576–580 (2015)
19. Zheng, Y., Yao, H., Zhao, S., Wang, Y.: Discovering discriminative patches for free-hand sketch analysis. Multimed. Syst. **23**(6), 691–701 (2017)

Joint $L1 - L2$ Regularisation for Blind Speech Deconvolution

Jian Guan[1], Xuan Wang[1]([✉]), Zongxia Xie[2], Shuhan Qi[1], and Wenwu Wang[3]

[1] Computer Application Research Center, Shenzhen Graduate School,
Harbin Institute of Technology, Shenzhen 518055, China
{j.guan,wangxuan,shuhanqi}@cs.hitsz.edu.cn
[2] School of Computer Software, Tianjin University, Tianjin 30072, China
caddiexie@hotmail.com
[3] Centre for Vision, Speech and Signal Processing, University of Surrey,
Guildford GU2 7XH, UK
w.wang@surrey.ac.uk

Abstract. The purpose of blind speech deconvolution is to recover both the original speech source and the room impulse response (RIR) from the observed reverberant speech. This can be beneficial for improving speech intelligibility and speech perception. However, the problem is ill-posed, which often requires additional knowledge to solve. In order to address this problem, prior information (such as the sparseness of signal or acoustic channel) is often exploited. In this paper, we propose a joint $L1 - L2$ regularisation based blind speech deconvolution method for a single-input and single-output (SISO) acoustic system with a high level of reverberation, where both the sparsity and density of the room impulse responses (RIR) are considered, by imposing an $L1$ and $L2$ norm constraint on their early and late part respectively. By employing an alternating strategy, both the source signal and early part in the RIR can be well reconstructed while the late part of the RIR can be suppressed.

Keywords: Blind deconvolution · Joint regularisation
Reverberation suppression · Acoustic channel estimation

1 Introduction

With the rapid development of internet and widespread use of intelligent terminals, speech becomes an important approach for human-machine interaction. However, speech intelligibility and speech quality are often degraded by room reverberation in an enclosed environment, which leads to the decrease of performance of many application systems, such as automatic speech recognition (ASR) [13], hands-free teleconferencing [12], and hearing-aids [9]. Moreover, reverberation has detrimental effects on listening comprehension and perception of affective speech signals with emotion and interest [11,15–18]. Therefore, speech dereverberation is of great importance in speech signal processing.

© Springer International Publishing AG, part of Springer Nature 2018
B. Zeng et al. (Eds.): PCM 2017, LNCS 10735, pp. 834–843, 2018.
https://doi.org/10.1007/978-3-319-77380-3_80

In our recent work, we focus on blind speech deconvolution for an SISO acoustic system, where the reverberant speech can be considered as the convolution of a source signal with the RIR. Our aim is to estimate both the source signal and the RIR from the reverberant speech, which is an ill-posed inverse problem. To solve this problem, we need to exploit prior information (e.g. sparsity) to reduce the possible solution space. However, speech signal is not naturally sparse in time domain unless converted to a transform domain by using the pre-defined dictionary (e.g. the DFT matrix) or the learned dictionary. In this paper, we instead take into account the prior information provided by the RIR of an acoustic system. The RIR usually includes three parts: direct path, early reflections and late reverberation, where the direct path and early reflections have a distinctive characteristic compared to the late reverberation, and can be considered as sparse in the time domain, whereas the late part of RIR is dense. A room that has a relatively low level of reflections can be assumed as a sparse acoustic system. In [8], we have proposed a sparse blind speech deconvolution method for such an acoustic system, where the sparsity of the RIR is exploited by imposing an $L1$ norm constraint on the RIR and a constraint on the dynamic range of the source speech in the cost function. An alternating minimisation strategy has been employed for the estimation of the source speech and the sparse RIR. Although the method in [8] works well for sparse RIR, it is limited in a relatively high level of reverberation, as the late part of the RIR has not been properly considered.

In this work, both the sparsity and density of RIR are taken into account as the prior information for blind speech deconvolution. We propose a joint $L1 - L2$ regularisation based blind deconvolution model, where an $L1$ norm constraint is imposed to exploit the sparsity of the early reflections, and an $L2$ norm constraint is used to capture the density of the late reflections. Moreover, an indicator function based regularisation is applied to the source signal to account for the dynamic range of the signal. A minimisation method is proposed to optimise the cost function, using two steps: *h-step* and *x-step*, by fixing one, updating the other, in an alternating manner.

This paper is organised as follows: Sect. 2 briefly reviews the previous work about sparse blind speech deconvolution; Sect. 3 describes the proposed joint $L1 - L2$ norm based method; Sect. 4 presents the evaluation results; and Sect. 5 gives the conclusion.

2 Background and Previous Work

2.1 Blind Speech Deconvolution

A reverberant speech $y \in \mathbf{R}^{N+L-1}$ can be considered as the convolution of the source speech signal $x \in \mathbf{R}^N$ and the RIR $h \in \mathbf{R}^L$, as follows

$$y = x * h, \tag{1}$$

where * denotes the convolution operator. Given y as an input, the aim of blind speech deconvolution is to estimate the unknown source x and the RIR h.

Equation (1) can be rewritten in a matrix form as

$$\boldsymbol{y} = \boldsymbol{Xh} = \boldsymbol{Hx}, \tag{2}$$

where $\boldsymbol{X} \in \mathbf{R}^{(N+L-1)\times L}$ and $\boldsymbol{H} \in \mathbf{R}^{(N+L-1)\times N}$ are the linear convolution matrices constructed from $\boldsymbol{x}$ and $\boldsymbol{h}$ respectively.

2.2   Previous Work

In [8], we assume that an acoustic system has a relatively low level of reflections, so that the RIR $\boldsymbol{h}$ can be considered as sparse.

By exploiting the sparsity of RIR $\boldsymbol{h}$, we proposed a blind speech deconvolution model as follows

$$F(\boldsymbol{x}, \boldsymbol{h}) = \|\boldsymbol{x} * \boldsymbol{h} - \boldsymbol{y}\|_2^2 + \gamma\|\boldsymbol{h}\|_1 + r(\boldsymbol{x}), \tag{3}$$

where $\|\boldsymbol{x} * \boldsymbol{h} - \boldsymbol{y}\|_2^2$ denotes the data fidelity term, $\gamma\|\boldsymbol{h}\|_1$ is the $L1$ norm constraint, which accounts for the sparsity of RIR $\boldsymbol{h}$, and γ is the regularisation parameter. Note that, only using sparsity prior is insufficient to guarantee the identifiability for the ill-posed blind deconvolution problem [3,4]. An additional regularisation $r(\boldsymbol{x})$ is considered to further reduce the solution space for the estimation of $\boldsymbol{x}$. Here, $r(\boldsymbol{x})$ is defined as an indicator function [6,14], which accounts for the dynamic range of the source signal.

An alternating optimisation strategy is adopted to address (3) in two steps: sparse RIR estimation and signal estimation, where $\boldsymbol{h}$ and $\boldsymbol{x}$ are estimated iteratively, by fixing one, and updating the other.

Sparse RIR estimation. In this step, given $\boldsymbol{x}$, $\boldsymbol{h}$ can be estimated by optimising the following problem

$$\boldsymbol{h}^{(k+1)} = \underset{\boldsymbol{h}}{\operatorname{argmin}} \|\boldsymbol{X}^{(k)}\boldsymbol{h} - \boldsymbol{y}\|_2^2 + \gamma\|\boldsymbol{h}\|_1, \tag{4}$$

where $\boldsymbol{X}^{(k)}$ is the linear convolution matrix constructed from $\boldsymbol{x}^{(k)}$ in the kth iteration. Here, (4) is an $L1$ regularised least-squares problem, which can be optimised by existing alogrithms, such as $l1\_ls$ [10], ADMM [2], and the CVX toolbox [7]. In [8], we use $l1\_ls$ to update $\boldsymbol{h}$ at each iteration, once we obtain $\boldsymbol{h}^{(k+1)}$, the convolution matrix $\boldsymbol{H}^{(k+1)}$ can then be constructed, and used to update $\boldsymbol{x}$ at this iteration.

Signal estimation. In this step, $\boldsymbol{x}$ is updated by minimising the following function

$$\boldsymbol{x}^{(k+1)} = \underset{\boldsymbol{x}}{\operatorname{argmin}} \|\boldsymbol{H}^{(k+1)}\boldsymbol{x} - \boldsymbol{y}\|_2^2 + r(\boldsymbol{x}), \tag{5}$$

where a variable metric forward-backward (VMFB) method [5] is applied to optimise (5).

As shown in [8], this method works well for sparse acoustic system, but is limited when dealing with late reverberation. In this paper, we propose a joint regularisation model by using an $L1$ and $L2$ norm constraint to exploit the sparsity and density of RIR, respectively, as detailed next.

3 Joint $L1 - L2$ Norm Based Blind Speech Deconvolution

We assume $\boldsymbol{h}_e$ and $\boldsymbol{h}_l$ are the early and late reflections of the RIR $\boldsymbol{h}$ of an acoustic system respectively, here the direct path of the RIR is included in $\boldsymbol{h}_e$. By taking into account the characteristics of both the early and late part of $\boldsymbol{h}$, our proposed joint $L1 - L2$ regularisation blind deconvolution model is formulated as follows

$$F(\boldsymbol{x}, \boldsymbol{h}) = \|\boldsymbol{x} * \boldsymbol{h} - \boldsymbol{y}\|_2^2 + \gamma\|\boldsymbol{h}_e\|_1 + \lambda\|\boldsymbol{h}_l\|_2^2 + \boldsymbol{r}(\boldsymbol{x}), \tag{6}$$

where $\|\boldsymbol{x} * \boldsymbol{h} - \boldsymbol{y}\|_2^2$ is the data fidelity term, the $L1$ and $L2$ norms account for the sparsity of $\boldsymbol{h}_e$ and the density of $\boldsymbol{h}_l$, and γ and λ are the regularisation parameters of these two terms respectively. $\boldsymbol{r}(\boldsymbol{x})$ is an indicator function considering the dynamic range of the source signal. As the source signal $\boldsymbol{x}$ is unknown, $\boldsymbol{r}(\boldsymbol{x})$ is approximated using the observation $\boldsymbol{y}$ as in [8].

Note that, it is reasonable to formulate the blind deconvolution problem by exploiting the early and late part of $\boldsymbol{h}$ separately as (6). The early reflections are usually caused by the speech signal arriving at the microphone within 5 ms to 100 ms after the direct sound. The length of $\boldsymbol{h}_e$ can be calculated once the sampling frequency is given, or estimated by some methods according to reverberation time RT60. In this paper, we simply assume that the early reflection is within the beginning 30 ms of $\boldsymbol{h}$. Typically, for a sampling frequency at 16 kHz, the length of $\boldsymbol{h}_e$ would be 480 samples.

The proposed joint norm model (6) can be expressed in matrix form as follows

$$F(\boldsymbol{x}, \boldsymbol{h}) = \|\boldsymbol{X}\boldsymbol{h} - \boldsymbol{y}\|_2^2 + \gamma\|\boldsymbol{h}_e\|_1 + \lambda\|\boldsymbol{h}_l\|_2^2 + \boldsymbol{r}(\boldsymbol{x}), \tag{7}$$

or, equally as

$$F(\boldsymbol{x}, \boldsymbol{h}) = \|\boldsymbol{H}\boldsymbol{x} - \boldsymbol{y}\|_2^2 + \gamma\|\boldsymbol{h}_e\|_1 + \lambda\|\boldsymbol{h}_l\|_2^2 + \boldsymbol{r}(\boldsymbol{x}). \tag{8}$$

Furthermore, Eq. (7) can be rewritten as

$$F(\boldsymbol{x}, \boldsymbol{h}) = \left\| \begin{bmatrix} \boldsymbol{X} \\ \boldsymbol{D}_l \end{bmatrix} \boldsymbol{h} - \begin{bmatrix} \boldsymbol{y} \\ \boldsymbol{0} \end{bmatrix} \right\|_2^2 + \gamma\|\boldsymbol{D}_e\boldsymbol{h}\|_1 + \boldsymbol{r}(\boldsymbol{x}), \tag{9}$$

where $\boldsymbol{D}_e \in \mathbf{R}^{L \times L}$ and $\boldsymbol{D}_l \in \mathbf{R}^{L \times L}$ are the matrices defined as $\boldsymbol{D}_e = \begin{bmatrix} \boldsymbol{I}_e & \boldsymbol{0} \\ \boldsymbol{0} & \boldsymbol{0} \end{bmatrix}$ and $\boldsymbol{D}_l = \sqrt{\lambda} \begin{bmatrix} \boldsymbol{0} & \boldsymbol{0} \\ \boldsymbol{0} & \boldsymbol{I}_l \end{bmatrix}$ respectively. Here, $\boldsymbol{I}_e$ and $\boldsymbol{I}_l$ are the identity matrices, which are designed according to the length of the early and late part of $\boldsymbol{h}$ respectively.

Let $\boldsymbol{\mathcal{X}} = \begin{bmatrix} \boldsymbol{X} \\ \boldsymbol{D}_l \end{bmatrix}$, and $\mathbf{y} = \begin{bmatrix} \boldsymbol{y} \\ \boldsymbol{0} \end{bmatrix}$, where $\boldsymbol{\mathcal{X}} \in \mathbf{R}^{(N+2L-1) \times L}$ and $\mathbf{y} \in \mathbf{R}^{N+2L-1}$, then we can recast (9) as the following cost function

$$F(\boldsymbol{x}, \boldsymbol{h}) = \|\boldsymbol{\mathcal{X}}\boldsymbol{h} - \mathbf{y}\|_2^2 + \gamma\|\boldsymbol{D}_e\boldsymbol{h}\|_1 + \boldsymbol{r}(\boldsymbol{x}). \tag{10}$$

It can be seen that the reformulated cost function (10) is similar to (3), so that a similar alternating optimisation method as in [8] can be used to optimise (10).

In *h-step*, x is fixed, by using (10), h is updated by minimising the following loss

$$h^{(k+1)} = \underset{h}{\text{argmin}} \, \|\mathcal{X}^{(k)}h - y\|_2^2 + \gamma\|D_e h\|_1, \tag{11}$$

where $\mathcal{X}^{(k)}$ is constructed by $X^{(k)}$ and D_l obtained in the kth iteration. Here, (11) can be seen as a special case of $L1$ norm regularised least-squares optimisation problem, hence we can use the CVX toolbox to optimise (11). After obtaining $h^{(k+1)}$, $H^{(k+1)}$ can be constructed for updating x at this iteration.

In *x-step*, h is fixed, by using (8), then x can be updated by using the same cost function as (5). So that, we can also use the VMFB algorithm as in [8] to optimise (5) for the estimation of signal x.

Algorithm 1

Input: y, γ, λ
Initialisation: initialise $x^{(0)}$ by using y, construct $X^{(0)}$ from $x^{(0)}$, construct D_e and D_l, initialise $\mathcal{X}^{(0)}$ and y as $\mathcal{X}^{(0)} = \begin{bmatrix} X^{(0)} \\ D_l \end{bmatrix}$ and $y = \begin{bmatrix} y \\ 0 \end{bmatrix}$ respectively, $I_K = 500$, $\epsilon = 10^{-6}$.
Iterations:
for $k = 1, \ldots, I_K$ do
  $h - step$:
  Update $h^{(k+1)}$ by solving (11), using CVX toolbox.
  Construct $H^{(k+1)}$ from $h^{(k+1)}$.
  $x - step$:
  Update $x^{(k+1)}$ by solving (5), using VMFB as in [8].
  Construct $X^{(k+1)}$ from $x^{(k+1)}$.
  Update $\mathcal{X}^{(k+1)}$, as $\mathcal{X}^{(k+1)} = \begin{bmatrix} X^{(k+1)} \\ D_l \end{bmatrix}$.
  Stopping criterion: If $\|x^{(k+1)} - x^{(k)}\|_2^2 <= \epsilon$, then $x_{opt} = x^{(k+1)}$, $h_{opt} = h^{(k+1)}$, and break, else continue.
end for
Output: x_{opt}, h_{opt}

Compared with the model (3), where only the $L1$ penalty parameter γ needs to be tuned, in (6), an additional parameter λ needs to be controlled. In this work, the penalty parameters are found empirically, and we will show how the penalty parameters impact on the estimation of x and h in Sect. 4. Here, the proposed algorithm is given in Algorithm 1.

4 Simulations and Results

4.1 Experimental Setup

Experiments were conducted to demonstrate the validity of the proposed method for speech dereverberation. The reverberant speech y was generated by the linear

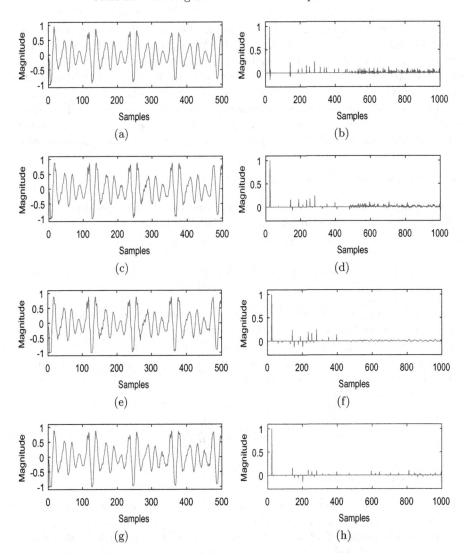

Fig. 1. Illustration of blind speech deconvolution by using the proposed method with different λ values, as compared with the method in [8]: (a) and (b) are the original signal and RIR respectively; (c) and (d) are the estimated source and RIR respectively, by the proposed method (for $\lambda = 0.005$); (e) and (f) are the estimated source and RIR respectively, by the proposed method (for $\lambda = 0.5$); (g) and (h) are the estimated source and RIR respectively, by the method in [8].

convolution of source speech x and RIR h, simulated in a $8 \times 10 \times 3$ m^3 room by a room image model [1]. The reverberation time is 900 ms, and the sampling frequency is 16 kHz. Here, we assumed that the early reflections were generated within 30 ms. Therefore, h_e was taken as the first 480 samples of h, and h_l was selected as the following 520 samples from h. The overall length of h was 1000 samples. Six speech signals (3 males and 3 females) from the TIMIT database were used as the source signals, each of length 500 samples. The observation y was used to initialise x by taking the first 500 samples from y (discounting the silence part) added with 0 dB white Gaussian noise. The maximum iteration number of the proposed method was set as 500, and the stopping criterion was $\|x^{(k+1)} - x^{(k)}\|_2^2 <= \epsilon$, where ϵ was set as 10^{-6}. The values of the penalty parameters γ and λ were set according to the experiments to be discussed later.

4.2 Performance Indices

The reconstruction error is used as the performance index to evaluate the estimation accuracy of the source signal and RIR, defined as

$$R_{err} = 20\log_{10} \left(\sqrt{\frac{1}{M} \sum_{i=1}^{M} (\hat{e}_i - \bar{e}_i)^2} \right), \tag{12}$$

where R_{err} represents the residual error (in decibels) between the original signal $\bar{e}$ and the estimated one $\hat{e}$ (both normalized as $e = \frac{e}{max(|e|)}$), and M is the length of the signal. Here, e can be either x or h.

In addition, a reverberation index is used to evaluate reverberation suppression by calculating the ratio of the energy in the early reflections to the energy in late reflections, which is

$$RR = 10log_{10} \frac{\|h_e\|_2^2}{\|h_l\|_2^2}. \tag{13}$$

4.3 Results and Analysis

First, experiments were conducted to illustrate the performance of the proposed method as compared with the method in [8], for deconvolving the reverberant speech as generated in Sect. 4.1. Here, two experiments were carried out to deconvolve the same reverberant signal by using the proposed joint norm method, where the $L1$ penalty parameter was set to be the same, which was $\gamma = 0.0038$; whereas the $L2$ penalty parameters were different, which were $\lambda = 0.005$ and $\lambda = 0.5$ respectively. With different values of λ, we are able to show how the $L2$ penalty parameter impacts on the deconvolution performance, especially, for RIR estimation. The result is given in Fig. 1.

From Fig. 1, we can see that both of the estimated source signals resemble the original source. The early parts of the estimated RIR (as shown in the subplots (d) and (f)) are also similar to that of the ground truth RIR in (b). It is worth noting that the late reflections are reduced to a lower level as shown in the subplot (f), which means the late reflections can be suppressed by increasing the $L2$ norm penalty parameter. This is beneficial for dereverberation or enhancement of an acoustic system. Also note that, the RIR can be well recovered by the

Table 1. Comparison of the reconstruction errors (dB) for different penalty parameters.

λ	0.0001	0.005	0.01	0.1	0.5	1	2
$\gamma = 0.0038$							
x error	−19.03	−19.11	−19.11	−18.97	−18.72	−18.53	−18.44
h error	−31.34	−31.46	−31.38	−30.94	−30.75	−30.77	−30.80
$\gamma = 0.01\gamma_{max}$							
x error	−18.94	−19.01	−18.99	−18.79	−19.76	−19.64	−19.28
h error	−30.22	−29.94	−29.47	−29.96	−31.12	−30.99	−30.69

proposed joint norm method with a smaller $L2$ penalty parameter as shown in the subplot (d), whereas the estimated RIR in the subplot (h) by the method in [8] is more sparse when compared with the original RIR in (b). This is because the method in [8] only used a sparsity constraint for the RIR h estimation.

Another experiment was carried out to show how the estimation results were influenced by the penalty parameters, where 6 source signals and one RIR as mentioned in Sect. 4.1 were used to generate 6 reverberant speech signals for the deconvolution tests. In order to see how λ influences the RIR estimation, especially for the suppression of the late part of the estimated RIR, the value of γ was fixed to $\gamma = 0.0038$ first, which was found empirically; then a warm starting strategy [14] was used for h estimation in each iteration, by setting $\gamma = 0.01\gamma_{max}$, where $\gamma_{max} = \|\mathcal{X}^{(k)^T} y\|_\infty$. Table 1 shows the comparison of the average reconstruction errors with different parameter values.

From Table 1, we can see that the signal reconstruction error is increasing when the parameter λ is increased from 0.005 to 2 for a fixed $L1$ parameter γ, meanwhile, the RIR reconstruction error is also increasing when λ is increased from 0.005 to 0.5, which indicates that λ is effective only in a certain range. When the warm starting strategy is used, the reconstruction errors of the source signal and RIR are fluctuating when λ is increasing, and the smallest reconstruction error can be obtained when $\lambda = 0.5$.

Note that, for a fixed γ, the variation of the RIR reconstruction error is larger than that of the signal within a certain range of λ (e.g. from 0.005 to 0.5). The increase in the reconstruction error is due to larger $L2$ penalty parameters used to suppress the late reflections.

In order to evaluate the suppression for late reflections in the estimated RIR h, we carried out another experiment on the same reverberant speech signals as used in the last experiment, where different penalty parameters were tested. Figure 2 shows the variation of the reverberation indices of the estimated RIRs with the change in λ. We can see from the figure that the reverberation indices are increasing when λ is increased, and all the reverberation indices of estimated RIRs are larger than that of the original RIR ($RR_{true} = 6.31$), which means the late part of the estimated h can be better suppressed by increasing the $L2$ norm penalty parameter. Note that, when λ is larger than a certain value, such as 0.5, the late reflections will be smoothed as shown in Fig. 1(f).

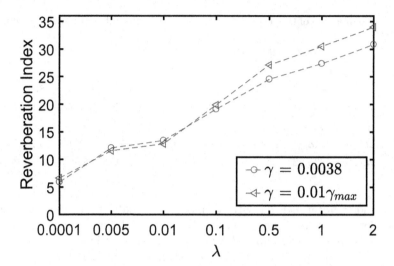

Fig. 2. The reverberation index variation for different penalty parameters, whereas the reverberation index of the original RIR is $RR_{htrue} = 6.31$.

5   Conclusions and Future Work

We proposed a joint $L1 - L2$ norm blind deconvolution method for reverberant speech deconvolution, where both the sparsity and density of RIR were taken into account. The experiments have shown that the proposed method can not only reconstruct the source speech and early part of RIR, but also suppress the late part of the estimated RIR. Future work will evaluate the method with noise interference, and also automate the selection of the penalty parameters based on the reverberation level.

Acknowledgements. The work was conducted when J. Guan visited the Centre for Vision, Speech and Signal Processing (CVSSP), the University of Surrey. This work was supported in part by International Exchange and Cooperation Foundation of Shenzhen City, China (No. GJHZ20150312114149569).

References

1. Allen, J.B., Berkley, D.A.: Image method for efficiently simulating small-room acoustics. J. Acoust. Soc. Am. **65**(4), 943–950 (1979)
2. Boyd, S., Parikh, N., Chu, E., Peleato, B., Eckstein, J.: Distributed optimization and statistical learning via the alternating direction method of multipliers. Found. Trends® Mach. Learn. **3**(1), 1–122 (2011)
3. Choudhary, S., Mitra, U.: Fundamental limits of blind deconvolution part I: Ambiguity kernel. arXiv preprint arXiv:1411.3810 (2014)
4. Choudhary, S., Mitra, U.: Fundamental limits of blind deconvolution part II: Sparsity-ambiguity trade-offs. arXiv preprint arXiv:1503.03184 (2015)

5. Chouzenoux, E., Pesquet, J.C., Repetti, A.: A block coordinate variable metric forward-backward algorithm. J. Glob. Optim. **66**(3), 457–485 (2016)
6. Combettes, P.L., Pesquet, J.C.: Proximal splitting methods in signal processing. In: Bauschke, H., Burachik, R., Combettes, P., Elser, V., Luke, D., Wolkowicz, H. (eds.) Fixed-Point Algorithms for Inverse Problems in Science and Engineering. SOIA, vol. 49, pp. 185–212. Springer, New York (2011). https://doi.org/10.1007/978-1-4419-9569-8_10
7. Grant, M., Boyd, S., Grant, M., Boyd, S., Blondel, V., Boyd, S., Kimura, H.: CVX: Matlab software for disciplined convex programming, version 2.1. In: Recent Advances in Learning and Control, pp. 95–110 (2008)
8. Guan, J., Wang, X., Wang, W., Huang, L.: Sparse blind speech deconvolution with dynamic range regularization and indicator function. Circ. Syst. Sig. Process. **36**(10), 4145–4160 (2017)
9. Hu, Y., Kokkinakis, K.: Effects of early and late reflections on intelligibility of reverberated speech by cochlear implant listeners. J. Acoust. Soc. Am. **135**(1), EL22–EL28 (2014)
10. Kim, S.J., Koh, K., Lustig, M., Boyd, S., Gorinevsky, D.: An interior-point method for large-scale l1-regularized least squares. IEEE J. Sel. Top. Sig. Process. **1**(4), 606–617 (2007)
11. Klatte, M., Lachmann, T., Meis, M., et al.: Effects of noise and reverberation on speech perception and listening comprehension of children and adults in a classroom-like setting. Noise Health **12**(49), 270 (2010)
12. Mosayyebpour, S., Esmaeili, M., Gulliver, T.A.: Single-microphone early and late reverberation suppression in noisy speech. IEEE Trans. Audio, Speech, Lang. Process. **21**(2), 322–335 (2013)
13. Nakatani, T., Miyoshi, M., Kinoshita, K.: One microphone blind dereverberation based on quasi-periodicity of speech signals. In: NIPS, pp. 1417–1424 (2003)
14. Parikh, N., Boyd, S.: Proximal algorithms. Found. Trends Optim. **1**(3), 127–239 (2014)
15. Schuller, B.: Affective speaker state analysis in the presence of reverberation. Int. J. Speech Technol. **14**(2), 77–87 (2011)
16. Zhao, S., Gao, Y., Jiang, X., Yao, H., Chua, T.S., Sun, X.: Exploring principles-of-art features for image emotion recognition. In: ACM International Conference on Multimedia, pp. 47–56 (2014)
17. Zhao, S., Yao, H., Gao, Y., Ji, R.R., Ding, G.: Continuous probability distribution prediction of image emotions via multi-task shared sparse regression. IEEE Transactions on Multimedia **PP**(99), 1 (2016)
18. Zhao, S., Yao, H., Jiang, X., Sun, X.: Predicting discrete probability distribution of image emotions. In: IEEE International Conference on Image Processing, pp. 2459–2463. IEEE (2015)

Multi-modal Emotion Recognition Based on Speech and Image

Yongqiang Li[1,2(✉)], Qi He[1], Yongping Zhao[1], and Hongxun Yao[2]

[1] School of Electrical Engineering and Automation,
Harbin Institute of Technology, Harbin 150001, China
liyongqiang@hit.edu.cn
[2] School of Computer Science and Technology,
Harbin Institute of Technology, Harbin 150001, China

Abstract. For the past two decades emotion recognition has gained great attention because of huge potential in many applications. Most works in this field try to recognize emotion from single modal such as image or speech. Recently, there are some studies investigating emotion recognition from multi-modal, i.e., speech and image. The information fusion strategy is a key point for multi-modal emotion recognition, which can be grouped into two main categories: feature level fusion and decision level fusion. This paper explores the emotion recognition from multi-modal, i.e., speech and image. We make a systemic and detailed comparison among several feature level fusion methods and decision level fusion methods such as PCA based feature fusion, LDA based feature fusion, product rule based decision fusion, mean rule based decision fusion and so on. We test all the compared methods on the Surrey Audio-Visual Expressed Emotion (SAVEE) Database. The experimental results demonstrate that emotion recognition based on fusion of speech and image achieved high recognition accuracy than emotion recognition from single modal, and also the decision level fusion methods show superior to feature level fusion methods in this work.

Keywords: Multi-modal emotion recognition · Feature level fusion
Decision level fusion

1 Introduction

Emotion is an intrinsic subjective experience, but always accompanied by certain external manifestations, such as changes in facial expressions, speech tones, rhythms, etc. Most traditional studies on emotion recognition focused on recognizing the current emotional state of human beings through single modal information, such as audio recognition. Cahn et al. [1] designed an emotional speech editor and analyzed the relationship between acoustic characteristics such as fundamental frequency, amplitude,

---

Electronic supplementary material The online version of this chapter (https://doi.org/10.1007/978-3-319-77380-3_81) contains supplementary material, which is available to authorized users.

© Springer International Publishing AG, part of Springer Nature 2018
B. Zeng et al. (Eds.): PCM 2017, LNCS 10735, pp. 844–853, 2018.
https://doi.org/10.1007/978-3-319-77380-3_81

formant and other emotional states; Tato et al. [2] found that sound quality not only expresses "Valence" information in the three-dimensional emotional space model, but also partly reflects its "control" information; Liu et al. [3] proposed a nonlinear method based on covariance descriptor and Riemannian manifold for audio emotion recognition. Some works [4–7] used speech spectral parameters LPC/LPCC/MFCC to study the short-term characteristics of speech signals. Besides, many scholars try to recognize facial expressions from images, such as Zeng et al. [8] used multi-scale and multi-directional Gabor wavelet to extract facial features for facial expression recognition; He et al. [9] used optical flow method with a priori knowledge of human face for facial expression recognition; Bouchra et al. [10] used the AAM model for the recognition and synthesis of facial expressions. Although emotion recognition based on single modal has made significantly progress, recognizing emotions from both image and speech will theoretically improve the recognition performance because of involving more information. Hence, more and more scholars turn to the field of multi-modal emotion recognition [11–16]. Some effects try to fuse the visual information obtained by the face image with the audio information obtained from the speech, to achieve a better recognition performance. In this paper, we explore the emotional recognition from multi-modal, i.e., speech and image. The target emotions include anger, disgust, fear, happiness, sadness, surprise and neutral. We extract 92-dimensional audio emotional features and 240-dimensional visual features, and make a systemic and detailed comparison among several feature level fusion methods and decision level feature fusion methods such as PCA based feature fusion, LDA based feature fusion, product rule based feature fusion, mean rule based feature and so on. All the compared methods are tested on the Surrey Audio-Visual Expressed Emotion (SAVEE) Database. A detailed comparison and analysis of the experimental results are provided.

2 Method

2.1 Database

The SAVEE emotional database, whose text material was selected from standard TIMIT database, was recorded from four native English male speakers, including postgraduate students and researchers at the University of Surrey aged from 27 to 31. There are seven emotional categories, namely anger, disgust, fear, happiness, neutral, sadness and surprise. Each emotion consists of 15 sentences: 3 common, 2 emotion-specific and 10 generic sentences that were different for each emotion and phonetically-balanced. There are also 30 sentences of neutral emotion. That is to say each recorder should speak 120 utterances, so there are 480 materials in total. The sampling rate was 44.1 kHz for audio and 60 fps for video.

To facilitate extraction of facial features, the actor's face was painted with 60 markers. After data capture, markers were manually labeled for the first frame of a sequence and then tracked for the remaining frames using a marker tracker. This stage created a set of 2D marker coordinates for each frame of the visual data.

Each actor's data were evaluated by 10 subjects, of which 5 were native English speakers and the rest of them had lived in UK for more than a year. Using the authoritative approach to evaluation, the final recognition results were audio 66.5%, visual 88.0%, Audio-visual 91.8%. The results showed that the database used for emotional recognition was effective.

2.2   Multi-modal Fusion Emotion Recognition

In this paper, SAVEE Database was selected to evaluate all the compared methods. We firstly extract the audio emotional features and visual emotional features from the data instances collected from SAVEE. All the compared methods are based on the same raw features. We test emotion recognition based on single modal, as well as based on multi-modal. The process of experiment is shown in Fig. 1.

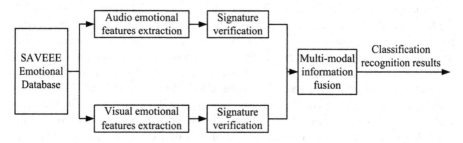

Fig. 1. Process of experiment

Specifically, 92-dimensional phonetic emotional features are extracted, including statistical parameters of short-term energy, duration of speech, pitch frequency, formants, and Mel Frequency Cepstral Coefficients (MFCCs). For visual features, we extract 240-dimensional features of the face image sequence by calculating the mean and standard deviation of the coordinates of 60 facial landmarks. The visual feature extraction flow is shown in Fig. 2. Then we use the "one-versus-one" strategy support vector machine (SVM) to perform emotional recognition experiments on the audio and visual features respectively, and we employ SVM as the classifier which is implemented using libsvm toolbox [17]. Finally, several the feature level fusion methods and the decision level fusion methods are implemented to fuse the audio modal information and the visual modal information, and then detailed comparison and analysis are provided.

PCA and LDA methods are used for feature level fusion and five rules are adopted for decision level fusion, including product rule, mean rule, summation rule, maximum rule and minimum rule. The general formula of decision level fusion is as follows:

$$\begin{cases} mid\_p_j(n) = rule(origin\_p_{ij}(n)) \\ new\_p_j(n) = \dfrac{mid\_p_j(n)}{\sum\limits_j mid\_p_j(n)} \end{cases} \quad , i = 1, 2, \ldots, k, j = 1, 2, \ldots, c \quad (1)$$

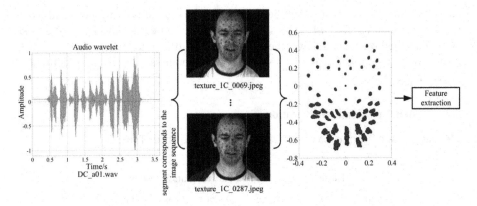

Fig. 2. Visual emotional feature extraction process

where $mid\_p_j(n)$ is the recognition probability matrix after the regular operation, *rule* denotes five rules as listed above, $origin\_p_{ij}(n)$ is audio emotional recognition probability matrix and visual emotional recognition probability matrix, and $new\_p_j(n)$ is the output recognition probability matrix, n is the current test sample, k denotes the number of emotional classifiers, c denotes the emotional category, and $k = 2$ and $c = 7$ in this paper. For data instance n, the final label is assigned to j where $new\_p_j(n)$ has its maximum value.

3　Experiments and Analysis

We tested all the compared methods on SAVEE database, from which we collect 480 data instances and randomly select 320 as training data and test the methods on the rest. The results of the experiments are analyzed below. Here we only gives out a brief experimental result, and for the whole confusion matrix, the readers are referred to the supplemental material.

3.1　Audio Emotional Recognition

Table 1 shows the recognition results based on audio data.

Table 1. Audio emotional recognition results

Emotion	Anger	Disgust	Fear	Happiness
Recognition accuracy	80.00%	70.00%	45.00%	35.00%
Emotion	Neutral	Sadness	Surprise	Average
Recognition accuracy	80.00%	70.00%	65.00%	65.63%

The average recognition accuracy is significantly higher than that in the work [18]. From Table 1 we can see that, recognition rates of anger and neutral have the highest accuracy. Anger is easily misidentified as disgust and neutral is easily misidentified as disgust and sadness. Disgust, sadness and surprise are all easily misidentified as sadness. Fear and happiness have the lowest recognition rate, where fear is easily misidentified as disgust, neutral or surprise, and happiness is easily misidentified as anger or fear.

3.2   Visual Emotional Recognition

The classification results based on visual data are shown in Table 2.

Table 2. Visual emotional recognition results

Emotion	Anger	Disgust	Fear	Happiness
Recognition accuracy	100.00%	70.00%	55.00%	95.00%
Emotion	Neutral	Sadness	Surprise	Average
Recognition accuracy	100.00%	100.00%	80.00%	87.50%

The average recognition accuracy based on visual data is higher than the speech emotional that of based on audio data. The recognition rates of anger, neutral and sadness are all 100%. Surprise is easily misidentified as fear, and disgust is easily misidentified as anger. Recognition rate of fear is higher than that on audio data, but is still the lowest, which is easily misidentified as surprise and sadness.

3.3   Feature Level Fusion Emotional Recognition

3.3.1   PCA Based Fusion

We feed all the 332 dimensional audio and visual features to PCA and 93 dimensional features were obtained. The classification results based on PCA based fusion are shown in Table 3.

Table 3. PCA fusion emotional recognition results

Emotion	Anger	Disgust	Fear	Happiness
Recognition accuracy	90.00%	85.00%	50.00%	95.00%
Emotion	Neutral	Sadness	Surprise	Average
Recognition accuracy	90.00%	85.00%	85.00%	83.75%

The average recognition accuracy is higher than that of audio emotional recognition but lower than that of visual emotional recognition, which is consistent with the conclusion of the paper [18]. Happiness, anger and neutral recognition accuracies are the highest. Disgust is easily misidentified as sadness, sadness is easily misidentified as fear, and surprise is easily misidentified as fear. Fear recognition accuracy is the lowest, which is easily misidentified as surprise and sadness.

3.3.2   LDA Based Fusion

We feed all the 332 dimensional audio and visual features to LDA and 6 dimensional features were obtained. The recognition results based on LDA based fusion are shown in Table 4.

Table 4. LDA fusion emotional recognition results

Emotion	Anger	Disgust	Fear	Happiness
Recognition accuracy	95.00%	90.00%	40.00%	95.00%
Emotion	Neutral	Sadness	Surprise	Average
Recognition accuracy	97.50%	100.00%	100.00%	89.38%

The average recognition accuracy is higher than that of audio emotional recognition and visual emotion recognition. The recognition accuracy of sadness and surprise recognition are the highest while that of fear is the lowest, which is easily misidentified as surprise and sadness.

3.4   Decision-Making Fusion Emotional Recognition

3.4.1   Product Rule

The recognition results of product rule based methods are shown in Table 5.

Table 5. Product rule based emotional recognition results

Emotion	Anger	Disgust	Fear	Happiness
Recognition accuracy	100.00%	95.00%	70.00%	95.00%
Emotion	Neutral	Sadness	Surprise	Average
Recognition accuracy	100.00%	100.00%	80.00%	92.50%

The average recognition accuracy of product rule based method is 92.5%, which is higher than that of feature level fusion methods, i.e., 83.75% for PCA based fusion and 89.38 for LDA based fusion. The recognition accuracies of surprise and fear were low, where surprise is easily misidentified as fear and fear is easily misidentified as surprise or disgust.

3.4.2   Mean Rule

The recognition results of mean rule based method are shown in Table 6. The average recognition accuracy of mean rule based method is 91.25%, which is higher than that of LDA based fusion but lower than the product rule based fusion. Anger, neutral and sadness have the highest recognition accuracies. Fear is also difficult to recognize since fear is easily misidentified as surprise, disgust or sadness.

Table 6. Mean rule fusion emotional recognition results

Emotion	Anger	Disgust	Fear	Happiness
Recognition accuracy	100.00%	90.00%	65.00%	95.00%
Emotion	Neutral	Sadness	Surprise	Average
Recognition accuracy	100.00%	100.00%	80.00%	91.25%

3.4.3 Summation Rule

The recognition results of summation based method are shown in Table 7. The average recognition accuracy is the same as the mean rule.

Table 7. Summation rule fusion emotional recognition results

Emotion	Anger	Disgust	Fear	Happiness
Recognition accuracy	100.00%	90.00%	65.00%	95.00%
Emotion	Neutral	Sadness	Surprise	Average
Recognition accuracy	100.00%	100.00%	80.00%	91.25%

3.4.4 Maximum Rule

The recognition results of maximum rule based methods are shown in Table 8.

Table 8. Maximum rule fusion emotional recognition results

Emotion	Anger	Disgust	Fear	Happiness
Recognition accuracy	100.00%	85.00%	70.00%	90.00%
Emotion	Neutral	Sadness	Surprise	Average
Recognition accuracy	100.00%	100.00%	75.00%	90.00%

The average recognition accuracy of maximum rule based method is 90.0%, which is lower than that of product rule based method. Surprise and fear are not well recognized, where surprise is easily misidentified as fear and fear is easily misidentified as surprise or sadness.

3.4.5 Minimum Rule

The recognition results of minimum rule based method are shown in Table 9.

Table 9. Minimum rule fusion emotional recognition results

Emotion	Anger	Disgust	Fear	Happiness
Recognition accuracy	100.00%	100.00%	70.00%	95.00%
Emotion	Neutral	Sadness	Surprise	Average
Recognition accuracy	100.00%	100.00%	85.00%	93.75%

The average recognition accuracy of minimum rule based method is 93.75%, which is higher than all other methods. Anger, disgust, neutral and sadness are all 100% accurately recognized. Fear is also difficult to recognize, where fear is easily misidentified as surprise or disgust.

3.5   Analysis of Experimental Results

The following is the detailed analysis of audio emotional recognition, visual emotional recognition and multi-modal fusion emotional recognition experimental results.

3.5.1   Comparison with State of the Art

The comparison of the recognition results of this work with that of work [18] is shown in Fig. 3. As shown in Fig. 3, blue bar indicates the evaluation results by ten evaluators, which indicates that the database is effective for emotional recognition. The green bar denotes the recognition results of paper [18] and brown bar is the recognition result of this paper. From Fig. 3 we can see that for audio recognition this paper achieved better performance, but for visual recognition and fused recognition the results of this paper is slightly lower than that of paper [18]. The reason is mainly because that the classifier used in this paper is different from that in paper [18], as well as some details for feature extraction, etc. In general, the recognition results obtained in this paper indicate that the fusion of multi-modal information can achieve better results than single-mode emotional recognition.

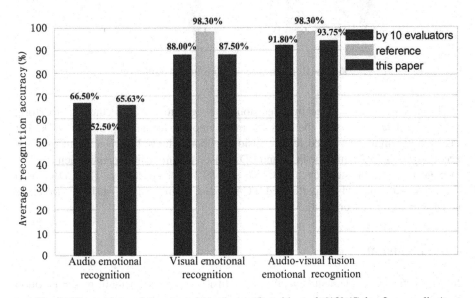

Fig. 3. Comparison of the recognition the results with work [18] (Color figure online)

3.5.2 Comparison of Feature Fusion Methods

In this paper, two different modal information fusion strategies are adopted, namely feature level fusion and decision level fusion. For feature level fusion, we employed PCA based feature fusion and LDA based feature fusion. For decision level fusion we adopt five different methods: product rule, mean rule, summation rule, maximum rule and minimum rule based feature fusion. The results of all these feature fusion methods are shown in Fig. 4.

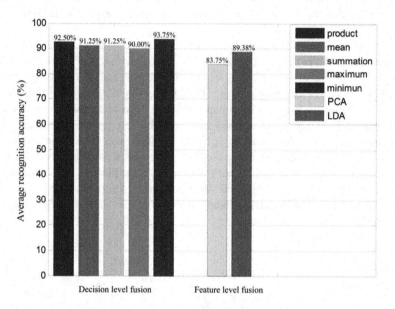

Fig. 4. Comparison of feature fusion methods.

From Fig. 4 we can see that decision level feature fusion methods outperform feature level feature fusion methods for multi-emotion recognition in this work. For instance, the minimum based feature fusion method achieved an average recognition accuracy of 93.75% while the PCA and LDA based feature fusion methods achieved an average recognition accuracy of 83.75% and 89.38% respectively. The LDA based feature fusion method outperformed PCA based feature fusion method, which is consistent with the work [18].

4   Conclusion

In this work, we implement several feature fusion methods for multi-modal emotion recognition, and evaluate all these methods on the SAVEE emotional database. The experimental results show that information fusion from multi-modal benefits the emotion recognition performance. And also, decision level feature fusion methods outperformed feature level feature fusion methods in this work.

Acknowledgements. This work is supported by National Natural Science Foundation of China Project (No. 61402219) and Postdoctoral Foundation Projects (Nos. LBH-Z14090, 2015M57 1417 and 2017T100243).

References

1. Cahn, J.: The generation of affect in synthesized speech. J. Am. Voice I/O Soc. **8**(1), 1–19 (1990)
2. Tato, R., Santos, R., Kompe, R., et al.: Emotional space improves emotion recognition. In: 7th International Conference on Spoken Language Processing, Denver, Colorado, pp. 2029–2032 (2002)
3. Liu, J., Chen, A., Ye, C.X., Bu, J.J.: Speech emotion recognition based on covariance descriptor and Riemannian manifold. Pattern Recogn. Artif. Intell. **05**, 673–677 (2009)
4. Bitouk, D., Verma, R., Nenkova, A.: Class-level spectral features for emotion recognition. Speech Commun. **52**(7–8), 613–625 (2010)
5. Bozkurt, E., Erzin, E., Erdem, Ē.: Formant position based weighted spectral features for emotion recognition. Speech Commun. **53**(9), 1186–1197 (2011)
6. Schuller, B., Batliner, A., Steidl, S., et al.: Recognising realistic emotions and affect in speech: state of the art and lessons learnt from the first challenge. Speech Commun. **53**(9), 1062–1087 (2011)
7. Koolagudi, S.G., Rao, K.S.: Emotion recognition from speech using source, system, and prosodic features. Int. J. Speech Technol. 1–25 (2012)
8. Zhang, Z., Lyons, M., Schuster, M., et al.: Comparison between geometry-based and Gabor-wavelets-based facial expression recognition using multi-layer perceptron. In: Third IEEE International Conference on Face and Gesture Recognition, Nara, Japan, pp. 454–459 (1998)
9. He, K., Wang, G., Yang, Y.: Optical flow-based facial feature tracking using prior measurement. In: 7th IEEE International Conference on Cognitive Informatics, Stanford, CA, pp. 324–331 (2008)
10. Abboud, B., Davoine, F., Dang, M.: Facial expression recognition and synthesis based on an appearance model. Sig. Process. Image Commun. **19**(8), 723–740 (2004)
11. Zhao, S., Gao, Y., Jiang, X., Yao, H., Chua, T., Sun, X.: Exploring principles-of-art features for image emotion recognition. In: ACM Multimedia, pp. 47–56 (2014)
12. Lee, C.M., Narayanan, S.: Toward detecting emotions in spoken dialogs. IEEE Trans. Speech Audio Process. **13**(2), 293–303 (2005)
13. Zhao, S., Yao, H., Sun, X.: Video classification and recommendation based on affective analysis of viewers. Neurocomputing 101–110 (2013)
14. Zhao, S., Yao, H., Gao, Y., Ji, R., Ding, G.: Continuous probability distribution prediction of image emotions via multi-task shared sparse regression. IEEE Trans. Multimedia 1 (2016)
15. Kudiri, K.M., Said, A.M., Nayan, M.Y.: Emotion detection through speech and facial expressions. In: 2014 International Conference on Computer Assisted System in Health (CASH), pp. 26–31. IEEE (2014)
16. Zhao, S., Yao, H., Jiang, X.: Predicting continuous probability distribution of image emotions in valence-arousal space. In: ACM Multimedia, pp. 879–882 (2015)
17. Chang, C.C., Lin, C.J.: LIBSVM: a library for support vector machines. ACM Trans. Intell. Syst. Technol. (TIST) **2**(3), 27 (2011)
18. Haq, S., Jackson, P.J.B., Edge, J.: Audio-visual feature selection and reduction for emotion classification. In: Proceedings of International Conference on Auditory-Visual Speech Processing (AVSP 2008), Tangalooma, Australia (2008)

Analysis of Psychological Behavior of Undergraduates

Chunchang Gao[⊠]

Information Office, University of Shanghai for Science and Technology,
Shanghai, China
gaocc@usst.edu.cn

Abstract. The study of psychological behavior of undergraduates is one of the key problems in modern teaching and has become a hot issue. This paper introduced the commonly psychological analysis methods in undergraduate education management. Analysis the psychological changes which thanks to daily data of students' actual life and learning. This paper puts forward the feasibility of analyzing the psychological behavior of students from the data level, and used the data of the psychological behavior of the students, to provide a reference for the teaching and management of the undergraduates.

Keywords: Undergraduates · Psychological behavior · Data analysis

1 Introduction

It has become one of the hot issues of common concern in society, the problem of psychological behavior of college students, and researchers study it in many ways [5]. Research in [1] shows that the mental health problems of contemporary college students including adaptability, interpersonal problems, love and sexual distress, emotional problems, academic problems, employment and development issues. These mental health problems affect the development of college students healthily in varying degrees. This paper analyzes the possible psychological behavior which come from college students' academic problems.

To the author's analysis, the current psychological behavior of college students performed in the following aspects: (a) positive behavior; (b) neutral behavior; (c) dilute (ignore) sexual behavior; (d) avoid behavior; (v) feared behavior. This paper is concerned about emotional and psychological abnormalities caused by abnormal behavior and performance is not ideal or academic cliff downward.

2 Objects of Study

2.1 Objects of Study

A college undergraduate students, selected part of the data of daily behavior of part student for the study, react the psychological behavior of students sideways.

© Springer International Publishing AG, part of Springer Nature 2018
B. Zeng et al. (Eds.): PCM 2017, LNCS 10735, pp. 854–860, 2018.
https://doi.org/10.1007/978-3-319-77380-3_82

2.2   Research Methods

Analyze the basic data of students' psychological behavior through data analysis and association analysis, which including consumer behavior, class behavior, academic performance, etc.

2.3   Statistical Methods

Collecting student basic data, and using Excel software to build a database, and then convert to visual reports, generate view files for educators as reference.

3   Research Process

3.1   Psychological Behavior of College Students

Psychological problems of students have great group differences. Research [1] shows that the psychological problems of freshmen, female college students and poor students are the most prominent. Outstanding psychological problems are learning problems, interpersonal and emotional problems, and personal development issues. And those questions reflected on daily life and behavior is the changes of track.

3.2   Analysis of the Causes of Psychological Vulnerability of College Students

College students are a group of people who have not really formed their own outlook on life, values. Their psychological process is almost a piece of white paper, no matter it is psychological pressure or heart accepted ability, are not left enough ink in the heart. As well the will is also not strong enough, mainly reflected in when they encountered setbacks or difficulties, the first thought is not solve it by themselves, but call for assistance of their loved ones, is not enough self-confidence from their own people. They are not enough self-confidence from their own people. For these who cannot get support, fear will follow. Especially these cannot effectively deal with the situation, evasion, fear and other psychological behavior follows.

3.3   The Psychological Problems Bring from the Student Online Behavior

Contemporary college students are the younger generation who rich in the inner world, full of vitality and pioneering spirit. The healthy and stability of each aspect of their mind is directly related to the personal growth, development, employment and talent, and even related to the construction of the rule of law and the realization of a harmonious society [13]. It is generally believed that the causes of college students' internet addiction are the following: (1) the contradiction between the interlocking and the intention of making friends, (2) the influence of sexual impulsivity and self-control, (3) to explore the psychological sense of curiosity and understanding of the contradiction between the impact, (4) the influence of ideals and reality in cognitive psychology (Fig. 1).

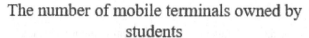

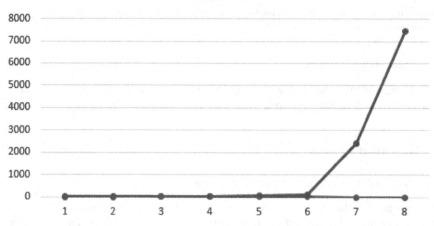

Fig. 1. The number of mobile terminals owned by students

Among the contemporary college students, more than 90% of students have computers, about 97% of college students have mobile phones. With such a large number of mobile terminals, the Internet behavior has become an inevitable event. And in the complicated network world [8], the not yet formed the concept of life, values, world view for student has been a serious challenge, psychological change is great. Once the lack of willpower and control, it is easy to fall into the network, cannot extricate themselves, and even abandoned school, adversely affected life [14].

Through the data generated by system shows students concentrated online hours is normal class time, but there are still some students concentrated online in the rest time or unconventional time, these may have psychological problem. So be very concerned about the abnormal behavior of Internet students and the behavior of these activities caused by changes in mental activity [10] (Fig. 2).

3.4 The Psychological Problem Brought from Results Fall of College Students

Study in [3] shows that the impact of adverse psychological status on college students' academic performance is there. The more serious adverse psychological status the more obvious of the impact [4].

The motivation of college students is derived from learning interest [15], which is the most intense and realistic psychological factors in students' learning life, to a large extent, learning achievement or learning effect is the internal factors that students generate motivation for learning [11]. Learning motivation is the psychological tendency to start and maintain learning activities, is the source of learning for students [12].

Internet Time Distribution

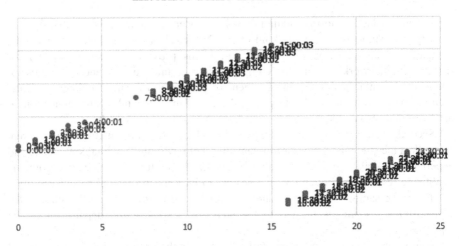

Fig. 2. Internet time distribution

3.5   The Psychology of the Consumption Behavior of College Students

College students in the economic independence is poor, no basis for consumption. The non-independence of the economy determines that college students have less experience in their own consumption and cannot rationally measure the value and cost of consumption. College students did not form a complete, stable consumption idea, self-control ability is not strong, the most consumption is the random consumption, impulse buying, which is induced by the media propaganda or affected by side classmates. All the above is also the result of the university student's consumption demonstration effect [9].

In the survey data, there was a link between some students' grades and the dining situations. For example, the student performance of a normal dining habit is relatively stable. But the abnormal dining ones, especially, non-dinner consumption behavior are not ideal for students. According to behavior data analysis, these students hold the enthusiasm psychology in learning, which should arouse the attention of relevant educators, thereby guide students remodel the motivation of learning from the psychological level.

In addition, studies [6] have shown that poor people with low consumption are likely to be driven from economic poverty to psychological poverty due to their poor experience in life. The so-called psychological poverty refers to the series of personality traits and negative changes in mental health caused by poor college students due to the stress of economic poverty. Most of the poor students do not do well in school. One reason is that poor students, due to economic pressures, it takes time to do part-time or work-study activities, which can take up time.

4 The Deficiency and Improvement of the Research

First, there is a lack of norms and definitions of concepts. There is no clear definition of what type of students exist what kind of psychological problems. Just from the side, reflected students may have psychological problems, providing a general direction for the educational worker. Only the comprehensive accurate understanding and establishment of mental health standards, when we solve the problem of college students' mental ability to achieve the target, college students' mental health education to achieve good results. This is a possible direction for future research.

Second, there is too much qualitative research and too little quantitative research. Just reflect the students' behavior problems in school, with the personal knowledge and experience to analyze it, with the subjective color. So the future research will combine qualitative research and quantitative research, to increase the reliability and validity.

Third, the sampling is narrow and the sample size is small. In all the studies, the scope of the research is limited to the area, the school or the department of the university.

Fourth, data analysis and correlation still stays in the shallow level, not associated with the psychological counseling of students, lack of innovative and forward-looking research, lack an widely evaluation index of psychological health of college students used in China.

Fifth, theoretical guidance and discipline basis are too monolithic [7]. Should strengthen the psychology, pedagogy, medicine, sociology, cultural science, anthropology, and other multi-disciplinary fusion and multidisciplinary personnel cooperation. In a comprehensive discipline, form a comprehensive research force.

5 Analysis and Discussion

Analysis from the level of student data, the system data shows that part of the student behavior may lead to mental health problems, and shows on the visual visualization. Some students are indulged in the online world and thus cannot form a good outlook on life or values, some students are lost learning motivation thanks to the effect of learning and pay are not proportional, while disgust, fear learning and even escape from learning, finally achieve the situation to ignore study. This article provides the educators a visual window through the system data. Give an early warning according to the details of the life of the students may have psychological changes. To explore a viable direction for student management, which can better education and teaching service. In short, in the college students' psychological health education, should according to different object, understand the psychological and emotional state in time [16–25], strengthen the psychological education training, targeted to carry out the deal with setbacks, improve cognitive function and social adaptation ability various training [26–28].

References

1. Zhang, D.: A summary of the research on psychological problems of contemporary college students. J. Graduates Sun Yat-Sen Univ. (Soc. Sci.) **28**, 136–141 (2007)
2. Ma, F.: Affect mental health of students on academic performance. China Health Ind. **3**, 174–175 (2015)
3. Chen, X.: Exploration on the psychological problems of contemporary university students. Sci. Educ. Art. Collect. **9**, 138–139 (2015)
4. Wu, P., Chen, F.G.: Investigation of psychological health condition of undergraduate students in Shanghai universities. J. Shanghai Jiaotong Univ. (Med. Sci.) **30**(8), 906–909 (2010)
5. Luo, S.: Theory and technology on affective computing. Syst. Eng. Electron. **7**, 905–909 (2003)
6. Bi, H.: From "Economic Poverty" to "Psychological Poverty". Vocat. Tech. Educ. **25**, 62–67 (2012)
7. Yan, G., et al.: The choice of the education practical path of college students' mental health at present stage in China. Theory Pract. Educ. **24**, 22–25 (2016)
8. Zhu, J.: The psychological health of college students in the network environment is education. J. Xinyang Normal Univ. (Philos. Soc. Sci. Ed.) **31**, 52–55 (2011)
9. Yao, J.: Discussion on the behavior of university students under the influence of the psychology of following the crowd. J. Gansu Lianhe Univ. (Soc. Sci. Ed.) **3**, 81–83 (2009)
10. Fu, H., et al.: Correlative analysis between college students' network behavior and academic record. Theory Mod. **3**, 37–43 (2014)
11. Xu, J., et al.: University students study and study and improve their strategies. High. Educ. Explor. **6**, 132 (2014)
12. Zhang, L.: The study of the behavior pattern of college students and the correlation of achievement. Heilongjiang Sci. Technol. Inf. **32**, 151–152 (2016)
13. Peng, X., et al.: The relationship between health related behavior and academic performance of college students. China J. Health Psychol. **4**, 582–584 (2012)
14. Zhou, M.: Current situation on internet addiction and its influencing factors among undergraduates in a compreliensive university. Chin. J. Health Educ. **4**, 416–418 (2015)
15. Shi, M.: Analysis of the reasons for low motivation of college students. Reform Open. **1**, 168–169 (2012)
16. Zhao, S., Yao, H., Gao, Y., Ji, R., Ding, G.: Continuous probability distribution prediction of image emotions via multi-task shared sparse regression. IEEE Trans. Multimedia **19**(3), 632–645 (2017)
17. Zhao, S., Yao, H., Gao, Y., Ding, G., Chua, T.-S.: Predicting personalized image emotion perceptions in social networks. IEEE Trans. Affect. Comput. (2017)
18. Zhao, S., Ding, G., Gao, Y., Han, J.: Approximating discrete probability distribution of image emotions by multi-modal features fusion. In: IJCAI (2017)
19. Zhao, S., Yao, H., Gao, Y., Ji, R., Xie, W., Jiang, X., Chua, T.-S.: Predicting personalized emotion perceptions of social images. In: ACM Multimedia, pp. 1385–1394 (2016)
20. Zhao, S., Yao, H., Jiang, X.: Predicting continuous probability distribution of image emotions in valence-arousal space. In: ACM Multimedia, pp. 879–882 (2015)
21. Zhao, S., Yao, H., Jiang, X., Sun, X.: Predicting discrete probability distribution of image emotions. In: IEEE ICIP, pp. 2459–2463 (2015)
22. Zhao, S., Gao, Y., Jiang, X., Yao, H., Chua, T.-S., Sun, X.: Exploring principles-of-art features for image emotion recognition. In: ACM Multimedia, pp. 47–56 (2014)

23. Zhao, S., Yao, H., Yang, Y., Zhang, Y.: Affective image retrieval via multi-graph learning. In: ACM Multimedia, pp. 1025–1028 (2014)
24. Zhao, S., Yao, H., Wang, F., Jiang, X., Zhang, W.: Emotion based image musicalization. In: IEEE ICMEW, pp. 1–6 (2014)
25. Zhao, S., Yao, H., Sun, X.: Affective video classification based on spatio-temporal feature fusion. In: ICIG, pp. 795–800 (2011)
26. Wang, F., Qi, S., Gao, G., Zhao, S., Wang, X.: Logo information recognition in large-scale social media data. Multimedia Syst. **22**(1), 63–73 (2016)
27. Zhao, S., Chen, L., Yao, H., Zhang, Y., Sun, X.: Strategy for dynamic 3D depth data matching towards robust action retrieval. Neurocomputing **151**, 533–543 (2015)
28. Chen, M., Ding, G., Zhao, S., Chen, H., Liu, Q., Han, J.: Reference based LSTM for image captioning. In: AAAI, pp. 3981–3987 (2017)

Sensor-Enhanced Multimedia Systems

Compression Artifacts Reduction for Depth Map by Deep Intensity Guidance

Pingping Zhang[1], Xu Wang[1(✉)], Yun Zhang[2], Lin Ma[3], Jianmin Jiang[1], and Sam Kwong[4]

[1] College of Computer Science and Software Engineering,
Shenzhen University, Shenzhen 518060, China
ppingyes@gmail.com, {wangxu,jianmin.jiang}@szu.edu.cn
[2] Shenzhen Institutes of Advanced Technology,
Chinese Academy of Sciences, Shenzhen 518055, China
yun.zhang@siat.ac.cn
[3] Tencent AI Lab, Shenzhen 518060, China
forest.linma@gmail.com
[4] Department of Computer Science,
City University of Hong Kong, Kowloon, Hong Kong
cssamk@cityu.edu.hk

Abstract. In this paper, we propose a intensity guided CNN (IG-Net) model, which learns an end-to-end mapping between the intensity image and distorted depth map to the uncompressed depth map. To eliminate the undesired blocking artifacts such as discontinuities around object boundary, two branches are designed to extract the high-frequency information from intensity image and depth map, respectively. Multi-scale feature fusion and enhancement layers are introduced in the main branch to strength the edge information of the restored depth map. Performance evaluation on JPEG compression artifacts shows the effectiveness and superiority of our proposed model compared with state-of-the-art methods.

Keywords: Convolutional neural network · Compression artifacts
JPEG Compression

1 Introduction

With the development of sensing technologies such as Microsoft Kinect, it is easy to capture the RGB-D data of 3D scene. Different from the traditional RGB image, the corresponding depth map is available for further applications such as object segmentation, classification [1]. The pixel of the depth map represents the distance information from the viewpoint to the surface of the objects, which can be used to render the virtual viewpoint, synthesize the 3D scene and provide users with immersive experience.

© Springer International Publishing AG, part of Springer Nature 2018
B. Zeng et al. (Eds.): PCM 2017, LNCS 10735, pp. 863–872, 2018.
https://doi.org/10.1007/978-3-319-77380-3_83

Due to the limitation of bandwidth and storage space, the color image and depth map need to be compressed and transmitted to client end for further processing. Thus, compression artifacts such as blockiness, blurring and ring artifacts are inevitably imposed to image, especially for low bit-rate compression condition. Different from the color image, degradation on the depth map will cause annoying virtual experience such as object offset, break boundary of object in the reconstructed 3D scene. Therefore, compression artifacts reduction for depth map is important for the success of 3D application.

Existing works on depth recovery such as super-resolution shows that color image can be used to guide the depth enhancement. Besides, the convolutional neural network (CNN) based models have shown excellent performance on image compression artifacts removal, which are focus on the color image restoration. Inspired by these, we proposed a intensity guided CNN (denoted as IG-Net) model, which avoids to introduce false boundary and strengths the edge information of the restored depth map. Up to now, there is rare published deep learning based work that aimed to reduce the compression artifacts of depth map. The main contributions are listed as follows:

- To eliminate the undesired blocking artifacts such as discontinuities around object boundary, two branches are designed to extract the high-frequency information from intensity image and depth map, respectively.
- Multi-scale feature fusion and enhancement layers are introduced in the model to strength the edge information of the restored depth map.
- The optimal setting of parameters such as filter numbers and patch sizes are discussed and determined in the experimental part.

The rest of this paper is organized as follows. Section 2 overviews the related works. In Sect. 3, the framework of proposed IG-Net model is introduced. Detailed description of experimental results are provided in Sect. 4. Finally, conclusions are given in Sect. 5.

2   Related Work

Image compression artifacts reduction has been widely investigated for number of years. In the early years, most of researchers tend to remove blocking artifacts in spatial or transform domain by designing smooth filters. For example, Luo and Ward [2] proposed an adaptive approach to reduce the block-to-block discontinuities in both the spatial and DCT domains. Singh et al. [3] modeled the blockness as a 2-D step functions between two neighboring blocks in DCT domain. Different filters are applied to smooth/non-smooth regions, respectively. Pointwise Shape-Adaptive DCT (SA-DCT) [4] maybe the most popular deblocking oriented method. SA-DCT can be computed on a support of arbitrary shape, thus, reconstructed edges are clean and have no ringing artifact. However, as most deblocking oriented methods, SA-DCT overly smooths texture regions, and results in losing sharp edges.

The state-of-the-arts methods of single image restoration are mostly sample-based. Inspired by the success of deep learning, Dong et al. [5] proposed a artifacts reduction convolutional neural network (AR-CNN) model with four convolutional layers, which is effective in reducing blocking artifacts while preserving edge and sharp details. To reduce the computation complexity and meet the requirement of real-time image processing, Yu et al. [6] formulate a compact and efficient network for seamless attenuation of different compression artifacts by introducing layer decomposition and joint using of large-stride convolutional and deconvolutional layers. Mao et al. [7] proposed a model that is composed of multiple layers of convolution and deconvolution operators and learned the end-to-end mappings from corrupted images to the original images. The convolutional layers capture the abstraction of image contents while eliminating corruptions. Deconvolutional layers have the capability to up-sample the feature maps and recover the image details.

Based on the above mentioned discussion, most of the CNN based works are designed for restoring the color images. However, the depth map represents the depth information of the scene, and their characteristics are different from the color image. Existing CNN models may not efficiency on removing compression artifacts of depth map since these models did not exploited the correlation between color and depth images. Existing works on depth recovery showed that there are local/non-local similarly between the depth map and the accompanied color image [8]. Inspired by this, we proposed an artifacts reduction model for depth map which is guided by the high-frequency information from depth map and its corresponding color image, respectively.

3   Intensity-Guided Compression Artifacts Reduction for Depth Map

Suppose we have compressed depth map D^q and its corresponding intensity image Y (luminance component of color image). The original depth map is denoted as D. The goal of compression artifacts reduction model is to learn an end-to-end mapping from D^q and Y to D. The compression of depth map will cause discontinuities and blur around block boundary. To strength the edge information of restored depth map, our proposed IG-Net model is consists of three branches, including Y branch, D branch and main branch as shown in Fig. 1. Y branch and D branch extract the high frequency information of the intensity image and depth map, respectively. The main branch is trained to restore the depth map with the high-frequency information from the Y and D branches.

3.1   Spectral Decomposition for Intensity Image and Depth Map

As we know, The color image and depth map have an extremely big difference, since the depth map record the distance information but the pixel value of corresponding color image indicates the intensity of luminance and color information. Thus, it is difficult to train the model without any preprocessing on color images.

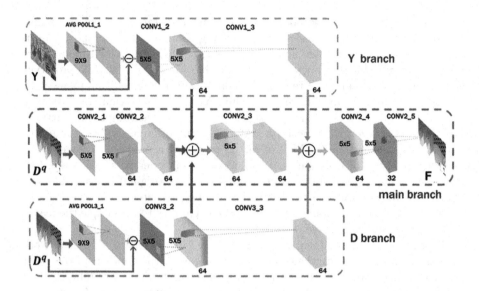

Fig. 1. The architecture of IG-Net. The proposed CNN model consists of three branches, including Y branch, D branch, and main branch. Y branch and D branch aim to strength the edge information with the guidance of color image and depth map, respectively. The learned features form these two branches is used to guide the artifacts reduction in the main branch. (Color figure online)

Based on our observation, we find that the edge of the depth image corresponds to the edge of the color image, since the pixels belong to the same object usually have the same depth. Different from the corresponding intensity image, depth maps are smooth in the object region and sharp around the object boundary. To reduce the interrupt of low frequency information, the spectral decomposition operation is introduced to extract the edge from color image and depth map in Y and D branches, respectively. Besides, using the high-frequency information of intensity image and depth map can speed up the training stage and guarantee the convergence of network training. This operation for Y and D branches can be expressed as:

$$F_0^Y = abs\,(Y - h(Y))$$ (1)

and

$$F_0^D = abs\,(D - h(D^q))\,,$$ (2)

where $h(.)$ is the operation of average pooling to extract low-frequency component.

3.2 Formulation

As shown in Fig. 1, our proposed IG-Net contains 5 convolutional layers in main brach (denoted as M) and 2 convolutional layers in both Y and D branches.

The detailed mathematical formula of IG-Net can be expressed as follows:

$$F_j^Y = max(0, W_j^Y * F_j^Y + B_j^Y), \quad j \in \{1,2\}, \quad (feature \quad extraction) \quad (3)$$

$$F_j^D = max(0, W_j^D * F_j^{D^q} + B_j^{D^q}), \quad j \in \{1,2\}, \quad (feature \quad extraction) \quad (4)$$

$$F_1^M = max(0, W_1^M * D^q + B_1^M), \quad (feature \quad extraction) \quad (5)$$

$$F_2^M = max(0, W_2^M * F_1^M + B_2^M), \quad (feature \quad enhancement) \quad (6)$$

$$F_3^M = F_2^M + F_1^Y + F_1^D, \quad (1st \quad feature \quad fusion) \quad (7)$$

$$F_4^M = max(0, W_3^M * F_3^M + B_3^M), \quad (nonlinear \quad mapping) \quad (8)$$

$$F_5^M = F_4^M + F_2^Y + F_2^D, \quad (2rd \quad feature \quad fusion) \quad (9)$$

$$F_6^M = max(0, W_4^M * F_5^M + B_4^M), \quad (nonlinear \quad mapping) \quad (10)$$

$$F = max(0, W_5^M * F_6^M + B_5^M), \quad (reconstruction) \quad (11)$$

where $*$ denotes the convolution operation. W_i^s is the filter of size $n_{i-1}^s \times f_i^s \times f_i^s \times n_i^s$ for Y, M and D branches, where the superscript $s \in \{Y, M, D\}$. n_{i-1}^s and n_i^s are the number of feature maps of input and output, respectively. B_i^s is a n_i^s-dimensional bias vector. For the top layer, it is scalar. The final output F is the restored depth map of the same size as the input compressed depth map.

In compressed depth map, the quantization error may blur the object boundary and introduce false edge or texture on smooth regions. The feature maps learned from high-frequency component of intensity image and depth maps can help to clean the noise. For better visualization, some feature maps of Y and D branches are randomly selected and provided as shown in Fig. 2. It is observed that these two branches provide useful high-frequency information to the main branch. Each convolutional layer learns different features, which will benefit to restore the depth image.

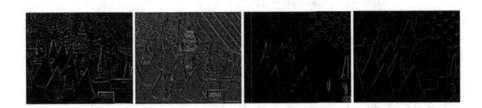

Fig. 2. Feature maps from Y branch and D branch (Visualization of learned feature maps from Y and D branches. From left to right, the feature maps are from CONV1_2, CONV1_3, CONV3_2, CONV3_3 respectively. For better, the intensity values of feature maps are mapped into range [0–255]).

Loss Function. Learning and end-to-end mapping from corrupted depth map and intensity image to clean depth map needs to estimate the weights $\Theta = \{W_i^s, b_i^s\}$. For a training set with n training sample pairs $<(Y_i, D_i^q), D_i>$, the Mean Squared Error (MSE) is employed as the loss function:

$$L(\Theta) = \frac{1}{N} \sum_{i=1}^{n} \|F(Y_i, D_i^q; \Theta) - D_i\|^2. \tag{12}$$

The loss function is minimized using the adaptive moment estimation (Adam) method to adaptively adjust the learning rate for model parameters, which converges faster than traditional optimization methods such as stochastic gradient descent (SGD) algorithm.

4 Experiments

To evaluate performance of proposed model, training and testing images are collected from existing RGB-D databases. In this paper, the training dataset is consist of 105 RGB-D scenes, including Middlebury dataset [9–12], MPI sintel depth dataset [1] and Multi Modal Stereo dataset [13]. The number of RGB-D scenes in test set is 12. Detailed information are provided in Table 1. Similar to the compression artifacts reductional model in ARCNN [5], the depth image is compressed by the MATLAB JPEG encoder with quality setting $q \in \{10, 20, 30, 40\}$ (from low quality to high quality). The corresponding color image in training/test set is keep uncompressed. Detailed information about the compression setting for color and depth images are provided in Table 2.

Table 1. Number of images in training/test dataset

Dataset	Training set	Test set
Middlebury dataset [9–12]	47	7
MPI sintel depth dataset [1]	36	4
Multi-modal stereo datasets [13]	22	1
Total	105	12

Instead of directly using the whole images for training, sub-images are extracted from the large size image in the training set. The uncompressed color image, uncompressed depth map and compressed depth map are decomposed into small overlapping sub-images with patch size $N \times N$ and stride 10, respectively. Final, we build four training sets $\{<(Y_i, D_i^q), D_i>\}_{i=1}^{l}$, where l is the number of samples in each training set.

The proposed model is trained and tested in tensorflow platform with a Tesla K80 GPU server. During the training stage, the base learning rate is set as 10^{-4} and Adam is enabled. Since depth image is not used for viewing, the criterion of

Table 2. Compression setting for color/depth images in training/test set

Training set		Test set	
Color	Depth	Color	Depth
Uncompress	$\{10, 20, 30, 40\}$	Uncompress	$\{10, 20, 30, 40\}$

performance evaluation in terms of root mean squared error (RMSE) is employed in the experiment. For simplify, we denote the trained model as IG-Net-q for the training set with quality setting q of depth image. The test set is denoted as TestSet-q where the test depth images are compressed with quality setting q. In this paper, the performance of model IG-Net-q will be evaluated on TestSet-q.

4.1 Influence of Model Parameter

To make our proposed model more flexible, the parameters such as patch size, filter numbers of each layer are not fixed in the experiment. In the following parts, we will discuss the influence of model parameters on the restoration performance.

Filter Number. To test the influence of filter numbers in each layer on the performance, we fix the patch size of train set as 32, and train the model with different filter number combinations. We fixed the number of filters as 64 except for the convolutional layer CONV2_4 and CONV2_5 in the main branch. In the experiment, our proposed IG-Net model is trained with three different setting for filter number of CONV2_4 and CONV2_5. As shown in Table 3, it is obviously that the model with more filters can significantly reduce the compression artifacts for all the quality level at the cost of increasing computational complexity. To make a balance between performance gain and computational complexity, we set the filter numbers of CONV2_4 and CONV2_5 as 64 and 32, respectively.

Patch Size. To evaluate the influence of patch size on the performance, we generate the training set with five different patch sizes, including 24×24, 32×32, 48×48, 64×64 and 80×80. The models are trained on training sets with $q = 10$ and $q = 40$. As shown in Fig. 3, the fluctuation trend of the training loss for

Table 3. The average result of RMSE on testing images with different filter number combinations

Model	JPEG	(32,16)	(64,32)	(128,64)
IG-Net-10	6.46	4.57	4.40	4.39
IG-Net-20	5.03	2.96	2.68	2.48
IG-Net-30	4.28	2.17	1.84	1.79
IG-Net-40	3.80	1.79	1.47	1.42

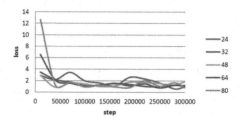

Fig. 3. The average performance of using different patch sizes.

Table 4. The average result of RMSE on test images with different patch size.

Model	JPEG	Patch size				
		24	32	48	64	80
IG-Net-10	6.46	4.96	5.02	4.96	5.01	4.98
IG-Net-40	3.80	1.85	1.48	1.45	1.44	1.51

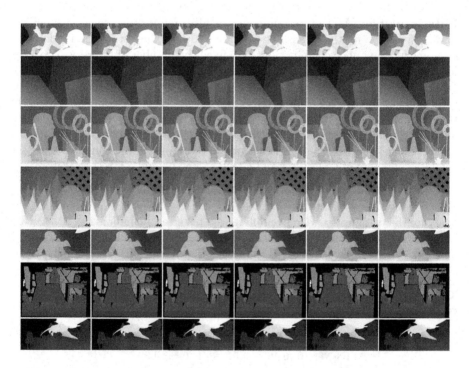

Fig. 4. Visualization of restored depth maps. (For left to right, the images are the ground-truth and JEPG compressed depth map with $q = 10$, restored depth maps by SA-DCT, ARCNN, RED-Net and IG-Net respectively.)

Table 5. Performance comparison of compression artifacts reduction algorithms on different test sets

	JPEG	SA-DCT	AR-CNN	RED-Net	IG-Net
TestSet-10	6.46	5.45	4.91	4.93	**4.37**
TestSet-20	5.03	4.13	3.45	3.39	**2.76**
TestSet-30	4.28	3.45	2.84	2.61	**1.94**
TestSet-40	3.80	3.00	2.53	2.27	**1.62**

models with different patch size are similar. The performance analysis on test set are provided in Table 4. For both IG-Net-10 and IG-Net-40 models, the average RMSE value of restored depth map are significantly reduced for all kind of patch size settings. There are no big performance gap between different patch sizes.

4.2 Performance Comparison with the State-of-the-Arts

To demonstrate the performance of our proposed model, we compare IG-Net with the state-of-the-arts algorithms, including SA-DCT, AR-CNN, RED-Net. All these models are designed for color image compression artifacts reduction. All the training and test stage of AR-CNN, RED-Net and proposed IG-Net models are same. The parameters of these models are set as default. Quantitative results evaluated on test set with different quality levels are shown in Table 5. We could find that our IG-Net achieves the smallest RMSE value and outperforms other models on all JPEG compression qualities, which means that IG-Net significantly reduce the blocking artifacts of JPEG compressed depth map. For better visualization, Fig. 4 provides some restoration results of different models on TestSet-10. From Fig. 4, we could see that the result of IG-Net could produce sharper edges with much less blocking artifacts compared with other models.

5   Conclusion

This paper proposed a proposed an artifacts reduction model for depth map which is guided by the high-frequency information from depth map and its corresponding color image, respectively. To strength the edge information of restored depth map, our proposed IG-Net model is consists of three branches, including Y branch, D branch and main branch. The optimal setting of parameters such as filter numbers and patch sizes are discussed and determined in the experimental part. Experimental results demonstrate that our model achieves high quality recovery from compressed depth map.

Acknowledgments. This work was supported in part by the National Natural Science Foundation of China under Grant 61501299, 61471348, 61672443 and 61620106008, in part by the Guangdong Nature Science Foundation under Grant 2016A030310058, in part by the Shenzhen Emerging Industries of the Strategic Basic

Research Project under Grants JCYJ20150525092941043, JCYJ20160226191842793, in part by the Project 2016049 supported by SZU R/D Fund, and in part by the Tencent "Rhinoceros Birds"-Scientific Research Foundation for Young Teachers of Shenzhen University.

References

1. McHenry, K., Bajcsy, P.: An overview of 3D data content, file formats and viewers. Natl Center Supercomput. Appl. **1205**, 22 (2008)
2. Luo, Y., Ward, R.K.: Removing the blocking artifacts of block-based DCT compressed images. IEEE Trans. Image Process. **12**(7), 838–842 (2003)
3. Singh, S., Kumar, V., Verma, H.K.: Reduction of blocking artifacts in JPEG compressed images. Digit. Signal Proc. **17**(1), 225–243 (2007)
4. Foi, A., Katkovnik, V., Egiazarian, K.: Pointwise shape-adaptive DCT for high-quality denoising and deblocking of grayscale and color images. IEEE Trans. Image Process. **16**(5), 1395–1411 (2007)
5. Dong, C., Deng, Y., Change Loy, C., Tang, X.: Compression artifacts reduction by a deep convolutional network. In: 2015 IEEE International Conference on Computer Vision (ICCV), pp. 576–584. IEEE, December 2015
6. Yu, K., Dong, C., Loy, C.C., Tang, X.: Deep convolution networks for compression artifacts reduction. arXiv preprint arXiv:1608.02778 (2016)
7. Mao, X.-J., Shen, C., Yang, Y.-B.: Image restoration using convolutional auto-encoders with symmetric skip connections. arXiv preprint arXiv:1606.08921 (2016)
8. Hui, T.-W., Loy, C.C., Tang, X.: Depth map super-resolution by deep multi-scale guidance. In: Leibe, B., Matas, J., Sebe, N., Welling, M. (eds.) ECCV 2016. LNCS, vol. 9907, pp. 353–369. Springer, Cham (2016). https://doi.org/10.1007/978-3-319-46487-9_22
9. Scharstein, D., Szeliski, R.: High-accuracy stereo depth maps using structured light. In: Proceedings of 2003 IEEE Computer Society Conference on Computer Vision and Pattern Recognition, vol. 1, p. I. IEEE Computer Society (2003)
10. Scharstein, D., Pal, C.: Learning conditional random fields for stereo. In: 2007 IEEE Conference on Computer Vision and Pattern Recognition, pp. 1–8. IEEE, June 2007
11. Hirschmuller, H., Scharstein, D.: Evaluation of cost functions for stereo matching. In: 2007 IEEE Conference on Computer Vision and Pattern Recognition, pp. 1–8. IEEE, June 2007
12. Scharstein, D., Hirschmüller, H., Kitajima, Y., Krathwohl, G., Nešić, N., Wang, X., Westling, P.: High-resolution stereo datasets with subpixel-accurate ground truth. In: Jiang, X., Hornegger, J., Koch, R. (eds.) GCPR 2014. LNCS, vol. 8753, pp. 31–42. Springer, Cham (2014). https://doi.org/10.1007/978-3-319-11752-2_3
13. Yaman, M., Kalkan, S.: An iterative adaptive multi-modal stereo-vision method using mutual information. J. Vis. Commun. Image Represent. **26**, 115–131 (2015)

LiPS: Learning Social Relationships in Probe Space

Chaoxi Li[1], Chengwen Luo[1(✉)], Junliang Chen[1], Hande Hong[2], Jianqiang Li[1], and Long Cheng[3]

[1] College of Computer Science and Software Engineering, Shenzhen University, Shenzhen, China
273626901@qq.com, {chengwen,lijq}@szu.edu.cn, jlchen0926@163.com
[2] National University of Singapore, Singapore, Singapore
honghand@comp.nus.edu.sg
[3] VirginiaTech, Blacksburg, USA
chengl@vt.edu

Abstract. Understanding users' social relationships plays an important role in many disciplines including marketing, management science, etc., and is the fundamental context information required in many context-aware applications. However, despite significant research progress in social learning, sensing and capturing users' daily social relationships in an accurate and non-obtrusive way is still a challenging open problem. In this paper, we propose LiPS, a social learning system that exploits wireless probes emitted by the smartphones carried by users to learn their social relationships. A novel probe filtering and Skipgram-based learning algorithm is adopted to automatically construct the social graph of users in an unobtrusive way. The evaluation results show that the LiPS system is able to accurately reflect the social relationships among smartphone users.

Keywords: Social learning · WiFi probe · Skipgram

1 Introduction

Understanding social relationships among users plays an important role in many commercial systems. The information of user interactions is essential in disciplines including management, business, psychology, etc. For example, using the social relationships among users shopping recommendations can be made automatically based on user interactions and similarities in order to increase sales. Knowing the value of social relationships, recently many research has been done to capture the offline social interactions automatically [1–4,6,8–10].

Despite significant research progress, obtaining such information often requires users to install additional softwares on their mobile devices, e.g., apps in the smartphones. The additional requirements and burdens placed onto the users make it harder to capture social relationships *in situ* since users usually become

© Springer International Publishing AG, part of Springer Nature 2018
B. Zeng et al. (Eds.): PCM 2017, LNCS 10735, pp. 873–882, 2018.
https://doi.org/10.1007/978-3-319-77380-3_84

less willing to cooperate if additional actions are required to take. SocialProbe [3] utilizes the passive WiFi probes emitted by smartphones carried by users to detect physical co-locations and infer user interactions based on their co-location information. The wireless packets sent unintentionally eliminate the need for app installation and make it possible to infer social interactions passively without explicit user cooperation. However, SocialProbe dose not provide an effective framework for social relationship learning based on the wireless probes captured. In this work, we learns users' offline interactions and infers social relationships automatically by capturing and analyzing the WiFi probes emitted by smartphones. Different from SocialProbe, we propose a system named *LiPS* which adopts an effective learning model that maps each user into a social space after learning a vector representation. The learned representation can be used to effectively interpret the user social relationships. We summarize our contribution as follows:

- We exploits WiFi probes to uniquely identify mobile devices attached to real users through MAC filtering to infer user relationships automatically.
- We combines WiFi probe capturing with the Skipgram-based learning model to effectively learn user representations in the social space. To the best of our knowledge, this is the first work that utilizes the Skipgram to learn users' offline social relationships.
- We design and implement LiPS, and evaluate its performance in real lab environment settings. The evaluation results further confirms that the social relationships can be learned effective through probe capturing and Skipgram-based representation learning.

The roadmap of this paper is as follows. We first introduce the technical backgrounds in Sect. 2. Section 3 discusses the detailed designed of LiPS, and Sect. 4 provides the evaluations. We finally conclude in Sect. 5.

2   Technical Background

2.1   WiFi Probe Sniffing

Probe Request Frame: A smartphone sends a Probe Request management frames frequently to detect what network is available within the WiFi range. These frames trigger responses from nearby APs, and as a result a smartphone can discovery surrounding APs efficiently. In order to have successful probe requests, network identifier (SSID) of the network should be included in the probe request frame. With SSID in probe request frames, APs can decide whether the senders of probe request can join the network or not. Besides, These frames also contain information such as MAC address, signal strength, and time stamps.

Smartphone users turn on WiFi interfaces on the phone to discover surrounding APs, no matter whether their smartphones are associated with any AP or not, the mobile devices can broadcast probe requests. The difference is

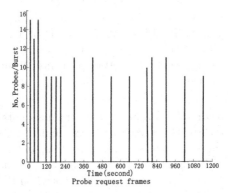

Fig. 1. The number of probes sent by a Xiaomi2A captured by a WiFi monitor. The phone is not associated to an AP.

that the number of probe requests are relatively smaller after they are already connected/associated to a WiFi network. And in a moving smartphone, there are relatively weak number of probe requests.

Figure 1 shows the number of probe request frames send over time observed for a Xiaomi2A smartphone. In this figure, we can see how often probe request send and how many times probe request in a second. In this case, a Xiaomi2A smartphone sends probe request frames in a burst of a few frames (9 to 15) each time, and there is a 30 s 120 s interval between two sends. The longest interval is a stable value of 120 s, it shows the smartphone cannot find available WiFi AP to connect after repeated attempts. The stable value shows that smartphone has been departured or no WiFi if the time difference between the current time and the last send is greater than 120 s.

Smartphone Probe Interval: In order to ensure the accuracy of the experiment results, and know what rules most phones send probe request frames, We conducted a experiment in a real environment by using 5 devices in the university, including dormitory, classroom, and laboratory. Figure 2 shows what rules most phones send probe request frames over a week period, from the figure, we

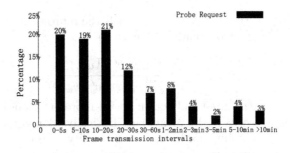

Fig. 2. Probe request captured by WiFi monitors over a week period.

can see clearly frame transmission intervals by most phones. For probe request frames, 87% of frames are sent within intervals of about 120 s and 93% of frames are sent within 5 min interval. According to the picture, we can conclude that smartphone has been departured or no WiFi if a inter-frame interval is greater than 5 min for most phones.

Received Signal Strength: Probe request frames contain many important informations, such as RSSI (Received Signal Strength Indication). In an IEEE 802.11 system, RSSI number shows received radio signal strength in a wireless environment, Thus, the higher the RSSI value, the stronger the signal. The distance between a AP and a phone is computed based on RSSI value, Therefore, the higher the RSSI value, the closer between a AP and a phone. RSSI value is known to be unreliable, it is often affected by the surrounding environment factors. A phone can also transmit at different power depending on the specific IEEE 802.11 version used [5].

RSSI value is noisy, but we can compute phones' approximate location based on it. In this system, we only study the sequential position of multiple mobile phones, so noisy signals have little effect on the experiment results.

2.2 Skipgram

In order to get users' social relationships, we need to use word representation represent users' social behavior. In many word representation methods, Skipgram [7] is suitable to get users' word representation in this system, because the Skipgram model's training objective is to learn word vector representations that are good at predicting the surrounding words in a context text.

Given a sequence of training words, large amounts of unstructured text data, such as $w_1, w_2, w_3, \ldots, w_T$, Skipgram learns the word representations explicitly encode linguistic regularities and patterns, after training, you will find many of these patterns can be represented as linear relationships, and simple word vector linear operations can often produce meaningful result. The objective of Skipgram is to maximize the following average log probability.

$$\frac{1}{T} \sum_{t=1}^{T} \sum_{-c \leq j \leq c, j \neq 0} log \; p\left(w_{t+j}|w_t\right) \tag{1}$$

where c is the size of the context window, w_t is the representation of the center word. The conditional probability is defined as $p\left(w_O|w_I\right)$ using the softmax function:

$$p\left(w_O|w_I\right) = \frac{exp\left(v'_{w_O}{}^\mathsf{T} v_{w_I}\right)}{\sum_{w=1}^{W} exp\left(v'_w{}^\mathsf{T} v_{w_I}\right)} \tag{2}$$

where v_w and v'_w are the input and output vector representations of word w, and W is the number of words in the vocabulary. Basically, Skip-gram tries to maximize the softmax probability, for learning high-quality vector representations by calculating the inner product of the center word's vector and its context word's vectors.

3 LiPS Design

In this section we provide a detailed description of each component of LiPS. Figure 3 shows the design overview of the LiPS system. The major components of the LiPS systems are:

- Passive WiFi Probe Sniffing. To deploy LiPS, multiple WiFi sniffers are deployed around the area of interest to capture the WiFi probes emitted by smartphones. Whenever a user carrying smartphones enters the area within the vicinity of WiFi sniffers, probes will be transmitted as long as the WiFi interfaces are on and will be captured by the deployed WiFi monitors.
- MAC filtering. The captured probes might be emitted by smartphones carried by real users, or by other devices that are not related to any real users. For example, WiFi enabled devices such as smart TVs will also transmit probes. The MAC addresses of such environmental devices should be filtered since they are not relating to the users and no social relationships should be inferred for such devices.
- Representation learning. LiPS is unique that it transfers the MAC address to a meaningful social representation, i.e., a high-dimensional vectors that uniquely characterize a user in the social space.
- Social interpretation. The social relationships such as social groups or social distance can then be discovered through the learned social representations of the smartphones.

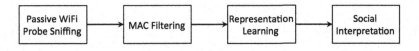

Fig. 3. Overview of LiPS

3.1 Probe Sniffing

In LiPS, WiFi monitors include Raspberry Pi 2B with two D-Link wireless USB adapters (DWA-137 and DWA-132). Each captured probe p_i consists of a MAC address MAC_i, a timestamp t_i, signal strength s_i, and monitor ID m_i. Hence:

$$p = (MAC_i, t_i, s_i, m_i).$$

To protect the privacy, each MAC is stored as a hashed value, therefore anonymity is achieved. The captured probes by all monitors are merged for further processing.

3.2 MAC Filtering

The key purpose of MAC filtering is to filter out probes that are emitted by devices which are not carried by real users, and only admitting probes that are emitted by smartphones of users for social learning. We introduce a hierarchical filtering mechanism in LiPS.

Filtering Based on MAC Address: In general, the MAC address is the unique identifier for the device, a MAC address is recognized as a person in system. We can get many MAC addresses from probe request frames, how to identify phones' mac address? we design a public database of data in a certain format, in which key is a 3 byte Organizationally (OUI) and value is a 3 byte Network Interface Controller Specific (NIC). In this way, we can protect the user's privacy, and we can identify smartphones carried by mobile users by matching between OUI and the first three bytes of MAC address. We collected 2973 OUI and NIC data, so we only process probe request frames by phone sends, which phone's type is contained in the database.

Filtering Based on Present Ratio: In this part, we design a filter method with a limited time. In Sect. 3, we analyze the rules most phones send probe request frames, and know a smartphone has been departured or no WiFi if a inter-frame interval is greater than 5 min for most phones. Besides, we design another way to determine which devices are left in the lab all the time, these devices without mobility can't be recognized as a person. If a inter-frame interval from a device are detected within 5 min and the device is no mobility, we delete its data from database.

In both methods, we can judge whether a smartphone is carried by a person. We analyze the filtered data, not including the smartphone is carried by humans who just stay the monitored area for a short time, it improves the accuracy of 7% in two ways, details in Sect. 5.

3.3   Representation Learning

We adopt the Skipgram learning model for representation learning for users. A representation v_i is a high dimensional vector that uniquely represents a user in certain space and can be used to characterize the users' co-existence relationships. Different from the MAC address which is also unique for each smartphone user, a learned representation by Skipgram captures the context of each user so that the distances measures the degree of intimacy between users. To learn the representation in the social space, the distances between different representations should reflect the probability that two users are co-location. That is, if two users are frequently co-located, their social distance should be closer in the space formed by the learned representations. In LiPS, we term the distance:

$$d_{ij} = \|v_i - v_j\| \tag{3}$$

as the *social distance*, where v_i and v_j are the learned representations of user i and user j respectively. And we term the space form by all representations as the *social space*.

To learn the representations in social space using Skipgram, the co-existence information must be captured. In LiPS, the co-existence can be naturally described as co-location in the physical locations. This can be interpreted as, if two users are frequently stay in the same location, their social distance should be smaller. As a result, we define a co-location index c_{ij} as:

$$c_{ij} = \sum_{k=1}^{n} \|s_i^{(k)} - s_j^{(k)}\| \tag{4}$$

where n is the number of deployed WiFi monitors, $s_i^{(k)}$ is the signal strength captured by monitor k for device i and $s_j^{(k)}$ is the signal strength for device j. A co-location event (i, j) is detected if and only if:

$$c_{ij} \leq \delta_c \tag{5}$$

where δ_c is an empirical threshold. The co-location event describes that two user are detected to be located at the same location in the physical space. In LiPS, we capture the co-location events continuously to form a sequence input $\{(i_1, j_1), (i_2, j_2), ..., (i_m, j_m)\}$, which is then fed to the Skipgram for representation learning for all users.

3.4   Social Interpretation

The learned representations capture the social relationships among users, and we can use them for social interpretation:

- **Social distance.** The social distance measures the social 'closeness' between two representations v_i and v_j for user i and j.
- **Social group.** The social groups can be defined as the clusters of the learned social representations.

4   Evaluation

4.1   System Implementation and Evaluation Setting

LiPS implementation consists of two parts: the frontend WiFi monitors and backend servers. In order to make sure that we have synchronized time in all monitors, we run NTP protocol every few hours for all monitors. We deployed the system in two lab environments and one dormitory environment, with more than 50 people moving around during the day.

4.2   Device Filtering

To evaluate the effectiveness of the device filtering, we perform a small control experiment by passive scanning devices for one week and use OUI and PR filter to identify valid devices. Since the experiment covers a relatively small area, we collect the ground-truth by manually collecting the real device presence.

Figure 4 shows the filtered devices detected for five days in one lab environment. The user changing trends can be seen obviously and the morning peak and

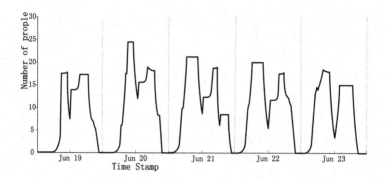

Fig. 4. Device number changing over time after MAC filtering

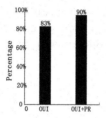

Fig. 5. Performance for MAC filter in LiPS

afternoon peak are present. The detected device number fits the ground-truth number of lab members, which shows the effectiveness of MAC filtering. Figure 5 shows the performance of MAC filtering mechanisms. With only OUI 83% precision is achieved, and 90% precision is achieved if OUI and PR mechanisms are combined.

4.3   Social Interpretation

The social relationships can be interpreted after the representations are learned using Skipgram. Figure 6 shows the 2D projection of the social representations learned for 21 users. The closer distance in the 2D plan represents a closer distance in the social space, hence indicating a 'closer' social relationship. As shown in Fig. 6, three social groups can be identifier, each with small social distance for intra-group members, and large social distance for inter-group members. Compared with the ground-truth, the three groups represent the dormitory members, and two separated lab members. Figure 7 shows the heatmap for each pair of 21 users. The deeper color represents a smaller social distance. It can be seen from the figure that user 1 has closer relationships to all users, indicating that he is the social center for all users, which also reflects the real social relationship well for all lab members.

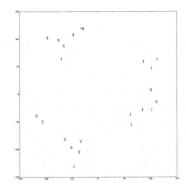

Fig. 6. Social distances projected onto a 2D space for 21 users

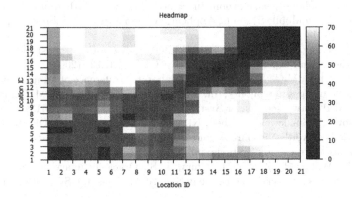

Fig. 7. Heatmap of the social distances detected for 21 users

5   Conclusion

In this paper, we propose LiPS, a passive social learning system that automatically learns social representations for mobile devices in the social space. The key novelty of LiPS is that it captures WiFi probes emitted by devices passively, incorporates novel MAC filtering mechanisms to identify real users, and seamlessly adopts Skipgram-based learning mechanisms for representation learning. The evaluations conducted in real lab environments show that the LiPS system can successfully detect social distances and reconstruct social groups by passive social learning.

References

1. Gan, T., Wong, Y., Mandal, B., Chandrasekhar, V., Kankanhalli, M.S.: Multi-sensor self-quantification of presentations. In: Proceedings of ACM International Conference on Multimedia, pp. 601–610 (2015)
2. Gan, T., Wong, Y., Zhang, D., Kankanhalli, M.S.: Temporal encoded F-formation system for social interaction detection. In: Proceedings of ACM International Conference on Multimedia, pp. 937–946 (2013)
3. Hong, H., Luo, C., Chan, M.C.: SocialProbe: understanding social interaction through passive WiFi monitoring. In: Proceedings of the 13th International Conference on Mobile and Ubiquitous Systems: Computing, Networking and Services (Mobiquitous), pp. 94–103. ACM (2016)
4. Lee, Y., Min, C., Hwang, C., Lee, J., Hwang, I., Ju, Y., Yoo, C., Moon, M., Lee, U., Song, J.: SocioPhone: everyday face-to-face interaction monitoring platform using multi-phone sensor fusion. In: Proceeding of the 11th Annual International Conference on Mobile Systems, Applications, and Services (MobiSys), pp. 375–388. ACM (2013)
5. Lim, H., Kung, L.-C., Hou, J., Luo, H.: Zero-configuration, robust indoor localization: theory and experimentation. In: INFOCOM. IEEE (2006)
6. Luo, C., Chan, M.C.: SocialWeaver: collaborative inference of human conversation networks using smartphones. In: Proceedings of the 11th ACM Conference on Embedded Networked Sensor Systems (SenSys), p. 20. ACM (2013)
7. Mikolov, T., Sutskever, I., Chen, K., Corrado, G.S., Dean, J.: Distributed representations of words and phrases and their compositionality. In: Advances in Neural Information Processing Systems, pp. 3111–3119 (2013)
8. Nie, L., Wang, M., Zha, Z.-J., Chua, T.-S.: Oracle in image search: a content-based approach to performance prediction. ACM Trans. Inf. Syst. 30(2), 13:1–13:23 (2012)
9. Nie, L., Wang, M., Zha, Z., Li, G., Chua, T.-S.: Multimedia answering: Enriching text QA with media information. In: Proceedings of the 34th International ACM SIGIR Conference on Research and Development in Information Retrieval, SIGIR 2011, pp. 695–704. ACM (2011)
10. Nie, L., Yan, S., Wang, M., Hong, R., Chua, T.-S.: Harvesting visual concepts for image search with complex queries. In: Proceedings of the 20th ACM International Conference on Multimedia, MM 2012, pp. 59–68. ACM (2012)

The Intelligent Monitoring for the Elderly Based on WiFi Signals

Nan Bao[1(✉)], Chengyang Wu[1], Qiancheng Liang[1], Lisheng Xu[1],
Guozhi Li[1], Ziyu Qi[1], Wanyi Zhang[1], He Ma[1], and Yan Li[2]

[1] Sino-Dutch Biomedical and Information Engineering School,
Northeastern University, Shenyang, Liaoning, China
{baonan,xuls,mahe}@bmie.neu.edu.cn,
wcymmm000@qq.com, hulklgz@qq.com, 595335816@qq.com,
843909302@qq.com, vin_liangqc@foxmail.com
[2] Troops 31411 of People's Liberation Army, Nanchang, China
xiaohair_99@163.com

Abstract. With the increasing aging population, the intelligent monitoring for the elderly living alone has become a hot research topic. As the universal of WiFi, the intelligent monitoring system based on WiFi Channel State Information (CSI) is proposed for elderly, including fall detection and sleep monitoring. The system is completely off-the-shelf and non-contact, which is more convenient and comfortable to users. The fall detection algorithm is based on phase difference and amplitude of CSI, whose features of different motions are extracted, and the falls are detected by machine learning algorithm. The sleep monitoring system only used phase difference changes of antennas; meanwhile, the respiration, turning over, and apnea will be detected, which can be used to evaluate sleep quality as well. According to the results of experiments, the accuracy of the system can reach 84.6% in fall detection. In sleep monitoring, the error of each breath is 0.337 s and the average accuracy is 89.9%.

Keywords: WiFi · CSI · Phase difference · Amplitude · Fall detection
Sleep monitoring

1 Introduction

With increasing aged population, the whole world is facing aging problems. Additionally, China is facing a more serious situation than western countries. According to reports, it is estimated that the number of people aged over 60 will be higher than 1/5 of the total population by 2050 [1]. With the population aging becoming tougher, the security of the elderly living alone has become a social problem. There are many factors affecting their health, such as the quality of sleep [2], sudden fallings [3], cardiovascular diseases, and so on. According to the report, about 50% of the falling accidents occur in their houses [4]. If the elderly falls alone at home and doesn't get first-aid treatment in time, it will threaten their lives [5]. Moreover, the quality of sleep is another major factor which affects their health, and the apnea caused by many reasons during sleeping also needs to be monitored. Therefore, in order to detect the fall

© Springer International Publishing AG, part of Springer Nature 2018
B. Zeng et al. (Eds.): PCM 2017, LNCS 10735, pp. 883–892, 2018.
https://doi.org/10.1007/978-3-319-77380-3_85

actions of the elderly living alone and monitor their sleep, this paper focuses on the design and implementation of the intelligent monitoring system.

There are several technologies for fall detection. Commonly, the wearable device, camera (vision) and ambiance sensor are used. Wearable devices use multiple sensors for collecting the data to detect falls, including pressure, acceleration, revolve, etc. [6]. Camera devices use several indoor cameras to obtain movement information or images of elderly for fall detection [7]. Moreover, ambiance devices can classify postures based on sensors, which can be set up around the room, such as fusing audio and visual data and even sensing through vibrational data [8].

Furthermore, the methods to estimate the sleep quality are generally based on RF-based devices, pressure sensors, and wearable sensor-based approaches. RF-based devices are set up around the bed, receiving respiratory signal data directly [9]. Pressure sensors are mounted on the mattress [10]. If there is a movement, the pressure is changed to detect turning action [11]. Wearable devices, like those for the fall detection, use multiple sensors for collecting the data when the elderly wear it and evaluate the sleep situation by the data [12].

So far as those methods above, the detection based on camera may expose people's privacy. Wearable devices will influence the comfort of elderly, causing their exclusion psychology, and RF-based devices need to buy additional equipment. To avoid these problems above, the intelligent monitoring systems based on WiFi signals are proposed. As the universal of WiFi, it is available for every family. WiFi signals are sensitive to the movements of the human body, and it is contactless. So, it is very convenient for elderly to utilize for fall detection and sleep monitoring in their daily lives. Above all, it is necessary to develop such intelligent monitoring system based on WiFi for elderly.

In the rest of the paper, methods and some principle details have presented in Sect. 2 .The results and evaluation are shown in Sect. 3, as well as the GUI of the system. The conclusion of this research will be provided in Sect. 4.

2 Method

2.1 Principle of CSI

The intelligent monitoring algorithm based on WiFi Channel State Information (CSI) has been designed in this paper. The relation between CSI, transmitter (WiFi router), and receiver(NIC) can be expressed as formula shown below:

$$Y = HX + n \tag{1}$$

In which X and Y represent vectors transmitted and received, and H is the channel matrix, and n is the additive white Gaussian noise vector. For each single subcarrier, the phase and amplitude can be described by the following formula:

$$H(f_k) = \|H(f_k)\| e^{j \sin \theta} \tag{2}$$

Where $H(f_k)$ is the CSI at the kth subcarrier with the frequency ω_k, $\| H_k \|$ and θ represent its amplitude and phase.

Signal phase shift can be caused by human's micro movement, and the measured phase of CSI has been computed by the following formula [13]:

$$\widehat{\phi}_f = \phi_f + 2\pi f_f \Delta t + \beta + Z_f \tag{3}$$

Where ϕ_f is the true phase, Δt is the time lag at the same antenna, β is an unknown constant phase offset, Z_f is environment noise, f_f is the carrier frequency offset at the receiver.

But raw phase is distributed and useless because a micro time lag change can cause the large phase offset. f_fs are of the same value in the same wireless device. So the phase difference between two antennae is regular in a stable environment. So the formula below can be calculated:

$$\Delta\widehat{\phi}_f = \Delta\phi_f + 2\pi f_f (\Delta t_1 - \Delta t_2) + \Delta\beta + \Delta Z_f \tag{4}$$

Where Δt_1 is the time lag at the first antenna, Δt_2 is the time lag at the second antenna. If the data is from the same device, then Δt_1 equals to Δt_2. So the phase difference can be calculated as followed:

$$\Delta\widehat{\phi}_f = \Delta\phi_f + \Delta\beta + \Delta Z_f \tag{5}$$

2.2 System Overview

The transmitter uses a router that can transmit 5 GHz band signals, and the receiver uses a computer with Intel 5300 wireless network card; meanwhile, the 5300 card comes with three high-gain antennas (see Fig. 1). To get WiFi CSI data, the project is powered by the Linux 802.11n CSI Tool. At the same time, the Ubuntu 10.04 LTS Linux system with 3.5.7 kernel has been selected to receive and deal with the data. The off-the-shelf devices have the good performance to detect fall and breath actions based on the amplitude and phase of the CSI. Both amplitude and phase difference are used for fall detection. However, the phase difference is more effective for sleep monitoring.

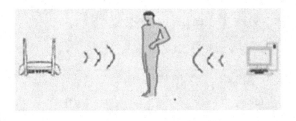

Fig. 1. System schematic diagram

2.3   Fall Detection Method

The fall actions are detected by the amplitude and phase of the CSI signals. Firstly, the amplitude and phase signals of the daily actions are collected. The daily actions are considered such as walking, standing, squatting, lying down, fall and other different actions for data collection. Taking the phase difference of the CSI signals in different actions as an example, the waveforms are shown in the following figures (see Fig. 2):

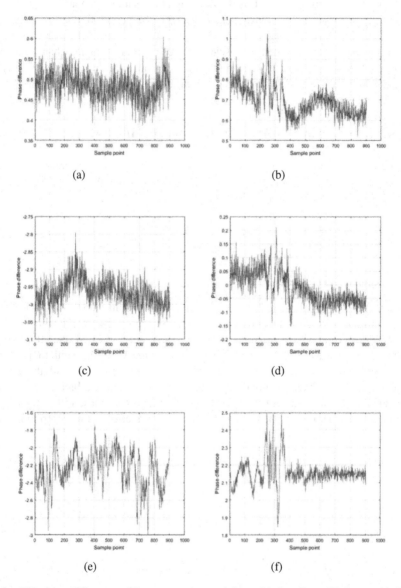

Fig. 2. CSI phase difference of human motion activities: (a) Standing. (b) Jump. (c) Squat. (d) Sit. (e) Walking. (f) Fall.

Then the feature extraction is applied to fall and non-fall movements. According to the analysis of them, 19 features are extracted. The phase difference features include normalized standard deviation, absolute median, signal strength offset, maximum differential value, quartile, signal entropy, signal delay, maximum power drop rate, high-frequency power maximum, high-Frequency power average, high-frequency dispersion, high-frequency power drop rate, and phase offset. Additionally, amplitude characteristics include: normalized standard deviation, absolute median, signal strength offset, maximum integral, quartile, and signal entropy. In addition, based on the 19 features extracted from all signals, the falling actions are detected.

Support Vector Machine(SVM) is used to train the fall detection classifiers. The positive sample set is fall actions, and the negative samples are non-fall movements. Based on the feature vectors calculated from 19 features of all signals, the fall detection classifier is trained with the positive and negative training sample sets.

2.4 Sleep Monitoring Method

There are three important indexes to evaluate the qualities of sleep, such as respiratory signals, turning, and apnea [14].

Respiratory Signal Analysis. The respiratory signal analysis is performed in terms of the effect of chest fluctuation on the phase difference of CSI signals when the human body breathed. To detect breath wave, the Discrete Wavelet Transform (DWT) is applied to denoising. It is calculated by a series of filters, which consist of a high pass filter h and a low pass filter g. The high pass filter h gives the detail coefficients and the low pass filter gives the approximation coefficients. First, samples are passed through a low pass filter:

$$y[n] = (x \times g)[n] = \sum_{k=-\infty}^{\infty} x[k]g[2n - k] \tag{6}$$

Thus, the signal is divided into two part:

$$y_{low}[n] = \sum_{k=-\infty}^{\infty} x[k]g[2n - k] \tag{7}$$

$$y_{high}[n] = \sum_{k=-\infty}^{\infty} x[k]h[2n - k] \tag{8}$$

Where $x[k]$ is the input signal, $y_{low}[n]$ and $y_{high}[n]$ is detail coefficients and the approximation coefficients, g and h are high pass filter and low pass filter.

As human breath 12–20 times per minute (0.2 Hz–0.33 Hz), we use a band-pass filter to denoise. And we find that the LF component of the 6th level decomposition consists of noise and breath signal, but the LF component of the 7th level decomposition only consists of noise. Thus, we use the HF component of the 7th level decomposition to detect the breath wave. Compared with another wavelet basis, db4

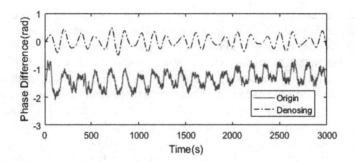

Fig. 3. De-noising and original waveforms

can provide a better performance. There is the respiration wave before using the filter and after using the filter (see Fig. 3).

In the following section, the accuracy of this system has been tested by comparison of bpm and respiration interval between our system and contacting monitor. Then, calculate the breath rate and the period of breath according to the extracted signals.

Turning Analysis. Turning is an indicator which reflects the user's sleep quality. Generally, turning actions may interfere the wireless signals. These actions cause large changes in CSI (see Fig. 4), which makes breathing difficult to sample. In the meanwhile,

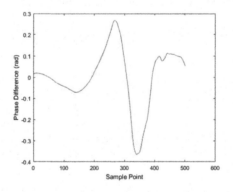

Fig. 4. Turning waveform

Thus, we monitor the DC component changes to indicate users turning. It can be described by following formula:

$$T = \begin{cases} 1, & \text{if } range > 0.2 \\ 0, & \text{if } range \leq 0.2 \end{cases} \tag{9}$$

where the range is the range of the 5 s window.

When we find out sudden changes, the time of turning is noted. However, it is also difficult to get breath wave from the signal without DC component. In this system, we set a minimum time to detect following breath after we get the previous one. Because the respiration rate of a normal person is between 12–20, the minimum time is 3 s to detect.

Apnea Detection. Apnea is a kind of breathing suspension caused by the airways block. During apnea, muscles of inhalation keep stationary for at least 10 s, which causes people cannot store enough oxygen. People who have apnea can occur up to 20–30 times each night. It often associated with high blood pressure, myocardial infarction, myocardial anoxia, and stroke. Thus, it is important to discovery and reports earlier to reduce the harm of patients.

Generally, a typical apnea wave is shown (see Fig. 5). When the apnea occurs, the system shows weak signals about 10 s. After this, the user has a strong breath and the strength of wave increases. Thus, we set a threshold θ to compare within the window.

The system notes the time when the window t appeared. The decision can be described as follows:

$$N_{apnea} = \begin{cases} 1, & if\ R_{t-1}R_{t+10} > \theta, R_t < \theta \\ 0, & if\ otherwise \end{cases} \tag{10}$$

where R_{t-1}, R_t is the range of 10 s waves around t.

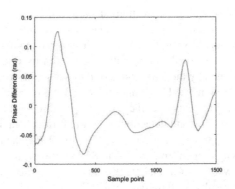

Fig. 5. Apnea waveform

3 Results and Evaluation

3.1 Monitoring System

The system includes two user interfaces, such as fall detection and sleep monitoring. The left side of the fall detection interface displays the waveform of the amplitude and phase difference of the CSI signals in real time, and the other side displays the values of 19 features. When fall actions take place, the button turns red and gives an alarm.

Meanwhile, the left side of the sleep monitoring interface displays phase difference wave form of the CSI signals and the value of calculated respiratory rate. It can also detect and show turning and apnea in the status bar. The right side is a report on the sleep status, suggesting the results of these related parameters (see Fig. 6).

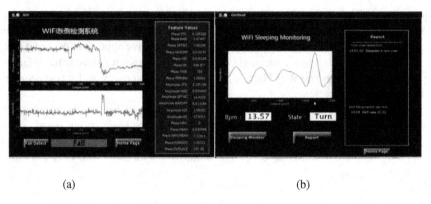

(a)   (b)

Fig. 6. (a) The interface of fall detection system (b) The interface of sleep monitoring system (Color figure online)

3.2 Fall Detection Experiment

In order to train and test, 600 sets of valid data, which includes 240 groups of fall data and 360 groups non-fall data, have been collected from four students (two male students and two female students) in this system. The experimental environment is 8 m * 8 m labs. The ten-fold cross-validation method has been used to test; in addition, the test data have been trained by the 540 groups of data which has been sampled randomly by the randperm function in MATLAB and the other 60 groups of the date were used to test. After a lot of measuring, the accuracy of the algorithm has been shown in Table 1.

According to the training and detection of non-real-time data, it has been found that the accuracy rate of the system ranged from 79.2% to 89.7%, the average accuracy rate is 84.6%; the sensitivity ranged from 78.8% to 85.1%, the average specificity is 81.1%; the specificity is between 84.4% and 93.9%, and the average sensitivity of is about 87.2%. Based on the results, walking-stop actions and fall-down actions are easy to be confused. To distinguish these two actions will be the important work in the future.

Table 1. The results of the cross-validation test

	Maximum	Minimum	Average
Accuracy (%)	89.7	79.2	84.6
Sensitivity (%)	85.1	78.8	81.1
Specificity (%)	93.9	84.4	87.2

3.3   Sleep Monitoring Experiment

The experimental environment is that setting 2.5 m between the transmitter and the receiver. Firstly, making a comparison between the WiFi-based respiratory waveform and bandage-based waveform. It took 200 min to measure the breathing rate and use the phase difference to measure data. The result is that error of each breath is 0.337 s and the average accuracy is 89.9%. Comparing with the banded respiratory monitoring device, this system shows a better result of the accuracy (see Fig. 7).

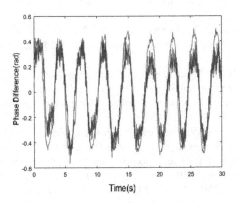

Fig. 7. Comparison of using bandage respiratory monitoring devices

In the turning tests, 100 groups of experiments have been finished, the accuracy of which is 92.1%. The symptoms of apnea are that the air stops flowing through mouse and nose lasting more than ten seconds [15]. As a result, another test is designed to imitate the breath state of apnea, which means that experimenters need to hold their breath for 10 s to test the accuracy of the system. The accuracy of this experiment is 93.2%. However, the respiratory rate cannot be obtained accurately in the turn action.

4   Conclusion

With the aging population increasing, the monitoring of the elderly who live alone becomes a social problem. In this paper, fall detection and sleep monitoring are implemented based on the CSI signals of WiFi. The amplitude and phase difference of the CSI signals are used to detect falls and the phase difference is used to monitor breath signals, turning over and apnea actions. The experiment results show the method has good performance, which can promote the use of home WiFi signals in the field of intelligent monitoring for the elderly. In addition, the future work will focus on the improvement of algorithm accuracy continually.

Acknowledgments. This research is financially supported under the Scientific Innovation and Venture Incubation.

References

1. WHO Homepage: http://www.portal.pmnch.org/mediacentre/factsheets/fs404/en/. Accessed 21 May 2017
2. Sullivan, C.E., Lynch, C.: Device and method for nonclinical monitoring of breathing during sleep, control of CPAP treatment and preventing apnea. US, US6398739 (2002)
3. Wang, H., Zhang, D., Wang, Y., Ma, J., Wang, Y., Li, S.: RT-Fall: a real-time and contactless fall detection system with commodity WiFi devices. IEEE Trans. Mob. Comput. **16**(2), 511–526 (2017)
4. Khan, S., Hoey, J.: Review of fall detection techniques: a data availability perspective. Med. Eng. Phys. **39**, 12–22 (2016)
5. Westergren, A., Hagell, P., Hammarlund, C.S.: Malnutrition and risk of falling among elderly without home-help service -a cross sectional study. J. Nutr. Heal. Aging **18**(10), 1–7 (2014)
6. Aziz, O., Musngi, M., Park, E.J., Mori, G., Robinovitch, S.N.: A comparison of accuracy of fall detection algorithms (threshold-based vs. machine learning) using waist-mounted tri-axial accelerometer signals from a comprehensive set of falls and non-fall trials. Med. Biol. Eng. Comput. **55**(1), 45–55 (2017)
7. Bourke, A.K., Ihlen, E.A., Van de Ven, P., Nelson, J., Helbostad, J.L., Bourke, A.K., et al.: Video analysis validation of a real-time physical activity detection algorithm based on a single waist mounted tri-axial accelerometer sensor. In: Conference Proceedings of IEEE Engineering in Medicine and Biology Society, vol. 2016, p. 4881 (2016)
8. Chen, K.H., Hsu, Y.W., Yang, J.J., Jaw, F.S.: Enhanced characterization of an accelerometer-based fall detection algorithm using a repository. Instrum Sci. Technol. **45**, 382–391 (2017)
9. Caccami, M.C., Mulla, M.Y.S., Di Natale, C., et al.: Wireless monitoring of breath by means of a graphene oxide-based radiofrequency identification wearable sensor. In: 2017 11th European Conference on Antennas and Propagation (EUCAP), pp. 3394–3396. IEEE (2017)
10. Gao, T., Bishop, W.E., Juang, R.R., et al.: Sensor-based adaptive wearable devices and methods. US, US7629881 (2009)
11. Nam, Y., Kim, Y., Lee, J.: Sleep monitoring based on a tri-axial accelerometer and a pressure sensor. Sensors **16**(5), 750 (2016)
12. Looney, D., Goverdovsky, V., Rosenzweig, I., et al.: Wearable in-ear encephalography sensor for monitoring sleep. Prelim. Obs. Nap Stud. **13**(12), 2229–2233 (2016). Annals of the American Thoracic Society
13. Sen, S., Radunovic, B., Choudhury, R.R., et al.: You are facing the Mona Lisa: spot localization using PHY layer information. In: International Conference on Mobile Systems, Applications, and Services, pp. 183–196. ACM (2012)
14. Schapire, R.E.: The boosting approach to machine learning: an overview. In: Denison, D.D., Hansen, M.H., Holmes, C.C., Mallick, B., Yu, B. (eds.) Nonlinear estimation and classification. Lecture Notes in Statistics, vol. 171, pp. 149–171. Springer, New York (2003). https://doi.org/10.1007/978-0-387-21579-2_9
15. Rechtschaffen, A., Kales, A.: A Manual of Standardized Terminology, Techniques and Scoring System for Sleep Stages of Human Subjects. US Government Printing Office, US Public Health Service, Washington DC (1968)

Sentiment Analysis for Social Sensor

Xiaoyu Zhu, Tian Gan[(✉)], Xuemeng Song, and Zhumin Chen

School of Computer Science and Technology, Shandong University, Jinan, China
xiaoyu_lorraine@163.com, {gantian,songxuemeng,chenzhumin}@sdu.edu.cn

Abstract. Every day, a huge number of information is posted on social media platforms online. In a sense, the social media platform serves as a hybrid sensor system, where people communicate information through the system just like in a sensor world (we call it Social Sensor): they observe the events, and they report it. However, the information from the social sensors (like Facebook, Twitter, Instagram) typically is in the form of multimedia (text, image, video, etc.), thus coping with such information and mining useful knowledge from it will be an increasingly difficult task. In this paper, we first crawl social video data (text and video) from social sensor Twitter for a specific social event. Then the textual, acoustic, and visual features are extracted from these data. At last, we classify the social videos into subjective and objective videos by merging these different modality affective information. Preliminary experiments show that our proposed method is able to accurately classify the social sensor data's subjectivity.

1 Introduction

With the development of the information age, social media has become a necessity in many people's lives. The social media like Twitter, Facebook, and Instagram, etc., has changed people's life. Twitter is one of the most popular social media platforms, it has more than 300 million active users every month[1]. Every moment, there have many users sent tweets to share information, and express their opinions, feelings etc. For this reason, we can take the social media platform as a hybrid sensor system, in which each user serves as a social sensor, that they observe the events and report to the system. Usually, users send a tweet with a special label to express their opinions, feelings or what they observed for a specific event. Meanwhile, more users tend to post their tweets in a variety of ways, such as text, picture, and video.

Subjective classification of tweet has been researched for many years. Many researchers have proposed different methods and systems to classify the text of tweet into subjective or objective automatically [1,7–11,13,17]. However, most of the research only focus on the analysis of the textual information. At the same time, the proportion of tweets that include pictures or video is increasing. The multimedia information gathered from the social sensors can help discover

---

[1] https://about.twitter.com/company.

© Springer International Publishing AG, part of Springer Nature 2018
B. Zeng et al. (Eds.): PCM 2017, LNCS 10735, pp. 893–902, 2018.
https://doi.org/10.1007/978-3-319-77380-3_86

breaking news early on, which would considerably facilitate the task of tracking social media for journalism practitioners, which has become paramount in their daily newsgathering process.

In this paper, we first crawl social video data (text and video) from social sensor Twitter for a specific social event. Textual, acoustic, and visual features are then extracted from these data. At last, we classify the social videos into subjective and objective videos by fusing these different modality affective information. Preliminary experiments show that our proposed method is able to accurately classify the social video's subjectivity.

The remainder of this paper is organized as follows. In Sect. 2, we review the previous work. We formulate our problem and introduce the features in Sect. 3. In Sect. 4, we introduce the dataset and the results of our experiments. Finally, we conclude in Sect. 5 with discussions on future work.

2   Related Work

2.1   Subjectivity Classification

Subjectivity classification has been a hot topic in the research community for years. In the earlier studies, the work on subjectivity classification mainly focuses on manually labelled documents, such as articles, reviews, and comments, etc. They proposed methods, concentrating on the text with different granularities like word [14], expression [13], sentence and document [17].

Wiebe [14] classified adjectives as subjective or objective by an unsupervised algorithm. The author used a small amount of detailed manual annotation seed words as subjective words, and expanded the subjective set of words by searching more similar words. Riloff and Wiebe [13] proposed a bootstrapping process that learns linguistically rich extraction patterns for subjective expressions. Yu and Hatzivassiloglou [17] separated opinions from fact, at both the document and sentence level. In sentence level, they measured the similarity of sentences, and took advantage of the Naive Bayes classifier with part-of-speech, polarity, and N-Gram, etc., as features to classify the sentence as subjective or objective. To separate documents that contain primarily opinions from documents that contain mainly facts, they utilized single words, without stemming or stopword removal, as features, to feed into the Naive Bayes classifier.

With the rise of social media in recent years, Twitter has become a popular online micro-blogging platform. Because almost all Twitter data are public, these rich data offer new opportunities for researchers to work on sentiment analysis. Due to the 140 characters limit, the Twitter text has its unique characteristic of short and always ambiguous. In addition, because the amount of tweets is huge, it is very time-consuming to manually label such large amounts of data. Therefore, more and more recent research learned the classifiers from data with noisy labels such as emoticons and hashtags. For example, to reduce the labeling effort in creating these classifiers, instead of using manually annotated data to compose the training data, Barbosa and Feng [1] leveraged sources of noisy labels as their training data. They classified the subjectivity of tweets with not only

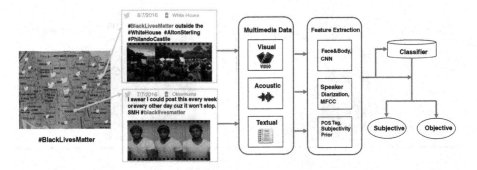

Fig. 1. An overview of our proposed method.

traditional features but also some tweet syntax features like retweets, hashtags, punctuation, emoticons etc. Similarity, Pak and Paroubek [11] collected negative and positive sentiments through the tweets consist of emoticons like ":" and ":(". They obtained objective data from the Twitter accounts of popular newspapers and magazines, such as "New York Time" etc. Then they used N-Grams with low entropy values as the feature and built a sentiment classifier using the multinomial Naive Bayes classifier. Liu *et al.* [7] utilized both manually labelled data and noisy labelled data for training. They established two models: a language model and an emoticon model. They used the noisy emoticon data to smooth the language model trained from manually labelled data, and seamlessly integrated both manually labelled data and noisy labelled data into a probabilistic framework.

2.2 Social Sensor Data Processing

Social media have drastically influenced the way of information dissemination, by empowering the general public to publish and distribute the user generated content [3]. In a sense, the social media makes every user a virtual sensor, which can contribute to the harvest of the information. Therefore, people can act as sensors to give us results in a timely manner, and can complement other sources of data to enhance our situational awareness and improve our understanding and response to such events [3–5]. In addition, the information gathered from the social sensors can help discover breaking news early on, which would considerably facilitate the task of tracking social media for journalism practitioners, which has become paramount in their daily newsgathering process.

3 Proposed Method

In this section, we first provide the problem formulation, followed by the details of each multi-modal feature representation. At last, we present our multimodal analytics module. Figure 1 shows the overview of our proposed method.

subjective	This is so true. #BLACKLIVESMATTER	You will respect us. #BlackLivesMatter	subjective
subjective			objective
objective	Speaker at #blacklivesmatter vigil in Liverpool	There is a protest in front of LA City Hall. #BlackLivesMatter	objective
subjective			objective

Fig. 2. The example of the Twitter posts which contains both text and video for the trending topic #BlackLivesMatter.

3.1   Problem Formulation

Textual information can be broadly categorized into two main types: facts and opinions [6,14–16]. Facts are objective expressions about entities, events and their properties. Opinions are usually subjective expressions that describe peoples sentiments, appraisals or feelings toward entities, events and their properties. Similarly, videos can also be classified as subjective and objective. We define video as *subjective* if the emphasis on video content reflects one or several people's point of view; *objective* if the video focuses on describing the situation and progress of the event.

Formally, suppose for the same trending topic T, we are given a collection of social media posts $P = \{P_1, \ldots, P_{|P|}\}$, where each post $P_i = \{T_i, V_i\}$ consists of two components: textual component T_i and visual component V_i. The objective of our framework is to automatically classify the visual component V_i as *subjective* or *objective*. Figure 2 shows an example of our problem, in which for the trending topic T #BlackLivesMatter, the same Twitter post P has textual component T and visual component V with different subjectivity labels.

3.2   Feature Representation

Textual Feature. For the problem of text subjectivity classification, the textual information plays an important role. In our work, we proposed to use two sets of textual features: Part-Of-Speech (POS) tags, and the prior polarity information from subjectivity lexicon.

The subjectivity of a sentence is highly related to the composition of the word in the sentence. For example, opinion messages are more likely contain adjectives or interjections [1]. Therefore, we annotated the POS tags for each sentence in the text, and chose the number of related tags as the textual feature. Specifically, we selected preposition, adjective, noun, pronoun, adverb, verb and hashtag from the standard treebank POS tags[2]:

$$\boldsymbol{x}^{T,POS} = [\#(prep), \#(adj), \#(noun), \#(pron), \#(adv), \#(verb), \#(ht)] \quad (1)$$

In addition to the composition of the sentence, the prior positive or negative effects of the word in the sentence are also good indicators of subjectivity classification [1,13,17]. Specifically, we utilized a $+/-$ Effect dictionary [2] to calculate the number of $+/-$ Effect words, together with the number of total words from the text (excluding the punctuations, expressions, and links), to characterize the prior subjectivity information:

$$\boldsymbol{x}^{T,+/-} = [\#(positive), \#(negative), \#(words)] \quad (2)$$

Visual Feature. In the social event scenarios, human are the main elements in the scene. In this work, we analyzed the face of people in the video. However, the size of face area varies and the frontal faces are not always shown, thus the performance of face detection is not good enough to analyze the people inside the scene, especially in the crowded or complex environments. Therefore, the human body was also considered as a feature to analyze human. Specifically, we calculated the minimum, the maximum, and the average number of face and body detected in each image for the video. In addition, the ratio of the area of the face and body versus the whole image was considered. By combining these information, we resulted in the following 12-dimension features for human in the visual scene:

$$\boldsymbol{x}^{V,human} = [\#(T)^{op}, ratio(T)^{op}], \quad (3)$$

where $T = \{face, body\}, op = \{min, max, average\}$.

Besides human analysis of the visual scene, we also took advantage of the deep convolutional neural networks, which is a state-of-the-art way for image representation. We adopted the pre-trained convolutional neural networks, obtaining a 4096-dimensional CNN features for each frame from the fc7 layer output. Then, we trained the visual codebook using the local CNN features with k-means, thus each cluster represents a unique visual word. Consequently, each local CNN feature in the convolutional layer is assigned its closest visual word in the learned codebook. At last, we obtained a visual feature for each video by calculating the frequency of each visual word C_v^k:

$$\boldsymbol{x}^{V,CNN-BoVW} = [C_v^1, C_v^2, \ldots, C_v^K] \quad (4)$$

---

[2] In total, there are 36 tags from standard treebank POS tags (https://www.ling.upenn.edu/courses/Fall_2003/ling001/penn_treebank_pos.html), together with four additional tags specific for twitter: URL, USR for user, RT for retweet, HT for hashtag.

Acoustic Feature. Thought audio information alone may not be sufficient for understanding the scene content, there is great potential to analyze the accompanying audio signal for video scene analysis [8,12]. In this work, we used the features in two layers: low-level acoustic characteristics, and high-level speaker diarization audio signature.

In the low-level layer, the audio signal was sampled at 1 KHz, divided into clips of 1 ms long. We sampled the 24-dimensional MFCC feature of each audio clips, and assumed that each MFCC descriptor represents an audio word. Then, we used a simple K-means method to cluster all the MFCC descriptors into N clusters, which is treated as the vocabulary size of an audio word. At last, we calculated the number of the MFCC features belong to each cluster. Therefore, for each audio segment, we obtained an N-dimensional vector:

$$x^{A,MFCC-BoAW} = [C_a^1, C_a^2, \ldots, C_a^N] \tag{5}$$

In the high-level layer, we applied the speaker diarization method to segment the audio clips into different clusters, which correspond to one or the same group of speakers. For example, for an audio A, it can be segmented into $A = \{a_{s1}, a_{s2}, a_{s1}, a_{s3}, a_{s2}\}$. We calculated the number of speaker changes along the temporal axis $Spk\_Change(x)$, the duration of the audio $Dur(x)$, and the number of unique speakers $Spk\_Num(x)$ as the feature:

$$x^{A,Spk} = [Spk\_Change(x), Dur(x), Spk\_Num(x)] \tag{6}$$

3.3 Multimodal Subjectivity Classification

For single-feature-based approach, we conducted the standard machine learning experiment to predict the subjectivity. The SVM with RBF kernel was utilized. For multiple features, the feature level fusion is conducted for the subjectivity prediction.

4 Experiment

In this section, we first introduce the multimodal social sensor dataset, followed by the quantitative results and discussions based on the evaluation metrics.

4.1 Dataset

In this work, we select "#BlackLiveMatter" as the trending topic T for our experiment. It is one of the Twitter Top 10 hashtags[3] in the year of 2016. It is a movement emerged in Year 2014 after high-profile police shootings of unarmed black men, and it ranked as Twitters Top News Hashtags of Year 2015 (13.3 million in total till Year 2016).

---

[3] The full list of Top 10 hashtags in the year of 2016 can be seen at https://blog.twitter.com/official/en_us/a/2016/thishappened-in-2016.html.

Table 1. The statistics of the social sensor data subjectivity.

Text		Video		#(Post)
Subj	Obj	Subj	Obj	
✓		✓		81
✓			✓	139
	✓	✓		40
	✓		✓	174

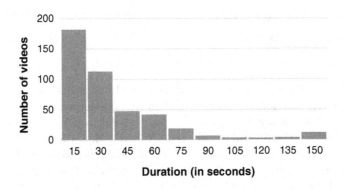

Fig. 3. The statistics of the duration of the 434 videos.

We first crawled all the tweets related to the event "#BlackLiveMatter" from July 7th 2016 00:00 to July 9th 2016 23:59 for three consecutive days, with the advanced search tool in Twitter. In total, we obtained 45570 Twitter posts, among which 3723 Twitter posts contain both text and video components. We randomly selected 200 Twitter posts everyday and applied duplicate removal, resulting in 434 unique Twitter posts. For each twitter post, we asked at least three human annotators to label the post as subjective or objective for both text and video components. The final groundtruth is determined by majority vote.

In the end, we obtained 220 pieces of textual information labelled as subjective, 214 pieces of textual information labelled as objective, 121 videos labelled as subjective, and 313 videos labelled as objective. The details of the statistics are shown in Table 1. In addition, we analyzed the statistics of the duration of the videos. As shown in Fig. 3, among 434 videos, more than 60% (295) of the videos are less than 30 s, which is different from the videos on other social video sharing platform like YouTube.

4.2 Experimental Results and Discussion

In all experiments, the classification performance is reported with 10-fold cross-validation. Table 2 shows our results with different feature configuration on both text and video subjectivity classification.

Table 2. Average classification accuracy (%) on video and text subjectivity. T, V, and A represent Textual, Visual, and Acoustic, respectively.

Modality	Video subjectivity	Text subjectivity
T	71.7	**76.5**
V	**88.2**	60.8
A	86.9	61.5
T + V	88.2	75.6
T + A	84.3	**77.0**
V + A	**90.3**	61.3
T + V + A	88.7	74.9

For single modality feature, we can see from Table 2 that visual feature and acoustic feature are significantly better than textual feature for video subjectivity classification. At the same time, for the text subjectivity classification, the performance with the textual feature is much better than that with the visual or acoustic feature. For multi-modal feature, it is interesting to find out that fusing all the three types of feature did not perform well. Instead, for video subjectivity classification, the visual feature combined with acoustic feature perform the best (with 90.3% accuracy); for text subjectivity classification, the textual feature together with acoustic feature perform the best (with 77.0% accuracy). One of the reasons for the results is that the subjectivity label for the video and text component of the same post are not consistent: as shown in Table 1, only 59% of the posts have the same subjectivity label for video component and text component. At the same time, the visual feature plays an important role in the video component subjectivity classification, same applies for the textual feature for text component subjectivity classification. Therefore, simply combine the visual feature and textual feature will not help. Another interesting finding is that acoustic feature indeed helps for both video and text subjectivity classification, which can be further explored.

5   Conclusions and Future Works

In this work, we have crawled social video data (text and video) from social sensor Twitter for a specific social event. We evaluated the performance of existing computational models and analyzed the efficacy by combining multiple features. Preliminary experiments show that our proposed method is able to accurately classify the social sensor data subjectivity. For the future work, we plan to explore the fusion method of different modalities. Also, other information from the social sensor, for example, geolocation of tweets, friendship of the user, and number of likes/retweets, etc. could be considered for the analysis.

Acknowledgments. This work was supported by the Natural Science Foundation of China (61672322, 61672324), the Natural Science Foundation of Shandong province (2016ZRE27468) and the Fundamental Research Funds of Shandong University (No. 2017HW001).

References

1. Barbosa, L., Feng, J.: Robust sentiment detection on Twitter from biased and noisy data. In: COLING International Conference on Computational Linguistics, pp. 36–44 (2010)
2. Choi, Y., Wiebe, J.: +/−EffectWordNet: sense-level lexicon acquisition for opinion inference. In: Conference on Empirical Methods in Natural Language Processing, pp. 1181–1191 (2014)
3. Crooks, A., Croitoru, A., Stefanidis, A., Radzikowski, J.: #Earthquake: Twitter as a distributed sensor system. Trans. GIS **17**(1), 124–147 (2013)
4. Gan, T., Wong, Y., Mandal, B., Chandrasekhar, V., Kankanhalli, M.S.: Multi-sensor self-quantification of presentations. In: Proceedings of ACM International Conference on Multimedia, pp. 601–610 (2015)
5. Gan, T., Wong, Y., Zhang, D., Kankanhalli, M.S.: Temporal encoded F-formation system for social interaction detection. In: Proceedings of ACM International Conference on Multimedia, pp. 937–946 (2013)
6. Liu, B.: Sentiment analysis and subjectivity. In: Handbook of Natural Language Processing, 2nd edn, pp. 627–666 (2010)
7. Liu, K., Li, W., Guo, M.: Emoticon smoothed language models for Twitter sentiment analysis. In: Proceedings of the AAAI Conference on Artificial Intelligence (2012)
8. Liu, Z., Wang, Y., Chen, T.: Audio feature extraction and analysis for scene segmentation and classification. VLSI Sig. Process. **20**(1–2), 61–79 (1998)
9. Luo, C., Chan, M.C.: SocialWeaver: collaborative inference of human conversation networks using smartphones. In: Proceedings of the ACM Conference on Embedded Networked Sensor Systems, p. 20. ACM (2013)
10. Nie, L., Yan, S., Wang, M., Hong, R., Chua, T.S.: Harvesting visual concepts for image search with complex queries. In: Proceedings of the ACM International Conference on Multimedia, pp. 59–68. ACM (2012)
11. Pak, A., Paroubek, P.: Twitter as a corpus for sentiment analysis and opinion mining. In: Proceedings of the International Conference on Language Resources and Evaluation (2010)
12. Rakotomamonjy, A., Gasso, G.: Histogram of gradients of time-frequency representations for audio scene classification. IEEE/ACM Trans. Audio Speech Lang. Process. **23**(1), 142–153 (2015)
13. Riloff, E., Wiebe, J.: Learning extraction patterns for subjective expressions. In: Proceedings of the Conference on Empirical Methods in Natural Language Processing, pp. 105–112 (2003)
14. Wiebe, J.: Learning subjective adjectives from corpora. In: Proceedings of the National Conference on Artificial Intelligence and Twelfth Conference on on Innovative Applications of Artificial Intelligence, pp. 735–740 (2000)
15. Wiebe, J., Riloff, E.: Creating subjective and objective sentence classifiers from unannotated texts. In: Gelbukh, A. (ed.) CICLing 2005. LNCS, vol. 3406, pp. 486–497. Springer, Heidelberg (2005). https://doi.org/10.1007/978-3-540-30586-6_53

16. Wiebe, J., Wilson, T., Bruce, R.F., Bell, M., Martin, M.: Learning subjective language. Comput. Linguist. **30**(3), 277–308 (2004)
17. Yu, H., Hatzivassiloglou, V.: Towards answering opinion questions: Separating facts from opinions and identifying the polarity of opinion sentences. In: Proceedings of the Conference on Empirical Methods in Natural Language Processing, pp. 129–136 (2003)

Recovering Overlapping Partials for Monaural Perfect Harmonic Musical Sound Separation Using Modified Common Amplitude Modulation

Yukai Gong, Xiangbo Shu, and Jinhui Tang[(⊠)]

Nanjing University of Science and Technology, Nanjing, China
{gyk,jinhuitang}@njust.edu.cn, shuxb104@gmail.com

Abstract. Monaural musical sound separation attempts to isolate one or more instrument sources from a mono-channel polyphonic mixture. The primary challenge is to accurately separate pitched musical sounds where their partials overlap with each other. In the general case, each source has one or more non-overlapping partials. However, there exists the case that no non-overlapping partial is available for at least one source, leading to a more complex problem. In order to address this problem, we propose a novel method named Modified Common Amplitude Modulation (Modified-CAM), which aims to separate monaural perfect harmonic musical sound (except the unison), especially for the perfect octave interval. The proposed system can accurately recover both the amplitudes and the phases of the perfect octave, which can be considered as the typical but the hardest condition. We evaluate the proposed system on the University of Iowa musical instrument sample database, and the experiment results show the system's superiority.

Keywords: Monaural perfect harmonic musical sound separation
Modified-CAM · Perfect octave · Overlapping partials

1 Introduction

In recent years, musical sound separation has arisen much attention as the demand for the singing-voice separation, music information retrieval, music mood analysis, automatic music note transcription, etc. When there has only one mono-channel, the problem called monaural musical sound separation is much harder to address [1].

It is well known that in musical signals, collision of partials from different sources with high chance [2]. When instruments play together, they share some frequency components, which is called overlapping partials [3]. When partials overlap, both the amplitude envelope and the phase of individual partials are unknown. To reconstruct the signals, there exists some monaural musical sound separation systems based on computational auditory scene analysis (CASA) [4], nonnegative matrix factorization (NMF) [5], sparse coding [6], independent subspace analysis (ISA) [7], etc. However, system based on CASA does not make any attempt to handle overlapping partials.

© Springer International Publishing AG, part of Springer Nature 2018
B. Zeng et al. (Eds.): PCM 2017, LNCS 10735, pp. 903–912, 2018.
https://doi.org/10.1007/978-3-319-77380-3_87

Despite systems based on NMF, sparse coding and ISA separate overlapping partials, they all ignore the phase which plays an important role in the amplitude spectrum.

Realizing the importance of the phase, several systems assume that the amplitude spectrum of each instrument partial is smooth [8]. Based on the assumption, Virtanen and Klapuri [9] estimate an overlapping partial by its neighboring non-overlapping partials through nonlinear interpolation, while Every and Szymanski [10] use the same information through linear interpolation. However, for real instruments, the smoothness assumption is often invalid. Bay and Beauchamp [11] propose a model that contains each instrument's partial amplitude and phase. However, the model's performance is quite limited due to the differences among various instruments, notes, velocities, playing styles, and diverse recording environments.

Although the amplitude ratio between an overlapping partial and its neighboring non-overlapping partial is difficult to calculate, the human ears have an important auditory perception [12] that the amplitude envelopes of different partials of the same instrument source are similar. It is known as common amplitude modulation (CAM). In [13], Li and Woodruff demonstrate how to recover overlapping partials by using CAM. In spite of accurate estimates of both the amplitude and the phase of an overlapping partial, they have a fatal defect that each instrument's pitch should be clean; otherwise at least one source does not have any non-overlapping partials as known, which makes the system result in failure.

As Western Music is subject to the twelve-tone equal temperament [16], in general, musical scale intervals have pitch frequencies close to small integer ratios, e.g. 3/2, 4/3, etc. When both the numerator and the denominator are smaller, the interval is more harmonious, and the chance of overlapping partials occurs more frequently. In theory, overlapping partials can be divided into three categories: First, all instrument sources' pitches are different, having no multiple relationships; Second, all instrument sources' pitches are different, but have multiple relationships; Third, all instrument sources' pitches are the same. Overlapping partials in the first one is the easiest for both human ears and algorithms to separate out. It is the general case which attracts previous scholars' most attentions. In the second one, overlapping partials is much harder to deal with by either human ears or an algorithm. To our knowledge, it has not been specially handled or well done without training in existing monaural musical sound separation systems. Han and Pardo [14] have taken a note, yet they need to learn partial models of each instrument throughout the recording, which is obviously unpractical. The sound of the last called unison is the hardest. In reality, human ears cannot distinguish in one mono-channel except asynchronous attack or asynchronous release. For algorithms, Ercan [15] have shown that performance of the system based on nonnegative tensor factorization (NTF) is limited in each instrument, and the similarity to the original of the best one is around 40% with poor decibel gains by the listening test, which indicates apparent noise artifacts.

In this paper, we put forward a new system for monaural perfect harmonic musical sound separation in a gradient-descent framework by a Modified-CAM form. The perfect octave interval is the typical but the hardest situation to handle in this case, thus our experiments specializes in this. Results show that our system's performance is well for recovering both the amplitudes and the phases of overlapping partials.

The organization of the paper is as follows. In Sect. 2, we introduce a sinusoidal model of harmonic instruments and the CAM assumption. Section 3 presents our Modified-CAM form and our solution of overlapping partials in the perfect harmonic case (except the unison) in detail. Section 4 shows the experimental results of our system. Finally, conclusions are drawn in Sect. 5.

2 Sinusoidal Modeling and CAM Assumption

2.1 Sinusoidal Modeling

A musical sound is composed of a series of periodic compound sounds. It can be described as the summation of partials with different frequencies, amplitudes and phases. Generally speaking, almost all pitched instruments' harmonics are multiples of their pitches. Within a period where sine waves are assumed constant, the sinusoidal model of an instrument source can be written as

$$x(t) = \sum_{h=1}^{H} a_h \cos(2\pi f_h t + \varphi_h) \tag{1}$$

where a_h, f_h, and φ_h are amplitude, frequency and phase, respectively of the h (th) partial of the instrument source. H denotes the number of partials in the source.

2.2 CAM Assumption

CAM assumes that all partials of a same instrument source have similar amplitude envelopes. [13] has shown that envelope similarity between the strongest partial and other partials reduces as other partial amplitudes decay. [3] has also stated that for real instruments, as the partial index increases, envelope similarity between the partial and the pitch decreases, yet it is still highly relative to the neighboring partial. Assuming the time frame t, the frequency band f, the amplitude $E(t,f)$, envelope similarity between partial A and B can be calculated by the inner product of their amplitudes:

$$Similarity(f_A,f_B) = \frac{\sum_{k=1}^{K} E(t_k,f_A) \cdot E(t_k,f_B)}{\sqrt{\sum_{k=1}^{K} E^2(t_k,f_A)} \cdot \sqrt{\sum_{k=1}^{K} E^2(t_k,f_B)}} \tag{2}$$

$Similarity(f_A,f_B)$ is between 0 and 1, where 1 means the partials are completely identical, which is the principle of CAM assumption, and 0 means they are irrelevant. The larger the $Similarity(f_A,f_B)$, the higher similarity among the partials.

3   Modified-CAM Form in the Perfect Harmonic Case (Except the Unison)

3.1   Limitations of CAM Assumption in the General Case

Li and Woodruff [13] have a system dealing with the general case by using CAM assumption. Each instrument source has some non-overlapping partials (including the pitch). For an overlapping partial, despite both the phase shift and the amplitude ratio to the pitch are unknown, the frequency and amplitude envelope can be inferred by the pitch, and the unknowns can be solved in a least-square framework. We make a refinement of their idea, which can be described as follows:

$$Mix_k = \sum_{i=1}^{k_x} c_{x_i^{non}} x_{ik}^{non} \cos\left(\frac{m \cdot \alpha_{m^*k}}{m^*} - \Delta\alpha_i^{non}\right) + \sum_{j=1}^{k_y} c_{y_j^{non}} y_{jk}^{non} \cos\left(\frac{n \cdot \beta_{n^*k}}{n^*} - \Delta\beta_j^{non}\right) \quad (3)$$

where the m (th) partial of source x and the n (th) partial of source y have collision. The two sources have k_x and k_y non-overlapping partials respectively. m^* is the index of the closest non-overlapping partial to x_m, and n^* is the index of the closest one to y_n. All non-overlapping partials of x and y are represented as x_i^{non} and y_j^{non}. In time frame k, each estimation of the phases of x_m and y_n is $\frac{m \cdot \alpha_{m^*k}}{m^*} - \Delta\alpha_i^{non}$ and $\frac{n \cdot \beta_{n^*k}}{n^*} - \Delta\beta_j^{non}$ respectively with shifts $-\Delta\alpha_i^{non}$ and $-\Delta\beta_j^{non}$ unknown, likewise, each estimation of the amplitudes is $c_{x_i^{non}} x_{ik}^{non}$ and $c_{y_j^{non}} y_{jk}^{non}$ respectively with ratios $c_{x_i^{non}}$ and $c_{y_j^{non}}$ unknown. Mix is the mixture signal.

In a general case that all instrument sources' pitches are different and do not have multiple relationships with each other, for example, two sources x and y which pitches are 220 Hz and 330 Hz respectively, the partials' relationships are shown in Table 1. Both two sources have some non-overlapping partials, including the pitches. All these partials can be used by Eq. (3) in CAM assumption.

However, when some sources' pitches have some multiple relationships, things are much more complicated. In a perfect harmonic case within one's pitch twice as the other's shown in Table 1, for example, x and y which pitches are 440 Hz and 880 Hz respectively, the amount of overlapping frequency regions is half partials of x with all partials of y overlapped. This time, Eq. (3) cannot be used obviously due to no partial of y is available. Therefore, new solutions need to be found.

3.2   Treatment by Combining Two Overlapping Frequency Regions

In the perfect octave condition, assuming the overlapping region of x_2 and y_1 is frequency band A, and the overlapping region of x_4 and y_2 is frequency band B. In spite of no clean partial of y, it is still a knowledge that y_2 has a similar amplitude envelope

Table 1. Two overlap examples of the general case and the perfect harmonic case respectively

Frequency/Hz	Partial index of x	Partial index of y	Frequency/Hz	Partial index of x	Partial index of y
220	1		440	1	
330		1	660		
440	2		880	2	1
660	3	2	1320	3	
880	4		1760	4	2
990		3	1980		
1100	5		2200	5	
1320	6	4	2640	6	3
1540	7		3080	7	
1650		5	3300		
1760	8		3520	8	4
1980	9	6	3960	9	
2200	10		4400	10	5
......			......		

to y_1. Hence, we assume that the amplitude envelopes are identical, and the frequency of y_1 is known with y_2 twice as y_1. In this way, a Modified-CAM form can be shown as the following simultaneous equations:

$$Mix_{Ak} = \sum_{i=1}^{k_x} c_{x_i^{non}}^A x_{ik}^{non} \cos\left(\frac{m_A \cdot \alpha_{m_A^* k}}{m_A^*} - \Delta\alpha_{Ai}^{non}\right) + y_{Ak}\cos(\beta_{Ak} - \Delta\beta_A)$$

$$Mix_{Bk} = \sum_{i=1}^{k_x} c_{x_i^{non}}^B x_{ik}^{non} \cos\left(\frac{m_B \cdot \alpha_{m_B^* k}}{m_B^*} - \Delta\alpha_{Bi}^{non}\right) + y_{Bk}\cos(\beta_{Bk} - \Delta\beta_B) \qquad (4)$$

$$y_{Bk} = c_{un}y_{Ak}$$

where the meaning of each scalar and vector is the same as it appears in the Sect. 3.1. y_{Ak} and y_{Bk} can be eliminated by these formulas, and then we can obtain

$$\left[Mix_{Ak} - \sum_{i=1}^{k_x}(Ec_iqc_{Ai} + Es_iqs_{Ai})\right](\cos\beta_{Bk}q_1 + \sin\beta_{Bk}q_2)$$
$$= \left[Mix_{Bk} - \sum_{i=1}^{k_x}(Fc_iqc_{Bi} + Fs_iqs_{Bi})\right](\cos\beta_{Ak}q_3 + \sin\beta_{Ak}q_4) \qquad (5)$$

where

$$
\begin{pmatrix} Ec_i \\ Es_i \\ Fc_i \\ Fs_i \end{pmatrix} = \begin{pmatrix} x_{ik}^{non} \cos \frac{m_A \cdot \alpha_{m_A^* k}}{m_A^*} \\ x_{ik}^{non} \sin \frac{m_A \cdot \alpha_{m_A^* k}}{m_A^*} \\ x_{ik}^{non} \cos \frac{m_B \cdot \alpha_{m_B^* k}}{m_B^*} \\ x_{ik}^{non} \sin \frac{m_B \cdot \alpha_{m_B^* k}}{m_B^*} \end{pmatrix}, \quad \begin{pmatrix} qc_{Ai} \\ qs_{Ai} \\ qc_{Bi} \\ qs_{Bi} \end{pmatrix} = \begin{pmatrix} c_{x_i^{non}}^A \cos \Delta\alpha_{Ai}^{non} \\ c_{x_i^{non}}^A \sin \Delta\alpha_{Ai}^{non} \\ c_{x_i^{non}}^B \cos \Delta\alpha_{Bi}^{non} \\ c_{x_i^{non}}^B \sin \Delta\alpha_{Bi}^{non} \end{pmatrix}, \quad \begin{pmatrix} q_1 \\ q_2 \\ q_3 \\ q_4 \end{pmatrix}
$$

$$
= \begin{pmatrix} c_{un} \cos \Delta\beta_B \\ c_{un} \sin \Delta\beta_B \\ \cos \Delta\beta_A \\ \sin \Delta\beta_A \end{pmatrix} \tag{6}
$$

Written by matrix representation as

$$
\begin{pmatrix} Ac_1 \, As_1 \ - Bc_1 \ - Bs_1 \ - E_1 \, F_1 \\ \cdots \\ Ac_k \, As_k \ - Bc_k \ - Bs_k \ - E_k \, F_k \\ \cdots \\ Ac_K \, As_K \ - Bc_K \ - Bs_K \ - E_K \, F_K \end{pmatrix} \begin{pmatrix} q_1 \\ q_2 \\ q_3 \\ q_4 \\ Q_A \\ Q_B \end{pmatrix} = \begin{pmatrix} 0 \\ \vdots \\ 0 \\ \vdots \\ 0 \end{pmatrix} \tag{7}
$$

It can be regarded as an over-determined system of homogeneous linear equations, where

$$
\begin{pmatrix} E_{ik} \\ F_{ik} \end{pmatrix} = \begin{pmatrix} Ec_i \cos \beta_{Bk} \ Es_i \cos \beta_{Bk} \ Ec_i \sin \beta_{Bk} \ Es_i \sin \beta_{Bk} \\ Fc_i \cos \beta_{Ak} \ Fs_i \cos \beta_{Ak} \ Fc_i \sin \beta_{Ak} \ Fs_i \sin \beta_{Ak} \end{pmatrix},
$$

$$
\begin{pmatrix} E_k \\ F_k \end{pmatrix} = \begin{pmatrix} E_{1k} & \cdots & E_{ik} & \cdots & E_{k_x k} \\ F_{1k} & \cdots & F_{ik} & \cdots & F_{k_x k} \end{pmatrix}, \quad \begin{pmatrix} Ac_k \\ As_k \\ Bc_k \\ Bs_k \end{pmatrix} = \begin{pmatrix} Mix_{Ak} \cos \beta_{Bk} \\ Mix_{Ak} \sin \beta_{Bk} \\ Mix_{Bk} \cos \beta_{Ak} \\ Mix_{Bk} \sin \beta_{Ak} \end{pmatrix},
$$

$$
Q_{Ai} = \begin{pmatrix} q_1 qc_{Ai} \\ q_1 qs_{Ai} \\ q_2 qc_{Ai} \\ q_2 qs_{Ai} \end{pmatrix}, \quad Q_{Bi} = \begin{pmatrix} q_3 qc_{Bi} \\ q_3 qs_{Bi} \\ q_4 qc_{Bi} \\ q_4 qs_{Bi} \end{pmatrix}, \quad Q_A = \begin{pmatrix} Q_{A1} \\ \vdots \\ Q_{Ai} \\ \vdots \\ Q_{Ak_x} \end{pmatrix}, \quad Q_B = \begin{pmatrix} Q_{B1} \\ \vdots \\ Q_{Bi} \\ \vdots \\ Q_{Bk_x} \end{pmatrix}, \tag{8}
$$

Considering the linear correlation among the items of Q_A and Q_B, and $q_3^2 + q_4^2 = 1$ in addition. In this case, the least-square framework is not applicable. We construct a gradient-descent framework, and solve the partial derivative of each unknown scalar:

$$
\begin{pmatrix}
\dfrac{\partial y}{\partial q_1} \\[4pt]
\dfrac{\partial y}{\partial q_2} \\[4pt]
\dfrac{\partial y}{\partial \Delta\beta_A} \\[4pt]
\vdots \\[4pt]
\dfrac{\partial y}{\partial qc_{Ai}} \\[4pt]
\dfrac{\partial y}{\partial qs_{Ai}} \\[4pt]
\dfrac{\partial y}{\partial qc_{Bi}} \\[4pt]
\dfrac{\partial y}{\partial qs_{Bi}} \\[4pt]
\vdots
\end{pmatrix}
=
\begin{pmatrix}
\displaystyle\sum_{k=1}^{K} S_k \left[Ac_k - \sum_{i=1}^{k_x}(Ec_i qc_{Ai} + Es_i qs_{Ai})\cos\beta_{Bk} \right] \\[10pt]
\displaystyle\sum_{k=1}^{K} S_k \left[As_k - \sum_{i=1}^{k_x}(Ec_i qc_{Ai} + Es_i qs_{Ai})\sin\beta_{Bk} \right] \\[10pt]
\displaystyle\sum_{k=1}^{K} S_k \left[Bc_k q_4 - Bs_k q_3 + \sum_{i=1}^{k_x} F_{ik}\begin{pmatrix} -q_4 qc_{Bi} \\ -q_4 qs_{Bi} \\ q_3 qc_{Bi} \\ q_3 qs_{Bi}\end{pmatrix} \right] \\[14pt]
\vdots \\[10pt]
\displaystyle\sum_{k=1}^{K} S_k(-Ec_i q_1 \cos\beta_{Bk} - Ec_i q_2 \sin\beta_{Bk}) \\[8pt]
\displaystyle\sum_{k=1}^{K} S_k(-Es_i q_1 \cos\beta_{Bk} - Es_i q_2 \sin\beta_{Bk}) \\[8pt]
\displaystyle\sum_{k=1}^{K} S_k(Fc_i q_3 \cos\beta_{Ak} + Fc_i q_4 \sin\beta_{Ak}) \\[8pt]
\displaystyle\sum_{k=1}^{K} S_k(Fs_i q_3 \cos\beta_{Ak} + Fs_i q_4 \sin\beta_{Ak}) \\[8pt]
\vdots
\end{pmatrix}
\tag{9}
$$

where

$$
S_k = Ac_k q_1 + As_k q_2 - Bc_k q_3 - Bs_k q_4 - E_k Q_A + F_k Q_B \tag{10}
$$

All partial derivatives should be 0. In the gradient-descent framework with the initial value 0, we iterate until the Euclidean distance between the next iteration and the previous is less than 10^{-3}, then we obtain all unknown scalars. The reconstruction of y_1 and y_2 can be done by subtractions. The envelope similarity between y_1 and y_2 is calculated by Eq. (2), and the residual sum of squares (RSS) is calculated by the quadratic sum of S_k.

According to the assumption, it can be inferred that the separation performance is well when we get high envelope similarity and low RSS is meanwhile, otherwise the performance is poor. We estimate the pitch of y by the equivalent of corresponding overlapping partial of x and the average of overlapping frequency bands from y_1 to y_{10} preliminarily. Each result shows that the similarity is a bit low and the RSS is a little high moreover. Therefore, it needs to re-estimate the pitch of y much more accurately to improve the similarity and the RSS.

3.3 Re-estimation of the Pitch of Source y

As is mentioned before, it is unable to get any partial frequency of y, due to all partials colliding with corresponding partials of x. According to limited separation performance of experiments, it is able to estimate y_1 by the first ten partials of y, regardless of the overlaps, in this way we obtain ten different estimations. Use these ten results in the gradient-descent framework, and iterate a certain number of times for each one, such as ten, and calculate each RSS of the last iteration. Then choose two estimations y_i and y_j, which having the lowest RSS, making several weighted means. After that, choose one weighted mean having the lowest RSS, iterating until the convergence. Finally, the pitch of y is estimated more reasonably with much higher similarity and much lower RSS moreover, and the Modified-CAM form for the perfect harmonic case is much more robust.

3.4 Treatment of the Rest Overlapping Frequency Regions

In the presented model of gradient-descend with the Modified-CAM form, we use two overlapping frequency regions each time for the perfect harmonic case, which is quite different from one overlapping frequency region each time for the general case. However, for example, the typical but the hardest condition, the perfect octave, when the first ten partials are taken from each instrument source, it needs to deal with at least five overlapping frequency regions of the mixture. This time how to handle the rest overlapping frequency regions after the first treatment is still a problem. If the recovered y_1 and the recovered y_2 are considered as known, then use the least-square framework to recover y_3, y_4 and y_5, the quadric error will be led into. Thus, for the rest overlapping regions, a cascade mode for the treatment of every two neighboring regions is designed. For five overlapping frequency regions, it should be four treatments in total. Because of repeated calculations of y_2, y_3 and y_4, we take the average of two reconstructions as their waveforms respectively. Corresponding x_4, x_6 and x_8 are recovered in the same way. Thus, y_1 and y_2, y_2 and y_3, y_3 and y_4, and y_4 and y_5 are all in accordance with the higher similarity between the two neighboring partials than two remote partials in the CAM assumption [3] (Fig. 1).

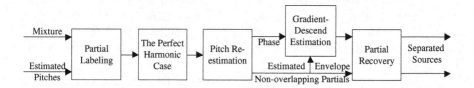

Fig. 1. System diagram for the perfect harmonic case (except the unison)

4   Experiments

4.1   Database and Samples

We use a database from the University of Iowa musical instrument sample database [17], which includes various kinds of western instruments, such as the woodwinds, the brass, the strings and the percussion. Considering the complexity of the percussion, in which most are unpitched, we discard all samples. We choose samples from nine instruments including Flute, Oboe, Clarinet, Horn, Trumpet, Trombone, Violin, Viola, and Cello. All samples are in the actual playing having shifts and fluctuations. Then we make mixtures of every two instruments according to the perfect octave interval, in this way the performance of the system can be tested straightly.

For each instrument, we choose five representative scales: C, D, E, G, and A. Each instrument has a range over two octaves. In our implementation, we have 95 clean samples and 430 two-instrument octave mixtures.

4.2   Results

We use signal-to-noise ratio (SNR) for evaluation. Results are shown in Table 2. The first row is the ΔSNR by forcing Li's system [13] with both the amplitude and the pitch of y estimated by the mean of overlapping bands from y_6 to y_{10}. The second row is the ΔSNR by baseline with the pitch of y estimated by equivalent of the pitch of x. The third row is the ΔSNR by baseline with the pitch of y estimated by the mean of overlapping bands from y_1 to y_{10}. The last row is the overall ΔSNR by our proposed system with re-estimation stage of the pitch of y. It is clear that the re-estimation stage is of great importance to our proposed system, which achieves 3.2 dB and 3.4 dB higher than the two baselines separately, and 5.8 dB higher than forcing Li's CAM system [13]. Moreover, partials higher than the first ten need to be taken from the mixture in the follow-up experiments.

Table 2. SNR improvement

Forced General CAM System	6.72 dB
Baseline 1	9.12 dB
Baseline 2	9.31 dB
Proposed System of Modified-CAM with Re-estimation	12.50 dB

5   Conclusion

In this paper, a monaural musical sound separation system is proposed to recover overlapping partials of perfect harmonic sound, especially handles the typical but the hardest condition of the case, the perfect octave interval. Our strategy is based on a Modified-CAM form in a gradient-descend framework using estimated pitches, which greatly relaxes the limitations of the CAM assumption. Experimental results also show that our proposed system achieves high improvements than that of predecessors. When each overlapping partial frequency is estimated accurately, the performance has significant SNR improvements. When an overlapping partial frequency cannot be inferred due to none of non-overlapping partials of the source, it can still be refined from a subset of the mixture's overlapping partials. And the re-estimation stage will achieve a decreased deviation from the truth and lead to improve the performance.

Acknowledgment. This research was supported in part by the 973 Program (Project No. 2014CB347600), the NSFC (Grant No. 61672304 and 61672285), and the NSF of Jiangsu Province (Grant BK 20140058, BK20170033 and BK20170856).

References

1. Virtanen, T.: Sound source separation in monaural music signals. Ph.D. dissertation, TUT (2006)
2. Li, Y.: Monaural musical sound separation. M.S. dissertation, OSU (2008)
3. Viste, H., Evangelista, G.: A method for separation of overlapping partials based on similarity of temporal envelopes in multichannel mixtures. IEEE TASLP **14**, 1051–1061 (2006)
4. Mellinger, D.K.: Event formation and separation in musical sound. Ph.D. dissertation, Stanford (1991)
5. Virtanen, T.: Monaural sound source separation by nonnegative matrix factorization with temporal continuity and sparseness criteria. IEEE TASLP **15**, 1066–1074 (2007)
6. Abdallah, S.A., Plumbley, M.D.: Unsupervised analysis of polyphonic music by sparse coding. IEEE TNN **17**, 1066–1074 (2007)
7. Casey, M.A., Westner, W.: Separation of mixed audio sources by independent subspace analasis. In: Proceedings of ICMC, pp. 154–161 (2000)
8. Klapuri, A.: Multiple fundamental frequency estimation based on harmonicity and spectral smoothness. IEEE TSAP **11**, 804–816 (2003)
9. Virtanen, T., Klapuri, A.: Separation of harmonic sounds using multipitch analysis and iterative parameter estimation. In: IEEE WASPAA, pp. 83–86 (2001)
10. Every, M.R., Szymanski, J.E.: Separation of synchronous pitched notes by spectral filtering of harmonics. IEEE TASLP **14**, 1845–1856 (2006)
11. Bay, M., Beauchamp, J.W.: Harmonic source separation using prestored spectra. In: Rosca, J., Erdogmus, D., Príncipe, J.C., Haykin, S. (eds.) ICA 2006. LNCS, vol. 3889, pp. 561–568. Springer, Heidelberg (2006). https://doi.org/10.1007/11679363_70
12. Bregman, A.S.: Auditory Scene Analysis. MIT Press, Cambridge (1990). 10
13. Li, Y., Woodruff, J.: Monaural musical sound separation based on pitch and common amplitude modulation. IEEE TASLP **17**, 1361–1371 (2009)
14. Han, J., Pardo, B.: Reconstructing completely overlapped notes from musical mixtures. In: ICASSP, pp. 249–252 (2011)
15. Ercan, M.B.: Musical instrument source separation in unison and monaural mixtures. M.S. dissertation, Bilkent (2014)
16. Rasch, R.A.: Description of regular twelve-tone musical tunings. JASA **73**, 1023–1035 (1983)
17. The University of IOWA Musical Instrument Sample Database. http://theremin.music.uiowa.edu/

Author Index

Printed in the United States
By Bookmasters